Lecture Notes in Computer Science 2736

Edited by G. Goos, J. Hartmanis, and J. van Leeuwen

T0100515

Springer
Berlin
Heidelberg
New York
Hong Kong
London
Milan
Paris
Tokyo

Vladimír Mařík   Werner Retschitzegger
Olga Štěpánková (Eds.)

Database and Expert Systems Applications

14th International Conference, DEXA 2003
Prague, Czech Republic, September 1-5, 2003
Proceedings

 Springer

Series Editors

Gerhard Goos, Karlsruhe University, Germany
Juris Hartmanis, Cornell University, NY, USA
Jan van Leeuwen, Utrecht University, The Netherlands

Volume Editors

Vladimír Mařík
Olga Štěpánková
Czech Technical University
Faculty of Electrical Engineering
Department of Cybernetics
Technicka 2, 16627 Prague 6, Czech Republic
E-mail:{marik/step}@labe.felk.cvut.cz

Werner Retschitzegger
University of Linz
Institute of Applied Computer Science
IFS - Department of Information Systems
Altenbergerstr. 69, 4040 Linz, Austria
E-mail: werner@ifs.uni-linz.ac.at

Cataloging-in-Publication Data applied for

A catalog record for this book is available from the Library of Congress

Bibliographic information published by Die Deutsche Bibliothek
Die Deutsche Bibliothek lists this publication in the Deutsche Nationalbibliografie;
detailed bibliographic data is available in the Internet at <http://dnb.ddb.de>.

CR Subject Classification (1998): H.2, H.4, H.3, H.5, I.2, J.1

ISSN 0302-9743
ISBN 3-540-40806-1 Springer-Verlag Berlin Heidelberg New York

Springer-Verlag Berlin Heidelberg New York
a member of BertelsmannSpringer Science+Business Media GmbH

http://www.springer.de

© Springer-Verlag Berlin Heidelberg 2003

Typesetting: Camera-ready by author, data conversion by PTP-Berlin GmbH
Printed on acid-free paper   SPIN 10929148   06/3142   5 4 3 2 1 0

Preface

The 14th DEXA 2003 International Conference on Database and Expert Systems Applications was held during September 1–5, 2003 at the Czech Technical University in Prague, Czech Republic. The DEXA line of conferences has already gained its own reputation and respected position as a platform for the exchange of ideas among theoreticians and practitioners in the wider area of computer science, but mainly in the areas of database and knowledge-based technologies.

Since DEXA 1993, which was held in Prague, DEXA has grown into a multiconference consisting of four more focused and specialized conferences besides DEXA itself, namely the DaWak conference, EC-Web conference, eGOV conference, and this year happening for the first time, the HoloMAS conference. In addition, the DEXA workshop is a special event offering enough space for specialized discussion, and acting – in a certain sense – as an incubator for new conferences.

The DEXA conference itself is growing in volume and quality each year. This time there were 236 papers submitted and reviewed and the program committee selected 91 of the best papers to be included in this volume. Each of the submitted papers was carefully reviewed by at least three independent PC members or external reviewers.

The DEXA proceedings quite clearly reflect the current trends in the database area and we are happy with the balanced content of both the conference and the proceedings.

We would like to express our thanks at this point to all the institutions that actively supported this event, namely:

- Czech Technical University, Prague, Czech Republic
- DEXA Association, Linz, Austria
- FAW, Johannes Kepler University, Linz, Austria
- Austrian Computer Society
- Microsoft Research, Cambridge, UK
- The Gerstner Lab, as part of the EU Center of Excellence MIRACLE at the Czech Technical University, Prague, Czech Republic

We would also like to thank the whole DEXA implementation team, especially the PC members and the reviewers who did a wonderful job in preparing the technical content of the conference. Special thanks go to Prof. Roland R. Wagner and Prof. A Min Tjoa, who remain persistently the main driving forces behind the DEXA line of events, and also to Gabriela Wagner, who dedicated all her efforts to the success of the DEXA event.

Prag, Linz   Vladimir Mařík

June 2003   Olga Stepankova

Werner Retschitzegger

Program Committee

General Chairperson

Valdimir Mařík, Czech Technical University, Czech Republic

Conference Program Chairpersons

Olga Stepankova, Czech Technical University, Czech Republic
Werner Retschitzegger, University of Linz, Austria

Workshop Chairpersons

A Min Tjoa, Technical University of Vienna, Austria
Roland R. Wagner, FAW, University of Linz, Austria

Program Committee Members

Michel Adiba, IMAG, Laboratoire LSR, France
Hamideh Afsarmanesh, University of Amsterdam, The Netherlands
Ala Al-Zobaidie, University of Greenwich, UK
Bernd Amann, CNAM, France
Frederic Andres, NII, Japan
Kurt Bauknecht, University of Zurich, Switzerland
Trevor Bench-Capon, University of Liverpool, UK
Alfs Berztiss, University of Pittsburgh, USA
Sourav S. Bhowmick, Nanyang Technological Univ., Singapore
Jon Bing, University of Oslo, Norway
Christian Böhm, UMIT, Austria
Alex Borgida, Rutgers University, USA
Omran Bukhres, Purdue University, USA
Luis Camarinah-Matos, New University of Lisbon, Portugal
Antonio Cammelli, IDG-CNR, Italy
Fabio Casati, HP Laboratories, USA
Wojciech Cellary, University of Economics at Poznan, Poland
Elizabeth Chang, Curtin University, Australia
Stavros Christodoulakis, Technical University of Crete, Greece
Panos Chrysanthis, Univ. of Pittsburgh, and Carnegie Mellon Univ., USA
Paolo Ciaccia, University of Bologna, Italy
Rosine Cicchetti, IUT, University of Marseille, France
Carlo Combi, University of Udine, Italy

Don Cowell, University of Greenwich, UK
John Debenham, University of Technology, Sydney, Australia
Misbah Deen, University of Keele, UK
Elisabetta Di Nitto, Politecnico di Milano, Italy
Nina Edelweiss, University of Rio Grande do Sul, Brazil
Johann Eder, University of Klagenfurt, Austria
Thomas Eiter, Technical University of Vienna, Austria
Gregor Engels, University of Paderborn, Germany
Peter Fankhauser, GMD-IPSI, Germany
Ling Feng, University of Twente, The Netherlands
Eduardo Fernandez, Florida Atlantic University, USA
Simon Field, Matching Systems Ltd., Switzerland
Burkhard Freitag, University of Passau, Germany
Mariagrazia Fugini, Politecnico di Milano, Italy
Antonio L. Furtado, University of Rio de Janeiro, Brazil
Georges Gardarin, University of Versailles, France
Alexander Gelbukh, CIC, IPN, Mexico
Parke Godfrey, York University, Canada
Paul Grefen, Eindhoven University of Technology, The Netherlands
William Grosky, Wayne State University, USA
Le Gruenwald, University of Oklahoma, USA
Abdelkader Hameurlain, IRIT, University of Toulouse, France
Igor T. Hawryszkiewycz, University of Technology, Sydney, Australia
Mohamed Ibrahim, University of Greenwich, UK
Yahiko Kambayashi, Kyoto University, Japan
Magdi N. Kamel, Naval Postgraduate School, USA
Nabil Kamel, American University in Cairo, Egypt
Gerti Kappel, University of Technology, Vienna, Austria
Dimitris Karagiannis, University of Vienna, Austria
Randi Karlsen, University of Tromsö, Norway
Rudolf Keller, Zühlke Engineering AG, Switzerland
Latifur Khan, University of Texas at Dallas, USA
Myoung Ho Kim, KAIST, Korea
Masaru Kitsuregawa, Tokyo University, Japan
Gary J. Koehler, University of Florida, USA
Donald Kossmann, Technical University of Munich, Germany
Petr Kroha, Technical University Chemnitz-Zwickau, Germany
John Krogstie, SINTEF, Norway
Josef Küng, University of Linz, Austria
Lotfi Lakhal, University of Marseille, France
Jiri Lazansky, Czech Technical University, Czech Republic
Michel Leonard, University of Geneva, Switzerland
Tok Wang Ling, National University of Singapore, Singapore
Mengchi Liu, Carleton University, Canada
Fred Lochovsky, Hong Kong Univ. of Science & Technology, Hong Kong

Peri Loucopoulos, UMIST, UK
Sanjai Kumar Madria, University of Missouri-Rolla, USA
Akifumi Makinouchi, Kyushu University, Japan
Simone Marinai, University of Florence, Italy
Heinrich C. Mayr, University of Klagenfurt, Austria
Subhasish Mazumdar, New Mexico Tech, USA
Dennis McLeod, University of Southern California, USA
Robert Meersman, Free University of Brussels, Belgium
Elisabeth Metais, CEDRIC/CNAM, Paris, France
Zoran Milosevic, University of Queensland, Australia
Mukesh Mohania, IBM-IRL, India
Tadeusz Morzy, Poznan University of Technology, Poland
Noureddine Mouaddib, University of Nantes, France
Günter Müller, University of Freiburg, Germany
Waseem Naqvi, Raytheon Inc., USA
Erich J. Neuhold, Fraunhofer-IPSI, Germany
Gultekin Ozsoyoglu, Case Western Reserve University, USA
Francois Pacull, Xerox Research Centre Europe, France
Georgios Pangalos, University of Thessaloniki, Greece
Stott Parker, University of Los Angeles (UCLA), USA
Oscar Pastor, Technical University of Valencia, Spain
Marco Patella, University of Bologna, Italy
Barbara Pernici, Politecnico di Milano, Italy
Günter Pernul, University of Regensburg, Germany
Gerald Quirchmayr, University of Vienna, Austria
Fausto Rabitti, CNUCE-CNR, Italy
Wenny Rahayu, La Trobe University, Australia
Isidro Ramos, Technical University of Valencia, Spain
P. Krishna Reddy, University of Science and Technology, Hong Kong
Harald Reiterer, University of Konstanz, Germany
Norman Revell, Middlesex University, UK
Sally Rice, University of South Australia, Australia
Jerome Robinson, University of Essex, UK
John Roddick, Flinders University of South Australia, Australia
Colette Rolland, University Paris I, Sorbonne, France
Elke Rundensteiner, Worcester Polytechnic Institute, USA
Domenico Sacca, University of Calabria, Italy
Simonas Saltenis, Aalborg University, Denmark
Marinette Savonnet, University of Bourgogne, France
Erich Schweighofer, University of Vienna, Austria
Ming-Chien Shan, HP Laboratories, USA
Keng Siau, University of Nebraska-Lincoln, USA
Michael H. Smith, University of California, USA
Giovanni Soda, University of Florence, Italy
Harald Sonnberger, CEC Brussels, Belgium

External Reviewers

Zaher Aghbari	Khalid Belhajjame	Pierluigi Plebani
Kunihiko Kaneko	Tania Cerquitelli	Chunsheng Liu
Seok Il Song	Anibal Arias	Shan Wei
Mohand Boughanem	Christian Koncilia	Wanjun Sun
Max Chevalier	Marek Lehmann	Qiong Ruan
Claude Chrisment	Harald Kosch	Masashi Toyoda
Franck Morvan	Roberto Tedesco	Noriko Imafuji
Josiane Mothe	Giuseppe Amato	Shingo Otsuka
Olivier Teste	Federica Mandreoli	Norio Katayama
Chun Tang	Pavel Zezula	Miyuki Nakano
Yong Shi	Franca Debole	Yitong Wang
Li Zhang	Chiara Renso	Mirella Moura Moro
Daxin Jiang	Jutta Willamowski	Renata de Matos Galante
Pengjun Pei	Damian Arregui	Carina Friederich Dorneles
Daoying Ma	Alessio Ceroni	Vanessa de Paula Braganholo
Dimitrios Theotokis	Andrea Passerini	Daniela Leal Musa
Anya Sotiropoulou	Sauro Menchetti	Jan Ma
Pierluigi Plebani	Samuil Angelov	Andreas Meissner
Barbara Oliboni	Hajo Reijers	Thomas Risse
Malu Castellanos	Alexander Hirnschall	Juan Carlos Casamayor
Christian Baumgartner	Wijnand Derks	Juan Sanchez
Angela Bonifati	Ednan Masovic	Vicente Pelechano
Mario Cannataro	Thosten Priebe	Patrick Lehti
Gianluigi Greco	Björn Muschall	Kaiyang Liu
Antonella Guzzo	Christian Breu	Jiying Wang
Giuseppe Manco	Eduardo Mena	Sven Van Acker
Riccardo Ortale	Isabel Diaz	Jan De Bo
Cristina Sirangelo	Javier Jaen	Majed AbuSafiya
Giorgio Terracina	Jennifer Pérez	Thomas Schlienger
Peter Fischer	Nieves R. Brisaboa	Andreas Erat
Andreas Grünhagen	Patricio Letelier	Martin Steinert
Steffen Rost	Morad Benyoucef	Erich Gstrein
Luciano Garcia Bañuelos	Sarita Bassil	Surya Nepal
Edgard Benitez Guerrero	Ting Chen	Wojciech Wiza
Vu-Tuyet Trinh	Liang Liang Fang	Jarogniew Rykowski

Table of Contents

Invited Talk

Policy Based Enterprise (Active) Information Integration 1
Mukesh Mohania, Inderpal Narang

XML I

SOFT – Generating Highly Flexible Object Code from
XML Specifications 8
Alun Butler, Liz Bacon, Mohamed Ibrahim

Querying Semistructured Data Efficiently 18
Hongsik Rho, Wen-Chi Hou, Dunren Che, Chih-Fang Wang

On the Optimality of Holistic Algorithms for Twig Queries............. 28
Byron Choi, Malika Mahoui, Derick Wood

AUSMS: An Environment for Frequent Sub-structures Extraction in a
Semi-structured Object Collection................................... 38
P.A Laur, M. Teisseire, P. Poncelet

Data Modeling

Defining Web Schema Transformers by Example 46
Stephan Lechner, Michael Schrefl

A Conceptual Framework for Spatiotemporal Data Modeling 57
Kuo Wang, Cristina Fierbinteanu, Mamoru Maekawa

Moa and the Multi-model Architecture: A New Perspective on NF^2 67
M. van Keulen, J. Vonk, A.P. de Vries, J. Flokstra, H.E. Blok

Entity Connectivity vs. Hierarchical Levelling as a Basis for
Data Model Clustering: An Experimental Analysis 77
Daniel L. Moody

XML II

An XML-Enabled Association Rule Framework 88
Ling Feng, Tharam Dillon, Hans Weigand, Elizabeth Chang

Validation of XML Document Updates Based on XML Schema in
XML Databases 98
Sang-Kyun Kim, Myungcheol Lee, Kyu-Chul Lee

XML Schemata Inference and Evolution 109
  Ismael Sanz, Juan Manuel Pérez, Rafael Berlanga,
  María José Aramburu

Spatial Database Systems I

Bulk Loading the MKL-Tree 119
  Annalisa Franco, Alessandra Lumini, Dario Maio

Bulk Insertion for R-Tree by Seeded Clustering 129
  Taewon Lee, Bongki Moon, Sukho Lee

Optimizing Both Cache and Disk Performance of R-Trees 139
  Myungsun Park, Sukho Lee

XML III

XML Views: Part 1 148
  Rajagopal Rajugan, Elizabeth Chang, Tharam S Dillon, Ling Feng

Partition Based Path Join Algorithms for XML Data 160
  Quanzhong Li, Bongki Moon

Representing and Querying Summarized XML Data 171
  Sara Comai, Stefania Marrara, Letizia Tanca

Storing and Querying XML Data in the Nested Relational Sequence
Database System 182
  Ho Lam Lau, Wilfred Ng

Spatial Database Systems II

Capturing Uncertainty in Spatial Queries over Imprecise Data 192
  Xingbo Yu, Sharad Mehrotra

Effective Load-Balancing via Migration and Replication in
Spatial Grids 202
  Anirban Mondal, Kazuo Goda, Masaru Kitsuregawa

Parallel Query Support for Multidimensional Data:
Intra-object Parallelism 212
  Karl Hahn, Bernd Reiner, Gabriele Höfling

Replicated Parallel I/O without Additional Scheduling Costs 223
  Mikhail Atallah, Keith Frikken

XML IV

XML Restructuring and Integration for Tabular Data 233
  Wei Yu, Z. Meral Ozsoyoglu, Gultekin Ozsoyoglu

Repairing Inconsistent Merged XML Data 244
  Wilfred Ng

XML and Knowledge Technologies for Semantic-Based Indexing of
Paper Documents 256
  Donato Malerba, Michelangelo Ceci, Margherita Berardi

Efficient Re-construction of Document Versions Based on
Adaptive Forward and Backward Change Deltas 266
  Raymond K. Wong, Nicole Lam

Mobile Computing I

Neighborhood-Consistent Transaction Management for
Pervasive Computing Environments 276
  Filip Perich, Anupam Joshi, Yelena Yesha, Timothy Finin

On Mining Group Patterns of Mobile Users 287
  Yida Wang, Ee-Peng Lim, San-Yih Hwang

Location Query Based on Moving Behaviors 297
  *Ming-Hui Jin, Eric Hsiao-Kuang Wu, Jorng-Tzong Horng,
  Cheng-Yan Kao, Yu-Cheng Huang*

Dynamic Splitting Policies of the Adaptive 3DR-Tree for
Indexing Continuously Moving Objects 308
  Bonggi Jun, Bonghee Hong, Byunggu Yu

Transactions

Comparing the Overhead Requirements of Database
Transaction Models 318
  Andrew G. Fry, Hugh E. Williams

Concurrent and Real-Time Update of Access Control Policies 330
  Indrakshi Ray, Tai Xin

Transactional Agent Model for Distributed Object Systems 340
  Masashi Shiraishi, Tomoya Enokido, Makoto Takizawa

Mobile Computing II

Incremental Query Answering Using a Multi-layered Database Model
in a Mobile Computing Environment 350
  Sanjay Kumar Madria, Yongjian Fu, Sourav Bhowmick

Environmental Noise Classification for Context-Aware Applications 360
  Ling Ma, Dan Smith, Ben Milner

An Access Time Cost Model for Spatial Range Queries on
Broadcast Geographical Data over Air 371
   Jianting Zhang, Le Gruenwald

Bioinformatics

Context-Aware Data Mining Framework for Wireless
Medical Application 381
   Pravin Vajirkar, Sachin Singh, Yugyung Lee

Data Management in Metaboloinformatics: Issues and Challenges 392
   Sourav S. Bhowmick, Dadabhai T Singh, Amey Laud

Mining the Risk Types of Human Papillomavirus (HPV) by AdaCost 403
   Seong-Bae Park, Sohyun Hwang, Byoung-Tak Zhang

Protein Structural Information Management Based on Spatial Concepts
and Active Trigger Rules.. 413
   Sung-Hee Park, Keun Ho Ryu, Hyeon S. Son

Mobile Computing III

ASOMNIA: A Service-Oriented Middleware for Ambient
Information Access... 423
   Karl Rehrl, Wernher Behrendt, Manfred Bortenschlager, Sigi Reich,
   Harald Rieser, Rupert Westenthaler

An Efficient Tree-Structure Index Allocation Method over Multiple
Broadcast Channels in Mobile Environments 433
   Byungkyu Lee, Sungwon Jung

DSTTMOD: A Future Trajectory Based Moving Objects Database 444
   Xiaofeng Meng, Zhiming Ding

Adaptive Peer-to-Peer Routing with Proximity 454
   Chu Yee Liau, Achmad Nizar Hidayanto, Stephane Bressan

Information Retrieval I

g-binary: A New Non-parameterized Code for Improved Inverted
File Compression 464
   Ilias Nitsos, Georgios Evangelidis, Dimitrios Dervos

Activation on the Move: Querying Tourism Information via
Spreading Activation 474
   Helmut Berger, Michael Dittenbach, Dieter Merkl

Similarity Join in Metric Spaces Using eD-Index 484
   Vlastislav Dohnal, Claudio Gennaro, Pavel Zezula

KeyQuery – A Front End for the Automatic Translation of Keywords
into Structured Queries 494
Martin Erwig, Jianglin He

Information Retrieval II

Supporting KDD Applications by the *k*-Nearest Neighbor Join 504
Christian Böhm, Florian Krebs

Approximate Query Processing for a Content-Based Image
Retrieval Method 517
*Paul W.H. Kwan, Kazuo Toraichi, Hiroyuki Kitagawa,
Keisuke Kameyama*

Query Algebra Operations for Interval Probabilities 527
Wenzhong Zhao, Alex Dekhtyar, Judy Goldsmith

Information Retrieval III

Tree Structure Based Parallel Frequent Pattern Mining on PC Cluster ... 537
Iko Pramudiono, Masaru Kitsuregawa

WebObjects: A New Approach for Querying the Web 548
Fábio Soares Silva, Marcus Costa Sampaio, Cláudio S. Baptista

Finding Neighbor Communities in the Web Using Inter-site Graph 558
Yasuhito Asano, Hiroshi Imai, Masashi Toyoda, Masaru Kitsuregawa

A Lesson for Software Engineering from Knowledge Engineering 569
John Debenham

Multimedia Database Systems

Image Retrieval by Web Context: Filling the Gap between Image
Keywords and Usage Keywords 579
Koji Zettsu, Yutaka Kidawara, Katsumi Tanaka

Query-by-Humming on Internet 589
Naoko Kosugi, Hidenobu Nagata, Tadashi Nakanishi

Efficient Indexing of High Dimensional Normalized Histograms 601
Alexandru Coman, Jörg Sander, Mario A. Nascimento

Implementation of a Stream-Oriented Retrieval Engine for Complex
Similarity Queries on Top of an ORDBMS 611
Andreas Henrich, Günter Robbert

Web Applications

GFIS Pro – A Tool for Managing Forest Information Resources 622
Thanh Binh Nguyen, Mohamed T Ibrahim

FDRAS: Fashion Design Recommender Agent System Using
the Extraction of Representative Sensibility and the Two-Way
Combined Filtering on Textile 631
Kyung-Yong Jung, Young-Joo Na, Jung-Hyun Lee

Ontologies I

An Explanation-Based Ranking Approach for
Ontology-Based Querying 641
Nenad Stojanovic

Visual Querying with Ontologies for Distributed
Statistical Databases 651
Yaxin Bi, David Bell, Joanne Lamb, Kieran Greer

Object-Oriented Database Systems I

DOEF: A Dynamic Object Evaluation Framework 662
Zhen He, Jérôme Darmont

Object Oriented Mechanisms to Rewriting Queries Using Views......... 672
Abdelhak Seriai

TVL_SE – Temporal and Versioning Language for Schema Evolution
in Object-Oriented Databases 683
Renata de Matos Galante, Nina Edelweiss, Clesio Saraiva dos Santos

Ontologies II

Building Conceptual Schemas by Refining General Ontologies 693
Jordi Conesa, Xavier de Palol, Antoni Olivé

Semantics for Interoperability 703
Trevor Bench-Capon, Grant Malcolm, Michael Shave

Object-Oriented Database Systems II

Multiple Views with Multiple Behaviours for Interoperable
Object-Oriented Database Systems................................ 713
M.B. Al-Mourad, W.A. Gray, N.J. Fiddian

Integrating Association Rule Mining Algorithms with
the F2 OODBMS 724
Lina Al-Jadir

Query Optimization I

Using User Access Patterns for Semantic Query Caching 737
Qingsong Yao, Aijun An

Exploiting Similarity of Subqueries for Complex Query Optimization 747
Yingying Tao, Qiang Zhu, Calisto Zuzarte

Workflow I

Process Data Store: A Real-Time Data Store for Monitoring
Business Processes 760
Josef Schiefer, Beate List, Robert M. Bruckner

Integrated Workflow Planning and Coordination 771
Hilmar Schuschel, Mathias Weske

Query Optimization II

Block Optimization in the Teradata RDBMS 782
Ahmad Ghazal, Ramesh Bhashyam, Alain Crolotte

Selecting Topics for Web Resource Discovery: Efficiency Issues in a
Database Approach 792
Abdullah Al-Hamdani, Gultekin Ozsoyoglu

Integrating Quality of Service into Database Systems 803
Haiwei Ye, Brigitte Kerhervé, Gregor v. Bochmann

Workflow II

Handling Dynamic Changes in Decentralized Workflow
Execution Environments 813
Vijayalakshmi Atluri, Soon Ae Chun

A QoS Oriented Framework for Adaptive Management of
Web Service Based Workflows 826
Chintan Patel, Kaustubh Supekar, Yugyung Lee

Discovering Role-Relevant Process-Views for Recommending
Workflow Information 836
Minxin Shen, Duen-Ren Liu

Knowledge Engineering I

Termination Analysis of Active Rules with Priorities 846
Alain Couchot

A Toolkit and Methodology to Support the Collaborative
Development and Reuse of Engineering Models 856
   Zdenek Zdrahal, Paul Mulholland, Michael Valasek, Phil Sainter,
   Matt Koss, Lukas Trejtnar

Security I

Secure Interoperability between Cooperating XML Systems by
Dynamic Role Translation 866
   Somchai Chatvichienchai, Mizuho Iwaihara, Yahiko Kambayashi

A Flexible Database Security System Using Multiple Access
Control Policies 876
   Min-A Jeong, Jung-Ja Kim, Yonggwan Won

Designing Secure Databases for OLS 886
   Eduardo Fernández-Medina, Mario Piattini

Knowledge Engineering II

CAML – A Universal Configuration Language for Dialogue Systems 896
   Gergely Kovásznai, Constantine Kotropoulos, Ioannis Pitas

NLC: A Measure Based on Projections 907
   Roberto Ruiz, José C. Riquelme, Jesús S. Aguilar-Ruiz

Security II

Decentralized Temporal Authorization Administration 917
   Chun Ruan, Vijay Varadharajan

Mobile Agent Watermarking and Fingerprinting:
Tracing Malicious Hosts 927
   Oscar Esparza, Marcel Fernandez, Miguel Soriano, Jose L. Muñoz,
   Jordi Forné

DEXA Position Paper

A Quick Review: What Have Been Presented at DEXA
International Conferences? 937
   Tran Khanh Dang, Roland Wagner, A Min Tjoa

Author Index 943

Policy Based Enterprise (Active) Information Integration

Mukesh Mohania[1] and Inderpal Narang[2]

[1] IBM India Research Lab,
I.I.T., Hauz Khas,
New Delhi, India
mkmukesh@in.ibm.com
[2] IBM Almaden Research Lab,
San Jose, CA, U.S.A.
narang@almaden.ibm.com

1 Introduction

For effective e-business, an enterprise must move business information among diverse sources to perform complex business transactions, and it must process business information through heterogeneous applications that may run on different platform and use different types of DBMS, etc. Moreover, to make the business processes more intelligent and reactive, an enterprise should integrate its information sources and also adapt the changes in a timely manner that might have detected automatically or semi-automatically by monitoring and analyzing the information sources, and by correlating events occurring in information sources so that timely business decision can be taken.

This timely (active) integration of information sources (or application databases) can be achieved by injecting intelligence into the information systems, and by defining the active functionality outside the information systems that describes the business logic or rules. This business logic description component is decoupled from the information sources and it describes the method of integration of information systems and how they can collaborate. For example, a business rule could be: "If a caller makes an international telephone call, then before connecting his call check whether the outstanding balance against his/her account is less than $200. If it is more, then convey the message to pay the outstanding balance before a call can be placed". This example shows the integration of two information systems (say, 'Call' database system and 'Payment' database system).

The integration of data sources is required for timely business information flow, timely business decisions, real-time consulting and marketing, etc. The solution areas that require (near) real time capabilities are (i) on-line transaction, especially in the financial sector, that require an integration of back-end operational system with the front-end information system, (ii) integration of enterprise applications with external applications (from supplier, marketing etc.), and (iii) on-line analytics integrated with operational transactions that improves the customer experience and the overall quality of transaction. Such integration will provide up-to-date, complete and consistent information for decision-making, and will reduce the operational cost, risk, and will allow greater scalability.

V. Mařík et al. (Eds.): DEXA 2003, LNCS 2736, pp. 1–7, 2003.

In this paper we discuss a framework for policy driven active integration of information sources. Policies are represented like Event-Condition-Action (ECA) rules [1] and these policies describe when to integrate data sources, under what conditions and what action need to be taken. Few examples of business policies are:

- "If the value of a transaction is less than $2 and this transaction is made by credit card, notify to the fraud detection system and send a notification to the customer service representative for calling the credit card holder immediately to check the validity of the transaction".
- If a customer has made at least 3 transactions or the total value of all transactions is more than $2000 during Christmas holidays, then offer 10% discount to the user between January 10-January 31.
- If the duration of a telephone call exceeds by more than 40 minutes, then send a notification to the fraud detection system.
- If less than 10% of the stock is sold in a retail store by the end of the week, offer a 20% discount on the non-luxury items for the next week.

In all these examples, the information flow between information systems starts based on the event occurrences. The events can be classified as customer-event (such as 1st purchase, new subscription, etc.), time-based event (such as, birthday, retirement, etc.), product-based (such as, launch of a new product, decline in sales, etc.), calendar-based (such as, Christmas, Diwali, etc.), etc.

The active functionality in the integration architecture can be seen as composition of various services, such as event composition and detection, analysis of condition, user-defined function (i.e. action) execution, information flow, triggering workflow, etc. These services can be defined in a policy that can be described using a declarative rule language, such as ECA rules [1,2].

The rest of the paper is organized as follows. There has been lot of work in active database systems, data integration and other related areas. Section 2 provides an overview of the related work. The proposed policy based information integration architecture is described in Section 3. Finally, the components of a policy are described in Section 4.

2   Related Work

Active database technology transforms passive database systems into reactive systems that respond to database and external events through the use of rule processing features [2]. Research issues for active database systems have focused on the development of active rule languages and the specification of execution models that define the semantics of rule execution [3]. Architectures for active environments have also been investigated, ranging from built-in rule processing components to layered approaches that add active capabilities to passive database systems. Active rule technology is now being extended for defining collaboration in distributed computing environments [4]. Limited versions of active rules also exist in commercial database products through the use of triggers. In [5], the authors have proposed architecture for an active data warehouse that automates the decision making of routine tasks by introducing analysis (active) rules in a data warehouse. These rules are fired at some fixed points in time or as a reaction to recent happenings.

In [6], the authors characterize four distinct types of integrations: portal integration, business-process integration, application integration, and information integration. Traditionally these integrations have been handled by custom codes. The custom-code solutions tend to be very expensive and are not flexible for future enhancements. Recently there has been a growth of middleware software, such as WebSphere MQ [7], Crosswords [8], BEA WebLogic Integrator, MS BizTalk, Web Methods Enterprise, etc in the area of business processes integration.

The problem of integration of heterogeneous databases has been addressed widely [9, 10, 11]. There are several approaches, such as the mediator approach or model-driven approach or metadata-driven approach, and all these approaches either define a global schema or model for abstracting the information content that provides a uniform interface to a collection of data sources and eliminates data model differences. A user poses the queries on the global schema to retrieve data, not to, typically, perform updates on the sources. Thus, this approach enables users to focus on specifying *what* they want rather than thinking about *how* to obtain the answers.

3 Policy Based Architecture for Information Integration

The policy based architecture for information integration is shown in Figure 1. Information integration involves the mediation of business data across multiple applications for timely business decisions. The timely integration is based on how efficiently these data sources can propagate the events that have occurred [12].

In an enterprise, typically the applications are heterogeneous in terms of the platform they run on, the type of DBMS they use, etc. Some of these applications may run on Data Stream Management System (DSMS) that allow some or all of the data being managed to come in the form of continuous, possibly very rapid, time varying, ordered data streams, or may run on XML databases, etc.Most of the time, data sources have the capabilities to define events that can be either published by the source or they can be subscribed. Some the databases on which these applications are running might not have the capability of defining triggers or publish events. In such cases, either the application code needs to be changed to detect events or to monitor the events outside the data source that are interest to integration of applications. Note that these events can be either database events or temporal events or user-defined events or external events.

Adapter and monitor are like a gateway, which on one side understands the application and on the other side understands the Integrator hub. One of the major tasks of an adapter is to exchange data between an application and the integration hub. It transforms data coming from an application in its native format to integration hub in a standard format, and vice versa. Note that a standard format is necessary to avoid all possible (i.e. n * (n-1), where n is the number of applications) transformations. The communication between an adapter and the application could be based on push or pull model. In the pull model, the adapter polls the application to catch the relevant event interest to integrator, while in the push model the application notifies of the event of interest to the adapter. The push model requires the application to be aware of event detection and notification to the adapter; in this case some changes need to be done at the application side. In the pull model, it is possible to avoid any changes in the application, however to take effective advantage of the enterprise application integration environment it may be necessary to make changes in an application.

The integration hub is responsible for executing a business task after the policy is triggered, for example change/edit a flight reservation, which could involve integration of two or more applications. It supports message routing to applications along with content transformation and formatting. A task can be either a short-running process or long-running process. The short-running process is once started it completes without any intervention (that is, the process of seamlessly passing information to all parties without manual handling or redundant processing), where as the long-running task may require human intervention and validation.

The integration hub has several components as shown in Figure 1. The event composer and detector sub-component detects events and composes the situation (composite event) as described in the event definition. Either information sources push these events to integration hub or they are polled periodically. Once an event is detected, it triggers the execution of all relevant policies. The action part of the policy describes the integration scenario, which requires interaction of different applications under certain rules. The description of an action could be in the form of a flow diagram or it could be in the form of a program. The policy execution engine executes the policy with the help of information flow engine that typically involves integrating information from different applications. The result of the policy execution is fed to the information integrator and decision analysis sub-component that may export decisions back to data sources depending on the decision rules [5].

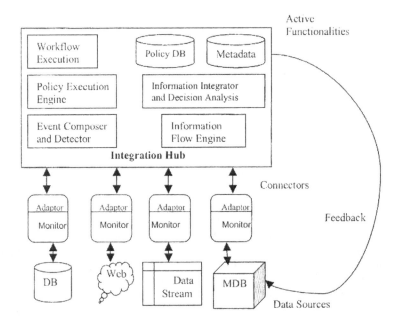

Fig 1. Information Integration Architecture

4 Policy Components

A policy driven integration framework provides effortless and autonomic integration of information, application databases and business processes. A policy can be defined using a declarative rule language that should have two different perspectives, one for the user to define policies in a very simple and intuitive way and the other for representing the policies internally for execution. As we discussed in the previous section, the policies can be defined at two levels, one at data source level and other at integrator hub level. Policies defined at data source level can be mapped to database triggers for detecting events that are interest to integration hub. When an event is happened, the data source notifies to the integrator hub via adaptor (if it is a subscription based model) about it. It may also send some data along with the event as per described in the action. Policies (i.e. business rules) defined at integration hub level trigger workflows that execute the conditional actions defined at various stages. For real-time integration, the system should have the support of advanced event definition functionalities, such as predefined external events, conditional events, rich set of database and temporal events, context based events, etc. An action in a policy can be either a user-defined or pre-defined function, such as simple message passing, to enable the automatic distribution of changes from one or more sources to one or more targets, to automate the process of archival of data, to monitor the business processes, etc.

We believe the policies can be represented using the extension of active rule language, such as of ECA (Event-Condition-Action) rules [13,14] that have been successfully introduced in operational databases as triggers for automating some tasks, where an action formulates the reaction to an event and is executed after the rule is triggered and the condition is evaluated to true. An event is defined as an instantaneous and atomic (either happens completely or not at all) point of occurrence within an application. Events can be classified as either database, temporal, or user-defined events and their type can be either primitive or composite. A context and/or lifespan can be associated with an event that describes the validity of that event and it can be specified either by time or with respect to another event. Events can be combined together using composition operators as defined in [1] to formulate complex events or situations. A time span can be associated with each composition operator within a complex event that denotes that all events combined with the operator should happen within the defined time-interval.

A policy is composed of three components:

- **Events (Detect-Evaluate)**: This consists of two sub-components namely, detection of events and condition checking on event parameters. Event condition checking is required if an event parameter is evaluated to determine whether the event is of interest to trigger an action or not. Note that this condition will be evaluated on the event parameters, not on the database states. For example, for every new transaction (event), if the transaction value is more than $20000 (condition on event parameter), send the transaction and customer details to product-promotion department.
- **Condition (Analyze-Evaluate)**: This consists of two sub-components, namely, analyze the database states and then evaluate it. All conditions must evaluate to true in order to take action. The condition expression can be either a simple expression or an SQL expression or any other user-defined function.

- **Action:** This component is responsible for defining the action (what needs to be performed) and determining the impact of the policy execution. Policies defined at data source level have simple action like message flow, etc., where as policies at integration hub level can have more complex actions that may have user-defined functions or stored procedures or workflow activation, etc. The action may utilize a set of conditions for analyzing data, which were otherwise carried out manually by analysts. These decisions may then be exported to the data sources for corrective actions.

Either the syntax of traditional ECA rules need to be extended to describe above integration policies or any other declarative rule language can be used to describe such policies. A policy is executed as follows: when a triggering event is detected at data source level, it is sent to the event composer module that composes a complex event and detects it within the time span defined for that event. Once the composite event is detected, it sends it to the policy execution engine that selects all the relevant policies from the policy database for that event. The policy execution engine executes a policy and the action part of this policy may trigger a workflow. The policy execution engine also identifies the dependencies among tasks, if any. The workflow engine executes the tasks as described in the workflow defined by the user. If it needs data from another information source for executing a task, the workflow engine sends a message (or a query) to the information flow engine that queries the respective information source through connector. In order to formulate a query, all data objects schemas and their properties are known at integration hub level and this information is stored in the metadata.

References

1. N. W. Paton and O. Diaz, "Active Database Systems", ACM Computing Surveys, 31(1): 63–103, March 1999
2. ACT-NET Consortium, "The Active Database Management System Manifesto: A Rulebase of ADBMS Features", ACM SIGMOD Record, vol. 25, no. 3, Sept 1996
3. E. Simon and A. Dittrich, "Promises and Realities of Active Database Systems", Proceedings of the 21ˢᵗ VLDB Conference, Zurich, 1995, pp. 642–653
4. G. Bultzingsloewen, A. Koschel, P. Lockemann, H. Walter, "ECA Functionality in a Distributed Environment", Proceeding of International Conference on Active Rules in Database Systems, Springer Verlag, 1999
5. T. Thalhammer, M. Schrefl, and M. Mohania, "Active Data Warehouses: Complementing OLAP with Active Rules", Journal of Data and Knowledge Engineering, 39(3): 241–268, December 2001
6. A.D. Jhingran, N. Mattos, and H. Pirahesh, "Information Integration: A Research Agenda", IBM Systems Journals, 41(4): 555–562, 2002
7. http://www-3.ibm.com/software/integration/wmqwf/
8. http://www-3.ibm.com/software/integration/cw/
9. Jeffrey D. Ullman, "Information integration using logical views", Journal of Theoretical Computer Science, 239(2): 189–210, 2000
10. D. Calvanese, G. De Giacomo, et al., "Integration in Data Warehousing", International Journal of Cooperative Information Systems, 10(3): 237–271, 2001
11. L. Jouise, K. Passi, S. Madria, and M. Mohania, "XML Schema Integration to Facilitate E-Commerce", (Book Chapter), Web-Enabled Systems Integration, published by Idea Group Publishing, pages 66–90, 2003

12. A. Carzaniga, "Architectures for an Event Notification Service Scalable to Wide-Area Network", Ph.D. thesis, Politecnico di Milano, Italy, 1998
13. U. Dayal, S. Chakravarthy et al., "The HiPAC project: Combining active databases and timing constraints", ACM SIGMOD Record 17(1): 51–70, March 1988
14. M. Cilia and A. Buchmann, "An Active Functionality Service for E-Business Applications", ACM SIGMOD Record 31(1): 24–30, March 2002

SOFT – Generating Highly Flexible Object Code from XML Specifications

Alun Butler[1,2], Liz Bacon[1], and Mohamed Ibrahim[1]

[1] University of Greenwich,
School of Computing and Mathematical Sciences,
London, SE10 9LS, United Kingdom
{E.Bacon,M.T.Ibrahim}@gre.ac.uk
[2] Abbtec Contract Ltd.,
12 Meadowcourt Road,
London, SE3 9DY, United Kingdom
abbtec@talk21.com

Abstract. Many code generation tools exist to aid developers in carrying out common mappings, such as from Object to XML or from Object to relational database. Such generated code tends to possess a high binding between the Object code and the target mapping, making integration into a broader application tedious or even impossible. In this paper we suggest XML technologies and the multiple inheritance capabilities of interface based languages such as Java, offer a means to unify such executable specifications, thus building complete, consistent and useful object models declaratively, without sacrificing component flexibility.

1 Introduction

Existing code generating tools attempt to move the developer from design to usable code in a single process. At the present time such tools typically generate code that is either so general as to be trivial or so highly bound to a particular purpose that utilising the generated code in any other context requires more work than would have been involved in simply hand crafting code from scratch.

Generating Tool
Design Specification $\longrightarrow$ Executable Specification

Fig. 1. A Design Specification is parsed by a Generating Tool which produces executable code.

During the process of attempting to design and build such a tool it was discovered that a number of approaches could significantly increase the flexibility and re-usability of the generated executable specifications. Once evolved, this flexibility also indicated some of the components an Object Oriented Design Specification Language would require to be truly useful in multiple contexts. Some of these approaches are the subject of this paper.

V. Mařík et al. (Eds.): DEXA 2003, LNCS 2736, pp. 8–17, 2003.

When coding an object Type, the Object Oriented developer will consider the Type's properties, behaviours and the Type's relationship to other Types in the whole system. Very often the developer will also be required to write code to persist and retrieve an object instance's properties to and from a relational database, or marshal and unmarshal the object from an XML document, or even display and gather those object properties in an HTML document or other GUI Form. In each of these various expressions, the developer must ensure suitable transformation and validation code is formulated and appropriate feed-back is provided in the event of error. Many of the constraints, relationships, trans-formations and validations associated with properties form part of the original Type design and should be mirrored across any property accesses in any context, but to enforce this will require that the developer does more than lift a finger.

Thus an `Order` Type with a public property `orderDate` is likely, *all things being equal*, to have a similarly named field defined in the database to which it will be saved and a similarly named attribute in a XML document. When displayed in a GUI Form, one might well expect a text box displaying the order date next to a label bearing the legend "Order Date". If the property cannot be set to null on the original object, a no nulls constraint should, *all things being equal*, form part of its relational database persistence specification.

Unfortunately rarely are "all things" equal. In the database or XML docu-ment the `orderDate` property may be represented by three fields for date, month and year. Language and other locale specific forces may alter the display repre-sentation of `orderDate` in an XML or HTML document. There are innumerable reasons why a particular property of an object should or should not be visible in any given context.

Related but distinct formats that have different concerns and priorities be-yond the initial object they reflect. Where this occurs there is said to be an "Impedance Mismatch" between the initial object format and the target repre-sentation [3]. The key example here is the persistence of an object instance in a relational database. Hand coding such translations is uninteresting, error prone and often application dependent (for example SQL that works in one RDMS (Relational Database Management System) will often not work in another).

In the second section of this paper we will discuss some existing tools designed to overcome these challenges and the limitations of current tools.

In section 3 we will discuss alternative approaches developed whilst designing a prototype code generation tool called "Entity Builder". Initially designed to ease the translation from an object to that object's XML representation, the authors have identified some ground rules for good generated code, that, if more widely adopted will substantially increase the interoperability, flexibility and power of all generated code. More substantially, these approaches, centred as they are around intrinsically structured, extensible extremely terse XML based specifications, allow a single point of contact between the developer's notion of the object class and its various representations (relational, XML, HTML, UML, ERD).

In section 3.1 we will look at how a XML based Object Design Specification must look to evolve usable executable code. In section 3.2 we briefly will consider how interface based generated code meets the desired goal of flexible reusable code. In section 3.3 we consider some of the inheritance possibilities working to interface allows, and some of the constraints good design imposes. In section 4 we will look at the limitations of the proposed model. In section 5 we will consider possible future work.

2   Existing Generators

Generational tools to create object code and/or aid mapping to external formats (such as XML or a relational database) are called Object Binding tools. They fall into three main categories.

– Graphical Tools (such as UML, ERD)
– Reflective Tools (reflecting on existing compiled code).
– Specification based Tool (often based on XML Schema or Database Schema).

Graphical approaches such as UML (Unified Modelling Language) and ERD (Entity Relationship Diagrams) aim to aid the developer in this process, and such tools will generate code for a prototype application based on the created diagram (for example Rational Software's *Rational Rose* and TogetherSoft's *Together*).

Graphical approaches tend to be somewhat heavyweight and as the hand written portions of the code increase, there is a tendency for the diagrams and the code to diverge. GUI based tools tend to lack terseness in the representation of the data model. Even simple UML diagrams can fill many virtual desktops – creating a complexity that fails to illuminate the underlying object metaphor. To make matters worse, no two UML tools (let alone an ERD or ORM tools) have any real degree of interoperability [6].

Reflective approaches rely on property naming semantics (as in JavaBeans) or defined properties such as in the .Net family of languages. Reflective techniques typically severely limit user configuration, or require a considerable degree of non terse user intervention to achieve configurable output.

The alternative approach – direct code generation – does not necessarily buy you any further abilities to configure output. JAXB (the Java™ API for XML Binding [http://java.sun.com/xml/jaxb/index.html].) generates object code that will produce one and one only XML-ised representation of the underlying object. Because of the structure of the generated code (the XML method is in a single code block), the only way to intervene in the output is to physically alter the generated code in situ, which means that each cycle of change (altering the XML specification and regenerating the code) will entail hand altering the new generated code. The design of the XML serialization code means it is not possible to override the key method in a subclass and – for example – exclude a field from output because the code directly accesses private member variables.

Similar problems occur with perhaps the most widely used XML to object binding tool for Java, Castor [http://castor.exolab.org/] and in Microsoft implementation for .Net, XSD [http://msdn.microsoft.com].

JAXB, Castor and .Net all use XML Schemas as their fundamental specification. In supporting the many XML Schema constructs this specification language is overly expressive in some areas – and fails in others (e.g. id reference pairs). XML Schemas were designed to specify and constrain XML documents, not Object Models, meaning the supplied schemas must be augmented with substantial further mark up to generate usable code. All are essentially serialisation mechanisms with inflexible support for alternative serialized representations.

3   Entity Builder – An Alternative Approach

Entity Builder was conceived as a code generation tool that generated JavaBeans classes and highly configurable Object to XML serialization code. Interfaces were deliberately designed to allow adjacent development of Object to SQL or to HTML (or other GUI) producing code. The generating specification should be written in XML so that amendments and additions could be made as simply as possible and to provide an inherent level of interoperability.

Consider a simple Bean centric interface with three properties (take Address to be a given complex object type).

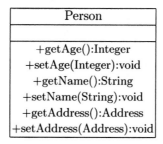

Person
+getAge():Integer
+setAge(Integer):void
+getName():String
+setName(String):void
+getAddress():Address
+setAddress(Address):void

There are many ways to represent this using XML (especially with respect to the distribution of attributes versus elements). Consider the table 1. In all cases the underlying model remains the same, but the expression is very different. This has been put forward as a reason for why XML/DTD are not suitable vehicles for Object Modelling [2].

Similarly, the specification language used by Entity Builder (henceforth referred to as EBS – for Entity Builder Specification [Language]) needed to be able to represent itself in various ways while the underlying model remained unambiguous. A number of procedures for designing EBS, and any other XML based Object Design Specification Language, simplified this process.

3.1   Guidelines for an XML Based Object Design Specification Language

Many of the guidelines given below reflect an object centric ambivalence with respect to document parsing efficiency in any EBS (a governing factor in the

Table 1. Possible XML representations of Person

DTD	Sample Output Document

`<!ELEMENT person (age, name, address)>`
`<!ELEMENT age (#PCDATA)>`
`<!ELEMENT name (#PCDATA)>`
	`<person>`
	`  <age>15</age>`
	`  <name>Harry Potter</name>`
	`  <address>... </address>`
	`</person>`

`<!ELEMENT person (address)>`
`<!ATTLIST person`
`   age  NMTOKEN #REQUIRED`
`   name CDATA   #REQUIRED>`
	`<person age="15"`
	`  name="Harry Potter">`
	`  <address>... </address>`
	`</person>`

design for XML Schema). In an EBS clarity, terseness and correctness should always take precedence over efficiency.

Guideline 1. Prefer attributes to elements when defining your model. Choose an element only when the data type of the underlying model is sufficiently compound that any alternative representation would entail rules that fall outside the scope of traditional DTD. Even then, if such rules are simple enough and greatly reduce document complexity, without sacrificing meaning, such a design may be accepted (see Guideline 2 and Guideline 3) with the following caveat – compound attributes with N compound properties – for example `occurs="1,2"` (meaning the element must occur between one and two times) must always have been defined elsewhere in terms of an element with N properties. In the example given a further construct for occurs, for which the instance document is `<occurs minOccurs="1" maxOccurs="2">`, would have been defined).

In EBS – unlike DTD and XML Schema – it is illegal to define core objects with identical attribute and element names *unless* they refer to the same underlying property. Within the Object world, where an object is constructed and then further properties and sub-properties set, such a construct mirrors common practice. Thus in EBS it is possible to specify an attribute with the same name as a sub element, but if both are present, the element will be providing additional information for the attribute – not denoting a separate object.

Guideline 2. Choose an Element when the one to many relationship between parent and child object is not confined to a unique scalar data type. Thus an attribute defined like this `years="1984,1905,1695"` would be acceptable because the construct defines a comma separated list of years (a single scalar data type).

Guideline 3. When specifying composite attributes, they must be unambiguously resolvable using named capturing blocks in regular expressions. An example of named capturing blocks along with a sample of a plausible prototype for EBS follows.

Named Capturing Blocks. Named capturing blocks do not form part of the default Regular Expression pattern matching API for Java (indeed the library known to the authors to support them natively is Microsoft's .Net R.E. Library).

Fortunately the algorithm for converting names to numbered capturing blocks is not onerous. Named capturing blocks are defined between an opening and closing bracket (indicating what is to be captured), are escaped by a "?" and the name itself is defined between '<' and '>' brackets "(?<[aCapturingName]>[aRegex])". Imagine we define in our specification language an item for "occurs" (indicating how often an element or attribute may occur). This is how it might look.

```
<elem name="occurs" children="maxOccurs?, minOccurs?"
pattern="^(?&lt;minOccurs&gt;[\d]+),(?&lt;maxOccurs&gt;[\d]+)$" >
    <att name="minOccurs?" classType="int"   defaultValue="1" />
    <att name="maxOccurs?" classType="int" defaultValue="1"/>
</elem>
```

The escaped '<' and '>' signs makes that pattern look unpleasant, but resolved the pattern is "^(?<minOccurs>[\d]+),(?<maxOccurs>[\d]+)$". The regular expression without capturing blocks is simply ^([\d]+),([\d]+)$ which means find the start of a string, find one or more numbers and save them, skip over a comma (which must be present), save one or more numbers which must be immediately followed by the end of the string. The ?<minOccurs> is a named capturing block and directs the application to take the contents of the captured block and apply it to the property of that name.

Now it is possible for the instance document to represent an Occurs in a number of ways. The traditional element.

```
<occurs>
      <minOccurs>0</minOccurs>
      <maxOccurs>10</maxOccurs>
</occurs>
```

As an inline element

```
<occurs>0,10</occurs>
```

Or even as a child attribute.

```
<elemNode name="upToTen" occurs="0,10" />
```

Questions of determinism and reversibility can arise in such cases, and mechanisms must exist to allow document only schemas passed to document parsers to restrict possibilities. Named capturing blocks can tempt users to effectively develop their own mark-up language, undermining the intrinsic advantages of XML as a generalized representational medium. With power comes responsibility – caveat emptor!

This open minded approach to XML means the specification language for the object model can be extremely terse. It means DTD like constructs such as '+' '*' and '?' can be included inline in the specification document. Named capturing blocks substantially diminish the tension caused by making the choice between attributes and elements. The choice between the two being decided broadly based on clarity and terseness – these two principles should always be fundamental building blocks for any declarative language. In either case the generated interface is the same.

Guideline 4. Recognise that in XML, some elements (and thus attributes) exist as naming placeholders, rather than as full blown objects in their own right.

This last guideline deserves some further explanation. The classic example is a DTD along these lines

```
<!ELEMENT order (deliveryAddress, customerAddress, orderItems) >
<!ELEMENT deliveryAddress (address) >
<!ELEMENT customerAddress (address) >
<!ELEMENT orderItems (orderItem+) >
<!-specification for orderItem and address would follow -->
```

Now a moments inspection indicates that `deliveryAddress` and `customer-Address` are merely placeholders for the true type of the element (which is `Address`). Each outer element acts as a convenient name to distinguish two instances of the same type. A similar example of this placeholder mechanism (this time for a collection) exists in the example orderItems element of the order specification. In the former case two bean methods would be generated – callable directly on the enclosing order instance.

```
public void setDeliveryAddress(Address address)
public Address getDeliveryAddress()
public void setCustomerAddress(Address address)
public Address getCustomerAddress()
```

In the latter case a single collection would be referenced – the default collection type being List – and associated bean methods would be generated and directly available to be called on the Order object.

```
public List getOrderItemsAsList();
public OrderItem getOrderItem(int index);
public OrderItem[] getOrderItems();
public boolean hasOrderItems(); //other list methods follow
```

It was discovered that identifying such "pass through" elements could be achieved entirely through introspecting on the XML specification without the need for any further clumsy mark-up.

Guideline 5. Where a one to one relationship exists between parent and child elements (attributes), the possibility of a shared interface comes into being. The implication of this is explored in sections 3.2 and 3.3.

In summary, the concentration of Guidelines 1 – 3 on attributes over elements effectively licence non atomic attributes. Now the term atomic is uncomfortable to us – as with others [5] – but only because what is atomic in one context is not in another (dates being examples of concepts that can be implemented from a single atomic field, but which are composite and complex). The true level of atomicity of any property will be application dependent, but it is an article of faith that any composite property within the realised context of an application will – in time – need to be broken into its composing structure. Attributes and Named Capturing Blocks encourage the designer to take this step early.

Attribute based property specification are more attuned to the Object Oriented way of looking at the world, where, in contrast to the relational model for example, one to one relationships are the rule and relationships are typically navigable parent to child rather than bi-directional.

3.2   Type Interfaces

Early in the design it became clear that the most flexible programming model exposed interfaces rather than concrete classes to client code. Thus a method returning the `Occurs` object, would appear to client code as an interface `Occurs` with two properties, rather than as a concrete class. This allowed a complete separation of concerns from representation specific implementation code.

Using Java's inner classes meant concrete classes could expose multiple interfaces (n for XML, n for SQL etc.). Shared code can be concentrated in superclasses, exposed through shared interfaces and implemented through private delegate inner classes. Java's forthcoming adoption of Generics (effectively C++ templates) has offered new opportunities and the authors plan to publish a separate paper shortly, describing their approach in the light of Generic facilities.

3.3   Inheritance

The issues arising from inheritance are still under investigation. The flexibility associated with multiple inheritance is often viewed with suspicion as the complexity of indirection acts as a barrier to bug tracking and general comprehension. In this case, the hackneyed nature of display code and the clarity added by clearly defined interfaces mitigate strongly against these issues. Nevertheless flexibility requires responsibility and a number of concerns are clear.

- The member variable holding the values exposed through public bean methods should be private access level e.g.

```
private int age; //this should be private - no excuses!
public int getAge(){ return age;    }
public void setAge(int age){ this.age = age;}
```

  No code – not even representation code – should have access to these private members. This is in sharp contrast to Sun's JAXB which, by default, leaves member access as 'protected' – this is bad practice with inevitable indeterminate consequences. See section 4.
- Representation code should be delineated down to the level of individual properties and have method visibility of at least protected, so that subclasses can intervene in a fine grained manner. Large blocks of persistence code (as in JAXB) are too inflexible.
- Generated object should fully implement the equals method contract based on the core property interface. Critically this means that if an attribute is added to the interface in a interface subclass e.g.

```
public interface Employee extends Person{
  public Job getJob();
  public void setJob(Job job);
} //Employee adds an aspect to Persons
```

then the implementing class cannot directly inherit from the implementing concrete class because this will force a breakdown of the transitivity of the equals contract [1]. Inheritance can still be achieved by allowing Interfaces inheritance and concrete implementing classes to delegate to contained classes (so Employee will delegate to a contained Person for all Person properties and methods). It should be noted that subclasses are free to add non aspect members (i.e. members that do not contribute to object equivalence). Similarly specific interface equivalence methods can be generated e.g.

```
public boolean personEquals(Person person).
```

– It is desirable to offer multiple interface inheritance to XML specified hierarchies. Experience demonstrated that using an XML based specification language meant that our object definitions became increasingly fine grained, with small groups of properties being associated with many object types. Where the relationship is one to one, it is often desirable for parent elements to implement the contained Types public interface, to simplify method calls. Thus if a Postcode class has these properties – postcodeString, mapRefX, mapRefY - it may be desirable for the owning Address class to fully implement the accessor interface for these properties, even if in fact all calls are passed directly down to a contained PostcodeType instance. In these cases the enclosing class must always act as a pure proxy, not persisting any member state in its own variables but always delegating to the owned class.

4 Limitations and Options

The gains of adopting the open architecture described are substantially increased flexibility within a type safe model. However such flexibility is not free – there may be performance costs associated with naive generated code. The quid pro quo is correctness.

JAXB directly accesses member variables. One can only imagine Sun's excellent programming team adopted this blunder because of performance concerns – but correctness should rarely be sacrificed for performance – and never in generated code. Adopters of a generating technology are always free to hand craft their own representation code if performance proves to be an issue. This is particularly true of representation code – where performance bottlenecks are far more likely to arise from IO operations than from costs associated with invoking method calls. Hot spot compilers can further optimize running code.

Generating against interfaces, leaves substantial freedom to change the implementation class logic. C.J. Date [3] has indicated how known constraints can give clues to optimisers, for example a field or collection of fields marked as "identity" means search and sort algorithms can be effectively indexed on those values. Similarly the structure of XML can give clues to representation coding design.

5 Conclusions and Future Work

Writers such as Date [4] have advocated applications driven purely on declarative languages (for example, variations on Date and Darwen's relationally correct SQL variant – Tutorial D [5]). Fully realised applications are always likely to depend on some custom coding, but that XML base specifications can move a long way towards the goal of declaratively mapped, enterprise level object tools.

At this time a prototype reference implementation has been built of a code generator capable of producing defined objects and their XML representations. Work is proceeding on producing SQL and HTML bound code, in codifying the specification language (EBS) and defining an effective inheritance model.

In the long run optimisation methods along the lines described in section 4 needs to be researched. Date's work is in the context of an object-like relational database. The authors believe more substantial progress may be made with an object-centric application layer that is more relational in its internal structure. In either case, an XML based declarative design language allows flexible and adaptable executable specifications with a high degree of internal structural correctness.

The main contribution of this paper is indicating how to generate flexible executable specifications. We have built a prototype as a proof of this concept. We have also proposed several guidelines for XML based Object Design Specification Languages. Future work will involve an investigation of multiple inheritance and related issues in the context of flexible generated code.

References

1. Bloch, Joshua.: Effective Java. Addison Wesley USA (2001).
2. Cover, Robin.: SGML/XML Elements versus Attributes, When Should I Use Elements, and When Should I Use Attributes? (2000). (Available from
   http://www.oasis-open.org/cover/elementsAndAttrs.html.
   Accessed 30th March 2002)
3. Date, C.J.: An Introduction to Database Systems (Seventh Edition). Addison-Wesley Publishing Company (2000).
4. Date, C.J.: What Not How. The Business Rules Approach to Application Development. Addison-Wesley Publishing Company (2000).
5. Date, C.J., Darwen, Hugh.: Foundation for Future Database Systems – The Third Manifesto (Second Edition). Addison-Wesley Publishing Company (2000).
6. Holub, Allen: When it comes to good OO design, keep it simple. JavaWorld (January 2002). (Available from
   http://www.javaworld.com/javaworld/jw-01-2002/jw-0111-ootools.html+.
   Accessed January 2003)

Querying Semistructured Data Efficiently

Hongsik Rho, Wen-Chi Hou, Dunren Che, and Chih-Fang Wang

Dept. of Computer Science
Southern Illinois University
Carbondale, IL 62901
{hou,dche,cfw}@cs.siu.edu

Abstract. In this paper, we address the issue of fast query processing of semistructured data. To this end, we propose a new index scheme, called the HQ-Index. The HQ-Index consists of two indexes, the H-Index and Q-Index. The H-Index is basically a hash table built upon the path expressions. It serves as a path index. The Q-Index facilitates fast traversal to the ancestor nodes in the graph and the retrieval of requested information. Not only the H-Index and Q-Index have very simple index structures, but also the combined use of them can effectively speed up the evaluation of ordinary path queries. The results of our experiments further confirm the advantage of our approach when compared with the Dataguide, one of the most referenced index schemes for XML and semistructured data.

1 Introduction

With increasing popularity of XML as a standard for data representation and exchange, XML data is drawing more and more attentions from the database community. XML documents are now an important and growing source of the semistructured data. In a semistructured data model, data is usually modeled as an edge-labeled graph in which nodes correspond to objects or values, and edges to elements or attributes. Therefore, in a native XML database, a document is usually stored as a tree (called the source database) as it is a natural realization of the data model. Consequently, queries on such databases often involve a great deal of path traversals (or graph navigation). To facilitate query processing, indexes on paths are often built to help find paths quickly. Some notable path indexes include Dataguide [5], 1-indexes [6], Index Fabrics [3], 2-indexes [6], and APEX [1].

In this paper, we address the issue of efficient query processing in semistructured databases, XML databases in particular. To achieve this, we propose a new index scheme, called the HQ-Index. The HQ-Index consists of two indexes, the H-Index and the Q-Index. The H-Index is basically a hash table built on path expressions. It summarizes the path structure of the database and serves as a path index. The Q-Index facilitates fast traversal to the ancestor nodes and the retrieval of requested information. In comparison, our H-Index is equivalent in function to Dataguide (Pindex) of LORE, while the Q-Index is similar to the value index (Vindex), label index (Lindex), and edge index (Bindex) of LORE [7] combined. Not only is our HQ-index simple, but it also adequately facilitates fast query evaluation.

V. Mařík et al. (Eds.): DEXA 2003, LNCS 2736, pp. 18–27, 2003.
© Springer-Verlag Berlin Heidelberg 2003

We have implemented the HQ-Index scheme and compared its performance with the Dataguide, the most referenced path index scheme, using different types of queries with both real world and synthetic data sets. The performance results showed that our HQ-Index is much faster and is not sensitive to changes of data.

The rest of the paper is organized as follows. Section 2 briefly reviews some current path index schemes, including the Dataguide, Naïve index, 1-index, and 2-index. Section 3 describes the structure of our HQ-Index, followed by experiments in Section 4. Section 5 discusses generalization of the HQ-index for dealing with regular path expressions, and Section 6 concludes this paper.

2 Related Work

In the following, we shall briefly describe some notable indexes for path expressions, which include the Naïve index, 1-index, and the Dataguide.

2.1 Naïve Index

The naïve guide classifies the nodes in the graph based on the concept of language equivalence relation. Let languages L_u and L_v be label paths from root to nodes u and v, respectively. Then, nodes u and v are in the language equivalence relation if $L_u = L_v$. The equivalence class of u, denoted by [u], is thus represented by the language L_u and the set of nodes v such that $L_u = L_v$. The latter is called the extent of [u], denoted by extent ([u]).

A Naïve index consists of the set of all distinct equivalence classes $[c_i]$, $1 \le i \le k \le$ n, where n is the total number of nodes in the source database and k is the total number of equivalence classes. A query is evaluated by simply iterating over all the classes $[c_i]$, $1 \le i \le k$, to see if a query label path is the same as the corresponding language Lc_i or not. One drawback of this approach is the high cost of index construction and index search.

2.2 Dataguide

LORE [5] [7] employs several indexes to facilitate query processing, which includes a Dataguide (Pindex), a value index (Vindex), a label index (Lindex), and an edge index (Bindex). The Dataguide [5] is developed to summarize the structure of the paths in a LORE database and used as the path index. The Dataguide is accurate in the sense that every label path in the data source appears in the Dataguide, and the converse is true, too. It is also concise because Dataguide describes every label path of the source exactly once. It is noted that each node in a Dataguide essentially corresponds to an equivalence class. Such a Dataguide can be built by going over the source database in a depth-first fashion.

Once candidate nodes are found using the Dataguide, LORE uses three other indexes to examine nodes and retrieve results. The Vindex is used to find atomic objects satisfying the conditions specified in the query. The Lindex finds all parents of an object via an edge with a given label, and the Bindex supports finding all parent-child object pairs connected by a specified label [McHu 99].

2.3 1-Index

The 1-index [6] is based on the concept of bisimulation. A binary relation ~ between two nodes v and v' is called a bisimulation, denoted v ~ v', and is defined as follows:(1) If v ~ v' and v is a root, then v' is a root, too. Conversely, if v ~ v' and v' is a root, then v is a root. (2) If v ~ v', then for any edge e from u to v, there exists an edge e from u' to v' such that u ~ u'. Conversely, if v ~ v', then for any edge e from u' to v', there exists an edge e from u to v such that u ~ u'.

The equivalence class based on the bisimulation needs to be computed for each node. It is noted that Dataguide and 1-index in many cases are identical even though different equivalence relation definitions are used. Therefore, the construction and computation cost is often the same or close to each other.

3 HQ-Index Scheme

In this section, we describe the HQ-Index scheme, which includes a hash index (H-Index) and a query index (Q-Index). Given a query, we first use the H-Index to find nodes matching the query paths in the source database. Then, we use the Q-Index to check if these nodes satisfy specified conditions and retrieve requested information.

3.1 The H-Index

The H-Index is a hash table. It serves as a path index. Each element of the table contains a status, a path name, and the set of nodes on that path (which is called the *target set* of the path). The H-Index can be easily built by traversing the source database in, say, pre- or post-order, and hashing each distinct path, along with the end nodes of the path, to an entry of the table. Figure 2 shows a snapshot of the H-Index derived from the data source in Figure 1.

Let us consider the query **"SELECT /University/Professor/Name WHERE /University/Professor/Dept. = 'Computer Science'"**, expressed in a relational query format with path expressions. Clearly, using the H-Index constructed from Figure 1, we can quickly find that nodes 7 and 10 are on the *condition path* University/Professor/Dept of the query. In addition, we also find nodes 6 and 9, called candidate result nodes, are on the *result path* University/Professor/Name of the query. The purpose of the H-index here is to find the two sets of nodes {7, 10} and {6, 9} quickly for further examination.

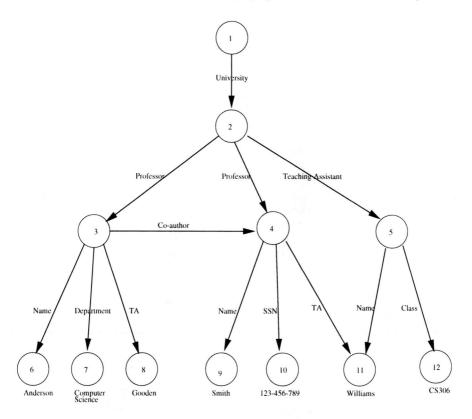

Fig. 1. An example OEM source university database

Status	Path Name	Node IDs
Occupied	University	2
Occupied	University /Professor/Name	6, 9
Occupied	University /Professor/Dept.	7, 10
Unoccupied		
Occupied	University /Professor	3, 4
Unoccupied		
Occupied	University/Professor/TA	8, 11
Occupied	University /Professor/Co-author	4

Fig. 2. H-Index

3.2 The Q-Index

Nodes 7 and 10 are further checked with the condition **University/Professor/Dept. = 'Computer Science'**. It is found that only node 7 satisfies the condition. To find the query result, we only need to identify nodes in {6, 9} that are "relevant" to node 7. This process requires backtracking to their respective ancestors at the University/Professor level, which is the common portion of the paths of University/Professor/Name and University/Professor/Dept (to decide which of the result candidates are related to node 7).

We propose the Q-Index to facilitate backward traversal and examination of node values. So, the Q-Index, as shown in Fig. 3, is essentially an array of backward pointers. Node ID (or number) is used as an index into the array. For each node, we store the parent IDs and a pointer to the text value of the node in the source database. For simplicity, we show the actual text value instead of the pointer to it in the Fig. 3.

After node 7 is identified from the H-Index, we locate the entry for node 7 in the Q-Index (using the node number as an index into the array). From the text value of this entry, node 7 is found satisfying the query condition (i.e., = 'Computer Science'). To find nodes relevant to node 7, we backtrack to University/Professor, which is the common portion of University/Professor/Dept and University/Professor/Name. From node 7, we backtrack to node 3; from nodes 6, and 9, we backtrack to nodes 3 and 4, respectively. So, we have found that node 7 and node 6 have the same parent (or ancestor, in general) at University/Professor. As a result, only node 6 qualifies as a result node, and the "Pointer to Text Value" of node 6 (i.e., 'Anderson') is returned.

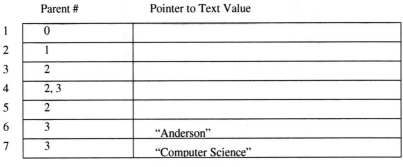

	Parent #	Pointer to Text Value
1	0	
2	1	
3	2	
4	2, 3	
5	2	
6	3	"Anderson"
7	3	"Computer Science"

Fig. 3. Q-index

3.3 Query Evaluation

In general, there are two types of queries, one with a WHERE conditional clause and the other without the WHERE clause. Some differences exist in the evaluation. In the above sections, we have demonstrated how a query of the first type is executed. Now, we shall consider a query without a WHERE clause.

Let us consider the query: "**SELECT /University/Professor/TA**" as an example. First, we find the entry in the H-Index for the path "**University/Professor/TA**". Through the "Node ID" field of the entry, we find nodes 8 and 11 are on this path.

Since no condition is specified, the text values of these nodes are returned as the query result (i.e., Gooden and Williams) after the simple look-up in the Q-Index.

The following algorithms summarize the evaluation of a query of the form "SELECT result-path WHERE condition". For simplicity, we assume there are no logical operators AND and/or OR in the WHERE clause.

Algorithm QEval (*result-path, condition*)
Begin
      find the set of nodes on the *result-path*, denoted **R**; //using the H-Index;
if(condition == NULL) then
      begin
      for each node in R
return its text value; //using the Q-Index;
end;
else
begin
      extract the path name from the *condition*, called *condition-path*;
      find the set of nodes that meet the *condition*, denoted **C**;
                //using the H-Index and Q-Index
      For each node in C
         find its nearest ancestor on the common portion of the
         condition-path and *result-path*, and add this node to **A**;
         //using the Q-Index
      For each node n in R
         Begin
            find its nearest ancestor on the common portion of the
            condition-path and *result-path*, denoted **a**;
            //using the Q-Index
        if (a is in A) return n;
    end
    end
    End.

For WHERE clauses that contain AND and/or OR logical operators, we can evaluate each condition separately and then use the intersection and/or union operations to obtain the results satisfying the overall conditions. For example, for a query like **"SELECT /University/Professor/Name WHERE /University/Professor/Dept.= 'Computer Science'** AND **/University/Professor/TA = 'Williams'** ", we shall get node 7 and node 11 for the two conditions in the WHERE clause, respectively. Since the query requests for University/Professor/Name, we backtrack to their parent nodes, (i.e., nodes 3 and 4, respectively) to see if there are any intersections between the two (sets) of parent nodes. Since there is no intersection, the query results in an empty set. If the intersection were not an empty set, then we shall go down the tree to get results following the "result-path". As for the OR operator, instead of taking an intersection, we shall perform a union operation.

4   Experiments

As explained earlier in Section 3.4, Dataguide and 1-index are faster than the naïve index and 2-index. Therefore, in the experimental study, we shall exclude the latter for comparisons. As for the Dataguide and 1-index, they basically behave the same due to similarity in structures, but the Dataguide is more concise. Therefore, in this section, we compare only with the Dataguide, which is also the most referenced path index in the literature. As for the Q-index, since it is much simpler and more efficient than the Lindex, Bindex, and Vindex combined, we shall not compare it with the combined scheme. To the best of our knowledge, there is no other data structure formally proposed for the same task. Therefore, we shall only show the performance of the Q-index here.

We have implemented the HQ-Index scheme and Dataguide in C++ programming language. For simplicity, all data structures are stored in memory. Experiments were performed on Pentium III 864 MHz CPU with 64 MB memory, running on a Microsoft Windows ME. The XML parser for the Windows version [8] was used to parse XML data, and the DOM (Document Object Model) API [4] from a W3C Recommendation is used to form the structure of documents.

In the following, we first describe the data sets used in the experiments, types of queries posed, and then the performance results.

4.1 Data Sets

Two different data sets have been used to evaluate the performance. One is a real world application data set from the plays of Shakespeare [2], and the other is a small synthetic data set, which we call Authors. The size of the Shakespeare play is 156 KB; the tags include <PLAY>, <ACT>, <TITLE>, <SCENE>, <SPEECH>, <SPEAKER>, <LINE>, <PERSONA>, <SUBHEAD>, and so on. As for the Authors data set, its initial size is 1.4 KB; the tags include <AUTHOR>, <FIRSTNAME>, <LASTNAME>, <LOCATION>, and <STATE>, where <LOCATION> has an attribute ZIP. While Shakespeare is deeply nested, the Authors is shallow and narrow in structure. In order to observe the effect of the structures of data, we expanded the original Authors data set "horizontally" and "vertically" later in the experiments. All data sets are stored as in-memory databases.

4.2 Types of Queries

A query may have a conditional WHERE clause or not. Here are some examples of the two types of query formulated to evaluate the performance.

Type I: Queries that do not have a WHERE clause.
(a).   Example 1: **SELECT /PLAY/ACT/SCENE/SPEECH/SPEAKER**
(b).   Example 2: **SELECT /AUTHORS/AUTHOR/LOCATION/ZIP**

Type II: Queries that have a WHERE clause.
(a).   Example 3: **SELECT /PLAY/ACT/SCENE/SPEECH/LINE WHERE
        PLAY/ACT/SCENE/SPEECH/SPEAKER='ADRIAN'.**

(b).   Example 4: **SELECT AUTHORS/AUTHOR/LOCATION/ZIP WHERE WHERE AUTHOR/LASTNAME='SMITH'.**

4.3 Performance Results

For each type of query, we generate multiple sample queries, and for each sample query we run 10,000 times to measure the performance. The average execution times for different types of queries obtained with the Dataguide, H-Index and Q-index on the Shakespeare data set are shown in the Table 1.

Table 1. Path Index Execution Time on Shakespeare Data Set

	Dataguide (μs)	H-Index (μs)	Q-Index (μs)
Type I Query	63	7	12
Type II Query	310	9	203

It is observed that our H-Index is 9 to 34 times faster than the Dataguide. The results show the effectiveness of our H-Index. Another factor that contributes to this huge disparity is the structure of the data, recalling that a deeply nested and wide structure could adversely affect the Dataguide, but not ours.

To examine nodes and retrieve final results using the Q-index, it took 9 and 203 μs for Types I and II queries, respectively. The Type II queries require significantly more time than Type I in traversal mainly due to the complexity of the queries itself, recalling that Type II has a WHERE statement and the result-path may be quite different from the condition-path.

The group of queries we tested with the synthetic Authors data set includes 10 different, carefully chosen queries, which are omitted herein due to space limitation. Table 2 shows the results on the Authors data set.

Table 2. Path Index Execution Time on Initial Authors Data Set

	Dataguide (μs)	H-Index (μs)	Q-Index (μs)
Type I Query	14	7	9
Type II Query	29	10	12

Again, the H-Index outperforms the Dataguide in all these types of queries. Note that since the data set is quite small and the structure of the data is simple, we outperform by only 2 to 3 times, not as much as with the Shakespeare data set, which is reasonably large and more complex. As for the Q-index, it took 9 and 12 μs for Types I and II, respectively. These results are very encouraging.

To investigate the effect of the structures of data, we added more elements to the original Authors data set horizontally (i.e., adding more leaf nodes to the data source).

For example, we added tags <AGE>, <SEX>, <SSN>, and <TITLE>. We also added seven more queries in addition to the queries used for generating Table 2 (again, these queries are omitted for space limitation). Table 3 shows the results.

Table 3. Execution time with horizontal change to the Authors data set.

	Dataguide (μs)	H-Index (μs)	Q-Index (μs)
Type I Query	19	7	9
Type II Query	41	10	17

As before, the H-Index outperforms Dataguide in all types of queries by 2.7 to 4 times. Comparing Table 2 and 3, we can see that the execution time for H-Index remains almost the same, but it increases for Dataguide as the source data has more leaves now. These results do not surprise us because it takes constant time to find a path through hashing, regardless of the data set, assuming no severe collisions have occurred. But for Dataguide, as more leaves are added, more paths need to be examined. Thus, it takes more time to find the desired path.

As for the Q-index, it took 9 and 17 μs for Types I and II, respectively. The slight increase in Type II queries, from 12 for the original data set to 17 now, is due to the added tags and nodes, which make the structure a little more complex.

Finally, we added more elements vertically (i.e., adding more non-leaf nodes) to the data source used to generate Table 3 to see how this change affects the performance.

Table 4. Execution time with vertical change to the Authors data set.

	Dataguide (μs)	H-Index (μs)	Q-Index (μs)
Type I Query	23	8	9
Type II Query	48	12	20

The H-Index outperforms Dataguide by about 3 to 4 times. Comparing Tables 3 and 4, we see that the execution times are almost the same for H-Index. The slight increases are due to the slight increases in the computation time on hashing keys (path names) as the structure gets more deeply nested. Note that it increases more for Dataguide as the data becomes more deeply nested, as explained earlier. For Q-index, it took 9 and 20 μs for Types I and II, respectively. The slight increase, from 17 to 20 for Type II queries, is due to the increased depth of the structure.

In summary, our experimental results have shown that the H-Index is more effective than the Dataguide because it is faster and less sensitive to the structure of the source database. In addition, our Q-index also demonstrates outstanding results due to its simplicity and efficiency. One can confidently speculate that when the data set gets reasonably larger and its structure gets more complex, the superiority of HQ-Index will be much amplified.

5   Conclusions

In this paper, we propose the HQ-Index scheme to facilitate fast query evaluation of semi-structured data. This index scheme consists of two indexes, the H-Index and the Q-Index. The H-Index serves as a path index and is implemented as a hash table. The Q-Index uses a simple array structure, where entries are indexed by nodes' IDs. Query processing in our setting consists of two major steps: first, all nodes on interested paths are identified using the H-Index; and then the Q-Index is used to examine all conditions posed by a query on those nodes and retrieves requested information.

We conducted experiments with different types of queries on both real world and synthetic data sets. The performance results show that the H-Index outperforms Dataguide on all types of queries on both data sets. We also verified another important advantage through experiments that HQ-Index is not sensitive to the changes of the structure of XML data while Dataguide is sensitive to those changes.

References

1. C. Chung, J. Min, K. Shim. APEX: An Adaptive Path Index for XML data. Proc. of the ACM SIGMOD conference on Management of data, June 2002.
2. R. Cover. The Cover Pages: XML. http://www.oasis-open.org/cover/xml.html, 2002.
3. B. Cooper, N. Sample, M. Franklin, G. Hjaltason, and M. Shadmon. A Fast Index for Semistructured Data. Proc. of the 27th VLDB Conference, pp. 341–350, September 2001.
4. Document Object Model (DOM). http://www.w3.org/DOM, 2002.
5. R. Goldman, and J. Widom. DataGuides: Enabling Query Formulation and Optimization in Semistructured Databases. Proc. of the 23rd VLDB Conference, pp. 436–445, 1997.
6. T. Milo, and D. Suciu. Index structures for path expressions. Proc. of the International Conference on Database Theory, pp. 277–295, 1999.
7. J. McHugh, J. Widom. Query Optimization for XML. Proc. VLDB Conf., pp. 315–326, 1999.
8. D. Veillard. Libxml Win32. http://www.fh-rankfurt.de/~igor/projects/libxml/index.html, 2002.

On the Optimality of Holistic Algorithms for Twig Queries

Byron Choi[1], Malika Mahoui[1], and Derick Wood[2]

[1] University of Pennsylvania
{kkchoi,mmahoui}@seas.upenn.edu
[2] HKUST
dwood@cs.ust.hk

Abstract. Streaming XML documents has many emerging applications. However, in this paper, we show that the restrictions imposed by data streaming are too restrictive for processing twig queries – the core operation for XML query processing. Previous proposed algorithm `TwigStack` is an optimal algorithm for processing twig queries with only descendent edges over streams of nodes. The cause of the suboptimality of the `TwigStack` algorithm is the structurally recursions appearing in XML documents. We show that without relaxing the data streaming model, it is not possible to develop an optimal holistic algorithm for twig queries. Also the computation of the twig queries is not memory bounded. This motivates us to study two variations of the data streaming model: (1) offline sorting is allowed and the algorithm is allowed to select the correct nodes to be streamed and (2) multiple scans on the data streams are allowed. We show the lower bounds of the two variations.

1 Introduction

As much database research has shifted its focus from relational systems to the extensions on semistructured data and XML [1], there is a growing need for processing XML document streams efficiently. Recently, streaming XML documents has many emerging applications, e.g. in monitoring stock markets and in managing the network traffic. In such applications, the systems do not know the size of the XML document streams and do not have the access to sort the items in the streams. Also, an item in a stream is either stored in the main memory or discarded once it has been processed. As a key step in developing a data stream management system, Arasu and his colleagues [2] study the theoretical issues of some important classes of relational queries over data streams. However, none of the previous work has studied some theoretical issues of the core operation – the twig queries – for XML query processing over data streams.

Recently, efficient algorithms [6,10,9,8] have been proposed to evaluate twig queries in XML-enabled relational databases. These algorithms typically decompose the queries into subqueries, evaluate the subqueries and combine the results of the subqueries. One drawback of this approach is that intermediate results can be large even though the results can be relatively small. In contrast, holistic

V. Mařík et al. (Eds.): DEXA 2003, LNCS 2736, pp. 28–37, 2003.

algorithms for twig queries evaluate a twig query *as a whole*. Hence, memory is not used unwisely to store irrelevant nodes. Algorithms as such are useful in data streaming since the sizes of the streams is usually not known in advance.

The holistic twig join algorithm called `TwigStack` was recently proposed by Bruno and his co-researchers [4]. It evaluates twig queries as a whole over streams of XML documents efficiently. Each node in the twig query is associated with a stream of nodes. The algorithm scans the streams only once and assigns constant memory only to the nodes that participate in at least one solution. Thus, the algorithm is asymptotically optimal among all sequential algorithms that read the entire input. However, the algorithm is suboptimal when the twig queries contain child edges.

We demonstrate that it is not possible to develop an optimal holistic algorithm for evaluating twig queries. This negative result implies that either the data streaming model [3] or our assumptions about the streams are too restrictive for processing twig queries. We consider two variations of the data streaming model. First, document preprocessing is allowed and the corresponding optimal holistic algorithm is allowed selecting the correct nodes to be streamed. Second, multiple scans of the data streams are allowed. We present some lower bounds for the two computation models.

1.1 Background and the Problem Statement

We describe the node representation and the assumptions about the streams of nodes that we use. We also briefly describe the syntax and the semantics of twig queries. Finally, we describe the technical problem that we investigate.

Fig. 1. An example XML document. **Fig. 2.** Graphical representation of $//A$
$(//B, //C (//D_1, //D_2))$.

Twig queries are applied to the XML documents represented as follows. A document is modeled as a label tree. Nodes are represented by (1) the preorder number, (2) the postorder number and (3) the depth of the node. An example is to be found in Fig. 1.

Assumptions. We assume that the preorder number, the postorder number, the depth and the label are the only accessible information of a node. These assumptions imply the followings:

1. Given any two nodes, one can compute the ancestor-descendent and parent-child relationship of the two nodes in constant time.
2. One can compute the depth of a node in constant time.

Definition 1. *The syntax of a twig query, Twig, is defined as follows in Backus-Naur Form:*

Step ::= / | //
NodeTest ::= label
Path ::= Step NodeTest | Step NodeTest Path
Twig ::= Path | Path (Twig, Twig, ..., Twig)

We first give the syntax of twig queries in Definition 1. The steps '/' and '//' denote advancing one step from a parent node to its children nodes and from an ancestor node to its descendent nodes, respectively. Given a set of nodes as input, a *NodeTest* returns the subset of nodes that have the same label as the *NodeTest*. A path is a sequence of alternating steps and node tests. A twig is path possibly followed by branches, that are also twigs. Fig. 2 graphically represents the twig query $//A$ ($//B$, $//C$ ($//D_1$, $//D_2$)). The subscript of the D-node test denotes its occurrence in the query. The *solution* of a twig query is the set of all node combinations that satisfy the query.

Since a stream contains only nodes with the same label, the partial ordering of two nodes in a stream is only defined if they have the same label. $a_1 < a_2$ is interpreted as node a_1 precedes node a_2 in the A-stream.

Our computation model assumes that there is a stream of nodes associated with a node test in the twig query such that the nodes satisfy the node test. A *stream* can be viewed as a pop-only stack. For example, given the document and the query shown in Fig. 1 and Fig. 2, respectively, A, B, C, D_1 and D_2 are associated with a stream of A-, B-, C-, and D-nodes, denoted by T_A, T_B, T_C, T_{D_1} and T_{D_2} and defined by $T_A = [a_1, a_2]$, $T_B = [b_1, b_2]$, $T_C = [c_1, c_2]$, $T_{D_1} = [$ $]$ and $T_{D_2} = [\ ]$. We will call the nodes that participate in at least one solution the *useful* nodes and the remaining nodes *useless* nodes.

Definition 2. *An algorithm for twig queries is asymptotically optimal if it returns the solution of the query by using: (1) a single forward scan of the streams, (2) constant memory for each useful nodes and (3) constant time processing each of the nodes in the streams.*

The problem statement is given as follows. *Given a twig query and its associated streams, is it possible to design an asymptotically optimal algorithm for all twig queries.*

1.2   The Suboptimality of the TwigStack Algorithm

The TwigStack algorithm [4] has been proved to be asymptotically optimal for evaluating descendent-edge-only twig queries. We demonstrate the relevant parts of the algorithm with two running examples. The first example show an optimal evaluation of a twig query and the second example shows a suboptimal evaluation of a twig query. In both cases, we use the TwigStack algorithm.

Example 1. We demonstrate the evaluation of the descendent-edge-only queries in this example. The query $Q_1 = //A$ ($//B$, $//C$) is applied to the document shown in Fig. 1. Nodes in a stream are given in preorder: $T_A = [a_1, a_2]$, $T_B = [b_1, b_2]$ and $T_C = [c_1, c_2]$. Initially, the nodes a_1, b_1 and c_1 are at the *top* of T_A, T_B and T_C, respectively. Since b_1 and c_1 are descendents of a_1, a_1 is a useful node because of the implications of Q_1. The stream T_A is advanced. The next A-node is a_2. We examine the node b_1 which is useful because of a_1. T_B is advanced and b_2 is the next B-node. Similarly, a_2 is also useful. Now there are no further A-nodes in T_A. The B-node b_2 is useful because of a_2. T_B is advanced. The stream T_C is advanced and c_2 is useful because of a_1. Hence the solution is returned by using one forward scan, constant memory for each useful nodes and constant time processing each of the nodes in the stream. We have skipped the details of the reconstruction of the result from the encoding of the intermediate results produced by the `TwigStack` algorithm.

Example 2. We demonstrate the evaluation of a twig query containing some child edges [4]. The `TwigStack` algorithm is suboptimal in this case. The query $Q_2 = //A (/B, /C)$ and the same streams as in the previous example. No algorithm can determine if a_1 is useful without advancing T_C. If T_C is advanced, however, c_1 is discarded and a_2 will be declared useless. If the A stream is advanced, a_1 is discarded. To ensure that all useful nodes are reported, a_1 must be stored in the main-memory. The `TwigStack` algorithm will process a_2 and then a_1. This shows the suboptimality of the algorithm.

Definition 3. *A label l is structurally recursive if $l \rightarrow \alpha$, where α is the content model of l in the DTD, and there is at least one occurrence of l in α directly or indirectly. A DTD is recursive if it contains a structurally recursive label.*

There are two important observations about the `TwigStack` algorithm. First, the nodes in a stream are sorted by the preorder numbering. Having this fact and the assumptions in Section 1.1, before the query evaluation, we have enough information answering the descendent-edge-only twig queries optimally. It is natural to order the nodes by some other sort keys. Second, the reason for suboptimality is that an A-node can have A-descendents; that is, the label A is *structurally recursive*.

The organization of the rest of the paper is as follows. We show in Section 2 that the data streaming model is too restrictive for processing the twig queries under the assumptions of Section 1.1. In Section 3, we show that when offline processing is allowed, optimal holistic algorithms become possible but the lower bound of offline processing is high. Section 4 shows that when multiple scans of the streams are allowed, the optimality becomes possible but the lower bound of the number of scans is high. We provide conclusions in Section 5.

2 First Few Questions on Optimality

Our first few questions on processing twig queries in the data streaming context are: (1) is it possible to design such algorithms and (2) do they use bounded memory. We argue that the answer to both questions is negative. In Theorem 1, we will show that the data streaming model is too restrictive for the holistic evaluation of twig queries.

Proposition 1. *To satisfy the memory requirement of data streaming, and to allow one scan of the streams, without loss of generality, if $a_i < a_j$ then for all b_i in N_i and b_j in N_j, $b_i < b_j$, where $N_i = a_i/p$ and $N_j = a_j/p$, p is a Path.*

Proof. Proof by a structural induction on *Path* and by contradiction.   □

Theorem 1. *Given the assumptions in Section 1.1, there is no ordering of nodes such that the holistic evaluation of all twig queries is optimal.*

Proof. Consider the complete binary tree with 15 A nodes shown in Appendix A. Proposition 1 implies that if $a_i < a_j$, then the descendent nodes of $a_i < $ the descendent nodes of a_j. Consider the query $//A\ (/A,\ /A)$. We have three streams of A nodes, T_{A_1}, T_{A_2} and T_{A_3}. Let the top node of the three streams are p_1, p_2 and p_3, respectively.

The possible partial ordering of a_1 and some other A-nodes are determined by performing a case analysis. Without loss of generality, assume that $a_2 < a_3$.

Case 1. Assume that $a_1 < a_2$. It implies that there must be a configuration (*) such that $p_1 = a_1$, $p_2 = a_2$ and $p_3 = a_3$. If the top of T_{A_3} is a_3, then a_2 and all of its descendents in T_{A_3} have been discarded. When p_1 is advanced to a_2, no solution is reported. Hence, the assumption is not valid.

Case 2. Assume that $a_3 < a_1$. The configuration (*) must occur. If the top of T_{A_2} is a_2, then a_3 and all of its descendents in T_{A_2} are not seen yet. If the top of T_{A_1} is a_1, then a_3 and all of its descendents in T_{A_1} have been discarded. Some solution is missed. Hence, the assumption is not valid.

Case 3. Assume that $a_2 < a_1 < a_3$. The configuration (*) must occur. Denote the set of nodes that are a left and right child of some node A_L and A_R, respectively. Among a_2 and its descendents, a_2 must be the last node in A_L. Otherwise, at least one solution will be missing. Similarly, a_3 must be the first node in A_R among a_3 and its descendents. Without loss of generality, assume that $a_4 < a_5$ and $a_6 < a_7$. There must not be useful descendent nodes of a_2 in the rest of T_{A_1} since $p_3 = a_3$. Therefore a_{11} is the only node which can follow a_1. Similarly, a_{12} is the only node which can precede a_1.

The possible orderings are $a_{11} < a_1 < a_{12}$, $a_{11} < a_{12} < a_1$ and $a_1 < a_{11} < a_{12}$.

Similarly, we argue about the position of a_2. The possible orderings are $a_9 < a_2 < a_{10}$, $a_9 < a_{10} < a_2$ and $a_2 < a_9 < a_{10}$. Since a_2 is the last A_L node among a_2 and its descendents, and a_{10} is in A_L, $a_9 < a_{10} < a_2$ is the only possible ordering.

However, this ordering causes the evaluation of some twig queries suboptimal. Consider a similar complete binary tree with all B-nodes except for a_{10}, a_2 and a_5. And the query is $//A/A$. We have $T_{A_1} = T_{A_2} = [a_{10}, a_2, a_5]$ and initially, $p_1 = a_{10}$ and $p_2 = a_{10}$. p_2 cannot be advanced until p_1 is advanced to a_5. That is, a_2 is discarded. Thus, the assumption is wrong. We conclude that it is not possible to have an ordering of nodes for optimal evaluation for all twig queries.   □

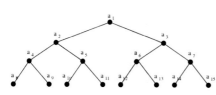

Fig. 3. A complete binary tree with 15 A nodes.

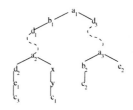

Fig. 4. Example used in Lemma 1 in Sec. 4.

Proposition 2. *Given the assumptions in Section 1.1, some twig queries are not computable with bounded memory for all possible document streams.*

Proof. The twig query $//A$ ($/A$, $/A$) is reduced to a SPJ query over streams of tuples. Assume a node is represented by a 3-ary tuple: $<preorder, postorder, depth>$. The corresponding SPJ query is $\pi_L(\sigma_P(T_{A_1} \times T_{A_2} \times T_{A_3}))$, where the predicate L is all the attributes of the three streams and P is $T_{A_1}.preorder < T_{A_2}.preorder \wedge T_{A_1}.postorder > T_{A_2}.postorder \wedge T_{A_2}.depth = T_{A_1}.depth + 1$ $T_{A_1}.preorder < T_{A_3}.preorder \wedge T_{A_1}.postorder > T_{A_3}.postorder \wedge T_{A_3}.depth = T_{A_1}.depth + 1 \wedge T_{A_2}.preorder \neq T_{A_3}.preorder$. We claim that the twig query is bounded memory computable if and only if the SPJ query is bounded memory computable. Given arbitrary node streams, all the preorder, postorder and depth attributes are not bounded [2]. Hence, there does not exist a constant M such that the evaluation of the SPJ query over all possible stream instances requires less than M. Therefore, the SPJ query is not memory bounded computable. □

3   Offline Sorting

In Theorem 1, we show that the data streaming model is too restrictive for optimal holistic evaluation. We consider a realistic variation in this section. We assume that a powerful server is available managing the XML documents. The client sends the twig query to the server, the server analyzes the query and sends the node streams to the client and the client evaluates the query.

Since we demonstrated that the suboptimality is caused by the structurally recursive labels, we assume that recursions are "removed" by offline sorting on the server side. We illustrate the idea by the following example. Consider the query $Q = //A$ ($/B$, $/C$). Now we sort the nodes by (1) the preorder number of a node's first A ancestor [1] and (2) the preorder number of a node. The streams become $[a_1, a_2]$, $[b_1, b_2]$ and $[c_2, c_1]$. Note that the subtree rooted at the a_1 node is read before that at the a_2 node. Locating the useful nodes of Q becomes straightforward. However, one can find a twig query which cannot be evaluated optimally by using this ordering. The natural question is to ask the number of necessary orderings for answering all twig queries optimally.

---

[1] 0 is assigned to the nodes that do not have an A ancestor.

We first define the smallest twig queries that may lead to the suboptimality of the `TwigStack` algorithm. We will use the queries to show the lower bound of the number of necessary orderings.

Definition 4. *A twig query is a simple child-edge query if descendent edges never follow child edges in the paths of the twig query.*

Fig. 5. (1) a twig query which is not a simple child-edge query; (2) a simple child-edge twig query; and (3) a twig query is a tree of simple child-edge twig queries connected by descendent edges.

A twig query is a set of simple child-edge queries in which queries are connected by descendent edges. (See Fig. 5.)

Theorem 2. *Let m be the number of structurally recursive labels in the DTD, d be the depth of the document and n is the number of nodes in the document. $\Omega(m^{min(d,m)} \times n)$ disk space is required to store the orderings of nodes for answering all twig queries optimally.*

Proof. Suppose a simple child-edge twig query Q (see Fig. 5 (1)) with the root A, where A is a structurally recursive label. We sort the nodes by two sort keys: (1) the preorder number of its first A-ancestor and (2) its preorder number. The visualization of this sorting is shown in Fig. 6. For each structurally recursive label X, one needs to spend n storing the nodes in which X-recursions are removed. Suppose m labels are structurally recursive, $m \times n$ space is required. These orderings produced by the sorting are all necessary because if one of these orderings is missing, then we can use the proof of Theorem 1 to show that optimality is not possible.

A twig query is a tree of simple child-edge queries. Hence, after sorting the nodes by X, we need to remove other recursions in each X subtree. The total number of orderings is $m^{min(d,m)}$. Therefore, if we store the nodes by $\Omega(m^{min(d,m)} \times n)$, optimal holistic algorithms become possible. □

3.1   A Restricted Case

In practice, the number of orderings of the nodes in a document is significantly smaller than the one in the worst case. This is due to the fact that structurally recursive labels are not always mutually recursive. Suppose some constraints on the XML document is given, there are some guarantees on the number of necessary orderings. The trivial case is that when the documents conform to a non-recursive DTD, the `TwigStack` algorithm returns all solution optimally. We also identify a restricted case in which the exponential blowup in the number of orderings does not occur.

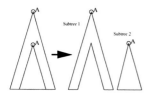
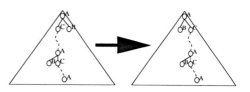

Fig. 6. Visualization of sorting nodes by (1) the preorder # of their first A ancestor and (2) their preorder #.

Fig. 7. The transformation described in the proof of Proposition 3

Definition 5. *A label l is* linearly recursive *if and only if $l \to \alpha$, where α is the content model of l in the DTD, and there is a single occurrence of l in α directly or indirectly. A label l is* non-linearly recursive *if and only if $l \to \alpha$ and there is more than one occurrences of l in α directly or indirectly.*

Proposition 3. *There is an ordering of nodes such that all twig queries on the documents conforming to a linearly recursive DTD can be evaluated asymptotically optimally.*

Proof. By definition, if the label of a node (say A) is linearly recursive, there is at most one child node which is an ancestor of its A-descendents. We cite a property of the `TwigStack` algorithm [5]: it guarantees that the ancestor nodes of a node n that uses a partial solution rooted at a are returned before a is returned by the core iterative procedure of the `TwigStack` algorithm. Suppose a_i is an immediate A-ancestor of a_j. Denote the descendents of a node n as `desc(n)`. If the document is transformed such that the nodes in `desc(a_i)` - `desc(a_j)` precedes the nodes in `desc(a_j)` (*), then the `TwigStack` algorithm returns all the solution due to the property. Consider a transformation as such: for each X-node, the child node that is an ancestor of some X-nodes is placed following other child nodes. The transformation is illustrated by the example in Fig. 7. Then we assign the numbers to the transformed document and sort the nodes by their preorder number. The transformed document always satisfies (*). □

A survey on real world DTDs [7] shows that non-recursive DTDs and linearly recursive DTDs are few in practice. In general, the optimal holistic evaluation for all twig queries requires at least an exponential number of orderings.

4 Multiple Scans

The second attempt on supporting more twig queries optimally is to allow multiple scans on the streams. We show that it is possible to return the solution by using the `TwigStack` algorithm repeatedly. However, the lower bound of the number of scan is rather high $\Omega(d^{\,t})$, where d and t are the depth of the document and the number of simple child-edge queries in the twig query, respectively.

Lemma 1. *The number of scans required by the stream evaluation of a simple child-edge query is $\Omega(d)$, where d is the depth of the document.*

Proof. We call an A subtree with k A ancestors an (A, k)-subtree. Assume the document contains an (A, k)-subtree and only m scans are allowed, where $m < k$. There must be a scan that processes some (A, i)-subtrees and some (A, j)-subtrees, where $i > j$. We argue that one scan is not sufficient to find all solution of these subtrees.

Consider the document shown in Fig. 4. Assume the a_1-subtree is an (A, i)-subtree and a_2-subtree and a_3-subtree are (A, j)-subtrees, where $i < j$ and a_1 is an ancestor of a_2 and a_3. Without loss of generality, assume that $a_2 < a_3$. By using Proposition 1, $\mathrm{desc}(a_2)$ precedes $\mathrm{desc}(a_3)$. Denote N to be nodes in a_1-subtree but not in a_2- and a_3-subtrees. (1) Nodes in N cannot follow $\mathrm{desc}(a_2)$ and $\mathrm{desc}(a_3)$ since given the query $//A//B//C$, either (a_1, b_1, c_1) (and c_3) or (a_3, b_2, c_2) is missed by using a scan. (2) Nodes in N cannot precede $\mathrm{desc}(a_2)$ and $\mathrm{desc}(a_3)$ since given the query $//A//D//E$, either (a_1, d_3, e_2) or (a_2, d_2, e_1) is missed by using a scan. (3) Nodes in N cannot be in between $\mathrm{desc}(a_2)$ and $\mathrm{desc}(a_3)$ since given the query $//A//D//C$, c_3 must precede c_1 since d_2 precedes d_1. Consider another document in which x and y are swapped with d_2 and e_1, respectively. Since c_3 precedes c_1 in the C-stream and (a_1, d_1, c_3) is missed.

Since a document with the depth d contains at most (A, d)-subtrees, the lower bound of the number of scans for simple child-edge query is $\Omega(d)$.   □

Theorem 3. *Given the assumptions in Section 1.1, except that multiple scans is allowed, the solution of a twig query is returned by using $\Omega(d^{\,t})$ scans on the data streams, where d is the depth of the document and t is the minimal number of simple child-edge queries in the twig query.*

Proof. Consider a twig query containing t simple child-edge queries, $q_1, q_2, ..., q_t$, with their root $r_1, r_2, ..., r_t$, respectively. We use a $t \times 1$ vector $(v_1, v_2, ... v_t)$ to denote the subtrees that a scan is processing. For example, consider the query $//A\,/B\,//C\,/D$. q_1 and q_2 are $A\,/B$ and $C\,/D$ and r_1 and r_2 are A and C, respectively. $V = (1, 1)$ means that the scan is processing the $(A, 1)$-subtrees and $(C, 1)$-subtrees. The number of possible values of V is $O(d^{\,2})$ although the scan is useless when $v_1 + v_2 > d$. In general, the number of possible values of V or the twig query containing t simple child-edge queries is in $O(d^{\,t})$.

Suppose the $(k_1, k_2, ..., k_t)$-th scan is not performed, there is a scan processing some (r_i, k_i)-subtrees and some (r_i, k)-subtrees for some k in one scan. By the same argument used in the proof of Lemma 1, we can construct a case such that some of the solution is not reported. Thus, all $O(d^{\,t})$ scans are necessary.   □

5   Conclusions

We studied processing twig queries – the core operation for XML query processing – over streams of XML documents. We showed that it is not possible to develop an asymptotically optimal holistic twig join algorithm in the context of data streaming. We also show that the computation of twig queries is not memory-bounded. These negative results indicate that the data streaming model is too restrictive for twig query processing. We locate that the cause of the suboptimality of the holistic evaluation of twig queries is the structurally recursive labels in the document. Two alternative computation models for twig query processing are presented: (1) offline sorting is allowed and the algorithm is allowed selecting the correct ordering of nodes to be streamed and (2) multiple scans is allowed. We show high lower bounds for the two models.

Acknowledgements. The work of Byron Choi was done while he was visiting HKUST. Byron Choi and Derick Wood were supported under a Research Grants Council Earmarked Research Grant. The authors owe Susan Davidson, Wilfred Ng and Jerome Simeon a large debt of gratitude for insightful discussions.

References

1. S. Abiteboul, P. Buneman, and D. Suciu. *Data on the Web: From Relations to Semistructured Data and XML.* Morgan Kaufmann, Los Altos, USA, 1999.
2. A. Arasu, B. Babcock, S. Babu, J. McAlister, and J. Widom. Characterizing Memory Requirements for Queries over Continuous Data Streams. In *PODS*, pages 221–232, Jun. 2002.
3. B. Babcock, S. Babu, M. Datar, R. Motwani, and J. Widom. Models and Issues in Data Stream Systems. In *PODS*, pages 1–16, Jun. 2002.
4. N. Bruno, N. Koudas, and D. Srivastava. Holistic Twig Joins: Optimal XML Pattern Matching. In *SIGMOD*, pages 310–321, Jun. 2002.
5. N. Bruno, N. Koudas, and D. Srivastava. Holistic Twig Joins: Optimal XML Pattern Matching. Technical Report. Columbia University, 2002.
6. S.-Y. Chien, Z. Vagena, D. Zhang, and V. J. Tsotras. Efficient Structural Joins on Indexed XML Documents. In *ICDE*, pages 141–154, Feb. 2002.
7. B. Choi. What Are Real DTDs Like. In *WebDB*, pages 43–48, Jun. 2002.
8. M. L. Lee, B. C. Chua, W. Hsu, and K.-L. Tan. Efficient Evaluation of Multiple Queries on Streaming XML Data. In *CIKM*, pages 118–125, Nov. 2002.
9. W. Wang, H. Jiang, H. Lu, and J. X. Yu. Containment Join Size Estimation: Models and Methods. In *SIGMOD*, Jun. 2003.
10. C. Zhang, J. Naughton, D. DeWitt, Q. Luo, and G. Lohman. On Supporting Containment Queries in Relational Database Management Systems. *ACM SIGMOD Record*, 30(2):425–436, 2001.

AUSMS: An Environment for Frequent Sub-structures Extraction in a Semi-structured Object Collection

Pierre-Alain Laur[1], Maguelonne Teisseire[1], and Pascal Poncelet[2]

[1] LIRMM,
161 rue Ada,
34392 Montpellier cedex 5, France
{laur,teisseire}@lirmm.fr
[2] EMA/LGI2P, Ecole des Mines d'Alès,
Site EERIE, Parc Scientifique Georges Besse,
30035 Nîmes cedex 1, France
Pascal.Poncelet@ema.fr

Abstract. Mining knowledge from structured data has been extensively addressed in the few past years. However, most proposed approaches are interested in flat structures. With the growing popularity of the Web, the number of semi-structured documents available is rapidly increasing. Structure of these objects is irregular and it is judicious to assume that a query on documents structure is almost as important as a query on data. Moreover, manipulated data is not static since it is constantly being updated. The problem of maintaining such sub-structures then becomes as much of a priority as researching them because, every time data is updated, found sub-structures could become invalid. In this paper we propose a system, called A.U.S.M.S. (Automatic Update Schema Mining System), which enables us to retrieve data, identify frequent sub-structures and keep up-to-date extracted knowledge after sources evolutions.

1 Introduction

The search for knowledge in structured data has been extensively addressed in the few past years. Most of the proposed approaches concern flat or highly structured structures. With the growing popularity of the World Wide Web, the number of semi-structured documents available is rapidly increasing. However in spite of this structural irregularity, structural similarities among semi-structured objects can exist and it is frequently noted that semi-structured objects which describe the same type of information have similar structures. The analysis of such implicit structures in semi-structured data can then provide significant information : to optimize requests evaluations, to obtain general information on the contents, to facilitate data integration resulting from various information sources, to improve storage, to facilitate index or views and to contribute to semi-structured documents classification. Applications fields are very numerous and gather, for example: bio-informatics, Web Content Mining and Web Usage Mining. Recently, new approaches were proposed to discover such sub-structures [4, 8, 11, 14, 15]. Unfortunately, handled data are not static

V. Mařík et al. (Eds.): DEXA 2003, LNCS 2736, pp. 38–45, 2003.

because new updates are constantly carried out. The problem of keeping such sub-structures up to date becomes very significant. As updates are carried out, the previously found sub-structures can become invalid. In this article we are interested in extraction of such sub-structures with a detailed attention for their evolution. We propose a system, called AUSMS (Automatic Update Schema Mining System), which allows collecting data, finding frequent sub-structures, and maintaining extracted knowledge during sources evolutions.

The article is organized in the following way. In section 2, we present the problems of searching frequent sub-structures and data maintenance. Section 3 presents the functional architecture of the system by detailing the various stages. A related work is proposed in section 4. Lastly, in section 5, we conclude.

2 Problem Statement

In this section, we give the formal definitions related to the problem of searching frequent sub-structures in semi-structured objects.

The goal of our proposal is to discover structural similarities among a set of semi-structured objects. Since in our context a cyclic graph can be transformed into an acyclic graph [14], we consider in the following a tree as an acyclic connected graph and a forest as a collection of trees where each tree is a connected component of the forest (rooted tree). Furthermore we consider that handled trees are ordered tree (a rooted tree in which the children of each node are ordered). The order is given according to the type of application and it follows either the lexicographical order (set-of), or the imposed order (list-of). To express the differences between orders in the following, we will respectively use the notations "{ }" to represent a "set of" and "< >" to represent a "list of". Due to lack of space, we do not define formally the inclusion of a structure in a tree. Nevertheless, we illustrate this notion by the following example

Example: for example, let us consider figure 1 and the structure [*address*: {*city*, *street*, *zipcode*}, *category*, *name*]. This structure is a sub-structure of the tree [*root*:{*address*: {*city*, *street*, *zipcode*}, *category*, *name*, *nearby*: {*category*, *name*, *price*}}]. However the structure [*address*: {*city*, *street*, *zipcode*}, *category*, *name*, *price*] is not a sub-structure of the tree since the element *price* is not on the same level in the graph.

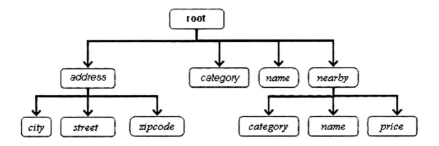

Fig. 1. Examples of sub-structures

Let us now consider DB a tree database also named structures, i.e. a forest where each tree T is composed of an identifier and a structure included in the forest. Let *supp (p)* be the support value for a structure corresponding to the number of occurrences of this structure in the database DB, i.e. the support of a structure *p* is defined as the percentage of all trees in the database which contain *p*. A tree of the database contains *p* iff *p* is a sub-structure of this tree. In order to decide whether a structure is frequent or not, a value of minimal support is specified by the user (*minSupp*) so a structure is frequent if the condition *supp (p)≥minSupp* holds. Being given a tree database DB, the problem of searching regularities in semi-structured data thus consists in finding all the maximum structures which are in DB and whose support is higher than minSupp.

Let us now consider the data sources evolutions. Let db the database increment where new information is added or removed. Let U=DB $\cup$ db, be the updated database holding all structures from DB and db. Let L^{DB} be the frequent sub-structures set in DB. The problem of keeping of up to date discovered knowledge is to seek the frequent sub-structures in U, noted L^{U}, by respecting the same support value without restarting mining algorithm from scratch.

3   The A.U.S.M.S. System

The aim of A.U.S.M.S. (Automatic Update Schema Mining System) is to propose an environment for knowledge discovery in semi-structured data from information recovery until the update of extracted knowledge. These general principles are illustrated in figure 2. The process can be broken into three main phases. First, starting from rough semi-structured data files, a pre-processing eliminates the irrelevant data and performs the transformation into the database. In a second phase, a knowledge extraction algorithm is used to find the frequent sub-structures which are stored into a database. Then, evolution of data sources is taken into account in order to update previously extracted knowledge. Finally, a visualization tool is provided to the end user.

In the following sections, we detail the extraction and the incremental process as well as the visualization tool.

3.1   Knowledge Extraction

We showed in [7] that there was a bijection between the problems of mining sub-structures such as we defined it and that of searching sequential patterns defined in [2]. To find the frequent structures we use a level-wize algorithm largely inspired by [2]. Interested reader may refer to [8]. In order to improve the candidate generation procedure as well as the management of candidate elements, we use a bitmap representation inspired by [3]. This structure offers the advantage of considerably reducing the storage space and the ability to easily generate candidates. Moreover it is particularly adapted in the long structures search. During the candidates search phase we also generate the negative border [10]. This is made up of all the structures which are not frequent but whose sub-structures are frequent. This negative border will be used in the following phase to take into account the data sources evolutions.

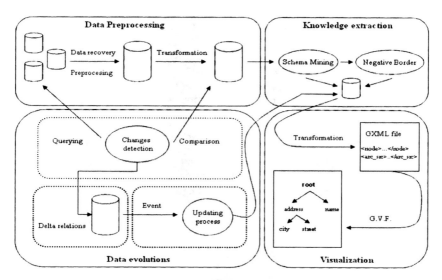

Fig. 2. General Architecture

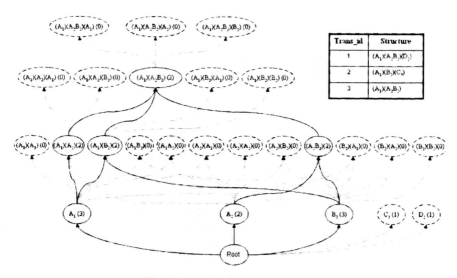

Fig. 3. Example of a negative border

Example: Let us consider figure 3 representing a lattice associated with a sample database. For a minimal support of 50 %, on level 1, only the A_1, A_2 and B_2 elements are frequent and can be used to create more complex structures. We thus store in the negative border, the C_3 and D_2 elements. On level 2, only (A_1) (A_2), (A_1) (B_2), $(A_2$ $B_2)$ are frequent, we preserve in the negative border those of the preceding level elements which were frequent.

42   P.-A. Laur, M. Teisseire, and P. Poncelet

3.2 Taking into Account Data Source Evolutions

The negative border obtained in the previous stage enables us to take into account updates and to maintain extracted knowledge. Indeed, to avoid applying the previous algorithm again at the time of each update, we store in the negative border the minimal information required to quickly compute the frequent sub-structures. The general principles are as follows:

Update algorithm

Input: S Set of data sources, BN the negative border, BN^{Limit}, L^{DB} the set of frequent structures, minSupp the minimal support specified by the user
Output: the updated sources S, BN updated and L^{DB} updated
while t ∈ delay *do*
foreach s ∈ S *do*
if $s_{new} \neq s_{old}$ *then*
    updateDeltaRelation (Δ_s, opmaj, t)
enddo

$$\Delta_S \leftarrow \bigcup_{i=0}^{S} \Delta_s$$

if Validate(Δ_s, BN^{Limit}) *then*
    Update (L^{DB})

From a date specified by the user (delay), the data sources are compared (as we maintain previous sources s_{old} stands for the initial data sources, i.e. during the last analysis, and s_{new} represents the data being analyzed, i.e. s). This operation is carried out in the AUSMS system by an agent which acts either in a temporal way (fixed time difference since last update), or in a direct way (user activation). The agent is in charge of comparing the data sources and propagating the modifications. Thus, if the data source was modified, the updates are stored as a Δs set which manages the history of the modifications (UpdateDeltaRelation procedure). This procedure, inspired from the delta relations, used in active rules, makes it possible to reflect the side effects of the structure modifications [5].

From the information contained as Δs set, a comparison is carried out, by the procedure Validate (Δ_s, BN^{Limit}), with the elements contained in the negative border which are likely to change quickly, i.e. those which can become frequent or not, up to one element. This procedure also takes into account the addition or the suppression of new sources which of course generate a modification of the support value. If one of the conditions is then verified the modifications are brought directly into the negative border to update the set of the frequent structures (procedure Update (L^{DB})). The first stage consists in deferring the modifications in the negative border as soon as structures are added or removed. Indeed, such an operation causes the calculation of the support value to be modified for the whole base. For each structure, we thus examine the support value in the negative border and if this one is lower than the support, the branches of the tree resulting from this structure are pruned. Otherwise the other elements are re-examined and the negative border is updated according to their frequency. When the operations consist in adding or removing elements in existing structures, we analyze the negative border while starting with level 1 so as to verify how frequently the elements appear. If elements become frequent the various levels of the lattice are built recursively with those which were already frequent. If frequent elements become infrequent, the various branches of the lattices resulting from the sub-structure are pruned. At the end of this phase, the frequent elements are extracted and L^{DB} is updated as well as the negative border.

3.3 Visualization

Whereas previous modules are charged to provide and maintain frequent sub-structures, this module makes it possible to visualize these structures and offers a formalism to describe them.

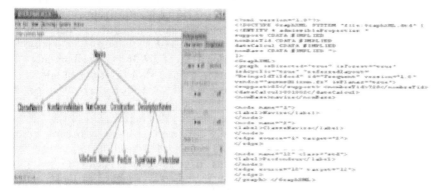

Fig. 4. Examples of extracted structures

For that, we use, initially, GraphXML [6] which is a graph description language in XML especially designed for drawing and display systems. In the second place, for visualizing extracted sub-structure as well as their implication in the date sources, we use the Graph Visualization Framework which proposes a set of java classes to visualize and handle the structures described by the GraphXML format.
We find at the left a frequent structure resulting from the frequent sub-structures search with at least 85% of a history of ships database displayed via GVF. On the right-hand side we have the same description within the GraphXML format.

4 Related Work

Our approach is very close to that proposed in [13, 14] for the search for structural association in semi-structured data. The authors propose a very effective approach and solutions based on a new representation of the search space. Moreover, by proposing optimizations based on pruning strategies, they considerably improve candidates' generation stage. In the same way, an approach suggested in [11] is rather similar to the previous approach and uses a particular tree called tag tree patterns. In [4], authors propose an algorithm called Find-Freq-Trees which also uses an approach based on a search by level as in the algorithm A-priori [1] and extends the proposal in order to discover sub-structures in long sequences. Finally in [15], author proposes two algorithms TreeMinerH and TreeMinerV for the search for frequent trees in a forest. TreeMinerH takes again the principle of the course in width of A-priori by improving candidates' generation and counting using the classes of equivalences, a structure of prefixed tree and "scope list". In TreeMinerV, a tree is described by a vertical structure. In these two algorithms, candidates' generation and counting are carried out by set operations on the "scope list"; the prefixed structure makes it possible to reduce the number of transactions to be traversed in the database. In our context, we are interested in the search for all the structures included in the base whereas they are interested only in search of tree-expression which are defined like trees going from the root to a final leaf of the tree. With this definition, they cannot find regularities of the form *[identity : [address : <street, zipcode>]]* which would be frequent but would be included in a longer transaction which is, itself, not frequent.

According to the maintenance of the extracted frequent sub-structures, there does not exist, to our knowledge, works in this field. We showed that the search for sub-structures could approach that of sequential patterns. In the continuation of our work, we will thus examine the work carried out around this field. In [12], authors propose an algorithm called ISM (Incremental Sequence Mining) which allows an update of the frequent sequences. The suggested approach builds a lattice of sequence which contains all the frequent and negative border elements [10]. When new information arrives, they are added to this lattice. The problem of this approach is obviously the increasing size of the negative border which in our case is minimized, because based on bit vectors. In [9], the ISE (Incremental Sequence Extraction) algorithm was proposed for the search for frequent patterns, it generates candidates in the entire database by attaching the sequences of the incremental database to those of the original base. This approach avoids keeping the sequences contained in the negative border and the recalculation of these sequences when the initial database has been updated. However, by not preserving the negative border, it is necessary to more often traverse the base to search for candidates. In [16] the algorithm proposed uses at the same time the concepts of negative border of the original data base and the concepts of suffixes and prefixes in the contrary of ISE. To control the size of this negative border, they introduce a minimum support for these elements thus reducing its size. Moreover this algorithm realizes an extension by prefix and suffix (using the negative border). The problem of this algorithm lies in the choice of the value of the minimum support for the negative border.

5 Conclusion

In this article, we proposed a functional architecture, AUSMS, of a system of extraction and maintenance of knowledge in semi-structured objects databases. The originality of the approach lies in the implementation of effective algorithms to extract the frequent sub-structures in the base from semi-structured objects but also in the taking into account of the handled data. The tests which we carried out on bases resulting from the Web show that the adopted approach is very useful to help the end-user in the analysis of the various handled elements. It offers solutions for the search of general information in the data sources, to contribute to the interrogation of semi-structured databases and to help building views and indexes.

References

[1]   R. Agrawal, T. Imielinski, and A. swami, "Mining Association Rules between Sets of Items in Large Databases", Proceedings of SIGMOD'93, pp. 2076, May 1993.

[2]   R. Agrawal and R. Srikant, "Mining Sequential Patterns", Proceedings of International Conference on Data Engineering (ICDE'95), pp. 3–14, Tapei, Taiwan, March 1995.

[3]   J. Ares, J. Gehrke, T. Yiu and J. Flannick, "Sequential Pattern Using Bitmap Representation", Proceedings of PKDD'02, Edmonton, Canada, July 2002.

[4]   T. Asai, K. Abe, and al., "Efficient substructure discovery from Large Semi-structured Data", Proceedings of the (ICDM'02) Conference, Washington DC, USA, April 2002.

[5]   S. Chawathe, S. Abiteboul and J. Widom, "Representing and Querying Changes History in Semistructured Data", Proceedings of ICDE'98, Orlando, USA, February 1998.

[6]   I. Herman and M.S. Marshall, "GraphXML An XML based graph interchange format", Centre for Mathematics and Computer Sciences (CWI), Technical Report Amsterdam, 2000.

[7]   P.A. Laur, F. Masseglia and P. Poncelet, "A General Architecture for Finding Structural Regularities on the Web", Proceedings of the AIMSA'00 Conference, September 2000.

[8]   P.A. Laur et P. Poncelet. "AUSMS : un environement pour l'extraction de sous-structures fréquentes dans une collection d'objets semi-structurées (in french)". Actes des Journées d'Extraction et Gestion des Connaissances (EGC'03), Lyon, France, 2003.

[9]   F. Masseglia, P. Poncelet and M. Teisseire, "Incremental Mining of Sequential Patterns in Large Database", Actes des Journées BDA'00, Blois, France, Octobre 2000.

[10] H. Mannila and H. Toivonen. "On an Algorithm for Finding all Interesting Sequences". In Proceedings of the 13th European Meeting on Cybernetics and Systems Research, Vienna, Austria, April 1996.

[11] T. Miyahara, T. Shoudai, T. Uchida, K. Takahashi and H. Ueda, "Discovery of Frequent Tree Structured Patterns in Semistructured Web Documents", Proceedings of PAKDD'01, pp. 47–52, Hong Kong, China, April 2001.

[12] S. Parthasarathy and M. J. Zaki, "Incremental and Interactive Sequence Mining", Proceedings of the CIKM'99 Conference, pp. 251–258, Kansas City, USA, November 1999.

[13] K. Wang and H. Liu, "Schema Discovery for Semi-structured Data", Proceedings of the KDD'97 Conference, pp. 271–274., Newport Beach, USA, August 1997.

[14] K. Wang and H. Liu, "Discovering Structural Association of Semistructured Data", In IEEE Transactions on Knowledge and Data Engineering , pp. 353–371, January 1999.

[15] M. Zaki, "Efficiently Mining Frequent Trees in a Forest", Proceedings of SIGKDD'02, Edmonton, Canada, July 2002.

[16] Q. Zheng, K. Xu, S. Ma and W. Lu, "The Algorithms of Updating Sequential Patterns", Proceedings of the International Conference on Data Mining (ICDM'02), April 2002.

Defining Web Schema Transformers by Example

Stephan Lechner and Michael Schrefl

Department of Information Systems,
University of Linz,
Austria
{lechner,schrefl}@dke.uni-linz.ac.at

Abstract. When defining a scheme of a web application (a web scheme)
using a conceptual modelling tool, modelers successively perform design
steps by extending or refining the scheme. Each design step is characterized by (i) the scheme to which the design step is applied (input scheme)
and (ii) the resulting scheme (output scheme). As modelers apply similar
design steps repeatedly, it would be convenient to have schema transformers that, when applied to an input scheme, generate an output scheme.
In this paper, we present a way of defining schema transformers by example. A transformer comprises an input and an output template that are
parameterized examples of an input and an output scheme, respectively.
Therefrom executable code necessary for performing transformations can
be generated automatically. A transformer is applied to an input scheme
by binding elements of the scheme to parameters. For each such application, a corresponding output scheme is then generated.
Our transformers can be introduced in various models/tools for web application modelling. We demonstrate this on the example of WebML.

1 Introduction

Conceptual modelling of web applications usually proceeds stepwise along the
axis "content, hypertext, and presentation scheme" [5,10,8,13]. However, as these
schemes are not independent and because they all become iteratively more and
more detailed, we will subsequently use the term "web scheme" (or simply
scheme) as for a web application as a whole.

With each design step, the scheme is extended or refined, for example, by
adding new scheme elements like page classes and links to existing scheme elements. Therefore, a design step is applied to an input scheme that is thereby
extended or refined and leads to an output scheme.

Yet typical "patterns" of extending or refining parts of schemes are repeatedly applied. Such "patterns" may be explicitly recommended by the provider of
the model/tool in use (e.g. [4,11,8]) but may also crystallize from the modeler's
experience. For example, having defined an entity type, often a page for displaying its members is added; this design step, which can be referred to as "create
page for entity type", is likely to be performed similarly for several entity types.

This suggests to enable modelers defining and applying schema transformers that can perform design steps such as that described above. Thereby, use

V. Mařík et al. (Eds.): DEXA 2003, LNCS 2736, pp. 46–56, 2003.
© Springer-Verlag Berlin Heidelberg 2003

and definition of such transformers should be easy as this would facilitate fast production of web application prototypes.

Transformers for particular models have already been introduced [8]. They are defined by specifying a sequence of schema modification operations, e.g. "*P.addLink (L)*" for adding a link represented by L to a page class represented by P. However, this approach has two disadvantages: (i) definition of transformers requires to understand the schema modification operations available, and (ii) transformers are difficult to use for average modelers as semantics is hidden in code.

In this paper, we present a way for defining schema transformers (or simply transformers) by example. Each transformer comprises two parameterized schemes (i.e. templates), whereby parameters are variables that represent scheme elements. Notably, these templates are defined with the same model/tool as used for defining schemes but have annotations, e.g. for identifying parameters. Therefrom a sequence of schema modification operations can be generated automatically such that definition and use of transformers does not require any knowledge about these operations.

The two templates of a transformer have the following purposes: (i) the *input template* is a parameterized example of an input scheme. It declares constraints over parameters and thereby specifies to which input schemes the transformer can be applied. Most of these constraints are expressed implicitly by the graphical arrangement of scheme elements. Explicit constraints, if required, can be annotated. (ii) the *output template* is a parameterized example of an output scheme. It represents new scheme elements by parameters and specifies derivation of values based on parameters of the input template. Again, this is mostly expressed implicitly by the graphical arrangement of scheme elements. Explicit derivations can be annotated.

With our approach, a transformer is easy to define because one has just to define an input scheme and an output scheme and then to annotate them in order to replace some concrete values with parameters. Moreover, these transformers are easy to understand because the templates denote examples of schemes. It is thereby intuitively clear (i) to which input schemes a transformer is applicable, and (ii) which result it will achieve.

Once defined, a transformer for a particular design step can be repeatedly applied in order to have the step performed. A transformer is applied to an input scheme by binding elements of the scheme to parameters of the transformer's input template. Thereby only a small set of parameters must be bound explicitly as the transformer can evaluate other parameter bindings due to constraint satisfaction. Each application then yields a result corresponding to the transformer's output template.

Use-cases for transformers are manyfold, supporting very small design steps as well as large ones. As transformers can be applied quickly, they facilitate everyday modelling tasks like, for example: (i) defining pages displaying the members of entity types; this will be the running example. (ii) adding content management operations like "delete" with corresponding success and error pages; this is shown in [9]. However, they can also capture complex design steps like (iii) generating a whole shopping cart application where users select products within a session. One has just to define entity types representing concrete products and users. A series of other scheme elements can then be generated, for example: an entity type "shopping cart" representing selected products, pages enabling users to select products and to view the shopping cart, as well as content management operations for adding/removing products and submitting an order.

Semantics of transformers is not specified based on schema modification operations of a particular model used for design such as WebML directly. Instead, we define a logical representation of such models that allows for precise definition of semantics and for a straight-forward implementation using a deductive engine such as FLORID [6]. Thus, transformers and the schemes to which they shall be applied are defined using a particular model/tool, yet they are mapped to logical representation before interpretation and execution. The result is then mapped back to the model in use.

Our approach can therefore be applied to various models/tools in the same way. In this paper, use of transformers is demonstrated with a small subset of WebML [5], though we could have supported full extent of WebML or other approaches like OO-H [7] or Araneus [10] as well. WebML has been chosen because it is available as commercial tool, WebRatio [1], which we prototypically extended by transformers.

The remainder of this paper is organized as follows. Section 2 introduces a small subset of WebML and motivates our transformers. Section 3 then defines the logical representation of this subset of WebML. Section 4 formally defines definition and application of transformers. In Sect. 5, related work is discussed before Sect. 6 concludes the paper.

2   Using a Simple Transformer in WebML

This section first defines a simple design step leading from a data scheme to a hypertext scheme. Thereby a subset of WebML, as far as required for this paper, is introduced informally. Then, we motivate how this design step could be performed by a transformer that will be the running example of this paper.

2.1   A Simple Design Step in WebML

We start with defining a WebML data scheme comprising entity types and relationships as depicted in Fig. 1(a) (please ignore the gray shaded part for the moment). It describes information about artists (entity type **Artist** with attribute **name**) and albums (entity type **Album** with attributes **title** and **published**). The undirected relationship between artists and albums is represented by a pair of directed relationships referred to as (relationship-) roles. Roles **Artist2Album** (0..N) and **Album2Artist** (1..1) state that an artist may author any number of albums and that an album is authored by exactly one artist, respectively. The values in parentheses (e.g. (ent1)) denote IDs for model elements like entity

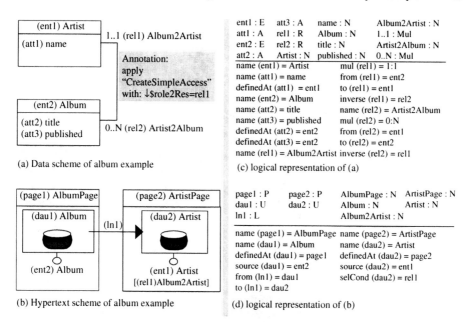

(a) Data scheme of album example

(b) Hypertext scheme of album example

(c) logical representation of (a)

(d) logical representation of (b)

Fig. 1. Left: (a)WebML data scheme, enhanced by (b)hypertext scheme, for albums example; Right: corresponding logical representations (c) and (d), resp.

types, attributes, etc. and are generated by WebML. Though these IDs are usually shown in separate forms, we have included them directly in the graphical representation for conciseness.

In our simple design step, the two connected entity types of the data scheme are complemented by linked pages in the hypertext scheme. The resulting hypertext scheme is depicted in Fig. 1(b) and comprises two pages **AlbumPage** and **ArtistPage**. These pages contain data units that define how to publish members of an entity type serving as source, whereby a data unit displays one member at a time. The source of unit **Album** is entity type **Album**, represented by ID **ent2**, and the source of unit **Artist** is entity type **Artist**, represented by ID **ent1**. Units may further define selectors (conditions) that identify the member that shall be displayed. This will be explained below.

Units are linked for navigation. Link **ln1** from unit **Album** to unit **Artist** specifies navigation from an album page to the page of its artist[1]. Which particular artist will be displayed depends on the album-object displayed in unit **Album** at the time the link is traversed. This is referred to as a contextual link that works as follows: the current album is passed as parameter along link **ln1**. Unit **Artist** uses this parameter for evaluating its selection condition in order to determine the artist that shall be displayed. This will be the album's artist as the selection condition refers to relationship role **rel1** (i.e. **Album2Artist**).

---

[1] To keep the example simple, we abandoned an index of albums and subsequently a link to the album page.

The next design step would then define a presentation scheme which specifies the arrangement of pages' content and the styles to use. However, because of limited space and because WebML emphasizes content and hypertext schemes [4], we will focus on these schemes as described so far, too.

2.2   An Example for Using a Transformer

Design steps as the one explained above, leading from a scheme with two entity types connected by a 1..1 relationship role to a scheme containing two pages with linked units that refer to the entity types, will probably arise many times. It would therefore be convenient to have them performed by a transformer. For example, a transformer "CreateSimpleAccess" could be defined that automatically generates a scheme like that of Fig. 1(b) when applied to a scheme like that of Fig. 1(a).

To get an impression of how a transformer is defined with our approach, the left hand side of Fig. 2 shows definition of transformer "CreateSimpleAccess". The input template shown in Fig. 2(a) looks quite the same as the scheme in Fig. 1(a). However, the template contains annotations like the $- and the ↓$-symbols denoting implicit and explicit parameters, respectively. Further, it abstracts from whether an entity type has attributes as well as from the name of the relationship role and its inverse role. These elements are not relevant for generating the pages and linked units as required. Analogously, the output template shown in Fig. 2(b) looks quite the same as the design step's result which is shown in Fig. 1(b). The ↑$-symbols denote scheme element construction.

Transformer "CreateSimpleAccess" is applied to a scheme by properly binding elements to explicit parameters as shown in the gray shaded area of Fig. 1(a). The relationship role to be resolved, `rel1`, is bound to parameter ↓ `$role2Res`. Note that ↓ `$role2Res` is the only parameter that has to be bound explicitly. All other parameters are bound implicitly by the transformer. For example, parameter `$tgtEnt` will be bound to `ent1` (i.e. entity type `Artist`) as this is the only entity type that is attached to the "to"-end of relationship role `rel1`. The result of this application will then be the scheme of Fig. 1(b).

3   Logical Representation of WebML Schemes

This section defines the logical representation of WebML schemes what will be the basis for defining transformers. Note that the formalization of a subset of WebML is required for demonstration but is not the focus of this paper.

In general, the logical representation of WebML-schemes comprises a set of universes $\widehat{U}$ of scheme elements and a set of single-valued functions $\widehat{\mathcal{F}}$ denoting relationships among scheme elements (sets of universes or functions are marked by a ^-symbol). Scheme elements are distinguished into literals and into tokens, i.e. IDs of scheme elements representing them. Correspondingly, the set of universes is divided into a set $\widehat{E}$ of token universes and a set $\widehat{\mathcal{L}it}$ of literal universes, $\widehat{\mathcal{L}it} = \widehat{U} \setminus \widehat{E}$. Each token universe $E \in \widehat{E}$ defines function $new(E)$ for generating new instances. For literal universes, a value stands for an instance.

The logical representation of WebML's content model consists of following universes and functions: Entity types, their attributes, and relationship roles are represented by universes E, $\mathcal{A}$, and $\mathcal{R}$, respectively. The names (literal universe $\mathcal{N}$) of these elements are defined by function $name : (E \cup \mathcal{A} \cup \mathcal{R}) \rightarrow \mathcal{N}$. Each attribute belongs to an entity type (function $definedAt : \mathcal{A} \rightarrow E$) and relationship roles are attached to a source and a target entity type (functions $from : \mathcal{R} \rightarrow E$, $to : \mathcal{R} \rightarrow E$). An undirected relationship is represented by a pair of directed relationship roles that refer to one another (function $inverse : \mathcal{R} \rightarrow \mathcal{R}$). Further, each role has a multiplicity (literal universe $\mathcal{M}ul = \{0..1, 1..1, 0..N, 1..N\}$ and function $mul : \mathcal{R} \rightarrow \mathcal{M}ul$).

The logical representation of WebML's hypertext model consists of following universes and functions: Pages, units, and links are represented by universes $\mathcal{P}$, $\mathcal{U}$, and $\mathcal{L}$, respectively. These elements have names (function $name : (\mathcal{P} \cup \mathcal{U} \cup \mathcal{L}) \rightarrow \mathcal{N}$). Units are components of pages (function $definedAt : \mathcal{U} \rightarrow \mathcal{P}$), and links connect one unit to another unit (functions $from : \mathcal{L} \rightarrow \mathcal{U}$ and $to : \mathcal{L} \rightarrow \mathcal{U}$). Each unit refers to its source entity type (function $source : \mathcal{U} \rightarrow E$) and may have a selection condition in form of a relationship role attached (function $selCond : \mathcal{U} \rightarrow \mathcal{R}$).

Example 1. Fig. 1(c) and (d) show the logical representations of the schemes in Fig. 1(a) and (b), respectively. A member m of a universe u is denoted as $m : u$. A function f relates its domain value x to its range value y and is denoted as $f(x) = y$. For example, function `name(ent1)=Artist` defines the name of entity type `ent1`. As WebML IDs represent scheme elements like entity types, they are directly used as tokens, e.g. *ent1* $: E$.

In these terms, each WebML scheme $S = (\widehat{\mathcal{U}}, \widehat{\mathcal{F}})$ is represented by a set of universes $\widehat{\mathcal{U}} = \widehat{\mathcal{L}it} \cup \widehat{E}$ with $\widehat{\mathcal{L}it} = \{\mathcal{N}, \mathcal{M}ul\}$, $\widehat{E} = \{E, \mathcal{A}, \mathcal{R}, \mathcal{P}, \mathcal{L}, \mathcal{U}\}$, and a set of functions $\widehat{\mathcal{F}} = \{name, definedAt, from, to, inverse, mul, source, selCond\}$.

For convenience, as we often use several schemes in different contexts, e.g. a scheme denoting an input scheme, we denote the particular context as x and the scheme as S_x. We then assume corresponding sets of universes $\widehat{\mathcal{U}}_x = (\widehat{E}_x \cup \widehat{\mathcal{L}it}_x)$ and functions $\widehat{\mathcal{F}}_x$ as defined.

4   Defining and Applying Transformers

This section formally defines transformers based on logical representations of schemes. We first specify how they are defined before we explain how they behave when applied to schemes.

4.1   Defining Transformers

A transformer is a parameterized description of (i) a scheme to which it may be applied, and (ii) how this scheme is extended or refined by new elements that are connected to existing or new elements. The first and the second property are specified by a transformer's input and output template, respectively.

Each *template* has, as usual for templates, a set of constant elements C as well as a set of variables V. Each variable represents a scheme element and denotes a parameter. Functions in templates are therefore defined over constant elements and variables. However, the semantics of constants, variables, and functions in an input template is different from that in an output template. Both templates will be explained now.

An *input template* S_{IT} of a transformer *trans* is a parameterized scheme and defines to which schemes *trans* can be applied. This is expressed by constraints over parameters (represented by variables) and constant elements. An input template is therefore defined with respect to a scheme S_i to which the transformer will later be applied and comprises following parts:

1. a set of *explicit parameters* $V_{expl} \subseteq V$, each being bound to an element of some universe $u \in \widehat{\mathcal{U}}_i$, denoted as $\downarrow \$ <name>: u$,
2. a set of *implicit parameters* $V_{impl} = V \setminus V_{expl}$, each ranging over a universe $u \in \widehat{\mathcal{U}}_i$, denoted as $\$ <name>: u$, and
3. a set of *constraints* over variables and constant elements denoted either (i) as $v_1 \ op \ (v_2 \mid c)$, whereby $\mid$ denotes a BNF-symbol separating alternatives, $op \in \{=, \neq\}$, $v_1, v_2 \in V$, and $c \in C$, or (ii) as $f(x_1, \ldots, x_{n-1}) = x_n$, for $i = 1..n, x_i \in (V \cup C), f \in \widehat{\mathcal{F}}_{IT}$.

Example 2. Fig. 2(c) shows the input template of transformer "CreateSimpleAccess", illustrated by depicting constraints and members of V_{expl}, V_{impl}, and C in sections named correspondingly. Constraint $name(\$srcEnt) = \$srcEntN$ restricts bindings of $(\$srcEnt, \$srcEntN)$ to those pairs of values $(e \in E_i, n \in N_i)$ where a function $name_i(e) = n$ is defined; constraint $\$srcEnt \neq \$tgtEnt$ states that the source and the target entity must be different.

In WebML, implicit parameters are denoted by symbol $\$$ preceding the scheme element's ID or literal value, explicit parameters additionally are preceded by symbol $\downarrow$. Constraints of the form $f(x_1, \ldots, x_{n-1}) = x_n$ are expressed implicitly by functions defined by the graphical arrangement of elements. Constraints of the form $v_1 \ op \ (v_2 \mid c)$ are annotated in comment fields and are extracted during the mapping to the logical representation of the template.

Example 3. Fig. 2(a) shows an input template and Fig. 2(c) its logical representation. The annotated constraint $\$srcEnt \neq \$tgtEnt$ has been taken over. The constraint $name(\$srcEnt) = \$srcEntN$ is implicitly defined by treating the corresponding function $name(\$srcEnt) = \$srcEntN$ as constraint.

Output Template. An output template S_{OT} is a parameterized description of new elements to be generated and of new connections between elements to be established and comprises following parts:

1. a set $\widehat{\mathcal{U}}_G = \widehat{E}_G \cup \widehat{\mathcal{L}it}_G$ of universes for generated elements, and a set of *new-element variables* $V_g \subseteq V$ for elements of a universe $u \in \widehat{\mathcal{U}}_G$, denoted as $\uparrow \$ <name>: u$,

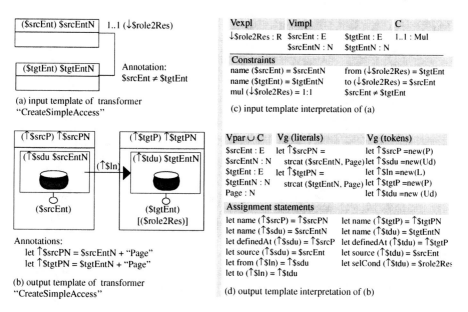

Fig. 2. (a) WebML input template and (b) output template for transformer "CreateSimpleAccess", correspondingly interpreted logical representations (c) and (d), resp.

2. a set of *parameters* $V_{par} = V \setminus V_g$ representing those explicit and implicit parameters that will be bound by the input template, denoted as $\$ $ <name>: u, $u \in \widehat{\mathcal{U}}_{OT}$,

3. a set of *construction expressions* for assigning values to each new-element variable $v_g \in V_g$. If v_g represents an element of some universe $u \in \widehat{E}_G$, the expression has the form `let` $v_g := $ `new` (u). Otherwise, v_g represents a literal and the expression has the form `let` $v_g := $ `exp`$(x_1, \ldots, x_n)$, whereby `exp` denotes an operation defined over particular universes[2] and for $i = 1..n$, $x_i \in (V_{par} \cup C)$, and

4. a set $\widehat{\mathcal{F}}_G$ of *generated functions* and a set of *assignment statements*, each defining the range value of a function $f_g \in \widehat{\mathcal{F}}_G$ for a particular domain value. This is denoted as *let* $f(x_1, \ldots, x_{n-1}) = x_n$, for $i = 1..n, x_i \in (V \cup C), f \in \widehat{\mathcal{F}}_G$.

Example 4. Fig. 2(d) depicts the output template of transformer "CreateSimpleAccess". Members of V_{par} and C are shown in section "$V_{par} \cup C$", literal and element constructions in "Vg (literals)" and "Vg (tokens)", respectively. Assignment statements are shown in section "Assignment statements". Literal construction `let` $\uparrow \$srcPN = $ `strcat`$(\$srcEntN, Page)$ denotes the call of

---

[2] Note that we do not provide predefined operations for `exp` as they are model-dependent. For example, operation $strcat(\mathcal{N}, \mathcal{N}) : \mathcal{N}$ concatenating two names is defined for WebML in particular.

model-dependent operation `strcat` concatenating two values of sort $\mathcal{N}$. Assignment statement `let` $source(\uparrow \$\text{tdu}) = \$\text{tgtP}$ lets the generated unit $\uparrow \$\text{tdu}$ refer to entity type $\$\text{tgtP}$ that is provided as parameter by the input template.

In WebML, parameters are denoted by symbol $ preceding the scheme element's ID or literal value, new-element variables additionally are preceded by symbol $\uparrow$. For each token element that is represented by a new-element variable, element constructions are denoted implicitly. Assignment statements are again denoted implicitly due to the graphical arrangement of scheme elements. Literal constructions are annotated explicitly.

Example 5. Fig. 2(b) depicts the output template of transformer "CreateSimpleAccess" in WebML. It should be self-explanatory as its logical representation is depicted to the right in Fig. 2(d).

4.2 Applying Transformers

A transformer *trans* is applied to a concrete scheme S_c by binding elements $e_i \in \widehat{\mathcal{U}}_c$, $i = 1..n$, to explicit parameters of *trans* and is denoted as $trans(S_c, v_{expl\_1} = e_1, \ldots, v_{expl\_n} = e_n)$. Such an application is *valid*, if (i) each explicit parameter is bound to an element of its type and (ii) a unique binding of implicit parameters exists such that all constraints defined by *trans* are satisfied.

Example 6. If transformer "CreateSimpleAccess" shown in Fig. 2(c) and (d) were applied to the scheme shown in Fig. 1(c) with relationship role `rel2` bound to explicit parameter $\downarrow \$\text{role2Res}$, the application would be invalid as constraint $mul(\downarrow \$\text{role2Res}) = 1..1$ would be violated.

In WebML, an application of a transformer is explicitly annotated and specifies the name of the transformer and the explicit parameter bindings.

Example 7. The gray shaded area of Fig. 1(a) specifies to apply transformer "CreateSimpeAccess" and binds relationship role `rel1` to $\downarrow \$\text{role2Res}$. This application is valid. Implicit parameter $\$\text{srcEnt}$ is bound to entity `ent2` as this is the only element of universe $E_c \in \widehat{\mathcal{U}}_c$ fulfilling constraint $from(\downarrow \$\text{role2Res}) = \$\text{srcEnt}$. Similarly, by evaluating all constraints, the transformer determines following bindings: $\$\text{srcEntN} = \text{Album}$, $\$\text{tgtEnt} = \text{ent1}$, and $\$\text{tgtEntN} = \text{Artist}$.

A valid application of transformer *trans* to scheme S_i generates new elements for each $v \in V_g$ and function assignments for each $f_g \in \widehat{\mathcal{F}}_G$ yielding a scheme-fragment $S_g = (\widehat{\mathcal{U}}_g, \widehat{\mathcal{F}}_g)$. Merging fragment S_g with S_i leads to the resulting scheme S_o. The merge is defined as follows: (1) for each kind of universe U, $U_o := U_i \cup U_g$, and (2) for each kind of model function F, $F_o := F_i \cup F_g$.

Example 8. Based on example 7, variable $\uparrow \$\text{srcPN}$ is assigned value "AlbumPage", variable $\uparrow \$\text{srcP}$ is assigned a new element p of universe $\mathcal{P}_g$, and the name of p is defined by function $name(p) = \text{AlbumPage}$. Unifying the set of all new elements and function assignments with the corresponding sets in S_i then yields the schemes depicted on the right hand side of Fig. 1. This logical representation then is mapped to the WebML-representation and leads to the schemes depicted on the left hand side of Fig. 1.

5   Related Work

This section describes approaches that partly have either motivation or realization common with transformers by example. Approaches closest to our's are explained first.

Transformation rules described in [8] define transformers by specifying a sequence of schema modification operations. This requires to understand operations like, for example, an expression "`addAPDPage (p)`" for creating a new page. In contrast, our approach is based on parameterized examples from which schema modification operations can be generated. However, iterative element construction as supported by transformation rules of [8] is not yet supported by our approach, although this is a problem of limited space rather than one of limited concept. Therefore, we cannot yet define a transformer that, for example, automatically collects all entity types of a scheme and generates a page class for each of them.

Visual query systems (VQS, surveyed in [3]) are graphical interfaces to databases. Some of them, e.g. QBE [14] and GQL [12], denote a query by specifying an example of the desired result. Their motivation is comparable to that of input templates. However, input templates offer (and require) less expressive power than query systems: in contrast to queries which yield a set of result tuples, input templates as described in this paper only yield one tuple, i.e. one unique binding of scheme elements. This allowed for precisely defining transformers' semantics, whereas a fully fledged query system would have gone beyond the scope of this paper.

Generic schema management as described in [2] provides a general and formal framework for specifying schema modification operations, and we could have used this framework for explaining our transformer's semantics. However, in our logical representation of schemes, there are only two sorts of schema modification operations, i.e. "generate new token" and "generate function instance". Therefore, for defining our transformer's semantics, the formal framework would have required much more explanation than reasonable.

6   Conclusion

We have presented a way for defining web schema transformers by example. As they are specified with the same model/tool as used for defining schemes, definition of transformers does not require to understand or define a sequence of various schema modification operations. Instead, a small set of generic constructs, which are denoted by annotating scheme elements, is sufficient to define and apply transformers. Modelers can therefore easily just use a repertoire of transformers, but they can also easily define their own transformers for various modelling tasks they perform repeatedly. This has been demonstrated on a use-case specified in WebML.

Semantics of transformers has been defined precisely with a logical representation of schemes independently of a particular model such as WebML. Therefore, enabling transformers in a particular model only requires (i) to define a universe for each different sort of the model's elements and (ii) to define a function for each different sort of relations among these elements. This has again been demonstrated with WebML.

The paper has focused on transformers for supporting design steps. Beside that, transformers could be beneficially used for generating hypertext views that adapt a base web application for particular front end devices. Similarly, transformers could also be used for generating personalized views for particular user groups on the fly. Describing these topics as well as improving expressive power of transformers to capture iterative construction of scheme elements will be subject of further work.

Acknowledgement. We are grateful for many helpful comments from Günter Preuner, Mathias Goller, Anne Hoffmann, and the anonymous referees.

References

1. *WebRatio Site Development Studio, Vers. 3.0.7.* http://www.webratio.com, 2002.
2. Suad Alagić and Philip A. Bernstein. A model theory for generic schema management. *Lecture Notes in Computer Science*, 2397:228–239, 2002.
3. T. Catarci, M.F. Costabile, S. Levialdi, and C. Batini. Visual query systems for databases: A survey. *Journal of Visual Languages and Computing*, 8(2), 1997.
4. S. Ceri, P. Fraternali, A. Bongio, M. Brambilla, S. Comai, and M. Matera. *Designing Data-Intensive Web Applications*. Morgan Kaufmann, 2003.
5. Stefano Ceri, Piero Fraternali, and Aldo Bongio. Web Modeling Language (WebML): a modeling language for designing Web sites. *Computer Networks (Amsterdam, Netherlands: 1999)*, 33(1–6):137–157, 2000.
6. J. Frohn, R. Himmeröder, P. Kandzia, G. Lausen, and C. Schlepphorst. FLORID: A prototype for F-logic. In *ICDE'97*, pages 583–. IEEE, April 1997.
7. Jaime Gómez, Cristina Cachero, and Oscar Pastor. Extending a conceptual modelling approach to web application design. In *CAiSE'00*, pages 79–93, 2000.
8. Jaime Gómez, Cristina Cachero, and Oscar Pastor. Conceptual modeling of device-independent Web applications. *IEEE MultiMedia*, 8(2):26–39, April 2001.
9. S. Lechner and M. Schrefl. *By-example schema transformers for supporting the process of conceptual web application modelling*. Technical Report TR0301, University of Linz, Austria, 2003.
10. G. Mecca, P. Atzeni, A. Masci, G. Sindoni, and P. Merialdo. The araneus web-based management system. In *ACM SIGMOD'98*, pages 544–546, 1998.
11. Marc Nanard, Jocelyne Nanard, and Paul Kahn. Pushing reuse in hypermedia design: golden rules, design patterns and constructive templates. In *9th ACM conference on Hypertext and hypermedia*, pages 11–20. ACM Press, 1998.
12. Anthony Papantonakis and Peter J. H. King. Gql, a declarative graphical query language based on the functional data model. In *Proceedings of the workshop on Advanced visual interfaces*, pages 113–122. ACM Press, 1994.
13. Daniel Schwabe and Gustavo Rossi. An object oriented approach to web-based application design. *Theory and Practice of Object Systems*, 4(4), 1998.
14. M. M. Zloof. Query-by-example: A database language. *IBM System Journal*, 16(4):324–343, 1977.

A Conceptual Framework for Spatiotemporal Data Modeling

Kuo Wang[1], Cristina Fierbinteanu[2], and Mamoru Maekawa[1]

[1] The Graduate School of Information Systems,
University of Electro-Communications,
Chofukaoka 1-5-1 Chofu,
Tokyo, Japan
{kuo,maekawa}@maekawa.is.uec.ac.jp
[2] Metroul S.A., Inc.,
Str. Gutenberg 3bis, sector 5 70626,
Bucharest, Romania
{cristina}@metroul.ro

Abstract. Conceptual data modeling of spatiotemporal applications is used to describe user's cognition of real world phenomena and must support adequate concepts and notations with accurate semantics to allow the developer to capture and present spatiotemporal information. In this paper we propose a conceptual framework for spatiotemporal geographic data modeling, which is based on the Object-Oriented concept and additionally provides an expression for capturing space, time and time-varying information. The framework is built around the concept of geographic theme. We focus on using operations to define a new theme based on already defined themes, the internal representation being completely hidden from the user.

1 Introduction

A conceptual model with precise semantics gives a high level abstraction representation of the real world and enables the system design to focus on the conceptual schema independently from the details of implementation. Conventional spatial applications are mostly concerned with 2-dimensional spatial information. However, spatial data changes in time, and corresponding spatial attributes also change values in time. There is at present a clear need for spatiotemporal information systems and high level models for the conceptual design of spatiotemporal application [15]. Good surveys for spatiotemporal conceptual models can be found in [16] [1] [10] [13] and the requirements and research issues are discussed in [6] [14] [9] in detail. So far, a number of conceptual models have been reported in the research literature [12] [15] [17] [3].

The concept of "Theme" is an essential part of the spatial data model to represent geographic phenomena in the real world. The theme is a view of the world from a user's perspective and is used to classify the reality objects and simplify the way of thinking and dealing with data [4]. For example, the real world's cities,

V. Mařík et al. (Eds.): DEXA 2003, LNCS 2736, pp. 57–66, 2003.

roads, rivers and buildings can be classified as cadastre, transportation, water system and building. Conventional spatial application usually perform specific analyses (e.g., buffer and overlay) or queries based on defined theme. The definition of new themes in current GIS requires knowledge of both the geographic data model used and database administration. The drawbacks carried by this process are (1)expert knowledge required for the design and manipulation of the system (2)consequently high development and maintenance costs.

However, the previous works which are relevant to conceptual data model have not considered the representation of the theme and their dependent relation, and thus lacked expressive power for defining the theme.

The GeoFrame [8] defines analysis patterns based upon the concept of the theme for geographic applications. Although GeoFrame-T, a temporal extension of GeoFrame has been proposed in [4], theme definition related to previously defined themes and their dependent relations have not been considered.

Glaucia Faria [7] et al. developed a framework based on extending an Object-Oriented database system with spatiotemporal classes, data structures and functions to provide support for the development of spatiotemporal applications. The basic operators are defined to perform all typical spatial and temporal queries (only valid time). Though these basic operators are similar to what we propose in this paper, our proposal is more flexible in handling with temporal information at different levels(e.g., geographic entity or theme) and is more suitable for definition of new themes.

In this paper, we propose an Object-Oriented conceptual framework for modeling spatiotemporal data in a spatiotemporal application. We especially focus on defining the theme and the dependent relations belonging to the themes at conceptual level. We represent the definition of new themes based on previously defined themes to allow the internal representation being completely hidden from the user. This will simplify the conceptual expression and facilitate the implementation of the system.

2   Essential Definition of Spatiotemporal Objects

We define the primitive spatiotemporal objects as follows:

`GeoEntity` is the true object in the real world. For example, a river, a road, a coastline, or a railway station. A geoentity must be assigned to one or more geoentity classes, for example, BUILDING, ROAD, UNIVERSITY or MUNICIPAL DISTRICT. A geoentity is a fundamental unit to represent geographic data and has its own inherent attributes (e.g., a MUNICIPAL AREA has name, area, population, population-density etc.). `GeoEntity` includes geometry information corresponding to geographic space (e.g., 3-dimension coordinates of buildings), thematic attributes describing qualitative or quantitative characteristics associated with geographic data (e.g., the owner name, building construction date are attributes of a building) and temporal information associated with timestamps.

`GeoEntity Class` is defined as a set of geoentities. A geoentity must be assigned to one or more geoentity classes. By assigning geographic entities to

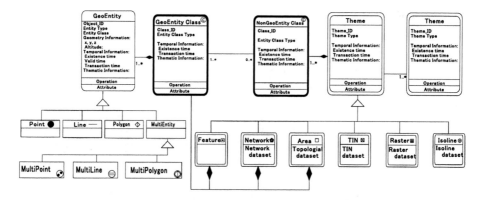

Fig. 1. Spatiotemporal abstract objects and themes

different geoentity classes, geoentities can be selectively manipulated. For example, the boundary of a county can be defined as a GeoEntity class which consists of several district line entities and at most one coastline entity. The coastline entity can be grouped with other coastline entities to compose a "Coastline" GeoEntity Class.

`NonGeoEntity Class` is defined as a class of nongeoentities. In spatiotemporal application there are also entities which have no geometric information. The NonGeoEntity can be associated with specific GeoEntity class.

`Theme` is defined as a set of geoentity classes and nongeoentity classes and has its specific attributes. A theme can be defined using only one geoentity class or more geoentity classes. Furthermore, a theme can be defined from other themes based on user-defined selection operations. For example, a new theme "University adjacent national road" can be defined by using an operation which selects the universities adjacent to national roads from theme "University" and theme "National Road".

We define BNF (Backus-Naur Form) of GeoEntity and Theme as follows:

GeoEntity := { Point | Line | Polygon | MultiPoint | MultiLine | MultiPolygon }

Theme := { Feature | Network | Area | Raster | TIN | Isoline }

The complete definitions of objects and hierarchy of theme are illustrated in Figure 1.

Note that Feature theme is a set of geoentity classes, for example triangulation point and building. A Network theme is a set of linear geoentity classes and has its own topological information, for example a highway network. Area theme is a set of polygonal geoentity classes, an Area theme has its own topological information holds among polygons (e.g., a Municipal District). We use Raster, TIN (Triangulated Irregular Network) and Isoline to represent field-based objects.

3   Representation of Temporal Information and Time-Varying Attributes

In a spatiotemporal database environment, the data values corresponding with geographic objects may vary with time. These changes include change of the geographic object's location or extent and change of its thematic property. For instance, the road network may change according to road construction process, municipal areas may have different boundaries following new urban planning. Road names, building owner names, etc. may change over time as well. We want to record the time related with these changes, such as existence time, valid time and transaction time [14].

The temporal information of geographic objects consists of Timestamp, Time Classification and temporal Granularity. Temporal information is a user-defined attribute for time-dependent properties.

The definitions of temporal information components are given in BNF as follows.

Temporal Information := {Timestamp | Time Classification | Granularity }
Timestamp := { instant | interval | temporal element}
Time Classification := { valid time | transaction time | existence time | user-defined time}
Granularity := { second | minute | day | month | year | user-defined }
Representation of spatiotemporal concepts is defined using symbols as follow:
Ⓢ : space-varying symbol
Ⓣ : time-varying symbol
The *space-varying* symbol represents the temporally change of geographic object on location or extent. The *time-varying* symbol represents the temporally change of thematic attribute associated with geographic object. We can use ⒮Ⓣ as a combination of Ⓢ and Ⓣ to represent that both space property and thematic attribute will change over time. These symbols can be used at different abstract levels, for example attribute level, as well as object level (see Figure 2).

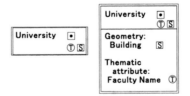

Fig. 2. Representing different abstract levels with spatiotemporal symbols

As an essential aspect of conceptual design, relationships should be represented precisely. The proposed conceptual model supports Object-Oriented relationships as well as spatial relationships and temporal relationships. We use Allen's definitions [2] to represent temporal relationships among timestamps.

Spatial relationships among geographic objects are more complex. According to [5], spatial relationships are classified into five categories: topological, direction, distance, fuzzy and comparative relations. For the sake of briefness, we defined topological and direction relationships. Furthermore, as geographic objects contain specific relationships (e.g., inside, above, below) in a three-dimension environment, the proposed model also defined some 3D-relationships which represent spatial relationships on Z-axis among geographic objects. These relationships are defined as follows:

Object-oriented relationship := { composition | inheritance | association }

Temporal relationship := { T-Before | T-Equal | T-Meets | T-Overlaps | T-During | T-Starts | T-Finishes | user-defined temporal relationship }

Spatial relationship := { Topological relationship | Direction relationship | 3D relationship | user-defined relationship}

Topological relationship := { Equal | Disjoint | Intersect | Touch | Cross | Within | Contains | Overlap | user-defined spatial relation}

Direction relationship := {North | South | West | East | in front of | to the left of | to the right of }

3D relationship := { Inside | Across | Higher | Under }

4   Theme-Dependent Properties and Operations

The classification of themes is based on user requests. For example, if according to user's need, superhighways have to be separated from "Main Road" theme, then a new theme "Superhighway" must be defined. Thus, it is better for the definition of a new theme to be based only on previously defined themes (if the new theme can be defined based on existing themes), and the details about theme, thematic attribute tables and related manipulation of database to be completely hidden from the user. We propose a unique method to represent theme-dependent definition at conceptual level. We defined operations to represent relationships among the new theme and previously defined themes. As these operations are representative queries in spatiotemporal, they can also be used to query spatial, temporal or spatiotemporal information.

Firstly, we give several examples to describe the definition of a new theme based on attribute-dependent, spatial-dependent, temporal-dependent and spatio-temporal-dependent operations among previously defined themes.

Example 1. The new theme "National Road" is defined by an operation which extracts the roads from theme "Road Network" with thematic attribute "Road.classification" = "National" (see Figure 3a).

This operation refers to specific attribute of theme and the attribute related with geographic object. We define this kind of operation as **Attribute-dependent Operation**. Actually, this kind of operation is used as an attribute condition to identify which geoentity should be the target of specific operation. For instance, "Road.classification" = "Superhighway" specifies that every road whose classification value is "Superhighway" will be a target of operation.

62   K. Wang, C. Fierbinteanu, and M. Maekawa

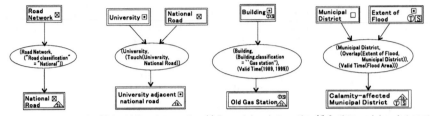

(a) Attribute-dependent operation (b) Spatial-dependent operation   (c) Temporal-dependent operation   (d) Spatiotemporal-dependent operation

Fig. 3. Examples for operations

Example 2. The new theme "University adjacent national road" is defined by an operation which extracts "the university which is adjacent to a national road" from two themes: "University" and "National Road" (see Figure 3b).

This operation requires a specific query about the spatial property of a geographic object within the theme. We define this kind of operation as Spatial-dependent Operation.

Example 3. The new theme "Old Gas Station" is defined by an operation which extracts "the gas station" according to "valid time from 1989 to 1999" from theme "Building" with thematic attribute "Building.classification" = "Gas Station" (see Figure 3c).

This operation requires a specific query about the temporal information of a geographic object within the theme. We define this kind of operation as Temporal-dependent Operation.

Example 4. The new theme "Calamity-affected Municipal District" is defined by an operation which extracts flooded municipal areas from themes "Municipal District" and "Extent of Flood". As "Extent of Flood" is a spatiotemporal theme, the properties of the new theme depend on the original theme not only spatially but also temporally (see Figure 3d). We define this kind of operation as Spatiotemporal-dependent Operation.

We defined theme-dependency symbol ⚠ to specify the relation of dependency between the new theme and previously defined themes.

⚠: = theme-dependency symbol

4.1 Spatial-Dependent and Temporal-Dependent Operations

As attribute-dependent operations are almost always defined by the user and depend on user-defined thematic attribute representation of the theme, we only consider spatial and temporal operations.

Spatial-dependent operations are defined as three types: operations based on spatial relations and spatial analysis and operations based on 3D relations. As there is still no consensus about spatial analysis, especially about field objects (or raster data), we only consider vectorial objects and vectorial themes.

We consider the following operations:

Spatial-dependent Topological Operations := { Disjoint | Intersect | Touch | Cross | Within | Contains | Overlap | user-defined Topological Operation }

Spatial-dependent Analysis Operations := {Area | Length | Perimeter | Distance | Shortest-path | Overlay | Buffer | ConvexHull | Intersection | Union | Difference | SymDiff | user-defined Analysis Operation }

3D Operations := { Altitude | Inside | Across | Higher | Under }

All above operations require a parameter (or parameters) holding geometric information. The parameter can be a geoentity, a geoentity class or a theme. As geoentity class and theme are defined as set of geoentities and set of geoentity classes respectively, the operation using theme or geoentity class as a parameter will return a list of tuples.

In our model, the time information is an intrinsic aspect of an entity, which describes the temporal properties of the entity. In this paper, we focus on three types of time information: *existence time*(when something exists), *valid time*(when something is true), *transaction time*(when something is recorded as current in the database) [11]. The geoentity has its lifespan defined as existence time which describes when a geoentity exists in the real world. Existence time is the valid time when the geoentity exists. For example, "Gas Station GS1" exists from 1982 to 1989. The valid time expresses when a fact is true. For example, "Farm FM1 extended and changed its shape in 1970". The transaction time shows when information is recorded in the database, for example the information that "Farm FM1 changed its extent and shape in 1970" is recorded as current in the database in 1992.

Table 1. Temporal operations

Operations	Operations description
Duration(T)	Returns duration of Time T
Existence-Time(E)	Returns existence time of object E
Valid-Time(E) Transaction-Time(E)	Returns valid time and transaction time of object E respectively
Valid-At(T)	Returns the concrete valid time value specified by Time T
Transaction-At(T)	Returns the concrete transaction time value specified by Time T
Existence-Time(T_s, T_e)	Returns the existence time interval specified by start time T_s and end time T_e
Valid-Time(T_s, T_e)	Returns the valid time interval specified by start time T_s and end time T_e
Transaction-Time(T_s, T_e)	Returns the transaction time interval specified by start time T_s and end time T_e

In addition to the operations based on conventional temporal relation, we also define some typical temporal operations required to define temporal-dependent operations (see Table 1). T_s and T_e denoting respectively start time and end time of the time interval. If $T_s = T_e$, the timestamp is treated as time point.

4.2   Spatiotemporal-Dependent Operations

The `spatiotemporal operations` are regarded as combinations of spatial operations and temporal operations. Assume that STO, SO, TO denote spatiotemporal operation, spatial operation and temporal operation respectively and E is a geoentity, then $STO(E, TO) = (SO(E), TO)$ returns a set of tuples $\{(SO(E)_i, T_i)\}$, where T_i are timestamps and $(SO(E)_i$ is the spatial operation corresponding to the timestamp. For example, assume Block B and convenience store S are two geographic entities, temporal operation is Valid-Time(1990, 1992), Blocks and Convenience stores are two themes. ST-Contains(Block B, Convenience store S, Valid-Time(1990, 1992)) = (Contains(Block B, Convenience store S), Valid-Time(1990, 1992)) will return true only if Block B contains a convenience store S in Valid time interval from 1990 to 1992. A part of Spatial-temporal operations are shown here:

Spatio-temporal Operations := { ST-Disjoint | ST-Intersect | ST-Touch | ST-Cross | ST-Within | ST-Contains | ST-Overlap | user-defined ST-Operation }

For representing theme definition at conceptual level, we define expression of spatiotemporal-dependent operations as below:

(*derived theme*,
 {([<*spatial operations*><comparison operator>
 <real number><logical operator>],...],
   [<*attribute operations*><comparison operator>
 <real number><logic operator>],...]),
 ([<*temporal operations*><comparison operator>
 <real number><logical operator>],...],
   [<*attribute operations*><comparison operator>
 <real number><logic operator>],...])}
 ,...)

The *derived theme* denotes the theme which is derived according to the identified condition. The parameter *spatial operations* describes specific predefined spatial-dependent operations. The attribute operations denote attribute-dependent operations defined by the user. The <comparison operator>, <real number>, <logic operator> are optional parameters which are used to allow formulation of the operation. The typical comparison operators are >, <, =, >=, <=, ≠. Three logic operators are defined: .AND. .OR. .NOT.

Next we show some examples of different operations. Assume Block, Building and Highway are themes in a map. "Building" consists of various buildings which are specified by their classification.

`attribute-dependent operation`: Find the buildings whose classification is "Gas station".

(Building, Building.classification = "Gas station")

`spatial-dependent operation`: Find the blocks which contain more than two buildings whose classifications are "convenience store".

(Block, (SUM(Overlay (Block, Building))) > 2, Building.classification = "convenience store")

Overlay is a spatial operation which derives all overlaid buildings and SUM gives the total of these buildings.

`temporal-dependent operation`: Find the buildings which existed during 1985-1990.

(Building,   T-During   (Existence   time   (Building),   Existence   Time (1985,1990)))

`spatiotemporal-dependent operation`: Find the blocks which contain more than two buildings whose classifications are "convenience store", according to valid time's timestamps of convenience store.

(Block, ((SUM(Overlay (Block, Building))) > 2, Building.classification = "convenience store"),

(Valid Time (Building), Building.classification = "convenience store"))

`spatiotemporal-dependent operation`: Find the forests whose area must be at least 5000 square meters according to valid time 1970-1998.

(Forest, (Area (forest) > 5000), (Valid Time(1970, 1998)))

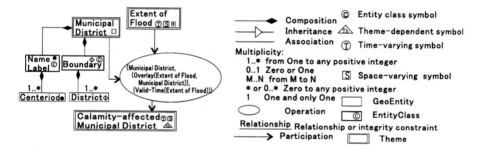

Fig. 4. Example of map definition

Figure 4 shows an example of map definition using our proposal. For the sake of simplicity, the internal details of geoentity, geoentity class and theme are omitted and only the conceptual structure and relations of dependency among themes are presented. The ellipse shows the definition of operations and the line with an arrow expresses which theme participates in an operation and links the result of an operation to a new theme.

5   Conclusions

This paper proposed a conceptual model for the development of spatiotemporal application. We focus on defining a new theme based on already defined themes and to represent their relations of dependency at conceptual level. The proposed model is based on our experience of implementing GIS applications and on the requirements for developing a new spatiotemporal GIS. We are implementing the system using C++ language and an extension query language and its visual interface are provided to support theme operation and spatiotemporal query.

References

1. T. Abraham and J. F. Roddick. Survey of spatio-temporal databases. *GeoInformatica*, 3(1):61–99, March 1999.
2. J. F. Allen. Maintaining knowledge about temporal intervals. *Communications of the ACM*, 26(11):832–843, November 1983.
3. K. A. V. Borges, A. H. F. Laender, and C. A. D. Jr. Spatial data integrity constraints in object oriented geographic data modeling. In *ACM GIS 99*, pages 1–5. ACM, 1999.
4. L. V. da Rocha, N. Edelweiss, and C. Iochpe. GeoFrame-T: A temporal conceptual framework for data modeling. In *ACM GIS '01, Proceedings of the 9th International Symposium on Advances in Geographic Information Systems, November 9–10, 2001, Atlanta, Georgia, USA*, pages 124–129. ACM, 2001.
5. M. J. Egenhofer and A. U. Frank. Towards a spatial query language: User interface considerations. In F. Bancilhon and D. J. DeWitt, editors, *Very large data bases: 1988, 14th VLDB, Los Angeles, USA, August 29–September 1: proceedings of the Fourteenth International Conference on Very Large Data Bases*, pages 124–133, Los Altos, CA 94022, USA, 1988. Morgan Kaufmann Publishers.
6. M. J. Egenhofer and A. U. Frank. Object-oriented modeling for GIS. *Journal of the Urban and Regional Information Systems Association*, 4:3–19, 1992.
7. G. Faria, C. B. Medeiros, and M. A. Nascimento. An extensible framework for spatio-temporal database applications. In *Statistical and Scientific Database Management*, pages 202–205, 1998.
8. J. L. Filho and C. Iochpe. Specifying analysis patterns for geographic databases on the basis of a conceptual framework. In C. B. Medeiros, editor, *ACM GIS '99, Proceedings of the 7th International Symposium on Advances in Geographic Information Systems, November 2–6, 1999, Kansas City, USA*, pages 7–13. ACM, 1999.
9. A. Friis-Christensen, N. Tryfona, and C. S. Jensen. Requirements and research issues in geographic data modeling. In *Proceedings of the ninth ACM international symposium on Advances in geographic information systems*, pages 2–8. ACM Press, 2001.
10. H. Gregersen and C. S. Jensen. Temporal entity-relationship models – A survey. *Transaction on Knowledge and Data Engineering*, 11(3):464–497, 1999.
11. C. S. Jensen, C. Dyreson, and et al. The consensus glossary of temporal database concepts (February 1998 version). In O. Etzion, S. Jajodia, and S. Sripada, editors, *Temporal Databases: Research and Practice*, volume 1399 of *Lecture Notes in Computer Science*, pages 367–405. Springer-Verlag, 1998.
12. C. Parent, S. Spaccapietra, and E. Zimanyi. Spatio-temporal conceptual models: Data structures + space + time. In *ACM GIS 99*, pages 26–33. ACM, 1999.
13. A. Pavlopoulos and B. Theodoulidis. Review of spatiotemporal data models. Technical report, TimeLab Technical Report TR-98-3, 1998.
14. D. Pfoser and N. Tryfona. Requirements, definitions and notations for spatiotemporal application environments. In *ACM GIS'98*, November 1998.
15. R. Price, N. Tryfona, and C. S. Jensen. A conceptual modeling language for spatiotemporal applications. Technical Report CH-99-20, CHOROCHRONOS, 1999.
16. B. Theodoulidis and et al. Review of temporal object-oriented approaches.
17. N. Tryfona and C. S. Jensen. Using abstractions for spatio-temporal conceptual modeling. In *Proceedings of the 2000 ACM symposium on Applied computing 2000*, pages 313–322. ACM Press, 2000.

Moa and the Multi-model Architecture: A New Perspective on NF²

M. van Keulen[1], J. Vonk[1], A.P. de Vries[2], J. Flokstra[1], and H.E. Blok[1]

[1] Center for Telematics and Information Technology (CTIT)
University of Twente,
Enschede, The Netherlands
{keulen,vonk,flokstra,blok}@eemcs.utwente.nl
[2] Centrum voor Wiskunde en Informatica,
Amsterdam, The Netherlands
arjen@cwi.nl

Abstract. Advanced non-traditional application domains such as geographic information systems and digital library systems demand advanced data management support. In an effort to cope with this demand, we present the concept of a novel multi-model DBMS architecture which provides evaluation of queries on complexly structured data without sacrificing efficiency. A vital role in this architecture is played by the Moa language featuring a nested relational data model based on XNF², in which we placed renewed interest. Furthermore, extensibility in Moa avoids optimization obstacles due to black-box treatment of ADTs. The combination of a mapping of queries on complexly structured data to an efficient physical algebra expression via a nested relational algebra, extensibility open to optimization, and the consequently better integration of domain-specific algorithms, makes that the Moa system can efficiently and effectively handle complex queries from non-traditional application domains.

1 Introduction

Advanced non-traditional applications, such as digital library systems (DL) and geographic information systems (GIS), place high demands on their data management components. Data in these areas is intrinsically complex and voluminous in nature and queries are computationally intensive. Researchers have sought to cope with these demands in different directions. In section 2, we explore these directions focussing on data model and DBMS architecture as a motivation for our multi-model DBMS architecture, as well as the particular role the logical algebra Moa plays in this architecture.

The multi-model DBMS architecture consists of three layers each supporting a different data model. In this way, the top conceptual layer provides a data model supporting complexly structured data, while in the logical and physical layers, a query on complexly structured data is gradually transformed to efficient storage-level operations. To be able to bridge the gap between a conceptual-level data model (e.g., a hierarchical or object-oriented data model) and a storage-level data model, we place renewed interest in Non First Normal Form (NF²) data models, which were popular in the 80s, but proved difficult to support efficiently with then available technology. The Moa data model, used in

V. Mařík et al. (Eds.): DEXA 2003, LNCS 2736, pp. 67–76, 2003.
© Springer-Verlag Berlin Heidelberg 2003

the logical layer of the architecture, is an adaptation and extension of $(X)NF^2$ for which we developed an approach towards efficient query evaluation. Another key feature of our approach is extensibility on all layers to be able to integrate domain-specific algorithms such that certain optimization obstacles concerning ADTs are avoided.

The strength of the Moa system lies in the combination of architecture, data models, the mappings between them, and the way extensibility is handled. This paper provides an overview of the entire concept necessarily leaving out much detail and focussing on architecture and data models. The more interested reader is referred to [21].

In Section 3, we present Moa's approach to query processing. The Moa language is illustrated by means of an example in Section 4. The ideas behind Moa have been validated and fine-tuned in various advanced application domains, such as GIS and multi-media retrieval, an overview of which is given in Section 5. Finally, we present our conclusions and future work in Section 6.

2 Motivation and Related Research

In the past decade, the following trade-off particularly eluded researchers when trying to make DBMS technology better suitable to non-traditional applications. On the one hand, it concerns *data model expressiveness*. The suitability of a DBMS for an application is closely related to the expressiveness of its data model. The data model of the conceptual level should fit the universe of discourse, since end-users have to understand this model of the real world in order to formulate their queries. To support the inherently complexly structure data of many application areas, advanced data models were proposed, such as the object-oriented and object-relational data models. On the other hand, *performance* is expected from the DBMS, which typically means that it should be able to effectively optimize queries. The more complex the data model, however, the harder it is to develop an effective optimizer, as research on OODBMSs clearly showed.

Garlic [8] is an example of a system that integrates special-purpose data servers using *object wrappers*. Unfortunately, even with its advanced optimizer that uses statistics from the wrappers, performing such processing outside the scope of the database system may cause serious performance degradation, see, e.g., [11]. *Full-fledged OODBMSs* do not meet demands either. Often data independence is not handled well: the application class structure dictates physical layout of data and user-interfaces were non-declarative. As known from RDBMSs, data independence is essential for scalability and data distribution. But even with a declarative query language and the ability to convert OO item-oriented thinking into set-oriented query plans, which O_2 [1] both mastered, OODBMSs never became the success as anticipated.

In the DBMS market today, the *object-relational (OR) data model* dominates claiming to be simple enough for query optimization, but expressive enough to handle advanced application areas. As Date and Darwen point out in [10], extensibility with user-defined data types does not require a new data model per se. However, as the Bucky benchmark has shown, room for improvement concerning performance exists [6]. Designed to evaluate especially the extra features of the OR data model, it

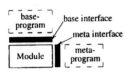

Fig. 1. Open implementation.

showed that a pure relational schema performed better in most cases than a schema using OR features such as set-valued attributes.

Furthermore, encapsulation of data and operations inside objects or ADTs affect query evaluation: optimization by the DBMS becomes infeasible, and query processing too often results in object-at-a-time evaluation. Predator's E-ADT concept [16] improves upon this by implementing an optimization interface to facilitate optimization of a query plan using its own algebraic operations. The E-ADT approach adheres to the *open implementation* approach, known from the software engineering field [14]. Instead of building an ADT as a black box, it provides a meta-interface (see Figure 1) allowing a client of the ADT to make certain performance choices. A typical example is a program's advice to the operating system to adjust its caching strategy to a (sequential) memory access pattern.

Multi-model DBMS architecture. To be able to deal with the trade-off between complex data model and performance, [22] introduces the multi-model DBMS architecture with different data models on different layers (see Figure 2) as opposed to ordinary relational systems, which use the relational model throughout the DBMS architecture. The conceptual layer typically has an OO data model or a hierarchical semi-structured one (e.g., XML). We choose other, 'simpler' data models for the logical and physical layers. Obviously, this comes at a cost, namely additional mappings between layers, that map a query expression from one language to another. A typical choice

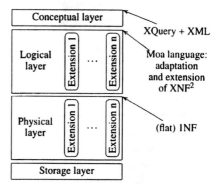

Fig. 2. The multi-model DBMS architecture and our choice for data models.

for a data model and algebra on the physical level, is one close to the machine, for example, relational algebra, or, what we have used in some cases, the binary relational data model of main-memory DBMS MonetDB [3].

The XNF^2-data model [15] is very suitable as intermediary data model for bridging the gap (logical layer) between a complex data model and a simple relational one. It handles complex data structures as nested relations, but still comes with an algebra that is not much more complex than an ordinary relational one. The idea of a DBMS based on XNF^2 [9] lost interest when it appeared too difficult to build one that performed well. In the sequel, we show our adaptation of the XNF^2 data model and its effective use in our multi-model DBMS prototype, called Moa.

Summarizing, the Moa DBMS prototype with its multi-model architecture has the potential of better meeting the demands of advanced application domains. By using different data models on different layers, it is possible to provide a complex data model at the top and still be able to evaluate queries efficiently. We achieve the latter through several provisions: (1) by utilizing an XNF^2-based algebra as an intermediary, queries on complexly structured data are gradually and effectively translated to efficient storage-level operations, (2) extensibility at all layers allows to better integrate domain-specific algorithms into the DBMS, thus improving the performance of domain-specific operations, and (3) extensibility in Moa is defined such that extensions are not black-boxes, but are open to the optimizer, hence, possible optimizations can be better exploited.

In the following section, we present Moa's approach to XNF^2-based query processing within the multi-model architecture.

3   Query Processing in Moa

As early as 1982, Schek and Pistor argued that the relational data model is inconvenient for a domain like information retrieval [15]. To overcome these shortcomings, they propose a NF^2 data model dropping the first normal form (1NF) requirement to allow non-atomic attribute domains such as sets of values. Many theoretical properties of the relational model also hold for NF^2. The main difference between NF^2 and eXtended NF^2 (XNF^2) data models such as that of the AIM DBMS [9], is that XNF^2 supports additional data types such as lists and allows for arbitrary nesting of type constructors.

The main part of the work on NF^2 concerns the *definition* of algebras, not their function: facilitate efficient query evaluation. With the latter, problems are encountered including inefficient nested-loop processing, data redundancy, restructuring overhead and the infamous *COUNT-bug* [18], since in the presence of empty subsets, unnest is not the inverse of nest. [17] has made a large contribution to the area of query optimization of nested relational algebras with, e.g., the introduction of a special *nestjoin*-operator.

Moa is an extension of XNF^2, where not only type constructors can be arbitrarily nested, but also new type constructors can be added. Moa additionally incorporates a solution to the mentioned NF^2 query processing problems. It does this by keeping an explicit structure definition in the form of type constructors connected to unnested (flat) data, and by having both nest/unnest operators as well as navigators, such as *map*. Furthermore, it deals with the COUNT-bug by explicitly generating counteracting operations where needed.

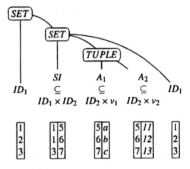

Example (see Figure 3). Suppose, our database

Fig. 3. Nested data and flat data.

db is structured as a set of sets of n-tuples: $db \in \mathcal{PP} V_1 \times \ldots \times V_n$ where $\mathcal{P}$ is the powerset operator and V_i are domains of atomic values. Choosing subsets of V_i as $v_1 = \{a, b, c\}$ and $v_2 = \{11, 12, 13\}$, a concrete db can look like $db = \{\{(a, 11), (b, 12)\}, \{\}, \{(c, 13)\}\}$. Our generic mapping represents db as type constructors (rounded rectangles) connected to the following flat data:

$$ID_1 = \text{set of as many unique id's as there are subsets in the database.} \quad (1)$$
$$ID_2 = \text{set of as many unique id's as there are } n\text{-tuples in the database.} \quad (2)$$
$$SI = \text{subset index as a set of pairs} \subseteq ID_1 \times ID_2 \quad (3)$$
$$A_i = \text{columns as a set of pairs} \subseteq ID_2 \times v_i \ (i \in \{1, 2\}) \quad (4)$$

The figure furthermore illustrates the distinction between a *value* and an *identified value set* (or *ivs*). A column does not represent one atomic value, but a *set* of atomic values. The TUPLE structure constructed from A_1 and A_2 represents a set of tuples, called

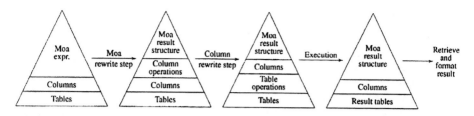

Fig. 4. Moa query evaluation steps.

an ivs, rather than one tuple value. The SET structure above it introduces a partitioning of this set of tuples according to SI, hence representing a set of sets, rather than one set, so it too is an ivs. The top-most SET doesn't introduce another partitioning, but only wraps things in a proper (nested) value and, therefore, is a value. All structures in Moa have a value and an ivs form.

Note that, based on SI alone, it is impossible to determine that one or more empty subsets exists. Part of solving the COUNT-bug is the representation of an empty subset as an occurrence in the third argument of SET ivs (ID_1) and no occurrence in the first (SI).

Each operator in our language is defined on structure and data level. For example, the *count* has the effect of converting a set-of-set-structured argument to a set-of-atomic-structured result (structure level), while at the same time generating a grouped count operation on the flat data connected to that result structure (data level). In other words, a query in Moa is translated into both a physical algebra expression on flat data, and an explicit conversion from argument to result structure.

This two-level approach to query evaluation is illustrated in Figure 4. The general form of a query is a *Moa expression* which uses columns from underlying tables[1] (the leftmost pyramid). In the first rewrite step, Moa operations are mapped onto their respective *column operations* and result structure (second pyramid). This step converts a query on a nested structure to operations on flat data, which, being a rewrite operation independent of data volume, causes only minimal overhead. In the third pyramid, the column operations have been translated to the *table operations* of the physical layer. The third step performs the actual execution of the table operations producing result tables connected to a Moa result structure. An example of the rewrite process is given at the end of the next section.

4   Moa Logical Language

As explained, the Moa logical language is based on XNF^2 and is described here by means of the well-known example of an organisation that has departments and employees that work in those departments. In terms of XNF^2, an organisation consists of a set of departments, which in turn consist of sets of employees.

---

[1] Until now, we have used relational tables as physical storage representation of a column, but this is theoretically not obligatory.

72   M. van Keulen et al.

A specific instantiation of such an organisation is shown in the organisation diagram presented in Figure 5. It contains three departments, one with three, another with two employees, and the technical healtcare department has no employees (yet), as it is a newly founded department. Each department has a name and address attribute. Each employee has a name and a salary attribute.

In traditional 1NF relational terms, the department entity has a multi-valued attribute (i.e., the employees), which requires a transformation into a seperate entity and relationship if stored in a strict 1NF relational database. In the Moa system however, the nested structure of the schema can be preserved. Figure 6 shows the entire structure specification of the example organisation in the Moa logical language. At first glance, without knowing the Moa language, one sees that the organisation is modeled more naturally, since the nesting is preserved and not flattened as in 1NF.

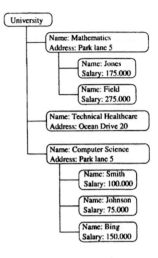

Fig. 5. Example organisation structure.

The structures Atomic, TUPLE, and SET in Figure 6 together form the kernel structures available in the Moa system. They constitute the NF^2 data model. Moa is open to the definition of additional structures, called extensions, that may support NF^2's arbitrary nesting. An example is the FV structure representing a feature vector intended for multi-media retrieval applications.

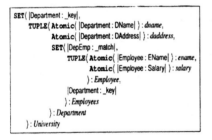

Fig. 6. Schema of University.

The syntax for type construction is a structure identifier, followed by a number of arguments and an optional label. The argument for Atomic is a column identifier which directly references the data stored in the underlying DBMS (cf., A_1 and A_2 in Figure 3). For example, |Department : DName| refers to the DName column of the Department table in an RDBMS. The label is used as a convenience mechanism to be able to reference the structure.

The **TUPLE** type constructor represents the theoretical notion of a product structure that consists of one or more Moa structures of any type. The **SET** type constructor represents a collection of Moa structures. The unrestricted nesting of type constructors makes it, in particular with this type constructor, possible to support the arbitrary nesting of the NF^2 data model. The arguments of SET include an index^2 mapping, the structure of the elements of this set, and the index of the set that encloses the specified set (cf., SI, TUPLE$\langle A_1, A_2 \rangle$, and ID_1 in Figure 3, respectively).

In the example above, the index mapping and enclosing set index are represented by |DepEmp : _match| and |Department : _key|, respectively. Those are special column identifiers disclosing database schema information. In this case, it maps primary keys of

---

^{2} In relational terms, an index is the same as the primary key of a table.

departments to primary keys of employees. Thus, the |DepEmp : _match| column contains the relationship (CS,Smith), (CS,Johnson), (CS,Bing), (M,Jones), and (M,Field), where CS is 'Computer Science' and M is 'Mathematics'.

Several operations are defined on the kernel structures, of which the most important ones are listed below.

- **select** [m] (op); The select-operation is similar to the select-operation of relational algebra. The modifier m specifies the selection criterion and the operand op specifies the argument on which the selection should be applied.
- **attr** (op, l); The attr-operation is Moa's equivalent of projection, i.e., it evaluates to the attribute referenced by label l of its tuple-valued argument. In a modifier, it can be abbreviated by '$\%l$'.
- **map** [m] (op); The map-operation is a navigational operator: it evaluates modifier m for each of the elements of operand op and collects the results in a SET structure.
- **join** [m_1, m_2] (op_1, op_2); The join-operation joins the two operands op_1 and op_2 based on equality of the modifiers m_1 and m_2, similar to the join-operation in relational algebra.
- **flatten** (op); The flatten-operation converts a set of subsets to one set by taking the union of all subsets, i.e., it removes one level of nesting.
- **count** (op); This is an example of an aggregate function and shown in the example of Figure 7 to illustrate that Moa correctly handles the COUNT-bug as explained in Section 3.

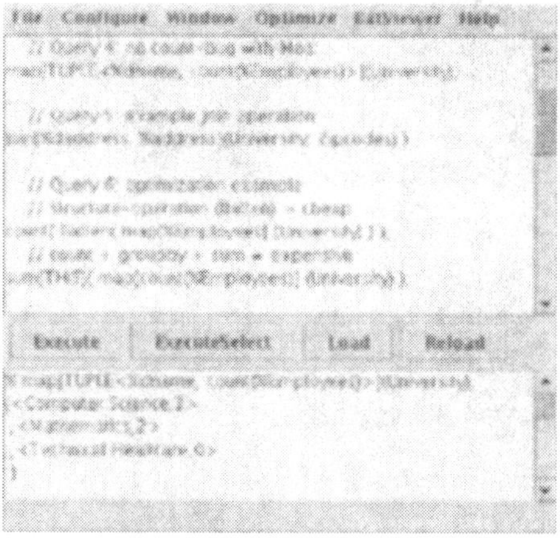

Fig. 7. Screendump of Moa System.

Note that the structure specification of Figure 6 is stored in the data dictionary of the system under the name "University" and can be used in queries directly.

Figure 7 shows a screen dump of the graphical user interface (GUI) of the Moa system. In the figure, the top-part of the GUI represents the input area and shows a number of example queries. The results of a query execution are presented in the bottom-part of the GUI. In this case, Query 4 has been executed. The resulting element ⟨"Technical Healthcare", 0⟩ illustrates the correct handling of the COUNT-bug, which would otherwise be missing from the result. Although without showing results, query 5 shows the use of the join-operation, and query 6 illustrates two equivalent expressions for the same query, hence offering an optimization opportunity. The underlying database used here is a relational DBMS.[3]

---

[3] The Moa system currently supports IBM DB2, PostgreSQL, MySQL, and MonetDB.

```
(query)   map|TUPLE( %dname, count(%employees) )|(University)
(step 1)  SET( C₁, TUPLE( Atomic( |Department : DName| ), Atomic( C₂ ) ) )
          C₁ = |Department : _key|
          C₂ = gbCount(outerJoin(|Department : _key|,|EmpDep : _inverse|))
(step 2)  SET{ |Department : _key|,
               TUPLE( Atomic( |Department : DName| ), Atomic( |tmp1 : _cnt| ) )
          }
          tmp0=outerjoin(Department.DNumber = Employee.DNO)
          tmp1=aggregate(count(tmp0.ENumber),tmp0.DNumber)
```

Fig. 8. Query rewrite steps for Query 4.

As an illustration of the rewrite steps of Figure 4, the rewrite process for example Query 4 is shown in Figure 8. The map and attr operations rewrite to the result structure representing a set of department tuples identified by C_1. The count operation rewrites to the column expression C_2. In the second step, column expression C_2 produces a column that takes the _cnt attribute from the result of the extended relational algebra (XRA) expression[4] tmp1 (table operation).

Besides the operations and structures described in this section, others are available in the Moa system, e.g., the nest and unnest operations. However, due to space limitations, it is infeasible to present an exhaustive list. The reader is referred to [21].

5   Application Areas and Context

The validity of the Moa concept described so far, can best be seen by looking at the various projects in which Moa played a central role. The ideas for Moa and multi-model architecture originate from the Magnum-project [5,4]. In this project, a structurally object-oriented DBMS was developed for the purpose of efficiently integrating spatial and thematic data in a single data manager. *Decomposition* and *extensibility* were the key features of this project. In terms of the multi-model architecture, the Magnum system consisted of two layers: the main-memory DBMS MonetDB as physical layer and Moa as logical layer. This architecture could be extended in two ways. First, new base types could be defined in MonetDB, e.g., polygon, together with a large set of spatial operators on these primitive base types. Secondly, Moa's structural extensibility was used to support structures like polygonal maps and triangulations, next to the conventional tuple and set. Moa mapped these structures to MonetDB's binary data model, meaning that the structured data was decomposed in binary tables. Experiments showed that the Magnum system performed well on the Sequoia benchmark [19].

The experiences with the Moa/MonetDB combination, especially with the combination of base type and structural extensibility, sparked off new efforts. In the Mirror and AMIS projects, the ideas for an extensible DBMS architecture based on Moa and MonetDB were further developed in the realm of text and multi-media retrieval. Mirror concentrated on a generic multi-media retrieval framework based on belief networks. Experiments showed its feasibility for content-based retrieval for text, images, and music [12,22]. Since parallelisation and fragmentation in the physical layer is orthogonal to the logical layer, the architecture design seems to be better

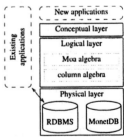

Fig. 9. SUMMER federated architecture.

---

[4] XRA [13] is a relational algebra extended with aggregates. The aggregate operation preforms the aggregate function in the first argument on the groups determined by the second argument.

prepared to scale up. The AMIS-project explored this idea by studying the optimization of top-N IR-queries in a fragmented context [2].

In all three projects described above, the integration of data and algorithms from non-traditional application domains in a single data manager was a central theme. Much thematic (tabular) data related to GIS or multi-media objects, however, resides in RDBMSs with existing applications running on them. Therefore, in the SUMMER-project [20], the multi-model architecture was taken one step further by using Moa as a kind of *data management middleware*, driving both MonetDB and 'normal' RDBMSs (see Figure 9) simultaneously. This allows the 'addition' of, for example, multi-media retrieval functionality to an existing federated information system. Also in SUMMER, we developed an XML-based conceptual layer providing a subset of XQuery [23]. This will make the DBMS suitable to be used in web-based environments, providing a more convenient way of managing large XML data volumes with, among others, integrated and efficient multi-media retrieval.

6   Conclusions and Future Work

In this paper, we presented the concepts behind the Moa system: the multi-model DBMS architecture and the Moa logical algebra which plays an important role therein. In order to support demanding applications like GIS or digital libraries, one needs an expressive conceptual data model supporting complexly structured data. Expressiveness is not the only requirement. Since the managed data is often voluminous and queries complex, performance is an important aspect as well. The multi-model architecture supports extensibility in all three layers thus enabling to integrate domain-specific algorithms in an effective way. Furthermore, the extensibility mechanism of the Moa language used in the logical layer, has been designed in such a way that optimization across extensions is possible. This alleviates the black-box ADT problem, which prohibits the optimizer, for example, to push projections and selections through ADT-operators.

To be able to bridge the gap between an expressive conceptual data model and an efficient simple physical data model, the nested relational intermediary proved effective. We placed renewed interest in XNF^2 algebra, adapted and extended it, and worked on new ways for efficient query evaluation. This resulted in the Moa language. We regard its role to be vital in the success of the multi-model architecture.

In several projects, a prototype DBMS evolved into what is now called the Moa system. The genericity, extensibility, and performance of the system were put to the test in real-life applications.

In current and future projects, the Moa system continues to be used as our experimentation platform, which imposes a ongoing demand for perfecting the extensibility and efficiency of the system. Moreover, we are exploring the realm of category theory in search for ways to fundamentally improve the Moa and column algebra. Further effort on distribution support is aimed at facilitating the construction of federated systems in more advanced ways. Finally, the focus of the CIRQUID-project [7] is the integration of information retrieval and databases to provide support for full text search in XQuery.

References

1. F. Bancilhon, C. Delobel, and P. Kanellakis, editors. *Building an Object-Oriented Database System : The Story of O_2*. Morgan Kaufmann Publishers, 1992.
2. H.E. Blok, A.P. de Vries, H.M. Blanken, and P.M.G. Apers. Experiences with IR Top N optimization in a main memory DBMS: Applying 'the database approach' in new domains. In *Procs of BNCOD 18*, LNCS 2097, pages 126–151, July 2001.
3. P.A. Boncz and M.L. Kersten. MIL primitives for querying a fragmented world. *VLDB Journal*, 8(2):101–119, 1999.
4. P.A. Boncz, W. Quak, and M.L. Kersten. Monet and its geographic extensions: A novel approach to high performance GIS processing. In *Procs of EDBT'96, Avignon, France*, LNCS 1057, pages 147–166, March 1996.
5. P.A. Boncz, A.N. Wilschut, and M.L. Kersten. Flattening an object algebra to provide performance. In *Procs of ICDE'98, Orlando, USA*, pages 568–577, February 1998.
6. M.J. Carey, D. J. DeWitt, J.F. Naughton, M. Asgarian, and et al. The BUCKY object-relational benchmark (experience paper). In *Procs of ACM SIGMOD'97, Tucson, Arizona, USA*, pages 135–146, May 1997.
7. The CIRQUID project website, 2003. http://www.cs.utwente.nl/~cirquid.
8. W.F. Cody, L.M. Haas, W. Niblack, M. Arya, and et al. Querying multimedia data from multiple repositories by content: the Garlic project. In *Procs of VDB 3, Lausanne, Switzerland*, IFIP 34, pages 17–35, March 1995.
9. P. Dadam, K. Küspert, F. Andersen, H.M. Blanken, and et al. A DBMS prototype to support extended NF^2 relations: An integrated view on flat tables and hierarchies. In *Procs of ACM SIGMOD'98, Washington, D.C., USA.*, pages 356–367, May 1986.
10. C.J. Date and H. Darwen. *Foundation for Object/Relational Databases: the Third Manifesto*. Addison-Wesley, 1998.
11. A.P. de Vries, B. Eberman, and D.E. Kovalcin. The design and implementation of an infrastructure for multimedia digital libraries. In *Procs of IDEAS'98, Cardiff, U.K.*, pages 103–120, July 1998.
12. A.P. de Vries, M.G.L.M. van Doorn, H.M. Blanken, and P.M.G. Apers. The Mirror MMDBMS architecture. In *Procs of VLDB'99, Edinburgh, U.K.*, pages 758–761, Sep. 1999.
13. Paul W. P. J. Grefen and Rolf A. de By. A multi-set extended relational algebra – a formal approach to a practical issue. In *Procs of ICDE'94, Houston, USA*, pages 80–88, Feb. 1994.
14. G. Kiczales, J. Lamping, C. Videira Lopes, C. Maeda, and et al. Open implementation design guidelines. In *Procs of ICSE'97, Boston, USA.*, pages 481–490, 1997.
15. H.-J. Schek and P. Pistor. Data structures for an integrated data base management and information retrieval system. In *Procs of VLDB'82, Mexico City*, pages 197–207, Sep. 1982.
16. P. Seshadri and M. Paskin. PREDATOR: An OR-DBMS with enhanced data types. In *Procs of ACM SIGMOD'97, Tucson, USA*, pages 568–571, May 1997.
17. H. Steenhagen. *Optimization of Object Query Languages*. PhD thesis, Uni. of Twente, 1995.
18. H.J. Steenhagen, P.M.G. Apers, and H.M. Blanken. Optimization of nested queries in a complex object model. In *Procs of EDBT'94, Cambridge, U.K.*, pages 337–350, 1994.
19. M. Stonebraker, J. Frew, K. Gardels, and J. Meredith. The Sequoia 2000 benchmark. In *Procs of ACM SIGMOD'93, Washington, D.C., USA.*, pages 2–11, May 1993.
20. The SUMMER project website, 2003. http://www.cs.utwente.nl/~summer.
21. M. van Keulen, J. Vonk, A.P. de Vries, J. Flokstra, and H.E. Blok. Moa: extensibility and efficiency in querying nested data. Technical Report 02–19, Centre for Telematics and Information Technology, University of Twente, The Netherlands, 2002.
22. A.P. de Vries. *Content and Multimedia Database Management Systems*. PhD thesis, University of Twente, 1999.
23. XQuery 1.0: An XML query language, 2003. http://www.w3.org/TR/xquery/.

Entity Connectivity vs. Hierarchical Levelling as a Basis for Data Model Clustering: An Experimental Analysis

Daniel L. Moody[1,2]

[1] Department of Software Engineering
Charles University
Prague, Czech Republic
moody@ksint.ms.mff.cuni.cz
[2] School of Business Systems,
Monash University
Melbourne, Australia 3800
dmoody@infotech.monash.edu.au

Abstract. Data model clustering is the process of dividing large and complex models into parts of manageable size, in order to improve understanding and simplify documentation and maintenance. Based on theories of human cognition, a previous paper proposed connectivity (defined as the number of relationships an entity participates in) as a basis for clustering data models. This paper describes a series of laboratory experiments which evaluate the validity of this metric as a basis for clustering compared to hierarchical levelling, which has been the predominant approach used in previous research. The first two experiments investigate the relationship between the metrics and perceptions of importance, while the third experiment investigates their relationship to how people intuitively cluster entities. The results show that connectivity provides an empirically valid basis for clustering data models, which closely matches human perceptions of importance and "chunking" behaviour. No significant results were found for hierarchical level in any of the experiments. The high levels of statistical significance and effect size of the results for connectivity, together with their consistency across different domains and sample populations, suggests the possible discovery of a natural "law" governing data models.

1 Introduction

1.1 The Entity Relationship Model

The Entity Relationship (ER) Model [6] is recognised world wide as the standard technique for data modelling in practice, and has been used to design database schemas for over two decades [32]. However while it has proven very effective as a technique for database design (as evidenced by its acceptance by IT practitioners), it has been far less effective for communication with users [17, 23, 28]. Empirical studies show that in practice, data models are poorly understood by users, and in most cases are not developed with direct user involvement [18].

V. Mařík et al. (Eds.): DEXA 2003, LNCS 2736, pp. 77–87, 2003.
© Springer-Verlag Berlin Heidelberg 2003

1.2   Complexity Effects on Data Model Understanding

One of the most serious theoretical practical limitations of the ER Model is that it lacks explicit constructs to manage complexity [1, 2, 3, 12, 15, 16, 24, 30, 31, 32, 33]. This provides a possible explanation for why Entity Relationship models are so poorly understood in practice. Psychological studies show that due to limits on short-term memory, humans have a strictly limited capacity for processing information – this is estimated to be "seven, plus or minus two" concepts at a time [22, 27]. If the amount of information received exceeds the limits of short term memory, information overload ensues and comprehension degrades rapidly [19]. Surveys of practice show that application data models consist of a mean of 95 entities, while enterprise data models consist of a mean of 536 entities [20]. Clearly, models of this size exceed human cognitive capacity many times over.

1.3   Data Model Clustering

According to Miller [22], human cognitive capacity can be increased by "chunking", or grouping concepts together. Thus large ER models may be divided into "chunks", each of which contains a subset of the entities and relationships in the original model, in order to improve understanding. This process is called *data model clustering* [1] or *data model decomposition* [25]. Decomposition is the process of breaking complex systems down into a set of smaller subsystems or modules, and is one of the most common ways of dealing with complexity in large and complex systems [13]. Experimental studies have shown that clustering data models can improve comprehension and verification of data models by more than 50% [26].

2   Previous Research

2.1   The Central Entity Concept

A number of approaches have been proposed in the literature for clustering ER models [e.g. 1, 5, 12, 14, 21, 31]. Most of these approaches rely on the concept of *central entities*, which act as anchor points or "nuclei" for forming clusters. These are variously called *major entities* [12], *dominant entities* [31], *root entities* [21] or *primary entities* [16]. In order to form clusters that are meaningful to people, central entities should represent the entities of greatest importance—the "core" business concepts in the model. Identification of appropriate central entities is critical to identifying meaningful "chunks" in data models. Most data model clustering approaches rely either on human judgement [16, 31] or hierarchical levelling [12, 21] to identify such entities.

2.2   Hierarchical Level as a Basis for Data Model Clustering

The most common approach to identifying central entities in previous research is to use hierarchical levelling. A data model can be organised into a set of overlapping hierarchies, each defined by a chain of one-to-many (parent-child) relationships. At the top of each hierarchy is a "root" entity – an entity with no many-to-one relationships. Clusters can then be formed using root entities as the centres of clusters and their descendants as cluster elements. Entities can be assigned level numbers based on their level in the hierarchy (the number of one-to-many relationships from a root entity). This defines a *partial ordering* on the entities in the model.

Hierarchical levelling provides a simple and deterministic way of clustering a data model. The use of one-to-many (functionally dependent) relationships as the basis for clustering entities can be understood as the logical extension of normalisation (which is used to cluster attributes into entities) to data model clustering. However while there is strong evidence that grouping attributes based on functional dependencies minimises redundancy [8], there is no evidence that clustering entities based on functional dependent relationships improves understanding. No theoretical justification is given in the literature for why it provides a useful basis for clustering, and this assumption has never been empirically tested.

2.3.   Connectivity as an Alternative Basis for Data Model Clustering

A previous paper [25] proposed the alternative concept of *connectivity* as a way of identifying central entities. The connectivity of an entity is defined as the number of relationships it participates in:

Connectivity (E_i) = no. of relationships R_j where E_i is one of the endpoints

Like hierarchical levelling, connectivity defines a *partial ordering* on the entities in a data model. Based on theories of human cognition, it was hypothesised that entities with the most relationships (regardless of their cardinality) would be perceived to be the most important. According to *semantic network theory* [10, 11], semantic memory is structured as a network of related concepts. The concept of *spreading activation* [4] says that nodes remain in a quiet state until they are activated or "primed". A node is primed whenever it is accessed, and results in the meaning of the concept being retrieved. The activation then spreads with decreasing intensity along all pathways connected to the initial node according to the following rules. Spreading activation theory predicts that recall accuracy will be highest and response latency will be lowest for concepts with large numbers of connections to other concepts, because they will receive higher levels of priming. In the case of a data model, which is structured as a network of concepts, entities with large numbers of relationships would therefore be more likely to be recalled. If we assume that "ability to recall" an entity is correlated with perceptions of its importance, we can conclude that entities with more relationships will be perceived to be more important.

2.4   Research Objectives

The research questions addressed by this paper are:
- Is connectivity an empirically valid basis for clustering ER models?
- Is hierarchical levelling an empirically valid basis for clustering ER models?

The empirical validity of these metric is assessed via three experiments. The first two experiments evaluate the metrics using perceptions of importance while the third experiment compares them to "natural" clustering as carried out by humans.

3   Experiment 1

3.1 Experimental Design

Nineteen subjects, all postgraduate students in Information Systems at the University of Melbourne, were given an example data model and a textual description of the problem domain. The experimental data model consisted of 23 entities and 29 relationships. Subjects were asked to identify the three most important entities in rank order, as this is the optimal number of subject areas in a model of this size.

3.2 Independent Variables

Connectivity
The primary independent variable in this experiment is Connectivity, which is the number of relationships an entity participates in. There are six levels of this variable, corresponding to the distinct values of Connectivity that exist in the experimental data model.

Hierarchical Level
The secondary independent variable in this experiment is Hierarchical Level. This is measured by the following empirical indicator:
- *Level Number*: this is defined as 1 for root entities and $x + 1$ for all other entities, where x is the number of many-to-one relationships between the entity and the nearest root entity [21].

There are three levels of this independent variable, corresponding to the distinct values of Hierarchical Level in the experimental data model.

3.3 Dependent Variable

The dependent variable in this experiment is Perceived Importance, which is defined as the relative importance of an entity as perceived by participants. This is measured by the following empirical indicator:
- *Mean Ranked Importance* $(E) = \sum_{i=1}^{n} \text{rank}(E_i)/n$ where $\text{rank}(E_i)$ represents the rank assigned by subject I to entity E and n = number of subjects.

3.4 Hypotheses

We have argued that the number of relationships an entity participates in will determine its perceived importance. We therefore propose the following hypothesis:

> **H1: Entities with more relationships will be perceived to be more important**

This will be measured by a positive relationship between Connectivity and Perceived Importance.

Clustering approaches based on the concept of hierarchical levelling implicitly assume that entities higher in the hierarchy are more important. We have argued that there is no sound theoretical basis for presuming that this is so. To test this assumption, we propose the following hypothesis:

> **H2: Entities higher in the hierarchy will be perceived to be more important**

This will be measured by a negative relationship between Hierarchical Level and Perceived Importance.

3.5   Results and Discussion

The effect of each independent variable on the dependent variable is evaluated using separate regression analyses, as the independent variables represent alternative explanations (rather than parallel determinants) of the dependent variable:

H1: Connectivity → Perceived Importance

In this stage, Connectivity was used as the independent (predictor) variable and Perceived Importance as the dependent (predicted) variable. The regression equation which results is:

Equation 1. Perceived Importance = 0.34 * Connectivity − 0.63

The regression was found to be highly significant, with p = 000. This means that H1 was strongly confirmed with $\alpha < .005$. The Pearson correlation coefficient (ρ) is .93, which represents a "large" effect [9]. This means that the relationship is practically meaningful as well as statistically significant.

H2: Hierarchical Level → Perceived Importance

In this analysis, Hierarchical Level was used as the independent variable and Perceived Importance as the dependent variable. The regression equation which results is:

Equation 2. Perceived Importance = 0.31 − 0.02 * Hierarchical Level

The regression was found to be non-significant with p = 0.887. This means that H2 is rejected. The Pearson correlation coefficient is −0.03, which is not a practically meaningful effect [9].

4   Experiment 2

This replicates the first experiment using a different experimental data model and a different sample population.

4.1 Experimental Design

Thirty nine subjects, all postgraduate students in Information Systems at Monash University, were given an example data model and a textual description of the problem domain. They were then asked to identify the seven most important entities in rank order. The experimental data model was an application data model for an airline reservation and scheduling system, which consisted of 53 entities and 73 relationships. This is a more realistic sized data model than the one used in the first laboratory experiment, and is close to the typical size for an application data model. A survey by Maier [20] found that the median size for an application data model was 60 entities. Subjects were asked to identify the seven most important entities, as this is the required number of subject areas in a model of this size, following the "seven, plus or minus two" principle [25].

4.2 Hypotheses

The same independent variables, dependent variable and hypotheses were used as in the first experiment, so are not repeated here.

4.3 Results and Discussion

As in the previous experiment, the hypotheses were tested using two separate regression analyses:

H1: Connectivity → Perceived Importance

A regression analysis was carried out using Connectivity as the independent variable and Perceived Importance as the dependent variable. The regression equation which results is:

Equation 3. Perceived Importance = 0.49 * Connectivity − 0.74

This is very similar to the regression equation found in the first experiment (Equation 1).

The regression was found to be highly significant with $p = 000$. This means that H1 was strongly confirmed. The Pearson correlation coefficient is .82, which represents a "large" effect [9].

H2: Hierarchical Level → Perceived Importance

In this stage, Hierarchical Level was used as the independent variable and Perceived Importance as the dependent variable. The regression equation which results is:

Equation 4. Perceived Importance = 0.38 * Hierarchical Level − .13

This is quite different to the regression equation found in the first experiment: the regression coefficient is almost twenty times the size and has the reverse sign.

As in the previous experiment, the relationship between the variables was found to be non-significant ($p = .095$). This means that H2 is rejected. The Pearson correlation coefficient is .23, which represents a small effect [9], but in the reverse direction to that predicted by the literature.

Comparison to Experiment 1 Results

A Chow test [7] was carried out to determine whether there was a significant difference between the results of the two experiments. The analysis showed that:

- There was no significant difference between the results for Connectivity → Perceived Importance between the two experiments ($\alpha = .113$)

- There was a significant difference between the results for Hierarchical Level → Perceived Importance between the two experiments ($\alpha = .000$)

This suggests that the relationship between Connectivity and Perceived Importance is a general "law" which applies across different data models and sample populations, while the relationship between Hierarchical Level and Perceived Importance is a more or less random effect.

5   Experiment 3

A final experiment was carried out to investigate the relationship between connectivity and clustering as performed by humans.

5.1   Experimental Design

Fourteen subjects, all undergraduate students in Information Systems at the University of Melbourne, were given an example data model and a textual description of the problem domain. They were then asked to cluster the entities into subject areas. The data model used was the same one as used in the second laboratory experiment. Participants were given the following instructions for performing the clustering task:

- Each entity must be assigned to one and only one subject area

- Each subject area should consist of an average of seven entities (excluding subtypes)

- Each subject area should be named after one of the entities on the subject area (the central entity)

No instructions were given about how to identify central entities – in particular, the concepts of "importance" or "connectivity" were not mentioned. The clusters produced therefore represent the result of "natural" clustering by subjects.

5.2   Independent Variables

The same independent variables were used as in the first two experiments.

5.3 Dependent Variable

The dependent variable in this experiment is Clustering Behaviour. This is calculated as the percentage of participants who identified a particular entity as the central entity of a subject area.

5.4 Hypotheses

Based on the results of the first two experiments, which showed that an entity's connectivity determines its perceived importance (H1), We argue that connectivity will in turn determine whether it is selected as a central entity. This is based on the assumption that people will form subject areas around the most important entities in the model. We therefore propose the following hypothesis:

> H3: Entities with more relationships will be more likely to be chosen as central entities

This will be measured by a positive relationship between Connectivity and Clustering Behaviour.

We also test whether an entity's hierarchical level has an effect on whether it is chosen as the centre of a cluster. Clustering approaches that are based on hierarchical ordering use root entities as the centres of clusters. We therefore propose the following hypothesis:

> H4: Entities higher in the hierarchy will be more likely to be chosen as central entities

This will be measured by a negative relationship between Hierarchical Level and Clustering Behaviour.

In formulating H3, we argued that Perceived Importance will determine Clustering Behaviour. This suggests that this assumption should be tested directly. Perceived Importance was not collected as part of this experiment, but we can analyse the relationship indirectly, by looking at the relationship between Clustering Behaviour in this experiment and the values of Perceived Importance found in the second laboratory experiment. This results in a further hypothesis:

> H5: Entities which are perceived to be more important will be more likely to be chosen as central entities

This will be measured by a positive relationship between Perceived Importance and Clustering Behaviour.

5.5 Results and Discussion

The theoretical model in this experiment is a three stage regression model, so the hypotheses are evaluated using three separate regression analyses:

H3: Connectivity → Clustering Behaviour

The objective of this analysis was to determine whether an entity's connectivity has an effect on whether it is chosen as a central entity. The regression equation which results is:

Equation 5. Clustering Behaviour = 14 * Connectivity − 23.2

The regression was found to be highly significant with p = .000. This means that H3 was strongly confirmed. The correlation coefficient is .91, which represents a "large" effect [9].

H4: Hierarchical Level → Clustering Behaviour

A regression analysis was then carried out using Hierarchical Level as the independent variable and Clustering Behaviour as the dependent variable. The regression equation which results is:

Equation 6. Clustering Behaviour = 4.3 * Hierarchical Level + 5.72

The relationship was found to be non-significant with p = 0.465. This means that H4 is rejected. The Pearson correlation coefficient is .1, which represents a small effect [9], but in the opposite direction to that predicted by the literature. This suggests that using hierarchical level as a basis for clustering is counter-intuitive, as it is the opposite to the way people cluster naturally.

H5: Perceived Importance → Clustering Behaviour

Finally, a regression analysis was carried out on the relationship between Perceived Importance and Clustering Behaviour. The regression equation which results is:

Equation 7. Clustering Behaviour = 22.6 * Perceived Importance − 1.26

The regression was found to be highly significant with p = .000. This strongly confirms H5. The Pearson correlation coefficient is .88, which represents a large effect [9].

6 Conclusion

The experiments described in this paper show that entity connectivity is strongly related to human perceptions of importance and also how people cluster entities into meaningful "chunks". This suggests that connectivity provides an empirically valid basis for clustering Entity Relationship models.

6.1 Theoretical Significance

The results of the experiments described in this paper contribute to our theoretical understanding of how people perceive data models and also how they perform the task of data model clustering. The high levels of statistical significance and effect size found for the relationship between Connectivity and Perceived Importance, and the consistency of the results using two different data models and sample populations, suggests the possible discovery of a natural "law" governing human perception of data models. Strong effects were found for the relationships Connectivity $\rightarrow$ Perceived Importance and Connectivity $\rightarrow$ Clustering Behaviour. Together these results suggest that connectivity plays an important part in understanding of data models, controlling attention and organisation into meaningful "chunks". These findings may well apply to other types of network structured models (e.g. UML class diagrams).

6.2 Practical Significance

The complexity of data models represents a major barrier to the effective understanding of data models in practice [2, 3, 12, 24, 29, 30]. Clustering provides a solution to this problem by dividing the model into conceptually "bite-sized" pieces. The practical significance of this research is that it provides the basis for automatically clustering Entity Relationship models around the most important entities. Most of the previous clustering approaches proposed either rely on human judgement to identify central entities, which means that they can only be partially automated, or on hierarchical leveling, which this paper has shown to be an invalid basis for clustering.

References

[1]   AKOKA, J. and I. COMYN-WATTIAU (1996): Entity Relationship And Object Oriented Model Automatic Clustering, Data And Knowledge Engineering, 20 (1).
[2]   ALLWORTH, S. (1996): Using Classification Structures To Develop And Structure Generic Industry Models, In D.L. Moody (Ed.) Proceedings Of The First Australian Data Management Conference, Melbourne, Australia: Australian Data Management Association (DAMA), December 2–3.
[3]   ALLWORTH, S. (1999): Classification Structures Encourage the Growth of Generic Industry Models, In D.L. Moody (Ed.) Proceedings of the Eighteenth International Conference on Conceptual Modelling (Industrial Track), Paris, France: Springer, November 15–18.
[4]   ANDERSON, J.R. and P.L. PIROLLI (1984): Spread Of Activation, Journal Of Experimental Psychology: Learning, Memory And Cognition, 10 (4).
[5]   BATINI, C., S. CERI, and S.B. NAVATHE (1992): Conceptual Database Design: An Entity Relationship Approach, Redwood City, California: Benjamin Cummings.
[6]   CHEN, P.P. (1976): The Entity Relationship Model: Towards An Integrated View Of Data, ACM Transactions On Database Systems, 1 (1), March: p. 9–36.
[7]   CHOW, G.C. (1983): Econometrics, New York: McGraw-Hill Book Company.
[8]   CODD, E.F. (1970): A Relational Database Model For Large Shared Data Banks, Communications of the ACM, 13 (6): p. 377–387.
[9]   COHEN, J. (1988): Statistical Power Analysis for the Behavioural Sciences (2nd ed.), 2nd ed, Hillsdale, NJ: Lawrence Earlbaum and Associates.
[10] COLLINS, A.M. and M.R. QUILLIAN (1969): Retrieval Time from Semantic Memory, Journal of Verbal Learning and Verbal Behaviour, 8.
[11] COLLINS, A.M. and M.R. QUILLIAN (1972): How To Make A Language User, In Organisation And Memory, E. Tulving and M. Donaldson (Eds.), Academic Press: New York.
[12] FELDMAN, P. and D. MILLER (1986): Entity Model Clustering: Structuring A Data Model By Abstraction, The Computer Journal, 29 (4).

[13] FLOOD, R.L. and E.R. CARSON (1993): Dealing With Complexity: An Introduction To The Theory And Application Of Systems Science: Plenum Press.

[14] FRANCALANCI, C. and B. PERNICI (1994): Abstraction Levels for Entity Relationship Schemas, In P. Loucopoulos (Ed.) Proceedings of the Thirteenth International Conference on the Entity Relationship Approach, Manchester, December 14–17.

[15] GANDHI, M., E.L. ROBERTSON, and D. VAN GUCHT (1994): Levelled Entity Relationship Models, In P. Loucopolous (Ed.) Proceedings Of The Thirteenth International Conference On The Entity Relationship Approach, Manchester, December 14–17.

[16] GILBERG, R.F. (1986): A Schema Methodology For Large Entity-Relationship Diagrams, In P.P. Chen (Ed.) Proceedings Of Fourth International Conference On The Entity Relationship Approach,

[17] GOLDSTEIN, R.C. and V.C. STOREY (1990): Some Findings On The Intuitiveness Of Entity Relationship Constructs, In F.H. Lochovsky (Ed.) Entity Relationship Approach To Database Design And Querying, Amsterdam: Elsevier Science,

[18] HITCHMAN, S. (1995): Practitioner Perceptions On The Use Of Some Semantic Concepts In The Entity Relationship Model, European Journal Of Information Systems.

[19] LIPOWSKI, Z.J. (1975): Sensory And Information Inputs Overload: Behavioural Effects, Comprehensive Psychiatry, 16 (3), May/June.

[20] MAIER, R. (1996): Benefits And Quality Of Data Modelling-Results Of An Empirical Analysis, In B. Thalheim (Ed.) Proceedings Of The Fifteenth International Conference On The Entity Relationship Approach, Cottbus, Germany: Elsevier, October 7–9.

[21] MARTIN, J. (1982): Strategic Data Planning Methodologies, Englewood Cliffs, N.J.: Prentice-Hall, xv, 236.

[22] MILLER, G.A. (1956): The Magical Number Seven, Plus Or Minus Two: Some Limits On Our Capacity For Processing Information, The Psychological Review, March.

[23] MOODY, D.L. (1996): Graphical Entity Relationship Models: Towards A More User Understandable Representation Of Data, In B. Thalheim (Ed.) Proceedings Of The Fourteenth International Conference On The Entity Relationship Approach, Cottbus, Germany, October 7–9.

[24] MOODY, D.L. (1997): A Multi-Level Architecture For Representing Enterprise Data Models, In D.W. Embley and R.C. Goldstein (Eds.), Proceedings Of The Sixteenth International Conference On Conceptual Modelling (ER'97), Los Angeles, November 1–3.

[25] MOODY, D.L. and A. FLITMAN (1999): A Methodology for Clustering Entity Relationship Models: A Human Information Processing Approach, In J. Akoka, et al. (Eds.), Proceedings of the Eighteenth International Conference on Conceptual Modelling, Paris, France: Springer, November 15–18.

[26] MOODY, D.L. (2001): Dealing with Complexity: A Practical Method for Representing Large Entity Relationship Models (PhD Thesis), Melbourne, Australia: Department Of Information Systems, University of Melbourne.

[27] NEWELL, A.A. and H.A. SIMON (1972): Human Problem Solving: Prentice-Hall.

[28] NORDBOTTEN, J.C. and M.E. CROSBY (1999): The Effect of Graphic Style on Data Model Interpretation, Information Systems Journal, 9.

[29] SHANKS, G.G. (1997): The Challenges Of Strategic Data Planning In Practice: An Interpretive Case Study, Journal Of Strategic Information Systems, 6.

[30] SIMSION, G.C. (1989): A Structured Approach To Data Modelling, The Australian Computer Journal, August.

[31] TEORY, T.J., G. WEI, D.L. BOLTON, and J.A. KOENIG (1989): ER Model Clustering As An Aid For User Communication And Documentation In Database Design, Communications Of The ACM, August.

[32] THALHEIM, B. (2000): Entity Relationship Modeling: Foundations of Database Technology, Berlin ; New York: Springer, xii, 627.

[33] WEBER, R.A. (1997): Ontological Foundations Of Information Systems, Melbourne, Australia: Coopers And Lybrand Accounting Research Methodology Monograph No. 4, Coopers And Lybrand.

An XML-Enabled Association Rule Framework

Ling Feng[1], Tharam Dillon[2], Hans Weigand[3], and Elizabeth Chang[4]

[1] University of Twente,
The Netherlands,
ling@cs.utwente.nl
[2] Faculty of Information Technology,
University of Technology Sydney,
Australia,
tharam5@fit.uts.edu.au
[3] Tilburg University,
The Netherlands,
weigand@uvt.nl
[4] Curtin University,
Australia,
ChangE@cbs.curtin.edu.au

Abstract. With the sheer amount of data stored, presented and exchanged using XML nowadays, the ability to extract knowledge from XML data sources becomes increasingly important and desirable. This paper aims to integrate the newly emerging XML technology with data mining technology, using association rule mining as a case in point. Compared with traditional association mining in the well-structured world (e.g., relational databases), mining from XML data is faced with more challenges due to the inherent flexibilities of XML in both structure and semantics. The primary challenges include 1) a more complicated hierarchical data structure; 2) an ordered data context; and 3) a much bigger data size. To tackle these challenges, in this paper, we propose an extended *XML-enabled association rule framework*, which is flexible and powerful enough to represent both simple and complex structured association relationships inherent in XML data.

Keywords: Association rule, semi-structure, XML.

1 Introduction

Currently, XML is penetrating virtually all areas of Internet application programming, and bringing about sheer amount of data encoded in XML. With the continuously growth in XML data sources, the ability to extract knowledge from them for decision support becomes increasingly important and desirable. Data mining, emerging during the late 1980s, has made great strides during the 1990s in transforming vast amounts of data into useful knowledge, and is expected to continue to flourish into the new millennium. However, compared to the fruitful achievements in mining well-structured data such as relational databases and

V. Mařík et al. (Eds.): DEXA 2003, LNCS 2736, pp. 88–97, 2003.

object-oriented databases, mining in the semi-structured XML world has received less exploration so far. The aim of this paper is to integrate the newly emerging XML technology into data mining technology, using association rule mining as a case in point.

Since the problem of mining association rules was first introduced in [1], a large amount of work has been done in various directions, including efficient, Apriori-like mining methods [2,4,7], mining generalized, multi-level, or quantitative association rules [6,3], and discovery of similar structures among a collection of semi-structured objects [8]. Under the traditional association rule framework, the basic unit of data to look at is database *record*, and the construct unit of a discovered association rule is *item* which has an *atomic value*. These lead us to the following two questions: 1) *what is the counterpart of record* and 2) *what is the counterpart of item* in mining association relationships from XML data?

In this study, we focus on rule detection from a collection of XML documents, which describe the same type of information (e.g., customer order, etc.). Hence, each of XML documents corresponds to a database record, and possesses a tree-like structure. Accordingly, we extend the notion of associated item to an XML fragment (i.e., tree), and build up associations among trees rather than simple-structured items of atomic values. For consistency, we call each such kind of trees a **tree-structured item** to distinguish it from the traditional counterpart *item*. With the above extended notions, we propose an **XML-enabled association rule framework** in the paper. From both structural and semantic aspects, XML-enabled association rules are more powerful and flexible than the traditional ones.

To our knowledge, the work reported here is the first attempt to integrate XML into the classic association rule mining framework. We believe that the synergy of the two areas has great potentials in delivering more desirable and self-describing knowledge in manifold application areas over the Internet. The remainder of the paper is organized as follows. A formal definition of XML-enabled association rules and related measurements is given in Section 2. We conclude the paper and outline future work in Section 3.

2 An XML-Enabled Association Rule Framework: Formulation

In this section, we define the XML-enabled association rule framework, starting with the tree structure of its associated items. The relationship among tree-structured items, as well as the containing relationship between a tree-structured item and an XML instance document, is then defined. They form the base for the definitions of XML-enabled association rules and related measurements.

2.1 Trees (Tree-Structured Items)

The basic construct in XML-enabled association rule framework is structured item, which can be described using a *rooted, ordered tree*. In the paper, we also refer to *tree-structured item* as *tree*, which is made up of a series of nodes that are connected to each other through directed labeled edges. In addition, constraints can be defined over the nodes and edges. At an abstract level, a tree consists of the following five components: a set of nodes, N_{ode}, representing XML elements or attributes; a set of directed edges, E_{dge}, representing *ancestor-descendant* or *element-attribute* relationships between the nodes; a set of labels, L_{abel}, denoting different types of relationships between the nodes; a set of constraints, $C_{onstraint}$, defined over the nodes and edges; and and a unique root node $n_{root} \in N_{ode}$ of the tree.

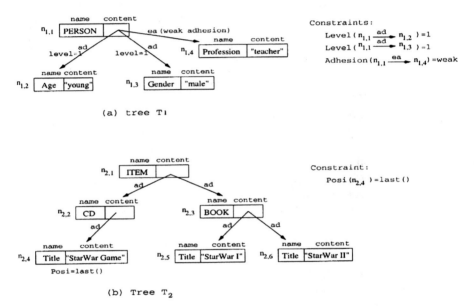

(a) tree T1

(b) Tree T_2

Fig. 1. Two tree examples

Nodes. We categorize nodes into *basic nodes* and *complex nodes*. Basic nodes have no edges emanating from them. They are the leaf nodes in the tree diagram. Complex nodes are the internal nodes in the diagram. Each complex node has one or more labeled directed edges emanating from it, each associated with a label, and each going to another node. Figure 1 gives two tree examples. The example tree T_1 contains one complex node $n_{1,1}$, and three basic nodes $n_{1,2}, n_{1,3}$ and $n_{1,4}$. The example tree T_2 has three complex node $n_{2,1}, n_{2,2}, n_{2,3}$, and three basic nodes $n_{2,4}, n_{2,5}$ and $n_{2,6}$.

Each basic node has a *simple content*, taking values from the domains of basic data types like string, integer and float. A wildcard value $*$ is allowed to denote any content including an empty one.

On the contrary, the content of a complex node called *complex content* refers to some other nodes through directed labeled edges. Each edge connects two nodes, with a label stating the relationship between the two nodes. Before giving the formal definition of complex content, let's first define the concepts of *connection*, *connection cluster* and *connection cluster set* using the *cableset* approach presented in [5].

Definition 1. *A **connection** of a node $n \in N_{ode}$ is a pair (l, n'), where l is a label in L_{able} and n' is a node in N_{ode}, representing that node n is connected to node n' via relation l.*   □

Definition 2. *A **connection cluster** of a node $n \in N_{ode}$ is a pair (l, ns), where l is a label in L_{able} and ns is a sequence of nodes in N_{ode}, representing that node n is connected to each node in ns via relation l.*   □

Definition 3. *A **connection cluster set** of a node $n \in N_{ode}$ is a set of connection clusters, $\{(l_1, ns_1), \ldots, (l_k, ns_k)\}$, where $\forall i \ \forall j \ (1 \leq i, j \leq k) \ (i \neq j \Leftrightarrow l_i \neq l_j)$.*   □

Definition 4. *A **complex content** of a complex node is a connection cluster set.*   □

Definition 5. *A **node** $n \in N_{ode}$ is a tuple $(n_{name}, n_{content})$, consisting of a node name n_{name} and a node content $n_{content}$.*   □

Example 1. In Figure 1 (a), the basic nodes $n_{1,2}$, $n_{1,3}$ and $n_{1,4}$ have simple contents of string data type, which are "young", "male" and "teacher". The complex node $n_{1,1}$ links to a sequence of nodes $\langle n_{1,2}, n_{1,3} \rangle$ via relationship "ad" (denoting ancestor-descendant), and to basic node $n_{1,4}$ via relationship "ea" (denoting element-attribute). It thus has a complex content $\{(ad, \langle n_{1,2}, n_{1,3} \rangle), (ea, \langle n_{1,4} \rangle)\}$.   □

Labeled Edges. Each edge in a tree links two nodes, with a label specifying their relationship. We consider two kinds of links, namely, *ancestor-descendant* and *element-attribute* relationships, abbreviated as "ad" and "ea", respectively. Thus, $L_{abel} = \{ad, ea\}$.

- An *antecedent-descendant* represents a structural relationship between an XML element and its nested subelement. It takes *parent-child* relationship as its special case.
- An *element-attribute* represents a relationship between an XML element and its attribute.

Definition 6. *An **edge** $e \in E_{dge}$ is a triple $(l, n_{source}, n_{target})$, consisting of a label $l \in L_{abel}$ stating the link type, the source node of the edge $n_{source} \in N_{ode}$ and the target node of the edge $n_{target} \in N_{ode}$. An edge e can also be pictorially denoted as "$n_{source} \xrightarrow{l} n_{target}$".*   □

Example 2. In Figure 1 (a), the edge "$n_{1,1} \xrightarrow{ea} n_{1,4}$" links PERSON element to its Profession attribute, and the edge "$n_{1,1} \xrightarrow{ad} n_{1,2}$" links *PERSON* element to its child element *Age*.   □

Constraints. The following three kinds of constraints can be imposed upon nodes and edges to enhance the expressiveness of tree structured items.

1) Level Constraint Over An ad-Labeled Edge $Level(e)$

For an *ancestor-descendant* relationship $e = n_{source} \xrightarrow{ad} n_{target}$, the level constraint $Level(e) = m$ (where m is an integer) indicates that n_{target} is the m-th descendant generation of n_{source}. When $m = 1$, it implies that n_{target} is a child of n_{source}. A wildcard level constraint value, denoted using *, (i.e., $Level(e) = *$) means any nested level among the ancestor and descendant nodes. In Figure 1 (a), the constraints $Level(n_{1,1} \xrightarrow{ad} n_{1,2}) = 1$ and $Level(n_{1,1} \xrightarrow{ad} n_{1,3}) = 1$ require that both *Age* and *Gender* are direct children of PERSON element. We simplify the constraint expression by attaching the level value directly with the edge in the figure. Unless explicitly specified, the default level constraint value over any *ad* relationship is *.

2) Adhesion Constraint Over An ea-Labeled Edge $Adhesion(e)$

Assume we have an edge $e = n_{source} \xrightarrow{ea} n_{target}$ pointing from an element node n_{source} to its attribute node n_{targe}. The adhesion constraint $Adhesion(e) = strong$ declares that n_{target} is a compulsory attribute node of element node n_{source}. An optional attribute node n_{target} of n_{source} can be specified using $Adhesion(e) = weak$. In Figure 1 (a), the weak adhesion constraint $Adhesion(n_{1,1} \xrightarrow{ea} n_{1,4}) = weak$ implies that *Profession* is an optional attribute of *PERSON* element. The default adhesion constraint over an element-attribute relationship is *strong*.

3) Position Constraint Over A Node $Posi(n)$

The position constraint over a node n states its contextual position among all the nodes sharing the same ancestor and meanwhile having the same node name as n. A position constraint has the form of $Posi(n) = last() - v \mid first() + v \mid v$ (where v is an non-negative integer). Taking T_2 tree in Figure 1 (b) for example, $Posi(n_{2,4}) = last()$ implies the *Title* of the last ordered CD. A constraint like $Posi(n_{2,4}) = last()$-1 means the title of the last to second ordered CD. By default, a node n is assumed to have the first occurrence position, i.e., $Posi(n) = first()$. Its next sibling node n' with the same node name as n is thus constrained by $Posi(n') = first()+1$ in turn.

Definition 7. *A **well-formed tree** T is a tree that satisfies the following three conditions:*

1) T has only one unique root node.

2) For any edge in T, it links two correctly-typed nodes. That is, if the link type is ea (element-attribute), the source is a complex node and the target is a basic node; and if the link type is ad (ancestor-descendant), the source is a complex node.

3) For any constraint in T, it is applied to a correctly-typed edged. That is, a level constraint only constrains an ad-labeled edge, and an adhesion constraint only constrains ea-labeled edge. □

In the paper, all the trees under discussion are assumed to be well-formed.

2.2   The Sub-tree (Sub-item) Relationship

We define the *sub-tree (sub-item) relationship* between two trees (tree-structured items) on the basis of *partial relationship* of tree nodes, which is defined as follows.

Definition 8. *Let $n = (n_{name}, n_{content})$ and $n' = (n'_{name}, n'_{content})$ be two nodes where $(n_{name} = n'_{name})$. n is a **part** of n', denoted as $(n \leq_{node} n')$, if and only if n and n' have the same position constraint $(Posi(n) = Posi(n'))$, and meanwhile satisfy one of the following requirements:*

[Case 1] n is a basic node with a wildcard content $*$ (i.e., $n_{content} = *$).

[Case 2] n and n' are basic nodes with the same simple content (i.e., $n_{content} = n'_{content}$).

[Case 3] n and n' are complex nodes, each with a connection cluster set as the content.

For $\forall (l, \langle n_1, \ldots, n_k \rangle) \in n_{content}$, there exists $(l, \langle n'_1, \ldots, n'_{k'} \rangle) \in n'_{content}$ and a subsequence $\langle n'_{m_1}, \ldots, n'_{m_k} \rangle$ of $\langle n'_1, \ldots, n'_{k'} \rangle$, such that $\forall i (1 \leq i \leq k)$ $((n_i \leq_{node} n'_{m_i}) \wedge (c(n \xrightarrow{l} n'_i) = c(n \xrightarrow{l} n'_{m_i})))$. Here, c denotes the level constraint if $l = ad$; and adhesion constraint if $l = ea$. □

Intuitively, all the information embedded within a partial node, including the nodes and edges, as well as the hierarchical ordered relationships of nodes and attached constraints, can also be found in its whole node.

Definition 9. *Given two trees (tree-structured items) whose root nodes are r and r', respectively. T is called a **sub-tree (sub-item)** of T', denoted as $(T \leq_{tree} T')$, if and only if there exists a node n' in T', such that $(r \leq_{node} n')$.* □

2.3   The Containing Relationship between an XML Document and a Tree (Tree-Structured Item)

Since an XML document possesses a hierarchical document structure, where an XML element may contain further embedded elements, and can be attached with a number of attributes, it is therefore frequently modeled using a labeled ordered tree. Here, we first define when the content of an element/attribute in an XML document contains a tree, including a single node tree. Based on this, the *containing relationship* between an XML instance document and and a tree (tree-structured item) can then be deduced.

Definition 10. *The **embedding** relationship between an XML element/attribute and a tree (tree-structured item) T, rooted at node $r = (r_{name}, r_{content})$, can be recursively defined as follows:*

[Case 1] r is a basic node (i.e., tree T has only one node) with a simple content.

*If a simple XML element/attribute 1) has a tag/attribute name r_{name}, 2) has a simple element/attribute value equal to $r_{content}$, and 3) satisfies the position constraint $Posi(r)$, i.e., the $Posi(r)$-th occurrence in the host XML document, then this element/attribute **embeds** T.*

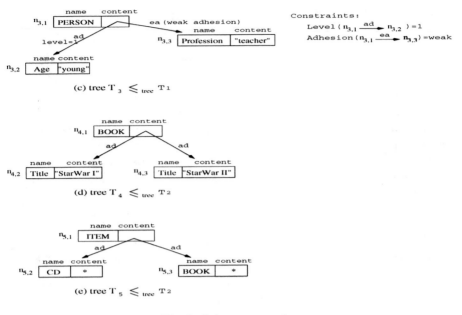

Fig. 2. Sub-tree examples

[*Case 2*] *r is a basic node (i.e., tree T contains only one node) with a wildcard content ٭.*

   *If a simple XML element/attribute 1) has a tag/attribute name r_{name}, and 2) satisfies the position constraint $Posi(r)$, then this element/attribute **embeds** T.*

[*Case 3*] *r is a complex node with a connection cluster set as its content.*

   *If an XML element 1) has a tag name r_{name}, 2) for any connection cluster $(l, \langle n_1, \ldots, n_k \rangle) \in r_{content}$ where $l = ea$, the element has a set of attributes which embed the trees rooted at $n_1, \ldots, n_k$ respectively; and 3) for any connection cluster $(l, \langle n_1, \ldots, n_k \rangle) \in r_{content}$ where $l = ad$, the element has a sequence of ordered subelements which embed the trees rooted at $n_1, \ldots, n_k$ respectively, then this element **embeds** T. Note that the appearance of these attributes or subelements in the XML document must conform to the constraints $Adhesion(r \xrightarrow{ea} n_i)$ and $Level(r \xrightarrow{ad} n_i)$ $(1 \le i \le k)$ defined in T.* $\square$

Definition 11. *An XML document doc **contains** a tree (tree-structured item) T rooted at node r, denoted as $(T \in_{tree} doc)$, if and only if it has an XML element or attribute which embeds tree T.* $\square$

Example 3. An XML instance document shown in Figure 3 contains all the example trees in Figure 1 and 2. Note that the order of CD and $BOOK$ elements, as well as the order of $Title$ subelements of $BOOK$ conform to the orders declared in T_2, T_5 and T_4. The position constraint over node $n_{2,4}$ $posi(n_{2,4}) = last()$ in T_2 is also satisfied by the given XML document. $\square$

```
<ORDER>
    <PERSON  Profession="teacher"  Address="NL">
        <Name> Martin Louis </Name>
        <Age> young </Age>
        <Gender> male </Gender>
    </PERSON>
    <ITEM>
        <CD>
            <Title> Pop Music </Title>
            <Title> StarWar Game </Title>
        </CD>
        <BOOK>
            <Title> StarWar I </Title>
            <Title> StarWar II </Title>
            <Title> Lost Space </Title>
        </BOOK>
    </ITEM>
</ORDER>
```

Fig. 3. An XML document example

2.4   A Formal Definition of XML-Enabled Association Rules

With the above notation, we are now in a position to formally define XML-enabled association rules and related measurements.

Definition 12. *Let $\mathcal{T}$ denote a set of trees (tree-structured items). An **XML-enabled association rule** is an implication of the form $X \Rightarrow Y$, which satisfies the following two conditions:*
  1) $X \subset \mathcal{T}$, $Y \subset \mathcal{T}$, and $X \cap Y = \emptyset$;
  2) *for $\forall T, T' \in (X \cup Y)$, there exists no tree T'' such that $(T'' \leq_{tree} T) \wedge (T'' \leq_{tree} T')$.* □

Different from classical association rules where associated items are usually denoted using simple structured data from the domains of basic data types, the items in XML-enabled association rules can have a hierarchical tree structure, as indicated by the first clause of the definition. Here, it is worth pointing out that when each of the tree-structured items contains only one basic root node, the XML-enabled association rules will degrade to the traditional association rules. The second clause of the definition requires that in an XML-enabled association rule, no common sub-trees exist within any two item trees in order to avoid redundant expression.

Figure 4 illustrates some XML-enabled association rule examples. Thanks to XML, XML-enabled association rules are more powerful than traditional association rules in capturing and describing association relationships. Such enhanced capabilities can be reflected from both a structural as well as a semantic point of view.

 – Association items have hierarchical tree structures, which are more natural, informative and understandable (e.g., Rule 1 & 2 in Figure 4).
 – Associated items inherently carry the *order* notion, enabling a uniform description of association and sequence patterns within one mining framework (e.g., Rule 1 states the sequence of books to be ordered, i.e., *"StarWar I"* proceeding *"StarWar II"* on a customer's order).

Rule 1: If a "male" person orders a CD entitled "StarWar Game", he will immediately
        order two books in the order of "StarWar I" and "StarWar II".

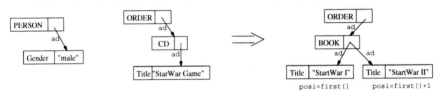

Rule 2: If a "student" living in "Tilburg" wants to order some flowers,
        s/he tends to go to a "small"-scaled shop located in "Tilburg South".

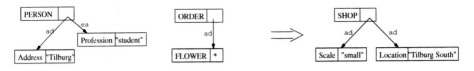

Fig. 4. XML-enabled association rule examples

- Associated items can further be constrained by their context positions, hierarchical levels, and weak/strong adhesion in the corresponding XML data to be mined. (e.g., Rule 1 indicates the contextual appearances of BOOKs on the order)
- Association relationships among structures and structured-values can also be captured and described (e.g., Rule 2 states that a student orders some flowers from a shop, and leaves detailed content of FLOWER element such as the kind of flowers and quantity, etc. aside).
- Auxiliary information which states the occurrence context of association relationships can be uniformly self-described in the mining framework (e.g., Rule 1 indicates that only *male* people have such as order pattern).

Similar to traditional association rules, we use *support* and *confidence* as two major measurements for XML-enabled association rules.

Definition 13. *Let $\mathcal{D}$ be a set of XML documents. The **support** and **confidence** of an XML-enabled association rule $X \Rightarrow Y$ are defined as: $support(X \Rightarrow Y) = \frac{|D_{xy}|}{|\mathcal{D}|}$, $confidence(X \Rightarrow Y) = \frac{|D_{xy}|}{|D_x|}$, where $D_{xy} = \{doc \mid \forall T \in (X \cup Y) \ (T \in_{tree} doc)\}$, and $D_x = \{doc \mid \forall T \in X \ (T \in_{tree} doc)\}$.* □

3   Conclusion

The paper presents an extended XML-enabled association rule framework, with the aim to discover associations inherent in massive amounts of XML data. We are currently developing practical algorithms for mining such kind of association rules from XML data.

References

1. R. Agrawal, T. Imielinski, and A. Swami. Mining association rules between sets of items in large databases. In *Proc. of the ACM SIGMOD Intl. Conf. on Management of Data*, pages 207–216, Washington D.C., USA, May 1993.
2. R. Agrawal and R. Srikant. Fast algorithms for mining association rules. In *Proc. of the 20th Intl. Conf. on Very Large Data Bases*, pages 478–499, Santiago, Chile, September 1994.
3. J. Han and Y. Fu. Discovery of multiple-level association rules from large databases. In *Proc. of the 21st Intl. Conf. on Very Large Data Bases*, pages 420–431, Zurich, Switzerland, September 1995.
4. J.-S. Park, M.-S. Chen, and P.S. Yu. An effective hash based algorithm for mining association rules. In *Proc. of the ACM SIGMOD Intl. Conf. on Management of Data*, pages 175–186, San Jose, CA, May 1995.
5. S.C. Shapiro. Cables, paths, and subconscious reasoning in propositional semantic networks (chapter). In Principles of Semantic Networks – Explorations in the Representation of Knowledge, Editor J.F. Sowa, 1991.
6. R. Srikant and R. Agrawal. Mining generalized association rules. In *Proc. of the 21st Intl. Conf. on Very Large Data Bases*, pages 409–419, Zurich, Switzerland, September 1995.
7. H. Toivonen. Sampling large databases for association rules. In *Proc. of the 22th Conference on Very Large Data Bases*, pages 134–145, Mumbai, India, September 1996.
8. K. Wang, Y. He, and J. Han. Mining frequent itemsets using support constraints. In *Proc. 26st Intl. Conf. Very Large Data Bases*, pages 43–52, Cairo, Egypt, September 2000.

Validation of XML Document Updates Based on XML Schema in XML Databases*

Sang-Kyun Kim[1], Myungcheol Lee[2], and Kyu-Chul Lee[1]

[1] Dept. of Computer Engineering,
Chungnam National University,
Korea
{skkim,kclee}@ce.cnu.ac.kr
[2] Computer System Department,
Computer & Software Research Laboratory,
Electronics and Telecommunications Research Institute,
Korea
mclee@etri.re.kr

Abstract. We study the validation of XML documents when they are updated in XML databases. An XML document can be verified by checking against an XML Schema, which contains structure and type information of XML documents. However, most of XML database systems just validate the whole XML document, but can not validate parts of it. If updates are very frequent, then validating the whole XML document will cause serious performance degradation. Furthermore, rollback should be performed if the updates result in an invalid document, because the updated document is usually validated after the update operation executed. In this paper, we propose an immediate and partial validation mechanism for solving these two problems, i.e the validity of an update operation is checked immediately before the actual update is applied to the database whether it causes invalidity, and validation is performed only on the updated parts of the XML document in the database. Consequently, XML database systems can maintain valid XML documents at any time. We already proposed an immediate and partial validation mechanism based on DTD[6], and we extend the mechanism based on XML Schema in this paper.

1 Introduction

Since XML has emerged as the Internet electronic document standard for neutral data representation and exchange, many researchers and database vendors have studied efficient ways to facilitate the task of storing and querying XML documents.

The next step to leverage XML into full-featured Internet data format is to support updates and their validation. Recently, several researches[1][2][3] have been performed for updating XML documents. These studies define update operations by extending XQuery and try to resolve semantic problems occurring during the process

---

* This work was partially supported by Brain Korea (BK) 21 and Software Research Center (SOREC) in Chungnam National University, Korea

V. Mařík et al. (Eds.): DEXA 2003, LNCS 2736, pp. 98–108, 2003.
© Springer-Verlag Berlin Heidelberg 2003

of the update operations. However, two or more update operations in a single update statement could cause several conflict problems in these approaches, because the update operation is usually validated after execution. For solving these conflicts, when an XML document in the database is updated, XML database systems must be able to validate immediately the update operation with respect to XML Schema before it is executed. Hence, only when the operation is valid, it is executed.

Whenever application programs modify an XML document, the XML parser must check the whole document for the validation. However, this is very inefficient in case that frequent updates occur upon small portions of documents. It becomes more serious when XML documents are stored in database than in a file. To validate an XML document modified by the update operations, we must take out the whole XML document and its schema information from the database, and then pass them to parser to check the validity so that validation time may result in serious performance degradation. However, most of the XML document update mechanisms use the full validation approach, because there have been few mechanism to support the partial validation until now.

Recently, several efforts have been progressed for more efficient handling of the XML document validation. Chen [4] provides a way to guarantee that valid XML views are defined, but updates and their validation for XML views are not considered. Papakonstantinou [5] suggests an incremental validation algorithm of XML documents. This mechanism enables the partial validation but it is problematic because the auxiliary structure must be recomputed whenever an update operation is performed. In section 4, we discuss this algorithm in detail.

We have already studied a validation mechanism based on DTD[6], which supports immediate validation of only updated parts when an XML document stored in the database is updated. In this paper, we extend our previous work to the validation mechanism based on XML Schema. Our approach is performed on inserts, deletes and updates of elements. For efficient validation, we translate XML schema information into a set of deterministic finite automaton (DFA)[7], and store DFAs into a database table. Thus, when an XML document stored in the database is updated, we can immediately check the validity of only updated parts using the stored schema information before it is actually applied to database.

The remainder of this paper is organized as follows. In section 2, we define the validation framework. In section 3, we present our mechanism to validate immediately parts of an XML document in the database. In section 4, we discuss prior efforts for the related subjects and compare our mechanism with them. Finally, in section 5, we summarize this paper.

2 Validation Framework

An XML document contains its own structural information. Therefore, before we store XML documents into the database or update them in applications, we must verify that the structural information is valid. In the following, we define the validation of XML documents based on validation granularity and validation time:

Definition 1. The validation based on validation granularity is defined as follows.
- The *full validation* of an XML document is to validate the whole document.
- The *partial validation* of an XML document is to validate only updated parts of the XML document

Definition 2. The validation based on validation time is defined as follows.
- The *deferred validation* of an XML document is to perform validation after updating.
- The *immediate validation* of an XML document is to perform validation before updating, and updates are executed only if it is valid.

Most of XML database systems use *deferred and full validation* method in case XML documents are updated. As we described in section 1, this method has conflicts and performance problems for update operations. Therefore, for solving these problems, XML database systems must be able to support *immediate and partial validation* method so that they can always maintain valid XML documents efficiently. Typically, these validation steps required for the immediate and partial validation in XML database systems are defined as follows:

Definition 3. The validation steps for the immediate and partial validation in XML database systems are defined as follows:
1. Parse XML Schema files and extract their information.
2. Store the extracted schema information into the database.
3. When an XML document updated, check its validity by referencing the stored schema information.
4. Perform the update operation or not according to the validity.

In the next section, we apply these validation steps to the validation of XML documents with respect to XML schema to perform the immediate and partial validation.

3   Immediate and Partial XML Schema Validation

3.1   Expression of the XML Schema Information

An XML document can be represented by an unranked tree[8] over a finite alphabet Σ. Unranked trees are finite labeled trees where nodes can have an arbitrary number of children. An unranked tree over Σ satisfies an XML Schema if the tree is a derivation tree of XML Schema's grammar, i.e. this tree is valid with respect to an XML Schema.

DTDs are extended context-free grammars (ECFG) [9][10][11] in which the right-hand sides of productions are regular expressions called content models. The productions of a DTD are called element type definitions. An ECFG is specified by a 3-tuple $G = (\Sigma, P, S)$ where Σ is a finite alphabet that consists of nonterminal symbols N and terminal symbols T, P is a finite set of production schemas, and the nonterminal S is the sentence symbol. Each production schema in an ECFG has the form $A \rightarrow E \in$

P, where $A \in N$, and E is a regular expression over the alphabet $\Sigma = N \cup T$. The language $L(G)$ of an extended context-free grammar G is the set of terminal strings derivable from the sentence symbol of G. Formally, $L(G)=\{w \in \Sigma^* | S \Rightarrow^* w\}$, where $\Rightarrow^*$ denotes the transitive closure of the derivability relation.

XML Schemas can be abstracted as specialized DTDs[12] that decouple the type of an element from its label. A specialized DTD is a 4-tuple $G'=(\Sigma,\Sigma',d,\mu)$ where Σ is a finite alphabet of labels, Σ' is a finite alphabet of types, d is a DTD over Σ' and μ is a mapping from Σ to Σ'. The language $L(G')$ of a specialized DTD G' is the set of terminal strings over the alphabet of types Σ with respect to extended context-free grammar G. Formally, $L(G')=\{w \in \Sigma^*, w' \in \Sigma'^* | \mu(w')=w\}$

In this paper, we use the DFA of finite automata to recognize the regular expression E. The finite automata are classified into nondeterministic finite automata(NFA) and DFA. Both can recognize exactly what regular expressions can denote through generalized transition diagrams. However, there is a difference in that a DFA has at most one transition while a NFA may have several transitions from each state on any input. Therefore, DFA is suitable rather than NFA to support the partial validation which only modified parts must be validated, since there is at most one path from the start state labeled by that string. We do not suggest here any concrete algorithms to express the mapping from Σ to Σ' in XML Schema. This could be implemented in various ways. For example, the type information of Σ' can be stored as the user-defined datatype of a database system, and validated by the own type-checking mechanism of the database system when an update operation occurs.

3.2 Construction of DFA

Many studies have been proposed for constructing finite automata from regular expressions[7][13][14][15]. To construct a DFA from a regular expression, we first could construct a NFA using Thompson construction[14] or Glushkov construction[15], and translate them into a DFA using Subset construction. Alternatively we could directly translate regular expression into a DFA[7]. A DFA constructed by above methods can recognize a string of a language, but can not recognize only the substring of a string. However, we need to recognize only the substring modified by updates to support efficient partial validation. Thus, we propose an algorithm to construct a DFA from a regular expression to support the partial validation. This algorithm uses the syntactic structure of regular expressions to guide the construction process. We show how to construct DFA for regular expressions that have alternation, concatenation and unary postfix operator.

Definition 4. If $a \in \Sigma$ and $b \in \Sigma$ are symbols, then a and b also could be regular expressions that denote $L(a)=\{a\}$ and $L(b)=\{b\}$ respectively.

Definition 5. Suppose a and b are regular expressions denoting the language $L(a)=\{a\}$ and $L(b)=\{b\}$ respectively, the language $L(E)$ defined by a regular expression E over Σ is defined inductively as follows:
- $L(ab) = L(a)L(b)$
- $L(a|b) = L(a) \cup L(b)$

- $L(a*) = \{v_1...v_n|v_1,...,v_n \in L(a),\ n \geq 0\}$
- $L(a^+) = \{v_1...v_n|v_1,...,v_n \in L(a),\ n \geq 1\}$
- $L(a?) = L(a) \cup \{\varepsilon\}$, where the symbol ε denotes the null string
- $L(a\{p,q\}) = \{v_1...v_n|v_1,...,v_n \in L(a),\ p \leq n \leq q\}$

Algorithm 1 : Constructing DFAs
Input : A regular expression E over an alphabet Σ
Output : A DFA D accepting $L(E)$
Steps :
1. Parse E into its constituent subexpressions.
2. For each of six operators in definition 5, construct DFAs as follows. (for each i, $0 < i < n$, $a \in \Sigma$ and $b \in \Sigma$ are symbols)

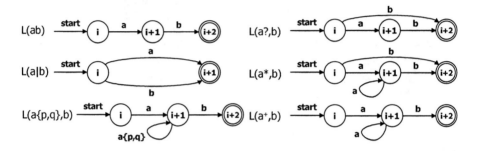

3. Combine DFAs whenever an operator occurs in an element declaration until we obtain the entire DFA. We just construct a DFA per an element declaration, and do not combine DFAs for each declaration.
4. Construct a DFA recursively for the parenthesized regular expression in an element declaration.

We use the following notation for DFA. A DFA is a 5-tuple $D = (S,\Sigma,s_0,F,\delta)$ where S is a set of states, Σ is a finite alphabet, $s_0 \in S$ is a start state, $F \subseteq S$ is the set of final states and δ is a mapping from $S \times \Sigma$ to $P(S)$. The above algorithm constructs a DFA for a regular expression of an element declaration, and a DFA for each operator is constructed according to the second step of the algorithm in each declaration. Note that all of elements with the same label in a DFA always arrive at the same state. Formally, $\delta(s_{j-1},i_j)=s_j$, for each i and j, $s \in S$, $i \in \Sigma$, $0 < j < n$. Therefore, this property enables us to identify the arrival state of an element in a DFA so that we can easily search a position of the substring in a string of a DFA. The partial validation uses this property. Fig. 1 shows an example of constructing a DFA for an element declaration in an XML Schema.

```
<xsd:complexType name="elementAType">
  <xsd:sequence>
    <xsd:element name="B" minOccurs="0" maxOccurs="5"
                 type="xsd:string" default="Title"/>
    <xsd:sequence minOccurs="0" maxOccurs="unbounded">
      <xsd:element name="C" type="xsd:integer" fixed="37"/>
      <xsd:element name="D" type="xsd:integer"/>
    </xsd:sequence>
    <xsd:element name="E" minOccurs="5" maxOccurs="10"/>
    <xsd:element name="F" minOccurs="0"/>
    <xsd:choice minOccurs="0" maxOccurs="unbounded">
      <xsd:element name="G" type="xsd:string"/>
      <xsd:element name="H" type="xsd:string"/>
    </xsd:choice>
  </xsd:sequence>
</xsd:complexType>
<xsd:element name="A" type="elementAType"/>
```

Fig. 1. An example of an XML Schema

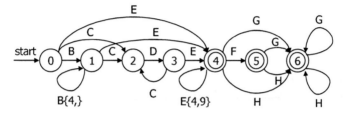

Fig. 2. An example of constructing a DFA from Fig. 1

3.3 Storing of DFA

The constructed DFAs have to be stored in the database for validating update operations. For example, a table storing the DFA constructed from an XML Schema of Fig. 2 is shown in Fig. 3. We may split all the transitions of a DFA for storing in a relational table. Each transition can be divided into beforeState, elementName, afterState, finalState, minOccurs and maxOccurs. Then, we store these with schemaId, elementName. By schemaId and elementName, it is easily identified to which XML Schema and element declaration each tuple relates respectively. Moreover, there could be other information like data values except that of DFA in an element declaration. However we ignore them because their validation is trivial.

schemaId	elementName	beforeState	tranName	afterState	finalState	minOccurs	maxOccurs
paper	A	0	B	1	false		
paper	A	1	B	1	false	4	unbounded
paper	A	0	C	2	false		
paper	A	0	E	4	true		
...	...	...	...	...	...	...	...
paper	A	4	E	4	true	4	9
...	...	...	...	...	...	...	...

Fig. 3. An example of storing a DFA diagram of Fig. 2

3.4   Validation of Update Operations

We introduce here an algorithm for validating an element update operation. This algorithm must be performed before updates. Consequently, if it is valid, the update operation will be executed.

When validating an element update operation, it needs not parse the whole document, but it is sufficient to examine only three elements, which are the new element to be inserted, a previous sibling and a next sibling of the new element. Because we organize the schema information as all of elements with the same name always arrive at the same state, we can easily identify the afterState of the previous sibling element of the new element. Then, we check whether the previous sibling element can be followed by the new element and the new element can be followed by the next sibling element. However, it is hard to search if there are two or more elements identical with a previous element of inserted element within an element declaration. Only in this situation, we examine whether all the children are valid.

Inserting an Element. Algorithm 2 is a validating algorithm for inserting an element.

Algorithm 2 : Validation for inserting an element
Input : a parent element *parentX*, a previous sibling element *previousX*, an inserted element *X*, a next sibling element *nextX*
Output : The answer "yes" if DFA accepts *X*; "no" otherwise
Steps :
if the datatype of an inserted element *X* is not valid **then return** "no";
if *X* is declared in an XML Schema **then**
   if the regular expression of *parentX* == "any" **then return** "yes";
   else
      if there are two or more elements having the same name with the *previousX* **then**
        previousX := a first child of the *parentX*; *X* := a next sibling of *previousX*;
        while all of children of *parentX* **do**
           if insertValidationProcess(*previousX*, *X*, *null*) == false **then return** "no";
           previousX := *X*; *X* := a next sibling of *X*;
        end
        return "yes";
      end if
      else return insertValidationProcess(*previousX*, *X*, *nextX*);
   end else
end if
else return "no";

SubAlgorithm : insertValidationProcess (check if there exists a transition in DFA)
Input : a previous element *previousX*, an inserted element *X*, a next element *nextX*
Output : The answer "yes" if there exists a transition; "no" otherwise
Steps :
if *previousX* can be followed by *X* **then**
   if *nextX* is exist **then**

      if *X* can be followed by *nextX* **then return** "yes";
        else return "no";
    end if
    else return "yes";
  end if
  else return "no";

Fig. 4 shows an example of the validating process that conforms to the above algorithm when an element is inserted according to the element declaration in the Fig. **1**.

1. "G" is an element declared in an XML Schema.
2. "A", a parent element, is not declared as "any".
3. "F", a previous element of the inserted element arrives at state "5".
4. "G", an element to be inserted, can transit from state "5" to state "6".
5. "G", just a next element, can not transit from current state "6".

This insert operation is not valid because it can not satisfy the condition 5.

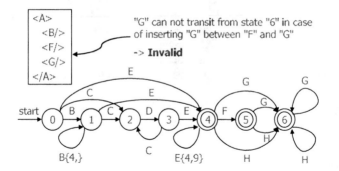

Fig. 4. An example of validating for inserting an element

Deleting an Element. A validating algorithm for deleting an element is similar to that for inserting. There is a difference in that a final state must be checked if an element to be deleted is a last element. If any siblings do not have a final state at least after deleting a last element, it is invalid.

Updating an Element. Updating an element can be simply regarded as the combination of two processes that insert an element after deleting it. Therefore, it is performed to delete first and insert an element in order.

4   Related Work

Researches[1][2] for updating XML documents have defined syntaxes for update operations and resolved semantic problems occurring during the process of the update operation. However, they do not consider how to validate update operations.

Recently, several efforts have been proposed for more efficient handling of XML document validation. Chen [4] provides a way to guarantee that valid XML views are defined. They transform an XML document into an Object-Relationship-Attribute model for SemiStructured data (ORA-SS) [16] schema diagram with necessary semantics and define a set of rules to guide the design of valid XML views. So, valid XML views could be designed according to the guideline, but updates and their validation for XML views are not considered.

Papakonstantinou [5] suggests an incremental validation algorithm of XML documents. The incremental validation is related with incremental parsing which have focused on LR parsing[17][18][19] and LL parsing[20][21]. The algorithm starts by parsing the input text and produces a parse tree, which is typically annotated with auxiliary information. The auxiliary information has minimal units of the parse tree that are affected by the updates so that the validity of the updates can be checked according to the auxiliary structures. This mechanism enables the partial validation, but it is problematic because the auxiliary structure must be recomputed whenever an update operation is performed. Therefore, we do not use the incremental parsing methods in our mechanism. Instead, we extract and store the XML Schema information through parsing an XML Schema file according to our DFA construction algorithm. This information is constructed only once when an XML Schema file is stored into a database and need not to be recomputed for validating update operations.

In addition, Papakonstantinou [5] provides a validation time of $O(m\log^2 n)$ for a specialized DTD using an auxiliary structure of size $O(n)$, where m is the number of updates in a NFA and n is the size of the document. We have already shown that our mechanism is always better than the full validating method regardless of the number of elements through analyzing the performance of update operations[6]. In this paper, we compare our mechanism with the incremental validation of Papakonstantinou [5]. Like Papakonstantinou [5], we assume that we can find the parent, the previous sibling and the next sibling of an updated element in $O(1)$. Then, the time required for validating an update operation using our mechanism just becomes $O(3)$, because it is sufficient to examine only three elements that consist of an updated element, a previous sibling and a next sibling of this updated element. However, if there are two or more elements identical with a previous one of inserting one within an element declaration, the time required for validating is $O(m)$, where m is the number of siblings of the updated element, which is equals to parameter m of Papakonstantinou [5]. Consequently, our mechanism shows much better performance than the incremental validation of Papakonstantinou [5]

5   Conclusion

In this paper, we proposed a validation mechanism, which supports immediate validation of only updated parts when an XML document stored in the database is updated. For this mechanism, we extract and store XML Schema information. Then, when users update an XML document stored in the database, we verify immediately whether the update operation is valid or not. Consequently, by using this mechanism for XML database systems, they can always maintain valid XML documents in the databases as well as resolve the conflict problems of update operations that could occur for performing update operations.

In addition, our mechanism validates three elements at most, a new element to be inserted, a previous sibling and a next sibling of this new element without validating the whole XML document. Therefore, the validation and update process is quite efficient regardless of the number of elements within an XML document.

Ultimately, if our mechanism is applied to XML database systems, it can satisfy users' various retrieval and updating requirements.

References

[1]   I.Tatarinov, Z.G.Ives, A.Y.Halevy, and D.S.Weld. Updating XML. Proceedings of ACM SIGMOD Conference, pp.413–424 (2001)
[2]   J.Robie and R.Lehti. Updates in XQuery. Proceedings of XML Conference (2001)
[3]   Software AG. QuiP: a prototype of XQuery, In
      http://www.softwareag.com/developer/quip/default.htm
[4]   Y.B.Chen, T.W.Ling and M.L.Lee. Designing Valid XML Views. Proceedings of the 21st International Conference on Conceptual Modeling, pp.463–478 Springer-Verlag (2002)
[5]   Y.Papakonstantinou and V.Vianu. Incremental Validation of XML Documents. Proceedings of the 9th International Conference on Database Theory, pp.47–63, Springer-Verlag (2003).
[6]   S.-K.Kim, M.-C.Lee and K.-C.Lee. Immediate and Partial Validation Mechanism for the Conflict Resolution of Update Operations in XML Databases. Proceedings of the 3rd Advances in Web-Age Information Management, pp.387–396, Springer-Verlag (2002)
[7]   A.V.Aho, R.Sethi, J.D.Ullman. Compilers Principles, Techniques, and Tools. Addison-Wesley (1986)
[8]   F.Neven. Automata theory for XML researchers. ACM SIGMOD Record, 31(3):39–46 (2002)
[9]   P.Kilpelainen and D.Wood. SGML and XML Document Grammars and Exceptions. Information and Computation, 169:230–252 (2001)
[10] A.Bruggemann-Klein. Regular expressions into finite automata. Theoretical Computer Science, 120:197–213 (1993)
[11] T.J.Sager. On the use of extended grammars. Proceedings of the 20th annual conference on Southeast regional conference, pp.246–252 (1982)
[12] Y.Papakonstantinou and V.Vianu. DTD inference for views of XML data. Proceedings of 20th Symposium on Principles of Database Systems (PODS 2001), pp.35–46, ACM Press (2001)
[13] G.Berry and R.Sethi. From regular expressions to deterministic automata. Theoretical Computer Science, 48:117–126 (1986)
[14] K.Thompson. Regular expression search algorithm. Communications of the ACM, 11:419–422 (1968)
[15] V.M.Glushkov. The abstract theory of automata. Russian Mathematical Surveys, 16:1-53 (1961)
[16] T.W.Ling, M.L.Lee and G.Dobbie. Application of ORA-SS: An Object-Relationship-Attribute Model for Semi-Structured Data. Proceedings of the 3rd International Conference on Information Integration and Web-based Applications & Services, pp.17–28 (2001)

[17] C.Ghezzi and D.Mandrioli. Augmenting parsers to support incrementality. Journal of the Association for Comupting Machinery, 27(3):564–579 (1980)
[18] T.Wagner and S.Graham. Efficient and flexible incremental parsing. ACM Transactions on Programming Languages and Systems, 20(2):980–1013 (1998)
[19] J.-M.Larcheveque. Optimal Incremental Parsing. ACM Transactions on Programming Languages and Systems, 17(1):1–15 (1995)
[20] A.Murching, Y.Prasant and Y.Srikant. Incremental recursive descent parsing. Computer Languages, 15(4) 1990
[21] W.Li. A simple and efficient incremental LL(1) parsing. 22nd Seminar on Current Trends in Theory and Practice of Informatics, pp.399–404 (1995)

XML Schemata Inference and Evolution

Ismael Sanz, Juan Manuel Pérez, Rafael Berlanga,
and María José Aramburu

Departament de Llenguatges i Sistemes Informàtics
Departament de Ingenieria y Ciencia de los Computadores
Universitat Jaume I,
E–12071 Castellón, Spain
{isanz,martinej,berlanga,aramburu}@uji.es

Abstract. This work addresses the automatic generation of conceptual models for XML-oriented databases, which in many cases have little or no support for schemata. Our techniques are based on both an incremental clustering algorithm, which groups together the incoming XML documents according to their structural similarities, and a schema inference method, which maintains dynamically the schema of each detected document cluster. Our proposal takes into consideration the schema evolution. For this purpose, we have adapted the TOODOR document model that describes the temporal properties of the XML document types.

Keywords: Schema Inference, Document Clustering, XML Databases.

1 Introduction

The fast-paced adoption of XML as a language for data interchange among diverse applications and web services, is opening the way towards the real integration of heterogeneous information sources. In our opinion, the success of this integration will reside in three key factors. Firstly, it will be necessary to develop repositories for the massive storage of XML data and documents coming from several sources (i.e. Web warehouses). Secondly, query languages providing homogeneous access to these data are also needed. Finally, the availability of (semi-)automatic methods for the creation, management and integration of the conceptual schemata that describe the data in XML repositories is also an important factor.

Regarding the first two factors, currently there exist several native XML-oriented databases, as well as extensions of commercial databases, that allow for the storage and retrieval of XML data. XQuery [7] and XML-QL [2] are two relevant proposals of query languages for this type of data. Nevertheless, not all of these approaches are valid for the integration of repositories in XML. An important requisite is that they should be flexible enough to accept any XML document, regardless of the existence of an accompanying type definition or schema. It should be taken into account that many XML documents come from applications that do not provide such definitions.

V. Mařík et al. (Eds.): DEXA 2003, LNCS 2736, pp. 109–118, 2003.

This requisite provides the rationale for the third key factor in the integration of information sources. The possible lack of typing, or the excessive presence of different type definitions, require the development of new mechanisms for the automatic definition of conceptual schemata. It should be noticed that current approaches to the semantic integration of data assume the existence of this kind of conceptual schemata (sometimes an ontology), and apply them to the search of relationships of equivalence or association; see [3,5] for some examples.

In this paper we address the issue of the automatic generation of conceptual schemata by discovering the structural similarities between XML documents, and their clustering into classes. Our proposal has been implemented over the G commercial database system [4], which has been designed for the development of web applications that integrate heterogeneous and highly dynamic information sources. The G system transforms the information extracted from different sources into linked XML documents, which are stored in a native format. The techniques discussed in this paper obtain, in a dynamic and incremental way, a conceptual schema for this database, and represents it by means of the XML Schema Language (XMLS) [6].

The remainder of the paper is organized as follows. Section 2 gives a brief description of the G system. In Section 3 we define a structural similarity measure for XML documents, a clustering algorithm based on this measure, and the XMLS generation mechanism for the classes obtained by the clustering algorithm. Section 4 shows some preliminary results of this approach, and in Section 5 some conclusions are presented.

2   Context of the Work

This work is part of a project with the objective of automatically generating web-based applications for integrated repositories of XML documents. The system is called *G*, and its architecture is shown in Figure 1. The main contribution of this paper is the *Schema Manager* module, which is depicted at the right side of the figure. This module is in charge of monitoring the input stream of documents in order to classify them by their structural properties, and of inferring for each detected class an XML schema.

One relevant feature of this process is that the inferred schemata can evolve along time so that only the up-to-date schemata must be regarded in the generation of the database indexes and their applications. The evolution of schemata is guided by the structural changes detected by the clustering algorithm. On the other hand, once a schema becomes historical, it will be not considered by the clustering routine anymore. In this way, the time and space complexity of this module is reduced considerably.

In the next sections we describe the two components of the *Schema Manager* module, namely: the clustering routine and the schema inference and evolution component.

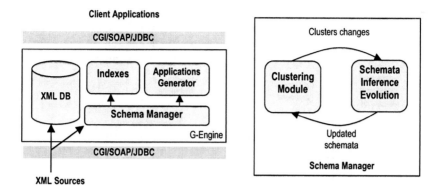

Fig. 1. Architecture of the G system.

3   The Clustering Module

The clustering module is in charge of classifying each incoming XML document according to its structural properties. We assume that this clustering process is mainly non-supervised, since most XML documents in the web do not provide a known schema nor DTD. Another important requirement for the clustering routine is that it must be incremental, that is, for each incoming document the algorithm must adjust the classes involved according to their structure.

In the next sections we first describe the similarity measure used to cluster documents by their structure, and then the clustering routine.

3.1   Structural Similarity

In the literature there exist several proposals to determine whether two documents have a similar structure or not. Most of these approaches rely on the tree edit distance [8] and usually have high complexity costs. In the context of our application, we need to evaluate this similarity function over a large set of documents. That is why we need to find out a new similarity function with a lower temporal cost.

Thus we propose a different approach based on the similarity between document paths. We consider that each document is represented by the set of all the paths that go from its root element to each one of its leaves (text or attribute). Let us denote this set as $pathSet(d)$, where d is an XML document.

We also define the similarity between two paths, p_1 and p_2 as follows:

$$pathSim(p_1, p_2) = \frac{|elements(p_1) \cap elements(p_2)|}{max(|elements(p_1)|, |elements(p_2)|)}$$

where the function *elements* returns the set of node elements of the given path.

As it would be expected, the more elements the paths share, the higher value the proposed measure returns. However, this measure does not take into account the relative order of the elements in the paths. With this simplification it is possible to return a high similarity value for a pair of incompatible paths (i.e. if the paths state different orderings for the same pair of elements). This drawback can be avoided by introducing the following compatibility function:

$$comp(p_1, p_2) = \begin{cases} false & \text{if } \exists e_1, e_2 \in elements(p_1) \cap elements(p_2) \\ & \text{such that } match(p_1, ``//e_1//e_2//") \\ & \wedge match(p_2, ``//e_2//e_1//") \\ true & \text{otherwise} \end{cases}$$

Here, the function $match(p, pe)$ returns $true$ if the path p matches the path expression pe.

Starting from these similarity and compatibility functions, we define the following global function to measure the similarity between the structure of two documents, d_1 and d_2:

$$Sim(d_1, d_2) = \frac{\sum_{p_i \in pathSet(d_1)} max_{p_j \in pathSet(d_2)}(pathSim(p_i, p_j))}{|pathSet(d_1)|}$$

$$docSim(d_1, d_2) = \begin{cases} 0 & \text{if } \exists p_1 \in d_1, p_2 \in d_2, \\ & \text{such that } \neg comp(p_1, p_2) \\ \frac{Sim(d_1,d_2)+Sim(d_2,d_1)}{2} & \text{otherwise} \end{cases}$$

With this formula, two documents have a similar structure if all their paths are compatible, and most of their paths are similar.

3.2   Clustering Routine

To describe the clustering routine, the following definitions are needed.

- Each document class C is a set of documents whose structural similarities with respect to the class representatives are greater than a given threshold β_{sim}. The class representatives, denoted $repSet(C)$, are themselves documents of the class. The similarity between two representatives of the class must not be greater than a given threshold β_{rep} ($\beta_{rep} \geq \beta_{sim}$). In this way, each class will represent a set of common structural properties, which are established by the intersection of all its representatives, as well as a set of structural particularities, which are stated by its representatives. Consequently, the threshold β_{sim} determines the degree of optionality of the associated class schema, whereas the number of representatives determines the degree of heterogeneity of the class schema.
- A document d *structurally subsumes* to another document d' if the path set of the former includes that of the latter, formally: $pathSet(d) \supset pathSet(d')$.
- The class to which a document d belongs is denoted with $class(d)$.

The clustering routine (see Algorithm 1) uses an inverted file over the representatives of the classes in order to efficiently calculate the structural similarity

---

Algorithm 1 Clustering Routine

Require: d_{new}, β_{sim}, β_{rep}, InvertedFile, Classes

    { d_{new}: new incoming document;

    β_{sim}: similarity threshold for documents;

    β_{rep}: similarity threshold for representatives;

    InvertedFile: inverted file for document class representatives;

    Classes: set of currently detected classes; }

Ensure: Classes, InvertedFile

 1: Select from the InvertedFile the representatives whose similarity with d_{new} is greater than β_{sim},
    and put them into the set *Docs*.

 2: $New = \emptyset$ {Auxiliary class that will contain the union of those classes similar to d_{new}}

 3: **for all** $d \in Docs$ **do**

 4:    **if** $New = \emptyset$ **then**

 5:       $New = class(d) \cup \{d_{new}\}$

 6:       $New.repSet = repSet(class(d))$

 7:    **else**

 8:       $New = New \cup class(d)$

 9:       $New.repSet = New.repSet \cup repSet(class(d))$

10:    **end if**

11:    **if** $\exists d' \in repSet(New)$ such that d_{new} subsumes d' **then**

12:       Remove all the representatives of New subsumed by d_{new}

13:       Add d_{new} to the set of representatives of New

14:    **end if**

15:    Remove the class $class(d)$ from Classes, and all its representatives from the InvertedFile.

16: **end for**

17: **if** $New = \emptyset$ **then**

18:    Add to Classes the new class $\{d_{new}\}$

19:    Update the InvertedFile with d_{new}

20: **else**

21:    **if** $\nexists d' \in repSet(New)$ such that $docSim(d', d_{new}) > \beta_{rep}$ **then**

22:       add d_{new} to the set of representatives of New

23:    **end if**

24:    Add to Classes the updated class New.

25:    Add the the representative set of New to InvertedFile.

26: **end if**

---

of each incoming document. Each entry of the inverted file represents a path element, and its associated value is the list of representatives having that path element.

The algorithm basically updates the inverted file and the set of current document classes according to the structure of each new incoming document. It takes into consideration the following situations:

- When the similarity between the new document and several representatives of different classes is greater than the given threshold β_{sim}, all the involved classes must be joined into one single class. The variable *New* is used for this purpose, which incrementally aggregates the involved classes (lines 3–16). Additionally, a representative set must be revised for the resulted class (lines 11–15 and lines 21–23).
- When the similarity between the new document and all the current representatives is not greater than the given threshold β_{sim}, the document belongs to a new class, whose representative is itself.
- The representative set of a class must be updated in the following two cases: when the new document structurally subsumes some of its current representatives, and when the similarity between the new document and all the class representatives is not greater than the threshold β_{rep}. In the first case,

the new document replaces all the representatives that are subsumed by it. In the second case, the new document becomes a new representative of the class.

4 Inference and Evolution of XML Schemata

The second module of the *Schema Manager* is in charge of inferring a schema for each document class, and of deciding how an existing schema evolves over time. This module deals with the small changes produced by the arrival of new documents into the system, as long as they do not alter the cluster structure. For instance, the appearance of a new optional attribute will probably not change the cluster representative set, but it needs to be taken into account when reporting the current cluster schema. In any case, the *Schema Inference and Evolution component* is tightly coupled with the Clustering Routine, since the schemata need to be refreshed each time some structural change occurs.

The type model we have adopted for schema modelling is an extension of the XML Schema standard to include the TOODOR model (Temporal Object Oriented Document Organization and Retrieval) [1]. More specifically, we have defined an RDF[1] notation for expressing the evolution of an XML Schema according to the rules of the TOODOR model.

TOODOR combines a static XML-like type system with a set of temporal primitives to represent the evolution of schemata. The model defines $\mathcal{CI}$ as a set of class identifiers, $\mathcal{OI}$ as a set of object unique identifiers and $\mathcal{AN}$ as a set of attribute names. As in other object-oriented data models, TOODOR allows class identifiers from $\mathcal{CI}$ to be used in the definition of types, being considered each class identifier as an object type. This type system is extended with two types for time expressions: *Time* to denote time instants, and *Period* to denote time periods. The document type system is denoted by $\mathcal{DOCTYPES}$, and the domain of time values is $\mathcal{PDATE}$.

In TOODOR a *class* is a 4-tuple whose components are as follows:

- *class_id* $\in \mathcal{CI}$ is the class identifier,
- *lifespan* $\in \mathcal{PDATE}$ is the time period during which the class is defined,
- *h_type* is a sequence of pairs (p_i, T_i) with $i \geq 1$, where $p_i \in \mathcal{PDATE}$ and $T_i \in \mathcal{DOCTYPES}$,
- and finally, *h_population* is a sequence of pairs (p_i, I_i) with $i \geq 1$, where $p_i \in \mathcal{PDATE}$ and I_i is the subset of $\mathcal{OI}$ that coincides with the set of the class's instances created during the time period p_i.

4.1 Inference of Types and Temporal Properties

The Schema Manager maintains one TOODOR schema for each cluster detected by the clustering routine. In order to keep these schemata up-to-date as new documents arrive to the system, the Schema Inference and Evolution component performs two tasks:

---
[1] http://krono.act.uji.es/toodor.rdfs

- The inference of types describing the static structure of the documents within a class at a given time.
- The tracking of the schema as it evolves along time, and in particular the *lifespan* of each static type.

In order to deal with the changes produced by the incoming documents, we use a label-relaxation algorithm. We represent TOODOR types as DAGs, in which nodes are class identifiers of $\mathcal{CI}$ and arcs are labelled to express the composition relationships between the types they represent. The allowed labels are analogous to those found in XML DTDSs: 1 (exactly one), ? (zero or one), * (zero or more) and + (one or more).

The process begins with an initial sample document, usually a representative chosen by the clustering routine, which is transformed into a labelled DAG. When new documents are added to a cluster, its schema is modified according to the label transition rules of Table 1. In order to update the DAG, these rules take into account the labels in the existing schema plus the multiplicity of the composition relationships $(0, 1$ or $N)$ of the new document.

Table 1. Label transition rules.

Initial label	Multiplicity	Resulting label
1	0	?
1	1	1
1	N	+
?	$0, 1$	?
?	N	*
+	0	*
+	$1, N$	+
*	$0, 1, N$	*

Additionally, the inference routine tries to infer the basic type of the elements of the class (e.g. numeric, date or string) by applying lexical patterns to their values.

All these changes are time-stamped and kept into a log. This will allow the Schema Manager to reconstruct a schema at any given time point. Note that no arcs or nodes are ever deleted in this phase, because nodes can only be added, and arcs only relaxed. Thus, the schema is just made more general.

A schema is considered completely evolved when the clustering routine detects a change in its structure (i.e. its representative set has changed). In this case the schema can no longer be considered valid, and it needs to be moved to a new *stable* state. For this purpose, the following procedure is applied:

- The schema is marked as obsolete and its associated change logs is closed.
- A new schema is created for the class according to the changes notified by the clustering routine.
- The new schema is initialized with a set of documents that the clustering routine has identified as belonging to its class. In order to create a schema that is as relevant as possible, these documents are chosen using a criterion

of temporal closeness, within a temporal window with a length that depends on the rate of change of the schema (that is, the frequency of changes as detected by the clustering routine).
– The resulting schema is stored and marked as current.

Summarizing, no all of the past states of a schema are actually stored in the database, only the *stable* states created after each change in the clustering are. It is possible to reconstruct any intermediate state by following the changes logs, applying the necessary steps in order to obtain the schema that was current at the given time.

5   Evaluation

In order to evaluate our automatic validation system for XML document schemata, various experiments were designed. In this section we explain one of these tests and how its results prove the effectiveness of the system. In this particular test we start from four different document types whose DTDs are presented in Table 2. As can be noted, DTDs 1 and 2 are very similar, so they could be integrated under the same schema. By analyzing DTD 3 we can see that it is incompatible with the previous two, so they should not be fused together. Finally, DTD 4 is completely different from the other three. The objective of the experiment is to start from a repository of documents with instances of these four DTDs to check whether our system is able to group them correctly, and to infer the proper schemata that defines their structure. Although our system is also able to infer XML Schemata, in order to simplify the example, here we prefer to express the structure of documents by using DTDs.

Table 2. DTDs of the input documents.

DTD 1	DTD 2
`<!ELEMENT term (code, lecturers)>`	`<!ELEMENT term (lecturers)>`
`<!ELEMENT code (#PCDATA)>`	`<!ELEMENT lecturers (lecturer+)>`
`<!ELEMENT lecturers (lecturer+)>`	`<!ELEMENT lecturer (name, subjects)>`
`<!ELEMENT lecturer (name, subjects)>`	`<!ELEMENT name (#PCDATA)>`
`<!ELEMENT name (#PCDATA)>`	`<!ELEMENT subjects (subject*)>`
`<!ELEMENT subjects (subject+)>`	`<!ELEMENT subject (#PCDATA)>`
`<!ELEMENT subject (#PCDATA)>`	
DTD 3	**DTD 4**
`<!ELEMENT term (code, subjects)>`	`<!ELEMENT book (code, authors, title, place,`
`<!ELEMENT code (#PCDATA)>`	`publisher)>`
`<!ELEMENT subjects (subject+)>`	`<!ELEMENT authors (name, address?)+>`
`<!ELEMENT subject (lecturers, code)>`	`<!ELEMENT code (#PCDATA)>`
`<!ELEMENT lecturers (lecturer+)>`	`<!ELEMENT title (#PCDATA)>`
`<!ELEMENT lecturer (name)>`	`<!ELEMENT place (#PCDATA)>`
`<!ELEMENT name (#PCDATA)>`	`<!ELEMENT publisher (#PCDATA)>`
	`<!ELEMENT name (#PCDATA)>`
	`<!ELEMENT address (#PCDATA)>`

To populate our repository with instances of the previous DTDs, we applied the IBM XML Generator[2]. With this tool we generated 20 document instances

---

[2] http://www.alphaworks.ibm.com/

of each DTD, so that in this experiment the input of the system consists of 80 documents. Table 3 presents the average similarity between the types of documents as returned by the system. Obviously, the table shows that the similarity rates between documents of the same DTD are very high. For documents of the DTDs 1 and 2 the returned similarity rates are also high as they share very similar structures. However, the returned similarity rates for any of the previous documents and the instances of the DTDs 3 (incompatible) and 4 (completely different) are null or nearly null.

Finally, the clustering and the schema inference modules were tested with two different similarity thresholds: $\beta_{sim} = \beta_{rep} = 0.7$ and $\beta_{sim} = \beta_{rep} = 0.95$. With the threshold of 0.7, the documents of DTDs 1 and 2 were grouped together, and a new DTD which integrated their schemata was inferred. However, the documents of DTDs 3 and 4 were not combined with the rest, and their inferred schemata were equivalent to those initially used for generating the document instances. In the case of the most restrictive similarity threshold (0.95), the documents of DTDs 1 and 2 were not grouped together and their schemata were separately inferred.

Table 3. Average similarity between the different types of documents.

	DTD 1	DTD 2	DTD 3	DTD 4
DTD 1	1	0.85	0	0.17
DTD 2	0.85	0.98	0	0.08
DTD 3	0	0	1	0.2
DTD 4	0.17	0.08	0.2	0.98

6 Conclusions

In this work we have presented some mechanisms for the automatic generation and upkeep of schemata for XML-oriented document repositories. Our approach assumes that there are no type or schema definitions available for the incoming XML documents, as occurs in many web-based applications. This paper describes two unsupervised algorithms for both, the *Clustering Routine* that detects significant changes in the structure of the repository, and for the *Schema Manager* that keeps the schemata up-to-date as new documents arrives to the system.

As future work, we need to assess the efficiency of the proposed solution; we also need to understand better how the arrival order of the documents affects the performance of the clustering routine. In addition to this, there are some useful applications that can be built on top of the foundations presented in this paper, such as the analysis of the changes in the schemata as they evolve over time. We are also considering the possibility of enhancing the system by means of semantic relationships defined in ontologies.

Acknowledgements. This work has been done with the support of Helide TI, S.A., Kodaima Europa, and the Spanish project CICYT TIC2002-04586-C04-03. We thank Alfonso Rios and Rolf Veen for their helpful comments and support.

References

1. M. J. Aramburu and R. Berlanga. A temporal object-oriented model for digital libraries of documents. *Concurrency: Practice and Experience*, 13(11), 2001.
2. D. Chamberlin, J. Robie, and D. Florescu. Quilt: An XML query language for heterogeneous data sources. In *WebDB 2000*, pages 53–62, 2000.
3. S. Cluet, P. Veltri, and D. Vodislav. Views in a large scale XML repository. In *VLDB 2001*, pages 271–280, 2001.
4. Hélide. The G Web Applications Platform. In http://www.helide.com, 2002.
5. E. Mena, A. Illarramendi, V. Kashyap, and A. P. Sheth. OBSERVER: An approach for query processing in global information systems based on interoperation across pre-existing ontologies. *Distributed and Parallel Databases*, 8(2):223–271, 2000.
6. W3C Consortium. XML schema. In http://www.w3.org/XML/Schema, 2002.
7. W3C Consortium. XQuery 1.0: An XML Query Language. In http://www.w3.org/xquery, 2002.
8. K. Zhang and D. Shasha. Simple fast algorithms for the editing distance between trees and related problems. *SIAM Journal of Computing*, 18(6):1245–1262, 1989.

Bulk Loading the MKL-Tree

Annalisa Franco, Alessandra Lumini, and Dario Maio

DEIS Università di Bologna,
viale Risorgimento 2,
40136 Bologna – Italy
{afranco,alumini,dmaio}@deis.unibo.it

Abstract. MKL-tree is a hierarchical, height-balanced structure for high dimensional data indexing. This structure is based on data representation in a lower dimensional space by means of the MKL transform, a multi-space generalization of the KL transform. A local dimensionality reduction is performed at each node of the tree, allowing more selective features to be extracted and thus increasing the discriminating power of the index. The dynamical version of MKL-tree presents two main drawbacks: first, the incremental loading of data points can determine very different structures and, as a consequence, different query performance, depending on the insertion order; second, the creation of the index can be very expensive, due to the high number of updating required. Since, in real applications, a large dataset is usually available at the tree creation time, we propose a new bulk loading technique for MKL-tree, based on a recursive clustering of data objects. The new algorithm searches for an optimal partitioning of data points, in order to calculate the most suitable KL-subspaces to represent the dataset.

Experimental results show that bulk loading can significantly improve the index performance with respect to the incremental insertion procedure, both in terms of effectiveness of similarity searches and of efficiency of the loading procedure.

1 Introduction

Similarity search in multidimensional databases is a problem widely discussed in the literature [5][15] and a variety of indexing data structures [10][11][16] for vector spaces has been proposed, where objects are usually represented as feature vectors belonging to high-dimensional spaces and are searched by similarity according to a given example.

Frequently, as the dimensionality grows, the number of possible structural relations exhibits a more-than-exponential increase, data points are rather scattered and are usually clustered in proper subspaces of the whole high-dimensional space (multicollinearity); as a consequence, for high-dimensional spaces (more than 20-30 dimensions), traditional data structures are outperformed by a simple sequential scan [16]. This problem, known as "dimensionality curse", is usually dealt with by reducing the dimensionality of the data to be indexed, by means of some dimensionality reduction techniques, such as the Karhunen-Loève transform (KL transform) [9][12], or the Discriminant Analysis [9][17]. These transformations

V. Mařík et al. (Eds.): DEXA 2003, LNCS 2736, pp. 119–128, 2003.

determine a subspace with a dimension much lower than the original space, by selecting only the components that are best suited to represent and discriminate the data points. This approach, usually referred to as Global Dimensionality Reduction (GDR), projects data in a single global space and uses a traditional structure to index them. Recently, a new indexing structure named MKL-tree has been presented [4]. MKL-tree performs a local dimensionality reduction by means of the MKL transform (Multi-space MKL) [3], a generalization of the KL transform where more subspaces are created to arrange the different patterns. Each subspace represents a subset of patterns that have similar characteristics, thus allowing more selective features to be extracted.

In this work, we present a new bulk loading technique for MKL-tree, based on a "partitional" clustering of the data objects. The clustering procedure starts with a single large cluster and ends when all the objects have been recursively partitioned in smaller sets so that all the maximum and minimum capacity constraints of the subsets at each level have been respected. Then each subset is associates to a leaf of the tree, and each "cluster" of leaves to an internal node. The aim of this new technique is to improve the query performance and to make the structure independent on the insertion order. Actually, the incremental algorithm proposed in [4], where points were added to the structure one by one, by updating internal nodes and leaves at each new insertion, could determine very different structures, depending on the insertion order and, as a consequence, different query performance. On the contrary, the new algorithm proposed in this work exploits the information given by the knowledge of a considerable dataset to generate an optimized structure, produced by an optimal clustering of the objects. The clustering algorithm produces more representative KL-subspaces within each node, improving the query performance. Moreover, although the incremental procedure has been speeded up by a KL-subspace updating procedure described in [8], the new bulk loading technique allows a large reduction of the execution time required to construct the structure, as each node is created once and no more updated.

The work is organized in 6 sections. Section 2 briefly summarizes the state of the art: the most common bulk loading techniques for indexing structures are reviewed. Section 3 describes the MKL-tree structure and section 4 presents the new algorithm for bulk loading thetree. Section 5 discusses experimental results and finally, in section 6, we draw our conclusions and include some proposals for future work.

2   Related Work

In the literature, a lot of structures are known that support random insertion, deletions and updates, but, recently, there has been an increasing interest in bulk operations, that is a series of operations executed atomically, without interruption. Among them, particularly interesting is the index creation from a given set of records, operation known as bulk loading. A great variety of bulk loading techniques has been proposed for R-trees, such as Hilbert R-tree [13] that sorts the dataset according to one-dimensional criteria, by means of space filling curves. A generic algorithm to bulk loading multidimensional index structures has been recently proposed in [18], but its performance still depends on the order in which data are inserted.

Finally, a lot of algorithms has been proposed [1][2] for clustering data points to be inserted in the structure. BIRCH [19], for example, clusters the data with a single scan of the space, since the assignment is based on some local characteristics, without considering the other clusters.

A main purpose for the problem we deal with is to discover data clusters that follow a gaussian distribution in a multi-dimensional space. Expectation-Maximization (EM) [7] is an algorithm particularly suited for this purpose; it operates iteratively, trying to find out a gaussian mixture that generated the dataset, on the basis of a maximum likelihood criterion. We tried to adopt this algorithm for our problem but, unfortunately, this method presents some problems in dealing with high-dimensional data points. For that reason we propose a new algorithm more suited for this kind of data.

3 MKL-Tree Structure

MKL-tree is a disk-based, height-balanced hierarchical structure for n-dimensional data points, where data are contained in the leaves, while internal nodes are used to route the search. Nodes are stored into disk blocks and represent the set of objects that are indexed by the corresponding subtree.

A KL subspace of the original space is associated to each node, root excepted. Each element of a leaf node is the projection into the corresponding KL subspace of an indexed object and the pointer to the disk block in which the object is stored. Each element of an internal node corresponds to the KL subspace associated to a child node. The KL subspace associated to each (internal or leaf) node is the subspace that better represents the points in the corresponding subtree (that is, the subspace that guarantees the minimum reconstruction error[1] for the points stored in the leaves of the subtree). The space associated to a node is characterized by a dimension k, markedly lower than the dimension n of the indexed data ($k \ll n$). The k value may vary among different nodes, although in our implementation it has been fixed to a constant value for the whole tree.

Internal nodes and leaves are characterized by a minimum and maximum capacity (fanout): respectively m_I e M_I for the internal nodes and m_L e M_L for the leaves; except the root which has at least two children. The minimum and maximum capacity of the leaves are related to the reduced dimension k of the corresponding KL subspace and the capacity of disk blocks in terms of data to be stored, respectively; in fact, in order to calculate the KL transform, at least $k+1$ elements must be present in a leaf, thus $m_L > k$. Moreover, the constraint $M_L \geq 2 \cdot m_L \geq 2 \cdot k$ is necessary to allow splitting of nodes. As far as internal nodes are concerned, the only constraint is $M_I \geq 2 \cdot m_I$.

Please refer to [4] for MKL-tree update, split and search algorithms.

---

[1] The reconstruction error is the approximation resulting from the projection/back-projection operations of a point **x** and it coincides with the distance of **x** from the KL subspace.

4 Bulk Loading MKL-Tree

Considering that, in real applications, a large dataset is usually available at the moment of the initial loading of the structure, in alternative to the original insertion technique proposed in [4] and referred to as *bottom-up* in the following, we propose a new loading procedure that adopts a *top-down* approach. The main benefit of this method is that points are analyzed as a whole. A global vision of the entire dataset allows to an optimal data partitioning to be obtained and the most suitable KL-subspaces to represent the dataset to be calculated. Please note that, whereas in the bottom-up approach the balancing of the structure is granted by the insertion and split procedures, in the top-down method the imposition of some constraints is required to maintain the tree height balanced and to fulfill minimum and maximum fanout of internal nodes and leaves.

The top-down procedure recursively applies a clustering algorithm to the dataset. At first, the entire dataset is partitioned, and then each subset is recursively partitioned until the capacity requirements of leaves are not fulfilled. The aim of this algorithm is to obtain a balanced tree by imposing some constraints on the maximum and minimum capacity of the clusters obtained.

Given an initial dataset P with m points and a maximum and minimum capacity for nodes (M_I and m_I for internal nodes and M_L and m_L for the leaves), the minimum height of the tree is obtained when all the nodes (internal or leaves, root included) are totally full.

$$(M_I)^h \geq \frac{m}{M_L} \quad \text{from which} \quad h_{min} = \left\lceil \log_{M_I} \frac{m}{M_L} \right\rceil$$

The maximum height is obtained when all the nodes (internal or leaves, root included) contain the minimum number of elements; as the minimum capacity for the root is 2, it results:

$$2 \cdot m_I^{h-1} \geq \frac{m}{m_L} \quad \text{from which} \quad h_{max} = \left\lceil \log_{m_I} \frac{m}{m_L} \right\rceil + 1$$

The height is fixed to a value h, $h_{min} \leq h \leq h_{max}$, and, as a consequence, all the other constraints for the clustering algorithm can be calculated at each step. The first constraint derives from the observation that, obviously, the number of points to be inserted in the structure must be comprised between the minimum (C_{min}) and maximum capacity (C_{max}) of the structure (evaluated with respect to h):

$$C_{min}(h) = m_I^{h-1} \cdot 2 \cdot m_L \qquad C_{max}(h) = (M_I)^h \cdot M_L$$

The minimum and maximum capacity of a subtree with height $l \in [0, h-1]$ are, respectively:

$$C_{min}(l) = (m_I)^l \cdot m_L \qquad C_{max}(l) = M_I^l \cdot M_L$$

At each level l, the minimum and maximum number of partitions to be obtained from clustering, depend on the actual number of points m' to be partitioned at such a level and on the maximum and minimum capacity of the nodes and of the subtrees, according to the following formulas:

$$NP_{min}(l) = \max\left(m_l, \frac{m'}{C_{max}(l)}\right) \quad NP_{max}(l) = \min\left(M_l, \frac{m'}{C_{min}(l)}\right)$$

At the first level above the leaves, the capacity constraint of leaves m_L e M_L have to be substituted to m_l and M_l in the formulas above. The creation procedure operates iteratively on the partition   obtained at the previous step, starting from the initial dataset P at the root level, and evaluating at each step the constraints depending on the current level and the number of points to be clustered.

As far as the clustering is concerned, in this work we analyzed three different algorithms: the K-Means algorithm [14] and the clustering algorithm for MKL [3] already known in the literature, and a third algorithm, appositely developed for this problem. The aim of this new algorithm is to join the advantages of both the previous solutions, that is to obtain compact clusters very representative of the points they contain.

The objective function to be minimized in this new algorithm is the weighted sum of two factors: the first is related to the distance of the points from the center of the cluster, the second is related to the reconstruction error of the points with respect to the KL-subspace associated to the cluster.

Formally the objective function to be minimized for the partitioning $= \{P_1,..,P_s\}$ of a set of points P, is:

$$J = \min. \; \alpha \sum_{i=1}^{s} \sum_{x \in P_i} \|x - \overline{x}_i\|^2 + \beta \sum_{i=1}^{s} \sum_{x \in P_i} d_{FS}(x, S_i).$$

where $\overline{x}_i$ and S_i are respectively the mean and the KL-subspace associated to the cluster P_i and α and β are two weight factors used to make the two terms "comparable". α and β have been estimated by adding all the distances, respectively from the center and from the space (d_{FS}), of the points in all the clusters.

In order to minimize the function J we propose an iterative procedure (algorithm KLC, described in figure 1) that, after an initialization step, assigns the points according to this criterion:

$$c = \min_{i=1..s}\left[\alpha \cdot \|x - \overline{x}_i\|^2 + \beta \cdot d_{FS}(x, S_i)\right]$$

The resulting partition is then submitted to a balancing procedure (function BALANCE), by reassigning part of the points in order to meet the capacity constraints (C_{max} and C_{min}) of each cluster.

The procedure ends when the maximum number of iterations is reached or the assignment of the previous step remains unchanged. As for K-Means, the number of partitions NP must be a priori set, consequently the optimization is carried out for each s in the interval [NP_{min}, NP_{max}] or until a solution   having a percentage mean-square reconstruction error $\xi(s, ,K)$ [3] lower then a fixed value ξ_{max} is found.

```
KLC (element set P, int NP_min , int NP_max , int C_min , int C_max , partition    , float
ξ_max, int k_max)
begin
    s = NP_min - 1; K = {k_1 = k_max, k_2 = k_max,...k_s = k_max};
    repeat
        s = s + 1;
            _1, _2,...  _w = INIT(s, P, K);              // Initialization
        for i = 0..w
            *_i = OPTIMIZE(s,   _i, K, C_min , C_max ); // Optimization
        end for
        z = arg  min (ξ(s, ℘*_i , K)); // Choice of the best partition
               i=1..w
    until (ξ(s,℘*_z,K)≤ξ_max  ∨  s = NP_max)
    return ( s,   *_z K);
end
OPTIMIZE (int s, partition    = { P_1, P_2,...P_s }, int K = {k_1, k_2, f  , k_s}, int C_min , int C_max )
begin
    iter = 0;
    repeat // Compute the set of subspaces S = {S_1, S_2,...S_s} starting from the
           // subsets P_1,...P_s of dimensionalities k_1..k_s
        _old =   ;
        P_1 = P_2 =... Ps = ∅;
        for each x∈ P      // Assignment
            c = min [α·‖x − x̄_i‖² + β·d_FS (x, S_i)] ;
                i=1..s
            P_c = P_c ∪{x};
        end for
            = BALANCE(   , C_min , C_max ) ;          // Balancing
        iter = iter + 1;
    until (   =   _old ∨ iter = iter_max);
    return (   );
end
```

Fig. 1. Pseudo-code for the clustering algorithm that minimizes the objective function J (KLC).

5 Experimental Results

In this section we present some experiments aimed to evaluate the three clustering algorithms presented in section 5 and to verify the efficiency of the structure created with the top-down procedure, in relation to the simple Linear Scan, to the MKL-tree created from scratch (bottom-up) and to other well known access methods: VA-File [6] and Global Dimensionality Reduction (GDR) where the dataset is previously projected into a lower dimensional space, by means of a global KL transform, and then indexed by an R-tree.

A real dataset (COLHIST) has been used as benchmark; it consists of about 70000 vectors of dimension $n=64$, taken from the database of color histograms from Corel images [15].

In the evaluation of the clustering algorithms, we considered two indicators: the *average distance from KL subspace* and the *average distance from the center* of the cluster. The experimental results (as reported in figure 3) show that the new algorithm is particularly suited for this problem, as it obtains the minimum reconstruction error after dimensionality reduction and a good value for the distance from the center of the cluster, i.e. compact clusters. Figure 2 reports a two-dimensional example of clustering: the good performance of algorithm KLC is visually confirmed as the subsets created give a good approximation of the original data distribution.

Fig. 2. Example of two-dimensional clustering obtained by MKL, K-Means and KLC.

The indicators used to measure the performance of the structures are:
- **Percentage of visited nodes:** used to compare the efficiency of MKL-tree top-down versus MKL-tree bottom-up;
- **I/O cost expressed in terms of random accesses**
  For each of the indexing techniques, we evaluated the number of random accesses as described below:
  Linear scan: in this technique each query requires the scan of the entire dataset.
  The number of disk blocks accessed is $\dfrac{m \times (n \times sizeof(float) + sizeof(id))}{PageSize}$. The term $sizeof(id)$ is a negligible factor and will be ignored. Considering that sequential I/O is about 10 time faster than random I/O, the cost in terms of random accesses is $\dfrac{m \times n \times sizeof(float)}{10 \times PageSize}$.
  GDR: in this case the I/O cost has two components: index access cost and post-processing cost for all the retained objects, for false positives elimination. The assumption that for each false positive an I/O operation is required is overly pessimistic, so that for this second component the I/O cost can be evaluated as $\dfrac{\# FalsePositives}{2}$.
  The total I/O cost is $\# AccessedIndexPages + \dfrac{\# FalsePositives}{2}$.
  VA-File: in this structure [6], a bit vector approximates each data point, based on

the quantization of the original feature vector. Each query requires the access to the whole file in order to individuate candidate vectors that are successively analyzed so that false positives can be discarded. The I/O cost has two components: file access cost and false positives elimination. The first can be evaluated as $\dfrac{\#VaFileBlocks}{10}$ and the second as $\dfrac{\#FalsePositives}{2}$. The total I/O cost is $\dfrac{\#VaFileBlocks}{10} + \dfrac{\#FalsePositives}{2}$.

MKL-tree: analogously to the GDR technique, the I/O cost is the sum of index access cost and post processing cost for false positive elimination: $\#AccessedIndexPages + \dfrac{\#FalsePositives}{2}$.

- **Precision:** it is defined as $\rho = |R_O|/|R_R|$, where R_o is the number of n-dimensional objects which satisfy the search condition and R_R is the number of objects returned by the search procedure on the reduced dimensional space. Please note that a distance evaluated in the reduced space is a lower bound to the real distance in the original space, thus $R_o \le R_R$ and $\rho \in [0, 1]$.

For each database, 100 range queries have been carried out. As described in [4], the search procedure of MKL-tree is approximated due to a probabilistic pruning criterion adopted in the range search algorithm. In the following experiments, the approximation error, that is the percentage of missed points with respect to the exact result, is also considered.

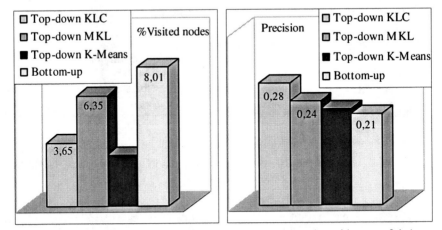

Fig. 3. Percentage of visited nodes and precision in range queries with range 0.1 (average selectivity factor of 0.02%) over 10000 vectors from the COLHIST dataset. For MKL-tree the approximation error is 7% for KLC and bottom-up, 8.1% for MKL and 9.4% for K-Means.

Figure 3 reports the results of range queries on the database COLHIST both in terms of percentage of visited nodes and precision. We compare different structures: three MKL-tree obtained by applying the three clustering algorithms (KLC, MKL and K-Means) and a bottom-up MKL-tree. The dimensionality of the reduced spaces (parameter k) is fixed to 8. The results show that the algorithm KLC allows the best trade-off between visited nodes and precision to be obtained. In the following all results for MKL-tree top-down refer to a structure created by applying the KLC algorithm.

Figure 4 compares different access methods (MKL-tree top-down, VA-File, GDR and Linear Scan) in the execution of range queries in terms of number of random accesses and precision of the result as a function of the dimension k of the reduced space. The graphs show that MKL-tree markedly outperforms all the other approaches. The loss of information is very low (about 2-3%, depending on the parameter k). For $k=14$ the loss is less than 1% and the result of the query is nearly exact.

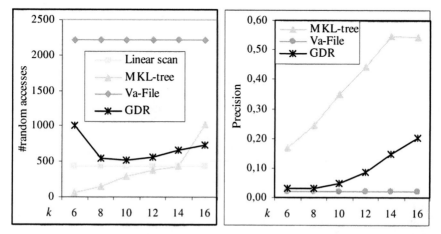

Fig. 4. Comparison of MKL-tree top-down, VA-File, GDR and Linear Scan in terms of I/O costs (expressed as number of random accesses) and precision of the result in the execution of range queries on the whole COLHIST dataset. The precision of Linear Scan is not reported because it is obviously 1. The average query selectivity is 0.02%.

6 Conclusions

In this work a novel technique for the construction of MKL-tree based on a top-down approach has been proposed, as an alternative to the bottom-up procedure [4]. This new method can be used when, at the moment of the creation of the structure, a large dataset is available. The main benefits of this approach, based on a recursive partitioning the data objects, are a resulting structure independent from the insertion order and a drastic reduction of the execution time for the construction of the tree. A new clustering algorithm has been presented, aimed to obtain compact clusters very representative of the points they contain; the comparison of the new algorithm with others well known in the literature shows that it is particularly suitable for our problem. Experimental results confirm the efficacy of the new technique when compared with MKL-tree bottom-up, with a traditional structure such as R-tree coupled with a global dimensionality reduction and with VA-Files. The poor performance of R-tree in terms of precision is not strictly related to the structure, but to the global dimensionality reduction required in order to index with a R-tree. Local dimensionality reduction is the main advantage in the use of MKL-tree because each point is inserted in the most suitable space.

Although MKL-tree is completely defined, many aspects can be optimized. The opportunity to manage outliers (i.e. points different from the majority of the objects in the dataset) should be analyzed. These elements could be recognized in the clustering phase and not inserted in the tree in order to obtain a more stable structure. As to node representation, a number of issues still remain open, such as the development of a technique to determine the optimal value for the subspaces dimensionality (parameter k) or to define a structure for which the dimensionality k is variable in different nodes.

References

[1] Aggarwal C.C., Procopiuc C., Wolf J. L., Yu P.S., Park J.S., "Fast Algorithms for Projected Clustering", Proc. of ACM SIGMOD '99.
[2] Agrawal R., Gehrke J., Gunopulos D., Raghavan P., "Automatic Subspace Clustering of High Dimensional Data for Data Mining Applications", Proc. of ACM SIGMOD '99.
[3] Cappelli R., Maio D., Maltoni D., "Multi-space KL for Pattern Recognition and Classification", IEEE Transactions on PAMI, vol.23, no.9, pp.977–996, September 2001.
[4] Cappelli R., Lumini A., Maio D., "MKL-tree: a hierarchical data structure for indexing multidimensional data", Proc. of *DEXA2002*, Aix en Provence (France), pp.914–924, September 2002.
[5] Cappelli R., Maio D., Maltoni D., "Similarity Search using Multi-space KL", Proc. of IWOSS'99, Florence (Italy), pp.155–160, 1999.
[6] Ferhatosmanoglu H., Tuncel E., Agrawal D., and El Abbadi A. "Vector approximation based indexing for non-uniform high dimensional data sets". In Proc. of the 9th ACM Int. Conf. on Information and Knowledge Management, pp. 202–209, McLean, Virginia, Nov. 2000.
[7] Figueiredo M., Jain A.K., "Unsupervised learning of finite mixture models", IEEE Transaction on PAMI, vol. 24, no. 3, pp. 381–396, March 2002.
[8] Franco A., Lumini A., Maio D., "Eigenspace merging for model updating", in Proc. of ICPR2002, Québec City (Canada), vol.2, pp.156–159, August 2002.
[9] Fukunaga K., Statistical Pattern Recognition, Academic Press, San Diego, 1990.
[10] Gaede V., Günther O., "Multidimensional Access Methods", ACM Computing Surveys, 30(2), 1998.
[11] Guttman A., "R-trees: A Dynamic Index Structure for Spatial Searching". Proc. ACM SIGMOD Int. Conf. On Management of Data, pp. 47–57, Boston, USA, 1984.
[12] Jolliffe I.T., "Principal Component Analysis", SpringerVerlag, New York, 1986.
[13] Kamel I., Faloutsos C., "Hilbert R-tree: An Improved R-tree using Fractals", Proc. of VLDB'94, pp.500–509.
[14] MacQueen J. "Some methods for classification and analysis of multivariate observations" Proc. of the Fifth Berkeley Symposium on Mathematical statistics and probability, v.1, pp 281–297, Berkeley. University of California Press, 1967.
[15] Ortega M., Rui Y., Chakrabarti K., Mehrotra S., Huang T.S., "Supporting similarity queries in MARS", ACM Conf. on Multimedia, Seattle, USA, November, 1997.
[16] Samet H., "The Design and Analysis of Spatial Data Structures", Addison Wesley, 1990.
[17] Swets D.L., Weng J., "Hierarchical Discriminant Analysis for Image Retrieval", IEEE Transactions on PAMI, 21(5), pp. 386–401, 1999.
[18] Van den Bercken J., Seeger B., Widmayer P., "A generic approach to bulk loading multidimensional index structures", Proc. of VLDB'97, Atene (Grecia) pp.406–415.
[19] Zhang T., Ramakrishnan R., Livny M., "BIRCH: A New Data Clustering Algorithm and its Applications", Data Mining and Knowledge Discovery 1(2), 1997.

Bulk Insertion for R-Tree by Seeded Clustering*

Taewon Lee[1], Bongki Moon[2], and Sukho Lee[1]

[1] School of Electrical Engineering and Computer Science
Seoul National University,
Seoul, Korea
{warrior@db,shlee@cse}.snu.ac.kr
[2] Department of Computer Science,
University of Arizona,
Tucson, AZ 85721
bkmoon@cs.arizona.edu

Abstract. In many scientific and commercial applications such as Earth Observation System (EOSDIS) and mobile phone services tracking a large number of clients, it is a daunting task to archive and index ever increasing volume of complex data that are continuously added to databases. To efficiently manage multidimensional data in scientific and data warehousing environments, R-tree based index structures have been widely used. In this paper, we propose a scalable technique called *Seeded Clustering* that allows us to maintain R-tree indexes by bulk insertion while keeping pace with high data arrival rates. Our approach uses a *seed tree*, which is copied from the top k levels of a target R-tree, to classify input data objects into clusters. We then build an R-tree for each of the clusters and insert the input R-trees into the target R-tree in bulk one at a time. We present detailed algorithms for the seeded clustering and bulk insertion as well as the results from our extensive experimental study. The experimental results show that the *bulk insertion by seeded clustering* outperforms the previously known methods in terms of insertion cost and the quality of target R-trees measured by their query performance.

1 Introduction

In many data-intensive applications, there has been an upsurge of interest in dealing with the problem of *bulk insertions* of new data into an existing database. It is important to add newly collected data into an existing database quickly, because data are continuously generated and added to databases. Construction of a new index structure each time from scratch for both the existing data as well as the new data is not likely to scale well.

In this paper, we present a bulk insertion technique using *Seeded Clustering* for an R-tree based index structure and show that it outperforms the previous

* This work was sponsored in part by the BK 21 Project from the Government of Korea. It was also sponsored in part by National Science Foundation CAREER Award (IIS-9876037), Grant No. IIS-0100436, and Research Infrastructure program EIA-0080123. The authors assume all responsibility for the contents of the paper.

V. Mařík et al. (Eds.): DEXA 2003, LNCS 2736, pp. 129–138, 2003.

bulk insertion methods in terms of insertion cost and query processing cost. Most of the previous work followed a common approach. They first group input data items into clusters and then insert each cluster one at a time in bulk [3, 4,6]. Under the approach, input data items that are spatially close are grouped into clusters. Although each cluster of data will cover a small extent of area, it is unlikely to guarantee the least of the dead space of existing R-tree nodes. This is because input data items clustered by themselves without considering the structure of a target R-tree. The query performance of the resulting target R-tree can be degraded.

Our *Seeded Clustering* utilizes the structure of a target R-tree in clustering input data items. We use the top k levels of a target R-tree as a guide to classify the input data items into clusters in a linear time. Then we build an input R-tree from each of the clusters and insert them into the target R-tree one at a time in bulk. However, the insertion of an input R-tree into the target R-tree is not such a simple process. The target R-tree should remain as a legitimate R-tree even after the insertion is done. This property is not guaranteed by some of the previous work.

There are two important aspects of bulk insertions. First, the bulk insertion itself should be fast enough to catch up with the rate of the data generation. Second, the query performance should not be compromised by bulk insertion. Since our approach attempts to reduce the overlap during the bulk insertion, the quality of the target tree is preserved or even better restructured so that the query performance can be improved.

For the performance evaluation, extensive experiments were conducted both with a real data set and various synthetic data sets. We used a TIGER/Line data set which is a popular data set for geographic information systems. One of the synthetic data sets was generated by a TPC/H data generator. We also used three more synthetic data sets, which are uniform distributed, skewed and clustered data set.

The paper is organized as follows. In section 2, we briefly overview the related work on bulk insertion. In section 3, the problem we are going to solve is described and the algorithm is presented roughly. In section 4, the structure of a seed tree is described. Classifying the input data items using a seed tree is also given. In section 5, the detailed algorithm of the bulk insertion is provided. In section 6, we show the result of performance evaluation and section 7 concludes this paper.

2   Previous Work

In an early piece of work on the bulk insertion for an R-tree, the data items to be inserted are first sorted by their spatial proximity (e.g., the Hilbert value of the center) and then packed into blocks of B rectangles [6]. These blocks are then inserted one at a time using standard insertion algorithm. Intuitively, the algorithm should give an insertion speed-up of B (as a block of B data items is inserted at a time), but it is likely to increase overlap and thus produces a worse index in terms of query performance. This can be explained as follows.

Although the block may contain data items that are spatially close, in the target tree's point of view, this block is randomly constructed against its nodes. Therefore a block and the nodes in the target tree are not guaranteed to be non-overlapping which might increase overlap between them. This can be supported by the empirical results [6].

There was another work on the bulk insertion which used a STLT (*small-tree-large-tree*) approach [3]. The STLT constructs an R-tree (*small tree*) from the data set and inserts it into the target R-tree (*large tree*). To insert a *small tree* into a *large tree*, it chooses an appropriate location to maintain the balance of the resulting *large tree*. However, this approach has the following shortcomings. In the STLT approach, a *small tree* is built from the input data items and inserted into the *large tree*. Therefore, if a *small tree* covers large area, the node into which a *small tree* is inserted needs to be enlarged for the *large tree* to enclose it. This means the STLT only works well for highly skewed data set [4]. And there is another restriction that the depth of a *small tree* must be smaller than the *large tree*.

A variant of STLT is the GBI (generalized bulk insertion) technique [4]. In this work, the input data set is partitioned into a number of clusters by grouping spatially close data items into the same cluster. After clustering, from each of these clusters, R-trees are built. Finally, these R-trees are inserted into the target tree one at a time. The data items not included in any cluster are classified as outliers and inserted one by one using normal R-tree insertion. This work alleviated the limitation of the STLT which depends on the data distribution. However, this has also the same problem that the R-trees being inserted may increase the overall overlap of the target R-tree for the same reason mentioned in the first paragraph of this subsection. In addition to this, GBI and STLT have a serious problem that the resulting tree may not be a legitimate R-tree by definition. From the properties of an R-tree, the root node of a *small tree* can have less than m entries(m is the minimum number of entries a node can have). However, after a *small tree* is inserted, the root of the *small tree* becomes an internal node of the *large tree*. The root node of the *small tree* having less than m entries breaks the property of an R-tree. This is not an easy issue to deal with but must be addressed properly. In section 5, we present how this problem is solved by our bulk insertion method.

The other class of algorithm presented a new buffer strategy for performing bulk operations on dynamic R-trees [1]. Their method uses the buffer tree idea, which takes advantage of the available main memory and the page size of the operating system. Although their bulk insertion strategy shows improved results over the normal insertion algorithm in terms of the insertion cost, it is conceptually identical to the repeated insertion algorithm that the query performance of the resulting tree shows no better than using repeated insertion.

3   Overview of Our Approach

We suppose there is a target R-tree indexing a large number of data objects. A number of new data items arrive and these items need to be inserted into the target R-tree. There is no pre-built index for these input data items. This should be done fast and the quality of the resulting target R-tree should be good enough in terms of query performance.

Our proposed work for bulk insertion algorithm is performed in two stages: *seeded clustering* and *bulk insertion*. First, we build a *seed tree* by taking a few top levels of nodes from a target R-tree. A seed tree guides the way the input data items are clustered. Then an R-tree is generated for each individual cluster. We call them *input* R-trees.

Next is the insertion step. During the insertion of an input R-tree, we attempt to reduce the overlapping area between the nodes of a target R-tree and an input R-tree to improve the query performance. Inserting an R-tree into another R-tree is described in Section 5 in detail.

4   Seeded Clustering

In the previous work, input data sets are partitioned into clusters using various clustering methods. Then an R-tree is built for each cluster. These R-trees are then inserted one at a time using a slightly modified standard insertion algorithm. This is the common way to perform bulk insertion [3,4,6].

Let us suppose that the input data items are located as in Fig. 1 (a) and the structure of the target R-tree is given as (b). Most of the known clustering

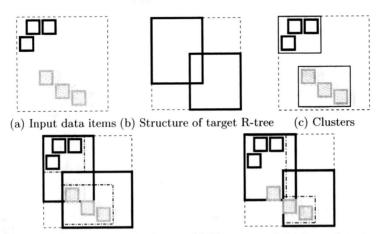

(a) Input data items (b) Structure of target R-tree   (c) Clusters

(d) Placement of the input data items (e) Placement of the input data items
          by standard insertions   by a seed tree

Fig. 1. Motivation of Seeded Clustering

methods may classify the data items as in (c). After building input R-trees from clusters and inserting them into the target R-tree as in (d), it is likely to increase the MBR of the nodes in the target R-tree since input R-trees are built independently from the target R-tree. However, we can utilize the structure of the target tree as shown in (e). If the structural information of the target R-tree can be exploited, we know in advance that the lower three rectangles should not be placed in the same cluster.

A *seed tree* is constructed by copying the top k levels of the target R-tree. We use this seed tree for clustering the input data set. In each level of a seed tree, an entry whose MBR fully encloses an input data item is chosen. If a data item can reach a leaf node of a seed tree, it is classified into the cluster that corresponds to the leaf node. By doing this, a seed tree guides an input data item to a node that would be chosen if an input data item were inserted in a normal way.

During the classification of input data items, there may be more than one entries that fully include an input data item. We can make a naïve selection by choosing the first entry that fully encloses an input data item. This is the fastest way possible. There may be other ways to choose an entry which might lead to the better index structure but we use this naïve method for simplicity.

If it fails to find an entry that encloses a data item in some internal node of a seed tree, a data item is classified as an *outlier* of the node. Outliers are inserted one by one using normal R-tree insertion method. For all the data sets we used in the performance evaluation, the proportion of outliers in the input data items was less than 0.1%.

In the following section, we will describe the insertion step of the algorithm in detail. Input R-trees are generated from the clusters and they are inserted into a target R-tree in the insertion step. Inserting an R-tree into a target R-tree is presented in detail.

5   Bulk Insertion

In this section, we describe the bulk insertion step of the *bulk insertion by seeded clustering*. Before we begin, let us define the leaf level of the R-tree as level 0. Therefore, the height of an R-tree is 1 + the level of the root node.

5.1   Inserting an Input R-Tree to the Target R-Tree

As described in section 4, we get a number of clusters and outliers after clustering. To perform bulk insertion, we first create an input R-tree from each of the clusters and insert them into the target R-tree one at a time in bulk. We use a bulk loading method (e.g., [7,8]) to build an input R-tree from each cluster.

Inserting an R-tree to another R-tree can be done in a similar way to inserting a data item into an R-tree except some post-processing. To insert an input R-tree into the target R-tree, we treat an input R-tree as if it were a data item whose MBR is that of the root of the input R-tree. However, to maintain the

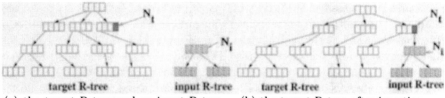

(a) the target R-tree and an input R-tree.   (b) the target R-tree after insertion.
The input R-tree is going to be inserted into
the node N_t

Fig. 2. inserting input R-tree into the target R-tree

property of an R-tree that all the leaf nodes must be in the same level, the root node should not be inserted into the leaf level of the target R-tree.

Suppose that the height of an input R-tree is h_i. For the target R-tree after insertion to be a legitimate R-tree, the root N_i of the input R-tree needs to be inserted into a node of level h_i of the target R-tree. This is depicted in Figure 2. By the definition of a seed tree, we already know where a particular input R-tree will be inserted.

There is another important property for the target R-tree to be a legitimate R-tree after the insertion. Every node except the root must have at least m entries [5]. *Node underflow* is the term used for the node with less than m entries [2]. Suppose the number of entries in the root node N_i of an input R-tree is less than m. By definition, this is a legal R-tree as the root can have less than m entries. However, the target R-tree after inserting this input R-tree becomes illegal because the root of the input R-tree is now an internal node of the target R-tree and the node has less than m entries.

We solve this problem by distributing all the entries of N_i among overlapping entries of the target node N_t. In other words, we reinsert the entries of the node N_i into the node N_t.

For the case where the node N_i has enough entries, we insert the input R-tree into the node N_t of the target R-tree. However, there can be some complicated problem in doing this. Suppose the level of N_t is h_t. For an input R-tree to be fit for the node N_t, it should be of height h_t. It is possible that the data items are skewed and as a result, the size of a cluster can be large such that the input R-tree generated from this cluster becomes of height greater than h_t. In this case, it is unfit for the node N_t. On the contrary, if the data items are so sparse that the cluster has a small number of data items, an input R-tree built from this cluster may be of height lower than h_t. In this case, it cannot be inserted as a direct entry of the node N_t. We deal with these three cases appropriately. However, we omit the discussion here for lack of space.

5.2   Repacking : Locally Reducing the Overlapped Area

Since there can be large overlap between the node N_i and the entries of the node N_t into which N_i is inserted, it is required to reduce overlap between them to make the target R-tree efficient for query processing. The *repacking* we describe

---

Algorithm 1: Post-process : reducing the overlap during the bulk insertion

Function post-process (N_t, N_i)

N_t : node into which N_i is inserted

N_i : the root of an input R-tree

begin

  $NoOvlp \leftarrow$ entries of N_t that do not overlap with N_i

  $Ovlp \leftarrow$ entries of N_t that overlap with N_i

  $RepackedNodes \leftarrow$ REPACK ($Ovlp$, N_i)

  return pack ($NoOvlp \cup RepackedNodes$)

end

Algorithm 2: Repack the node N_{input} and the nodes in the set N_{set}

Function REPACK (N_{set}, N_{input})

N_{set} : a set of nodes whose parent nodes overlap with the node N_{input}

N_{input} : a node from an input R-tree

begin

1   $ent \leftarrow$ entries of each elements of N_{set}

2   $NoOvlp \leftarrow$ subset of ent that do not overlap with any entry of N_{input}

3   $Repacked \leftarrow \emptyset$

4   **if** N_{input} *is a leaf node* **then**

5   **return pack** ($ent \cup$ entries of N_{input})

  else

6   **foreach** $e \in$ *entries of* N_{input} **do**

7       $entOvlp \leftarrow$ find elements of ent that overlap with e

8   **if** $entOvlp \neq \emptyset$ **then**

9         $Repacked \leftarrow Repacked \cup$ REPACK ($entOvlp$, e)

      else

10         $Repacked \leftarrow Repacked \cup e$

      endif

    endfch

  endif

11   **return pack** ($NoOvlp \cup Repacked$)

end

---

in this section is the post-processing step of our algorithm that locally minimizes overlap between nodes.

Basic idea of the repacking is as follows. We take the entries out of the largely overlapped nodes and rebuild MBRs that enclose those entries. Detailed algorithms are given through Algorithm 1 to 3.

For lack of space, we briefly describe the algorithm. The entries of the target node N_t, into which N_i is inserted, can be divided into two groups. The entries

---

Algorithm 3: Pack the entries to create node(s) that contain all of them

---

Function pack (N_{set})
N_{set} : set of nodes to pack
begin
| **return** create nodes that enclose the elements of N_{set} using bulk loading
| method
end

---

that do not overlap with the node N_i, and the entries that overlap with the node N_i. We repack the latter group with N_i. Before repacking them, we first repack their child entries. This can be recursively defined and is given in Algorithm 2.

6   Experiment

In this section, we present the result of an extensive experimental study to show the validity and the effectiveness of our approach. We have implemented a disk based R-tree in C++ on the linux machine. A node corresponds to a 4KB-disk block and can hold approximately 100 entries per node. We compared our experimental results with the repeated insertion method of an R-tree (OBO; *one by one*) and GBI. We presented the insertion cost and the query cost in average number of disk I/O. From now on, we will use SCB to represent our bulk insertion by seeded clustering algorithm.

We used a number of synthetic data sets having different characteristics as well as real data set. For the real data set, the standard benchmark data used in spatial databases, namely rectangles obtained from the TIGER/Line data set was used [9]. We extracted about 2,600,934 line objects from the states of Arizona, New Mexico, Utah and Colorado. For synthetic data sets, we used a data set from TPC-H, an ad-hoc, decision support benchmark [10] and three other data sets that have different distribution characteristics. They are uniform, zipfian(for skewed data set) and clustered data set, respectively. Each data set has 1,000,000 data items.

6.1   Insertion Cost and Query Cost for the Different Data Sets

We evaluated the performance of SCB as compared to OBO and GBI, for all the data sets described formerly. The size of an input data set was 5% of the size of the target R-tree. A seed tree for each data set was generated initially by copying the top 2 levels of the target R-tree which was of height 4. The target R-tree was initially built using the repeated insertion method. We measured the query cost for 5,000 random point queries. The insertion cost for each data set is given in Table 1 and the query cost is given in Table 2.

The result shows that the SCB we proposed in this paper outperforms the OBO and GBI in both insertion and query performance. Although it does not show extremely high gain in insertion cost, we can still see high gain from the

Table 1. Insertion Costs for various data set(# of I/Os)

	SCB	GBI	OBO
TIGER/Line data	36263	80757	151689
TPC-H data	18752	53021	108018
Uniform distributed data	16443	49855	103809
Zipfian distributed data	13247	43724	98096
Clustered data	11607	25351	56945

Table 2. Query Costs for various data set (# of I/Os). Point queries were used

	Initially	SCB	OBO	GBI
TIGER/Line	2.665	2.496	3.034	3.215
TPC-H	2.111	1.547	2.234	2.561
Uniform	5.446	4.313	5.678	5.941
Zipfian	4.442	3.733	4.645	5.018
Clustered	4.234	3.471	4.523	4.833

result. This is mainly because our approach is designed to perform insertion in bulk.

An important result is that our method decreases not only the insertion cost, but also the query cost. We are targetting application areas where it is almost impossible to rebuild an index from scratch. Until now, OBO showed the best query performance. Previous work on bulk insertion showed no improvements in query performance compared to OBO [1,4]. However, SCB showed better query performance than OBO after the insertion. This is because SCB tries to reorganize the target tree to reduce overlap between the nodes.

6.2 Repeated Insertion with Time Interval

In this experiment, we performed an experiment to see if the target tree maintains acceptable query performance after successive insertion of data with time gap. For a target R-tree to handle the continuously added data, the insertion method should maintain the quality of a target R-tree. The result is given in Figure 3.

7 Conclusion

In this paper, we have proposed an effective bulk insertion method in the environment where data are continuously added to databases. We have presented the *Seeded Clustering* technique which utilizes the structure of the target R-tree to quickly and effectively cluster the input data objects. By clustering, input data objects are grouped with their locality and from each of the clusters, input R-trees are built and inserted one at a time in bulk. We also have presented a local overlap minimizing algorithm called *repacking* which reorganizes nodes of the target R-tree and an input R-tree during the insertion to minimize the

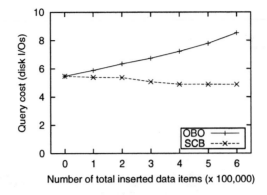

Fig. 3. Repeated insertion with time interval

overlapped area. This makes our algorithm scalable. As the data items are continuously added, our method yields a good quality tree to a certain point that it outperforms previous bulk insertion methods in terms of query performance.

References

1. L. Arge, K. H. Hinrichs, J. Vahrenhold, and J. S. Vitter. Efficient Bulk Operations on Dynamic R-Trees. *Algorithmica*, 33(1):104–128, 2002.
2. Norbert Beckmann, Hans-Peter Kriegel, Ralf Schneider, and Bernhard Seeger. The R*-tree: an efficient and robust access method for points and rectangles. In *Proceedings of the 1990 ACM SIGMOD international conference on Management of data*, pages 322–331, 1990.
3. Li Chen, Rupesh Choubey, and Elke A. Rundensteiner. Bulk-insertions into R-trees using the small-tree-large-tree approach. In *Proceedings of the sixth ACM international symposium on Advances in geographic information systems*, pages 161–162, 1998.
4. Rupesh Choubey, Li Chen, and Elke A. Rundersteiner. GBI: A Generalized R-tree Bulk-Insertion Strategy. In *Advances in Spatial Databases*, pages 91–108, 1997.
5. Antonin Guttman. R-Trees: A dynamic index structure for spatial searching. In *Proceedings of the 1984 ACM-SIGMOD Conference*, pages 47–57, June 1984.
6. I. Kamel, M. Khalil, and V. Kouramajian. Bulk insertion in dynamic R-trees. In *Proceedings of the 4th International Symposium on Spatial Data Handling (SDH'96)*, pages 3B.31–3B.42, 1996.
7. Ibrahim Kamel and Christos Faloutsos. On packing R-trees. In *Proceedings of the second international conference on Information and knowledge management*, pages 490–499, 1993.
8. S. T. Leutenegger, J. M. Edgington, and M. A. Lopez. STR: A Simple and Efficient Algorithm for R-Tree Packing. In *Proceedings of the IEEE Data Engineering*, pages 497–506, 1997.
9. TIGER/Line Files, 2000 Technical Documentation, U.S. Bureau of Census, Washington DC, accessible via URL `http://www.census.gov/geo/www/tiger/tigerua/ua_tgr2k.html`.
10. TPC-H, Transaction Processing Performance Council, accessible via URL `http://www.tpc.org/tpch/`.

Optimizing Both Cache and Disk Performance of R-Trees*

Myungsun Park and Sukho Lee

School of Electrical Engineering and Computer Science
Seoul National University ENG4190
Seoul 151-744, Korea
mspark@db.snu.ac.kr
shlee@cse.snu.ac.kr

Abstract. R-Trees have been traditionally optimized for I/O performance with disk pages as tree nodes. Recently, researchers have proposed cache-conscious variations of R-Trees optimized for CPU cache performance in main memory environments, where the node size is wider than the cache line size and more entries are packed in a node by compressing MBR keys. However, because there is a big difference between the node sizes of two types of R-Trees, disk-optimized R-Trees show poor cache performance while cache-optimized R-Trees exhibit poor disk performance. In this paper, we propose a cache and disk optimized R-Tree, called the TR-Tree (Two-way optimized R-Tree). We evaluate the in-page leaf and non-leaf node sizes and the height of the in-page tree to minimize the cache miss cost for searching a TR-Tree. In addition, we fit nodes into disk pages to maximize the disk I/O performance. Our implementation achieves better cache and disk performance than disk-optimized R-Trees: a factor of 6-28 improvement for insertions and a factor of 1.28-2.00 improvement for range queries.

1 Introduction

As the gap between processor speed and DRAM speed continues to grow exponentially, it becomes an important issue to make effective use of caches to achieve high performance on database management systems [3]. Recently, several studies have improved the cache effectiveness of previous index structures. There are some studies that set the B-Tree node size to be the cache line size, which reduces cache miss latency [8], [9]. Using prefetch ability of modern processors, [4] reduces B-Tree height and speeds up the range scan operation. [5] arranges in-page nodes to disk pages, which achieves both cache and disk I/O performance gains. To pack more entries in an R-Tree node in main memory environments, CR-tree [7] compresses MBR keys and reduces the tree height and the number of cache misses. However, because there is a big difference between the node sizes of two types of R-Trees, disk-optimized R-Trees show poor cache performance while cache-optimized R-Trees exhibit poor disk performance.

---

* This work was supported by the Brain Korea 21 Project.

V. Mařík et al. (Eds.): DEXA 2003, LNCS 2736, pp. 139–147, 2003.

In this paper, we propose a cache and disk optimized variation of the R-Tree, called the TR-Tree (Two-way optimized R-Tree). To improve cache performance, we make nodes wider than a cache line size and call prefetch functions to pre-load data in memory into CPU caches. In addition, we fit memory nodes into disk pages to maximize the disk I/O performance. Moreover, we exhibit a metric for determining the leaf and non-leaf node sizes and the height of the in-page tree to minimize the cache miss cost for searching TR-Trees. We show the possible enumeration of all combinations of disk page sizes and node sizes. We implement TR-Trees and experiment on various node sizes. Our implementation achieves better cache and disk performance than disk-optimized R-Trees: a factor of 6-28 improvement for insertions and a factor of 1.28-2.00 improvement for range queries.

Our contributions are as follows. First, we propose and evaluate the TR-Tree (Two-way optimized R-Tree) that optimizes both cache and disk performance. Second, we represent the detailed analysis for the search operation of TR-Trees. We evaluate the number of in-page non-leaf and leaf nodes as a search operation continues, and calculate the cache miss latency considering the prefetch operation. Third, we implement the TR-Tree and experiment on every possible combination of in-page non-leaf and leaf node size. We show that the TR-Tree achieves better cache and disk performance than the disk-optimized R-Tree.

This paper is organized as follows. In section 2, we present previous work. Section 3 shows the page structure and algorithms of the TR-Tree. In section 4, we present the cache performance metric of our work. Section 5 exhibits the experimental results, and section 6 concludes this paper.

2   Related Work

In order to enhance the performance of main memory indexes, the node size and specific CPU cache instructions are considered in several studies. To minimize the cache miss latency, the node sizes of main memory B-Trees are the same as the CPU cache line size in [8], [9], where the cache line is a data transfer unit between the CPU and the memory. In [4], they propose Prefetching B^+-Trees (pB^+-Trees). Using prefetch instructions, they can create wider nodes than the data transfer size. By these wider nodes, the height of the B-Tree is reduced; thereby decreasing the number of cache misses to search a key. To accelerate the range scan, they implement jump-pointer arrays. In [5], they show fractal prefetching B^+-Trees (fpB^+-Trees) which are the disk I/O optimized variations of pB^+-Trees, To optimize disk performance, fpB^+-Trees fit nodes into disk pages.

The CR-tree [7] is a cache-optimized version of the R-Tree. To pack more entries in a node, the CR-tree compresses MBR keys. It represents the coordinates of an MBR key relatively to the lower left corner of its parent MBR. The compression is the elimination of leading 0's from the relative coordinate representation. Consequently, the CR-tree becomes wider and smaller than the R-tree.

3   The TR-Tree

The TR-Tree is a cache and disk I/O optimized version of the R-Tree. Here, the TR-Tree is the disk-first optimized version. It is because the disk-first version is general in most cases [5]. We do not need to consider range scans in the TR-Tree, so we can use a simple node allocation strategy. We do not use the MBR key compression technique of the CR-tree, because it can be smoothly adapted to our work.

3.1   Structure

Figure 1 shows a disk page whose in-page tree height is two. The outer rectangle in the figure represents a disk page. It has an in-page tree that is a part of the whole TR-Tree. To fit nodes into a disk page for maximizing disk usage, the sizes of leaf and non-leaf nodes may differ from each other. Figure 2 shows the data structure of a disk page. Figure 2 (b) and (c) are non-leaf and leaf node entries, respectively. As non-leaf nodes contain pointers to other in-page nodes within the same disk page, 2 byte offset is enough. While leaf nodes contain pointers to in-page root nodes in other disk pages, they have 4 byte page ID.

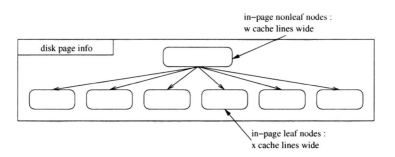

Fig. 1. Page structure

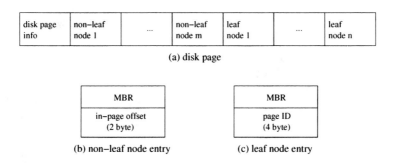

Fig. 2. Data structure of a disk page

3.2   Algorithms

All nodes of a TR-Tree are stored in disk pages at first. When a node is requested, if its disk page is not in memory, the disk page is loaded into a buffer page of the buffer pool. TR-Tree operations such as search, insertion, and deletion are the same as those of R-Trees except that child pointers of non-leaf and leaf nodes differ from each other. When the current node has an in-page offset, it just follows the offset to access its child node. While the current node has a page ID, it loads the disk page with the page ID, and then follows the in-page root node of the newly loaded page.

When a node splits, the newly created node is placed in the disk page that holds the original node if that disk page has room for the new node. If the new node is in the same page as the original node, we can minimize the number of disk accesses for searching. Otherwise, a new disk page is allocated, and the new node is placed in the new disk page. Then the in-page root node is also split explicitly. When an in-page root node splits, a new disk page is allocated, and then the new in-page root node is placed in the new disk page, and finally all descendent nodes of the new in-page root node in the original disk page are moved into the new disk page.

4   Analysis

A search operation in a TR-Tree accesses one or more nodes in each level. Therefore, in order to evaluate cost for searching, we count accessed nodes as follows. Without loss of generality, we assume the data domain of a unit hyper-cube. For simplicity, we assume the data objects are uniformly distributed point data in the domain, and the query MBRs are hyper-cubes. In addition, we assume that the TR-tree nodes of the same height have square-like MBRs roughly of the same size as in other analytical work.

4.1   Number of Accessed Cache Lines

Let h denote the height or level of a TR-Tree node assuming that the height of leaf nodes is one. Let n denote the height of a disk page and H_D the height of the root page which contains the root node of the TR-Tree. For example, when $L = 2$ and $h = 3, 4$ then $n = 2$. Here, $h = nL, nL+1, \ldots, nL+(L-1), n = 1, 2, \ldots, H_D$. Therefore, $n = \lfloor (h-1)/L \rfloor + 1$. Assume L is the number of levels in an in-page tree, w is the number of cache lines of a non-leaf node, x is the number of cache lines of a leaf node, and f is the fan-out of a cache-line-sized node. Then, wf and xf are the fan-outs of non-leaf and leaf nodes, respectively.

Let N denote the total number of data objects. Let M_h denote the number of nodes at the height of h. Then, from the above assumption,

$$M_h = \left\lceil \frac{N}{(xf)^n (wf)^{h-n}} \right\rceil$$

Let a_h denote the average area that a node of height h covers. Then, a_h is $1/M_h$. Using the Minkowski sum technique [6] [2], the probability that a node of height h overlaps a given query rectangle is $\left(\sqrt[d]{s} + \sqrt[d]{a_h}\right)^d$, where s denotes the size of the query rectangle. Then, the number of the height-h nodes that overlap the query rectangle is $M_h \left(\sqrt[d]{s} + \sqrt[d]{a_h}\right)^d$ or

$$\left(1 + \sqrt[d]{\left\lceil \frac{N}{(xf)^n (wf)^{h-n}} \right\rceil \cdot s}\right)^d$$

Assume T_1 is the full latency of a cache miss, T_{next} is the latency of an additional pipelined (prefetched) cache miss. The cache latency cost of searching through a TR-tree composed of L-level in-page trees is

$$cost = N_w \left[T_1 + (w-1)T_{next}\right] + N_x \left[T_1 + (x-1)T_{next}\right] \tag{1}$$

N_w and N_x are the number of in-page non-leaf nodes and in-page leaf nodes accessed by the query, respectively. The height of the disk page is $H_D = \lceil \log_{xf(wf)^{L-1}} N \rceil$. The number of in-page leaf nodes of the height-H_D disk page is

$$M_{L(H_D-1)+1} = \left\lceil \frac{N}{(xf)^{H_D-1}(wf)^{(H_D-1)(L-1)+1}} \right\rceil$$

The root level of the TR-Tree is $H = L(H_D - 1) + 1 + \lceil \log_{wf} M_{L(H_D-1)+1} \rceil$. Then, N_w and N_x are evaluated as follows.

$$N_w = \sum_{h=1,n=1}^{h\neq nL+1, h\leq H, n\leq H_D} \left(1 + \sqrt[d]{\left\lceil \frac{N}{(xf)^n (wf)^{h-n}} \right\rceil \cdot s}\right)^d$$

$$N_x = \sum_{n=1}^{h=nL+1, n\leq H_D} \left(1 + \sqrt[d]{\left\lceil \frac{N}{(xf)^n (wf)^{h-n}} \right\rceil \cdot s}\right)^d$$

4.2   Determining Optimal Sizes of In-page Leaf and Non-leaf Node

Our goals are to optimize search performance and I/O performance. For search performance, we minimize the number of cache miss cost of equation 1. For I/O performance, we maximize the fan-out of the disk page.

To achieve the optimal solution of two goals, we enumerate all the possible combinations of w and x. Hence, we set the following restrictions for the TR-Tree of two dimensional data; $L \geq 2$, $w \geq 64B$, $x \geq 64B$, and L, w, x have the possible upper bound that utilizes the most space in the page, where the disk page sizes are 4KB, 8KB, 16KB, and 32KB. The actual evaluations are shown in figure 3. Table 1 depicts the optimal node widths where we choose the maximum disk page fan-out whose evaluated cache latency cost is within 0.01% of the optimal. In table 1, keys are 4 byte, dimension is 2, $s = 0.0001$, $T_1 = 150$, $T_{next} = 10$.

Table 1. Optimal node width selections

Page size	non-leaf node	Leaf node	cost/optimal	Disk page fan-out
4KB	96	1312	1	123
8KB	96	2688	1.00001	252
16KB	96	5376	1.00005	504
32KB	256	4000	1.00009	1000

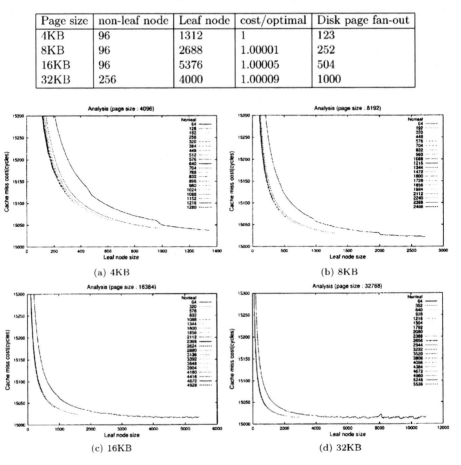

(a) 4KB   (b) 8KB

(c) 16KB   (d) 32KB

Fig. 3. Cache miss cost analysis

In figure 3, from left top to right bottom, there are analysis results of page sizes of 4KB, 8KB, 16KB and 32KB. We drew only 20 lines of possible in-page non-leaf node sizes. X-axis represents the in-page leaf node size and y-axis the cache miss cost in cycles. In every graph, the execution time decreases steeply and then decreases gently. As the disk page size becomes bigger, graphs show better performance. Comparing with figure 5 in section 5, this figure does not exhibit the limit of the prefetch operation of a real CPU.

5   Experimental Results

In this section, we evaluate cache and I/O performance of the TR-Tree. We use CLOCK algorithm for the page replacement strategy with simple locking mechanism that locks the current node and its ancestors to the root node. We

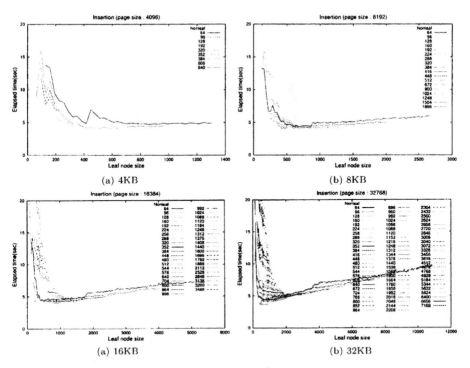

Fig. 4. Insertion performance

use 4 byte keys, 4 byte page IDs, and 2 byte in-page offsets. The machine used for experiments has Intel Pentium III 1GHz CPU whose both L1 and L2 cache are 32B wide, a 40GB IDE hard disk with 5400 rpm, 768MB memory, and Red Hat Linux as operating system. The time we measure is wall-clock time. We implemented and evaluated TR-Trees for disk page sizes of 4KB, 8KB, 16KB, 32KB and possible combinations of w, x and L. Each experiment had the same number of buffer pages. The prefetch routine was macro-coded for each w and x. We compiled TR-Trees by GCC version 3.2.1 without any optimization options.

In figure 4, from left top to right bottom, there are insertion results of page sizes of 4KB, 8KB, 16KB and 32KB. We inserted 100,000 two-dimensional point data one by one. The data inserted to TR-Trees are pseudo-random floating-point values from 0 to 1. Each line in figure represents the size of an in-page non-leaf node. X-axis represents the in-page leaf node size and y-axis the execution time. In every graph, the execution time decreases steeply and then increases gently. As the page size becomes bigger, the prefetch operation seems to cause additional overheads.

In figure 5, we searched TR-Trees with query rectangle whose sides had the same length (0.3) in each axis. We got the average execution time of 1,000 pseudo-random range queries. Like figure 4, graphs represent the execution time per non-leaf and leaf node. As the disk page size becomes bigger, the range query performance becomes better.

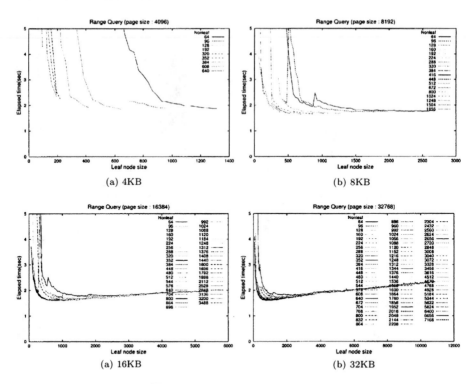

(a) 4KB   (b) 8KB

(a) 16KB   (b) 32KB

Fig. 5. Range query performance

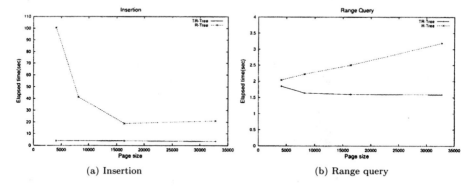

(a) Insertion   (b) Range query

Fig. 6. Performance comparison between TR-Trees and R-Trees

In figure 6, we compare the performance of TR-Trees with R*-Trees [1]. We used Stefan Berchtold's R*-Tree implementation. We inserted the same data to both trees, and then gave 1000 range queries, as described in the above paragraph. In figure 6, the TR-Tree graph has the best performance combinations of w, x, L for each page size. The R-Tree becomes worse as the page size becomes bigger. It seems that the bigger page size causes worse cache performance. This figure shows that the TR-Tree is better than the R*-Tree from 6 to 28-fold improvement for insertions and a factor of 1.28-2.00 improvement for range queries.

6   Conclusions

Previous studies on improving R-Tree index performance have concentrated either on optimizing the I/O performance of disk resident databases traditionally, or on optimizing the cache performance of main memory databases. Because there is a big difference between the node sizes of two types of R-Trees, disk-optimized R-Trees show poor cache performance while cache-optimized R-Trees exhibit poor disk performance. In this paper, we propose a cache and disk optimized R-Tree, called the TR-Tree. We use the prefetch ability of modern CPUs for cache optimization and fit nodes into disk pages for disk I/O optimization. We exhibit a metric for determining the in-page leaf, non-leaf node size and the height of the in-page tree to minimize the cache miss cost for searching TR-Trees. We evaluate the possible enumerations of all combinations of disk page sizes and node sizes. Our implementation achieves better cache and disk performance than disk-optimized R-Trees: a factor of 6-28 improvement for insertions and a factor of 1.28-2.00 improvement for range queries.

References

1. Beckmann, N., Kriegel, H.-P., Schneider, R., Seeger, B.: The R*-Tree: An Efficient and Robust Access Method for Points and Rectangles. In Preceedings of the 1990 ACM SIGMOD International Conference (1990) 322–331
2. Berchtold, S., Böhm, C., Kriegel, H.-P.: The Pyramid-Tree: Breaking the Curse of Dimensionality. In Proceedings of the 1998 ACM SIGMOD International Conference (1998) 142–153
3. Boncz, P., Manegold, S., Kersten, M.: Database Architecture Optimized for the new Bottleneck: Memory Access. In Proceedings of 25th International Conference on Very Large Data Bases (1999) 54–65
4. Chen, S., Gibbons, P. B., Mowry, T. C.: Improving Index Performance through Prefetching. In Proceedings of the 2001 ACM SIGMOD International Conference (2001) 235–246
5. Chen, S., Gibbons, P. B., Mowry, T. C., Valentin, G.: Fractal Prefetching B^+-Trees: Optimizing Both Cache and Disk Performance. In Proceedings of the 2002 ACM SIGMOD International Conference (2002) 157–168
6. Kamel, I., Faloutsos, C.: On Packing R-trees. In Proceedings of the 1993 ACM CIKM Conference (1993) 490–499
7. Kim, K., Cha, S., Kwon, K.: Optimizing Multidimensional Index Trees for Main Memory Access. In Proceedings of the 2001 ACM SIGMOD International Conference (2001) 139–150
8. Rao, J., Ross, K. A.: Cache Conscious Indexing for Decision-Support in Main Memory. In Proceedings of 25th International Conference on Very Large Data Bases (1999) 78–89
9. Rao, J., Ross, K. A.: Making B^+-Trees Cache Conscious in Main Memory. In Proceedings of the 2000 ACM SIGMOD International Conference (2000) 475–486

XML Views: Part 1

Rajagopal Rajugan[1], Elizabeth Chang[2], Tharam S Dillon[1],
and Ling Feng[3]

[1] Faculty of Information Technology, UTS,
Sydney, Australia
rajugan@computer.org
tharam@it.uts.edu.au
[2] School of Information Systems,
Curtin University of Technology,
Australia
ChangE@cbs.curtin.edu.au
[3] Faculty of Computer Science,
University of Twente,
The Netherlands
ling@cs.utwente.nl

Abstract. The exponential growth and the nature of Internet and web-based applications made eXtensible Markup Language (XML) as the de-facto standard for data exchange and data dissemination. Now it is gaining momentum in replacing conventional data models for data representation. XML with its self-describing hierarchical structure and its associated XML Schema (XSD), provide the flexibility and manipulative power needed to accommodate distributive, heterogeneous data. But due to XML's non-scalar, set-based semi-structured nature and ambiguity, traditional data design models lack the capability to conceptually model, design and successfully implement a data model. Due to this, organising and extracting information of XML documents with their conceptual and operational semantics intact is still a challenging task. In this paper, we propose a generic, language independent conceptual view mechanism for XML documents (*XML View*) to enhance conceptual modelling and designing capabilities of XML based information systems. We focus view definition at the conceptual level and the semantics required in accommodating such view mechanism at this higher level of abstraction.

1 Introduction

XML has emerged as the de-facto standard for data exchange and is gaining momentum in replacing conventional data models for data representation. This is mainly due to increase in distributed heterogeneous data (Internet and web applications) sources which are mostly semi-structured and/or unstructured in nature. XML documents which are tag-based and self-describing data documents represent a hierarchical tree structure [RDEL02]. At the conceptual level, they can be visualised as hierarchical trees or graphs. An XML document is usually associated with a Document Type Definition (DTD) or XML Schema [XSW3C] which is used to define

V. Mařík et al. (Eds.): DEXA 2003, LNCS 2736, pp. 148–159, 2003.

and constrain the syntax and structure of a document. In this paper, we only consider XML documents and their associated schemas, as XML schema provides more rich facilities for descriptive user-defined elements and attributes specification, with the flexibility of re-use and flexible constraint definitions. XML schema, which itself is a XML document can be also represented as a hierarchical tree/graph structure.

The rest of the paper is organized as follows. Section 1 looks at early data models for XML, classical view definitions, related work and an outline of our own work. Section 2 presents the XML view, its concept, definition and its characteristics. Different XML view types are discussed in Section 3, while Section 4 concludes the paper.

1.1 XML and Data Models

Models are developed to understand a certain domain (concepts and data) by abstraction. The relational model and OO models have been widely used for modelling and structuring data. These relational and OO models have been extended to accommodate semi-structured data models to support growing Internet and web-based heterogenous data requirements.

W3C proposed a few document structure models to help users to work with XML documents at an abstract level like DOM, OEM and RDF to name a few. Although they provide a certain degree of abstraction for the underlying XML document structures, they are more exposed to implementation-specific and/or implementation-oriented abstraction rather than domain specific conceptual level semantics [LDESN01].

Only recently work has been carried out to incorporate "top-down" conceptual level semantics directly into XML documents/Schema [RDEL01, LDESN01, RDEL02, Sch-LED02]. This gives the user the power to model XML at a higher-level of abstraction using proven methodologies such as Object-Oriented conceptual models using industry standard notations, namely, the Unified Modeling Language (UML™ 1.4) and transform these conceptual models directly into the XML model.

For the purpose of our work, an OO conceptual model can be represented using any of the following notations; Dillon & Tan [DT93], UML[1] or semantic nets [LDESN01]. Since our work is independent of any specific notations above, our personal belief is that semantic nets offer more flexibility and a range of abstract constructs [LDHE02] that is of interest to our future work. Semantic nets are discussed briefly in Section 3. For the purpose of this paper, we use UML notation for the ease of understanding. In a complementary paper [RETL03+] we explain semantic nets [LDESN01] for modeling conceptual views.

1.2 Views and Data Models

Since the early days of data models, the concepts of views were used to give different perspectives and abstraction for underlying base data, for different users and uses. Its usefulness was proven again and again in commercial database systems in the form of security, data reuse and later for performance and abstraction in dimensional data

---

[1] Object Management Group (OMG) Specifications on UML™ 1.4

modeling (data warehouse, OLAP etc.) and distributed data models (Internet, user portals, profiles, etc.). The core definition of views has been carried out from relational database systems, to OO and Object-Relational (O-R) systems. These view definitions have heavily relied on the underlying schema, data model and the data manipulation language used to access the data in the database/(s).

The classical definition of view is based on the three-schema architecture[2] (storage/internal schema, conceptual schema and external schema) of the relational models [WW95]. The relational view is treated as a virtual relation, constructed by a query executed on one or more stored relations. During the early stages of the relational model, the presumed usage for these virtual relations is to provide data protection against unauthorized user access. Later the concept of view was extended to support complex queries and/or aggregate/summary queries.

View definitions were extended to OO data models by Abiteboul et al. [SA91] and Won Kim et al. [W90][WW95]. These were defined in a synonymous manner to the relational model and/or extending the relational definition [W90]. They included the idea of the *virtual class*. Both relational and OO view concepts make two implicit assumptions, that the underlying data is structured and there exists a fixed data model and a data access/query language. Since the emergence of the Internet and XML, the need for semi-structured data models, which have to be independent of fixed data models and data access, violates fundamental properties of persistent data models. Many researchers are attempting to solve these issues by using graph based [YH98] and/or semi-structured data models [SRJMVY].

One of the early discussions on XML view was by Serge Abiteboul [SA99] and later more formally by Sophie Cluet et al. [SPD01]. They proposed a declarative notion of XML views. Abiteboul pointed out that, a view for XML, unlike classical views, should do more than just providing different presentation of underlying data [SA99]. This, he argues, arises mainly due to the nature (semi-structured) and the usage (primarily as common data model for heterogenous data on the web) of XML. Also he argues that, an XML view specification should rely on a data model (like ODMG model) and a query language. Later, keeping the growing web data in mind, Sophie Cluet et al. formally provided an XML view definition as

"....A view defined by a set of pairs <p,p'>, called mappings, where p is a path in the abstract DTD and p' a path in some concrete DTD....." [SPD01].

In the paper [SPD01], they discuss in detail on how abstract paths/DTDs are mapped to concrete paths/DTDs. These concepts, which are implemented in the Xyleme[3] project [Xyleme02], provide one of the most comprehensive mechanisms to construct an XML view to-date. The Xyleme project uses an extension of ODMG Object Query Language (OQL) to implement such an XML view.

Our approach to XML view is complementary in that it is based on an XML view mechanism which provides a higher level of abstraction of the underlying XML domain would be of more useful, as it can provide an abstract definition of a view at early stages of analysis and design, independent of the underlying storage/physical schema. To do so, we provide a view definition at the conceptual level that maps user requirement/perception to that of an XML View document.

Our work differs from previous work done in the following three aspects; (1) Conceptual Views: *XML View* concept is tightly coupled to the conceptual model. In

---

[2] The 3-Schema Architecture or ANSI/SPARC Architecture [Tsichritzis & Klug 1978].

[3] Xyleme Project: A warehouse for web XML documents.

contrast to traditional query based XML views [SA99] or node-to-node or path-to-path mappings [SPD01] between the base document/(s) and the views, we consider mapping of *"conceptual view"* (discussed in detail in Section 2) in base XML domain/(s) to that of an *Imaginary XML document (XML View)*. Here the *XML View* mechanism serves more than just providing simplified and/or optimised query support for the underlying composite base documents/(s) (2) Language independent: The *XML View* is adaptable to any data language, as its definition semantics [RETL03*] are defined at a higher level (3) The *XML View* we propose **may** have an extra sematic net layer [RETL03+] which provides additional constructs for defining view specific and/or design specific syntax (discussed in Section 2.2).

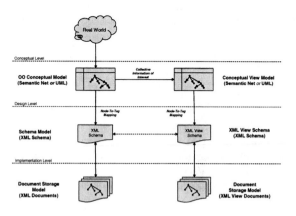

Fig. 1. Deriving Conceptual View & XML View

Our concept of XML view is that, it is defined at the conceptual level using abstract constructs such as semantic nets rather than at ANSI standard external schema level using data definition/manipulation constructs. The main advantage of having such a view mechanism is that, in some complex data domains such as dimensional modelling, OLAP etc. there exists a requirement to model views (for user, performance, analysis) depending on its usage.

In addition, an abstract notation of views is also important in the design of user and web interfaces that are independent of the implementation tool [CD94, Chang96]. Another advantage of having the view definition at this higher level helps to reduce the loss of conceptual semantics as well as gives flexibility in defining a view at a high level of abstraction, unconstrained by any specific data manipulation language. Also defining a conceptual level XML view can be more responsive to both domain/schema level changes as well as document level changes.

2 Imaginary XML Document

In comparison to relational databases where a view is defined as a *virtual relation*, or a virtual class (in OODB), with XML, we define the XML view to be an ***imaginary***

XML document; i.e. the XML document doesn't exist on its own, but is derived from one or more of the physical XML document/(s) and/or pre-derived XML views of an XML domain. We use the term *imaginary* document rather than virtual document because this has been widely used to mean any electronic and/or dynamic HTML documents.

>   **Note:** In this paper we use the terms *imaginary* XML document and *XML View* document interchangeably. They all refer to the same concept, XML View.

A valid XML document is a document, which is correct in syntax, well formed and is constraint by a valid XML schema. Similarly, an *XML View* document should behave as any other stored valid XML document. It may be dynamically created and deleted, support queries issued against it, presentation constraints may applied against it and one or more views may be defined on it. The *conceptual view* is the abstraction of the *imaginary XML document*, represented at the conceptual level.

2.1 Conceptual View

Definition: *Conceptual View*
*A **conceptual view** is an XML View, which is defined at the conceptual level with higher level of abstraction. A **conceptual view** is such that, it has (1) a view document name (2) a valid conceptual schema definition which constrains and validates the document (3) a collection of tags and their namespaces (or domain) (4) new tags and their namespaces which are derived from others and (5) a constructor (that is specified at the conceptual level) defines how the document will be materialised.*

This implies that, an *XML View* document should include the following characteristics.

- The *conceptual view* definition includes a view name, a valid conceptual schema definition which constrains and validates the view, a collection of tags and their namespaces (or domain), new tags (and their namespaces) which are derived from other base domain tags and an optional constructor (that is specified at the conceptual level) that defines how the document will be materialised.
- The query part of the conceptual view definition is optional. In relational view definition, they involve typical SPJ (Select-Project-Join) operations or summarizations. Since the conceptual view is defined at a higher level (conceptual), they can be specified using abstract syntax such as SDX or omitted.
- A tag specification in conceptual view is similar to that of a tag specification of the stored XML document, defined and constrained in the XML schema (view schema). In the case of a derived (new) tag, which is not present or defined in the stored XML domain, the tag specifications are defined only in the XML schema of the *conceptual view*.
- A newly defined/derived XML tag in the conceptual view, is a tag that may be derived from one or more tag/(s) in the stored XML schema/namespace.
- Additional constraints (pattern, restriction, scope, default values) can be defined for tags in the conceptual view.
- For a conceptual view, only the specification is defined using a given declarative notation (Semantic nets / UML). It serves *only* as a blueprint for the construction of *XML View* documents, i.e. there exists a 1:1 mapping between a conceptual view and an *XML View*.

In simple terms, a *conceptual view* describes how a collection of XML tags make sense to a domain user[4] at the conceptual/abstract level. A typical XML domain may contain few XML documents to many thousands of semantically related, clusters of XML documents (and their related schemas) depending on the real world requirement. At a given instant, only a subset of these cluster of XML tags, its specification and their data values (information) may be of use or required by a domain user. This subset of XML tags, collectively form a conceptual view which is of interest to the domain user at a point in time.

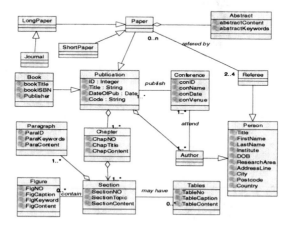

Fig. 2. UML Class Diagram of a simple conference system (Conceptual Level)

In order to illustrate the conceptual view mechanism, we divided the domain user's view requirements into three groups, namely new user requirement, user perception, and user query. Also we use the conceptual level class diagram of a simple Conference System (CS) to include real world concrete examples.

– New User Requirement *Conceptual View*

An example of a new user requirement conceptual view is an ADDRESS_BOOK of the CS system, where all person and their contact details in the CS are pulled out to form a *conceptual view*. This includes person's name (first, middle, last), street address, postcode, country, phone numbers and email. These types of *conceptual views* are very useful in modeling dimensional data models, where complex new data definitions are derived from one or more existing data definitions at higher levels of abstraction.

```
"ADDRESS_BOOK= Author (Title, FirstName, LastName, AddressLine,
City, Postcode, Country) UNION
Referee (Title, FirstName, LastName, AddressLine,
City, Postcode, Country)"
```
(1)

– User Perception as Conceptual Views

For example, there may exist a user perception "BOOKS" (independent of how the conceptual model is implemented in the storage model) of the CS, where the individual components of a book (i.e. publication, chapter, section, paragraph,

---

[4] Domain User: Here we use this term very generally to refer to all people who are working in a particular domain and not to task specific people.

figure, tables) *"assembled"* behaves as if it is one component. Therefore BOOKS may form a *conceptual view*, independent of the storage/implementation model.

```
BOOKS = {Publication(*), Chapter(ChapTitle, ChapContent),
Section (SectionTitle, SectionContent),
Paragraph (ParaContent), Figure (FigCaption, FigContent),
Tables (TableCaption, TableContent)}                        (2)
```

– User Trigger as a *Conceptual View*

In the CS, there may exist a requirement that, based on some change/(s) (trigger) in the underlying XML documents, a view has to be constructed. For example,

```
"Re-Build Publication List when any of the
submitted abstract content changed"                         (3)
"Build Publication Abstract list when
paper due date is 'today'".                                 (4)
```

– User Query as Conceptual View

These types of *conceptual views* are analogous to that of a relational view, where a view is used as shorthand for a frequently executed and/or complex query. In the case of *conceptual view*, this is defined using the higher level syntax of the conceptual modelling language extended with view operators (similar to that of a pseudo code or semantic net) than in a specific data manipulation/query language. For example, in the CS, some of the individual XML document may be Journal, ShortPaper, Author etc. There may exist a requirement that,

```
"Set higher "priority code" to all ShortPaper to be
published in Conference='DEXA03'".                          (5)
```

This *conceptual view* can be made more expressive or complex by refining or adding extra requirements.

```
"Get all higher priority code of Publications to be
published in Conference during 2003 academic year".        (6)
"Get all Publications of authors who are members of
the Institute 'La Trobe University, Australia'".           (7)
```

2.2   From Conceptual View to XML View

Definition: *XML View*

*An **XML View** is an imaginary XML document which points to a collection of semantically related XML tags from an XML domain and satisfies a **Conceptual View** definition from the target XML conceptual domain.*

An imaginary XML document is said to be an XML View if and only if, it has a document name, a valid schema definition (which constrains and validates the document), a collection of semantically related tags and their namespaces (or domain), (if any) a set of new tags and their namespaces which are derived from others and a constructor that defines how the document will be materialised.

Since an *XML View* document may result in a few collections of XML tags to that of a whole semantically related cluster of XML tags, for the user, the resulting *XML View* document behaves as another XML document. In addition, an *XML View* has the following properties.

– An *XML View* definition includes a view name, a valid schema definition which constrains and validates the view, a collection of tags and their namespaces (or domain), new tags (and their namespaces) which are derived from other base domain tags and a constructor that defines how the document will be materialised.

- The query part of the *XML View* definition is any arbitrary query or transformation of the abstract syntax of the conceptual view query using any query language for XML with language specific syntax (e.g. XPath, XQuery) issued against one or more stored XML document/(s). This is normally a SPJ (Select-Project-Join) operation/(s) or summarization queries.
- A tag specification in *XML View* is similar to that of a tag specification of the stored XML document, defined and constrained in the XML schema (view schema). In the case of a derived (new) tag, which is not present/defined in the stored XML domain, the tag specifications are defined only in the XML schema of the *XML View*.
- A newly defined/derived XML tag in the conceptual view, is a tag that may be derived from one or more tag/(s) in the stored XML schema/namespace.
- Additional constrains (pattern, restriction, scope, default values) can be specified in *XML View* schema (which is syntax specific).
- An *XML View* is a template for the creation of new view instances.

2.3 Mapping of Conceptual View to *XML View*

The relationship between a conceptual view and that of its *XML View* is that; they have a 1:1 mapping between them. The only difference is the level abstraction at which they are derived or defined. A similarity is the difference between a conceptual level class diagram and its design level equivalent. The following tables outline how a conceptual view (Table 1, using UML and Table 2, using sematic nets) is mapped to the resulting *XML View*.

Table 1. Mapping between Conceptual View (UML) and *XML View*.

View Property	Conceptual View (Using UML)	XML View
Representation	Class	XML document
View Name	Valid UML class name.	Document name (XML specific syntax)
Schema	List of attribute specification (name, type, constraints etc.)	XML Schema
Domain	Class domain	XML Namespace
Data	Attribute value	XML Tag encapsulated value
Constructor	Class Method/function specification (Optional)	Language specific (E.g. XPath, XQuery, SQL)

Table 2. Mapping between Conceptual View (Semantic Net) and *XML View*.

View Property	Conceptual View (Semantic Net)	XML View
Representation	Rooted collection of nodes and edges	XML document
View Name	Label of the root node	Document name (XML specific syntax)
Schema	Connected collection of nodes and labelled edges.	XML Schema
Domain	Sematic net domain	XML Namespace
Data	Leave nodes	XML Tag coded values
Constructor	Semantic net operators (Set/Unary operators) (Optional)	Language specific (E.g. XPath, XQuery, SQL)

2.4 Stored XML Documents and Imginary XML Documents

A class in OO system has both attributes (may be nested or set valued) and methods. A class can also form complex hierarchies (inheritance, part-of, etc) with other classes. Owing to these complexities, definition of views for OO systems is not straightforward. In one of the early discussions on OO data models, Won Kim argues that, an OO data model should be considered as one kind of extended relational model [W90]. Naturally, this statement reflected on early discussions of OO views [W90, SA91, WW95, Chang96]. In general, the concept of *virtual class* is considered as the OO equivalent of a relational view.

Abiteboul and Bonner 1991 argue that *virtual classes* and stored classes are interchangeable in a class hierarchy [SA91]. They also state that, virtual classes are populated by creating new objects (imaginary objects) and from existing objects of other classes (virtual objects).

But Won Kim et al. and Chang et al. argue that, in contrast to relational models, class hierarchy and view (virtual) class hierarchy should be kept separate [WW95, Chang96]. It is inappropriate to include the view virtual class in the domain inheritance hierarchies because (1) a view can be derived from an existing class by having fewer attributes and more methods. It would be inappropriate to treat it as a subclass unless one allow for the notion of selective inheritance of attributes. (2) Two views could be derived from the same subclass with different groups of instances. However the instances from one view definition could be overlapping with the other and non-disjoint. (3) View definitions, while useful for examining data, might give rise to classes that may not be semantically meaningful to users [BE92]. (4) Effects of schema changes on classes are automatically propagated to all subclasses. If a view is considered as a subclass, this could create problems [WW95] in requiring the changes to be propagated to the view as it might be appropriate or inappropriate. (5) An inappropriate placement of the view in the inheritance hierarchy, could lead to the violation of the semantics because of the extent of overlapping with an existing class [WW95, Chang96].

In continuing the above discussion, to avoid confusion, we need to clarify the issue of the relationship between *stored* XML documents and *XML View* documents. As in relational and OO systems, modelling of XML documents share some relational and many OO features. Naturally, new *XML View documents* may form new document hierarchies (inheritance, aggregation, nested etc.), may extend the existing namespace of the stored XML namespace/(s) and may be used to provide dynamic windows to one or more stored heterogenous XML domains. XML views may also be used to provide imaginary schema changes (such new simple/complex tags, new document hierarchy, restructuring etc.). But, keeping in line with the arguments presented for OO views in [WW95, Chang96, W90], we believe that the stored XML documents hierarchy and the *XML View* documents hierarchy should be kept separate. Many of the points made by Won Kim and Chang & Dillon [DT93] for OO views apply to XML views.

At a given instant, in an XML domain, users can add new documents, modify/delete old documents, modify structures/schema of stored documents, create new schemas/hierarchies or create new XML view definitions based on stored documents and/or existing XML views. But, at any given instant, users *cannot* create new *stored XML document/schema* based on existing *XML View* document(s)/schema(s).

3 XML View Types

XML view can be used for many purposes from simple projection of selected XML tags to providing dynamic window into complex heterogenous XML documents. Based on how these *XML View* documents are constructed/behave we classify them into three categories, namely Derived Imaginary XML document (***DIX***) Constructed Imaginary XML document (***CIX***) and Triggered Imaginary Document (***TIX***). The following sections discuss these views and their characteristics.

3.1 *XML View*: Derived Imginary XML Document (DIX)

A *Derived Imaginary XML Document* (DIX) is an XML view, which is derived from an existing XML document called *base document*. This is done without violating the original hierarchical structure of the base document. This derivation is similar to that of a XSL transformation, applied on XML documents. The derived documents are as a result of vertical partitioning (projection) or horizontal partitioning (selection) and/or both (incl. simple join operation within an XML document) of the physical XML documents. The resulting document is derived virtually when required and only the view definition is persistence in the form of XML schema.

Deduction: *DIX is a shallow copy of its original base document.*

This view is very similar to that of SPJ (Select, Project Join) views in relational data model. The difference being, the SPJ operations are done with in a single XML document. The resulting document is derived virtually when required and only the view definition is persistence in the form of XML schema. Good examples of such XML view types are Example (5), (6) and (7) above in Section 2.1.

3.2 *XML View*: Triggered Imginary XML Document (TIX)

A Triggered *Imaginary XML Document* (TIX) is an XML view, where the resulting XML document is *triggered* from existing base XML document/(s) and their associated XML schema/(s) when a certain "change" or "condition" is satisfied in the XML domain. The trigger which initiates the creation of the *XML View* is defined as part of the *XML View* definition, which is unique to TIX view definition. This is the only difference between the other two *XML Views* mentioned in sections above.

These types of view are very useful in defining an *event based* XML views, where the creation of an *XML View* document depends on a change in the underlying base XML domain (e.g. user action, value change, state change, version change etc.). Example (3) and (4) in Section 2.1 above are examples of such XML view types.

3.3 *XML View*: Constructed Imginary XML Document (CIX)

A *Constructed Imaginary XML Document* (CIX) is an XML view, where the resulting XML document is *constructed* from existing base XML document/(s) and their associated XML schema/(s) by manipulating their structure/elements to form a new virtual/abstract XML document hierarchy. The construction is done by partitioning (similar to derived XML documents) and/or by re-arranging the XML element information (by hierarchy, order, add, remove etc). The result is a new imaginary/abstract *XML document* with its associated *XML schema*.

This view is similar to that DIX, but the base document/(s) can be cluster of semantically related XML documents. In other words CIX can satisfy a *conceptual view*, which may span across one or more base document and/or XML schema/(s). Example (1) and (2) in Section 2.1 above are examples of such XML view types.

4 Conclusion and Future Work

XML is becoming increasingly popular in web and e-Commerce applications, as a data exchange medium and a replacement persistence data store. But it lacks proper modelling techniques and high level abstraction that is needed to describe and accommodate complex systems. XML schema language tries to address few of the issues defining constraining XML documents, but it still lacks proper modelling semantics.

Due to these factors, we propose a conceptual level definition of XML views for the underlying XML documents and their associated schemas. This approach, in our view will improve the level of abstraction provided by an XML domain. This level of abstraction is very helpful in complex domains such as e-commerce, data warehouse, OLAP or SCM applications where XML is gaining its ground. Developers of such domains can define complex heterogenous document views without constrained by lower level document structure or data models, and derived explicit information systems.

Our future work includes extending the view definition to accommodate summarization and grouping mechanism at conceptual level. And later we plan to utilize XML views in manipulating large volume of XML documents to provide semantic aware information queries.

References

[BE92].   Bertino, Elisa; "A View Mechanism for Object-Oriented Databases"; Proc. 3rd Int. conf. on Extending Database Technology (EDBT92), Austria, 1992, pp 136–151.
[CD94].   E. Chang, T. Dillon; "Integration of User Interfaces with Application Software and Databases Through the Use of Perspectives"; Proceedings of the 1st Int. Conf. on Object-Role Modeling, ORM-1, Magnetic Island, Australia, 4–6 July 1994.
[Chang96]. E.J. Chang, "Object Oriented User Interface Design and Usability Evaluation", Department of Computer Science & Computer Engineering, La Trobe University, Australia, 1996.
[DT93].   T S Dillon, P.L Tan; "Object-Oriented Conceptual Modeling"; Prentice Hall, Australia, 1993.
[LDE02].   Ling Feng, Tharam Dillon & E Chang; "Schemata Transformation of Object Inheritance to XML; Web Information System Engineering (WISE 02) 2002, Singapore.

[LDESN01]. Ling Feng, Tharam Dillon & E Chang; "A Semantic Network Based Design Methodology for XML Documents"; ACM Trans. on Info. Sys., Volume 20, No. 4, August 2002; pp 390–421.

[LDHE02]. Ling Feng, Tharam Dillon, Hans Weigand, & E Chang; "An XML-Enabled Association Rule Framework"; Database & Expert Systems Applications (DEXA) 2003.

[RDEL01]. Renguo Xiao, Tharam S Dillon, E Chang & Ling Feng; "Modeling and Transformation of Object-Oriented Conceptual Models into XML Schema"; Database & Expert Systems Applications (DEXA) 2001; Springer, 795–804, 2001.

[RDEL02]. Renguo Xiao, Tharam S Dillon, E Chang & Ling Feng; "Mapping Object Relationships into XML Schema"; OOPSLA Workshop on Objects, XML & Databases, USA, October 2001.

[RETL03+]. R Rajugan, E Chang Thram S Dillon & Ling Feng; "XML Views Part II: Conceptual Modeling of XML Views Using Semantic Nets"; (To be Submitted).

[RETL03*]. R Rajugan, E Chang Thram S Dillon & Ling Feng; "XML View: A Declarative View Specification"; (To be Submitted).

[SA91]. Serge Abiteboul, Anthony Bonner; "Objects and Views"; ACM SIGMOD Record, Proceedings of the 1991 ACM SIGMOD Int. Conf. on Mgt of data; 1991, Volume 20 Issue 2.

[SA99]. Serge Abiteboul; "On Views and XML"; PODS '99; Philadelphia PA, 1999.

[SPD01]. Sophie Cluet, Pierangelo Veltri, Dan Vodislav; "Views in a Large Scale XML Repository"; Proceedings of the 27th VLDB Conference, Roma, Italy, 2001.

[SRJMVY]. Serge Abiteboul, Roy Goldman, Jason McHugh, Vasilis Vassalos, Yue Zhuge; "Views for Semistructured Data"; Wkshp on Mgt of Semistructured Data 1997, USA.

[W90]. Won Kim; "Research Directions in Object-Oriented Database Systems"; Proceedings of the ninth ACM SIGACT-SIGMOD-SIGART symposium on Principles of database systems,1990, Nashville, Tennessee, USA; pp 1–15, ACM Press New York, NY, USA.

[WW95]. Won Kim, William Kelly; "On View Support in Object-Oriented Database Systems"; Modern Database Systems; Addison-Wesley Publishing Company, Chapter 6, pp 108–129; 1995.

[XSP01-1]. W3C Consortium; "XML Schema Part 0: Primer"; http://www.w3.org/TR/xmlschema-0/.

[XSP01-2]. W3C Consortium; "XML Schema Part 1: Structures"; http://www.w3.org/TR/xmlschema-1/.

[XSP01-3]. W3C Consortium; "XML Schema Part 2: Datatypes"; http://www.w3.org/TR/xmlschema-2/.

[XSW3C]. W3C Consortium; "XML Schema"; http://www.w3c.org/XML/Schema.

[Xyleme02]. Xyleme Project; Publications; http://www.xyleme.com/ .

[YH98]. Yue Zhuge, Hector Garcia-Molina; "Graph structured Views and Incremental Maintenance"; Proceeding of the 14th IEEE Conference on Data Engineering, ICDE 1998, USA 1998.

Partition Based Path Join Algorithms for XML Data*

Quanzhong Li and Bongki Moon

Department of Computer Science,
University of Arizona,
Tucson, AZ 85721
{lqz,bkmoon}@cs.arizona.edu

Abstract. Path expression is an important component in querying XML data. The extended preorder numbering scheme enables us to quickly determine the ancestor-descendant relationship between elements in the hierarchy of XML data. Using the numbering scheme, a path expression can be evaluated by join operations to avoid potentially high cost of tree traversals. In this paper, we first formulate XML path queries as range-point join queries. Then we discuss the partition based algorithms that can utilize the *range containment property* to efficiently process the range-point join queries. Under the partition based framework, we propose three algorithms, namely *Descendant partition join*, *Segment-tree partition join* and *Ancestor Link partition join*, which can be chosen by a query optimizer for different input data characteristics. The experimental results show that the partition based algorithms can make better use of the buffer memory than sort-merge algorithms, and the proposed *Ancestor Link join* algorithm yields the best performance by using small in-memory data structures and by taking advantage of unevenly sized inputs.

1 Introduction

With the popularity of XML as a new standard for information representation and exchange on the Internet, the problem of managing and querying XML data is becoming more and more important. Various work has been done to efficiently evaluate queries on XML data. In graph-based data models, a path expression is evaluated through tree traversal according to the shape of the data [8,3]. With the introduction of the numbering scheme on XML data [6], a path expression can be processed using join algorithms [6,13,12]. *Path Join* algorithms [6] (e.g. $\mathcal{EE}$-**Join** and $\mathcal{EA}$-**Join**) are sort-merge based algorithms to process ancestor-descendant type expressions. *Structural Joins* [12] (tree-merge and stack-tree algorithms) optimizes the join performance by introducing in-memory stacks.

Sort-merge based algorithms assume the inputs are in sorted order of assigned numbers, but this order is not always guaranteed. For example, an input may be sorted by data values, or it may be the result from operations using hash indexes. In this paper, we discuss the use of partition based algorithms to process XML join queries. When the descendant input is used as the outer set in the join, the *Descendant Partition Join* algorithm can be used to process join operations. When the ancestor input is used as

---

* This work was sponsored in part by the National Science Foundation CAREER Award (IIS-9876037), NSF Grant No. IIS-0100436, and NSF Research Infrastructure program EIA-0080123. The authors assume all responsibility for the contents of the paper.

V. Mařík et al. (Eds.): DEXA 2003, LNCS 2736, pp. 160–170, 2003.

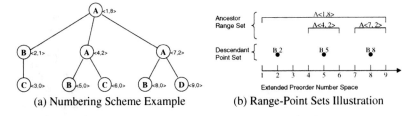

(a) Numbering Scheme Example   (b) Range-Point Sets Illustration

Fig. 1. Numbering Scheme and Range-Point Sets

the outer set, we propose the *Segment-tree Partition Join* and the *Ancestor Link Partition Join* algorithms. The experimental results show that the Ancestor Link algorithm can make the best use of memory buffer and take advantage of unevenly sized inputs. We believe that these algorithms are necessary choices for query optimizers to consider during XML query processing for different input characteristics.

The rest of the paper is organized as follows. In Section 2, we will introduce the numbering scheme and three partition based join algorithms. Section 3 presents the performance results. After the brief survey in Section 4, we conclude the work of this paper in Section 5.

2 Partition Based Path Join Algorithms

Since the extended preorder numbering scheme is the basis for path join algorithms, we will briefly introduce it next.

2.1 Extended Preorder Numbering Scheme

XML data objects are commonly modeled by a tree structure, where nodes represent elements, attributes and text data, and parent-child node pairs represent nesting between XML data components. The *Extended Preorder Numbering Scheme* captures this tree structure and assigns each node a pair of numbers, $<order, size>$. The *order* is similar to the preorder, and the *size* is the number of descendants. This pair of numbers should satisfy the following conditions:

- For a tree node y and its parent x, $order(x) < order(y)$ and $order(y) + size(y) \leq order(x) + size(x)$. In other words, y's range $[order(y), order(y) + size(y)]$ is contained in x's range $[order(x), order(x) + size(x)]$.
- For two sibling nodes x and y, if x is the predecessor of y in preorder traversal, $order(x) + size(x) < order(y)$. In other words, x's and y's ranges are disjoint.

For example, Figure 1(a) shows a tree labeled with these pairs of numbers. The ancestor-descendant relationship can be determined in constant time by examining these numbers. That is, for two given nodes x and y of a tree T, x is an ancestor of y if and only if $order(x) < order(y) \leq order(x) + size(x)$. To process path expressions, we can gather two node sets, the ancestor set and the descendant set, and join them together using the above condition.

According to the numbering scheme, we can treat the ancestor set as a range set and the descendant set as a point set. In Figure 1(a), suppose we are going to find all the paths of the pattern "A//B", which is to get all the "B" descendants of "A". We can first gather the ancestor set, which is $\{< 1, 8 >, < 4, 2 >, < 7, 2 >\}$. Then, we obtain the descendant point set, which is $\{2, 5, 8\}$. By the numbering scheme, the ancestor set corresponds to the range set: $\{[1, 9], [4, 6], [7, 9]\}$. Now, the task to find "A//B" is the same as to find the pairs of range and point, where the point is contained in the range. Figure 1(b) illustrates this range set and point set relationship. After mapping ancestor sets to range sets and mapping descendant sets to point sets, the problem of finding path pattern is reduced to computing the join between a range set and a point set, which will be referred as *range-point join* in this paper.

The ancestor range set is generated from a document tree using the numbering scheme, where each range corresponds to a sub-tree in the document tree. Since there is no partial overlap between any two sub-trees, there is no partial overlap among ranges. We formalize this property as *range containment property*, which is defined as follows:

Range Containment Property: For any two ranges in the range set, either one range is contained in the other or they are disjoint.

It is this property that provides us the opportunity and basis to deal with this special type of join operation. In the following section, we will describe how this property can be exploited to make the join algorithms more efficient.

2.2   Partition Based Algorithms

Data Partitioning. The first step in partition join is to partition both input data sets that need to be joined. Each pair of corresponding partitions from both sets need to be joined. In order to avoid data reread, at least one partition of the pair should fit in memory. If no information about the data distribution is available, sampling data can help to determine the partition boundaries. There has been some research work addressing the random sampling problem [1,7]. We have chosen a similar algorithm to "determinePartIntervals" algorithm [11] to determine the partition intervals. This partition algorithm considers partition cost, sampling cost and join cost to minimize the total I/O. The cost of sampling is computed based on the Kolmogorov test statistic [2]. During sampling, we clustered disk page reads such that sample pages close enough are read sequentially instead of several random reads. If one partition is larger than memory size, further partitioning can be applied recursively. In this paper, we assume that each outer partition can fit in memory, which is also true in our experiments.

Range Partition and Range Cache. Unlike the point set, for a range set, there is a possibility that some ranges can overlap with multiple partitions, no matter how the partition boundaries are determined. Which partition should we put those long ranges in? A straightforward solution is to replicate the ranges to all partitions it overlaps. This requires additional disk I/O to handle replicates. Instead, we adopted the solution proposed in [11], where the partitioning is performed using only the start point of each range. A range is put in the partition, where the start point of the range falls in. One requirement of this method is that the partition join should be evaluated in increasing order of partitions. When the current partition is done, the ranges that cross the next partition boundary are kept in memory cache. These ranges in cache will participate in the join of the next partition.

One nice property of the XML data range set is that the number of ranges crossing any partition boundary is bounded by the height of the document tree. Thus, we can

---

Algorithm 1: Descendant Partition Join

    Input: (ancestor range set, descendant point set)

1 Set range cache to be empty;
2 Determine partition boundaries according to the descendant point set;
3 Partition both range and point sets;
4 **for** *Each partition pair in increasing order* **do**

5   Load descendant partition in memory;
6   **for** *Each range in range cache* **do**

7   Join the range with descendant partition;
8   Remove the range if it doesn't cross the next partition boundary;
      end
9   **for** *Each page of range partition* **do**

10   Load the range set page in memory;
11   **for** *Each range in the page* **do**

12   Join the range with descendant partition;
13   Put the range in the range cache if it crosses the next partition boundary;
        end
     end
  end

---

pre-allocate the in-memory cache to hold those crossing boundary ranges according to the tree height. A possible improvement is to use the maximum level difference of the ranges plus one as the cache upper bound. This upper bound can be obtained before sampling and partition. We can take the size of this in-memory range cache out from the total memory buffer size before partitioning. So, the partitioning can be done as normal point data partitioning without considering the boundary crossing problem.

Descendant Partition Join. In the *descendant partition join* algorithm, which is shown in Algorithm 1, the descendant point set is the outer set. The sampling and partitioning is based on the point set. During the join phase, each point partition is loaded in memory to be joined with the corresponding range partition and the cached ranges from previous range partitions.

In line 7 and line 12, the join operation is to join one range with all the descendant points in a partition. Since it is an in-memory operation, at first, we directly used the nested loop join. From our preliminary experimental results, we found that the performance of the nested loop join was very bad due to the high CPU and memory access cost. So, we changed the nested loop to binary search. The descendant point partition is sorted after it is loaded in memory. When a range is to be joined with the points partition, a binary search is used to locate the first point in the range. Then, we scan the sorted point set until we reach the last point in this range.

In line 13, after the join of each range, we put the range in the range cache if it crosses the next partition boundary. At the beginning of the join, the ranges in the range cache are joined with points first (see line 7). At the same time, we try to eliminate the ranges that do not cross the next partition boundary, which is shown in line 8. Thus, the range cache is maintained in such a way that only the ranges crossing the next partition boundary are kept in memory, and are used in the join of the next partition.

In a partition join, either join input data set can be chosen as the outer set to determine the partition boundaries. However, partitioning based on the larger input produces more

---

Algorithm 2: Segment Tree Partition Join

    Input: (ancestor range set, descendant point set)

1 Set range cache to be empty;
2 Determine partition boundaries according to the ancestor range set;
3 Partition both range and point sets;
4 **for** *Each partition pair in increasing order* **do**

5   Load ancestor range partition in memory;
6   Build a segment tree for ranges in the partition and the range cache;
7   **for** *Each page of point partition* **do**

8   Load the point set page in memory;
9   **for** *Each point in the page* **do**

10   Join the point using the segment tree;
            end
      end
11   Dispose the segment tree;
12   Remove from range cache the ranges not crossing the next boundary;
13   Put ranges crossing the next boundary from range partition to range cache;
    end

---

partitions than partitioning based on the smaller input. With the smaller input set as the outer set, we can have smaller number of partitions and more sequential I/O. If the smaller input can totally fit in memory, there is no partitioning needed at all. Usually, in XML data, the size of the descendant point set is larger than that of the ancestor range set. So, partitioning based on the ancestor range set could produce better performance. We next introduce two partition join algorithms using the ancestor range set as the outer set. They are named *Segment Tree Partition Join* and *Ancestor Link Partition Join* based on their in-memory join algorithms.

Segment Tree Partition Join. In partition join algorithms using the ancestor range set as the outer set, the partitioning is based on the ancestor range set. As in the *descendant partition join* algorithm, a range cache is also used. During the join phase, each range partition is first loaded into memory. These ranges in the partition and the ranges in the range cache are together to be joined with each descendant point from the inner partition. Because the nested loop join is inefficient, in the segment tree partition join algorithm, which is shown in Algorithm 2, the segment tree [10] is used as the in-memory algorithm to quickly find a set of ranges containing a point. The worst case space complexity of the segment tree is $O(N \cdot logN)$, where N is the number of ranges [10]. In our implementation, we used several techniques to minimize the size of the segment tree data structure. In this in-memory join context, the ranges and their end-points are already known. No insertion and deletion of end-points is required after the tree is built. We can utilize this property to build a static segment tree, which is more compact than a dynamic one.

    The first step of building a segment tree is to sort the end points of the ranges in memory (duplicate points should be eliminated). Let us suppose the number of ranges is N. Because the start point of each range is a unique preorder ID number, there are at least N points in the segment tree. After sorting, an *virtual* empty segment tree is there, because the parent-child relationship in the segment tree can be determined by the array index calculation. There is no additional space needed for the structure pointers of the

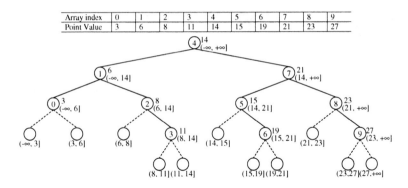

Fig. 2. End Point Array and Its Segment Tree

tree. However, the number of segment tree nodes is twice the size of the point array. When a range is inserted to the segment tree, a pointer is needed to store the linked list for each segment tree node. So, at least $2N$ pointers are needed. For each range, at least one linked list record is associated with it. Each linked list record contains the range ID and the next link pointer. In total, we need at least $3N$ pointers, and N range ID's. If pointers and ID's are represented by integers, then at least $4N$ integers are required for the segment tree. This is a large memory requirement, since in our implementation, each XML element node record only uses four integers. In this case, half of the memory is used for the segment tree.

As an example, the table in Figure 2 shows a set of point values along with their index in an array. In the segment tree illustrated below, the number in a node circle is the index value. It is empty for leaf nodes, since they are virtual nodes. The point value and the node range are labeled near each node. The root index value of each sub-tree is the middle index value of the index range of the sub-tree. That is $tree\ root = \lfloor (start\ index + end\ index)/2 \rfloor$. For example, index value 4 is the root of the index range [0,9], which is the whole tree.

Since memory size is limited, the more memory used for in-memory index like segment tree, the smaller memory is left for partitions. To solve the large memory occupation problem of the segment tree, we propose to use *Ancestor Link* algorithm for in-memory join, which is described in the next section.

Ancestor Link Partition Join. The control flow of the *Ancestor Link Partition Join* algorithm is the same as the segment tree partition join algorithm (Algorithm 2), except that the in-memory join is now the *ancestor link join*. Instead of building a segment tree, an ancestor link data structure is used. Each descendant point is joined with all the in-memory ranges using this ancestor link data structure.

According to the *range containment property*, for any two ranges, either one range contains the other range, or they are disjoint. We can build a *range tree* according to the containment relationship. In the range tree, a child range is directly contained in the parent range, which is the smallest range containing the child. If a descendant point p is contained in a range R in the range tree, then this point p is also contained in all the ancestor ranges of range R in the range tree. Using this range tree, we can efficiently perform the join between a point and a set of ranges.

Since all range records to be joined are already in the buffer memory, no additional range information needs to be duplicated again in the range tree. In our implementation,

---

Algorithm 3: Build Ancestor Link

  Input: (sorted range array, range tree array)

1 Initialized pointer stack to be empty;
2 **for** *Each range in the range array* **do**

3   **while** *pointer stack is not empty and the top of pointer stack is not the parent of the current range* **do**

4   Pop the pointer stack;
      end
5   **if** *pointer stack is empty* **then**

6   Set the current range tree pointer to be null;
      else

7   Set the current range tree pointer to be the top of the pointer stack;
      end
8   Push the current range pointer to the pointer stack;
  end

---

the range tree is only a pointer array, which has the same size as the number of the ranges in memory. The positions of pointers correspond to the positions of the ranges in the range array. The content of a pointer is the array index of the parent range. So, an edge in the range tree is pointing from a child node to a parent node. To build the range tree, we first sort all the ranges by the start points. After the sorting, the ranges are also in sorted preorder with respect to the range tree. Then we scan the range array once with a pointer stack to find the parent of each range and update the ancestor pointer array. This algorithm is shown in Algorithm 3.

Next, we show how to find the first (smallest) range containing a given point p in the range tree. Since the range array is sorted by the start point, we can use binary search to find the range R_p that may contain the point p. That is R_p is the first range whose start point is smaller than p. If R_p contains p, then all the ancestors of R_p in the range tree also contain p. If R_p does not contain p, we can follow the ancestor link of R_p to find the ranges that contain p. The main advantage of the ancestor link is its small memory requirement. The whole structure is only an array of pointers. The size is at least less than one fourth of the segment tree. So, more memory can be used for partitions.

3 Experiment

We implemented these three partition join algorithms discussed in the paper. They are referred to as *partition-d*, *partition-s* and *partition-a* for Descendant partition join, Segment-tree partition join and Ancestor-link partition join algorithms respectively. For performance study, we also implemented the sort-merge based algorithms similar to the Stack-Tree join algorithm (Stack-Tree-Desc) [12]. Two variations of sort-merge join algorithms, *sortmerge-s* and *sortmerge-m*, were implemented. Sortmerge-s sorts each input into a single run before the join phase, while sortmerge-m combines the last merge phase of sorting with the join phase.

The above algorithms were all implemented on top of a paged file layer, which also provides buffer management functionality. In our experiments, the page size was 4K bytes. The input files were paged files, and were directly generated from the data-set in

Table 1. Queries and Description

Data Set	Query	Ancestor		Descendant	
		Record#	Page#	Record#	Page#
Shakespeare	ACT//SPEECH	185	1	31028	122
	SPEECH// LINE	31028	122	107833	423
DBLP	dblp//author	783	4	320300	1257
	inproceedings//author	140936	553	320300	1257

random order. We have chosen two data sets, Shakespeare and DBLP, to demonstrate the performance. The Shakespeare data set is the Shakespeare's plays in XML format. The DBLP data set is a computer science bibliography [9]. In our experiment, we used the conference portion with a raw data size 58MB.

In the experiments, we measured the elapsed time (both CPU and IO) of query processing. For fair comparison, the sorting cost for sort-merge based algorithms, and the sampling cost for partition based algorithms were both counted in the performance measure. Since the cost of output generation is the same regardless of algorithms applied, the output cost was not included in the measurements. Experiments were performed on an Intel workstation with a Pentium 4 1.6GHz CPU running Solaris 8 for Intel platform. This workstation has 512M bytes of memory and a 40GB EIDE disk drive (with 7200 RPM and 8ms average seek time). The disk is locally attached to the workstation and used to store XML data. We used the direct I/O feature of Solaris for all experiments to avoid operating system's cache effects.

3.1 Query Performance and Analysis

Table 1 describes the queries we used in the experiments. It also provides the ancestor range set size and the descendant point set size information. All queries are of the form "$E_A//E_B$", which is to find the ancestor-descendant element pairs.

Figure 3 shows the performance for two queries on the Shakespeare data and Figure 4 shows the performance for the DBLP data. The performance measure is elapsed time in seconds with different number of memory buffer pages. Although the size of the DBLP data is much larger than that of the Shakespeare data, we observed similar performance trends.

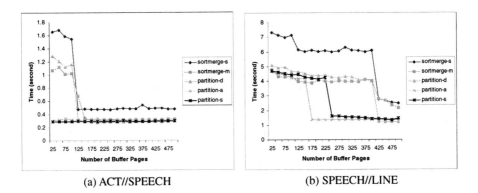

(a) ACT//SPEECH   (b) SPEECH//LINE

Fig. 3. Shakespeare Data Queries

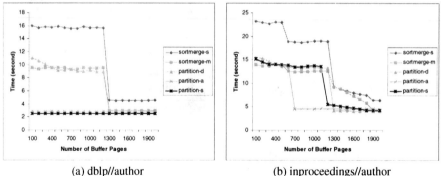

(a) dblp//author   (b) inproceedings//author

Fig. 4. DBLP Data Queries

In Figure 3(a) and Figure 4(a), the ancestor set size is small. Since the partition-a and the partition-s algorithms use the ancestor set as the outer set, there is no need to do partitioning at all if the memory can hold the outer set. So, their performances are better than others when the total buffer size is small.

For both sort-merge join and partition join algorithms, if memory buffer can hold both sets, there is only one scan of the input files needed to load data in memory. That is the minimum cost for the query processing. So, when the memory buffer size is large enough, there is a sharp performance increase. After this, the performance remains almost constant. This trend can be seen from Figure 3(a) and Figure 4(a).

In the sortmerge-m algorithm, the last merge phase of sorting is combined with the join phase, so the last merge scan is saved. On the other hand, for the sortmerge-s algorithm, the last sorting merge scan of input files is always needed. It increases both the I/O and the CPU cost. Among these algorithms, the sortmerge-s algorithm is the worst, which is clearly shown in Figure 3 and Figure 4.

In Figure 3(b) and Figure 4(b), the ancestor set is large. When neither join set can fit in memory, all algorithms have to scan the input files at least twice. In this case, the partition join algorithms (partition-d, partition-a and partition-s) and the sortmerge-m algorithm have similar performance. From this result, we can also see that the sampling cost for the partition based algorithms is low. The reason is that the number of samples is small compared to the whole set, and we also optimized the sampling process using clustered read technique as described in Section 2.2.

With the memory size getting larger, the performances of the partition join algorithms improve faster than the sortmerge-m algorithm, since the partition join algorithms can avoid partitioning when one join set can fit in memory. For the sortmerge-m algorithm, it can keep all runs in memory only if the memory is large enough to hold both join sets. Otherwise, additional I/O for runs is unavoidable. Among the partition join algorithms, the performance of the partition-a algorithm is the best. The in-memory join data structure *ancestor link* requires less memory than *segment tree*. So, more memory can be used to hold partitions.

The above experimental results provide useful information for query optimization. If one of the two join sets is much smaller that the other, using the partition join algorithms require less memory. The query optimizer can choose the smaller set as outer set and the corresponding partition join algorithm.

4 Previous Work

Sort-merge join has been widely used in relational database. For equality queries, hash-based join can be used as an alternative to sort-merge join. Comparisons of sort-based and hash-based algorithms show that many dualities exist between the two types of algorithms and both should be available in a query-processing system [4]. There are a large amount of work has been done in the temporal database area to process temporal intersection joins [5], in which join predicates over time attributes are mostly of the inequality type. To process valid-time joins, a partition-based evaluation algorithm has been proposed [11]. This algorithm utilizes in-memory cache to store "long-lived" tuple and avoids the replication of tuples in multiple partitions. For XML data, with the introduction of *the extended preorder numbering scheme* [6], XML path queries can be processed using traditional relational database techniques. For example, sort-merge based algorithms like $\mathcal{EE}$-**Join**, $\mathcal{EA}$-**Join** and *Structure join* [12] have been proposed. *Stack-Tree Join* [12] algorithms utilizing in-memory stack to hold ancestor nodes have been proposed to deal with structural join [12].

5 Conclusion

In this paper, we have proposed partition based algorithms, which can be chosen by query optimizer according to the characteristics of the inputs. An in-memory range cache is used to hold ranges crossing partition boundaries. In the Ancestor Link partition join algorithm, we propose to use the *Ancestor Link* data structure, which is much smaller in size compared to the segment-tree. So, more memory can be used for holding partitions. The experimental results show that the Ancestor Link algorithm can make the best use of memory buffer and take advantage of the uneven sized inputs. We believe that those algorithms are necessary choices for query optimizer to consider during XML query processing.

References

[1] Surajit Chaudhuri, Rajeev Motwani, and Vivek R. Narasayya. Random sampling for histogram construction: How much is enough? In *SIGMOD 1998, June 2–4, 1998, Seattle, Washington, USA*, pages 436–447, 1998.

[2] David J. DeWitt, Jeffrey F. Naughton, and Donovan A. Scheneider. An evaluation of non-equijoin algorithms. In *VLDB 1991*, Barcelona, Spain, September 1991.

[3] Roy Goldman and Jennifer Widom. DataGuides: Enabling query formulation and optimization in semistructured databases. In *VLDB 1997*, Athens, Greece, September 1997.

[4] Goetz Graefe, Ann Linville, and Leonard D. Shapiro. Sort versus hash revisited. *IEEE Transactions on Knowledge and Data Engineering*, 6(6):934–944, 1994.

[5] Himawan Gunadhi and Arie Segev. Query processing algorithms for temporal intersection joins. In *ICDE 1991*, Kobe, Japan, April 1991.

[6] Quanzhong Li and Bongki Moon. Indexing and querying xml data for regular path expressions. In *VLDB 2001*, Rome, Italy, September 2001.

[7] Richard J. Lipton, Jeffrey F. Naughton, Donovan A. Schneider, and S. Seshadri. Efficient sampling strategies for relational database operations. *Theoretical Computer Science*, 116:195–226, 1993.

[8] Jason McHugh and Jennifer Widom. Query optimization for XML. In *VLDB 1999*, pages 315–326, Edinburgh, Scotland, September 1999.

[9] Michael Ley. DBLP Computer Science Biblography.
http://www.informatik.uni-trier.de/~ley/db/index.html, February 2003.

[10] Franco P. Preparata and Michael Ian Shamos. Computational Geometry - An Introduction. Springer-Verlag, Berlin/Heidelbrg, Germany, 1985.

[11] Michael D. Soo, Richard T. Snodgrass, and Christian S. Jensen. Efficient evaluation of the valid-time natural join. In *ICDE 1994, February 14-18, 1994, Houston, Texas, USA*, 1994.

[12] Divesh Srivastava, Shurug Al-Khalifa, H.V. Jagadish, Nick Koudas, Jignesh M. Patel, and Yuqing Wu. Structural joins: A primitive for efficient xml query pattern matching. In *ICDE 2002*, San Jose, California, February 2002.

[13] Chun Zhang, Jeffrey Naughton, David DeWitt, Qiong Luo, and Guy Lohman. On supporting containment queries in relational database management systems. In *SIGMOD 2001*, Santa Barbara, CA, May 2001.

Representing and Querying Summarized XML Data

Sara Comai, Stefania Marrara, and Letizia Tanca

Politecnico di Milano,
Dipartimento di Elettronica e Informazione
Piazza L. Da Vinci 32,
I-20133 Milano, Italy
{comai,marrara,tanca}@elet.polimi.it

Abstract. In the last few years several repositories for storing XML documents and languages for querying XML data have been studied and implemented. All the query languages proposed so far allow to obtain *exact* answers, but when applied to large XML repositories or warehouses, such precise queries may require high response times. To overcome this problem, in traditional relational warehouses fast *approximate* queries are supported, built on concise data statistics based on histograms or sampling techniques. In this paper we propose a novel approach to *summarize an XML document collection* taking into account the hierarchical structure of XML documents, which makes the summarization process substantially more difficult than in case of flat, relational data.

1   Introduction

In the last few years XML [Con98] has spread in many applications putting forth a strong demand both for repositories storing XML documents, and for XML querying capabilities.

In response to the former demand, some repositories have been implemented: Tamino [TAM98] and Excelon [EXC] are two examples of XML repositories storing native XML documents, Xyleme [CVV] is a warehouse for the storage of heterogeneous huge sets of XML documents, and new academic prototypes are under development (e.g., Virtuoso [VIR] and Timber [JAKL+02]).

In response to the latter demand, several languages for querying XML data have been suggested [QL9] and among them XQuery [SS01] is emerging as the standard XML query language. All the proposed languages allow to obtain *exact* answers to queries posed over XML data. However, when applied to large XML repositories or warehouses, such precise queries may require high response times. To overcome this problem, in traditional relational warehouses fast *approximate* queries are supported, built on concise data statistics based on histograms or sampling techniques [GM99]. The basic idea for approximate answers is to store pre-computed summaries of the XML warehouse, also called *synopses* (concise data collections), and to query them instead of the original database, thus saving time and computational costs.

V. Mařík et al. (Eds.): DEXA 2003, LNCS 2736, pp. 171–181, 2003.

We believe that the current trend of XML claims for the extension of such approaches also to query massive XML data-sets. However, due to the intrinsically hierarchical structure of XML documents, summarizing a large XML database is substantially more difficult than constructing synopsis for flat, relational data [PG02].

A first approach in this direction is given by XSchetch [PG02], a graph model addressing the optimization of XML queries posed over large volumes of XML data: in [PG02] the authors construct synopsis structures for enabling the estimation of the path and branching distribution in the data graph to be used for the optimization of the original query.

With a different approach, we propose to summarize an XML document collection with the main aim to permit quick and approximate answers to queries. For this reason we attempt to obtain a synopsis with a structure as similar as possible to the original document, in order to combine conciseness of the data set and easiness of query formulation.

While our whole research involves techniques for such transparent query transformation, as well as methods for estimating the error produced by the evaluation of the query on the synopsis instead of the original data, in this paper we concentrate on document transformation criteria and methods, in order to summarize information in a way as close as possible to the original data intention.

This paper is organized as follows: in Section 2 we analyze the construction of the XML synopsis and outline an algorithm for its automatic computation. We first determine the synopsis structure expressed by its DTD, and then compute the summarized XML collection. In Section 3 we show some examples of query transformations at work. Finally, in Section 4 we draw the conclusions.

2   Representing Summarized XML Data

Following a common use, we represent XML documents as labelled trees $T = (V, E)$, where V is the node set comprising both nodes representing tags and nodes representing text content and attributes[1], and $E \subseteq V \times V$ represents elements and text containment arcs. The structure description of a document (i.e., its DTD) is also described as a labelled graph G_D using the same notation, while $\mathcal{G}_D = \{G_D^j\}$ is the set of graphs representing the DTD's of the whole document collection.

Given a set $\mathcal{T} = \{T_i\}$ of XML documents, an *XML synopsis* is obtained as a transformation $XMLtransf : \{T_1, ..., T_h\} \in \mathcal{P}(\mathcal{T}) \rightarrow \{T'_1, ..., T'_k\} \in \mathcal{P}(\mathcal{T})$, $k \leq h$ (often it will be $k \ll h$), where $\{T_1, ..., T_h\}$ share the same DTD. Their summarization produces a (small) number of documents conforming to one or more new DTDs, which we call *synopsis DTDs* (DTD_{syn}). They can be obtained

---

[1] Attributes will not be explicitly handled in this paper: however, if a literal semantics [GR99] for the representation of XML documents is adopted, they can be treated as a particular case of PCDATA elements.

as a transformation $DTDtransf : \mathcal{G}_\mathcal{D} \to \mathcal{P}(\mathcal{G}_\mathcal{D})$ on the DTD of the initial set of documents.

2.1 Computation of the Synopsis DTD

An XML synopsis is composed by a small collection of documents that store histograms instead of the data composing the original data-set. Each histogram stores the statistical distribution of the values of a certain element divided into disjoint sets called *buckets*, each one characterized by a frequency value (i.e., the number of elements falling in each bucket), and a boundary value(i.e., the highest value of each set, the data of the element are supposed ordered), which are different for each histogram type. The computation of (each) DTD_{syn} requires a *preliminary phase* aimed at analyzing the application aspects of the collection: the type of histogram for the current application and the set of elements to be summarized must be chosen.

Type of Histogram. The type of histogram to use for summarizing the content of a collection of XML documents (such as, for example, the *equi-width* or the *equi-height* histogram [BD01]) must be chosen according to the application and to the kind of data contained in the XML documents collection. For example, if XML data describe categories such as names, colors etc. the equi-width histograms represent the most appropriate choice because each category may be represented by one bucket of the histogram.

The choice of the type of histogram impacts the resulting synopsis DTDs and also their computation. Indeed, depending on the type of histogram different data need to be stored in the XML synopsis. For example, in case of equi-height histograms the frequency value must be fixed; then, the number of buckets of the corresponding histogram and the boundary value of the bucket bv can be automatically computed[2]. Instead, in case of equi-width histograms, the designer has to decide how many buckets compose the histogram, by fixing the boundaries of each bucket. This kind of statistics is not significant if the boundaries are set automatically: usually, specific criteria are adopted to classify the population.

According to the data to be stored in the synopsis a *DTD of the histogram* DTD_H ($\subset DTD_{syn}$) can be defined, dictating the form of the histogram data that collects the statistics of the XML elements. For example, two different possible DTD_H, for the equi-height and for the equi-width histogram, respectively are:

DTD of an equi-height histogram:	DTD of an equi-width histogram:
`<!ELEMENT hist (frequency, bucket+)>`	`<!ELEMENT hist (bucket+)>`
`<!ELEMENT frequency (PCDATA)>`	`<!ELEMENT bucket (frequency, bv)>`
`<!ELEMENT bucket(bv)>`	`<!ELEMENT frequency (PCDATA)>`
`<!ELEMENT bv (PCDATA)>`	`<!ELEMENT bv (PCDATA)>`

---

[2] In most applications, if many buckets have the same boundary values, the equi-height histogram can be transformed into a *compressed* histogram, by collecting these buckets together.

In the DTD_H for the equi-height histogram, the <hist> node contains the elements for storing the buckets of the histogram and a single value for recording the frequency value, which is equal for all the buckets. Each bucket contains the element <bv>, which is its boundary value. On the other hand, in case of equi-width histograms DTD_H contains one frequency node for each bucket node.

Set of Elements to Summarize. The second decision to take in the preliminary analysis step consists in the identification of the set $E_s \subseteq E$ of elements to summarize.

We represent XML elements with their paths from the root of the document using a XPath [W3C99] notation, in order to distinguish elements with the same tag name but with different internal meaning (e.g., a person's home address is different from the address of the company the person belongs to).

Elements can be summarized in two different ways:

1. we can summarize each element content independently of the content of the other elements (*assumption of element independence*) or
2. we can summarize element values taking into account the values of other (related) elements (*assumption of dependent data*).

For example, we could summarize the content of the elements tagged "age" assuming that the age does not depend on any other value, or we could summarize them relating people's ages to the city where they live. Operationally, we will treat this second case by grouping the dependent elements w.r.t. the elements which they depend on and by calculating the statistics for the separate groupings.

Taking into account this distinction, each element $e \in E_s$ is formally represented as a pair $(pathe, \{pathg\})$, where $pathe$ is the path expression of the element to be summarized, and $\{pathg\}$ is a set of path expressions of the elements whereof $pathe$ is grouped in the summarization process. In case of element independence we have $\{pathg\} = \emptyset$. Usually, $pathe$ and $pathg$ will be leaf nodes, otherwise they will be considered as a shortcut for all their leaf descendant nodes (i.e., a non leaf element $pathe$ represents the set of all the paths $\{pathe\prime\}$, such that $pathe\prime$ is a leaf node and is a descendant of $pathe$). In the sequel we always consider the expanded version of E_s containing only leaf nodes.

E_s affects the structure of DTD_{syn}: for example, in case of independence assumption, a single histogram will be created for all the values of each given element in the document collection; in case of summarization with grouping, for each element a set of histograms will be collected, one for each grouping value.

Computation of the Synopsis DTD. After performing the two choices described above, DTD_{syn} can be computed by the algorithm (see Fig. 1)

$$\text{compute\_DTD}(DTD_{in}, E_{si}, \text{histType}) \rightarrow DTD_{syn},$$

where histType is the histogram type chosen for the application, while $E_{si} \subseteq E_s$ is a set of elements to be summarized, for which a single XML document is created.

$compute\_DTD(DTD_{in}, E_{si}, \text{histType})$
begin
   $DTD_{syn} = DTD_{in} \cup DTD_H(histType);$
   $DTD_{syn} = set\_card\_1(DTD_{syn}, e);$
   for each $(e \in E_{si})$
   {
      $patha = find\_lowest\_common\_ancestor(pathe, \{pathg\});$
      $DTD_{syn} = set\_card\_n(DTD_{syn}, patha);$
      $DTD_{syn} = convert\_leaves(pathe, DTD_{syn});$
   }
   for each ($path \in DTD_{syn}$)
   {
      if $(NOT(contains(E_{si}, path))ANDNOT(descendent(E_{si}, path)))$
      {
         $DTD_{syn} = \text{delete}(path, DTD_{syn});$
      }
   }
end.

Fig. 1. Algorithm for the construction of DTD_{syn}

The algorithm produces a single DTD_{syn} containing all the histograms produced by the different groupings specified in E_{si}. Usually the number of grouping criteria could be too high to summarize all the data into a single document in a readable and effective way. A better solution is to store separately different documents containing all the histograms produced by a grouping criterion, i.e., to break E_s into several subsets $E_{si} \subseteq E_s$, where each E_{si} contains *compatible* or *nested* $\{pathg\}$. The algorithm is applied to each E_{si} and generates a DTD_{syn} for each grouping criterion. Two grouping paths $Pathg' = \{pathg'_1, ...pathg'_k\}$ and $Pathg'' = \{pathg''_1, ...pathg''_m\}$, with $k < m$, are compatible if $Pathg' \subseteq Pathg''$. Now we are ready to define synopsis compatibility: two synopsis subgraphs represented by $e' = (pathe', Pathg')$ and $e'' = (pathe'', Pathg'')$ are *compatible* if and only if $pathe''$ is a descendant of $pathe'$ and $Pathg'$ is compatible with $Pathg''$.

The algorithm compute_DTD(DTD_{in}, E_{si}, histType) outlined in Fig. 1 computes the DTD_{syn} by modifying the structure of DTD_{in}. Indeed, due to the semi-structured nature of XML, the documents conforming to a given DTD may differ considerably one from another: there may be optional elements (whole branches may be absent in some documents) or repeatable elements that allow the presence of multiple branches. This multi-shape structure is the great difficulty to overcome when we try to summarize data from different documents. Consequently, the structure of the resulting DTD may slightly change. In particular some branches, which are present in DTD_{in}, may not appear in DTD_{syn}, while multiple branches are returned into one branch or some other branches change their cardinality from 1 to N. The algorithm starts by considering the original DTD and the structure of the histogram chosen for the application (DTD_H). Then, function set_card_1 sets all the cardinalities of the elements to 1. The other cardinalities are correctly set according to the elements in E_{si}: for each element $e \in E_{si}$, function find_lowest_common_ancestor identifies the lowest common ancestor *patha* among *pathe* and the elements in {*pathg*} and function `set_card_n` sets its cardinality to N, because one histogram for each grouping must be calculated. Notice that if {*pathg*} is empty, the cardinality of the element *pathe* remains equal to 1: indeed, only one histogram must be created. Then, function `convert_leaves` substitutes the PCDATA content of the element *pathe* with the `hist` node (and consequently the whole structure of DTD_H). Finally, the algorithm deletes each element in DTD_{syn} that does not belong to E_{si} and that is not an ancestor of an element in E_{si}: this means that the synopsis DTD will keep only the elements belonging to the paths of some *pathe* and *pathg*, while all the other elements can be ignored and are therefore deleted from the synopsis DTD.

Notice that the algorithm does not change the general structure of the resulting DTD: only cardinalities are modified and some elements that do not affect the summarization are deleted.

Running example. As an example consider the following DTD (DTD_{in}) describing a car store: cars are characterized by their model and color, and for each car the details of the customers who bought it are listed:

```
<? xml version = "1.0" ?>
<!ELEMENT store (car+)>
<!ELEMENT car(model, color, customer*)>
<!ELEMENT model (PCDATA)>
<!ELEMENT color (PCDATA)>
<!ELEMENT customer (name, payment, city, card)>
<!ELEMENT name (PCDATA)>
<!ELEMENT payment (PCDATA)>
<!ELEMENT city (PCDATA)>
<!ELEMENT card (PCDATA) #implied>
```

Suppose to use equi-width histograms (which are appropriate since most XML data represent categories such as colors, models, etc.) and that the set of elements E_s to summarize be: E_s={(store/car/color, {store/car/model}), (store/car/customer/city, {store/car/model}), (store/car/customer/payment, {store/car/model})}. so that colors, cities and payments be grouped by car model. Then, the execution of the algorithm produces the following synopsis DTD:

```
<? xml version = 1.0 ?>
<!ELEMENT store (car+)>
<!ELEMENT car (model, color, customer)>
<!ELEMENT model (PCDATA)>
<!ELEMENT color (hist)>
<!ELEMENT customer (city, payment)>
<!ELEMENT payment (hist)>
<!ELEMENT city (hist)>
<!ELEMENT hist (bucket+)>
<!ELEMENT bucket (frequency, bv)>
<!ELEMENT frequency (PCDATA)>
<!ELEMENT bv (PCDATA)>
```

Notice that the original path `store/car/model` (i.e., *pathg*) which is used to group colors, cities and payments has not been changed w.r.t. the original DTD and still contains PCDATA; instead, the contents of the elements in *pathe* (color, city and payment) have been replaced with the histogram element `hist`. The elements composing the histogram structure (buckets, frequency and bv) have also been added to DTD_{syn}.

According to the algorithm, the cardinality of element `car` in the synopsis DTD has been set to n (i.e., there is a subgraph for each value of `model`), the cardinality of `customer` has been set to 1, whereas elements name and card have been discarded.

Indeed, the algorithm fixes the correct cardinalities of the elements of the collection. If $Pathg \neq \emptyset$, elements must be collected with respect to the grouping element: a set of collections, one for each group, must be obtained and therefore the original cardinality of the element collection of these groups must be modified accordingly. In this example, the grouping element is `model`, but the element to be repeated is the common ancestor between this element and the elements `color`, `city` and `payment`, to be grouped: in all the three kinds of grouping the common ancestor is `car` and therefore its cardinality is set to N.

The elements which have been discarded belong neither to elements to be summarized nor to grouping elements. The only exception in the running example is represented by the `customer` elements: these are kept because they belong to the path of `payment`. Its original path is kept also in DTD_{syn}: unchanged paths help query formulation.

2.2 Synopsis Creation

Also the computation of the document synopsis, $DATA_{syn}$, requires a preliminary step, since the actual summarization depends on the application data: for each element in E_s the *parameters* needed to compute the histogram (e.g., the number of buckets or the frequency value) must be defined.

The parameters depend, of course, on the kind of histogram: in case of equi-height histogram the frequency value, i.e., the number of elements falling in each bucket, must be chosen. Then, the number of buckets of the corresponding histogram is obtained as n_b =(population of the element) / (number of items per bucket).

The highest value of each set (the collection is supposed to be ordered) is the boundary value of the bucket *bv*, which can be automatically computed.

Instead, in case of equi-width histograms the designer has to decide how many buckets compose the histogram, by fixing the boundaries of each bucket.

Given DTD_{syn}, the original data collection, and the parameters of the histograms, the synopsis can be automatically created.

The parameters of the histograms to be computed for each element $e \in E_{si}$ are represented by a set of tuples $P = \{(e, \{f^j\}, n_b, \{bv^j\})\}$, where $1 < j < n_b$, f is the frequency of the element e in bucket j, n_b is the number of its buckets and $\{bv^j\}$ is the set of n_b boundary values of the buckets of the element.

Computation of the Synopsis. For each element in E_{si} statistics are computed and the corresponding data are inserted in the synopsis, according to the structure defined by DTD_{syn}. The transformation is represented by the algorithm $compute\_synopsis(DATA_{in},\ P,\ E_{si}) \rightarrow DATA_{syn}$ in Fig. 2, where $DATA_{in}$ is the original data collection and P is the set of parameters necessary to construct the histograms required by the elements contained in E_{si}. First, the algorithm creates an empty XML document, then for each element $e \in E_{si}$ to be summarized, the function `extract_possible_g_values` creates a set of tuples: each tuple is a possible combination of values of the elements $\{pathg\}$. For each tuple of grouping values the function `collect_data` collects together the data of the collection of documents that correspond to e. Then, this data set (set_data) is used by the function `build_hist` to create the histogram according to the parameters $\in P$ corresponding to e and the values selected for $\{pathg\}$. Finally, the histogram data are added to $DATA_{syn}$ below the element with path $pathe$. Function `buildTree` adds to the tree also the paths $\{pathg\}$ with the values (set_values) that generated the histogram of $pathe$. An example of synopsis creation an be found in [CMT03].

```
compute_synopsis(DATA_in, P, E_i s) → DATA_syn
begin
DATA_syn = ∅;
for each (e ∈ E_si)
{
    set_values = extract_possible_g_values(DATA_in,{pathg});
    for each (tuple ∈ set_values)
    {
        set_data = collect_data(DATA_in, pathe, tuple);
        hist = build_hist(set_data, n_b, {f}, {bv});
        DATA_syn = buildTree(DATA_syn, pathe, {pathg}, tuple, hist);
    }
}
end.
```

Fig. 2. $compute_{doc}$ **algorithm**

3   Querying Summarized XML Data

The XML synopsis is created with the goal to facilitate query formulation. A query in our scenario is always expressed using the standard language XQuery, and the goal of our work is to develope an automatic transformation from an XQuery query specified over the original documents to the corresponding transformed XQuery query on the synopsis. We present the approach at work showing some query examples. Consider the query: *What is the average prize for a "Fiat Brava"?*

The query, formulated knowing only DTD_{in} and using the standard language XQuery is:

```
LET $p:=document("www.store.it")/store/car/model[text()="Fiat
    Brava"]/customer/payment
RETURN avg($p)
```

The query retrieves all the payment elements of the cars whose model is "Fiat Brava" and returns the average value of the set of payment values.

The query to be applied to the synopsis data does not change, except for the structure of the function *avg*, which must be computed on the histograms (*avg_hist*). The resulting query is, intuitively enough:

```
LET $p:=document("www.store.it")/store/car/model[text()="Fiat
    Brava"]/customer/payment
RETURN avg_hist($p)
```

Another example, a little more complicated than the previous one, is represented by: *Which is the city where we sold the largest amount of "Fiat Brava"?*

The query, formulated knowing only DTD_{in} and using the standard language XQuery is:

```
<list-cit-max-fiat-brav>
 let $distcit:= distinct-values(//store/car/customer/city)
 for $cit in $distcit
  let $brvcnt:=count(//store/car/model[text()="Fiat Brava"
                  and customer/city=$cit])
  where $brvcnt=max( for $c in $distcit
  return count(//store/car/model[text()="Fiat Brava" and
                  customer/city=$c]))
 return \$cit
</list-cit-max-fiat-brav>
```

The automatically transformed query is:

```
<list-cit-max-fiat-brav>
 let $distcit := distinct-values(//store/car/customer/city_hist)
 for $cit in $distcit
  let $brvcnt := count_hist(//store/car[model/text()="Fiat Brava" and
      customer/city_hist =$cit]/customer/city)
  where $brvcnt = max_hist( for $c in $distcit return
      count_hist(//store/car[model/text()="Fiat Brava" and
      customer/city_hist =$cit]/customer/city))
 return $cit
</list-cit-max-fiat-brav>
```

In the transformed query city_hist is a function that retrieves the value necessary inside the histogram. The function count_hist is created to compute the aggregate inside the histogram as $\sum_{bucket/bv} bucket/freq$ while the function max_hist returns the bucket with the highest frequency.

The transformation of the second query is not obvious as the first one. Our current work aims at capturing all these more complex cases in a uniform transformation algorithm.

4   Conclusions

In this paper we have proposed an approach to construct a synopsis of a huge set of XML documents, in order to reduce query computation time to the price of some impreciseness. The main idea of this approach is to construct a synopsis with a structure as similar as possible to the original documents structure, in order to facilitate and automate the query transformation from the original dataset to the synopsis. The paper focuses on the construction of the synopsis DTD and of the summarized collection itself and presents the querying problem at work. The approach has recently been tested using a data set generated by the benchmark XBench [XB] freely available on the Internet. Among the number of benchmarks for XML databases recently proposed such as XMach-1, XMark, X007 etc., which allow to capture different application characteristics, we chose to use XBench because it is a family of benchmarks studied to be application independent. The XBench database generator can generate databases ranging from 10MB to 10GB in size. As future work we plan to formalize the architecture of a demo prototype, to formalize and implement the automatic transformation of the query and its optimization, and to estimate the error resulting for query applied to summarized data.

References

[BD01]   Q. A. Bamboat and O. Dunemann. Obtaining quick results for approx-
           imate answers. In *Proc. of SCI 2001 and ISAS 2001*, Orlando, Florida,
           2001.
[CMT03]   S. Comai, S. Marrara, and L. Tanca. Representing and querying summa-
           rized xml data. Technical report, Politecnico di Milano, 2003.
[Con98]   W3C Consortium. Xml 1.0, Feb. 1998. http://www.w3.org/XML.
[CVV]   http://www.xyleme.com.
[EXC]   http://www.excelon.com.
[GM99]   Phillip B. Gibbons and Yossi Matias. Synopsis data structures for mas-
           sive data sets. *DIMACS: Series in Discrete Mathematics and Theoretical
           Computer Science: Special Issue on External Memory Algorithms and Vi-
           sualization*, A, 1999.
[GR99]   Widom J. Goldman R., McHugh J. From semistructured data to xml:
           Migrating the lore data model and query language. In *Proc. WebDb*,
           pages 25–30, 1999.
[JAKL⁺ 02] H. Jagadish, S. Al-Khalifa, L. Lakshmanan, A. Nierman, S. Paparizos,
           J. Patel, D. Srivastava, and Y. Wu. Timber: A native xml database,
           2002.
[PG02]   N. Polyzotis and M. Garofalakis. Statistical synopses for graph-structured
           xml databases. In ACM, editor, *Proc. ACM SIGMOD Conference*, Madi-
           son,Wisconsin,USA, 2002.
[QL9]   Ql'98 query languages 1998. http://www.w3.org/TandS/QL/QL98.
[SS01]   D. Chamberlin D. Florescu J. Robie J. Simeon and M. Stefanescu.
           Xquery: A query language for xml., 2001.
           http://www.w3.org/TR/xquery/.

[TAM98]   1998. http://www.tamino.com.
[VIR]   Virtuoso. http://www.openlinksw.com/virtuoso.
[W3C99]   W3C. Xml path language (xpath) version 1.0, 1999.
           http://www.w3.org/TR/xpath.
[XB]   http://db.uwaterloo.ca/ ddbms/projects/xbench/index.html.

Storing and Querying XML Data in the Nested Relational Sequence Database System

Ho Lam Lau and Wilfred Ng

Department of Computer Science
The Hong Kong University of Science and Technology
{lauhl,wilfred}@cs.ust.hk

Abstract. We developed the Nested Relational Sequence Database System (NRSD System), which is built upon the Nested Relational Sequence Model (NRSM). The NRSM eliminates a substantial amount of redundancy embedded in XML documents and preserves the order of XML data. In this paper, we demonstrate that the storing and querying of XML data are desirable over an NRS relation, which we incorporate an index system into the NRSD System. We introduce a set of NRS operations which allow users to manipulate the XML data effectively and demonstrate how to use NRS operations to query the XML data stored in the NRSD System. Our experimental results confirm that the NRSD System substantially reduces the storage size of data. We also study the performance of the select and project operations having path expressions at different nested levels.

1   Introduction

We have proposed the Nested Relational Sequence Model (NRSM) in [3,4], which is an extension of the well-established Nested Relational Data Model (NRDM) [2,6] in order to cater for nesting structure and node ordering of XML data. The NRSM supports composite and multi-valued attributes, which are essential for representing hierarchically structured data objects in XML documents. In addition, the NRSM extends the NRDM to support ordering of XML data elements and allows nested tuple sequences to be defined in an NRS relation.

We developed the NRS Database System (NRSD System) [3,4], which is built upon the NRSM. An important feature of the system is that XML data that share the same path expression can be merged together and store in the same *index table*, and thus, eliminates a substantial amount of redundancy in XML documents. Another feature of the NRSD System is that it preserves the value, sibling and ancestor orders which are illustrated in Figure 1. In the sequel we will explain how these features are preserved in the NRSD System by using an indexing scheme. We also present the experimental results concerning the resources needed for storing XML documents and the performance of the *select* and *project* operations on various path expressions.

V. Mařík et al. (Eds.): DEXA 2003, LNCS 2736, pp. 182–191, 2003.

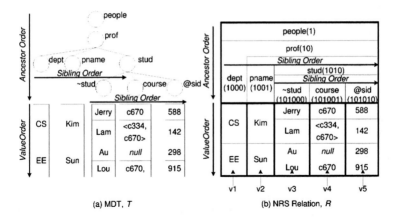

Fig. 1. (a)A MDT and (b) its corresponding NRS relation

2   The Nested Relational Data Model

Like the NRDM, the NRSM supports composite and multi-valued attributes, which are essential for representing hierarchically structured information such as XML data. In the NRSM, XML data are stored in the NRS relations. The representation of NRS relations is similar to the Nested Tables (NTs) of the NRDM, which contains multiple rows and columns. The NRS relations inherit the desirable features of the NTs, such as minimizing redundancy of XML data in a document and having more expressive power than conventional relations. We represent an XML document as a *merged data tree* (MDT), where leaf nodes are sequences of data values, called the *data nodes*, and non-leaf nodes are the labels of the XML tags and attributes, called the *label nodes*. The MDT is different from the DOM tree proposed in [8] in the following way: the information in a MDT with the same tags are grouped together and the values are stored under the same label node.

The NRSM incorporates three types of order: (1) the value order resulting from the sequence of data elements in a data node; (2) the sibling order resulting from the left to right sides for those label nodes which share the same parent; (3) the ancestor order resulting from the tree levels of the label nodes. Figure 1 portrays the three types of orders in a MDT.

The NRSM preserves the original structure of XML documents, in general, they can be retrieved from NRS relations without loss of information. Descriptive information such as *comments* and *processing instructions* can also be stored in an NRS relation. The proposed mapping algorithms [3,4] between XML documents and NRS relations are straightforward enough to implement on Oracle, as adopted in our NRSD System. If an XML document is not associated with a DTD, we extract an approximated DTD from the input XML document. The extracted DTD provides a basis for constructing the corresponding NRS schema. A benefit resulting from this approach is that if several XML documents of simi-

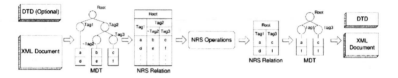

Fig. 2. Mapping an XML document into an NRS relation and retrieve XML data using NRS operations

lar structures are combined into a single NRS relation, we are able to generate an optimized DTD for them. Figure 2 demonstrates the mapping between an XML document and an NRS relation. After we have mapped an XML document into a MDT, we can generate the corresponding NRS relation. The XML semantics and the order of the document structure are preserved in both MDTs and NRS relations and the mapping between MDTs and NRS relations is reversible. After an XML document is transformed into its corresponding NRS relation, we can then apply a sequence of NRS operations on the relations for retrieving the data.

3   Formulating Queries in the NRSD System

The target of the proposed XML query languages, such as XQuery [8] and XML-QL [1], is to query XML documents and they are not designed for the information stored in XML databases. We introduce a set of operations for the NRSM, called the *NRS operations*, which is a combination of the refinements of existing nested relation algebra [2,6] together with some newly defined operations such as the *rearrange* and *swap* operations in order to cater for order.

An *NRS expression*, denoted by *NRS Expr*, is defined by the following BNF syntax:

$NRS\ Expr ::= Op_{[Arugment]}(Range)$
$Op ::= \pi \mid \sigma \mid \eta \mid \mu \mid \uplus \mid \oplus \mid \ominus \mid \odot \mid \omega \mid \kappa \mid \chi \mid \varsigma \mid \Sigma \mid \alpha \mid \bot \mid \top \mid \cup \mid - \mid \times \mid \bowtie$
$PathExpr ::= PathExpr/Tag \mid PathExpr//Tag$
$Tag ::= tag\ labels \mid *$
$Argument ::= PathExpr \mid (ArgumentList) \mid Cast(Argument)$
$ArgumentList ::= PathExpr \mid ArgumentList, PathExpr$
$Cast ::= INT \mid CHAR \mid DATE$
$Range ::= PathExpr \mid BETWEEN\ PathExpr\ AND\ PathExpr$

Since all XML data are considered as strings in a document, we use the *Cast* function to convert the values from strings to other data types such as integers or dates. The NRS expressions do not have the *For-Each* clause, instead, the NRS expressions loop through each tuple specified by the *Range* argument. In the *Range* argument, the expressions *BETWEEN* and *AND* can be used to limit the range of a query in a declarative way. A set of NRS operations for manipulating the XML data stored in the NRSM is introduced in [3,4]. The operations are classified into the following six categories: (1) Nesting operations, (2) Ordering operations, (3) Basic operations, (4) Structure operations, (5) Binary operations, and (6) Aggregate operations.

3.1 Translating XQuery into NRS operations

The flexible and structured facilities of XQuery [8] have been recognized as an effective way to query XML data. Currently, we are able to translate the XQuery of the form "FOR-WHERE-RETURN", which is a fundamental form of XQuery expressions, into sequences of NRS operations. We now use the following XQuery expression to illustrate the translation.

```
FOR $b1 IN path1,
    $b2 IN path2,
    ...
    $bn IN pathn,
WHERE condition 1, condition 2,..., condition m
RETURN
<tag1>
{
    <tag2>$b1/resultPath1</tag2>
    <tag3>$b2/resultPath2</tag3>
    ...
}
</tag1>
```

Since a query may involve several XML documents, we need to map them into their corresponding NRS relations, $R_1, R_2, \ldots, R_n$, before we apply the NRS operations. After the mapping, the following query expressions are performed:

1. $S_1 \leftarrow \pi_{[path_1]}(R_1), S_2 \leftarrow \pi_{[path_2]}(R_2), ..., S_n \leftarrow \pi_{[path_n]}(R_n)$
2. $T_1 \leftarrow \sigma_{[condition_1]}(S_{i1}), T_2 \leftarrow \sigma_{[condition_2]}(S_{i2}), ..., T_m \leftarrow \sigma_{[condition_m]}(S_{im})$
3. $U \leftarrow \uplus_{(tag1(tag2,tag3))}$
4. $R_{result} \leftarrow \oplus_{(tag2=T1/path3,tag3=T2/path4,...)}(U)$

First, we translate the XQuery expression "FOR $\$b_i$ IN $path_i$" into a sequence of "π" operation and store the result into intermediate NRS relations $S_1, S_2, \ldots, S_n$. Then, based on the conditions stated in the clauses "WHERE $condition_1, condition_2, \ldots, condition_m$", we perform the "$\sigma$" operation on the involved intermediate NRS relations $S_1, S_2, \ldots, S_n$ and store the required data in the intermediate NRS relations $T_1, T_2, \ldots, T_m$. For example, if "$condition_i$" is equal to "$\$b/name = $ "abc"", we know that S_1 is involved and we perform the "σ" operation on S_1. The last step is to return the results in the specified format stated in the "RETURN" expression. To achieve this, we perform the "$\uplus$" operation to create a new NRS relation using the schema corresponding to the one stated in the XQuery "RETURN" expression and perform the "$\oplus$" operations to insert the corresponding results into the NRS relation.

3.2 Query Examples

We now give examples to demonstrate how to formulate queries using the NRS operations.

stud*		
~stud	course*	@sid
Jerry	c670	588
Lam	<c334, c670>	142
Au	-	298
Lou	c670	915

stud*		
~stud	course*	@sid
Jerry	c670	588
Lam	<c334, c670>	142
Lou	c670	915

stud*
~stud
Jerry
Lam
Lou

S T R_{result}

Fig. 3. Intermediate NRS relations for answering the query Q_1

Q_1. Return the names of the students who take the course "c670".
The query Q_1 can be formulated by the XQuery expressions as follows:

```
FOR $s IN document("sample.xml")people/prof/stud
WHERE $s/course = "c670"
RETURN $s/text()
```

We first transform the XML document "*sample.xml*" and its DTD into the corresponding NRS relation, R, which is shown in Figure 1 (b). Then we perform the following sequence of NRS expressions:

1. $S \leftarrow \pi_{(/people/prof/stud)}(R)$
2. $T \leftarrow \sigma_{(/stud/course="c670")}(S)$
3. $R_{result} \leftarrow \pi_{(/stud/\sim stud)}(T)$

For the sake of clarity, we use the intermediate NRS relations, S and T, to show the results in each processing step, as shown in Figure 3. We first perform the "π" operation "*people/prof/stud*" over R. Then we perform the "σ" operation according to the condition "*/stud/course = "c670""* over S. Finally, we perform the "π" operation "*/stud/~stud*" over T, which generates the required results R_{result} and transform it into the corresponding valid XML document as follows:

```
<!ELEMENT stud(#PCDATA)>
<stud>Jerry</stud>
<stud>Lam</stud>
<stud>Lou</stud>
```

Q_2. Create a new XML document with the format given below, where X is the number of professors, Y is the number of students in the department, and Z is the name of the department:

```
<university>
   <dept numP="X" numS="Y">Z</dept>
</university>
```

University		
Dept		
~dept	@numP	@numS

S

University		
Dept		
~dept	@numP	@numS
CS		
EE		

T

University		
Dept		
~dept	@numP	@numS
CS	1	2
EE	1	2

R_{result}

Fig. 4. Intermediate NRS relations for answering the query Q_2

The query Q_2 is formulated as the following sequence of NRS operations:

1. $S \leftarrow \uplus_{(university(dept(\sim dept,@numP,@numS))}$;
2. $T \leftarrow \oplus_{(university/dept/\sim dept=R/people/prof/dept)}(S)$;
3. $R_{result} \leftarrow \oplus_{(university/dept/@numP=\zeta(/people/prof/pname)(U))}(T)$
   $R_{result} \leftarrow \oplus_{(university/dept/@numS=\zeta(/people/prof/stud/\sim stud)(U))}(R_{result})$;
   where $U = \sigma_{(R/people/prof/dept=university/dept)}(R)$.

First, we create a new and empty NRS relation with the schema $university(dept(\sim dept, @numP, @numS))$ using the "$\uplus$" operation. Second, we insert the value of $dept$ corresponding to the $dept$ of R. Final, we use the "ζ" operation to find out the number of professors and students in the $dept$ and insert it into R_{result} using the "$\oplus$" operations. The intermediate NRS relations, S and T, are shown in Figure 4.

4   Developing the Indexing Scheme in the NRSD System

An NRS relation is stored as a set of *index tables (ITs)* in the NRSD System. The schema of the NRS relation is mapped to a *global index table (GIT)* and the data value are mapped to various *value index tables (VITs)*. For example, the MDT and NRS relation R_{sample} shown in Figure 1 is mapped into the ITs $= \{g, v_1, \ldots, v_5\}$ shown in Figure 5, where g is the GIT and $v1, \ldots, v5$ are the VITs.

In the NRSD System, we capture different kinds of order by representing order using index values, which further reduce the storage size. We use the *prefix matching* and the *dot-notation indexing strategies* to handle the orders of XML data in the NRSD System.

Prefix matching indexing is used in the GIT. We assign the root attribute with index 1 and for each child attribute, we assign $\lceil log_2 k \rceil$ bits to represent its sibling order, where k is the number of its sibling nodes, and concatenate it after the index of its parent. For example, in Figure 1, attribute *stud*, whose index is 1010, has three children, we assign two bits for each of its child attributes. The indexes of its children are coded as 101000(40), 101001(41) and 101010(42), which are shown in g of Figure 5. We apply the *longest bit match algorithm* to search for the parent of a sequence of nodes. The essential idea of the algorithm is to find out the *longest common prefix* of the indexes in an incremental manner.

g

index	name	child
1	people	2
2	prof	8,9,10
8	dept	v1
9	pname	v2
10	stud	41, 42, 43
33	~stud	v3
34	course	v4
35	@sid	v5

GIT = g

v1

index	name
1.1.1	CS
1.1.2	EE

v2

index	name
1.1.1	Kim
1.1.2	Sun

v3

index	name
1.1.1.1	Jerry
1.1.1.2	Lam
1.1.2.1	Au
1.1.2.2	Lou

v4

index	name
1.1.1.1	c670
1.1.1.2.1	c334
1.1.1.2.2	c670
1.1.2.2	c670

v5

index	name
1.1.1.1	588
1.1.1.2	142
1.1.2.1	298
1.1.2.2	915

VITs = {v1, v2, v3, v4, v5}

Fig. 5. The ITs developing for R_{sample}

In the VITs, the indexes are assigned by using the dot notation indexing. For example, the index for the *stud Lam* in $v3$ is 1.1.1.2. From table g, the path expression of $v3$ is "*people/prof/stud/~stud*". It represents the fact that *Lam* is the second *stud* of the first *prof*, who is the first *people* in the XML document.

Basically, we implement the NRS operations in the NRSD System following a sequence of generic actions. (1) Lookup the corresponding child attributes from the GIT by tracing the path expressions. (2) Perform queries over the corresponding VITs stated in the child attributes of the GIT. (3) Return the data required. For example, if we perform the "π" operation on *stud*, $\pi_{[/prof/stud]}(people)$. We lookup the GIT for the path *people/prof/stud* and know that it has three corresponding VITs having indexes: 40, 41 and 42. Therefore, we join the values from these three VITs according to their longest common prefix and return them into tuples. The two *course* of *stud Lam* are assigned with indexes 1.1.1.2.1 and 1.1.1.2.2, the longest common prefix is 1.1.1.2, which is in the same tuple of *stud Lam*. In order to avoid heavy overhead of the machine arising from referencing the GIT extensively. An in-memory tree is built for storing the global information for performing quick reference. In general, the size of the GIT is less then 0.1% of a given XML document and it does not impose significant burden on the main memory.

5   Preliminary Experimental Results

In order to show the effectiveness of the NRSD System, we have been running experiments using real life *DBLP* XML data [7] on the NRSD System. The data has maximum twelve child tags per element and four nesting levels in DBLP XML documents. The experiments are conducted on a computer of *Pentium III 550MHz* with 256MB RAM and 30GB hard disk.

Table 1. Experimental results of the NRSD System with different XML document sizes

Size of NRS schemas (bytes)	Number of all tables in Oracle DBMS	Table space including schema and table over-heads (kilobytes)	Input XML file size (kilobytes)	Percentage of table space re-quired
414	23	1,987	2,404	82.65%
1368	61	8,159	9,318	87.56%
1380	63	12,399	14,251	87.00%
1404	66	16,722	18,817	88.87%
1425	67	24,076	28.791	83.62%

5.1   Results for Storing XML Documents in the NRSD System

In the experiment, we load XML documents having different sizes into the NRSD System. Table 1 shows the results of our experiments, from which we can check that the table space required for storing an XML document is approximately 85% of its original size. With the growth of document size, the number of the ITs and the size of the GIT become stable. It is due to the fact that the NRSD System groups and stores the tags which share the same path expression, and represents orders using indexes. We remark that the size reduction is obtained without performing any compression on the database. This work can serve as a starting point for applying existing XML data compression technology [5] on the NRS relations. However, we are able to formulate queries in the NRSD System by using a set of NRS operations, which is difficult to perform such algebraic operations in a compressed domain. We are improving the grouping algorithm and trying to further decrease the table space for storing XML data in the NRSD System. The data size reduction in the NRSD System is useful in practice for exporting and exchanging XML database objects on the Web.

5.2   Results for Performing Select and Project Queries

In order to study the query performance of the NRSD System, we run six queries (E_1 to E_6) over three sample DBLP XML documents of sizes 8.8MB, 24MB and 36MB. The objective of the experiment is to test how path expressions affect the performance of the "π" and "σ" operations in the NRSD System, since they are fundamental in NRS query expressions. By studying their performance, we can understand how to optimize more complex queries. The queries used in the experiment are formulated as follows.

$$E_1 = \pi_{/dblp/inproceedings/author}(R)$$
$$E_2 = \pi_{//author}(R)$$
$$E_3 = \pi_{//inproceedings/}(R)$$
$$E_4 = \sigma_{/dblp/inproceedings/year='2000'}(R)$$
$$E_5 = \sigma_{//year='2000'}(R)$$
$$E_6 = \sigma_{[//year='2000',//author='Sun']}(R)$$

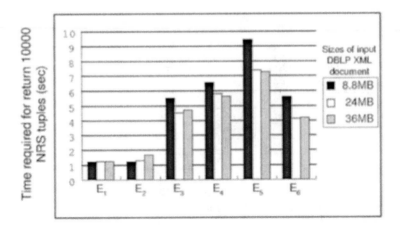

Fig. 6. Performance of the queries E_1 - E_6

E_1 and E_2 evaluate the performance of the "π" operation on full path expression and recursive path expression ($//$) respectively. E_3 evaluates the performance of the "π" operation that requires several outer join operations. E_4 and E_5 evaluate the performance of "σ" operation with a condition specified with full path expression and recursive path expression respectively. E_6 evaluates the "σ" operation with multiple conditions specified with recursive path expressions. We plot in Figure 6 the average time required for the NRSD System to output 10000 NRS tuples. From E_1 and E_2, we can see that the number of nesting levels does not significantly affect the running time of the queries. This is because the structure of the XML document stored as an in-memory tree saves the time for looking up the corresponding indexes from the GIT from the database. The NRSD System requires more time to return the results for queries E_3 - E_6. This is due to the fact that the NRS relation are stored in several VITs in the underlying Oracle DBMS, where join operations are performed to retrieve the data from the NRSD System. This finding urges us on further studying the issues of query optimization of the join operation. The select operation requires more time than the project operation, since we need to return the indexes that satisfied the select conditions. We also notice that from E_4 to E_6, when the document size is small, the ratio of the selecting overhead is high, since the number of tuples returned is small compared with large documents. One interesting observation is that, in E_6, we have two conditions and the number of returned tuples is limited, although the fraction of selecting overhead is still high, but the number of join operations required are smaller and therefore the results can be efficiently obtained.

6   Conclusions and Future Work

In this paper, we introduce the storage and manipulation of XML data in the NRSD System. The NRS relations are useful in storing XML data while allowing users to manipulate the structure and order of the XML documents. We also demonstrate with examples how to formulate XML queries in terms of NRS operations and to translate XQuery into a sequence of NRS operations. We believe that a more user-friendly and high level language similar to standard SQL can be developed on the basis of NRS operations. We also discuss the experimental results of the NRSD System and show that the table space required for storing XML data with the NRSD System is significantly less than the size of the original XML documents, which is mainly due to the fact that NRSM eliminates redundant data from the XML documents. We believe that compression can be further applied on the NRSM such that the storage size can be further reduced while preserving the querying facilities. We are improving the grouping algorithm on data nodes which have the same labels. We are still investigating the performance of other NRS operations apart from the project and select operations over NRS databases.

References

1. A. Detsch, M. Fernandez, D. Florescu, A. Levy and D. Suciu. *A Query Language for XML.* In: http://www.research.att.com/ mff/files/final.html, (1998).
2. H. Kitagawa and T. L. Kunii. *The Unnormalized Relational Data Model.* Springer-Verlag, (1989).
3. H. L. Lau and W. Ng. *Querying XML Data Based on Nested Relational Sequence Model.* In: Poster Proc. of WWW, (2002).
4. H. L. Lau and W. Ng. *The Development of Nested Relational Sequence Model to Support XML Databases.* In: Proc. of the International Conference on Information and Knowledge Engineering (IKE'02), pp. 374–380, (2002).
5. H. Liefke and D. Suciu, *XMILL: An efficient compressor for XML data.* In: Proc. of SIGMOD, vol. 29, pp. 153–164, (2000).
6. M. Levene. *The Nested University Relation Database Model.* Springer-Verlag, (1992).
7. M. Ley. *Digital Bibliography & Library Project.* In: http://dblp.uni-trier.de/, (2002).
8. World Wide Web Consortium. In: http://www.w3.org/, (2002).

Capturing Uncertainty in Spatial Queries over Imprecise Data

Xingbo Yu and Sharad Mehrotra

Shcool of Information and Computer Science,
University of California
Irvine, CA 92697, USA
{xyu,sharad}@ics.uci.edu

Abstract. Emerging applications using miniature electronic devices (e.g., tracking mobile objects using sensors) generate very large amounts of highly dynamic data that poses very high overhead on databases both in terms of processing and communication costs. A promising approach to alleviate the resulting problems is to exploit the application's tolerance to bounded error in data in order to reduce the overheads. In this paper, we consider imprecise spatial data and the correlation between the data quality and precision requirements given in user queries. We first provide an approach to answer spatial range queries over imprecise data by associating a probability value with each returned object. Then, we present a novel technique to set the data precision constraints for the data collecting process, so that a probabilistic guarantee on the uncertainty in answers to user queries could be provided. The algorithms exploit the fact that objects in two-dimensional space are distributed under certain distribution function. Experimental results are also included.

1 Introduction

With the rapid development of wireless communication devices and sensor networks, wide variety of applications that require efficient access to and management of dynamic spatial-temporal data have emerged. Examples include traffic control, vehicle navigation, battle field monitoring and mobile communication analysis. Due to the dynamic nature of the data, many issues [2] arise on collection, storage and query of such data.

In many such applications, data is generated at a rapid rate(often continuously). It raises significant challenge for the database server where data is stored, as well as the communication networks through which the data flows to the server. Existing data management systems, as well as communication networks do not possess the bandwidth and capability required to sustain the data generating rate. The problem is further exacerbated when bandwidth is limited or network wireless electronics(e.g. sensors) have limited resource(e.g. power). Recent research has provided various techniques, including compression and model adaptation [3]. Deliberately accepting approximate data is another important

V. Mařík et al. (Eds.): DEXA 2003, LNCS 2736, pp. 192–201, 2003.

approach to reduce data size and associated cost, if the imprecision could be tolerated by user applications posed on the collected data.

In this paper, we consider the situation in which users have specific requirements on the accuracy/certainty of the answers. The problem we address is how data precision can be set during data collection so as to meet the application requirement. Other issues related to how the spatial-temporal data can be stored at the server(see [10] and [11]) or indexing approaches to optimize query performance(see [14], [15] and [13]) are not considered.

The rest of the paper is organized as follows: In next the section, we provide a formal description on the problems we are going to address. Section 3 illustrates how uncertainty from imprecise data could be propagated to and presented in query answers. In section 4, we present our proposed algorithms on setting precision requirements to guarantee small uncertainty in answering user queries. Experimental results are presented in section 5. Section 6 concludes the paper.

2   Problem Formulation

The first problem we will discuss deals with answering range queries with imprecise cached data. Let e represent the imprecision of a object location. If we know from the database the object location at certain time instant, its real physical location may be at any point within a distance of e from that cached location. Thus, an object location could be represented graphically using a circle area(referred as "uncertain area" henceforth). In another word, a point object will be represented by an object with physical extent. The probability density distribution of the exact object location in the circle area should be decided by the data collection process. In this paper, we make the assumption that a given object is equally likely to be anywhere in its uncertain area.

Let R represent a query region. A typical range query is "return all the objects that are located in R". A $COUNT$ query is "return the number of objects that are located in R". Due to the fact that there exists uncertainty with the exact location of objects, it is impossible to provide exact answers to these queries. In section 3 we discuss how to process these queries. Here we introduce a couple of more concepts to facilitate later discussions.

$MUST$ set: The set of objects that "must" be located within the query range.
MAY set: The set of objects that "may" be located within the query range.
ANS set: It is the approximate answer set of objects whose cached locations are in the query region.

We further represent the number of objects in a $MUST$ set as N_s, number of objects in a MAY set as N_m, and number of objects in an ANS set as N_q.

Absolute Uncertainty δ_a: δ_a is the size of MAY set ($\delta_a = N_m$).
Relative Uncertainty δ_r: δ_r is the ratio of N_m to N_q ($\delta_r = \frac{N_m}{N_q}$).

In our second problem, we assume that there is a requirement on the degree of uncertainty that could appear in answering user queries. The task is to set precision constraints to all location data(e.g. using a quality-aware data collection middleware), so that the specified requirement is satisfied. Formally, the problem can be stated as:

Given a requirement that the answer to a random range COUNT query on objects in a two-dimensional space should have uncertainty $\delta \leq \delta_0$ with probability $P \geq P_0$, find the largest possible imprecision value e for all location data.

δ_0 and P_0 are constants specified by users or database servers. Some times, we also refer to P_0 as the confidence level. Although in this paper we address how to solve the above problem based on *COUNT* queries, other type of aggregate queries could be handled in a similar way. We solve this problem using probabilistic analysis in section 4.

3   Answer Range Queries over Imprecise Data

In this section, we show how to answer the two range queries described earlier. Although the process is straightforward, the format of results is important for further discussions in the later sections. Here different objects may have different imprecision e. Note although we assume a uniform probability distribution of object location across the uncertain area, any type of known probability distribution is applicable.

3.1   Return Objects in a Given Range

The task of returning objects within a given query range can be accomplished by modifying the traditional spatial query processing technique that deploys tree structures. The first modification is that the point objects are now represented by objects with non-zero extents—the uncertain area with radius e(see figure 1). To handle the fact that some objects are not fully contained in the region, another modification is needed to associate each returned object with a probability value(p_i) to indicate how likely the object can really be in the query region.

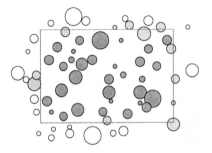

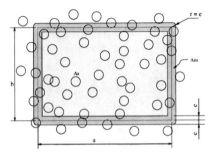

Fig. 1. Range Query over Imprecise Data (sets differentiated by colors)

Fig. 2. Effect of Imprecision e in Range Query

Probability value p_i is 1.0 for those objects whose uncertainty area is completely contained by the given query region. For objects whose uncertainty areas overlap with query region, p_i could be computed as the cumulative probability represented by the overlapping area. Under the assumption of uniform probability distribution, we have: $p_i = \frac{A_i}{\pi e^2}$, where A_i is the overlap area that can be computed from geometric parameters.

3.2   Return $COUNT$ of Objects in a Given Range

To answer $COUNT$ queries, the format of answers needs to be specified first. Possible options are $\{min, max\}$, $\{min, max, mean\}$, $\{min, max, mean, var\}$, and $\{(min, P_{min}), (min + 1, P_{min+1}), ..., (max, P_{max})\}$. Note that here we use upper case P to represent the probability that $COUNT$ takes a specific value. Lower case p is used to represent the probability with which an object could be in a query region. A server can produce all the information needed in the above answer formats, given its capability to answer the query discussed in section 3.1. Here we summarize the process to compute the above answers.

Let the first N_s objects in the answer set be the ones from $MUST$ set. Then, we know $p_i = 1$ for all $1 \le i \le N_s$. An immediate result is that $min = |MUST| = N_s$ and $max = |MUST| + |MAY| = N_s + N_m$. $Mean$ is summation of p_i's of all relevant objects. And $variance$ can be evaluated as:

$$variance = \sum_{k=0}^{N_s+N_m} P(COUNT = k)(k - mean)^2 \qquad (1)$$

The probability for individual $COUNT$ value can be computed by summation of probabilities of events that yield the $COUNT$. For example, below is the probability that $COUNT$ takes value of $min + 1$.

$$P(COUNT = N_s + 1) = \sum_{i,j=N_s+1}^{N_s+N_m} p_i[\prod_{j \neq i}(1 - p_j)] \qquad (2)$$

Among the four answer formats, the more detailed formats require more computation as well as larger answer sizes. Choosing a proper format should be a task of database server based on user requirements. In next section, we base our discussion on the second format.

4   Set Data Precision Constraints to Meet Application Requirements

As shown in the previous section, aggregate range queries can be answered in form of $\{min, max, mean\}$. For $COUNT$ query, $max - min$ is determined by information on the size of query range, object density in the area of interest, and the location data precision. Figure 2 illustrates the above factors under a typical query scenario. Intuitively, the smaller e is, the smaller the shaded area A_m is and thus the smaller the absolute uncertainty is. In this section, we develop a precision constraint on e so that we can have a probabilistic guarantee on uncertainty. Usually, high confidence on small uncertainty is desired.

There are many factors in the real world that complicate the problem. Certain assumptions have to be made to simplify the problem. First, we assume objects are uniformly distributed on the space of interest, with density known as d. In another word, any object is equally likely to appear anywhere in a given space. In most applications, locations of moving objects may display certain pattern(e.g., many vehicles are on highway 405). However, a space could be partitioned into different areas that approximately have uniform densities. For example, density of mobile phone users in a community area can be different from that on a campus. With the partitioning, data imprecision can be set differently for different areas. For the regions that contain parts of neighboring areas, data precisions can be set with the density that can provide conservative result. It is also possible for a specific application to estimate the upper and lower bound of object densities in the application scenario and choose a conservative bound for analysis. Density can be estimated by sampling the interested area. Second, we will set the same imprecision e to all location data. Although it could be more beneficial to set different imprecision to different object location data, the problem with various data precision will become very complicated. And that remains a topic of future work. We also assume a typical range query is over a range with dimension $a \times b$. And it could be positioned anywhere in the space.

4.1   Geometric Representation and Probabilistic Properties

We can visualize the MAY set and $MUST$ set in the answer to a range query by areas in figure 2. The inner rectangle area A_s in the figure corresponds to $MUST$ set. Similarly, the shaded area A_m corresponds to MAY set. All the objects falling outside of these areas are irrelevant. These conclusions are based on the observation that any circle centered within A_m must intersect with query window and the corresponding object has non-zero probability of both being within query region and being outside the region. Also notice that ANS set is represented by the query window R. Geometric calculations yield the following results: $A_s = (a - 2e)(b - 2e)$ and $A_m = 4(a + b)e - (4 - \pi)e^2$.

Corresponding to N_s, N_m, and N_q introduced earlier, we use n_s, n_m, and n_q to denote variables (not actual outcomes) of number of objects with cached locations in A_s, A_m, and query region respectively. From probability theory [1], we know that they are Poisson variables, with means of $\lambda_s = A_s d$, $\lambda_m = A_m d$, and $\lambda_q = abd$. In the following analysis, we first make an assumption that n_m and n_q are independent variables. This is valid when the overlap(hence, correlation) between A_m and R is small. When the assumption is not valid, we use heuristic method to improve the performance.

4.2   Probabilistic Guarantee on Absolute Uncertainty

The problem to be solved here is *"Find a constraint on e, such that with probability $P \geq P_0$, a randomly positioned range$(a \times b)$ COUNT query will be answered with $\delta_a \leq \delta_0$."*. The desired solution should be some constraint on e, such that $P(n_m \leq \delta_0) \geq P_0$. Since n_m is a Poisson variable with mean $\lambda_m = A_m d$, its probability density function and cumulative probability distribution function are:

$$P_{n_m} = \frac{e^{-\lambda_m} \lambda_m^{n_m}}{n_m!} \tag{3}$$

$$P(n_m \leq \delta_0) = \sum_{n_m=0}^{\delta_0} \frac{e^{-\lambda_m} \lambda_m^{n_m}}{n_m!} \tag{4}$$

We observe [1] that when λ_m becomes smaller, $P(n_m \leq \delta_0)$ gets larger. This observation of monotonicity tells us that if e_0 is the value of e such that $P(n_m \leq \delta_0) = P_0$, we will guarantee $P(n_m \leq \delta_0) \geq P_0$ when $e \leq e_0,$. Now the problem becomes to find the λ_m that enables $P(n_m \leq \delta_0) = P_0$. There exist many approaches to deal with this problem, including programs implementing numerical methods or employing Poisson Cumulative Probability Table. With λ_m computed, e_0 can be obtained by solving the equation: $[4(a+b)e - (4-\pi)e^2]d = \lambda_m$.

$$e_0 = \frac{4(a+b) - \sqrt{16(a+b)^2 - 4(4-\pi)\frac{\lambda_m}{d}}}{2(4-\pi)} \tag{5}$$

We conclude that $e \leq e_0$ is the desired constraint that guarantee, with probability P_0 or higher, a random COUNT query will be answered with absolute uncertainty $\delta_a \leq \delta_0$. Since we exploited the exact Poisson cumulative distribution in the above process, the e_0 so obtained is the optimal tight bound on e that satisfies the uncertainty constraint.

4.3   Probabilistic Guarantee on Relative Uncertainty

In this subsection, we will try to *"find a constraint on e, such that with probability $P \geq P_0$, a randomly positioned range$(a \times b)$ COUNT query will be answered with $\delta_r \leq \delta_0$."*. In a random query, δ_r is represented by $\frac{n_m}{n_q}$. The problem becomes to find a constraint on e such that $P(\frac{n_m}{n_q} \leq \delta_0) \geq P_0$. Since n_m and n_q are Poisson variables, we can develop cumulative probability function for $\frac{n_m}{n_q}$:

$$P(\frac{n_m}{n_q} \leq \delta_0) = \sum_{n_q=0}^{\infty} \sum_{n_m=0}^{\delta_0 n_q} p(n_m, n_q) \tag{6}$$

---

[1] One easy way to look at this is to use figures of cumulative functions with different means.

When n_m and n_q are independent, we can express $p(n_m, n_q)$ as $p(n_m)p(n_q)$:

$$P(\frac{n_m}{n_q} \leq \delta_0) = \sum_{n_q=0}^{\infty} \left(\frac{e^{-\lambda_q} \lambda_q^{n_q}}{n_q!} \cdot \sum_{n_m=0}^{\delta_0 n_q} \frac{e^{-\lambda_m} \lambda_m^{n_m}}{n_m!} \right) \tag{7}$$

Since n_q goes up to infinity, it is impossible to evaluate for exact cumulative probability $P(\frac{n_m}{n_q} \leq \delta_0)$. But we can approximate the value by observing the fact that when n_q becomes large, the element to be summed in the outer summation becomes very small. It is smaller than Poisson probability at value n_q. Obviously, the larger the upper bound of n_q, the more accurate the approximation is. Also note that the standard deviation of Poisson variable is square root of its mean $\sigma = \sqrt{\lambda}$. Then using $c\lambda_q$ as upper bound, where c is a constant larger than 1, should yield a good approximation that is *smaller* than exact value.

$$P(\frac{n_m}{n_q} \leq \delta_0) \cong \sum_{n_q=0}^{c\lambda_q} \left(\frac{e^{-\lambda_q} \lambda_q^{n_q}}{n_s!} \cdot \sum_{n_m=0}^{\delta_0 n_q} \frac{e^{-\lambda_m} \lambda_m^{n_m}}{n_m!} \right) \tag{8}$$

With this approximation, we can find λ_m that will guarantee $P(\frac{n_m}{n_q} \leq \delta_0) \geq P_0$. And the corresponding $e = e_0$ can be evaluated using formula 5. Again, numerical method should be deployed for finding $\lambda_m(e_0)$. In our experiment, we search for $\lambda_m(e_0)$ starting from $\lambda_m = \delta_0 \lambda_q$ when $P_0 \geq 0.5$. This is enabled by the fact that the cumulative probability function is a monotonic function of λ_m(hence, e_0).

We have so far showed how to set imprecision constraints on location measurements so that a probabilistic guarantee could be provided on the answers to random user queries. Between the two uncertainties we have defined, since approximation is applied and correlation plays a role in developing bound with relative uncertainty, the bound is not as tight as the one for absolute uncertainty. On the other hand, relative uncertainty guarantee could still be preferred by users, since people tend to have a percentage concept in mind.

5   Empirical Evaluation

In this section, we study the performance of the proposed algorithms for providing probabilistic guarantees through simulation. We compare the simulation results of probability that a random query will be answered under given uncertainty constraints with desired confidence values.

Data: In the simulation, we set the space of interest to be 100×100 in two dimensions. The unit is not specified and it could vary from application to application. Queries are randomly positioned in the 100×100 space and they are all in same size—10×10. However, we change the object density(which is uniform) from 0.05/square unit to 10/square unit. From statistics point of view, changing query window size and changing object density have the same effect on theoretical analysis, since both result in a change in the mean value.

Experiments on Various Densities: Our first experiment is done by varying the density, while fixing the uncertainties at 10 or 10% and fixing the confidence requirement at $P_0 = 0.90$, and computing tolerated imprecision value e. Then simulations are conducted to count the numbers of returned objects in different sets, N_m and N_q, for each randomly generated query. The number of trials is set to be 10000. This simulation gives us insight about how the algorithms behave with different densities(thus, mean λ_q). Figure 3 shows the computed

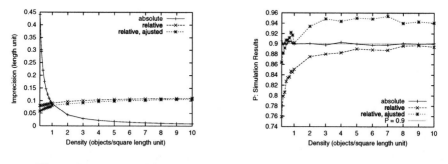

Fig. 3. Imprecision Values   **Fig. 4.** Simulation Results

imprecision values and figure 4 shows the simulation results. It is easy to see that the algorithm performs extremely well for absolute uncertainty constraint. But for relative uncertainty constraint, the result is good only for large density values and deteriorate when the density becomes smaller and smaller. This can be understood, however, with a re-examination of the independence assumption between n_m and n_q. The assumption is valid only when the overlap between MAY region and query region R is small and there are large number of objects in query region. But when λ_q is small, the correlation between n_m and n_q becomes too significant to be ignored. We adopt heuristic methods to improve the performance. The curve "relative, adjusted" in above figures show the effect of an adjustment, which is to use $P_0 \geq 0.95$ for constraint requirement $P_0 \geq 0.90$. After this adjustment, for most of the densities larger than 0.5/square unit yield good results. Experimental results show that a very small decrease in e will produce significant improvement on the confidence level. Although the results from adjustments are not optimal, they are very close to optimal (which should be a curve between the two "relative" curves) as shown in figure 3.

Experiments on Different Confidence Levels: Figure 5 and figure 6 show us empirical results on different confidence levels ranging from 0.80 to 1 with fixed uncertainties ($\delta_a = 10$ or $\delta_r = 10\%$) and density ($d_0 = 1$). Again, results for absolute uncertainty are very good. The adjusted experiments are done by increasing the confidence level by 5% percent for P_0 values below 0.90 and increasing less(up to $0.96, 0.97, 0.98, 0.99, 0.995, 1$, respectively) for other confidence values. And the results are conservative after the adjustments.

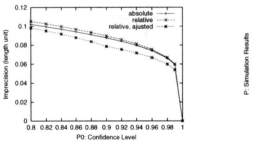
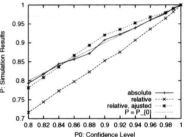

Fig. 5. Imprecision Values   **Fig. 6.** Simulation Results

6   Related Work

The authors are not aware of any work on calibrating data for probabilistic uncertainty guarantees in the domain of spatial range query. There are two closely related areas, uncertainty management in information system and quality-aware data collection, where substantial amount of research work has been conducted.

Uncertainty management in information system([5], [4]) deals with the uncertainty management and reasoning in an information system. The work in section 3 of this paper can be viewed as a specific example of uncertainty management in the domain of spatial range queries using probabilistic method. As a contrast, [12] handled uncertainty in spatial database domain using method of fuzziness. But the major contribution of this paper is on how to control the introduction of uncertainty into an information system, which has not been addressed in the area.

Quality-aware data collection is the most closely related work to this paper. In this area, quality/precision requirements of query answers and quality in raw data are connected, with the ultimate goal of satisfying query requirements while minimize certain cost. For example, Yu et al. [6] addressed network monitoring problems in which certain aggregate values in a network are approximated. Olston et al. [9] provided an adaptive data collection protocol to collect data with certain precision requirements so that the application quality requirements of a set of continuous queries could be met and the total communication cost for collecting the data is minimized. However, most of the works in this area have been concentrated on deterministic guarantees of user requirements. Usually in the context of real time applications, more accurate data is available with more cost. In contrast, in our problem, queries are on data collected before and thus the precisions have been fixed.

There are also some other uncertainty-related works in literature. Schneider [7] introduced fuzziness into the modeling of spatial data. Pfoser et al. [8] addressed a problem in which the uncertainty is caused by low sampling rate. These works are all different from our approach or our problem setting.

7   Conclusion

In this paper, we first described a query processing technique for aggregate range queries over imprecise data. Then we presented algorithms to set precision constraints on spatial data collection process to meet uncertainty constraints when the data are used to answer user queries. The guarantees are probabilistic and are discussed under the scenarios of using either absolute uncertainty or relative uncertainty. Both theoretical analysis and experimental results showed that the probabilistic guarantee based on absolute uncertainty yields a tighter bound which enables larger tolerated data imprecision. And simple adjustments on relative uncertainty method can be applied to improve its performance.

Acknowledgments. Our work was supported by the National Science Foundation (Awards IIS-9996140, IIS-0086124, CCR-0220069, IIS-0083489) and by the United States Air Force (Award F33615-01-C-1902).

References

1. S. Ross. A First Course in Probability. *Prentice Hall*, 2002.
2. O. Wolfson, B. Xu, S. Chamberlain, L. Jiang. Moving Objects Databases: Issues and Solutions. *SSDBM* 1998: 111–122.
3. I. Lazaridis, S. Mehrotra. Capturing Sensor-Generated Time Series with Quality Guarantees. *International Conference on Data Engineering (ICDE)*, March, 2003.
4. F. Sadri. Modeling Uncertainty in Databases. *Proceedings of the Seventh IEEE International Conference on Data Engineering*, April, 1991.
5. C. E. Dyreson. A Bibliography on Uncertainty Management in Information Systems. *Uncertainty Management in Information Systems: From Needs to Solutions, Kluwer Academic Publishers*, 1997: 415–458.
6. H. Yu, A. Vahdat. Efficient Numerical Error Bounding for Replicated Network Services. *VLDB* 2000: 123–133.
7. M. Schneider. Uncertainty Management for Spatial Data in Databases: Fuzzy Spatial Data Types. *SSD* 1999: 330–351.
8. D. Pfoser, Christian S. Jensen. Capturing the Uncertainty of Moving-Object Representations. *SSD* 1999: 111–132.
9. C. Olston, J. Jiang, and J. Widom. Adaptive Filters for Continuous Queries over Distributed Data Streams. *To appear: SIGMOD* 2003.
10. M. Erwig, R. Hartmut, M. Schneider, M. Vazirgiannis. Spatio-Temporal Data Types: An Approach to Modeling and Querying Moving Objects in Databases. *GeoInformatica 3(3)*, 1999: 269–296.
11. M. Vazirgiannis, O. Wolfson. A Spatiotemporal Model and Language for Moving Objects on Road Networks. *SSTD* 2001: 20–35.
12. M. Vazirgiannis. Uncertainty Handling in Spatial Relationships. *SAC (1)* 2000: 494–500.
13. S. Saltenis, C. S. Jensen, S. T. Leutenegger, M. A. Lopez. Indexing the Positions of Continuously Moving Objects. *SIGMOD* 2000: 331–342.
14. Y. Theodoridis, T. K. Sellis, A. Papadopoulos, Y. Manolopoulos. Specifications for Efficient Indexing in Spatiotemporal Databases. *SSDBM* 1998: 123–132.
15. G. Kollios, D. Gunopulos, V. J. Tsotras. On Indexing Mobile Objects. *PODS* 1999: 261–272.

Effective Load-Balancing via Migration and Replication in Spatial Grids

Anirban Mondal, Kazuo Goda, and Masaru Kitsuregawa

Institute of Industrial Science
University of Tokyo,
Japan
{anirban,kgoda,kitsure}@tkl.iis.u-tokyo.ac.jp

Abstract. The unprecedented growth of available spatial data at geographically distributed locations coupled with the emergence of *grid computing* provides a strong motivation for designing a *spatial grid* which supports fast data retrieval and allows its users to *transparently* access data of *any* location from *anywhere*. This calls for efficient search and load-balancing mechanisms. This paper focusses on dynamic load-balancing in spatial grids via data *migration/replication* to prevent degradation in system performance owing to severe load imbalance among the nodes. The main contributions of our proposal are as follows. First, we view a spatial grid as comprising several clusters where each cluster is a local area network (LAN) and propose a novel *inter-cluster load-balancing* algorithm which uses migration/replication of data. Second, we present a novel scalable technique for dynamic data placement that not only improves data availability but also minimizes disruptions and downtime to the system. Our performance study demonstrates the effectiveness of our proposed approach in correcting workload skews, thereby facilitating improvement in system performance. To our knowledge, this work is one of the earliest attempts at addressing load-balancing via both *online* data migration and replication in grid environments.

1   Introduction

Spatial data occurs in several important and diverse applications associated with resource management, development planning, emergency planning and scientific research. Given the unprecedented growth as well as the growing importance of available spatial data at geographically distributed locations and the tremendous increase in globalization, the need for efficient networking of such data with a view towards increased data availability has never been greater. Interestingly, the emergence of *grid computing*[5] coupled with large and powerful computer networks, which have the capability to connect thousands of geographically distributed computers worldwide, has opened a world of opportunities for such networking. Grid computing relates to the massive integration and virtualization of geographically distributed computing resources, thereby enabling a grid user to see a unified image of a single *powerful* virtual computer. Scientific applications

V. Mařík et al. (Eds.): DEXA 2003, LNCS 2736, pp. 202–211, 2003.

that require virtual collaboration across the globe would benefit tremendously by deploying grids. For example, if Earth scientists could have better access to data at geographical locations that are thousands of kilometres away from their current location, their ability to compare and contrast data from distant locations would facilitate optimal exploitation of the Earth's resources. This provides a strong motivation for designing a *spatial grid* which provides acceptable response times for user queries and allows its users to access data of *any* location from *anywhere* without having to bother about the details of the procedures that mediate their access to the data.

However, several challenging issues need to be addressed for the spatial grid to work efficiently in practice. In particular, mechanisms for efficient search and effective load-balancing need to be in place. This paper focusses on dynamic load-balancing in spatial grids via *data movement* to prevent degradation in system performance owing to severe load imbalance among the nodes. (By *data movement* we mean *data migration/replication*). *Online* load-balancing strategies are preferable for availability reasons. Incidentally, issues concerning load-balancing are more complex in case of grids than for traditional domains primarily because a grid usually spans across several administrative domains. The implication is that the data at each administrative domain are likely to be managed by different administrators, thereby possibly signifying different administrative policies for indexing, load-balancing and detection of hotspots at different domains, thus exacerbating the problems associated with load-balancing. For search in grids, we adopt the technique that we had proposed in [9]. However, any existing search mechanism for grids (with possibly some modifications) may be used in conjunction with our load-balancing strategy.

Incidentally, our problem of load-balancing via data movement in spatial grids differs significantly from that of load-balancing in peer-to-peer (P2P) systems. First, moving one tuple of a spatial database entails data movement *at most* in the Kilobyte range, while P2P data movements are usually in the Megabyte range or even in the Gigabyte range, the implication being that the cost of data movement is different in these two cases. Second, for spatial grids, hot regions of data need to be moved for load-balancing purposes with a view towards preventing *scattering* of data, while in case of P2P systems, individual hot data items need to be moved and *data scattering* is not really a concern. Third, in case of spatial grids, individual nodes are usually dedicated and they may be expected to be available most of the time, while for P2P systems, nodes may join or leave arbitrarily at any point of time. Fourth, there is some degree of control over the individual clusters in spatial grids since it is likely that they are owned by the same organization, while for P2P systems, the individual nodes in the clusters are usually distributively owned, thereby precluding the possibility of any kind of centralized control.

The main contributions of our proposal are as follows.

- We view a spatial grid as comprising several clusters where each cluster is a local area network (LAN) and propose a novel inter-cluster load-balancing algorithm which uses migration/replication of data.

– We present a novel scalable technique for dynamic data placement that not only improves data availability but also minimizes disruptions and downtime to the system.

Our performance study demonstrates the effectiveness of our proposed approach in correcting workload skews, thereby facilitating improvement in system performance. To our knowledge, this work is one of the earliest attempts at addressing load-balancing via both *online* data migration and replication in grid environments. The remainder of this paper is organized as follows. Section 2 provides a brief overview of related work, while Section 3 presents an overview of our proposed system framework. Issues concerning data movement are presented in Section 4. The proposed load-balancing strategy is discussed in Section 5, while Section 6 reports our performance evaluation. Finally, we conclude in Section 7.

2   Related Work

Representative examples of important ongoing grid computing projects include the Earth Systems Grid (ESG)[6], the NASA Information Power Grid (IPG)[8], the Grid Physics Network (GriPhyN)[11] and the European DataGrid[2]. While the ESG project aims at facilitating detailed analysis of huge amounts of climate data by a geographically distributed community via high bandwidth networks, the IPG project attempts to improve existing systems in NASA for solving complex scientific problems efficiently. The GriPhyN project and the European DataGrid project both aim at employing grid systems for improving scientific research which require efficient distributed handling of data in the petabyte range. Keeping in mind the demanding I/O needs of grid applications, the work in [14] proposes the binding of execution and storage sites together into I/O communities that participate in the wide area system. The proposal in [13] describes a data-movement system (Kangaroo) which makes opportunistic use of resources (disks and networks), while hiding network storage devices behind memory and disk buffers such that background processes handle data movements.

Static load-balancing approaches [1] typically attempt to perform an intelligent initial declustering of data. Incidentally, the tile technique [10] is a commonly used declustering method for performing static load-balancing of spatial data. It works as follows. Assuming that there are P nodes in the system, the universe is first decomposed into P partitions and each of these P partitions is assigned to a different node. Then the universe is divided into T rectangular tiles of equal size such that $T \geq P$ and each tile is mapped to a partition using a hash function. Note that disjoint regions may be assigned to the same node. Several dynamic load-balancing techniques [9,15], which adaptively balance the system load across the nodes during runtime, have also been proposed. However, *none* of these works are adequate for load-balancing in heterogeneous grid environments since they do *not* take into account grid-specific issues such as heterogeneity. A notable exception to these works is the Condor system [4] which uses job (process) migration for load-balancing purposes via a 'flocking' mechanism in which multiple Condor clusters worldwide collaborate in load-sharing activities.

However, process migration necessitates overheads (e.g., saving the status of a process) and can be expected to be extremely challenging, especially when the movement happens to be across different operating systems, which is often the case for grid environments. Note that our strategy differs from that of Condor since we load-balance via data migration/replication as opposed to job (process) migration.

3   System Overview

This section discusses an overview of the proposed system. In the interest of amenability, we envisage the spatial grid as comprising several clusters, where each cluster is a LAN. (Nodes are assigned to clusters such that the clusters are mutually disjoint.) This facilitates the separation of concerns between intra-cluster and inter-cluster load-balancing issues. At the very outset, we define *distance* between two clusters as the communication time τ between the cluster leaders and if τ is less than a pre-specified threshold, the clusters are regarded as *neighbours*. (Since cluster leaders will collaborate, their communication time is critical.) Also, we define a node P_i as *relevant* to a query Q if it contains at least a non-empty subset of the answers to Q, otherwise P_i is regarded as *irrelevant* w.r.t. Q. Additionally, we define a cluster as being *active* with respect to Q if *at least* one of its members is still processing Q. Notably, unlike replication, migration implies that once hot data have been transferred to a destination node, they will be **deleted** at the source node.

Most existing works define a node's load as the number of requests directed to that node, the implicit assumption being that *all* requests are of equal size, but this does *not* always hold good in practice. To take varying request sizes as well as the variations in processing capacity of different nodes into account, we define the load of node P_i, L_{P_i}, as follows.

$$L_{P_i} = D_i \times (CPU_{P_i} \div CPU_{Total}) \tag{1}$$

Here, D_i represents the number of disk I/Os at node P_i during a given time interval T_i, CPU_{P_i} denotes the CPU power of P_i and CPU_{Total} stands for the total CPU power of the cluster in which P_i is located. Also, we define the load of a cluster $L_{Cluster}$ as $\sum L_{P_i}$ i.e, the sum of the loads of its individual members.

Each node in the grid is assigned a unique identifer *node_id* and every incoming query is assigned a unique identifier *Query_id* by the node P_i at which it arrives. *Query_id* consists of *node_id* and *num* (a distinct integer generated by P_i). Every node keeps track of the *Query_ids* that it has recently processed in order to ascertain whether it has already processed a specific query before. Also, each node maintains information concerning the regions that it indexes and we shall refer to such information as *region-based information*. A node may store data from multiple and disjoint[1] regions in space. Moreover, every node maintains its own access statistics i.e., the number of disk accesses made for each

---

[1] This is similar to existing work [9,10].

of its data regions *only* during the *recent* time intervals[2] for hotspot detection purposes. Notably, we use only recent access statistics to detect hotspots. We leave issues concerning the optimal granularity at which statistics concerning data regions should be maintained to further study.

Each cluster is randomly assigned a leader. The job of the cluster leaders is to coordinate the activities (e.g., load-balancing, searching) of the nodes in their clusters. Additionally, each cluster leader maintains region-based information concerning the data stored both in its own cluster as well as in its neighbouring clusters. This facilitates effective pruning of the search space as it enables a cluster leader to decide quickly whether its cluster members contain the answer to a particular user query. Updates to region-based information are periodically exchanged between neighbouring cluster leaders preferably via piggybacking onto other messages.

4   Data Movement in Grids

This section discusses issues concerning inter-cluster data movement in grids. (For intra-cluster data movement, we adopt the approach that we had proposed in [9].)

Migration vs. Replication

Now let us study the trade-offs between migration and replication. If replication is used, in spite of the existence of several replicas of a specific data item D_i, a specific replica may keep getting accessed a disproportionately large number of times because the search is completely decentralized, thereby providing no absolute guarantee of load-balancing[3]. However, replication increases data availability albeit at the cost of disk space. In contrast, migration ensures reasonable amount of load-balancing and prevents wastage in disk space albeit at the cost of possible decreased data availability since the node to which data have been migrated may encounter failure (e.g., communication link failure, machine failure). For predicting the availability of a given node, every cluster leader monitors its nodes' availability over a period of time. If the probability of failure of a node P_i is very low, hot data should be migrated to P_i, otherwise hot data should be replicated for availability reasons. In essence, we propose that decisions concerning migration/replication should be taken during **run-time** since both migration and replication have their own inherent advantages and disadvantages.

Dealing with Heterogeneity of Clusters

Clusters in grid environments are highly likely to be heterogeneous in terms of processing power, available disk space, administrative policies (e.g., security,

---

[2] Time is divided into equal pre-defined intervals at design time.

[3] If the same query is issued from different nodes, randomness may guarantee a certain amount of load-balancing.

data access) and data management techniques (e.g., indexing, hotspot detection, load-balancing) since grids usually span across several administrative domains. Heterogeneity across clusters has significant implications for inter-cluster data movements.

Variations in indexing mechanisms: Spatial data being typically huge, it is almost always true that indexing mechanisms are used to facilitate speedy retrieval of such data. When moving data across clusters, the indexes associated with the data also need to be moved. However, variations in indexing mechanisms across clusters precludes the possibility of migrating the indexes across clusters. For example, when data are moved from a node X (which uses an R-tree [7] for indexing) to a node Y (where indexing is performed by a UB-tree [12]), the indexes of the relevant data cannot be moved *directly* from X to Y. Moreover, it may *not* be possible to integrate the moved data smoothly into Y's index structure.

We address this problem by extracting data from the index at the source node and transferring the data to the destination node. At the destination node, there are two different indexes, one for organizing the dedicated data at that node and another for the moved data. Note that at the destination node, the moved data are indexed by the indexing mechanism of the destination node itself, irrespective of the indexing mechanism at the source node of the data. This is important because the destination node may *not* have the indexing software that was being used to index the data at its source node. Interestingly, moving data as opposed to moving indexes also solves problems associated with *porting*. In retrospect, it is clear that in practice, we *cannot* impose our grid-related policies on any cluster, thereby indicating that our policies should be aimed at *supplementing* a given cluster's policies as opposed to interfering with them.

Variations in available disk space: Given the implications of significant variations in available disk space of different nodes in a grid, we adopt the following strategy.

- 'Pushing' non-hot data (via migration for large-sized data and via replication for small-sized data) to large capacity nodes as much as possible.
- Replicating small-sized hot data at small capacity nodes (smaller search space expedites search operations).
- Large-sized hot data are migrated to large capacity nodes only if such nodes have low probability of failure, otherwise they are replicated at large capacity nodes, an upperlimit being placed on the number of replicas to save disk space.

5   Load-Balancing

This section discusses inter-cluster load-balancing via migration and replication of data. We propose that such load-balancing should be performed *only* between neighbouring clusters by means of collaboration between the cluster leaders, the reason being that moving data to distant clusters may incur too high a communication overhead to justify the movement.

Cluster leaders periodically exchange load information *only* with their neighbouring cluster leaders. If a cluster leader α detects that its load exceeds the average loads of the set β of its neighbouring cluster leaders by more than 10% of the average load, it first ascertains the hot data regions that should be moved and sends a message concerning each hot region's space requirement to each cluster leader in β in order to offload some part of its load to them. The leaders in β check the available disk space in each of their cluster members and if their disk space constraint is satisfied, they send a message to α informing it about their total loads and their total available disk space. α first removes those cluster leaders from the set β whose loads exceed its own load and then sorts the willing leaders of β in $List_1$ such that the first element of $List_1$ is the least loaded leader.

The number of hot data regions to be moved depends upon load imbalance i.e, if the load imbalance is severe, more data regions need to be moved, while in case of lesser load imbalance, lesser data regions are moved. Assume the hot data regions to be moved are numbered as $h_1, h_2, h_3, h_4...$ (h_1 is the hottest element). Let the number of willing nodes in β and the number of hot data regions to be moved be denoted by b and h respectively. If $b < h$, h_1 is assigned to the first element in $List_1$, h_2 is assigned to the second element and so on in a round-robin fashion till all the hot regions have been assigned. If $b \geq h$, the assignment of hot data to elements of $List_1$ is done similarly, but in this case some elements of $List_1$ will *not* receive any hot data. After the hot data arrives at the destination cluster's leader, the leader creates a sorted list $List_2$ (in ascending order according to load) of its nodes and assigns the hot data to elements of $List_2$ in the manner described above. Note that the data movement associated with our load-balancing strategy is based solely upon the respective loads and disk space availability at the destination clusters. In particular, in this paper, we do *not* specifically look at issues concerning whether a specific data movement will *really* be able to reduce user response times. In the near future, we intend to design a more sophisticated data movement technique (for our proposed load-balancing strategy) based on a cost-benefit analysis which attempts to predict whether a specific data movement will be beneficial in reducing user query response times.

6   Performance Study

This section reports the performance evaluation of our proposed inter-cluster load-balancing technique via data migration[4]. Note that we consider performance issues associated *only* with inter-cluster load-balancing since a significant body of research work pertaining to efficient intra-cluster load-balancing algorithms already exists. Our test environment comprises a cluster of 16 SUN workstations, each of which is a 143 MHz Sun UltraSparc I processor (256 MB RAM) running Solaris 2.5.1 operating system. These are connected by high speed switch (200 Mbyte/s), the APnet. Each cluster is modeled by a workstation node

---

[4] Owing to constraints concerning available disk space, we could not investigate replication in our performance study.

in our experiments. Hence, throughout this section, we shall be using the term 'cluster' to refer to such a workstation node. From this perspective, such a workstation node may be viewed as the cluster leader which is representative of its entire cluster. The implication is that there are 16 neighbouring clusters among which we attempt to provide inter-cluster load-balancing. Additionally, to model inter-cluster communication in a wide area network environment, we simulated a transfer rate of 1 Mbit/second among the respective clusters.

We implemented an R-tree on each of the clusters to organize the data allocated to each cluster. For all our experiments, we assumed that one R-tree node fits in a disk page (page size = 4096 bytes). Hence, R-tree node capacity is the same as page size in our case. The height of each of the R-trees at each node was 3 and the fan-out was 64. We have used the tile technique [10] as reference. We divided the universal space into 48 tiles and the tiles were assigned to the 16 clusters. We shall henceforth refer to this approach as **TM** (tile method). Also, we shall refer to our proposed strategy as **DILBM** (dynamic inter-cluster load-balancing via migration). A real dataset (Greece Roads [3]) was enlarged and used for our experiments. The enlargement was done by translating and mapping the data. Each cluster contained more than 200000 spatial data rectangles. In order to model skewed workloads, we have used the well-known Zipf distribution to decide the number of queries to be directed to each cluster. Note that this is only an approximate manner of generating skewed workloads since queries may vary in selectivity.

6.1   Performance of Our Proposed Scheme

Now let us investigate the effectiveness of our proposed scheme in improving the system performance. For this purpose, an experiment was performed using 90000 spatial select (window) queries, the value of the zipf factor being set at 0.1, which indicates a highly skewed workload. Figure 1a displays a time line indicating the progress of the queries over time by presenting the wall-clock execution times of queries as a function of the time intervals during which the queries were executed, while Figure 1b presents the disk I/O of the hot cluster for the same experiment. Figure 1a indicates that initially during certain intervals, the performance of DILBM is slightly worse than that of TM. This occurs owing to migration-related overheads and disturbances. However, once the migration has been completed, DILBM significantly outperforms TM. This is possible because of the reduction in the load of the hot cluster as demonstrated in Figure 1b. Such reduction occurs as a result of the effective load-balancing provided by DILBM as depicted in Figure 1c.

6.2   Variations in Workload Skew

Now we shall examine the performance of DILBM for varying skews in the workload. For this purpose, we used zipf factors of 0.5 and 0.9 to model medium-skewed workload and low-skewed workload respectively. Figure 2a depicts the wall-clock completion time of *all* the queries when the zipf factor was varied,

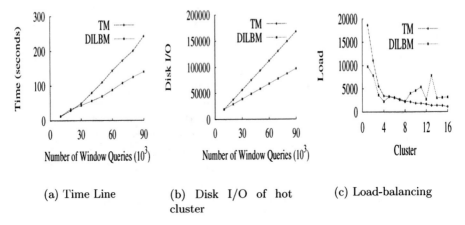

(a) Time Line

(b) Disk I/O of hot cluster

(c) Load-balancing

Fig. 1. Performance of our proposed scheme

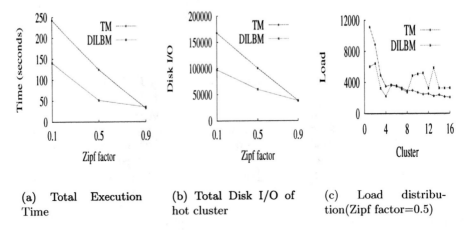

(a) Total Execution Time

(b) Total Disk I/O of hot cluster

(c) Load distribution(Zipf factor=0.5)

Fig. 2. Effect of varying skew in the queries

while Figure 2b shows the total disk I/Os incurred by the hot cluster during the same experiment. Interestingly, the gain in execution time is significantly more in the case of highly skewed workloads than for low-skewed workloads, the reason being that the need for load-balancing reduces as the workload skew decreases. Note that at a value of 0.9 for the zipf factor, there is no significant difference in performance between DILBM and TM since the workload in this case was too lowly skewed to necessitate migrations. Figure 2c demonstrates that DILBM performs good load-balancing for medium-skewed workloads.

7 Conclusion

Huge amounts of available spatial data at geographically distributed locations coupled with the growth of powerful computer networks provides a strong motivation for designing a spatial grid. Efficient search and load-balancing mechanisms are essential for the grid to work efficiently in practice. Incidentally, issues concerning indexing and load-balancing are more complex in case of grids than in case of traditional domains primarily because a grid usually spans across several administrative domains. We have proposed a dynamic strategy for inter-cluster load-balancing in spatial grids via data migration/replication and analyzed the trade-offs between migration and replication. Our performance study has demonstrated that our proposed technique is indeed feasible for providing load-balancing in spatial grids. Currently, we are investigating performance issues concerning replication in spatial grids and the applicability of our data movement strategy to P2P systems.

References

1. H. Boral, W. Alexander, L. Clay, G. Copeland, S. Danforth, M. Franklin, B. Hart, M. Smith, and P. Valduriez. Prototyping Bubba, a highly parallel database system. Proc. IEEE TKDE, 2(1), March 1990.
2. European DataGrid. http://eu-datagrid.web.cern.ch/eu-datagrid/.
3. Datasets. http://dias.cti.gr/~ytheod/research/datasets/spatial.html.
4. D.H.J Epema, M. Livny, R.V. Dantzig, X. Evers, and J. Pruyne. A worldwide flock of Condors : Load sharing among workstation clusters. Journal on Future Generations of Computer Systems, 12, 1996.
5. I. Foster and C. Kesselman. The grid: Blueprint for a new computing infraestructure. Morgan-Kaufmann, 1999.
6. Earth Systems Grid. http://www.earthsystemgrid.org/.
7. A. Guttman. R-trees: A dynamic index structure for spatial searching. In Proc. ACM SIGMOD, pages 47–57, 1984.
8. NASA IPG. http://www.ipg.nasa.gov/.
9. A. Mondal, M. Kitsuregawa, B.C. Ooi, and K.L. Tan. R-tree-based data migration and self-tuning strategies in shared-nothing spatial databases. Proc. ACM GIS, 2001.
10. J. Patel and D. DeWitt. Partition based spatial-merge join. Proc. ACM SIGMOD, pages 259–270, 1996.
11. GriPhyN Project. http://www.griphyn.org/index.php.
12. F. Ramsak, V. Markl, R. Fenk, M. Zirkel, K. Elhardt, and R. Bayer. Integrating the UB-tree into a database system kernel. Proc. VLDB, pages 263–272, 2000.
13. D. Thain, J. Basney, S.C. Son, and M. Livny. The Kangaroo approach to data movement on the grid. Proc. HPDC, 2001.
14. D. Thain, J. Bent, A. Arpaci-Dusseau, R. Arpaci-Dusseau, and M. Livny. Gathering at the well: Creating communities for grid I/O. Proc. SC, 2001.
15. Gerhard Weikum, Peter Zabback, and Peter Scheuermann. Dynamic file allocation in disk arrays. Proc. ACM SIGMOD, pages 406–415, 1991.

Parallel Query Support for Multidimensional Data: Intra-object Parallelism

Karl Hahn, Bernd Reiner, and Gabriele Höfling

FORWISS,
Bavarian Research Center for Knowledge Based Systems,
Munich, Germany
{hahnk,reiner,hoefling}@forwiss.tu-muenchen.de
http://www.wibas.forwiss.tu-muenchen.de

Abstract. Intra-query parallelism is a well-established mechanism for achieving high performance in (object-) relational database systems. However, the methods have yet not been applied to the upcoming field of multidimensional array databases. Specific properties of multidimensional array data require new parallel algorithms. This paper focuses on the parallel execution of expensive multidimensional operations on a single very large multidimensional object. Experiences of the ESTEDI project have shown that this scenario is very typical for the database-supported analysis of large multidimensional data. In the paper we concentrate on data parallelism and investigate multidimensional operations concerning their capability to be executed on parts of a multidimensional object. Furthermore, we introduce different possibilities of splitting multidimensional objects for parallel processing and merging the results, which affects the architecture of the parallel query execution. Intra-operator parallelism was implemented in the Array DBMS RasDaMan.

1 Introduction

Arrays of arbitrary size and dimensionality appear in a large variety of database application fields, e.g., medical imaging, geographic information systems [6], scientific simulations, etc. Current scientific contributions in this area mainly focus on an algebra for *multidimensional discrete data (MDD)* and specialized storage architectures [1] [2] [3]. Since MDD objects may have a magnitude of several megabytes and much more and, compared to scalar values, operations on these values can be very complex, their efficient evaluation becomes a critical factor for the overall query response time. Beyond query optimization, parallel query processing is the most promising technique to speed up complex operations on large data volumes. One of the outcomes of the predecessor project of *ESTEDI* (http://www.estedi.org), called *RasDaMan* (funded by the European Commission under grant no. 20073), in which the *Array DBMS RasDaMan* [2] has been developed, was the awareness that most queries on multidimensional array data are in fact CPU-bound [10]. Therefore, one major research issue of the succeeding project *ESTEDI* is the parallel processing of queries which is the topic of this paper. In [7] we discussed the transfer of relational parallel concepts to array data. Inter-object parallelism (in contrary to intra-object parallelism) distributes complete multidimensional objects which is

V. Mařík et al. (Eds.): DEXA 2003, LNCS 2736, pp. 212–222, 2003.

comparable to data parallelism in the relational counterpart. The main advantages of array data distribution which arise from the magnitude of a single data element and the expensive operations performed were load balancing and lacking data skew. One of the disadvantages we discussed in the paper was the fact that a typical query class could not be parallelized, i.e., operations on one single (possibly very large) object. In this paper we concentrate on such single data objects and how to parallelize very expensive multidimensional operations on them. Therefore, we have to analyze each multidimensional operation if it can be processed on a fragment of the multidimensional object. In a second step, we investigate how to split multidimensional arrays, distribute them to processes and collect and combine intermediate results.

The remainder of the paper is organized as follows: in chapter 2 we discuss the data model and query tree. Chapter 3 will analyze multidimensional operations regarding usability for distributed processing. Furthermore, the adaptation of the query tree using split and merge operations which encapsulate the inter-process communication will presented. The basic concept of the adaptation is the forming of operation chains to be executed by the internal processes without further redistributing the multidimensional data within. How to split the data object and collect and merge the results is the content of chapter 4. In chapter 5 we finalize with a conclusion and summary.

2 Processing Multidimensional Data: The Array DBMS RasDaMan

2.1 Logical Data Model

The fundamental concept of the RasDaMan data model is *Multidimensional Discrete Data (MDD) with value $\underline{m}$ of type [[D, T]]and dimensionality $d(\underline{m})$*. This is defined as the multidimensional array $\underline{m}$ with

1. a *spatial domain D (having a dimensionality d) over points $\underline{l}$, $\underline{h}$* with $\underline{l}$, $\underline{h} \in Z^d$, $l_i < h_i$ for i=1, …, d is defined as

$$D := \underset{i=1}{\overset{d}{X}} \{x \mid l_i < x < h_i, x \in Z\} = [l_1:h_1] \times … \times [l_d:h_d] = [l_1:h_1, …, l_d:h_d].$$

2. a specific *cell base type T*, consisting of a single scalar value or a complex type structure.

An MDD value $\underline{m}$ maps a value of base type T to each point of the spatial domain D.

In Fig. 1, left, we can see an example of a 3D MDD with spatial domain of 128 pixels in the first dimension, 64 cells for the second dimension, and 2880 values in the third dimension. The cell type consists of double values for temperature, and two components of wind speed. An *MDD collection* (relation) holds an unordered set of MDD with the same spatial domain (and therefore same dimensionality) and cell base type. In the example above, the collection can combine different MDD of different runs of the simulation. The definition of collection sets allows for relational operations on the data sets (see chapter 2.4). Further details of the multidimensional data model of RasDaMan can be found in [3] and [10].

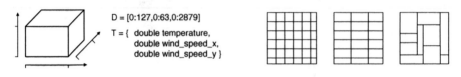

$D = [0:127,0:63,0:2879]$

$T = \{$ double temperature,
        double wind_speed_x,
        double wind_speed_y $\}$

Fig. 1. Example of 3D MDD (left). Example of a 2D storage layout (right).

2.2 Physical Data Model

The potentially huge size of MDD values demands specialized physical storage structures for their efficient access. In order to minimize the number of pages read when operations are executed on parts of MDD, tiling has been integrated into RasDaMan. This is a subdivision into rectangular tiles with the following conditions

1. $\displaystyle\bigcup_{i=1}^{n} D_i = D$ 2. $D_i \cap D_j = \varnothing$ for $i, j \in \{1, ..., n\}, i \neq j$

RasDaMan supports different tiling layouts, e.g., regular tiling, irregular (aligned) tiling, and arbitrary tiling. Regular tiling splits the data in storage units all having the same extent in each dimension. Only tiles reaching the boundary of the object can differ in their spatial extent. Using irregular tiling the spatial extent of the chunks can be different for the dimensions, and therefore, special query behavior can be supported. In arbitrary tiling, each tile can be defined separately. Regular, irregular and arbitrary tiling is shown for the 2D case in Fig. 1, right. The tiles are stored in a relational DBMS as binary large data objects (BLOBs) and are accessed using a multidimensional index, i.e., an R^+ tree. Details about tiling concepts can be found in [10].

2.3 Multidimensional Array Operations

Array operations for multidimensional data can be divided into four basic classes:
1. *Elementary array constructor and condenser*
   The *marray constructor* allows to create arbitrary multidimensional arrays by iterating with a point variable $\underline{x}$ through a pre-defined spatial domain D evaluating a given cell expression e_x: $marray_{D,\underline{x}}(e_{\underline{x}}) := \{ (\underline{x}, e_{\underline{x}}) \mid \underline{x} \in D \}$.
   The *condense* operation on the contrary iterates through a given MDD $\underline{m}$ evaluating an expression $e_{m, \underline{x}}$ and results in a scalar value. $\circ$: T×T→T is a commutative and associative operation: $cond \;\circ_{D, \underline{x}}(e_{m, \underline{x}}) := \underset{x \in D}{O} \; e_{m, \underline{x}} = e_{m, \underline{x}1} \circ ... \circ e_{m, \underline{x}n}$

   The elementary marray constructor and condense operation allow for powerful data transformations but are of less importance in real data analysis especially because of their inherent complexity. For all typical specific condense operations exist pre-defined condensers called aggregation operations (described in 4).
2. *Geometric operations*
   The *trimming* operation specifies a sub-array with the same dimensionality:
   $trimming(\underline{t}) := \underline{u} \subset \underline{t}$, $D_u \leq D_t$, i.e. the extent of D_u is in all dimensions less equal the extent of D_t. A *section* operation reduces the dimensionality by one, i.e. the data is projected to a hyper plane: $section(\underline{t}) := \underline{u} \subset \underline{t}$, $d(\underline{u}) = d(\underline{t}) - 1$.

3. *Induced operations.* Operations which are defined on the base cell type are also defined on multidimensional arrays. The definition of a binary induced operation is $\underline{m} \oplus \underline{n} := v_t(\underline{m}) \oplus v_t(\underline{n})$ *for the value v of each point t* $\in D(m) = D(n)$.

4. *Aggregation operations* An MDD $\underline{n}$ is reduced to an MDD $\underline{m}$ with $D(\underline{m}) \leq D(\underline{n})$ or to a single scalar value. Operations of this class are quantifiers, maximum, minimum, average, scale, etc. The definition is equal to the definition of the elementary condenser with the condense function e_m being a pre-defined function.

2.4 Relational Operations

As described in 2.1 the data model distinguishes between multidimensional arrays called MDD objects and sets (relations) of equal structured objects called collections. There are different relational-like operations which allow for the iteration over collections R and S of multidimensional objects $\underline{t}$.

1. *Collection access* ω iterates over a collection and returns (an identifier of) the next MDD of the named collection with each invocation: $\omega(R) := \{ \underline{t} \mid \underline{t} \in R \}$

2. *Repartitioning iterator* ϕ which returns partitions of a given MDD. This operation is used if partitions of an object are analyzed (selection and application operation are based on collections): $\phi(R, \underline{t}, D) := \{ \underline{u} \mid \underline{u} < \underline{t} \}, \cap(D_{ui}) = \varnothing \wedge \cup(D_{ui}) = D$

3. *Cross product* $\times$ delivers the cross product of objects of all referenced collections. The basic (binary) definition is: $\times(R,S) := \{ (\underline{r},\underline{s}) \mid \underline{r} \in R \wedge \underline{s} \in S \}$

4. *Selection* σ_{cond} evaluating a condition tree of multidimensional operations. All multidimensional data objects for which the condition tree evaluates true are returned: $\sigma_{cond}(R) := \{ \underline{t} \mid \underline{t} \in R, cond(\underline{t}) \}$

5. *Application* α_{op} returning a set of MDD or scalars. The operation tree executes array operations on the multidimensional data sets. The application α_{op} is defined as $\alpha_{op}(R) := \{ \underline{t} \mid \underline{t} = op(\underline{u}), \underline{u} \in R \} \vee \{ i \mid i = op(\underline{u}), i \in S, \underline{u} \in R \}$

2.5 Query Language and Query Execution

In order to invoke operations on array data and specify the multidimensional interval to be accessed, RasDaMan provides a query language RasQL which is derived from standard SQL. The simplified structure of such a RasQL query is

```
SELECT <array operation> FROM collection 1, ..., collection n
WHERE <condition operation>
```

The from-clause specifies the cross product $\times$ of the accessed collections (operator ω for each collection) which can previously be repartitioned (ϕ operation). In the where-clause a multidimensional condition is evaluated on the collection of MDD. Further multidimensional operations can be applied in the select-clause which represents the application α. The operation tree and condition tree consist of complex multidimensional array operations described in 2.3. The array operations in fact build a query tree on themselves, like it can be seen in Fig. 2. The relational operations (left part of Fig. 2) which are working on data sets are implemented using the well known iterator concept. The operation tree of application α and the condition tree of selection σ which are the most expensive operations of array query execution do not correspond to the iterator concept. In this case the complete result (evaluating one tuple of the cross product at a time) is evaluated with a single procedure call.

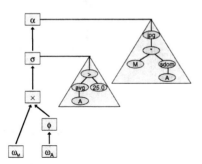

Fig. 2. Example of a query tree for a RasQL statement

In this example, only partitions (operation φ) of the collection A with an average value larger than 25.0 will be selected. The remaining objects will be restricted in their spatial domain and combined with a mask collection M using the induced multiplication. Finally, the result is converted to a JPEG image (which is only possible with 2D objects). Details on query optimization and execution can be found in [10].

3   Parallel Processing of Multidimensional Array Operations

Parallel processing in the context of array DBMS means data parallelism (data distribution, intra-operator parallelism). Pipeline parallelism which is a widely used concept in RDBMS will lead to major problems with array data as a data object (and therefore the granularity of query execution) is much larger. A pipeline buffer filled with multidimensional objects of several GB will soon lead to main memory shortage; intermediate results have to be written to disc; speed-up will decrease. The distribution of array data to processes can rely on the logical data model which is based on its relational counterpart. In this case a set of unordered objects (MDD of a collection; tuples of a relation) is evaluated by processes. A description of the methods as well as implementation notes and measurements can be found in [7]. The basic concept is to let condition $\sigma_{cond}(R) := \{ \underline{t} \mid \underline{t} \in R, cond(\underline{t}) \}$ and application $\alpha_{op}(R) := \{ \underline{t} \mid \underline{t} = op(\underline{u}), \underline{u} \in R \} \vee \{ i \mid i = op(\underline{u}), i \in S, \underline{u} \in R \}$ be executed on several processes as $cond(\underline{u})$ and $op(\underline{u})$ always are evaluated on a MDD $\underline{u}$ which is independent of the other objects in its collection. Helper processes administer the tuples which are returned by the cross product operator × to assure mutual exclusion of the processes while requesting a data element. One single master process manages the workload and transmits combined query results to the clients. Intra-object parallelism distributes array data in finer granules based on the physical model of the data parallelizing the array operations. Splitting one single data element and processing the fragments in several processes requires the analysis of each array operation that should be executed in parallel. This is discussed in 3.1 while the adaptation of the query tree is the content of section 3.2.

3.1   Evaluation of Operations for Parallel Execution

Multidimensional array operations can be divided into four classes: elementary array constructor and condensers, geometric operations, induced operations, and aggregation operations. In chapter 2.3 we gave a formal definition, here we will discuss their capability to be executed in parallel.

3.1.1 Elementary Array Constructor and Condenser

Both, marray constructor and condenser, create a new array evaluating a given expression which references a point variable iterating a spatial domain. We will demonstrate the difficulty of parallelizing these operations on the marray constructor. As defined in 2.3 the marray constructor is $marray_{D,x}(e_x) := \{ (\underline{x}, e_x) \mid \underline{x} \in D \}$. I.e., each point of the result array is computed by evaluating the function e_x. The value of e_x can depend on various positions in the base array with domain D: Let $v(\underline{x}_i)$ be the value of point $\underline{x}_i$ in the input array and $v(\underline{x}_o)$ be the value of point $\underline{x}_o$ in the result array then $v(\underline{x}_o) = e\{ (v(x_i) \mid x_i \in D) \}$. In this generic case each parallel process which builds a partial of the result array needs the complete input array as one result cell is computed evaluating arbitrary input cells. Considering the fact that these elementary operations are more of theoretical interest we abandoned the parallelization of these operations.

3.1.2 Geometric Operations

Geometric operations change the spatial domain of the multidimensional objects. They are not well suited for parallel execution for two reasons: first, these operations are typically I/O bound. Second, these operations change the spatial domain of the object. Data distribution is based on splitting the objects' spatial domain in order to distribute the resulting partial objects to different processes (see chapter 3.2). Changing the spatial domain while the object is processed by different processes will result in data skew. Thus, geometric operations should never be executed in parallel. However, a common optimization of multidimensional operations is to push down all geometric restrictions which leads to query trees with geometric operations at the bottom and CPU-bound operations above. This results in the parallelization algorithm described in chapter 3.2 to split the data objects exactly below geometric operations.

3.1.3 Induced Operations

Induced operations (binary example is $\underline{m} \oplus \underline{n} := v_i(\underline{m}) \oplus v_i(\underline{n})$) are the perfect candidates for parallel execution. Each cell of the result object is computed by evaluating the corresponding cell(s) (cell(s) with same coordinates) of the input object(s): let v_i be the value of the input array at a given point $\underline{t}$ and v_o the corresponding output array value then $v_o(\underline{t}) = f(v_i(\underline{t}))$. Thus, no matter how the input object is partitioned and distributed to processes there are absolutely no dependencies of the partitions and therefore of the processes. If parallelizing binary induced operations we have to assure that both input objects are split in exactly the same objects, i.e., each process must have objects with exactly the same spatial domain as a binary operation $\underline{m} \oplus \underline{n}$ is defined only if $D(\underline{n}) = D(\underline{m})$.

3.1.4 Aggregation Operations

Typical queries on multidimensional data often include aggregation operations as data is often analyzed on server side instead of retrieving the complete object at client side. Mathematically spoken, an aggregation operation is a function of all cells of an input array returning an aggregated array or (more often) a scalar value $s = f(\{\forall v_i(\underline{t}) \mid \underline{t} \in D\})$. Thus, the complete input array has to be evaluated if computing the output. Parallel computation of an aggregation requires a two-phase approach to avoid this problem: in the first phase the processes evaluating partials of the input return the aggregated value of this partial input. In the second phase a master process collects the pre-aggregated values and combines them to an overall result. This leads to various problems: first, the merge operation has to be executed immediately after such an aggregation operation as the combined value has to be built from the partial results before doing further computations. Second, the merging operation has to execute functionality on the intermediate results which are actually part of the operation below. This problem is sketched in Fig. 3: intermediate results which hold the average value of partials of the original object must be merged right after the aggregation operation. The master process has to finalize the operation by building the average from the intermediate results.

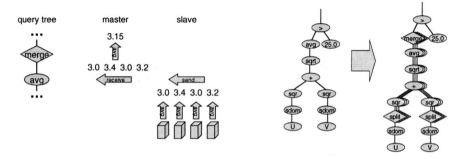

Fig. 3. Merging aggregation operations (left). Example for query tree adaptation (right).

The first problem which means that each aggregation operation has to be followed by a merge operation in the query tree is not a constraint but actually suits very well to the typical structure of the query tree. Expensive operations which should be evaluated in parallel are operations on multidimensional arrays. If we have an aggregation operation in the query tree there is typically no array operation above. The second problem is no restriction of the functionality but leads to the only exception of the implementation concept to separate the parallel functionality from the array operations. If the implementation of aggregation operations will change or new operation will be added the merge operation has to be adapted accordingly.

3.2 Adaptation of the Query Tree: Avoidance of Data Transfer

Adapting the query tree for intra-object parallelism results in a top-down traversal of each condition tree (selection σ_{cond}) and operation tree (application α_{op}) in the overall query tree. The algorithm used is equal for condition and operation tree. As discussed above data streams in the operation and condition trees can be classified into scalar and array streams. Expensive operations which are well suited for parallelization always have multidimensional array data as input. Therefore, the query tree is analyzed top-down until an operation with array data input is found. The merge operation is placed above this operation which can be an induced operation or an aggregation operation. Operations of other type are not parallelized and the algorithm continues with the node(s) below in this case.

If a merge node was set the method continues the traversal of the tree searching for the appropriate position for the split operation(s). The split node(s) is set as deep as possible in the query tree but above collection access, geometric operation, or elementary marray constructors and condense operations. Binary operations in the tree can lead to more than one split node. In this case the implementation of the split node has to assure that the data is partitioned using the same strategy for the different multidimensional objects.

Using this algorithm operations chains are built which can be distributed in parallel avoiding data transfer within. Furthermore, as RasDaMan actually loads data as late as possible (in the operation where the data is processed in any way) we distribute persistent data which includes metadata (cell type, spatial domain, etc.). This assures minimal data transfer between processes which has to be proven the primary bottleneck of the speedup in the parallel server. The same concept is used for the merge operation: intermediate data is collected by the master process preferably after aggregations have been done on the data. This again results in minimal data transfer. Fig. 3 (right) depicts the method for query tree parallelization in an example showing a condition tree: *...where avg(sqrt(sqr(a[sdom])+sqr(v[sdom])))>25.0.* Two data objects of collection U and V are split after restricting the data to a new spatial domain (geometric operation). At this stage not the complete data is transferred but only persistent data which is metadata and a pointer to the underlying RDBMS. The split node has to assure that objects of collection U and V are split in the same way, i.e., each process has to process the same spatial domain of its objects. Above, the parallel operation chain begins: unary induced square operation executed on both objects, binary induced sum combining the two inputs, unary induced square root, and aggregation operation average. Results are sent to the master process which combines them to an overall average value.

4   Splitting and Merging of Multidimensional Objects

This chapter describes in detail how the data is actually split and merged. First, we introduce operations encapsulating the parallel query execution. Then, three methods for the partitioning of data are discussed. Te first two methods have been implemented while the third method is not at the moment. Finally, we will discuss the merging of array data and scalar values which (following the parallelizing algorithm) always occur after an aggregation operation and therefore executes functionality of this operation.

4.1   Split and Merge Operations: Encapsulating the Parallel Functionality

Operations of the optimized query tree should not be changed in order to execute them in parallel. Instead, we insert special operators in the query tree which are responsible for the splitting and merging of data, and encapsulate the inter-process communication, i.e. the transfer of requests and intermediate data.

1. $split(\underline{m}) := \{ \underline{n}_n \mid \underline{n}_n \subset \underline{m} \}$, $\cup D(\underline{n}_n) = D(\underline{m})$, $D_i \cap D_j = \emptyset$ for $i, j \in \{1, ..., n\}$, $i \neq j$

The split operation returns a set of (disjoint) multidimensional object: The number of objects created corresponds to the number of processes n which are available for the computation. In the implementation the split operation also encapsulates the inter-process communication, i.e., the master process sends one of the objects created to each worker (slave) process, and the slave processes receive this object and returns it to the operation above in the query tree.

2. $merge(\{\underline{n}_n\}) := m$, $D(\underline{m}) = \cup D(\underline{n}_n)$, $D_i \cap D_j = \emptyset$ for $i, j \in \{1, ..., n\}$, $i \neq j$

The merge operation collects a set of (disjoint) multidimensional objects and combines them to a new object. In the implementation this operation also sends (for the slaves) and receives (master process) the intermediate results before combining them.

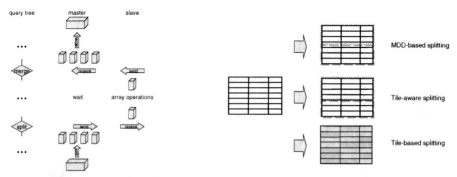

Fig. 4. Split and merge operations for the master and slave processes (left). Concepts for splitting multidimensional objects (right).

In Fig. 4 (left) the implementation for split and merge operations regarding master and slave processes are sketched.

4.2 Three Concepts for Splitting

We can distinguish three basic concepts to split multidimensional data. The first two methods return multidimensional objects, i.e., multidimensional rectangles. In the current implementation of RasDaMan this is the transfer structure between the nodes of the operation and condition tree. The third concept partitions the object in different set of tiles which are the storage structure for multidimensional arrays. The operations are typically computed tile by tile although data within the query tree is transferred in the granularity of objects. Thus, the possibility to distribute data tile-based is discussed here but contradicts the current implementation of RasDaMan. *MDD-based splitting*: The input is partitioned to objects of equal (or almost equal) size avoiding data skew. The disadvantage is that data will be split within its storage layout, i.e. tiles. This typically leads to tiles which are loaded by different processes as each process is doing computations on parts of these tiles. The larger the object is and the smaller the tiles are chosen (at insertion of the data) the less serious will be the redundant loading of data. Furthermore, the quota of the redundantly loaded data can be reduced by choosing the 'right' dimension to split. In regular tiling, the dimension to split makes no difference whereas in irregular (aligned) tiling the dimension is chosen which has the largest extent regarding tiling layout. In arbitrary tiling the redundant data has to be analyzed for each dimension. In Fig. 4 (right) a 2D object having an aligned tiling is split using this first concept. The object is partitioned in the first dimension (x-axis) because the tiles are aligned in this direction, therefore, the redundant loaded tiles will be less. *MDD-aware splitting*: The second possibility is to be more aware of the tiling structure and exploit this knowledge. Thus, the data object is split at tiling boundaries which avoids redundant loading of data completely. The disadvantage is that this method typically creates data skew. This concept is sketched for aligned tiling in Fig. 4 (right). Arbitrary tiling can in most cases not be split avoiding redundancy completely but can minimize it choosing this strategy. This concept will show better performance than the first method if the query response time is still dependant on the I/O and not dominated by CPU limitations. *Tile-based splitting*: Theoretically, an input object can also be split using the storage layout of the data which is tiling. This implies the data transfer between operation tree nodes on the basis of tiles and therefore, the realization of a finer iterator concept within the operation and condition trees. Such a complete redesign of the RasDaMan execution engine would result in many advantages: first, redundant data loading is avoided (in most cases) in the parallel server. Second, data can be sent on demand avoiding data skew and assuring load balancing. Third, pipeline parallelism is only possible if the intermediate results have an inherent granularity. On the other hand, if tile-based splitting is done for binary operations working on arrays of different tiling layout, redundant loading can not be avoided while the algorithm of finding minimal coverage is more complex.

4.3   Merging Arrays and Combining Scalar Results

The result of the condition tree always is a boolean value which indicates an aggregation operation in the tree. Thus, parallelizing the condition tree leads to a merge operation which combines scalars. An operation tree can produce a scalar value or an array as result. The creation of a new MDD from partials which were received from the internal processes can be achieved by dynamically augmenting the spatial domain of the first received partial MDD by the domains of the following intermediate results. The data (tiles) can then be inserted in the enlarged multidimensional object. The combination of scalar values which occurs after aggregation operations requires knowledge about the aggregation operation because the merge operation has to finalize the aggregation. An example for this two-phase merging approach was already given in Fig. 3. This leads to the only exception of the implementation concept to separate the parallel functionality from the array operations. If aggregation operations will change or new operations will be added the merge operation has to be adapted accordingly.

5   Conclusions

Parallel processing of multidimensional array data in an array DBMS has attracted minor attention in database research so far, although query execution time for processing this kind of data is mostly determined by CPU resources. Our goal was the utilization of parallel hardware in order to speed up CPU-bound queries, especially very expensive queries with execution times of several minutes or even hours. We designed a concept to dynamically split up the computational work on multidimensional objects between multiple processes. This required an adaptation of the query tree to allow parts of the query tree to be executed by different processes. In order to achieve good speed-up we minimized data transfer and inter-process communication.

Our concept of data parallelism partitions data in subsets of multidimensional objects. In contrary to relational techniques where data is distributed in granularity of complete objects (relational tuples) this concept is especially well suited for array queries which often compute extremely expensive operations on single objects of extreme size. The concept described was fully implemented in the RasDaMan server kernel. Extensive test scenarios were performed regarding the structure of the resulting query tree and the intermediate results that have to be transmitted.

First performance measurements prove the validity of our concept. On a two processor machine we observed an increase in speed by a factor of up to 1.82 which is an extremely good result. Performance measurements on computers with more processors and workstation clusters will follow. We expect a good performance on these architectures as the concept implemented makes no assumptions regarding the number of processes or cluster nodes.

References

1. Agrawal, R., Gupta, A. Sarawagi, S.: Modeling Multi-dimensional Databases. Research Report, IBM Almaden Research Center, San Jose, USA, 1995
2. Baumann, P., Furtado, P., Ritsch, R., Widmann, N.: Geo/Environmental and Medical Data Management in the RasDaMan System. In Proc. of the Int. Conf. on Very Large Data Bases (VLDB), Athens, Greece, 1997
3. Baumann, P.: A Database Array Algebra for Spatio-Temporal Data and Beyond. In Proc. of the 4th International Workshop on Next Generation Information Technologies and Systems (NGITS), Zikhron Yaakov, Israel, 1999
4. Bouganim, L., Florescu, D., Valduriez, P.: Dynamic Load Balancing in Hierarchical Parallel Database Systems. In Proc. of the Int. Conf. on Very Large Data Bases (VLDB), Mumbai (Bombay), India, 1996
5. DeWitt, D.J., Gray, J.: Parallel Database Systems: The Future of High Performance Database Systems, Communication of the ACM, Volume 35, 1992
6. DeWitt, D.J., Kabra, N., Luo, J., Patel, J., Yu, J.: Client Server Paradise. In Proc. of the Int. Conf. on Very Large Data Bases (VLDB), Santiago, Chile, 1994
7. Hahn, K., Reiner, B., Höfling, G., Baumann, P.: Parallel Query Support for Multidimensional Data: Inter-object Parallelism. DEXA 2002: 820–830
8. Nippl, C., Mitschang, B.: TOPAZ: a Cost-Based, Rule-Driven, Multi-Phase Parallelizer. In Proc. of the Int. Conf. on Very Large Data Bases (VLDB), p. 251–262, 1998
9. Rahm, E.: Dynamic Load Balancing in Parallel Database Systems. In Proc. of EURO-PAR, Lyon, Springer-Verlag, Lecture Notes in Computer Science 1123, S. 37–52, 1996
10. Ritsch, R.: Optimization and Evaluation of Array Queries in Database Management Systems, PhD Thesis, Technical University Munich, 1999
11. Tamer Özsu, M., Valduriez, P.: Principles of Distributed Database Systems, Second Edition. Prentice-Hall 1999

Replicated Parallel I/O without Additional Scheduling Costs*

Mikhail Atallah and Keith Frikken

Purdue University

Abstract. A common technique for improving performance in a
database is to decluster the database among multiple disks so that data
retrieval can be parallelized. In this paper we focus on answering range
queries in a multidimensional database (such as a GIS), where each of its
dimensions is divided uniformly to obtain tiles which are placed on different disks; there has been a significant amount of research for this problem (a subset of which is [1,2,3,4,5,6,7,8,9,11,12,13,14,15]). A declustering
scheme would be optimal if any range query could be answered by doing
no more than ⌈# of tiles inside the range/# of disks ⌉ retrievals from
any one disk. However, it was shown in [1] that this is not achievable in
many cases even for two dimensions, and therefore much of the research
in this area has focused on developing schemes that performed close to
optimal. Recently, the idea of using replication (i.e. placing records on
more than one disk) to increase performance has been introduced. [7,
12,13,15]. If replication is used, a retrieval schedule (i.e. which disk to
retrieve each tile from) must be computed whenever a query is being processed. In this paper we introduce a class of replicated schemes where
the retrieval schedule can be computed in time O(# of tiles inside the
query's range), which is asymptotically equivalent to query retrieval for
the non-replicated case. Furthermore, this class of schemes has a strong
performance advantage over non-replicated schemes, and several schemes
are introduced that are either optimal or are optimal plus a constant additive factor. Also presented in this paper is a strictly optimal scheme for
any number of colors that requires the lowest known level of replication
of any such scheme.

1 Introduction

A typical bottleneck in many systems is I/O; to reduce the effect of this bottleneck data can be declustered onto multiple disks to facilitate parallel retrieval of
the data. In a multi-dimensional database, such as a GIS or a spatio-temporal
database, the dimensions can be tiled uniformly to form a grid, and when answering a range query in such a system, only the tiles that contain part of the

* Portions of this work were supported by Grants EIA-9903545 and ISS-0219560 from
the National Science Foundation, Contract N00014-02-1-0364 from the Office of Naval Research, by sponsors of the Center for Education and Research in Information
Assurance and Security, by Purdue Discovery Park's e-enterprise Center, and by the
GAANN fellowship.

V. Mařík et al. (Eds.): DEXA 2003, LNCS 2736, pp. 223–232, 2003.
© Springer-Verlag Berlin Heidelberg 2003

query need to be retrieved. In such an environment, a declustering scheme attempts to place the tiles on disks in such a way that the average range query is answered as efficiently as possible. If the database is treated like a grid and the disks as colors, then this can be stated as a grid coloring problem. For the rest of the paper we use record and tile synonymously and likewise use declustering and coloring interchangeably.

Given a database declustered on k disks and a range query Q contained on m tiles, Q is answered optimally if no more than $\lceil \frac{m}{k} \rceil$ tiles are retrieved from any one disk. A declustering is called strictly optimal if all range queries can be answered optimally, however it was shown in [1] that this is not achievable except in a few limited circumstances. Thus there has been a significant amount of work to develop declustering schemes that have close to optimal performance, a sampling of which are in [2,3,4,5,6,9,11,14].

To improve performance further the idea of using replication (i.e. placing each tile on multiple disks) has been introduced [7,12,13,15]. When replication is used each tile in a query can be retrieved from multiple places which allows greater flexibility when answering the query. In order to use replication an algorithm for computing an optimal retrieval schedule is required (i.e. which disk do you retrieve each tile from). Algorithms for computing this schedule are given in [7, 12,13,15]. The most general of these runs in time $O(rm^2 + mk)$ where r is the most number of disks that a tile is stored on, m is the number of tiles to be retrieved, and k is the number of disks. (For more information on work using replication see Section 2). One problem with replication is that it adds a non-negligible overhead to query response. In this paper we define a class of coloring techniques, which we call the grouping schemes, for which a schedule of retrievals can be computed in time $O(\#$ of tiles to be retrieved$)$ (from here on we refer to this as $O(\#$ of tiles$)$), which is asymptotically equivalent to the time required to compute a schedule for a non-replicated scheme. This technique essentially transforms existing coloring schemes into replicated schemes by placing disks into groups and placing tiles on all disks in a group; when the group size is two this is equivalent to RAID level 1. Previously, the only general strict optimal solution for any number of disks was the Complete Coloring [7,15], which places each tile on every disk. We introduce several new schemes that are either have strictly optimal performance for all queries or will answer any query in no more time than a strictly optimal scheme plus an additive constant; these new schemes have the lowest known level of replication for such performance bounds. Furthermore, these grouping schemes are shown to have stronger experimental performance than schemes without replication.

The outline of this paper is as follows: Section 2 discusses previous work in this area, in Section 3 the grouping schemes are introduced and schemes that achieve strictly optimal performance or are a constant additive factor above an optimal solution, Section 4 contains experimental data showing the performance of the grouping schemes, and Section 5 concludes the paper.

2   Related Work

Given an n-dimensional database with each dimension divided uniformly to form tiles, if tiles are placed on different disks, then the retrieval of records during query processing can be parallelized. The I/O time in such a system is time that it takes to retrieve the maximum number of tiles stored on the same disk. The problem of placing the records so that the response times for range queries is minimized has been well studied; this section presents a survey of this work.

Given a database declustered onto k disks and a range query Q contained on m tiles, an optimal tile declustering would require no more than $\lceil \frac{m}{k} \rceil$ retrievals from any one disk. It was shown in [1] that this bound is unachievable for all range queries in a grid except in a few limited circumstances. Since there are many cases where no scheme can achieve this optimal bound, several schemes have been developed to achieve performance that is close to optimal. To quantify "close to optimal", define the additive error of a declustering scheme to be the maximum over all range queries Q of the value $(rettime(Q) - \lceil \frac{m}{k} \rceil)$, where $rettime(Q)$ is defined as the retrieval time for query Q (i.e. it is the maximum number of tiles in Q retrieved from a single disk). These schemes include Disk Modulo DM [6], Fieldwise eXclusive (FX) or [9], the cyclic schemes (including RPHM, GFIB, and EXH) [11], GRS [4], a technique developed by Atallah and Prabhakar [2] which we will call RFX, and several techniques based on discrepancy theory [5,14] (for an introduction to discrepancy theory see [10]). Note that these are just a subset of the declustering techniques that have been developed for this problem.

Suppose we are given k colors. The DM approach [6] assigns tile (x, y) to $(x + y) \bmod k$. The FX approach [9] assigns tile (x, y) to $(x \oplus y) \bmod k$. Cyclic allocation schemes [11] choose a skip value s such that $gcd(k, s) = 1$ and assigns tile (x, y) to $(x + sy) \bmod k$. The choice of the skip value, s, is what defines the scheme. In RPHM (Relatively Prime Half Modulo), s is defined to be the integer nearest to $\frac{k}{2}$ that is relatively prime to k. The GFIB (Generalized FIBonacci) scheme defines s to be an approximate of the previous Fibonacci number (by using the closed formula) that is relatively prime to k. The EXH (Exhaustive) scheme takes all values of s where $gcd(s, k) = 1$ and finds the one that optimizes a certain criterion, for example minimizing the additive error is a possible criterion. Another class of schemes are the permutation schemes [4], in these schemes a permutation ϕ of the numbers in $\{0, ..., k - 1\}$ is chosen and then tile (x, y) is assigned color $(x - \phi^{-1}((y) \bmod k))$. Examples of permutation schemes are DM, the cyclic schemes, and GRS. In the GRS scheme [4] the permutation is computed as follows: i) $\forall i \in \{0, ..., k - 1\}$ compute the fractional part of $\frac{2i}{1+\sqrt{5}}$, and call it k_i and then ii) sort the values k_i and use this to define the permutation. A scheme based on the Corput set is defined in [14] that is similar to GRS except that the k_i values are $\frac{a_0}{2} + \frac{a_1}{4} + \frac{a_2}{8} + ... + \frac{a_{k-1}}{2^k}$ where $a_{k-1}...a_1 a_0$ is the binary representation of i. In [2], the RFX scheme was presented that was later found in [3] to be equivalent to $(x \oplus y^R) \bmod k$, where y^R is the $(\lceil \log k \rceil)$-bit reversal of y. For brevity, the details of higher dimensional schemes are not provided.

It was shown in [14] that the additive error for k colors in two dimensions is $\Omega(\log k)$, and that in $d(\geq 3)$ dimensions it is $\Omega(\log^{\frac{d-1}{2}} k)$. In two dimensions, schemes have been developed (RFX, GRS, and schemes based in discrepancy theory [2,14]) that have a provable upper bound of $O(\log k)$ on additive error. For higher dimensions $d(\geq 3)$, two schemes are given in [5] with additive error $O(\log^{(d-1)} k)$, which are the schemes with the lowest proven asymptotic bound on additive error. A recent trend has been to use replication [7,12,13,15] to increase performance further. Several query scheduling algorithms have been given in previous work, but the only general algorithm that works for any type of replication is in [7] and runs in time $O(rm^2 + mk)$ where r is the most number of disks that a tile is stored on, m is the number of tiles to be retrieved, and k is the number of disks. In [12,13] it was proven that if tiles are stored on two random disks then the probability of requiring more than ($\lceil$ (# of tiles/# of disks) $\rceil$ +1) retrievals from a single disk for a random query approaches 0 as the number of disks gets large. In [15] replication was used to achieve optimal solutions for up to 15 disks. A strictly optimal scheme, called Complete Coloring (CC), for any number of disks by storing all tiles on all disks was introduced in [7,15]. The SRCDM scheme was introduced in [7], and has an additive error no larger than 1, but requires the number of disks be a perfect square (n^2) and requires that each tile is placed on n disks.

3   Grouping Replication Scheme

In this section the grouping schemes are introduced. Section 3.1 defines some notations that will be needed before defining this class of schemes. In Section 3.2, the grouping schemes are defined along with an algorithm that computes the retrieval schedule in time $O(\#\text{of tiles})$. Section 3.3 contains several schemes that have an additive error that is 0 or is $O(1)$. Finally, in Section 3.4 we provide a strictly optimal coloring scheme that works for any number of colors.

3.1   Notations and Terminology

Before we can formally define the grouping schemes we need to define some notation and terminology. A *non-replicated coloring function* C for d dimensions and m disks is a function $C : \aleph^d \to \{0, ..., m-1\}$, essentially C maps a tile to a disk. A *replicated coloring function* C with *level of replication* r for d dimensions and m disks is a function $C : \aleph^d \to \bigcup_{i=1}^{r} \{0, ..., m-1\}^i$, essentially C maps a tile to the set of disks (with size no more than r) that contain the tile. Since the replicated coloring function is a generalization of the non-replicated coloring function, we assume all coloring functions are replicated for the rest of the paper. A convenient shorthand notation for coloring schemes is (C, m, r, d) which states the coloring function C declusters a d dimensional grid onto m disks with a level of replication r. Two coloring schemes (C, m, r, d) and (D, m, r, d) are said to be *equivalent* if and only if there is a bijection $f : \{0, ..., m-1\} \to \{0, ..., m-1\}$ such that $i \in C(x_1, ..., x_d)$ iff $f(i) \in D(x_1, ..., x_d)$. Essentially schemes are equivalent if there is a rearrangement of the colors that will make them identical, and it is obvious that equivalent schemes have identical retrieval time for any query.

3.2   Definition of Grouping Schemes

A scheme is considered to be *formed with groups* if the colors are partitioned into sets and tiles are assigned to partitions where assigning a partition to a tile is equivalent to placing it on all disks in that partition. The motivation for this class of schemes is to be able to distribute the additive error of the coloring that assigns tiles to partitions among the different members of the partition. Hence, the additive error of any one member of the partition will be smaller, and thus reducing the additive error of the scheme.

Formally, a coloring scheme (C, m, r, d) is considered formed by groups if the colors can be partitioned into sets $S_1, S_2, ..., S_k$ with at least one set where $|S_i| > 1$ such that if $C(x_1, x_2, ..., x_d) = S$ and the following holds: if $(S_i \cap S) \neq \emptyset$, then $S_i \subseteq S$. Such a scheme is called *simple* if the last constraint is changed to: if $(S_i \cap S) \neq \emptyset$, then $S_i = S$. A scheme formed by groups is said to have *equal partitions* if each partition S_i is identical in size, or equivalently $|S_i| = \frac{m}{k}$ for all i.

It is possible to transform any coloring scheme (C, m, r_1, d) into a scheme formed by groups with equal partitions (of size r_2) (C', mr_2, r_1r_2, d), where C' is defined as: $C'(x_1, ..., x_d) = \bigcup\limits_{s \in C(x_1, ..., x_d)} \{im + s | 0 \leq i < r_2\}$, we denote this transformation process by $GROUP((C, m, r_1, d), r_2)$ ((C, m, r_1, d) is referred to as the *base scheme* in what follows). A scheme defined with $GROUP$ is simple if $r_1 = 1$. Now any scheme defined with $GROUP$ is a scheme formed by groups with equal partitions, but any scheme formed by groups with equal partitions is equivalent to a scheme that can be defined with $GROUP$ (proof omitted). We call the set of schemes defined by $GROUP$ the *grouping schemes*.

There have been scheduling algorithms defined for any replicated algorithm that will work for any replicated scheme, but for simple grouping schemes (represented by $GROUP((C, m, 1, d), r)$) there is a scheduling algorithm that runs in time $O(m)$ and executes with one pass over the tiles (see **RetrieveTiles** below). The algorithm uses a function **SetSchedule**(*tile*,*disk*) which sets the schedule to retrieve *tile* from *disk*.

begin RetrieveTiles(Query, $(C, mr, r, d) = GROUP((D, m, 1, d), r)$)
    $A[]$:= array initialized to 0 of size m.
    forall $t = (t_1, ..., t_d)$ **in** Query **do**
        $c := C(t)$
        SetSchedule(*t*,$c + A[c]$)
        $A[c] := ((A[c] + m) \bmod (mr))$
    endfor
end RetrieveTiles

Thus simple grouping schemes can be used without having to incur the additional scheduling costs of other replicated schemes. In addition to this, the additive error of a grouping scheme with level of replication l is bounded by the $\lceil \frac{o}{l} \rceil$ where o is the additive error of the base scheme (see Theorem 3-3). Before this can be proven we need Lemmas 3-1 and 3-2.

Lemma 3-1: If the coloring scheme (C, m, r, d) has an additive error of o, then $GROUP((C, m, lr, d), l)$ will have a response time no larger than $\lceil \frac{\lceil \frac{x}{k} \rceil + o}{l} \rceil$ for x records.

Proof: For the x records the original coloring scheme will have at most $(\lceil \frac{x}{k} \rceil + o)$ instances of any one color which means there will be at most $(\lceil \frac{x}{k} \rceil + o)$ instances of any group. These values can be distributed equally among the l colors in that group to obtain a maximum response time of $\lceil \frac{\lceil \frac{x}{k} \rceil + o}{l} \rceil$. **QED**

Lemma 3-2: $\lceil \frac{\lceil \frac{x}{k} \rceil + o}{l} \rceil \leq \lceil \frac{x}{kl} \rceil + \lceil \frac{o}{l} \rceil$

Proof: Let $x = a(kl) + bk + c$, where $0 \leq b < l$ and $0 \leq c < k$. There are two cases to consider: $(b = 0$ and $c = 0)$ or $(b \neq 0$ or $c \neq 0)$.

Case 1: $(b = 0$ and $c = 0)$: $\lceil \frac{\lceil \frac{x}{k} \rceil + o}{l} \rceil = \lceil \frac{\lceil \frac{a(kl)}{k} \rceil + o}{l} \rceil = \lceil \frac{al + o}{l} \rceil = a + \lceil \frac{o}{l} \rceil = \lceil \frac{a(kl)}{kl} \rceil + \lceil \frac{o}{l} \rceil = \lceil \frac{x}{kl} \rceil + \lceil \frac{o}{l} \rceil$

Case 2: $(b \neq 0$ or $c \neq 0)$: $\lceil \frac{\lceil \frac{x}{k} \rceil + o}{l} \rceil = \lceil \frac{\lceil \frac{akl + bk + c}{k} \rceil + o}{l} \rceil = \lceil \frac{al + b + \lceil \frac{c}{k} \rceil + o}{l} \rceil \leq a + \lceil \frac{b + 1 + o}{l} \rceil \leq a + \lceil \frac{l + o}{l} \rceil = a + 1 + \lceil \frac{o}{l} \rceil = \lceil \frac{a(kl) + bk + c}{kl} \rceil + \lceil \frac{o}{l} \rceil = \lceil \frac{x}{kl} \rceil + \lceil \frac{o}{l} \rceil$.

In either case $\lceil \frac{\lceil \frac{x}{k} \rceil + o}{l} \rceil \leq \lceil \frac{x}{kl} \rceil + \lceil \frac{o}{l} \rceil$. **QED**

Theorem 3-3: If the coloring scheme (C, m, r', d) has an additive error of o, then $GROUP((C, m, r', d), r)$ will have an additive error no larger than $\lceil \frac{o}{r} \rceil$.

Proof: Follows directly from Lemma 3-1 and Lemma 3-2. **QED**

This last theorem implies that the additive error for a coloring scheme can be reduced by using this grouping method. Since the additive error can be reduced the expected value above optimal will also be reduced. To summarize this section, a class of replicated schemes can be defined with the $GROUP$ transformation, which we call the grouping schemes. A subset of these schemes are simple and for this subset there are two significant benefits compared to non-replicated schemes including: i) queries can be processed in time proportional to the number of records which is asymptotically optimal, and ii) there is a performance increase.

3.3   Achieving Optimal and Constant Additive Error

In this section schemes with 0 and $O(1)$ additive error are introduced.

Corollary 3-4: If a scheme (C, m, r_1, d) is strictly optimal so is $GROUP((C, m, r_1, d), r_2)$.

Proof: Since (C, m, r_1, d) is strictly optimal the additive error will be 0, and thus by Theorem 3-3, the additive error of $GROUP((C, m, r_1, d), r_2)$ will also be 0, and thus is strictly optimal. **QED**

The previous corollary implies that any scheme with level of replication r that is optimal for c disks can be transformed using $GROUP$ into a scheme that is optimal for ck disks with level of replication kr. It is possible to color a two dimensional grid optimally with 1, 2, or 3 (or 5 in 2-D) colors using RPHM in two dimensions and DM in higher dimensions. Hence, it is possible to color a grid with r, $2r$, or $3r$, (or $5r$ in 2-D) with level of replication r in a strictly optimal fashion (by Corollary 3-4). Furthermore, these schemes are simple and so **RetrieveTiles** can be used to retrieve the tiles in time proportional to the number of records. The CC scheme described in [7,15] is the scheme defined above that uses a base scheme with only 1 color. In addition to these optimal schemes there are grouping schemes that achieve an additive error that is $O(1)$.

Corollary 3-5: If a scheme (C, m, r_1, d) has an additive error of $O(f(m))$ for some function f then is $GROUP((C, m, r_1, d), x)$, where $x > f(m)$ has an additive error that is $O(1)$.

Proof: Since the scheme (C, m, r_1, d) has an additive error of $O(f(m))$, then the additive error is bounded by $af(m)$ for some constant a. Now by theorem 3-3, $GROUP((C, m, r_1, d), x)$ will have an additive error no larger than $\lceil \frac{af(m)}{x} \rceil \leq a$ and thus is $O(1)$. **QED**

The following is a table of grouping schemes with base schemes with m colors that have an additive error which is $O(1)$ but can be scheduled with **RetrieveTiles** (it is assumed m is a power of 2 for the RFX scheme):

Base Scheme	Dimensions	Level of Replication	Additive Error
LHDM [8]	d	$(m-1)^{d-1} - 1$	1
RFX, GRS, and other schemes [2,3,14]	2	$\log m$	$O(1)$
RFX [2,3]	2	$2\log m - 3$	1
Schemes in [5]	d	$\log^{d-1}(m)$	$O(1)$

3.4   Generalizing Optimal Additive Error

In the previous section schemes were introduced that were strictly optimal, but these schemes are applied in the situation where the number of colors was a multiple of the number of colors in a base scheme that is optimal (i.e. 1, 2, or 3 (or 5 in 2-D)). The CC coloring is an instance of the previous scheme and is strictly optimal for any number of colors, but it requires that the level of replication be the number of colors, which may be unreasonable for many applications. In this section a strictly optimal scheme for any number of colors is given with a level of replication close to half the number of colors.

The scheme presented here is a generalization of $GROUP((C, 2, 1, d), k)$ where C is the DM coloring scheme that is strictly optimal for any number of colors. In the case, where the number of colors is even, we are trivially done using schemes discussed in the previous section. Suppose the number of colors is odd (i.e. $m = 2k + 1$), to create a scheme for m colors place $2k$ of the colors using the grouped DM scheme with level of replication k and then place the entire database on the last disk. Note that the level of replication for such a scheme for m disks is $\lfloor \frac{m}{2} \rfloor + (m \bmod 2)$ which is about $\frac{m}{2}$. It can be proven that this scheme is strictly optimal, but we omit this proof due to space constraints.

A possible criticism of this scheme is that if you can place the entire database on a single disk, then why not use the CC mechanism for simplicity. However, in this case it is only required that a single disk be large enough to hold the entire database. This may not be reasonable for large databases, but is reasonable in some situations.

This generalized approach can be extended to grouping schemes with base schemes with 3 (and 5 in 2-D) disks in a similar fashion (we omit the details due to space constraints). It is not true however that if you have an optimal scheme for k colors that if you put all tiles on another disk that the solution will be optimal for $k + 1$ disks.

The scheme defined in this section constitutes a general strictly optimal schemes with the lowest known level of replication. With some modification to our scheduling algorithm the schedule can be computed in time $O(\# \text{ of records})$. We give a verbal description of the algorithm here for when there are $2k + 1$ colors and the scheme described above is used. Essentially there are two groups of k colors and 1 extra color. We know that an optimal schedule is achievable so we determine what optimal is, and call it o. Assign up to the first ko tiles of each group to disks in that group, such that no more than o tiles are assigned to any one disk, and if there are any tiles remaining after this has been done to both groups assign these leftovers to the last disk which is not in either group.

4   Experiments

For this section, experiments were performed to compare the performance between grouped schemes with level of replication as 2 and non-grouped schemes. The comparison criterion that is used is the expected deviation from optimal for all queries. To compute the expected deviation from optimal for a coloring scheme (C, m, r, d) we compute the expected value from optimal of all wraparound queries in an d dimensional grid with side lengths equal to m. There is a finite number of queries in such a grid so this value can be computed exactly for smaller m values, but is estimated for larger values. This estimation is done by taking a random sampling of queries and computing the expected deviation from optimal of these queries. It is worth noting that when an exact value is computed that the maximum additive error found will be the maximum additive error in any grid (see [8], which can be generalized to grouping schemes, but this generalization is omitted). To perform the comparison between the replicated and non-replicated schemes we use a hybrid coloring. Given a set of colorings this hybrid coloring uses the coloring that minimizes the expected deviation from optimal for a specific number of disks, i.e. the hybrid coloring uses the best coloring in the set for a specific situation. The comparison is figure 1 is between the hybrid coloring of a set of non-replicated schemes and the hybrid coloring for these schemes transformed with $GROUP$ using level of replication of 2.

The set of non-replicated coloring schemes used are DM [6], FX (for powers of 2) [9], RFX (for powers of 2) [2], RPHM [11], GFIB [11], GRS [4], and a scheme

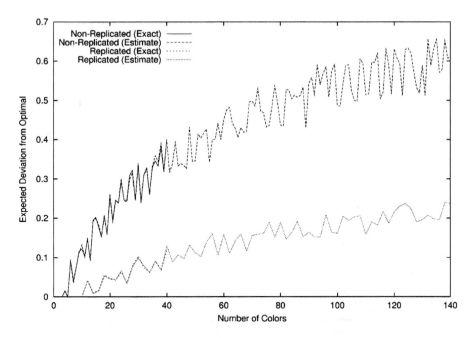

Fig. 1. Expected Deviation from Optimal for 2-D Schemes

based on the Corput set [14]. For the grouping schemes we use the grouped
version of these schemes with level of replication 2. When the number of disks
is no more than 40, exact values were computed, but estimates were used for
up to 140 disks. These estimates were made by looking at 5000 queries (chosen
randomly with uniform distribution) in the grid using the mean deviation as the
estimate. The results are displayed in Figure 1.

Figure 1 is interesting for several reasons. First, it shows that the estimate is
accurate for predicting the expected deviation for values up to 40. Also, it shows
that the grouping schemes perform far better than the non-replicated schemes,
since the expected deviation from optimal is 2-3 times larger for non-replicated
colorings than for grouping schemes. Thus if a replication level of 2 is used, then
range query performance will be improved substantially.

5   Conclusions

When declustering data, there are three inhibiting factors that may prevent the
usage of replication: i) there is not enough disk space on each disk to contain
enough information, ii) the slow down that occurs with query scheduling for
replication is too overwhelming, and iii) the benefit from replication is not significant. We have introduced a class of schemes, called the grouping schemes,
which eliminate conditions (ii) and (iii). Condition (ii) is eliminated because the
grouping schemes can be scheduled in time O(number of tiles), and it was shown

in Section 4, that these techniques perform extremely well even if the level of replication is 2 which eliminates condition (iii). Thus an important conclusion about the usage of replication can be stated: If there is enough room on the disks to facilitate replication, then replication should be used. Furthermore, a strictly optimal scheme for any number of colors with the lowest known level of replication for such a solution was presented along with several schemes with additive error that is $O(1)$ were given that have fewer restrictions on the number of disks and have a lower level of replication than previous schemes that achieve an $O(1)$ bound on additive error (the authors know of only one such previous scheme, which is SRCDM).

References

1. K. Abdel-Ghaffar and A. E. Abbadi. Optimal allocation of two-dimensional data. In *International Conference on Database Theory*, pages 409–418, 1997.
2. M. J. Atallah and S. Prabhakar. (almost) optimal parallel block access to range queries. In *Proceedings of the nineteenth ACM SIGMOD-SIGACT-SIGART symposium on Principles of database systems*, pages 205–215. ACM Press, 2000.
3. R. Bhatia, R. Sinha, and C.-M. Chen. Hierarchical declustering schemes for range queries. In *In 7th Int'l Conf. on Extending Database Technology*, 2000.
4. R. Bhatia, R. K. Sinha, and C.-M. Chen. Declustering using golden ratio sequences. In *ICDE*, pages 271–280, 2000.
5. C.-M. Chen and C. T. Cheng. From discrepancy to declustering: near-optimal multidimensional declustering strategies for range queries. In *Proceedings of the twenty-first ACM SIGMOD-SIGACT-SIGART symposium on Principles of database systems*, pages 29–38. ACM Press, 2002.
6. H. Du and J. Sobolewski. Disk allocation for cartesian product files on multiple disk systems. *ACM Transactions on Database System*, pages 82–101, 1982.
7. K. Frikken, M. Atallah, S. Prabhakar, and R. Safavi-Naini. Optimal parallel i/o for range queries through replication. In *Proceedings of 13th Intl. Conf. on Database and Expert Systems Application (LNCS 2453)*, pages 669–678.
8. B. Himatsingka, J. Srivastava, J.-Z. Li, and D. Rotem. Latin hypercubes: A class of multidimensional declustering techniques, 1994.
9. M. H. Kim and S. Pramanik. Optimal file distribution for partial match retrieval. In *Proceedings of the 1988 ACM SIGMOD international conference on Management of data*, pages 173–182. ACM Press, 1988.
10. J. Matousek. *Geometric discrepancy, an illustrated guide*. Springer-Verlag, 1999.
11. S. Prabhakar, K. Abdel-Ghaffar, D. Agrawal, and A. E. Abbadi. Cyclic allocation of two-dimensional data. Technical Report TRCS97-08, 1, 1997.
12. P. Sanders. Reconciling simplicity and realism in parallel disk models. In *Proceedings of the twelfth annual ACM-SIAM symposium on Discrete algorithms*, pages 67–76. ACM Press, 2001.
13. P. Sanders, S. Egner, and J. Korst. Fast concurrent access to parallel disks. In *Proceedings of the eleventh annual ACM-SIAM symposium on Discrete algorithms*, pages 849–858. ACM Press, 2000.
14. R. K. Sinha, R. Bhatia, and C.-M. Chen. Asymptotically optimal declustering schemes for range queries. In *International Conference on Database Theory*, 2001.
15. A. Tosun and H. Ferhatosmanoglu. Optimal parallel i/o using replication. Technical Report OSU-CISRC-11/01-TR26, 2001.

XML Restructuring and Integration for Tabular Data

Wei Yu, Z. Meral Ozsoyoglu, and Gultekin Ozsoyoglu

Electrical Engineering and Computer Science Department,
Case Western Reserve University,
Cleveland, Ohio 44106, U.S.A.
{wyu,ozsoy,tekin}@eecs.cwru.edu

Abstract. We study the data integration and restructuring issues of tabular data. We consider the case where the same set of data is collected from independent sites, stored in different DBMSs or other repositories, organized in different tabular or equivalent semi-structured formats, and published on the web. These sites transform tabular data into XML data with possible syntactic discrepancies in their original tabular structures. Data integration refers to the task of creating an integrated XML view with a pre-specified format by restructuring and integrating different XML documents. Existing XML query algebras are not sufficient for tabular conversions. We propose the XML-T model and the restructuring and integration operators for tabular data. We show with examples the uses of our operators to create "views".

1 Introduction

In many scientific research communities, the same set of data is collected from independent sites, stored in different DBMSs or other repositories, organized in different tabular or equivalent semi-structured formats, and published in XML on the web. Such transformations from local tabular data into XML data inevitably inherit the syntactic discrepancies that originally exist in local tabular formats. In this paper, we investigate the data integration issues involved in creating an integrated XML tabular view with a pre-specified format by restructuring and integrating the tabular data obtained from the web sites.

1.1 An Example: Metabolic Pathway Data

Consider metabolic pathway results in bioinformatics such as those in [6], where data about molecules, processes (metabolic reactions), and pathways (graph-structured organizations of pathways) are maintained as illustrated in Fig 1 (a), Fig 2 (a), Fig 3 (a), and Fig 4 (a). Metabolic pathways represent the sequential and cumulative actions of genetically distinct, but functionally related molecules. A pathway consists one or more processes, each of which begins with input molecules, called substrates, uses various combinations of other input molecules such as cofactors, activators and inhibitors, and ends with product molecules (output) that are chemically modified substrates. Molecules are identified by unique *id* numbers and, sometimes, are

V. Mařík et al. (Eds.): DEXA 2003, LNCS 2736, pp. 233–243, 2003.

(a) Relational Tables:

Molecules

ID	NAME
999	OPQ

Processes

MOLECULE	PROCESS	TYPE
999	004	T1

Pathways

MOLECULE	PATHWAY
999	P2
999	P3

(b) Relational View Query:

```
CREATE VIEW Molecules_View AS
(SELECT id, name, process, p_type, pathway
 FROM Molecules m, Processes p, Pathways w
 WHERE m.id = p.molecule AND
       m.id = w.molecule)
```

(c) View Table

Molecules_View

ID	NAME	PROCESS	P_TYPE	PATHWAY
999	OPQ	004	T1	P2
999	OPQ	004	T1	P3

(d) XML DTD:

```
<DOCTYPE  SITE1_DTD [
<!ELEMENT  molecule_view (row*)>
<!ELEMENT  row ( id, name?, process,
                 p_type, pathway )>
<!ELEMENT  id (#PCDATA)>
<!ELEMENT  name (#PCDATA)>
<!ELEMENT  process (#PCDATA)>
<!ELEMENT  p_type (#PCDATA)>
<!ELEMENT  pathway (#PCDATA)>]>
```

(e) XML Instance:

```
<molecule_view>
  <row>
    <id>999</>
    <name>OPQ</>
    <process>004</>
    <p_type>T1</>
    <pathway>P2</></>
  <row>
    <id>999</>
    <name>OPQ</>
    <process>004</>
    <p_type>T1</>
    <pathway>P3</></></>
```

Fig. 1. Relational tables and their exported view at Site #1, and XML DTD and XML instance mapped to the view.

(a) Hierarchical Tables:

Molecules

PROCESSES	ID	NAME	PATHWAYS
●	123	XYZ	●

PROCESS	TYPE
001	T1
002	T2

PATHWAY
P1

(b) XML DTD:

```
<DOCTYPE  SITE2_DTD [
<!ELEMENT  molecules (row*)>
<!ELEMENT  row ( processes, id, name?,
                 pathways )>
<!ELEMENT  processes ( process_row+ )>
<!ELEMENT  process_row ( process, type )>
<!ELEMENT  process (#PCDATA)>
<!ELEMENT  type (#PCDATA)>
<!ELEMENT  id (#PCDATA)>
<!ELEMENT  name (#PCDATA)>
<!ELEMENT  pathways ( pathway_row* )>
<!ELEMENT  pathway_row ( pathway )>
<!ELEMENT  pathway (#PCDATA)>]>
```

(c) XML Instance:

```
<molecules>
  <row>
    <processes>
      <process_row>
        <process>001</>
        <type>T2</> </>
      <process_row>
        <process>002</>
        <type>T3</></></>
    <id>123</>
    <name>XYZ</>
    <pathways>
      <pathway_row>
        <pathway>P1</></>
    </></></>
```

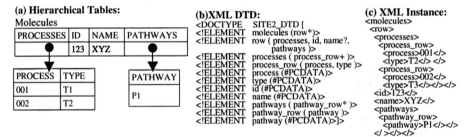

Fig. 2. Nested tables, XML DTD and instance at Site #2. (a) represents a set of hierarchical tables, that have other nested tables as attribute values; (b) and (c) present the XML DTD and data that are transformed from the hierarchical tables.

classified by types. There are many-to-many relationships between pathways, processes, and molecules. The collected data is usually organized in tables of users' choices. *Tables* are the two-dimensional representations of data. A table consists of (a) a table name, (b) a set of column names (entries) which define attributes and their formats: atomic value set of values, or table of values, (c) a set of row entries each of which represents an ordered list of occurrences of attribute values. The *tabular format* defines how the data are organized in tables.

Regular tabular format is one where table column values are of single type. Examples of tables with a regular tabular format include (1) relational tables of relational DBs (Fig 1 (a)), (2) nested tables of hierarchical DBs (Fig 2 (a)) or OODBs where an object ID is treated as a pointer to another table, and (3) spreadsheet tables commonly used in non-database repositories produced by, say, MS Excel (Fig 3 (a)) etc. An attribute value in relational tables is atomic; in nested tables, it is either atomic or another nested table; and, in spreadsheet tables, it is either atomic, a set, or another nested table.

(a) Spreadsheet Table:

Molecules

PROCESSES NUM	TYPE	ID	NAME	PATHWAYS
002 003	T2 T3	321	ABC	P1, P2

(b) XML DTD:

```
<DOCTYPE  SITE3_DTD [
<!ELEMENT  molecules ( row* )>
<!ELEMENT  row ( processes, id, name?,
                      pathways* )>
<!ELEMENT  processes ( process_row+ )>
<!ELEMENT  process_row ( num, type )>
<!ELEMENT  num (#PCDATA)>
<!ELEMENT  type (#PCDATA)>
<!ELEMENT  id (#PCDATA)>
<!ELEMENT  name (#PCDATA)>
<!ELEMENT  pathways (#PCDATA)>]>
```

(c)XML Instance:

```
<molecules>
 <row>
  <processes>
   <process_row>
    <num>002</>
    <type>T2</></>
   <process_row>
    <num>003</>
    <type>T3</></></>
  <id>321</>
  <name>ABC</>
  <pathways>P1</>
  <pathways>P2</></></>
```

Fig. 3. Spreadsheet tables, XML DTD and instance at Site #3. (a) represents a spreadsheet table which allows a nested table and a set of values; (b) and (c) present the XML DTD and data that are transformed from the spreadsheet table.

(a) Irregular Tables:

Molecules

PROCESS	ID	NAME	PATHWAYS
TYPE 002 T2 003 T3	321	ABC	P1, P2
005	999	OPQ	P1

(b) XML DTD:

```
<DOCTYPE  SITE4_DTD [
<!ELEMENT  molecules ( row* )>
<!ELEMENT  row ( processes | process, id,
                      name?, pathways* )>
<!ELEMENT  processes ( process_row+ )>
<!ELEMENT  process_row ( num, type )>
<!ELEMENT  num (#PCDATA)>
<!ELEMENT  type (#PCDATA)>
<!ELEMENT  process (#PCDATA)>
<!ELEMENT  id (#PCDATA)>
<!ELEMENT  pathways (#PCDATA)>
<!ELEMENT  name (#PCDATA)>]>
```

(c) XML Instance:

```
<molecules>
 <row>
  <processes>
   <process_row>
    <process>002</>
    <type>T2</></>
   <process_row>
    <process>003</>
    <type>T3</></></>
  <id>321</>
  <name>ABC</>
  <pathways>P1</>
  <pathways>P2</></>
 <row>
  <process>005</>
  <id>999</>
  <name>OPQ</>
  <pathways>P1</></></>
```

Fig. 4. Irregularly-formatted tables, XML DTD and instance at Site #4.

Irregular tabular format is one where table column values are of multiple formats. For example, Fig 4 (a) shows that the *PROCESS* column is either an atomic value or a nested table. Occasionally, an irregular tabular-formatted data is stored as semi-structured data.

XML document type definition (DTD) describes the structure of XML data. Three useful DTD constructs are: (a) repetition structure, denoted by '+' or '*', that shows multiple occurrences of the structure ('+' indicates one or more occurrences, and '*' indicates zero or more occurrences); (b) option structure, denoted by '?', that describes an optional occurrence of the structure; and (c) alternation structure, denoted by '|', that allows an item to take either one structure or the other.

To be able to define XML transformations among tables with regular /irregular formats, we propose a *Table-to-XML transformation* that maps a table into a three-level XML tree structure, and transforms differently-formatted column values (e.g. atomic value, set of values, nested table, and alternative attributes) into the corresponding XML structures. Now, we are in a position to define the problem that this paper solves.

Problem. Given a set D of XML documents obtained through a Table-to-XML transformation from regular/irregular formatted tables of data in the same set of attributes, the integrated view is a mapping function over D in algebra with operators. The problem is to define a highly expressive XML algebra that generates an integrated view of the set D of documents.

The rest of the paper is organized as follows. Section 2 introduces transformations from regular/irregular tables to XML and the *XML-T*, an XML model for tables. Section 3 defines the XML tabular restructuring and integration operators. Section 4 presents, with examples, the uses of the proposed operators to create an XML integrated view. Section 5 briefly surveys the relevant studies, and compares our approach to others.

2   XML Model for Tables: XML-T

XML-T represents XML documents that are transformed from tables. We use XML DTD to describe the structures of XML-T. Given an XML document *Doc*, we use *I(Doc)* and *DTD(Doc)* to denote the instance and its DTD. An *XML-T document* has a table element as the root, which has one or more row elements as children, and each row element has one or more column elements as children. The column element may contain a data item or another nested table element. The hierarchical structure is described by the following recursive definition:

   tab_elem ← begin(tab_elem tag) row_elem* end(tab_elem tag);
   row_elem ← begin(row_elem tag) col_elem$_1$,...,col_elem$_k$ end(row_elem tag);
   col_elem ← begin(col_elem tag) data end(col_elem tag) or tab_elem.

where *tab_elem tag*, *row_elem tag*, *col_elem tag* denote tags for tables, rows, and columns, respectively; and *begin(tag)*, the concatenation of '<' | *tag* | '>', denotes the beginning mark of tag; and *end(tag)*, the concatenation of '</' | *tag* | '>' or '</>', denotes the end mark of tag.

Every XML-T document has an associated DTD. In an XML-T document, each element except the root has exactly one parent so that the graphical representation of XML-T document is a tree. XML data that is transformed from tables using methods discussed in 2.1 conforms to the XML-T model.

An *XML-T tree* is a node-labeled and rooted tree that highlights the nested structure of the relevant XML-T document instance. Each *tag* in the XML-T instance is mapped to an internal node labeled by the string of that tag, and each *data* is mapped to a leaf node labeled by the string of the associated data value.

2.1   Rules for Transforming Regular/Irregular Tables into XML-T Documents

Rule 1. Any table is mapped to a three-level XML tree structure: (i) the name of the table is mapped into an XML element called the table element; (ii) the rows of the table are mapped to the table element's child elements, called row elements; and (iii) the attributes of rows are mapped to child elements of row elements. Because a table contains zero and more rows, the row element has the repetition structure. For example, the (relational view) table *Molecule_View* and its row entries in Fig 1 (c) are mapped to the XML table element *molecule_view* and XML row element *row* in Fig 1 (d) and (e). The columns of row entries *id, name, process, p_type,* and *pathway* in Fig 1 (c) are mapped to XML column elements *id, name, process, p_type,* and *pathway* in Fig 1 (d) and (e), respectively.

Rule 2. Different formats of column values are mapped to the corresponding XML structures:

- Atomic values are mapped to XML leaf elements that have the singleton structure. For example, relation attribute values of *id, name, process, p_type,* and *pathway* in Fig 1 (c) are mapped to the corresponding XML data enclosed by *id, name, process, p_type,* and *pathway* in Fig 1 (d) and (e) respectively. And, the relational constraint NULL or NOT NULL on a column sets on or off the structure option on the corresponding XML element. Generally, the XML column element that is mapped to the column of a relational table may have the option structure, but never has any the repetition, alternation, or nested structures.
- The 'table inside table' structure of nested tables is mapped to the 'table element inside table element' nested structure in XML. For example, the columns *PROCESSES* and *PATHWAYS* in Fig 2 (a) contain tables; so are mapped into two table elements in XML *processes* and *pathways* in Fig 2 (b) and (c). Assume that the row element of *processes* cannot be empty, but the row element of *pathways* may be empty. The *process_row* has '+' to indicate one and more occurrences, while the *pathway_row* has '*' to indicate zero or more occurrences. Generally, the XML element that is mapped to a column of nested tables is either a singleton element or a nested table element.
- Set of values is mapped to the XML element that has the repetition structure. For example, the *PATHWAYS* column in Fig 3 (a) is mapped to the XML element *pathways** in Fig 3 (b) and (c). Generally, the XML element that is mapped to a column of spreadsheet tables is a singleton element, a nested table element, or the repetition element.
- Alternative column attributes in irregular tabular formats are mapped to the alternation structure of several corresponding XML elements. For example, the *PROCESS* attribute in Fig 4 (a) takes two alternative formats: a nested table containing *process ids* and *types* or an atomic value of a *process id*. The *PROCESS* attribute is mapped to the alternation structure of the two corresponding XML elements *processes* | *process* in Fig 4 (b) and (c).

3   XML-T Operators

The restructure and integration operators manipulate instances (node-labeled trees) of the XML-T model. In XML-T model, two instances are the same if and only if there is an isomorphism between them. An *isomorphism* between two rooted trees T_1 and T_2 is a bijection (one-to-one and onto) function between the nodes of T_1 and T_2 that maps the root of T_1 to the root of T_2 and preserves the edges. For node-labeled rooted trees, the isomorphism must also match the labels of corresponding nodes. The comparison of our operators with other related algebra operators is briefly presented in section 5.

3.1   Restructure Operators

XML-T restructure operators perform table structure conversions. *XSplit* and *XMerge* enable the structure conversions of column elements from the repetition (multi-values) to the singleton (atomic value), and vice verse. *XNest* and *XUnnest* create and remove nested XML table elements. Formal definitions of the operators are presented in [11].

XSplit. *XSplit* operator takes the parameter *Target* as the column element of a repetition structure, and converts the repetition structure into a singleton structure by duplicating the row elements to hold a set of values in the original target column elements. *XSplit* operation of a target T on an XML-T document I is denoted by $S^x_T I$. Fig 5 (a) illustrates the *XSplit* operation. Fig 6 (a) shows the result of applying *XSplit* of *pathways* on the data from Site #3.

XMerge. *XMerge* operator is the reverse of *XSplit*, and takes the parameter *Target* as the column element of a singleton structure. *XMerge* merges the values of *Target* to form a repetition structure based upon the tree isomorphism of the rest of the structures. *XMerge* operation of a target T on an XML-T document I is denoted by $M^x_T I$. Fig 5 (b) illustrates the *XMerge* operation. Fig 6 (b) shows the result of applying *XMerge* of *pathway* on the data from Site #1.

XNest. *XNest* operator is used to create nested table elements, and takes three required parameters: (1) *Target* as one or more singleton column elements of a row element to be nested, (2) label of the nested table element to be created and (3) label of row elements of the nested table element to be created. *XNest* groups the row elements based upon the tree isomorphism of the structure of all non-Target columns, and creates a nested table element for each group to hold the Target columns. *XNest* operation of targets T_1, …, T_m on an XML-T document I with N and E being the labels of the nested table element and its row elements to be created, is denoted by $N^x_{(T\_1,...T\_m),\ N,\ E} I$. Fig 5 (c) illustrates the *XNest* operation. Fig 6 (c) shows the result of applying *XNest* of *process* and *t_type* on the data from Site #1. The nested table element and its row elements are labeled as *processes* and *process_row*, respectively.

XUnnest. *XUnnest* removes nested table elements by replacing the nested table element with its column elements. It takes one required parameter *Target* as the nested table element to be removed. *XUnnest* removes the nested table elements by duplicating the row elements that contains the nested table elements to hold each of row elements contained in the original nested table elements. *XUnnest* operation of a nested table element N on an XML-T document I is denoted by $U^x_N I$. Fig 5 (d) illustrates the *XUnnest* operation. Fig 6 (d) shows the results of applying *XUnnest* of *processes* on the data from Site #3.

3.2 Binary Operators

XUnion, XDiff, and XIntersection. Binary operators combine two *XML-T* instances in a way analogous to the set union, difference and intersection, and therefore are named as *XUnion, XDiff,* and *XIntersect*. They differ from the traditional counterparts in that they operate on two sets of tree structures instead of two sets of values. In *XUnion, XDiff,* and *XIntersect,* two tree structures are considered as duplicates of each other if and only if they are isomorphic. Fig 6 (e), (f), and (g) show the results of applying *XUnion, XDiff* and *XIntersection* to the data from Site #3 and Site # 4, respectively. Formally, given two XML-T instances: I(1) whose root is R and I(2) whose root S:

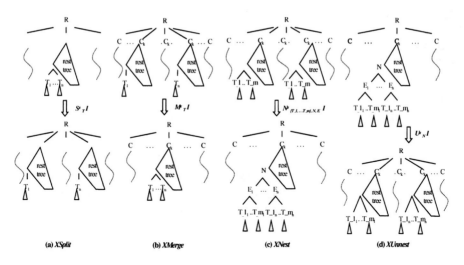

Fig. 5. Graphical explanations of (a) XSplit, (b) XMerge, (c) XNest, and (d) XUnnest

- *XUnion* operation on I(1) and I(2), denoted by $I(1) \cup^x I(2)$, attaches root's direct children in I(2) to the root of I(1), removes the duplications, and returns I(1);
- *XDiff* operation on I(1) and I(2), denoted by $I(1) -^x I(2)$, removes the root's child in I(1) if there exists a root's child in I(2) which is isomorphic to it, and returns I(1);
- *XIntersection* operation on I(1) and I(2), denoted by $I(1) \cap^x I(2)$, removes the root's direct child in I(1) if there does not exist a root's direct children in I(2) which is isomorphic to it, and returns I(1).

(a) $S^x_{<pathways>}$ I(site#3):
```
<molecules>
 <row>
  <processes>
   <process_row>
    <num>002</>
    <type>T2</></>
   <process_row>
    <num>003</>
    <type>T3</></></>
  <id>321</>
  <name>ABC</>
  <pathways>P1</></>
 <row>
  <processes>
   <process_row>
    <num>002</>
    <type>T2</></>
   <process_row>
    <num>003</>
    <type>T3</></></>
  <id>321</>
  <name>ABC</>
  <pathways>P2</></></>
```

(i) $T^x_{<process>, <t_type>}$ I(site#1):
```
<molecule_view>
 <row>
  <id>999</>
  <name>OPQ</>
  <pathway>P2</></>
 <row>
  <id>999</>
  <name>OPQ</>
  <pathway>P3</></></>
```

(b) $M^x_{<pathway>}$ I(site#1):
```
<molecule_view>
 <row>
  <id>999</>
  <name>OPQ</>
  <processes>004</>
  <p_type>T1</>
  <pathway>P2</>
  <pathway>P3</></></>
```

(f) I(site#4) $-^x$ I(site#3) :
```
<molecules>
 <row>
  <process>005</>
  <id>999</>
  <name>OPQ</>
  <pathways>P1</></></>
```

(g) I(site#4) $\cap^x$ I(site#3) :
```
<molecules>
 <row>
  <processes>
   <process_row>
    <process>002</>
    <type>T2</></>
   <process_row>
    <process>003</>
    <type>T3</></></>
  <id>321</>
  <name>ABC</>
  <pathways>P1</>
  <pathways>P2</></></>
```

(c) $N^x_{[<process>, <t_type>], <processes>, <process_row>}$ I(site#1):
```
<molecule_view>
 <row>
  <id>999</>
  <name>OPQ</>
  <processes>
   <process_row>
    <process>004</>
    <p_type>T1</></></>
  <pathway>P2</></>
 <row>
  <id>999</>
  <name>OPQ</>
  <processes>
   <process_row>
    <process>004</>
    <p_type>T1</></></>
  <pathway>P3</></></>
```

(h) $R^x_{<molecules>=<molecule_view>, <type>=<t_type>}$ I(site#1):
```
<molecules>
 <row>
  <id>999</>
  <name>OPQ</>
  <process>004</>
  <type>T1</>
  <pathway>P2</></>
 <row>
  <id>999</>
  <name>OPQ</>
  <process>004</>
  <type>T1</>
  <pathway>P3</></></>
```

(d) $U^x_{<processes>}$ I(site#3):
```
<molecules>
 <row>
  <num>002</>
  <type>T2</>
  <id>321</>
  <name>ABC</>
  <pathways>P1</>
  <pathways>P2</></>
 <row>
  <num>003</>
  <type>T3</>
  <id>321</>
  <name>ABC</>
  <pathways>P1</>
  <pathways>P2</></></>
```

(e) I(site#4) $\cup^x$ I(site#3):
```
<molecules>
 <row>
  <processes>
   <process_row>
    <process>002</>
    <type>T2</></>
   <process_row>
    <process>003</>
    <type>T3</></></>
  <id>321</>
  <name>ABC</>
  <pathways>P1</>
  <pathways>P2</></>
 <row>
  <process>005</>
  <id>999</>
  <name>OPQ</>
  <pathways>P1</></></>
```

Fig. 6. Examples of (a) XSplit, (b) XMerge, (c) XNest, (d)XUnnest, (e) XUnion, (f) XDiff, (g) XIntersection, (h) XRename, and (i) XTrim

3.3 Accessory Operators

Accessory operators rename, and trim an element. If the XML algebra being complemented has the abilities to rename, select, and project elements, these accessory operators are not necessary.

XRename. *XRename* solves XML tag conflicts by renaming a set of XML tags. It takes a set of pairs of *old* and *new* tags as parameters. Given an XML-T document instance I and a set of n pairs of *old* and *new* tags, *XRename* operation on I is denoted by $R^x_{new1 = old1, ..., newn = oldn}$ *I*. Fig 6 (h) shows the result of applying *XRename* of *molecule_view* and *t_type* to *molecules* and *type* on the data from Site #1.

XTrim. *XTrim* removes given elements. Elements being removed are specified as parameters. Given an XML-T instance I and n target elements to be trimmed: T_1, ..., T_n, *XTrim* operation on I is denoted by $T^x_{T1, ..., Tn}$ *I*. Fig 6 (i) shows the result of applying *XTrim* of *process* and *t_type* on the data from Site #1.

3.4 Expressive Power for Restructuring XML-T Data

Canonical representation (schema) of XML-T data is the simplest *XML-T* tree structure that contains a root table element with its row elements and singleton column elements. In canonical representation, there is no nested table element, and the *data* under each row element encodes the data occurrence on all the attributes in other *XML-T* representations.

Lemma 1. Let D be an XML-T schema. There exists a transformation Γ in algebra with the proposed operators, only on D, such that for every instance I with D, Γ generates the canonical representation of I, denoted by Can(I).

Lemma 2. Let D_1 and D_2 be two different XML-T schemas for the same data. For XML instances I_1 with D_1 and I_2 with D_2, there exists a function *f* in algebra that renames elements in either Can(I_1) or Can(I_2) such that Can(I_1) and Can(I_2) are isomorphic.

Proofs of Lemmas are given in [11]. It is easy to show that the algebra with proposed operators is sufficient to restructure an XML-T data from an arbitrary XML-T schema D' to another arbitrary schema D. Let R be such a restructuring algebra expression. By lemma 1, we can use an algebra transformation Γ" to compute Can(I') from I' with D', and use another algebra transformation Γ to compute Can(I) from I with D. In order to obtain the restructuring algebra expression R, we consider the composition of Γ" $\circ$ f $\circ$ Γ^{-1} to compute R. By lemma 2, the algebra function f exists.

4 Typical Examples on the Uses of Proposed Operators

The proposed *XML-T* operators can be incorporated into existing XML query algebras in two ways: (a) they generate the integrated XML view so that the user query refers to the view instead of individual source sites; and (b) they perform the tabular structure conversions to the results of XML queries so that the output conforms to a given structure. Due to space limitations, we only show (a).

4.1 Creations of the Integrated View

Example 1. Create an integrated view v_1 over Site #1 using the XML DTD in Site #3 as the view structure. The answer is:

$$v_1': N^x_{\{<process>,<p\_type>\},<processes>,<process\_row>} (R^x_{<pathways>=<pathway>} (M^x_{<pathway>} I(site\#1)));$$

$$v_1: R^x_{<molecules>=<molecule\_view>,<num>=<process>,<type>=<t\_type>} v_1'.$$

Example 2. Create an integrated view v_2 over Site #2 using the XML DTD in Site #3 as the view structure. The answer is:

$$v_2: R^x_{<pathways>=<pathway>,<num>=<process>} (M^x_{<pathway>} (U^x_{<pathways>} I(site\#2))).$$

Example 3. Create an integrated view v_3 over Site #1, Site #2, and Site #3 using the XML DTD in Site #3 as the view structure such that we combine the data that exist in Site #1 and Site #3, but not in Site #2. Given $v1$ and $v2$ in example 1 and 2, the answer is:

$$v_3: (v_1 \cap^x I(site\#3)) -^x v_2.$$

Example 4. Create the integrated view w over Site #1, Site #2, Site #3, and Site #4 with the view structure as the following XML DTD:

```
<DOCTYPE  DTD_W [
<!ELEMENT  molecules (row*)>
<!ELEMENT  row ( process*, id, pathway )>
<!ELEMENT  process (#PCDATA)>
<!ELEMENT  id (#PCDATA)>
<!ELEMENT  pathway (#PCDATA)>]>
```

This view can be created as follows:

Step 1. Combine data from site#3 and site#4, remove the alternation structure, trim off the irrelevant elements and solve the label conflictions, and finally split pathways element:

$$w_{34}: R^x_{<process>=<num>} (T^x_{<type>} (U^x_{<processes>} (I(site\#3) \cup^x I(site\#4))));$$

$$w_{34}: R^x_{<pathway>=<pathways>} (S^x_{<pathways>} w34');$$

Step 2. Convert data from site #2 and combine it with data from site #1:

$$w_{12}: (T^x_{<t\_type>,<cname>} I(site\#1)) \cup^x (U^x_{<pathways>} (U^x_{<processes>} (T^x_{<type>,<cname>} I(site\#2))));$$

Step 3. Combine two groups, and create the repetition structure on *process*:

$$w: M^x_{<process>} (w_{12} \cup^x w_{34}).$$

4.2 Incorporation of the View to XML Query

Using integrated views greatly simplifies the specifications of users' query. We show an example to incorporate the integrated view w to XQuery query.

Example 5. Find, from all four sites, the molecule that appears in pathway $P1$ and is involved in at least two processes (as a substrate or a product). The answer is:

```
FOR $row IN document (w)
LET $process1 := $row/process, $process2 := $row/process
WHERE $process1/data() <> $process2/data() AND $row/pathway/data() = 'P1'
RETURN <result> {$row/id} </>
```

In addition to solving structure conflicts, the integrated view also fuses data from different sites. For example, the data related to molecule *999* is stored in both sites #1 and #4. In site #1, this molecule appears in process *004* and pathways *P2* and *P3*. In site #4, it appears in process *005* and pathway *P1*. The view w fuses processes *004* and *005* together with molecule *999*, and relates it to pathways *P1*, *P2*, and *P3*.

5   Related Work

Our algebra operators are influenced by many previous studies. Algebras for non-1NF model, such as [9] etc., support transformations between 1NF relation and nested relations. Algebras for OODB model such as [7] and [10] explore hierarchical structures and their restructurings. Gyssens et al [4] proposes algebra for querying and restructuring tabular data. However, the proposed algebra does not support structure conversions between a table allowing multiple-valued entries and another allowing only atomic-value entries, as well as conversions between tables allowing and disallowing nested-table entries. Madhavan et al [8] discusses data transformations between different data models through mappings between them. Their operators manipulate the metadata of models and their mappings, but do not create the mappings.

We compare in [11] our operators with the XML query algebras of YATL [1], Niagara [3], TAX [5], and XQuery [2]; none of these algebras has the equivalent operators and the expressive power of our tabular restructuring operators. For example, transformations of data between two XML DTDs in Fig 1 (d), Fig 2 (b), Fig 3 (b), and Fig 4 (b) are independent of the data, and are not expressible in these algebras. In general, the existing XML query algebras can not handle the following situations: (1) partition XML elements based on their tree structures, rather than values; (2) select a target substructure and compare all the other parts of an XML element except the given target; (3) select or partition elements based on the matching of their isomorphic structures, rather than exact structures; and (4) each occurrence of a repetition structure has to be individually referred. In addition, binary operators in YALT and Niagara are value-based, instead of structure-based. Union in XQuery, written by user-defined functions, combines XML elements, but does not remove duplicates. Binary operators in TAX are structure-based, and remove the duplicates. However, they combine two sets of trees in which each tree must have a user-defined ordering number for determining the duplicates.

6   Conclusions

In this paper, we have discussed an XML-based solution to restructuring and integration of tabular data, stored in different systems. We have introduced the XML-T model for the representation of tabular data as XML documents. We have discussed three regular tabular formats and the irregular tabular format, and provided methods to transform data from regular/irregular tables to XML-T data. We have proposed a set of algebra operators for restructuring and integrating XML-T data, and shown that the proposed operators are sufficient for XML-T structure conversions. We have presented, with examples, the use of the proposed operators to create XML integrated views, and to incorporate the integrated view into XML queries.

Partitioning XML trees by their isomorphic structures is the key to implementing our algebra operators. In [11], we propose and simulate an $O(n*m)$ isomorphic tree partition algorithm for m XML trees, each of which has n nodes in the average.

References

1. Christophides, V. et al.: On Wrapping Query Languages and Efficient XML Integration. ACM SIGMOD'00. (2000)
2. Fankhauser, P. (ed): XQuery 1.0 Formal Semantics. W3C XML Query Working Gr. Note. (2002)
3. Naughton, J. (ed): The Niagara Internet Query System. IEEE Data Eng. Bulletin, Vol. 24. No. 2.
4. Gyssens, M. et al: Tables As a Paradigm for Querying and Restructuring. ACM PODS'96. (1996)
5. Jagadish, H., Lakshmanan, L., Srivastava, D., Thompson K.: TAX: a Tree Algebra for XML. Proc. DBPL Conf. Rome, Italy (2001)
6. Krishnamurthy, L., Nadeau, J., Ozsoyoglu, G., Ozsoyoglu, M. (ed.): Pathways database system: an integrated system for biological pathways. *Bioinformatics* (2003).
7. Lin, J., Ozsoyoglu, M.: Processing OODB Queries by O-algebra. CIKM'96. (1996)
8. Madhavan, J., Bernstein, P., Rahm, E.: Generic Schema Matching with Cupid. In Proc. of VLDB Conf., Rome, Italy (2001)
9. Ross, M., Korth, H., Silberschatz, A.: Extended Algebra and Calculus for −1NF Relational Databases. ACM TODS, Vol. 13, No. 4. (1988)
10. Shaw, G., Zdonik, S.: A Query Algebra for Object Oriented Databases. IEEE ICDE Conf. (1990)
11. Yu, W., Ozsoyoglu, M., Ozsoyoglu, G.: XML-T Algebra Operators and Implementation Issues. Tech. Report. Case Western Reserve University, Cleveland, U.S.A (2002)

Repairing Inconsistent Merged XML Data

Wilfred Ng

Department of Computer Science
The Hong Kong University of Science and Technology
Hong Kong, China
wilfred@cs.ust.hk

Abstract. XML is rapidly becoming one of the most adopted standard for information representation and interchange over the Internet. With the proliferation of mobile devices of communication such as palmtop computers in recent years, there has been growing numbers of web applications that generate tremendous amount of XML data transmitted via the Internet. We therefore need to investigate an effective means to handle such ever-growing XML data in various merging activities such as aggregation, accumulation or updating, in addition to storing and querying XML data. Previously, we recognized that FDs are an important and effective means to achieve consistent XML data merging, which we restricted data consistency for leaf nodes in an XML data tree. In this paper we further extend FDs to be satisfied in an XML document by comparing subtrees in a specified context of an XML tree. Given an XML tree T and a set of FDs F defined over a set of given path expressions, called targeted functional path expressions, we tackle the problem of repairing the inconsistency with respect to F in the most concise merged format of T.

1   Introduction

There is now little debate that XML (eXtensible Markup Language) [1] will play an ever increasing role in web data specification and exchange. This increasing use of XML in web data specification and interchange increases the need for better tools and techniques to maintain the ever-growing XML data. Merging can be applied to XML documents in order to aid appending XML fragments/documents, accumulating XML data streams and to combining partial results for incremental querying. In this paper we develop the notion of merged XML trees and extend conventional FDs [7] being satisfied in XML trees in order to generate the most concise merged XML trees.

We follow the assumptions in our previous work (c.f. for details see [8]) when discussing the application of FDs to maintain data consistency in an XML setting and assume that DTD is absent in XML documents and that a pre-defined set of element labels (or tag names in common terms) is available to "spell" the path languages. The contribution of this work is that we generalise the notions of merged XML trees in [8] and extend the semantics of an FD being satisfied in

V. Mařík et al. (Eds.): DEXA 2003, LNCS 2736, pp. 244–255, 2003.
© Springer-Verlag Berlin Heidelberg 2003

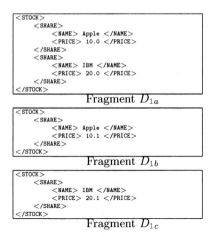

Fragment D_{1a}

Fragment D_{1b}

Fragment D_{1c}

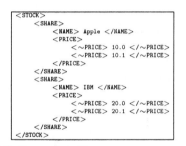

(a) A document is formed by direct combining the document fragments D_{1a}, D_{1b}, D_{1c} − such naive merging is not concise and inconsistent although individual fragments are concise and consistent.

(b) Document D_2 − a more concise merging at the STOCK level but the result is still inconsistent.

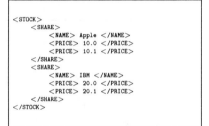

(c) Document D_3 − an even more concise merging at the SHARE level than D_2 but still inconsistent with respect to g.

(d) Document D_4 − an even more concise merging at the PRICE level and is consistent with respect to both f and g.

Fig. 1. Satisfaction of FDs in XML documents.

an XML tree in order to cater for the situation when information are obtained from different XML data sources and therefore merging is necessary.

As a motivating example consider an XML document formed by a naive merging of three XML fragments D_{1a}, D_{1b} and D_{1c} given in Figure 1(a), which has *STOCK* as a *context* node, and (share) name and (share) price as data nodes, all of these nodes are represented as their corresponding tags in D_1. In addition, we suppose that the FDs $f = SHARE.NAME \rightarrow SHARE$ and $g = SHARE.NAME \rightarrow SHARE.PRICE$ are specified as constraints, implying that *each share name has a unique piece of share information* and *each share has a unique price in the context of stock*. We assume that the current price information may be obtained from the three different XML data fragments D_{1a}, D_{1b} and D_{1c} as shown in Figure 1(a). Thus at any given time the naive *merging* of such information may be inconsistent. We now suppose that at some later stage the three fragments are merged at the STOCK level to be the document

D_2 as shown in 1(b). It can be easily verified that D_2 satisfy neither f nor g, and is therefore inconsistent. However, it is *less verbose* and thus it is a *more concise* representation than a direct merging of D_{1a}, D_{1b} and D_{1c}. These fragments can be merged at the SHARE level to generate an even more concise representation D_3, which is consistent with respect to f but is still inconsistent with respect to g, since we have more than one price element for each share. We propose to further fix this problem by "degenerating" the price node as shown in Figure 1. It can be easily verified that D_4 satisfies both f and g, and therefore the document is thus consistent. We will justify that the document D_3 is in fact the most concise representation of merged XML documents D_{1a}, D_{1b} and D_{1c} with respect to f, and D_4 is in fact the most concise representation of merged XML documents D_{1a}, D_{1b} and D_{1c} with respect to *both f and g*.

We adopt the usual notation in set theory and organise the rest of the paper as follows. In Section 2 we formalise the notion of merging in XML trees. In Section 3 we define the semantics of a functional dependency being satisfied in a merged XML tree and adapt the classical chase procedure in the context of XML, which is called XChase, for maintaining the consistency of an XML tree. In Section 4 we establish the notion of repairing and show that the output of XChase is always the consistent and most concise for merging a set of XML trees. Finally, in Section 5 we give our concluding remarks.

2   Merged XML Documents

In this section we formalise the notion of a merged XML document. We adopt the usual view that a document D is modeled as a node-labeled data tree T_D (or simply T whenever D is understood). In the sequel, we assume that (1) only two disjoint finite sets of labels exist in T as follows: $\mathbf{E}$ being the set of labels for element nodes (i.e. tag names) and S being a label denoting text nodes (i.e. PCDATA in XML documents), (2) an element node is either followed by a sequence of element nodes or is terminated with a text node, and (3) a countably infinite set of nodes $\mathbf{V}$ and a countably infinite domain of strings $\mathbf{S}$ exist.

Definition 1. (Merged XML Tree) A *merged XML node-labeled data tree* T_D corresponding to an XML document D (or simply an XML tree T) is defined by $T = (V, \lambda, \eta, \delta, r)$, where (1) $V \subseteq \mathbf{V}$ is a finite set of nodes; (2) λ is a mapping $V \to \mathbf{E} \cup \{S\}$ which assigns a label l to each node n in V; a node n in V is called an *element node* if $\lambda(n) \in \mathbf{E}$, and a *text node* if $\lambda(n) = S$; (3) η is a partial mapping that defines the edge relation of T as follows: if n is an element node in V then $\eta(n)$ is either a set of element nodes or a set of text nodes in V, and if n is a text node then $\eta(n)$ is undefined; and for each $n' \in \eta(n)$, n' is called a child of n, and we say that there is an edge from n to n', and n in V is called a *leaf node* if n' is a text node; (4) δ is a partial mapping that assigns a string to each text node: for any node n in V, if n is a text node then $\delta(n) \in \mathbf{S}$, and $\delta(n)$ is undefined otherwise; (5) $r \in V$ is a unique and distinguished *root* node.

It follows from Definition 1 that when given an XML tree for each $n \in V$, there is a *unique set of edges* (or *paths*) from root r to n. In addition, XML

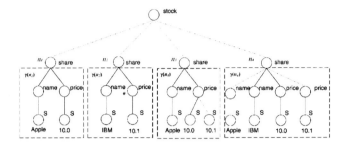

Fig. 2. Overlapping and containment of financial data

trees are finite due to the fact that V contains a finite number of nodes. In subsequent discussion, the terms XML documents and XML trees will be used interchangeably, though we remark that the order of tags in an XML document is ignored in a tree representation according to Definition 1. Given T and $n \in V$ we denote by $\gamma(n)$ the subtree of T, which takes n as the root. Clearly, we have the special case $\gamma(r) = T$. We now introduce the useful notions related to comparing two subtrees in our context.

Definition 2. (Equality, Overlapping and Containment of XML Subtrees) Let $\gamma(r_1) = (V_1, \lambda_1, \eta_1, \delta_1, r_1)$ and $\gamma(r_2) = (V_2, \lambda_2, \eta_2, \delta_2, r_2)$ be two XML subtrees of a given tree T. Let $V_i \subseteq V$ be the set of nodes in $\gamma(n_i)$; λ_i, η_i and δ_i be the mappings *restricted* on the domain V_i for $i \in \{1, 2\}$. The XML trees $\gamma(r_1)$ and $\gamma(r_2)$ is said to be *equal*, denoted as $\gamma(r_1) \approx \gamma(r_2)$, if there exists a bijective mapping ρ from V_1 to V_2 satisfying that $r_2 = \rho(r_1)$, and for all $n'_1 \in V_1$, $\lambda_1(n'_1) = \lambda_2(\rho(n'_1))$, $\rho(\eta_1(n'_1)) = \eta_2(\rho(n'_1))$ and $(\delta_1(n'_1)) = \delta_2(\rho(n'_1))$. We say $\gamma(r_1)$ and $\gamma(r_2)$ are *overlapping* if there exists nodes $m_1 \in \eta_1(r_1)$, $m_2 \in \eta_2(r_2)$ such that $\gamma(m_1) \approx \gamma(m_2)$, or else we say $\gamma(r_1)$ and $\gamma(r_2)$ are *non-overlapping*. We say $\gamma(r_1)$ *contains* $\gamma(r_2)$ if for all nodes $m_2 \in \eta_2(r_2)$, there exists $m_1 \in \eta_1(r_1)$ such that $\gamma(m_1) \approx \gamma(m_2)$, or equivalently $\gamma(r_2)$ is contained in $\gamma(r_1)$.

Informally, two subtrees in T are equal if they are (1) isomorphic in structures and (2) identical in their corresponding element names and leaf values. Two subtrees are overlapping if they have equal children as their immediate subtrees. In our approach we consider only the immediate children for comparison, since we use the functional path as a means to specify the necessary depth involved, which will be explained in detail in Section 3. We also remark that using Definition 2 we can compare element nodes based on their subtree equality, overlapping and containment. In the special case of leaf nodes being the roots of the subtrees, the equality in our definition reduces to the equality of their respective sets of data values given by δ. Trivially, if two subtrees $\gamma(r_1)$ and $\gamma(r_2)$ are equal then they are overlapping. However, the converse may not be true.

Example 1. In Figure 2, the subtrees $\gamma(n_1)$ and $\gamma(n_2)$ are non-overlapping, the subtrees $\gamma(n_1)$ and $\gamma(n_3)$ are overlapping since they have common children of name nodes, and the subtree $\gamma(n_4)$ contains both $\gamma(n_1)$ and $\gamma(n_2)$.

Definition 3. (Mutating a Subtree and Joining of Two Subtrees) Let $\gamma(r_1) = (V_1, \lambda_1, \eta_1, \delta_1, r_1)$ and $\gamma(r_2) = (V_2, \lambda_2, \eta_2, \delta_2, r_2)$ be two trees of T. Given a subtree $\gamma(r_1)$, we define a *mutate operator*, denoted as μ, to generate a new subtree which is equal to $\gamma(r_1)$ but has a distinct set of nodes from those in $\gamma(r_1)$. Formally, $\mu(\gamma(r_1)) = (V_3, \lambda_3, \eta_3, \delta_3, r_3)$ such that $V_1 \cap V_3 = \emptyset$ and there exists a bijective mapping ρ from V_3 to V_1 satisfying that for all $n_1' \in V_3$, $\lambda_3 = \lambda_1 \circ \rho$, $\eta_3 = \rho^{-1} \circ \eta_1 \circ \rho$ and $\delta_3 = \delta_1 \circ \rho$. We define the *join* of two distinct subtrees $\gamma(r_1)$ and $\gamma(r_2)$ (where $r_1 \neq r_2$) by $\gamma(r_1) \sqcup \gamma(r_2) = (V_1 \cup V_2', \lambda_1 \cup \lambda_2', \eta_1 \cup \eta_2', \delta_1 \cup \delta_2', r_1)$ where $\mu(\gamma(r_2)) = (V_2', \lambda_2', \eta_2', \delta_2', r_1)$ and $V_1 \cap V_2' = r_1$.

The join operation provides us a basis for merging trees with respect to Ω which will be elaborated later on. Note that the mutation operation is necessary for technical reasons since the nodes used by $\gamma(r_2)$ cannot be used again in merging with $\gamma(r_1)$ according to Definition 3. The join operation essentially collects the children the under the two given subtrees under the root of the first subtree. Referring to Figure 2 it can be easily checked that $\gamma(n_4) = \gamma(n_1) \sqcup \gamma(n_2)$. The following propositions can be deduced from Definition

Proposition 1. The following statements are true.

1. $\mu(\gamma(r_1)) \approx \gamma(r_1)$.
2. $\gamma(x_1) \sqcup \gamma(x_2) \approx \gamma(x_2) \sqcup \gamma(x_1)$.
3. $\gamma(x_1) \sqcup (\gamma(x_2) \sqcup \gamma(x_3)) \approx (\gamma(x_1) \sqcup \gamma(x_2)) \sqcup \gamma(x_3)$. $\square$

We also need to use the concepts of a path expression, reachable nodes and the most distant node set (c.f. for details see [8], which are fundamental concepts prior to formalise the notion of XML document merging and the semantics of FDs in the context of XML trees. Essentially, a path expression in an XML tree T is essentially a special class of *regular expression*, which specifies a set of paths in T. For example, $node(FINANCE, STOCK.SHARE.NAME)$ means all the nodes of share names and $node(FINANCE, *.NAME)$ means all the nodes of (share, currency or brokers) names in the $FINANCE$ tree. In Figure 2, we can verify that all the $NAME$ nodes of shares are reachable from the root $FINANCE$ by following the path expression $STOCK.SHARE.NAME$ and all the $NAME$ nodes of currency are reachable from the root $FINANCE$ by following the path expression: $FOREIGN\_EXCHANGE.CURRENCY.NAME$.

3   Chasing XML Trees

We formalise the notion of an FD being satisfied in an XML tree, which is evolved from the one proposed in [8] as follows. We allow FDs to be defined for non-leaf nodes of an XML tree.

A *functional dependency* (FD) f over an XML tree T is a statement written in a triplet as follows, $(Q, Q', \{P_1, \ldots, P_m\} \to \{P_{m+1}, \ldots, P_n\})$, where Q, Q' and P_i are definite path expressions such that, for all $1 \leq i \leq n$, $Q.Q'.P_i$ is a valid path expression. The expression Q is called the *context path expression*, which specifies a set of paths starting from r; the expression $Q.Q'$ is called

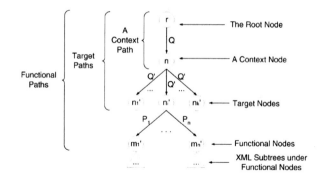

Fig. 3. Path expressions for reasoning FDs in an XML tree

the *target path expression*, which specifies a set of paths within the context following Q; and finally the expression $Q.Q'.P_i$ is called the *functional path expression*. We emphasize that a functional path expression specifies a set of paths which can reach functional nodes. We denote the *targeted functional path set* $\Omega(Q, Q')$ the collection of all possible P_i that follows the path specified the target path expressions $Q.Q'$ (i.e. $\Omega(Q, Q') = \{P_i \mid Q.Q'.P_i$ is a functional path expression $\}$). We assume throughout the paper Q and Q' denoting the context path expression and the target path expression and simplify the notations of targeted functional path set as Ω and the FD f as $P_1 \cdots P_m \rightarrow P_{m+1} \cdots P_n$. Using different path terminologies we have introduced for an XML tree and shown in Figure 3, we now define the semantics of FDs in an XML tree T.

Definition 4. (Functional Dependency Satisfaction) Let T be an XML tree, $X = P_1 \cdots P_m$ and $Y = P_{m+1} \cdots P_n$. Then the FD $X \rightarrow Y$ is satisfied in T (or alternatively holds in T), denoted by $T \models X \rightarrow Y$, if, for any node $n \in node(r, Q)$, for any $n'_1, n'_2 \in node(n, Q')$ such that (1) $node(n'_1, P_i)$ and $node(n'_2, P_i)$ are non-empty for $i \in I_m$, and (2) for any two functional nodes $x_1 \in node(n'_1, P_i)$ and $x_2 \in node(n'_2, P_i)$, such that $\gamma(x_1)$ and $\gamma(x_2)$ are non-overlapping, it is also the case that, for $j \in \{m + 1, \ldots, n\}$, if $node(n'_1, P_j)$ and $node(n'_1, P_j)$ are non-empty, then for any two functional nodes $y_1 \in node(n'_1, P_j)$ and $y_2 \in node(n'_2, P_j)$, $\gamma(y_1)$ and $\gamma(y_2)$ are non-overlapping.

Informally, along any two target paths (not necessarily to be distinct) specified by $Q.Q'$ in T which reach nodes n'_1 and n'_2 respectively, whenever *all* the children subtrees that follow the paths $P_1 \cdots P_m$ starting from n'_1 and n'_2 exist and overlap, then there exists corresponding subtrees specified by the path $P_{m+1} \cdots P_n$ also overlap if they exist. Note that there are three essential differences between the satisfaction of FDs in the context of an XML tree and a usual relation. First, the validity of the constraint holds only within the scope following the context path specified by Q and thus is only localized within the region of the subtree under a given node in $node(r, Q)$. Second, the semantics of FDs take into account of the fact that some path specified by the expressions in XY may have none or more than one occurrences. Third, the comparison

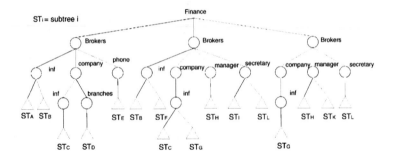

Fig. 4. An example of FD satisfaction in an XML tree

is based on overlapping of subtrees under the corresponding functional nodes rather than equality of attribute values.

Example 2. In Figure 4, we show an XML tree (possibly) contains the information of a broker and the broker's company (labeled as *inf*), phone numbers, the corresponding details of the manager and the secretary. A company may have none or more than one secretary. It can be verified that the tree T with target node $BROKERS$ satisfies the following set of FDs: $\{NAME \rightarrow COMPANY.NAME, PHONE;$ $COMPANY.NAME \rightarrow MANAGER;$ $MANAGER \rightarrow SECERTARY\}$.

We now ready to formalise the concept of merging by making use of a targeted functional path set. Let $P \in \Omega$. For any $n \in node(r, Q)$ and any $n'_1, n'_2 \in node(n', Q')$ and for any two functional nodes $x_1 \in node(n'_1, P)$ and $x_2 \in node(n'_2, P)$, if there does not exist $r_1 \in \eta(x_1)$ and $r_2 \in \eta(x_2)$ such that $\gamma(r_1)$ and $\gamma(r_2)$ are overlapping, we define $\gamma(x_1)$ to be $\gamma(x_1) \sqcup \gamma(x_2)$ and $\gamma(x_2)$ to be $\gamma(x_2) \sqcup \gamma(x_1)$. We extend the joining of subtrees to be induced by the nodes in $node(n', P)$ for all $n' \in node(n, Q')$ and all $P \in \Omega$, and define a *merging* operation which replaces the children (i.e. the subtrees) following the functional paths specified by $Q.Q'.P$ by the joining of subtrees induced by $node(n', P)$.

Definition 5. (Merge Operation) The *merge* of an XML tree T with respect to a given Ω, denoted by $merge(T, \Omega)$, is the XML tree resulting from executing the following two steps.

1. **FOR** each $P \in \Omega$, any $n \in node(r, Q)$, and any pair of $n'_1, n'_2 \in node(n, Q')$, **WHILE** there are any two functional nodes $x_1 \in node(n'_1, P)$ and $x_2 \in node(n'_2, P)$ such that if $\gamma(x_1)$ and $\gamma(x_2)$ are overlapping, **DO** $\gamma(x_1) := \gamma(x_1) \sqcup \gamma(x_2)$ and $\gamma(x_2) := \gamma(x_2) \sqcup \gamma(x_1)$.
2. If there exists $n'_1, n'_2 \in node(n, Q')$ such that $\gamma(n'_1) \approx \gamma(n'_2)$ then remove $\gamma(n'_2)$.

Essentially, the first step in $merge(T, \Omega)$ replaces iteratively any pair of subtrees for functional nodes having the same expression by their merged set whenever an overlapping occurs. The second step remove some redundant subtrees

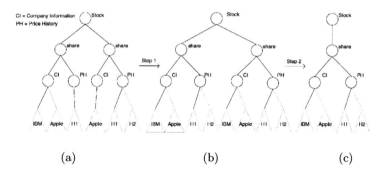

Fig. 5. An example of running the merge operation on an XML tree

following $Q.Q'$. As an example, it can easily be verified that in Figure 5, the XML tree is $merge(T, \Omega)$ where $\Omega = \{CI$ (Company Information), PH (Price Histories)$\}$. The tree is obtained first by replacing the children of share names (CI and PH) by the join of their overlapping subtrees in the first step. Then, we remove the second occurrence of the share nodes in the second step, since they are duplicated under share nodes.

Let $n \in node(r, Q)$. The XML tree resulting from $merge(T, \Omega)$ can be computed in polynomial time in the sizes of $node(n, Q')$, $node(r, Q)$ and Ω. We present in Algorithms 1 the pseudo-code for XChase(T, F), which is used for repairing inconsistency of an XML tree.

Algorithm 1 (XChase(T, F))

1.   **begin**
2.   Result := T ;
3.   Tmp:= $\emptyset$;
4.   **while** Tmp $\neq$ Result **do**
5.   Tmp := Result;
6.   **if** $\exists\ X \to Y \in F$, for any $n \in node(r, Q)$ where r is the root of Result, for any $n'_1, n'_2 \in node(n, Q')$ such that for all $i \in I_m$
                (1) $node(n'_1, P_i)$ and $node(n'_2, P_i)$ are non-empty, and
                (2) for $x_1 \in node(n'_1, P_i)$ and $x_2 \in node(n'_2, P_i)$,
                    $\gamma(x_1)$ and $\gamma(x_2)$ being overlapping,
            but $\exists j \in \{m+1, \ldots, n\}$ such that $node(n'_1, P_j)$ and $node(n'_1, P_j)$ are non-empty, and for $y_1 \in node(n'_1, P_j)$ and $y_2 \in node(n'_2, P_j)$, $\gamma(y_1)$ and $\gamma(y_2)$ being non-overlapping
7.   **then** $\gamma(y_1) := \gamma(y_1) \sqcup \gamma(y_2), \gamma(y_2) := \gamma(y_2) \sqcup \gamma(y_1)$;
8.   **end while**
9.   **return** $merge($Result$, \Omega)$;
10.   **end**.

Example 3. In Figure 6 we see that the XML tree T at (a) is inconsistent with respect to $F = \{P_1 \to P_2 P_3, P_3 \to P_1\}$. We use the symbol $ST_{i_1, \ldots, i_n}$ to represent a set of the instances of n subtrees $ST_{i_1}, \ldots, ST_{i_n}$ under a functional node. The reader can also verify that the XML tree at (b) output from XChase(T, F) satisfies F, i.e. XChase(T, F) is consistent.

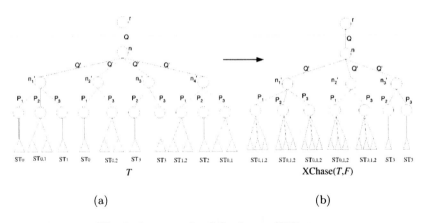

$$T \qquad\qquad \text{XChase}(T,F)$$

(a)   (b)

Fig. 6. An example of chasing an XML tree

XChase possesses the following desirable properties: (1) it outputs a consistent XML tree, (2) it is unique and can be computed in polynomial time in the sizes of T and F, and (3) it commutes with the merge operation. The next theorem shows that the chase procedure outputs a consistent XML tree and commutes with the merge operation.

Theorem 1. Let Ω be a targeted set of functional paths over T. Then the following statement is true. $\text{XChase}(T, F) = \text{XChase}(merge(T, \Omega), F)$. $\square$

4   A Concise Semantic-Preserving XML Forests

In this section we assume throughout all XML trees are maximally merged, formally $T = merge(T, \Omega)$ and justify, by using a formal notion of repairing, that XChase generates the most concise merged XML tree that is semantic-preserving with respect to F. Using the notion of conciseness restricted to Ω we define an XML forest as a *conciseness-equivalent* class of XML trees and the *join* operation of two XML forests. Then we define the concepts of *semantic-preserving forest* for T with respect to a set of FDs F to be the *join* of all consistent XML forests which are less concise than the forest consisting T.

Definition 6. (Conciseness-Equivalent XML Trees) Let Ω be a targeted functional set. An XML tree T_1 is *less concise* than another XML tree T_2 with respect to Ω, written $T_1 \sqsubseteq_\Omega T_2$ (or simply $T_1 \sqsubseteq T_2$ whenever Ω are understood from the context), if, for any node $n_1' \in node(r_1, Q.Q')$ in T_1, there exists a node $n_2' \in node(r_2, Q.Q')$ in T_2 such that for all $i \in I_n$, for any two functional nodes $x_1 \in node(n_1', P_i)$ and $x_2 \in node(n_2', P_i)$, $\gamma(x_2)$ contains $\gamma(x_1)$. We say that T_1 and T_2 are *conciseness equivalent* with respect to Ω (or simply Ω-equivalent), written $T_1 \equiv_\Omega T_2$ (or simply $T_1 \equiv T_2$), if $T_1 \sqsubseteq_\Omega T_2$ and $T_1 \sqsubseteq_\Omega T_2$.

We call a collection of Ω-equivalent XML trees an *XML forest* with respect to Ω and denote it by $\Upsilon(\Omega)$. We say that T_1 *semantically preserves* T_2 if $T_2 \models f$ then $T_1 \models f$. The following result follows from Definition 6, which means our

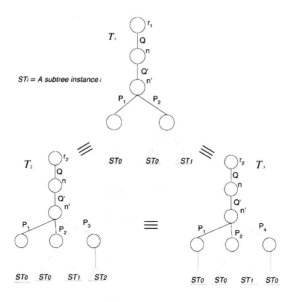

Fig. 7. A forest of Ω-equivalent trees

definition of conciseness preserve the semantics of XML data trees. The converse of the proposition is clearly not true, since two trees being mutually semantic-preserving may not be comparable with respect to $\sqsubseteq$.

Proposition 2. If $T_1 \equiv T_2$, then T_1 (or respectively T_2) semantically preserves T_2 (or respectively T_1).   □

Figure 7 illustrates a simple forest having $\Omega = \{P_1, P_2\}$. Using the notion of conciseness, we are able to compare XML trees in some accurate sense and to define a semantic characterization of XChase later on. The following lemma shows that XChase result is less or equally concise as the original XML tree T.

Lemma 1. Let F be a set of FDs, Ω be a targeted functional set, and T be an XML tree. The statement XChase$(T, F) \sqsubseteq merge(T, \Omega)$ is true.   □

Let $FOR(\Omega)$ be the collection of all XML forests w.r.t. Ω. The following proposition confirms that an XML forest is *uniformly concise and consistent*.

Proposition 3. Let $\Upsilon_1, \Upsilon_2 \in FOR(\Omega)$, $T_1, T_1' \in \Upsilon_1$, and $T_2, T_2' \in \Upsilon_2$. Then the following statements are true.

1. $T_1 \sqsubseteq T_2$ if and only if $T_1' \sqsubseteq T_2'$ for all $T_1' \in \Upsilon_1$ and $T_2' \in \Upsilon_2$.
2. $T_1 \models F$ if and only if $T_1' \models F$ for all $T_1' \in \Upsilon_1$.   □

From Proposition 3 we are able to extend some concepts defined for an XML tree in Definition 6 to an XML forest. First, the partial order $\sqsubseteq_\Omega$ on $FOR(\Omega)$ is defined as follows: $\Upsilon_1 \sqsubseteq \Upsilon_2$ if $T_1 \sqsubseteq T_2$ where $T_1 \in \Upsilon_1$ and $T_2 \in \Upsilon_2$. Second, the satisfaction for an XML forest Υ with respect to F is defined by $\Upsilon \models F$ if, for all $T_1' \in \Upsilon_1$, $T_1' \models F$. We denote by $SAT(F)$ the set of all XML forests that satisfy

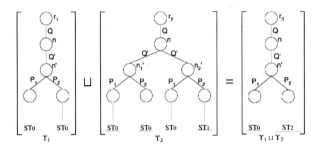

Fig. 8. A counter-example to the converse of Theorem 2

F. Finally, a merged XML forest is defined by $merge(\Upsilon, \Omega) = \{merge(T, \Omega) \mid T \in \Upsilon\}$. We now define the *join* operation on $FOR(\Omega)$ which returns a more concise forest than two given XML forests.

Definition 7. (Join of Two XML Forests) The *join* of two forests, $\Upsilon_1, \Upsilon_2 \in FOR(\Omega)$, denoted by $\Upsilon_1 \sqcup \Upsilon_2$, is defined by the set of XML trees that are Ω-equivalent to an XML tree T such that for any node $n_1' \in node(r_1, Q.Q')$ in $T_1 \in merge(\Upsilon_1, \Omega)$, and $n_2' \in node(r_2, Q.Q')$ in $T_2 \in merge(\Upsilon_2, \Omega)$, there exists a node $n' \in node(r, Q.Q')$ in T such that for all $P \in \Omega$, $\gamma(x) \equiv \gamma(x_1) \sqcup \gamma(x_2)$, where $x \in node(n, P)$, $x_1 \in node(n_1', P)$ and $x_2 \in node(n_2', P)$.

It is easy to see that the join of two merged XML forests is also a merged XML forest. The next theorem shows the fact that the join operation preserves the satisfaction of FDs.

Theorem 2. Let $\Upsilon_1, \Upsilon_2 \in SAT(F)$. Then $(\Upsilon_1 \sqcup \Upsilon_2) \in SAT(F)$.   □

The converse of Theorem 2 is false as shown in Figure 8 where $ST_2 = ST_0 \sqcup ST_1$. Let $f = P_1 \to P_2$ be an FD. It can be verified that $\Upsilon_1 \sqcup \Upsilon_2 \models f$ but $\Upsilon_2 \not\models f$. We now formalise the concept of repairing an XML forest. A *repairing* for a given Υ is a less concise but still consistent forest. The *best possible repaired XML forest* for Υ with respect to a set of FDs F over Ω is the join of all consistent forests Υ' (i.e. $\Upsilon' \models F$) such that Υ' is less concise than Υ.

Definition 8. (Repaired XML Forest) Given Υ. A *repaired XML forest* for Υ with respect to F over Ω is an XML forest Υ' such that $\Upsilon' \sqsubseteq_\Omega \Upsilon$ and $\Upsilon' \in SAT(F)$. Let $REP(\Upsilon)$ be the set of all repaired XML forests for Υ. The *best possible repaired XML forest* for Υ with respect to F over Ω (or simply the repairing of Υ if F and Ω are understood from the context), denoted by $repair(\Upsilon, F)$, is given by $\bigsqcup_{\Upsilon' \in REP(F)} \Upsilon'$.

We note that the join of XML forests is well-defined, since the join operator is commutative and associative as shown in Proposition 1. The next theorem shows the main result in this section. It shows that the output of the XChase procedure is the best possible repairing, since the XML forest formed by the collection of all XML trees that are Ω-equivalent to XChase(T, F) is equal to $repair(\Upsilon, F)$, where $T \in \Upsilon$.

Theorem 3. Let $T \in \Upsilon$. Then XChase$(T, F) \in repair(\Upsilon, F)$.   □

5   Concluding Remarks

We have defined the notion of a merged XML tree T with respect to a given set of FDs F over a targeted set of possible functional paths Ω specified by a contextual path Q and a target path Q' in T. The notion of an FD was extended to merged XML trees in Definition 4, whose satisfaction is defined by using overlapping immediate children subtrees of corresponding functional nodes over T, which is different from the usual way of defining FDs. We then defined XChase over XML trees in Algorithm 1 as a means of repairing inconsistency of an merged XML tree with respect to a set of FDs F. In addition, we established the desirable properties in Theorem 1 that XChase outputs a consistent XML tree and commutes with the merge operation. We further proposed to view the XML trees that are equivalent in conciseness over Ω as an XML forest in Definition 6 and defined the concept of the best possible repaired XML forest with respect to a set of FDs F in Definition 8. By using the join operation on merged XML forests we are able to show that if two XML forests are consistent then their join is also a consistent XML forest in Theorem 2. The best possible repaired XML forest for Υ with respect to F is the join of all consistent XML forests that are less concise than Υ, in this sense we presented our final result in Theorem 3, which shows that the chase procedure XChase(T, F) outputs the best possible repairing of T with respect to F.

References

1. S. Abiteboul, P. Buneman and D. Suciu. *Data on the Web*. Morgan Kaufmann Publishers, (2000).
2. P. Buneman, W. Fan, and S. Weinstein. *Interaction Between Path and Type Constraints*. Proc. of the 18th ACM Symposium on Principles of Database Systems (PODS'99), pp. 56–67, (1999).
3. Peter Buneman, Susan B. Davidson, Wenfei Fan, Carmem S. Hara, and Wang Chiew Tan. *Keys for XML*. Proc. of WWW10, pp. 201–210, (2001).
4. W. Fan, G.M. Kuper and J. Siméon. *A Unified Constraint Model for XML*. Proc. of WWW10, pp. 179–190, (2001).
5. W. Fan and L. Libkin. *On XML Integrity Constraints in the Presence of DTDs*. Proc. of the 20th ACM Symposium on Principles of Database Systems, (PODS'01), (2001).
6. M. Levene and G. Loizou. Maintaining consistency of imprecise relations. *The Computer Journal* **39**, pp. 114–123, (1996).
7. H. Mannila and K-J Raiha. *The Design of Relational Databases*. Addison-Wesley, (1992).
8. W. Ng. *Maintaining Consistency of Integrated XML Trees*. LNCS Vol. 2419: Proc. of WAIM, Beijing, China, pp. 145–157, (2002).
9. J. Wijsen. *Condensed Representation of Database Repairs for Consistent Query Answering* LNCS Vol. 2572: Proc. of 9th ICDT, Seina, Italy, pp. 378–393, (2002).

XML and Knowledge Technologies for Semantic-Based Indexing of Paper Documents

Donato Malerba, Michelangelo Ceci, and Margherita Berardi

Dipartimento di Informatica,
Università degli Studi
via Orabona, 4
70126 Bari - Italy
{malerba,ceci,berardi}@di.uniba.it

Abstract. Effective daily processing of large amounts of paper documents in office environments requires the application of semantic-based indexing techniques during the transformation of paper documents to electronic format. For this purpose a combination of both XML and knowledge technologies can be used. XML distinguishes between data, its structure and semantics, allowing the exchange of data elements that carry descriptions of their meaning, usage and relationship. Moreover, the combination with XSLT enables any browser to render the original layout structure of the paper documents accurately. However, an effective transformation of paper documents into XML format is a complex process involving several steps. In this paper we propose the application of knowledge technologies to many document processing steps, namely rule-based systems for semantic indexing of documents and the extraction of the necessary knowledge by means of machine learning techniques. This approach has been implemented in the system Wisdom++, which is currently used in the European project COLLATE (Collaboratory for Annotation, Indexing and Retrieval of Digitized Historical Archive Material) to provide film archivists with a tool for the automated annotation of historical documents in film archives.

1 Introduction

The increasingly large amount of paper documents to be processed daily in office environments requires new document management systems with abilities to catalog and organize these documents automatically on the basis of their contents. Personal document processing systems that can provide functional capabilities like classifying, storing, retrieving, and reproducing documents, as well as extracting, browsing, retrieving and synthesizing information from a variety of documents are in continual demand [5]. However, they operate on electronic documents and not on the more common paper documents. This issue is considered in the area of Document Image Analysis (DIA), which investigates the theory and practice of recovering the symbol structure of digital images scanned from paper or produced by computer.

The representation of extracted information in some common data format is a key issue. Some general data formats (e.g. DAFS [11]) and many ad-hoc formats have been developed for this purpose, but none of them is extensible and general enough to

V. Mařík et al. (Eds.): DEXA 2003, LNCS 2736, pp. 256–265, 2003.

hold for all different situations. This variety of formats prevents the easy exchange of data between different environments. A solution to this problem could lie in XML technology. XML has been proposed as a data representation format in general, but it was originally developed to represent (semi-) structured documents, therefore it is a natural choice for the representation of the output of DIA systems. XML is also an Internet language, a characteristic that can be profitably exploited to make information present on paper more quickly web-accessible and retrievable than distributing the bitmaps of document images on a web server. Moreover, it is possible to define some hypertext structures which improve document reading [16]. Finally, in the XML document, additional information on the semantics of the text can be stored in order to improve the effectiveness of the retrieving. This is a way to reduce the so-called *semantic gap* in document retrieving [17], which corresponds to the mismatch between the user's request and the way automated search engines try to satisfy these requests.

Commercial OCR systems are still far from supporting the XML format generation satisfactorily. Most of them can save scanned documents in HTML format, but generally their appearance on the browser is not similar to the original documents. Rendering problems, such as missing graphical components, wrong reading ordering in two-columned papers, missing indentation and broken text lines, are basically due to poor layout information extracted from the scanned document. In addition, no information on the semantics of some content portions is associated to documents saved in HTML format.

The extraction of information from the document image requires knowledge technologies, which offer various solutions to the knowledge representation problem and automated reasoning, as well as to the knowledge acquisition problem, by means of machine learning techniques. The importance of knowledge technologies has led some distinguished researchers to claim that document image analysis and understanding belongs to a branch of artificial intelligence [12], despite the fact that most of the contributions fall within the area of pattern recognition [10].

In this paper we present the multi-page DIA system WISDOM++ (http://www.di.uniba.it/~malerba/wisdom++/), whose architecture is knowledge-based and supports all the processing steps required for semantic indexing and storing in XML format [1]. More precisely, the transformation process performed by WISDOM++ consists of the preprocessing of the raster image of a scanned paper document, the segmentation of the preprocessed raster image into basic layout components, the classification of basic layout components according to the type of content (e.g., text, graphics, etc.), the identification of a more abstract representation of the document layout (layout analysis), the classification of the document on the basis of its layout and content, the identification of semantically relevant layout components, the application of OCR only to those textual components of interest and the storing in XML format providing additional information on the semantics of the text.

Four of these processing steps are knowledge-based, namely:

1. classification of basic-blocks,
2. layout analysis,
3. automatic global layout analysis correction,
4. semantic indexing (document image classification and understanding).

The knowledge technologies used in these four steps are:

- a knowledge-based system which contains explicitly represented rules and supports inference by resolution (used for document classification and understanding);
- a production-system which operates with a forward-chaining control structure and is used for global layout analysis correction;
- the decision tree learning system ITI [14] (used for block classification);
- the inductive logic programming system ATRE [7] (used to learn rules for layout analysis correction and for semantic indexing);
- the logic programming system for the implementation of several modules of WISDOM++.

In this paper, we briefly describe the current architecture of the WISDOM++ system (next section), and then focus our presentation on the rule-based semantic indexing step (Section 3). The transformation process in XML format is described in Section 4. Finally, in Section 5 a real-world application to censorship documents in film archives is described.

2   System Architecture

The general architecture of WISDOM++, shown in Figure 1, integrates several components to perform all the steps reported in the previous section.

The *System Manager* manages the system by allowing user interaction and by coordinating the activity of all other components. It interfaces the system with the data base module in order to store intermediate information. The *System Manager* is also able to invoke the OCR on textual layout blocks which are relevant for the specific application (e.g., title or authors).

The *Image Processing Module* is in charge of the image preprocessing facilities. Preprocessing consists of a series of image-to-image transformations, which do not increase the system's knowledge of the contents of the document, but may help to extract it. One basic preprocessing step is the detection of the skew angle, which is defined as the orientation angle of the baselines of text blocks. Once the skew angle has been estimated the document image can be rotated to a reference direction to facilitate further format analysis and OCR. Additional preprocessing steps are noise filtering, such as removal of salt-and-pepper noise, and resolution reduction.

The *Layout Analysis Module* supports the separation of text from graphics and the layout analysis. The separation of text from graphics is performed into two steps: the segmentation detects non-overlapping rectangular blocks enclosing content portions, while the block classification identifies the content type (e.g., text, drawings, pictures and horizontal/vertical lines). WISDOM++ segments the reduced document image into rectangular blocks by means of an efficient variant of the Run Length Smoothing Algorithm [15]. The smoothing thresholds used in the segmentation are adaptively defined depending on a spread factor which is computed during the skew evaluation step. The classification of blocks is based on the description of some features of each block. In WISDOM++ only geometrical (e.g., width, height, area, and eccentricity) and textural features are used to describe blocks. The classification of blocks as text, horizontal line, vertical line, picture (i.e., halftone images) and graphics (e.g., line drawings) is performed by means of the decision tree learning system ITI.

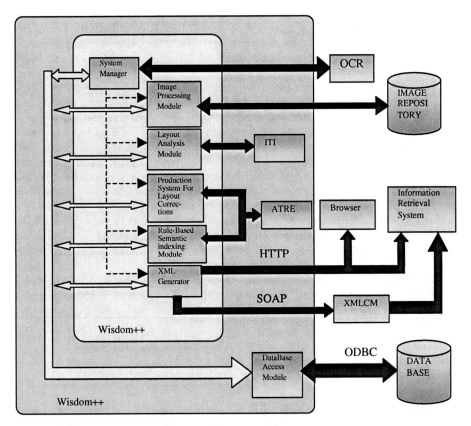

Fig. 1. Wisdom++ architecture

The *layout analysis* detects structures among blocks extracted during the segmentation step. It generates a hierarchy of abstract representations of the document image, the *geometric* (or *layout*) *structure*, which can be modeled by a *layout tree*. It is performed in two steps: firstly, the global analysis determines possible areas containing paragraphs, sections, columns, figures and tables, and secondly, the local analysis groups together blocks that possibly fall within the same area.

Once the layout analysis has been performed and the layout tree has been generated, the user can manually modify the layout tree by performing three different types of actions: vertical or horizontal split of a component in the layout tree, and grouping of two components. WISDOM++ stores both the result of corrective actions and the actions themselves. In this way it is possible to learn corrective layout operations from user interaction [9]. These operations are expressed as a set of "production" rules in the form of an antecedent and a consequent, where the antecedent expresses the precondition to the application of the rule and the consequent expresses the action to be performed in order to modify the layout structure. Production rules are then used by the *Production System for Layout Analysis Module*, which operates with a forward-chaining control structure. The production system is implemented with a theorem prover, using resolution to do forward chaining over a full first-order knowledge base. The system maintains a knowledge base (the working memory) of ground literals describing the layout tree. Ground literals are automatically generated by WISDOM++ after the execution of an operation. In each cycle, the system computes the subset of rules whose condition part is satisfied by the current contents of the working memory (*match phase*). Conflicts are solved by selecting the first rule in the subset.

The *Rule-based Semantic Indexing Module* performs the document classification and the document understanding tasks. Document classification automatically identifies the membership class of a document with respect to a user-defined set of document classes. Document understanding aims at automatically associating some layout components with components of a logical hierarchy. By performing document image classification and understanding, WISDOM++ actually replaces the low-level image feature space (based on geometrical and textural features) with a higher-level semantic space. Query formulation can then be performed using these higher level semantics, which are much more comprehensible to the user than the low level image features [2]. Rules for document classification and understanding are learned by means of the inductive logic programming system ATRE [7], as explained in the next section.

The *XML Generator Module* is used to save the document in XML format. It transforms document images into XML format by integrating textual, graphical, layout and logical information extracted in the document analysis and understanding processes.

3   Rule-Based Semantic Indexing

Semantic-indexing of a document image is based on a mapping of the *layout structure* into the *logical structure* of a (multi-page) document. The former associates the content of a document with a hierarchy of layout components, such as blocks, lines, and paragraphs. It is related to the presentation of the document on some media. On the other hand, the logical structure associates the content of a document with a hierarchy of logical components, such as sender/receiver of a business letter, title/authors of a scientific article, and so on. It is related to the organization of the content. Luckily, in many documents the two structures are strongly related. This means that layout clues can be profitably used to reconstruct the logical structure of the document without "reading" the document itself.

The general process of defining the mapping is called *document image understanding*[1] (or *interpretation*) [13], while the specific association of the whole document (root of the layout tree) with some class (root of the logical structure) is called *document image classification* [3]. This mapping is usually represented as a labeled layout tree, where each layout component is associated with zero, one or more logical components (the semantics). This association can theoretically affect layout components at any level in the *layout tree*. However, in WISDOM++ only the most abstract components in the *layout tree* are associated with some component of the *logical hierarchy*. Moreover, only layout information is used in document image

---

[1] This process is distinct from *document understanding* which is related to natural language aspects of one-dimensional text flow.

understanding. This approach differs from that proposed by other authors [6] which also makes use of textual information (e.g. text pattern), font information (e.g. style, size, boldness, etc.) and universal attributes (e.g. number of lines) given by the OCR. This diversity is due to a different opinion on when an OCR should be applied. We believe that only some layout components of interest for the application should be subject to OCR (e.g., title and authors, but not figures and tables of a scientific paper), hence document understanding should precede text reading and cannot be based on textual features.

Procedurally, the mapping is determined by means of a set of rules expressed in a first-order logic language. The antecedent of a rule describes both spatial and aspatial properties that should hold between layout components in a page. The consequent specifies the semantics of some layout components involved in the antecedent part. The matching between the antecedent of a rule and the description of the page layout determines the association between the layout structure and the logical structure.

In order to express spatial relations properly, WISDOM++ resorts to first-order definite clauses, such as rule representation formalism. Therefore, the induction of these rules from a set of labeled layout trees requires the application of an inductive logic programming system that can learn logic theories (i.e., sets of definite clauses). The learning system embedded in WISDOM++ is ATRE and a full description is reported in [7]. We limit ourselves to observing that two important features of ATRE for this specific application domain are its ability to discover concept dependencies [8] and to handle both symbolic and numerical attributes and relations [4].

4   Generating a Document in XML Format

Data concerning the result of document processing can be stored in XML format so that the resulting XML document, which includes semantic information extracted in the document analysis and understanding processes, is accessible via web through queries at a high level of abstraction.

The simplest transformation consists in attaching document images to XML pages, after having converted bitmaps into a format supported by most browsers (e.g. GIF or JPEG). Nevertheless, this approach presents at least four disadvantages. First, compressed raster images are still quite large and their transfer can be unacceptably slow. Second, the original document can only be viewed and not edited. Third, in the case of multi-page documents, pages can be presented only in a sequential order, thus missing the advantages a hypertext structure which supports document browsing. Fourth, additional information about the semantics of the content cannot be represented, hence no semantics-based retrieval facility can be supported. Therefore, it is important to transform document images into XML format by integrating textual, graphical, layout and semantic information extracted in the document analysis and understanding processes. Moreover, the XML specification includes a facility for physically isolating and separately storing any part of a document, for example, storing data without contamination of formatting information.

A *DTD* is associated to each document class and the XML document refers to the appropriate *DTD*. In the following, an example of a *DTD* generated by WISDOM++ for the class "faa_cen_decision" is reported.

```
<!-- standard DTD file for faa_cen_decision class -->
<!ELEMENT faa_cen_decision (logic-structure?, geometric-structure)>
<!ELEMENT logic-structure (registration-au|undefined|date-
place|department|applicant|reg-number|film-genre|film-length|film-
producer|film-title)*>
<!ELEMENT      registration-au (paragraph)*>
<!ATTLIST      registration-au ID      NMTOKEN         #IMPLIED>
<!ELEMENT      undefined (paragraph)*>
<!ATTLIST      undefined ID            NMTOKEN         #IMPLIED>
<!ELEMENT      date-place (paragraph)*>
<!ATTLIST      date-place ID           NMTOKEN         #IMPLIED>
<!ELEMENT      department (paragraph)*>
<!ATTLIST      department ID           NMTOKEN         #IMPLIED>
...
<!ELEMENT      paragraph (#PCDATA|TAB)*>
<!ELEMENT TAB EMPTY>
<!ELEMENT geometric-structure (image, blocklevels)>
<!ELEMENT image      EMPTY>
<!ATTLIST image      urlimage          CDATA           #REQUIRED
                     length            NMTOKEN         #REQUIRED
                     width             NMTOKEN         #REQUIRED
                     formatimage       NMTOKEN         #REQUIRED
                     resolution        NMTOKEN         #REQUIRED>
<!ELEMENT blocklevels (basic-block, line, setofline, frame1, frame2)>
<!ELEMENT basic-block (block+)>
...
<!ATTLIST      basic-block    numBB   NMTOKEN          #REQUIRED>
<!ATTLIST      line           numL    NMTOKEN          #REQUIRED>
...
<!ELEMENT block      EMPTY>
<!ATTLIST block      indexblock NMTOKEN       #REQUIRED
                     top               NMTOKEN        #REQUIRED
                     bottom            NMTOKEN        #REQUIRED
                     left              NMTOKEN        #REQUIRED
                     right             NMTOKEN        #REQUIRED
                     physical-type     NMTOKEN        #REQUIRED
                     subblockslist     CDATA          #IMPLIED
                     label          (registration-au|undefined|date-
place|department|applicant|reg-number|film-genre|film-length|film-
producer|film-title) "undefined" >
```

The keyword ELEMENT introduces an element declaration which represents the information on the semantics of the content (e.g. registration-au, date-place, department, applicant, reg-number, film-genre, film-length, film-producer, film-title, undefined[2]). An element may have no content at all, may have a content of only text, of only child element, or of a mixture of elements and text. For example, in the DTD presented the content of the element `faa_cen_decision` is a child element, which is structured. An attribute may be associated with a particular element in order to provide refined information on an element. Examples of attributes are the URL, the height, the width, the format and the resolution of a document image. All the attributes are declared separately from the element, but are usually declared together, in the *attribute list declaration*. It is also noteworthy that the DTD generated by WISDOM++ distinguishes the logical structure (`logic-structure`) from the

---

[2] The element *undefined* refers to all those logical components of no specific interest for the application.

layout structure (`geometric-structure`). The layout structure is used for storing purposes, in particular it is used to build XSL specifications in order to render the document similar in appearance to the original document, since XML language is not concerned with visualization aspects.

The XML document generated can be stored in an XML-based Content Management System (XMLCM), which is the back-end of WISDOM++. XMLCM uses the XML language to represent/manage documents, structured data and metadata (DTD or XML Schema) and to exchange them over Internet. Because Internet-based applications deal with complex, heterogeneous and worldwide information, the XMLCM is based on basic open communication standards for information processing, such as HTTP, XML and SOAP.

5   Application to Censorship Decisions

Document images processed in the European project COLLATE (http://www.collate.de/) are provided by three national film archives, namely Deutsches Filminstitut (DIF), Filmarchiv Austria (FAA) and Národní Filmový Archiv (NFA). Generally, documents are multi-page, where each page is an RGB 24bit color image representing either a censorship card or, in the case of DIF, a newspaper article. An example of a document is reported in Figure 2.

Table 1. Main features of processed documents

Source	Type	No of documents	Tot No of pages	Size (pixel)	Resolution (dpi)	Image size (mm)
FAA	Censorship cards	29	60	4836×3408	600	204,72 ×144,27
DIF	Censorship cards	6	18	1710×1212	300	144,78 × 102,62
DIF	Censorship cards	30	360	2460×3474	300	208,28 × 294,13
DIF	Newspaper articles	19	57	Not fixed	Not fixed	Not fixed
NFA	Censorship cards	24	72	2528×3988	300	214,05 × 337,66

To investigate the applicability of the solution proposed we considered 108 multi-page documents belonging to 5 classes (see Table 1). We applied WISDOM++ to 567 document images in all.

As regards the extraction of semantic information on the class of the document, the rule learned by ATRE for the faa_cen_decision class is the following:

```
class(X1)=faa_cen_decision←image_width(X1)∈[4832..4992].
```

where X1 denotes the whole page. This rule is simple and its interpretation is straightforward. The paper document is considered as a `faa_cen_decision` if the image width is between 4832 and 4992 pixels. The simplicity of the rule depends on the standard dimension of the images. In particular, the learning system is able to classify the document without ambiguity by considering only dimensions, rather than additional information on the internal layout structure.

As regards the extraction of semantic information on the logical components of the document, some examples of rules learned by ATRE for the faa_cen_decision class are reported:

```
film_genre(X2)  ← y_pos_centre(X2)∈[452..472],
                  to_right(X2,X1), width(X2)∈[182..881]
```

This rule expresses the condition that a possibly large layout component (width between 182 and 881) with its baricentre at a point between 452 and 472 on the y-axis and to the left of another block (X1) is the genre of the film. An example of the mapping of the layout structure into the logical structure is reported in Figure 3.

Fig. 2. The original scanned document   **Fig. 3.** The labeled image. This is the result of the document unterstanding process.

6 Conclusions and Challenging Problems

This work presents the integration of knowledge and XML technologies for semantic indexing of paper documents. Semantic-indexing is the result of a complex process, involving, among other things, the document classification and understanding steps and the application of machine learning techniques. The proposed approach has been investigated in the context of a European project on annotation, indexing and retrieval of digitized historical archive material.

This work can be extended in several directions. In particular, the project requires more complex document preprocessing and layout analysis techniques. Moreover, text extracted by the OCR enables the investigation of the integration of DIA techniques with both text mining and information extraction techniques. Finally, we intend to extend the system WISDOM++ presented in the paper with information retrieval facilities, based both on semantic annotations and OCRed text and on graphical (layout) information.

Acknowledgements. This work partially fulfills the research objectives set by the IST-1999-20882 project COLLATE (Collaboratory for Automation, Indexing and Retrieval of Digitized Historical Archive Material) funded by the European Union (http://www.collate.de). The authors also wish to thank Lynn Rudd for her help in reading the manuscript.

References

1. Altamura O., Esposito F., & Malerba D.: Transforming paper documents into XML format with WISDOM++, *International Journal on Document Analysis and Recognition*, 4(1), (2001), pp. 2–17.
2. Bradshaw, B.: Semantic based image retrieval: a probabilistic approach. *ACM Multimedia 2000*, (2000), pp. 167–176.
3. Esposito F., Malerba D., Semeraro G., Annese E., and Scafuro G.: An experimental page layout recognition system for office document automatic classitication: An integrated approach for inductive generalization. *In Proc. of the 10th Int. Conf on Pattern Recognition*, (1990), pp. 557–562.
4. Esposito, F.; Malerba, D. & Lisi, F.A.: Machine Learning for intelligent processing of printed documents. *Journal of Intelligent Information Systems* 14(2/3), (2000), pp. 175–198.
5. Fan X., Sheng F., Ng P.A.: DOCPROS: A Knowledge-Based Personal Document Management System. *Proc. of the 10th International Workshop on Database & Expert Systems Applications*, DEXA Workshop. (1999), pp. 527–531.
6. Klink S., Dengel A., and Kieninger T.: Document structure analysis based on layout and textual features. In *Proc. of Fourth IAPR International Workshop on Document Analysis Systems, DAS2000*, Rio de Janeiro, Brazil, (2000), pp. 99–111.
7. Malerba D., Esposito F., and Lisi F.A.: Learning recursive theories with ATRE, in H. Prade (Ed.), *Proceedings of the 13th European Conference on Artificial Intelligence*, John Wiley & Sons, Chichester, England, (1998), pp. 435–439.
8. Malerba D., Esposito F., Lisi F.A. and Altamura O.: Automated Discovery of Dependencies Between Logical Components in Document Image Understanding. *Proceedings of the Sixth International Conference on Document Analysis and Recognition*, Seattle (WA), (2001), pp. 174–178.
9. Malerba D., Esposito F., Altamura O., Ceci M., and Berardi M.: Correcting the Document Layout: A Machine Learning Approach. *Proceedings of the Seventh International Conference on Document Analysis and Recognition*, Edinburgh (UK), (2003), to appear.
10. Nagy, G.: Twenty Years of Document Image Analysis in PAMI. *IEEE Transactions on Pattern Analysis and Machine Intelligence*, 22 (1), (2000), pp. 38–62.
11. RAF Technology, Inc. *DAFS Library, Programmer's Guide and Reference*, August (1995).
12. Tang Y.Y., Yan C. D., Suen C. Y.: Document Processing for Automatic Knowledge Acquisition, *in IEEE Trans. on Knowledge and Data Engineering*, 6(1), (1994), pp.3–21.
13. Tsujimoto S., Asada H.: Understanding Multi-articled Documents, *in Proceedings of the 10th International Conference on Pattern Recognition*, Atlantic City, N.J., (1990), pp. 551–556.
14. Utgoff P.E.: An improved algorithm for incremental induction of decision trees. *Proc. of the Eleventh Int. Conf. on Machine Learning*, San Francisco, CA: Morgan Kaufmann, (1994).
15. Wong K.Y., Casey R.G., and Wahl F.M.: Document analysis system. *IBM Journal of Research Development* 26(6), (1982), pp. 647–656.
16. Worring M., Smeulders A.W.M.: Content based Internet access to scanned documents. *Int J. Doc. Anal. Recognition* 1(4), (1999).
17. Zhao R., Grosky W. I.: Narrowing the Semantic Gap Improved Text-Based Web Document Retrieval Using Visual Features, *in IEEE Trans. on Multimedia*, 4(2), (2002), pp. 189–200.

Efficient Re-construction of Document Versions Based on Adaptive Forward and Backward Change Deltas

Raymond K. Wong and Nicole Lam

School of Computer Science & Engineering,
University of New South Wales,
Sydney 2052, Australia,
wong@cse.unsw.edu.au

Abstract. This paper presents an efficient content-based version management system for managing XML documents. Our proposed system uses complete deltas for the logical representation of document versions. This logical representation is coupled with an efficient storage policy for version retrieval and insertion. Our storage policy includes the conditional storage of complete document versions (depending on the proportion of the document that was changed). Based on the performance measure from experiments, adaptive scheme based on non-linear regression is proposed. Furthermore, we define a mapping between forwards and backwards deltas in order to improve the performance of the system, in terms of both space and time.

1 Introduction

With the increasing popularity of storing content on the WWW and intranet in XML form, there arises the need for the control and management of this data. As this data is constantly evolving, users want to be able to query previous versions, query changes in documents, as well as to retrieve a particular document version efficiently. A possible solution to the version management of data would be to store each complete version of data in the system. Although this would maintain a history of the data stored on the system so far, the performance of such a system would be poor. This leads to the use of change detection mechanisms to identify the differences between data versions. The storage of these differences may provide an increased performance of the system, especially in relation to its space requirements.

Change detection algorithms have been proposed by [CAM02] and [WDC01]. In each case, the algorithm utilises the concept of persistent identifiers and node signatures in order to find matchings between nodes of the 2 input documents. We adopt a similar approach. An alternative solution to the change detection problem is via object referencing as suggested by [CTZ01a]. Marian et. al. [MACM01] developed a change-centric method for version management, which is similar to our approach. In [MACM01], the system stores the last version of a document and the sequence of forward completed deltas. In contrast to

V. Mařík et al. (Eds.): DEXA 2003, LNCS 2736, pp. 266–275, 2003.

the approach by [MACM01], we also store intermediate complete versions of the document. A disadvantage of [MACM01] is: if we have already stored 100 versions of a document, retrieving the 3rd version would involve applying 97 deltas to the curent version - a very inefficient process. On the other hand, by storing intermediate versions, our system is likely to result in a more efficient retrieval of the 3rd version (for example, by working forward from the initial version).

In this paper, we present an adaptive selection scheme between forward and backward deltas for an efficient content-based version management system that have been previously proposed in [WL02]. The system is primarily designed for managing and querying changes on XML documents based on update logging. The proposed system uses complete deltas for the logical representation of document versions. Our storage policy includes the conditional storage of complete document versions (depending on the proportion of the document that was changed). Furthermore, we define a mapping between forwards and backwards deltas in order to improve the performance of the system, in terms of both space and time. We also adapt a set of basic edit operations, which provide the necessary semantics to describe the changes between documents, from our previous work regarding the extensions of XQL with a useful set of update operations [WON01]. Although these operations are based on XQL, since they are designed and implemented based on regular path expressions, they can easily be extended as other query languages such as XPath or XQuery. The prototype of our proposed Version Management System has been integrated with a native XML database system called SODA3 that is available at [SODA3].

2   System Model

This section defines a system model for version management. The logical model of the system consists of the representation of intermediate versions similar to the notion of Complete Deltas in the style of [MACM01]. Different from [MACM01], we here define an efficient storage policy for the document versions to reduce the storage requirements of the system. The system also maintains the time at which the document was loaded into the system in order to perform time related queries on this data.

2.1   Complete Deltas

Our proposed system uses the concept of Complete Deltas to store the different versions of a document in the database. That is, instead of storing the complete versions of all documents in the system, we chose to represent only the differences between versions to conserve storage space.

The Complete Deltas used here are representations of the differences between versions. They are termed 'Complete' as it is possible, given two versions, V_i and V_j and their Complete Delta $\Delta_{i,j}$ to reconstruct either document version. That is, given V_i and $\Delta_{i,j}$, we can reconstruct V_j; and given V_j and $\Delta_{i,j}$, we can reconstruct V_i.

2.2 Storage Policy

We define an efficient storage policy for our proposed system. Suppose there are many differences between two versions of a document, it may be more efficient to store the complete version of the more recent document, rather than storing the large complete delta. This is the intuition behind the storage policy defined.

Depending on the relative size of a complete delta, as compared to the complete document version, we either store the complete delta or the complete version. This reduces the storage requirements of the system significantly. However, due to this unconventional storage policy, there arises the need to define new query mechanisms in order to efficiently query these document versions.

2.3 Representing Time

We associate with each version of data (i.e. a complete delta or a complete version) a time value, also called a *timestamp*. This *timstamp* represents the time that the version was entered into the system. This facilitates the processing of time related queries, detailed in the next section.

2.4 Edit Operations

In addition to the two basic operations: Insert and Delete, there are three more main operations supported by SODA3 [SODA3]: Update, Move and Copy. Although the Insert and Delete operations are sufficient to describe the differences between two versions, we find that the three additional operations provide a more meaningful and intuitive approach to the description of differences. Moreover, for the insert, delete, move and copy operations, it is necessary to include the element's final index as this facilitates the inversion of the operations. The operations also contain some redundant information (for example the *oldvalue* in Update operation) so as to aid in the mapping between forward and backward deltas. The detailed semantics of these operations [WL02] and the version index can be found at [LW03].

3 Main Algorithms

In this section, we consider the major parts of the system and present their key algorithms.

global:
    currentVersion ← 1

    // flag to indicate if the complete version of
    // (*currentVersion* - 1) should be stored
    storeComplete ← false

    // stores the delta between

```
// (currentVersion - 2) and (currentVersion - 1)
prevDelta ← null

// list of version numbers that have
// their complete versions stored
fullVersion ← []

// hash table or stucture to store the number of
// operations associated with each delta stored
numOp ← φ
```

insertNewVersion(File *version*) :
```
1  delta ← version;
2  operations ← countOperations(delta);
3  write 'version' out to disk ;
4  if !storeComplete ∧ !prevDelta :
5      write prevDelta out to disk;
6      delete complete version of 'currentVersion';
7      prevDelta ← null;
8  if operations > MAX_RATIO * size(version) :
9      fullVersion.append(currentVersion++);
10     storeComplete ← true;
11 else :
12     numOp{currentVersion++} ← operations;
13     prevDelta ← delta;
14     storeComplete ← false;
```

getVersion(int *ver*) :
```
1  i ← complete version closest and > ver
2  prev ← complete version closest and < ver
3  uBound ← fullVersion[i];
4  lBound ← fullVersion[prev];
5  for j ← lBound to ver do :
6      lowerOps ← lowerOps + numOp{j};
7  for k = uBound to ver do :
8      if upperOps > (lowerOps * FORWARD_CONSTANT) :
9          break;
10     upperOps ← upperOps + numOp{k};
11 if upperOps < (lowerOps * FORWARD_CONSTANT) :
12     cVersion ← complete file, 'uBound';
13     constructBackwards(uBound, ver, cVersion);
14 else :
15     cVersion ← complete file, 'lBound';
16     contructForwards(lBound, ver);
```

constructBackwards(int *upper*, **int** *version*, **File** *f*) :
```
1  if upper != version :
2      delta ← retrieve delta file, 'version';
3      applyDelta(delta, f);
```

```
4    constructBackwards(upper-1, version, f);
5  return;

constructForwards(int lower, int version, File f):
1  if lower != version :
2      applyForwardDelta(lower, f);
3      constructForwards(lower+1, version, f);
4  return;

applyForwardDelta(int version, File fileSoFar):
1  backwardDelta ← retrieve delta file, 'version';
2  forwardDelta ← convertToForward(backwardDelta);
3  applyDelta(forwardDelta, fileSoFar);
4  return;

applyDelta(File deltaFile, File fileSoFar):
1  for each e ∈ fileSoFar do:
2      apply e to fileSoFar;

convertToForward(File backwardDeltaFile):
1  File forwardDeltaFile;
2  for each e ∈ backwardDeltaFile do :
3      apply rules in Section 2: Edit operations
4      to obtain the inverse of e;
5      store the inverse operation e¹in
6      reverse order in forwardDeltaFile ;
7  return forwardDeltaFile;
```

To insert a new version of a document into the system, we firstly process the new version - by storing it in its entirety into the system. Next, we process the previous version of the document using Eq. (1). This determines whether the backward delta of the previous version or the complete version of the document is stored.

For the retrieval of a given version, we have to iterate through the complete versions of the document stored in the system, in order to identify the version that can be used to most efficiently reconstruct the required version. This can be achieved by applying the backward deltas directly to a complete version of the document, or inverting the backward deltas and then applying the operations to the complete version.

We define a function `applyDelta` which applies the edit operations to its argument file. `convertToForward` is a function that converts each operation to its inverse.

4 Adaptive Parameters

This section proposes an alternative to the adaptive parameters FOR-WARD_CONSTANT and MAX_RATIO in an attempt to automate the process of version management, without having the user specify the value of the respective parameters.

4.1   FORWARD_CONSTANT

We first consider the parameter FORWARD_CONSTANT. We propose another equation which takes into account the extra computation cost associated with inverting a forward complete delta to a backward complete delta.

Suppose the total number of operations that have to be performed on a complete document version stored in the system (using forward deltas) is l, while the total number of operations using backward deltas is u. The cost ($cost_l$) of using forward deltas is:

$$cost_l = T_l \tag{1}$$

where T_l represents the cost of performing all l operations on the complete version. We estimate the cost of T_l using the formula:

$$T_l = l * \frac{i + d}{2} \tag{2}$$

where i represents the cost of applying an insert operation to a document and d represents the cost of applying a delete operation to a document. Here, we assume that the time complexity for move (m), update (up) and copy (c) are such that:

$$m < d + i \tag{3}$$

$$c < i \tag{4}$$

$$up < d + i \tag{5}$$

This assumption is valid because, for example, if Eq. 3 was not true, we could replace the move operation to a delete and insert operation to improve the time complexity. Similarly for Eq. 4 and 5.

The cost ($cost_u$) of using backward deltas is:

$$cost_u = u + T_u \tag{6}$$

where T_u represents the cost of performing all u operations on the complete version. We estimate the cost of T_u using the formula:

$$T_u = u * \frac{i + d}{2} \tag{7}$$

Note that in contrast to $cost_l$, $cost_u$ includes an additional u to the cost of retrieval. This is because the forward complete deltas that are stored explicitly in the system have to be converted to their inverse (i.e. backward complete deltas). It takes constant time to invert each operation in a complete delta, hence to invert u operations, it costs u.

Hence, the final cost is

$$\frac{cost_u}{cost_l} > 1 \quad or \quad \frac{u(\frac{i+d}{2})}{l + l(\frac{i+d}{2})} > 1 \tag{8}$$

The intuition behind the above equation is: if the cost of using backward deltas is higher than the cost of using forward deltas, it is more efficient to use a forward delta to retrieve the document version.

4.2 MAX_RATIO

By analysing the adaptive parameter MAX_RATIO, we find that the main issue involves the efficient retrieval of the version being inserted. The factors that affect whether a complete delta or the complete version, V_x of a document is stored in the system include:

1. cost of executing the edit operations, $E = \frac{i+d}{2}$;
2. the size of the complete delta, $| \Delta_x |$;
3. the size of the current version being inserted, $| V_x |$;
4. the size of the previous complete version stored in the system, $| V_{x-1} |$;
5. number of operations in each complete delta stored in the system, $Ops(\Delta_i)$; and
6. total number of operations since the last complete version.

Hence, by analysing the costs associated with retrieving version, V_x, in the long run, we are able to identify a meaningful relationship between the factors listed above and whether a complete delta or document version of V_x is stored in the system.

More precisely, we divide the problem into two sections: (i) the cost of retrieving the current version using forward deltas (C_f); and (ii) the cost of retrieving the current version using backward deltas (C_b).

Hence, the cost is:

$$\frac{min(C_f, C_b)}{| V_x |} > K \quad where \quad K \in INT, K \geq 1 \tag{9}$$

This inequality represents the relationship between the cost of version retrieval and the size of the current complete document version. It indicates that if the cost of version retrieval using complete deltas is large relative to the size of the actual document, the system should store the complete version of the document rather than the complete delta. Here, K is a system-defined constant.

Cost to retrieve a version with forward deltas (C_f): The cost associated with retrieving a version using forward deltas (which are stored explicitly in the system) is mainly attributed to the total number of operations since the last complete version. Hence,

$$C_f = \Sigma_{i=m}^{x-1} Ops(\Delta_i) * E \tag{10}$$

In the above equation, m represents the previous closest complete version stored in the system.

Cost to retrieve a version with backward deltas (C_b)**:** Given that we are currently performing the version insertion of V_x, it would be impossible to determine accurately the cost associated with retrieving V_x using backward deltas. This is because it would involve having some knowledge of the document versions that are yet to be stored in the system. Hence, the best approach to determining a cost value would be to approximate the costs associated with retrieval by predicting the the number of edit operations contained in future complete deltas $(Op(\Delta_i'))$ to be stored in the system.

We use nonlinear regression to predict $Op(\Delta_i')$ on the basis that V_x is not stored as a complete version. Hence we are able to identify whether a subsequent document version is stored as a complete version (using the threshold, T, presented in next section). We consider all subsequent document versions up to the version specified by the cost equation, such that using backward complete deltas to retrieve the current version is more efficient than using forward complete deltas.

Also, as backward deltas are not stored explicitly in the system, we have to consider the extra computational cost associated with converting a forward complete delta to a backward complete delta.

$$C_b = \Sigma_{i=x}^{k} Ops(\Delta_i') + \Sigma_{i=x}^{k-1}(Ops(\Delta_i') * E) \tag{11}$$

In the equation above, k represents the predicted version number which is the closest complete version of the document stored in the system, such that x $\leq$ k. That is, $Ops(\Delta_i') < T$, $\forall i \in \{x..(k-1)\}$ and $Ops(\Delta_k') \geq T$. Hence, C_b represents the predicted cost associated with retrieving V_x using backward deltas in an efficient manner.

5   Adaptivity

The adaptivity of the system is defined by a nonlinear regression model detailed in this section. This model enables the system to operate autonomously, without any user input specifying the value of MAX_RATIO. In addition, this model is adaptive in terms of being able to modify its storage plan based on the version history of the documents that are currently stored in the system. This results in a highly efficient version management system, especially for the retrieval of a given document version.

By comparing the estimated number of operations in the next delta: $Op(\Delta_x')$ (using nonlinear regression) with a probability threshold: T, we can predict if the complete version of x will be stored in the system. These concepts will be presented in this section.

5.1   Nonlinear Regression

We use nonlinear regression to estimate the number of operations in each subsequent delta to be entered into the system.

$$Op(\Delta_y') = (A * Op(\Delta_x) + B \mid V_x \mid)^C \quad where \quad A, B, C \geq 1 \tag{12}$$

This equation forms the model for the nonlinear regression. We observe that the number of operations in a subsequent delta is largely dependant on the number of operations in each previous delta stored in the system, together with the size of each complete version of the document stored in the system. The equation above contains variables A, B and C that vary independantly. In particular, C represents the *order* of the equation. The value of C is adjusted accordingly, based on the percentage error on a given prediction.

Error. Each prediction of $Op(\Delta'_y)$ is verified when version y of the document is loaded into the system by the user. Hence, it is possible to verify the accuracy of the regression, especially with regard to the *order* variable C. Initially, we set the value of C to be 1. However, as the user loads more versions of the document into the system, the value of C adapts accordingly. This enables a more accurate equation for regression, and hence provides a more accurate prediction on the number of operations contained in the subsequent deltas and improves the efficiency of the system.

More specifically, the system allows a minimal error rate before adjusting the value of C in order to improve performance. For example, if C = 2 and regression has predicted the wrong size of subsequent deltas for the last 4 out of 5 document versions loaded into the system, we increase the value of C to 3 in an attempt to obtain a more accurate estimate for the size of a delta. Once the error rate converges to a specific range, we increment the value of C by smaller amounts, as this range is the most appropriate for regression.

5.2 Threshold

We define a threshold, T, that specifies the maximum probability to store a complete delta in the system (rather than a complete version) based on the number of edit operations in the deltas currently stored in the system.

$$T = \frac{\sum_{i=1}^{x-1} Pr_i * Op(\Delta_i)}{x-1} \tag{13}$$

Pr_i indicates the probability that the number of operations for a delta stored in the system is equal to $Op(\Delta_i)$. It is based on the version history of the document stored in the system.

From the equations in last section,

$$l < u * \left(\frac{i+d}{2+i+d}\right) \tag{14}$$

We use this equation to limit the number of deltas the system attempts to predict the size of, using nonlinear regression. Therefore, while the above equation is true, the system estimates the number of operations in the next delta that is to be stored in the system. This process continues until the estimated number of edit operations in a subsequent delta exceeds the threshold, T, resulting in a complete version of the document being stored in the system.

6 Conclusion

In this paper, we have addressed the problem of content-based version management of XML data. We presented a system which had an efficient logical representation and storage policy for managing changes of such data, which involved the storage of intermediate complete versions, together with complete deltas. Automatic conversion between the forward and backward deltas was also defined, which can be used to derive the complete deltas without storing both types of deltas. Finally adaptive selection between forward and backward deltas based on the justifications from the experimental performance data was presented.

References

[CAM02]   G. Cobena, S. Abiteboul, and A. Marian. Detecting changes in xml documents. In *ICDE (San Jose)*, 2002.

[CAW98]   S. Chawathe, S. Abiteboul, and J. Widom. Representing and querying changes in semistructured data. In *Proceedings of the International Conference on Data Engineering*, February 1998.

[CTZ01a] S-Y. Chien, V. Tsotras, and C. Zaniolo. Copy-based versus edit-based version management schemes for structured documents. In *RIDE-DM*, pages 95–102, 2001.

[CTZ01b] S-Y. Chien, V.J. Tsotras, and C. Zaniolo. Efficient management of multiversion documents by object referencing. In *Proceedings of VLDB*, September 2001.

[LW03]   N. Lam and R.K. Wong. A fast index for xml document version management. In *Proceedings of the Asia Pacific Web Conference (APWEB)*, September 2003.

[MACM01] A. Marian, S. Abiteboul, G. Cobéna, and L. Mignet. Change-centric management of versions in an xml warehouse. In *Proceedings of VLDB*, September 2001.

[W3C99]   W3C Recommendation. Xml path language (xpath) version 1.0. *http://www.w3.org/TR/xpath*, November 1999.

[SODA3]   Soda Technologies. Soda3 xml database management system version 3.0. *URL: http://www.sodatech.com*.

[WDC01]   Y. Wang, D. J. DeWitt, and J-Y. Cai. X-diff: An effective change detection algorithm for xml documents. Technical report, University of Wisconsin, 2001.

[WL02]   R.K. Wong and N. Lam. Managing and querying multi-version xml data with update logging. In *Proceedings of the ACM International Symposium on on Document Engineering (DocEng)*, November 2002.

[WON01]   R.K. Wong. The extended xql for querying and updating large xml databases. In *Proceedings of the ACM International Symposium on on Document Engineering (DocEng)*, November 2001.

Neighborhood-Consistent Transaction Management for Pervasive Computing Environments*

Filip Perich, Anupam Joshi, Yelena Yesha, and Timothy Finin

Department of Computer Science and Electrical Engineering
University of Maryland Baltimore County
1000 Hilltop Circle,
Baltimore, MD 21250, USA
{fperic1,joshi,yeyesha,finin}@csee.umbc.edu

Abstract. This paper examines the problem of transaction management in pervasive computing environments and presents a new approach to address them. We
represent each entity as a mobile or static semi-autonomous device. The purpose
of each device is to satisfy user queries based on its local data repository and interactions with other devices currently in its vicinity. Pervasive environments, unlike
traditional mobile computing paradigm, do not differentiate between clients and
servers that are located in a fixed, wired infrastructure. Consequently, we model
all devices as peers. These environments also relax other assumptions made by
mobile computing paradigm, such as the possibility of reconnection with a given
device, support from wired infrastructure, or the presence of a global schema.
These fundamental characteristics of pervasive computing environments limit the
use of techniques developed for transactions in a "mobile" computing environments. We define an alternative optimistic transaction model whose main emphasis
is to provide a high rate of successful transaction terminations and to maintain a
neighborhood-based consistency. The model accomplishes this via the help of active witnesses and by employing an epidemic voting protocol. The advantage of
our model is that it enables two or more peers to engage in a reliable and consistent transaction while in a pervasive environment without assuming that they can
talk to each other via infrastructure such as base stations. The advantage of using
active witnesses and an epidemic voting protocol is that transaction termination
does not depend on any single point of a failure. Additionally, the use of an epidemic voting protocol does not require all involved entities to be simultaneously
connected at any time and, therefore, further overcomes the dynamic nature of
the environments. We present the implementation of the model and results from
simulations.

1 Introduction

Maintaining data consistency between devices in distributed mobile environments has
always been, and continues to be, a challenge. These environments represent networks
composed of stationary and mobile nodes that share a subset of a global data repository.
The devices use their network connectivity to exchange data with other nodes in the

---

* This work was supported in part by NSF awards IIS 9875433 and 0209001, and DARPA contract
F30602-00-2-0591.

V. Mařík et al. (Eds.): DEXA 2003, LNCS 2736, pp. 276–286, 2003.

network. In order to operate correctly, devices involved in a transaction must ensure that their data repositories remain in a consistent state. While stationary nodes often embody powerful computers located in a fixed, wired infrastructure, mobile nodes represent devices with low-bandwidth communication, limited battery life and with limitation to other resources. Consequently, transacting devices must accommodate mobility and, in turn, possible failures due to a network disconnection. The challenge of providing data consistency is especially substantial for pervasive computing environments.

Pervasive computing environments extend the traditional concept of mobile networks [10,18]. Mobile devices in pervasive computing environments consist of hand helds, wearables, computers in vehicles, computers embedded in the physical infrastructure, and (nano) sensors. A device satisfies user queries by relying on its local data repository and data available in other devices in its vicinity. Additionally, every device is equipped with short range ad-hoc networking technologies such as Bluetooth [3]. The ad-hoc networking technology allows mobile devices to spontaneously interact with other devices, both fixed and mobile, in their vicinity. For example, two cars passing each other on the street can establish a network connection and exchange data while within range of each other. At the same time, pervasive computing environments do not guarantee any infrastructure support, a crucial requirement for traditional mobile systems [6,7,24]. Hence unlike traditional mobile computing, the pervasive environment does not differentiate between mobile clients and servers located in a fixed, wired infrastructure. Instead we model all devices as peers and any two devices may engage in a transaction, a case not covered by traditional mobile computing paradigm. In the mobile computing paradigm, only one transacting device, the mobile client, is allowed to move during a transaction. This allowed previous solutions to rely on the help of the infrastructure by using mobile support stations as proxies; however, there is no default infrastructure support in pervasive computing environments. Additionally, pervasive environments relax other assumptions made in mobile computing paradigm. As all devices may be mobile, the vicinity of each device is likely to change in both spatial and temporal dimensions. This not only limits data and data source availability but the serendipitous nature of the environment also limits the possibility of reconnection between transacting devices. In pervasive computing environments, there is no guarantee that all devices wishing to transact may be concurrently available and that two disconnected devices will *meet* again. For example, when two people serendipitously meet at an airport and agree to exchange a song for a micro-payment, their electronic wallets must be updated correctly even when one person leaves the airport before the transaction completes [1]. Consequently, transacting peers must either trust each other or rely on a third party. In a traditional mobile paradigm, the third party is a server located in a fixed, wired infrastructure. In that case, transacting peers must send all relevant data to the server before they disconnect. This may not always be possible in pervasive environments. Instead, an alternative approach is to use other peers in the environment as third parties. This raises the issue of trust since there is no guarantee that these peers will behave correctly. We address the issue via the use of a random witness selection policy which reduces the probability of obtaining malicious witnesses. In summary, the change in perception of mobile devices, together with other characteristics of pervasive computing environments, limits the use of traditional mobile transactions.

To address the problem, we present a novel transaction model designed for use in pervasive computing environments. We focus on maintaining consistency of transactions, which has generally been termed as the most important ACID property of transactions for mobile environments [9]. Consistency is, however, not critical in read only transactions [18]. Our *Neighborhood-Consistent Transaction* model (NC-Transaction) provides a higher rate of successful transactions in comparison to models designed for traditional mobile computing environments. NC-Transaction maintains neighborhood consistency among devices in the vicinity. It does not ensure global consistency, a task often impossible since there is no guarantee that two devices will ever reconnect in a pervasive computing environment. NC-Transaction accomplishes neighborhood consistency and high successful termination rate by employing active witnesses and an epidemic voting protocol. NC-Transaction defines witnesses as devices in a vicinity that can *hear* both transacting devices and agree to monitor the status of a transaction. Each witness can cast a vote to commit or abort a transaction. A transacting device must collect a quorum of the votes, defined as a percentage of all witness votes, to decide on the final termination action for a transaction. By using a voting scheme and redundancy of witnesses, NC-Transaction ensures that transacting devices terminate in a consistent state. Additionally, information stored by each witness can be used to resolve conflicts between devices involved in a transaction.

The remainder of the paper is structured as follows: We present related work in Section 2. In Section 3, we define the NC-Transaction model and the generic consistency protocol in the context of MoGATU [18]. In Section 4, we present our experimental setup. We empirically show how the NC-Transaction model improves successful transaction termination rate and how it affects the computing cost for all entities in the environment. We conclude and describe directions for future work in Section 5.

2   Related Work

The NC-Transaction model is designed within the context of MoGATU [18] – a lightweight architecture for profile–driven data management in pervasive computing environments. The work on MoGATU spans research areas on both data management and ad-hoc networking technologies. MoGATU is currently implemented both as a prototype running on Linux based computers with support for Bluetooth and Ad–Hoc 802.11 [11] and as an extension of the GloMoSim simulator [23].

The problem of transaction management in wireless networks has drawn a significant degree of attention. Most of the proposed solutions are based a client/proxy/server model. These solutions place primary data on servers located within the wired infrastructure and treat mobile devices solely as clients. Using this approach, the solutions assume that mobile devices are only one-hop away from a wired network and attempt to overcome issues caused by the characteristics of the one-hop wireless link. The solutions accomplish their task by relaxing some of the ACID properties, by enabling a non-blocking execution in a disconnected mode and by adapting commit protocols [5, 8,15,9,20]. For example, Kangaroo Transaction [9] model addresses mobility of mobile hosts (MH) that hop from one mobile support station (MSS) to another. The model exploits the concept of split transactions. Each MSS acts as a proxy between a server

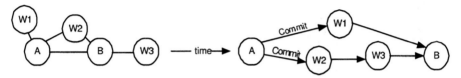

Fig. 1. Help of Witnesses in NC-Transaction

and a mobile client and manages all sub-transactions for the time period it serves as a proxy. PRO-MOTION [22] is a mobile transaction processing system that also exploits the concept of nested-split transactions by relaxing the atomicity restriction and using *compacts*, a local cache of objects with additional state information. These objects are synchronized upon a reconnection. In contrast, the Bayou architecture [8] uses an epidemic protocol for synchronizing objects; however, objects must be first committed on a primary copy. An alternative solution is presented in the context of Deno [13], which is also a replicated-object system for mobile environments. Unlike in Bayou, every replica in Deno has an equal chance of committing an update whenever it can obtain a voting quorum. Each replica obtains a quorum by gathering weighted votes from other replicas in the system and by providing its vote to others. Similarly, Coda [14] and Ficus [17] provide support for disconnected operations in the domain of distributed file systems. Each mobile device can modify its cached files while disconnected. Upon a reconnection to the network, the device connects to a subset of replica holders, the so-called AVSG in Coda, in order to commit its updates. These servers then propagate updates to the remaining nodes. Unlike the NC-Transaction, however, most of these solutions either depend on infrastructure support or require reconnection in order to synchronize *dirty* data, an option not guaranteed in pervasive computing environments.

3   Neighborhood-Consistent Transaction Model

The NC-Transaction model is defined in terms of a session among multiple devices in a vicinity that wish to transact with each other. A session extends the classical concept of a transaction defined for distributed database systems [16]. Traditionally, transactions consist of three phases – *start*, *execution* and *end*. In the first phase, S, all devices are synchronized. In the next step, each device executes a sequence of read and write operations, $\{R/W\}$. Finally, in the last step, all devices synchronize themselves to either unilaterally commit or abort the transaction, denoted as C/A. Formally, a transaction is defined as:

$$T = (S, \{R/W\}, C/A) \tag{1}$$

Similarly, a session in NC-Transaction consists of three phases: (i) negotiation, (ii) execution and (iii) termination. The most important part of NC-Transaction is to terminate in a consistent state. Transacting devices in a NC-Transaction achieve this goal by soliciting and relying on the help of other devices in the vicinity that agree to serve as active witnesses. The use of witnesses has traditionally been a social device to ensure the fairness and correctness of an event involving two parties [4]. Witnesses are requested to monitor an event and provide testimony that can help decide its outcome.

NC-Transaction abstracts the notion of witnesses for a similar purpose; to ensure consistency via fairness and correctness. In our model, transacting devices request other

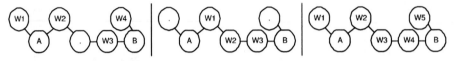

Fig. 2. Alternative Witness Selection Protocols for NC-Transaction

devices in their vicinity to monitor their transaction and these witnesses are responsible for voting on the veracity of the transaction's outcome. The advantage of using
witnesses for transactions is threefold: (i) In traditional mobile computing paradigms,
commit protocols, such as 2PC [16], depend on network reliability and the existence of
a wired infrastructure, neither of which is guaranteed in pervasive computing environments. As we will show, witnesses mitigate the negative impacts on transactions within
pervasive computing environments by serving as intermediaries. As illustrated in Figure 1, witnesses can propagate intentions to abort or commit from one transacting device
to another. (ii) Witnesses provide redundancy, increasing the probability of a consistent
outcome of a transaction because they do not rely on each other. Each witness monitors
transacting devices independently. It attempts to collect enough information to decide
whether a transaction should be committed or aborted. Transacting devices can then
choose the number of witness' votes necessary for a forming a quorum to decide on the
terminating action. (iii) Witnesses provide a higher level of assurance on fairness and
correctness than transacting devices would have otherwise. This is due to the fact that
the decision to commit or abort does not depend on a single device, rather it must be a
collective decision.

Negotiation Phase – In the initial phase of NC-Transaction, a device wishing to
transact with other devices first negotiates the query terms that each should execute,
the planned duration of a transaction and the set of active witnesses. The negotiation
is based on the principles of Contract Nets [21]. NC-Transaction supports any type of
a query that can be decomposed into a sequence of reads and writes over a local data
repository for each transacting device. In addition, the query may include operations
for exchanging data between multiple devices. Mobile peers also negotiate the planned
duration of the transaction to provide a default fall-back for terminating a transaction by
aborting it. Each transacting device must gather enough votes from witnesses to commit
a transaction before the time period elapses in order to commit the results locally.

Witness Selection Protocols – During the *negotiation* phase, transacting devices
also select other devices in the vicinity as active witnesses. The transacting devices
attempt to collect at least three witnesses by employing the principles of Contract Nets.
Each node in the vicinity is presented with a list of transacting devices, terms of queries
and the planned duration period. A possible witness evaluates the terms and decides to
accept or reject the task. The transacting devices determine the list of devices that agree
to witness a transaction and choose at most n witnesses, a variable parameter for NC-
Transaction. We define three methods for selecting witnesses in pervasive computing
environments and illustrate them in Figure 2. In the first method, each transacting device
attempts to use only its current one-hop neighbors as witnesses. The advantage of this
approach is that mobile nodes in a human environment move as a group in a predictable
manner. For example, many cars on a street travel in the same direction. This improves the
chances that witnesses and transacting devices are able to *hear* each other. Alternatively,

transacting devices attempt to use only those devices that route packets between them. The advantage of this approach is that the underlying routing protocol may utilize a majority of the route for most of the transaction, and thus the devices are guaranteed to *hear* each other for most of the time. The third method combines the other two approaches by selecting witnesses on the route and those currently around each transacting device.

Execution Phase – In this phase, each transacting device begins to execute the negotiated sequence of reads and writes over its local data repository. Given the ad-hoc nature of the pervasive computing environments, the device may not be able to obtain "locks" on all replicas in the environment. Instead, we assume an optimistic concurrency control which allows each device to modify its data independently from others. When a device either completes or has to abort its part of the transaction, it attempts to inform as many witnesses as possible about its intention. In contrast, each witness uses the *execution* phase to collect evidence in order to monitor the progress of the transaction and intentions about a commit/abort by transacting devices. Once a witness has enough knowledge to decide on an outcome, it attempts to send a commit or abort message to all transacting devices.

Termination Phase – In the *termination* phase each transacting device either commits or aborts the transaction. A device can commit a transaction only when it is able to gather a quorum of commit votes from witnesses [13]. In NC-Transaction, a voting quorum represents a predefined percentage of votes cast by all witnesses and can range from at least one vote to all 100% votes from all witnesses.

4   Performance Experiments

The primary goal of NC-Transaction is to provide a high rate of successful transaction terminations while maintaining neighborhood-based consistency. Consequently, in this section we focus on the following properties: (i) performance of NC-Transaction compared to that of a representative of traditional mobile transaction models, (ii) the appropriate number of witnesses per NC-Transaction and (iii) the effects of different percentages for voting quorums on transaction termination and neighborhood consistency. We use Kangaroo Transaction [9] as the representative of traditional mobile transaction models but have modified it in order to suit the experimental environment by allowing the server to be represented by a mobile device. We have implemented both transaction models within the context of the MoGATU framework using the GloMoSim simulator [23].

We employ a spatio-temporal environment that consists of a 200 x 200m field and 100 nodes – 36 stationary and 64 mobile nodes – for a period of 50 minutes. The stationary nodes represent a variable infrastructure support, which is required for the traditional mobile transaction model. In contrast, the mobile nodes represent devices in a pervasive computing environment. The mobile devices move according to a random waypoint mobility model [2]. Using this model, a device chooses a random point within the field and a random speed. Next, the device moves using the chosen speed and direction until it reaches its target location. The device then waits for a predefined time period and repeats the process. In our experiments, we have set the waiting period to 5 seconds and varied the speed from 1m/s, 3m/s to 9m/s to simulate different mobile environments. All devices in the environment employ the AODV protocol [19] for routing packets at the network level.

To study the performance of NC-Transaction, we concentrate on transactions initiated by a mobile device A. A attempts to initiate a transaction with another mobile device B at one minute intervals, a total of 50 transactions per simulation run. Each transaction is negotiated to last from 10 to 20 seconds, after which both devices must commit the transaction based on the voted received from witnesses or, by default, abort. We vary the probability of infrastructure support from 0% to 100%, in order to compare the performance to that of Kangaroo Transactions. Complete, 100%, infrastructure support represents an environment where each mobile device is in the range of a stationary node. For lesser probability values, the number of stationary nodes decreases accordingly from 36 to 0, thus creating areas of no support. We differentiate among three types of NC-Transaction based on the different witness selection policies specified in Section 3. Using these policies, witnesses to a transaction between A and B can include only their one-hop peers or only those devices on the route between A and B or a combination of both. Additionally, we vary the number of witnesses that A and B must gather in order to start executing a transaction from 3 to 33. Finally, we vary the number of votes required for quorum from 0% to 100%.

4.1   Infrastructure Support vs. Transaction Success and Consistency

In the first experiment, we compare the performance of NC-Transaction against that of a traditional mobile transaction. We differentiate among three versions of NC-Transaction based on a witness selection policy: (i) one-hop peers O NC-T, (ii) routing peers R NC-T, and (iii) both one-hop and routing peers $O+R$ NC-T. Figure 3 shows the empirical results for different levels of infrastructure, base station type support. For traditional transactions, only infrastructure nodes can route between A and B. For NC-Transactions every device, mobile or within the infrastructure, can provide routing functionality for any other device. Each stacked bar represents the average distribution of initiated transactions given a transaction model and infrastructure support. We differentiate among five cases: (i) a transaction is successfully executed and terminated by both A and B, (ii) a transaction is aborted in a consistent state by both A and B, (iii) a transaction does not start because A or B cannot be reached and, hence, leaves both A and B in a consistent state, (iv) a transaction does not start because A and B are unable to obtain enough witnesses, again resulting in a consistent state, and (v) a transaction leaves A and B in an inconsistent state. Accordingly, a transaction model should maximize the amount of transactions falling into the first category and minimize all other cases. Due to the limited amount of space, we report only a subset of our results. Specifically, we have fixed the witness size to 5 and the voting quorum percentage to 66%, which yielded optimal results against other witness group sizes and voting quorums in our experiments.

As depicted in Figure 3, NC-Transaction performs better than the traditional mobile model. This is expected because NC-Transaction was defined specifically for the pervasive computing environment. The NC-Transaction model using broadcast-based witness selection protocol performs the best. On average, 75% of transactions successfully executed and only 0.3% of transactions resulted in an inconsistent state. This may be because some witnesses travel in a similar direction as A or B and are, therefore, able to

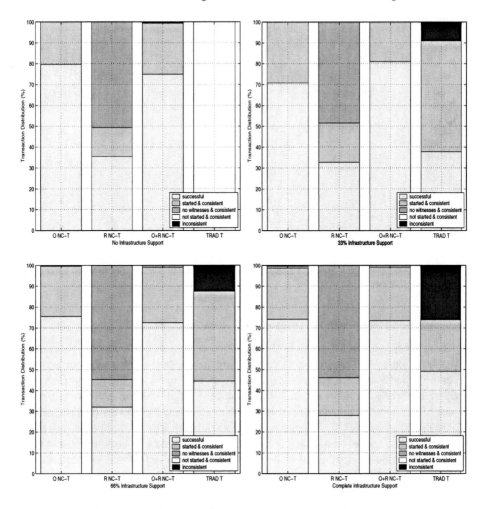

Fig. 3. Infrastructure Support vs. Transaction Success and Consistency

monitor the ongoing transactions. NC-Transaction using routing-peer witness selection protocol does not perform as well because, 51.9% of the time on average, the model was unable to collect enough witnesses. This may be because A and B were often only 3 hops away during transaction initiation. NC-Transaction combining one-hop and routing-peer witness selection protocols performs similar to the O NC-T model. As expected, in environments without infrastructure support, no Kangaroo Transaction could be initiated because A and B could not communicate with each other. As infrastructure support was increased, A and B were able to exchange messages and initiate transactions; however, many of the transactions gracefully aborted or created inconsistency between A and B. This is due to the fact, that B committed and informed A to also commit; however, A did not receive the instruction since it had moved out of the range and could not connect to the infrastructure.

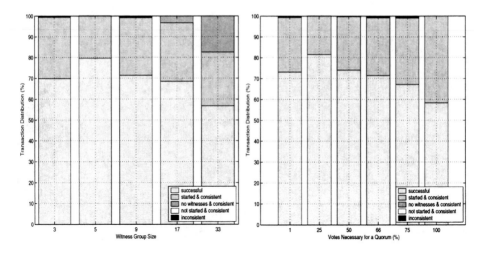

Fig. 4. (a) Witness Group Size vs. Transaction Execution. (b) Voting Quorum vs. Successful Transaction Execution.

4.2 Witness Group Size vs. Transaction Execution

In the next experiment, we study the effect of witness group size on transaction execution. We use only the NC-Transaction model utilizing the one-hop witness selection protocol because it performed the best in the previous experiment. We set the voting quorum to 66%, requiring a device to obtain at least two thirds of all votes in order to commit or abort before a transaction deadline, and exponentially vary the number of witnesses, K, from 3 to 33. As depicted in Figure 4 (a), we see that for a small number of witnesses, *i.e.*, $K<5$, message loss can cause inconsistency on or aborts by both A and B. This is because in these cases a transaction depends on every witness. Optimal performance was obtained for $K=5$ as suggested in the previous experiment. For larger groups of required witnesses, we see that the number of successfully executed transactions decreases. This is because many witnesses were unable to cast a vote or that transacting devices were unable to collect enough votes. In addition, for very large groups, we also see that A and B are unable to obtain enough witnesses, 17.7% for $K=33$, in order to start executing a transaction.

4.3 Voting Quorum vs. Successful Transaction Execution

In this experiment, we again study the performance of the NC-Transaction model utilizing a one-hop witness selection protocol; however, we fix the size of the required witness group K to 9. We use this base size in order to better illustrate the effects of different voting quorums, Q, on transaction execution. We vary Q from 0% to 100% and measure its effects on consistency and transaction execution. As shown in Figure 4 (b), the best performance was obtained for $Q=25\%$, which is not as good as the performance for $K=5$ and $Q=66\%$ from the first experiment. For higher values of Q, we see that the number of gracefully aborted transactions increases as the transacting devices A and B were unable to obtain enough votes matching the voting quorum level.

5 Conclusions and Future Work

We have presented the design of the NC-Transaction model and its implementation in the context of the MoGATU framework. We have shown that NC-Transaction, using one-hop witness selection protocol, radically increases the number of successfully executed transactions and at the same time decreases the number of inconsistent transactions. NC-Transaction accomplishes this via the help of active witnesses and by employing an epidemic voting protocol. The role of each witness is to monitor an ongoing transaction and gather enough information to assist in terminating the transaction. In turn, each transacting device serendipitously collects votes from witnesses in order to successfully commit or abort. In this manner, a device does not depend on a single controller and is, therefore, less prone to errors due to the nature of pervasive computing environments. We have measured the effects on transaction execution and consistency for different witness group sizes, K, and the number of votes required to form a quorum, Q. Our measurements suggest best performance for $K=5$ and $Q=66\%$. Our measurements also suggest that both K and Q play an important role in NC-Transaction performance.

We have not addressed the issues related to trust. In our initial design, we have assumed that all devices are reliable and, therefore, each transacting or witnessing device behaves correctly. This clearly may not be the case of a *real-world* pervasive environment where any device possessing ad-hoc network connectivity may choose to interact with its peers. We will address this issue in future work by incorporating distributed trust mechanisms discussed in [12].

References

1. S. Avancha, P. D'souza, F. Perich, A. Joshi, and Y. Yesha. P2P M-Commerce in Pervasive Environments. In *ACM SIGEcom Exchanges*, 2003.
2. C. Bettstetter. Smooth is Better than Sharp: A Random Mobility Model for Simulation of Wireless Networks. In *MSWiM'01*, 2001.
3. Bluetooth SIG. Specification. `http://bluetooth.com/`.
4. A. Borr. Transaction Monitoring in Encompass: Reliable Distributed Transaction Processing. In *VLDB*, 1981.
5. O. Bukhres, S. Morton, P. Zhang, E. Vanderdijs, C. Crawley, J. Platt, and M. Mossman. A Proposed Mobile Architecture for Distributed Database Environment. Technical report, Indiana University, Purdue University, 1997.
6. M. Cherniak, E. Galvez, D. Brooks, M. Franklin, and S. Zdonik. Profile Driven Data Management. In *VLDB*, 2002.
7. P. Chrysanthis and E. Pitoura. Mobile and Wireless Database Access for Pervasive Computing. In *ICDE*, 2000.
8. A. J. Demers, K. Petersen, M. J. Spreitzer, D. B. Terry, M. M. Theimer, and B. B. Welch. The bayou architecture: Support for data sharing among mobile users. In *IEEE Workshop on Mobile Computing Systems & Applications*, 1994.
9. M. Dunham, A. Helal, and S. Balakrishnan. A Mobile Transaction Model that Captures Both the Data Movement and Behavior. *ACM MONET*, 1997.
10. M. Franklin. Challenges in ubiquitous data management. In *Informatics*, 2001.
11. IEEE 802.11 Working Group. Ad-hoc 802.11. `http://ieee802org/11`.
12. L. Kagal. Rei : A Policy Language for the Me-Centric Project. Technical report, HP Labs, 2002.

13. P. Keleher and U. Cetintemel. Consistency Management in Deno. *ACM MONET*, 1999.
14. J. Kistler and M. Satyanarayanan. Disconnected Operation in the Coda File System. *ACM Transactions on Computer Systems*, 1992.
15. S. Lauzac and P. Chrysanthis. Utilizing versions of views within a mobile environment. In *Conference on Computing and Information*, 1998.
16. M. Oezsu and P. Valduriez. *Principles of Distributed Database Systems*. Prentice Hall, Inc., New Jersey, 2nd edition edition, 1999.
17. T. Page, R. Guy, J. Heidemann, D. Ratner, P. Reiher, A. Goel, G. Kuenning, and G. Popek. Perspectives on Optimistically Replicated Peer-to-Peer Filing. In *Software – Practice and Experience*, 1998.
18. F. Perich, S. Avancha, D. Chakraborty, A. Joshi, and Y. Yesha. Profile Driven Data Management for Pervasive Environments. In *DEXA*, 2002.
19. C. Perkins and E. Royer. Ad hoc on-demand distance vector routing. In *IEEE Mobile Computing Systems and Applications*, 1999.
20. E. Pitoura. A Replication Schema to Support Weak Connectivity in Mobile Information Systems. In *DEXA*, 1996.
21. R. Smith. *Readings in Distributed Artificial Intelligence*, chapter The Contract Net Protocol: High-Level Communication and Control in a Distributed Problem Solver. 1988.
22. G. Walborn and P. Chrysanthis. Transaction Processing in PRO-MOTION. In *ACM Symposium on Applied Computing*, 1999.
23. X. Zeng, R. Bagrodia, and M. Gerla. GloMoSim: A Library for Parallel Simulation of Large-Scale Wireless Networks. In *Workshop on Parallel and Distributed Simulation*, 1998.
24. Y. Zhang and O. Wolfson. Satelitte-Based Information Services. *ACM MONET*, 2002.

On Mining Group Patterns of Mobile Users

Yida Wang[1], Ee-Peng Lim[1], and San-Yih Hwang[2]

[1] Centre for Advanced Information Systems,
School of Computer Engineering
Nanyang Technological University,
Singapore 639798, Singapore
wyd66@pmail.ntu.edu.sg
aseplim@ntu.edu.sg
[2] Department of Information Management
National Sun Yat-Sen University,
Kaohsiung, Taiwan 80424
syhwang@mis.nsysu.edu.tw

Abstract. In this paper, we present a *group pattern mining* approach to derive the grouping information of mobile device users based on the spatio-temporal distances among them. Group patterns of users are determined by a distance threshold and a minimum duration. To discover group patterns, we propose the AGP and VG-growth algorithms that are derived from the Apriori and FP-growth algorithms respectively. We further evaluate the efficiencies of these two algorithms using synthetically generated user movement data.

1   Introduction

In our daily activities, we are affiliated to groups of many different sorts. Group dynamics and its influence on individual decision making have been well studied by sociologists[6], and it has been shown that peer pressure and group conformity can affect the buying behaviors of individuals. With a good knowledge of groups a customer belongs to, one can derive common buying interests among customers, develop group-specific pricing models and marketing strategies, and provide personalized services. For example, venders may offer discounts or recommend products to groups so as to encourage more purchases with a higher success rate.

There are many ways one can determine the groups a person belongs to, e.g., partitioning people into groups based on past purchases of same product items, similar occupations, incomes, etc.. In this paper, we aim to derive group knowledge of users using their spatio-temporal information, namely their movement data. The grouping knowledge derived from these movement data is unique compared to the previous approaches in several ways:

- *Physical proximity between group members*: The group members are expected to be physically close to one another when they acts as a group. Such characteristics are common among many types of groups, e.g., shopping pals, game partners, etc..

V. Mařík et al. (Eds.): DEXA 2003, LNCS 2736, pp. 287–296, 2003.

– *Temporal proximity between group members*: The group members are expected to stay together for some meaningful duration when they acts as a group. Such characteristic distinguishes an ad hoc cluster of people who are physically close from a group of people who come together for some planned activity(ies).

Unlike the existing techniques that partition people into groups based on other factors, the above two characteristics ensure that members of the derived groups are aware of and maintain contact with one another. Hence, the group members are expected to exert much stronger influence on one another.

Related Work

In this research, we assume that the user movement data can be collected by logging location data emitted from mobile devices. This logging facility provides time series of locations for each user. This assumption is technically feasible since mobile devices are becoming more and more location-aware using positioning technologies [3,15], which has become more affordable and even more so in the future. To keep a focused discussion, we shall keep the privacy and legal issues out the scope of this paper.

Group pattern mining deals with time series of user location information involving temporal and spatial dimensions. We observe that previous temporal and spatial data mining research mostly focus either on temporal or spatial mining[4, 10,12], not both. There are also significant work in periodicity analysis for time series data [7,13,14]. Nevertheless, these time series data usually do not involve spatial information. Although there has been some work on spatial-temporal mining [11,5] that considers both temporal and spatial aspects of information, they mainly focus on the models and structures for indexing the moving objects.

2   Problem Definition

The *user movement database*, D, consists of a set of time series of locations, one for each user. Assume that there are M distinct users $u_1, u_2, \cdots, u_M$. D is defined as the union of time series of locations belonging to all the users, i.e., $D = \cup_{i=1}^{M} D_i$. Each D_i is a time series containing triplets (t, x, y) denoting the x- and y-coordinates respectively of user u_i at time t. For simplicity, we assume that the all user locations are known at every time point, and the interval between every t and $t + 1$ is fixed.

Definition 1. *Given a group of users G, a maximum distance threshold max_dis, and a minimal time duration threshold min_dur, a set of consecutive time points $[t, t + k]$ is called a **valid segment** of G if*

1. *All users in G are not more than max_dis apart at time t, $t + 1$, $\cdots$, and $t + k$;*
2. *Some users in G are more than max_dis apart at time $t - 1$;*

Table 1. User Movement Database D

u_1			u_2			u_3			u_4			u_5			u_6		
t	x	y	t	x	y	t	x	y	t	x	y	t	x	y	t	x	y
0	68	41	0	73	41	0	73	46	0	81	39	0	80	43	0	99	43
1	72	75	1	72	69	1	79	71	1	71	67	1	71	71	1	61	97
2	79	51	2	80	52	2	82	59	2	81	53	2	73	51	2	34	45
3	80	50	3	84	52	3	81	53	3	85	57	3	80	11	3	42	96
4	62	56	4	59	10	4	50	63	4	60	53	4	58	9	4	7	80
5	45	65	5	24	49	5	49	61	5	22	45	5	20	48	5	29	54
6	67	58	6	39	19	6	36	27	6	40	19	6	40	19	6	39	61
7	73	53	7	68	52	7	72	52	7	74	53	7	72	53	7	88	35
8	75	51	8	72	51	8	69	54	8	73	53	8	75	53	8	62	70
9	73	53	9	64	56	9	62	50	9	74	51	9	79	53	9	7	59

3. Some users in G are more than max_dis apart at time $t + (k + 1)$;
4. $(k + 1) \geq min\_dur$;

Consider the user movement database in Table 1. For $min\_dur = 3$ and $max\_dis = 10$, $[5, 8]$ is a valid segment of the user group $\{u_2, u_4\}$.

Definition 2. *Given database D, a group of users G, thresholds max_dis and min_dur, we say that G, max_dis and min_dur form a **group pattern**, denoted by $P = < G, max\_dis, min\_dur >$, if G has a valid segment.*

The valid segments of the group pattern P are therefore the valid segments of its G component. We also call a group pattern with k users a **k-group pattern**.

The thresholds max_dis and min_dur are used to define the spatial and temporal proximity requirements between members of a group. By choosing appropriate thresholds, we can define the minimum duration a set of users must "stay close together" before we consider them as a meaningful group.

In a user movement database, a group pattern may have multiple valid segments. The combined length of these valid segments is called the *weight count* of the pattern. We quantify the significance of the pattern by comparing its weight count with the overall time duration.

Definition 3. *Let P be a group pattern with valid segments $s_1, \cdots, s_n$, and N denotes the number of time points in the database, the **weight** of P is defined as:*

$$weight(P) = \frac{\sum_{i=1}^{n} |s_i|}{N} \qquad (1)$$

Since weight represents the *proportion* of the time points when the group of users stay close, the larger the weight, the more significant is the group pattern. If the weight of a group pattern exceeds a threshold min_wei, we call it a **valid group pattern**, and the corresponding group of users a **valid group**. For example, if $min\_wei = 50\%$, the group pattern $P = < \{u_2, u_3, u_4\}, 10, 3 >$ is a valid group pattern, since it has valid segments $\{[1, 3], [6, 8]\}$ and weight $6/10 \geq 0.5$.

Definition 4. *Given a database D, and thresholds max_dis, min_dur, and min_wei, the problem of finding all valid groups (or valid group patterns) is called **valid group (pattern) mining problem**.*

3   AGP: Algorithm Based on Apriori Property

In this section, we present the AGP (**A**priori-like algorithm for mining valid **G**roup **P**atterns) algorithm, which is derived from the well known Apriori algorithm[1] as the Apriori property also holds for group patterns.

Definition 5. *Given two group patterns, $P =< G, max\_dis, min\_dur >$ and $P' =< G', max\_dis, min\_dur >$, P' is called a **sub-group pattern** of P if $G' \subseteq G$.*

Property 1. [Apriori property for group patterns]: Given database D and thresholds max_dis, min_dur, and min_wei, if a group pattern is *valid*, all of its *subgroup patterns* will also be valid.

This property can be proven quite easily and we shall leave out the proof in the interest of space.

Based on the Apriori property, we develop the AGP algorithm as shown in Figure 1[1]. In the algorithm, we use C_k to denote the set of candidate k-groups, and use $\mathbb{G}_k$ to denote the set of valid k-groups. From $\mathbb{G}_1$, the set of all distinct users, the algorithm first computes $\mathbb{G}_2$, which is in turn used to compute $\mathbb{G}_3$. The process repeats until no more valid k-groups can be found. In each iteration, AGP performs *join* operation to generate candidate k groups from $\mathbb{G}_{k-1}$, and the generated candidates are further pruned using Apriori property.

Input: D, max_dis, min_dur, and min_wei
Output: all valid groups $\mathbb{G}$
01    $\mathbb{G}_1$ = all distinct users;
02   **for** $(k = 2; \mathbb{G}_{k-1} \neq \varnothing; k++)$
03        $C_k = $ **Generate_Candidate_Groups**$(\mathbb{G}_{k-1})$;
04   **for** $(t = 0; t < |D|; t++)$ // scan D to compute the "weight"
05   **for each** candidate k-group $c_k \in C_k$
06   **if Is_Close**(c_k, t, max_dis) **then**   // check closeness of candidate group c_k
07                    $c_k.cur\_seg + +$;
08   **else**
09   **if** $c_k.cur\_seg \geq min\_dur$ **then**
10                        $c_k.weight = c_k.weight + c_k.cur\_seg$;
11                    $c_k.cur\_seg = 0$;
12        $\mathbb{G}_k = \{c_k \in C_k \mid c_k.weight \geqslant min\_wei \times N\}$;
13        $\mathbb{G} = \mathbb{G} \cup \mathbb{G}_k$;
14   return $\mathbb{G}$;

Fig. 1. Apriori-like Algorithm AGP for Mining Group Patterns.

Let M be the number of distinct users and N be the number of time points in D. The time complexity of AGP algorithm is $O(\ \Sigma_k\{k \cdot |\mathbb{G}_{k-1}|^3,\ M \cdot N,\ N \cdot |C_k| \cdot k^2\ \}\ )$ (please refer to [9] for a detailed discussion on the time complexity of Apriori-like algorithm).

---

[1] Some functions are not shown to save space.

4   VG-Growth: An Algorithm Based on Valid Group Graph Data Structures

AGP, similar to the Apriori algorithm, incurs large overheads in candidate k-group pattern generation and database scans to check if the candidates are valid. In order to reduce such overheads, we propose a divide-and-conquer algorithm *VG-growth* using a novel data structure known as *VG-graph*. VG-growth and VG-graph are designed based on the principle similar to that of FP-growth and FP-tree (Frequent Pattern tree) for association rule mining[8].

Definition 6. *A **valid group graph** (or **VG-graph**) is a directed graph* (V, E), *where V is a set of vertices representing users in the set of valid 2-groups, and E is a set of edges representing the set of valid 2-groups. Each edge is also associated with the valid segments of the corresponding valid 2-group pattern.*

To construct a VG-graph, a complete scan on D is required to compute the valid 2-group patterns using the AGP algorithm. The users represented by V in the VG-graph are called the **valid users**. For easy enumeration of all the edges in a VG-graph, the edge linking two users in a valid 2-group pattern always origins from the user with a smaller id. Consider the movement database D in Table 1. Given $max\_dis = 10$, $min\_dur = 3$ and $min\_wei = 60\%$, we construct the corresponding VG-graph based on the set of valid 2-groups associated with valid segments, as shown in Figure 2.

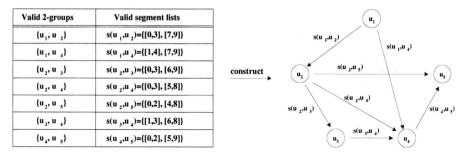

Valid 2-groups	Valid segment lists
$\{u_1, u_2\}$	$s(u_1, u_2) = \{[0,3], [7,9]\}$
$\{u_1, u_4\}$	$s(u_1, u_4) = \{[1,4], [7,9]\}$
$\{u_2, u_3\}$	$s(u_2, u_3) = \{[0,3], [6,9]\}$
$\{u_2, u_4\}$	$s(u_2, u_4) = \{[0,3], [5,8]\}$
$\{u_2, u_5\}$	$s(u_2, u_5) = \{[0,2], [4,8]\}$
$\{u_3, u_4\}$	$s(u_3, u_4) = \{[1,3], [6,8]\}$
$\{u_4, u_5\}$	$s(u_4, u_5) = \{[0,2], [5,9]\}$

Fig. 2. The VG-graph for Table 1

Note that VG-graph only contains the valid users involved in valid 2-groups. Thus, the number of vertices in the VG-graph will be no more than the total number of users. Suppose that on average, each user belong to k valid 2-groups. It can be shown that VG-graph will take smaller space than the original database if each user participates in less than $2 \times min\_dur$ valid 2-groups.

Based on the VG-graph data structure, we develop the VG-growth algorithm presented as follows.

If $(u \rightarrow v)$ is a directed edge in a VG-graph, u is called the **prefix-neighbor** of v. For example, in Figure 2, u_2, u_4 are the prefix-neighbors of u_5.

Consider the VG-graph in Figure 2. We can mine the valid group patterns by traversing the VG-graph. In the following, we illustrate how u_4 in the VG-graph can be traversed.

Input: VG-graph, max_dis, min_dur, and min_wei
Output: all valid groups
Method: call procedure VG-$growth(VG$-$graph, null)$.
Procedure: VG-$growth(Graph, \alpha)$
01   for each vertex u in Graph
02   generate the condition group $\beta = \{u\} \cup \alpha$;
03   select all prefix-neighbors of u, denoted by V_β;
04   if $V_\beta \neq \varnothing$ then
05   for each vertex v in V_β
06   output a valid group: $\{v\} \cup \beta$;
07   select the directed edges on V_β, denoted by $E(V_\beta)$;
08   if $E(V_\beta) \neq \varnothing$ then
09   for each directed edge $(v_i \rightarrow v_j)$ in $E(V_\beta)$
10                    $s(v_iv_j) = s(v_iv_j) \cap s(v_iu) \cap s(v_ju)$;   // adjust against u
11   if $s(v_iv_j)$ does not satisfy min_dur and min_wei then
12   remove edge $(v_i \rightarrow v_j)$ from $E(V_\beta)$;
13   if $E(V_\beta) \neq \varnothing$ then
14   construct the conditional VG-graph of β, $VG(\beta)$;
15   call procedure VG-$growth(VG(\beta), \beta)$;

Fig. 3. VG-growth Algorithm.

- Select all prefix-neighbors of u_4, $V_{u_4} = \{u_1, u_2, u_3\}$. Three valid 2-groups, $\{u_1, u_4\}$, $\{u_2, u_4\}$, $\{u_3, u_4\}$, are generated. Next, select the directed edges on V_{u_4}, $E(V_{u_4}) = \{(u_1 \rightarrow u_2), (u_2 \rightarrow u_3)\}$ with associated segment lists, $s(u_1, u_2) = \{[0, 3], [7, 9]\}$, $s(u_2, u_3) = \{[0, 3], [6, 9]\}$. Adjust the two segment lists against u_4 as follows.
  - $s(u_1, u_2) = s(u_1, u_2) \cap s(u_1, u_4) \cap s(u_2, u_4) = \{[0, 3], [7, 9]\} \cap \{[1, 4], [7, 9]\} \cap \{[0, 3], [5, 8]\} = \{[1, 3], [7, 8]\}$
  - $s(u_2, u_3) = s(u_2, u_3) \cap s(u_2, u_4) \cap s(u_3, u_4) = \{[0, 3], [6, 9]\} \cap \{[0, 3], [5, 8]\} \cap \{[1, 3], [6, 8]\} = \{[1, 3], [6, 8]\}$

  Check these adjusted segment lists against min_dur and min_wei, and remove those edges that does not meet the threshold requirements. The edge $(u_1 \rightarrow u_2)$ is therefore removed.

  The prefix-neighbors V_{u_4} and $E(V_{u_4})$ (after adjustment and checking) form u_4's **conditional group base**. From the u_4's conditional group base (involving u_1, u_2, and u_3 and an edge between u_2 and u_3), we derive the the **conditional VG-graph** of u_4, denoted by $VG(u_4)$, which contains two vertices $\{u_2, u_3\}$ and an edge $(u_2 \rightarrow u_3)$ with associated segment list $\{[1, 3], [6, 8]\}$.

  We perform mining recursively on $VG(u_4)$ and any valid groups generated from $VG(u_4)$ will involve u_4 as a member. We compute $V_{u_3u_4} = \{u_2\}$ and the valid 3-groups $\{u_2, u_3, u_4\}$ is generated. Since u_2 has no prefix-neighbors, the mining process for u_4 terminates.

Given a vertex u, let V_u denote the set of prefix-neighbors of u, and $E(V_u)$ be the set of directed edges after adjustment against u. V_u and $E(V_u)$ form a small database of groups which co-occur with u in some valid groups, known as u's **conditional group base**. We can compute all the valid groups associated with u in u's conditional group base by creating a smaller VG-graph, known as

u's **conditional VG-graph** and denoted by $VG(u)$. The mining process can be recursively performed on the conditional VG-graph. The complete VG-growth algorithm is given in Figure 3.

5   Evaluation

In this section, we evaluate and compare the performance of AGP and VG-growth algorithms based on their execution time. The experiments have been conducted using synthetically generated user movement databases on a Pentium-IV machine with a CPU clock rate of 2.4 GHz, and 1 GB of main memory. Note that both AGP and VG-growth are implemented to run in main memory to give a direct comparison between them.

5.1   Methodology

Performance Study. In the performance study experiment, we measure the execution times of AGP and VG-growth on three synthetic datasets (see Table 3) for different min_wei thresholds (from 0.1% to 10%). The thresholds max_dis and min_dur are fixed as 50 and 4 respectively. The execution time for VG-growth includes the time for constructing VG-graph.

Scale-up Performance. In scale-up experiment, we study the scale-up features of VG-growth against both the number of users (M) and the number of time points in the database (N). We use different M values from 1000 to 5000 with N fixed as 1000. We also vary N from 1000 to 10,000 keeping M fixed as 1000. The min_wei threshold varies from 0.5% to 10%. The thresholds max_dis and min_dur are fixed as 50 and 4 respectively. The scale-up feature of AGP is not included as in the performance study we have found that VG-growth always outperforms AGP.

5.2   Datasets

Since real datasets are not available, we have implemented a synthetic user movement database generator for our experiments. Our data generation method extends that for transaction databases described in [1,2]. The process of generation can be divided into 2 steps:

1. Generate a set $\mathbb{G}$ of maximal valid groups[2];
2. Pick groups from $\mathbb{G}$ and "assign" them to each time point by giving them locations that are close at the time point.

Due to space constraint, we shall not elaborate the detailed steps of database generation. Table 2 shows the parameters used for synthetic database generation. Table 3 summarizes the parameter settings for performance study and scale-up performance.

---

[2] Given a set $\mathbb{G}$ of group patterns and a group pattern $P \in \mathbb{G}$, we call P a **maximal group pattern**, and the group in P a **maximal group**, if P is not a sub-group pattern of any other group pattern in $\mathbb{G}$.

Table 2. Parameter List

M	The number of distinct users
N_G	The number of potentially maximal valid groups in the set $\mathbb{G}$
A_G	The average size of the potentially maximal valid groups
N	The number of time points(i.e., the whole time span)
A_t	The average number of groups involved in each time point
A_d	The average time duration of each group

Table 3. Parameter Settings

Performance Study & Scale-up against N						
Name	M	A_G	N_G	N	A_d	A_t	Size in Megabytes
DBI	1,000	5	1,000	1,000	6	100	15.4
DBII	1,000	5	1,000	5,000	6	100	81.5
DBIII	1,000	5	1,000	1,0000	6	100	164
Scale-up against M						
Name	M	A_G	N_G	N	A_d	A_t	Size in Megabytes
DBIV	1,000	5	1,000	1,000	6	100	15.4
DBV	3,000	5	3,000	1,000	6	300	46.3
DBVI	5,000	5	5,000	1,000	6	500	77.3

5.3   Results

Performance Study. The results of performance study are shown in Figure 4, in which the Y-axis has a log scale. It is observed that VG-growth outperforms AGP for all the datasets, especially when min_wei becomes smaller ($< 1\%$). When min_wei is small, there will be more valid groups as shown in Figure 5. The cost of candidate groups generation in AGP will become very high due to multiple database scans to check the closeness of members in the candidate groups.

We also observe that the time to find valid 2-groups is significant compared to the total execution time. In particular, for large min_wei values, VG-growth spends almost all the time finding valid 2-groups as shown in Figures 4 and 5. When the proportion of valid 2-groups is large, VG-growth takes almost the same time as AGP. This does not come as a surprise since VG-growth uses the same method as AGP to find valid 2-groups. Hence, reducing the cost of finding valid 2-groups is an important topic for our future work. Nevertheless, considering that the same VG-graph can be used for different runs of group pattern mining, the effective execution time of VG-growth is actually much less if we amortise the construction time of VG-graph over the runs.

In the performance study, we also examine the size of VG-graphs. Assuming an adjacency list structure, we compute the estimated size of VG-graph. Figures 6 and 7 give the sizes of VG-graphs in KB for different min_wei, and the compression ratios respectively. Although the actual sizes of VG-graphs are different for each min_wei, the compression ratios are almost the same and the compression ratios range from $0.5\% \sim 5\%$. This shows the compactness of the VG-graphs.

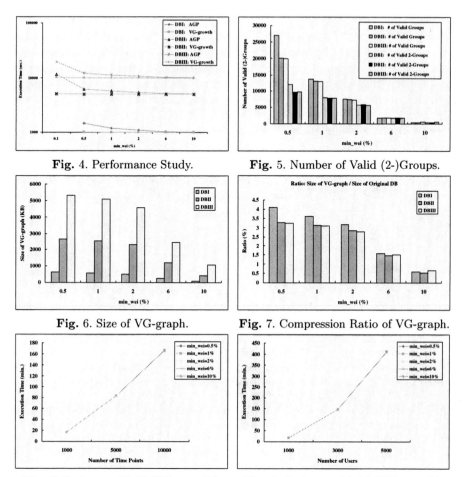

Fig. 4. Performance Study.

Fig. 5. Number of Valid (2-)Groups.

Fig. 6. Size of VG-graph.

Fig. 7. Compression Ratio of VG-graph.

Fig. 8. Scale-up with N (VG-growth).

Fig. 9. Scale-up with M (VG-growth).

Scale-up Performance. The results of scale-up performance experiments for VG-growth are shown in Figures 8 and 9. The performance curves for different *min_wei* in each figure are almost identical. The execution time is almost linear with the number of time points, N, and is almost linear with M^2, where M is the number of distinct users. This due to the fact that (1) the time required for finding valid 2-groups occupies a large proportion of the total execution time; and (2) most of the time required to find valid 2-groups is spent on scanning the database to compute the weights of candidate 2-groups, which is roughly determined by $N \cdot \binom{M}{2}$.

6   Conclusions

This paper reports a innovative approach to mine user group patterns from their movement data. The discovered group patterns, satisfying both spatial and temporal proximity requirements, could potentially be used in target marketing and personalized services. We formally define the notion of group patterns and develop two algorithms (AGP and VG-growth) for mining valid group patterns. The performance of these two algorithms has been reported using synthetically generated user movement databases. It has been shown that the cost of mining group patterns is mainly due to the computation of valid-2 group patterns as the number of larger group patterns reduces. Hence, the performance gain of VG-growth algorithm is most apparent when the *min_wei* is small. However, considering that VG-graphs can be stored beforehand and its construction cost can be amortised over multiple runs of group pattern mining, the savings of VG-growth algorithm will be more significant.

References

1. R. Agrawal and R. Srikant. Fast Algorithms for Mining Association Rules. In *Proc. of the 20th VLDB*, 1994.
2. R. Agrawal and R. Srikant. Mining Sequential Patterns. In *Proc. of 11th ICDE*, 1995.
3. B.Hofmann-Wellenhof, H.Lichtenegger, and J.Collins. *Global Positioning System: Theory and Practice*. Springer-Verlag Wien New York, third revised edition, 1994.
4. S. Chakrabarti, S. Sarawagi, and B. Dom. Mining Surprising Patterns using Temporal Description Length. In *Proc. of 24th VLDB*, 1998.
5. L. Forlizzi, R. H. Guting, E. Nardelli, and M. Schneider. A Data Model and Data Structures for Moving Objects Databases. *ACM SIGMOD Record*, 2000.
6. D.R. Forsyth. *Group Dynamics*. Wadsworth, Belmont, CA, 1999.
7. J. Han, G. Dong, and Y. Yin. Efficient Mining of Partial Periodic Patterns in Time Series Database. In *Proc. of 15th ICDE*, 1999.
8. J. Han, J. Pei, and Y. Yin. Mining Frequent Patterns Without Candidate Generation. In *Proc. of ACM SIGMOD*, 2000.
9. J. Han and A.W. Plank. Background for Association Rules and Cost Estimate of Selected Mining Algorithms. In *Proc. of the 5th CIKM*, 1996.
10. K. Koperski and J. Han. Discovery of Spatial Association Rules in Geographic Information Databases. In *Proc. of 4th Int. Symp. on Advances in Spatial Databases*, 1995.
11. J. F. Roddick and B. G. Lees. Paradigms for Spatial and Spatio-Temporal Data Mining. *Geographic Data Mining and Knowledge Discovery*, 2001.
12. J. F. Roddick and M. Spiliopoulou. A Survey of Temporal Knowledge Discovery Paradigms and Methods. *IEEE Trans. on Knowledge and Data Engineering*, 2002.
13. Wei Wang, Jiong Yang, and P.S. Yu. InfoMiner+: Mining Partial Periodic Patterns with Gap Penalties. In *Proc. of the 2nd ICDM*, 2002.
14. Jiong Yang, Wei Wang, and Philip Yu. Mining Asynchronous Periodic Patterns in Time Series Data. *IEEE Transaction on Knowledge and Data Engineering*, 2002.
15. Paul Zarchan. *Global Positioning System: Theory and Applications*, volume I. American Institute of Aeronautics and Astronautics, 1996.

Location Query Based on Moving Behaviors

Ming-Hui Jin[1], Eric Hsiao-Kuang Wu[1], Jorng-Tzong Horng[1],
Cheng-Yan Kao[2], and Yu-Cheng Huang[2]

[1] Department of Computer Science and Information Engineering
National Central University,
Chungli Taiwan
{jinmh,horng}@db.csie.ncu.edu.tw
hsiao@csie.ncu.edu.tw
[2] Department of Computer Science and Information Engineering,
National Taiwan University,
Taiwan
{cykao,r91021}@csie.ntu.edu.tw

Abstract. The importance of location prediction is rapidly increasing with the current trend of database applications in mobile computing environment. However, current personal communication services (PCS) could only provide currently maintained location information of non-idle mobile terminals. In this study, we explore the possibility of querying the future location of mobile terminals through their moving behavior which could be mined from their long-term moving history. Location prediction based on moving behavior requires no power consumption, and the prediction results are effective for a long period of time without requiring the queried clients to be non-idle. With the help of moving behavior, several location prediction operators for location query were proposed. The accuracy of the location query operators were verified through simulation statistics. The experimental results show that the predictions are accurate enough for regular moving mobile terminals.

1 Introduction

Under the sharply developing wireless communication technologies, more and more mobile terminals will access information instantly anytime, anywhere through the wireless radio. The mobile computing environment no longer enforces users to stay at fixed and universally known position and enables unrestricted mobility of the users [1, 5]. In this situation more and more mobile terminals will become the data sources, or furthermore, the mobile terminals themselves become the queried information. This phenomenon indicates that the mechanisms of querying the location information about mobile terminals are urgent for applications in the mobile computing environment.

Most cellular systems such as the GSM adopt the fixed paging area strategies [1, 5, 6] to maintain the location of their mobile subscribers. In the fixed paging area strategy, the coverage of the PCS is divided into several cells and the set of all cells were partitioned into several paging areas (PA). Whenever the current location of a mobile terminal is queried, the paging procedure will page the last known PA of the

V. Mařík et al. (Eds.): DEXA 2003, LNCS 2736, pp. 297–307, 2003.
© Springer-Verlag Berlin Heidelberg 2003

mobile terminal so that the exact cell of the mobile terminal could be retrieved. To ensure the creditability of the PA, each mobile terminal is required to inform the PCS its new location via location update procedures whenever it moves to another PA.

Although the PCS provides means for capturing the current location of each mobile terminal, the decision makers of many applications still desire information about the future location of them. For example, the handover functions of each base station would like to know how many mobile terminals would move into its cell in the next time interval so that it could reserve appropriate channel resources for them [3, 7, 8]. A businessman is finding a storefront that most of people usually walk randomly there. The fact that existing PCS could provide only the current location of mobile terminals and the desires of learning futures location from decision makers make location prediction urgency.

Pertinent researches about location prediction were based on the current position and velocity of each mobile terminal and they use tangent velocity to predict future location [3, 7, 10]. To get accurate position of a mobile terminal for prediction, each mobile terminal is required to calculate its exact position through the help of GPS or other position mechanisms [9] and then answer its position.

Rapidly growing load for personal communication network has strengthened the poverty of limited bandwidth resource. To satisfy the eagerness of profuse bandwidths under limited resource, diminishing the coverage area of cells to reduce the clients for each base station seems to be the ultimate solution. In this trend, it is expectable that the location information presented by cell ID will be accurate enough to fit the requirement of most applications. Based on this idea, we proposed a data model called moving behavior in [5], which describes the moving paths of each mobile terminal associate with the corresponding information about time and probability. In this paper, we propose several location prediction functions to facilitate the design of location queries for many applications.

In comparison with the tangent velocity approaches, the advantages of location prediction based on moving behaviors are summarized below. 1) The prediction is not only effective within a short time interval, but also is effective in the time intervals of long time future. 2) Our approach is much cheaper because our approach does not require mobile terminal to estimate its location and keep on communicating to system through expensive wireless channels. 3.) Our approach also works for mobile terminals which are in idle mode but the tangent velocity approaches are effective only in the situation that the mobile terminals are in ready mode [2].

This paper is organized as follows. In Section 2, we briefly introduce the concept of the moving behavior and propose a data model for it. In Section 3, we propose several location prediction functions from moving behavior and then make some location queries in SQL. Experiments and simulation results are presented in Section 4. Conclusion is drawn in Section 5.

2   The Moving Behavior

If a mobile terminal possesses regular moving behavior, then it often moves on the same set of paths, and the arrival times to individual location points of the paths are similar. Therefore, the moving behavior of a mobile terminal should contain not only the vertices of the moving paths where the mobile terminal often passes through, but also the information about the time at which the mobile terminal visits each vertex.

Fig. 1 shows an example of a mobile terminal's moving behavior. In this example, the moving period of the mobile terminal is a day. In most days, the mobile terminal follows one of the two paths to move from l_1 at about 7:00AM to l_8 at about 8:30AM, stays there until about 12:00PM and then goes to an unpredictable location (break time for lunch with random walk mobility model). At about 13:30PM, it returns to l_8 and stays there until about 17:30PM. At that time, it chooses one of the original two paths to go back to l_1 at about 19:30PM. In real cases, the arrival time to each position is not always the same. Specifically, the arrival time to each location could be represented by a random variable.

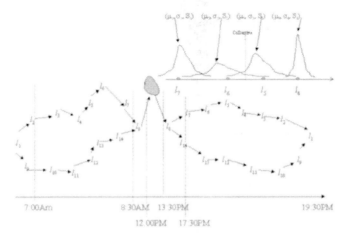

Fig. 1. A moving behavior example

Based on the concept above, in [5], we defined the moving behavior of each mobile terminal to be a partial ordered set $<V, E, C_E>$ to describe their mobility model as follows, and provided a set of data mining procedures to derive the moving behavior from their long-term moving history.

♦ $V \subseteq \{(l, t, s) \in L \times T \times N\}$ is the set of all moving states in which L is the set of all cells, T is the set of all normal distributed random variables and N is the set of all nature numbers. We denote, for each moving state $C_i = (l_i, t_i, s_i) \in V$, l_i is the cell ID of C_i, t_i is the time at which the corresponding mobile terminal arrives in l_i, μ_i and σ_i^2 are the mean and standard deviation of t_i, and s_i is the support of C_i.

♦ E is a subset of $V \times V$.

♦   For each $e = (C_i, C_j) \in E$, $C_E(e)$ is defined to be the confidence that the mobile terminal will change its moving state to C_j given the mobile terminal is in the moving state C_i.

For convenience, we say that moving stat $C_j < C_i$ if there is a path in the moving behavior which pass from C_j to C_i.

3 Location Query Based On Moving Behavior

3.1 Schema for Moving Behavior

The moving behavior could be maintained by a relational database. In Fig. 2, the schema for moving behavior contains two relations. The first relation called "Edges" which maintains the direct edges of the moving behavior of all mobile terminals. A tuple (X, C_1, C_2, P) in the relation Edges presents the fact that if mobile terminal X is in node C_1, then C_2 has probability P to be the next node of X. The second relation called "Nodes" which maintains the nodes of moving behavior. The tuple $(C, l, \mu, \sigma, S_1, S_2)$ in the relation Nodes shows that the support of node C is S_1, the mean and standard deviation of the time that mobile terminal X move into node C are μ and σ, respectively. And the node contains S_2 cells. The key of the relation "Edges" is (Mobile-ID, Current) and the key of the relation "Nodes" is (Node). Current is a foreign key of relation Edges referring to the relation Nodes.

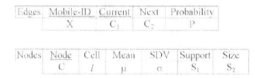

Fig. 2. A schema for moving behavior maintenance

3.2 Functions for Location Queries

Besides the mobile ID, all parameters that involve in a location query on the moving behavior could be decomposed and then be classified into the following five categories. They are 1) a node, 2) an order pair of nodes (edge), 3) a certain time, 4) a time interval and 5) probability. In the five categories, it is clear that parameters in category 3 could not be calculated from the moving behavior and hence it can only be specified by the query designers. Finding appropriate time interval is in general an optimization problem and hence we do not provide functions for finding time intervals. Due to this reason, we propose only the location prediction functions, which estimate the corresponding probabilities from moving behavior, and then the query designers can design their queries in SQL with the help of our proposed functions; they are *InNode*, *MV* and *EP*.

Given a mobile ID X, a specific time t and a node C, the function *InNodel*(X, t, C) returns the probability that X will be in node C at time t. Given a mobile ID X, a time interval (t_0, t) and a node C, the function $EP(X, t_0, t, C)$ returns the average probability that X will be in node C in the time interval (t_0, t). Given a mobile ID X, a time interval (t_0, t_1) and an order pair of nodes (C_0, C_1). $MV(X, t_0, t_1, C_0, C_j)$ returns the conditional probability that X will move into node C_1 in time interval (t_0, t_1) given X is in the node C_0 at time t_0. Besides the previous three functions, we assume that the system provides a function $C\_Cell(X)$ which returns the current cell ID of X.

3.3 Implementing the Location Query Functions

Function InNode and EP
Assume the last known location of the mobile terminal is l_1 and there exists no fork in the path $l_1 \rightarrow \ldots \rightarrow l_j \rightarrow \ldots \rightarrow l_i \rightarrow \ldots l_n$. If the mobile terminal follows its moving behavior, then the probability that the mobile terminal stays l_i at time t could be estimated by Lemma 1 below. Due to the page limitation, we ignore the proof of lemma 1, 2, theorem 1 and theorem 2 in this paper since the proofs are stated in [5, 8].

Lemma 1: If the moving behavior of a mobile terminal is a directed path $C_1 \rightarrow C_2 \rightarrow \ldots C_n$ satisfying $C_E(C_i, C_{i+1}) = 1$ for all $1 \le i < n$ and $l_i \ne l_j$ if $i \ne j$, then $CP(C_i, C_1, t)$, the probability that the mobile terminal stays l_i at time t given it is in node C_1, is

$$CP(C_i, C_1, t) = \int_{-\infty}^{t} \left(\rho(\mu_i, \sigma_i, x) - \rho(\mu_{i+1}, \sigma_{i+1}, x) \right) dx \qquad (1)$$

Where $\rho(\mu_i, \sigma_i, x)$ is the density function of the arrival time random variable of C_i.

The probability that the mobile terminal X will stay in C_j not only depends on the last known node, say C_i, of X, but also depends on the probability that X will choose a path from C_i to C_j. We denote the probability to be $Path(C_j, C_i)$ and estimate it by Lemma 2.

Lemma 2: If C_i and C_j are two nodes of the moving behavior of the mobile terminal X, then $Path(C_j, C_i)$, the probability that the mobile terminal will pass through C_j given X is in C_i, is

$$Path\left(C_j, C_i\right) = \sum_{P \text{ is a path from } C_i \text{ to } C_j} \left(\prod_{(u, v) \text{ is in } P} C_E(u, v) \right) \qquad (2)$$

Theorem 1: Let MB be the moving behavior of mobile terminal X, C_{min} be the set of all minimal nodes of MB and $S(C)$ be the support for node $C \in MB$, then

$$InNode(X, t, C) = \begin{cases} Path(C, C_f) \times CP(C, C_f, t) & \text{if the last know location } l_f \\ & \text{and its associated arrival} \\ & \text{time } t_f \text{ exists with } (l_f, t_f) \in C_f \\ \dfrac{\sum\limits_{u \in C_{min}} Path(C, u) \times CP(C, u, t) \times S(u)}{\sum\limits_{v \in C_{min}} S(v)} & \text{Otherwise} \end{cases} \qquad (3)$$

With the help of the function *InNode*, the function *EP* could be calculated by the equation below

$$EP(X, C, t_0, t) = \frac{1}{t - t_0} \int_{t_0}^{t} InNode(X, C, y) dy \qquad (4)$$

Function MV
Let $P_{X,j}$ be the probability that N_j will be the next node of mobile terminal X, $\mu_{X,i}$ and $\sigma_{X,i}$ are the mean and standard deviation of the arrival time that the mobile terminal X will move into node N_j given it is in the node N_0 at time t_0, then the function $MV(X, t_0, t, N_0, N_j)$ could be calculated by Theorem 2 below when $N_0 \ne N_j$. Here we define $MV(X, t_0, t, N_0, N_j) = 0$ if $N_0 = N_j$.

Theorem 2: If mobile terminal X stays in N_0 at time t_0 and X follows its moving behavior which contains the vertex N_0, and if $N_0 \neq N_j$ then

$$MV\left(X,t_0,t,N_0,N_j\right) = \begin{cases} 0 & \text{if } t \le t_0 \\ \dfrac{\varPhi\left(\dfrac{t-\mu_{X,j}}{\sigma_{X,j}}\right) - \varPhi\left(\dfrac{t_0-\mu_{X,j}}{\sigma_{X,j}}\right)}{1 - \varPhi\left(\dfrac{t_0-\mu_{X,j}}{\sigma_{X,j}}\right)} \times C_e\left(N_0,N_j\right) & \text{otherwise} \end{cases} \tag{5}$$

Where

- $\mu_{X,j}$ and $\sigma_{X,j}$ are the mean and standard derivation of the arrival time that X will move into N_j.

- $\varPhi()$ is the c.d.f. of the standard normal random variable.

Node-ID Determination

Although we have proposed the formulas for implementing the three location query functions, however, most query designers have no idea about how to choose appropriate nodes for their queries. This shows us that we should provide a function to select appropriate node whenever the end users have specified a set of cells and a specific time or a specific time interval.

If the cell ID appeared in a query is l_0, then, according to the definition of moving behavior, there may exist zero, one or more than one vertex in the moving behavior which contains cell l_0. If there is no vertex containing cell l_0, then the three proposed functions should not be called because their parameters could not be specified. This situation is seldom occurs for mobile terminal X since no vertex contains cell l_0 in the moving behavior of X implies X never or seldom visited l_0. If there exists more than one vertex which contains cell l_0, than we need to choose the most appropriate one for the proposed functions.

Let $MB_X = <V_X, E_X, C_{E,X}>$ be the moving behavior of mobile terminal X and $V_X(l_0) = \{v = (l, t, s) \in V_X \mid l = l_0\}$, we assume that $V_X(l_0) = \{v_1, v_2, ..., v_n\}$ for some $n \geq 1$ and ignore the condition that $V_X(l_0) = \phi$. If the fact that X stays inside cell l_0 at time t_0 is specified, then we could find the most appropriate node for the corresponding query as follows. Assume that, for each $v_j \in V_X(l_0)$, $\{v_{j,1}, ..., v_{j,n(j)}\} = \{v_{j,k} = (l_{j,k}, t_{j,k}, s_{j,k}) \in V_X \mid (v_j, v_{j,k}) \in E_X\}$ is the set of all next nodes of v_j, then the probability that $(l_0, t_0) \in v_j$ is[+]

$$P\left(\{l_0,t_0\} \in v_i\right) = \sum_{k=1}^{n(i)} \varPhi\left(\frac{t_0-\mu_i}{\sigma_i}\right) \times \left(1-\varPhi\left(\frac{t_0-\mu_{i,k}}{\sigma_{i,k}}\right)\right) \times C_E\left(v_i,v_{i,k}\right) \tag{6}$$

Finding the vertex $v_i \in V_X(l_0)$ such that $P\{(l_0, t_0) \in v_i\} \geq P\{(l_0, t_0) \in v_k\}$ for all $v_k \in V_X(l_0)$ and then the appropriate node could be determined. To facilitate the implementation of the location query functions, propose a function CTN as follow.

[+] Due to the page limitation, we ignore the proof of the equation since they are stated in [8].

$$CTN\left(X,l,t\right)=\begin{cases}\phi & if\ l\notin v\ \forall v\in V_{X}\\ v & if\ P\left\{(l,t)\in v\right\}\geq P\left\{(l,t)\in v\text{'}\right\}\\ & for\ all\ v\text{'}\in V_{X}\left(l\right)\end{cases} \tag{7}$$

3.4 Queries in SQL

In Section 3.3, we propose three functions which returns only the probabilities of given location and time parameters, however, many decision maker would like to know more about future locations given constraints about certain mobile terminals, time or probability. Fortunately, many location queries could be made by SQL, which is the most popular database query language. In this section, we design several useful location queries in SQL and the proposed location prediction functions.

Querying a Specific Mobile Terminal

For a mobile terminal Jimmy whose mobile ID is "0953-927547", a client may wish to make the following queries to learn the future location about Jimmy. Where is Jimmy? What is the possibility that Jimmy will appear somewhere near the Taipei train station at 14:20 tomorrow? Where will Jimmy appear in the time between 14:00 and 14:20 tomorrow? The first query could be answered by the function C_Cell easily and we design queries Q1 – Q2 for the remaining questions in SQL as follows. The words in bold form are the reserved words where the reserved word **NOW** is the time the query is applied.

Q 1: Tell me the possibility that Jimmy will stay somewhere in the set of cells $\{l_1, l_2, ..., l_k\}$ at 14:00 PM tomorrow (Assume that there is a view "SetL" which contains only an attribute "Cell" maintaining all the cells $\{l_1, l_2, ..., l_k\}$).

SELECT   **InNode**("0953-927-547", 14:00)/Size
FROM   Nodes, SetL
WHERE   Nodes.Node = **CTN**("0953-927547", SetL.Cell, 14:00)

Q 2: Show the place where Jimmy will appear in the time interval (14:00PM, 14:20PM) tomorrow with associated to their corresponding probabilities?

SELECT   Cell, **SUM(EP**("0953-927547", Current, 14:00, 14:30)/Size)
FROM   Nodes, Edges
WHERE   Edges.Mobile-ID = "0953-927547" **AND EP**("0953-927547", Edges.Current, 14:00, 14:30) > 0 **AND** Edges.Current = Nodes.Node.
GROUP BY Cell

Query for Mobile Transaction

Seamless handover is helpful for mobile transactions [4, 11]. To reach the goal of seamless handover for mobile transaction, requiring each base station to reserve channels for the coming mobile terminals is an effective approach. Thus, a mobile transaction could require appropriate base stations to reserve channels for it according to the query results of Q3 below.

Q 3: For each the cells *l* adjacent to the current cell of Jimmy, list the corresponding
        probability that Jimmy will move into *l* in the next 30 seconds.

CREAT VIEW V1 (Next, MV) **AS**
  SELECT Next, **MV**("0953-927547", **NOW, NOW**+30, Current, Next)
    FROM   Edges
  WHERE   Edges.Mobile-ID = "0953-927547" **AND** Edges.Current = **CTN**(C_**Cell**(0953-
              927547), **NOW**)

(**SELECT** Cell, MV/Size
FROM   V1, Nodes
WHERE   V1.Next = Nodes.Node) **UNION**
(**SELECT**   Cell, (1-**SUM**(MV))/Size
FROM   Nodes, V1
WHERE   Nodes.Node = **CTN**(C_**Cell**("0953-927547"), **NOW**))

4   Experiments and Comparisons

4.1 Simulation Design

In the simulations, the radius of the transmission coverage area for each base station is 500 meters and the individual mobile terminal moves by the rules defined in its corresponding moving schedule. A moving schedule of a mobile terminal is a lattice in which each vertex has three attributes: the location, the expected arrive time and the expected leave time. The exact leave time is decided according to the following rules: (1) If the exact arrive time is earlier than the expected leave time, then the leave time is normal distributed with mean = expected leave time and variance = 1. The time unit is minute. (2) If the exact arrive time is later than the expectative leave time, than the mobile terminal will leave this vertex immediately when it arrives this vertex.

Each edge of a moving schedule has 9 attributes. They are the start and the end vertex of the path, the width of the path, the maximum, average, minimum and diffusion of the moving speed, the probability that the path will be chosen and whether the moving is returnable or not. The mobile terminal moves on each path in Brownian motion by the rules defined in the path.

4.2 Experimental Results

In this subsection, we compare the location prediction results to the simulation statistics. All the location predictions are made from the moving behavior generated from moving history of the first 30 days' simulation and we then apply the statistic results from the next 100 day's simulations to evaluate the accuracy of our predictions.

Accuracy of InNode
Fig. 3 shows the average number of the cells (100 days' simulation records) that the mobile terminal goes through. The time unit is 5 minutes. In this figure, the mobile terminal moves faster in the time intervals (80, 100) and (210, 235) and moves much

slower in other time intervals. To show the accuracy of our predictions, we compare the query results of Q2 at time 95 to the statistical results that are generated from the next 100 days' simulations. The cells are chosen according to the probabilities that the mobile terminal will visit there at time 95 and we choose the most possible k cells for k = 1, 2, …, 14.

In Fig. 4, we observe that the statistical results for the next 100 days' simulation converges faster than then query results of Q2. It is because our prediction considers not only the probability of each cell for the time interval, but also considers the probability outside this interval. This is the main reason why our prediction converges slower than the statistical results of the samples. Because the time for the comparison is 95 at which the mobile terminal moves fast, we could expect that our prediction would be much accurate at other time.

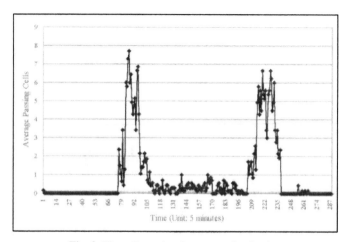

Fig. 3. The cell-passing frequency distribution

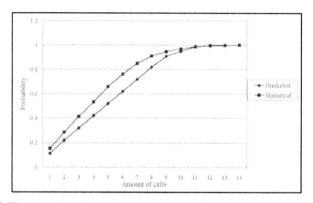

Fig. 4. The comparison between our prediction of Q2 and the simulation results

The Function MV

To show the accuracy of function *MV*, we need to specify a location l and a time t_0 at which the mobile terminal X stays in l at time t_0 in all days. In Fig 5 we focus on the moving behavior around the home of the mobile terminal X and we choose $t_0 = 78$ (t_1 and t_2 are normal distributed random variables with mean = 81 and standard deviation = 2). According to Fig. 3 and Fig. 5, the mobile terminal X will leave l_0 after time t_0 and goes to l_1 or l_2 (with the same probability). In the simulation we remove 7 samples from the simulation results of 100 days since X had left l_0 at time t_0 in the samples. In Fig. 6 we compare the results of $MV(X, 78, t, l_0, l_1) + MV(X, 78, t, l_0, l_2)$ to the statistical results under several time t. Fig. 7 shows that our prediction is accurate.

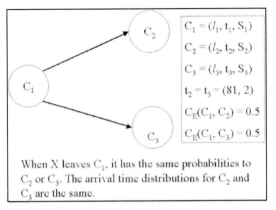

Fig. 5. The moving behavior of X near by l1 at time about t0

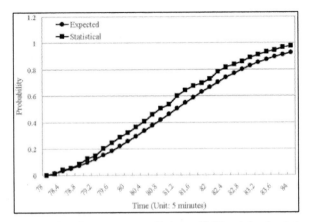

Fig. 6. The comparison between our predictions of MV and the simulation results

5   Conclusions and Future Work

In this paper, we propose propose several location prediction functions which enable the ability for querying the future location information. We implement several useful location queries in SQL, which is the most popular query language for database designers. According to the experimental results, we find our approach is promising for querying the future location information.

Finding the primitives of location prediction language is an interesting and important research for extending the ability of location query. In this paper, we ignore some function of location predictions. For example, given a set of cells S and a real value $\alpha \in (0, 1)$, find a shortest time interval (t_i, t_j) in which the corresponding mobile terminal has probability greater than or equal to α to stay somewhere in S. We will also investigate on stating a set of primitives for location query.

Acknowledgement. This research was supported by the Wireless Advanced Portable Bio-Diagnosis System project of Ministry of Economic Affairs, R.O.C

References

1. Datta, D. E. Vandermeer, A. Celik, and V. Kumar, "Broadcast Protocols to Support Efficient Retrieval from Databases by Mobile Users", ACM transactions on Database Systems, Vol. 24, No. 1, pp. 1–79, March 1999
2. Bettstetter, H. J. Vögel and J. Eberspächer, "GSM Phase 2+ General Packet Radio Service GPRS: Architecture, Protocols, And Air Interface", IEEE Communications Surveys, vol. 2, no. 3, third quarter, 1999
3. A. Levine, I. F. Akyldiz, and M. Naghshineh, "A resource estimation and cell admission algorithm for wireless multimedia networks using the shadow cluster concepts," IEEE/ACM Trans. on Networking, vol. 5, pp. 1–12, Feb. 1997
4. G. C. Chen and S. Y. Lee, "Modeling the Static and Dynamic Guard Channel Schemes for Mobile Transactions", International conference on Parallel and Distributed System, pp. 258–265, 1998
5. H. K. Wu, M. H. Jin, J. T Horng, and C.Y. Ke, "Personal Paging Area Design Based On Mobile's Moving Behaviors", will appear in Proc. of INFOCOM. 2001
6. Ian F. Akyildiz and Joseph S. M. Ho, "On Location Management for Personal Communications Networks", IEEE Communications Magazine, pp. 1380150145, Sep. 1996
7. M. H. Chiu and M. A. Bassiouni, "Predictive Schemes for Handoff Prioritization in Cellular Networks Based on Mobile Positioning", IEEE JSAC, vol. 18, no, 3, pp. 5100150522, Mar. 2000
8. M. H. Jin, J. T. Horng and H. K. Wu, "An Intelligent Handoff Scheme Based On Location Prediction Technologies", in Proc. of the IEEE European Wireless 2002. pp. 551–557, Feb. 2002
9. M. Hellebrandt, R. Mathar and M. Scheibenbogen, "Estimating Position and Velocity of Mobiles in a Cellular Radio Network," IEEE Trans. on Vehicular Technology, vol. 46, No. 1, Feb, 1997
10. S. Šaltenis, C. S. Jensen, S. T. Leutenegger, and M. A. Lopez, "Indexing the Positions of Continuously Moving Objects", In Proc. of the ACM SIGMOD Conf., pp. 331–342, 2000
11. V. C. S. Lee, K. W. Lam, S. H. Son, "Real-time Transaction Processing with Partial Validation at Mobile Clients", The 7th international conference on Real-Time Computing Systems and Applications, pp. 473–477, 2000

Dynamic Splitting Policies of the Adaptive 3DR-Tree for Indexing Continuously Moving Objects

Bonggi Jun[1], Bonghee Hong[1], and Byunggu Yu[2]

[1] Department of Computer Engineering,
Pusan National University
30 Jangjeon-dong, Geumjeong-ku,
Busan, 609-735, Republic of Korea
{bgjun,bhhong}@pusan.ac.kr
[2] Department of Computer Science,
University of Wyoming
Laramie, WY82071, U.S.A
yu@uwyo.edu

Abstract. Moving-objects databases need a spatio-temporal indexing scheme for moving objects to efficiently process queries over continuously changing locations of the objects. A simple extension of the R-tree that employs time as the third dimension of the data universe shows low space utilization and poor search performance because of overlapping index regions. In this paper, we propose a variant of the 3-dimensional R-tree called the Adaptive 3DR-tree. The dynamic splitting policies of the Adaptive 3DR-tree significantly reduce the overlap rate, and this, in turn, results in improved query performance. The results of our extensive experiments show that the Adaptive 3DR-tree outperforms the original 3D R-tree and the TB-tree typically by a big margin.

1 Introduction

Moving-objects databases should efficiently support database queries that refer to the trajectories and positions of continuously moving data objects. To improve the performance of these queries, an efficient indexing scheme for continuously moving objects is required. We assume that the movement of each moving object is represented as a sequence of line segments each of which is represented by two consecutively sampled positions. Each of the sampled positions is represented as a 3-dimensioal point: two space dimensions and one time dimension.

Among many issues related to indexing spatio-temporal data, we focus on the issues of minimizing the overlap of index regions in the index structures, since this is one of the most important known factors that determine the query performance [6,9]. A spatio-temporal index should be able to efficiently answer the range queries of the type "report all objects located within a specific area during the given period of time". For this type queries, several indexing schemes, such as the 3D R-tree[2], the HR-tree[3], the MV3R-tree[4], the TB-tree[5] and the STR-tree[7] have been developed based on the R-tree[1]. Since the R-tree structure is a hierarchy of possibly overlapping index regions, the R-tree variants are often called *region-overlapping*

V. Mařík et al. (Eds.): DEXA 2003, LNCS 2736, pp. 308–317, 2003.

schemes. The region overlap in R-tree variants leads to the traversal of a larger number of index paths, which increases the number of accessed index pages.

The 3D R-tree is a simple extension of the original R-tree and views time as another dimension. Although the 3D R-tree showed the best performance for range queries among the above mentioned indexing schemes, it can suffer from bad search performance due to high overlap of index regions. There is room for significant performance improvement: The smaller the region overlap is, the better the query performance becomes. The HR-tree and MV3R-tree are very efficient for time-slice queries, but the performance of range queries is not better than the 3D R-tree. While the TB-tree for processing trajectories queries outperforms the 3D R-tree, the performance for processing range queries is not better than the 3D R-tree.

The above mentioned index structures suffer from the fact that they cannot efficiently process range queries. To address this issue, we propose an access method, called the Adaptive 3DR-tree (or just A3DR-tree), which is based on the original 3D R-tree method. The 3D R-tree is not adequate for indexing continuously moving objects because the amount of region overlap in these structures is relatively very large when trajectories of moving objects are indexed. Unlike typical regional data, trajectories of moving objects tend to be clustered since they usually move along existing geographic features - e.g., roads. This results in a higher overlap rate in the index structure. In addition, the space utilization of the 3D R-tree is less than 60%, since any insertion does not occur in the old node split along the time axis under the balanced splitting policy of the original R-tree method.

The A3DR-tree is equipped with a specially designed splitting-merging policy. The splitting-merging policy of the A3DR-tree minimizes region overlap and increases space utilization to enhance the performance of range queries. This splitting-merging policy consists of the following sub-policies: *forced merging policy* that reduces the overlap and *unbalanced splitting policy along time axis* that increases page utilization. We present *the unbalanced splitting policy along time axis* to assign more entries to the old node. To achieve the optimal shape of bounding boxes, we define the cubical bounding box in 3-dimensional space by means of both the number of sampling positions for each object and the number of moving objects.

The rest of the paper is organized as follows. Section 2 defines the problems of indexing moving objects based on the original 3D R-tree. Section 3 presents the forced merging policy and gives the definition of high overlap of index regions. Section 4 introduces a new criterion for choosing the split axis and the unbalanced splitting policy along time axis. Section 5 contains experiments that compare the performance of the Adaptive 3DR-tree with the 3D R-tree and the TB-tree. Finally we summarize our contributions and provide directions for future work in Section 6.

2   The Problems of the 3D R-Tree

In this section, we discuss two major problems of the original 3DR-tree: One is high overlap of index regions and the other is low page utilization. The overlap rate between the adjacent index regions depends on the moving patterns and the distribution of moving objects. Low space utilization of the old node after splitting is due to biased insertion to new nodes.

We assume that the movement of each moving object is represented as a sequence of connected line segments each of which consists of two end points, (x_1, y_1, t_1) and (x_2, y_2, t_2). When a new sampled point is inserted, the line segment that connects the previous sampled point and the new sampled point is inserted into a specific leaf node, and the MBB(Minimum Bounding Box) of the leaf node is enlarged to include this new line segment. The enlargement of an MBB possibly increases the overlap.

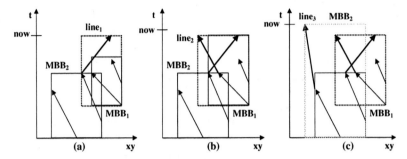

Fig. 1. The problem of enlargement of bounding boxes. (a) the enlargement of MBB_1, after inserting $line_1$. (b) the enlargement of MBB_1, after inserting $line_2$. (c) the enlargement of MBB_2, after inserting $line_3$

In Figures 1(a) and (b), if two line segments, $line_1$ and $line_2$ are inserted, the algorithm ChooseSubtree of the original R-tree chooses the leaf-level MBB_1 for inserting the line segments. For choosing the best leaf, the R-tree uses the least area enlargement policy. The insertion of $line_2$ results in the enlargement of MBB_1 as shown in Figure 1(b). Finally, the insertion of $line_3$ requires the enlargement of MBB_2. Figure 1(c) shows high overlap of MBB_1 with MBB_2. The high overlap of leaf nodes can deteriorate the performance of index structures.

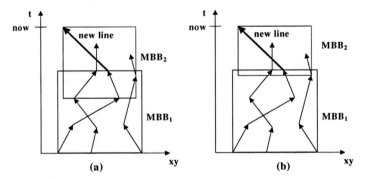

Fig. 2. The problem of the balanced splitting policy along time axis. (a) the balanced splitting along time axis in the R-tree. (b) the unbalanced splitting along time axis in the A3DR-tree

In order to add a new entry to a full node containing the maximum number of entries M, it is necessary to distribute M + 1 entries into two nodes. In the R-tree, each of two nodes must contain at least m entries, where m ∈ [0, M/2]. In many studies related to the R-tree, it proposed that m = 40% was a suitable value for the split algorithm. Suppose that two split nodes along time axis are an old node MBB_1

and a new node MBB_2. The R-tree performs the balanced splitting as shown in Figure 2(a). MBB_1 will not be chosen to insert the new line segment by means of the least area enlargement policy. In this case, the balanced splitting along the time axis will degrade space utilization. In section 4.3, we propose a new unbalanced splitting policy to improve the page utilization of the old leaf node that will not grow any more.

3 The Forced Merging Policy

In this section, we introduce a new method of reducing the overlap of index regions by merging adjacent nodes sharing a large overlapping region. The R*-tree[6] uses the policy of minimum overlap enlargement to choose the leaf node to be inserted. The R*-tree, however, cannot avoid overlapping of index region of leaf nodes. The Adaptive 3DR-tree proposed in this paper differs in that the forced merging policy reduces a high degree of overlap of leaf nodes.

Let the intersection of two bounding boxes of two leaf nodes, E_i and E_j, be the overlapping area. The rate of overlapping area is defined as follows:

OverlapRate$(E_i,\ E_j)$ = area$(E_i.MBB\ \cap\ E_j.MBB)$ / min(area$(E_i.MBB)$, area$(E_j.MBB)$), where E_i and E_j are leaf nodes. If this overlap rate is greater than some HRO(High Rate of Overlap), it is said that E_i highly overlaps E_j, and the two leaf nodes should be merged. HRO was tested from 20% to 60%. Our experiments show that HRO = 40% yields the best performance.

Suppose E_j is overlapped with E_i , where E_i and E_j are leaf nodes. High overlap of MBB, called HOMBB is defined as follows:

If OverlapRate(E_i, E_j) > HRO, E_i has high overlap of MBB, namely HOMBB, for the overlapping node, E_j.

We assume that three leaf nodes, E_i, E_j and E_k initially do not have any HOMBB. By inserting a new line segment LS to E_k, the MBB of E_k, $E_k.MBB$, is enlarged to include LS. This extended MBB is denoted by $E_k.EMBB$. If the overlap of $E_k.EMBB$ and $E_i.MBB$ is greater than the threshold HRO, the leaf nodes E_i and E_k should be merged by the forced merging policy. Let E_m be a merged node obtained by the function merge(E_i, E_k). If E_m has high overlap with E_j, the two nodes E_m and E_j also should be merged by the same policy.

The forced merging policy has the following rules.
1)   Any two nodes having high overlap of MBBs should be merged.
2)   IF a node has two or more HOMBBs, the node is merged with an overlapping node having the largest HOMBB of which OverlapRate is maximum.
3)   IF the result of merging two nodes is overflow THEN the merged node should be re-split.
4)   IF the merged node becomes HOMBB with another nodes (the cascading of HOMBB) THEN HOMBBs should be merged again.

The forced merging policy has the two advantages: (1) the overlap between leaf nodes can considerably be reduced. (2) the index structures are gradually improved by means of the policy of merging and re-splitting.

4 Two Kinds of Splitting Policies along Spatial or Time Axis

In this section, we introduce a new criterion based on the number of moving objects and the number of sampling positions for defining the optimal shape of bounding boxes. We also present different splitting policies along spatial or time axis.

4.1 Comparing the Size of Time Domain with Spatial Domain

In order to compare the time domain with the spatial domain, this paper uses new measurement by means of both the number of sampling positions for each object and the number of moving objects. In three-dimensional space, it does not make sense to directly compare the time unit of time domain with the spatial distance of the spatial domain(x or y axis). For example, you cannot say that 10m are larger than 1hour. Table 1 summarizes several symbols used in the paper.

Table 1. Summary of symbols and definitions

Symbols	Definitions
Nls	the number of all line segments
Nln	the number of leaf nodes
Cnode	the effective capacity of the node
Nmo	the number of all moving objects
Tsampling	the number of sampling positions for each moving object
X, Y, T	the length of domain
x_i, y_i, t_i	the size of a leaf node LN_i
Nmo_i	the number of moving objects in a leaf node LN_i
Ts_i	the number of sampling positions for each object in a leaf node LN_i

By analyzing the relation between the number of moving objects and the number of sampling positions for each object, we derive the cubical bounding box. First we introduce three assumptions to get an optimal condition of leaf nodes.

Assumption 1) Moving objects are uniformly distributed in leaf nodes, and all leaf nodes have the same size and do not have any overlap.

$$Nln = Nls / Cnode \tag{1}$$
$$Nln = (X * Y * T) / (x_i * y_i * t_i) \tag{2}$$
$$Nls * (x_i * y_i * t_i) = (X * Y * T) * Cnode \quad \text{(3), by (1) and (2)}$$

Assumption 2) The number of moving objects is constant within a leaf node, and moving objects report their location at the same time interval.

$$Nls = Nmo * Tsampling \tag{4}$$
$$Nmo * Tsampling * (x_i * y_i * t_i) = (X * Y * T) * Cnode, \quad \text{by(3) and (4)}$$
$$Nmo * (x_i * y_i) * Ts_i = (X * Y) * Cnode, \quad \text{since } Tsampling/Ts_i = T/t_i$$
$$Nmo * Ts_i = (X * Y) / (x_i * y_i) * Cnode \tag{5}$$

Assumption 3) The maximum number of line segments in a leaf node is determined by the number of sampling position per object and the number of moving objects. The number of moving objects in a leaf node, Nmo_i can be expressed as follows:

$$Nmo_i = Nmo * (x_i * y_i) / (X*Y) \tag{6}$$
$$Nmo * Ts_i = Nmo / Nmo_i * Cnode, \qquad \text{by (5) and (6)}$$
$$Ts_i * Nmo_i = Cnode \tag{7}$$

Expression 7 shows a relation for an optimal leaf node under three assumptions.

Let x_i, y_i, t_i be the size of each domain in a leaf node(LN_i), and $LS_j.x$, $LS_j.y$, $LS_j.t$ be the projection of LS_j along x,y,t axis, respectively, in 3-dimensional space, where LS_j is a line segment in LN_i. The function sum_covered( ) returns the minimally covered line of a collection of line segments.

$$x_i = sum\_covered(LS_j.x), \, y_i = sum\_covered(LS_j.y), \, t_i = sum\_covered(LS_j.t)$$
$$\text{where } j = 1 \dots Cnode \tag{8}$$

Since, in each leaf node, moving objects are uniformly distributed and do not overlap, the projection of entries has the same size, denote by $|LS_1.x| = |LS_2.x| = \dots = |LS_{Cnode}.x|$. The size of leaf node is defined as follows:

$$x_i = Nmo_i * |LS_j.x|, \, y_i = Nmo_i * |LS_j.y| \text{ and } t_i = Cnode/Nmo_i * |LS_j.t|, \text{ where } Nmo_i$$
is the number of moving objects in a leaf node. $\tag{9}$

If we assume that the cubical bounding box has the same size for each axis, denoted by $x_i = y_i = t_i$, then it is derived by expression 9:

$$Nmo_i * |LS_j.x| = Nmo_i * |LS_j.y| = Cnode/Nmo_i * |LS_j.t|$$
$$Nmo_i = Cnode/Nmo_i, \qquad \text{since we assume } |LS_j.x| = |LS_j.y| = |LS_j.t|$$
$$Nmo_i = Cnode^{1/2} \tag{10}$$

The condition of the cubical bounding box is derived by expression 7 and 10 as follows:

$$Ts_i = Nmo_i = Cnode^{1/2} \tag{11}$$

4.2 The Condition of Choosing a Split Axis

In order to select a suitable split axis, we use a new criterion that is based on the number of moving object(Nmo_i) and the number of sampling positions(Ts_i). The new criterion is explained as follows:

```
IF Ts_i >= Nmo_i  THEN split along t axis                              // condition(1)
ELSE IF Nmo_i >= 2 * Cnode^{1/2} THEN split along x, y axis            // condition(2)
    ELSE IF √2 * Cnode^{1/2} <= Nmo_i < 2 * Cnode^{1/2}
            AND 1/2 * Cnode^{1/2} < Ts_i <= 1/√2* Cnode^{1/2}          // condition(3)
    THEN split along x, y axis
    ELSE split along t axis
```

Let $Nmo_i = Ts_i$ be a split condition that maximizes the search performance. If $Ts_i \geq Nmo_i$ (condition 1), the split should be performed along time axis. The reason is that the optimal shape of bounding box should be cubical, where it is based on $Nmo_i = Ts_i$. Let E_i be an overfull node, and E_i is split into two nodes, E_{i1} and E_{i2}. If there are split along time axis, E_{i1} corresponds to the old node, and E_{i2} becomes the new node, that is, $E_{i1}.t < E_{i2}.t$.

In condition 1) If $Ts_i \geq Nmo_i$, then $Ts_i \geq Cnode^{1/2}$ and $Nmo_i \leq Cnode^{1/2}$. If the unbalanced splitting(explained in the next section) occurs along time axis, the old node E_{i1} keeps at most Ts_i of E_i, where is $Ts_{i1} \cong Ts_i >= Cnode^{1/2}$ and $Nmo_{i1} <= Cnode^{1/2}$. The condition of a new node E_{i2} is $Ts_{i2} < Cnode^{1/2}$ and $Nmo_{i2} <= Cnode^{1/2}$.

In condition 2) If $Nmo_i >= 2 * Cnode^{1/2}$, then $Ts_i <= 1/2 * Cnode^{1/2}$. If the balanced splitting occurs along x, y axis, then Nmo_{i1}(or Nmo_{i2}) $>\cong Cnode^{1/2}$ and Ts_{i1}(or Ts_{i2}) $<= 1/2 * Cnode^{1/2}$.

In condition 3) The following expression is a condition, which is not satisfied with two previous conditions, that is, $Ts_i < Nmo_i$ and $Nmo_i < 2 * Cnode^{1/2}$. By $Ts_i = Cnode / Nmo_i$, it is derived as follows:

$$Cnode^{1/2} < Nmo_i < 2 * Cnode^{1/2} \text{ AND } 1/2 * Cnode^{1/2} < Ts_i < Cnode^{1/2} \qquad (12)$$

When it is split along x, y axis, the side along the spatial dimension becomes half, i.e. $Nmo_{i1} \cong 1/2 * Nmo_i$, but the side along the time dimension is not changed. In order to make a cubical bounding box, the condition for spatial split is $Nmo_{i1} >= Ts_{i1}$, and it is derived as $1/2 * Nmo_i >= Ts_i$. By $Ts_i = Cnode/Nmo_i$, it is finally derived as $Nmo_i >= \sqrt{2}* Cnode^{1/2}$. The final spatial split condition satisfying the expression (12) is as follows.

$$\sqrt{2} * Cnode^{1/2} <= Nmo_i < 2 * Cnode^{1/2} \qquad (13)$$

4.3 The Splitting Policy along Time Axis

The continuous growth of trajectories requires enlargement of MBB along time axis. This leads to splitting of overfilled nodes along time axis. The old leaf node among two split nodes shows low space utilization because insertions into the old leaf much less frequently occur. We propose a new splitting policy to improve space utilization of split nodes.

The term UC (abbreviation of "until changed") is used for representing the most recently reported position of an object. The line segment whose one end is the UC of the corresponding object is called as the UC line segment. Let $UCLine_i$ be a UC line segment of a moving object O_i. Each MBB that contains one or more UC line segments is declared to be a UC MBB. The fixed MBB means the MBB that does not contain any $UCLine_i$.

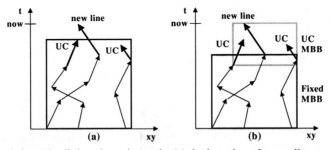

Fig. 3. The unbalanced splitting along time axis. (a) the insertion of a new line segment. (b) the unbalanced split along time axis

Figure 3 shows an example of unbalanced splitting along time axis. The results of unbalanced splitting are a UC MBB and a fixed MBB. While the UC MBB contains both UC lines and non-UC lines, the fixed MBB does not include any UC line. In order to increase space utilization, we assign as many lines to the fixed MBB as possible. The fixed MBB is allowed to contain more than half of the maximum number of entries of a leaf node within the upper bound of Cnode defined in section 4.1. Every UC lines should be assigned to the UC MBB.

When an overfilled node is split into a UC MBB and a fixed MBB along time axis, the fixed MBB must contain more than Cnode/2 non-UC lines. If the fixed MBB is assigned fewer than Cnode/2 lines, the splitting should be canceled and performs the split along a spatial axis. On the other hand, the lower bound of an UC MBB can be less than Cnode/2. Nevertheless, space utilization will not degrade because every UC MBB will continuously grow.

5 Experiments

In order to evaluate the performance of our Adaptive 3DR-tree, we compared it with the 3D R-tree and the TB-tree, well known indexing schemes for continuously moving objects. We used the GSTD generator[8] to generate test datasets for the experiments. The initial distribution of objects was Gaussian, and the movement of objects was random.

Because the splitting algorithm used in the Adaptive 3DR-tree is very simple, the time of index creation for the Adaptive 3DR-tree is lower than the original 3DR-tree and the TB-tree. The forced merging policy increases the number of node accesses, but the number of performing the forced merging is 0.25%~0.1% for the total number of inserting line segments.

5.1 Comparison of Space Utilization

The A3DR-tree using the unbalanced splitting policy for the time domain has the average space utilization varying between 68% and 77%. The space utilization of the TB-tree is over 94%. However, the improved page utilization comes at high overlap of leaf nodes. The space utilization of the R-tree is usually about 58%. Although the R*-tree[6] increases the space utilization up to 63% with the forced reinsertions, the performance improvement of range queries over the R-tree is marginal.

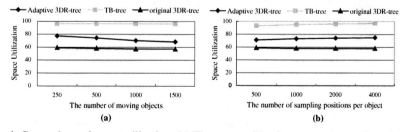

Fig. 4. Comparison of space utilization. (a) The space utilization versus the number of moving objects. (b) The space utilization versus the number of sampling positions

Figure 4(a) shows space utilization with the number of moving objects varying between 250 and 1500. The number of sampling positions per object was 2000 in the dataset. Our experiments show that the space utilization of the Adaptive 3DR-tree deteriorates as the number of moving objects increases. In Figure 4(b), we examined the space utilization versus the number of sampling positions for the different data set in which the number of sampling positions per object was between 500 and 4000. The number of moving objects was 500 in the dataset. As the number of sampling positions increases, the space utilization of the Adaptive 3DR-tree becomes better.

5.2 Performance Evaluation for Variable Numbers of Moving Objects

The number of disk accesses for processing range queries depends on the number of moving objects. Figure 5 shows the number of total node accesses for various range queries on the dataset. In Figure 5, we used the dataset containing between 250 and 1500 moving objects. The number of sampling positions per object was 2000 in the dataset. As for the queries, we used three kinds of query windows whose lengths are, respectively, 5%, 10% and 20% of each dimension, i.e., 0.0125%, 0.1%, and 0.8% of the universe. Each query set includes 1000 randomly generated query windows.

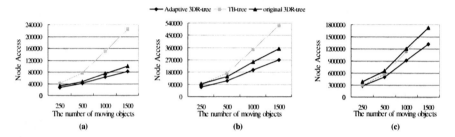

Fig. 5. Number of node accesses versus the number of moving objects : various range, (a) 5%, (b) 10% and (c) 20% in each dimension

The experimental results (Figure 5) show that the Adaptive 3DR-tree outperforms the 3D R-tree as well as the TB-tree for all range queries. The experiments show that the Adaptive 3DR-tree considerably can reduce the overlap between nodes by using the forced merging policy. For range queries with a large query region, the performance of 3D R-tree is similar to the TB-tree. Since the space utilization of the TB-tree is better than the others, the TB-tree is the best method for lowering the height of the tree.

6 Conclusions

This paper has addressed the region-overlap problem of the indexing schemes designed for continuously moving data objects, which is aggravated by the continuous growth of moving-object trajectories. We introduced two insertion policies: the forced merging policy and two kinds of splitting policies. Our experimental results showed that these policies can effectively reduce the overlap. In addition, to improve the space utilization of index nodes, we developed the unbalanced splitting policy for dividing an overfilled node along time axis. To determine the optimal shape of bounding boxes of index nodes, we introduce a criterion of a cubical bounding box for approximating the movement of moving objects. By virtue of the unbalanced splitting along time axis, the Adaptive 3DR-tree has better space utilization than the 3D R-tree. The TB-tree is more efficient than the Adaptive 3DR-tree in terms of the space utilization, but the performance of range queries is not desirable compared to the 3D R-tree and Adaptive 3DR-tree because of high overlap between nodes. The Adaptive 3DR-tree's space utilization is better than 3D R-tree, and the performance of range queries is also better. Although the Adaptive 3DR-tree improves the performance of the 3D R-tree and TB-tree, indexing of current positions remains unsolved. We are currently developing a unified spatio-temporal indexing for querying on current, future and past positions.

Acknowledgement. This work was supported by grant No.C1-2002-058-0-4 from the University Fundamental Research Program of Ministry of Information & Communication in republic of Korea.

References

1. A. Guttman, "R-trees: A dynamic index structure for spatial searching," Proceedings of ACM SIGMOD Conference, p47–54, 1984.
2. Y. Theodoridis, M. Vazirgiannis, and T. K. Sellis, "Spatio-Temporal Indexing for Large Multimedia Applications," IEEE International Conference on Multimedia Computing and Systems, p441–448, 1996.
3. M. A. Nascimento and J. R. O. Silva, "Towards historical R-trees," ACM symposium on Applied Computing, p235–240, 1998.
4. Y. Tao and D. Papadias, "MV3R-Tree: A Spatio-Temporal Access Method for Timestamp and Interval Queries," Proceedings of the VLDB Conference, p431–440, 2001.
5. D. Pfoser, C.S. Jensen, and Y. Theodoridis, "Novel Approaches in Query Processing for Moving Objects," Proceedings of the VLDB Conference, p395–406, 2000.
6. N. Beckmann and H. P. Kriegel, "The R*-tree: An Efficient and Robust Access Method for Points and Rectangles," Proceedings of ACM SIGMOD Conference, p332–331, 1990.
7. D. Pfoser, Y. Theodoridis, and C.S. Jensen, "Indexing Trajectories in Query Processing for Moving Objects", Chorochronos Technical Report, CH-99-3, 1999.
8. Y. Theodoridis, J. R. O Silva and M.A Nascimento, "On the Generation of Spatiotemporal Datasets," SSD, LNCS 1651, Springer, p147–164, 1999.
9. T. K. Sellis, N. Roussopoulos and C. Faloutsos, "The R+-Tree: A Dynamic Index for Multi-Dimensional Objects", Proceedings of the VLDB Conference, p507–518, 1987.

Comparing the Overhead Requirements of Database Transaction Models

Andrew G. Fry and Hugh E. Williams

School of Computer Science and Information Technology,
RMIT University,
GPO Box 2476V,
Melbourne 3001, Australia
andrewfry@acm.org
hugh@cs.rmit.edu.au

Abstract. A transaction model defines the behaviour, constraints, integrity, inter-relationships, and robustness of database transactions. Such models are generally evaluated indirectly, often by experiments on a database monitor that implements the model, or by workload simulation. In this paper, we propose a novel method of comparing transaction models based on functions of architectural- and isolation-work. Using these functions, we show the complexity of ten transaction models and discuss the relationship between them. We conclude that our architectural- and isolation-work functions can be used to reason about transaction models and as one measure for selecting the model appropriate to specific applications.

1 Introduction

Database systems are an essential software tool for most organisations. The prevalence of large databases and simultaneous access by many users necessitated the provision of concurrency control. Moreover, such size and complexity has made it necessary to control and limit the effects of errors and failures. Failure management and *concurrency control* have been research focuses in databases for more than twenty years [1].

To manage concurrent access and failure, most database systems support a *transaction* mechanism. A *transaction model* describes the requirements on application programs and the behaviours and guarantees provided by the database *monitor*. A model can usually be implemented using several different protocols and algorithms. Many transaction models have been devised according to changing requirements. For example, the need to control update conflicts lead to access locks; error recovery requirements to the inclusion of update logging; and the characteristics of locks and logs prompted the design of optimistic, nested, and multi-value transactions. Gray and Reuter discuss the evolution of transaction processing concepts and systems [2].

Evaluating a database system typically requires simulating the behaviour of the system, or measuring the performance of an implementation, while variables

V. Mařík et al. (Eds.): DEXA 2003, LNCS 2736, pp. 318–329, 2003.

such as the degree of concurrency or the size of the transactions are altered. The results are used to argue the benefits of one system under specific conditions, or to explore the behaviour of the system under varying conditions. The overwhelming factors in database performance have been storage speed (for example, disk speed and cache behaviour) and conflict management (for example, wait delays and transaction retries), so the amount of work performed by the database monitor has been largely ignored. However, as the character of applications changes from large monolithic transactions towards fine-grained distributed transactions, the overhead of the transaction monitor is becoming a more important factor in overall system performance.

In this paper, we propose a function of database model overhead useful for discussion and comparison of general transaction models. The function provides a measure of the theoretical overhead of a transaction monitor, independently of an implementation or simulation. Our method of comparison is coarse-grained, that is, it does not compare protocols or optimisations but provides a simple, practical framework for considering the complexity of transaction models.

Our overhead function is derived from the number and type of object-states that occur during execution of transactions. Using it, we show the relative complexity of ten well-known transaction architectures. Our analysis allows a ranking of the architectures based on complexity and reveals, for example, similarity of the Epsilon and Escrow transaction models. We argue that our function is a useful tool for selecting the least-complex transaction architecture for a database system and may facilitate the rational design of new transaction architectures.

2   Background

Concurrency control has been a requirement for simultaneous access to shared data in multi-user concurrent database systems for more than twenty years [3]. In most applications, it is agreed that concurrent database *transactions* must be *serialisable* [4].

Database transactions are commonly characterised by the ACID properties: conventionally *Atomicity, Isolation* and *Durability* are guaranteed by a *transaction monitor* and *Consistency* by requiring that applications never *commit* inconsistent transactions [2,5].

A *transaction model* describes the structure that is imposed on transactions, that is, the rules which govern their execution and interaction. The simplest transaction model is one that does not provide for concurrency, allowing a single active transaction. A more complex model permits concurrency and uses locks to enforce mutual exclusion and provide isolation. Additional complexity provides rollback, allowing transactions to be committed or undone, so providing atomicity and durability; a formal description of many models and mechanisms can be found elsewhere [6,7]. Other complex properties solve problems such as spatial distribution, replication, and time distribution [8,9,10]. We discuss the complexity of selected models in Section 3.

The early analysis of database systems centred on concurrency control and the behaviour of locking mechanisms [11,12,13,14,15], and on the effect of factors such as transaction size [16,17]. Strict two-phase-locking is widely accepted as the standard for concurrency-control because interleaved transactions appear to have executed in a serial order [5].

As the behaviour of locking systems became better understood, investigations looked to architectural variations. Agrawal et al. discuss a scheme for rewriting transactions into sub-transactions that execute with increased levels of parallelism while retaining existing atomicity [18,19]. Similarly, though of more limited applicability, time-stamp ordering has been considered as a replacement for locking [18,20]. Interesting variations on exclusive access theme include the separately developed Epsilon and Escrow transactions. The Epsilon model [21] permits limited conflict and allow transactions knowledge of the degree of uncertainty. In contrast, the Escrow model [22] permits a transaction to reserve some subrange of a value.

Given the number of architectural variations, there has been surprisingly little investigation into the structure of transaction models. ACTA [23,24] is a formal framework for describing architectures, and it has been used to specify transaction behaviour and discuss variations. An alternative framework based on formal automata is used by Lynch [7]. A range of correctness criteria have categorised by Ramamritham and Chryanthis [25].

3   A Novel Method of Comparing Transaction Models

In this section, we propose a novel method of comparing the relative complexity of transaction models. Our method produces a function of two transaction architecture features: first, *architectural work*, a measure of the amount of overhead performed by an architecture; and, second, *isolation work*, a function of the difficulty of isolating one transaction from all others or providing as much isolation as given by the transaction model. We discuss these two features throughout this section.

Consider the life-cycle of a database run. Initially, when the database is dormant, we are certain of the entire database state; every object can be represented by a single object-state with a known value. As transactions grow the state of the database becomes less certain: object o_1 might have two potential values depending on whether transaction t_1 commits or aborts; these two values can be represented by two concurrently existing object-states. Finally, when all transactions have completed, we are again certain of every object value. *Architectural work* is a measure of object states that were constructed by the monitor although they were not usable by application transactions. *Isolation work* measures the proportion of object states hidden from application transactions.

We propose a tuple $\mathcal{M}(\mathcal{M}_W, \mathcal{M}_R, \mathcal{M}_I)$ to describe a transaction model. The values $\mathcal{M}_W$ and $\mathcal{M}_R$ are an upper bound on the number of *architectural object-states* (that provide no useful information to other transactions) produced as a transaction performs write and read operations respectively. Collectively,

$\mathcal{M}_W$ and $\mathcal{M}_R$ are a measure of the work performed for the architecture, not the applications.

The third component, $\mathcal{M}_I$, indicates the work associated with isolating concurrent transactions. To find $\mathcal{M}_I$ we classify object-states as *visible*, *importable* or neither. An object-state is *visible* to transaction t if its existence could influence the behaviour of t; both locked and committed object-states are visible. An object-state is *importable* if a transaction can extract a value from it; the locked object-state is usually not importable. $\mathcal{M}_I$ is an upper bound on the ratio of visible to importable object-states.

Smaller values of $\mathcal{M}_W$ and $\mathcal{M}_R$ indicate a transaction model with lower upper-bounds on overhead work. In contrast, $\mathcal{M}_I$ indicates isolation that must be provided, and we expect that smaller values of $\mathcal{M}_I$ indicate models that have lower bounds on the cost of conflict management.

3.1 $\mathcal{M}_W$ and $\mathcal{M}_R$ – Architectural Work

Transaction execution produces and destroys object-states, the number and type varying with the architecture. Figure 1 shows simple transaction t_1 executing under a simple commit-only architecture. Object X exists in a *committed* state prior to the transaction; *committed* is the default state and the means for storing object values. The *write( )* operation causes a second, *uncommitted* object state to be constructed.

The *uncommitted* state exists concurrently with the *committed* state, revealing the updated value to the application transaction and the monitor. The *uncommitted* state is removed by a commit or abort and does not exist outside the lifetime of the transaction that created it, so it provides no information to subsequent transactions; thus *uncommitted* is an architectural state—an artifact of the architecture.

Figure 2 shows the same transaction t_1 executing under an optimistic database model. The model is slightly more complex (and will involve a correspondingly greater level of work by the monitor) and in return permits concurrent access.

We categorise the object-states created by transaction t into two sets: *(user) application object-states*, S_U, which potentially provide information to applications; and *architectural object-states*, S_A, which are not directly useful to applications but are needed by the monitor.

To illustrate how different architectures might involve dissimilar overhead, consider two architectures $\mathbb{X}$—a conventional locking architecture—and $\mathbb{Y}$—an optimistic architecture. The two architectures have only the *committed* state in common and both architectures provide all the operations required by application t_2. If we execute an t_2 under both the $\mathbb{X}$ and $\mathbb{Y}$, we have two processes that necessarily have no view of the workings of the monitor but that performed the same function. In this example, all object-state types except *committed* are architectural, they do not contribute to the application logic and to the application are overhead.

We consider below a formal definition of architectural work.

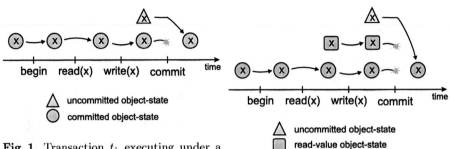

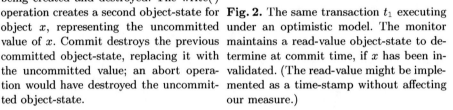

Fig. 1. Transaction t_1 executing under a commit-only model, showing object-states being created and destroyed. The write( ) operation creates a second object-state for object x, representing the uncommitted value of x. Commit destroys the previous committed object-state, replacing it with the uncommitted value; an abort operation would have destroyed the uncommitted object-state.

Fig. 2. The same transaction t_1 executing under an optimistic model. The monitor maintains a read-value object-state to determine at commit time, if x has been invalidated. (The read-value might be implemented as a time-stamp without affecting our measure.)

A *database* D is a set of uniquely addressable *objects* $\mathcal{O}$, each existing as one or more *object-states* which may have an associated value. Access to the database is managed by a *monitor* program

An application performs *operations* within a *transaction*. We consider only well-formed transactions, those conforming to architectural requirements

Operations revealing a value to the application belong to the set of *read operations*, O_R. Those that change the value of an object are members of the set O_W, *write operations*

An *operation-history*, H, is the set of all operations invoked by all transactions ordered by time of invocation; operations of concurrent transactions are interleaved. The *state-history*, H_S, is the ordered set of object-states created by the execution of H

The set of all legal histories is $\mathcal{H}$

The *lifetime*, L_t, of a transaction is the maximal contiguous subset of H, from the first operation invoked by t, to the last operation invoked by t

When the value of object o could be revealed differently to distinct concurrent transactions, each value is associated with a distinct *object-state* instance. Likewise when the monitor distinguishes between multiple possible values, each is a distinct object-state. States are identified by a mnemonic *state-type*, such as *committed* or *uncommitted*. $\mathcal{S}$ is the set of all state-types constructed by an architecture. Every object has at least one *default-object-state* (eg. *committed*) that exists over the lifetime of the object. Most states have an associated value but some (eg. *locked*) may not

Every instance of an object-state $\sigma \in H_S$ (except for default object-states) has one or more *creator* transactions, σ_t, being those transactions that when removed from the operation-history produce a state-history that does not include σ

For all state-types $s \in \mathcal{S}$; if there exists any object-state σ of state-type s, and σ's value is revealed to any transaction in $\mathcal{H}$ outside the lifetime of σ's creator σ_t, then s is a member of the set of *(user) application-states*, S_U. All other state-types are members of S_A, the *architectural-states*

Architectural work, S_A, is the number of architectural object-states that are created by the transaction architecture performing a particular operation. $\mathcal{M}_W$ is the architectural work associated with an attempt by a transaction to update an object's value and $\mathcal{M}_R$ is the work associated with a transaction obtaining an object's value.

S_R, the set of *read-state* state-types, is all members of $\mathcal{S}$ which do not exist except when the operation-history includes some read operations O_R. Similarly, S_W, the *write-states*, is those states which exist only in the presence of write operations, O_W

$\mathcal{M}_W$ is an upper bound defined as the number of state-types that are members of both S_W, the write-states, and S_A, the architectural-states

$\mathcal{M}_R$ is similarly defined as the upper bound of the number of state-types that are members of both S_R, read-states, and S_A, architectural-states

3.2 $\mathcal{M}_I$ – Isolation

One primary function of a database model is to provide a specific level of isolation between concurrent transactions. Conventionally, this is complete isolation, where no transaction can read any uncommitted value, but this may be weakened by design, contingence, or providence. The $\mathcal{M}_I$ function expresses the size of the problem domain of providing the degree of isolation specified by the transaction model.

H^t, the *operation-history* of transaction t, is the projection of an operation history H where the transaction is t. The *state history* of t, H_S^t, is similarly the projection of the state history H_S for transaction t

Given a history h, the associated *potential conclusions*, $\mathcal{H}^h$, is the set of all legal histories $\mathcal{H}$ that contain h

An object-state, o, is *importable* to transaction t if there exists some some history amongst all the potential conclusions $\mathcal{H}^h$ in which t reads value associated with o

An object-state, o, is *visible* to t if t's state history H_S^t in the presence of o is different to its history H_S^t in the absence of o; that is, if the existence of o affects the behaviour of t

S_V, the set of visible state-types, contains all state-types $\mathcal{S}$ that are visible to any transaction in any of the legal histories $\mathcal{H}$

S_I, the set of importable state types, similarly contains all state-types for which a value could be read (imported) in any $\mathcal{H}$

To illustrate isolation in terms of object-states, consider a conventional locking database that includes the object-states *committed, uncommitted* and *locked*.

Both *committed* and *locked* are visible to non-creator transactions, and can affect the behaviour of non-creator transactions. Only the *committed* state is importable (and can be read), so the *locked* states must be hidden from other transactions; for a database of N_O objects, the monitor hides at most N_O instances of *locked* states.

The $\mathcal{M}_I$ function provides a measure of the object-states that must be hidden from any particular transaction. $\mathcal{M}_I$ is defined as an upper bound being the ratio of visible object-states S_V to the number of importable states S_I, and the number of objects involved, that is, an upper bound of that architecture's isolation problem.

N_I is the cardinality of S_I; N_V is the cardinality of S_V

Transaction u *overlaps* transaction t in history h if there exists any any operation in u that appears after t's first operation and any of u's operations appear before the last operation in t

Given a transaction t, the *potential overlapping objects*, Q^t, is the set of all objects that are accessed in any potential history $\mathcal{H}$ by any transaction u where u overlaps t

N_Q is the maximum cardinality of the set of potential overlapping objects objects Q^t, for all transactions t. For conventional architectures all states potentially overlap, so $Q^T = \mathcal{O}$ and $N_Q = N_O$

$\mathcal{M}_I$ is defined as the function $\frac{N_V}{N_I}N_Q$. Where all database objects are potentially overlapping (the normal case) we do not specify N_Q but show $\mathcal{M}_I$ as $\frac{N_V}{N_I}$

3.3   Example – The Unix File System

A derivation outline of the "Locking-Only" transaction model is included as representative of the simplest non-trivial transaction model[1]. As the simplest common transaction model with concurrency control, this permits explicit object locking but does not include any rollback functionality. This transaction model is that used in Unix file locks and Pick databases.

Set of object states $\mathcal{S}$ = {current, locked}   (Well-formed transactions lock before read or write.)

Architectural states S_A = {locked}   (The *locked* state ceases to exist when the transaction completes, either by committing or aborting.)

Architectural update states S_{AW} = {locked} so $M_W = 1$ (Both reading and writing lock objects.)

Architectural read states S_{AR} = {locked} so $M_R = 1$.

Visible states S_V = {current, locked}, cardinality $N_V = 2$ (*Current* is visible because its value can be read, *locked* is visible because its presence may change the behaviour of other transactions.)

---

[1] The derivation of the remaining nine transaction models is excluded from this manuscript, but is available as
http://www.cs.rmit.edu.au/~hugh/derivation.pdf

Importable states $S_I = \{\text{current}\}$, so cardinality $N_I = 1$ (Only *current* has a readable value.)

The isolation-function $\mathcal{M}_I = N_V/N_I = 2$

Overhead: $\mathcal{M}(1, 1, 2)$

4   Application of $\mathcal{M}(\,)$ to Selected Transaction Models

This section gives the overhead function for selected transaction models and illustrates how they match our intuitive measures of transaction model complexity. Note that $\mathcal{M}(\,)$ expressions are all upper bounds, and not specific values for any individual transaction or implementation. The term N_T is the total number of concurrent transactions; N_C is the number of nested child transactions; and N_S is the number of cooperating sub-transactions in a Saga-style group.

Isolated Execution $\mathcal{M}(0, 0, 1)$

This simplest transaction model permits only a single process without aborts or locks. While it could be argued that this is not a transaction model at all, we include it to represent the simplest case.

The values for $\mathcal{M}_W$ and $\mathcal{M}_R$ indicate that the monitor adds no overhead to write and read operations; this does not imply that there is no cost but that the transaction mechanism did not add to that cost. $\mathcal{M}_I$ is the ratio of accessible to potentially accessible object-states; $\mathcal{M}_I = 1$ means as all potentially accessible object-states are immediately accessible, that is, there is no overhead in hiding inconsistent states.

Locking Only $\mathcal{M}(1, 1, 2)$

The simplest transaction model with concurrency control, this permits explicit object locking but not rollback (see Section 3.3). As we would expect, using locks to isolate concurrent transactions adds complexity to both the read and write operations, and requires the monitor to perform some isolation management.

Locking with Commit $\mathcal{M}(2, 1, 2)$

Adding the ability for a transaction to commit/abort requires an additional object-state for the uncommitted/rollback value. $\mathcal{M}(\,)$ shows the complexity of the locking and commit model is greater than simple locking. Note the commit functionality does not increase isolation; the uncommitted state is invisible to other transactions and need not be hidden.

Commit Only $\mathcal{M}(2, 1, 1)$

A transaction that can abort or commit but cannot explicitly lock may be handled using optimistic techniques [2]. Our method ranks the optimistic model as less complex than conventional lock and commit models because the monitor need not isolate locked objects from other transactions.

One cost of this strategy is that we have to abort an entire transaction when we might have detected the conflict earlier and waited for the conflict to disappear. Empirical observation of optimistic monitors supports this: detecting conflict is conceptually simpler than maintaining locks and wait-tables, but unsuited to volatile environments.

Multi-version Transactions $\mathcal{M}(N_T, 0, N_T)$

Multi-version transaction models [20] retain past object-values, permitting a transaction t to consistently read an object that has been updated since t began, t is serialised into the past. Variations which handle updating transactions exist, for simplicity we show $\mathcal{M}()$ without waiting and rollback.

$\mathcal{M}(N_T, 0, N_T)$ illustrates the trade-off between architectural and isolation overhead. An architecture where old states are retained, reduces read overhead (by making all states accessible) but results in a large isolation problem: of all the object-states representing object o, only one has a time-stamp that provides transaction t with a consist view.

Epsilon Transactions $\mathcal{M}(1 + 2N_T, 1, 1 + N_T)$

An epsilon transaction [21] reveals a primary object-value and a range which is guaranteed to include the object's quiescent value. The architecture requires an object-state to represent each change being performed.

Closed Nested Transactions $\mathcal{M}(2 + N_C, 1, 2 \rightarrow 1)$

Similar to locking and committing transactions, these include nesting of child transactions [2] which are dependent on the parent transaction; if the parent aborts, so do the children. $\mathcal{M}_I$ isolation tends from 2 when $N_C = 0$, to 1 as N_C approaches infinity; the trade-off is $\mathcal{M}_W$ complexity increases with N_C.

Open Nested Transactions $\mathcal{M}(2 + N_C, 1, 2 \rightarrow 1)$

Similar to the closed nested transaction model, open nested transactions can invoke sub-transactions but changes are committed by child transactions independently of the parent [9]. The same function value describes open-nested and closed-nested transactions because the interactions between child and parent uncommitted states are similar. In practice, closed nested transactions hold locks for longer but open nested transactions require the application designer to handle the child-commit and parent-abort case.

Escrow Transactions $\mathcal{M}(1 + 2N_T, 1, 1 + N_T)$

Transactions operating under the Escrow model [22] can 'reserve' some portion of an object's value, leaving the remainder available for other transactions. Escrow was inspired by financial transactions and was designed with account balances in mind. This analysis provides for multiple transaction access to each object and shows the similarity of Epsilon and Escrow architectures.

Cooperating Transactions $\mathcal{M}(1 + N_S, 1, 2)$

In this category, we include the work-group and work-flow database models such as Sagas [23,26], ConTracts [27] and Split [28] and Flex [29] transactions. These are based on defined sets of relatively independent sub- transactions, allow sub-transactions to commit and reveal their results, and rely on compensating transactions to complete aborts. The underlying transaction models are similarly based on sets of nested sub-transactions and provide control of various combinations open- and closed-sub-transactions. The $\mathcal{M}()$ value shown is representative of the general class.

Table 1. Transaction models ranked from least- to most-complex using $\mathcal{M}(\ )$, the function permits an objective selection of a least-complex model.

Architecture	Complexity Function	Architecture	Complexity Function
Isolated	$\mathcal{M}(0,0,1)$	Locking	$\mathcal{M}(1,1,2)$
Commit Only	$\mathcal{M}(2,1,1)$	Locking-Commit	$\mathcal{M}(2,1,1)$
Open nested	$\mathcal{M}(2+N_C,1,2\to1)$	Closed nested	$\mathcal{M}(2+N_C,1,2\to1)$
Cooperating	$\mathcal{M}(1+N_S,1,2)$	Multi-version	$\mathcal{M}(N_T,0,N_T)$
Epsilon	$\mathcal{M}(1+2N_T,1,1+N_T)$	Escrow	$\mathcal{M}(1+2N_T,1,1+N_T)$

5   Interpretation

From the $\mathcal{M}(\ )$ values in Section 4 we make selected observations on transaction models. We note that $\mathcal{M}(\ )$ values are upper-bounds functions and that actual behaviour would not normally approach the upper-bounds, but that our intention is to reveal differences and similarities of transaction models.

Table 1 shows the models ranked from least- to most-complex under $\mathcal{M}(\ )$. While practical architectural differences depend on implementations, increasing $\mathcal{M}(\ )$ values correspond to increasingly complex transaction models. Moreover, increasing $\mathcal{M}(\ )$ values correspond to larger problem domains, so more complex architectures solve larger problems. Given a specific problem domain, the $\mathcal{M}(\ )$ function permits selection of the least-complex transaction model that meets application requirements.

We observe the relationship between the open- and closed-nested models and the various cooperating (Saga) models. The $\mathcal{M}(\ )$ function highlights that moving responsibility for rollback from the monitor to compensating sub-transactions has not produced a conceptually simpler system (although there are advantages to revealing partial results). We could reasonably expect monitors for nested and cooperating models to behave similarly and for differences in overall behaviour to be factors of transaction mix.

The $\mathcal{M}(\ )$ function shows how some models are more closely related than may be initially obvious. The Epsilon and Escrow models, while developed separately and providing apparently different functions to the application, show high similarity under $\mathcal{M}(\ )$. Investigations from this perspective showed that Escrow and Epsilon transactions are equivalent; in different ways, both architectures reveal run-time value uncertainty. Similarly, the open and closed nested transaction models are intuitively distinct but have very similar architectural complexity.

Table 2 draws attention to the common factors in the $\mathcal{M}(\ )$ values: isolated transactions add no overhead; simple locking and commit architectures add a constant bounded overhead; the nested architectures add an N_C bounded overhead; and, the multi-version architecture adds N_T overhead in two distinct areas. We plan to further investigate architectures in each class.

The isolation domain $\mathcal{M}_I$ is based on the number of database objects N_O, for these models $\mathcal{M}_I$ ranges from 1 to $1+N_T$. For models where N_T is a factor (such as multi-version transactions) reducing the number of visible transactions will have

Table 2. Transaction models grouped by the dominant factors in $\mathcal{M}(\ )$. Members of each class are likely to show similar overhead trends with database size, number of concurrent transactions, etc.

Class	Dominant Factors	Architectures
0	0	Isolated
1	K	Locking, Commit Only, Locking with Commit
2	N_C	Open nested, Closed nested, Cooperating
3	$N_T \cdot N_T$	Multi-version, Epsilon, Escrow

a corresponding effect on $\mathcal{M}_I$. For example, nested multi-version transactions (where N_T is limited to the number of child transactions N_C) would demonstrate a reduced isolation domain but at the cost of increasing $\mathcal{M}_R$ or $\mathcal{M}_W$.

6   Conclusion

Transaction models define the structure of protocols for concurrency control in database systems. We have proposed a novel function to categorise transaction models by two measures that we call architectural- and isolation-complexity. We have applied this function to selected transaction models and shown ranking of the models by complexity and reasoning about their performance. We have shown the close complexity relationship between Epsilon and Escrow transactions, and we have confirmed the intuitive relative complexity of simple database models.

Our overhead function is a practical measure of the complexity and theoretical overhead of transaction management; it can be used as one measure for selecting transaction models for database systems. It is likely that the function will also permit reasoning about novel models and may aid in reasoning about the features of new transaction systems. Using the function, we plan to investigate new transaction models and have already begun this work [30].

References

1. Bhargava, B.: Concurrency control in database systems. IEEE Trans. on Knowledge and Data Engineering **11** (1999) 3–16
2. Gray, J., Reuter, A.: Transaction Processing: Concepts and Techniques. Morgan Kaufmann (1993)
3. Thomasian, A.: Concurrency control: Methods, performance and analysis. ACM Computing Surveys **30** (1998) 70–119
4. Elmasri, R., Navathe, S.B.: Fundamentals of Database Systems. 2nd edn. Benjamin-Cummings, Redwood City (1994)
5. Bernstein, P.A., Newcomer, E.: Principles of Transaction Processing. Morgan Kaufmann (1997)
6. Elmagarmid, A.K., ed.: Database Transaction Models for Advanced Applications. Volume 1. Morgan Kaufmann (1995)

7. Lynch, N., Merritt, M., Weihl, W., Fekete, A.: Atomic Transactions. Morgan Kaufmann (1994)
8. Barghouti, N.S., Kaiser, G.E.: Concurrency control in advanced database applications. ACM Computing Surveys 23 (1991) 269–317
9. Weikham, G., Schek, H.J.: 13. [6]
10. Climent, A., Bertran, M., Nicolau, M.: Database concurrency control on a shared-nothing architecture using speculative lock modes. In: Advances in Database and Information Systems, Proc. 5th East European Conf. (2001)
11. Franaszek, P., Robinson, J.T.: Limitations of concurrency in transaction processing. ACM Trans. on Database Systems 10 (1985) 1–28
12. Tay, Y.C., Goodman, N., Suri, R.: Locking performance in centralized databases. ACM Trans. on Database Systems 10 (1985) 415–462
13. Tay, Y.C., Suri, R., Goodman, N.: A mean value performance model for locking in databases: The no-waiting case. Journal of the ACM 32 (1985) 618–651
14. Tay, Y.C., Suri, R., Goodman, N.: A mean value performance model for locking in databases: The waiting case. Journal of the ACM 31 (1984) 311–322
15. Thomasian, A.: Two-phase locking performance and its thrashing behavior. ACM Trans. on Database Systems 18 (1993) 579–625
16. Ryu, I.K., Thomasian, A.: Analysis of database performance with dynamic locking. Journal of the ACM 37 (1990) 491–523
17. Yu, P.S., Dias, D.M., Lavenberg, S.S.: On the analytical modeling of database concurrency control. Journal of the ACM 40 (1993) 831–872
18. Agrawal, D., Abbadi, A.E., Jeffers, R.: An approach to eliminate transaction blocking in locking protocols. In: Proc. ACM Principles of Database Systems. (1992) 223–235
19. Agrawal, D., Bruno, J.L., Abbadi, A.E., Krishnaswamy, V.: Relative serializability: An approach for relaxing the atomicity of transactions. In: Proc. ACM SIGMOD Int. Conf. Management of Data. (1994) 139–149
20. Reed, D.P.: Naming and synchronization in a decentralized computer system. Tech. Report MIT/LCS/TR-205, MIT Laboratory for Computer Science, Cambridge, Massachusetts (1978)
21. Ramamritham, K., Pu, C.: A formal characterisation of Epsilon serializability. IEEE Trans. Knowledge and Data Engineering 7 (1995) 997–1007
22. O'Neil, P.E.: The Escrow transactional method. ACM Trans. on Database Systems 11 (1986) 405–430
23. Chrysanthis, P.K., Ramamritham, K.: ACTA: A framework for specifying and reasoning about transaction structure and behavior. In: Proc. ACM SIGMOD Int. Conf. Management of Data. (1990) 194–203
24. Chrysanthis, P.K., Ramamritham, K.: 10. [6] 349–398
25. Ramamritham, K., Chryanthis, P.K.: A taxonomy of correctness criteria in database applications. VLDB Journal 5 (1996) 85–97
26. Chrysanthis, P.K., Ramamritham, K.: Synthesis of extended transaction models using ACTA. ACM Trans. on Database Systems 19 (1994) 450–491
27. Wächter, H., Reuter, A.: 7. [6] 219–264
28. Kaiser, G.E., Pu, C.: 8. [6] 265–296
29. Kühn, E., Puntigam, F., Elmagrmid, A.K.: 9. [6] 297–348
30. Fry, A.G.: Expressing database transactions as atomic-operations. In: Seventh International Database Engineering and Applications Symposium. (2003)

Concurrent and Real-Time Update of Access Control Policies*

Indrakshi Ray and Tai Xin

Department of Computer Science
Colorado State University
{iray,xin}@cs.colostate.edu

Abstract. Access control policies are security policies that govern access to resources. *Real-time update* of access control policies, that is, updating policies
while they are in effect and enforcing the changes immediately, is necessary for
many security-critical applications. In this paper, we consider real-time update
of access control policies in a database system. We consider an environment in
which different kinds of transactions execute concurrently some of which are policy update transactions. Updating policy objects while they are deployed can lead
to potential security problems. We propose two algorithms that not only prevent
such security problems, but also ensure serializable execution of transactions. The
algorithms differ on the degree of concurrency provided.

1 Introduction

An enterprise security policy is subject to adaptive, preventive and corrective maintenance. Since security policies are extremely critical for an enterprise, it is important to
control the manner in which policies are updated. Updating policy in an adhoc manner
may result in inconsistencies and problems with the policy specification; this, in turn,
may create other problems, such as, security breaches, unavailability of resources, etc.
In other words, policy updates should not be through adhoc operations but done through
well-defined *transactions* that have been previously analyzed.

An important issue that must be kept in mind about policy update transactions is that
some policies may require *real-time updates*. We use the term real-time update of a policy
to mean that the policy will be changed while it is in effect and this change will be enforced
immediately. An example will help motivate the need for real-time updates of policies.
Suppose the user *John*, by virtue of some policy *P*, has the privilege to execute a long-
duration transaction that prints a large volume of sensitive financial information kept in
file *I*. While *John* is executing this transaction, an insider threat is suspected and the policy
P is changed such that *John* no longer has the privilege of executing this transaction. Since
existing access control mechanisms check *John*'s privileges *before John* initiates the
transaction and not *during* the execution of the transaction, the updated policy *P* will not
be correctly enforced causing financial loss to the company. In this case, the policy was
updated correctly but not enforced immediately resulting in a security breach. Real-time
update of policies is also important for environments that are responding to international

---

* This work was done in part while the author was working as a Visiting Faculty at Air Force
Research Laboratory, Rome, NY in Summer 2002.

V. Mařík et al. (Eds.): DEXA 2003, LNCS 2736, pp. 330–339, 2003.

crisis, such as relief or war efforts. Often times in such scenarios, system resources need reconfiguration or operational modes require change; this, in turn, necessitates policy updates.

In this paper we consider real-time policy updates in the context of a database system. A database consists of a set of objects that are accessed and modified through transactions. Transactions performing operations on database objects must have the privilege to execute those operations. Such privileges are specified by access control policies; access control policies are stored in the form of *policy objects*. Transactions executing by virtue of the privileges given by a policy object is said to *deploy* the policy object. In addition to being deployed, a policy object can also be accessed and modified by transactions. We are considering an environment in which different kinds of transactions execute concurrently some of which are policy update transactions. In other words, a policy may be updated while transactions are executing by virtue of this policy. We propose two different algorithms that allow for concurrent and real-time updates of policies. The algorithms differ with respect to the degree of concurrency achieved.

The rest of the paper is organized as follows. Section 2 introduces our model. Section 3 describes a simple concurrency control algorithm for policy updates. Section 4 illustrates how the semantics of the policy update operation can be exploited to increase concurrency. Section 5 highlights the related work. Section 6 concludes our paper with some pointers to future directions.

2   Our Model

A *database* is specified as a collection of objects together with a set of *integrity constraints* on these objects. At any given time, the *state* of the database is determined by the values of the objects in the database. A change in the value of a database object changes the state. Integrity constraints are predicates defined over the state. A database state is said to be *consistent* if the values of the objects satisfy the given integrity constraints.

A *transaction* is an operation that transforms the database from one consistent state to another. To prevent the database from becoming inconsistent, transactions are the only means by which data objects are accessed and modified. A transaction can be initiated by a user, a group, or another process. A transaction inherits the access privileges of the entity initiating it. A transaction can execute an operation on a database object only if it has the privilege to perform it. Such privileges are specified by access control policies.

In this paper, we consider only one kind of access control policies: authorization policies[1]. An authorization policy specifies what operations an entity can perform on another entity. We focus our attention to systems that support positive authorization policies only. This means that the policies only specify what operations an entity is *allowed* to perform on another entity. There is no explicit policy that specifies what operations an entity is *not allowed* to perform on another entity. The absence of an explicit authorization policy authorizing an entity A to perform some operation O on another entity B is interpreted as A not being allowed to perform operation O on entity B.

We consider simple kinds of authorization policies that are specified by *subject*, *object*, and *rights*. A subject can be a user, a group of users or a process. An object, in

---

[1] Henceforth, we use the term policy or access control policy to mean authorization policy.

our model, is a data object, a group of data objects, or an object class. A subject can perform only those operations on the object that are specified in the rights.

Definition 1. *A* policy *is a function that maps a subject and a object to a set of access rights. We formally denote this as follows:* $P : S \times O \rightarrow \mathbb{P}(R)$ *where P represents the policy function, S, represents the set of subjects, O represents the set of objects, $\mathbb{P}(R)$ represents the power set of access rights.*

In a database, policies are stored in the form of policy objects.

Definition 2. *A* policy object P_i *consists of the triple* $< S_i, O_i, R_i >$ *where S_i, O_i, R_i denote the subject, the object, and the access rights of the policy respectively. Subject S_i can perform only those operations on the object O_i that are specified in R_i.*

Example 1. Let $P = < John, FileF, \{r, w, x\} >$ be a policy object. This policy object gives subject John the privilege to Read, Write, and Execute *FileF*.

Before proceeding further, we discuss how to represent the access rights. The motivation for this representation will be clear in Section 4.

Definition 3. *Let* $\mathbf{O}_i = \{o_1, o_2, \ldots, o_n\}$ *be the set of all the possible operations that are specified on Object O_i. The set of operations in $\mathbf{O_i}$ are ordered in the form of a sequence* $< o_1, o_2, \ldots, o_n >$. *We represent an access right on the object O_i as an n-element vector* $[i_1 i_2 \ldots i_n]$. *If $i_k = 0$ in some access right R_j, then R_j does not allow the operation o_k to be performed on the object O_i. $i_k = 1$ signifies that the access right R_j allows operation o_k to be performed on the object O_i. The total number of access rights that can be associated with object O_i equals 2^n.*

Example 2. Let $< r, w, x >$ be the operations allowed on a file F. The access right $R_1 = [001]$ signifies that r, w operations are not allowed on the file F but the operation x is permitted on File F. The access right $R_2 = [101]$ allows r and x operations on the file F but does not allow the w operation.

Definition 4. *The set of all access rights associated with a object O_i having n operations forms a* partial order *with the ordering relation $\geq_{O_i}$. The ordering relation is defined as follows: Let $R_j[i_k]$ denote the i_k-th element of access right R_j. Then $R_p \geq_{O_i} R_q$, if $R_p[i_k] = R_q[i_k]$ or $R_p[i_k] > R_q[i_k]$, for all $k = 1 \ldots n$.*

Definition 5. *Given two access rights R_p and R_q associated with an object O_i having n operations, the* least upper bound *of R_p and R_q, denoted as $lub(R_p, R_q)$ is computed as follows. For $k = 1 \ldots n$, we compute the i_k-th element of the least upper bound of R_p and R_q: $lub(R_p, R_q)[i_k] = R_p[i_k] \vee R_q[i_k]$. The n-bit vector obtained from the above computation will give us the least upper bound of R_p and R_q.*

Definition 6. *Given two access rights R_p and R_q associated with an object O_i having n operations, the* greatest lower bound *of R_p and R_q, denoted as $glb(R_p, R_q)$ is computed as follows. For $k = 1 \ldots n$, we compute the i_k-th element of the greatest lower bound of R_p and R_q: $glb(R_p, R_q)[i_k] = R_p[i_k] \wedge R_q[i_k]$. The n-bit vector obtained from the above computation will give the greatest lower bound of R_p and R_q.*

Since each pair of access rights associated with an object have a unique least upper bound and a unique greatest lower bound, the access rights of an object can be represented as a lattice.

Definition 7. *The set of all possible access rights on an object O_i can be represented as a lattice which we term the* access rights lattice *of object O_i. The notation $ARL(O_i)$ denotes the set of all nodes in the access rights lattice of object O_i.*

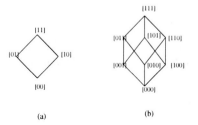

(a)   (b)

Fig. 1. Representing Possible Access Control Rights of Objects

Figure 1(a) shows the possible access rights associated with a file having only two operations: Read and Write. The most significant bit denotes the Read operation and the least significant bit denotes the Write operation. The lower bound labeled as Node 00 signifies the absence of Read and Write privilege. The Node 01 signifies that the subject has Write privilege but does not have Read privileges. The Node 10 signifies that the subject has Read privilege but no Write privilege. The Node 11 indicates that the subject has both Read and Write privileges. Figure 1(b) shows the possible access rights associated with a object having three operations.

Next we define a policy in terms of the access rights lattice.

Definition 8. *A policy P_i maps a subject S_i's access privilege to a Node j in the access rights lattice of the object O_i. Formally, $P : S \to (ARL(O))$.*

Definition 9. *A policy update is an operation that changes some policy object $P_i =< S_i, O_i, R_i >$ to $P_i' =< S_i, O_i, R_i' >$ where P_i' is obtained by transforming R_i to R_i'. Let R_i, R_i' be mapped to Node j, Node k of $ARL(O_i)$ respectively. The update of policy object P_i changes the mapping of the subject S_i's access privilege from Node j to Node k in the access rights lattice of object O_i.*

Having given some background on the policies, we are now in a position to discuss policy objects. Recall from Definition 2 that policies are stored in the database in the form of policy objects. Next we describe the operations associated with the policy objects. Policy objects, like data objects, can be read and written. However, unlike ordinary data objects, policy objects can also be *deployed*.

Definition 10. *A policy object P_j is said to be* deployed *if there exists a subject in P_j that is currently accessing an object in P_j by virtue of the privileges given by policy object P_j.*

Example 3. Suppose the policy object P_i allows subject S_j to read object O_k. Subject S_j initiates a transaction T_l that reads O_k. While the transaction T_l reads O_k, we say that the policy object P_i is deployed.

The environment we are considering is one in which multiple users will be accessing and modifying data and policy objects, while the policy objects are deployed. To deal with this scenario, we need some concurrency control mechanism. The objectives of our concurrency control mechanism are the following: (1) Allow concurrent access to data objects and policy objects. (2) Prevent security violations arising due to policy updates.

3   A Simple Algorithm for Policy Updates

In our model, each data object is associated with Read and Write operations. A policy object is associated with three operations: Read, Write and Deploy. We now give some definitions.

Definition 11. *Two operations are said to* conflict *if both operate on the same data object and one of them is a Write operation.*

Definition 12. *A transaction T_i is a partial order with ordering relation $<_i$ where*

1. $T_i \subseteq \{r_i[x], w_i[x] \mid x \text{ is a data or policy object } \} \cup \{d_i[x] \mid x \text{ is a policy object } \} \cup \{a_i, c_i\};$
2. $a_i \in T_i$ *iff* $c_i \notin T_i;$
3. *if t is c_i or a_i, for any other operation $p \in T_i$, $p_i <_i t$; and*
4. *if $r_i[x]$, $w_i[x] \in T_i$, then either $r_i[x] <_i w_i[x]$ or $w_i[x] <_i r_i[x]$.*
5. *if $d_i[x]$, $w_i[x] \in T_i$, then either $d_i[x] <_i w_i[x]$ or $w_i[x] <_i d_i[x]$.*

Condition 1 defines the different kinds of operations in the transactions ($r_i[x]$, $w_i[x]$, $d_i[x]$, a_i, c_i denote Read operation on object x, Write operation on x, Deploy operation on x, Abort or Commit operation respectively). Condition 2 states that this set contains an Abort or a Commit operation but not both. Condition 3 states that Abort or Commit operation must follow every other operation of the transaction. Condition 4 requires that the partial order $<_i$ specify the order of execution of Read and Write operations on a common data or policy object. Condition 5 requires that the partial order $<_i$ specify the order of execution of Deploy and Write operations on a common policy object.

Table 1. Locking Rules for Policy Objects

Has	Wants		
	RL	WL	DL
RL	Yes	No	Yes
WL	No	No	No
DL	Yes	Signal	Yes

(a)   Syntax-Based Algorithm

Has	Wants			
	RL	WXL	WSL	DL
RL	Yes	No	No	Yes
WXL	No	No	No	No
WSL	No	No	No	No
DL	Yes	Yes	Signal	Yes

(b)   Semantics-Based Algorithm

Each data object O_i in our model is associated with two locks: read lock (denoted by $RL(O_i)$) and write lock (denoted by $WL(O_i)$). The locking rules for data objects are the same as the standard two-phase locking protocol [3]. A policy object P_j is associated with three locks: read lock (denoted by $RL(P_j)$), write lock (denoted by $WL(P_j)$) and deploy lock (denoted by $DL(P_j)$). The locking rules for the policy objects are given in Table 1(a). *Yes* entry in the lock table indicates that the lock request is granted. *No* entry indicates that the lock request is denied. *Signal* entry in the lock table indicates that the lock request is granted, but only after the transaction currently holding the lock is aborted and the lock is released.

Definition 13. *A transaction is* well-formed *if it satisfies the following conditions.*

1. *A transaction before reading or writing a data or policy object must deploy the policy object that authorizes the transaction to perform the operation.*
2. *A transaction before deploying, reading, or writing a policy object must acquire the appropriate lock.*
3. *A transaction before reading or writing a data object must acquire the appropriate lock.*
4. *A transaction cannot acquire a lock on a policy or data object if another transaction has locked the object in a conflicting mode.*
5. *All locks acquired by the transaction are eventually released.*

Definition 14. *A well-formed transaction T_i is* two-phase *if all its lock operations precede any of its unlock operations.*

Example 4. Consider a transaction T_i that reads object O_j (denoted by $r_i(O_j)$) and then writes object O_k (denoted by $w_i(O_k)$). Policies P_m and P_n authorize the subject initiating transaction T_i, the privilege to read object O_j and the privilege to write object O_k respectively. An example of a well-formed and two-phase execution of T_i consists of the following sequence of operations: $< DL_i(P_m), RL_i(O_j), d_i(P_m), r_i(O_j), DL_i(P_n),$ $WL_i(O_k), d_i(P_n), w_i(O_k), UL_i(P_m), UL_i(P_n), UL_i(O_j), UL_i(O_k) >$, where $DL_i, RL_i, WL_i,$ d_i, r_i, w_i, UL_i denote the operations of acquiring deploy lock, acquiring read lock, acquiring write lock, deploy, read, write, lock release, respectively, performed by transaction T_i.

Definition 15. *A transaction is* policy-secure *if for every operation that a transaction performs, there exists a policy that authorizes the transaction to perform the operation.*

Note that, all transactions may not be policy-secure. For instance, suppose entity A can execute a long-duration transaction T_i by virtue of policy P_x. While A is executing T_i, P_x changes and no longer allows A to execute T_i. In such a case, if transaction T_i is allowed to continue after P_x has changed, then T_i will not be a policy-secure transaction.

We borrow the definitions of *history*, and *serializable history* from Bernstein et al. [3]. Next we define what we mean by a *policy-secure* history.

Definition 16. *A history is* policy-secure *if all the transactions in the history are policy-secure transactions.*

The lock based concurrency control approach provides policy-secure and serializable histories.

4   Concurrency Control Using the Semantics of Policy Update

The approach presented in Section 3 is overly restrictive. A change of policy may result in increased access privileges; in such cases terminating valid access will result in poor performance. This motivates us to classify a policy update operation either as a *policy relaxation* or as a *policy restriction* operation. Policy relaxation causes increase in subject's access rights; transactions executing by virtue of a policy need not be aborted when the policy is being relaxed. On the other hand, a policy restriction does not increase the access rights of the subject. To ensure policy-secure transactions, we must abort the transactions that are executing by virtue of the policy that is being restricted. Before going into the details, we first give the definitions of policy relaxation and policy restriction.

Definition 17. *A* policy relaxation operation *is a policy update that increases the access rights of the subject. Let the policy object* $P_i =< S_i, O_i, R_i >$ *be changed to* $P_i' =< S_i, O_i, R_i' >$. *Let Let* R_i, R_i' *be mapped to the nodes* k, j *respectively in* $ARL(O_i)$. *A policy update operation is a policy relaxation operation if* $lub(k, j) = j$.

Example 5. Let the operations allowed on *FileF* be $< r, w, x >$. Suppose the policy $P_i =< John, FileF, [001] >$ is changed to $P_i' =< John, FileF, [101] >$. This is an example of policy relaxation because the access rights of subject John has increased. Note that $lub([001], [101]) = [101]$. Thus, this is a policy relaxation.

Definition 18. *A* policy restriction operation *is a policy update operation that is not a policy relaxation operation. Let the policy object* $P_i =< S_i, O_i, R_i >$ *be changed to* $P_i' =< S_i, O_i, R_i' >$. *Let Let* R_i, R_i' *be mapped to the nodes* k, j *respectively in* $ARL(O_i)$. *A policy update operation is a policy restriction operation if* $lub(k, j) \neq j$.

Example 6. Let the operations allowed on *FileF* be $< r, w, x >$. Suppose the policy $P_i =< John, FileF, [001] >$ is changed to $P_i' =< John, FileF, [110] >$. This is an example of policy restriction because the access rights of subject John has not increased. Note that, $lub([001], [110]) = [111]$. Since $lub([001], [110]) \neq [110]$, this is an example of policy restriction.

4.1   Concurrency Control Based on Knowledge of Policy Change

We now give a concurrency control algorithm that uses the knowledge of the kind of policy change. Distinguishing between policy restriction and relaxation will increase concurrency. A policy object is now associated with four operations: Read, Deploy, WriteRelax, WriteRestrict. The Read and Deploy operations are similar to those specified in Section 3. The Write operations on policy object are classified as WriteRelax or WriteRestrict. A WriteRelax operation is one in which the policy gets relaxed. All other write operations on the policy object are treated as WriteRestrict. Since the operations are different than those discussed in Section 3, we modify the definitions of transaction and well-formed transaction (Definitions 12 and 13).

Definition 19. *A transaction T_i is a partial order with ordering relation $<_i$ where*

1. $T_i \subseteq \{r_i[x], w_i[x] \mid x$ *is a data object* $\} \cup \{d_i[x], r_i[x], ws_i[x], wx_i[x] \mid x$ *is a policy object* $\} \cup \{a_i, c_i\}$;
2. $a_i \in T_i$ *iff* $c_i \notin T_i$;
3. *if t is c_i or a_i, for any other operation $p \in T_i$, $p_i <_i t$; and*
4. *if $r_i[x]$, $w_i[x] \in T_i$, then either $r_i[x] <_i w_i[x]$ or $w_i[x] <_i r_i[x]$.*
5. *if $d_i[x]$, $ws_i[x] \in T_i$, then either $d_i[x] <_i ws_i[x]$ or $ws_i[x] <_i d_i[x]$.*
6. *if $d_i[x]$, $wx_i[x] \in T_i$, then either $d_i[x] <_i wx_i[x]$ or $wx_i[x] <_i d_i[x]$.*

Condition 1 is changed from that in Definition 12 to reflect that the operations allowed on data objects are Read and Write and the operations allowed on policy objects are Read, Deploy, WriteRelax (denoted by wx), and WriteRestrict (denoted by ws). Conditions 2,3, and 4 are the same as given in Definition 12. Condition 5 given in Definition 12 is no longer applicable as there is no simple Write operation on policy objects; this condition is replaced by two conditions (Conditions 5 and 6 in Definition 19). Condition 5 specifies that if there is a Deploy operation on a policy object and a WriteRestrict operation on the same object, then the ordering relation $<_i$ must specify the order of the operations. Condition 6 specifies a similar condition for Deploy and WriteRelax operation.

Now we give the details of the locking rules. The locking rules for data objects are as given in Section 3. Corresponding to the four operations on the policy object, we have four kinds of locks associated with policy objects: read locks (RL), deploy locks (DL), relax locks (WXL) and restrict locks (WSL). The locking rules are given in the table 1(b).

Definition 20. *A transaction is* well-formed *if it satisfies the following conditions.*

1. *A transaction before reading or writing a data object must deploy the policy object that authorizes the transaction to perform the operation.*
2. *A transaction before reading, write relaxing or write restricting a policy object must deploy the policy object that authorizes the transaction to perform the operation.*
3. *A transaction before reading or writing a data object must acquire the appropriate lock.*
4. *A transaction before deploying, reading, write relaxing, or write restricting a policy object must acquire the appropriate lock.*
5. *A transaction cannot acquire a lock on a policy or data object if another transaction has locked the object in a conflicting mode.*
6. *All locks acquired by the transaction are eventually released.*

To ensure serializable and policy-secure histories, we require each transaction to be well-formed (Def. 20) and two-phase (Def. 14).

5   Related Work

Although a lot of work appears in the area of security policies [6], policy updates have received relatively little attention. Some work has been done in identifying interesting adaptive policies and formalization of these policies [7,13]. A separate work [12] illustrates the feasibility of implementing adaptive security policies. The above works pertain to multilevel security policies encountered in military environments; the focus is in protecting confidentiality of data and preventing covert channels. We consider a more general problem and our results will be useful to both the commercial and military sector.

Automated management of security policies for large scale enterprise has been proposed by Damianou [5]. This work uses the PONDER specification language to specify policies. The simplest kinds of access control policies in PONDER are specified using a *subject-domain, object-domain* and *access-list*. The subject-domain specifies the set of subjects that can perform the operations specified in the access-list on the objects in the object-domain. This work allows new subjects to be added or existing subjects to be removed from the subject-domain. The object-domain can also be changed in a similar manner. But this work does not allow the policy specification itself to change. An example will help illustrate this point. Suppose we have a policy in PONDER that is implementing Role-Based Access Control: *subject-domain = Manager, object-domain = /usr/local, access-list = read, write*. This policy allows all *Managers* to *read/write* all the files stored in the directory */usr/local*. Now the toolkit will allow adding/removing users from the domain *Manager*, adding/deleting files in the domain */usr/local*. However, it will not allow the policy specification to be changed. For example, the subject-domain cannot be changed to *Supervisors*. Our work, focuses on the problem of updating the policy specification itself and complements the above mentioned work.

Concurrency control in database systems is a well researched topic. Some of the important pioneering works have been described by Bernstein et al. [3]. Thomasian [14] provides a more recent survey of concurrency control methods and their performance. The use of semantics for increasing concurrency has also been proposed by various researchers [1,2,8,9,10,11].

6   Conclusion and Future Work

Real-time updates of policy is an important problem for both the commercial and the military sector. In this paper we focus on real-time update of access control policies in a database system. We propose two algorithms for real-time update of access control policies. The algorithms generate serializable and policy-secure histories and provide different degrees of concurrency.

A lot of work still remains to be done. In this work we assume there exists exactly one policy by virtue of which any subject has access privilege to some object. In a real-world scenario multiple policies may be specified over the same subject and object. The net effect of these multiple policies depend on the semantics of the application. Changing the policies in such situations is non-trivial. In future we plan to extend our approach to handle more complex kinds of authorization policies, such as, support for negative authorization policies, incorporating conditions in authorization policies, support for specifying priorities in policies. Specifically, we plan to investigate how policies specified in the PONDER specification language [4] can be updated.

References

1. P. Ammann, S. Jajodia, and I. Ray. Applying Formal Methods to Semantic-Based Decomposition of Transactions. *ACM Transactions on Database Systems*, 22(2):215–254, June 1997.
2. B.R. Badrinath and K. Ramamritham. Semantics-based concurrency control: Beyond commutativity. *ACM Transactions on Database Systems*, 17(1):163–199, March 1992.
3. P. A. Bernstein, V. Hadzilacos, and N. Goodman. *Concurrency Control and Recovery in Database Systems*. Addison-Wesley, Reading, MA, 1987.
4. N. Damianou, N. Dulay, E. Lupu, and M. Sloman. The Ponder Policy Specification Language. In *Proceedings of the Policy Workshop*, Bristol, U.K., January 2001.
5. N. Damianou, T. Tonouchi, N. Dulay, E. Lupu, and M. Sloman. Tools for Domain-based Policy Management of Distributed Systems. In *Proceedings of the IEEE/IFIP Network Operations and Management Symposium*, Florence, Italy, April 2002.
6. N. C. Damianou. *A Policy Framework for Management of Distributed Systems*. PhD thesis, Imperial College of Science, Technology and Medicine, University of London, London, U.K., 2002.
7. J. Thomas Haigh et al. Assured Service Concepts and Models: Security in Distributed Systems. Technical Report RL-TR-92-9, Rome Laboratory, Air Force Material Command, Rome, NY, January 1992.
8. H. Garcia-Molina. Using semantic knowledge for transaction processing in a distributed database. *ACM Transactions on Database Systems*, 8(2):186–213, June 1983.
9. M. P. Herlihy and W. E. Weihl. Hybrid concurrency control for abstract data types. *Journal of Computer and System Sciences*, 43(1):25–61, August 1991.
10. H. F. Korth and G. Speegle. Formal aspects of concurrency control in long-ouration transaction systems using the NT/PV model. *ACM Transactions on Database Systems*, 19(3):492–535, September 1994.
11. Nancy A. Lynch. Multilevel atomicity – A new correctness criterion for database concurrency control. *ACM Transactions on Database Systems*, 8(4):484–502, December 1983.
12. E. A. Schneider, W. Kalsow, L. TeWinkel, and M. Carney. Experimentation with Adaptive Security Policies. Technical Report RL-TR-96-82, Rome Laboratory, Air Force Material Command, Rome, NY, June 1996.
13. E. A. Schneider, D. G. Weber, and T. de Groot. Temporal Properties of Distributed Systems. Technical Report RADC-TR-89-376, Rome Air Development Center, Rome, NY, September 1989.
14. A. Thomasian. Concurrency Control: Methods, Performance and Analysis. *ACM Computing Surveys*, 30(1):70–119, 1998.

Transactional Agent Model for Distributed Object Systems

Masashi Shiraishi, Tomoya Enokido, and Makoto Takizawa

Tokyo Denki University,
Japan
{shira,eno,taki}@takilab.k.dendai.ac.jp

Abstract. A transactional agent is a mobile agent which manipulates objects in multiple object servers with some constraint. There are other constraints like majority constraint where a transaction can commit if more than half of the object servers are successfully manipulated. An agent leaves a surrogate agent on an object server on leaving the object server to hold objects manipulated by the agent. A surrogate recreates an agent if the agent is faulty. We discuss how transactional agents with types of constraints can commit. We discuss implementation and evaluation of transactional agents for multiple database servers.

1 Introduction

In peer-to-peer (P2P) applications [3], huge number of peer computers are interconnected to cooperate in networks. Here, the computers are mainly PCs which are not so reliable as server computers. In order to reduce the power consumption and due to communication noise, connections with mobile computers are often disconnected. Thus, it is not easy to reliably perform application programs in P2P platforms even if servers are reliable. The two-phase commitment (2PC) protocol [2,6] is widely used to realize the atomic manipulation of multiple database servers. The 2PC protocol supports robustness against server faults but not against application faults, i.e. servers may block due to application faults [13]. Thus, application programs cannot be reliably performed in client-server model even if servers are reliably realized like database servers [9,16].

Another computation paradigm on distributed systems is mobile agent-based computation. A *mobile agent* [5] locally manipulates objects on an object server by moving to the object server. An object is an encapsulation of data and methods for manipulating the data. After manipulating all or some object servers, an agent makes a decision on *commit* or *abort* based on its own commitment condition like ACID (atomicity, consistency, isolation, and durability) [2,8,7] and at-least-one commitment [12]. A concept of transactional agent is generally discussed by Nagi [8]. In this paper, a *transactional* agent is defined to be a mobile agent which manipulates one or more than one object server with some type of commitment constraint. In addition, an agent negotiates with another agent if the agent manipulates objects in a conflicting manner. Through the negotiation,

V. Mařík et al. (Eds.): DEXA 2003, LNCS 2736, pp. 340–349, 2003.

each agent autonomously makes a decision on whether the agent still holds or releases the objects. A transactional agent autonomously finds another destination object server if a current destination object server is faulty. An agent leaves its *surrogate* agent which holds objects in an object server when the agent departs at the object server for a destination object server. The surrogate agent holds objects until the agent commits or aborts. The agent is faulty due to the fault of a current object server. A surrogate agent recreates another incarnation of the agent. We discuss how transactional agents manipulate objects in multiple object servers in presence of object server and application faults. We evaluate performance of a transactional agent compared with a client-server implementation.

In section 2, we present a system model. In section 3, we discuss transactional agents. In section 4, we discuss how to implement transactional agents by using database servers. In section 5, transactional agents are evaluated compared with traditional client-server applications.

2   System Model

A system is composed of object servers $D_1, \ldots, D_m$ ($m \geq 1$), which are interconnected with reliable communication networks. Each object server supports a collection of objects and methods for manipulating the objects. If result obtained by performing a pair of methods op_1 and op_2 on an object depends on a computation order of op_1 and op_2, op_1 and op_2 are referred to as *conflict* on the object. For example, a pair of methods *increment* and *reset* conflict on a *counter* object. On the other hand, *increment* and *decrement* do not conflict, i.e. are *compatible*. If a method op_1 from a transaction T_1 is performed before a method op_2 from another transaction T_2 where the methods op_1 and op_2 conflict, every method op_3 from T_1 is required to be performed before every method op_4 from T_2 conflicting with the method op_3. This is a *serializability* property [2,4]. Locking protocols [2,4,6] are widely used to realize the serializability.

A mobile agent is an autonomous program which moves around multiple object servers and locally manipulates objects in each object server. A *home* computer of an agent is one where the agent is initiated. A *current* object server is one where the agent exists. An agent locally issues methods to the current object server. Every object server is assumed to support a platform to perform agents. First, an agent is autonomously initiated and moves to an object server. If an agent moves to an object server D_j from a current object server, D_j is a *destination* object server. In D_j, an agent A is allowed to be performed on the object server D_j if there is no agent on an object server D_j which conflicts with an agent A.

An agent A can be replicated in multiple replicas $A_1, \ldots, A_m$ ($m \geq 2$). Each replica A_i is autonomously performed. By replicating an agent, parallel and fault-tolerant computing of the agent can be realized. Even if some replica is faulty, other replicas is being performed. An agent autonomously finds a destination object server. If the destination object server is faulty, the agent finds another destination object server which is operational. As long as an agent is operational, the agent can try to find an operational destination object server. Thus, an agent can be operational by escaping from faulty servers.

3   Transactional Agents

A *transactional* agent locally manipulates objects in object servers by moving around the object servers with some *commitment* constraint $Com(A)$. A scope $Scp(A)$ of an agent A means a set of object servers which the agent A possibly manipulates. There are following commitment conditions [12]:

[Commitment Conditions]

1. *Atomic commitment*: an agent is successfully performed on all the object servers, i.e. all-or-nothing principle. This is a commitment condition used in the traditional two-phase commitment protocols [4,13].

2. *Majority commitment*: an agent is successfully performed on more than half of the object servers.

3. *At-least-one commitment*: an agent is successfully performed on at least one object server.

4. $\binom{n}{n}$ *commitment*: an agent is successfully performed on more than r out of n object servers ($r \leq n$). □

Generalized consensus conditions with preference are discussed in a paper [11]. A commitment condition $Com(A)$ is specified for each agent A by an application. There are still discussions on when the commitment condition $Com(A)$ to be checked while an agent A is moving around object servers. Let $H(A)$ be a *history* of an agent A, i.e. a set of object servers which an agent A has so far manipulated ($H(A) \subseteq Scp(A)$). For example, the atomic commitment condition $Com(A)$ can hold only if all the object servers to be manipulated are successfully manipulated, i.e. $H(A) = Scp(A)$.

When an agent A leaves an object server D_i, a *surrogate* agent A_i is created on D_i by the agent A [Figure 1]. Even if the agent A leaves the object server D_i, the surrogate agent A_i still holds objects manipulated by the agent A on behalf of the agent A. A surrogate agent releases objects depending on the isolation level of the agent A. The surrogate does not release objects until the agent A commits or aborts at the highest isolation level, i.e. strict level [2]. A surrogate agent releases objects just after an agent leaves at the weakest isolation level. Surrogate agents created by an agent A are referred to as *sibling* surrogates.

Suppose another agent B arrives at an object server D_j after the agent A leaves the object server D_j. Here, the agent B negotiates with the surrogate agent A_i of the agent A if the agent B conflicts with the agent A. After the negotiation, the agent B might take over the surrogate A_i. Thus, when the agent A finishes visiting all the object servers, some surrogate may not exist due to the fault and abortion in negotiation with other agents. The agent A starts the negotiation procedure with its sibling surrogates $A_1, \ldots, A_m$. If a commitment condition $Com(A)$ is satisfied, the agent A commits. For example, an agent commits if all

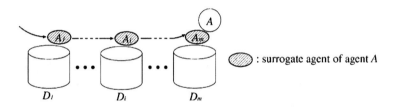

Fig. 1. Surrogate agents

the sibling surrogates in the history $H(A)$ safely exist in the atomic commitment condition. If all the object servers in the history $H(A)$ are manipulated but the commitment condition $Com(A)$ is not satisfied, the agent A aborts. Then, all the surrogate agents created by the agent A are annihilated.

Suppose an agent A moves to an object server D_j from another object server D_i. An agent A cannot be performed on an object server D_j if there is an agent or surrogate agent B conflicting with the agent A. Here, the agent A can take one of the following actions:

1. *Wait*: The agent A in the object server D_i *waits* until all the conflicting agents commit or abort in an object server D_j.
2. *Escape*: The agent A *finds another* object server D_k which has objects to be possibly manipulated before the object server D_j.
3. *Abort*: The agent A *aborts*.
4. *Negotiate*: The agent A *negotiates* with the conflicting agent B in the object server D_j. After the negotiation, the agent A can hold objects if B releases the objects. Otherwise, the agent takes one of the actions 1, 2, and 3.

An agent A blocks as long as some agent B holds an object in the first action with the agent A. If the agent B waits for release of an object held by the agent A, a pair of the agents A and B are deadlocked. Thus, deadlock among agents may occur. If the timer expires, the agent A takes a following way:

1. The agent A *retreats* to an object server D_j in the history $H(A)$, i.e. object server which A has passed over. The surrogates of the agent A which have been performed before the object server D_j are aborted.
2. Then, the surrogate A_j on D_j recreates a new incarnation of the agent A. The agent A finds another destination object server D_h.

The surrogate A_j to which the agent A retreats plays a role of *checkpoint*. Differently from traditional checkpointing protocols [10], the agent A retreating to some surrogate A_j autonomously finds a destination object server which may be different from one which A has visited.

4 Implementation

4.1 Object Servers

A transactional agent is implemented in a mobile agent of Aglets [5] for manipulating multiple object servers. Each object server is realized by using a relational

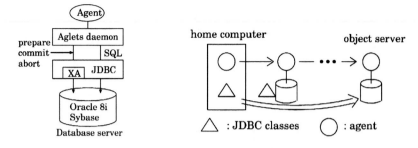

Fig. 2. Object server   **Fig. 3.** Loading of JDBC classes

database server [Figure 2]. Two types of relational database systems, Sybase [16] and Oracle8i [9] are used on types of platforms Solaris, Linux, and Windows2000. Object servers are interconnected with a 100base local area network. Each object server supports an XA interface [17] for agents' performing the two-phase commitment (2PC) protocol [2,6] [Figure 2]. Agents atomically manipulate objects in multiple object servers by using the XA interfaces. An agent can commit or abort on multiple object servers by issuing *prepare*, *commit*, and *abort*. A transactional agent manipulates table objects in multiple object servers by issuing SQL [1] commands like **select** and **update**. An Aglets agent cannot bring the state to other object servers, just text and heap area are transferred. If an agent leaves an object server, a transaction for the agent automatically terminates, i.e. commits or aborts on the object server.

JDBC (Java database connectivity) [15] classes provide agents with a program interface on an object server. An agent manipulates objects in an object server by using JDBC classes, e.g. open a database, start a transaction, and issue SQL commands. JDBC classes are required to be loaded to an Aglets agent when the agent issues database operations on an object server to open and close an object server and manipulate objects through SQL. In order to load JDBC classes to an agent on an object server, JDBC classes are required to exist on the home computer or the current object server. Unless JDBC classes exist on the current object server, JDBC classes on the home computer are transfered to the current object server [Figure 3]. The sizes of JDBC classes of Oracle8i and Sybase are 1.1MB and 0.9MB, respectively. It takes about 10 seconds to transfer and load JDBC classes in the 100base local area network. In the Internet, it takes about 30 to 40 seconds to transfer JDBC classes. It takes time to transfer JDBC classes. The loading time of JDBC classes depends how many JDBC classes an agent uses since only JDBC classes used in an agent are transferred from the home computer to the current object server.

Each type of object server, i.e. Oracle and Sybase, requires an agent to use its own type of JDBC. For example, an agent cannot be performed on an Oracle server if neither the server has JDBC classes nor the home computer has Oracle JDBC classes. An agent cannot move to an object server if neither the object server nor the home computer supports JDBC classes. Next, suppose the home

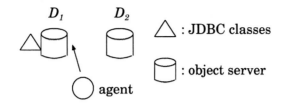

Fig. 4. Destination object server

computer supports JDBC classes for the type of the object server. An agent moves to one of object servers D_1 and D_2. Here, suppose one object server D_1 has JDBC classes but the other object server D_2 does not. It takes the agent a longer time to move to the object server D_2 than D_1 because JDBC classes have to be transferred to the object server D_2 in addition to transferring the agent. Hence, an agent moves to the object server D_1. Thus, it is an important decision factor to select a destination object server from the performance point of view whether an object server supports JDBC classes or not.

4.2 Surrogate Agents

As presented before, when an agent leaves an object server, a surrogate agent is created for the agent. The surrogate agent stays on the object server after the agent leaves the object server. The surrogate agent holds objects manipulated by the agent after the agent leaves. The surrogate agent does not release the objects until the agent commits or aborts. Here, suppose an agent A manipulates objects in an object sever D_i by issuing SQL commands with some isolation level and commitment condition. In this implementation, an agent A behaves on a current object server D_i as follows [Figure 5]:

[Behaviour of Agent]
1. An agent A manipulates objects in an object server D_i.
2. A *clone* A' of the agent A is created if the agent A finishes manipulating objects in the object server D_i. The clone A' leaves the object server D_i for another object server D_j as an agent A. The agent A itself stays on the object server D_i and plays a role of surrogate.
3. The surrogate agent A' holds objects manipulated by the agent until the agent terminates while negotiating with other agents. □

A clone of an agent A is created on a current object server and moves to another object server as an agent A while the agent A stays on the current object server as a surrogate. The agent A is just performed on the object server D_i and then is changed to the surrogate agent. If an agent leaves the object server D_i, every lock on objects held by the agent is released. Thus, an agent cannot leave the object server. Hence, an agent has to stay to hold objects on an object server D_i while a clone leaves the object server D_i for a destination object server D_j as an agent [Figure 5]. A surrogate agent communicates with

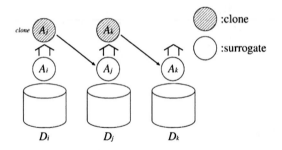

Fig. 5. Surrogate and agent

other agents. Through the negotiation, the surrogate agent might be aborted as presented in the preceding subsection.

If all the object in object servers required by the commitment condition are successfully manipulated, an agent makes a decision on whether to commit or abort by communicating with the surrogates as discussed in this paper. If the agent decides to *commit* according to the commitment condition, a surrogate agent commits on an object server D_i. Otherwise, a surrogate aborts.

4.3   Conditional Commitment

An agent A can commit if all or some of the surrogate agents commit depending on the commitment condition $Com(A)$. A commitment protocol for sibling surrogate agents is realized by using the XA interface [17] on each object server which supports the two-phase commitment protocol. The commitment protocol named conditional one is shown as follows:

[Conditional Commitment Protocol]

1. An agent sends a *prepare* message to every surrogate agent.
2. Each surrogate agent issues a *prepare* request to an object server on receipt of a *prepare* message from the agent.
3. If *prepare* is successfully performed, the surrogate sends a *prepared* message to the agent. Here, the surrogate is referred to as *committable*. Otherwise, the surrogate aborts after sending *aborted* to the agent.
4. The agent receives responses from surrogate agents after sending *prepare*. On receipt of responses from surrogates, the agent makes a decision on *commit* or *abort* based on the commitment condition.   □

In the atomic commitment, an agent sends a *commit* message to all the surrogates only if *prepared* is received from every surrogate. The agent sends an *abort* message to all committable servers if *aborted* is received from at least one surrogate. On receipt of *abort*, a committable surrogate aborts. In the at-least-one commitment condition, the agent sends *commit* to all committable servers only if *prepared* is received from at least one object server [Figure 6]. The agent A sends *commit* or *abort* depending on the commitment condition $Com(A)$.

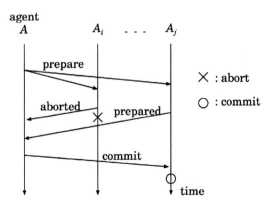

Fig. 6. Conditional commitment

Next, we discuss how to support robustness against agent faults. Suppose a surrogate agent A_i of an agent A is faulty after sending *prepared*. Here, the surrogate is committable. On recovery of the committable surrogate, the surrogate unilaterly commits if the surrogate is committable in the at-least-one transaction condition. In the atomic condition, the surrogate agent A_i asks the other surrogates if they had committed. Suppose the surrogate A_i is faulty before receiving *prepared*. Here, the surrogate A_i is abortable. If a faulty surrogate A_i is recovered, A_i unilaterly aborts without communicating with other surrogates.

5 Evaluation

We evaluate performance of a transactional agent in terms of access time compared with client-server model. In the evaluation, three object servers D_1, D_2, and D_3 are realized in Oracle database management system which are in a Sun workstation (SPARC 900MHz x 2) and a pair of Windows PCs (Pentium3 1.0GHz x 2 and Pentium3 500MHz), respectively, interconnected with 100base Ethernet. JDBC classes are initially loaded in each object server. An application program A updates table objects by first issuing **select** and then **update** to some number of object servers at the highest isolation level, i.e. **select for update** in Oracle. The program is implemented in Java for Aglets with a client-server model. In the client-server model, the application program A is realized in Java on a client computer. A transactional agent A is realized in Aglets.

The computation of Aglets agent is composed of five computation steps, moving, class loading, manipulation of objects, creation of clone, and commitment. In the client-server model, there are four computation steps of program initialization, class loading to client, manipulation of objects, and two-phase commitment. Figure 7 shows how long it takes to perform each step for two cases, one for manipulating one object server and another for manipulating two object servers, in client-server (CS) and transactional agent (TA) models. In

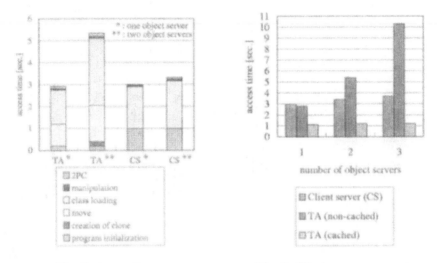

Fig. 7. Access time   **Fig. 8.** Client server vs. agent

the transactional agent (TA) model, Aglets classes are loaded to each object server before an agent is performed. Since Java classes are loaded to clients in the client-server model, time for loading the classes is in variant for any number of object servers. As shown in Figure 7, it takes a shorter time to manipulate objects in a transactional agent than the client-server model because there is no communication between agent and object server. The time to load Aglets classes in each object server is about half of the total computation time in the transactional agent.

Next, access time from time when the application program starts until time when the application program ends, is measured for transactional agent (TA) and client-server (CS) models. Figure 8 shows the access time for number of object servers. Aglets classes are required to be loaded in addition to JDBC classes to perform an agent on an object server. The *non-cached Aglets* shows that Aglets classes are not loaded when an agent A arrives at an object server. Here, the agent can be performed after Aglets classes are loaded. The *cached Aglets* means that an agent manipulates objects in each object server where Aglets classes are already loaded, i.e. the agent comes to the object server after other agents have visited the object server. As shown in Figure 8, the client-server model is faster than the transactional agent. However, the transactional agent is faster than the client-server model if object servers are frequently manipulated, i.e. cashed Aglets classes are a priori loaded. On the other hand, Aglets classes have to be loaded in the transactional agent. It takes about two seconds to load Aglets classes.

6   Concluding Remarks

A mobile agent model for processing transactions which manipulate multiple object servers is discussed in this paper. An agent first moves to an object server and then manipulates objects. The agent autonomously moves around object servers. If the agent conflicts with other agents in an object server, the agent negotiates with the other agents. The negotiation is done based on the commitment conditions like at-least-one conditions. We implemented a transactional agent on multiple relational database servers in a mobile agent. We evaluated a mobile agent-based transaction agent on Oracle servers. If Aglets classes are *a priori* loaded, the transactional agents can manipulate object servers faster than the client-server model.

References

1. American National Standards Institute: Database Language SQL. Document ANSI X3.135 (1986)
2. Bernstein, P. A., Hadzilacos, V., Goodman, N.: Concurrency Control and Recovery in Database Systems. Addison Wesley (1987)
3. Gong, L.: JXTA: A Network Programming Environment. IEEE Internet Computing Vol. 5 No. 3 (2001) 88–95
4. Gray, J., Reuter, A.: Transaction Processing : Concepts and Techniques. Morgan Kaufmann (1993)
5. IBM Corporation: Aglets Software Development Kit Home. http://www.trl.ibm.com/aglets/
6. Korth, F. H.: Locking Primitives in a Database System. Journal of ACM Vol. 30 No. 1 (1989) 55–79
7. Lynch, N. A., Merritt, M., Weihl, W., Fekete, A., Yager, R. R.: Atomic Transactions. Morgan Kaufmann (1994)
8. Nagi, K.: Transactional Agents : Towards a Robust Multi-Agent System. Lecture Notes in Computer Science, Springer-Verlag No.2249 (2001)
9. Oracle Corporation: Oracle8i Concepts Vol. 1. Release 8.1.5 (1999)
10. Pamula, R. S., Srimani, P. K.: Checkpointing strategies for database systems. Proceedings of the 15th annual conference on Computer Science (1987) 88–97
11. Shimojo, I., Tachikawa, T., Takizawa, M.: M-ary Commitment Protocol with Partially Ordered Domain. Proc. of the 8th Int'l Conf. on Database and Expert Systems Applications (DEXA'97) (1997) 397–408
12. Shiraishi, M., Enokido, T., Takizawa, M.: Fault-Tolerant Mobile Agent in Distributed Objects Systems. Proc. of the Ninth IEEE Int'l Workshop on Future Trends of Distributed Computing Systems (FTDCS 2003) (2003) 145–151
13. Skeen, D.: Nonblocking Commitment Protocols. Proc. of ACM SIGMOD (1982) 133–147
14. Sun Microsystems Inc.: The Source for Java (TM) Technology. http://java.sun.com/
15. Sun Microsystems Inc.: JDBC Data Access API. http://java.sun.com/products/jdbc/
16. Sybase Inc.: SYBASE SQL Server. http://www.sybase.com/
17. X/Open Company Ltd.: X/Open CAE Specification Distributed Transaction Processing: The XA Specification. Document number XO/CAE/91/300 (1991)

Incremental Query Answering Using a Multi-layered Database Model in a Mobile Computing Environment

Sanjay Kumar Madria[1], Yongjian Fu[1], and Sourav Bhowmick[2]

[1] Department of Computer Science,
University of Missouri-Rolla,
Rolla, MO 65401
{madrias,yongjian}@umr.edu
2 School of Computer Engineering,
Nanyang Technological University,
Singapore
assourav@ntu.edu.sg

Abstract. In this paper, we present incremental and intelligent query answering techniques using a multi-layered database (MLDB) in a mobile environment. We discuss static and dynamic ways of generating MLDB and explore the issues of join and updates in maintaining MLDB. We explore various issues in answering queries incrementally and intelligently.

1 Introduction

In a mobile environment, it is not always possible or desired to generate an exact answer to a database query due to various mobile constraints [MBMB]. In fact, a user may be interested in knowing some snapshot of the results and if she gets interested may request some more details. From a system's perspective, a summarized result may be provided due to non-availability of bandwidth required to transfer bulky data or restricted storage available at the client side. For example, a moving object such as a user traveling in a car would like to get a summarized result of her query due to some time constraint, bandwidth available, storage restriction, or due to location based query. Also, due to some failure, a query that needs to be answered using two different databases, may not be answerable. Therefore, in cases, where one has some hard-deadline constraint, a delayed result produced may be of no use and may result in some undesired consequences. Thus, generating some intelligent answers to queries may be worthwhile due to lack of time, bandwidth or inaccessibility of data due to failure or poor connection. When the connection and bandwidth improves, a query can be answered using more detailed data. Querying using a mobile device with bandwidth constraints will likely to jam the communication and thus, will be very slow.

In this paper, we present a multi-layered database model (MLDB) to incrementally and intelligently process queries in mobile databases. The incremental query answering approach is to feed the information progressively as the client refines the query. Queries can be answered efficiently and intelligently using the one or multiple layers in MLDB based on the current scenario. The MLDB is constructed using a

V. Mařík et al. (Eds.): DEXA 2003, LNCS 2736, pp. 350–359, 2003.

series of generalized operators and can be constructed on-the-fly or in advance. The intelligent query answering is provided by feeding the information progressively using different layers of MLDB. This avoids the communication bottleneck by abstracting information into multiple layers, providing different levels and quality of data depending on the query, user profiles, different devices and the mobile constraints.

1.1 Related Work

Our MLDB model extends the concepts proposed in [HFN,HHCF,MMR] which give the general ideas about MLDB for intelligent query answering. These models are limited as they use only one generalization operator called concept hierarchy climbing. Our MLDB model is also different from the other models proposed where restrictions are placed on attributes and tuples, however, the schema, instance values and attribute types remain the same at all levels. In our model, relations at different levels have different schemas and values. Approximate query processing [V,VL] provides useful approximate answers to database queries if exact answers cannot be produced in time, or if the needed data is not available. However, their model has no concept of multi-layered database model and they mainly considered numeric attributes. Also, the discussion is not focused on how to make use of the model for mobile computing. In [RFS], authors extended the relational data model to support multi-resolution data retrieval and gave algebra using a sandbag operator. Our model extends these ideas by introducing formally different types of generalization operators.

2   Multi-layered Database Model (MLDB)

In this section, we define a multi-layered database (MLDB) model, a database composed of several layers of information, with the lowest layer corresponding to the primitive data stored in a conventional database, and with higher layers storing more general information extracted from one or more lower layers. The basic motivation of MLDB is to use a series of generalization operators to provide different levels of the generalized relations that are smaller in size. Queries will be answered first by higher layer relations that are smaller in size and can be downloaded faster on mobile devices. The information in lower layers is not transmitted to clients until it is requested and permitted.

Definition: A multi-layered database (MLDB) consists of 5 major components: <S,O,C,D,U>, defined as follows:

1.   S: a database schema, which contains the meta-information about the layered database structures;
2.   O: a set of generalization operators, which are used to construct higher layer relations from lower layer ones;
3.   C: a set of integrity constraints,
4.   D: a set of database relations, which consists of all the relations (primitive or generalized) in the multi-layered database, and
5.   U, a set of user profiles, which includes device configuration.

MLDB is constructed by the generalization of the layer 0 (original) database. Since there are many possible ways to generalize a relation, it is practically impossible to store all possible generalized relations. Too many layers will cause excessive interactions between clients and server that will increase the communication cost.

2.1 Generalization Operators

We are investigating several generalization operators listed below to create different levels in MLDB.

Sampling: A sample of an attribute value is returned, for example, giving a sample picture of an attraction or part of a video. This will help in maintaining security of data and at the same time queries return partial results.

Transformation: High-resolution pictures may not be accessible to the user, as they consume more storage and bandwidth. Therefore, it is desirable to lower the resolution of the images, or reduce the number of colors used in the visual objects. One other way is to transform the pictures into thumbnail images.

Concept Hierarchy Climbing: A primitive concept is replaced by a more general concept using a concept hierarchy, which organized concepts according to their generality levels.

Categorization: In some cases, a user may request for a price of an item or cost of a service and if such data are sensitive and available only to authorized users then instead of giving an exact price, a category of the items in that range can be given.

Aggregation: Aggregate functions such as min, max, count, sum, and average can be applied on the collection of objects at higher level.

Deletion: Depending on the users query, we can delete some attributes that are rarely queried or attribute which are highly secured. The attribute can be simply removed when generalizing from a lower layer relation to a higher layer relation.

Summary: Summarize the contents of a text attribute. For example, an unpublished paper can be replaced by its short abstract.

Infer: In some cases, for example, after retrieving the qualification of an employee, one may infer his job type.

Different generalization operators may be selected for different attributes and operators may be applied more than once.

Example: Suppose a tourist database contains the following three relations. A number of operators can be applied to generalize relations based on various heuristics.

1. *Attractions* (name, state, city, address, {telephones}, {map}, {pictures}, services)
2. *Hotels* (name, address, {telephones}, review, rates, reservation, {rooms}, {map}, {pictures}, {video})
3. *Restaurants* (name, description, address, telephone, review, {menu}, reservation, {order}, {business_hours}, {map}, {pictures})

Operator 1: Sample less frequently queried attributes or attributes, which don't have access restrictions.

Level 1: Attractions[1] (name, state, city, address, {telephones}, map, picture, services)

Operator 2: Transform bulky attributes into smaller size attributes.
Level 1: Hotels[1] (name, address, {telephones}, review, rates, reservation, {rooms}, {map},{thumbnails}, {compressed_video})
Operator 3: Delete less frequently queried attributes or highly secured attributes.
Level 2: Attractions[2] (name, state, city, address, {telephones})
Level 2: Hotels[2] (name, address, {telephones}, review, rates)
Operator 4: Categorize attributes with continuous values.
Level 3: Hotels[3] (name, address, {telephones}, review, rate_ranges)
Operator 5: Aggregate attribute to hide individual values.
Level 1: Restaurants[1] (name, description, address, telephone, review, no_items_in_menu)

3   Construction of MLDB Using Generalization Operators

There are two ways of building the MLDB: Static_MLDB and Dynamic_MLDB. Static_MLDB is to be build and store data based on one or more generalized operators discussed before. The number of levels of schema in MLDB is decided based on the application and the operators used at each level and is independent of the query patterns. The database expert decides on which generalization operators to use at each layer when building the MLDB.

3.1   Building MLDBs Using Static Summarization

The attributes in the relations can be classified as:
1.   Infrequently queried attributes by users
2.   Bulky attributes which stores data such as images and videos
3.   Continuous values for some attributes
4.   Discrete values and small size attributes

According to the classification of attributes, we now give the following algorithm to build MLDB using different generalized operators.
Algorithm: Construction of MLDB.
Input: A relational database, a set of concept hierarchies, and a set of frequently referenced attributes, a set of bulky attributes, a set of continuous valued attributes and a set of mechanisms for generalization.
Output: A multi layered database
Method. MLDB is constructed in the following steps.
1.   The attribute referenced infrequently is simply removed using the deletion operator at the beginning when generalizing from the lower layer relation to a higher layer relation.
2.   The bulky attribute is summarized using the operators such as selection, sampling, resolution, transformation, discoloration, summary and even possible deletion.
3.   The attribute that has continuous values can be grouped into categories using the categorization operator.

4.   After the step 3, the attributes left will have only discrete and small size values. We use concept hierarchy climbing operator to further summarize the tables.

Repeat 1~4 to construct the higher levels.

3.2   Building MLDBs Using Dynamic Summarization

In our model, each MSS will contain a query processing agent called QP. The QP receives the queries from the mobile hosts located in its cell. The QP will keep a log of the continuous queries for a certain period of time. After each interval of time, QP will generate different levels of MLDB.

The QP resides at MSS. MSS receives the continuous queries and pass them to the QP. QP will save each query in its log and try to find an answer from the higher levels of the MLDB. If the answer is not found, the QP will search the lower levels of the MLDB.

Algorithm: Here, we study the steps in building the MLDB dynamically depending on users' queries. We give some examples of SQL queries and then we build the MLDB using these queries. Suppose a tourist database contains the following three relations.

Attractions (name, state, city, address, {telephones}, {map}, {pictures}, services)

Hotels (name, address, {telephones}, review, rates, reservation, {rooms}, {map}, {pictures}, {video})

Restaurants (name, description, address, telephone, review, {menu}, reservation, {order}, {business_hours}, {map}, {pictures})

Example: Consider the following SQL queries, which users have posed.

Select name, state, city From Attractions Where state = "Missouri"	Select name, city, telephone From attractions Where city = "Rolla"
Select name, state, city, map From Attractions Where state = "California"	Select name, state, city, picture From Attractions Where city = "Rolla"

Method 1: Sample less frequently queried attributes.

From the above queries, we notice that the attributes such as telephones, maps, pictures, services, are not frequently queried. Users for example, are not always interested in multimedia views such as maps, pictures, or videos. Hence, the QP can build the first level (i.e., level 1) by using the **sampling** generalization operator. Instead of showing a slide show, showing one picture may be enough, or showing a part of the video clip.

Level 1: *Attractions^1 (name, state, city, address, telephone, map, picture, services)*

Method 2: Delete less frequently queried attributes.

From the SELECT part we know the set of attributes that are most frequently queried. The QP adds these attributes to the higher level (i.e., level 2).

Level 2: *Attractions^2 (name, state, city)*

In the above example, we considered all the queries generated answers from one table. In the next example, we show how dynamic MLDB can be built by joining two tables.

Example: In this example, we consider joining two tables. Suppose a user is looking for any restaurant that is located in a hotel. This query can be written in SQL as following:

Select	restaurants.name, restaurants.address
from	hotels, restaurants
where	hotels.address = restaurants.address

Method 3: Join similar attributes of higher level from Table A and Table B.

Assume that *hotels* relation is summarized to *hotels^1* (name, address, tel, review, thumbnail) and *restaurants* is summarized to *resturants^2* (name, description, address). If the previous query could be answered from the highest level of hotels and the highest level of restaurants, then we can join the two relations using the attributes name and address.

Level 3: *Rest-Hotel^3 (rest_name, hotel_name, address)*

This table will contain all the restaurants that are located in hotels.

Dynamic_MLDB is to build depending on the query patterns. An agent is responsible to keep track of different attributes users request as part of their queries. The agent determines and generates different levels of MLDB at different time periods. Some guidelines for building the MLDB are discussed below:

1. The appropriate generalization layers of the databases may be based on the applications, access restrictions, users profiles, device configuration, etc.
2. In general, the layers can be constructed based on the heuristics and domain knowledge. It should also be noted that the high layers should be adaptive since users interests, their queries and access permissions change over time.
3. With attribute generalization techniques available, the important question is how to selectively perform appropriate generalizations to form useful layers of database. In principle, there could be a large number of combinations of possible generalizations by selecting different sets of attributes to generalize and selecting the levels for the attributes to reach in the generalization. However, in practice, few layers containing most frequently referenced attributes and patterns will be sufficient to balance the implementation efficiency and practical usage.
4. Frequently used attributes and patterns should be determined before generation of new layers of a MLDB by the analysis of the statistics of query history or by receiving instructions from users or experts. The following guidelines may be used:
   A) It is wise to remove rarely used attributes or highly secured attributes.
   B) More secure attributes may need to be removed at higher layers.
   C) Retain frequently referenced ones in higher layers.
   D) Similar guidelines apply when generalizing attributes to a more general concept level.

3.3 Maintenance of MLDB

When base relations (at level 0) in MLDB are modified by insertion, deletion, or update, the corresponding higher levels will be updated after the update at level 0. In case of an insertion, the generalization operator generalizes the new tuple before it can be inserted into higher layer relations. In case of deletion, the deleted tuple is first generalized and then deleted from higher layer relations. In case of update, the corresponding tuple in the higher layer relations is updated. It should be noted that an operation in a base relation might has no effect at some of the higher layers. When updates are arrived at MSS from MH, these updates can be grouped together and can be applied at later time and most of the queries answered using higher layers are not going to affected by new updates. This is an advantage over the flat database, as concurrency control will delay execution of queries.

4   Intelligent Query Answering in MLDB

We will explore the following ideas for intelligent query answering in MLDB. A query processing algorithm will be designed for each of these cases.

1.   When a query reaches the query processor, the query processor will decide whether to answer the query using level 0 or higher levels according to different parameters, such as the connection bandwidth, security requirement for the MLDB and the user's profile, the given time limit for the query to return the answer and the nature for the query.
2.   The system will always start querying the highest level in the MLDB that is consistent with the requirements. If the user is not satisfied with the results, the system will further query using lower layers in the MLDB. If in the lowest layer also can't get the complete answer, system will answer the query only approximately.
3.   If the query answer is incomplete, intelligent query answering will give the best possible answer with the explanation.
4.   If the query answering returns too many results, it gives only partial results to the users with the option of getting more results later.
5.   If the query can't get answer from any level in MLDB, the query will be rewritten by relaxing the query conditions.

4.1   Criteria Used for Answering the Queries

In our model, each MSS maintains three parameters for each user type or query type. These parameters are: *Quality of Service (QoS), bandwidth connection, and Security requirements*. Query Processor (QP) at the MSS will decide the quality of answer to be returned depending on the parameter values. For example, in a high bandwidth connection, QP will answer the MH's query from the level 0 in MLDB.

Security parameter is the most important parameter. In some queries, the QP will only answer the query from the higher levels of the MLDB even if both the bandwidth connection and QoS availability are high. This is because based on the user's profile and security access granted, the system can determine what quality of data to be returned in response to the query.

Some queries need a high QoS such as audio/video data. In this case the QP answers should be returned within real time and therefore, can be critical. Hence, the query will be directly sent to level 0 in MLDB.

When a query arrives at the query processor, the query processor will decide based on the bandwidth available whether the query will be directly sent to level 0 or any other higher level. If the current bandwidth connection is high or the user is entitled to high quality data, the query will be directly sent to the level 0.

4.2   How to Get Query Answering Using Higher Levels in MLDB?

As we know, a query consists of query conditions and query return attributes. Both of them are attributes for a specific table in a database. Now, we try to find the highest level in MLDB, which includes all these attributes. If the query answering using the highest level is not complete, we will query the lower level relations.

Example: Suppose an e-book database contains the following data relations.

For level 0: e-book(ISBN, title, author, year, price, cover(picture))

For level 1 shown below, we remove the owner attribute from house (level 0).

e-book' (ISBN, title, author, year, price)

For level2: e-book" (title, year)

Example Query: Select author

       From e-book"

       Where title="Ad Hoc Networking"

Case1: Suppose we want to find author's name of the book title Ad Hoc Networking. Our goal is to try to query the higher layers of MLDB. Here, the query condition is attribute title, which is present in e-book" relation. The e-book" relation is the highest level where this attribute appears in this MLDB. However, the query return information is the attribute author, which doesn't present in the e-book" relation. So, we cannot get retrieve the query results from the highest-level e-book" relation. In this case, the query will go to the lower level e-book' relation. In this level, the attributes title and author both are present.

Case 2: Suppose we want to find the book "Ad Hoc Networking" which is published in 2000. In this case, the answer for this query is incomplete from the highest level (e-book" relation) because only one book is returned but actually there may be many books which should be returned from MLDB. So, to get the complete information, the query will move on to the lower level.

5   Query Processing in MLDB Using Join

As we know, most joins on several relations are performed on the key or foreign key attributes. However, some higher levels may have already lost the key or foreign key while creating MLDB.

For such MLDB, we have the following rule to use for join among multi level relations:

If a query involves a join of two or more relations, the highest possible layer consistent with the query should be:

1.   This level has the key or foreign key, performed as join attributes
2.   This level should be the highest layer including the all attributes for the corresponding relation.

Example: Suppose the query on the Customer and e-book MLDB is to describe the relationship between customer and e-book. In this example, the foreign key for ebook' and customer' is title. In the customer" and e-book", the foreign key values have been generalized.

Consider the schemas:

Customer' (Name, Title, Age)

e-book' (ISBN, Title, Author, Year, Price)

Customer' (smith, Neural Network, 46)

Customer' (Mike, Ad Hoc Network, 23)

e-book' (099999999, Neural Network, John, 1997, 80)

e-book' (012345678, Ad Hoc Networking, Smith, 2000, 40)

After generalization, we get

Customer" (smith, Science, 46)

Customer" (Mike, Science, 23)

e-book" (099999999, Science, John, 1997, 80)

e-book" (012345678, Science, Smith, 2000, 40)

The query involves a join of Customer and E-book relations. We try to use the higher levels to join [SY] these relations. Here, the highest level is Customer" and E-book". However, join cannot be performed on these two higher layer relations as the join attributes (title) of Customer" and e-book" have been generalized. So, we have to move to lower layer to join the Customer and e-book relations. Therefore, we have to use Customer' and e-book' to do the join operator.

5.1   Updating the MLDB

The level 0 in MLDB will be updated when you insert, delete or update tuples in the database. The corresponding higher levels will be updated after the update of level 0.

In case of inserting a new tuple into level 0 in MLDB, the query processor will insert this tuple to the corresponding higher levels. While inserting the new tuple to the higher levels, we should generalized the attribute values in the higher level database using same generalized operators as used before. We will search the schema tree for the mechanism of summarization (generalized operators used) and use the mechanism for every attribute to insert the tuple into the higher level. It is also possible that inserting a tuple in base relation has no effect at some of the higher layers. In such cases it is important to add cardinality of each tuple in higher order relations.

In case of deleting a tuple from level 0, the query processor will search this tuple in the corresponding higher levels and delete it. If the attribute name has been changed in the higher level, the deletion condition will be changed correspondingly using the other attribute. It is also possible that deleting a tuple from a base relation has no effect in some of the higher layers.

In case of updating a tuple from level 0, the query processor will search this tuple in the corresponding higher level and update the tuple with the corresponding attributes in the higher levels.

6   Conclusions and Future Work

A multiple layered database (MLDB) model is proposed and examined in this study, which demonstrates the usefulness of MLDB in incremental query answering in a mobile environment. MLDB can be constructed by dynamic or static data generalization. Data generalization and layer construction methods using different operators have been developed in this study to guarantee new layers can be constructed efficiently, effectively and consistently with the primitive information stored in the database. Incremental and intelligent query answering using join are studied. However, more studies are needed in the construction and utilization of multiple layered databases in intelligent query answering in the future. Access control and cost models are under investigation currently.

Acknowledgement. We thank Malik AlJarad and Jian Yan for their contributions during the progress of this paper.

References

[HFN]   Han, J., Fu, Y., and Ng, R., Cooperative Query Answering Using Multiple Layered Databases, Second International Conference on Cooperative Information System(COOPIS'94), Toronto, Canada, pages 47–58, May 1994.

[HHCF] Han J., Huang Y., Cercone N., and Fu Y., Intelligent Query Answering by Knowledge Discovery Techniques, IEEE Transactions on Knowledge and Data Engineering, 8(3): 373–390, 1996.

[MMR]   Madria, S.K., Mohania, M., Roddick, J., Query Processing in Mobile Databases Using Concept Hierarchy and Summary Database, in Proc. of 5th International Conference on Foundation for Data Organization (FODO'98), Kobe, Japan, Nov., 1998.

[MBMB] S K Madria, B Bhargava, M Mohania, S S Bhowmick. Data and Transaction Management in a Mobile Environment. To appear as a book chapter in Mobile Computing: Implementing Pervasive Information and Communication Technologies, Kluwer Academic Publishers, 2002.

[RFS]   Robert L. Read, Donald S. Fussell, Abraham Silberschatz: A Multi-Resolution Relational Data Model. VLDB 1992: 139–150.

[SY]   Mukesh Singhal, Yuping Yang, Fast Join Execution Using Summary Information in Large Databases (1997), Technical Report, Ohio State University (Also in CAMM NSF workshop, Brown University, 2002)

[V]   Vrbsky S. V., A Data Model for Approximate Query Processing of Real-time Databa se, Data & Knowledge Engineering 21 (1997) 79–102.

[VL]   Vrbsky S. V., Liu J. , APPROXIMATE: A Query Processor that Produces Monotonically Improving Approximate Answers, IEEE Trans. On Knowledge and Data Engineering, 5(6) (Dec. 1993) 1056–1058.

Environmental Noise Classification for Context-Aware Applications

Ling Ma, Dan Smith, and Ben Milner

School of Computing Sciences,
University of East Anglia
Norwich, NR4 7TJ, UK
{ling.ma,dan.smith,b.milner}@uea.ac.uk

Abstract. Context-awareness is essential to the development of adaptive information systems. Much work has been done on developing technologies and systems that are aware of absolute location in space and time; other aspects of context have been relatively neglected. We describe our approach to automatically sensing and recognising environmental noise as a contextual cue for context-aware applications. Environmental noise provides much valuable information about a user's current context. This paper describes an approach to classifying the noise context in the typical environments of our daily life, such as the office, car and city street. In this paper we present our hidden Markov model based noise classifier. We describe the architecture of our system, the experimental results, and discuss the open issues in environmental noise classification for mobile computing.

1 Introduction

Traditional computer systems run with explicit input and output, such as mouse clicks, keyboard presses and on-screen displays. Users must provide explicit information to the computer and the computer only can give explicit results. Nowadays, mobile computing is increasingly important and people want to access information anytime and anywhere. To exploit this mobility requires systems that can sense appropriate context information and adapt their operation automatically without involving direct user interaction. This information may include location, time, weather, co-located objects, noise, recent events, etc., although many definitions of context have been proposed [10]. Context information is especially important in the mobile computing area where the context and the user's needs change rapidly. We define time, location/co-location and discourse (including environmental noise) as three dimensions of context in mobile computing area of principal interest.

The challenge for context-aware computing is the complexity of capturing, representing, processing, adapting and recording of context information. In a context-aware application, contexts can be captured via different sensors; user feedback can confirm context and be used to improve the model; services can be provided according to the current context and user preferences; finally, context information can be tagged for later retrieval [16]. The notion of context-aware computing was

V. Mařík et al. (Eds.): DEXA 2003, LNCS 2736, pp. 360–370, 2003.

proposed about a decade ago. The Active Badge system [24] - probably the first context-ware application – was published in 1992 and Schilit [22] first introduced the term "context-aware" in 1994. Subsequent work has concentrated on time, identity and location.

Environmental noise can be a rich source of information about the current situation. For example, we often infer the situation of a respondent in a mobile phone conversation by identifying the background noise and adjusting our response accordingly. The noise classification system described here classifies the audio context in the typical environments of our daily life, such as the office, bar, and city street, to identify the scenes in order to predict the user's needs and adjust the mode of operation accordingly. This work is part of a larger investigation into the integration of multiple sources of context information in a unified framework.

This paper describes the overall design of the context system and is focused on the development and evaluation of an environmental noise classifier. It is organised as follows. In section 2, we review related work in the area of mobile context-aware applications and audio scene classification. Section 3 describes our approach to building an environmental noise classification system, and the methodology to classify auditory scenes into predefined classes. Section 4 presents the experimental results and discussion. In section 5, we describe the overall architecture of the application system. Conclusions and future work are discussed in section 6.

2   Related Work

Most existing context-aware applications are location-based, augmented with timestamp information. The sensors mainly used are short range IR and RF signals, and GPS. Those applications include services, e.g. "Conference assistant" [8], "Office Assistant" [25], or guides, such as "Cyberguide" [1], "Shopping Jacket" [20], and memory aids, e.g. "Stick-e notes" [4], "Memoclip" [2] and "CybreMinder" [9]. Recent surveys [10] [5] [15] show that most existing context-aware applications use identity, time, and location, which are all important and are can be obtained using current technology.

Couvreur [7] has introduced three classifiers (statistical classifiers, adaptable and adaptive classifiers, hidden Markov model based classifiers) to be used in separated noise event recognition (car, truck, airplane etc.) and the attempt to develop a classifier for multiple simultaneous signals. Statistical classifiers have the major drawback of their sensitivity to variations in utilization conditions. Adaptable and adaptive classifiers that adapt to changes in spectra can solve this problem, but do not take the advantage of the time evolving structure of the spectra. Hidden Markov model based classifiers provide a dynamic solution. Gaunard et al. [12] have implemented a HMM-based classifier to recognise five noise events (car, truck, moped, aircraft, train). They observed that the frame length in noise recognition is larger than in speech recognition. Their best results are from a five-state HMM using LPC-cepstral features, which they report gives better results than human listeners. Much work has been done on separating speech from background noise, following

[3]; we are interested in recognising everyday scenes (office, car, etc.) rather than sound events.

The above classifiers recognise individual sound events. Only a few classification systems have been proposed to recognise auditory scenes. Peltonen *et al.* [17] demonstrated that mel-frequency cepstral coefficients out-performed other feature representations. Sawhney [21] classified five everyday noise types, comparing several approaches, of which filterbank with Nearest Neighbour (NN) clearly outperformed the others. Their results indicate that frequency bands generated from filterbank analysis of frame-by-frame audio windows provide robust features. Other work (e.g. [6], [11]) has been directed toward recognising both the scene and sound subjects in it, focusing on exhaustively identifying sound events and their relationships in a continuous classifier.

Our approach differs from previous work with its emphasis on rapid, lightweight classification for mobile applications and an adaptive short-duration sampling strategy.

3 HMM-Based Noise Classification

This section describes a hidden Markov model (HMM) framework for classifying a range of different environmental noises. Classification is based on combining digital signal processing (DSP) technology with pattern recognition methods that have been central to progress in automatic speech recognition [14] over the last 20 years. However there are subtle difference between recognising speech and identifying environmental noises. For example speech is produced from a single source (the human vocal system) which is well modelled, has limitations on the character of sound it can produce and is also constrained to a single location in an environment. Environmental noise, however, has none of these constraints and is a complex sound made up of a mixture of different events. There is no constraint on what these sounds can be and they may emanate from many different localities in the environment. For example consider an office environment; a stationary component may come from an air conditioning fan, a quasi-stationary component from keyclicks, and non-stationary events from people moving around, opening doors and talking.

In this paper, we are interested only in modelling slow-changing attributes of the environmental noise in the audio signal. This means the focus is on recognising the context, or environment, instead of analysing and interpreting discrete sound events.

This section describes four phases which have been used to construct a set of environmental noise models suitable for classification. These are environmental noise database capture via portable recording devices, pre-processing (digitisation, segmentation and labelling), feature exaction using mel-frequency cepstral coefficients (MFCCs) and finally training and testing a set of hidden Markov models (HMMs). Figure 1 shows the overall process for feature extraction and classification of the noise data. These experiments have been performed using the HTK (Hidden Markov Model Toolkit) developed at the Speech, Vision and Robotics Group of the Cambridge University Engineering Department (CUED) [23].

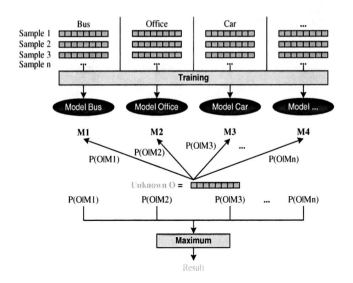

Fig. 1. Overall process for feature extraction and classification of noise data

3.1 Data Collection

A high quality microphone and two portable recording devices (Sony MD and Sony micro cassette) were used to capture the auditory contexts from different scenes. The recordings were designed to cover a range of everyday environments from where Fig. 1. Overall process for feature extraction and classification of noise data users would be accessing information services from mobile devices. The recordings took place in and around the University of East Anglia during the spring and summer of 2002. All data were then labelled manually. Based on the length and quality of the recordings 11 different noise contexts were chosen for initial classification experiments. These are shown in table 1.

Table 1. Description of the scenes

Scene	Location
Office	Wolfson Lab at UEA
Bus	Across a range of buses
Football match	Football match at Norwich City
Bar	Graduate student bar in UEA
Beach	Great Yarmouth beach
Railway station	Norwich railway station
Car	Small car in urban driving
Laundrette	Laundrette at UEA
Street	Norwich city centre on a Saturday
Lecture	UEA
Silence	–

3.2 Data Pre-processing and Analysis

Following data collection the audio data was digitised and divided into short duration segments. Digitisation was achieved by sampling the analogue data at 22.050kHz using 16-bit quantisation. The recordings were then segmented into 3 second duration audio files. This duration was chosen as it is likely to be the length of noise data from which the system would operate in practical applications. Associated with each of these 3 second audio files is a manually created label file which contains information regarding the scene.

Pre-processing resulted in a set of 80 examples for each scene. Of these, 60 examples were used for training and 20 for testing. Therefore, for the 11 scenes (including silence), 880 noise examples were used for the initial experiments (660 examples for training and further 220 for testing).

For example, figure 2 shows the spectrogram of the one of the office noise samples. The spectrogram shows time along the abscissa and frequency along the ordinate. Darker regions show more energy present at a particular point in time-frequency.

The spectrogram of the office noise displays a number of distinctive characteristics. For example the vertical lines result from the impulsive noise of keyboard clicks – a feature very characteristic of an office environment. The continuous horizontal line comes from the air conditioning fan which provides another important cue to underlying environment. Other noises also displayed similar identifiable characteristics.

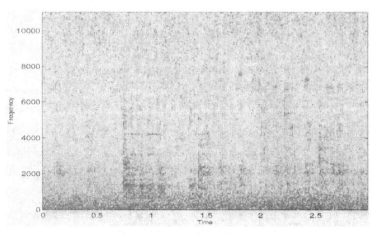

Fig. 2. Spectrogram of office noise

3.3 Feature Extraction

The purpose of feature extraction is to extract useful discriminative information from the time-domain waveform which will result in a compact set of feature vectors. Researchers have experimented with many different types of feature for use in speech recognition [7][14][17]. The most popular feature used for speech recognition is currently Mel-Frequency Cepstral Coefficients (MFCCs). Peltonen [17] implemented a system for recognising 17 sound events using 11 features individually and obtained the best result with the MFCC features.

MFCC feature extraction begins by estimating the magnitude spectrum of a short duration frame of speech (conventionally using a Fast Fourier Transform, FFT). The magnitude spectrum is then non-linearly quantised using a mel-scale filterbank which models the psychoacoustic properties of the human ear. From this a logarithm is taken and then a discrete cosine transform (DCT) applied [23],

$$c_i = \sqrt{\frac{2}{N}} \sum_{j=1}^{N} m_j \cos(\frac{\pi i}{N}(j - 0.5))$$

where c_i is the ith MFCC, N is the number of filterbank channels and m_j the output of the jth mel-scale filterbank channel. This results in the MFCC vector.

For the experiments used in this work the speech was first pre-emphasised and then a Hamming window used to extract 25ms duration frames of audio. These frames were extracted every 10ms. A 23-channel mel filterbank was applied to the resultant magnitude spectrum. Following the DCT, truncation resulted in a 12-D MFCC vector. This was augmented by a log energy term to give a 13-D static feature vector. To improve performance both the velocity and acceleration were computed and this resulted in a 39-D feature vector which was used for training and testing.

3.4 HMM Training and Testing

For modelling the different environmental noises a set of HMMs has been created. These provide a powerful statistical method of dynamically characterizing the observed noise samples in time and frequency. The HMM has also been very successful in automatic speech recognition applications [19].

A HMM consists of a series of stationary states which are connected together by a Markov chain. This allows the time-varying nature of signals to be modelled as a progression through a series of stationary states. This makes the HMM an appropriate model for representing the non-stationary behaviour of environmental noises. More detailed HMM theory is given in [19]. For noise modelling a left-to-right HMM topology was used (figure 3). This model topology has a self-transition and a left-to-right transition to the next state. The self-transition is used to model contiguous features in the same state. The left-to-right transition enables a progression when the next quasi-stationary segment evolves. In such a topology, each state has a state-dependent output probability distribution that is used to interpret the observable noise signal. Progression through the states is described by a transition probability matrix.

For the left-to-right HMM, an important parameter to determine is the number of states. To a certain extent the choice of model topology depends on the amount of available training data and the signal to be modelled. For the time-varying nature of environment noise, more states are generally required and this also depends on the duration of the signal. For our three second noise signal, we have implemented from 3 to 21 state HMMs.

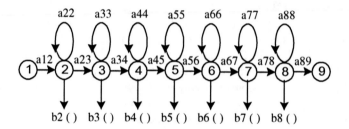

Fig. 3. A nine-state left-to-right HMM model topology

4 Experimental Results

The HMMs were trained using the 60 noise examples from each of the 11 different noise scenes to give a set of 11 HMMs. A preliminary test was performed to identify the optimal number of states for the models. Ten different numbers of states were tested; 3, 5, 7, 9, 11, 13, 15, 17, 19 and 21 states. The classification performance for each number of states in the HMM is shown in figure 4.

From the figure we see that accuracy of the 3-state HMM is 80.00% and as the number of states increases the accuracy is improved up to a maximum of 92.27% at 11, 13 and 15 states. At higher numbers of states the accuracy begins to reduce. This indicates that the number of states in the HMM has a significant impact on the overall classification accuracy. In general, more states in the HMM does allow better modelling of the underlying noise characteristics. On the other hand, a model with more states will have more parameters which will requires more training data to estimate accurately. In addition, the duration of our samples is 3 seconds and too many states in the HMM may cause overfitting. Therefore the limited amount of training data and relatively short duration of the samples cause the accuracy to decrease with a number of states higher than 15.

Using the result from the 11-state HMM topology, the accuracy of the individual scenes is shown in table 2. These ranged from 75% to 100%, with the office, football match, beach, laundrette and silence giving 100% classification accuracy for the 20 examples tested of each. Worst performance was obtained for identifying street noise. This attained only 75% accuracy but can be attributed to the fact the this is probably the most diverse noise type.

The accuracy of noise recognition depends on a number of factors such as the amount and coverage of the training data, the feature extraction component, the allowable computational complexity, and the model parameters. The noise classifier designed in this system is not capable of recognising multiple and simultaneously occurring environmental noises. For example sitting in an office with a car is passing by would cause a conflict. Similar problems also occur when identifying similar noise scenes.

For simultaneous classification and to get improved discrimination when classifying similar scenes, we may consider how humans solve these sorts of classification problems. Peltonen's [18] human listening test shows that humans distinguish similar scenes by catching pieces of sound events in them (e.g. music, clinking glasses and conversation in a bar). Previous research has successfully modelled distinct sound events [12] [17]. The short sampling strategy we use does not require a dedicated audio channel and can obtain noise samples during periods of speech inactivity. A dedicated noise channel would facilitate alternative recognition strategies.

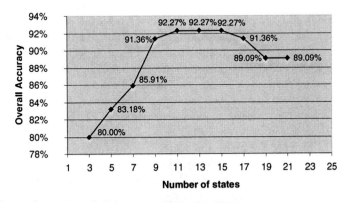

Fig. 4. Overall accuracy from 3 to 21 states

Table 2. Noise classification results and confusion matrix

Result and Confusion matrix for 11 scenes										
Accuracy %	Bus	Office	Football Match	Bar	Beach	Car	Laundrette	Rail Station	Street	Lecture	Silence
Bus	95	0	5	0	0	0	0	0	0	0	0
Office	0	100	0	0	0	0	0	0	0	0	0
Football Match	0	0	100	0	0	0	0	0	0	0	0
Bar	15	0	0	85	0	0	0	0	0	0	0
Beach	0	0	0	0	100	0	0	0	0	0	0
Car	0	0	0	0	10	85	0	0	5	0	0
Laundrette	0	0	0	0	0	0	100	0	0	0	0
Rail Station	0	0	0	0	0	0	0	90	10	0	0
Street	0	0	0	0	0	0	10	15	75	0	0
Lecture	0	0	0	0	0	0	0	0	15	85	0
Silence	0	0	0	0	0	0	0	0	0	0	100
Overall accuracy: 92.27%										

5 Context System Design

The basic context-aware application framework has a client-server architecture, shown in figure 5. The server side comprises a set of noise models, a database of new samples, a noise classification application and a web application server. The current client application, mostly written in Java, consists of an audio recorder, noise recogniser, noise analyser, context logger, browser and update connection. These are lightweight processes which can easily run on limited capacity devices. The audio recorder periodically samples the environmental noise (3 seconds per minute by default). The noise recogniser classifies the noise. The noise analyser reads the result file and initiated any actions required. The context logger writes each captured context to an XML record. The browser is used as a memory aid, by recalling context details. The update connection updates the HMM definitions.

The current system senses two contexts, environmental noise and time. The microphone is a sensor to sense the environmental noise. The built-in clock is the time sensor. The time is automatically called updated every time a new noise context is captured. If a changed or uncertain context is detected, samples are taken more frequently until the change is confirmed or the context is clarified. The values read from sensors periodically are continually fed to an extensible log in XML format. The state of the system and a number of sampling parameters can be controlled by the user. The log can be used for later analysis to refine the classifier's performance and to detect longer duration events.

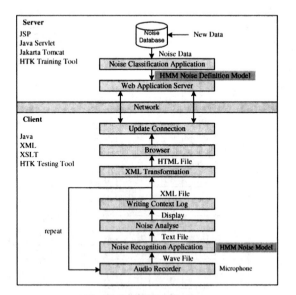

Fig. 5. System architecture

6 Conclusions and Future Work

We have described our HMM-based environmental noise classifier which we trained on a database of manually gathered samples. The overall recognition accuracy of 11 typical scenes in our daily life (including silence) is 92.27%. The recognition accuracy of individual scenes ranged from 75% to 100%. We intend undertaking further experiments, using more samples and more scenes from different locations, to compare the result of using different features, classification methods and algorithms.

We have described our initial client-server context-aware application. The current version of this system is able to capture, recognise and track environmental noise changes as a user changes locations. We are developing this system to provide: a range of customisable output responses and modalities appropriate to the user's situation, extending the range of input modalities, and to increasing the range of context data.

References

[1]   Abowd G. D., Atkeson C. G., Hong J., Long S., Kooper R., and Pinkerton M., *Cyberguide: A mobile context-aware tour guide*, ACM Wireless Networks, 1997.
[2]   Beigl M. MemoClip: A Location based Remembrance Appliance, Personal Technologies, 4(4): 230–233, September 2000.
[3]   Brown G.J. and Cooke M. P., *Computational Auditory Scene Analysis*. Computer Speech and Language, 8, pp. 297–336, 1994.
[4]   Brown P. J., *STICK-E NOTES: changing notes and contexts – the SeSensor module and the loading of notes*, EP-odd, January 1996.
[5]   Chen G., Kotz D., *A Survey of Context-Aware Mobile Computing*, Research Dept. of Computer Science, Dartmouth College, 2000.
[6]   Clarkson B., Sawhney N. and Pentland A., *Auditory Context Awareness via Wearable Computing*, Proc. of the 1998 Workshop on Perceptual User Interfaces (PUI'98), San Francisco, CA, USA, November 1998.
[7]   Couvreur C., *Environmental Sound Recognition: A Statistical Approach*, PhD thesis, Faculte Polytechnique de Mons, Belgium, June 1997.
[8]   Dey A. K., Salber D., Abowd G. D. and Futakawa M., *The Conference Assistant: Combining Context-Awareness with Wearable Computing*, The Third International Symposium on Wearable computers, 1999.
[9]   Dey A. K. and Abowd G. D., *CybreMinder: A Context-Aware System for Supporting reminders*, In Proceeding of the Second International Symposium on Handheld and Ubiquitous Computing, HUC 2000.
[10] Dey A.K., Abowd G. D., *Towards a Better Understanding of Context and Context-Awareness*, CHI 2000 Workshop on the What, Who, Where, When, and How of Context-Awareness, 2000.
[11] Ellis D., *Prediction-Driven Computational auditory Scene Analysis For Dense Sound Mixtures*, the ESCA workshop on the Auditory Basis of Speech Perception, Keele UK, July 1996.
[12] Gaunard P., Mubikangiey C. G., Couvreur C. and Fontaine V., *Automatic Classification Of Environmental Noise Events By Hidden Markov Models*, Applied Acoustics, 1998.
[13] Harter A., Hopper A., Steggles P., Ward A. and Webster P., *The Anatomy of a Context-Aware Application*, ACM/IEEE Mobile Computing and Networking, 2002.
[14] Huang X., Acero A. and Hon H., *Spoken Language Processing*, Prentice Hall, 2001.

[15] MIT media Lab, http://cac.media.mit.edu:8080/contextweb/jsp/projects.jsp
[16] Pascoe, J., *The Stick-e Note Architecture: Extending the Interface Beyond the User*, International Conference on Intelligent User Interfaces, Orlando, Florida, USA. ACM. pp. 261–264, 1997.
[17] Peltonen V., Tuomi J., Klapuri A., Huopaniemi J. and Sorsa T., *Computational Auditory Scene Recognition*. In Proc. International Conference on Acoustic, Speech and Signal Processing, Orlando, Florida, May 2002.
[18] Peltonen V.T.K., Eronen A.J., Parviainen M. P. and Klapuri A.P., *Recognition of Everyday Auditory Scenes: Potentials, Latencies and Cues*, 110th Convention Audio Engineering Society, 2001.
[19] Rabiner L. R., *A tutorial on hidden Markov models and selected application in speech recognition*, Proc. IEEE, vol. 77, no. 2, pp. 257–286, Feb. 1989.
[20] Randell C., Muller H., *The Shopping Jacket: Wearable Computing for the Consumer*, Personal Technologies vol.4 no.4.
[21] Sawhney N., *Situational Awareness from Environmental Sounds*, 1997.
[22] Schilit B., Adams N., Want R., *Context-Aware Computing Applications*, IEEE Workshop on Mobile Computing Systems and Applications, 1994.
[23] The HTK Book Version 3.1, Cambridge University Engineering Department, December 2001, http://htk.eng.cam.ac.uk.
[24] Want R., Hopper A., Falcao V., Gibbons J., *The Active Badge Location System*, ACM Transactions on Information Systems, 10(1) 1992.
[25] Yan H. and Selker T., *Context-aware office assistant*, In Proceedings of the 2000 International Conference on Intelligent User Interfaces, New Orleans, LA, January 2000.

An Access Time Cost Model for Spatial Range Queries on Broadcast Geographical Data over Air

Jianting Zhang and Le Gruenwald

School of Computer Science,
University of Oklahoma
200 Felgar Street
Norman, OK, 73072, USA
{jianting,ggruenwald}@ou.edu

Abstract. Wireless data broadcasting is well known for its excellent scalability. Most geographical data, such as weather and traffic, is public information and has a large number of potential users. Broadcast is a good mechanism that can be used to transmit the data to users at this scale. In this paper, we propose a cost model for access time in processing spatial range queries on broadcast geographical data over air. We also propose heuristics in generating orderings of broadcast sequences and evaluate their performances based on the cost model.

1 Introduction

Data broadcasting is well known for its excellent scalability (*Imielinski, 1997*). Most geographical data, such as weather and traffic, is public information and has a large amount of potential users. Thus it is attractive to broadcast geographical data in metropolitan areas to reduce the increasing demands for wireless bandwidth resources. Furthermore, for users that are able to be aware of their locations by using Global Position System (GPS), network infrastructures or their combinations (Konig-Ries, 2002), they can perform Location Dependent Queries (LDQ, Seydim, 2001) to request Location Dependent Services (LDS). It is easy to see that LDQ on broadcast geographical data over air is particular interesting in the context of large-scale resource-efficient data dissemination in mobile computing. Spatial range query (Rigaux, 2002) processing on broadcast geographical data will be one of the most popular techniques to provide LDS.

The performance of a data broadcast system is characterized by two parameters (*Imielinski, 1997*), tune-in time (TT) and access time (AT). TT is defined as the time for a client to download data from a broadcast sequence. During this time the client has to be in active mode and consumes more energy than in doze/sleep mode. AT is defined as the time a client begin to access the broadcast sequence to the time all the requested data items are downloaded. A client may switch to doze mode in between two active downloading where usually less energy is consumed. In Fig. 1, TT is equal to the total of the length of required data items (shaded) while AT is the duration between the first and the last required data items.

V. Mařík et al. (Eds.): DEXA 2003, LNCS 2736, pp. 371–380, 2003.

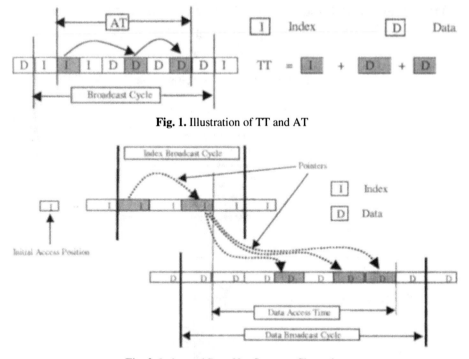

Fig. 1. Illustration of TT and AT

Fig. 2. Index and Data Use Separate Channels

In this paper, we aim at providing a cost model of access time for spatial range queries on broadcast geographical data. We assume a client has already had an ordered set of pointers to data items in the broadcast channel by performing a spatial range query on index segments which are either in the same channel with the data or in a separate index channel. Currently we focus on the data access time only and leave the index access for future work. The scenario we consider is that index and data are broadcast using separate channels where a client may begin to access the data channel randomly (Fig.2).

The rest of this paper is arranged as follows. Section 2 is an overview of related work. We propose our cost model for range queries over broadcast geographical data in Section 3. We present several ordering heuristics and evaluate their performances based on the cost model using a real data set in Section 4. Finally Section 5 concludes the paper with summary and future work directions

2   Related Work

Range queries are the most frequently used spatial queries and have been extensively studied in disk-resident data management research. Several cost models have been proposed for measuring the performance of spatial indexing on range queries (Pagel, 1993; Theodoridis, 1996; Theodoridis, 2000). The measurement used is the number of disk accesses which is equivalent to tune-in time in broadcasting without considering paging and buffering effects. However, to the best of our knowledge, there is no previous work done on access time for spatial range queries on broadcast data.

There have been several studies on general data broadcast. Many of them focus on indexing techniques to make tradeoffs between TT and AT, such as tree-indexing (Imielinski, 1994a), hashing (Imielinski, 1994b), signature (Lee, 1996) and hybrid (Hu, 2001a). They can support only queries on one-dimensional data and can search only one data item in a query result. Although (Imielinski, 1997) proposed to chain data items that have the same values in different meta-segments in its nonclustering index and multi-index methods, it cannot be applied to data items that have different values but are often in the same query results. Furthermore, in its performance analysis, it assumes that it takes a whole broadcast cycle to retrieve non-clustered data items of a particular value. That is an unnecessary overestimation. The issue of multi-attribute data broadcast and query was first addressed in (Hu, 2001b). However, this work can handle only conjunction/disjunction queries that involve fewer than three attributes. They are not suitable for range queries on geographical data.

Recent works on object-oriented database broadcast (Chehadeh, 1999) and relational database broadcast (Lee, 2002) allow multiple data items to be accessed in a query. However, they assumed the access to data items had predefined orders. They are not suitable for spatial range queries since data items in a query result do not necessarily have a predefined order. The work presented in (Chung, 2001) is essentially similar to our cost model of data access time. However, it excluded the tune in time from access time for the items in the query result set which makes the total access time a summation of multiple quadratic terms. To simplify the result, it used a linear function to approximate the quadratic cost, which makes the model inaccurate. Furthermore, its proof of the approximation is incorrect. We believe that our result in which the access time for a single query is linear with respect to a single quadratic term (see Section 3.2 for details) is more concise and accurate. None of the above cost models are designed for spatial range queries.

The only previous work on geographical data broadcast we know is (Hambrusch, 2001). It studied the execution of spatial queries on broadcast tree-based spatial index structures. Their work assumed the client had very limited memory that the whole R-tree cannot be fit into the client memory and the client has to discard some retrieved R-Tree nodes to hold more useful ones during the query process. Their work focused on reducing extra access time incurred by having to access multiple broadcast cycles due to the discard and replacement. Our cost models assume that a client has already have the pointers to data items in the data channel, either from another separate index channel or from the same channel that combines both data and index. A client can sort the values of the pointers and thus only one scan of data channel is sufficient to retrieve all the data items. We believe that our assumption that a client can hold the entire index segments related to a spatial range query is more realistic for LDQs.

3 The Cost Model

3.1 Preliminaries

Let DS=[x1,x2)× [y1,y2) be the data space that defines all the geographical data items. Suppose the size of a range query window is (q_x, q_y).

We define an Extended Region R_u of data item P_u as the rectangle of (q_x,q_y) centered at P_u. As shown in Fig. 3, the distribution of the centers of query window (q_x,q_y) that contains data item P_u is the extended region of R_u. Furthermore, from Fig. 4 we can see that the distribution of the centers of query window (q_x,q_y) that contains both data items P_u and P_v is the intersection of their extended regions R_u and R_v. This relationship can be extended to higher orders, i.e., up to the intersected region among all n extended regions where n is the number of points in the data set to broadcast.

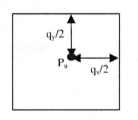 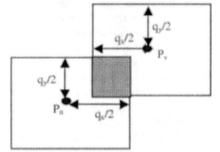

Fig. 3. The Distribution of Centers of Query Window (q_x,q_y) that Contains P_u

Fig. 4. The Distribution of Centers of Query Window (q_x,q_y) that Contains both P_u and P_v (Shaded Area)

Before presenting our cost model, we define the following symbols. Let A_i be the area of R_i, $A_{i,j}$ be the intersection area of R_i and R_j, ... $A_{1,2...n}$ be the intersection area of R_1, R_2...R_n. Let $\tilde{A}_i$ be the part of A_i that solely contains one point for all i where $0 \leq i < n$, $\tilde{A}_{i,j}$ be the part of $A_{i,j}$ that solely contains two points for all i and j where $0 \leq i < j < n$, ... $\tilde{A}_{1,2...n}$ be the part of the intersection area of R_1, R_2...R_n that contains solely n points. Note $\tilde{A}_{1,2...n} = A_{1,2...n}$.

Under the assumption that all the locations inside the study region are equally likely to be the locations where users request spatial range queries, the number of expected requests from a region is the multiplication of the area of the region and a constant c, the number of requests per unit area. For the sake of simplicity we omit the constant factor and only use $\tilde{A}_i$, $\tilde{A}_{i,j}$ ... $\tilde{A}_{1,2...n}$ as the access frequencies for the corresponding query result sets in the following sections.

3.2   Access Time for Processing a Single Query

Let function $\pi(u)$ maps point u to its position in the broadcast sequence. Suppose the single query result set contains k data items n_1, n_2 ... n_k. Assume the data broadcast cycle length is L. Let L_2 denote the access time of a query result set with a query window size of (q_x, q_y). Let L_1 and L_3 denote the time before L_2 and after L_2 (Fig. 5). It is easy to see that $L=L_1+L_2+L_3$, $L_1 = \min\{ \pi(n_1), \pi(n_2),... \pi(n_k) \}$, and

$L_2 = \max\{ \pi(n_1), \pi(n_2),... \pi(n_k) \} - \min\{ \pi(n_1), \pi(n_2),... \pi(n_k) \}$.

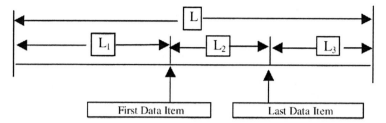

Fig. 5. Illustration of L_1, L_2 and L_3

Since a client might begin to access data channel at any position (between 0 and L), we need to consider the following three cases separately. We first compute the total access time in these three cases and then compute the average.

Case1: Begin access in L_1, the total access time is the sum of the rest of L_1 and the whole L_2:

$$\sum_{i=0}^{L_1-1} (L_1 - i + L_2) = \frac{L_1(L_1 + 1)}{2} + L_1 * L_2$$

Case 2: Begin access in L_2, the total access time is equivalent to the whole broadcast cycle regardless of the access position:

$$\sum_{i=0}^{L_2-1} L = L * L_2$$

Case 3: Begin access in L_3, the total access time is equal to the rest of L_3 in the current broadcast cycle plus $L_1 + L_2$ in the next broadcast cycle:

$$\sum_{i=0}^{L_3-1} (L_3 - i + L_1 + L_2) = \sum_{i=0}^{L_3-1} (L - i) = L_3 * L - \frac{L_3(L_3 - 1)}{2}$$

The average access time is :

$$\frac{1}{L} [\frac{L_1(L_1 + 1)}{2} + L_1 * L_2 + L * L_2 + L_3 * L - \frac{L_3(L_3 - 1)}{2}]$$

$$= \frac{1}{L} [\frac{(L_1 + L_3)(L_1 - L_3 + 1)}{2} + L_1 * L_2 + L * (L_2 + L_3)]$$

$$= \frac{1}{L} [\frac{(L - L_2)(L_1 - L_3 + 1)}{2} + L_1 * L_2 + L * (L - L_1)]$$

$$= \frac{1}{L} [L^2 - L_1 * (L - L_2) + \frac{(L - L_2)(L_1 - L_3 + 1)}{2}]$$

$$= \frac{1}{L} [L^2 - \frac{(L - L_2)(2 * L_1 - L_1 + L_3 - 1)}{2}]$$

$$= \frac{1}{L} [L^2 - \frac{(L - L_2)(L_1 + L_3 - 1)}{2}]$$

$$= \frac{1}{L} [L^2 - \frac{(L - L_2)(L - L_2 - 1)}{2}]$$

From the result we can see that the average access time to the data channel is determined only by L and L_2. We can rewrite the average data access time as follows:

$$\frac{1}{L}[L^2 - \frac{(L-L_2)^2 - (L-L_2)}{2}]$$

$$= \frac{1}{L}[L^2 - \frac{(L-L_2)^2 - 2*(\frac{L-L_2}{2}) + (\frac{1}{2})^2 - \frac{1}{4}}{2}]$$

$$= \frac{1}{L}[L^2 + \frac{1}{8} - \frac{(L-L_2 - \frac{1}{2})^2}{2}]$$

Since $L_2 < L$, the average access time of a range query decreases monotonically as L_2 decreases. Since the number of data items in a query is usually much smaller than the number of data items to broadcast, we assume $L - L_2 >> 1$. Thus the formula can be simplified as

$$\frac{L}{2} + L_2 - \frac{L_2^2}{2L}.$$

3.3 Access Time for Processing All Queries

Let function $g(L_2)$ be $g(L_2) = \frac{L}{2} + L_2 - \frac{L_2^2}{2L}$. The total data access time for a query window (q_x, q_y) can be written as follows by summarizing the access time over all possible query result sets. Substituting L_2 back with

$\max\{ \pi(n_1), \pi(n_2),... \pi(n_k) \} - \min\{ \pi(n_1), \pi(n_2),... \pi(n_k) \}$, we have

$$Cost^{(q_x,q_y)}$$

$$= \sum_{1 \leq i < j \leq n} \tilde{A}_{ij}^{(q_x,q_y)} * g(|\pi(i) - \pi(j)|)$$

$$+ \sum_{1 \leq i < j \leq k \leq n} \tilde{A}_{i,j,k}^{(q_x,q_y)} * g(\max(\pi(i),\pi(j),\pi(k)) - \min(\pi(i),\pi(j),\pi(k)))$$

$$+ ...$$

$$+ \tilde{A}_{1,2,...n}^{(q_x,q_y)} * g(\max(\pi(1),\pi(2)...\pi(n)) - \min(\pi(1),\pi(2)...\pi(n)))$$

The final total access time will be the summation of $Cost^{(q_x,q_y)}$ over all possible query windows Q, i.e.,

$$Cost = \sum_{(qx,qy) \in Q} Cost^{(q_x,q_y)}$$

$$= \sum_{(qx,qy) \in Q} [\sum_{1 \leq i < j \leq n} \tilde{A}_{ij}^{(q_x,q_y)} * g(|(\pi(i) - \pi(j)|)]$$

$$+ \sum_{(qx,qy) \in Q} [\sum_{1 \leq i < j \leq k \leq n} \tilde{A}_{i,j,k}^{(q_x,q_y)} * g(\max(\pi(i),\pi(j),\pi(k)) - \min(\pi(i),\pi(j),\pi(k)))]$$

$$+ ...$$

$$+ \sum_{(qx,qy) \in Q} \tilde{A}_{1,2...n}^{(q_x,q_y)} * g(\max(\pi(1),\pi(2)...\pi(n)) - \min(\pi(1),\pi(2)...\pi(n)))$$

Let

$$w_{i,j} = \sum_{(qx,qy)\in Q} \tilde{A}_{i,j}^{(q_x,q_y)}$$

$$w_{i,j,k} = \sum_{(qx,qy)\in Q} \tilde{A}_{i,j,k}^{(q_x,q_y)}$$

$$\ldots$$

$$w_{1,2,\ldots n} = \sum_{(qx,qy)\in Q} \tilde{A}_{1,2,\ldots n}^{(q_x,q_y)}$$

Then

$$Cost =$$

$$\sum_{1\le i<j\le n} w_{i,j} * g(|\pi(i)-\pi(j)|)$$

$$+ \sum_{1\le i<j\le k\le n} w_{i,j,k} * g(\max(\pi(i),\pi(j),\pi(k)) - \min(\pi(i),\pi(j),\pi(k)))$$

$$+ \ldots$$

$$+ w_{1,2,\ldots n} * g(\max(\pi(1),\pi(2)\ldots\pi(n)) - \min(\pi(1),\pi(2)\ldots\pi(n)))$$

It is easy to observe that the cost model we have developed is similar to the Minimum Linear Arrangement (MinLA) problem in graph theory defined as follows (Daíz, 2002):

$$la(G) = \sum_{(u,v)\in E} w(u,v) * |\pi(u)-\pi(v)|$$

There are two differences between MinLA and our cost model. First, there are multiple data items in a query result set and a hyper-graph representation is more appropriate for our cost model than a graph representation for MinLA. Second, our cost model is quadratic with respect to the differences in the positions of the beginning and ending nodes in a hyper-edge while it is linear in MinLA. It might be interesting to extend the existing low computation cost approximation methods for MinLA (Bar-Yehuda, 2001; Koren, 2002) to optimise access time based on our cost model which we leave for our future work.

4   Experiments and Results

4.1   Ordering Heuristics

The order of the geographical data items in a broadcast channel determines the total access time of spatial range queries on such data items. Space Filling Curves (SFC,

Gade, 1998), such as row-wise enumeration of the cells, Peano curve or Z-Ordering, Hilbert-Ordering and Gray-Ordering, which transforms multi-dimensional data into one-dimension can be used to generate orderings by comparing the SFC codes. Although spatial index trees such as R-Tree family (Guttman, 1984; Sellis, 1987; Beckmann, 1990) are not originally designed to be aware of the order of data items, traversals of these trees do generate orderings that can be used to sequence the data items. Since spatial indexing methods usually maintain spatial adjacencies, the orderings generated by SFCs and spatial index tree traversals are good candidates with low computation costs. We will evaluate the performances of the two heuristics based on our cost model using a real data set.

4.2 Experiments Setup

We use a data set from the MapInfo census 2000 data samples ([HREF 1]). There are 586 points in the area representing service locations, such as hospitals and parks. The data set is shown in Fig. 6. We choose four query window sizes with $q_x=q_y$ (We thus use q_x to denote the query window size hereafter). The sizes of the query windows are 0.5, 1.0, 2.5 and 5.0 miles respectively. We believe they are meaningful in practice. The C program from ([HREF 2]) was used to generate the Hilbert codes for all the points. The codes are then sorted to generate the Hilbert ordering. We also obtain the code from ([HREF 3]) to generate the R-trees and their traversal orderings. To investigate the effect of the branch factor in generating R-Tree traversal ordering, we vary its value factor from 4 to 19.

4.3 Results and Discussion

The results of the total access times versus the branch factors for the four query window sizes are shown in Fig 7. Note that the absolute access time values presented in this section does not reflect the constant factor as discussed in Section 3.1.

Fig. 6. The Data Set

From the results we can see that the totalaccess time does not have a perceivable relationship with the R-Tree branch factor. An obvious pattern in the results is that the total access time has a strong relationship with the query window size. Interestingly the total access times reach their maximum for the query window size of 2.5 miles. We suspect that this pattern is rather data-dependent.

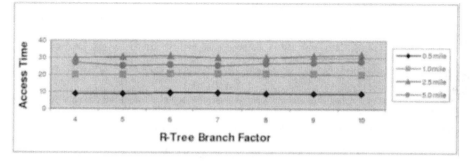

Fig. 7. Access Time vs. R-Tree Branch Factor

By comparing the result of Hilbert ordering and R-Tree traversal orderings we can see that Hilbert ordering is generally better than the best R-tree orderings. In Table 1the access time of Hilbert ordering is compared with the minimum access times of R-tree orderings for all the four window sizes. The result suggests that the Hilbert ordering is about 9% better than the R-Tree traversal ordering on average.

Table 1. Comparison of Hilbert and Best R-Tree Traversal Orderings

Query Window Size (Miles)	Hilbert (A)	Best R-Tree (B)	(B-A)/A (%)
0.5	8.33124	8.92838	7.17%
1.0	18.03957	20.12991	11.59%
2.5	27.09348	30.08675	11.05%
5	23.51733	25.49852	8.42%

5   Conclusions and Future Work Directions

We believe we are the first to address the problem of spatial range queries over broadcast geographical data. We developed a precise and concise cost model for data access time in processing spatial range queries on broadcast geographical data. We also presented several heuristics in generating orderings and evaluate their performances based on the cost model.

For future work, we first would like to extend our cost models to handle the access time both to the data channel and the index channel. Second, we want to optimise the access time by generating better orderings based on our cost model. Finally we would like to do more experiments using real data sets as well as synthetic data sets to evaluate the cost models, ordering heuristics and optimization methods.

References

N.Beckmann, H.-P. Kriegel, R.Schneider, B.Seeger, The R*-tree: An efficient and robust access method for points and rectangles. SIGMOD Conference, 1990:322–331

Y. C. Chehadeh, A. R. Hurson, Mohsen Kavehrad: Object Organization on a Single Broadcast Channel in the Mobile Computing Environment. Multimedia Tools and Applications 9(1): 69–94 (1999)

Josep Daíz and Jordi Petit and María Serna: A Survey on Graph Layout Problems. *ACM* Computing Surveys, 34(3): 313–356 (2002)

Yon Dohn Chung, Myoung-Ho Kim: Effective Data Placement for Wireless Broadcast. Distributed and Parallel Databases 9(2): 133–150 (2001)

V.Gaede, O.Günther: Multidimensional access methods. ACM Computing Survey, 30(2):170–231 (1998)

A.Guttman, R-trees: A dynamic index structure for spatial searching. SIGMOD Conference, 1984:47–54

S. Hambrusch, C.-M. Liu, W. Aref, S. Prabhakar: Query Processing in Broadcasted Spatial Index Trees. SSTD,2001: 502–521

Qinglong Hu, Wang-Chien Lee, Dik Lun Lee: A Hybrid Index Technique for Power Efficient Data Broadcast. Distributed and Parallel Databases, 9(2): 151–177 (2001)

Qinglong Hu, Wang-Chien Lee, Dik Lun Lee: Indexing Techniques for Power Management in Multi-Attribute Data Broadcast. MONET 6(2): 185–197 (2001)

T. Imielinski, S. Viswanathan, B. R. Badrinath: Energy Efficient Indexing On Air. SIGMOD Conference, 1994:25–36

T. Imielinski, S. Viswanathan, B. Badrinath: Power Efficient Filtering of Data on Air. EDBT, 1994: 245–258

T. Imielinski, S. Viswanathan, B. R. Badrinath, Data on Air: Organization and Access. IEEE Transactions on Knowledge and Data Engineering, 9(3): 353–372 (1997)

Birgitta König-Ries, etc.: Report on the NSF Workshop on Building an Infrastructure for Mobile and Wireless Systems. SIGMOD Record 31(2): 73–79 (2002)

Y. Koren, D. Harel: A Multi-Scale Algorithm for the Linear Arrangement Problem, Lecture Notes in Computer Science, Vol. 2573, Springer Verlag, 2002:293–306

Guanling Lee, Shou-Chih Lo, Arbee L. P. Chen: Data Allocation on Wireless Broadcast Channels for Efficient Query Processing. IEEE Transactions on Computers 51(10): 1237–1252 (2002)

Wang-Chien Lee, Dik Lun Lee, Using Signature Techniques for Information Filtering in Wireless and Mobile Environments. Distributed and Parallel Databases, 4(3): 205–227 (1996)

Bernd-Uwe Pagel, Hans-Werner Six, Heinrich Toben, Peter Widmayer: Towards an Analysis of Range Query Performance in Spatial Data Structures. PODS 1993: 214–221

Philippe Rigaux, Michel O. Scholl, Agnes Voisard, Spatial Databases: With Application to GIS, San Diego, CA: Academic Press 2002

T. Sellis, N. Roussopoulos and C. Faloutsos. The R+-Tree: A Dynamic Index for Multi-Dimensional Objects. VLDB Journal, 1987:507–518

Ayse Y. Seydim, Margaret H. Dunham, Vijay Kumar: Location dependent query processing. MobiDE, 2001: 47–53

Yannis Theodoridis, Timos K. Sellis: A Model for the Prediction of R-tree Performance. PODS 1996: 161–171

Yannis Theodoridis, Emmanuel Stefanakis, Timos K. Sellis: Efficient Cost Models for Spatial Queries Using R-Trees. TKDE 12(1): 19–32 (2000)

Reuven Bar-Yehuda, Computing an optimal orientation of a balanced decomposition tree for linear arrangement problems. Journal of Graph Algorithms and Applications, 5(4): 1–27 (2001)

[HREF 1] Http://www.mapinfo.com

[HREF 2] http://www.caam.rice.edu/~dougm/twiddle/Hilbert/

[HREF 3] http://www.cs.ucr.edu/~marioh/rtree/index.html

Context-Aware Data Mining Framework for Wireless Medical Application

Pravin Vajirkar, Sachin Singh, and Yugyung Lee

School of Computing and Engineering,
University of Missouri–Kansas City,
Kansas City, MO 64110 USA.
{ppv22e,sbs7vc,leeyu}@umkc.edu

Abstract. Data mining, which aims at extracting interesting information from large collections of data, has been widely used as an effective decision making tool. Mining the datasets in the presence of context factors may improve performance and efficacy of data mining by identifying the unknown factors, which are not easily detectable in the process of generating an expected outcome. This paper proposes a Context-aware data mining framework, by which contexts will be automatically captured to maximize the adaptive capacity of data mining. Context could consist of any circumstantial factors of the user and domain that may affect the data mining process. The factors that may affect the mining behavior are delineated and how each factor affects the behavior is discussed. It is also observed that a medical application of the model in wireless devices offers the advantages of Context-aware data mining. A Context-aware data mining framework is quantified through a partial implementation that would be used to test the behavior of the mining system under varied context factors. The results obtained from the implementation process are elucidated on how the prediction output or the behavior of the system changes from the similar set of inputs in view of different context factors.

1 Introduction

Context-awareness computing work has been carried out by many researchers [4, 2,1]. Many of them have been worked on defining Context-awareness and some of them are mainly focusing on building Context-aware applications. However, little has been done in building a framework which supports data mining based on Context awareness leading to useful and accurate information extraction.

Context is a powerful, long-standing concept. In computer-human interaction it can be mostly captured via explicit models of communication (e.g., user query inputs). However, implicit context factors (e.g., physical environmental conditions, location, time etc.) are normally ignored due to absence of knowledge base or appropriate model. We believe implicit context-aware factors could be used to interpret and enhance explicit user inputs and thereby affecting data mining results to deliver accurate and precise prediction results.

V. Mařík et al. (Eds.): DEXA 2003, LNCS 2736, pp. 381–391, 2003.
© Springer-Verlag Berlin Heidelberg 2003

Nowadays, huge volume of data is available. This data-rich environment does not guaranty for information-rich environment. Data mining is a process that discovers patterns in data that may be used for valid predictions [6]. We focus on building a context-aware data mining framework that can filter useful and interesting context factors, produce accurate and precise prediction using those factors.

This framework was designed keeping the medical applications in mind, even though it is generic in nature and can be used in any domain. Medical professionals are always on-the-go. The use of decision support PDA supported by data mining facility can be of great asset to the medical professionals while working on an emergency or while rushing to attend an emergency. Even in other domains, getting the data mining based services on a mobile device can be of substantial utility, like a stock broker getting the predicted value of stocks on his PDA. Presenting the information on a PDA deals with a set of constraints due to its restricted resources like memory, screen and CPU power. Providing Data Mining services on a PDA is a case of a very *thin* client communicating with a very *fat* server, required a huge amount of processing. Despite the technical challenges that one faces due to the limited computing power of mobile devices, it provides a great deals of portability, mobility and practical usage to the proposed context-aware data mining framework.

2   What Is Context-Awareness?

The concept of *Context* have often been interwoven and used in many different applications. Depending upon the application an information may be interpreted as a *meaningful* but in another context, as a meaningless. Thus, when the information has to be conveyed from one element to another, the interpretation of information can be changed particularly depending on the context of the information.

Dey and Abowd [4] defined *context* as a piece of information that can be used to characterize the situation of participants in an interaction. Similarly, [2,1] defined context as information on the location, environment, identity of people in a certain situation. By sensing context information, context enabled applications can present context information to users, or modify their behavior according to changes in the environment [8]. Chen and Kotz [3] defined *context* as the set of environmental states and settings that either determines what an application behavior is or where the event occurs. Schilit and Theimer [10] emphasized the importance of applications which adapt themselves to context.

There are some definitions which were too broad to apply to any application while some are too specific to certain domains. In real-world datasets, the context-aware factors that constitute context-awareness change rapidly and therefore the factors tend to become subjective and very domain specific. Our challenge in this paper is to make the concept *hybrid* (combining generic and domain specific). From our point of view on context, lack of context-awareness leads to missing a lot of critical and useful information that would affect the data mining process and thereby, affecting the data mining results. Our definition of the context is the information regarding objects (including actors) which supports the entire process from the user query to the mining. More importantly, the context will provide the system the ability to adapt to a changing environment during the data mining process and thereby providing the users with a time sensitive data accurately, efficiently and in a precise manner.

We now define the types of context factors:

User Context: *User Identity Context* describes the information of user responsible for the query including his/her field of expertise, authorization of tasks or datasets, his/her team members and their expertise fields. *User History Context* describes the history (i.e., user-profiling) built up for each user when he/she queries for a particular information. This helps when the user frequently queries with a similar query or uses the same piece of information.

Application Context describes the evolving context with the application specific and wireless features. *Joint Conference Context*: A specific query on patient can perform jointly to combine related information, such as a conference with neuro-surgeon and diabetics specialist. The context-ware data mining enables all related areas of work related to the patient to be covered and ensure for the patient's well-being as developed at Future Computing Environment [5]. *Time Context*: Time is an important aspect to certain domains such as stock market, war planning or medicine. Considering an example of diagnosis of diabetics, the sugar level tends to drop at night than in day time. It is also higher an hour after meals than before meal. We can have different datasets on the bases of at what period of time the blood sample was collected to get better prediction outputs.

Data Context. *Domain Context* describes domain specific context. In our medical application, it is *Patient Context* which captures the personal and medical history of the patient. It also records the immediate family members and their medical history. *Location Context:* The importance of this context lies in the fact that it can be used to cluster datasets. For example, assume that we have collected the dataset from different zone/states/countries etc. If the patient under consideration falls in any one of these parameters, then the system should extract a set of records, which correspond to the particular zone and then use this subset for mining. The datasets primary formed from the population living near a certain location as living area is related to health issues. For example, people living in coastal regions have less probability of getting goiter. Similar, people living in the country side have less tendency to get high blood pressure as compared to suburban folks. It would be a good idea to pick the datasets depending on the location context of the patient. This may improve the accuracy of the system, wherein we just concentrate on the data more relevant to him/her than the generic data. If the patient doesn't fall in any one of the zones, then the system can approximate his datasets to the zone closest to him/her or use the default datasets or combination of two zones etc.

Data Mining Context describes attributes related to the data-mining query: *Data Context* As the data is distributed in a typical domain, it is im-

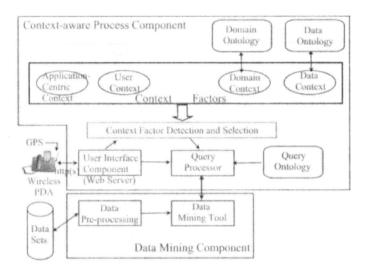

Fig. 1. System Architecture

portant to determine which dataset to be mined for a given context. *Attribute Context* The classification of Data mining [11,7,6] builds a model (e.g., a decision tree in C4.5) as a prediction model and querying this tree based on the user inputs leads to predicting the value of desired information. Since these models are built with the attributes whose prediction is to be made, it is important to identify which attributes should be chosen for a query in a given context. *Performance Context* describes the time taken for data mining process. This addresses the classic question of speed vs. accuracy issue in data mining. Certain applications would require faster responses for multiple attributes even if the accuracy is not the best. For example, stock applications which predict stock prices of numerous companies pretty quickly with reduced accuracy. Certain applications, however, would require highest accuracy even if it takes time. Medical applications where the prediction values would be critical for a future course of treatment to be given to a patient has to be accurate even if it takes more time. Thus, depending on the context the framework may choose an appropriate algorithm for the mining process.

3   Context-Aware Data Mining Framework

We propose a context-aware framework which considers context factors during data mining process. As a proof of concept, we have implemented a decision support system for wireless medical applications. Figure 1 shows the system architecture of the Context-aware data mining framework.

Context-aware Process Component handles context factors for Data mining and Query processor components. In this component, Context factors such as *Application Context, User Context, Domain Context, Data Context* are defined as described in Section 2. In order to identify context factors from the implicit information of the user's query, we perform the processes including checking the attributes of the user query; learning about the entities of the query context. For instance, Heather has an allergic symptom and is living in Huntsville, AL. The model can analyze Huntsville's pollen grain content at that period of the year and season and invokes subsequent processes such as selecting the desired datasets for the data mining component; discovering missing entities: Comparing with the datasets, missing entities that might help in mining the data accurately can be identified; classifying the discovered entities based on the Context-Aware factors; resolving any missing, ambiguous and conflicting information with minimum user's involvement.

Ontology Component defines a high level meta-data information about the existing datasets, users, and mining tools. For instance, the domain ontology stores knowledge about the existing datasets like relationships between datasets at structural level and also at the semantic level. For example, if one gives queries for diabetics datasets with a missing parameters for say, blood pressure. The missing value can be predicted from the blood pressure dataset. Interestingly, we may mine more datasets to fill in the missing attributes.

Data-mining Component consists of two subcomponents. The first one is a preprocessing component which converts the existing datasets format into the format acceptable by the data mining tool. The second subcomponent is the actual data mining tool (Weka3[1]) which requires ARFF format as input. The tool mines the datasets, given the input parameters, like the datasets name, query elements and values, etc. This subcomponent accepts the preprocessed datasets and the query parameters and returns the queried result.

User Interface Component is a Web Server component which interacts with the client subsystems on the PDA over HTTP(S). Once it receives a request from the user, it forwards it to the Query Processor. At the same time, it also passes the query to the Context Factor component that determines which context factors are applicable for the given query. After determining which ones are applicable it extracts the relevant information from the query and passes it to the Query Processor.

Query Processor has all the information explicitly given by the user in the form of the query and all implicit information from the Context component. The Query Processor may use the output of one query as an input to other query and so on till it gets all the inputs required for the original query that the user had requested. In case of still-missing attributes, user input will be requested. Thus the Query Processor can be considered as a Meta task manager, managing multiple atomic tasks which are part of the same high level task. After the Meta task is executed the final result is returned to the user over HTTP(S) to the PDA as the prediction or query results. Using appropriate domain-specific query ontology it will construct an appropriate query/set of queries.

---

[1] http://www.cs.waikato.ac.nz/ ml/weka/index.html

4   Medical Scenarios

The usage of Context-aware factors tends to change the data mining behavior by the pruning the user query by attaching its context factors. These factors could affect the change by picking different and the correct datasets, changing its query values itself, attaching missing query values to its attributes, and/or affecting the change using different data mining algorithms, etc.

Case 1: Diabetes Treatment. Dr. Smith is a female diabetics specialist. He has a patient named Martha whose report show a high level of sugar in blood. Dr. Smith can always rely on his experience and prudence, though he would like to explore the advantages of data mining techniques which can derive some useful information from historical data. For this scenario, we have selected a diabetes dataset[2]. The attributes from 1st - 8th are the patients inputs while 9th (Class) is the output results which supports his treatment decision for Martha. The dataset attributes for the Diabetics are follows: [min, max, mean, SD].

1. Number of times pregnant [0, 17, 3.84, 3.36]
2. Plasma glucose concentration a 2 hours in an oral glucose tolerance test [0, 199, 120.89, 31.97]
3. Diastolic blood pressure (mm Hg) [0, 122, 69.10, 19.35]
4. Triceps skin fold thickness (mm) [0, 99, 20.53, 15.95]
5. 2-Hour serum insulin (mu U/ml) [0, 846, 79.79, 115.24]
6. Body mass index (weight in kg/(height in $m)^2$) [0, 67.1, 31.99, 7.88]
7. Diabetes pedigree function [0.078, 2.42, 0.471, 0.331]
8. Age (years) [21, 81, 33.24, 11.76]
9. Class variable (0 or 1) [Discrete][500-negative, 268-positive]

Table 1 shows the interpretation of the given diabetes dataset from the perspective of our context-aware model.

Case 2: Heart Attack Risk. In this scenario Dr. Smith is interested in determining whether the major blood vessel is <50% or >50% narrowed as a measure of a probable heart attack risk. This could form the basis of further action that he may take in treating the patient. The effect of context factors can be explained in the light of a carefully selected scenario. The datasets we have chosen is the heart datasets[3] as our proof-of-concept. This real-life datasets was customized to make use of other related datasets and to prove the validity of our context factors. Let us consider the datasets attributes first.

1. (age) Age in years
2. (sex) Sex (1: Male; 0: Female)
3. (chest_pain) chest pain type (1: Typical angina; 2: Atypical angina; 3: Non-anginal pain, Value 4: Asymptomatic)
4. (trestbps) resting blood pressure (in mm Hg on admission to the hospital)
5. (chol) Serum cholestoral in mg/dl

[2] http://kdd.ics.uci.edu/
[3] http://kdd.ics.uci.edu/

Table 1. Case1: Interpretation of Context-Aware Factors

Location Context	The record history used in diabetes dataset is explicitly from the area near Phoenix, Arizona. The user has a choice to pick location specific if he believes that the problem has no regard to location change. Some results are more location sensitive than the other. Here in this case, there is no direct relation to location.
Application Context	Dr. Smith may want to discuss the discovered result with gynecologist (if Martha is pregnant), or with a blood pressure expert to jointly come to an effective diagnostic treatment.
User Context	According to user's specified area of interest, a user profile can be developed. For an advanced user, his various query records and statistics allow him know about the risk factors of the results. In this case, he may query diabetes dataset, jointly with other datasets (e.g. blood pressure, pregnancy, etc). The selecting these datasets can be done by analyzing Dr. Smith's profile and a flavored output can be generated.
Data Mining Context	Five of input details about Martha are known and rest are unknown or uncertain. The application would try to fill in the void data by asking relative queries to the model and using the supporting dataset. The input attribute 7 from the diabetes which asks the user about the pedigree value for Martha. The application would very closely speculate the value based on family history, genetic history, and nursing assessments.

6. (fbs) (Fasting blood sugar >120 mg/dl) (1: True; 0: False)
7. (restecg) resting electrocardiographic results (0: Normal; 1: ST-T wave abnormality; 2: Definite left ventricular hypertrophy)
8. (thalach) Maximum heart rate achieved
9. (exang) Exercise induced angina (1 = yes; 0 = no)
10. (oldpeak) ST depression induced by exercise relative to rest
11. (slope) The slope of the peak exercise ST segment (1: upsloping; 2: flat; 3: downsloping)
12. (ca) Number of major vessels (0-3) colored by flourosopy
13. (thal) the heart status (3: Normal; 6: Fixed defect; 7: Reversible defect)
14. (Family-Hist) - History of any heart disease within immediate family (1: True; 0: False)
15. (Smoke-Disease) - Symptoms of smoke disease
16. (Location) - Location of the person where he lives.
17. (num) Diagnosis of heart disease (angiographic disease status) (0: <50% Diameter narrowing; 1: >50% Diameter narrowing)

We have selected attribute 17 as the pivot element to form the prediction value in the classification tree. Apparently, we need a few more factors to determine the value of our pivot element. Most of the elements from attribute 4 through attribute 13 are standard clinical tests and should be available to doctor. Table 2 shows the interpretation of the given heart attack risk datasets from the perspective of our context-aware model.

It is worthwhile to note that though this scenario brings up the possible uses of different context factors, it also highlights the different behavior of the

Table 2. Case 2: Interpretation of Context-Aware Factors

Data Context	This parameter refers to any health affects caused by say, smoking. Determining whether a person has smoking ill effects is in itself a sub-problem. Here we refer to dataset which has information like (1) Smoking since (2) Cigarettes per day (3) Quitting period. Based on these input parameters from the user, the system picks up another dataset referring to smoking, say *Smoking Effects*. We perform mining with this dataset to build the classification tree and thereby to predict the person's smoking problems. Using the input parameter for the given patient, the system will query the above tree and predict whether the patient has smoking problems. The predicted output is the input to the original user query and is used to plug in the smoking attribute to the original classification tree for the heart disease. It is so because one of the inputs to the original query is output after the system selects related datasets. In this case, the system will select the auxiliary datasets only if the patient ever smoked. Thus based on the context different datasets are picked up to query and used in plug-in the missing attribute value(s).
Patient Context	The system knows the patient's immediate family members. For each of these members it can access the *Historical patient repository*. We are assuming that hospitals maintain some medical record of each patient in history about what disease they had in past, etc. If any one of these members had any such a medical condition, it can be picked up as input.
Location Context	Location is less likely affect to the data mining behavior because Location here is not an input to the system. But there are cases that a context factor can affect the output given the same input parameters.

system. First, the system picks up a data value from a record to plug in to another datasets. The idea is the system to *know* where to pick and plug the data. Second, the system *trims* or *customizes* the data. For instance, the system can filter relevant datasets attributes for mining. Third, the system picks up related auxiliary datasets, mines it, and grabs a predicted value to use this output for querying the main datasets classification tree. Finally, we also think of *hybrid* behavior, where the system picks values as combination of all approaches discussed above and then computes the values by using some domain-specific formulae. Example, for height/weight ratio parameter, we can grab height and weight as two different values and then compute its ratio.

5   Implementation and Experimental Results

The proposed framework has been implemented in a wireless J2ME[4] enabled, CLDC[5] (Connected-Limited Device Configuration) complaint PDA (Personal Digital Assistant). The communication from PDA to the server is made through HTTPS connection, so make the connection secure. The connection is established at the physical layer and the user is given the desired output on his/her

---

[4] http://java.sun.com/j2me/
[5] http://0511704376-0001.bei.t-online.de/seiten/indexeh.htm

PDA screen. The application contains palm-sized PDA that would communicate with the computer, enabling *Context-aware data mining framework*. The wireless component is assumed to have following capabilities and features.

Now we will show the experimental results regarding the heart attack risk case. The dataset selected is the heart dataset[6] that stores the history of patients with heart diseases. The dataset consists of following attributes:

- Personal details: *age* in years and *sex* (1 = male; 0 = female)
- Cardiac Details: *painloc* : chest pain location (1: substernal; 0: otherwise)
- The prediction output for this dataset is *num*: the diameter of the artery (angiographic disease status) (0: < 50% diameter narrowing; 1: > 50% diameter narrowing)

The user requests a query, which consists of inputs. He/she expects an outcome prediction value *num*. The system performs data mining using all attributes and entire datasets to construct the model. Using this model, it will apply the query variables to get the prediction result. We applied the J48 algorithm [11] and build a decision tree using C4.5 [7] on the heart dataset. Figure 2 (Case 1) shows the classification tree generated using the decision tree.

Case 1: Classification Tree
exang= no
   oldpeak _ 1: < 50 (190.0/27.0)
   oldpeak > 1
      slope = down: > 50 1 (0.0)
      slope= flat
         sex = female: < 50 (3.0/1.0)
         sex = male: > 50 1 (8.0)
      slope = up: < 50 (3.7)
   exang = yes: > 50 1 (89.3/19.3)

Case 3: Classification Tree
exang = no: < 50 (64.82/4.0)
exang = yes
   thalach _ 108: > 50 1 (3.04/0.04)
   thalach> 108
      chol _ 254: < 50 (4.0)
      chol > 254
   thalach _ 127: < 50 (4.08/1.0)
   thalach > 127: > 50 1 (3.06/0.06)

Case 2: Classification Tree
exang= no
   oldpeak _ 1: < 50 (129.0/24.0)
   oldpeak > 1
      slope = down: > 50 1 (0.0)
      slope = flat: > 50 1 (8.0)
      slope = up: < 50 (2.0)
exang= yes
   chest pain = typ angina: > 50 1 (0.0)
   chest pain = asympt: > 50 1 (62.0/6.0)
   chest pain = non anginal
      age _ 55: > 50 1 (3.0/1.0)
      age > 55: < 50 (2.0)
   chest pain = atyp angina
      oldpeak _ 1.5: < 50 (4.0/1.0)
      oldpeak > 1.5: > 50 1 (3.0)

Fig. 2. The Experimental Results

Using the meta-level understanding, we know that the personal detailed attributes can be patient-contexts. In our case, we considered *Sex* as a context factor. We will use the same query inputs to analyze the change. The application is now *context-aware* so it knows that part of the query where the *Sex* variable is actually a context input. Male persons can have different factors affecting more predominantly as compared to female ones. If we mine the datasets differently we may get interesting results. So if the user query variable is *Sex=male*, then it may not make sense to mine the entire dataset and then query the model and get the results. We have retrieved only those records that are males, and then mine

---

[6] http://www.cs.waikato.ac.nz/ ml/weka/arff.html

the dataset excluding the *Sex* column. We performed a vertical and horizontal trimming of dataset. The data model mined out of this could be called as *specialized* dataset. In our experiments we mined the datasets separating on basis of *Sex* as context information. Figure 2 (Case 2) shows the C4.5 tree corresponding to males. As is evident from the figure the new model shows emergence of some new factors in the decision making tree which were not appearing in the non Context-aware factor domains. The Context-aware factors can achieve different results and also give more insight of the trend in the dataset and their interrelations. Figure 2 (Case 3) shows the classification tree when entering a constraint *Sex = female*.

Thus, we can improve the accuracy of the data mining process or simple bring out the "suppressed" trends within the data by suitably applying context factors to the data mining process.

6   Conclusion

In this paper we have introduced an application model for providing accuracy and precision to data-mining prediction results based on context-aware factors. The model is wrapped on a wireless framework to provide user-friendliness, mobility and practical usage. The model proposed is generic in nature and can be applied to most of the fields. Two scenarios were provided as a proof of concept to our proposed model. Much of the work is focused on combining Context-aware, data-mining and wireless communication and towards feasibility of such a model. The model is tested and implemented with live and customized medical datasets to make the model efficient.

References

1. Brown, P.J.: The Stick-e Document: a Framework for Creating Context-Aware Applications. Electronic Publishing '96 (1996) 259–272
2. Brown, P.J., Bovey, J.D., Chen, X.: Context-Aware Applications: From the Laboratory to the Marketplace. IEEE Personal Communications, **4(5)** (1997) 58–64
3. Chen, G., Kotz, D.: A Survey of Context-Aware Mobile Computing Research. Dartmouth Computer Science Technical Report TR2000-381
4. Dey, A.K., Abowd, G.D.: Towards a better understanding of Context and Context-Awareness. GVU Technical Report GITGVU-99-22, College of Computing, Georgia Institute of Technology. **2** (1999) 2–14
5. Dey, A.K., Futakawa, M., Salber, D., Abowd, G.D.: The Conference Assistant: Combining Context-Awareness with Wearable Computing. In Proceedings of the 3rd International Symposium on Wearable Computers (ISWC '99), 21–28, San Francisco, CA, October 1999. IEEE Computer Society Press.
6. Edelstein, H. A.: Introduction to Data Mining and Knowledge Discovery, Two Crows Corporation, 1999. ISBN: 1-892095-02-5
7. Ragone, A.: Machine Learning C4.5 Decision Tree Generator
8. Salber, D., Dey A.K., Orr, R.J., Abowd, G.D.: Designing For Ubiquitous Computing: A Case Study in Context Sensing, GVU Technical Report GIT-GVU 99-29, (http://www.gvu.gatech.edu/)

9. Schilit, B., Adams, N., Want, R.: Context-Aware computing applications. In Proceedings of IEEE Workshop on Mobile Computing Systems and Applications, 85–90, Santa Cruz, California, December 1994. IEEE Computer Society Press.
10. Schilit, B., Theimer, M.: Disseminating Active Map Information to Mobile Hosts. IEEE Network,**8(5)** (1994) 22–32
11. Witten, I.H., Frank, E.: Data Mining: Practical Machine Learning Tools and Techniques with Java Implementations. Morgan Kaufmann, 1999.

Data Management in Metaboloinformatics: Issues and Challenges

Sourav S. Bhowmick[1], Dadabhai T Singh[1], and Amey Laud[2]

[1] School of Computer Engineering
Nanyang Technological University
Singapore 639798
assourav@ntu.edu.sg
[2] HeliXense Pte Ltd
73 Science Park Drive
02-05 Science Park 1
Singapore 118254
{dtsingh,alaud}@helixense.com

Abstract. *Metaboloinformatics* can be considered as derivation of knowledge from computer analysis of *metabolomite* resources. *Metabolomics* is the systematic analysis of thousands of non peptide small compounds such as sugars, fatty acids, vitamins etc. at the cellular and tissue level of a living organism. Using metabolomic technologies, researchers are able to systematically determine metabolite concentration in a sample. These developing technologies have the potential of being applied in the areas of drug discovery and development and preventive screening/diagnostics. In this paper, we identify the issues and challenges in metaboloinformatic data management. We also discuss how the *gRNA* can be used to address some the challenges in this field.

1 Introduction

Metaboloinformatics may be considered as derivation of knowledge from computer analysis of *metabolomite* resources. *Metabolomics* is the systematic analysis of thousands of non peptide small compounds such as sugars, fatty acids, vitamins etc. at the cellular and tissue level of a living organism [17]. Traditionally metabolites are studied at individual level or at the most at the concerned pathway level. These small molecules constitute the metabolome of an organism and metabolome is the natural successor of genome, transcriptome and proteome. However, unlike the other "omes" the study of metabolome as an integrated science is only couple of years old.

Biochemical pathways are analyzed, traditionally, at two levels: molecular genetic and biochemical. The importance of metabolic pathways combined with the recent advances in metabolic pathway engineering has stimulated the development of famous databases like KEGG [18], Ex Pasy [12], Brenda [9] etc. and a plethora of pathway analysis tools like Pathway tools [10], Gene networks [8] etc. All these developments are driven by the spectacular advances in molecular genetics and information technology over the past one decade.

V. Mařík et al. (Eds.): DEXA 2003, LNCS 2736, pp. 392–402, 2003.

The analysis of the intermediate compounds (biochemicals) of these pathways has been the main stream of biochemical research for ages. However, these intermediate metabolites were studied more from an academic point of view. The industrial exploitation of these intermediates, especially amino acid production, is well established. An industrial level microbial transformation system for efficient and large scale production of specific rare compounds such as flavins is also well established and is a multimillion dollar industry. Despite being studied and utilized in biochemical and pharmaceutical industries for decades at individual level, a systematic effort to visualize and exploit metabolome at organism level for human welfare has begun only recently.

There are two major reasons for this lack of effort at an "omics" level: lack of appropriate software tools and the lack of other relevant databases that need to be integrated and mined in conjunction with the biochemical data. Metabolites are frequently measured to provide information about system's response to environmental or physiological stresses. By systematic profiling, this information can be used for system response analysis at organism level. The natural extension of this study would be to integrate measurements of metabolites into a multiplayer characterization of system response. The first step towards understanding system response is to carry out a systematic analysis of all of the metabolites in the concerned pathways during a transient state where the fluxes are altered in response to various stimuli. Computational analysis of such metabolome data including polar and non polar metabolites in conjunction with global gene expression data and other relevant data would pave the way for the much promised and eagerly awaited era of "personalized" genomic medicine.

2 Issues in Metabolomics

In this section, we discuss various issues related to metabolomics. We first discuss the importance of metabolomics in disease diagnosis. Then, we discuss various sources of metabolomics data. Finally, we relate metabolomics and natural product research.

2.1 Metabolomics and Disease Diagnostics

A comparative analysis of the metabolome profiles between a normal tissue and a diseased tissue can be used to identify the biochemical pathways that are perturbed under diseased conditions. The identification of perturbed pathways greatly facilitates to pinpoint the defective gene or gene product. For example, simple blood sugar levels can lead to the diagnosis of diabetes, that of cholesterol to cardiovascular diseases etc. However, neither all disease diagnostics are that simple nor all diseases are biochemical pathway based. Improper analysis and interpretation of such individual metabolite based results can lead to fatal results.

Metabolomics has an equally important role in understanding and tracking an unwanted perturbation in related biochemical pathways subsequent to drug administration. Adverse drug reactions are known to cause more than two million hospitalizations and nearly 100,000 deaths in US alone [16]. It should be noted that despite the stringent measures being imposed by bodies like FDA, the increased time (from eight years in sixties to more than sixteen years today) and money (few million dollars in sixties to more than 800 million dollars today) spent [6], no clinical trial can be foolproof for prescribing a drug to general public at large. Ethnic and individual variations to drug response largely determine the success or a failure of an approved drug in the open market. Identification and utilization of toxicity biomarker data developed using metabolome data for patient screening during and after clinical trials may also rescue several drugs withdrawn from the market for wrong reasons.

The study of Metabolomics also helps in understanding the molecular basis of effective drugs whose targets/mechanism of action are unknown. Nearly 7% of the drugs in the market today belong to this class. Computational analysis of the changes in the metabolome profile of an organism subsequent to the administration of such drugs, can lead to valuable insights into the mechanism of action and target identification. This reverse pharmacology technique is also known as *chemical genetics* [21] and is rapidly gaining ground, especially in understanding the molecular mechanisms of natural products as potential drugs.

Increased biochemical awareness amongst the health care professionals and the rapid advances in biomedical sciences has resulted in a systematic analysis of all the related data for disease diagnostics. These efforts are rapidly taking the shape of invaluable databases. These databases are still at a very early stage of development and various international platforms have recognized the critical importance of these databases. However, the field of Medical informatics [5] is still in a transition stage and may take some more time to mature from patient records to metabolome databases. Such transition is evident in many developed and developing nations. Many research institutes, universities and pharmaceutical companies are in the process of developing these metabolomics databases and the development of software tools to mine and integrate these databases with other relevant databases is of prime importance today.

2.2   Sources of Metabolomics Data

Conventionally, metabolite analysis is the stronghold of the "chemists" in the biochemistry divisions. These chemists are well versed with the classical analytical chemistry techniques such as chromatography, colorimetry, spectrophotometry etc. Accordingly the sources of metabolome data is the output of related techniques like GC, GCMS, HPLC, NMR etc. Depending on the number of samples and tissues analyzed and the analytical complexity required in the lab involved, the data source may scale up from a simple gas chromatograph level to a highly complex NMR level. Each of these instruments is equipped with proprietary software to capture the analytical data and display the output either in the form of graphical data or tabular data or both. The molecular "signatures" obtained are rapidly compared against a reference data set and the results constitute the "raw" metabolome data. This process is also generally referred as *metabolite profiling* [22].

Many a time the software bundled along with the equipment is generally a stand alone application and does not interface with the outputs from other related equipments such as a spectrophotometer. Any high throughput lab uses robotic sample handling for efficient sample preparation. Sample preparation is a very complicated task in metabolite research as there a plethora of samples some of which are polar and some non polar. Hence, the solubility, extraction and analysis is a challenge for any analytical chemist.The samples thus prepared need to be tracked as they are processed through the processing pipeline. Hence, most of the high throughput labs employ a customized LIMS (Laboratory Information Management System) for the smooth flow and tracking of samples.

It is also often the case that different labs analyzing the same set of samples using different analytical techniques and different analytical instruments may need to complement their data sets with each other for a comprehensive analysis. The data generated under such disparate circumstances also need to be captured and made a part of the database.

The lack of standards in bioinformatics research is a much debated topic. One of the massive community efforts to impose standards in the microarray gene expression data submission has resulted in the development of a universally acceptable MAGE-ML [4] format now. Similar efforts are underway for the representation of proteome data, SNP data etc. Unfortunately, there are no such standards are readily available for the metabolite data. However, a growing metabolome community is becoming aware of these basic necessities and before long, it may be possible to have a standard format for the representation of metabolome data in databases.

The raw metabolome data available in several public and private research organizations needs to be converted and populated in commercial databases. There are a handful of software tools available commercially (Eclipse [3] from Chemonx Inc.) which specialize in capturing raw data from high throughput analytical techniques like NMR and populate in a commercial RDBMS. However, these tools are not useful for the creation of "meta" databases. The utility of metabolite databases can be fully realized only when these databases are integrated with other relevant databases such as global gene expression databases to form metadatabase.

2.3 Metabolomics and Natural Product Research

Metabolomics and the natural product research are intertwined in a way as most of the effective natural products are *secondary metabolites*, mostly from wild plants. Nearly 40,000 compounds have been identified from plants and more than 100,000 compounds are yet to be discovered. This multitude of compounds with different carbon skeletons and physicochemical properties makes plants, a rich source of pharmaceuticals in the form of lead compounds, health promoting compounds, flavor and fragrance compounds, toxins etc. The other well known sources for effective natural products are: marine organisms and micro organisms.

The drug discovery process starts with identification and sample collection from world wide resources. Sample storing and tracking is very critical at this stage and the role of LIMS starts as soon as samples are received in the lab. The next step is the sample preparation which involves use of high throughput robotics as the samples include a wide variety of compounds. Screening thousands of samples per day and determining their chemical structure is a very successful business model for many industries involved in *bioprospecting* [23]. The libraries of compounds thus generated are the sources for natural products databases. Several such databases exist both in public and private domain. However, unlike the other public domain databases, most of these databases have restricted access for obvious reasons.

The next step in the drug discovery process is the most critical *bioassay analysis*. The active ingredients identified and characterized may be single entity pharmaceutical ingredients or multicomponent botanical compounds. The bioassays to discover promising lead compounds may be a combination of mechanism blind and mechanism specific biological assays to detect agents that show novel activity against selected infectious diseases, cancer, and immunological targets. The promising single entity compounds form another rich database which is mined and used for the synthesis of analogues. The multicomponent botanical compounds are subjected to further reverse pharmacology tests as mentioned earlier. These formulations with novel pharmaceutical activity are further processed in the drug discovery pipeline involving the following studies: preclinical, analytical, preformulation, formulation and stability analysis.

At this stage a lot of software packages dedicated to the elucidation of structure activity relationship are used. Since most of these packages are commercial entities with proprietary formats, researchers have very little flexibility in extending the capabilities of these packages and also it often becomes impossible to make these packages interact with another set of tools.

2.4   Natural Products as Agrochemicals

The most important economic stabilization factor for any nation is its food security achieved through sustainable agriculture. The dramatic increase in crop productivity in several developed and developing nations over the past several decades can be mainly attributed to the development of high yielding crop varieties responsive to high nitrogenous fertilizer usage under irrigated conditions and the use of chemical pesticides to control insect pests, pathogens and weeds. However, excessive use and abuse of these chemicals have wrecked havoc on the environment and made agriculture unsustainable for many agrarian societies worldwide. Irresponsible use of pesticides has resulted in the development of insect pests and pathogens resistant to many chemical pesticides.

The global market for fertilizers in 2001 was about $50 billion [7]. Many crop plants are limited by their ability to utilize the added fertilizer. Agronomic practices which include the utilization of natural product formulations such as neem cake, castor cake etc. have been reported to enhance the ability of crop plants to utilize the fertilizer added besides providing pest control activity. Several agrobusiness giants like Monsanto, CIBA etc. are investing heavily in R&D to identify the natural products that can add value to their products.

The global sales of chemical based pesticides in 2001 was more than $100 billion with herbicides like Roundup and fungicides like Tilt and Ridomil accounting for nearly $20 billion [7]. Conventionally, researchers have discovered new herbicide products by spraying various chemicals on weeds in the hope of finding a chemical that kills weeds without killing crops. Once a promising chemical is discovered, researchers use labour-intensive genetics, physiology and biochemistry techniques to determine the protein in the weed that the chemical affects. This conventional approach is expensive and slow and has a low success rate. Typically, researchers must screen 80,000 chemicals to find a commercial product. It is estimated that there are only 23 known mechanisms of herbicide action [7].

As with herbicides, researchers conventionally have discovered fungicides by spraying various chemicals on crops in the hope of finding a chemical that inhibits fungal infections on crops without killing the crops themselves. Until recently, researchers had not used an approach based upon the determination of gene function for fungicide discovery.

The use of natural products as insect repellents is gaining a lot of ground in view of the notorious ability of insects to develop resistance to chemical based insecticides and even to *transgenic Bt toxin* [20]. The ability of the natural products to repel the insect with out killing it may not force the insect to develop resistance. Thus several leading research groups are creating databases consisting of libraries of such chemicals which can be used in conjunction with the conventional chemical pesticides, so as to increase the efficiency of insect pest management. At the same time the dependency on hazardous chemical sprays will be lessened leading to sustainable agriculture. Hence, computer aided modelling and analysis of the data should rapidly be able to determine the chemicals that specifically target genes/ gene products in weeds/pathogens/insect pests, thus increasing the success rate of herbicide/ fungicide/insecticide discovery which are more environmental friendly. In order to achieve this efficiency it is inevitable to use database integration, querying and mining techniques.

2.5   Natural Products as Herbal Products

Many of the botanical formulations mentioned above can be treated as minimally processed herbal products. The herbal products industry is one of the fastest growing industries in the world with billions of dollars turnover. They are increasingly used as dietary supplements, phytomedicines and neutraceuticals. Unfortunately, there is no system in place at present to distinguish high quality products from low quality products as most of these are formulations developed based on traditional knowledge which is more subjective than objective.

Keeping the rapid growth in sales and the lack of standards in view, USDA (United States Department of Agriculture) recently has launched a massive programme for the genetic profiling of the important medicinal plants most commonly used in these herbal products. This data in conjunction with the metabolome data of these plants will definitely yield rich dividends.

3   Challenges

It is evident from the discussions in the preceding sections that this latest "omics" revolution and the related field of Natural Products Research are severely constrained at the moment for the following reasons:

*Lack of standards:*It is a common knowledge that several research groups involved in metabolite profiling and/ or natural products research build their own databases, sometimes meant exclusively for internal drug discovery programs. However, several public domain databases are also available. Unfortunately, most of them are cluttered with lot of unwanted data and images with out following any industrial standard guidelines. Such lack of standards and the non-implementation of the guidelines impede the accessibility of these databases sitting in "ivory towers".

Lack of database integration: As mentioned earlier, the dawn of the personalized genomic medicine heavily depends on the ability of the health care professional in the field to integrate the metabolite profile, global gene expression profile and phenomics profile of the patient. In addition to these databases, molecular marker data in the form of SNPs or *Hap map data* [19] may also be required for predicting drug efficacy and/or the possibility of adverse drug reaction. In order to realize the dream of personalized genomic medicine efforts should be made right now to make the relevant databases amenable for database integration. Similarly, a drug discoverer working on potassium channel inhibitors has to integrate the chemical database with gene expression profiles and toxicogenomic data for making faster and more accurate research progress.

Lack of a common querying language: The establishment of "metadatabases" becomes meaningful only when these databases can be queried across by biologists in the field. A health care professional in the hospital should be able to query the above mentioned databases seamlessly to understand the health status of a given patient before embarking upon any treatment. A drug discoverer has to query the metabolome data in conjunction with the structure activity relationship data and bioassay data before he can proceed to preclinical trial level. At every advancing step in the drug discovery program new sets of data are generated which needs to be constantly analyzed in conjunction with the data generated earlier. Such an automated computer aided pipelines are very rare and expensive at present.

Lack of dedicated application development: Each project involving Metabolomics and Natural Products Research is unique and specific target oriented. The target identification and validation along with the implementation of the software has to go on in parallel. This process involves the best of the brains from disparate fields and demands the development customized workflows and dedicated software applications. The applications to mine a C15 compound library may not work very efficiently for mining a formulation library unless some basic modifications

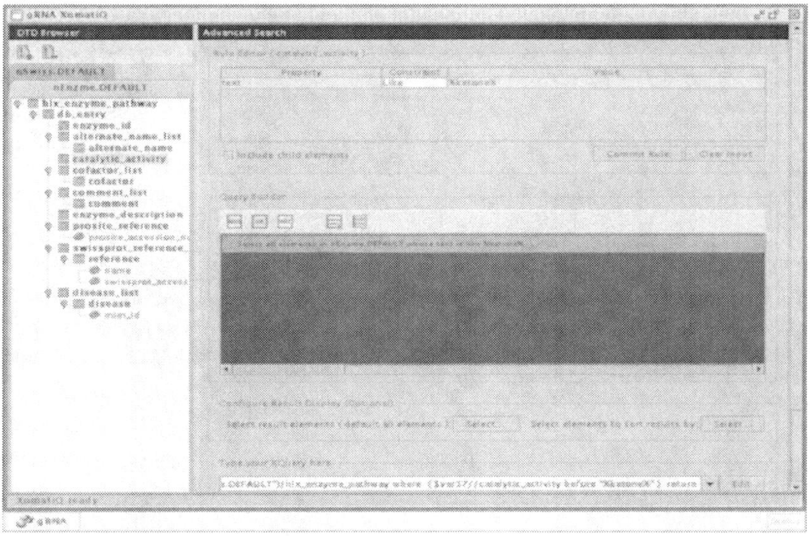

Fig. 1. XomatiQ GUI.

are made. Unfortunately, many developers embark upon writing a suite of Perl or Python scripts to meet the immediate requirements. These programmers often shy away from writing dedicated programs and developing customized software applications for the lack of a proper developer oriented software infrastructure. *Lack of a repository of tools developed:* The suites of perl scripts written are often forgotten once the fire fighting is done! It also happens that the person who has written the script has moved and the successor has no idea of using these scripts to any other scenario. Since there is no infrastructure available to take an algorithm to a full-fledged software application, many clever algorithms are routinely neglected. The customized software applications developed also are not freely exchanged because of the lack of a system in place.

4   The gRNA

In this section, we discuss how the *Genomics Research Network Architecture* (gRNA) [15] which was designed and developed at HeliXense Pte Ltd, Singapore [1] to address some of the challenges in metaboloinformatics. The gRNA provides a *development environment* and a *deployment framework* in which to maintain distributed warehouses, and to model, query and integrate disparate sources of biological data. The gRNA provides a framework to quickly develop new bioinformatics applications. We highlight some of the components of the gRNA that can be used to address some of the challenges discussed in the preceding section.

Data Hounds: The problem of integrating metabolite data along with other relevant data sources can be addressed using the *Data Hounds* component [13] in

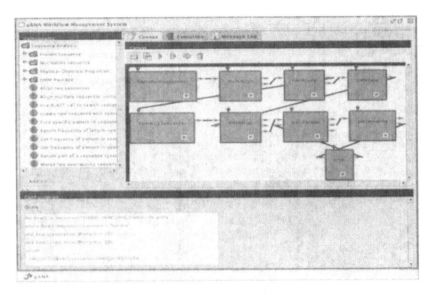

Fig. 2. HyperThesis GUI.

the gRNA. The Data Hounds [13] enable us to efficiently harness heterogeneous biological data from disparate sources warehouse them locally. In Data Hounds we first generate a relational schema. Second, we transform data from various sources to XML format by creating valid XML documents of the corresponding data. Third, we parse XML documents created from the previous step and load them into tuples of relational tables in a standard commercial DBMS.

XomatiQ: The problem of querying various metabolite data along with other relevant data sources can be addressed using the *XomatiQ* component [13] in the gRNA. The XomatiQ component supports a visual XML-based query interface to query the warehoused data (Figure 1. Through the interface, DTD structures of stored XML documents are displayed, and users can formulate queries by clicking the relevant data elements and entering conditions. Such queries are specified in a language similar to XQuery [11] and are transformed into SQL queries over the corresponding relational data as biological data is transformed and stored in relational format in the gRNA. The results are formatted as XML documents (if necessary) and returned back to the user or passed to another application for further processing.

HyperThesis: The gRNA provides the facility to take the results of one analysis in metabolomics as the basis for conducting further downstream analysis in a manageable, efficient way. Specifically, HyperThesis [14] is a graphical workflow management system in the gRNA designed to perform such analysis (Figure 2. HyperThesis provides a large repository of interconnectable, parameterized workflow components that opens a wide range of possibilities for processing and relating diverse biological data. Each workflow component in HyperThesis is designed to perform a specific task such as reading a sequence from a file, performing alignment on a given set of sequences, etc. Using an assortment of them, one can then weave together a metaboloinformatic workflow that performs a particular task as desired by the user. The components are arranged and connected based on experimental logic, not on programming logistics. One can also expand the range of functionalities available in HyperThesis simply by creating user-defined workflow components into this repository.

5   Conclusions

Metabolomics and Natural Products Research are in a state of transition and convergence at present. Instead of simply catering to the organic chemists' community for the synthesis of millions of analogues which need to be tested in a conventional and expensive way of drug design and development, a serious effort is needed to bring the voluminous data accumulated over decades of Natural Products Research into the arena of database integration so as to analyze it in conjunction with Metabolomics data and gene expression data using the modern software tools like gRNA. Only such efforts can augment the ushering in of the era of personalized genomic medicine for better health and human welfare.

References

1. Helixense Pte Ltd. www.helixense.com.
2. Interoperable Informatics Infrastructure Consortium (I3C). www.i3c.org.
3. Eclipse, a software tool for Metabolomics.
   http://www.chenomx.com/technology/technology.htm.
4. MAGE-ML: MicroArray Gene Expression Markup Language.
   http://www.mged.org/Workgroups/MAGE/MAGEdescription2.pdf.
5. Electronic Medical Records: Can They Revolutionize Health Care?
   http://www.tech-forum.org/, Feb 13, 2003.
6. http://www.fda.gov/oc/gcp/default.htm.
7. http://www.paradigmgenetics.com/ag/crop_production.asp.
8. http://www.gene-networks.com/informatics.html.
9. http://www.brenda.uni-koeln.de/.
10. The Pathway Tools Software. *Bioinformatics*, 2002.
11. XQuery 1.0: An XML Query Language.
    www.w3.org/TR/2001/WD-xquery-20011220.
12. A. BAIROCH, R. D. APPEL, M. C. PEITSCH. Protein Data Bank Quat. *Newsletter*, 81:5–7, 1997. 5.
13. S. S. BHOWMICK, P. CRUZ, A. LAUD. XomatiQ: Living with Genomes, Proteomes, Relations and a Little Bit of XML. *Proceedings of the 19th International Conference on Data Engineering (ICDE 2003)*, Bangalore, India, 2003.
14. S. S. BHOWMICK, V. VEDAGIRI, A. LAUD. HyperThesis: The gRNA Spell on the Curse of Bioinformatics Applications Integration. *Submitted for publications* .
15. A. LAUD, S. S. BHOWMICK, P. CRUZ ET AL. The gRNA: A Highly Programmable Infrastructure for Prototyping, Developing and Deploying Genomics-Centric Applications. *Proceedings of the 28th International Conference on Very Large Databases (VLDB 2002)*, Hong Kong, China, 2002.

16. D. C. CLASSEN, S. L. PESTOTNIK, R. S. EVANS ET AL. Adverse drug events in hospitalized patients: excess length of stay, extra costs, and attributable mortality. *JAMA*, 277:301–6, 1997.

17. R. HALL ET.AL. Plant Metabolomics: The missing link in Functional Genomics Strategies. *The Plant Cell*.Vol.14, pp:1437–1440.

18. M. KANEHISA, S. GOTO. KEGG for computational genomics. *Current Topics in Computational Molecular Biology* (Jiang, T., Xu, Y., and Zhang, M.Q., eds.), pp. 301–315, MIT-Press, Cambridge, MA, 2002.

19. D. E. REICH ET AL. *Nature 411*, 199–204, 2001.

20. D. T. SINGH ET AL. Pathway engineering: Towards the development of a smart Rice plant. *Proc.Intl. Symp. On Rice Biotechnology (Rockefeller meeting)*, 1997.

21. B. R. STOCKWELL. Nature Reviews Genetics, 1(2): 116–25,2000.

22. R. N. TRETHEWEY, A. J. KROTZKY, L. WILLMITZER. Metabolic profiling: A Rosetta Stone for Genomics? *Curr Opin Plant Biol*, 2(2):83–5, 1999.

23. HOWARD G. WILDMAN. Pharmaceutical Bioprospecting and its Relationship to the Conservation and Utilization of Bioresources. http://www.iupac.org/symposia/proceedings/phuket97/wildman.html, 1997.

Mining the Risk Types of Human Papillomavirus (HPV) by AdaCost

S.-B. Park, S. Hwang, and B.-T. Zhang

School of Computer Science and Engineering
Seoul National University
151-742 Seoul, Korea
{sbpark,shhwang,btzhang}@bi.snu.ac.kr

Abstract. Human Papillomavirus (HPV) infection is known as the main factor for cervical cancer, where cervical cancer is a leading cause of cancer deaths in women worldwide. Because there are more than 100 types in HPV, it is critical to discriminate the HPVs related with cervical cancer from those not related with it. In this paper, we classify the risk type of HPVs using their textual explanation. The important issue in this problem is to distinguish false negatives from false positives. That is, we must find out high-risk HPVs though we may miss some low-risk HPVs. For this purpose, the AdaCost, a cost-sensitive learner is adopted to consider different costs between training examples. The experimental results on the HPV sequence database show that considering costs gives higher performance. The F-score is higher than the accuracy, which implies that most high-risk HPVs are found.

1   Introduction

Human papillomavirus (HPV) is a double-strand DNA tumor virus that belongs to the papovavirus family, and there are more than 100 types in HPV that are specific for epithelial cells including skin, respiratory mucosa, and the genital tract. Especially, the genital tract HPV types are classified by their relative malignant potential into low-, and high-risk types [6]. The common, unifying oncogenic feature of the vast majority of cervical cancers is the presence of high-risk HPV. Therefore, the most important thing for diagnosis and therapy is discriminating what HPV types are high-risk.

One way to discriminate the risk types of HPVs is using a text mining technique. Since a great number of research results on HPV have been already reported in biomedical journals [4,5], they can be used as a source of discriminating HPV risk types. One problem in discriminating the risk types is that it is important to distinguish false negatives from false positives. That is, it is not critical to classify the low-risk HPVs as high-risk ones, because they can be investigated by further empirical study. However, it is fatal to classify the high-risk HPVs as low-risk ones. In this case, dangerous HPVs can be missed, and there is no further chance to detect cervical cancer by them.

V. Mařík et al. (Eds.): DEXA 2003, LNCS 2736, pp. 403–412, 2003.

Most machine learning algorithms for classification problems have focused on minimizing the number of incorrect predictions. However, this kind of learning algorithms ignores the differences between different types of incorrect prediction cost. Thus, recently, there has been considerable interest in cost-sensitive learning [11]. Ting and Zheng proposed two related but different cost-sensitive boosting approaches for tree classification [13]. Their approaches can be applied only to situations where the costs change very often. To apply boosting to situations where misclassification costs are relatively stable, Fan et al. proposed the AdaCost algorithm [2].

In this paper, we propose a cost-sensitive learning method to classify the risk types of HPVs using their textual explanation. In classifying their risk types, we consider the learning costs of each example, because it is far more important to reduce the number of false negatives[1] than to reduce that of false positives. For this purpose, we adopt AdaCost as a learning algorithm and prove empirically that it shows great performance in classifying the HPV risk types.

The rest of this paper is organized as follows. Section 2 explains how the HPV dataset is generated. Section 3 describes the cost-sensitive learning to classify HPV risk types. Section 4 presents the experimental results. Finally, section 5 draws conclusions.

2   Dataset

In general, the research in biomedical domain starts from investigating previous studies in PubMed designed to provide access to citations from biomedical literature. And, most bioinformatics research on text mining has focused on PubMed as its resource, because it includes most summaries and citations about biomedical literature. However, learning HPV risk types from PubMed is not an easy work. The difficulties can be summarized with two reasons.

- **The PubMed data are too sparse**
  For example, there are 3,797 articles about HPV and cervical cancer in PubMed, but most of them do not discuss the risk of HPV directly. Thus, it is difficult to capture the risk of HPV from the articles. In addition, the term distribution is totally different according to the interest of the articles.
- **Poor performance of NLP techniques**
  The current natural language processing (NLP) techniques are not for text understanding yet. The best thing we can expect from NLP techniques is morphological analysis and part-of-speech tagging. Thus, the articles need to be refined for further study.

In this paper, we use *the HPV Sequence Database* in Los Alamos National Laboratory as a dataset. This papillomavirus database is an extension of the HPV compendiums published in 1994 – 1997, and provides the complete list of 'papillomavirus types and hosts' and the records for each unique papillomavirus

---

[1] In this paper, *false negative* implies that high-risk HPV is misclassified as low-risk. Similarly, *false positive* means low-risk HPV that is misclassified as high-risk.

<definition>
Human papillomavirus type 80 E6, E7, E1, E2, E4, L2, and L1 genes.
</definition>
<source>
Human papillomavirus type 80.
</source>
<comment>
The DNA genome of HPV80 (HPV15-related) was isolated from histologically normal skin, cloned, and sequenced. HPV80 is most similar to HPV15, and falls within one of the two major branches of the B1 or Cutaneous/EV clade. The E7, E1, and E4 orfs, as well as the URR, of HPV15 and HPV80 share sequence similarities higher than 90%, while in the usually more conservative L1 orf the nucleotide similarity is only 87%. A detailed comparative sequence analysis of HPV80 revealed features characteristic of a truly cutaneous HPV type [362]. Notice in the alignment below that HPV80 compares closely to the cutaneous types HPV15 and HPV49 in the important E7 functional regions CR1, pRb binding site, and CR2. HPV 80 is distinctly different from the high-risk mucosal viruses represented by HPV16. The locus as defined by GenBank is HPVY15176.
</comment>

Fig. 1. An example description of HPV80.

Fig. 2. Neighbor joining phylogenetic tree of 106 PVs based on CPR region of L1.

type. An example of the data from this database is given in Figure 1. This is for HPV80 and consists of three parts: definition, source, and comment. The definition indicates the HPV type, the source explains where the information for this HPV is obtained, and the comment gives the explanation for this HPV.

To measure the performance of the results in the experiments below, we manually classified HPV risk types using the 1997 version of HPV compendium

Table 1. The manually classified risk types of each HPV.

Type	Risk	Type	Risk	Type	Risk	Type	Risk
HPV1	Low	HPV2	Low	HPV3	Low	HPV4	Low
HPV5	Low	HPV6	Low	HPV7	Low	HPV8	Low
HPV9	Low	HPV10	Low	HPV11	Low	HPV12	Low
HPV13	Low	HPV14	Low	HPV15	Low	HPV16	High
HPV17	Low	HPV18	High	HPV19	Low	HPV20	Low
HPV21	Low	HPV22	Low	HPV23	Low	HPV24	Low
HPV25	Low	HPV26	Don't Know	HPV27	Low	HPV28	Low
HPV29	Low	HPV30	Low	HPV31	High	HPV32	Low
HPV33	High	HPV34	Low	HPV35	High	HPV36	Low
HPV37	Low	HPV38	Low	HPV39	High	HPV40	Low
HPV41	Low	HPV42	Low	HPV43	Low	HPV44	Low
HPV45	High	HPV47	Low	HPV48	Low	HPV49	Low
HPV50	Low	HPV51	High	HPV52	High	HPV53	Low
HPV54	Don't Know	HPV55	Low	HPV56	High	HPV57	Don't Know
HPV58	High	HPV59	High	HPV60	Low	HPV61	High
HPV62	High	HPV63	Low	HPV64	Low	HPV65	Low
HPV66	High	HPV67	High	HPV68	High	HPV69	Low
HPV70	Don't Know	HPV72	High	HPV73	Low	HPV74	Low
HPV75	Low	HPV76	Low	HPV77	Low	HPV80	Low

and the comment in the records of HPV types. The classifying procedure is as follows. First, we divided roughly HPV types by the groups in the 1997 version of HPV compendium. These groups are shown in Figure 2. This tree, which contains 108 Papillomavirus (PV) sequences, was computed for the L1 consensus primer region (CPR) using neighbor joining method and a distance matrix calculated with a modified Kimura 2-parameter model (transition/transversion ratio 2.0). Neighbor-joining analysis is a convenient and rapid way to get an initial estimate of branching relationships, especially when a large number of taxa are involved. In the figure, the outermost wide gray arcs show the five PV supergroups (A-E). Each tree branch is labeled with an abbreviated sequence name. For HPVs the 'type' number alone is given in most cases, so the branch labeled 40 is that of HPV40.

Second, if the type of the group is skin-related or cutaneous HPV, the members of the group are classified into low-risk type. Third, if the group is known to be high-risk type of cervical cancer-related HPV, the members of the group are classified into high-risk type. Lastly, we used the comment of HPV types to classify some types difficult to be classified. Table 1 shows the summarized classification of HPVs according to its risk.

In the all experiments below, we used only `comment` part. The comment for a HPV type can be considered as a document in text classification. Therefore, each HPV type is represented as a vector of which elements are $tf \cdot idf$ values. In $tf \cdot idf$, the weight of a word w_j appeared in the document d_i is given as

$$N(w_j, d_i) = tf_{ij} \cdot \log_2 \frac{m}{n}, \tag{1}$$

where tf_{ij} is the frequency of w_j in d_i, m is the total number of documents, and n is the number of documents where w_j occurs at least once. When we stemmed the documents using the Porter's algorithm and removed words from the stoplist, the size of vocabulary is just 1,434. Thus, each document is represented as a 1,434-dimensional vector.

3   Classifying by Cost-Sensitive Learning

3.1   AdaCost Algorithm

In order to consider the misclassification cost of HPV risk types, we adopt the AdaCost algorithm [2]. Let $S = \{(x_1, c_1, y_1) \ldots, (x_m, c_m, y_m)\}$ be a training set where $c_i \in \mathcal{R}^+$ is a cost factor and is additionally given to the normal $x_i \in \mathcal{X}$ and $y_i \in \{-1, +1\}$. First of all, the distribution of each example is set to $D_1(i) = c_i / \sum_{j=1}^{m} c_j$. When t is an index to show the round of boosting, $D_t(i)$ is the weight given to (x_i, c_i, y_i) at the t-th round. And, $\alpha_t > 0$ is a parameter as a weight for weak learner h_t at the t-th round, and its value is given as

$$\alpha_t = \frac{1}{2} \ln \frac{1+r}{1-r},$$

where $r = \sum_i D(i) y_i h_t(x_i) \beta(i)$. And, $\beta(i)$ is a cost adjustment function with two arguments, $sign(y_i h_t(x_i))$ and c_i. If $h_t(x_i)$ is correct, then $\beta(i) = 0.5c_i + 0.5$, otherwise $\beta(i) = -0.5c_i + 0.5$.

The main difference between AdaBoost and AdaCost is how the distribution D_t is updated. AdaCost has an additional cost adjustment factor in updating D_t. As AdaBoost does, the weight of an instance will be increased if it is misclassified. Similarly, its weight will be decreased otherwise. However, the weight change is affected by the value of the cost factor. When an instance has a high cost factor, the weight change will be greater than that with a low cost factor.

3.2   Naive Bayes Classifier as a Weak Learner

Kim et al. proposed the BayesBoost algorithm and showed that it gives great efficiency in text filtering [7]. It uses naive Bayes classifiers as its weak learner within AdaBoost. Assume that a document d_i is composed of a sequence of words which is $w_{i1}, w_{i2}, \ldots, w_{i|d_i|}$, and the words in a document are mutually independent one another and the probability of a word is independent of its position within the document. Though these assumptions are not true in real situations, naive Bayes classifiers showed rather good performance in text classification [8].

Due to the independence assumption, the probability that a document d_i is generated from the class y_j can expressed as

$$P(d_i | y_j; \hat{\theta}) = P(|d_i|) \prod_{k=1}^{|d_i|} P(w_{d_{ik}} | y_j; \hat{\theta})^{N(w_{d_{ik}}, d_i)},$$

Table 2. The contingency table to evaluate the classification performance.

	Answer should be *High*	Answer should be *Low*
The classifier says *High*	a	b
The classifier says *Low*	c	d

where $w_{d_{ik}}$ denotes the k-th word in the document d_i, $N(w_{d_{ik}}, d_i)$ given by Equation (1) denotes the weight of word $w_{d_{ik}}$ occurring in document d_i, and $|d_i|$ is the number of words in the document. Thus, when assuming $P(|d_i|)$ is uniform, the best class y^* of a document d_i is determined by

$$y^* = \arg\max_{y_j \in \{-1,+1\}} P(y_j|d_i; \hat{\theta}),$$

where

$$P(y_j|d_i; \hat{\theta}) = \frac{P(y_j|\hat{\theta})P(d_i|y_j; \hat{\theta})}{P(d_i|\hat{\theta})}$$

$$= \frac{P(y_j|\hat{\theta}) \prod_{k=1}^{|d_i|} P(w_{d_{ik}}|y_j; \hat{\theta})^{N(w_{d_{ik}}, d_i)}}{\sum_{r=1}^{2} P(y_r|\hat{\theta}) \prod_{k=1}^{|d_i|} P(w_{d_{ik}}|y_r; \hat{\theta})^{N(w_{d_{ik}}, d_i)}}. \quad (2)$$

In order to calculate this probability, we need to determine $P(w_k|y_j; \hat{\theta})$ and $P(y_j|\hat{\theta})$. These two values can be estimated as

$$P(w_k|y_j; \hat{\theta}) = \frac{1 + \sum_{i=1}^{m} N(w_k, d_i)P(y_j|d_i)}{|V| + \sum_{k=1}^{|V|} \sum_{i=1}^{m} N(w_k, d_i)P(y_j|d_i)},$$

$$P(y_j|\hat{\theta}) = \frac{\sum_{i=1}^{m} P(y_j|d_i)}{m}.$$

Here, $|V|$ is the size of vocabulary.

One of the advantages of using naive Bayes classifier as a weak learner is that the naive Bayes utilizes term weights such as term frequency naturally. Moreover, because it is a probabilistic model, it provides a natural measure for calculating confidence ratios in AdaBoost. Thus, in this paper, we also use naive Bayes classifier as a weak learner of AdaCost.

4   Experiments

4.1   Evaluation Measure

In this paper, we evaluate the classification performance using the contingency table method. In this method, recall and precision are defined as follows:

$$recall = \frac{a}{a+c} \cdot 100\%$$

$$precision = \frac{a}{a+b} \cdot 100\% \quad (3)$$

$$accuracy = \frac{a+d}{a+b+c+d} \cdot 100\%,$$

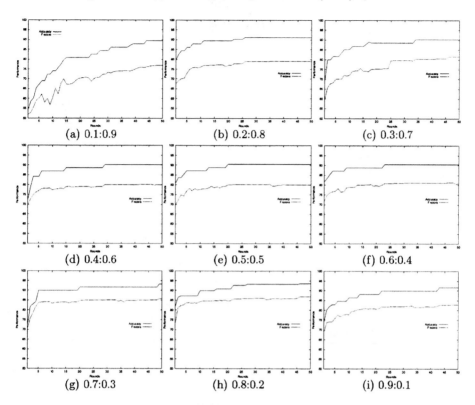

(a) 0.1:0.9   (b) 0.2:0.8   (c) 0.3:0.7

(d) 0.4:0.6   (e) 0.5:0.5   (f) 0.6:0.4

(g) 0.7:0.3   (h) 0.8:0.2   (i) 0.9:0.1

Fig. 3. Performance of AdaCost on HPV risk classification with various costs.

where a, b, c and d are defined in Table 2. The F_{β}-score which combines precision and recall is defined as

$$F_{\beta} = \frac{(\beta^2 + 1) \cdot recall \cdot precision}{\beta^2 \cdot recall + precision},$$

where β is the weight of recall relative to precision. We use $\beta = 1$ in all experiments, which corresponds to equal weighting of the two measures.

4.2   Experimental Results

Since we have only 72 HPV types except "Don't Know"s and the explanation of each HPV is relatively short, *leave-one-out* (LOO) *cross validation* is used to determine the performance of the proposed method. We normalized each cost c_i to [0, 1]. That is, the cost for low-risk HPVs is set to 0.1 when the cost for high-risk HPVs is set to 0.9.

Figure 3 demonstrates the performance of AdaCost. The graphs in this figure show the accuracy and F-score according to the round of AdaCost. Each graph represents the ratio of costs for high-risk and low-risk HPVs. For instance, figure

Table 3. The performance comparison of AdaCost and AdaBoost on HPV risk classification.

	AdaCost	AdaBoost	naive Bayes
Accuracy (%)	93.05	90.55	81.94
F-score	86.49	80.08	63.64

(a) imposes 0.1 on high-risk HPVs and 0.9 on low-risk HPVs. Because the costs in figure (e) are both set to 0.5, it is the performance of the AdaBoost. Figures (a)–(d) plot the performance when lower costs are imposed on high-risk HPVs than those on low-risk HPVs. And, figures (f)–(i) plot the performance when higher costs are imposed on high-risk HPVs.

Generally, when we set higher cost to high-risk HPVs than to low-risk HPVs, we obtained higher performance than AdaBoost shown by figure (e). When we impose lower cost to high-risk HPVs than to high-risk HPVs, the performance gets lower than AdaBoost except figure (c). These results coincide with the intuition that we should set higher costs to high-risk HPVs. It is also interesting to see that figure (a) shows the worst performance. Therefore, if we impose wrong cost, we may obtain worse result. Among nine graphs, figure (h) shows the best performance. It implies that 0.8 is the best cost for high-risk HPVs.

The final classification performance is given in Table 3. It compares three learning methods: AdaCost, AdaBoost, and naive Bayes classifier which is used as a weak learner in AdaCost and AdaBoost. AdaCost shows 93.05% of accuracy and 86.49 of F-score, while AdaBoost gives only 90.55% of accuracy and 80.08 of F-score. Especially, naive Bayes classifier reported 26 high-risk HPVs. Among 26 high-risk HPVs reported by naive Bayes classifier, only fourteen are correctly predicted. Thus, it shows only 81.94% of accuracy and 63.64 of F-score. As shown in Equation (3), F-score is closely related with the number of found high-risk HPVs while accuracy is related with the number of correctly predicted HPVs including both low-risk and high-risk HPVs.

In our previous study, we showed that even AdaBoost has an implicit ability of cost learning [12]. That is, AdaBoost can show higher F-score than naive Bayes classifier. In our experiments, the F-score of AdaCost and AdaBoost is actually far higher than that of naive Bayes classifier. And, this result supports our goal to reduce false negatives. In addition, when we strongly pose cost factors as in AdaCost, it shows higher F-score than AdaBoost. The difference in accuracy between AdaCost and AdaBoost is just 2.5%, but the difference in F-score is 6.41. This implies that more high-risk HPVs found by AdaCost than by AdaBoost.

This can be found also in Figure 4 which depicts the receiver operating characteristic (ROC) curves of AdaCost. In this figure, the dotted line plots the ROC curve of AdaBoost, while the thick line plots that of AdaCost when the cost of 0.8 is imposed on high-risk HPVs. Since two curves do not intersect and the curve of AdaCost is above that of AdaBoost, the performance of AdaCost is superior under all relative weightings of true positive and false positive rates.

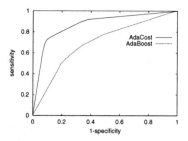

Fig. 4. ROC curve of AdaCost.

Table 4. The risk type predicted by the proposed method for four HPVs whose risks are not known exactly.

HPV Types	Risk Type
HPV26	Low
HPV54	Low
HPV57	High
HPV70	Low

Table 4 shows the predicted risk type for the HPV types whose risks are not known exactly. These HPVs are described as "Don't Know" in Table 1. According to previous research on HPV [3,1,9,10], only HPV70 seems to be misclassified. This is because the comment for HPV70 does not describe its risk but because of its lack of biomedical research it explains only that it is found at the cervix of patients and its sequence is analyzed.

5   Conclusions

This paper proposed a practical method to determine the risk type of human papillomaviruses. In classifying their risk type, it is important to distinguish false negatives from false positives, where false-negatives are high-risk HPVs that are misclassified as low-risk and false positives are low-risk HPVs misclassified as high-risk.

For this purpose, we set different costs for low-risk and high-risk HPVs. As a learning algorithm, we adopted *AdaCost* and showed empirically that it outperforms AdaBoost which does not consider learning cost. In addition, the experimental results gave higher improvement on F-score than that on accuracy, and it means that more high-risk HPVs are found by AdaCost. This result is important because high-risk HPVs, as stated above, should not be missed. Since HPV is known as the main cause of cervical cancer, high-risk HPVs must not be missed for further medical investigation of the patients.

Our results can be used as fundamental information to design the DNA-chips for diagnosing the presence of HPV in cervical cancer patients. Because the cost is too high to test all HPV types, the results presented in this paper reduce time and monetary cost to know their relation with cervical cancer.

412   S.-B. Park, S. Hwang, and B.-T. Zhang

Acknowledgements. This research was supported by the Korean Ministry of Education under the BK21-IT Program, and by the Korean Ministry of Science and Technology under BrainTech and NRL programs.

References

1. S. Chan, S. Chew, K. Egawa, E. Grussendorf-Conen, Y. Honda, A. Rubben, K. Tan, and H. Bernard, "Phylogenetic Analysis of the Human Papillomavirus Type 2 (HPV-2), HPV-27, and HPV-57 Group, Which is Associated with Common Warts," *Virology*, Vol. 239, pp. 296–302, 1997.
2. W. Fan, S. Stolfo, J. Zhang, and P. Chan, "AdaCost: Misclassification Cost-Sensitive Boosting," In *Proceedings of the 16th International Conference on Machine Learning*, pp. 97–105, 1999.
3. M. Favre, D. Kremsdorf, S. Jablonska, S. Obalek, G. Pehau-Arnaudet, O. Croissant, and G. Orth, "Two New Human Papillomavirus Types (HPV54 and 55) Characterized from Genital Tumours Illustrate the Plurality of Genital HPVs," *International Journal of Cancer*, Vol. 45, pp. 40–46, 1990.
4. H. Furumoto and M. Irahara, "Human Papilloma Virus (HPV) and Cervical Cancer," *The Jounral of Medical Investigation*, Vol. 49, No. 3–4, pp. 124–133, 2002.
5. T. Ishiji, "Molecular Mechanism of Carcinogenesis by Human Papillomavirus-16," *The Journal of Dermatology*, Vol. 27, No. 2, pp. 73–86, 2000.
6. M. Janicek and H. Averette, "Cervical Cancer: Prevention, Diagnosis, and Therapeutics," *Cancer Journal for Clinicians*, Vol. 51, pp. 92–114, 2001.
7. Y.-H. Kim, S.-Y. Hahn, and B.-T. Zhang, "Text Filtering by Boosting Naive Bayes Classifiers", In *Proceedings of the 23rd Annual International ACM SIGIR Conference on Research and Development in Information Retrieval*, pp. 168–175, 2000.
8. A. McCallum and K. Nigam, "Empolying EM in Pool-based Active Learning for Text Classification," In *Proceedings of the 15th International Conference on Machine Learning*, pp. 350–358, 1998.
9. T. Meyer, R. Arndt, E. Christophers, E. Beckmann, S. Schroder, L. Gissmann, and E. Stockfleth, "Association of Rare Human Papillomavirus Types with Genital Premalignant and Malignant Lesions," *The Journal of Infectious Diseases*, Vol. 178, pp. 252–255, 1998.
10. G. Nuovo, C. Crum, E. De Villiers, R. Levine, and S. Silverstein, "Isolation of a Novel Human Papillomavirus (Type 51) from a Cervical Condyloma," *Journal of Virology*, Vol. 62, pp. 1452–1455, 1988.
11. F. Provost and T. Fawcett, "Analysis and Visualization of Classifier Performance: Comparison Under Imprecise Class and Cost Distributions," In *Proceedings of the Third International Conference on Knowledge Discovery and Data Mining*, pp. 43–48, 1997.
12. S.-B. Park and B.-T. Zhang, "A Boosted Maximum Entropy Model for Learning Text Chunking," In *Proceedings of the 19th Internatinal Conference on Machine Learning*, pp. 482–489, 2002.
13. K.-M. Ting and Z. Zheng, "Boosting Trees for Cost-Sensitive Classifications," In *Proceedings of the 10th European Conference on Machine Learning*, pp. 190–195, 1998.

Protein Structural Information Management Based on Spatial Concepts and Active Trigger Rules*

Sung-Hee Park[1], Keun Ho Ryu[1], and Hyeon S. Son[2]

[1] Database Laboratory,
Chungbuk National University,
Hungduck-ku,
Cheongju, 360-763, Korea
{shpark,khryu}@dblab.chugnbuk.ac.kr
[2] Center for Computational Biology & Bioinformatics,
Korea Institute of Science and Technology Information,
Eoeun-dong 52, Yuseong-gu,
Daejeon city, 305-600, Korea.
hss@kisti.re.kr

Abstract. A protein structure has four different levels of structures with spatial conformation and arrangement of peptide chains. Features of newly emerging protein structure data are extremely complex, large, multidimensional and incomplete. Therefore, it is necessary to develop approaches to manage protein structure data compared with management of conventional data in order to provide protein structural information for analysis applications.

We propose a new approach to manage protein structural information by using spatial object management and active database techniques. We introduce data modeling for protein structures using a geographic object model and version management of a protein sequence with trigger rules and show analysis structural information using topological and geometric operators.

Our experimental results show that applying spatial models and an active trigger to manage protein structure can efficiently support fast protein structure analysis by using spatial operations and a filter–refinement processing with a multi dimensional index.

1 Introduction

Since the first draft of Human Genome Project published, a large volume of protein structure data have been offered on the web, and need of systems to analyze structure data has been raised. However, the analysis and the management of protein structure data are more complicated and more difficult due to their characteristics of protein structures, which have four distinct levels and, of which features are various such as geometry, topology and physico-chemical properties.

---

* This work was supported by Bioinformatics Center of Korea Institute of Science and Technology Information, University IT Research Center for Project, and KOSEF RRC(ChongJu Univ. ICRC) in Korea.

V. Mařík et al. (Eds.): DEXA 2003, LNCS 2736, pp. 413–422, 2003.

To date, PDB(protein data bank)[5] has been the most popular protein structure database and has been distributed and arranged flat files containing protein str and experimental information since 1990. There have been many studies on similarity and homology search [15] geared toward finding the methods to predict the 2D[10,12] or 3D structure[8, 9, 11] of protein from sequences and structures.

These conventional researches have focused on analyzing specific properties, but have not considered integrated analysis approaches to combine spatial characteristics of protein structure and physico-chemical properties. Furthermore, the analysis of protein structures such as prediction and comparison needs fast filters to generate candidate set for further refinement step from the large volume of protein structural data increased tremendously.

In this paper, we propose a protein structural information management system by using spatial object management and an active database. We introduce integrated data modeling for geometric(2D and 3D) and thematic(chemical or physical) properties of protein structures based on a geographic object model. We show how to analysis of the structural information by using topological and geometric operators based on implementation of proposed modeling in ORACLE 8i Spatial DBMS. For the management of protein sequences, we employ ECA(Event-Condition-Action) rules to detect versions of protein sequences.

This paper is contributed to provide the method to manage the newly emerging complex protein structures based on the existing technology of spatial databases and active databases. It can provide structural and chemi-physic properties to applications of protein structure analysis. Furthermore, it can efficiently retrieve the structural information by using a filter–refinement processing and a multi dimensional index for analyzing protein structures.

2   Structural Features and Extraction

A protein structure has four different dimensions and their structural features are various. Each application for structure analysis uses different structure level similarities(e.g. atom, group, residue, fragment, secondary structures) and different features(e.g. geometry, topology, physico-chemical properties). This section describes structural features used in prediction, comparison and pattern discovery from PDB flat files and shows what geometry, topology and properties are extracted from flat files for modeling.

Structural features of protein will consist of geometry, topology and physico-chemical properties. These features include as follows:

- Geometry: coordinates or relative positions of atoms, fragments or SSEs
- Topology: the elements' order along the backbone, spatial connection, adjacencies and intersection of fragments or SSEs
- Physico-Chemical properties: atom type, residue type, partial charge, hydrophobicity

We extracted the identification, geometry and topology of protein structure from flat files in feature extraction step. The identification information of protein structures is PDB identifier, molecule name and chain identifier. The geometry of protein structures is diverse from that of each structure level. We consider relative positions of central atoms of a residue in a sequence, coordinates of central atoms, and SSEs (secondary structure elements) which include between the start and the end position of SSEs. Topology of protein structures, which presents element's order along the backbone and connectivity of residue (consecutive order of residue) in a sequence, is extracted.

The amino acid sequence as primary structure is extracted from SEQRES record in flat files. SEQRES contains the amino acid in macromolecule. In Helix record, chain identifier, identifier of Helix, residue name and residue position (residue number) where helix starts and ends are extracted. Sheet identifier, strand identifier, residue name and residue position (residue number) where strand starts and ends, are also obtained from flat files. Structural information related to Turn and Loop is extracted in the same manner with Helix and Sheet.

Chain identifier, residue number, atom number, and 3D coordinates of atoms are extracted as 3D structural information. Fields of a flat file for geometry or topology of protein structure show in the Fig. 1.

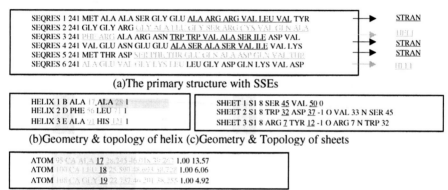

(a)The primary structure with SSEs

(b)Geometry & topology of helix (c)Geometry & Topology of sheets

(d) Geometry & Topology of atom

Fig. 1. Extracted structural features in PDB flat file

3 Protein Structure Modeling

In this section, we describe data modeling for geometric(2D and 3D) and thematic(chemical or physical) properties of protein structures based on a geographic object model. We also depict representation of the geometry and topology of protein structures to spatial types in a spatial network model.

3.1 Protein Structure Modeling Based on a Geographic Object Model

In aspects of management of geographic information, a geographic object has two components: (1) description and (2) spatial object which corresponds to the shape and location of the object in the embedding space. Geographic information gathers within a spatial object points of the embedding space sharing the description. A lot of thematic information is used to describe spatial objects. Similarly in protein database, the structural features of protein mentioned in section 2 include spatial features such as geometry and topology and non-spatial description like physico-chemical properties. Therefore, a new approach to manage thematic information along with spatial properties is provided by applying geographic object modeling to protein structures. The abstract definition is a mean to show intuitively the protein structures as geographic objects.

> Protein structure object ={identifiers, description, spatial objects of structural elements}

> Spatial objects of structural elements ={point, arc, node, polygon, region}

> Description={physico-chemical properties, author information, references, experiment information, Taxonomy, annotation}

The protein structure object as mentioned above consists of description and spatial object. In this case the description includes the thematic information of the protein structure(e.g physico-chemical properties and etc.). The spatial objects represent the topology and geometry of the protein structure with spatial data types such as a point, a line, and a polygon. In section 3.2 we show representation of protein structures with spatial types as spatial objects.

3.2   Representation of Protein Structures with Spatial Types

Each atom in a protein molecule has three dimensional coordinates, and arrangement of atoms in space and connection between them generate topological relationship. The spatial features of protein structures can be represented by geometric types in spatial databases.

The protein 3D molecule can be divided into one or more rigid substructures. Thus, if we consider a molecule as a three dimensional graph, each atom is a node, each bond is an edge, and substructure is a block of the graph. This graph can be represented with a spatial network model[2] which was first designed for representing the networks in graph-based application such as transportation services or utility management. In Fig. 2 tuples are denoted by [], lists by<>, and set by { }. Using this notation, protein structures can be summarized in Fig. 2.

In primary structure of a protein, a sequence can be defined as the polyline which is a finite set of line segments, such that end point of each segment is shared by exactly two segments if a residue corresponds to a point in spatial types. A point corresponds to a amino acid molecule in the backbone. Coordinates of the point are those of the C^α atom in a residue.

The elements of secondary structures of a protein such as α-helix and β-sheet are represented with polylines which can have topologies and differ from polylines of the primary structure. The details are omitted here and are referred to[2]. In the spatial network model[3], polylines including an spatial topology denote arcs which start at a node and end at a node, and include a finite set of point. A node is a distinguished point that connects a list of arcs.

A start node corresponds to the C^α atom of a starting residue in a SSEs and an end node to the the C^α atom of a starting residue in a SSEs. If the secondary structures can be defined to polylines, the tertiary structure can be defined as a finite set of the elements of the secondary structures and there can be spatial topology relationships among them. Thus, the tertiary structure can denote a finite set of points, nodes, and arcs in the spatial network model. We implemented the spatial network model with oracle spatial types. Details are shown in Park's work[1, 2].

- primary structure of protein:
  < residue> = <polyline>
  <polyline> = <line-segment>
  <line-segment>=<start-point, end-point>
  <point> =[x:real, y:real, z:real]

- secondary structure of protein:
  <α-Helix| β-Sheet> = <arc>
  <arc> =< [node-start, node-end, <point>] >
  - node-start: Cα Atom of starting residue in an α-Helix
  - node-end : Cα Atom of ending residue in an α-Helix
  - point : Cα Atoms between starting residue and ending

- tertiary structure of protein:
  <node| arc| point >

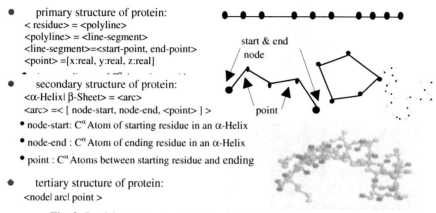

start & end
node

point

Fig. 2. Spatial geometries and topological relationship of protein structures

4 The Management for Versions of Sequences with Active Rules

There often occur changes of a sequence from producing the same piece of protein due to biological mutation through evolution history, variables of experimental environment factors, uncertainty of measurement and unknown flaws of program algorithms concerned with sequencing process. In this section we introduce management of sequence versions which is a representative operation to manipulate sequences as a primary structure of a protein by using a trigger.

Storing protein sequences: A sequence is stored in database as an attribute of a relation, and the domain of the attribute sequence is treated as a variable character. The length of variable character in ORACLE can be taken up to a maximum size of 4000 bytes. The sequence that is longer than 4K is divided into two tuples. The strength of storing sequence data as a variable character is that the operator LIKE in SQL can be used, which performs the pattern match operations to a string type.

A mechanism for detecting version sequences with using an active trigger:
The order of amino acids or composition of them in a sequence is different from those of other sequences which are repeatedly produced from the same organism. We named variant sequences of source sequence as versions. The versions of the sequence is defined as follows:

❑ Let $SS = \{S_1, S_2, ..., S_l\}$ denote a finite set of sequences produced from a protein sample and l is total number of sequences($l=|SS|$) , where $S_i=\{a_1, a_2...a_k...a_n\}$ and a_k represent a character which is a amino acid of a sequence S_i and $n=|S_i|$ represents length of the sequence S_i. Also, let $Sid(S_i)$ denote a unique identifier of the sequence S_i.

❑ Definition 1. Given a sequence $S_i' = \{ a_1', a_2'...a_j'...a_m' \}$ and $Sid(S_i')$ obtained from the same piece of protein sequence in the same protein sample(SS'), a version sequence, S_i^v, satisfies as follows :

❏ $Sid(S_i) = Sid(S_i')$, Length(S) = Length(S_i'), Order$(S) \neq$ Order(S_i') and Composition $(S) \neq$ Composition(S_i''), where D is a sequence database, $SS \subseteq D$ and $S_i' \notin D$.

When a new sequence is inserted, we automatically detect a sequence on a table SEQUENC of a database, which has the same identifier with it and is inconsistent with the inserted sequence using a trigger[13] of active databases. If there is the match sequence with queried one, then the algorithm moves to change detection. In the step of change detection, a trigger finds existing version sequences on a table VERSION with the same identifier of the queried sequence and compares the composition and length of queried sequence to those of version sequences with the string matched operation SQL provides. If the queried sequence is satisfied with conditions of the version sequence, the trigger executes action that the queried sequence is inserted into the table VERSION and then increases the number of version on the table SEQUENCE using update operation. Fig. 3 describes a trigger for detecting a version of a sequence.

5   Analyzing Protein Structures Using Spatial Operators

This section describes that geometric operators and topological operators which lead to spatial relationship between spatial objects are applied to retrieve of structural relationship among proteins.

Geometric operators to query structural distance: Calculation of the residue-residue(C^{alpha} atom-C^{alpha} atom) distance is a primitive operation for determining RMSD(Root Mean Squared Distance) at the aligning step for comparing rigid structures of proteins. Measuring RMSD is by far more costly than simple scalar comparison because a protein structure has at least 10,000 number of atoms. Therefore, the optimization of CPU cost is an important factor to execute comparison algorithms efficiently. In this paper, before calculation of RMSD is called, we compute distance between center atoms of residues in back born of protein after the protein structures are stored in database.

Geometric operators such as SDO_DISTANCE, SDO_WITHIN_DISTANCE and SDO_LENGTH calculate an Euclidean distance between two spatial objects and select spatial object within distance range. We analyzed RMSD of secondary structure elements(SSEs) using spatial geometric operators and other relational operators supported by Oracle Spatial 8i DBMS.

Topological operators to query superposition : To compare two protein structures, the superposition between two protein structures is examined[6]. Finding the superposition of SSEs between protein is executed by using topological operators which evaluated intersection of spatial geometry of spatial object represented the SSEs of protein. Topological operators[4] on spatial objects defined by Clementini can be used to find superposed SSEs, and can be used for fast filtering many candidate protein objects at the comparison. Oracle 8i Spatial includes 9IM(Intersection Matrix)[14] which implemented the topological operators. SDO.GEOM.RELATE operator provided by ORACLE 8i Spatial is used for this purpose.

[Query 1] Find α-helices of protein, which superpose those of protein 1DHR.
SELECT H1.PDB_IDCODE, H1.SSENUM, H2.PDB_IDCODE, H2.SSENUM;

FROM LHELIX H1, LHELIX H2
WHERE SDO_RELATE(H1.HARC, H2.HARC, 'mask=ANYINTERACT
        querytype=JOIN')='TRUE'
AND H1.PDB_IDCODE!=H2.PDB_IDCODE
AND H1.HELIXNUM != H2.HELIXNUM AND H1.PDB_IDCODE='1DHR'
ORDERBY H1.PDB_IDCODE, H1.SSENUM, H2.PDB_IDCODE, H2.SSENUM;

```
CREATE OR REPLACE TRIGGER DetectingVerionSequence
AFTER INSERT ON TempSeq //A Triger event occurs when a new sequence is inserted
REFERENCING
  OLD ROW as oldrow
  NEW ROW as newrow
FOR EACH ROW
DECLARE  // Declaration variables
  Maxvid INTEGER;Duple INTEGER;Seqtrue INTEGER;Vertrue INTEGER;Firstver INTEGER;
BEGIN
  SELECT COUNT(*) INTO Duple FROM Sequence
  WHERE Sid = newrow.Sid AND Sseq= newrow.Sseq;
   IF Duple = 0 THEN // A condition of the trigger  to check whether there are duplicated identifier of the
                    // sequence
  SELECT COUNT(*) INTO Seqtrue FROM Sequence   WHERE Sid = newrow.Sid;
  IF Seqtrue = 0 THEN // A condition of the trigger  to check the first insertion of the input  sequence
   INSERT INTO Sequence VALUES  (newrow.Sid, newrow.SPid, newrow.Sseq,
   newrow.Slength, newrow.Stype, newrow.Sdate, newrow.Smachine, 0, 0, newrow.SsPos,
   newrow.SePos, newrow.SnumA, newrow.SnumT, newrow.SnumC, newrow.SnumG);
    ELSE  // A condition of the trigger  to check whether the input sequence may be version or not
      SELECT COUNT(*) INTO Firstver FROM VersionSeq
  WHERE VSid = newrow.Sid;
  IF Firstver = 0 THEN // A condition of the trigger to be the first version of a sequence
   INSERT INTO VersionSeq // Action of  the trigger to insert the first version of the sequence
      VALUES (newrow.Sid,1, newrow.SPid, newrow.Sseq,newrow.Slength, newrow.Sdate);
     ELSE
   SELECT COUNT(*) INTO Vertrue FROM VersionSeq
   WHERE VSid = newrow.Sid AND Vseq = newrow.Sseq;
    IF  Vertrue = 0 THEN // A condition of  the trigger to be a new version of the sequence
         SELECT MAX(Vid) INTO Maxvid FROM VersionSeq WHERE VSid = newrow.Sid;
     INSERT INTO VersionSeq  // Action of  the trigger to insert a version of the sequence
         VALUES (newrow.Sid,Maxvid+1,newrow.SPid,newrow.Sseq, newrow.Slength,newrow.Sdate);
     ELSE // A condition of  the trigger to be the same base composition with existing versions
     RAISE_APPLICATION_ERROR(-20000, 'WARNING! DUPLECATED VERSION!!!');
    END IF;
   END IF;
  END IF;
 ELSE // A condition of  the trigger  when a existing sequence is inserted into a table SEQUENCE
    RAISE_APPLICATION_ERROR(-20000,'WARNING! DUPLECATED ID AND SEQUENCE!');
    END IF;
END;
```

Fig. 3. The source of a trigger to detecting a version of sequences

Query 1 performs a spatial join operation with two common attributes of spatial relation, i.e., H1.HARC and H2.HARC. In addition, ANYINTERACT finds spatial objects that do not disjoint from H1.HARC to H2.HARC, and returns resulting objects sorted by the order of columns in ORDER BY clause. This query generates the candidate set for a refinement step of comparison with simple use of topological operators and without taking high cost.

6   Experimental Results

In this section, we describe performance analysis for an operation to manage version sequences and structural information based on spatial modeling. We implemented the proposed protein structure modeling using spatial types of ORACLE 8i spatial with java language on a Compaq ProliantML330e server.

6.1   Experiment 1: Detecting a Version of a Sequence Using a Trigger

Fig. 4 shows the execution time results for retrieving tuples including matched sequences with a queried sequence or a subsequence using a LIKE operator as the number of sequences is increased from 2000 to 10000. Average size of sequences in the database is 4KBytes and size of total database is 1.431GBytes. The execution time in the Fig. 4 is increased in proportion to the number of sequences. However, its results are quite reasonable to be accepted.

Fig. 5 shows the execution time results for determining whether a new sequence can be a new version of a sequence when it is inserted into a database. We evaluate detection of a version in two cases: 1) using a trigger 2) without a trigger. In case of using the trigger we implemented a trigger into a database proposed in section 4 and in the other case we implemented an application which includes the same algorithm of detection of a version without using the trigger.

As shown in Fig. 5 detecting the version of a sequence using the trigger has better performance than the application implementing the same algorithms. Increasing the number of sequences in the database, variation of a tilt of the graph present with using trigger in Fig. 5 is low, and its shape is almost constant. The sequence identifier as a primary key indexed in the table can be efficiently used to access a sequence in the trigger for detecting the version of the sequence.

6.2   Experiment 2: Querying Topological Relation of Protein Structures

Our second experiment query is "To find topological equivalent atom pairs in the α-Helix of the protein 1K6Y of HIV" using topological operator ANYINTERACT like Query1. This experiment restricts to N-terminal Zn binding domain of HIV integrase family which belongs to DNA/RNA-binding 3-helical bundle fold and all alpha class in the SCOP. We queried all the proteins within N-terminal Zn binding domain of HIV integrase family using ANYINTERACT topological operator. As a result the matched protein has the same as that of the SCOP except the 1K6Y PDB entry. In our result with Table1, 1K6Y PDB entry did not match with any protein in DNA/RNA-binding 3-helical bundle fold and 1K6Y matched with 1A00 PDB entry. The following Table 1 shows the same matched proteins between the SCOP and our results.

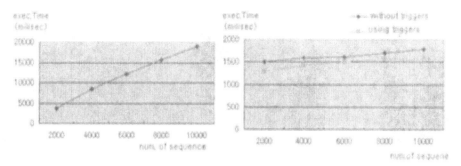

Fig. 4. Execution time to retrieve sequences
sequences using LIKE

Fig. 5. Execution time to check a new version of
a sequence using trigger

Table 1. The result of query with a topological operator

Fold : DNA/RNA-binding 3-helical bundle			
Family: N-terminal Zn binding domain of HIV integrase Num. of atoms=136,352 Num of atom in helix=6,055 Num. of helix=1,625 Execution time=3.687 seconds			
SCOPE	This	SCOPE	This
1K6Y	**1A00**	1WJD	1WJD
1WJA	1WJA	1WJE	1WJE
1WJB	1WJB	1E0E	1E0E
1WJC	1WJC		

7 Conclusions

This paper described the protein structure modeling based on a geographic object
model and spatial types and showed manipulation of structural information using
spatial operators and active ECA(Event-Condition-Action) rules. Structural
relationship among proteins was retrieved using spatial operators for comparison of
protein structures.

Geometric and topological operators can generate small candidate set to use at
structural alignment step to filter unrelated structures. Applying the trigger of active
database system to detect the versions of a sequence can maintain integrity and
consistency between versions of a sequence and origin without the interference of
applications.

To manage the protein structure using technology of the spatial database can
facilitate to analyze protein structures with spatial primitive functions and index
structures. Thus, advanced conventional data management system such as spatial and
active database can be applied to manage the newly emerging protein structures data.
The proposed modeling can be applied for classifications of 3D structures of proteins
and structure prediction. In future work, the spatial operation can be extended to
classify the similar 3D structures of proteins.

References

1. S. H. Park, K. H. Ryu, H. S. Son, Modeling Protein Structures with Spatial Model for Structure Comparison, Lecture Notes in Computer Science, Vol. Springer-Verlag, Berlin Heidelberg New York (2003)
2. S. H. Park, R. H. Li, K. H. Ryu, B. J. Jeong, H. S. Son, Modeling and Querying Protein Structure Based on Spatial Model, Proc. of Int. Conf. on Computer and information Science, Korea Information Processing (2002) 773–778.
3. P. Rigaus, M. School, A. Voisard: Spatial Databases with application to GIS. Academic Press San Diego (2002) 29–61
4. Oracle Spatial User's Guide and Reference: Loading and Indexing Spatial Object Types. Release8.1.5, Oracle (2001)
5. H. M. Berman, J. Westbrook, Z. Feng, G. Gilliland, T. N. Bhat, H. Weissig, I. N. Shindyalov, P. E. Bourne: The Protein Data bank. J. Nucleic Acids Research., Vol. 28. Oxford University Press New York (2000) 235–242
6. D. Higgins, W. Tailor: Bioinfomatics: Sequence, Structure, and databanks, 1ˢᵗ edn. Oxford University Press New York (2000)
7. K. H. Ryu: Genome database & EST database. J. Scientific & Technological Knowledge Infrastructure, Vol.10. KORDIC (2000)48–61
8. L. Holm , C. Sander: Dali/FSSP classification of three-dimensional protein folds. Nucleic Acids Research., Vol. 25. Oxford University Press New York (1997) 231–234
9. M. Levitt: Competitive assessment of protein fold recognition and alignment accuracy. Int. J. Proteins Struct. Funct. Genet. 1 (1997) 92–104
10. M. Stultz, R. Nambudripad, H. Lathrop, V. White: Predicting protein structure with probabilistic models. Int. J. Adv. Mol. Cell Biol. 22B (1997)447–506
11. N. Alexandrov, R. Nussinov, .M. Zimmer: Fast Protein fold recognition via sequence to structure alignment and contact capacity protentials. In: Proc. of Pac. Symp on Biocomput. (1996) 53–72
12. J. Garnier, J.-F. Gibrat, B. Robson: GOR method for predicting protein secondary structure from amino acid sequence. J. Method Enzymol. 266 (1996) 540–553
13. J. Widom, S. Ceri, Introduction to Active Database Systems. Active Database Systems: Triggers and Rules For Advanced Database Processing, Morgan Kaufmann (1996)1–41
14. E. Clementini, P. Felice, P. van Oostrom: A small set of formal topological relationships suitable for end-user interaction. In: Proc. of Spatial Databases Symp., Singapore (1993) 277–295
15. S. F. Altschul, R. J. Carrol, D. J. Lipman: Basic local alignment search tool. J. Mol. Biol. 215 (1990) 403–410

ASOMNIA: *A Service-Oriented Middleware for Ambient Information Access*

Karl Rehrl, Wernher Behrendt, Manfred Bortenschlager, Sigi Reich,
Harald Rieser, and Rupert Westenthaler

Salzburg Research
Jakob Haringer Straße 5/III
5020 Salzburg, Austria
{krehrl,wbehrendt,mborten,sreich,hrieser,rwestenthaler}
@salzburgresearch.at

Abstract. With the growing pervasiveness of information systems we are increasingly confronted with integrating heterogeneous end-user devices into existing information infrastructures. However, most existing middleware platforms either focus on plug & work functionalities or on multimedia streaming capabilities. ASOMNIA is a service-oriented middleware that combines the needs of plug & work infrastructures with the necessities of delivering multimedia contents. We describe ASOMNIA's service-oriented architecture and show how it can be applied in different scenarios.

1 Introduction

With the advent of pervasive information delivery and consumption, we increasingly face the issue of having to integrate various new types of end-user devices into existing information infrastructures. New middleware platforms are necessary in order to prepare the transition from PC based client/server computing to pervasive information systems, thus leading to ubiquitous information access and the convergence of multimedia content delivery, peer-to-peer networks and heterogeneous, context-aware devices.

The application scenario we are addressing is concerned with information systems for travellers in the area of public transport. As passengers we are all accustomed to textual information informing us about departure times, delays, etc. Furthermore, we are often confronted with the fact that the information provided is not up-to-date.

In this paper we argue for a convergent service-oriented middleware platform that allows for multimedia information to be displayed with arbitrary devices; by focusing on plug & work integration of devices in ad-hoc networks we are able to provide the necessary communicative hooks for enabling display devices to be closely connected to the information systems in the back-end in order to provide up-to-date information.

This paper is structured as follows. Section 2 outlines the requirements that lead to the design of ASOMNIA. Next, Section 3 provides a description of related

V. Mařík et al. (Eds.): DEXA 2003, LNCS 2736, pp. 423–432, 2003.

work. Following on to that, Section 4 describes ASOMNIA's system architecture. We continue with sample scenarios in Section 5 and conclude in Section 6.

2 Requirements for Service-Oriented Middleware Infrastructure

In this section we list the requirements from an infrastructure point of view. The latter sections will refer to these requirements.

R1 Openness with respect to devices and networks. A key requirement for pervasive infrastructures is the openness for heterogeneous devices. In the area of public transport we are confronted with different multimedia displays such as video walls, information kiosks or also end-user devices like PDAs or smart phones. This means, that more and more future devices will be connected over standard wireless networks like WLAN or Bluetooth. To assist a broad variety of devices, we argue for building the middleware architecture upon widely adopted device and network standards.

Moreover, in order to allow for situation aware information delivery [17,8, 3,4], we are increasingly forced to integrate devices with low processing power, like sensors, micro-controllers or RFID-Tags, which require a conceptual bridge in order to seamlessly communicate between devices.

R2 Simple construction and reconfiguration of services. One of the most important aspects of a service-oriented architecture is the modular design, which enables a developer to easily integrate new functionality into existing applications. This means that

1. The developer of new services is encouraged to concentrate on the development of functionality rather than struggling with protocol details.
2. Distribution and installation of new services can be accomplished on-the-fly.
3. Services can be reconfigured (i.e., activated/deactivated/moved) within a running middleware infrastructure.

R3 Location independent service provision. Any device in need of a certain functionality should be able to find an appropriate service irrespective of its location. In [5] this feature is referred to as "virtualization of resources", in *Centaurus* [9] a XML based ontology is used for exchanging service capabilities. The concept of "virtualization of resources" is particularly useful for travellers or public transport vehicles, using the same services in local networks at different stations.

R4 Flexible discovery mechanisms for ad-hoc networks. Especially for ad-hoc networks in pervasive settings, the reliable discovery of newly or sporadically available services and devices is a crucial requirement for middleware platforms [2,1]. Public transport vehicles arriving at a station should be able to find the necessary services to acquire new data or to announce their arrival. Travellers with mobile devices can use services available at a station or in a vehicle. Mobile peers, i.e., devices temporarily connected with each other, should enable arbitrary pairs of services to communicate [5].

R5 Plug & work functionality. In order to support ad-hoc networks, it is a key requirement for a middleware architecture to make the connection process for new peers as simple as possible. This implies that new peers should be able to get their configuration and service implementations or updates from decentralised plug & work servers.

R6 Support for different communication modes. Due to the mostly disconnected mode of mobile devices, communication heavily depends on the current connection status. Existing middleware systems typically depend on one specific communication mode. Object oriented middleware systems such as CORBA, DCOM or RMI are mainly based on synchronous remote procedure calls and provide transaction processing functionality; event distribution systems mainly depend on message passing; other communication modes include the usage of virtual shared memory, e.g. [12,14]. In pervasive applications, in case a device is connected to a network, synchronous communication is possible, whereas a disconnected device can only make use of asynchronous communication.

R7 Grouping of services. In service-oriented architectures it is often difficult to structure, combine or administer services running at different locations. Thus, it is a key requirement to provide mechanisms for a virtual grouping of services, which allows for allocation of access rights, multicast communication and easier administration and monitoring.

3   Related Work

In this section we categorise existing work by providing typical examples for the various middleware platforms. Furthermore, we point out additional examples of middleware architectures related to our approach.

Concerning the category of service-oriented middleware we consider the following examples as important to our work: *Jini* [18], *Cooltown* [10] and the *Open Grid Services Architecture* (OGSA) [5] by the Global Grid Forum. *Jini* uses the abstraction of a federated group of resources, which can be hardware devices or software programs. Using *Jini*, services can be dynamically added and deleted during runtime in a flexible way to reflect the dynamic nature of distributed systems. *Cooltown* influenced our work because of the possibility to virtually represent physical entities, whereas *OGSA* is driven by the idea of providing a higher-level concept of services for grid computing infrastructures. Especially important to our approach are concepts for standard interface definition, local/remote transparency and uniform service semantics.

Besides service-oriented middleware architectures other architectural styles include peer-to-peer(P2P) middleware, distributed event systems and virtual shared memory (VSM) middleware. *JXTA* [6], for instance, is a P2P platform targeted at the development of P2P networking and it is composed of a set of open protocols. The *Hermes* event-based middleware architecture [15] uses a type- and attribute-based publish/subscribe model to build large-scale distributed systems. The *EQUIP* platform [7] provides a middleware infrastructure for exploring the relationship between physical and digital artefacts. The main characteristics are cross language integration, modularisation, extensibility, dynamic loading of code, state sharing and support for heterogeneity of devices and networks.

One important issue considering pervasive applications is the convergence of multimedia content delivery, P2P networks and heterogeneous, context-aware devices. Most of the middleware systems discussed above only focus on one aspect, not considering the necessary convergence of technologies. *JXTA* primarily addresses P2P functionality and the building of ad-hoc networks, whereas *Cooltown* or *EQUIP* provide context information but do not care about the integration of heterogeneous devices or plug & work functionality. When it comes to the assistance of different communication modes, *Jini* is not suitable to offline devices because of its synchronous communication mode. *Hermes* provides asynchronous communication modes and event distribution but it lacks plug & work functionalities and the support for heterogeneous devices.

In general, most systems provide only low level data or event distribution mechanisms, but they do not provide higher level services including dynamic configurability, plug & work functionality or the infrastructure for adaptive multimedia based content delivery. In the following sections we will describe how we addressed these issues in designing and implementing the service-oriented platform ASOMNIA.

4 System Architecture

Based on an application scenario in the area of public transport and the requirements outlined in previous sections, we have defined an appropriate network structure for an ASOMNIA network (Fig. 1) and also an architecture for middleware services running on ASOMNIA devices.

The network structure shown in Figure 1 reflects our approach to a 2-layered, hierarchical overlay network scheme. The network is logically divided into one global domain (first layer) and a number of local domains (second layer). There is one central device, called the control center, which is logically the root of the system, hosting some root services like the central registry or a global messaging service. This central device is the only well-know device in the ASOMNIA network, all others are discovered dynamically. Devices can either register at the global registry, or discover a local registry within their local network by IP-multicast. Therefore, devices are able to use only local services available in their actual local domain.

In order to be integrated in the network, each device is running a set of middleware services responsible for certain tasks. Services on devices are using a service infrastructure, which is defined in the device architecture. The device architecture is mainly focused on the following goal: to provide a set of higher level system services and an abstract concept for re-usable service components in order to enable application developers to easily build their application services

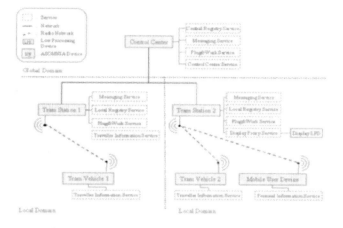

Fig. 1. The network structure of a typical application scenario

on top of the infrastructure. Therefore, important issues are the abstraction of the underlying devices, the provision of different communication modes, the easy building and integration of new services and the support of plug & work functionality. Consequently, Asomnia's device architecture consists of the following key components

- A small runtime environment, which is a combination of a core module called Core and a communication subsystem called CoSu. With the provision of a runtime environment, less effort has to be invested into porting Asomnia's service infrastructure to new devices. By implementing the communication functionalities in a dedicated module a changing of the underlying communication protocols can be achieved by modifying simply the CoSu (cf Requirement R1).
- The ServiceManager component is responsible for registering and controlling the services of an Asomnia device. At startup services are registered with the ServiceManager which takes care of them until they are unregistered. The ServiceManager provides access methods to other local/remote services. With its knowledge of local and remote services, the ServiceManager is able to use *either* local *or* remote calls for executing service methods (thus improving performance and off-line work capabilities).
- Services in Asomnia are rather coarse-grained functional entities, which are based on an abstract service definition (cf R2). Internally, services are built of fine-grained functional units to allow for component reuse and modular design. However, the functional units are encapsulated behind the service facade and can only be access via the public interface.
- The functionality of a service is defined by supporting a list of events, which was chosen as an abstraction to allow for different communication modes. Events can be activated from functional units or from other services by RPC or messaging, depending on the underlying CoSu. Only the event list

of a service is used as an interface by other services for interacting with the service (cf R3), therefore allowing for easy changing of implementations.

4.1 Communication Modes

As a key requirement we have defined the availability of different communication modes, ranging from synchronous communication to asynchronous messaging mechanisms. The actual communication mode used should be determined by the applications' needs (e.g. reliability of communication) and the connection state of the device. In fact, we have defined the following communication modes (cf R6):

Table 1. Communication modes

Connection state/reliability	Communication Modes
Online/reliable	Synchronous RPC/Asynchronous reliable messaging
Online/unreliable	Asynchronous unreliable messaging
Off-line/reliable	Asynchronous reliable messaging
Off-line/unreliable	No communication necessary

ASOMNIA by now supports these different communication modes on top of a Web Services CoSu. We believe that Web Services will play a major role in service-oriented architectures within the next few years [5,6,13]. Furthermore, the key features of Web Services e.g., openness to different platforms and heterogeneous devices and widely adopted standards, meet our requirements (cf R1) defined in Section 2. To provide the different communication modes, we made the following technical decisions:

- Synchronous, reliable communication between online devices is accomplished by the use of SOAP-RPC, for asynchronous reliable messages between online devices SOAP Messaging is used.
- If the receiver of an event is off-line, SOAP messages are stored at the central messaging service, by using a local messaging service to forward the message to the central messaging service. The messaging service is responsible for reliable delivery and handling acknowledgements as well as timeouts.

4.2 Plug & Work

On the path to ubiquitous computing, it is a key requirement to provide access to ad-hoc networks in a convenient way. For example, people who permanently change location and networks [11], are not likely to configure their devices and applications constantly. Thus, we think that pervasive middleware platforms have to provide the appropriate mechanisms for a convenient and ubiquitous access to information systems, independent of underlying network technologies or specific device configurations. We refer to this mechanism as plug & work and define the following key concepts:

- Services are provided in a subdomain or specific location (cf R3). Thus, wireless devices can always use local services in their current subdomain.
- Registry and discovery of services is based on a hierarchical concept, preferring local registries and services to more general ones (cf R4).
- Connecting new devices to the Asomnia network requires only little configuration settings on the device (e.g. a unique ID, the type of the device and optionally the central registry). All other configuration settings are loaded from the nearest plug & work service. Local plug & work services use the central plug & work service to get configuration settings from a centralised database server.
- Services do not have to be installed manually but can be loaded, updated and configured from plug & work access points if necessary (cf R5).
- Specific configuration settings of devices and services can be changed remotely by the system operator via the control center.

4.3 Proxy Services

In some cases it is necessary to integrate a device which is not able to provide the processing power needed to run the Asomnia middleware (or simply cannot offer the necessary software prerequisites to execute the middleware platform, e.g. a Java platform). Micro-controllers or sensors are examples for such devices. In order to integrate these devices a proxy service can be used (cf R1). The proxy service is able to communicate with the low-processing device via an appropriate interface and a specific – often proprietary – protocol.

4.4 Member of Groups and Service for Groups

Traveller information networks in the area of public transport are typically structured hierarchically, defining groups for different kinds of transport means and describing the dependencies between groups. Hierarchical structuring supports the system operator in controlling, monitoring and administrating, e.g. specifying access rights for services, or defining the different groups of services and devices. Therefore, a concept for structuring services is required. Asomnia is based on two key concepts for hierarchically structuring services (cf R7):

- A service can be a member of one or more groups by adding the service in the "Member of Group" set property of the service.
- A service can offer its functionality to other groups by adding the services to the "Service for Groups" set property.

5 Prototype and Sample Applications

As a proof-of-concept and demonstration of the practical applicability in real world scenarios, we have built a prototype based on the Java 2 platform and the the Apache AXIS toolkit.

5.1   Controlling the "Schmunzel" SMIL Player with a Conrad C2-Unit

In our test scenario, we have built a simple demonstration network to simulate a realistic application scenario. PC devices with "Schmunzel" SMIL players [16] were used to emulate multimedia displays. On each PC we installed a service component which was designed as a control interface for the SMIL player. A simple control GUI on another PC was used as control center. Additionally, a Conrad C2-Unit (a micro-controller based on the Infineon C164CI) connected via the RS232 interface was integrated in the middleware infrastructure via a proxy service thus demonstrating the possibility to integrate devices with low processing power. The C2-Unit provides a small display for showing a few characters and a numbed for entering data. This simple interface can be used for controlling the SMIL player.

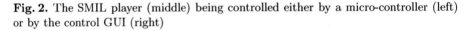

Fig. 2. The SMIL player (middle) being controlled either by a micro-controller (left) or by the control GUI (right)

Another service component on a PC simulated a simple multimedia repository with SMIL presentations. With the use of the Conrad controller we could choose a SMIL presentation in the repository and tell the SMIL players to play this presentation. The setting was perfectly suited as a showcase for the traveller information scenario. Moreover, with SMIL as an open standard for the presentation of multimedia assets and Java as an open platform for mobile computing, the key requirement for open standards has been fulfilled (cf R1).

5.2   Experiences and Discussion

The prototype implementation of ASOMNIA's service-oriented architecture was perfectly suited to fulfill the requirements defined in section 2. The following findings can be reported:

- The construction of the necessary services was carried out with little effort because of the concept of abstract services and the simple event-based interaction model. Because of the abstractions defined in the service runtime environment, the service developer is not longer bothered with communication details like building SOAP messages or making remote procedure calls.

- Although Web Services are not yet fully standardised, many concepts were adopted to the communication layer in ASOMNIA. In fact, Web Services turned out to be well suited for this task because of their assistance of different communication modes. However, Web Service technology lacks an appropriate runtime infrastructure and the concept of higher level services.
- Especially the concept of proxy services has turned out to be a powerful tool for integrating devices with low processing power like sensors. Devices with low processing power are considered a necessity on the way to ambient intelligence.
- Plug & work functionality is an important feature in pervasive computing scenarios. The high amount of heterogeneous devices connected to the network can only be managed by reducing configuration effort on the devices. On ASOMNIA devices at least only the type of the device or a unique ID has to be configured, which is considered as true plug & work functionality.

6   Summary and Conclusion

In this paper we have argued for the need of convergent middleware infrastructures for pervasive information systems. We have shown that existing systems do not provide the necessary assistance for different communication modes, ad-hoc networks and heterogeneous devices. In fact, many of the systems only provide low level communication, without providing the necessary abstractions.

Thus, in our paper we have defined the key requirements for a middleware infrastructure, which provides convergence between multimedia content delivery, ad-hoc networks and heterogeneous, context-aware devices. We have shown the system architecture and we have demonstrated a proof-of-concept closely related to our real application scenario.

In conclusion, we believe that ASOMNIA can bridge the gap between pure network connectivity (as provided by Bluetooth, etc.) and existing information systems (ranging from enterprise application solutions to peer-to-peer like applications). Therefore, middleware infrastructures such as ASOMNIA will enable the full potential of ubiquitous information access.

Acknowledgements. This work has been supported in part by the ASCOM Center of Competence, Salzburg, and the Austrian Forschungsförderungsfonds.

References

1. Dipanjan Chakraborty, Filip Perich, Anupam Joshi, Timothy Finin, and Yelena Yesha. Middleware for mobile information access. In *DEXA Workshops*, pages 729–733, 2002.

432   K. Rehrl et al.

2. Harry Chen, Anupam Joshi, and Timothy W. Finin. Dynamic service discovery for mobile computing: Intelligent agents meet jini in the aether. *Cluster Computing*, 4(4):343–354, 2001.
3. A. Ferscha, S. Vogl, and W. Beer. Ubiquitous context sensing in wireless environments. In 4th DAPSYS *(Austrian-Hungarian Workshop on Distributed and Parallel Systems)*. Kluwer Academic Publishers, 2002.
4. Sebastian Fischmeister, Guido Menkhaus, and Wolfgang Pree. Context-awareness and adaptivity through mobile shadows. Technical report, Software Research Lab, University of Salzburg, 2002.
5. Ian Foster, Carl Kesselman, Jeffrey M. Nick, and Steven Tuecke. The physiology of the grid: An open grid services architecture for distributed systems integration. Draft 5, Mathematics and Computer Science Division, Argonne National Laboratory and Department of Computer Science, University of Chicago and Information Sciences Institute, University of Southern California and IBM Corporation, November 2002.
6. Li Gong. Jxta: A network programming environment. *IEEE Internet Computing*, V 5:88–95, 2001.
7. Chris Grennhalgh. Equip: a software platform for distributed interactive systems. Technical report, The Mixed Reality Laboratory, University of Nottingham, 2001.
8. M. Beigl und A. Schmidt H-W. Gellersen. Sensor-based context-awareness for situated computing. In *Workshop on Software Engineering for Wearable and Pervasive Computing SEWPC00 at the 22nd Int. Conference on Software Engineering ICSE 2000, Limerick, Ireland*.
9. L. Kagal, V. Korolev, H. Chen, A. Joshi, and T. Finin. Centaurus: A framework for intelligent services in a mobile environment. In *Proceedings of the International Workshop on Smart Appliances and Wearable Computing (IWSAWC)*, 2001.
10. Tim Kindberg, John J. Barton, Jeff Morgan, Gene Becker, Debbie Caswell, Philippe Debaty, Gita Gopal, Marcos Frid, Venky Krishnan, Howard Morris, John Schettino, Bill Serra, and Mirjana Spasojevic. People, places, things: Web presence for the real world. In*MONET 7(5)*, pages 365–376.
11. Leonard Kleinrock. Nomadicity: Anytime, anywhere in a disconnected world. In *Mobile Networks and Applications 1*, pages 351–357, 1996.
12. E. Kühn and G. Nozicka. Post client/server coordination tools. In *Proceedings of Coordination Technology for Collaborative Applications, Springer Series Lecture Notes in Computer Science*, 1997.
13. Tobin J. Lehman and Allessandro Garcia. Tspaces services suite, 2001. See http://www.almaden.ibm.com/cs/TSpaces/services.html.
14. Tobin J. Lehman, Stephen W. McLaughry, and Peter Wycko. T spaces: The next wave. In HICSS, 1999.
15. Peter R. Pietzuch and Jean M. Bacon. Hermes: A distributed event-based middleware architecture. In Proceedings of the 1st International Workshop on Distributed Event-Based Systems (DEBS'02), 2002.
16. Siegfried Reich, Martin Schaller, and Rupert Westenthaler. Developing advanced multimedia presentations with Java. Technical report, Sun Microsystems, June 2001. Presentation T541 at JavaOne, San Francisco, June 2001.
17. Albrecht Schmidt, Michael Beigl, and Hans-W. Gellersen. There is more to context than location. Computers and Graphics, 23(6):893–901, 1999.
18. Jim Waldo. Jini™technology architectural overview. Technical report, Sun Microsystems, Inc., 901 San Antonio Road, Palo Alto, CA 94303 U.S.A., 1999. Available as http://www.sun.com/jini/whitepapers/architecture.html.

An Efficient Tree-Structure Index Allocation Method over Multiple Broadcast Channels in Mobile Environments*

Byungkyu Lee and Sungwon Jung

Department of Computer Sciences,
Sogang University
1 Shinsoo-Dong, Mapo-Ku,
Seoul 121-742, Korea
bkblue@sogang.ac.kr
jungsung@ccs.sogang.ac.kr

Abstract. Broadcast has been often used to disseminate the frequently requested data efficiently to a large volume of mobile units over a single or multiple channels. Since the mobile units have limited battery power, the minimization of the access time for the broadcast data is an important problem. In this paper, we studied an efficient index allocation method for the broadcast data over multiple physical channels to minimize the access time. Previously proposed index allocation techniques either require the equal size of index and data or have a performance degradation problem when the number of given physical channels is not enough. To cope with these problems, we propose an efficient tree-structured index allocation method for the broadcast data with different access frequencies over multiple physical channels.

1 Introduction

In mobile environment, organizing massive amount of data on wireless communication networks to provide fast and low power access to users equipped with palmtops, is a new challenge to the data management and telecommunication communities[1]. To cope with this problem, broadcasting has been suggested as a possible solution in wireless environment[2]. There have been many research efforts reported in the literature that focus on the improvement of the broadcast method by providing indexes[3,4,6]. Indexes will allow mobile clients to slip into the doze mode most of the time and come into the active mode only when the data of interest arrives on the broadcast channel. Most works on the improvement of data broadcast methods aim to enhance the quality of service for two performance metrics: tuning time and access time. Imielinski and et al. propose

---

* This research was supported by the next-generation new technology development program of Ministry of Commerce, Industry and Energy in Korea, and in part by Institute for Applied Science and Technology of Sogang University

V. Mařík et al. (Eds.): DEXA 2003, LNCS 2736, pp. 433–443, 2003.

a tree-structured index allocation technique on the broadcast data over a single wireless channel, where each data item is considered to have same access frequency[3].

Prabhakara and et al. studied efficient ways of broadcasting data to mobile users over multiple physical channels which cannot be coalesced into a lesser number of high-bandwidth physical channels [5]. In their scheme, they use flat-structured indexes which have access and tuning times larger than the tree-structured indexes. Two different approaches have been studied on tree-structured indexing techniques for broadcast data over multi-channel environments[4,6]. One approach is to use multi-channels such that data and index nodes are interleaved over each channel[6]. This approach has a problem since it requires the equal size of index and data nodes. Note that the sizes of data nodes are usually larger (i.e., 10-50 times) than their index nodes. Thus, the index node size becomes unnecessarily large, which will in turn dramatically increase the tuning and access times for the broadcast data. The other approach is to partition the multi-channels into dedicated data and index channels so that data(index) channels carry only data (index) nodes[4]. Due to the separation of the index and data channels, this approach does not have the same serious problem as above. However, this approach is not efficient when the number of physical index channels is less than the depth of the index tree.

In this paper, we propose a new tree-structured index allocation method for the broadcast data with different access frequencies over multi-channels. Our method minimizes the average access time by broadcasting hot data and their indexes more frequently than the less hot data and their indexes. This is not possible in the two methods proposed in [4,6]. Furthermore, our method does not have the above two problems due to the following two reasons. First, we adopt the approach proposed in [4] to avoid the equal size requirement of index and data nodes. Secondly, our method does not require having the index channels as many as the depth of the index tree in [6].

The rest of the paper is organized as follows. In section 2, we provides a data broadcast method over data channels. We then propose a new tree-structured index allocation method for the broadcast data with non-uniform access frequencies over index channels in section 3. Section 4 discusses how we can access data nodes on data channels from index nodes on index channels. Performance analysis of our method is given in section 5. Finally, section 6 gives concluding remarks.

2   Data Broadcast Method over Data Channels

We propose a new tree-structured index allocation method that partitions the multiple wireless channels into the index and data channels. Note that the channels in consideration are all symmetric, physical channels with same bandwidth. The index and data channels are dedicated to broadcast index nodes and data nodes respectively. In this section, we first discuss the algorithm to broadcast data nodes over the data channels. It is shown in Figure 1. It assumes that each

```
/* INPUT:
    D = {d_1, d_2, ..., d_n} be a set of data nodes to broadcast;
    Temperature(d_i) = Temperature of data d_i for i = 1 to n;
    DC = {DC_1, DC_2, ..., DC_k} be a set of given data channels
    k = the number of data channels
    OUTPUT:
    the data broadcast program for the data nodes in D over data channels in DC. */

Step 1:
    Sort the data d_i in D by Temperature(d_i) in descending order;
    Let d'_i represent i^th sorted data in descending order;
Step 2:
    ave_channel_temperature = sum_{i=1}^{n} Temperature(d'_i)/k ; j = 0;
    for (i = 1; i <= k; i + +) {
      do {
        j = j + 1;
        Allocate data d'_j to the data channel DC_i;
      } while (the sum of temperatures of all data allocated to the data channel DC_i < ave_channel_temp); }
```

Fig. 1. Data Broadcast Algorithm over Data Channels

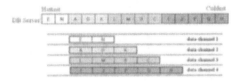

Fig. 2. An Example of Data Broadcast Schedule

data has its temperature. Data with hot (cold) temperatures mean they have high (low) access frequencies. Without loss of generality, we assume that data channel i accommodates the hotter data than data channel $i + 1$ does[1].

An example of the algorithm is illustrated in Figure 2 where the number of data channels is 4.

It has 14 data sorted in descending order of their temperatures(i.e. access frequencies) such that $E, N, A, D, K, L, M, B, C, I, J, F, G, H$ where $temperature(E)$ and $temperature(H)$ is the hottest and the coldest respectively. At step 2, we compute the average data channel temperature, which we assume 70. Then, we allocate E and N to data channel 1 such that the sum of the temperatures of E and N is not less than 70. [A, D, K], [L, M, B, C] and [I, J, F, G, H] are respectively allocated data channel 2, 3, and 4 in a similar fashion. Note that the broadcast cycle of [E,N] over channel 1 is shorter than those over data channel 2, 3, and 4.

---

[1] Note that data channel i is named a higher channel than data channel $i + 1$.

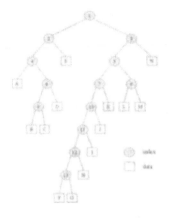

Fig. 3. An Example of Alphabetic Huffman Tree

3   Index Allocation Method over Index Channels

In this section, we discuss our index allocation method that reflects the data broadcast schedule generated by Algorithm in Figure 1. To reflect the data broadcast schedule, our index allocation method requires that the broadcast frequencies of the indexes for data over the data channel i be the same as the broadcast frequencies of the data over the data channel i.

3.1   Existing Tree-Based Index Allocation Methods

Two different approaches have been studied on tree-structured indexing techniques for broadcast data with non-uniform access frequencies over multi-channel environments[4,6]. These techniques use Alphabetic Huffman tree for indexing the data[4]. The depth of each data node in Alphabetic Huffman tree reflects its relative temperature compared to other data nodes. That is, the depth of hot data is low whereas the depth of the less hot data is high. This property makes the data at the low depths of the tree have less tuning and access times than those at the high depths of the tree.

    An example of Alphabetic Huffman Tree constructed over the set of data nodes {A,B,C,D,E,F,G,H,I,J,K,L,M,N} in Figure 2 is shown in Figure 3. The set of index nodes created are {1, 2, 3, ..., 11, 12, 13}. In the Figure, the data nodes E and N have the hottest temperatures and the data nodes F and G have the coldest temperatures. The Alphabetic Huffman tree in Figure 3 will be used as a running example throughout the paper.

    In [4], Shivakumar and Venkatasubramanian partition the multi-channels into dedicated data channels and index channels so that data(index) channels carry only data (index) nodes. They assign one index channel to each level of the Alphabetic Huffman tree. This method has a performance degradation problem when the number of physical index channels is less than the depth of the Alphabetic Huffman tree. Figure 4-(a) shows an example of index allocation

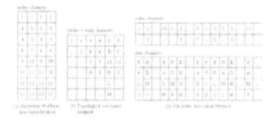

Fig. 4. Examples of Index Allocation Methods

method of [4] for the Alphabetic Huffman tree shown in Figure 3. Since the depth of the tree in Figure 3 is 8, it has 8 index channels where each channel has the index nodes at each level of the tree.

In [6], Lo and Chen use multi-channels such that data and index nodes are interleaved over each channel. They create an Alphabetic Huffman Tree for the broadcast data and then create the topological tree adapted for the given multi-channels by using the Alphabetic Huffman Tree. Lastly, they assign index and data nodes of the topological tree to the given multi-channels. Figure 4-(b) shows its example. Their approach has a problem since it requires the same size of index and data nodes. Note that the size of data nodes are usually larger (i.e., 10-50 times) than their index nodes[9,10]. Thus, the index node size becomes unnecessarily large wasting the bandwidth of channels, which will in turn dramatically increase the tuning and access times for the broadcast data. Our method overcomes the two problems occurred in [4,6]. Figure 4 -(c) shows an example of our index allocation method where 2 index and 4 data channels are given.

3.2   Our Tree-Structure Index Allocation Method

In this section, we first give the assumptions and the terminologies, and the definitions that will be used to explain our method.

- The channels in consideration are assumed to be all symmetric, physical channels with same bandwidth.
- The sizes of data and index nodes need not to be equal. However, data nodes are assumed to be all equi-sized and index nodes are assumed to be all equi-sized.
- An index node is assumed to have the information about the channel number and the time offset for the next index or data nodes.
- Access time is the time elapsed from the initial probe to the point when all required data is downloaded by the mobile client.
- Index broadcast cycle : A index broadcast cycle is the one period of index broadcast.

Definition 1. *Let DC_i be the ith data channel. IS_1 denotes the 1st index set that contains the sequence of index nodes along the path from the root of an Alphabetic Huffman tree to the data in DC_1. Then, IS_i ($2 \leq i \leq$ the number of*

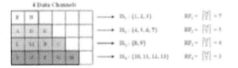

Fig. 5. Index Set & Repetition Frequency

data channels) represents the ith index set which contains the sequence of index nodes along the path from the root of an Alphabetic Huffman tree to the data in DC_i excluding all the index nodes in IS_j for $j = 1, i - 1$.

Note that we have to create index set IS_i before creating IS_{i+1} due to the above definition 1. The indexes in IS_i point to the hotter data nodes than those in IS_{i+1}, because the data at DC_i are hotter than those at DC_{i+1}. Furthermore, we need to broadcast the indexes in IS_i as frequently as the corresponding data in DC_i. For this, we need to compute the repetition frequency RF_i that IS_i have to be broadcast in a single index broadcast cycle.

Definition 2. *Let IS_i be the index set corresponding to the ith data channel DC_i. Let BD and DX_i be the number of data to broadcast and the number of data indexed by the index nodes in IS_i. Then, $RF_i = \lceil \frac{BD}{DX_i} \rceil$ represents the repetition frequency that IS_i have to be broadcast.*

Figure 5 shows the examples of IS_i and RF_i obtained from the Alphabetic Huffman tree in Figure 3where $BD = 14$, $DX_1 = 2, DX_2 = 3, DX_3 = 4$, and $DX_4 = 5$.

Definition 3. *Let IS_i be the index set corresponding to the ith data channel DC_i. Assume that k be the number of index channels. From IS_i, a sequence of its subsets $S_{i1}, S_{i2}, ..., S_{in}$ is defined as the index block IB_i for IS_i. And S_{ip} is named as the pth member of the index block IB_i where $1 \le p \le n$. The index block IB_i must meet the following 4 requirements:*

1. $IS_i = \bigcup_{j=1}^n S_{ij}$
2. $S_{ip} \cap S_{iq} = \emptyset$ for $1 \le p, q \le n$ and $p \ne q$
3. All the indexes in S_{ip} should not be related to each other in an ancestor-descendent relationship.
4. For $1 \le p \le n$, make $|S_{ip}|$ be k where $|S_{ip}|$ represents the size of S_{ip}. If $|S_{ip}| < k$, then put a **null index** into S_{ip} until its size becomes k.

Figure 6 shows an example of the index blocks for the index sets $IS_1 = \{1, 2, 3\}$, $IS_2 = \{4, 5, 6, 7\}$, $IS_3 = \{8, 9\}$, and $IS_4 = \{10, 11, 12, 13\}$ obtained from the Alphabetic Huffman tree in Figure 3 when the number of index channels is 2. Since we have two index channels, the size of each member of the index block must be 2 and all the elements in each member should not be related to each other in an ancestor-descendent relationship. These requirements enforce $S_{11} = \{1\}$, $S_{41} = \{10\}$, $S_{42} = \{11\}$, $S_{43} = \{12\}$, and $S_{44} = \{13\}$ to include the *null index* as their element.

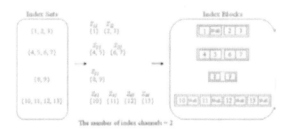

Fig. 6. Examples of Index Blocks

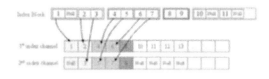

Fig. 7. Allocation of Indexes from Index Blocks to 2 Index Channels

We now discuss our index allocation scheme. Assume that $S_{ip} = \{I_1, I_2, \ldots, I_k\}$ be a member of the index block for an index set IS_i from definition 3. Here, k represents the number of index channels and I_1, I_2, ..., I_k represents indexes[2]. Since the k indexes are not related to each other by an ancestor and descendant relationship, they don't need to be accessed in any order for accessing data. This property allows us to broadcast the k indexes to the k index channels simultaneously. That is, we allocate the index I_j to the index channel j for j=1 to k.

Figure 7 shows an example of how we allocate the indexes of the index blocks in Figure 6 to the two index channels. Figure 8 gives the formal description of our algorithm over k multi-channels. To show how the above algorithm works, we give an example in Figure 9 where 4 data channels and 2 index channels are physically available. We assume the data broadcast schedule in Figure 2 and the Alphabetic Huffman tree in Figure 3. Based on the above assumption, the example shows the index allocation to 2 index channels. As the repetition frequencies in 5 represent, the index sets IS_1, IS_2, IS_3, and IS_4 appears 7, 5, 4, and 3 times in the first index broadcast cycle in Figure 9.

3.3   Accessing Data Nodes from Index Nodes

In this section, we discuss how we can access data nodes over data channels from index nodes over index channels. An index node y needs to have the following information to compute the position of its child data node x over a data channel i.

- *DSize*: the size of a data node
- *Bcast(i)*: the number of data nodes that constitute a broadcast cycle over data channel i

---

[2] A sequence of indexes $I_k, I_{k-1}, I_{k-2}, \ldots, I_d$ may be *null indexes* by the *4th* requirement of definition 3 where $1 \le d \le k$.

```
/* INPUT:
   AHT = Alphabetic Huffman Tree created for the broadcast data
   ND = the number of data channels
   IC = {IC_1, IC_2, ..., IC_k} be a set of k index channels
   DBP = the data broadcast program computed by the algorithm in Figure 1
   OUTPUT:
   Index Allocation Program over k Index Channels in IC for DBP. */
Step 1: Create Index Sets
       for(i = 1; i ≤ ND; i + +) Create IS_i from AHT and DBP by definition 1;
Step 2: Compute Repetition Frequencies for Index Sets
       for(i = 1; i ≤ ND; i + +) Compute RF_i from IS_i by definition 2;
Step 3: Create Index Blocks for Index Sets
       for(i = 1; i ≤ ND; i + +) Create Index Block IB_i for IS_i by definition 3;
Step 4: Allocate Indexes to k index channels in IC;
       count = 0;
       for(i = 1; i ≤ ND; i + +) count = count + RF_i;
       while (count > 0) {
          for(i = 1; i ≤ ND; i + +) {
          if (RF_i ≥ 0) {
             Let IB_i consists of S_{i1}, S_{i2}, ..., S_{in};
             for(j = 1; j ≤ n; j + +) {
                Assume that S_{ij} = {I_1, I_2, ..., I_k};
                for p = 1 to k, allocate the index I_p to the index channel IC_p;
             }
             RF_i = RF_i - 1;
             count = count - 1;
          } } }
```

Fig. 8. Index Allocation Algorithm to k Index Channels

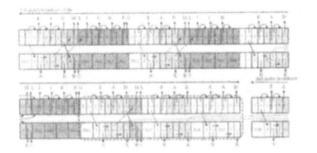

Fig. 9. An Example of Index Allocation Generated by the Algorithm in Figure 8

- $Size\_of\_Data\_Channel(i)$: $Bcast(i) \times DSize$ for the data channel i
- $Relative\_Data\_Position(x, i)$: the time offset of the data node x from the beginning of the data broadcast cycle over data channel i

Based on the above information, we describe an algorithm in Figure 10 that computes the current position of the data node x over data channel i from an index node y.

4   Performance Analysis

In this section, we analyze the performance of our method in comparison with the topological tree based method proposed. The topological tree based method is quite relevant to our method due to the following two reasons. The first is that both methods adapt to a given number of channels easily without requiring

```
/* INPUT:
   x = data node that needs to be accessed;
   y = index node that points to data node x;
   i = data channel number over which data node x is being broadcast;
   current_index_position = the current position of index node y;
   Size_of_Data_Channel(i) = Bcast(i) × DSize;
   OUTPUT:
   position = the current position of data node x over data channel i from index node y */

   period_number = ⌊current_index_position/DSIZE⌋;
   position = Size_of_Data_Channel(i) × period_number + Relative_Data_Position(x, i)
   while (current_index_position > position) {
      period_number + +;
      position = Size_of_Data_Channel(i) × period_number + Relative_Data_Position(x, i); }
```

Fig. 10. Accessing a Data Node from an Index Node

additional channels for the index allocation[3]. The second is that both methods use Alphabetic Huffman Tree for their index tree. For convenience, we call our method as SIME (Separated Indexing in Multiple Channel Environments) and the topological tree-base method as TOPO (TOPOlogical) for the rest of this paper.

We carried out the simulation for the performance comparison on a Pentium-III 866EB with 512MB memory. The simulator was implemented using CSIM 18 simulation language[8]. To model the non-uniform (or skwed) data access pattern of mobile clients, we use a Zipf distribution with a parameter θ. Note that the Zipf distribution is typically used to model non-uniform access patterns[7]. It produces access patterns that becomes increasingly skewed as θ increases. In this simulation, we set the value of θ to 0.95 to model a skewed access pattern. This access pattern is common in broadcasting environments. The various parameters used in the simulation are as follows:

- the number of data channels = 8, the number of index channels = 2, $\Theta = 0.95$
- the total number of channels = 10, the number of broadcast data = 2000
- R = ratio of a data node size and an index node size = 1-50

We chose an average access time of a mobile client as our primary performance metric. The average access time is measured by averaging the access times of a mobile client over 20000 simulation runs. Note that we measure the access time in terms of broadcast units. A broadcast unit represents an amount of time taken to broadcast a single index node. For example, it will take 20 broadcast units to broadcast a single data node when R is 20. Since the size of a data node is usually very large (i.e., 10-50 times) compared to that of an index node[9,10], their size difference will affect on the performances of SIME and TOPO. Thus, we first analyze its effect on the performance of $SIME$ and $TOPO$ by varying R from 1 to 50. This is shown in Figure 11.

Figure 11 shows the average access time of TOPO is less than that of SIME only when R is less than 3. Note that the average access time of SIME increases very slowly whereas that of TOPO increases rapidly as R increases. As a result,

---

[3] Since this is not possible in Huffman tree-based method, Huffman tree-based method is not considered in our performance analysis.

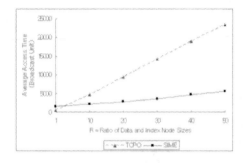

Fig. 11. Performance of SIME and TOPO when varying R

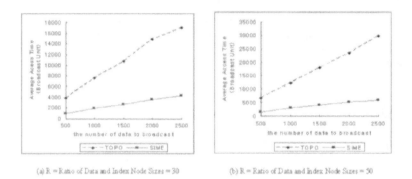

(a) R = Ratio of Data and Index Node Sizes = 30   (b) R = Ratio of Data and Index Node Sizes = 50

Fig. 12. Performance of SIME and TOPO when varying the number of broadcast data

the average access time of SIME is getting a lot less than that of TOPO as R increase from 4 to 50. In TOPO, as R increases, the size gap between the data and index nodes is getting bigger, thus wasting the bandwidth of channels allocated to index nodes. This will in turn increase the access time of TOPO method. However, this problem does not occur in SIME method since we partition the wireless channels into index and data channels. Next, we study how increasing the number of broadcast data will affect the the performances of SIME and TOPO methods. For this experiment, we fix R to 30 and 50 and varies the number of broadcast data from 500 to 2500. The results are illustrated in Figure 12 (a) and (b).

They show that the access time of SIME method is much better than TOPO as the number of broadcast data increases. This is because the skewed data access patterns severely deteriorate the performance of TOPO as the number of broadcast data becomes large. In TOPO method, the broadcast frequencies of hot data and their corresponding index nodes are not high enough to reflect the skewed data access patterns. As a result, the access times of TOPO method in Figure 12 (a) and (b) increase rapidly. On the contrary, SIME method overcomes this problem by broadcasting hot data and their index nodes more frequently than the less hot data and their index nodes in a single broadcast cycle. Thus, the access times of SIME in Figure 12 (a) and (b) increase very slowly. From these two experiments, we conclude that SIME method is much better than TOPO method in mobile environments with multi-channels.

5   Conclusion

In this paper, we proposed an efficient index allocation method for broadcast data with non-uniform access patterns over multiple broadcast channels in mobile environments. Our method minimizes an average access time by broadcasting hot data and their indexes more frequently than the less hot data and their indexes over dedicated index and data channels. Our method further reduces the average access time by not wasting the bandwidth of channels caused by the size difference between an index node and a data node. This is achieved by allocating index and data nodes to dedicated index and data channels respectively.

We then analyzed the performance of our method by comparing it with a topological tree based method. The simulation results show that our method performs far better than the topological tree based method. Our method is also shown to be scalable when the number of broadcast is increased.

References

1. T. Imielinski and B. Badrinath, "Wireless Mobile Computing : Challenges in Data Management", *Comm. of ACM*, Vol 37, No. 10, pp. 18–28, 1994.
2. S. Acharya, M. Franklin, S. Zdonik, and R. Alonso, "Broadcast Disks : Data Management for Asymmetric Communication Environment", *Proc. ACM SIGMOD International Conf. on Management of Data*, pp. 199–210, 1995.
3. T. Imielinski, S. Viswanathan, and B. R. Badrinath, "Data on Air: Organization and Access", *IEEE Trans. on Knowledge and Data Engineering*, Vol. 9, No. 3, pp. 353–372, May/June 1997.
4. Narayanan Shivakumar, Suresh Venkatasubramanian, "Efficient indexing for Broadcast Based Wireless Systems", *Mobile Networks and Applications*, pp. 433–446, 1996.
5. K. Prabhakara, K. Hua, and J. Oh, "Multi-Level Multi-Channel Air Cache Design for Broadcasting in a Mobile Environment", *Proceedings. 16th International Conference on Data Engineering*, 2000.
6. S. Lo and A. Chen, "Optimal Index and Data Allocation in Multiple Broadcast Channels", *In proceedings. 16th international conference on Data Engineering*, 2000
7. D. Knuth, "The Art of Computer Programming Second Edition", Vol, *Addison Wesley*, 1998.
8. H. D Schwetman, "CSIM: A C-based process oriented simulation language", *Proceeding 1986 Winter Simulation Conference*, 1986
9. Ni, W., S. Vrbsky, Q. Fang and J. Zhang, "Concurrency Control for Mobile Real-Time Databases Using Adaptive Broadcasting", *20th IASTED International Conference on Applied Informatics*, Feb. 2002, pp. 425–430.
10. Hong V. Leong , Antonio Si, "Data broadcasting strategies over multiple unreliable wireless channels", *Proc of the fourth international conference on Information and knowledge management*, December 1995

DSTTMOD: A Future Trajectory Based Moving Objects Database

Xiaofeng Meng[1] and Zhiming Ding[2]

[1] Institute of Data and Knowledge Engineering
Renmin University of China,
Beijing China,100872
xfmeng@mail.ruc.edu.cn
[2] Praktische Informatik IV
Fernuniversität Hagen,
D-58084 Hagen, Germany
zhiming.ding@fernuni-hagen.de

Abstract. In this paper, a new moving objects database model - Discrete Spatio-Temporal Trajectory Based Moving Objects Database (DSTTMOD) model, is put forward. Trajectories are used to represent dynamic attributes of moving objects, including the past, current, and future location information. Moving objects can submit moving plans of different length according to their moving patterns. Moreover, they can divide the whole moving plan into multiple sections, and submit each section only when it is about to be used. Different moving objects can set up different threshold to trigger location updates. When a location update occurs to a moving object, not only its future trajectory is updated, but also the corresponding index records are adjusted. The model can support three kinds of queries (point queries, range queries, and K-nearest neighbor (KNN) queries) for location information in not only the near future, but also the far future. In order to evaluate the performance of the DSTTMOD model, a prototype system is developed and a series of experiments are conducted which show promising performance.

1 Introduction

With the development of wireless communications and positioning technologies, the concept of moving objects databases (MOD) has become increasingly important, and has posed a great challenge to the database community. Existing DBMS's are not well equipped to handle continuously changing data, such as the location of moving objects [1]. Therefore, new location modeling methods are needed to solve this problem.

Recently, a lot of research has been focused on MOD technology, and many models and algorithms have been proposed. O. Wolfson *et al.* in [1-4] have proposed a Moving Objects Spatio-Temporal (MOST) model which is capable of tracking not only the current, but also the near future position of moving objects. L. Forlizzi *et al.* in [5] have proposed a data model to describe the trajectories of moving objects, but their work has not discussed the location update problem, which limits the adaptability of the model. H. D. Chon *et al.* in [6] have proposed a Space-Time Grid

V. Mařík et al. (Eds.): DEXA 2003, LNCS 2736, pp. 444–453, 2003.

Storage model for moving objects, which mainly deals with the storage problem and discusses the Ripple Effect. Besides, C. S. Jensen *et al.* in [7-8] have discussed the indexing problem for moving object trajectories. In their work, however, the trajectories are mainly used to represent the history information.

When querying moving objects, the users may be interested in the past or current position information. However, in many circumstances, location information in the future, especially in the far future, may be more attractive to querying users. For instance, the driver of a broken car would be more interested in service cars that will arrive within the next 20 minutes. In this case, the previously proposed models are not well equipped to provide this kind of information.

In order to solve the above problem, we put forward a new MOD model - Discrete Spatial-Temporal Trajectory Based Moving Object Database (DSTTMOD) model, in this paper. Our aim is to support queries for location information not only in the past and at present, but also in the future.

Compared with other previously proposed MOD models, DSTTMOD has the following features. (1) Trajectories are used to represent dynamic attributes of moving objects, including the past, current, and future location information. (2) Moving objects can submit moving plans of different length according to their moving patterns. Moreover, they can divide the whole moving plan into multiple sections, and submit each section only when it is to be used. (3) Different moving objects can set up different threshold to trigger location updates. When a location update occurs to a moving object, not only its future trajectory is updated, but also the corresponding index records are adjusted. (4) The model can support three kinds of queries (*point queries*, *range queries*, and *K-nearest neighbor* (*KNN*) *queries*) for location information covering a large time range from the past into the future.

2 DSTTMOD: The System

Figure 1 depicts the architecture of the DSTTMOD system we have implemented. The system consists of five components: Route Map Generator, Moving Object Generator and Manager, Moving Object Indexer, Moving Object Simulator, and Query Processor.

Route Map Generator is responsible for generating route maps (road networks) on which moving objects move. There are two different ways to generate route maps: automatic and user interactive. The generated route map will be stored in the database.

Moving Object Generator and Manager generates moving objects according to a specified route map. The user can choose to create a moving object either automatically or manually. Information concerning each moving object includes an identifier and a moving plan. The system then generates the corresponding trajectory according to the moving plan, which will be stored in the database.

Moving Object Indexer generates a spatial-temporal index for the moving objects managed by the system. In DSTTMOD, we use a Grid-file based indexing structure which is called GMOI to index moving object trajectories. We have made two major modifications to the original Grid-file based method [9] in order to reduce location update costs (see Section 4).

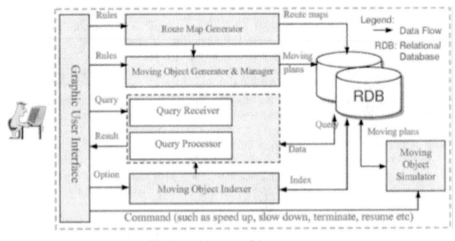

Fig. 1. Architecture of the system

Moving Object Simulator is responsible for simulating the running of moving objects. During its life time, a moving object can change its moving plan proactively, and it may also deviate from the predefined moving plan due to unforeseeable events (say traffic congestions). Both cases will trigger location updates. The system allows users to define parameters which will then affect the frequency of location updates and the uncertainty of the system.

Query Processor can support 3 kinds of queries concerning past, current, or future location information. Results of *Point queries* such as "tell me the current location of MO01" can be directly computed from the trajectories of moving objects. *Range queries* and *KNN queries* can be supported by the index structure of DSTTMOD. The system provides a GUI to interact with querying users.

3 Modeling Moving Objects with Future Trajectories

In the DSTTMOD model, we use a discrete method to describe the location information of moving objects. The whole trajectory of a moving object is represented by a set of line segments in the spatial-temporal space (For simplicity, we suppose that moving objects move on the two-dimensional X×Y plane. Thus, the spatio-temporal trajectory is a curve in three-dimensional X×Y×T space). Within each line segment, the movement of a moving object has the following properties:

   a) Spatially, the moving object moves along a straight line;
   b) The speed of the moving object keeps constant.

The whole complicated trajectory of a moving object can be represented by a set of such relatively simple line segments, and these line segments are then saved into the indexing structure so that they can be quickly retrieved. Since these line segments form a polyline in the X×Y×T space, we can simply use a set of vertexes to represent the whole trajectory, as defined below.

Definition 1(Trajectory): Suppose M is a moving object whose identifier is *MID*, then, its **Spatio-Temporal Trajectory**, denoted by $\overline{\xi}(MID)$, is defined as a finite sequence of points in the X×Y×T space:

$$\overline{\xi}(MID) = ((x_i, y_i, t_i))_{i=1}^{n}$$

The expression $(x_i, y_i, t_i)(1 \leq i \leq n)$ is called the *i*th **key point**, denoted by $\overline{\xi}(MID) \cdot \rho(i)$. And the line segment $[(x_i, y_i, t_i), (x_{i+1}, y_{i+1}, t_{i+1})]$ is called the *i*th **spatio-temporal segment**, denoted by $\overline{\xi}(MID) \cdot Seg(i)$.

Definition 2: Suppose M is a moving object whose identifier is *MID*, $\overline{\xi}(MID)$ and $\overline{\xi}(MID) \cdot \rho(i)$ are its spatio-temporal trajectory and the *i*th key point respectively. We define that:

$\overline{\xi}(MID) \cdot \rho(i) \cdot \varphi$ is the element of $\overline{\xi}(MID) \cdot \rho(i)$ in φ-direction, $\varphi \in \{x, y, t\}$;

$\overline{\xi}(MID) \cdot CurSeg$ is the **serial number** of the spatio-temporal segment on which M is currently moving;

$\overline{\xi}(MID) \cdot SumSeg$ is the **total number** of spatio-temporal segments in $\overline{\xi}(MID)$.

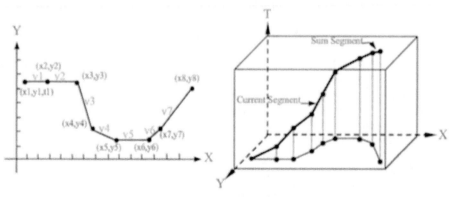

(a) moving plan of a moving object

(b) corresponding trajectory in the spatial-temporal space

Fig. 2. Location model of DSTTMOD

The spatio-temporal trajectory can represent not only the historical and current location of moving objects, but also the future locations. In order to get this information, moving objects need to submit their moving plans to the system in advance. During the process of moving, when the deviation of the actual location from the anticipative location exceeds a certain threshold, a location update is triggered. In this case, both the current and the subsequent segments of the trajectory need to be updated and the corresponding indexing structures must also be modified to reflect the up-to-date situation. Figure 2 illustrates the location model of DSTTMOD.

4   Indexing Moving Objects with Low Updating Cost

The index of moving object trajectories is essentially a spatial index in the three-dimensional space X×Y×T, and we can adopt conventional spatial indexing methods to index moving objects. However, this is not the best solution. In moving objects databases, location updates can cause the index structure to be updated frequently. As a result, special considerations should be taken to reduce the updating cost.

There are three main indexing methods for spatial or spatio-temporal data: R-tree and its variation, Quad-tree and its variation, and Grid-file and its variation. R-tree and Quad-tree are both multilevel nested structures in essential. As stated earlier, in MOD, moving objects are subject to frequent location updates, and when location updates occur, the whole indexing structure should be adjusted. Therefore, the index structure must provide optimal updating performance. It is obvious that these two methods are not proper for frequent location updates. In addition, in the process of updating, deleting former trajectory segments and inserting new ones may result in multilevel merges and splits, which can affect the performance enormously. However, it is different for Grid File. The index structure of Grid File is flat and the way of splitting is flexible. So Grid File is more suitable for the case of frequent location updates.

Based on the above analysis, we adopt a Grid-file based indexing method, which is called Grid File based Moving Objects Index (GMOI for short), to organize the trajectories of moving objects. In this section we describe the indexing structure and the corresponding algorithms.

Suppose that the indexed space is X×Y×T*, in which X×Y represents the geographic space of the application and T* represents a section of T axis. Because time extends infinitely, we deal with the period around current time instant when building index and make parallel translation of the indexed space along with time.

Definition 3 (Partition): A **Partition**, denoted by P, in the space of X×Y×T* is expressed as $P = P_x \times P_y \times P_t$. $P_x = (x_0, x_1, ..., x_l)$, $P_y = (y_0, y_1, ..., y_m)$ and $P_t = (t_0, t_1, ..., t_n)$ are sub-partitions in three directions, in which x_i $(0 \leq i \leq l)$, y_j $(0 \leq j \leq m)$ and t_k $(0 \leq k \leq n)$ are successive end-to-end sections in the dimension of X, Y, and T respectively.

In GMOI, we make a partition in the three-dimensional indexed space and derive a set of Grid blocks, as shown in Figure 3. Each of these Grid blocks contains a pointer leading to a certain Grid bucket in the storage, whose size equals to that of the basic I/O units. What stored in the Grid buckets are the indexed records.

In the process of operation on GMOI, insertion and deletion of records may cause dynamic change of the Grid partition, i.e., splits and merges of Grid blocks. For example, as shown in Figure 3, the broken line divides the section x_2 into two in the x dimension. Dynamic partition of X×Y×T* space and the maintenance of the relation between Grid blocks and buckets are accomplished by managing a Grid directory. In the Grid directory, every item contains the boundary of the block and a pointer leading to the corresponding bucket.

In GMOI, the trajectories of moving objects are stored in the forms of trajectory segments. Considering trajectory segment $SEG=[(x_i, y_i, t_i), (x_{i+1}, y_{i+1}, t_{i+1})]$, if it goes through a Grid block, with the pointer in the block, the entire information of *SEG* can be found in the corresponding Grid bucket, including its identifier and the vertex information. Because *SEG* is essentially a line segment in the three-dimensional space, it is quite easy to find out all Grid blocks intersected by *SEG*.

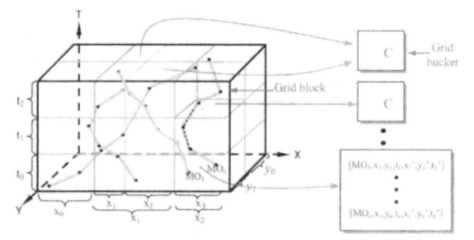

Fig. 3. The Grid partition in three-dimensional spatio-temporal space

5 Querying Moving Objects in DSTTMOD

In MOD, most queries fall into the following three categories: point query, range query and k-nearest neighbor (KNN) query. In this section, we present the processing approaches of these queries based on GMOI.

5.1 Point Queries

Point queries search for the location of a certain moving object at a given time instant, e.g., "find the location of MOq at tq". When processing such a query, the system can get the result directly from the trajectory information without searching the index. Suppose that the starting and ending points of the corresponding trajectory segment is $(x0, y0, t0)$ and $(x1, y1, t1)$ $(t0 \leq tq \leq t1)$. Then the location of MOq at time instant tq, denoted by (xq, yq), can be computed by the following formula:

$$\begin{cases} xq = \varepsilon \times (x1 - x0) + x0 \\ yq = \varepsilon \times (y1 - y0) + y0 \end{cases}, \text{ in which } \varepsilon = \frac{tq - t0}{t1 - t0}$$

5.2 Range Queries

Range queries search moving objects that cross a given geographic region in a given time period, e.g., "find all the objects passing the region A in the next 10 minutes". Such a query returns objects whose trajectory goes through a querying box in X×Y×T space, i.e. the cubic range covers a geographic region and a time period. When processing such queries, first the Grid directory is looked up to find all the Grid blocks that has common part with the querying box. Then for each block, find the corresponding Grid bucket and retrieve the desired records.

For Grid blocks which are totally contained in the querying box, the records in the corresponding bucket are sure to be desired and can be output directly. For other cases, further calculation is performed to determine whether the trajectory segment stored in the bucket is really in the querying box. For example, suppose G is a Grid block intersecting with the querying box Q. Q is determined by three sections: $[qx_1, qx_2]$ in x-direction, $[qy_1, qy_2]$ in y-direction, and $[qt_1, qt_2]$ in t-direction. Assume $[MO, x_0, y_0, t_0, x_1, y_1, t_1]$ is one of the records in the corresponding bucket. It represents a trajectory segment $[(x_0, y_0, t_0), (x_1, y_1, t_1)]$ of MO. Through some simple mathematical computation, the two intersecting points of G with $[(x_0, y_0, t_0), (x_1, y_1, t_1)]$ can be figured out, denoted by (x_m, y_m, t_m) and (x_n, y_n, t_n). If $[qx_1, qx_2]$ intersects with $[x_m, x_n]$, $[q_{y1}, q_{y2}]$ intersects with $[y_m, y_n]$, and $[qt_1, qt_2]$ intersects with $[t_m, t_n]$ simultaneously, MO is output. Otherwise, MO is ignored.

5.3 K-Nearest Neighbor Queries

An example k-nearest neighbor query is "find k moving objects which are closest to (x_q, y_q) around time t_q". Different from range queries, KNN queries are evaluated by incremental searching. Originally the searching box is a small circular range surrounding the given point, and then gradually expanded by extending the radius until k nearest objects are found. That is, at first, find the moving objects in the searching box with (x_q, y_q, t_q) as the center. If the number of the found objects $m>k$, select k nearest ones from them as the result. If m is equal to k, just output these objects. Otherwise, i.e., $m<k$, extend the searching radius to find the remaining k-m objects. The increase of searching radius follows a kind of strategy, such as linear increase. Because some Grid blocks have been checked in last round, the remaining k-m objects are searched only in the Grid blocks which are involved because of the expansion of the searching radius.

6 Performance Evaluation

In order to evaluate the performance of the proposed data structures and algorithms, we have developed a prototype system. Based on the system, we have carried out a series of performance experiments to compare the Grid-File based Moving Objects Indexing (GMOI) method with other indexing methods. Since the GMOI method is a HDD-based solution, we choose R-tree based Moving Objects Indexing (RMOI) method [6], which has the same feature, as the control of the experiments. Table 1 summarizes the parameters used in the experiments.

6.1 Index-Create Performance

As shown in Figure 4(a), when the number of moving objects is small, it will take more time for Grid-File to create the index structure than for the R-Tree method. This is because the inserting of the Grid records will lead to the Grid block's splitting and merging based on the actual state. However, with the number of the moving objects increasing, the R-tree's increment of the creating time will be larger than that of the Grid-File, and will finally exceed Grid-File.

Table 1. Main parameters in the experiment

Parameter	Value	Meaning
A	1000*1000*1000	size of indexed space (X×Y×T*)
M	50-300	number of moving objects
N	32	number of moving objects generated/expired per second
C	(50, 25), (25, 12)	maximal/minimal number of records in one data block of R-tree
U	500	frequency of location updates for moving objects
R	100*100*10	size of querying box in range queries
T	2000	number of range query issued per second
S	10	average number of the segments in each Spatio-Temporal trajectory
W	500	average size of active window with moving plans

From Figure 4(b), we can see that the storage consumption for Grid-File is greater than for R-Tree. In order to implement the flat structure of the Grid bucket and speed up querying and updating, a number of navigation pointers are used in the nodes of the Grid-File. On the contrary, there is no redundancy in R-Tree. The nodes of R-Tree only store location information.

6.2 Update Performance

In this experiment, we compare GMOI and RMOI in terms of the time of processing U (U=500) update operations for the objects.

As shown in Figure 4(c), there is an obvious difference between the Grid-File and R-Tree in location updating performance. The reason is that the R-Tree has a nested structure, when updating, it will lead to nested merges and splits of the tree node and nested adjustment of MBR's because of the delete and insert operations. On the contrary, the Grid-File method has a flat structure, which will not lead to such actions. At the same time, the choice of splitting point is flexible in Grid-File method. So the latter will cost much less in terms of location updating.

6.3 Query Performance

Figure 4(d) shows the time elapsed from the issuing of a query to the returning of the result. We can see that Grid-File has a little bit better query performance than R-Tree. This is because the scope overlap of the R-Tree's nodes will be more serious with the number of the moving object increasing, and in most cases it will be necessary to look through the whole tree structure to find the objects that match the query. All the above will not occur while using Grid-File indexing method.

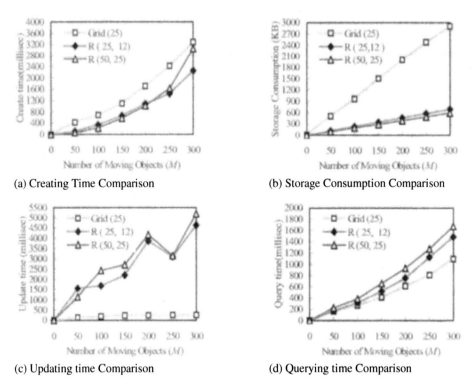

(a) Creating Time Comparison

(b) Storage Consumption Comparison

(c) Updating time Comparison

(d) Querying time Comparison

Fig. 4. Performance comparisons between GMOI and RMOI

7 Conclusion

The key research issue with moving objects databases (MOD) is the modeling of location information. In this paper, we put forward a new MOD model - Discrete Spatio-Temporal Trajectory Based Moving Objects Database (DSTTMOD) model. Our aim is to support queries for location information not only in the past and at present, but also in the future (including the near and far future). To obtain this goal, we use a trajectory based method to represent moving objects and a Grid-file based indexing method to organize these trajectories. We have also developed a prototype system and conducted a series of experiments which show promising performance results.

Acknowledgements. This research was partially supported by the grants from 863 High Technology Foundation of China (2002AA116030), the Natural Science Foundation of China (60073014, 60273018), the Key Project of Chinese Ministry of Education (03044) and the Excellent Young Teachers Program of MOE, P.R.C (EYTP). We would also like to thank Yun Bai, Chen Wu and Xiaoqing Wu of Renmin University of China for their valuable help in the detailed implementation of the prototype system.

References

[1] Wolfson O., Xu B., Chamberlain S., Jiang L., Moving Object Databases: Issues and Solutions. *Proceedings of the 10th International Conference on Science and Statistical Database Management*, Capri, Italy, July 1998:111–122.

[2] Wolfson O., Chamberlain S., Dao S., Jiang L., Location Management in Moving Objects Databases. In *Proceedings of WOSBIS'97*, Budapest, Hungary, Oct. 1997.

[3] Sistla A.P., Wolfson O., Chamberlian S., Dao S.. Modeling and querying Moving Objects. In: *Proceedings of ICDE* 1997.

[4] Wolfson O., Chamberlain S., Dao S., Jiang L., Mendez G. Cost and Imprecision in Modeling the Position of Moving Objects. In: *Proceedings of ICDE* 1998.

[5] Forlizzi L., Guting R. H., Nardelli E., Schneider M. A Data Model and Data Structures for Moving Objects Databases. *In Proc. of ACM SIGMOD 2000*, Texas, USA, 2000.

[6] Chon H. D., Agrawal D., Abbadi A. E. Query Processing for Moving Objects with Space-Time Grid Storage Model. *In Proceedings of the 3rd International Conference on Mobile Data Management (MDM2002)*. Hong Kong. Jan. 2001.

[7] Pfoser D., Jensen C. S., Theodoridis Y. Novel Approach to the Indexing of Moving Object Trajectories. *Proceedings of the 26th VLDB*, Cairo, Egypt, 2000.

[8] Saltenis S., Jensen C. S., Leutenegger S. T., Lopez M. A. Indexing the Position of Continuously Moving Objects. *In Proc. of ACM SIGMOD 2000*, Dallas, TX, USA, 2000.

[9] J. Nievergelt, H. Hinterberger, and K. C. Sevcik, The grid file: An adaptable, symmetric multikey file structure, *ACM Trans. on Database Sys.* 9(1), 1984:38–71.

Adaptive Peer-to-Peer Routing with Proximity

Chu Yee Liau[1], Achmad Nizar Hidayanto[2], and Stephane Bressan[1]

[1] School of Computing,
Department of Computer Science,
National University of Singapore
{liaucy,steph}@comp.nus.edu.sg
[2] Faculty of Computer Science,
University of Indonesia
nizar@cs.ui.ac.id

Abstract. In this paper, we presented a routing strategy for requests in unstructured peer-to-peer networks. The strategy is based on the adaptive routing Q-routing. The strategy uses reinforcement learning to estimate the cost of routing a request. Such a strategy is scalable only if the routing indices are of reasonable size. We proposed and comparatively evaluated three methods for the pruning for the pruning of the routing indices. Our experiments confirm the validity of the adaptive routing and the scalability of a pruning approach based on a pruning strategy considering the popularity of the resources.

1 Introduction

Peer-to-peer networks constitute an architectural revolution that may, if the managerial and economical conditions are met, replace the traditional client server approaches to information management. Potentially, peer-to-peer may solve the scalability issues as raised by the advent of a global information infrastructure. This infrastructure has millions of users exchanging large amounts of information from computers of all sorts and kinds across the Internet for all kinds of purpose ranging from leisure to business and government.

Yet, peer-to-peer technology is not yet mature and does not offer satisfactory and sustainable solutions to the scalability issues on all its aspects. We are concerned in this paper with the efficient retrieval of documents in a peer-to-peer network.

In general, peer-to-peer can be divided into two main classes according to its data organization, namely structured and unstructured architecture. In the structured peer-to-peer architecture such as [1,2], peers are connected to each other and resources or the records are moved to a peer according to some mapping techniques. For example, Chord employs a hashing technique to map resources to a key and peers to a key range. Peers host resources whose keys fall into their key range. In the unstructured peer-to-peer architecture [3,4], peers are connected to each other as they join the network and resources are not being moved to other peers but hosted on site. Hence, searching for a resource requires to either broadcast the request or use routing information.

V. Mařík et al. (Eds.): DEXA 2003, LNCS 2736, pp. 454–463, 2003.

Searching strategies that have been proposed so far for most peer-to-peer architectures do not take into account the geography and the load of the physical network. Most of the current proposed peer-to-peer systems use application-level hops when measuring the performance of their searching mechanism. While the hop measurement is straightforward and easy to understand, it does not guarantee reflect actual routing time. This is due to the various factors that affect the routing time such as the physical network topology, its bandwidth, and local processing power available. For example, a hop between two peers that reside on a local area network usually take lesser time than two peers that reside on a wide area network. Furthermore, a slower machine or a popular peer might cause delay in the actual transmission time due to a longer queue. We will employ actual time as our performance measurement.

Our contribution in this paper is twofold: a general approach to indexed routing, and the presentation and comparative evaluation of three strategies to prune the information to be maintained. We first propose in this paper a solution to the creation and maintenance of indices based on the adaptive Q-routing algorithm. The algorithm maintains at each peer a table, we call the index, of the estimates of the time to reach a given resource from this peer using reinforcement learning.

Yet, given the large amount of resources to index, it is unrealistic to assume that every peer can index every resource. Therefore we propose three strategies that allow pruning of the index according to the topology of the network of peers and the popularity of the resources, respectively. We empirically analyze the respective performance of the three strategies and compare them. We show that popularity is the best criterion.

2   Related Works

In this section, we look at some of the structured (Chord [1] and CAN [2]) and unstructured (Gnutella [3] and Freenet [4]) decentralized peer-to-peer systems. Chord is a distributed lookup protocol that stores (key, value) pair for distributed data items. Each data item will be associated with a key using hash function and will be stored at the node to which key mapped. Each key k is stored on the first node whose identifier id is equal to or follows k in the identifier space. Each node maintains a routing table with information for only about O(logN) nodes. With a high probability, the number of nodes that must be contacted to resolve a query in an N-node network is O(logN).

CAN is a distributed hash-based infrastructure that provides fast lookup functionality on internet-like scales. It maintains virtual space based on "d-torus". The virtual space is partitioned into many small d-dimensional zones. Keys are mapped into zones and a zone will be split whenever a node requests to join that zone. Routing is performed by forwarding requests to the regions closest to the position of the key. In this way the expected number of hops for a search is $O(N^{1/d})$, where d is the chosen dimensionality.

Gnutella system is a decentralized file-sharing system whose participants form a virtual network communicating in peer-to-peer fashion via the Gnutella protocol which consists of 5 basic message types: ping, pong, query, queryHit and push. These messages are routed to their destination using constrained broadcast by decrementing the message's time-to-live field. A simplified HTTP GET interaction will be run to retrieve the file after requestor received location of the file from another peers.

Freenet, an anonymous peer-to-peer storage system, is decentralized, symmetric and automatically adapts when host leave and join. Freenet does not assign responsibility for documents to specific servers; instead, its lookups take the form of searches for cached copies. This allows Freenet to provide a degree of anonymity, but prevents it from guaranteeing retrieval of existing documents or from providing low bounds on retrieval costs.

In [5], the authors introduced the concept of Routing Indices (RI) in unstructured peer-to-peer network. The RI allows nodes to forward queries to the neighbors that are likely to have the needed answers. When a query arrived at a node, the node will use the RI to select a neighbor nodes and forward the query to it. The authors proposed 3 different types of RI: Compound RI, Hop-count RI and Exponential RI. Compound RI provides number of resources that can be obtained if a query were to be forwarded to a selected neighbor. While Compound RI provides only information about the quantity of resources, it provides no distance information. Hop-count RI added the distance information to the RI. Exponential RI also provides the two information but present it in a different way from Hop-count RI. The RI are constructed by propagating local information to neighboring peers at a fixed interval or when the changes in the local indices have reached a certain threshold. In the proposed scheme, resources in the network is classified into different classes and indexing is done with these classes. While this reduces the size of the index, it prevents finer granularity.

3   Background

3.1   Peer-to-Peer Search and Routing Indices

Generally, searching mechanism in a peer-to-peer system can be divided into two main components: resource locating and routing. In resource locating, given a resource id, the challenge is to locate the resource in a minimal time to yield better performance and response time. In routing, the challenge is to efficiently route a resource request to the next peer in order to achieve the minimal time. This is usually done with the help of Routing Indices. Routing indices, which is maintained at each peer, store the cost of routing requests for resources via each of its neighbors.

There might be multiple copies of similar resources scattered in the network. Successfully locating the resources within minimal time will increase the responsiveness of the system and hence making it more reliable and usable. A straightforward solution to these challenges is a centralized management model

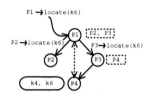

Fig. 1. An example of searching in peer-to-peer

of resource sharing such as Napster [6]. However, there are several problems with using a centralized server such as the notorious single point of failure and congestion. In additional, maintaining a unified view in single node is expensive and poses scalability problems.

In this work, we focus on routing and searching strategies in totally decentralized environment. We define the routing and searching problem in peer-to-peer networks as follows (see figure 1). We consider a set of peers, $P = p_1, ..., p_n$, and a set of resources, $R = r_1, ..., r_m$, located on the peers and identified by the set of keys $K = k_1, ..., k_m$. Given a request of the form $locate(k_I)$, i.e. a request to locate resource r_i, a peer receiving this request must make a local decision as to which of its neighbors to forward the request.

3.2   Reinforcement Learning

In a reinforcement learning (RL) model [7], an agent learns by interacting with its environment and observing the results of these interactions. This interaction occurs as a result of the agent's capacity to perceive current environment conditions and to select the actions that should be performed in that environment. An action that is carried out changes the environment, and the agent becomes aware of these changes through a scalar reinforcement signal that is supplied by the environment. The objective of RL is to learn the mapping of states into action. The scalar reinforcement value obtained from a reinforcement function represents the system's immediate objective. The agent makes use of value function to represent the quality of the actions in the long-term. The decision to take special action when it faces a given status depends on the policy that represents the agent's behaviour. By performing actions, and observing the resulting reward, the policy used to determine the best action for a state can be fine-tuned. Eventually, if enough states are observed an optimal decision policy will be generated and we will have an agent that performs perfectly in that particular environment. RL agent learns by receiving a reward or reinforcement from its environment, without any form of supervision other than its own decision making policy. Figure 2 depicts the general model of reinforcement learning.

4   Design

We propose to use an adaptive routing strategy for the routing of requests in a peer-to-peer network. This routing strategy is based on reinforcement learning: the Q-routing. At each peer, we maintain routing indices, which consist

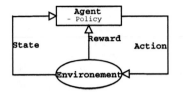

Fig. 2. Reinforcement learning model

of estimates for the routing time to resources via each of the peers' immediate neighbor. We define various strategies for selecting resources to be maintained in the routing indices and analyze the startegies in the next section.

4.1   Routing Strategy

We employ Q-Routing [8] as our routing technique. Q-Routing is an adaptive routing strategy that uses Q-learning, a reinforcement learning algorithm. Q-Routing has been studied in various network routing literatures and the performance studies showed that it is able to adapt to the network traffic.

In Q-learning [9], the states and the possible actions in a given state are discrete and finite in number. It uses a set of values termed Q-values when learning. Each Q-value is denoted by $Q(s, a)$ where s is a given state and a is the action taken. In general, Q-value represents the expected reinforcement yield when the action a is being taken in a state s.

Given the current state of the network, Q-Routing algorithm learns and finds an optimal routing policy from the Q-values distributed over all peers in the network. Each peer p in the network represents its own view of the state of the network through a table that stores all the Q-value, $Q_p(p', r)$, where $r \in R$, a set of resource objects in the peer-to-peer network and $p' \in N(p)$ the set of all neighbours of peer p. $Q_p(p', r)$ is defined as the best estimated time that a query take to reach the peer that host the resource r from peer p through its neighbor p'.

The Q-value, $Q_p(p', r)$ can be represented by the following mathematical equation:

$$Q_p(p', r) = q_{p'} + \delta + Q_{p'}(p'', r) \tag{1}$$

From the equation we can derive that the minimum time needed to locate a resource r in the peer-to-peer network from the peer p through its neighbour p', is affected by 3 components:

1. The time the query spends in peer p', $q_{p'}$.
2. The transmission delay between p and p'.
3. The best estimation time for $Q_{p'}(p'', r)$.

Once we are clear what the Q-values stored at each peer stand for, it is easy to see how they can be used for making locally optimal routing decisions. When a peer p receives a query $q(s, r)$ looking for resource r, peer p will lookup its Q-value table $Q_p(*, r)$ to select the neighboring peer p' with the minimum $Q_p(p', r)$

value. With this mechanism being used in every peer in the network, the query will be answered in a minimal time.

4.2   Updates of Q-Value

The performance on the routing strategy depends on all the Q-values in the path taken by the query. The closer these Q-values are to the actual time needed, the closer the routing strategy reflects the actual optimal time. Therefore, the process of updating the Q-value in a peer is very important.

Recall that when peer p receives a query $q(s, r)$, it will find a peer in the neighbour list such that Q_p fulfills the following condition:

$$Q_p(p', r) = \min_{p' \in N(p)} Q_p(p', r) \tag{2}$$

Once p' is chosen, p will then forward the query $q(s, r)$ to p'. Upon receiving the query, p' will first search if it has the requested resource r. If the requested r is not in the shared list of p', it will have to forward the query to its neighbour. For both cases, p' will have to send the Q-value back to p. In the first case, since the query can be answered by p', no further routing of the query $q(s, r)$ is needed and the Q-value returned to p is 0. While in the second case, the Q-value, $Q_{p'}(p'', r)$, returned will be according to equation 2.

The Q-value returned by p' is essentially its estimation of how long a query will be answered after p' has processed the query. The estimation returned is excluded the queuing time at p' and the transmission delay, δ, for the query to travel from p to p'. Based on the estimated value, peer p will calculate the new Q-value for $Q_p(p', r)$ with the following equation:

$$Q_p(p', r)^{new} = Q_p(p', r)^{old} + l(Q_{p'}(p'', r)^{new} + q_{p'} + \delta - Q_{p'}(p'', r)^{old}) \tag{3}$$

where l is the learning rate with $0 \leq l \leq 1$. When l is set to 1, the equation will become:

$$Q_p(p', r) = Q_{p'}(p'', r) + q_{p'} + \delta \tag{4}$$

However, since the new Q-value send back by p' is the propagation of estimated values, the Q-value is not necessary accurate. Therefore, in order to reflect the possibly error caused by estimation in the learning process, the learning rate should always be set to a value less than 1 {eg. 0.7 has been a suggested learning rate on previous network routing studies}.

4.3   Pruning of Routing Indices

Figure 3 depicts the structure of the Routing Indices (RI) that store Q-values.

Each resource r is a record row in the RI. For each resource, there will be corresponding Q-value for each neighbor. Since the number of resources in the network determine the number of rows, therefore, the size of the RI is proportional to the resources shared in the network and it can be potentially big. In this work, we study 3 mechanisms to maintain the size of the Q-value table: Near-Method, Far-Method and Popularity-Method.

Resources	Neighbour Q-value			
	p1	p2	...	pn
r1	12	6	...	8
r2	10	12	...	7
r3	4	10	...	9
rn	3	4		9

Fig. 3. Q-value table for peer p

Near-Method. In near-method, we prune the routing indices according to the proximity. Initially we set the capacity of the routing indices in terms of number of entries, n, that can be stored by a peer. We prune the routing indices and store only the first n entries that have the smallest value. This method allows us to index only those resources that are closest to the peer. When the routing indices exceeded n, we remove the most distant resource in the routing indices. With this, when a peer receives a query requesting for resources that is close to the peer, the peer will be able to route the query to the neighbor that is able to answer the query within a minimal time.

Far-Method. In far-method, we keep the resources in the routing indices that are furthest from the peer. Similar to near-method, we keep only maximum of n entries in the routing indices. Once routing indices overflowed, we remove the resource entry that are nearest to the peer. This allows us to index the resources that are furthest from a peer, giving more efficient routing when answering a request especially for distant resources.

Popularity-Method. The third pruning method is according to popularity of resources. This method index resources that are most requested in local view. In this work, we assume the knowledge of the popular resource beforehand in order to study this pruning method. With the popularity knowledge, we apply the learning on the popular resources. Those resources that are not listed in the popularity list will be ignored.

5   Performance Analysis

We simulate the peer-to-peer network to study the performance of Q-routing and the three proposed strategies for pruning the routing indices.

The network is a randomly re-wired ring lattice. A ring lattice is a graph with n vertices, each of which is connected to its nearest k neighbors. In our experiments, we use a k value of 4. The rewiring is done by randomly choosing m vertices to connect with each other. In our experiments, we use an m value of 10% of n. This relatively small number compared to n is meant to reflect the small world effect [10].

We randomly assign the d resources to the n peers according to a uniform distribution.

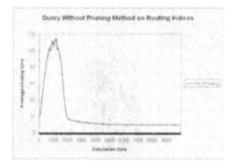

Fig. 4. Query result with Q-Routing

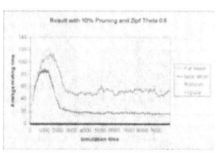

Fig. 5. 10% Pruning with Zipf θ 0.6

Fig. 6. 50% Pruning with Zipf θ 0.6

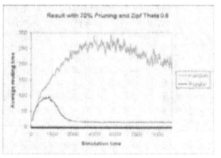

Fig. 7. 70% Pruning with Zipf θ 0.6

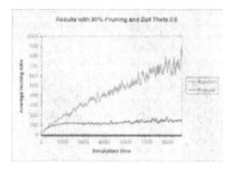

Fig. 8. 90% Pruning with Zipf θ 0.6

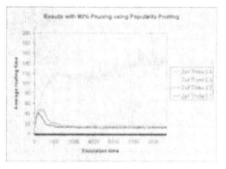

Fig. 9. 90% Popularity Pruning for various Zipf θ

The workload is determined by a Zipfian distribution corresponding to the popularity of the resources. Requests for a resource are generated according to this distribution. Requests originate from a random peer chosen uniformly.

Figure 4 shows the average routing time of the requests reaching destination at each unit of simulation time for a strategy using routing indices containing an entries for each resource and using Q-routing to estimate the cost of reaching the resource. The result of this experiment confirms the adaptive property of Q-routing. Indeed, after an initial unstable learning phase, the average routing time continuously converges toward a minimum.

The result of this experiment confirms the adaptive property of Q-routing. Indeed, after an initial unstable learning phase, the average routing time continuously converges toward a minimum.

Figures 5, 6, 7, 8, and 9 show the average routing time of the requests reaching destination at each unit of simulation time for several strategies using pruned routing indices.

In Figures 5, 6, 7, and 8, we first compare the performance of the near-method, the far-method, the popularity-method as well as, for reference, the performance of a method randomly pre-selecting the resources to be kept in every routing index. For these three figures, the popularity of the resources is determined by a Zipfian with a θ coefficient of value 0.6. We fix the number of entries pruned from the routing indices to 10%, 50%, 70%, and 90%, for each figure respectively.

We only present the performance of the near- and far- methods on the first two figures since it immediately appears that these methods do not scale up as they cannot route efficiently with 50% and less of the documents in the routing indices. This phenomenon is not only due to the possible irrelevance of the entries in the routing indices but also to their high instability and therefore to the inaccuracy of the content of the routing indices under these two approaches. Indeed the two approaches are outperformed by the random-method. The popularity-method, on the contrary, continues to outperform the random-method and to stabilize to a reasonable routing time up to 90% pruning.

Figure 9 shows the average routing time of the requests reaching destination at each unit of simulation time for the popularity-method with a varying skewedness of the popularity distribution. We control this aspect by choosing different values of the θ parameter. The smaller θ, the skewer the distribution. We present the results for four values of θ: 0.5, 0.3, 0.2, and 0.1. Skewer popularity improves the convergence of the popularity-method. Indeed as there are fewer more popular documents, more requests find appropriate and more accurate entries in the routing indices.

6   Conclusion and Future Works

We have presented a routing strategy for requests in peer-to-peer networks based on adaptive routing in routing indices Q-routing. The strategy uses reinforcement learning to estimate the cost of routing a request. Yet such a strategy is scalable only if the routing indices are of reasonable size. It is not realistic to consider maintaining at each peer a complete routing index of all the resources in the network. We proposed and comparatively evaluated three methods for the pruning for the pruning of the routing indices.

Our experiments confirm the validity of the adaptive routing and the scalability of a pruning approach based on popularity of the resources.

Our analysis, however, relies on a predetermined popularity. We are currently extending this work and devising a strategy in which peers adaptively learn the resource popularity based on the requests they route. In such a strategy, reinforcement learning is used twice: for estimating the cost of routing, and for estimating the popularity, forward, and backward, respectively. Such a method would constitute a complete, effective, and efficient routing solution for unstructured peer-to-peer networks

References

1. D. Karger F. Kaashoek I. Stoica, R. Morris and H. Balakrishnan. Chord: A scalable Peer-To-Peer lookup service for internet applications. In *Proceedings of the 2001 ACM SIGCOMM Conference*, pages 149–160, 2001.
2. M. Handley R. Karp S. Ratnasamy, P. Francis and S. Shenker. A scalable content addressable network. In *Proceedings of the 2001 ACM SIGCOMM Conference*, 2001.
3. GNUTELLA. http://gnutella.wego.com.
4. B. Wiley I. Clarke, O. Sandberg and T. W. Hong. Freenet: A distributed anonymous information storage and retrieval system. In *Lecture Notes in Computer Science*, 2001.
5. J. Kubiatowicz et al. Routing indices for peer-to-peer systems. In *Proceedings International Conference on Distributed Computing Systems*, July 2002.
6. NAPSTER. http://www.napster.com.
7. Leslie Pack Kaelbling, Michael L. Littman, and Andrew P. Moore. Reinforcement learning: A survey. In *Journal of Artificial Intelligence Research*, volume 4, pages 237–285, 1996.
8. Michael Littman and Justin Boyan. A distributed reinforcement learning scheme for network routing. In *Proceedings of the International Workshop on Applications of Neural Networks to Telecommunications*, 1993.
9. Sutton R. S. and Barto A. G. *Reinforcement learning: An introduction.* MIT Press, 1998.
10. A. Oram, editor. *Peer-to-Peer : Harnessing the Power of Disruptive Technologies.* O'Reilly & Associates, 2001.

g-binary: A New Non-parameterized Code for Improved Inverted File Compression

Ilias Nitsos[1], Georgios Evangelidis[1], and Dimitrios Dervos[2]

[1] Department of Applied Informatics,
University of Macedonia
156 Egnatia Str.,
54006 Thessaloniki, Greece
{nitsos,gevan}@uom.gr
[2] Department of Information Technology,
TEI
P.O. Box 14561,
54101 Thessaloniki,
Greece
dad@it.teithe.gr

Abstract. The inverted file is a popular and efficient method for indexing text databases and is being used widely in information retrieval applications. As a result, the research literature is rich in models (global and local) that describe and compress inverted file indexes. Global models compress the entire inverted file index using the same method and can be distinguished in parameterized and non-parameterized ones. The latter utilize fixed codes and are applicable to dynamic collections of documents. Local models are always parameterized in the sense that the method they use makes assumptions about the distribution of each and every word in the document collection of the text database. In the present study, we examine some of the most significant integer compression codes and propose *g-binary*, a new non-parameterized coding scheme that combines the Golomb codes and the binary representation of integers. The proposed new coding scheme does not introduce any extra computational overhead when compared to the existing non-parameterized codes. With regard to storage utilization efficiency, experimental runs conducted on a number of TREC text database collections reveal an improvement of about 6% over the existing non-parameterized codes. This is an improvement that can make a difference for very large text database collections.

1 Introduction

Among the numerous schemes that have been developed for indexing text databases the most popular is the inverted file [4], [15], [14]. The success of the inverted file is closely related to the great advances in the field of integer compression codes [7], [3], [6], [9], [1], [10]. There exist several such codes that allow the average pointer (an integer value) inside an inverted file to be stored in less than 1 byte [14], thus producing very compact indexes. Compressed indexes are

V. Mařík et al. (Eds.): DEXA 2003, LNCS 2736, pp. 464–473, 2003.
© Springer-Verlag Berlin Heidelberg 2003

also fast, because the required number of disk accesses is small and the decompression CPU cost is low [13].

In the present paper we consider a number of compression codes and focus mainly on the Golomb code [9], [6], [15], [10] and the binary representation of integers. There exist two major categories of compression models for inverted files: the *global* and the *local* models. Global models are further divided into *parameterized* and *non-parameterized*. The former involve some parameter that reflects the distribution of the integers inside the inverted files. Non-parameterized models produce fixed codes and are useful when dynamic collections of documents are stored. On the other hand, local models are always parameterized.

In Section 2 we examine several codes that have been developed for compressing integers inside the inverted files and the models they are based on. In Section 3 we introduce a new non-parameterized code, g-binary, that comprises a combination of the Golomb code and the binary representation of integers. The performance of the new code against some TREC text database collections is tested in Section 4. In Section 5, we perform an analysis on the length of the codes for all integers obtained by the coding schemes we examine in this paper. We show that g-binary is always equal or better in compression efficiency than the popular non-parameterized codes for certain integer intervals. Finally, in Section 6 we present our conclusions.

2   Codes for Compressing Inverted Files

In the inverted file index, each one of the N (say) text database documents is represented by a positive integer $d \in [1, \dots, N]$. For each distinct word t, an inverted list is created that stores all the document numbers d containing t. Inverted lists are stored in a single file, known as the inverted file [4].

The integer numbers are stored in the inverted file in a way suitable for allowing compression by means of run length encoding [6]: instead of storing the absolute numbers d of the documents containing a word, inverted lists store their differences. For example, instead of storing the d list $\{2, 9, 10, 15, 16, 20\}$, for word t, one could store the corresponding d-gap list $\{2, 7, 1, 5, 1, 4\}$. This results in storing smaller (in value) and more frequently occurring integers, in general. The initial list may easily be reconstructed from the d-gap list.

In the subsections that follow, a number of popular compression codes are considered that utilize run length encoding to implement compression. The codes are based on models that take into consideration the probability distribution of d-gap sizes. In this respect, small bit codes are assigned to frequent d-gap sizes and larger bit codes to rare ones. Depending on whether they involve or not the storage of some kind of parameter, the models and their codes are categorized as being *parameterized* or *non-parameterized*, respectively.

2.1   Non-parameterized Codes

Unary Code. In the unary coding scheme each positive integer x is represented by x-1 ones followed by a zero. For example, integer 5 is stored as 11110. This

Table 1. Examples of codes for integers

				Golomb			g-binary	
x	unary	γ code	δ code	b=2	b=3	b=4	b=2	b=3
1	0	0	0	00	00	000	00	00
2	10	100	1000	01	010	001	010	0100
3	110	101	1001	100	011	010	011	0101
4	1110	11000	10100	101	100	011	10000	01100
5	11110	11001	10101	1100	1010	1000	10001	01101
6	111110	11010	10110	1101	1011	1001	10010	01110
7	1111110	11011	10111	11100	1100	1010	10011	01111
8	11111110	1110000	11000000	11101	11010	1011	101000	100000
9	111111110	1110001	11000001	111100	11011	11000	101001	100001
10	1111111110	1110010	11000010	111101	11100	11001	101010	100010

means that the bit length of integer x in unary is $len_u(x) = x$. A list of the unary codes for the first ten positive integers is shown in Table 1. The unary code is equivalent to assigning a probability of 2^{-x} to gaps of length x [14].

Elias Codes. Two popular non-parameterized codes for compressing integers, that result in significant savings, are the γ and δ codes introduced by Elias in [3]. In the γ coding scheme each positive integer x is encoded as follows:

- store integer $1 + \lfloor log_2 x \rfloor$ in unary.
- store the remainder $x - 2^{\lfloor log_2 x \rfloor}$ in binary using $\lfloor log_2 x \rfloor$ bits.

It follows that the bit length of integer x in γ code is $len_\gamma(x) = 2\lfloor log_2 x \rfloor + 1$. In the δ coding scheme each positive integer x is encoded as follows:

- store integer $1 + \lfloor log_2 x \rfloor$ using γ code.
- store the remainder $x - 2^{\lfloor log_2 x \rfloor}$ in binary using $\lfloor log_2 x \rfloor$ bits.

It is shown [14] that the bit length of integer x in δ code is $len_\delta(x) = \lfloor log_2 x \rfloor + 2\lfloor log_2(1 + \lfloor log_2 x \rfloor) \rfloor + 1$. A list of the γ and δ codes for the first ten positive integers is shown in Table 1. The γ code is equivalent to assigning a probability of $\frac{1}{2x^2}$ to gap x, whereas, the δ code assigns a probability of $\frac{1}{2x(logx)^2}$ [14].

Golomb Code. In this coding scheme, for a given parameter b, each positive integer x is encoded as follows:

- store integer $q + 1$ in unary, where $q = \lfloor (x - 1)/b \rfloor$.
- store the remainder $r = x - q \times b - 1$ in binary using either $\lfloor log_2 b \rfloor$ or $\lceil log_2 b \rceil$ bits [14].

It follows that the bit length of integer x in Golomb code is at most $len_g(x) = \lfloor (x-1)/b \rfloor + 1 + \lceil log_2 b \rceil$. A list of Golomb codes for the first ten positive integers, for some values of the parameter b, is shown in Table 1. At the decompression phase, the original integer is computed as $x = r + q \times b + 1$.

2.2   Parameterized Codes

One can find many parameterized codes in the literature, e.g., the Golomb code for the global Bernoulli model [6], the Golomb code for the local Bernoulli model [2], the skewed Bernoulli model [12], [9], the local hyperbolic model [11], and the interpolative method [8].

In the following, we emphasize on the Bernoulli models. The Golomb code for the local Bernoulli model is preferred in the case of static document collections as it combines acceptable compression with fast decoding. We also include it in the performance results of Section 4 as a measure of comparison between our non-parameterized code and a popular parameterized code, that is expected to achieve better compression, but is not suitable for dynamic text databases.

Golomb Code for the Global Bernoulli Model. Let us suppose, that we have an N-document text database that contains n distinct words and f index pointers (i.e., f distinct *"document, word"* pairs). The global Bernoulli model assumes that the words are distributed uniformly across the N documents. This, in turn, implies that the probability of a randomly selected word to appear in any one randomly selected document is $p = f/(N \times n)$. It has been shown that the d-gaps in this case can be efficiently represented by the Golomb code [6]. The Golomb coding method can satisfy the probabilities generated by the global Bernoulli model when b is is chosen to be $b = \lceil \frac{log_2(2-p)}{-log_2(1-p)} \rceil$ [5].

Golomb Code for the Local Bernoulli Model. The difference between the global and the local Bernoulli model is that the latter does not assume uniformity in the distribution of words across the N-document text database. This in turn implies that in general a different b parameter is associated to each one list [2]. The value of b for the d-gap list of word t is calculated as in the case of the global Bernoulli model, except that now $p = f_t/N$, where f_t is the number of documents containing t. This implies that for each distinct word t in the text database, the value for f_t must also be stored alongside with the inverted list of the word in order to be possible to compute the value of b at decoding time. The value for f_t is stored at the head of each list, using the γ code [14]. During the inverted list decompression phase, the f_t value is decoded first, then the b parameter is calculated and decompression continues with the rest of the list.

3   g-binary

In this section we introduce g-binary, a combination of the Golomb code and the binary representation of an integer. The aim is to produce a non-parameterized code that reduces the number of bits used to store a d-gap. The main idea behind the proposed new code is to store an integer using its exact binary representation. The problem is that the length of the binary representation must also be stored so that decoding is possible. After experimenting with all the popular codes for integers and examining the lengths of the bit sequences produced, we came down to the conclusion that the best code for storing the above lengths is the Golomb code for certain global values of b. In g-binary, for a given b value, each positive integer x is encoded as follows:

- store the length m of the binary representation of x using the Golomb code for the globally selected parameter b.
- store the exact binary representation of x excluding its most significant bit (which is always 1).

Essentially, the g-binary code of an integer is the concatenation of the Golomb code that represents the length of the binary representation of the integer and the actual binary representation of that integer (without its most significant bit). Thus, the compression and decompression algorithms share the same complexity with the other codes (γ, δ and Golomb).

We use the notations len_b and len_{gb} for the lengths of the exact binary and g-binary representations respectively. The length of the exact binary representation for any integer $x > 0$ is $len_b(x) = \lfloor log_2 x \rfloor + 1$ bits. For example, the exact binary representation of integer 9 is 1001 and requires $\lfloor log_2 9 \rfloor + 1 = 4$ bits. In g-binary, we omit the first bit of this representation which is always 1, thus, we are left with $\lfloor log_2 x \rfloor$ bits. In order to store $m = \lfloor log_2 x \rfloor + 1$ (i.e., the length of the exact binary representation of x) using the Golomb coding scheme, we need at most $len_g(m) = \lfloor (m-1)/b \rfloor + 1 + \lceil log_2 b \rceil$ bits (see Section 2.2). This means that the total number of bits used by g-binary adds up to at most

$$len_{gb}(x) = len_g(m) + len_b(x) - 1 = \lfloor (m-1)/b \rfloor + 1 + \lceil log_2(b) \rceil + \lfloor log_2(x) \rfloor \quad (1)$$

or

$$len_{gb}(x) = \lfloor \lfloor log_2(x) \rfloor / b \rfloor + 1 + \lceil log_2(b) \rceil + \lfloor log_2(x) \rfloor \quad (2)$$

We will use an example to demonstrate the coding and decoding stages for the g-binary code. Let us suppose that we have to code the following integer list: 12 (1100), 19 (10011), 75 (1001011), 1 (1). We will use Golomb ($b = 2$) for the coding of the lengths of the binary representations of the integers.

The exact binary representation for integer 12 is 1100. The length of the binary representation is 4 and it is encoded using the Golomb code (b=2) as 101 (see Table 1). Eventually, 12 is stored as 101,100 where the first part is the length of the exact binary representation of 12 and the second part is the binary representation of 12 itself without its most significant bit. The comma between the length and the binary representation is not stored; we use it here to facilitate our presentation. The rest of the integers are encoded in a similar way as [19: 1100,0011], [75: 11100,001011] and [1: 00]. In the case of the last integer 1, it is only the length of the binary representation that is stored; the decoding process stage proceeds without any problem, since 1 is the only integer that is represented with just one bit.

During decompression, the Golomb value is decoded first and reveals m, the length of the binary representation of the integer we try to decode. Next, the m-1

Table 2. Testbed collection profiles

Collection	Size (MB)	Distinct words (n)	Total documents (N)	Total pointers (f)
LAT	475	288823	130472	31193292
FBIS	470	247563	131167	34982316
LATFBIS	945	437864	261639	66175608

bits of the remaining bit sequence are retrieved. By adding 1 in the beginning of the m-1 bits we obtain the exact binary representation of the integer in question. Decompression continues with the rest of the bit sequence.

Several g-binary versions can be obtained by assigning different values to b. Any single version can be regarded as a non-parameterized code. Table 1 lists the g-binary codes for the first ten positive integers, when b=2 and b=3. In the next section, we examine whether some of these versions produce bit sequences for integers that result in better compression ratios, compared to the existing non-parameterized codes.

4 Experimental Results

The fifth volume of the TREC collection comprises the testbed for the storage utilization efficiency measuring test runs that we present in this section. The volume contains 475MB of articles from the Los Angeles Times (LAT), published during the January 1, 1989 – December 31, 1990 period, plus 470MB of documents of the Foreign Broadcast Information Service (FBIS) from 1994. The profiles for the LAT and FBIS collections as well as of their concatenation (LATFBIS) are shown in Table 2.

We implemented and compared the following codes:

- "γ-**code**": Elias γ code for all the gaps in all the lists of the inverted file.
- "δ-**code**": Elias δ code for all the gaps in all the lists of the inverted file.
- "**Golomb**": Golomb code for the local Bernoulli model. An inverted list is created for every word in the collection. Each list also stores the value for f_t (document frequency for term t) using the γ code. The f_t overhead for each word is included in the final results.
- "**g-binary**": The g-binary code for various values of the b parameter.

Figure 1 illustrates the results obtained for the LAT, FBIS, and LATFBIS collections. In each graph, the average number of bits per pointer is plotted as a function of b and this is why the curves for "γ-code", "δ-code" and "Golomb" are horizontal lines. For the "Golomb" code, in particular, it has to be stated that it is a local, parameterized code involving a number of b values that are calculated and stored alongside each inverted list inside the inverted file, according to the model discussed in Section 2. In this respect, the "Golomb" line represents the average bit size per pointer and it is not affected by the b values of the x-axis. The latter are used to differentiate the g-binary code versions and for each such version they are applied globally on the entire inverted list.

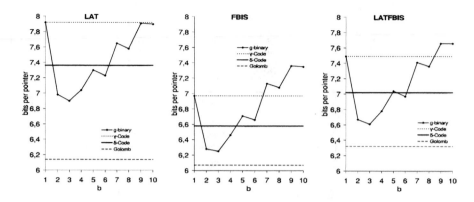

Fig. 1. Comparison of the γ, δ, Golomb and g-binary codes using the LAT, FBIS and LATFBIS collections

A first observation is that the "γ-code" line is always above the "δ-code" line. This means that the γ code produces larger indexes than the δ code, when applied globally on an entire inverted file. This finding confirms similar results presented in [9]. Another observation is that the "γ-code" compression ratio is equal to the "g-binary" compression ratio when $b=1$. This is expected because for $b=1$, g-binary is identical to γ code: they both produce the same bit sequences for all integers. Another expected result is that the "Golomb" code achieves the best compression among the existing codes, because it is a local, parameterized code. Unfortunately, such codes are not suitable for dynamic document collections.

The results demonstrate that the compression efficiency of "g-binary" is maximized when b is 2 and 3 and that in general it decreases as b increases beyond 4. More specifically, "g-binary" performs better than the "γ-code" and "δ-code" when the value of the b parameter is set to 2 or 3. The gain achieved ranges from 0.3 to 0.4 bits per 7-bit (average) pointer. This is about half the gain achieved by the popular parameterized Golomb code. It represents a significant gain since the two "g-binary" code versions are non-parameterized and they can be used to compress dynamic text database collections.

5   Analysis

In this section we follow an analytic approach and try to investigate the conditions under which g-binary for $b = 2$ and 3 achieves better compression than γ and δ code. To achieve this we examine the code lengths we obtain when we code all integers using these three methods.

For any integer $x > 0$ the length difference between the γ and g-binary codes is at least:

$$len_\gamma(x) - len_{gb}(x) = \lfloor log_2(x) \rfloor - \lfloor \lfloor log_2(x) \rfloor / b \rfloor - \lceil log_2(b) \rceil \qquad (3)$$

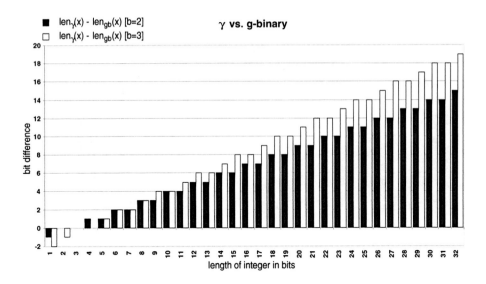

Fig. 2. Comparing γ code and g-binary

For any integer $x > 0$ the length difference between the δ and g-binary codes is at least:

$$len_\delta(x) - len_{gb}(x) = 2\lfloor log_2(1 + \lfloor log_2 x \rfloor) \rfloor - \lfloor \lfloor log_2(x) \rfloor / b \rfloor - \lceil log_2(b) \rceil \quad (4)$$

We can substitute $\lfloor log_2(x) \rfloor + 1$, that is equal to the number of bits used for the binary representation of integer x, with y. The above equations are respectively transformed into

$$len_\gamma(x) - len_{gb}(x) = y - 1 - \lfloor (y-1)/b \rfloor - \lceil log_2(b) \rceil \quad (5)$$

and

$$len_\delta(x) - len_{gb}(x) = 2\lfloor log_2 y \rfloor - \lfloor (y-1)/b \rfloor - \lceil log_2(b) \rceil \quad (6)$$

Apparently, the latter equations are functions of y, i.e., the number of bits that are used for the binary representation of the integers. Figures 2 and 3 are the graphical representation for equations 5 and 6 respectively.

The results demonstrate (see Figure 2) that the g-binary code for $b = 2$ has equal or better compression efficiency than the γ code for all integers except 1.

Also, the g-binary code for $b = 3$ has equal or better compression efficiency than the γ code for all integers except 1, 2 and 3. That explains the improved performance of g-binary when compared to γ code.

The results demonstrate (see Figure 3) that the g-binary code for $b = 2$ has equal or better compression efficiency than the δ code for all integers in $[2 \ldots 2^{12} - 1]$ or $[2 \ldots 4095]$. Also, the g-binary code for $b = 3$ has equal or better compression efficiency than the δ code for all integers in $[2 \ldots 2^{21} - 1]$ or $[2 \ldots 2097151]$. This is an important observation for g-binary, because large gaps

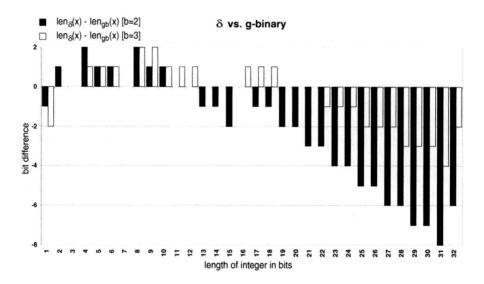

Fig. 3. Comparing δ code and g-binary

inside the inverted lists only occur in the case of rare terms. This means that large integers are not very frequent and that the majority of the integers stored are relatively small. Moreover, very small d-gap values (1 or 2) only occur in the case of very frequent terms. The latter may appear in stop-word lists, i.e., lists of words such as "the", "a", "of", etc., that are usually not indexed. In our experiments we did not take into consideration such lists, because we did not want to favor our method in any way. In other words, we indexed all words.

6   Conclusion

In the present study we consider the problem of integer number encoding in the context of index compression for dynamic document collections. The relevant research literature suggests that the γ and δ codes comprise the preferred choice for index compression.

We introduce g-binary, a new group of codes, involving a tunable parameter b that determines the Golomb code version used to store the length of the binary representation of an integer. A g-binary code consists of the length of the binary representation of an integer stored using Golomb code and the exact binary representation of the integer itself (without its most significant bit that is always 1). Experimental runs of the proposed group of codes conducted against two TREC collections reveal that by setting $b = 2$ and 3 we obtain two global non-parameterized codes that improve the size of the encoded index file by nearly 6% when compared to the size obtained by δ codes. Moreover, by construction the g-binary code does not introduce any extra CPU overhead during the encoding and decoding phases when compared to the γ and δ codes.

References

1. Blandford, D., Blelloch, G.: Index Compression through Document Reordering. Proceedings of the Data Compression Conference. (2002)
2. Bookstein, A., Klein, S.T., Raita, T.: Model based concordance compression. In Storer and Cohn. (1992) 82–91
3. Elias, P.: Universal codeword sets and representations of the integers. IEEE Transactions on Information Theory, Vol. IT–21. (1975) 194–203
4. Fox, E., Harman, D., Baeza-Yates, R., Lee, W.: Inverted Files. In: Frakes, W., Baeza-Yates, R. (eds): Information Retrieval: Data Structures and Algorithms. Prentice-Hall, Englewood Cliffs, NJ, Chapter 3. (1992) 28–43
5. Gallager, R.G., van Voorhis, D.C.: Optimal source codes for geometrically distributed alphabets. IEEE Transactions on Information Theory, Vol. IT–21. (1975) 228–230
6. Golomb, S.W.: Run-length Encodings. IEEE Transactions on Information Theory, Vol. IT–21. (1966) 399–401
7. Huffman, D.A: A method for the construction of minimum redundancy codes. Procedures IRE, Vol.40(9). (1952) 1098–1101
8. Moffat, A., Stuiver, L.: Exploiting clustering in inverted file compression. In Storer and Cohn. (1996) 82–91
9. Moffat, A., Zobel, J.: Paremeterised Compression for Sparse Bitmaps. 15th Ann Int'l SIGIR, Denmark (1992) 274–285
10. Scholer, F., Williams, H.E., Yiannis, J., Zobel, J.: Compression of Inverted Indexes for Fast Query Evaluation. SIGIR, Finland (2002) 222–229
11. Schuegraf, E.J.: Compression of large inverted files with hyperbolic term distribution. Information Processing and Managemant Vol 12. (1976) 377–384
12. Teuhola, J.: A compression method for clustered bit-vectors. Information Processing Letters, Vol 7(2). (1978) 308–311
13. Williams, H. E., Zobel, J.: Compressing Integers for Fast File Access. The Computer Journal, Vol. 42. (1999) 193–201
14. Witten, I.H., Moffat A., Bell T.C.: Managing Gigabytes. Compressing and Indexing Documents and Images. Academic Press (1999)
15. Zobel, J., Moffat, A., Ramamohanarao K.: Inverted Files Versus Signature Files for Text Indexing. ACM Transactions on Database Systems, Vol. 23. (1999) 369–410

Activation on the Move: Querying Tourism Information via Spreading Activation

Helmut Berger[1], Michael Dittenbach[1], and Dieter Merkl[1,2]

[1] E-Commerce Competence Center – EC3,
Donau-City-Straße 1,
A–1220 Wien, Austria
{helmut.berger,michael.dittenbach,dieter.merkl}@ec3.at
[2] Institut für Softwaretechnik,
Technische Universität Wien,
Favoritenstraße 9–11/188,
A–1040 Wien, Austria

Abstract. In this paper, we present an information retrieval system for tourism information that allows query formulation in natural language. We describe a knowledge representation model, based on associative networks, for defining semantic relationships of terms. The relatedness of terms is taken into account and we show how a fuzzy search strategy, performed by a constrained spreading activation algorithm, yields beneficial results and recommends closely related matches to users' queries. Thus, spreading activation implicitly implements query expansion.

1 Introduction

How to determine the real intention of a user, when she or he is forced to choose from a fixed set of options available to her or him? The importance of understanding what users really want to know from information retrieval systems remains a crucial task in the field of information retrieval. An approach leaving the means of expression in users' hands, narrows the gap between users' needs and interfaces used to express these needs. Therefore, a natural language interface allows for easy and intuitive access to information sources. Fesenmaier et al. give an example of a recommendation system in the tourism domain [8] allowing to choose, inter alia, from a fixed set of attributes represented by option sets or dropdown lists. The diversity of terms results in a dramatically overloaded search interface. The avoidance of such overloaded interfaces is an argument in favor of query formulation in natural language. Moreover, as O'Brian pointed out in [9], a sophisticated recommendation of, for instance, accommodations goes hand in hand with the ability of expressing intentions in *own* words.

Furthermore, how to get notion of newly appearing trends if users are not able to express them via the search interface? A field trial based on a natural language search interface providing access to tourism data throughout Austria, revealed the willingness of users to provide much more information than they are able to express by conventional means. Thus, analyzing natural language queries

V. Mařík et al. (Eds.): DEXA 2003, LNCS 2736, pp. 474–483, 2003.

provides a starting point for determining changes of user interests and conveniently provides a means to identify new domain-relevant information. Hence, the application of natural language interfaces assists in gathering information about users' real interests and in expanding and refining the vocabulary of the domain according to zeitgeist.

The core element remains the underlying knowledge representation model. On the one hand, the conceptual model has to offer adequate performance during the search process and, on the other hand, the knowledge representation model must allow for easy integration of additional domain relevant information. To achieve this, we use an approach based on associative networks reflecting the relationship of information items in the tourism domain. Thus, the approach described in this paper, first, extends traditional search interfaces by integrating a natural language interface, second, incorporates a means for knowledge representation allowing for the definition of semantic relationships of domain-intrinsic information. Finally, due to the network structure of the knowledge representation model, implicit query expansion enriches the result set with additional recommendations.

2   A Natural Language Information Retrieval System

The software architecture of our natural language information retrieval system is designed as a pipeline structure. Hence, successively activated pipeline elements apply transformations on natural language queries that are posed via arbitrary client devices, such as, for instance, web browsers, PDAs or mobile phones.

First, the natural language query is evaluated by an automatic language identification module based on an n-gram text classification approach [2]. Next, the system corrects typographic errors and misspellings to improve retrieval performance. The spell-checking module uses the metaphone algorithm [10] to transform words into their soundalikes and suggests words that are likely to be the correct substitution from the orthographic or phonetic point of view. Subsequently, a phrase recognizer inspects the query and identifies multi-word denominations, as, for instance *Kirchberg am Wechsel*. Before adding grammar rules and semantic information to the query terms, a converter transforms numerals to their numeric equivalents. Depending on the rules assigned to the query terms, a mapping process associates these terms with SQL fragments that represent the query in a formal way. Due to the fact that the system uses a relational database as backend this mapping process is crucial. In a next step the SQL fragments are combined according to the modifiers (e.g. *and, or, near, not*) identified in the query and we obtain a single SQL statement that reflects the intention of the query. Finally, the system determines the appropriate result and generates an XML representation for further processing. The XML result set is adapted to fit the needs of the client device.

A major component of the system is the knowledge base that stores domain knowledge. During query processing the pipeline elements work hand in hand with the knowledge base. The synonym ontology, for instance, is used to identify relevant terms of the query and rewrites them to a preferred, semantically equivalent representation. For a detailed system description see [1,7].

A field trial was carried out from March 15 to March 25, 2002. During this time our interface was promoted on and linked from the homepage of the largest Austrian tourism platform, *Tiscover* [12]. We obtained 1,425 unique queries through our interface. The results of the field trial show that the level of sentence complexity is moderate, which suggests that shallow language processing should be sufficient within a limited domain. Users show that they are willing to type grammatically correct natural language sentences. This might be because they are able to express their intentions in their own words without the need of reducing them to a set of possible keywords or options.

Additionally, regions or local attractions are important information that have to be integrated into the system. Furthermore, users' queries contained vague or highly subjective criteria like *romantic* or *wellness*. For a detailed exposition of our findings we refer to [6].

Basically, the system fulfilled its intended purpose but we recognized several flaws that implied a redevelopment of parts of the system. Strictly speaking, the underlying knowledge base reached its limitations as the integration of semantic relations between information items is difficult in the non-hierarchic structure of our original prototype. Regarding the queries obtained during the field trial, we realized that this flat structure limits the power of the system and, therefore, restricts the ability of providing appropriate recommendations. Furthermore, the integration of subjective criteria, region and location dependent information implies the use of an alternative approach that combines the features of the original system with the demands derived from the results of the field trial.

3   Associative Networks

Quillian introduced the basic principle of a semantic network [13] and it played, since then, a central role in knowledge representation. The building blocks of semantic networks are, first, nodes that express knowledge in terms of concepts, second, concept properties, and third, the hierarchical sub-super class relationship between these concepts. Each concept in a semantic network represents a semantic entity; the associations between concepts describe the hierarchical relationship between these semantic entities via *is-a* or *instance-of* links. The higher a concept moves up in the hierarchy along *is-a* relations, the more abstract is its semantic meaning. Properties are attached to concepts, and therefore, properties are also represented by concepts and linked to nodes via labeled associations. Furthermore, a property that is linked to a high-level concept is inherited by all descendants of the concept. Hence, it is assumed that the property applies to all subsequent nodes. An example of a semantic network is depicted in Figure 1.

Semantic networks initially emerged in cognitive psychology and the term itself has been used in the field of knowledge representation in a far more general sense than described above. In particular, the term semantic network has been commonly used to refer to a conceptual approach known as associative network.

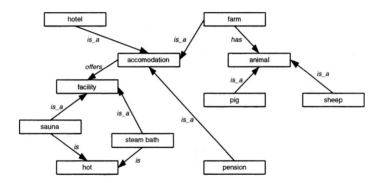

Fig. 1. A semantic network example of tourism-related terms

An associative network defines a generic network which consists of nodes representing information items (semantic entities) and associations between nodes, that express relations among nodes. Links between particular nodes might be weighted to determine the strength of connectivity.

In contrast to the knowledge base of the original system, associative networks assist in inferring similar or related semantic entities. Thus, the network structure provides a means of exact search strategies and suggests results that are closely related or at least similar. Furthermore, the integration of *abstract* terms, linked via accordingly weighted associations, allows the definition of subjective criteria. Different people might associate different meanings with the concept of *wellness*, for instance. Personalized associative networks accomplish this requirement. The integration and, therefore, the task of associating newly acquired semantic entities with already existing ones can be accomplished by exploiting their semantic relatedness. Moreover, associative networks provide a means for incorporating predefined scenarios, e.g. winter holiday. More precisely, the approach allows the definition of networks that favor certain semantic entities.

A commonly used technique for implementing information retrieval on semantic or associative networks is referred to as *spreading activation* (SA). The SA paradigm is tight-knit with the supposed mode of operation of human memory. The algorithm underlying SA is based on a simple approach and operates on a data structure reflecting the relationships between information items. Nodes model real world entities and weighted links define the relatedness of entities. We shall note that SA has some tradition in information retrieval [3,5,14].

The idea, underlying SA, is to propagate activation starting from source nodes via weighted links over the network. More precisely, the process of propagating activation from one node to adjacent nodes is called a *pulse*. The SA algorithm is based on an iterative approach that is divided into two steps: first, one or more pulses are triggered and second, a termination check determines if the process has to continue or to halt. A comprehensive overview of methods for SA can be found in [11]. Spreading activation works according to the formula:

$$I_j(p) = \sum_i^k (O_i(p-1) \cdot w_{ij}) \tag{1}$$

Each node j determines the total input I_j at pulse p of all linked nodes. Therefore, the output $O_i(p-1)$ at the previous pulse $p-1$ of node i is multiplied with the associated weight w_{ij} of the link connecting node i to node j and the grand total for all k connected nodes is calculated.

Inputs or weights can be expressed by binary values (0/1), inhibitory or reinforcing values (-1/+1), or real values defining the strength of the connection between nodes. The first two options are used in the application of semantic networks. The latter one is commonly used for associative networks and is used to express the relationship between nodes. Furthermore, the output value of a node has to be determined. In most cases, no distinction is made between the input value and the activation level of a node, i.e. the input value of a node and its activation level are equal. Before firing the activation to adjacent nodes a function calculates the output depending on the activation level of the node: $O_i = f(I_i)$. Various functions can be used to determine the output value of a node, for instance the sigmoid function, or a linear activation function. Most commonly used is the threshold function which determines if a node is considered to be active or not. If the activation level exceeds the threshold, the state of the node is set to active. Subsequent to the calculation of the activation state, the output value is propagated to adjacent nodes. Normally, the same output value is sent to all adjacent nodes. The process described above is repeated, pulse after pulse, and activation spreads through the network and activates more and more nodes until a termination condition is met. Finally, the SA process halts and a final activation state is obtained. Depending on the application's task the activation levels are evaluated and interpreted accordingly.

Unfortunately, the basic approach of SA entails some major drawbacks. Without appropriate control, activation might be propagated all over the network. To overcome these undesired side-effects the integration of constraints helps to tame the spreading process [4]. Constraints commonly used are described as follows.

- **Fan-out constraint:** Nodes with a broad semantic meaning posses a vast number of links to adjacent nodes. This circumstance implies that such nodes activate large areas of the network. Therefore, activation should diminish at nodes with a high degree of connectivity to avoid this unwanted effect.
- **Distance constraint:** The basic idea underlying this constraint is that activation ceases when it reaches nodes far away from the activation source. Thus, the term *far* corresponds to the number of links over which activation was spread, i.e. the greater the distance between two nodes, the weaker is their semantic relationship.
- **Activation constraint:** Threshold values are assigned to nodes (it is not necessary to apply the same value to all nodes) and are interpreted by the threshold function. Moreover, threshold values can be adapted during the spreading process in relation to the total amount of activity in the network.
- **Path constraint:** Usually, activation spreads over the network using all available links. The integration of preferred paths allows to direct activation according to application-dependent rules.

```
<concept id="ferienwohnung" role="concrete" initial="1.0">
  <connectedTo id="pension" weight="w1"/>
  <connectedTo id="bauernhof" weight="w2"/>
  <lang id="de">
    <syn>Ferienwohnung</syn>
    <syn>Ferienhaus</syn>
  </lang>
  <lang id="en">
    <syn>holiday flat</syn>
  </lang>
</concept>
```

Fig. 2. XML representation of an information item in the associative network

4   Recommendation via Spreading Activation

Basically, the knowledge base of our system is composed of two parts: first, a relational database that stores information about domain entities and, second, a data structure based on an associative network that models the relationships among terms. The associative network consists of three logical layers:

- **Abstraction layer:** One objective of the redevelopment of the knowledge base was to integrate information items with abstract semantic meaning. More precisely, in contrast to the knowledge base used in the original system which only supported modeling of entity attributes, the new approach allows the integration of a broader set of terms, e.g. terms like *wellness* or *summer activities* that virtually combine several information items.
- **Conceptual layer:** The conceptual layer is used to associate entity attributes according to their semantic relationship and each entity attribute has a representation at this layer. The strengths of the relationships between information items are expressed by a real value associated with the link.
- **Entity layer:** Finally, the entity layer associates entities with information items (entity attributes) of the conceptual layer, e.g. an entity possessing the attribute *sauna* is associated with the *sauna*-node of the conceptual layer.

The building blocks of the network are concepts. A concept represents an information item possessing several semantically equivalent terms, i.e. synonyms, in different languages. Figure 2 depicts an example of an XML representation of the concept *ferienwohnung*. Each concept is described by a unique id (e.g. id="ferienwohnung") and an initial activation level (e.g. initial="1.0"). Furthermore, each concept has a tag named *role*. We distinguish three different role types: *concrete*, *abstract* and *modifier*. Concrete concepts represent information items at the conceptual layer, i.e. entity attributes. Abstract concepts refer to terms at the abstraction layer and modifier concepts alter the processing rules for abstract or concrete concepts. More precisely, a modifier like, for instance, *not* allows the exclusion of concepts by negation of the *initial* tag's value.

Moreover, concepts provide, depending on their role, a method for expressing relationships among them. The *connectedTo* relation defines a bidirectional weighted link between two concrete concepts, e.g. the concept *pension* is linked

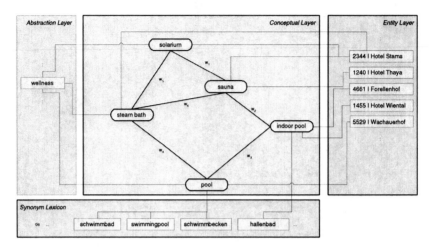

Fig. 3. Knowledge base architecture

to *ferienwohnung*. Weights associated with links are, on the one hand, determined during a manual tuning process and, on the other hand, influenced by subjective preferences of users. The second relation used to associate information items is the *parentOf* association and is used for abstract concepts only. These relations will be detailed later in this section.

A set of concepts representing a particular domain is described in a single XML file and act as input source for the retrieval system. During initialization, the application parses the XML file, instantiates all concepts, generates a list of synonyms pointing at corresponding concepts, associates concepts according to their relations and, finally, links the entities to concrete concepts. Currently, the associative network consists of about 2,200 concepts, 10,000 links and more than 13,000 entities. The concept network includes terms that describe the tourism domain as well as towns, cities and federal states throughout Austria.

Due to the adaptivity of the original system, the integration of the redesigned parts has been accomplished with relatively little effort. In particular, the existing knowledge base has been replaced by the associative network and we incorporated new pipeline elements to implement spreading activation.

Figure 3 depicts the redeveloped knowledge base on which the processing algorithm operates. The conceptual layer stores concrete concepts and the weighted links among them. Associating abstract concepts with concrete concepts is done at the abstraction layer. Each entity has a unique identifier that is equivalent to the entity identifier stored in the relational database. Furthermore, entities are connected to concepts at the conceptual layer. More precisely, an entity is connected to all attributes it possesses. As an example consider the entity *Hotel Stams* as depicted in Figure 3. This hotel offers a *sauna*, a *steam bath* and a *solarium* and is linked to the corresponding concepts at the conceptual layer.

First, a user's query, received by the retrieval system, is decomposed into single terms. After applying an error correction mechanism and a phrase detection algorithm (cf. [7]) to the query, terms found in the synonym lexicon are linked to their corresponding concept at the abstract or conceptual layer. These concepts act as activation sources and subsequently, the activation process is initiated and activation spreads according to the algorithm as outlined below.

At the beginning, the role of each concept is evaluated and different initialization strategies are applied, respectively:

- **Modifier role:** In case of the *not* modifier, the initialization value of the following concept is multiplied by a negative number. Due to the fact that the *and* and *or* modifiers are implicitly resolved by the associative network, they receive no special treatment. Furthermore, the *near* modifier reflecting locational dependencies, is automatically resolved by associating cities or towns within a circumference of 15km. Depending on the distance, the weights are adapted accordingly, i.e. the closer they are together, the higher is the weight of the link in the associative network.
- **Abstract role:** If a source concept is *abstract*, the set of source concepts is expanded by resolving the *parentOf* relation between parent and child concepts. This process is repeated until all abstract concepts are resolved, i.e. the set of source concepts contains only concepts of the conceptual layer. The initial activation value is propagated to all child concepts, with respect to the weighted links.
- **Concrete role:** The initial activation level of concrete concepts is set to the value defined in the *initial* tag of the concept (cf. Figure 2). Spreading activation takes place at the conceptual layer, i.e. the *connectedTo* relations between concepts are used to propagate activation through the network.

After the initialization phase has completed, the iterative spreading process is activated. During a single iteration one pulse is performed, i.e. the number of iterations equals the number of pulses. Starting from the set of source concepts determined during initialization, in our current implementation activation is spread to adjacent nodes according the following formula:

$$O_i(p) = \begin{cases} 0 & \text{if } I_i(p) < \tau, \\ \frac{F_i}{p+1} \cdot I_i(p) & \text{otherwise, with } F_i = (1 - \frac{C_i}{C_T}) \end{cases} \quad (2)$$

The output, $O_i(p)$, sent from node i at pulse p, is calculated as the fraction of F_i, which limits the propagation according to the degree of connectivity of node i (i.e. fan-out constraint), and $p + 1$, expressing the diminishing semantic relationship according to the distance of node i to activation source nodes (i.e. distance constraint). Moreover, F_i is calculated by dividing the number of concepts C_i directly connected to node i by the total number of nodes C_T building the associative network. Note, τ represents a threshold value.

Simultaneously with calculating the output value for all connected nodes, the activation level $I_i(p)$ of node i is added to all associated entities. More precisely, each entity connected to node i receives the same value and adds it to an internal variable representing the total activation of the entity. As an example, if the concept node *sauna* is activated, the activation potential is propagated to the

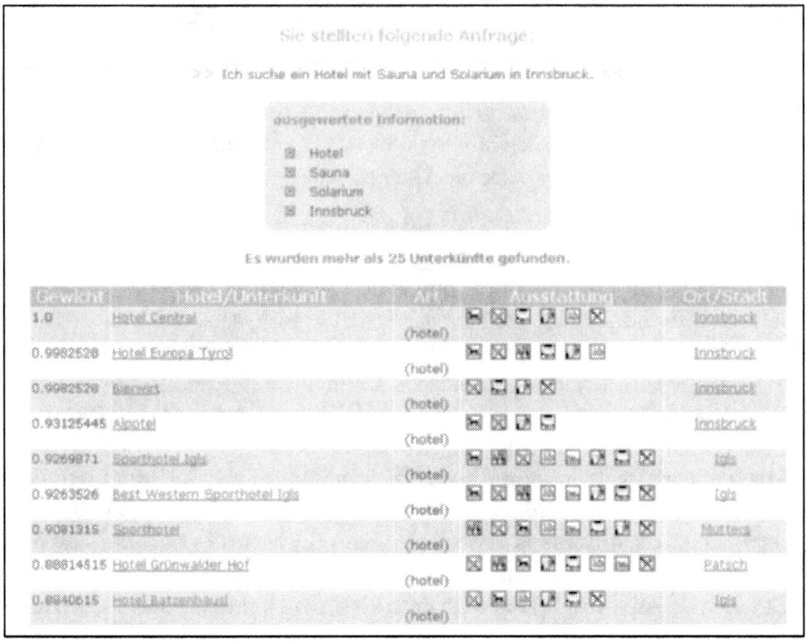

Fig. 4. Weighted result set determined by constrained spreading activation

entities *Hotel Stams* and *Hotel Thaya* (cf. Figure 3). Next, all newly activated nodes are used in the subsequent iteration as activation sources and the spreading process continues until the maximum number of iterations is reached.

After the spreading process has terminated, the system inspects all entities and ranks them according to their activation. Figure 4 depicts the results determined for the query *"Ich suche ein Hotel mit Sauna und Solarium in Innsbruck"*. In this case, the entity *Hotel Central* located in *Innsbruck* is suggested to be the best matching answer to the query. Moreover, the result set includes matches closely related to the user's query. Thus, depending on the relations stored in the associative network, entities offering related concepts are activated accordingly. More precisely, not only the attributes *hotel, sauna* and *solarium* are taken into account, but also all other related entity attributes (e.g. *steam bath*) have some influence on the ranking position. Furthermore, accommodations in cities in the vicinity of *Innsbruck* providing the same or even better offers are also included in the result set. Thus, the associative network allows exact information retrieval and incorporates a fuzzy search strategy that determines closely related matches to the user's query.

5   Conclusion

In this paper, we described a search interface providing natural language access to tourism information. A field trial revealed the necessity of redeveloping the knowledge base underlying the system. Therefore, we replaced the knowledge base of the original system with an approach based on associative networks. As a means for determining the appropriate results to a user's query, we use constrained spreading activation. Generally, the combination of the associative nature of the underlying knowledge base and the constrained spreading activation approach implements a search algorithm that evaluates the relatedness of terms and, therefore, provides a means for implicit query expansion. Furthermore, the flexible method of defining relationships between terms unleashes the ability to recommend highly associated results as well as results that are predefined due to personal preferences. Moreover, specially designed associative networks can be used to model scenarios, as, for instance, a winter holiday scenario that favors accommodations offering winter sports activities by adapting the weights of links accordingly.

References

1. H. Berger. Adaptive multilingual interfaces. Master's thesis, Vienna University of Technology, 2001.
2. W. B. Cavnar and J. M. Trenkle. N-gram-based text categorization. In *Int'l Symp. on Document Analysis and Information Retrieval*, Las Vegas, NV, 1994.
3. P. R. Cohen and R. Kjeldsen. Information retrieval by constrained spreading activation in semantic networks. *Information Processing and Management*, 23(4):255–268, 1987.
4. F. Crestani. Application of spreading activation techniques in information retrieval. *Artificial Intelligence Review*, 11(6):453–582, 1997.
5. F. Crestani and P. L. Lee. Searching the web by constrained spreading activation. *Information Processing and Management*, 36(4):585–605, 2000.
6. M. Dittenbach, D. Merkl, and H. Berger. What customers really want to know from tourism information systems but never dared to ask. In *Proc of the 5th Int'l Conf. on E-Commerce Research (ICECR-5)*, Montréal, Canada, 2002.
7. M. Dittenbach, D. Merkl, and H. Berger. A natural language query interface for tourism information. In *Proc of the 10th Int'l Conf. on Information Technologies in Tourism (ENTER 2003)*, pages 152–162, 2003.
8. D. R. Fesenmaier, F. Ricci, E. Schaumlechner, K. Wöber, and C. Zanella. DIETORECS: Travel Advisory for Multiple Decision Styles. In *Proc of the 10th Int'l Conf. on Information Technologies in Tourism*, pages 232–241, 2003.
9. P. O'Brian. Dynamic travel itinerary management: The ubiquitous travel agent. In *Proc of the 12th Int'l Australasian Conf. on Information Systems*, Coffs Harbour, Australia, 2001.
10. L. Philips. Hanging on the metaphone. *Computer Language Magazine*, 7(12), 1990.
11. S. Preece. *A spreading activation model for Information Retrieval*. PhD thesis, University of Illinois, Urbana-Champaign, USA, 1981.
12. B. Pröll, W. Retschitzegger, R. Wagner, and A. Ebner. Beyond traditional tourism information systems: TIScover. *Information Technology and Tourism*, 1, 1998.
13. M. R. Quillian. Semantic memory. In M. Minsky, editor, *Semantic Information Processing*, pages 227–270. MIT Press, 1968.
14. G. Salton and C. Buckley. On the use of spreading activation methods in automatic information retrieval. In *Proc of the 11th Int'l Conf. on Research and Development in Information Retrieval*, 1988.

Similarity Join in Metric Spaces Using eD-Index

Vlastislav Dohnal[1], Claudio Gennaro[2], and Pavel Zezula[1]

[1] Masaryk University
Brno, Czech Republic
{xdohnal,zezula}@fi.muni.cz
[2] ISTI-CNR
Pisa, Italy
{gennaro}@isti.pi.cnr.it

Abstract. Similarity join in distance spaces constrained by the metric postulates is the necessary complement of more famous similarity range and the nearest neighbor search primitives. However, the quadratic computational complexity of similarity joins prevents from applications on large data collections. We present the eD-Index, an extension of D-index, and we study an application of the eD-Index to implement two algorithms for similarity self joins, i.e. the range query join and the overloading join. Though also these approaches are not able to eliminate the intrinsic quadratic complexity of similarity joins, significant performance improvements are confirmed by experiments.

1 Introduction

Contrary to the traditional database approach, the Information Retrieval community has always considered search results as a ranked list of objects. Given a query, some objects are more relevant to the query specification than the others and users are typically interested in the most relevant objects, that is the objects with the highest ranks. This search paradigm has recently been generalized into a model in which a set of objects can only be pair-wise compared through a distance measure satisfying the *metric space* properties [1].

For illustration, consider the text data as the most common data type used in information retrieval. Since text is typically represented as a character string, pairs of strings can be compared and the *exact match* decided. However, the longer the strings are the less significant the exact match is: the text strings can contain errors of any kind and even the correct strings may have small differences. According to [8], text typically contain about 2% of typing and spelling errors. This gives a motivation to a search allowing errors, or *approximate search*, which requires a definition of the concept of *similarity*, as well as a specification of algorithms to evaluate it.

Though the way how objects are compared is very important to guarantee the search effectiveness, indexing structures are needed to achieve efficiency of searching large data collections. Extensive research in this area, see [1], have produced a large number of index structures which support two similarity search conditions, the range query and the k-nearest neighbor query. Given a reference (query) object, the *range queries* retrieve objects with distances not larger than a user defined threshold, while the *k-nearest neighbors* queries provide k objects with the shortest distances to the reference.

V. Mařík et al. (Eds.): DEXA 2003, LNCS 2736, pp. 484–493, 2003.
© Springer-Verlag Berlin Heidelberg 2003

In order to complete the set of similarity search operations, *similarity joins* are needed. For example, consider a document collection of books and a collection of compact disk documents. A possible search request can require to find *all pairs of books and compact disks which have similar titles*. But the similarity joins are not only useful for text. Given a collection of time series of stocks, a relevant query can be: *report all pairs of stocks that are within distance μ from each other*. Though the similarity join has always been considered as the basic similarity search operation, there are only few indexing techniques, most of them concentrating on vector spaces. In this paper, we consider the problem from much broader perspective and assume distance measures as metric functions. Such a view extends the range of possible data types to the multimedia dimension, which is typical for modern information retrieval systems.

The development of Internet services often requires an integration of heterogeneous sources of data. Such sources are typically unstructured whereas the intended services often require structured data. Once again, the main challenge is to provide consistent and error-free data, which implies the *data cleaning*, typically implemented by a sort of *similarity join*. In order to perform such tasks, similarity rules are specified to decide whether specific pieces of data may actually be the same things or not. A similar approach can also be applied to the *copy detection*. However, when the database is large, the data cleaning can take a long time, so the processing time (or the performance) is the most critical factor that can only be reduced by means of convenient similarity search indexes.

The problem of approximate string processing has recently been studied in [4] in the context of data cleaning, that is removing inconsistencies and errors from large data sets such as those occurring in *data warehouses*. A technique for building approximate string join capabilities on top of commercial databases has been proposed in [6]. The core idea of these approaches is to transform the difficult problem of approximate string matching into other search problems for which some more efficient solutions exist.

In this article, we extend the existing metric index structure, D-index [2], and compare two algorithms for similarity join built on top of this extended structure. In Section 2, we define principles of the similarity join search in metric spaces and describe the extension of the D-index. Performance evaluation of proposed algorithms is reported in Section 3.

2   Similarity Join

A convenient way to assess similarity between two objects is to apply metric functions to decide the closeness of objects as a distance, which can be seen as a measure of the objects *dis-similarity*. A *metric space* $\mathcal{M} = (\mathcal{D}, d)$ is defined by a domain of objects (elements, points) $\mathcal{D}$ and a total (distance) function d – a *non negative* ($d(x,y) \geq 0$ with $d(x,y) = 0$ iff $x = y$) and *symmetric* ($d(x,y) = d(y,x)$) function, which satisfies the *triangle inequality* ($d(x,y) \leq d(x,z) + d(z,y), \forall x, y, z \in \mathcal{D}$).

In general, the problem of indexing in metric spaces can be defined as follows: *given a set $X \subseteq \mathcal{D}$ in the metric space $\mathcal{M}$, preprocess or structure the elements of X so that similarity queries can be answered efficiently*. Without any loss of generality, we assume that the maximum distance never exceeds the distance d^+. For a query object $q \in \mathcal{D}$, two fundamental similarity queries can be defined. A *range query* retrieves all elements within distance r to q, that is the set $\{x \in X, d(q,x) \leq r\}$. A *k-nearest neighbors*

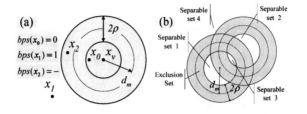

Fig. 1. The *bps* split function (a) and the combination of two *bps* functions (b).

query retrieves the k closest elements to q, that is a set $R \subseteq X$ such that $|R| = k$ and $\forall x \in R, y \in X - R, d(q, x) \leq d(q, y)$.

2.1 Similarity Join: Problem Definition

The *similarity join* is a search primitive which combines objects of two subsets of $\mathcal{D}$ into one set such that a similarity condition is satisfied. The similarity condition between two objects is defined according to the metric distance d. Formally, the similarity join $X \overset{sim}{\bowtie} Y$ between two finite sets $X = \{x_1, ..., x_N\}$ and $Y = \{y_1, ..., y_M\}$ ($X \subseteq \mathcal{D}$ and $Y \subseteq \mathcal{D}$) is defined as the set of pairs: $X \overset{sim}{\bowtie} Y = \{(x_i, y_j) \mid d(x_i, y_j) \leq \mu\}$, where the threshold μ is a real number such that $0 \leq \mu \leq d^+$. If the sets X and Y coincide, we talk about the *similarity self join*.

2.2 eD-Index

The eD-Index is an extension of the D-Index [5,2] structure. In the following, we provide a brief overview of the D-Index, we then present the eD-Index and show the differences to the original D-Index structure.

D-Index: An Access Structure for Similarity Search. It is a multi-level metric structure, consisting of *search-separable* buckets at each level. The structure supports easy insertion and bounded search costs because at most one bucket needs to be accessed at each level for range queries up to a predefined value of search radius ρ. At the same time, the applied *pivot-based strategy* significantly reduces the number of distance computations in accessed buckets. In the following, we provide a brief overview of the D-Index, more details can be found in [5] and the full specification, as well as performance evaluations, are available in [2].

The partitioning principles of the D-Index are based on a multiple definition of a mapping function, called the ρ-split function. Figure 1a shows a possible implementation of a ρ-split function, called the *ball partitioning split* (*bps*), originally proposed in [10]. This function uses one reference object x_v and the *medium distance* d_m to partition a data set into three subsets. The result of the following *bps* function gives a unique identification of the set to which the object x belongs:

$$bps(x) = \begin{cases} 0 & \text{if } d(x, x_v) \leq d_m - \rho \\ 1 & \text{if } d(x, x_v) > d_m + \rho \\ - & \text{otherwise} \end{cases}$$

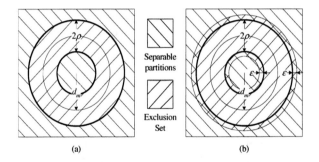

Fig. 2. The modified *bps* split function: (a) original ρ-split function; (b) modified ρ-split function.

The subset of objects characterized by the symbol '−' is called the *exclusion set*, while the subsets of objects characterized by the symbols 0 and 1 are the *separable sets*, because any range query with radius not larger than ρ cannot find qualifying objects in both the subsets.

More separable sets can be obtained as a combination of *bps* functions, where the resulting exclusion set is the union of the exclusion sets of the original split functions. Furthermore, the new separable sets are obtained as the intersection of all possible pairs of the separable sets of original functions. Figure 1b gives an illustration of this idea for the case of two split functions. The separable sets and the exclusion set form the separable buckets and the exclusion bucket of one level of the D-index structure, respectively.

Naturally, the more separable buckets we have, the larger the exclusion bucket is. For the large exclusion bucket, the D-index allows an additional level of splitting by applying a new set of split functions on the exclusion bucket of the previous level. The exclusion bucket of the last level forms the exclusion bucket of the whole structure. The ρ-split functions of individual levels should be different but they must use the same ρ. Moreover, by using a different number of split functions (generally decreasing with the level), the D-Index structure can have different number of buckets at individual levels. In order to deal with overflow problems and growing files, buckets are implemented as *elastic buckets* and consist of the necessary number of fixed-size blocks (pages) – basic disk access units.

Due to the mathematical properties of the split functions, precisely defined in [2], the range queries up to radius ρ are solved by accessing at most one bucket per level, plus the exclusion bucket of the whole structure. This can intuitively be comprehended by the fact that an arbitrary object belonging to a separable bucket is at distance at least 2ρ from any object of other separable bucket of the same level. With additional computational effort, the D-Index executes range queries of radii greater than ρ. The D-index also supports the nearest neighbor(s) queries.

eD-Index: An Access Structure for Similarity Self Join. The idea behind the eD-Index is to modify the ρ-split function so that the exclusion set and separable sets overlap of distance ϵ. Figure 2 depicts the modified ρ-split function. The objects which belong to both the separable and the exclusion sets are replicated. This principle, called the *exclusion set overloading*, ensures that there always exists a bucket for every qualifying pair $(x, y)\,|\,d(x, y) \leq \mu \leq \epsilon$ where the pair occurs. As explained later, a special algorithm is used to efficiently find these buckets and avoid access to duplicates. In this way, the eD-Index speeds up the evaluation of similarity self joins.

2.3   Similarity Self Join Algorithm with eD-Index

The outline of the similarity self join algorithm is following: execute the join query independently on every separable bucket of every level of the eD-Index and additionally on the exclusion bucket of the whole structure. This behavior is correct due to the exclusion set overloading principle – every object of a separable set which can make a qualifying pair with an object of the exclusion set is copied to the exclusion set. The partial results are concatenated and form the final answer.

The similarity self join algorithm which processes sub-queries in individual buckets is based on the *sliding window algorithm*. The idea of this algorithm is straightforward, see Figure 3. All objects of a bucket are ordered with respect to a pivot p, which is

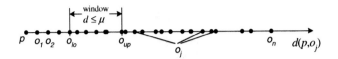

Fig. 3. The Sliding Window algorithm.

the reference object of a ρ-split function used by the eD-Index, and we define a sliding window of objects as $[o_{lo}, o_{up}]$. The window always satisfies the constraint: $d(p, o_{up}) - d(p, o_{lo}) \leq \mu$, i.e. the window's width is $\leq \mu$. Algorithm 21 starts with the window $[o_1, o_2]$ and successively moves the upper bound of the window up by one object while the lower bound is increased to preserve the window's width $\leq \mu$. The algorithm terminates when the last object o_n is reached. All pairs (o_j, o_{up}), such that $lo \leq j < up$, are collected in each window $[o_{lo}, o_{up}]$ and, at the same time, the applied pivot-based strategy significantly reduces the number of pairs which have to be checked. Finally, all qualifying pairs are reported.

Algorithm 21 *Sliding Window*

$lo = 1$
for $up = 2$ **to** n
    # move the lower boundary up to preserve window's width $\leq \mu$
    increment lo **while** $d(o_{up}, p) - d(o_{lo}, p) > \mu$

        for $j = lo$ **to** $up - 1$ # for all objects in the window
            if *PivotCheck()* = *FALSE* **then**   # apply the pivot-based strategy
                compute $d(o_j, o_{up})$
                if $d(o_j, o_{up}) \leq \mu$ **then**
                    add pair (o_j, o_{up}) **to result**
                end if
            end if
        end for
    end for

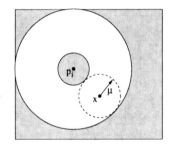

Fig. 4. Example of pivots behavior.

The eD-Index structure stores distances between stored objects and reference objects of ρ-split functions. These distances are computed when objects are inserted into the structure and they are utilized by the pivot-based strategy. Figure 4 illustrates the basic principle of this strategy, the object x is one object of an examined pair and p_i is the reference object, called pivot. Provided that the distance between any object and p_i is known, the gray area represents the region of objects y that do not form a qualifying pair with x. This assertion can easily be decided without actually computing the distance between x and y. By using the triangle inequalities $d(p_i, y) + d(x, y) \geq d(p_i, x)$ and $d(p_i, x) + d(p_i, y) \geq d(x, y)$ we have that $|d(p_i, x) - d(p_i, y)| \leq d(x, y) \leq d(p_i, y) + d(p_i, x)$, where $d(p_i, x)$ and $d(p_i, y)$ are pre-computed. It is obvious that, by using more pivots, we can improve the probability of excluding an object y without actually computing its distance to x. Note that we use all reference objects of ρ-split functions as pivots.

The application of the exclusion set overloading principle implies two important issues. The former one concerns the problem of duplicate pairs in the result of a join query. This fact is caused by the copies of objects which are reinserted into the exclusion set. The described algorithm evades this behavior by coloring object's duplicates. Precisely, each level of the eD-Index has its unique color and every duplicate of an object has colors of all the preceding levels where the replicated object is stored. For example, the object is replicated and stored at levels 1, 3, and 6. The object at level 1 has no color because it is not a duplicate. The object at level 3 has color of level 1 because it has already been stored at level 1. Similarly, the object at level 6 receives colors of levels 1 and 3, since it is stored at those preceding levels. Before the algorithm examines a pair it decides whether the objects of the pair share any color. If they have at least one color in common the pair is eliminated. The concept of sharing a color by two objects means that these objects are stored at the same level thus they are checked in a bucket of that level.

The latter issue limits the value of parameter ρ, that is $2\rho \geq \epsilon$. If $\epsilon > 2\rho$ some qualifying pairs are not examined by the algorithm. In detail, a pair is missed if one object is from one separable set while the other object of the pair is from another separable set. Such pairs cannot be found by this algorithm because the exclusion set overloading principle does not duplicate objects among separable sets. Consequently, the separable sets are not contrasted enough to avoid missing some qualifying pairs.

3   Performance Evaluation

In order to demonstrate suitability of the eD-Index to the problem of similarity self join, we have compared several different approaches to join operation. The *naive* algorithm strictly follows the definition of similarity join and computes the *Cartesian product* between two sets to decide the pairs of objects that must be checked on the threshold μ. Considering the similarity self join, this algorithm has the time complexity $O(N^2)$, where $N = |X|$. A more efficient implementation, called the *nested loops*, uses the symmetric property of metric distance functions for pruning some pairs. The time complexity is $O(\frac{N \cdot (N-1)}{2})$. More sophisticated methods use pre-filtering strategies to discard dissimilar pairs without actually computing distances between them. A representative of these algorithms is the *range query join* algorithm applied on the eD-Index. Specifically, we assume a data set $X \subseteq \mathcal{D}$ organized by the eD-Index with $\epsilon = 0$ (i.e., without overloading exclusion buckets) and apply the search strategy as follows: for $\forall o \in X$, perform $range\_query(o, \mu)$. Finally, the last compared method is the *overloading join* algorithm which is described in Section 2.3.

We have conducted experiments on two real application environments. The first data set consisted of sentences of Czech language corpus compared by the *edit distance* measure, so-called Levenshtein distance [9]. The most frequent distance was around 100 and the longest distance was 500, equal to the length of the longest sentence. The second data set was composed of 45-dimensional vectors of color features extracted from images. Vectors were compared by the *quadratic form distance* measure. The distance distribution of this data set was practically *normal distribution* with the most frequent distance equal to 4,100 and the maximum distance equal to 8,100.

In all experiments, we have compared three different techniques for the problem of the similarity self join, the *nested loops* (NL) algorithm, the *range query join* (RJ) algorithm applied on the eD-Index, and the *overloading join* (OJ) algorithm, again applied on the eD-Index.

Join-Cost Ratio. The objective of this group of tests was to study the relationship between the query size (threshold, radius, or selectivity) and the search costs measured in terms of distance computations. The experiments were conducted on both the data sets each consisting of 11,169 objects. The eD-Index structure used on the text data set was 9 levels and 39 buckets. The structure for the vector data collection was 11 levels and 21 buckets. Both the structures were fixed for all experiments.

We have tested several query radii upto $\mu = 28$ for the text set and upto $\mu = 1800$ for the vector data. The similarity self join operation retrieved about 900,000 text pairs for $\mu = 28$ and 1,000,000 pairs of vectors for $\mu = 1800$, which is much more than being interesting. Figure 5 shows results of experiments for the text data set. As expected, the number of distance computations performed by RJ and OJ increases quite fast with growing μ. However, RJ and OJ algorithms are still more than 4 times faster then NL algorithm for $\mu = 28$. OJ algorithm has nearly exceeded the performance of RJ algorithm for large $\mu > 20$. Nevertheless, OJ is more than twice faster than RJ for small values of $\mu \leq 4$, which are used in data cleaning area. Figure 6 demonstrates results for the vector data collection. The number of distance computations executed by RJ and OJ has the similar trend as for the text data set – it grows quite fast and it nearly exceeds the performance of NL algorithm. However, the OJ algorithm performed even better than

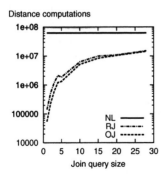

Fig. 5. Join queries on the text data set.

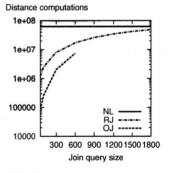

Fig. 6. Join queries on vectors.

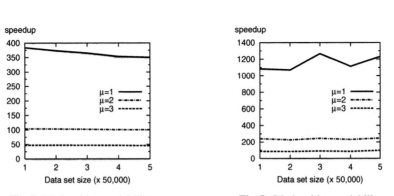

Fig. 7. RJ algorithm scalability.   **Fig. 8.** OJ algorithm scalability.

RJ comparing to the results for the text data. Especially, OJ is 15 times and 9 times more efficient than RJ for $\mu = 50$ and $\mu = 100$, respectively. The results for OJ are presented only for radii $\mu \leq 600$. This limitation is caused by the distance distribution of the vector data set. Specifically, we have to choose values of ϵ and ρ at least equal to 1800 and 900, respectively, for join queries with $\mu = 1800$. This implies that more than 80% of the whole data set is duplicated at each level of the eD-Index structure, this means that the exclusion bucket of the whole structure contains practically all objects of the data set, thus, the data set is indivisible in this respect. However, this behavior does not apply to small values of μ and ϵ where only a small portion of data sets were duplicated.

Scalability. The scalability is probably the most important issue to investigate considering the web-based dimension of data. In the elementary case, it is necessary to study what happens with the performance of algorithms when the size of a data set grows. We have experimentally investigated the behavior of the eD-Index on the text data set with sizes from 50,000 to 250,000 objects (sentences).

We have mainly concentrated on small queries which are typical for data cleaning area. Figure 7 and Figure 8 report the *speed-up* (s) of RJ and OJ algorithms, respectively. The speed-up is defined as follows:

$$ s = \frac{N \cdot (N-1)}{2 \cdot n}, $$

where N is the number of objects stored in the eD-Index and n is the number of distance evaluations needed by the examined algorithm. In fact, the speed-up states how many times the examined algorithm is faster than the NL algorithm. The results indicate that both RJ and OJ have practically constant speedup when the size of data set is significantly increasing. The exceptions are the values for $\mu = 1$ where RJ slightly deteriorates while OJ improves its performance. Nevertheless, OJ performs at least twice faster than RJ algorithm.

In summary, the figures demonstrate that the speedup is very high and constant for different values of μ with respect to the data set size. This implies that the similarity self join with the eD-Index, specifically the overloading join algorithm, is also suitable for large and growing data sets.

4   Conclusions

Similarity search is an important concept of information retrieval. However, the computational costs of similarity (dis-similarity or distance) functions are typically high – consider the edit distance with the quadratic computational complexity. We have observed by experiments that a sequential similarity range search on 50,000 sentences takes about 16 seconds. But to perform the nested loops similarity self join algorithm on the same data would take 25,000 times more, which is about 4 days and 15 hours. In order to reduce the computational costs, indexing techniques must be applied.

Though a lot of research results on indexing techniques to support the similarity range and nearest neighbors queries have been published, there are only few recent studies on indexing of similarity joins. In this article, we have analyzed several implementation strategies for similarity join operation. We have applied the eD-Index, a metric index structure, to implement two similarity join algorithms and we have performed numerous experiments to analyze their search properties and suitability for the similarity join implementation.

In general, we can conclude that the proposed overloading join algorithm outperforms the range query join algorithm. In [3], authors claim that the range query join algorithm applied on the D-index structure is never worse in performance that the specialized techniques [4,6]. The eD-Index is extremely efficient for small query radii where practically on-line response times are guaranteed. The important feature is that the eD-Index scales up well to processing large files and experiments reveal linear scale up for similarity join queries.

We have conducted some of our experiments on vectors and a deeper evaluation has been performed on sentences. However, it is easy to imagine that also text units of different granularity, such as individual words or paragraphs with words as string symbols, can easily be handled by analogy. However, the main advantage of the eD-Index is that it can also perform similar operations on other metric data. As suggested in [7], where the problem of similarity join on XML structures is investigated, metric indexes can be applied for approximate matching of tree structures. We consider this challenge as our future research direction.

References

1. E. Chavez, G. Navarro, R. Baeza-Yates, and J. Marroquin: Searching in Metric Spaces. *ACM Computing Surveys*, 33(3):273–321, 2001.
2. V. Dohnal, C. Gennaro, P. Savino, P. Zezula: D-Index: Distance Searching Index for Metric Data Sets. To appear in *ACM Multimedia Tools and Applications*, 21(1), September 2003.
3. V. Dohnal, C. Gennaro, P. Zezula: A Metric Index for Approximate Text Management. Proceedings of *IASTED International Conference on Information Systems and Databases* (ISDB 2002), Tokyo, Japan, 2002, pp. 37–42.
4. H. Galhardas, D. Florescu, D. Shasha, E. Simon, and C.A. Saita: Declarative Data Cleaning: Language, Model, and Algorithms. Proceedings of *the 27th VLDB Conference*, Rome, Italy, 2001, pp. 371–380.
5. C. Gennaro, P. Savino, and P. Zezula: Similarity Search in Metric Databases through Hashing. Proceedings of *ACM Multimedia 2001 Workshops*, October 2001, Ottawa, Canada, pp. 1–5.
6. L. Gravano, P.G. Ipeirotis, H.V. Jagadish, N. Koudas, S. Muthukrishnan, and D. Srivastava: Approximate String Joins in a Database (Almost) for Free. Proceedings of *the 27th VLDB Conference*, Rome, Italy, 2001, pp. 491–500.
7. S. Guha, H.V. Jagadish, N. Koudas, D. Srivastava, and T. Yu: Approximate XML Joins. Proceedings of *ACM SIGMOD 2002*, Madison, Wisconsin, June 3–6, 2002
8. K. Kukich: Techniques for automatically correcting words in text. *ACM Computing Surveys*, 1992, 24(4):377–439.
9. G. Navarro: A guided tour to approximate string matching. *ACM Computing Surveys*, 2001, 33(1):31–88.
10. P. N. Yianilos: Excluded Middle Vantage Point Forests for Nearest Neighbor Search. Tech. rep., NEC Research Institute, 1999, Presented at Sixth DIMACS Implementation Challenge: Nearest Neighbor Searches workshop, January 15, 1999.

KeyQuery – A Front End for the Automatic Translation of Keywords into Structured Queries

Martin Erwig and Jianglin He

School of EECS,
Oregon State University,
Corvallis, OR 97331
{erwig,heji}@cs.orst.edu

Abstract. We demonstrate an approach to transform keyword queries automatically into queries that combine keywords appropriately by boolean operations, such as **and** and **or**. Our approach is based on an analysis of relationships between the keywords using a taxonomy. The transformed queries will be sent to a search engine, and the returned results will be presented to the user. We evaluate the effectiveness of our approach by comparing the precision of the results returned for the generated query with the precision of the result for the original query. Our experiments indicate that our approach can improve the precision of the results considerably.

1 Introduction

The most common way to find information on the Internet is to use a search engine and provide a list of keywords describing the sought information. A problem with keyword-based search is that it often returns too many irrelevant results. The use of boolean operators can improve the preciseness of queries considerably. However, there is strong empirical evidence that end users, who are by far the largest group of users of search engines, are not able to use Boolean operators correctly. For instance, Pane and Myers found that sometimes, when people say **and**, they actually mean **or** [11] (for example, "I am interested in blue *and* red cars" usually expresses the interest in cars that are red *or* blue.) This and/or confusion happens very frequently when keywords are used that are closely related in a concept hierarchy (for example, red and blue are both colors).

Based on this observation, we have designed and implemented a front end for search engines, called *KeyQuery*, which groups keywords based on their similarity and inserts the Boolean operator **or** between keywords in one group and connects different groups by **and**. Our approach is based on identifying the relations among the keywords used in a query by using a taxonomy. The transformed structured queries produce more relevant results, in particular, in the first couple of returned pages.

For example, a user wants to buy a Honda car and he likes red and blue colors. So he might input "red blue Honda" to search the Internet to find some information. The default relation between keywords for most search engines is **and**. So the web pages that contain all the three words "red", "blue", and "Honda" will be returned as a

V. Mařík et al. (Eds.): DEXA 2003, LNCS 2736, pp. 494–503, 2003.

result. Other useful pages, which contain only "red" and "Honda", or only "blue" and "Honda", but not all the three words, will not be in the results. The user might miss a lot of useful information. Aa another example, suppose a user wants to find the biographies of some classical musicians, and he types "biographies Mozart Debussy Beethoven Liszt Tchaikovsky" on the Internet, he may get only a few web pages because only a few web pages contain all the keywords. In fact, there are many web pages on the Internet that contain information about biographies of one or several of the musicians. All keywords except the first are related by the category "musician". Therefore, our goal is to add the boolean operator **or** between these keywords, and transform the whole query into "biography **and** (Mozart **or** Debussy **or** Beethoven **or** Liszt **or** Tchaikovsky)". This query returns more relevant information, in particular, on the first two pages of results.

The query interface is shown in Figure 1 on the left. A list of entered keywords will be transformed behind the scenes into a structured query, which will then be executed by a search engine capable of dealing with boolean operators (we are currently using Google [7]). The results will then be presented to the user in the same browser window. For example, Figure 1 shows on the right the result of the above musician/biography query.

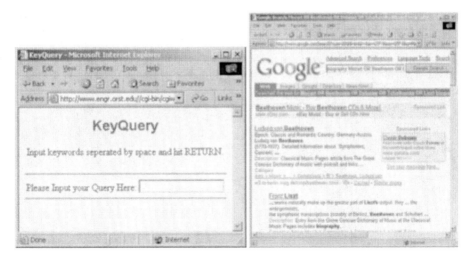

Fig. 1. User interface and example query results

The rest of this paper is structured as follows. In Section 2 we discuss the general approach and give an overview over the query system. In Section 3 we introduce our similarity measures for keywords and describe the concept of a distance matrix, which is used by the algorithm to form groups of similar keywords, introduced in Section 4. In Section 5 we evaluate our approach by comparing search results for keyword queries with the results for the transformed queries. We draw some conclusions and give remarks on future work in Section 6.

2 System Overview

Our system KeyQuery can be considered as query preprocessing front end for web browsers. We require access to the taxonomy WordNet [14], either installed locally or through the Internet. The query processing is performed in several steps. Step 1: In a dedicated user interface, users can input a query that consists of one or more keywords. We call this query Q. Step 2: The user interface sends the query Q to the "Word Finder", which sends all the keywords to WordNet and obtains a classification file C for each keyword. Step 3: The "Sense retriever" extracts all the senses S for each keyword from the classification files obtained from WordNet. Step 4: The "Categorizer" calculates similarity between every pair of keywords and categorizes them based on these similarities by using a threshold-based algorithm. A new query Q', combined with boolean operators **and** and **or,** will be generated based on the categorized keywords. Step 5: The "Redirector" sends Q' to a search engine that supports Boolean operators. It obtains the results R from the search engine and sends the results back to the user interface. The system architecture is summarized in Figure 2.

To categorize a list of keywords into different groups, we use WordNet's lexical database as the taxonomy in a semantic similarity measurement task. WordNet was developed by the Cognitive Science Laboratory at Princeton University and has been used in many different projects [2, 8, 13]. WordNet essentially provides information regarding four relationships [9]: 1. Synonymy, 2. Antonymy, 3. Meronymy, and 4. Hyponymy. Our system currently exploits only the hponymy/hypernymy relationship, which basically represents an IS-A relationship. For example, "sedan" is a kind of "car".

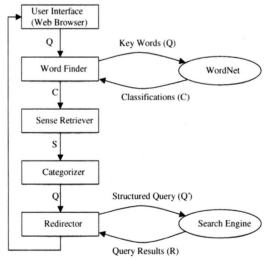

Q	Original keyword query
C	Classification files downloaded from WordNet for each keyword
S	The senses of all the keywords
Q'	Transformed query
R	The results returned by the search engine

Fig. 2. System structure

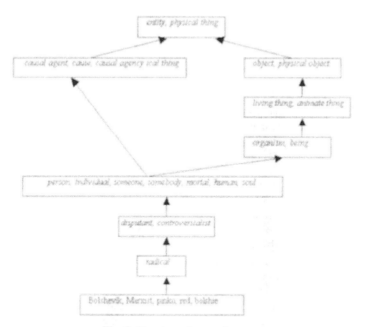

Fig. 3. Structure of a word sense

In the IS-A hierarchy provided by WordNet, each word has one or several *senses*. A *sense* is one meaning of a word. As an example, we show sense 3 of the word "red" in Figure 3. We can see that the structure of a word sense is a DAG.

3 Similarity

The groups that are derived from a list of keywords depend on the similarity between those words. The degree of similarity of two words A and B is determined by their *conceptual distance*, which we define as follows.

Definition 1 (*Conceptual Distance*): If there is not any common ancestor for word A and word B, then $D_{AB} = D_{max}$, where D_{max} is the maximal value of conceptual distance; otherwise, if there is a common ancestor at level i of sense m in word A's ancestors and level j of sense n in word B's ancestors, then we define:

$$D_{AB} = C * (m + n - 2) + i + j$$

It is easy to verify that if the distance between A and B is D_{AB}, the distance between B and A is also D_{AB}. For every pair of common ancestors, we apply this formula and get the conceptual distances $D_1, D_2, D_3, ..., D_p$. Let $D_{AB} = min (D_1, D_2, D_3, ..., D_p)$. C is a constant, called "sense amplifier", used to enlarge the conceptual distance of two words linearly with the sense levels. We use this sense amplifier to penalize similarity in later senses since WordNet orders senses by their frequencies of usage.

The presented formula presents a compromise between simplicity and expressiveness; our experiments have shown that it yields good results. In particular, we have found that C = 4 is a good choice. Let us explain the use of C by the following example. Consider the query "red blue black coat". We can find that level 1 of sense 1 of the word "red" has a common ancestor "chromatic color" with level 1 of sense 1 of the word "blue". So by definition, their conceptual distance is 2. However, the conceptual distance between the word "red" and the word "black" is 4 since the closest ancestor of "black" is "achromatic color". Both, "red" and "black", are expected to be in the same category "color" by most people. By our definition, the conceptual distance between "blue" and the word "coat" is 8. If we do not introduce the sense amplifier and consider all senses have the same role and only count the level difference, the distance between "Blue" and "coat" is also 2. However, "blue" is not similar to "coat" because most people will think that "blue" is a kind of "color" like "red" while "coat" is a kind of "clothing". Thus we need a sense amplifier to enlarge the distance if two words have no common ancestor in their first senses.

WordNet lists as the first sense the most often used meaning for a word. WordNet ranks senses of a word by the frequency of usage of that sense. To determine if two words are similar, we also need a threshold value. We call this value *group distance* and write Δ for it. Only if the conceptual distance between two words is less than Δ, they should be in the same group and we say that they are "similar"; otherwise, they are called "different". It is very important to choose an appropriate group distance. If the group distance is too small, then a lot of similar words will not be correctly grouped. If the group distance is too large, then more words will be similar to each other than normally considered by users. The group distance also depends on the value of the sense amplifier, which must, in particular, allow similarity between words on second-level senses. The key point is that we must find a balance that can fairly treat the weight of senses as well as the group distance. For C = 4 we have found that $\Delta = 7$ yields good results.

We can calculate the conceptual distance between each pair of keywords by using the definition of conceptual distance. Given a list of keywords K_1, K_2, ..., K_n, we can put the distances into a so-called "distance matrix". (Since the conceptual distance is symmetric, we need only half of the matrix.)

Distance	K_1	K_2	...	K_n
K_1	0	D_{12}	...	D_{1n}
K_2		0	...	D_{2n}
...			0	...
K_n				0

4 Keyword Categorization

In grouping similar words together, we have to resolve the following ambiguity. Consider the keyword query "yellow orange apple" and assume $D_{max} = 99$, $\Delta = 7$, and C = 4. The conceptual distance between "yellow" and "orange" is 6, so "yellow" and "orange" are similar and *could* be in the same group. Meanwhile, the conceptual distance between "orange" and "apple" is 3, so "orange" and "apple" are also similar and also *could* be in the same group. The problem is, "orange" could be in the same group with "yellow" and also could be in the same group with "apple". But "yellow" and "apple" could not be in the same group since their conceptual distance is 99 and greater than the group distance. To solve this conflict, we employ the following rule:

Priority Grouping Rule: Words with smaller conceptual distance have a higher priority to be grouped.

This priority grouping rule is realized in the following algorithm by sorting the keyword pairs that are to be grouped by their conceptual distances and processing them in order of increasing distance. We write $S \oplus X$ for $S \cup \{ X \}$.

Categorization Algorithm:

Input: A list of keywords $K = \{K_1, K_2, ..., K_n\}$
Output: A set of groups $G = \{ g_1, g_2, ..., g_s \}$
Method: First, we determine the distance matrix D for K, with entries $D_{12}, D_{13}, ..., D_{1n}, D_{23}, ..., D_{(n-1)n}$. Let L be the sorted list that contains the $(n^2 - n) / 2$ elements (the upper right half of the matrix) in D.
If $n = 1$, there is only one element, so we get only one group, i.e., let $G = \{\{K_1\}\}$.
If $n > 1$, we proceed as follows:

    Let $G = \varnothing$.

    For every element in L do

        If $D_{ij} < \Delta$ then S

            Consider the following cases:

                Case 1: $\forall\, g \in G, K_i, K_j \notin g$. Then let $G = G \oplus \{ K_i, K_j \}$
                Case 2: $\exists\, g_m \in G, K_i \in g_m$ and $\forall\, g \in G, K_j \notin g$.
                    If $\forall\, K_a \in g_m, D_{aj} < \Delta$ then let $G = G - \{ g_m \} \oplus (g_m \oplus K_j)$
                                    else let $G = G \oplus \{K_j\}$
                Case 3: Symmetric to Case 2 with K_i, K_j swapped.
                Case 4: $\exists\, g_m \in G, K_i \in g_m$ and $\exists\, g_r \in G, K_i \in g_r$ and $g_m \bullet g_r$.
                    If $\forall\, K_a \in g_m, D_{ai} < \Delta$ and $\forall\, K_h \in g_r, D_{rj} < \Delta$ then
                            let $G = (G - \{g_m, g_r\}) \oplus (g_m \cup g_r)$

        If $D_{ij} \geq \Delta$ then

            If $\forall\, g \in G, K_i \notin g$ then let $G = G \oplus \{K_i\}$
            If $\forall\, g \in G, K_j \notin g$ then let $G = G \oplus \{K_j\}$

Sort all the groups in G by the smallest indices of their keywords in ascending order. Return G.

Here is an example for case 2 when $D_{ij} < \Delta$. Consider the query "yellow orange apple". According this algorithm, "orange" and "apple" will be grouped first since they have the smallest conceptual distance 3. Then we find that the conceptual distance between "orange" and "yellow" is smaller than Δ. But because the conceptual distance between "yellow" and "apple" is 99 and is greater than Δ, the word "yellow" will be placed in another group. Cases 3 and 4 are very similar to case 2.

So far, we can categorize a list of keywords into different groups based on the distance matrix. We also sort these groups by the smallest indices of their keywords in ascending order since in some search engines, such as Google and Yahoo, the order of the keywords will affect the results. We try to preserve the original order of the keywords. Finally, the groups of keywords will be transformed into a query by inserting **or** between all keywords in a group and **and** between all groups.

5 Evaluation

The two most common measures of retrieval effectiveness are *recall* and *precision*. Recall measures the percentage of relevant documents in a collection that are actually found by a retrieval system – i.e., the ratio of the number of relevant retrieved documents over the total number of relevant documents contained in the collection. Precision measures the percentage of retrieved documents that are judged to be relevant to the original request – i.e., the ratio of the number of relevant retrieved documents over the total number of retrieved documents. Normally there is a trade-off between recall and precision.

It is very common that a user gets millions of results returned from a keyword search. However, most users only go over the first one or two pages. Therefore, precision in the first two pages is crucial to search engines. The ranking of results by search engines has an influence on the precision in the first pages. In particular, ranking pages by their popularity yields much better results than by using just a count of number of contained keywords (cf. Google's PageRank™ [16] techonology).

For our system we can observe that if no two keywords are similar in a query, KeyQuery will **and** all the keywords, so the results will be the same as for the original query because the boolean operator **and** is the default relation between keywords for most search engines. From this it follows that in these cases the recall and precisions of KeyQuery and the other search engines are the same since KeyQuery does not change the original query. But if some keywords are similar to each other, KeyQuery will insert the relation **or** between those keywords. The transformed query will be different from the original query. Since we add the **or** operator between keywords, the infamous trade-off between precision and recall will hit: if the overall recall is increased, then the overall precision will be decreased as we retrieve more results than the original ones.

If we redirect our transformed query to Google, what will happen? Let us consider a query "A1 A2 B1". We assume that A1 and A2 are similar words and are grouped together by our algorithm. B1 is in a different group. The original results from Google are 'ranked web pages that contain "A1 A2 B1" by their popularity. The new results are 'ranked web pages that contain "A1 B1" or "A2 B1" by their popularity'. Do we improve the precision for the first two pages?

We explain the effect of our approach for this example in Figure 4. Assume that a user looks only at the first five results. Table 1 holds the results of original query. We assume that R1, R2, R3, R4 and R5 are the ranked results and 2100, 1300, 900, 500 and 300 are their PageRank values, respectively. Now we reorganize the query into two queries: "A1 B1" and "A2 B1". Table 2 and 3 hold envisioned results of the queries "A1 B1"and "A2 B1", respectively. Table 4 holds the results of the transformed query "(A1 **or** A2) **and** B1" that we get from our KeyQuery system. All the results in these tables are ranked by their corresponding PageRank values. Some of the original query results are in the results for the reorganized queries. For example, R1 = L2 = K4. The results in table 4 are those results with highest PageRank values chosen from table 2 and table 3. We can observe that the constraint of three keywords prevents some of the possibly more relevant results, i.e., the results with larger PageRank values, from appearing in the initial part of the result list for the original query. From these tables, we can conclude that the first five results for the transformed query are possibly more relevant than those for the original query.

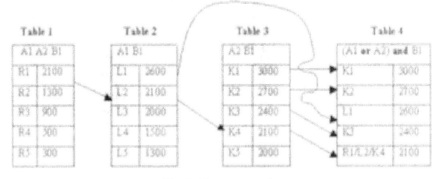

Fig. 4. Abstract example

As another example, consider again the query "biography Mozart Debussy Beethoven Liszt Tchaikovsky" (This is query 1). Since Google supports boolean operators, we have used Google as our back end search engine, and we have checked the relevance of the first 20 returned links. A group of students from different departments have judged the search engine results for relevance. We have averaged all the precision rates. We have obtained an average of 9.2 relevant links with the original query, which means the precision is 46%. With the transformed query, the precision is 96%. As another example, consider the query "admission engineering MIT Stanford". With the original query, the precision is only 26%. However, the transformed query obtained by our system yields a precision of 98%. Other queries used in our evaluation are:

3. California Hawaii Vacation package

4. Seattle Chinese Japanese Mexican restaurant

5. Red blue Honda coupe

6. Diamond ruby emerald wedding ring

7. Smoked pork beef recipe

8. How to plant apple pear orange tree

9. Cat dog training program

10. BMW convertible sedan dealer Portland

The results are shown in Figure 5.

Query#	Precision (%)		
	Original Query	Transformed Query	Improvement
1	46	96	109
2	26	98	277
3	87	95	9
4	69	94	36
5	60	93	55
6	78	97	24
7	85	100	18
8	50	57	14
9	63	69	10
10	35	95	171
Avg. Precision (%)	60	89	72

Fig. 5. Comparison table

6 Conclusions and Future Work

We have developed the system KeyQuery that can improve the precision of search results for keyword queries considerably. The approach taken was to use a taxonomy to automatically insert boolean operators **and** and **or** between keywords. Since the generated queries are in boolean form, we can apply our approach to any search engine or database that support boolean operators.

One of the next steps is to perform a systematic study of the precision improvements that can be achieved by our system. Moreover, the system can be improved in several ways. One route for future work is to include adjectives and adverbs from WordNet.

Another area of future work is to construct a taxonomy besides WordNet. The reason is that WordNet does not include many common words, like brand names, such as Honda. However, since manually maintaining such taxonomies is almost impossible, we currently consider a strategy of generating and updating these taxonomies by web queries themselves.

References

[1]   AltaVista, http://www.altavista.com.
[2]   E. Agirre and G. Rigau, "Word Sense Disambiguation Using Conceptual Density", In Proceedings of the 16th International Conference on Computational Linguistics (Coling '96), Copenhagen, Denmark, 1996.
[3]   N.J. Belkin, R.N. Oddy, and H.M. Brooks, "ASK for information retrieval: Part 1. Background and theory", Journal of Documentation, 38, pp. 61–71, 1982.

[4]   C. Silverstein, M. Henzinger, H. Marais, and M. Moricz, "Analysis of a very large web search engine query log", SIGIR Forum, 33 (1): 6–12, 1999. Previously available as Digital System Research Center TR 1998–014 at http: //www.research.digital.com/SRC

[5]   D.D. Lewis and K. Sparck Jones, "Natural Language Processing for Information Retrieval", Comm. ACM, Vol. 39, No. 1, Jan. 1996, pp. 92–101.

[6]   M. Erwig. and M.M. Burnett, "Adding Apples and Oranges", 4th Int. Symp. on Practical Aspects of Declarative Languages, LNCS 2257, 173–191, 2002.

[7]   Google, http://www.google.com.

[8]   J.J. Jiang and D.W. Conrath, "Semantic Similarity Based on Corpus Statistics and Lexical Taxonomy", in Proceedings of ROCLING X (1997) International Conference on Research in Computational Linguistics, Taiwan, 1997.

[9]   G. Miller, (1990) "Five papers on WordNet", Special Issue of International Journal of Lexicography 3(4).

[10] N. Guarino, C. Masolo, and G. Vetere, "OntoSeek: Content-Based Access to the Web", IEEE Intelligent Systems, 14(3), 70–80, (May 1999).

[11] J.F. Pane and B.A. Myers, "Tabular and Textual Methods for Selecting Objects from a Group", VL 2000: IEEE International Symposium on Visual Languages. IEEE Computer Society, September 10–13 2000, pp. 157–164. Seattle, WA.

[12] R. Prieto-Diaz, "Implementing Faceted Classification for Software Reuse", Comm. ACM, Vol. 34, No. 5, May 1991, pp. 88–97.

[13] P. Resnik, "Using Information Content to Evaluate Semantic Similarity in a Taxonomy", Proceedings of the 14th International Joint Conference on Artificial Intelligence, Vol. 1, 448–453, Montreal, August 1995.

[14] WordNet, http://www.cogsci.princeton.edu/~wn/

[15] N. Kurtonina and M. de Rijke, "Classifying description logics", In Proceedings DL'97, 1997.

[16] PageRank, http://www.google.com/technology/PageRank.html

Supporting KDD Applications by the *k*-Nearest Neighbor Join

Join

Christian Böhm and Florian Krebs

University for Health Informatics and Technology,
Innrain 98,
6020 Innsbruck,
Austria
Christian.Boehm@umit.at
Krebs.Florian@symplex.de

Abstract. The similarity join has become an important database primitive to support similarity search and data mining. A similarity join combines two sets of complex objects such that the result contains all pairs of similar objects. Well-known are two types of the similarity join, the *distance range join* where the user defines a distance threshold for the join, and the *closest point query* or *k-distance join* which retrieves the *k* most similar pairs. In this paper, we propose an important, third similarity join operation called *k-nearest neighbor join* which combines each point of one point set with its *k* nearest neighbors in the other set. We discover that many standard algorithms of *Knowledge Discovery in Databases (KDD)* such as *k*-means and *k*-medoid clustering, nearest neighbor classification, data cleansing, postprocessing of sampling-based data mining etc. can be implemented on top of the *k*-nn join operation to achieve performance improvements without affecting the quality of the result of these algorithms. Our list of possible applications includes standard methods for all stages of the KDD process including preprocessing, data mining, and postprocessing. Thus, our method is turbo charging the complete KDD process.

1 Introduction

Knowledge Discovery in Databases (KDD) is the non-trivial process of identifying valid, novel, potentially useful, and ultimately understandable patterns in data [12]. The KDD process [3] is an interactive and iterative process, involving numerous steps including preprocessing of the data (data cleansing) and postprocessing (evaluation of the results). The core step of the KDD process is *data mining*, i.e. finding patterns of interest such as *clusters*, *outliers*, *classification rules* or *trees*, *association rules*, and *regressions*.

KDD algorithms in multidimensional databases are often based on similarity queries which are performed for a high number of objects. Recently, it has been recognized that many algorithms of similarity search [2] and data mining [4] can be based on top of a single join query instead of many similarity queries. Thus, a high number of single similarity queries is replaced by a single run of a *similarity join*. The most well-known form of the similarity join is the distance range join $R \bowtie_\varepsilon S$ which is defined for two finite sets

V. Mařík et al. (Eds.): DEXA 2003, LNCS 2736, pp. 504–516, 2003.
© Springer-Verlag Berlin Heidelberg 2003

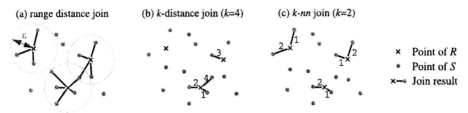

Fig. 1. Difference between similarity join operations

of vectors, $R = \{r_1,...,r_n\}$ and $S = \{s_1,...,s_m\}$, as the set of all pairs from $R \times S$ having a distance of no more than ε:

$$R \bowtie_\varepsilon S := \{(r_i,s_j) \in R \times S \mid \|p_i - q_j\| \leq \varepsilon\}$$

E.g. in [4], it has been shown that density based clustering algorithms such as DBSCAN [21] or the hierarchical cluster analysis method OPTICS [1] can be accelerated by high factors of typically one or two orders of magnitude by the range distance join. Due to its importance, a large number of algorithms to compute the range distance join of two sets have been proposed, e.g. [23, 18, 6]

Another important similarity join operation which has been recently proposed is the incremental distance join [15]. This join operation orders the pairs from $R \times S$ by increasing distance and returns them to the user either on a give-me-more basis, or based on a user specified cardinality of k best pairs (which corresponds to a k-closest pair operation in computational geometry, cf. [19]). This operation can be successfully applied to implement data analysis tasks such as noise-robust catalogue matching and noise-robust duplicate detection [10].

In this paper, we propose a third kind of similarity join, the k-nearest neighbor similarity join, short k-nn join. This operation is motivated by the observation that a great majority of data analysis and data mining algorithms is based on k-nearest neighbor queries which are issued separately for a large set of *query points* $R = \{r_1,...,r_n\}$ against another large set of *data points* $S = \{s_1,...,s_m\}$. In contrast to the incremental distance join and the k-distance join which choose the best pairs from the complete pool of pairs $R \times S$, the k-nn join combines each of the points of R with its k nearest neighbors in S. The differences between the three kinds of similarity join operations are depicted in figure 1.

Applications of the k-nn join include but are not limited to the following list: k-nearest neighbor classification, k-means and k-medoid clustering, sample assessment and sample postprocessing, missing value imputation, k-distance diagrams, etc. We briefly discuss using these algorithms on top of a join operation in section 4.

Our list of applications covers all stages of the KDD process. In the preprocessing step, data cleansing algorithms are typically based on k-nearest neighbor queries for each of the points with NULL values against the set of complete vectors. The missing values can be computed e.g. as the weighted means of the values of the k nearest neighbors. A k-distance diagram can be used to determine suitable parameters for data mining. Additionally, in the core step, i.e. data mining, many algorithms such as clustering and classification are based on k-nn queries. As such algorithms are often time consuming and have at least a linear, often $n \log n$ or even quadratic complexity they typically run on a sample set rather than the complete data set. The k-nn-queries are used to assess the quality of the sample set (preprocessing). After the run of the data mining algorithm, it is necessary to relate the result to the complete set of database points [9]. The typical method for doing that is again a k-nn-query for each of the database points with respect to the set of classified sample points.

In all these algorithms, it is possible to replace a large number of k-nn queries which are originally issued separately, by a single run of a k-nn join. Therefore, the k-nn join gives powerful support for all stages of the KDD process.

The remainder of the paper is organized as follows: In section 2, we give a classification of the well-known similarity join operations and review the related work. In section 3, we define the new operation, the k-nearest neighbor join. Section 4 is dedicated to applications of the k-nn join. We show exemplary, that typical data mining methods can be easily implemented on top of the join. The experimental evaluation of our approach is presented in section 5 and section 6 concludes the paper.

2   Related Work

In the relational data model a join means to combine the tuples of two relations R and S into pairs if a *join predicate* is fulfilled. In multidimensional databases, R and S contain points (feature vectors) rather than ordinary tuples. In a *similarity join*, the join predicate is similarity, e.g. the Euclidean distance between two feature vectors.

2.1   Distance Range Based Similarity Join

The most prominent and most evaluated similarity join operation is the distance range join. Therefore, the notions *similarity join* and *distance range join* are often used interchangeably. Unless otherwise specified, when speaking of *the similarity join*, often the distance range join is meant by default. For clarity in this paper, we will not follow this convention and always use the more specific notions.

As depicted in figure 1a, the distance range join $R \bowtie_\varepsilon S$ of two multidimensional or metric sets R and S is the set of pairs where the distance of the objects does not exceed the given parameter e. Formally:

Definition 1 Distance Range Join (e-Join)

The distance range join $R \bowtie_\varepsilon S$ of two finite multidimensional or metric sets R and S is the set

$$R \bowtie_\varepsilon S := \{(r_i, s_j) \in R \times S : \|r_i - s_j\| \le \varepsilon\}$$

The distance range join can also be expressed in a SQL like fashion:

SELECT * FROM R, S WHERE $\|R.\text{obj} - S.\text{obj}\| \le \varepsilon$

In both cases, $\|\cdot\|$ denotes the distance metric which is assigned to the multimedia objects. For multidimensional vector spaces, $\|\cdot\|$ usually corresponds to the Euclidean distance.

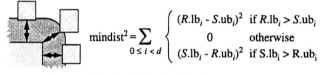

$$\text{mindist}^2 = \sum_{0 \le i < d} \begin{cases} (R.lb_i - S.ub_i)^2 & \text{if } R.lb_i > S.ub_i \\ 0 & \text{otherwise} \\ (S.lb_i - R.ub_i)^2 & \text{if } S.lb_i > R.ub_i \end{cases}$$

Fig. 2. mindist for the similarity join on R-trees

The distance range join can be applied in density based clustering algorithms which often define the local data density as the number of objects in the e-neighborhood of some data object. This essentially corresponds to a self-join using the distance range paradigm.

Like for plain range queries in multimedia databases, a general problem of distance range joins from the users' point of view is that it is difficult to control the result cardinality of this operation. If ε is chosen too small, no pairs are reported in the result set (or in case of a self join: each point is only combined with itself). In contrast, if ε is chosen too large, each point of R is combined with every point in S which leads to a quadratic result size and thus to a time complexity of any join algorithm which is at least quadratic; more exactly $o\,(|R|\cdot|S|)$. The range of possible ε-values where the result set is non-trivial and the result set size is sensible is often quite narrow, which is a consequence of the curse of dimensionality. Provided that the parameter h is chosen in a suitable range and also adapted with an increasing number of objects such that the result set size remains approximately constant the typical complexity of advanced join algorithms is better than quadratic.

Most related work on join processing using multidimensional index structures is based on the *spatial join*. The spatial join operation is defined for 2-dimensional polygon databases where the join predicate is the intersection between two objects. This kind of join predicate is prevalent in map overlay applications. We adapt the relevant algorithms to allow distance based predicates for multidimensional point databases instead of the intersection of polygons.

The most common technique is the *R-tree Spatial Join (RSJ)* [8] which processes R-tree like index structures built on both relations R and S. RSJ is based on the lower bounding property which means that the distance between two points is never smaller than the distance (the so-called mindist, cf. figure 2) between the regions of the two pages in which the points are stored. The RSJ algorithm traverses the indexes of R and S synchronously. When a pair of directory pages (P_R, P_S) is under consideration, the algorithm forms all pairs of the child pages of P_R and P_S having distances of at most ε. For these pairs of child pages, the algorithm is called recursively, i.e. the corresponding indexes are traversed in a depth-first order. Various optimizations of RSJ have been proposed.

Recently, index based similarity join methods have been analyzed from a theoretical point of view. [7] proposes a cost model based on the concept of the Minkowski sum [5] which can be used for optimizations such as page size optimization. The analysis reveals a serious optimization conflict between CPU and I/O time. While the CPU requires fine-grained partitioning with page capacities of only a few points per page, large block sizes of up to 1 MB are necessary for efficient I/O operations. The authors propose the *Multipage Index (MuX)*, a complex index structure with large pages (optimized for I/O) which accommodate a secondary search structure (optimized for maximum CPU efficiency). It is shown that the resulting index yields an I/O performance which is similar (*equal*, up to a small additional overhead by the more complex structure) to the I/O optimized R-tree similarity join and a CPU performance which is close to the CPU optimized R-tree similarity join.

A join algorithm particularly suited for similarity self joins is the ε-*kdB-tree* [23]. The basic idea is to partition the data set perpendicularly to one selected dimension into stripes of width ε to restrict the join to pairs of subsequent stripes. The join algorithm is based on the assumption that the database cache is large enough to hold the data points of two subsequent stripes. In this case, it is possible to join the set in a single pass. To speed up the CPU operations, for each stripe a main memory data structure, the ε-kdB-tree is constructed which also partitions the data set according to the other dimensions until a defined node capacity is reached. For each dimension, the data set is partitioned at most once into stripes of width ε. Finally, a tree matching algorithm is applied which is restricted to neighboring stripes.

Koudas and Sevcik have proposed the *Size Separation Spatial Join* [17] and the *Multidimensional Spatial Join* [18] which make use of space filling curves to order the points in a multidimensional space. Each point is considered as a cube with side-length ε in the multidimensional space. The cube is assigned a value l (level) which is essentially the size of the largest cell (according to the Hilbert decomposition of the data space) that contains the point. The points are distributed over several *level-files* each of which contains the points of a level in the order of their Hilbert values. For join processing, each subpartition of a level-file must be matched against the corresponding subpartitions at the same level and each higher level file of the other data set.

An approach which explicitly deals with massive data sets and thereby avoids the scalability problems of existing similarity join techniques is the *Epsilon Grid Order (EGO)* [6]. It is based on a particular sort order of the data points which is obtained by laying an equi-distant grid with cell length h over the data space and then compares the grid cells lexicographically.

2.2   Closest Pair Queries

It is possible to overcome the problems of controlling the selectivity by replacing the range query based join predicate using conditions which specify the selectivity. In contrast to range queries which retrieve potentially the whole database, the selectivity of a (*k-*) closest pair query is (up to tie situations) clearly defined. This operation retrieves the *k* pairs of $R \times S$ having minimum distance. (cf. figure 1b) Closest pair queries do not only play an important role in the database research but have also a long history in computational geometry [19]. In the database context, the operation has been introduced by Hjaltason and Samet [15] using the term (*k-*) *distance join*. The (*k-*)closest pair query can be formally defined as follows:

Definition 2 (*k-*) Closest Pair Query $R \bowtie_{k\text{-}cp} S$

$R \bowtie_{k\text{-}cp} S$ is the smallest subset of $R \times S$ that contains at least
k pairs of points and for which the following condition holds:

$$\forall (r,s) \in R \bowtie_{k\text{-}cp} S, \ \forall (r',s') \in R \times S \setminus R \bowtie_{k\text{-}cp} S: \|r-s\| < \|r'-s'\| \tag{1}$$

This definition directly corresponds to the definition of (k-) nearest neighbor queries, where the single data object o is replaced by the pair (r,s). Here, tie situations are broken by enlargement of the result set. It is also possible to change definition 2 such that the tie is broken non-deterministically by a random selection. [15] defines the closest pair query (non-deterministically) by the following SQL statement:

SELECT * FROM R, S
ORDER BY $\|R.\text{obj} - S.\text{obj}\|$
STOP AFTER k

We give two more remarks regarding self joins. Obviously, the closest pairs of the selfjoin $R \bowtie_{\text{k-cp}} R$ are the n pairs (r_i, r_i) which have trivially the distance 0 (for any distance metric), where $n = |R|$ is the cardinality of R. Usually, these trivial pairs are not needed, and, therefore, they should be avoided in the **WHERE** clause. Like the distance range selfjoin, the closest pair selfjoin is symmetric (unless nondeterminism applies). Applications of closest pair queries (particularly self joins) include similarity queries like

- find all stock quota in a database that are similar to each other
- find music scores which are similar to each other
- noise-robust duplicate elimination of any multimedia application

For plain similarity search in multimedia-databases, it is often useful to replace k-nearest neighbor queries by ranking queries which retrieve the first, second, third,... nearest neighbor in a one-by-one fashion. The actual number k of nearest neighbors to be searched is initially unknown. The user (or some application program on top of the database) decides according to a criterion which is unknown to the DBMS whether or not further neighbors are required. This kind of processing called *incremental* distance join can also be defined on top of the closest pair query, e.g. by cancelling the STOP AFTER clause in the SQL statement above. The query results are passed to the application program using some cursor concept. It is important to avoid computing the complete ranking in the initialization phase of the cursor, because determining the complete ranking is unnecessarily expensive if the user decides to stop the ranking after retrieving only a few result pairs. Hjaltason and Samet [15] also define the distance semijoin which performs a GROUP BY operation on the result of the distance join. All join operations, k-distance join, incremental distance join and the distance semijoin are evaluated using a pqueue data structure where node-pairs are ordered by increasing distance.

The most interesting challenge in algorithms for the distance join is the strategy to access pages and to form page pairs. Analogously to the various strategies for single nearest neighbor queries such as [20] and [14], Corral et al. propose 5 different strategies including recursive algorithms and an algorithm based on a pqueue [11]. Shin et al. [22] proposed a plane sweep algorithm for the node expansion for the above mentioned pqueue algorithm [15, 11]. In the same paper [22], Shim et al. also propose the *adaptive multi-stage algorithm* which employs aggressive pruning and compensation methods based on statistical estimates of the expected distance values.

3   The *k*-Nearest Neighbor Join

The range distance join has the disadvantage of a result set cardinality which is difficult to control. This problem has been overcome by the closest pair query where the result set size (up to the rare tie effects) is given by the query parameter k. However, there are only few applications which require the consideration of the k best pairs of two sets. Much more prevalent are applications such as classification or clustering where each point of one set must be combined with its k closest partners in the other set, which is exactly the operation that corresponds to our new k-nearest neighbor similarity join (cf. figure 1c). Formally, we define the k-nn-join as follows:

Definition 3 k-nn-Join $R \underset{k\text{-}nn}{\bowtie} S$

$R \underset{k\text{-}nn}{\bowtie} S$ is the smallest subset of $R \times S$ that contains for each point of R at least k points of S and for which the following condition holds:

$$\forall\,(r,s) \in R \underset{k\text{-}nn}{\bowtie} S,\ \forall\,(r,s') \in R \times S \setminus R \underset{k\text{-}nn}{\bowtie} S: \|r-s\| < \|r-s'\| \tag{2}$$

In contrast to the closest pair query, here it is guaranteed that each point of R appears in the result set exactly k times. Points of S may appear once, more than once (if a point is among the k-nearest neighbors of several points in R) or not at all (if a point does not belong to the k-nearest neighbors of any point in R). Our k-nn join can be expressed in an extended SQL notation:

SELECT * FROM R,
   (**SELECT * FROM** S
      ORDER BY $\|R.\text{obj} - S.\text{obj}\|$
      STOP AFTER k)

The closest pair query applies the principle of the nearest neighbor search (finding k best *things*) on the basis of the pairs. Conceptually, first all pairs are formed, and then, the best k are selected. In contrast, the k-nn join applies this principle on a basis "per point of the first set". For each of the points of R, the k best join partners are searched. This is an essential difference of concepts.

Again, tie situations can be broken deterministically by enlarging the result set as in this definition or by random selection. For the selfjoin, we have again the situation that each point is combined with itself which can be avoided using the WHERE clause. Unlike the ε-join and the k-closest pair query, the k-nn selfjoin is not symmetric as the nearest neighbor relation is not symmetric. Equivalently, the join $R \underset{k\text{-}nn}{\bowtie} S$ which retrieves the k nearest neighbors for each point of R is essentially different from $S \underset{k\text{-}nn}{\bowtie} R$ which retrieves the nearest neighbors of each S-point. This is symbolized in our symbolic notation which uses an *asymmetric* symbol for the k-nn join in contrast to the other similarity join operations.

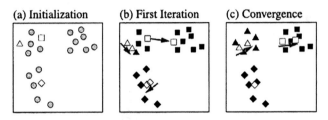

Fig. 3. k-Means Clustering

4   Applications

4.1   k-Means and k-Medoid Clustering

The k-means method [13] is the most important and most widespread approach to *clustering*. For k-means clustering the number k of clusters to be searched must be previously known. The method determines k cluster centers such that each database point can be assigned to one of the centers to minimize the overall distance of the database points to their associated center points.

The basic algorithm for k-means clustering works as follows: In the initialization, k database points are randomly selected as tentative cluster centers. Then, each database point is associated to its closest center point and, thus, a tentative *cluster* is formed. Next, the cluster centers are redetermined as the means point of all points of the center, simply by forming the vector sum of all points of a (tentative) cluster. The two steps (1) point association and (2) cluster center redetermination are repeated until convergence (no more considerable change). It has been shown that (under several restrictions) the algorithm always converges. The cluster centers which are generated in step (2) are artificial points rather than database points. This is often not desired, and therefore, the k-medoid algorithm always selects a database point as a cluster center.

The k-means algorithm is visualized in figure 3 using k = 3. At the left side (a) k = 3 points (white symbols ◇ △ □) are randomly selected as initial cluster centers. Then in figure 3(b) the remaining data points are assigned to the closest center which is depicted by the corresponding symbols (◆ ▲ ■). The cluster centers are redetermined (moving arrows). The same two operations are repeated in figure 3(c). If the points are finally assigned to their closest center, no assignment changes, and, therefore, the algorithm terminates clearly having separated the three visible clusters. In contrast to density-based approaches, k-means only separates compact clusters, and the number of actual clusters must be previously known.

It has not yet been recognized in the data mining community that the point association step which is performed in each iteration of the algorithm corresponds to a ($k = 1$) nearest neighbor join between the set of center points (at the right side) and the set of database points (at the left side of the join symbol) because each database point is associated with its nearest neighbor among the center points:

$$\text{database-point-set} \bowtie_{1\text{-NN}} \text{center-point-set}$$

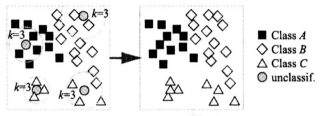

Fig. 4. k-Nearest Neighbor Classification

During the iteration over the cursor of the join, it is also possible to keep track of changes and to redetermine the cluster center for the next iteration. The corresponding pseudocode is depicted in the following:

```
repeat
  change := false ;
  foreach (dp,cp) ∈ database-point-set ⋈₁₋ₙₙ center-point-set do
    if dp.center ≠ cp.id then change := true ;
    dp.center := cp.id ;
    cp.newsum := cp.newsum + dp.point ;
    cp.count := cp.count + 1 ;
  foreach cp ∈ center-point-set do
    cp.point := cp.newsum / cp.count ;
  until ¬ change ;
```

4.2 k-Nearest Neighbor Classification

Another very important data mining task is classification. Classification is somewhat similar to clustering (which is often called *unsupervised classification*). In classification, a part of the database objects is assigned to class labels. For classification, also a set of objects without class label (new objects) is given. The task is to determine the class labels for each of the unclassified objects by taking the properties of the classified objects into account. A widespread approach is to build up tree like structures from the classified objects where the nodes correspond to ranges of attribute values and the leaves indicate the class labels (called *classification trees* [13]). Another important approach is k-nearest neighbor classification [16]. Here, for each unclassified object, a k-nearest neighbor query on the set of classified objects is evaluated (k is a parameter of the algorithm). The object is assigned to the class label of the majority of the resulting objects of the query. This principle is visualized in figure 4. As for each unclassified object a k-nn-query on the set of classified objects is evaluated, this corresponds again to a k-nearest neighbor join:

$$\text{unclassified-point-set} \underset{k\text{-}nn}{\bowtie} \text{classified-point-set}$$

4.3   Sampling Based Data Mining

Data mining methods which are based on sampling often require a k-nearest neighbor join between the set of sample points and the complete set of original database points. Such a join is necessary, for instance, to assess the quality of a sample. The k-nearest neighbor join can give hints whether the sample rate is too small. Another application is the transfer of the data mining result onto the original data set after the actual run of the data mining algorithm [9]. For instance, if a clustering algorithm has detected a set of clusters in the sample set, it is often necessary to associate each of the database points to the cluster to which it belongs. This can be done by a k-nn join with $k = 1$ between the point set and the set of sample points:

$$\text{sample-set} \underset{k\text{-nn}}{\bowtie} \text{point-set}$$

4.4   k-Distance Diagrams

The most important limitation of the DBSCAN algorithm is the difficult determination of the query radius e. In [21] a method called k-distance diagram is proposed to determine a suitable radius e. For this purpose, a number of objects (typically 5-20 percent of the database) is randomly selected. For these objects, a k-nearest neighbor query is evaluated where k corresponds to the parameter MIN_PTS which will be used during the run of DBSCAN. The resulting distances between the query points and the k-th nearest neighbor of each are then sorted and depicted in a diagram (cf. figure 5). Vertical gaps in that plot indicate distances that clearly separate different clusters, because there exist larger k-nearest neighbor distances (inter-cluster distances, noise points) and smaller ones (intra-cluster distance). As for each sample point a k-nearest neighbor query is evaluated on the original point set, this corresponds to a k-nn-join between the sample set and the original set:

Fig. 5. k-Distance Diagram

$$\text{sample-set} \underset{k\text{-nn}}{\bowtie} \text{point-set}$$

If the complete data set is taken instead of the sample, we have a k-nn self join:

$$\text{point-set} \underset{k\text{-nn}}{\bowtie} \text{point-set}$$

5   Experimental Evaluation

We implemented a k-Means clustering algorithm and a k-Nearest Neighbor classification algorithm in both versions traditionally with single similarity queries (nearest neighbor queries) as well as on top of our new database primitive, the similarity join. Our k-NN similarity join algorithm used the Multipage Index [7] which allows a separate optimization of CPU and I/O performance. The competitive technique, the evaluation on top of single similarity queries, was also supported by the same index structure which is traversed using a variation of the nearest neighbor algorithm by Hjaltason and Samet [14] which has been shown to yield an optimal number of page accesses.

All our experiments were carried out under Windows NT4.0 SP6 on Fujitsu-Siemens Celsius 400 machines equipped with a Pentium III 700 MHz processor and at least 128 MB main memory. The installed disk device was a Seagate ST310212A with a sustained transfer rate of about 9 MB/s and an average read access time of 8.9 ms with an average latency time of 5.6 ms. We allowed about 20% of the database size as cache or buffer for either technique and included the index creation time for our k-nn join and the hs-algorithm. We used large data sets from various application domains, in particular:

- 5-dimensional feature vectors from earth observation. These data sets have been generated from the well known SEQUOIA benchmark
- 20-dimensional data from astronomy observations
- 64-dimensional feature vectors from a color image database (color histograms)

In our first set of experiments, we tested the k-nearest neighbor classification method where we varied the number of training objects (cf. figure 6) as well as the number of objects which have to be classified (cf. figure 7). The superiority of our new method becomes immediately clear from both experiments. The improvement factor over the simple k-NN approach is high over all measured scales. It even improves for an increasing number of training objects or classified objects, respectively, and reaches a final factor of 9.1 in figure 6 (factor 2.0 in figure 7).

Figure 8 varies over our various data sets and shows that the improvement factor also grows with increasing data space dimension. Our new database primitive outperforms the well-known approach by factors starting with 1.8 at the 5-dimensional space up to 3.2 at the 64-dimensional space. In our last experiment, depicted in figure 9, we tested the k-nearest neighbor clustering method. In the depicted experiment, we varied the number of clusters to be searched. Again, the improvement factor grows from 1.4 for the smallest number of clusters to 5.1 for our largest number of clusters.

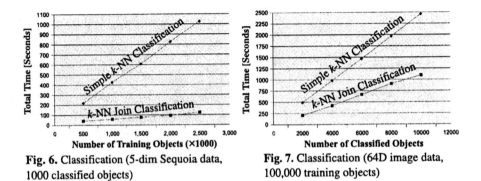

Fig. 6. Classification (5-dim Sequoia data, 1000 classified objects)

Fig. 7. Classification (64D image data, 100,000 training objects)

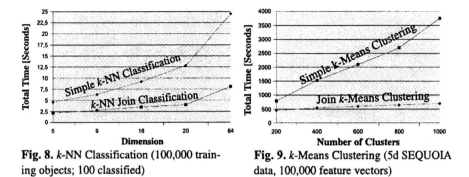

Fig. 8. k-NN Classification (100,000 training objects; 100 classified)

Fig. 9. k-Means Clustering (5d SEQUOIA data, 100,000 feature vectors)

6   Conclusions

In this paper, we have proposed a new kind of similarity join which is based on a k-nearest neighbor join predicate. In contrast to other types of similarity joins such as the distance range join, the k-distance join (k-closest pair query) and the incremental distance join, our new k-nn join combines each point of a point set R with its k nearest neighbors in another point set S. We have demonstrated that many standard algorithms of *Knowledge Discovery in Databases (KDD)* such as k-means and k-medoid clustering, nearest neighbor classification, data cleansing, postprocessing of sampling-based data mining etc. can be implemented on top of the k-nn join operation to achieve performance improvements without affecting the quality of the result of these algorithms. Our list of possible applications includes standard methods for all stages of the KDD process including preprocessing, data mining, and postprocessing. In our experimental evaluation, we have demonstrated the performance potential of the new database primitive. The results yield high performance gains for classification and clustering algorithms.

References

1   Ankerst M., Breunig M. M., Kriegel H.-P., Sander J.: *OPTICS: Ordering Points To Identify the Clustering Structure*, ACM SIGMOD Int. Conf. on Management of Data, 1999.

2   Agrawal R., Lin K., Sawhney H., Shim K.: *Fast Similarity Search in the Presence of Noise, Scaling, and Translation in Time-Series Databases*, Int. Conf on Very Large Data Bases (VLDB), 1995.

3   Brachmann R., Anand T.: *The Process of Knowledge Discovery in Databases*, in: Fayyad et al.: *Advances in Knowledge Discovery and Data Mining*, AAAI Press, 1996.

4   Böhm C., Braunmüller B., Breunig M. M., Kriegel H.-P.: *Fast Clustering Based on High-Dimensional Similarity Joins*, Int. Conf. on Information Knowledge Management (CIKM), 2000.

5   Berchtold S., Böhm C., Keim D., Kriegel H.-P.: *A Cost Model For Nearest Neighbor Search in High-Dimensional Data Space*, ACM Symposium on Principles of Database Systems (PODS), 1997.

6 Böhm C., Braunmüller B., Krebs F., Kriegel H.-P.: *Epsilon Grid Order: An Algorithm for the Similarity Join on Massive High-Dimensional Data*, ACM SIGMOD Int. Conf. on Management of Data, 2001.

7 Böhm C., Kriegel H.-P.: *A Cost Model and Index Architecture for the Similarity Join*, IEEE Int. Conf on Data Engineering (ICDE), 2001.

8 Brinkhoff T., Kriegel H.-P., Seeger B.: *Efficient Processing of Spatial Joins Using R-trees*, ACM SIGMOD Int. Conf. on Management of Data, 1993.

9 Breunig M. M., Kriegel H.-P., Kröger P., Sander J.: *Data Bubbles: Quality Preserving Performance Boosting for Hierarchical Clustering*, ACM SIGMOD Int. Conf. on Management of Data, 2001.

10 Böhm C.: *The Similarity Join: A Powerful Database Primitive for High Performance Data Mining*, tutorial, IEEE Int. Conf. on Data Engineering (ICDE), 2001.

11 Corral A., Manolopoulos Y., Theodoridis Y., Vassilakopoulos M.: *Closest Pair Queries in Spatial Databases*, ACM SIGMOD Int. Conf. on Management of Data, 2000.

12 Fayyad U. M., Piatetsky-Shapiro G., Smyth P.: *From Data Mining to Knowledge Discovery: An Overview*, in: Fayyad et al.: *Advances in Knowledge Discovery and Data Mining*, AAAI Press, 1996.

13 Han J, Kamber M.: *Data Mining: Concepts and Techniques*, Morgan Kaufmann, 2000.

14 Hjaltason G. R., Samet H.: *Ranking in Spatial Databases*, Int. Symp. on Large Spatial Datab. (SSD), 1995.

15 Hjaltason G. R., Samet H.: *Incremental Distance Join Algorithms for Spatial Databases*, SIGMOD Int. Conf. on Management of Data, 1998.

16 Hattori K., Torii Y.: *Effective algorithms for the nearest neighbor method in the clustering problem*. Pattern Recognition, 26(5), 1993.

17 Koudas N., Sevcik C.: *Size Separation Spatial Join*, ACM SIGMOD Int. Conf. on Managem. of Data, 1997

18 Koudas N., Sevcik C.: *High Dimensional Similarity Joins: Algorithms and Performance Evaluation*, IEEE Int. Conf. on Data Engineering (ICDE), Best Paper Award, 1998.

19 Preparata F. P., Shamos M. I.: *Computational Geometry*, Springer 1985.

20 Roussopoulos N., Kelley S., Vincent F.: *Nearest Neighbor Queries*, ACM SIGMOD Int. Conf. on Management of Data, 1995.

21 Sander J., Ester M., Kriegel H.-P., Xu X.: *Density-Based Clustering in Spatial Databases: The Algorithm GDBSCAN and its Applications*, Data Mining and Knowledge Discovery, Kluwer Academic Publishers, Vol. 2, No. 2, 1998.

22 Shin H., Moon B., Lee S.: *Adaptive Multi-Stage Distance Join Processing*, ACM SIGMOD Int. Conf. on Management of Data, 2000.

23 Shim K., Srikant R., Agrawal R.: *High-Dimensional Similarity Joins*, IEEE Int. Conf. on Data Engin. 1997.

Approximate Query Processing for a Content-Based Image Retrieval Method

Paul W.H. Kwan[1]*, Kazuo Toraichi[2], Hiroyuki Kitagawa[2],
and Keisuke Kameyama[2]

[1] Core Research for Evolutional Science & Technology Program,
Japan Science & Technology Corporation
Hongou 6-17-9, Bunkiyou-ku,
Tokyo 113-0033, Japan
kwan@ieee.org
[2] Institute of Information Sciences and Electronics,
University of Tsukuba
1-1-1 Tennodai, Tsukuba-shi,
Ibaraki 305, Japan
{toraichi,kitagawa}@is.tsukuba.ac.jp
kame@tara.tsukuba.ac.jp

Abstract. An approximate query processing approach for a content-based image retrieval method based on probabilistic relaxation labeling is proposed. The novelty lies in the inclusion of a filtering mechanism based on a quasi lower bound on distance in the vector space that effectively spares the matching between the query and a number of database images from going through the expensive step of iterative updating the labeling probabilities. This resembles the two-step filter-and-refine query processing approach that has been applied to k-nearest neighbor (k-NN) retrieval in database research. It is confirmed by experiments that the proposed approach consistently returns a close "approximation" of the accurate result, in the sense of the first k' in the top k output of a k-NN search, while simultaneously reduces the amount of processing required.

1 Introduction

Content-based Image Retrieval (CBIR) is a technique for retrieving images based on features automatically derived such as color, texture, shape, and their spatial locations [1]. In a related research, we developed a CBIR method based on matching the shape of object contours between the query and every database image in succession, and ranked them by a computed distance function [2]. The matching algorithm made use of probabilistic relaxation labeling that had been successfully applied in a number of image processing applications [3]. In our formulation, the query image S represents the set of objects while a database image V the set of labels of the labeling problem.

---

* Corresponding author. Phone: +81-298-53-6798, Fax: +81-298-52-6333

V. Mařík et al. (Eds.): DEXA 2003, LNCS 2736, pp. 517–526, 2003.

While our retrieval method achieved promising results as supported by experiments on a database of trademark images (refer to Table 1), the need for matching the query against the entire database before the final ranking is determined incurs a potential loss in processing. One possible solution would be to apply an indexing structure on the underlying vector space as adopted by a number of distance-based similarity retrieval method in order to narrow down to a subset of candidate images. In applying such an indexing structure, however, it is commonly assumed that the vector space is also a metric space in that distances between data points obey an L_p-metric distance function such as Euclidean (L_2-metric), etc. On input, the query is similarly cast as a data point in the vector space, and the indexing structure coupled with the metric distance function quickly narrow down a subset of data points for subsequent matching.

In our retrieval method, however, the underlying vector space is not formed until the query is entered, and serves as the reference point from which distances to other data points are calculated. This is due to the fact that the distance function involves probabilistic variables whose values are not known until after the iterative probability updating has converged. Moreover, the vector space itself is not a metric space in the sense of obeying the triangle inequality on distances, rendering it difficult to designate one of the database images as the reference point for a possible index.

As a solution to address the problem of sequential matching in our CBIR method, we propose in this paper an approach based on the current method that is able to return a close "approximation" of the result obtained at present while simultaneously reduces the amount of processing required. By close "approximation", we are referring to the likelihood of ensuring that the first k' in the top k output of a k-nearest neighbor (or k-NN) search are always returned. Here, k and k' are integers with $k' < k$.

The remaining of this paper is organized as follow. In Section 2, the CBIR method on which the research reported in this paper was based is briefly explained. In Section 3, the proposed approximate query processing approach is described. In Section 4, comparisons with the accurate (i.e., the current) method are conducted for evaluation. Finally, conclusions are drawn in Section 5.

2   A Content-Based Image Retrieval Method

The CBIR method explained briefly here was based on an application of probabilistic relaxation labeling in matching a pair of images. Here, we will first summarize the main ideas behind probabilistic relaxation labeling, and point out its connection to the matching algorithm in our CBIR method. An example of the retrieval results is given towards the end to illustrate the method's effectiveness.

In probabilistic relaxation labeling, a set of n objects $A = \{a_1,...,a_n\}$ and a set of m labels $\Lambda = \{\lambda_1,..., \lambda_m\}$ are initially assumed. The assignment of labels to object i are expressed in a vector of assignment probabilities as $p_i = [p_i(1),...,p_i(m)]^T \in R^m$, where "$T$" denotes the transpose. The elements of p_i meets the usual condition of $\Sigma_{\lambda=1,m}\, p_i(\lambda) = 1$. The set of p_i for all the n objects constitute $p = [p_1,...,p_n]^T \in R^{mn}$, which is the state vector of the relaxation labeling system.

For updating the state vector p, a four dimensional matrix $R = [r_{ij}(\lambda,\mu)] \in R^{mn \times nn}$ is defined, and the state vector will be updated according to,

$$p(t + 1) = f(p(t), q(t)), \tag{1}$$

$$f(p, q) = [f_1(1), \dots, f_n(m)]^T, \tag{2}$$

$$f_i(\lambda) = q_i(\lambda) p_i(\lambda) / \Sigma_{\lambda'=1,m} \, q_i(\lambda') \, p_i(\lambda'), \tag{3}$$

and

$$q(t) = Rp(t), \tag{4}$$

where t denotes the time. It has been shown in [4] that the relaxation labeling system with symmetric R will possess a Liapunov (energy) function defined as,

$$-A(p(t)) = -p(t)^T Rp(t), \tag{5}$$

which is guaranteed to decrease by the iterative transition of p until one of the local minima of $-A(p)$ is reached (i.e., at convergence).

In our formulation, contour segments extracted from the query and a database image represent the objects and labels of the labeling problem. Each contour segment is denoted by a feature vector with attributes including both start and end points in x-y coordinates, the segment length, a pair of start point 1/3 and end point 1/3 gradients (or angle of inclination), lists of neighboring segments, and the segment type (i.e., line, arc, or curve).

Here, we will not explain the steps of the matching algorithm in details [2], other than pointing out that an initial pairing process aimed in reducing the size of the labeling problem through enforcing compatibility constraints between objects and labels based on their respective feature vectors precedes the step on iterative probability updating. At the convergence of iterative probability updating, the distance used in similarity ranking is computed by using the minimized $-A(p)$ attained, which involves probabilistic values.

Lastly, Table 1 shows the 10 most similar images to a sample query retrieved from a database of 3,000 trademark images. The response time is 6.5 seconds on a Pentium IV 1.2GHz PC with 256MB memory running on Windows XP. The software was written in C++.

Table 1. The 10 most similar images of a sample query image

Query				
Rank: 1 [same]	2	3	4	5
Distance: 0.0	2.97	3.51	4.06	4.35

6	7	8	9	10
4.69	5.08	5.77	5.78	6.27

3 Approximate Query Processing

In this section, the proposed filtering mechanism that is novel in this research is explained first, followed by a description of the modifications made in the main CBIR method that accomplish this filtering.

3.1 Filtering by a Quasi Lower Bound on Distance

The approximate query processing approach introduced here resembles the two-step filter-and-refine approach in [5][6][7] that made use of a lower bound of the actual distance function to filter out irrelevant database objects from the step of computing actual distances from the query. Since a lower bounding distance is used, no relevant objects will be discarded by the filtering step. However, as some objects that remain might not be included in the final retrieval result, a further refinement step based on the actual distances computed is necessary for eliminating these false alarms.

While the lower bounding distances used in [5][6][7] are "true" lower bounds in the sense of Lp-metric between the query and a data point, the distance function used in our CBIR method involves probabilistic values that might not allow for a lower bound on the distance between a data point and the query in the vector space being confidently determined without having to go through the expensive iterative probability updating process until convergence. To address this problem, the concept of a *quasi lower bound on distance* is introduced here. This quasi lower bound on distance is computed based on the *same* distance function. However, rather than at convergence, it is computed at the point where the initial pairing process finished, but before the iterative probability updating process has commenced.

In developing such an approach for approximate query processing, two important assumptions are made:

☐ First, the amount of processing spent on the initial pairing of objects and labels is far less than that of the iterative probability updating process.

☐ Second, the quasi lower bound on distance computed between the query and a data point in the vector space based on the *same* distance function should be close enough to the actual distance (which is computed after iterative probability updating has converged) so that false dismissals will seldom occur. Ideally, the quasi lower bound on distance should not be too much smaller than the actual distance in order that excessive false alarms will not occur, thereby fulfilling the function of a close "approximation" to the true lower bound used for filtering.

Furthermore, in calculating the quasi lower bound on distance, another concept known as the *confidence factor* is introduced. To facilitate explanation, the following notations are used:

D_{initp} ≡ Distance calculated after the initial pairing process
D_{actual} ≡ Distance calculated after the iterative probability updating
D_{quasi} ≡ The quasi lower bound on distance
c ≡ The confidence factor

The following condition holds throughout the entire retrieval process:

$$D_{actual} \leq D_{initp} \qquad (6)$$

The function of the confidence factor "c" is to facilitate the adjustment of D_{initp} in order to minimize the chance of false dismissals while avoiding excessive false alarms as explained in the second assumption earlier. It is used in the context of the following equation when computing the quasi lower bound on distance, D_{quasi}.

$$D_{quasi} \; = \; c * D_{initp}, \text{ and } 0.0 < c \le 1.0 \qquad (7)$$

An illustration might be useful in explaining why it is being called the confidence factor. For example, if the level of confidence is high regarding D_{initp} computed right after the initial pairing process is already close enough to D_{actual}, then the value for "c" should be large such as in the interval [0.9, 1.0], but without causing the problem of false dismissals. However, if the level of confidence is low regarding whether D_{initp} is close enough to D_{actual}, then the value for "c" should be smaller, but not too much, otherwise excessive false alarms will occur.

Two questions are expected to arise naturally. First, how to determine the value of "c" suitably in order that the function of filtering is effective via D_{quasi}? Second, is there a procedure to determine this confidence factor automatically without the need for manual adjustment?

To address these two questions, a heuristic procedure is devised to determine the value of the confidence factor dynamically by treating it as a discrete random variable that takes the value of the mean of the cumulative sum of the quantity, D_{actual} / D_{initp}, averaged by the number of times that D_{actual} has computed. In other words, the confidence factor "c" is a running average determined based on the ratio between D_{actual} and D_{initp}. Taken over an infinite time interval, this running average approximates the expected mean, $E[c]$, of the confidence factor.

3.2 Modifications in Main Method

Modifications in the main CBIR method are made in two crucial places. The first modification is made within the initial pairing process, while the second modification concerns the filtering step that is enabled based on D_{quasi} calculated dynamically using the product of "c" and D_{initp}. This filtering step decides whether or not the matching between the query and a database image could avoid the iterative probability updating. These two modifications are summarized as follows.

- ☐ The "initial pairing" process is carried out between the query and every database image. For each of these processes, a D_{initp} is calculated based on the initial "highest" labeling probability for each object (i.e., the best matched label initially). The distance function used in computing D_{initp} is the same as the one used after iterative probability updating to compute the actual distance, D_{actual}. This differs from the main method where the "initial pairing" process is immediately followed by iterative probability updating for every (query, database image) pair.
- ☐ In the filtering step, the quasi lower bound on distance, D_{quasi}, is calculated by taking the product of D_{initp} and the current value of "c". A database image is a candidate wherever less than k nearest neighbors have been found so far or when the following condition is satisfied:

$$D_{quasi}(\text{db}[i]) \le D_{actual}(\text{current } k\text{th-nearest neighbor}) \qquad (8)$$

Here, db([*i*]) refers to the current database image (i.e., *i*th image) being compared to. Only those database images that satisfy the above condition at their respective turn of comparison will have iterative probability updating carried out and D_{actual} calculated. The value of D_{actual} computed is used in comparing the distances of the k nearest neighbors in order to update the k-*NN* list. Furthermore, the ratio D_{actual} / D_{initp} is used in updating the running value of the confidence factor "c" to be used in the matching with the next database image.

A high-level pseudo code of the approximate query processing is presented as follow:

```
[BEGIN]
float mean_c_factor = 0.0;
float sum_c_factor = 0.0;
int   cumulative_count = 0;

for (i : [1,NUMBER_DB_IMAGES]) {
    D_initp[i] = initial_pairing(Query, DB_Image[i]);
}

for (i : [1,NUMBER_DB_IMAGES]) {
   if (Less than k-NN images) {
       D_actual = relax_matching(Query, DB_Image[i]);
       Update NN-List;
       cumulative_count = cumulative_count + 1;
       sum_c_factor += (D_actual / D_initp[i]);
       mean_c_factor = sum_c_factor / cumulative_count;
   } else {
       D_quasi = mean_c_factor * D_initp[i];
       if (D_quasi <= kth-NN-distance) {
          D_actual = relax_matching(Query, DB_Image[i]);
          Update NN-List;
          cumulative_count += 1;
          sum_c_factor += (D_actual / D_initp[i]);
          mean_c_factor = sum_c_factor / cumulative_count;
       }
   }
}

Result <- NN-List of images
[END]
```

4 Experimental Evaluation

In this section, a group of preliminary experiments aimed at comparing the performance and accuracy in retrieval by the approximate query processing with that of the main CBIR method described in Section 2 are performed. For ease of explanation, the main method is also called the "accurate" query processing here.

In this group of experiments, two trademarks (one of which have been used in experiments reported in [2]) are chosen as query images as shown in Table 2. Two parameters are used to affect the result of a retrieval query, namely a choice of whether or not a "segment type" constraint is enabled, and a choice of whether the confidence factor is set manually or calculated automatically. In the case where the confidence factor is to be set manually, a value in the range of (0.0,1.0] is specified.

In all of the retrieval queries performed, the 10 most similar images are returned. In other words, this is a k-nearest neighbor search with $k = 10$. The program used in these experiments has been modified from that used in the main method which was written in the C++ language. The computer on which these experiments are performed is identical to the one used for the "accurate" query processing experiments.

These experiments are briefly summarized as follows:

☐   First, for each of the two test images, the "accurate" query processing is performed twice, one with the "segment type" constraint enabled and another without. Altogether, results from four retrieval queries are obtained.

☐   Second, based on the approximate query processing, two batches of experiments for each test image are carried out, first involving the "type" queries and then the "no-type" queries.

☐   For the initial batch of experiments involving the "type" queries, the first ten experiments are run by varying the confidence factor manually from 0.1~ 1.0 respectively, which is followed by an experiment based on automatic calculation of the confidence factor. Similar steps are carried out for the second batch of experiments in which the segment "type" constraint is not involved. Altogether, 22 different query results are obtained for each of the test images.

In terms of evaluation, the proposed approximate query processing approach is compared with the accurate query processing based on two criteria, namely performance and accuracy.

☐   **Performance**
This is in relation to how efficient the filtering by the quasi lower bound on distance can be achieved in terms of the (1) Reduction in processing time when handling the same retrieval query, and (2) Reduction in the number of database images that actually have to go through the iterative probability updating. Here, two reduction ratios (abbreviated as R.R.) are introduced, namely reduction ratio in processing time and reduction ratio in number of images matched:

R.R. (Processing time) = Approximate retrieval time / Accurate retrieval time   (9)

R.R. (Images matched) = # images relaxed match / # total database images   (10)

Table 2. Two test images used in the approximate query processing experiments

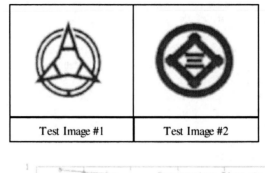

| Test Image #1 | Test Image #2 |

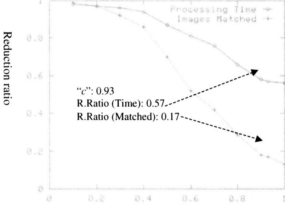

Fig. 1. Reduction Ratios vs. Confidence Factor for Test Image #1

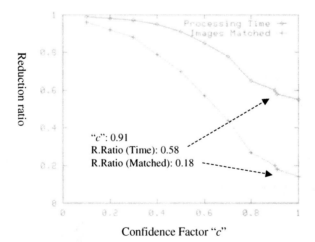

Fig. 2. Reduction Ratios vs. Confidence Factor for Test Image #2

Table 3. Effect of confidence factor on precision P' of approximate query processing

P' \ "c"	Test Image #1		P' \ "c"	Test Image #2	
	Type	No-Type		Type	No-Type
0.1	10/10	10/10	0.1	10/10	10/10
0.2	10/10	10/10	0.2	10/10	10/10
0.3	10/10	10/10	0.3	10/10	10/10
0.4	10/10	10/10	0.4	10/10	10/10
0.5	10/10	10/10	0.5	10/10	10/10
0.6	10/10	10/10	0.6	10/10	10/10
0.7	10/10	10/10	0.7	10/10	10/10
0.8	10/10	10/10	0.8	10/10	10/10
0.9	10/10	10/10	0.9	10/10	10/10
0.965	10/10	10/10	0.953	10/10	10/10
1.0	9/10	10/10	1.0	10/10	9/10

These reduction ratios are plotted against the confidence factor "c" for each of the two test images (without using "type" constraint), and shown in Figures 1 and 2 respectively. It is apparent from these figures that there is a steady reduction in both processing time and number of images matched as the value of the confidence factor "c" increases from 0.1 to 1.0. At the value where the confidence factor is computed automatically, that is 0.93 for test image #1 and 0.91 for test image #2, the reduction ratio in number of images matched are respectively less than 20%, highlighting a considerable reduction in processing by the approximate query processing.

Between these two reduction ratios, the reduction ratio in number of images matched reflects more accurately the filtering achieved by the approximate query processing approach as it is not influenced by external factors such as the current processing load of the computer and sub-optimal program implementation.

□ **Accuracy**

In terms of evaluating the accuracy of the approximate query processing approach, a slightly modified definition of "precision" often used in information research is employed here. The usual definition of precision P of a retrieval method adopted in information retrieval research is defined as:

$$P = \text{\# correct responses} / \text{\# responses} \qquad (11)$$

Here, as the comparison is between the approximate query processing approach and the main method, which is assumed to be the "accurate" query processing, the definition of precision P' is being defined as:

$$P' = \text{\# "accurate" responses in the "approximate" result} / \text{\# responses returned} \quad (12)$$

Here, the denominator is 10, as the number of responses to return for every query is 10. This precision P' is simply the percentage of "accurate" responses that are included in the "approximate" result. For each value of the confidence factor measured, the precision P' is computed. Results for the test images are summarized in Table 3.

It is noteworthy that even if the approximate query processing is considerably faster than the accurate query processing, but results in a significant percentage of the accurate answers being missed (i.e., false dismissals), then the question of whether such an approximate query processing approach should be used is still questionable. In the experimental results as shown in Table 3, it is clear that for the two test cases, the precision is 100% at the place where the confidence factor is calculated automatically. However, in the case of test image #1, simply filter by D_{initp} after the initial pairing is not sufficient to achieve a 100% precision for the "type" query, while for test image #2, filtering by D_{initp} after the initial pairing is similarly not sufficient to achieve a 100% precision for the "no-type" query. In other words, simply relying on D_{initp} calculated after the initial pairing alone might not be sufficient to return the accurate answer as exemplified by the main CBIR method. A certain amount of probability updating, albeit small, is nevertheless needed to facilitate the quasi lower bound on distance to accomplish its filtering function.

5 Conclusions

An approximate query processing approach for a content-based image retrieval method based on probabilistic relaxation labeling is introduced. The novelty lies in the inclusion of a filtering mechanism based on a quasi lower bound on distance in the vector space that effectively spares the matching between the query and a number of database images from the expensive iterative probability updating. Experimental results are promising in that the approach consistently returns a close "approximation" of the accurate result while reducing the amount of processing required.

References

1. Aigrain, P., Zhang, H.J., Petkovic, D.: Content-based representation and retrieval of visual media – a state-of-the-art review. *Multimedia Tools and Applications*, 3(3): (1996) 179–202
2. Kwan, P.W.H., Kameyama, K., Toraichi, K.: On a relaxation-labeling algorithm for real-time contour-based image similarity retrieval. *Image and Vision Computing* Vol. 21(3), 2003, pp.285–294
3. Rosenfeld, A., Hummel, R.A., Zucker, S.W.: Scene labeling by relaxation operations. *IEEE Trans. Systems Man Cybernetics*, 6(6): (1976) 420–433
4. Pelillo, M. and Refice, M.: Learning compatibility coefficients for relaxation labeling processes. *IEEE Trans. Pattern Anal. Machine Intell.*, Vol.16, No.9, 1994, pp.933–945.
5. Hafner, J., Sawhney, H.S., Equitz, W., Flickner, M., Niblack W.: Efficient Color Histogram Indexing for Quadratic Form Distance Functions. *IEEE Trans. Pattern Anal. Machine Intell.*, Vol.17, No.7, 1995, pp.729–736.
6. Korn, P., Sidiropoulos N., Faloutsos, C., Siegel E., Protopapas Z.: Fast and Effective Retrieval of Medical Tumor Shapes. *IEEE Trans. Knowledge and Data Eng.*, Vol.10, No.6, 1998, pp.889–904
7. Ciaccia P. and Patella M.: Searching in Metric Spaces with User-Defined and Approximate Distances. *ACM Transactions on Database Systems*, Vol.27, No.4, Dec 2002, pp.398–437.

Query Algebra Operations for Interval Probabilities

Wenzhong Zhao, Alex Dekhtyar, and Judy Goldsmith

Department of Computer Science
University of Kentucky
Lexington,
KY40503, USA
{wzhao0,dekhtyar,goldsmit}@cs.uky.edu

Abstract. The groundswell for the '00s is imprecise probabilities. Whether the numbers represent the probable location of a GPS device at its next sounding, the inherent uncertainty of an individual expert's probability prediction, or the range of values derived from the fusion of sensor data, probability intervals became an important way of representing uncertainty. However, until recently, there has been no robust support for storage and management of imprecise probabilities. In this paper, we define the semantics of traditional query algebra operations of selection, projection, Cartesian product and join, as well as an operation of conditionalization, specific to probabilistic databases. We provide efficient methods for computing the results of these operations and show how they conform to probability theory.

1 Introduction

Reasoning with common sense leads to attempts to make decisions and inferences with incomplete information about the real world. This process, whether applied to medical decision-making [17] or pure logical reasoning [16,17] or to other applications such as network modeling [2] or reasoning about databases [15], can be implemented effectively using probability intervals. Models were proposed for computations with interval probabilities [4,18,19] recently, but there has been little work on incorporating management of interval probability distributions into databases.

Many research areas deal with discrete random variables with finite domains. Probability distributions of such random variables are finite objects, as probabilities need to be specified only for a finite number of instances. Thus, representations of probability distributions can be stored as database objects. A number of database models suitable for storing probability distributions has been proposed recently [5,10,13,14].

The issue of querying *interval* probability distributions is independent of the choice of representation. As previous research on probabilistic databases has established [1,5,7,13], any manipulation of probabilities in a database must be consistent with probability theory, and classical relational algebra operations fail

V. Mařík et al. (Eds.): DEXA 2003, LNCS 2736, pp. 527–536, 2003.

to take this into account. Even in the case of point probabilities, one must define
the semantics of database operations carefully, as is the case in previously proposed probabilistic relational algrebras [1,3,7]. In order to define query algrbra
operations on interval probability distributions we must define the semantics
of the underlying interval probability computations. Until recently, no formal
semantics for interval probabilities provided a clear and convenient way to compute marginal or conditional probability distributions. In [4], we have introduced
a possible-world semantics (a generalization of a special-purpose model from [6])
for interval probability distributions which provides closed-form solutions for
such computations.

This work builds upon the semantics of [4] (briefly summarized in Section 2)
to introduce query algebra operations of selection, projection, conditionalization
[5,7], Cartesian product and join in databases that store interval probability
distributions of discrete random variables (Section 3). The query algebra introduced in this paper is independent of any specific data model. Its operations
have already been implemented in at least two (to our best knowledge) different
frameworks [9,10].

1.1   Related Work

Relational probabilistic database models were first proposed by Cavallo and
Pittarelli [3] and Barbara, Garcia-Molina and Proter [1] in late-80s/early-90s.
The former framework considered a single probability distribution as a complete relation; the latter used non-1NF tuples to store probability distributions.
Dey and Sarkar [7] proposed a 1NF approach to storing probabilistic data and
first introduced the operation of conditionalization. Kornatzky and Shimony [12]
introduced the first object-oriented model for probabilistic data. All these frameworks assumed point probabilities and in all but [1] a database record/object
represented information about a probability of a single event, rather than a
probability distribution.

Interval probabilities were introduced to databases by Lakshmanan et. al
in their ProbView [13] framework, which also used 1NF relation semantics to
store probability intervals for individual events. ProbView was a predecessor of
another object-oriented approach by Eiter et. al [8].

Probability distributions, rather than probabilities of individual events, became the basis of the Semistructured Probabilistic Object model introduced by
Dekhtyar, Goldsmith and Hawkes [5]. In this framework, diverse discrete point
probability distributions are represented as database objects. To query these
objects, [5] introduced Semistructured Probabilistic Algebra. After that, Nierman and Jagadish [14] and Hung, Getoor and Subrahmnian [10] also represented
probabilistic information in semistructured (XML) form.

In parallel with the development of approaches to probabilistic databases,
imprecise probabilities have attracted the attention of AI researchers, as doc-
umented by the Imprecise Probability Project [11]. Walley's seminal work [18]
made the case for interval probabilities as the means of representing uncertainty.

2 Semantics of Interval Probabilities

This section briefly summarizes the possible worlds semantics for interval probability distributions described in [4]. We consider the probability space $\mathcal{P} = \mathsf{C}[0,1]$,
the set of all subintervals of the interval $[0, 1]$. The rest of this section introduces
the formal semantics for the probability distributions over $\mathcal{P}$ and the notions of
consistency and *tightness* of interval distributions.

Definition 1. *Let V be a set of random variables. A **probabilistic interpretation (p-interpretation)** over V is a function $I_V : dom(V) \to [0, 1]$, such
that $\sum_{\bar{x} \in dom(V)} I_V(\bar{x}) = 1$.*

The main idea of our semantics is that a probability distribution function
$P : dom(V) \to \mathsf{C}[0,1]$ represents a **set of possible point probability distributions** (a.k.a., **p-interpretations**). Given a probability distribution function
$P : dom(V) \to \mathsf{C}[0,1]$, for each $\bar{x} \in dom(V)$, we write $P(\bar{x}) = [l_{\bar{x}}, u_{\bar{x}}]$. Whenever
$dom(V) = \{\bar{x}_1, \ldots \bar{x}_m\}$, we write $P(\bar{x}_i) = [l_i, u_i]$, $1 \leq i \leq m$.

Definition 2. *Let V be a set of random variables and $P : dom(V) \to \mathsf{C}[0,1]$
a (possibly incomplete)[1] interval probability distribution function (ipdf) over V.
A probabilistic interpretation I_V satisfies P ($I_V \models P$) iff $(\forall \bar{x} \in dom(V))(l_{\bar{x}} \leq
I_V(\bar{x}) \leq u_{\bar{x}})$.*

*An interval probability distribution function $P : dom(V) \to \mathsf{C}[0,1]$ is **consistent** iff there exists a p-interpretation I_V such that $I_V \models P$.*

Theorem 1. *Let V be a set of random variables and $P : dom(V) \to \mathsf{C}[0,1]$
be a complete interval probability distribution function over V. Let $dom(V) =
\{\bar{x}_1, \ldots, \bar{x}_m\}$ and $P(\bar{x}_i) = [l_i, u_i]$. P is **consistent** iff the following two condi-
tions hold: (1) $\sum_{i=1}^{m} l_i \leq 1$; (2) $\sum_{i=1}^{m} u_i \geq 1$.*

*Let $P' : X \to \mathsf{C}[0,1]$ be an incomplete interval probability distribution func-
tion over V. Let $X = \{\bar{x}_1, \ldots, \bar{x}_m\}$ and $P'(\bar{x}_i) = [l_i, u_i]$. P' is **consistent** iff
$\sum_{i=1}^{m} l_i \leq 1$.*

Consider the two interval probability distributions P and P' shown on Figure 1.(b,c) and the four p-interpretations over the same random variables from
Figure 1.(a): We can see that $I_1 \models P$ and $I_1 \models P'$; $I_2 \models P$ but $I_2 \not\models P'$; $I_3 \models P'$
but $I_3 \not\models P$ and I_4 does not satisfy either P or P'.

Definition 3. *Let $P : X \to \mathsf{C}[0,1]$ be an interval probability distribution function over a set of random variables V. Let $X = \{\bar{x}_1, \ldots, \bar{x}_m\}$ and $P(\bar{x}_i) = [l_i, u_i]$.
A number $\alpha \in [l_i, u_i]$ is **reachable** by P at $\bar{x}_i$ iff there exists a p-interpretation
$I_V \models P$, such that $I(\bar{x}_i) = \alpha$.*

We observe that all points between any pair of reachable probability values
are themselves reachable. Intuitively, points *unreachable* by an interval probability distribution do not provide any additional information about *possible* point

---

[1] "Incomplete", in this context means that the function need not be defined on each
instance of its domain.

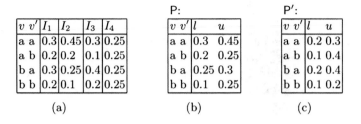

Fig. 1. Interval Probability Distributions

probabilities. Of the possible interval probability distributions, of primary interest are those with no unreachable points. These distributions are called **tight**.
We can show that for each interval probability distribution, one can find an
equivalent tight probability distribution.

Definition 4. *Let* $P : X \rightarrow C[0,1]$ *be an interval probability distribution over
a set* V *of random variables.* P *is called* **tight** *iff* $(\forall \bar{x} \in X)(\forall \alpha \in [l_{\bar{x}}, u_{\bar{x}}])$
$(\alpha$ *is reachable by* P *at* $\bar{x})$.

Let P' *be an interval probability distribution function. An interval probability
distribution function* P *is its* **tight equivalent** *iff (i)* P *is* **tight** *and (ii) For
each p-interpretation* I, $I \models P'$ *iff* $I \models P$.

Each complete interval probability distribution P has a **unique** tight equivalent. It can be efficiently computed using

Theorem 2. *Let* $P : dom(V) \rightarrow C[0,1]$ *be a complete interval probability distribution function over a set of random variables* V. *Let* $dom(V) = \{\bar{x}_1, \ldots, \bar{x}_m\}$
and $P(\bar{x}_i) = [l_i, u_i]$. *Then* $(\forall 1 \leq i \leq m)$

$$ \mathcal{T}(P)(\bar{x}_i) = \left[\max \left(l_i, 1 - \left(\sum_{j=1}^{m} u_j - u_i \right) \right), \min \left(u_i, 1 - \left(\sum_{j=1}^{m} l_j - l_i \right) \right) \right]. $$

3   Query Operations

Consider a finite collection $P_1, \ldots, P_M$ of interval probability distributions over
the set of random variables V. The semantics of the operations we discuss below
is independent of the representation of interval probability distributions in the
database. The operations described below are applicable to any representation
that has the following properties: *(i)* it is possible to retrieve/construct an individual interval probability distribution from the representation and *(ii)* there
exists an efficient procedure for converting an interval probability distribution
of discrete random variables into the representation. In what follows, we assume
that the collection $\mathcal{D} = \{P_1, \ldots, P_M\}$ is the database.

3.1 Selection

In the relational model, selection is applied to flat tuples and its result is a collection of flat tuples. When probability distributions of discrete random variables are the database objects they can be viewed as tables in which each row describes the probability of a particular instance. Thus, selection operations on probability distributions can do two things: (i) select a subset of the input set of probability distributions and (ii) select a subset of rows in each input probability distribution. In particular, we consider three separate types of selection conditions:

Selection on participating random variables. Given a list $\mathcal{F} = \{v_1, \ldots, v_s\}$ of random variables, $\sigma_{\mathcal{F}}(\mathcal{D})$ returns the set of probability distributions that contain **all** variables in $\mathcal{F}$. The probability distributions are returned unchanged.

Selection on random variable values. Given a condition $v = x$, where $v \in \mathcal{V}$ is a random variable name and $x \in dom(v)$, $\sigma_{v=x}(\mathcal{D})$ will return the set of probability distributions which contain v as a participating random variable. In each distribution returned, *only the rows* satisfying the $v = x$ condition will remain.

Selection on probability. Given a condition $c = l$ op x or $c = u$ op x where x is a real number, op $\in \{=, \neq, <, >, \leq, \geq\}$ and l and u represent lower and upper bound of the probability interval, $\sigma_c(\mathcal{D})$ will return the set of probability distributions which contain at least one row satisfying the condition c. In each probability distribution returned, *only the rows* satisfying c will remain.

These operations can be illustrated on the following example. Consider the database $\mathcal{D} = \{P, P'\}$ consisting of the two probability distributions shown in Figure 1. Figure 2 shows the result of the following queries: (a) $\sigma_{\{v\}}(\mathcal{D})$ (find all distributions involving random variable v; returns both P and P' unchanged); (b) $\sigma_{v'=a}(\mathcal{D})$ (find all probabilities involving the value a of random variable v' in the database; returns two rows from each distribution); (c) $\sigma_{u=0.4}(\mathcal{D})$ (find all probability table rows with upper bound equal to 0.4; returns two rows from P').

Despite having different effects on the database, selection operations of different types commute.

Theorem 3. *Let c_1 and c_2 be two selection conditions and $\mathcal{D}$ be a database of interval probability distributions. Then $\sigma_{c_1}(\sigma_{c_2}(\mathcal{D})) = \sigma_{c_2}(\sigma_{c_1}(\mathcal{D}))$.*

3.2 Projection

As described earlier, interval probability distributions have one column per participating random variable and two additional columns for lower and upper probabilities. Here, we only consider the semantics of the projection operation that removes random variables from distributions Given a joint probability distribution of two or more random variables, the operation of obtaining a probability distribution for a proper subset of them is called in probability theory *computing the marginal probability distribution* or *marginalization*. We use the terms

$\sigma_{\{v\}}(\mathcal{D})$:

v v'	l	u
a a	0.3	0.45
a b	0.2	0.25
b a	0.25	0.3
b b	0.1	0.25

v v'	l	u
a a	0.2	0.3
a b	0.1	0.4
b a	0.2	0.4
b b	0.1	0.2

$\sigma_{v'=a}(\mathcal{D})$:

v v'	l	u
a a	0.3	0.45
b a	0.25	0.3

v v'	l	u
a a	0.2	0.3
b a	0.2	0.4

$\sigma_{u=0.4}(\mathcal{D})$:

v v'	l	u
a b	0.1	**0.4**
b a	0.2	**0.4**

(a)   (b)   (c)

Fig. 2. Selection on interval probability distributions.

projection and *marginalization* interchangeably. Marginalization is a straightforward operation on point probability distribution functions [5]: given a p-interpretation I over set V of random variables and a random variable $v \in V$, the marginal probability distribution I' over set $V - \{v\}$ can be computed as follows: $\pi_{V-\{v\}}(I)(\bar{y}) = I'(\bar{y}) = \sum_{x \in dom(v)} I(\bar{y}, x)$. But when probabilities are expressed as intervals, what is a reasonable definition of the marginal probability distribution?

Recall that an interval probability distribution P is interpreted as a set of p-interpretations I satisfying it. So, when trying to represent the result of projection, we have to describe the set $\{\pi_{V-\{v\}}(I) | I \models P\}$. This intuition is captured in the following definition.

Definition 5. *Let P be an ipdf over the set V of random variables and let $U \subset V$. The result of projection (marginalization) of P onto U, denoted $\pi_U(P)$, is defined as*

$$\pi_U(P)(\bar{x}) = [\min_{I \models P}(\sum_{\bar{y} \in dom(V-U)} I(\bar{x}, \bar{y})), \quad \max_{I \models P}(\sum_{\bar{y} \in dom(V-U)} I(\bar{x}, \bar{y}))]$$

Definition 5 specifies precisely the result of the projection operation, but does not provide an algorithm for computing it. The following theorem presents a straightforward way to compute the projection based on a search over the space of all p-interpretations that satisfy P.

Theorem 4. *Let P be an ipdf over the set V of random variables and let $U \subset V$. Let $P'' : U \longrightarrow C[0,1]$ be*

$$P''(\bar{x}) = [\min(\sum_{\bar{y} \in dom(V-U)} l_{(\bar{x}, \bar{y})}, 1), \quad \min(\sum_{\bar{y} \in dom(V-U)} u_{(\bar{x}, \bar{y})}, 1)].$$

Then $\pi_U(P) = \mathcal{T}(P'')$.

The process of computing the projection $\pi_{\{v\}}(P)$ is shown below. First the random variable v' is removed from the probability distribution function. Then a new probability distribution function P'' is formed for the variable v, and the intervals $P''(a)$ and $P''(b)$ are computed as the sums, i.e. $P''(a) = [l_{(a,a)} + l_{(a,b)}, u_{(a,a)} + u_{(a,b)}]$ [2] and $P''(b) = [l_{(b,a)} + l_{(b,b)}, u_{(b,a)} + u_{(b,b)}]$. Observe that P''

---

[2] $l_{(x,y)}$ denotes the lower bound for $v = x$ and $v' = y$; $u_{(x,y)}$ denotes the upper bound for $v = x$ and $v' = y$.

is not tight: the upper bound of both probability intervals for $P''(a)$ and $P''(b)$ are not reachable. Thus, the final probability distribution function $\pi_{\{v\}}(P)$ is computed by applying the tightening operation on P''.

P:

v v'	l	u
a a	0.3	0.45
a b	0.2	0.25
b a	0.25	0.3
b b	0.1	0.25

$\Longrightarrow$

v	l	u
a	0.3	0.45
a	0.2	0.25
b	0.25	0.3
b	0.1	0.25

$\Longrightarrow$

P'' :

v	l	u
a	0.5	0.7
b	0.35	0.55

$\Longrightarrow$

$\pi_v(P) = \mathcal{T}(P'')$

v	l	u
a	0.5	0.65
b	0.35	0.5

Fig. 3. Projection for interval probability distributions.

3.3 Conditionalization

Given a joint probability distribution of random variables, *selection* operation can return certain rows of its probability table and *projection* operation will compute marginal probability distributions. There is, however, another important operation on probability distributions, namely, computation of conditional probability distribution, for which no existing classical relational algebra operation seems an appropriate match. Recognizing this, Dey and Sarkar [7] proposed a new query algebra operation, *conditionalization*, which they denoted as μ.

When point probability distributions are considered, conditionalization is a straightforward operation: given a p-interpretation I over the set of random variables V, the conditional probability $\mu_{v=x}(I)$ of I under the assumption $v = x$ is computed as $\mu_{v=x}(I)(\bar{y}) = \frac{I(\bar{y},x)}{\sum_{\bar{y}' \in dom(V - \{v\})} I(\bar{y}',x)}$. When defining conditionalization on interval probability distribution functions, we follow the same intuition as with the projection operations.

Definition 6. *Let* $V = (v_1, \ldots, v_n)$ *be a sequence of random variables,* $V^* = \{v_k, \ldots, v_n\}$, $k > 1$ *and* $V' = V - V^*$. *Let* C *be a conditionalization constraint* $\bar{v} = \bar{X}$, *where* $\bar{v} = (v_k, \ldots, v_n)$. *The conditionalization is defined as*

$$\mu_C(P)(\bar{y}) = \left[\min_{I \models P} \left(\frac{I_{\bar{X}}(\bar{y})}{\sum_{\bar{y}' \in dom(V')} I_{\bar{X}}(\bar{y}')} \right), \quad \max_{I \models P} \left(\frac{I_{\bar{X}}(\bar{y})}{\sum_{\bar{y}' \in dom(V')} I_{\bar{X}}(\bar{y}')} \right) \right].$$

We provide a closed-form formula in [4,9] for computing it. Notice that there are some problems inherent in this definition, as discussed in [4,9], but that we have implemented the operation in the database with a user-beware warning.

3.4 Cartesian Product and Join

In order to consider operations that combine different interval probability distributions into one, we must first consider an issue of computing the probability of conjunctions.

Probabilistic Conjunctions. Consider two events e_1 and e_2 with known probabilities $p(e_1)$ and $p(e_2)$. When no additional information about the relationship between e_1 and e_2 is available, the probability of $e_1 \wedge e_2$ lies in the interval $[\max(0, p(e_1) + p(e_2) - 1), \min(p(e_1), p(e_2))]$. Specific assumptions about the relationship between the events may help us determine a more exact probability.

More formally, a *probabilistic conjunction* operation is a function $\otimes_\alpha : [0, 1] \times [0, 1] \rightarrow$ C[0,1] that is *commutative*, *associative* and *monotonic* ($a \otimes_\alpha b \subseteq a \otimes_\alpha c$ iff $b \leq c$) and satisfies the following conditions: (i) $a \otimes_\alpha 0 = 0$; (ii) $a \otimes_\alpha 1 = a$; and (iii) $a \otimes_\alpha b \leq \min(a, b)$. Probabilistic conjunctions were introduced in ProbView [13] and used in other probabilistic database frameworks [6,8]. Some examples of probabilistic conjunctions are shown in the table below:

α	$\otimes_\alpha$
independence	$a \otimes_{ind} b = [a \cdot b, a \cdot b]$
ignorance	$a \otimes_{ig} b = [\max(0, a + b - 1),\ \min(a, b)]$
positive correlation	$a \otimes_{pc} b = [\min(a, b), \min(a, b)]$
negative correlation	$a \otimes_{nc} b = [\max(0, a + b - 1),\ \max(0, a + b - 1)]$

Cartesian Product The Cartesian product of two interval probability distributions P and P' can be viewed as the joint probability distribution of the random variables from both P and P'. The resulting probability distribution will have one row $(\bar{x}, \bar{y})$ for each pair of rows $\bar{x}$ from P and $\bar{y}$ from P'. Given a relationship α together with $\otimes_\alpha$, we can define the corresponding Cartesian product of two *ipdfs*. Notice that for the Cartesian product to be defined for two distributions P and P', their sets of participating random variables V and V' *must be disjoint*.

Definition 7. *Let* $P : dom(V) \rightarrow$ *C[0,1] and* $P' : dom(V') \rightarrow$ *C[0,1] be two interval probability distributions such that* $V \cap V' = \emptyset$. *Let* $\mathcal{I} = \{I'' : dom(V) \times dom(V') \rightarrow [0, 1] | (\forall \bar{x} \in dom(V))(\forall \bar{y} \in dom(V'))(\exists I \models P)(\exists I' \models P')I''(\bar{x}, \bar{y}) \in I(\bar{x}) \otimes_\alpha I'(\bar{y})$. *The* Cartesian product $P \times_\alpha P'$ *under assumption* α *is defined as* $(P \times_\alpha P')(\bar{x}, \bar{y}) = [\min_{I'' \in \mathcal{I}}(I''(\bar{x}, \bar{y})),\quad \max_{I'' \in \mathcal{I}}(I''(\bar{x}, \bar{y}))]$.

The result of Cartesian product can be computed directly.

P:

v v'	l	u
a a	0.3	0.45
a b	0.2	0.25
b a	0.25	0.3
b b	0.1	0.25

P'':

v''	l	u
a	0.5	0.6
b	0.4	0.5

$P \times_{ind} P''$:

v v' v''	l	u
a a a	0.15	0.27
a a b	0.12	0.225
a b a	0.1	0.15
a b b	0.08	0.125
b a a	0.125	0.18
b a b	0.1	0.15
b b a	0.05	0.15
b b b	0.04	0.125

Fig. 4. Cartesian Product for interval probability distributions.

Theorem 5. *Let* $P : dom(V) \to C[0,1]$ *and* $P' : dom(V') \to C[0,1]$ *be two interval probability distributions such that* $V \cap V' = \emptyset$. *Then*
$$(P \times_\alpha P')(\bar{x}, \bar{y}) = [l_{\bar{x}} \otimes_\alpha l_{\bar{y}}, u_{\bar{x}} \otimes_\alpha u_{\bar{y}}].$$

Figure 4 depicts the process of computing the Cartesian product $P \times P'$ under the assumption of independence.

Join. When two *ipdfs* P and P' contain common variables, the computation of the joint distribution must ensure that the influence of common variables is accounted for only once.

Consider two interval probability distributions P and P' over sets of random variables V and V' respectively, and assume that $V \cap V' = V^*$ and $\emptyset \subset V^* \subset V \cup V'$. In what follows, let $\bar{x} \in dom(V-V^*)$, $\bar{y} \in dom(V'-V^*)$ and $\bar{z} \in dom(V^*)$.

Our goal is to define interval probability distribution $P'' : dom(V - V^*) \times dom(V^*) \times dom(V' - V^*) \to C[0,1]$, given P and P'. Consider the instance $(\bar{x}, \bar{z}, \bar{y})$ of $dom(V-V^*) \times dom(V^*) \times dom(V'-V^*)$. We can compute $P''((\bar{x}, \bar{z}, \bar{y}))$ from $P((\bar{x}, \bar{z}))$ and $P'((\bar{z}, \bar{y}))$, but with some extra effort. Direct computation of $P((\bar{x}, \bar{z})) \times_\alpha P'((\bar{z}, \bar{y}))$ is not meaningful because $\bar{z}$ affects probabilities in both P and P'. In order to be able to apply cartesian product computation, $\bar{z}$ must be factored out of one of the two distributions.

To do this, we verbalize the problem of computing $P''((\bar{x}, \bar{z}, \bar{y}))$ as "compute the joint probability of $(\bar{x}, \bar{z})$ from P and $\bar{y}$ from P', *given that* V^* *takes the values of* $\bar{z}$". This, in turn, suggests the use of conditionalization to factor $\bar{z}$ out of $P'((\bar{z}, \bar{y}))$. We note that in the same manner we could have attempted to factor $\bar{z}$ out of P. This leads to two families of join operations (left join and right join).

Definition 8. *Let* $P : dom(V) \to C[0,1]$ *and* $P' : dom(V') \to C[0,1]$, *and* $V \cap V' = V^*$, *where* $\emptyset \subset V^* \subset V \cup V'$. *Let* α *be a(n assumed) relationship between variables in* V *and variables in* $V' - V^*$ *and* β *be a(n assumed) relationship between variables in* $V - V^*$ *and* V'. *The operations of left and right join are defined as follows.*
$$(P \ltimes_\alpha P')((\bar{x}, \bar{z}, \bar{y})) = P((\bar{x}, \bar{z})) \times_\alpha \mu_{V^*=\bar{z}}(P'((\bar{z}, \bar{y}))).$$
$$(P \rtimes_\beta P')((\bar{x}, \bar{z}, \bar{y})) = \mu_{V^*=\bar{z}}(P((\bar{x}, \bar{z}))) \times_\beta P((\bar{z}, \bar{y})).$$

4   Conclusions

Given the increasing interest in the use of interval probability distributions, there is a clear and present need for database methods to handle the managmenet of large collections of such data. This paper has presented the results of an initial investigation into the semantics of traditional database operations on interval probability distributions. The operations presented here are independent of any representation of the distributions in the database.

Initial implementations of these operations are being implemented by the authors of this paper as an extension of the SPO model described in [5]. This is presented in [9]. Hung, Subrahmanian and Getoor use the semantics of some of the operations presented here in their work on probabilistic XML [10].

References

1. D. Barbara, H. Garcia-Molina, and D. Porter. The management of probabilistic data. *IEEE Trans. on Knowledge and Data Engineering*, 4:487–502, 1992.
2. M. Braun and Gabriele Kotsis. Interval based workload characterization for distributed systems. In *Computer Performance Evaluation*, pages 181–192, 1997.
3. R. Cavallo and M. Pittarelli. The theory of probabilistic databases. In *Proc. VLDB'87*, pages 71–81, 1987.
4. Alex Dekhtyar and Judy Goldsmith. Conditionalization for interval probabilities. In *Proc. Workshop on Conditionals, Information, and Inference'02*, LNAI, Berlin, 2003. Springer.
5. Alex Dekhtyar, Judy Goldsmith, and Sean Hawkes. Semistructured probabilistic databases. In *Proc. Statistical and Scientific Database Management Systems*, 2001.
6. Alex Dekhtyar, Robert Ross, and V.S. Subrahmanian. Probabilistic temporal databases, I: Algebra. *ACM Transactions on Database Systems*, 26(1):41–95, 2001.
7. D. Dey and S. Sarkar. A probabilistic relational model and algebra. *ACM Transactions on Database Systems*, 21(3):339–369, 1996.
8. T. Eiter, J. Lu, T. Lukasiewicz, and V.S. Subrahmanian. Probabilistic object bases. *ACM Transactions on Database Systems*, 26(3):313 –343, 2001.
9. Judy Goldsmith, Alex Dekhtyar, and Wenzhong. Can probabilistic databases help elect qualified officials? In *Proc. FLAIRS'2003*, 2003.
10. Edward Hung, Lise Getoor, and V.S. Subrahmanian. Probabilistic interval XML. In *Proc. International Conference on Database Theory*, 2003.
11. H. E. Kyburg Jr. Interval-valued probabilities. In G. de Cooman, Peter Walley, and F.G. Cozman, editors, *Imprecise Probabilities Project*, 1998.
12. E. Kornatzky and S.E. Shimony. A probabilistic object data model. *Data and Knowledge Engineering*, 12:143–166, 1994.
13. V.S. Lakshmanan, N. Leone, R. Ross, and V.S. Subrahmanian. Probview: A flexible probabilistic database system. *ACM Transactions on Database Systems*, 22(3):419–469, 1997.
14. Andrew Nierman and H. V. Jagadish. ProTDB: Probabilistic data in XML. In *Proceedings of the 28th VLDB Conference*, pages 646–657, 2002.
15. Thomas Rölleke and Norbert Fuhr. Probabilistic reasoning for large scale databases. In *Dittrich, K.R.; Geppert, A. (eds.). Datenbanksysteme in Büro, Technik und Wissenschaft (BTW'97)*, pages 118–132. Springer, 1997.
16. M. Schramm and W. Ertel. Reasoning with probabilities and maximum entropy: The system PIT and its application in LEXMED. In *Symposium on Operations Research 1999*, 1999.
17. S. Sundaresh, T. Leong, and P. Haddawy. Supporting multi-level multi-perspective dynamic decision making in medicine. In *Proc. AMIA Annual Fall Symposium*, 1999.
18. Peter Walley. *Statistical Reasoning with Imprecise Probabilities*. Chapman and Hall, 1991.
19. K. Weichselberger. The theory of interval-probability as a unifying concept for uncertainty. In *Proc. 1st International Symp. on Imprecise Probabilities and Their Applications*, 1999.

Tree Structure Based Parallel Frequent Pattern Mining on PC Cluster

Iko Pramudiono and Masaru Kitsuregawa

Institute of Industrial Science,
The University of Tokyo
4-6-1 Komaba, Meguro-ku,
Tokyo 153-8505, Japan
{iko,kitsure}@tkl.iis.u-tokyo.ac.jp

Abstract. Frequent pattern mining has become a fundamental technique for many data mining tasks. Many modern frequent pattern mining algorithms such as FP-growth adopt tree structure to compress database into on-memory compact data structure. Recent studies show that the tree structure can be efficiently mined using frequent pattern growth methodology. Higher level of performance improvement can be expected from parallel execution. In particular, PC cluster is gaining popularity as the high cost-performance parallel platform for data extensive task like data mining. However, we have to address many issues such as space distribution on each node and skew handling to efficiently mine frequent patterns from tree structure on a shared-nothing environment. We develop a framework to address those issues using novel granularity control mechanism and tree remerging. The common framework can be enhanced with temporal constrain to mine web access patterns. We invent improved support counting procedure to reduce the additional communication overhead. Real implementation using up to 32 nodes confirms that good speedup ratio can be achieved even on skewed environment.

1 Introduction

Frequent pattern is defined as the pattern, which can be a set of items or a sequence, that occurs together in a database frequent enough to satisfy a certain minimum threshold [1,3]. The frequent pattern is important since it indicates a certain regularity in the database. The frequent pattern mining is also the key step in many data mining tasks such as association rule mining, sequence pattern mining etc.

Recently a paradigm has become a new trend in the field of frequent pattern mining research. The paradigm is often called pattern growth or divide-and-conquer. The main idea of the paradigm is the projection of database into a compact on-memory data structure and then use divide-and-conquer method to extract frequent patterns from the data structure. One of the most successful pioneering algorithms is FP-growth [5]. FP-growth devises a data structure called FP-tree that collects all information required to mine frequent patterns.

V. Mařík et al. (Eds.): DEXA 2003, LNCS 2736, pp. 537–547, 2003.

The need for faster frequent pattern mining has motivated the development of parallel algorithms [8,2,10,7]. In addition, parallel platforms have become more affordable. In particular, PC cluster that composed of commodity components is a promising high cost-performance platform. However the development of parallel algorithms for PC cluster has to face many hurdles such as the relatively poor network latency and bandwidth, and memory constraint. Recently some works also address the heterogeneity of PC cluster configuration [6]. Since the life cycle of PCs has been becoming very short, upgrading a PC cluster means adding newer generation of PCs to existing configuration. A parallel execution on such mixed environment needs adaptive parallel algorithm to balance the workload.

Here we report the development of tree structure based parallel frequent pattern mining algorithm for parallel execution on heterogenous PC cluster. We also address some methods for load balancing and better memory space utilization since complex data structures like tree tend to increase processing skew. Other contribution is that our framework of parallelization can be easily adapted for other tree structure based algorithms. We show that by the implementation of parallel web access pattern mining [4,9]. Optimization to reduce the intercommunication is also proposed.

2   FP-Growth

The FP-growth algorithm can be divided into two phases : the construction of the FP-tree and mining frequent patterns from the FP-tree [5].

2.1   Construction of FP-Tree

The construction of the FP-tree requires two scans of the transaction database. The first scan accumulates the support of each item and then selects items that satisfy minimum support, i.e. frequent 1-itemsets. Those items are sorted in frequency descending order to form F-list. The second scan constructs the FP-tree.

First, the transactions are reordered according to the F-list, while non-frequent items are stripped off. Then reordered transactions are inserted into the FP-tree. If the node corresponding to the items in transaction exists the count of the node is increased, otherwise a new node is generated and the count is set to one.

The FP-tree also has a frequent-item header table that holds the head of the node-links, which connect nodes of same item in FP-tree. The node-links facilitate item traversal during mining of frequent patterns.

2.2   FP-Growth

Input to the FP-growth algorithm are the FP-tree and the minimum support. To find all frequent patterns whose support are higher than minimum support,

FP-growth traverses nodes in the FP-tree starting from the least frequent item in F-list.

While visiting each node, FP-growth also collects the prefix-path of the node, that is the set of items on the path from the node to the root of the tree. FP-growth also stores the count on the node as the count of the prefix path. The prefix paths form the so-called *conditional pattern base* of that item.

The conditional pattern base is a small database of patterns that co-occur with the item. Then FP-growth creates small FP-tree from the conditional pattern base called *conditional FP-tree*. The process is recursively iterated until no conditional pattern base can be generated and all frequent patterns that contain the item are discovered.

3   Parallel Execution of FP-Growth

From Lemma 1, it is natural to consider the processing of conditional pattern base as the execution unit for the parallel processing.

Lemma 1. *The processing of a conditional pattern base is independent from other conditional pattern base.*

Proof. From the definition of the conditional pattern base, item a's conditional pattern base generation is only determined by existence of the item a in the database. The conditional pattern base is generated by traversing the node-links. The resulting conditional pattern base is unaffected by node-links of other items since node-link connects nodes of same item only and there is no node deletion during the processing of the FP-tree.   □

3.1   Trivial Parallelization

The basic idea is that each node accumulates a complete conditional pattern base and processes it independently to the completion before receiving other conditional pattern bases. Pseudo code for this algorithm is depicted in Fig. 2 (right) and the illustration is given in Fig. 1.

Basically, we need two kind of processes : SEND process and RECV process. After the first scan of transaction database, SEND process exchanges the support count of all items to determine globally frequent items. Then each node builds F-list since it also has global support count. Notice that each node will have the identical F-list. At the second database scan, SEND process builds a local FP-tree from the local transaction database with respect to the global F-list.

From the local FP-tree, local conditional pattern bases are generated. SEND process use hash function to determine which node should process it, instead of processing conditional pattern base locally. The RECV process at the destination node will collect the conditional pattern bases from all SEND processes and then executes the FP-growth. We can do this because of the following lemma :

Lemma 2. *Accumulation of local conditional pattern bases results in the global conditional FP-tree.*

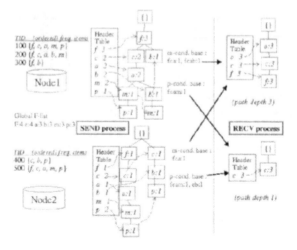

Fig. 1. Illustration of trivial parallel execution

Proof. When a prefix-path in the global conditional FP-tree already exists, the counts of prefix-paths in the other conditional pattern bases are simply added to the path in the tree. Thus the final global conditional FP-tree is not affected by how the prefix-paths are contained in the conditional pattern bases.   □

The lemma also automatically leads to the following lemma that will be useful when we are discussing how to handle the memory constraint.

Lemma 3. *The way to split the branches of FP-tree does not affect the resulting conditional pattern bases.*

3.2   Path Depth

It is obvious to achieve good parallelization, we have to consider the granularity of the execution unit or parallel task. Granularity is the amount of computation done in parallel relative to the size of the whole program.

Lemma 4. *Path depth can be calculated when creating FP-tree.*

Proof. FP-tree contains all the frequent patterns, thus the depth, the distance of a node from the root, of an item is also preserved in the tree structure. Thus, it can be collected during or after the generation of FP-tree.   □

When the execution unit is the processing of a conditional pattern base, the granularity is determined by number of iterations to generate subsequent conditional pattern bases. The number of iteration is exponentially proportional with the depth of the longest frequent path in the conditional pattern base. Thus, here we define *path depth* as the measure of the granularity.

Definition 1. *Path depth is the longest path in the conditional pattern base whose count satisfies minimum support count.*

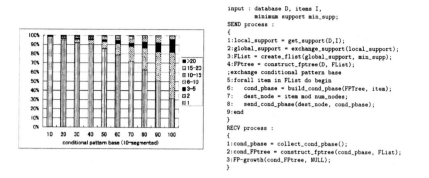

```
input : database D, items I,
        minimum support min_supp;
SEND process :
{
1:local_support = get_support(D,I);
2:global_support = exchange_support(local_support);
3:FList = create_flist(global_support, min_supp);
4:FPtree = construct_fptree(D, FList);
;exchange conditional pattern base
5:forall item in FList do begin
6:    cond_pbase = build_cond_pbase(FPTree, item);
7:    dest_node = item mod num_nodes;
8:    send_cond_pbase(dest_node, cond_pbase);
9:end
}
RECV process :
{
1:cond_pbase = collect_cond_pbase();
2:cond_FPtree = construct_fptree(cond_pbase, FList);
3:FP-growth(cond_FPtree, NULL);
}
```

Fig. 2. Path depth distribution (left) Trivial parallel pseudo code (right)

Example. In Fig. 1, the longest pattern that satisfies the minimum support count when processing m's conditional pattern base is <acf> then the path depth of m's conditional pattern base is three.

Typical path depth distribution of conditional pattern base is given in Fig. 2 (left). When the items following F-list order are divided into ten equal segments, the vertical axis represents the distribution of path depth for each segment. For example if F-list contains 100 items from 1 to 100, the third segment contains items range from 71 to 80. Most of conditional pattern base have small path depth, but some have very large path depth. Since the granularity differs greatly, many nodes with smaller granularity will have to wait busy nodes with large granularity.

To achieve better parallel performance, we have to split parallel tasks with large granularity. Since the path depth can be calculated when creating FP-tree, we can predict in advance how to split the parallel tasks.

Here we use the iterative property of FP-growth that a conditional pattern base can create conditional FP-tree, which in turn can generate smaller conditional pattern bases. Note that at each iteration, the path depths of subsequent conditional pattern bases are decremented by one.

Therefore, we can control the granularity by specifying a *minimum path depth*. Any conditional pattern base whose path depth is smaller than the threshold will be immediately executed until completion; otherwise, it is executed only until the generation of subsequent conditional pattern bases. Then the generated conditional pattern bases are stored, some of them might be executed at the same node or sent to other idle nodes. Since node with heavy processing load can split the load and disperses it to other nodes, path depth approach can also absorb the processing skew among nodes to some extent. Complete pseudo code of this mechanism is depicted in Fig. 3 (left).

3.3   Memory Constraint

As the data is getting bigger, one of the first resources to get exhausted is local memory. Distributed memory helps alleviate. However, the distribution of

```
SEND process :
{
1:cond_pbase = get_stored_cond_pbase();
2:if(cond_pbase is not NULL) then
3:  send_cond_pbase(cond_pbase);
4:end if
}
RECV process :
{
1:cond_pbase = get_stored_cond_pbase();
2:if(cond_pbase is NULL) then
3:  cond_pbase = receive_cond_pbase();
4:end if
5:cond_FPtree = construct_fptree(cond_pbase, FList);
6:FP-growth(cond_FPtree, cond_pbase.itemset);
}
procedure FP-growth(FPtree, X);
input : FP-tree Tree, itemset X;
{
1:for each item y in the header of Tree do {
2:  generate pattern Y = y U X with
      support = y.support;
3:  cond_pbase = construct_cond_pbase(Tree, y);
4:  if (cond_pbase.path_depth < min_path_depth) then
5:     Y-Tree = construct_fptree(cond_pbase,Y-FList);
6:     if (Y-Tree is not NULL) then
7:        FP-growth(Y-Tree, Y);
8:     end if
9:  else
10:    store_cond_pbase(cond_pbase, Y);
11:  end if
12:end for
}
```

```
construct_fptree(database D, flist FList)
input : database D, F-list FList;
output : FP-tree FPtree;
{
1:while not eof(D) do
2:  line = read_trans(D);
3:  o_trans = get_ordered_trans(line);
4:  if available_memory() < mem_lim then
5:     mig_item_lim = next_branch_migration(FPtree);
6:     dest_node = hash(mig_item_lim);
7:     migrate_tree_branch(dest_node, FPtree);
8:  end if
9:  if head_of(o_trans) > mig_item_lim then
10:    dest_node = hash(head_of(o_trans));
11:    migrate_trans(dest_node, o_trans);
12: else
13:    insert_fptree(FPtree, o_trans);
14: end if
15: receive_trans(o_trans);
16: if (o_trans is not NULL)
17:    insert_fptree(FPtree, o_trans);
18:end while
19:mig_plan = balancing_tree_size(FPtree);
20:reallocate_branch(FPtree, mig_plan);
}
```

Fig. 3. Pseudo code : path depth (left) remerging tree (right)

FP-tree over nodes is also accompanied by space overhead since some identical prefix-paths are redundantly created at different nodes.

We can eliminate the space redundancy if the branches of FP-tree are re-merged, i.e. each branch of FP-tree is allocated exactly to only one node. Lemma 3 guarantees that we can safely modify the way to split FP-tree.

As depicted in Fig. 3 (right), when we detect that the available memory drops below *mem_lim* threshold, we pick next larger branch in FP-tree for migration. Here the notion branch means all prefix paths with the same root item. The variable *mig_item_lim* now holds the last migrated item. The destination node is decided with hash function. Then we migrate the whole branch to the destination node. The destination node receives all prefix paths with the same root item from all nodes. In other word, the branches of the item are *remerged* from all local FP-trees to a particular destination node.

Then while reading the transaction database, if the head of the ordered transaction *o_trans* is one of the migrated items, the ordered transaction is sent to appropriate node, otherwise it is inserted to the local FP-tree.

At the end, we have to examine whether the size of local FP-trees is fairly balanced among the nodes. If there is significant skew of FP-tree size distribution, a migration plan of FP-tree branches is derived to balance the skew.

4   Mining Web Access Patterns

Essentially, a web access pattern is a sequential pattern in a large set of parts of a web log, which is pursued frequently by users. The problem of mining sequential patterns was first addressed by AprioriAll algorithm [4].

Here our parallel algorithm is based on WAP-mine. WAP-mine also uses a tree data structure called WAP-tree to register access sequences and corresponding counts compactly [9].

With little modification described here, our common framework for tree data structure can be applied for parallel execution of WAP-mine.

4.1   WAP-Mine

Since the order of the sequence has to be preserved, WAP-mine does not need to sort the items, thus it does not create F-list. WAP-mine also differs from FP-growth in the way of support counting.

In a web access sequence, there are many occasions where the same page is visited more than once. For example in the sequence <abacad>, the page a is visited three times. However the support of the item in the sequence is only one.

To avoid double counting, WAP-mine devises an unsubsumed count property. For each prefix sequence of item a with count c, inserted into a-conditional pattern base, all of its sub-prefix sequences are inserted also but with count -c.

4.2   Intercommunication Reduction

The unsubsumed count property correctly counts the support of items in the sequences, the size of conditional pattern base increases linearly with the number of the item duplications in the sequences. Since our parallelization scheme exchanges the conditional pattern bases, a lot of data has to be sent through the network.

To reduce the size of conditional pattern bases, we use a *direct count decrement* method. While traversing the path from the node to the root in order to collect the prefix-sequence of item a with count c, we simply decrement c from the count of the duplicate nodes directly. The duplicate node here is the node on the path with the same item label a. Thus we do not have to generate the sub-prefix sequences. In addition, if the count of a duplicate node becomes zero, we do not have to generate the conditional pattern base starting from the node.

Our method significantly saves both time to generate the conditional pattern base and the required network bandwidth. We omit the proof of the correctness and efficiency analysis here due to the space limitation.

5   Implementation and Performance Evaluation

Here we give the detail of implementation and the results of experiments.

5.1   Implementation

As the shared nothing environment for this experiment we use a PC cluster of 47 nodes that are interconnected by a 100Base-TX Ethernet Switch. There are two types of configuration : (A) older 32 nodes have 800MHz Pentium III and

128 MB of main memory, and (B) newer 15 nodes have a 1.5 GHz Pentium4 and 384 MB of main memory. The operating system is Solaris 8. The programs are developed in C using native socket library.

Three processes are running on each node :

(1) SEND process

creates FP-tree, and sends conditional pattern bases.

(2) RECV process

receives the conditional pattern bases, and processes conditional pattern bases after exchanging phase finishes.

(3) EXEC process

processes the conditional pattern bases in background during the exchanging phase.

There are also small COORD processes that receive requests for the conditional pattern bases from idle nodes and coordinate how to distribute them.

5.2   Performance Evaluation

For performance evaluation, we use several types of datasets. However due to the space constraint, we only pick some representative results.

We use synthetically generated datasets as described in Apriori and AprioriAll papers[3,4]. The web sequences are treated as customer sessions. The term transaction here is used also to represent a sequence. The following notions are used for data generation : the number of transactions (D), the number of items (i), the average transaction size (T) and the average of maximal potentially frequent itemset (I). For example T25.I20.D100K.i10K means that in the dataset, number of transactions in the dataset is set to 100K with 10K items. And the average transaction size and average maximal potentially frequent itemset size are set to 25 and 20 respectively.

Comparison with HPA. First we compare the performance of our parallel FP-growth with that of Hash Partitioned Apriori(HPA), a variant of parallel Apriori with better memory utilization schema[10]. HPA improves the Apriori by partitioning the candidate patterns among the member nodes in the cluster using hash function. To count the support of all candidate itemsets, each node reads its local transactions data and applies the same hash function to determine where to send the item combinations.

The dataset is T15.I4.D1M.i5k. he experiments are conducted on 2, 4, 8, and 15 nodes of configuration B. The execution time for minimum supports of 0.03% and 0.05% are shown in Fig. 4 (left). Notice that the execution time (y-axis) is log scale. The results show that the parallel FP-growth outperforms HPA at least an order of magnitude for this dataset.

Speedup Ratio. We also measure the speedup ratio that is the ratio of performance gain when more processing nodes are used. Here we show the results with up to 32 nodes of configuration A. The dataset is T25.I20.D100K.i5K.

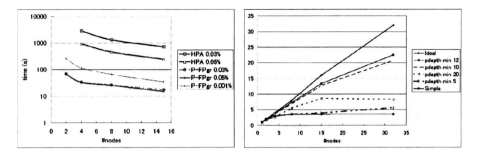

Fig. 4. Execution time T15.I4.D1M.i5k(left) Speedup ratio T25.I20.D100K.i5K 0.1%(right)

Fig. 4 (right) shows that path depth greatly affects the speedup achieved by the parallel execution. The trivial parallelization, denoted by "Simple", performs worst since almost no speedup achieved after four nodes. This is obvious since the execution time is bounded by the busiest node, that is node that has to process conditional pattern base with highest path depth.

When the minimum path depth is too low such as "pdepth min = 5", the speedup ratio is not improved because there are too many small conditional pattern bases that have to be stored thus the overhead is too large. On the other hand, when the minimum path depth is too high, as represented by "pdepth min = 20", the granularity is too large so that the load is not balanced sufficiently.

When the minimum path depth is optimum, sufficiently good speedup ratio can be achieved. For "pdepth min = 12", parallel execution on eight nodes can gain speedup ratio of 7.3. Even on 16 nodes and 32 nodes, we still can get 13.4 and 22.6 times faster performance respectively.

However finding the optimal value of minimum path depth is not a trivial task yet, and it is becoming one of our future works.

Heterogeneous Environment. We set up a heterogeneous environment with three nodes of the configuration B and one node of the slower configuration A. We also allocate more data on the slowest node to mimic data skew. 70.000 transactions of T25.I10.D100K.i10K dataset are stored in that node while the rest 30.000 transactions are distributed evenly among other nodes.

The execution trace in the left part of Fig. 5 (left) shows that without path depth, the faster nodes are left idle before the node pc025 (the bottom graph) finishes. After employing the path depth adjustment, we get a more balanced execution as shown in right part of Fig. 5 (left). The overall time is improved from 400s to 317s. The minimum path depth here is 12.

Remerging FP-Tree. Here we show that remerging FP-tree such as depicted in subsection 3.3 can help relaxing the memory constraint of parallel FP-growth. It is important since if on memory FP-tree consumes too much memory space, further processing will be inflicted by memory thrashing. Figure 5 (right) shows

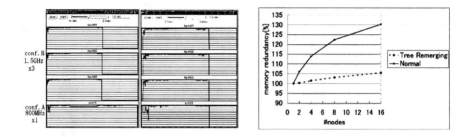

Fig. 5. Execution trace, heterogeneous (left) Global memory consumption(right)

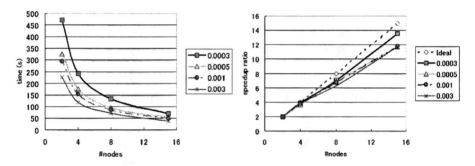

Fig. 6. Execution time (left) Speedup ratio (right) for T20.I10.D1M.i10K

the total number of nodes in the all FP-trees relative to those in single node. The horizontal axis represents the number of processing nodes while the vertical axis represents the memory redundancy. For this experiment, we remerge all branches of FP-tree except the largest one whose root is the most frequent item. The dataset is T25.I20.D100K.i10K with minimum support 0.1%.

One can infer that without remerging FP-tree, 30% more memory is needed by all nodes for parallel execution with 16 nodes. When we employ the remerging FP-tree only 5% of memory is wasted globally. One can also observe that the space saving is becoming more significant when the number of processing nodes is increasing. Thus, the remerging FP-tree potentially can leverage the execution of very large scale data on massive array of processing nodes.

Mining Web Access Patterns. We have varied the minimum support to see how it affects performance. The experiments are conducted on 2, 4, 8 and 15 nodes of configuration B with dataset T20.I10.D1M.i10K. The execution time for minimum support of 0.0003%, 0.00005%, 0.001% and 0.003% is shown in Fig. 6 (left).

Figure 6 (right) shows that good speedup ratio is achieved for all minimum support. When the minimum support is set to 0.0003%, 15 processing nodes gain 13.6 times faster performance. Our algorithm suitably balances the processing load and keeps the intercommunication overhead low. When the minimum support is lower, the overhead is relatively smaller, thus the speedup is improved.

6 Conclusion

The development of tree structure based parallel algorithm has to address several issues. We have used the FP-growth as the underlying algorithm and proposed *path depth* based mechanism to break down the granularity of parallel processing. The parallel execution on a PC cluster proves that it is much faster than other parallel algorithm called HPA and it also achieves sufficient speedup ratio up to 32 nodes.

Skew handling is also important on heterogenous environment where the configuration of each node is different. We have shown that the path depth can handle such mixed configuration.

We also showed that the way to partition the FP-tree among nodes does not affect the final result of FP-growth. Based on the observation we proposed a method to remerge FP-tree among nodes to save global memory consumption. In particular, parallel execution with many processing nodes will be benefited from remerging FP-tree.

Our parallel framework has the potential to enhance the performance of other pattern-growth paradigm based modern algorithms. We have shown that mining web access patterns can be implemented efficiently using the framework. We are planning to implement other algorithms on our framework.

References

[1] R. Agrawal, T. Imielinski, A. Swami. "Mining Association Rules between Sets of Items in Large Databases". In *Proc. of the ACM SIGMOD Conference on Management of Data*, 1993.

[2] R. Agrawal and J. C. Shafer. "Parallel Mining of Associaton Rules". In *IEEE Transaction on Knowledge and Data Engineering*, Vol. 8, No. 6, pp. 962–969, December, 1996.

[3] R. Agrawal and R. Srikant. "Fast Algorithms for Mining Association Rules". In *Proceedings of the 20th Int. Conf. on VLDB*, pp. 487–499, September 1994.

[4] R. Agrawal and R. Srikant. "Mining Sequential Patterns". In *Proc. of International Conference of Data Engineering*, pp. 3–14, March 1995.

[5] J. Han, J. Pei and Y. Yin "Mining Frequent Pattern without Candidate Generation" In *Proc. of the ACM SIGMOD Conf. on Management of Data*, 2000

[6] K. Goda, T. Tamura, M. Oguci, and M. Kitsuregawa "Run-time Load Balancing System on SAN-connected PC Cluster for Dynamic Injection of CPU and Disk Resource" In *Proc of 13th Int. Conf. on Database and Expert Systems Applications (DEXA'02)*, 2002

[7] S. Orlando, P. Palmerini, R. Perego, and F. Silvestri "Adaptive and Resource-Aware Mining of Frequent Sets" In *Proc. of the Int. Conf. on Data Mining*, 2002

[8] J.S.Park, M.-S.Chen, P.S.Yu "Efficient Parallel Algorithms for Mining Association Rules" In *Proc. of 4th Int. Conf. on Information and Knowledge Management (CIKM'95)*, pp. 31–36, November, 1995

[9] J. Pei, J. Han, B. Mortazavi-asl and H. Zhu "Mining Access Patterns Efficiently from Web Logs" In *Proc. of fourth Pacific-Asia Conference in Knowledge Discovery and Data Mining(PAKDD'00)*, 2000.

[10] T. Shintani and M. Kitsuregawa "Hash Based Parallel Algorithms for Mining Association Rules". In *IEEE Fourth Int. Conf. on Parallel and Distributed Information Systems*, pp. 19–30, December 1996.

WebObjects: A New Approach for Querying the Web

Fábio Soares Silva[1], Marcus Costa Sampaio[2], and Cláudio S. Baptista[2]

[1] Universidade Tiradentes,
55 (79) 218-2121
300 Murilo Dantas – Farolândia,
Aracaju, Sergipe, Brazil
fabio_soares@unit.br
[2] Universidade Federal de Campina Grande,
55 (83) 310 1119
Av. Aprígio Veloso, 882 Bodocongó,
Campina Grande, Paraíba, Brazil
{sampaio,baptista}@dsc.ufcg.edu.br

Abstract. Although there is a great effort on the development of Web search engines, search results are still poor in terms of precision and recall. This paper presents *WebObjects*, a new approach for querying the Web. *WebObjects* consists of a framework which enables Web searching using OQL queries according to the ODMG 3.0 standard. By using this query language we obtain high expressiveness on Web searching and it maximizes precision. Moreover, *WebObjects* validates the result set in order to avoid broken links. Finally, experimental results using the framework are reported.

1 Introduction

Although there is a great effort on the development of searching tools for the Web, high level tools, which maximize precision and recall, are still demanded. Nowadays, there are many search engines for querying the Web, but most of them are restricted to keyword matches and their interfaces are too limited ([1], [2]).

Moreover, an increasing number of Database Management Systems (DBMS) are connected to the Web. Hence, we need an integrated tool, which is able to query these structured data stored in DBMS and non-structured or semi-structured data stored in the Web.

This paper proposes *WebObjects* which is a new approach for querying the Web. *WebObjects*. is a framework that contains a virtual data scheme to represent the Web, and a declarative query language. Therefore, *WebObjects* enables searching the Web with high expressiveness, without requiring a previous knowledge of the complex Web structure.

The *WebObjects* main features include ODMG 3.0 standard compliance [3]; independence of platform; access to structured and semi-structured data; an Application Programming Interface (API) to be used by other applications; and optimization of OQL/ODMG queries.

Therefore, *WebObjects* can be used either by end-users who produce queries over the Web, or by applications which use the provided API. The rest of this paper is

V. Mařík et al. (Eds.): DEXA 2003, LNCS 2736, pp. 548–557, 2003.

structured as follows. Section 2 discusses related work. Section 3 describes the *WebObjects* framework. Section 4 focuses on the framework architecture. Experimental results are the subject of section 5. Finally, section 6 concludes the paper and discusses further work to be undertaken.

2 Related Work

Many related works have been presented in the literature. In this section we briefly discuss some of them such as WebSQL [4], WebOQL [5], WSQ/DSQ [2], XML-QL [6], Squeal [7].

WebSQL models the Web as a relational schema. Queries on this scheme are specified using an SQL-like language. However, the query language uses many elements from the SQL standard, which makes difficult its use and assimilation.

WebOQL maps the Web in a hierarchical scheme, using an OQL/ODMG-like query language. The main characteristic of this solution is the ability to represent structured and semi-structured data. Nevertheless, the use of a non object-oriented model imposes the addition of several elements to the language, dismissing it from the OQL/ODMG standard. Besides, its use becomes difficult due to the language complexity.

WSQ/DSQ proposes a solution that uses the SQL language for querying structured and non-structured data available on the Web. In addition, it offers Web-DBMS integration. Unfortunately, WSQ/DSQ does not offer mechanisms to Web topology exploration. Moreover, it does not lead with search engines in a transparent way.

The XML/QL language provides extraction, restructuring and integration of XML files. However, XML/QL has many restrictions including limited use of the Web topology and searching restricted to XML files.

Squeal is an extension of WebSQL data scheme, once it extends the number of available information to users. The main drawbacks of this solution include the restrictions imposed by the relational model, and its lack of support for the dynamic nature of the web data.

3 The WebObjects Framework

The *WebObjects* framework consists of a software layer which uses traditional search engines for querying Web content. However, it implements a query processor which validates the result set obtained from search engines, maximizing precision.

The implementation of a query processor for the Web involves the representation of the Web as a generic, flexible and extensible database schema which offers support for a query language with high expressiveness. In addition to that, the complexity of query processing is associated essentially to the following factors: the diversity of patterns, types and technologies used in the Web, and both the huge volume and physical distribution of data. The combination of the last two factors requires interaction with a diversity of services and data, supported by several servers, with autonomous management and administration.

In the *WebObjects* framework, the Web is modeled as a virtual database – a Web view –, i.e., without any physical and local data storage. Queries are written according

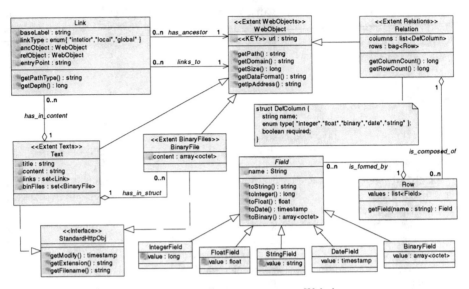

Fig. 1. UML class diagram to represent Web data

to this Web view and, then, mapped and submitted to search engines. The query processor validates each retrieved URL. The latter will be part of the result set if it exists and its content is according to the query criteria. This strategy allows eliminating from query answer inaccurate results due to the use of search engine off-line catalogues. Thus, *WebObjects* provides more accurate results.

Complex objects are an excellent way to represent the great diversity of Web data. *WebObjects* follows the object-oriented data model standard proposed by the ODMG (Object Data Management Group) committee in its 3.0 version [3]. This data model is composed basically by the ODL textual language (Object Data Language) for data schema definition, and by OQL (Object Query Language). ODL is complemented by UML (Unified Modeling Language) diagrams .

Currently, *WebObjects* consider the Web as composed by HTML documents, relational tables and image files related to HTML documents. Fig. 1 presents the UML class diagram that represents the Web in *WebObjects*.

According to Fig. 1, Web content is modeled as virtual extents of classes *WebObject*, *Relation*, *Text* and *BinaryFile*. The *Relation*, *Text* and *BinaryFile* are subclasses of *WebObject* class. Hence, the *WebObjects* extent comprehends the whole query space of *WebObjects* framework

The *WebObject* class defines general features – attributes and relationships – of any Web object (e.g. HTML documents, relational tables or image files) which is handled by the framework. Through inheritance and polymorphism, this class is extended to define specialized behavior. This feature provides extensibility to the *WebObjects* data schema. Fig. 2 contains a representation of a hypothetic university website: "www.unit.br".

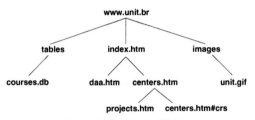

Fig. 2. A University Website

WebObjects supports link redundancy, which facilitates a search language that does not support recursion, such as OQL . According to Mendelzon et al. [10], the exploration capacity of a hyperlink structure is fundamental to any Web search mechanism. Besides the mentioned redundancy, the WebObjects framework offers the linkType attribute and the getPathType() and getDepth()methods.

As an example of the *Link* class, consider an object with the following URL: "http://www.unit.br/index.htm". In Fig. 2 , it can be noticed the direct links "daa" and "centers", and the transitive and redundant links "projects" and "courses".

The *linkType* attribute represents the relation of localization between a text object and an object addressed by the *refObject* attribute of its hyperlinks. This attribute contains one of the following values: *interior*, which indicates that the pointed object is in the same document of the object (e.g. the document "courses" is inside the document "centers"); *local*, which indicates that the pointed object is in the same server of the object (e.g. "centers" and "projects" are in the same server of "index"); and *global*, which indicates that the pointed object is in a different server from that where the object is located (e.g."daa" is not in the same server of "index").

The getPathType() method of the *Link* class retrieves the relation of localization between the object and the hyperlinks accessed up to the mentioned object. As illustration, getPathType() to the *Link* "courses" into "index" returns "local;interior", showing that, to access "courses" from "index", an hyperlink must be accessed to a "local" object related to "index", which has as inside attribute the value "courses". In the previous example, the getDepth() method would return 2, which is the number of accessed objects.

Finally, the hyperlinks that point to a document anchor, are mapped by the *Link* class using the *entryPoint* attribute. When the target is the beginning of the page, this attribute has null value (nil), otherwise, it has the HTML tag that represents the document anchor.

3.1 Querying the Web

This section presents two query examples using the OQL syntax in *WebObjects*. The database instance is the one presented in Fig. 2.

Query 1: Retrieve all text documents in the "www.unit.br" domain that have at least one hyperlink and also have some images in gif, jpeg or jpg format.

```
select distinct t.url
  from Texts t, t.binFiles f
  where t.getDomain() = "www.unit.br" and
        t.links != nil and t.binFiles != nil and
        f.getExtension() in( "gif", "jpeg", "jpg" );
```

In this example, two OQL interesting features are used. The first one allows the searching of the whole collection of binary elements joined to each text document (Text class), through the t.binFiles construction specified in the FROM statement clause. The f variant verifies if a pointed object is an image.

Query 2: Obtain the domain, the IP address of the server and the size of UNIT professor home pages entailed to center 01.

```
select r.urlProf, w.getDomain(), w.getIpAddress(),
       w.getSize()
  from Relations r, WebObjects w
  where (r.url="http://www.unit.br/professors.db") and
        (r.urlProf=w.url ) and ( r.centerCod=01 );
```

This example evidences the WebObjects framework capacity of joining data derived from relational tables with Web data.

4 Architecture and Implementation

The core of the *WebObjects* framework is the query processor which is implemented by a Java class library. This processor is able to recognize, interpret and execute queries written in OQL using an UML/ODL conceptual data schema. Any application written in Java can use the services offered by the framework, through its API. The application can interact with the user, capture her requests, and convert them into an OQL query that will be submitted to the framework. The framework processes the request and returns either a collection of objects which satisfy the user request, or an error message, in case of an exception in the query is launched.

Fig. 3 shows the *WebObjects* framework architecture, its components and the interaction among them. The lexical-syntactic analyzer is the framework component that starts the query execution process. Its basic tasks include the parsing of the OQL statement as a valid constructor for the language; running the types validation and generating an intermediary code that will serve as a base for the query processor to solve the request. This intermediary code consists of a data structure built from the analysis and decomposition of the original OQL statement. If there are errors during this parsing process, an error massage is generated by the framework.

The next step is the use of two components: the code generator and the *WebObjects* virtual machine. The code generator is responsible for analyzing the symbols table, and for creating a query execution plan with specific instructions of the *WebObjects* virtual machine. During this process, the dependence between the access to several extents of data schema is analyzed, and the sequence through which the data will be accessed is defined. The code generator also performs a very simple analysis of query costs, which interrupts the execution of those the cost of which is considered prohibitive to be solved. Basically, this cost analysis verifies the query capacity of filtering Web elements.

Once the execution plan is defined, the *WebObjects* virtual machine begins the query execution itself. The virtual machine is composed by an instruction set; an interpreter, which is able to execute those instructions; and a class set, which is able to access Web information, instanciating the data schema objects with the collected information.

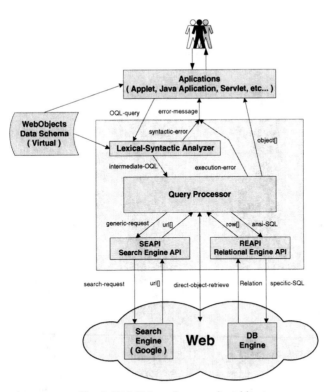

Fig. 3. WebObjects framework architecture

The Web data can be captured by two different ways: either by using the direct access to the objects through http protocol or by calling SEAPI and REAPI API. Direct access can be performed by using a Java API which obtains available information from Web servers. The framework API was developed basically to make possible the communication with search engines (SEAPI) and the access to relational database systems (REAPI).

The SEAPI (Search Engine API) is responsible for the integration of *WebObjects* with several search engines. This feature is implemented by SEAPI as a generic interface that is used by the query process to generate the requests. Once the search is executed, the SEAPI converts the request into a proprietary format, and send it to the search engine. The result set consists of URLs that satisfy the search condition. Thus, in order to incorporate a new search engine into the framework it is necessary to extend the SEAPI.

The same principle is used in the REAPI (Relational Engine API), which receives the requests to access the relational databases in SQL-ANSI and convert them into an SQL owner format. Again, the extensibility provided by the SEAPI is applied to REAPI, so that different DBMS can be integrated into the framework.

In the analysis and retrieval process, the *WebObjects* framework uses the principle of accessing data only when they are effectively necessary. For that, it uses a technique of condition evaluation in curt circuit, besides the validations in the URLs which avoid trying to retrieve unavailable data. The capture classes of Web data are implemented to retrieve information only when they are really needed. For instance, a Text object does not need to have its content retrieved and processed if the user wants to know just the file size where the object is stored.

5   Experimental Results

The experimental assessment of the framework was performed through the creation of some Java applications that use the main features offered by *WebObjects*. In this paper, we will describe shortly two 3-tier applications using the JSP technology.

The first application is the htmlExplorer. This tool enables the retrieval of structured data of an HTML document. This permits, among other things, the investigation of hyperlinks that are pointing to unavailable documents. The user may enter an URL and the htmlExplorer retrieves the basic data from that page, such as the title and size in bytes, the existent hyperlinks – the unavailable ones appear explicitly – and the image files related to the page.

In the implementation of this application, the most complicated task was associated with the development of the user interface. Indeed, regarding the retrieval process, only the following code was necessary:

```
Query q = new Query(
    "select t from Texts t " +
    "where t.url=\"" + urlDesc + "\";" );
```

This program code uses the *Query* class for the query execution in the *WebObjects* framework. This class receives an URL as a parameter – urlDesc – and retrieves the respective Text object. Then, by calling the class methods, all the information for the page mounting is retrieved.

The other JSP application, the *webExplorer*, implements a query tool to the Web such as the one supplied by the conventional DBMS. It offers to users the possibility of specifying an OQL query and obtaining the result set. This application has also used the *Query* class, but the OQL statement is passed as a parameter. The query result is processed through the calls to hasMoreElement() – which returns true if there are still elements to be returned – and nextElement() methods – which returns a vector of objects for each element of the result set.

5.1   Comparison between the webExplorer and the Google

We will use the webExplorer application to compare *WebObjects* framework with the Google search engine. However, the comparison between these tools is limited to the retrieval of Web documents content. It is important to mention that apart from searching Web page content, webExplorer offers mechanisms for topology exploration, and the possibility of querying both relational databases and Web documents.

In order to proceed with the comparison, let us use an example. Suppose an user wants to find pages about the best soccer player of the last Word Cup. Also, she wants to filter documents located in a specific server and wih a specific size. For that, a search using the words "best soccer player", "Oliver Kahn" e "world cup" was submitted to Google. In webExplorer, the query was performed using the following statement:

```
select t.url as URL, t.getSize() as Size,
       t.getIpAddress() as IP, t.getModify() as Date
from Texts t
where ( t.getIpAddress() like "66.%" or
        t.getSize() > 50000 ) and
      ( t.content like "World Cup" ) and
      ( t.content like "Oliver Kahn" ) and
      ( t.content like "Best Soccer Player" );
```

The first point to observe is the semantic wealth of the OQL statement compared to the search using only keywords. Particularly, Google does not allow the use of complex boolean conditions. Besides, the webExplorer permits the capture of any document data that interest the user.

Table 1 shows a parallel between the information retrieved by Google and webExplorer.

The analysis of the results of both applications shows clearly the improved precision offered by *WebObjects* framework. In the example, three of the URLs that are not according to the query specification are eliminated automatically from the result by webExplorer, while in Google this task would be made by the user.

Moreover, the example demonstrates the capacity of data capture offered by the framework, such as IP address; document hyperlinks and binary files; and updated date of the last modification. This information can not be retrieved by search engines such as Google.

Other point to be mentioned is the accuracy offered by the *WebObjects* framework when compared to search engines. As the catalogues used by search engines are off-line, websites that were changed or that are unavailable when the search was performed will be returned continually by Google. However, using the WebObjects framework, data are checked in order to assure that they are still available, avoiding broken links.

Obviously, the Google performance was better than the webExplorer one, as the former does not have the overhead associated with the validation of data on the Web. For the query example, the Google wasted about 3.5 seconds, while the webExplorer wasted about 11 seconds for mounting a page with 10 hits. However, the webExplorer answer time should not be considered too bad. Moreover, we should consider the low processing capacity of the computer used to assess the framework: a Pentium II 400 Mhz, 256 Mb of RAM memory, IDE disk and internet channel with 1 Mbps.

The performance obtained by *WebObjects* was improved due to the concurrent process of several documents (asynchronous iteration). This concurrent process balanced the latency in data capture. In the performance evaluation, the use of Java threads reduced 50% the average time of query execution, but in some cases the improvement was up to 85%. Of course, when the size of the result set increases, better are the results obtained through the asynchronous iteration. In small URL collections the query execution time generally was based on the retrieval of the highest latency document.

Finally, one of the greatest advantage of *WebObjects* framework compared to search engines is the facility offered by its features which enables programmers to create new applications that access the Web as a real database.

Table 1. Documents retrieved in Google (Goo) and WebExplorer (wExp)

Documents on result			Retrieved	
URL	Bytes	IP	Goo	wExp
http://cbc.ca/sports/soccer/playerprofile_beckham.html	21846	159.33.3.85	Yes	No
http://missouri.asfm.edu.mx/events/webfolders_5th/5h/webpages5h/rodrigo_e_5h_folder/rodrigo_5h.htm	2931	200.36.49.71	Yes	No
http://news.bbc.co.uk/sport3/worldcup2002/hi/sports_talk/newsid_2069000/2069337.stm	140377	212.58.240.131	Yes	Yes
http://bulletin.ninemsn.com.au/bulletin/edesk.nsf/All/49FF2EB1DDBF930DCA256BE80078D0B6	34660	203.41.45.3	Yes	No
http://www.geometry.net/athletes_soccer/nesta_alessandro_page_no_3.html	13232	66.13.172.114	Yes	Yes
http://www.geometry.net/athletes_soccer/rivaldo_page_no_2.html	17504	66.13.172.114	Yes	Yes
http://germany.newstrove.com/	245695	66.12.80.59	Yes	Yes

6 Conclusions and Future Work

WebObjects requirements have been fulfilled, among them we emphasize:
- it follows exactly the ODMG standard;
- it uses the OQL language, which has a high capacity of expression;
- it is independent of platform; it deals with relational tables, HTML documents and image files; and
- it has an extensible data schema for treating other data standards and data structures.

Concerning the framework evolution, there is still work to be accomplished. The first task is associated with the query optimization. Another task is to incorporate support for XML documents.

References

1. Manocha, Nitish, Cook, Diane J., Holder, Lawrence B.: Structural Web Search Using a Graph-Based Discovery System, in Proceedings of the Florida Articial Intelligence Research Symposium, Florida, USA (2001)
2. Goldman, Roy, Widom, Jennifer: WSQ/DSQ: A Pratical Approach for Combined Querying of Databases and the Web, in SIGMOD/PODS, Dallas, USA (2000)
3. Cattell, R. G. G., Barry, Douglas, Berler, Mark, Eastman, Jeff, Jordan, David, Russel, Craig, Schadow, Olaf, Stanienda, Torsen, Velez, Fernando: The Object Data Standard: ODMG 3.0. San Diego: Academic Press (2000)

4. Mihaila, George A. WebSQL: An SQL-like Query Language for the World Wide Web. MSc Thesis - Department of Computer Science in the University of Toronto (1997), Canada.
5. Arocena, Gustavo O., Mendelzon, Alberto O.: WebOQL: Reestructuring Documents, Databases e Webs, in 14th Intl. Conf. on Data Engineering (ICDE 98), Florida, USA (1998)
6. Deutsch, Alin, Fernandez, Mary, Florescu, Daniela, Levy, Alon, Suciu, Dan: XML-QL: A Query Language for XML, in 8th Internacional Conference on the World Wide Web, Toronto, Canada (1999)
7. Spertus, Ellen, Stein, Lynn A.: Squeal: A Structured Query Language for the Web, in Proceedings of the 9th International World Wide Web Conference, Amsterdam, Netherlands (2000)
8. Lakshmanan, Laks V. S., Sadri, Fereidoon, Subramanian, Iyer N.: A declarative Language for Querying and Restructuring the Web, in 6th Workshop on Research Issues in Data Engineering, New Orleans, USA (1996)
10.Mendelzon, Alberto O., Mihaila, George A., Milo, Tova: Querying the World Wide Web, in Journal of Digital Libraries 1 (1997):54–67

Finding Neighbor Communities in the Web Using Inter-site Graph

Yasuhito Asano[1], Hiroshi Imai[2], Masashi Toyoda[3],
and Masaru Kitsuregawa[3]

[1] Graduate School of Information Sciences,
Tohoku University
[2] Graduate School of Information Science and Technology,
The University of Tokyo
[3] Institute of Industrial Science,
The University of Tokyo

Abstract. In recent years, link-based information retrieval methods from the Web are developed. A framework of these methods is a Web graph using pages as vertices and Web-links as edges. In the last year, the authors have claimed that an inter-site graph using sites as vertices and global-links (links between sites) as edges is more natural and useful as a framework for link-based information retrieval than a Web graph. They have proposed *directory-based sites* as a new model of Web sites and established a method of identifying them from URL and Web-link data. They have examined that this method can identify directory-based sites almost correctly by using data of URLs and links in `.jp` domain. In this paper, we show that this framework is also useful for information retrieval in response to user's query. We develop a system called **Neighbor Community Finder** (NCF, for short). NCF finds Web communities related to given URLs by constructing an inter-site graph with neighborhood sites and links obtained from the real Web on demand. We show that in several cases NCF is a more effective tool for finding related pages than Google's service by computational experiments.

1 Introduction

In recent years, information retrieval methods from the Web using characteristic graph structures of the Web-links are developed. HITS proposed by Kleinberg [9] and Trawling proposed Kumar et al. [10] are examples of well-known such methods. Such information retrieval methods are based on the following idea: if page u has a link to page v, then page v is considered to contain valuable information by the author of u. Thus, these methods are considered to be algorithms running on a Web graph which consists of the pages as the vertices and the links as the edges, and it can be said that they treat a page as a unit of information.

If we consider a Web graph as a framework for link-based information retrieval as above, the following natural question arises: can we handle every link equally? The answer is probably no, since humans frequently consider a Web site as a unit of information. That is, for a link from a page u to a page v, if u

V. Mařík et al. (Eds.): DEXA 2003, LNCS 2736, pp. 558–568, 2003.

and v are in different Web sites then v will be valuable for u as described above, but otherwise (i.e. if u and v are in the same Web site), the link may be made for convenience of navigation or browsing.

A practical example is a *mutual-link*. It is known that a mutual-link between two sites A and B (i.e. there are a link from a page in A to a page in B and a link from a page B to a page in A) is made when these sites are related and authors of the sites know each other. However, if we consider a page as a unit, we cannot find a mutual-link between site A and B when no pair of page (u, v) for $u \in A$ and $v \in B$ links each other. Such a case frequently occurs, for example, when the top page and a page for links to other sites are different.

Therefore, we claim that *inter-site graph*, which consists of sites as vertices and links between sites as edges, is a more natural framework for link-based information retrieval than a Web graph. Since a method of identifying Web sites from URLs or HTML files had not been established, several researches have used a Web server instead of a Web site. Actually, HITS and Trawling use only links to pages in other servers or domains. This idea works relatively well when a Web site corresponds to a server such as official Web sites made by companies, governments or other social organizations, but works poorly when multiple Web sites correspond to a server such as personal Web sites on a server of internet service providers (ISPs) or universities, or rental servers and so on. This seems to be wasting valuable information, since information about relatively minor and specialized topics including important scientific results is frequently laid on such personal Web sites.

In 2002, the authors proposed a new model of Web sites, called a *directory-based site* model to deal with typical personal sites [2], [3]. In the directory-based site model, we regard a set of pages in a directory and all its subdirectories, and therefore if we can find directories corresponding to users' sites correctly from the Web, we can treat personal sites well. They have also proposed a method of identifying directory-based sites. It consists of several procedures called *filters* and an error correction phase. Each filter finds some Web servers and determines whether they contain only one site or multiple sites (i.e. two or more sites), and transfers the remaining servers to the next filter. They have examined that this method can determine whether Web servers contain only one site or multiple sites almost correctly (more than 90%) and extracts about five times as many directory-based sites as Web servers by using data sets of URLs and links in .jp domain crawled in 2000 and 2002 by Toyoda and Kitsuregawa.

They have shown that an inter-site graph is more suitable for finding communities (i.e. sets of related sites) containing personal sites than a Web graph or an inter-server graph by using Trawling. They have also proposed a new information retrieval method utilizing mutual-links and shown that maximal cliques of mutual-links correspond to communities. These cliques contain a large number of communities of personal sites, although Trawling could find a small number of such communities. See [2].

Since Trawling and enumerating maximal cliques described above are not suitable for information retrieval in response to user's query such as Google's

"Similar Pages" service, in this paper we present a new information retrieval tool, called a **Neighbor Community Finder** (NCF, for short), to find related communities in the neighborhoods of given URLs by users. This system first constructs an inter-site graph containing neighbor sites of the given sites, by crawling required Web pages, and obtaining in-links by search engines, and identifying directory-based sites by the filters.

Then this system enumerates maximal cliques in this inter-site graph to find neighbor communities related to the given sites. We show that NCF is a more effective tool for finding related pages than Google's service in several cases by computational experiments.

The rest of this paper is organized as follows. In Section 2, we describe a new framework of link-based information retrieval using a site as a unit and a method of implementing this framework. In Section 3, we propose NCF and describe how it works. In Section 4, we show several results of NCF and compare them with results of Google's service. In Section 5, we describe concluding remarks.

2   Site-Oriented Framework for Information Retrieval

In this section, we describe our site-oriented framework for information retrieval from the Web proposed in [2]. First, we describe a new model of Web sites, called *directory-based sites*, since a phrase "Web site" is used ambiguously in our daily life, and therefore it is hard to present a unique definition of the Web site. For example, the following definition which seems not to be apart from the concept used in our daily life. Note that similar definition is found in [1] and [6], although they did not find sites from the whole Web according to their definition.

Definition 1. *A Web site is a set of Web pages that are written by a single person, company, or group.*

If every Web page includes Meta information about its authors, this definition will be well-defined and we can compute Web sites easily according to this definition. Unfortunately, such information does not exist in the real Web and therefore it is hard to compute Web sites according to this definition. Thus, we have to consider a method of estimating Web sites under a restricted situation, such as our directory-based sites described below.

Next, we describe our method of identifying directory-based sites, called *filters*, and summarize the results for the jp-domain data sets collected in 2000 and 2002 by Toyoda and Kitsuregawa. Then, we describe the definition of an *inter-site graph* with directory-based sites as vertices.

2.1   Directory-Based Site

Definition 2. *[2]: For a Web server, let $\{d_1, ..., d_k\}$ be a given set of directories in the server such that d_i $(1 \leq i \leq k)$ is neither the root directory of the server nor a subdirectory of any other d_j $(j \neq i)$. Then, for each i, a directory-based site whose top directory is d_i denoted by D_i is defined to be the set of Web pages* *in the directory d_i and all its subdirectories. That is, D_i consists of pages such of which is contained in d_i or a subdirectory of d_i. On the other hand, the set of Web pages in the server but not in $\{d_1, ..., d_k\}$ (and their subdirectories) is called a directory-based site of the administrator of the server. For convenience, a directory-based site different from the directory-based site of the administrator is called a user's directory-based site.*

If all pages in a given server are in the site of the administrator of the server (i.e. $k = 0$ in Definition 3), the Web server is called a *single-site server*. Otherwise (i.e. $k \geq 1$ and at least one directory is given), the server is called a *multi-site server*.

2.2 Filters

We now describe an outline of our method of identifying directory-based sites. It consists of a filtering phase and an error correction phase (error correction of filters using clique, ECFC for short). In the filtering phase, there are seven filter steps and we call the i-th filter step is called Filter i ($0 \leq i \leq 6$). Note that the remaining Web servers after these filters are regarded as single-site servers.

Filter 0: by using our knowledge for a level of directories corresponding to users' Web sites on each famous rental Web server or ISP, find directory-based sites in multi-site servers. For example, it is well-known that in `geocities.co.jp` the 3rd level directories are the top directories of sites of users. **Filter 1:** by using a *tilde*-symbol in a URL as a symbol representing directories corresponding users' Web sites, find directory-based sites in multi-site servers. **Filter 2:** by using our knowledge of famous companies and organizations, find single-site servers. For example, it is well-known that `www.sony.co.jp` is a single-site server. **Filter 3:** considers any server having at most one directory as a single-site server. **Filter 4:** considers any server which has at most 20 pages as a single-site server. **Filter 5:** for each server, we consider its associated graph with pages in the server as vertices and links between these pages as edges, and decompose it into the connected components. Then, regarding each component as a site, determine whether the server is a multi-site server or a single-site server. **Filter 6:** by using information about the numbers of back-links and directories, find multi-site servers and a level of directories corresponding to top directories of sites of users. Frequently, these directories have few back-links and a number of these directories are much larger than a number of parent directories of them. **ECFC:** it enumerates maximal cliques of the directory-based sites found in Filters 5 and 6, and finds any clique such that every directory-based site in the clique belongs to one server. It removes such servers from the results of Filters 5 and 6, then regards them single-site servers.

The authors have examined this method by using the `jp`-domain URL data sets. The filters and ECFC have identified 74,441 servers among 112,744 servers and found 563,611 directory-based sites for the data set in 2000. For the data set in 2002, they have identified 299,785 servers among 373,737 servers and found 1,975,087 directory-based sites. They have also estimated error rate of this method by sampling 150 servers randomly from the identified servers by each filter and ECFC. As a result, the estimated error rate is about 6.8% for the data set in 2000, and 4.5% for the data set in 2002, and therefore it can be said that this method identifies directory-based sites almost correctly, in practice.

The details of the filters, ECFC, and the estimation of the error rate are described in [2]. The filters are also described in [4], [3].

2.3   Inter-site Graph

Now, as a framework for information retrieval, we can use an inter-site graph or a mutual-link graph defined as follows. For convenience, we also define an inter-server graph and an intra-server graph here.

Definition 3. *Let A and B be two distinct directory-based sites. (1) If there is a link from a page v in A to a page w in B, we say there is a* **global-link** *from A to B. (2) A link from a page v to a page w with v and w in A is called a* **local-link** *inside A.*

Definition 4. *(1) A graph which consists of directory-based sites as vertices and global-links as edges is called an* **inter-site graph**. *(2) For each site, a graph which consists of pages in the site as vertices and local-links in the site as edges is called an* **intra-site graph** *for the site. (3) A graph which consists of sites as vertices and mutual-links as edges is called a* **mutual-link graph**. *(4) A graph which consists of servers as vertices and links between servers as edges is called an* **inter-server graph**. *(5) For each server, a graph which consists of pages in the server as vertices, and links in the server as edges is called an* **intra-server graph**.

3   Neighbor Community Finder

3.1   Outline of the System

We describe the outline of NCF. As an input, receive at least one URL from the user. Let these URLs be $\{u_1, ..., u_h\} = U$ and S_i be the server containing u_k for $1 \le k \le h$. The detail of each step is described in Section 3.2 to 3.4.

1. Construct a *seed graph G*. A seed graph is the inter-site graph which consists of directory-based sites in $\{S_1, ..., S_h\}$ and global-links between them.
2. By repeating a *growth step*, grow G. A growth step finds directory-based sites adjacent to sites in G and adds them to G.
3. Enumerate maximal cliques formed by mutual-links in G and output them as neighbor communities.

We also prepare a filter database describing our knowledge used in Filters 0 and 2 for NCF. This filter database consists of pairs of a string corresponding to a suffix of the name of a server and integer corresponding to the level of top directories of users' directory-based sites in servers whose names contain the suffix. For given URL u, a function $db(u) \geq 0$ for this database returns an integer. If $db(u) > 1$, the $db(u)$-th slash symbol in the URL represents the top directory of user's directory-based site, otherwise, the server with u is regarded as a single-site server. Otherwise $(db(u) = 0)$, it means that the database cannot determine which slash symbol is so. If such a slash symbol is found, we can find a name of the directory-based site induced from the URL. Let $sitename(u)$ be the name of the directory-based site, that is, a prefix part of u starts from the first character and ends at the slash symbol. Let $pagename(u)$ be a suffix part of u starts from the character just behind the slash symbol. For example, if u is "`http://www.geocities.co.jp/Playtown-Denei/1722/src/SRC.html`", $sitename(u)$ is "`http://www.geocities.co.jp/Playtown-Denei/1722/`" and $pagename(u)$ is "`src/SRC.html`".

3.2 Constructing a Seed Graph

When NCF receives seed URL set U, NCF begins to construct a *seed graph* and *neighbors set* N_v, that is a set of URLs { u } such that $u \notin S_k$ (for $1 \leq k \leq h$) and the page of u is adjacent to a page in the seed graph by a Web-link. Let $G = (V, E)$ be an empty graph, R be an empty set of graphs, N_v be an empty set of URLs, and N_e be an empty set of Web-links. Each vertex $v \in V$ has a label $label(v)$ corresponding to some part of its URL.

Construct-Seedgraph(U, G, R, N_v, N_e)

1. For each URL $u \in U$, do the following "new URL addition" procedure:
   a) If $db(u) > 0$, do the following "create intra-site graph" procedure:
      i. If there is no vertex in V whose label equals to $sitename(u)$: Create a new intra-site graph $G_i = (V_i, E_i)$, where $i = |V| + 1$ and add a vertex with label $pagename(u)$ to V_i. Then, add a vertex with label $sitename(u)$ to V and add G_i to R.
      ii. Otherwise: Let $v \in V$ with a label $sitename(u)$ and G_i be the corresponding intra-site graph. If there is no vertex in V_i with a label $pagename(u)$, add a vertex with a label $pagename(u)$ to V_i. (Otherwise, do nothing.)
   b) Otherwise: Do a "create intra-site graph" procedure, by using $servername(u)$ instead of $sitename(u)$. The graphs created here called *temporary intra-server graphs*.
2. For each graph $G_i \in R$, call **crawling(G, G_i, N_v, N_e)** procedure described below.
3. For each temporary intra-server graph G_t, do the following.
   a) By using Filters 1 and 3 to 6, and ECFC, compute $a > 0$ such that the a-th slash symbol represents the top directory of user's directory-based site in the server and add this result (i.e. the name of the server and the integer a) to the filter database.
   b) Divide G_t into the multiple intra-site graphs correctly by using the above result of the filters.
4. Output G, G_i $(1 \leq i \leq |V|)$, and N_v.

Crawling(G, G_i, N_v, N_e)

1. Set $S = V_i$, and for each $s \in S$, let u_s be the URL corresponding to s.
2. For each u_s, properly add new vertices and edges to G_i by doing the breadth first search. Note the following:
   - When $|V_i| \geq M$, terminate the search. We set $M = 600$ for intra-site graphs and $M = 300$ for temporary intra-server graphs.
   - When the search visits v and if there is a page with URL w in the neighborhood of v such that w does not belong to the directory-based site corresponding to G_i, do the following:
     a) If there is no vertex in V with a label equal to a prefix part of w: Then add w to N_v and a new pair of URLs (v, w) to N_e.
     b) Otherwise: Let G_j be the intra-site graph containing w. If there is no vertex in V_j with a label equal to $pagename(w)$, add a vertex with label $pagename(w)$ to V_j. Moreover, if $(i, j) \notin E$, add a new edge (global-link) (i, j) to E.

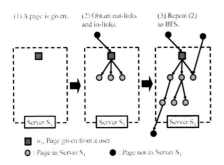

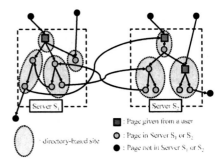

Fig. 1. Crawling pages in a server

Fig. 2. Identifying directory-based sites

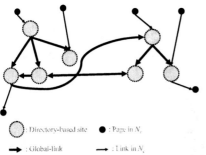

Fig. 3. A seed graph (the inter-site graph and the neighbors set are shown)

Figures 1 to 3 illustrate the outline of the construction of a seed graph. Note that we use an existing search engine, such as Google or Altavista, in order to find pages linked to u_s (i.e. in-link) and we use "libwww-perl" presented by W3C as a HTML parser in order to find pages links from u_s.

3.3   Growth of Seed Graph

By using the following *growth* procedure, NCF adds sites containing URLs in the neighbor sets (i.e., sites adjacent to sites in the seed graph) to G in order to grow the seed graph G. The inputs of the growth procedure are G, $R = \{G_i \mid 1 \leq i \leq |V|\}$, N_v and N_e.

Growth

1. Set N_v' and N_e' to be empty.
2. Set $G' = G$, and $\{G_i'\} = \{G_i\}$.
3. Call **Construct-seedgraph**$(N_v, G', \{G_i'\}, N_v', N_e')$.
4. Update G, $\{G_i\}$, N_v and N_e by G', $\{G_i'\}$, N_v' and N_e', respectively.

Repeating the procedure can grow the seed graph by one hop of global-link, and therefore our system is considered to grow the initial subgraph on the basis of the inter-site graph, in contrast, the previous works (HITS [9], Companion [7], and so on) grow a graph by one hop of a Web-link on the basis of the Web graph. This difference would be significant for information retrieval, because growth by one hop of local-link yields no effect to results of HITS or Companion, but growth of one hop of global-link would affect the results. Note that the two kinds of growth cannot be distinguished unless we identify sites according to some proper model.

3.4   Enumerating Maximal Cliques

After the growth procedures, NCF finds neighbor communities in G by enumerating maximal cliques formed of mutual-links.

By using the jp-domain URL data sets, the authors have shown that maximal cliques in the mutual-link graph correspond to communities (even a K_2 corresponds to a community) and communities of personal sites occupy relatively large amount. Note that such communities are very few in the results of Trawling using the same data. They have also shown in [2] that a Web graph and an inter-server graph are not good for this method. This fact has also shown that mutual-links are useful for information retrieval only when sites are obtained according to some proper model.

3.5   Experiments and Comparison with Google's Similar Pages Service

We also compare communities obtained by NCF with pages obtained by Google's "Similar Pages" service. Our NCF can use multiple seed URLs as an input and this fact will be useful for finding communities related to user's interests since multiple seeds are more reliable data than a single seed. However, we use results for sets which consist of only one seed to compare with Google's service in fairness, since Google's service allows only a single URL as an input.

Table 1. Comparison with Google's "Similar Pages" service.

ID	Cliques		Google	
	Number	Quality of samples	Number	Quality of samples
1	6	6/6	16	0/16
2	83	19/20	16	0/16
3	9	8/9	0	0/0
4	156	17/20	0	0/0
5	15	15/15	15	13/15
6	13	10/13	3	0/3
7	28	15/20	5	3/5
8	5	5/5	25	16/20
9	12	11/12	0	0/0
10	7	7/7	30	13/20
11	24	15/20	0	0/0
12	3	3/3	7	5/7
13	5	5/5	0	0/0
14	14	13/14	0	0/0
15	149	19/20	24	19/20
16	139	20/20	28	18/20
17	8	8/8	0	0/0
18	46	20/20	24	20/20
19	16	15/16	25	10/20

Table 1 shows comparisons of the communities (i.e. maximal cliques) obtained by NCF with the pages obtained by Google's "Similar Pages" service. "Number" column in "Cliques" columns (or "Google" columns) shows the number of cliques (or pages, respectively) obtained. "Quality of samples" column in "Cliques" columns (or "Google" columns) shows the number of cliques which consist of related sites (or the number of related pages, respectively) to the seed URL in 20 samples (if obtained cliques or pages are less than 20, we use all of the cliques or pages).

The seeds corresponding to IDs 1 to 7 are personal sites given by voluntary users and the topics of them are mainly specialized hobbies and so on. IDs 1 and 2 (3 and 4) uses the same seed URL, but the number of applied growth procedures is one for ID 1 (3) and two for ID 2 (4, respectively). The details of the results for IDs 1 to 7 (e.g. sizes of graphs) are shown in [2]. The seeds of IDs 8 to 19 are sites registered on Yahoo! Japan for 10 topics. For each topic, we select one public site and one personal site. IDs of even (odd) numbers are corresponding to public (personal) sites. IDs 8 and 9 are sites about cooking, 10 and 11 are sites about news, 12 and 13 are about investment, 14 and 15 are about movies, 16 and 17 are about models, 18 and 19 are about armies.

As a result, in several cases our NCF returns better results than Google's service in both quantity and quality. In particular, when seeds are personal sites, the results of NCF are much better. For IDs 1 and 2, Google's service returns 16 pages, but there are no related pages in them, in contrast to most of the maximal cliques represent communities having the same topic as the seed. For

ID 6, a similar result can be seen. For IDs 3, 4, 9, 11, 12, 13, and 17, Google's service returns no pages, while most of the maximal cliques (i.e. results of NCF) have good quality. These bad results of Google's service will be due to that these seed pages are personal sites having relatively specialized topics or they contains many pictures and illustrations instead of poor text information. (Note that contents of these sites have good quality for their topics) However, NCF returns good results by using link information even under such difficult situations.

On the other hand, for IDs 8, 10, and 12, Google's service returns better results than NCF. Google's service returns as good results as NCF in quality for IDs 5, 7, 15, 16, and 18. The seeds for these IDs are well-known sites for given topics and contain plenty of text information, but having very few mutual-links. These results have shown that such situations are advantageous to Google's service, and it will be a future work to improve NCF by combining with our ideas using mutual-links and the ideas used by HITS or Trawling.

As a result, we conclude that our NCF is a useful tool to find communities in response to user's query (i.e. seed pages). In particular, it is shown that NCF is suitable for finding communities of personal sites and specialized topics.

4   Concluding Remarks

In conclusion, we have shown that our site-oriented framework is useful for information retrieval in response to user's query by developing **Neighbor Community Finder**, a tool to find communities related to given URLs by users. We have also shown comparison with Google's service. More experiments compared to other methods of finding related pages (e.g. [8], [11]) will be a future work.

On the other hand, we also consider other applications of our site-oriented framework to several research fields based on graph structures of Web-links. We have shown that distinguishing global-links from local-links is useful for constructing more reasonable drawing of the Web graph than existing tools. We have presented **Web-Linkage Viewer**, a visualization system drawing Web-links understandably by drawing sites and global-links on a spherical surface and drawing pages and local-links in cones emanating from a point representing a site on the surface. We examined that our Web-linkage Viewer produces more understandable drawing of structures in the Web graph than existing tools using several examples. See [2] and [5].

References

1. B. Amento, L. G. Terveen, and W. C. Hill. Does "authority" mean quality? Predicting expert quality ratings of web documents. In *Proceedings of SIGIR'00*, pages 296–303, 2000.
2. Y. Asano. *A New Framework for Link-based Information Retrieval from the Web.* PhD thesis, The University of Tokyo, December 2002.
3. Y. Asano, H. Imai, M. Toyoda, and M. Kitsuregawa. Applying the site information to the information retrieval from the Web. In *Proceedings of the 3rd International Conference on Web Information Systems Engineering*, pages 83–92, 2002.

4. Y. Asano, H. Imai, M. Toyoda, and M. Kitsuregawa. Focusing on Sites in the Web. In *Proceedings of IASTED International Conference Information Systems and Databases 2002*, pages 154–159, 2002.

5. Y. Asano, H. Imai, M. Toyoda, and M. Kitsuregawa. The Web-Linkage Viewer: Finding graph structures in the Web. In *Proceedings of the 3rd International Conference on Web-Age Information Management*, pages 441–442, 2002.

6. N. Craswell, D. Hawking, and S. Robertson. Effective site finding using link anchor information. In *Proceedings of SIGIR'01*, pages 250–257, 2001.

7. J. Dean and M. R. Henzinger. Finding related pages in the World Wide Web. In *Proceedings of the 8th International World Wide Web Conference*, 1999.

8. G. W. Flake, S. Lawrence, and C. L. Giles. Efficient identification of Web communities. In *Proceedings of the Sixth International Conference on Knowledge Discovery and Data Mining (ACM SIGKDD-2000)*, pages 150–160, 2000.

9. J. Kleinberg. Authoritative sources in a hyperlinked environment. In *Proceedings of the 9th Annual ACM-SIAM Symposium on Discrete Algorithms*, pages 668–677, 1998.

10. R. Kumar, P. Raghavan, S. Rajagopalan, and A. Tomkins. Trawling the Web for emerging cyber-communities. In *Proceedings of the 8th International World Wide Web Conference*, 1999.

11. T. Murata. Finding related Web pages based on connectivity information from a search engine. In *Poster Proceedings of the 10th International World Wide Web Conference*, 2001.

A Lesson for Software Engineering from Knowledge Engineering

John Debenham

University of Technology, Sydney,
Faculty of Information Technology,
PO Box 123, NSW 2007, Australia
debenham@it.uts.edu.au

Abstract. Knowledge engineering has developed fine tools for maintaining the integrity of knowledge bases. These tools may be applied to the maintenance of conventional programs particularly those programs in which business rules are embedded. A unified model of knowledge represents business rules at a higher level of abstraction than the rule-based paradigm. Representation at this high level of abstraction enables any changes to business rules to be quantified and tracked through to the imperative programs that implement them. Further, methods may be applied to simplify the unified model so that the maintenance of the imperative implementation too is simplified.

1 Introduction

A very simple example motivates this discussion. Consider the business rule: [K1]
• The sale price of a part is the cost price of that part marked up by the markup rate for that part . This rule is not in if-then form. Its form is that of a simple statement of fact. It could give rise to the following simple Java program:

```
public int part_sale_price( int part_no, int part_cost_markup[][],
                 int no_of_part_nos ) {
    if (no_of_part_nos < 1 ) return -1;
    for ( int count = 0; count < no_of_part_nos; count++ ) {
        if ( part_cost_markup[count][0] == part_no ) {
            return part_cost_markup[count][1] *
                    part_cost_markup[count][2] / 100;
        }
    }
    return -2;
}                                                              [P1]
```

that returns the sale_price of a given part_no. There is no immediate issue here. But if the wisdom in [K1] finds its way into other imperative representations then some machinery is required to acknowledge that those representations are linked. Further, as we will see, [K1] may contain within it other business rules that may also be buried in yet others. The argument presented here is that these links are revealed by applying knowledge engineering tools to the construction of a conceptual model

V. Mařík et al. (Eds.): DEXA 2003, LNCS 2736, pp. 569–578, 2003.
Springer-Verlag Berlin Heidelberg 2003

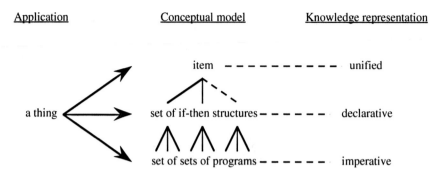

Fig. 1. A thing and its representation in the unified representation, a declarative representation and an imperative interpretation.

that is employed as a specification of the imperative implementations derived from it. Further, methods may be applied to convert the conceptual model into a model in which the original implicit links become explicit. This exposes the maintenance structure so that it may then form an integral part of either a declarative or an imperative implementation.

To illustrate the complexity present in this very simple example, consider also the business rules: [K2] "The profit on a part is the difference between the marked-up cost price and the cost price", and [K3] "The profit on a part is the difference between the sale price and the cost price of that part". [K2] may be derived from both [K1] and [K3]. Why does this present a problem? If the knowledge in either [K1] or [K3] becomes invalid and so is modified then [K2] should be modified as well to preserve consistency. The relationship between these three chunks is not difficult to identify given the raw chunks, but, given only implementations as programs—even with documentation—the relationship becomes more obscure.

An abstract conceptual model that describes the knowledge embedded in a set of programs is used to drive the maintenance process for those programs. The maintenance problem is to determine which programs should be checked for correctness in response a change in the application [1]. This model is at a very high level of abstraction. In it each chunk of knowledge is represented directly as a single 'item'. Each item may be interpreted as a number of declarative if-then rules. Each rule may be interpreted as a number of imperative programs. So in the model an item will correspond to a number of programs each of which implements an imperative interpretation of the original chunk of knowledge. This abstraction hierarchy is represented in Fig. 1.

In the above example, business rule [K1] admits three different declarative if-then interpretations:

part/sale-price(x, y) ← part/cost-price(x, z),
  part/mark-up(x, w), y = (z × w)   [C1.1]
part/cost-price(x, z) ← part/sale-price(x, y),
  part/mark-up(x, w), y = (z × w)   [C1.2]
part/mark-up(x, w) ← part/sale-price(x, y),
  part/cost-price(x, z), y = (z × w)   [C1.3]

part/sale-price		part/cost-price		part/mark-up	
1234	1.44	1234	1.20	1234	1.2
2468	2.99	2468	2.30	2468	1.3
3579	4.14	3579	3.45	3579	1.2
1357	10.35	1357	4.50	1357	2.3
9753	12.06	9753	6.70	9753	1.8
8642	12.78	8642	8.52	8642	1.5
4321	5.67	4321	2.70	4321	2.1

Fig. 2. Value set for a knowledge item.

and each of these admit a number of imperative interpretations. Program [P1] is but one interpretation of [C1.1]. Note that [C1.1] as a Prolog program can find a part_number with a given cost—a task that [P1] can not do directly.

Given any form of conceptual model *maintenance links* are introduced that join two things in that model if a modification to one of them means that the other must necessarily be checked for correctness, and so possibly modified, if consistency of that model is to be preserved. If that other thing requires modification then the links from it to yet other things are followed, and so on until things are reached that do not require modification. If node A is linked to node B which is linked to node C then nodes A and C are *indirectly* linked. In a *coherent* model of an application everything is indirectly linked to everything else. A good conceptual model for maintenance will have a low density of maintenance links [2]. Ideally, the set of maintenance links will be *minimal* in than none may be removed. Informally, one conceptual model is •better than another if it leads to less checking for correctness. The aim of this work is to generate a good conceptual model. A classification of maintenance links into four classes is given here. Methods are given for removing two of these classes of link so reducing the density of maintenance links in the resulting model. In this way the maintenance problem is simplified.

Approaches to the maintenance of declarative conceptual models are principally of two types [3]. First, approaches that take a model •as is• and then try to *control* the maintenance process [4]. Second, approaches that *engineer* a model so that it is in a form that is inherently easy to maintain [5] [6]. The approach described here is of the second type because maintenance is driven by a maintenance link structure that is simplified by transforming the model.

2   Representing Knowledge

Consider again the chunk of knowledge [K1]. Suppose that that chunk is represented as an *item*—with the name *[part/sale-price, part/cost-price, part/mark-up]*. The data associated with this item may be presented as a rather messy relation; such a relation is called the *value set* of the item, a possible value set is shown in Fig. 2.

The meaning of an item A—called its *semantics* S_A—is an expression that recognises the members of that item•s value set. For the item considered above the semantics could be:

$$\lambda x_1 x_2 y_1 y_2 z_1 z_2 \bullet [(\ S_{part/sale\text{-}price}(x_1, x_2) \wedge S_{part/cost\text{-}price}(y_1, y_2) \wedge$$
$$S_{part/mark\text{-}up}(z_1, z_2)\ ) \wedge ((x_1 = y_1 = z_1) \rightarrow (x_2 = z_2 \times y_2))] \bullet$$

where $S_{part/sale\text{-}price} = \lambda xy \bullet [\ S_{part}(x) \wedge S_{sale\text{-}price}(y) \wedge \text{sells-for}(x, y)\ ] \bullet$
and where $S_{part} = \lambda x \bullet [\text{is-a}[x{:}P]] \bullet$ for some suitable domain P where:

$$\text{is-a}[x{:}P] \begin{cases} = \mathbf{T} \ \ if \ x \ is \ in \ P \\ \\ = \mathbf{F} \ \ otherwise \end{cases}$$

In general, an *item* is a named triple $A[\ S_A, V_A, C_A]$ with *item name* A, S_A is called the *item semantics* of A, V_A is called the *item value constraints* of A and C_A is called the *item set constraints* of A. The item semantics, S_A, is a λ-calculus expression that recognises the members of the value set of item A. The expression for an item's semantics may contain the semantics of other items $\{A_1,..., A_n\}$ called that item's *components*:

$$\lambda y_1^1...y_{m_1}^1...y_{m_n}^n \bullet [S_{A_1}(y_1^1,...,y_{m_1}^1) \wedge...\wedge S_{A_n}(y_1^n,...,y_{m_n}^n) \wedge J(y_1^1,...,y_{m_1}^1,...,y_{m_n}^n)] \bullet$$

The item value constraints, V_A, is a λ-calculus expression:

$$\lambda y_1^1...y_{m_1}^1...y_{m_n}^n \bullet [V_{A_1}(y_1^1,...,y_{m_1}^1) \wedge...\wedge V_{A_n}(y_1^n,...,y_{m_n}^n) \wedge K(y_1^1,...,y_{m_1}^1,...,y_{m_n}^n)] \bullet$$

that should be satisfied by the members of the value set of item A as they change in time; so if a tuple satisfies S_A then it should satisfy V_A [7]. The expression for an item's value constraints contains the value constraints of that item's *components*. The item set constraints, C_A, is an expression of the form:

$$C_{A_1} \wedge C_{A_2} \wedge...\wedge C_{A_n} \wedge (L)_A$$

where L is a logical combination of:
• Card lies in some numerical range;
• Uni(A_i) for some i, $1 \le i \le n$, and
• Can(A_i, X) for some i, $1 \le i \le n$, where X is a non-empty subset of $\{A_1,..., A_n\} - \{A_i\}$;

subscripted with the name of the item A, "Uni(a)" means that "all members of the value set of item a must be in this association". "Can(b, A)" means that "the value set of the set of items A functionally determines the value set of item b". "Card" means "the number of things in the value set". The subscripts indicate the item's components to which that set constraint applies.

For example, each *part* may be associated with a *cost-price* subject to the "value constraint" that parts whose part-number is less that 1,999 should be associated with a cost price of no more than \$300. A set constraint specifies that every part must be in this association, and that each part is associated with a unique cost-price. The information item named *part/cost-price* then is:

part/cost-price[$\lambda xy \bullet [\ S_{part}(x) \wedge S_{cost\text{-}price}(y) \wedge \text{costs}(x, y)\ ] \bullet$,

$\lambda xy \bullet [\ V_{part}(x) \wedge V_{cost\text{-}price}(y) \wedge ((x < 1999) \rightarrow (y \le 300))\ ] \bullet$,

$C_{part} \wedge C_{cost\text{-}price} \wedge (\text{Uni}(part) \wedge \text{Can}(cost\text{-}price, \{part\}))_{part/cost\text{-}price}$]

Rules, or knowledge, can also be defined as items, although it is neater to define knowledge items using "objects". "Objects" are item building operators. The knowledge item [K1] *[part/sale-price, part/cost-price, part/mark-up]* which means "The sale price of a part is the cost price of that part marked up by the markup rate for that part" is:

[part/sale-price, part/cost-price, part/mark-up][

$$\lambda x_1 x_2 y_1 y_2 z_1 z_2 \bullet [(\ S_{part/sale-price}(x_1, x_2) \wedge S_{part/cost-price}(y_1, y_2) \wedge$$
$$S_{part/mark-up}(z_1, z_2)\ ) \wedge ((x_1 = y_1 = z_1) \rightarrow (x_2 = z_2 \times y_2))]\bullet,$$

$$\lambda x_1 x_2 y_1 y_2 z_1 z_2 \bullet [\ V_{part/sale-price}(x_1, x_2) \wedge V_{part/cost-price}(y_1, y_2) \wedge$$
$$V_{part/mark-up}(z_1, z_2)\ ) \wedge ((\ x_1 = y_1\ ) \rightarrow (\ x_2 > y_2\ ))]\bullet,$$

$$C_{[part/sale-price,\ part/cost-price,\ mark-up]}\ ]$$

What have we achieved with the representation of our business rule [K1]? All of what it says plus additional constraints is represented above as an item. The formal notation is not particularly "user friendly". An alternative schema notation is more palatable for practical use [1]. But the item above is a complete formal representation of the business rule. Further we will show that items may be modified so as to simplify the maintenance links in the conceptual model and so too the links from the model to an imperative program implementation of it.

Two different items can share common knowledge and so can lead to a profusion of maintenance links. This problem can be avoided by using objects. An n-adic *object* is an operator that maps n given items into another item for some value of n. Further, the definition of each object will presume that the set of items to which that object may be applied are of a specific "type". The *type* of an m-adic item is determined both by whether it is a data item, an information item or a knowledge item and by the value of m. The type is denoted respectively by $\mathbf{D}^m$, $\mathbf{I}^m$ and $\mathbf{K}^m$. Items may also have unspecified, or free, type which is denoted by $\mathbf{X}^m$. The formal definition of an object is similar to that of an item. An *object* named A is a typed triple $A[E,F,G]$ where E is a typed expression called the *semantics* of A, F is a typed expression called the *value constraints* of A and G is a typed expression called the *set constraints* of A. For example, the *part/cost-price* item can be built from the items *part* and *cost-price* using the **costs** operator:

part/cost-price = **costs**(*part, cost-price*)
$$\mathbf{costs}[\lambda P{:}\mathbf{X}^1 Q{:}\mathbf{X}^1 \bullet \lambda xy \bullet [\ S_P(x) \wedge S_Q(y) \wedge \mathbf{costs}(x,y)\ ]\bullet\bullet,$$
$$\lambda P{:}\mathbf{X}^1 Q{:}\mathbf{X}^1 \bullet \lambda xy \bullet [V_P(x) \wedge V_Q(y) \wedge ((1000 < x < 1999) \rightarrow (y \leq 300))\ ]\bullet\bullet,$$
$$\lambda P{:}\mathbf{X}^1 Q{:}\mathbf{X}^1 \bullet [\ C_P \wedge C_Q \wedge (\text{Uni}(P) \wedge \text{Can}(Q, \{P\}))_{\Psi(\mathbf{costs},P,Q)}\ ]\bullet]$$

where $\Psi(\mathbf{costs}, P, Q)$ is the name of the item **costs**(P, Q).

Data objects provide a representation of sub-typing. Rules are quite clumsy when represented as items; objects provide a far more compact representation. For example, consider the *[part/sale-price, part/cost-price, part/mark-up]* knowledge item which represents the rule "parts are marked-up by a universal mark-up factor". This item can be built by applying a knowledge object **mark-up-rule** of argument type $(\mathbf{I}^2, \mathbf{I}^2, \mathbf{I}^2)$ to the items *part/sale-price*, *part/cost-price* and *part/mark-up*. That is:

[part/sale-price, part/cost-price, mark-up] =
    mark-up-rule(*part/sale-price, part/cost-price, part/mark-up*)

Objects also represent value constraints and set constraints in a uniform way. A decomposition operation for objects is defined in [1].

A *conceptual model* consists of a set of items and a set of maintenance links. The items are constructed by applying a set of object operators to a set of fundamental items called the *basis*. The *maintenance links* join two items if modification to one of them necessarily means that the other item has at least to be checked for correctness if consistency is to be preserved. Item join provides the basis for item decomposition [8]. Given items A and B, the item with name $A \otimes_E B$ is called the *join* of A and B on E, where E is a set of components common to both A and B. Using the rule of composition $\otimes$, knowledge items, information items and data items may be joined with one another regardless of type. For example, the knowledge item:

$$[cost\text{-}price,\ tax]\ [\lambda xy\bullet[S_{cost\text{-}price}(x) \wedge S_{tax}(y) \wedge x = y \times 0.05]\bullet,$$
$$\lambda xy\bullet[V_{cost\text{-}price}(x) \wedge V_{tax}(y) \wedge x < y]\bullet,$$
$$C_{[cost\text{-}price,\ tax]}]$$

can be joined with the information item *part/cost-price* on the set {*cost-price*} to give the information item *part/cost-price/tax*. In other words:

$$[cost\text{-}price,\ tax] \otimes_{\{cost\text{-}price\}} part/cost\text{-}price =$$
$$part/cost\text{-}price/tax[\ \lambda xyz\bullet[\ S_{part}(x) \wedge S_{cost\text{-}price}(x) \wedge S_{tax}(y) \wedge costs(x,y) \wedge$$
$$z = y \times 0.05\ ]\bullet,$$
$$\lambda xyz\bullet[\ V_{part}(x) \wedge V_{cost\text{-}price}(x) \wedge V_{tax}(y) \wedge$$
$$((1000<x<1999) \rightarrow (0<y\leq300)) \wedge (z<y)\ ]\bullet,$$
$$C_{part/cost\text{-}price/tax}]$$

In this way items may be joined together to form more complex items. The $\otimes$ operator also forms the basis of a theory of decomposition in which each item is replaced by a set of simpler items. An item I is *decomposable* into the set of items $D = \{I_1, I_2,..., I_n\}$ if: I_i has non-trivial semantics for all i, $I = I_1 \otimes I_2 \otimes ... \otimes I_n$, where each join is *monotonic*; that is, each term in this composition contributes at least one component to I. If item I is decomposable then it will not necessarily have a unique decomposition. The $\otimes$ operator is applied to objects in a similar way [2]. The rule of decomposition is: "Given a conceptual model discard any items and objects which are decomposable". For example, this rule requires that the item *part/cost-price/tax* should be discarded in favour of the two items *[cost-price, tax]* and *part/cost-price*.

3   Maintenance Links

So far we have shown how business rules such as [K1] may be represented, manipulated and decomposed. We now address the maintenace of the conceptual model. A *maintenance link* joins two items in the conceptual model if modification of one item means that the other item must be checked for correctness, and maybe modified, if the consistency of the conceptual model is to be preserved [9]. The number of maintenance links can be very large. So maintenance links can only form the basis of a practical approach to knowledge base maintenance if there is some way of reducing their density on the conceptual model [10].

For example, given two items A and B, where both are n-adic items with semantics S_A and S_B respectively, if π is permutation such that:

$$(\forall x_1 x_2 ... x_n)[\ S_A(x_1,x_2,...,x_n) \leftarrow S_B(\pi(x_1,x_2,...,x_n))\ ]$$

then item B is a *sub-item* of item A. These two items should be joined with a maintenance link. If A and B are both data items then B is a *sub-type* of A. Suppose that:

$$X = E\ D; \quad \text{where} \quad D = C\ A\ B \tag{1}$$

for items X, D, A and B and objects E and C. Item X is a sub-item of item D. Object E has the effect of extracting a sub-set of the value set of item D to form the value set of item X. Item D is formed from items A and B using object C. Introduce two new objects F and J. Suppose that object F when applied to item A extracts the same subset of item A's value set as E extracted from the "left-side" (ie. the "A-side") of D. Likewise J extracts the same subset of B's value set as E extracted from D. Then:

$$X = C\ G\ K; \quad \text{where} \quad G = F\ A \quad \text{and} \quad K = J\ B \tag{2}$$

so G is a sub-item of A, and K is a sub-item of B. The form (2) differs from (1) in that the sub-item maintenance links have been moved one layer closer to the data item layer, and object C has moved one layer away from the data item layer. Using this method repeatedly sub-item maintenance links between non-data items are reduced to sub-type links between data items.

It is shown now that there are four kinds of maintenance link in a conceptual model built using the unified knowledge representation. Consider two items A and B, and suppose that their semantics S_A and S_B have the form:

$$S_A = \lambda y_1^1 ... y_{m_1}^1 ... y_{m_p}^p \bullet [S_{A_1}(y_1^1,...,y_{m_1}^1) \wedge\ ......\ \wedge$$
$$S_{A_p}(y_1^p,...,y_{m_p}^p) \wedge\ J(y_1^p,...,y_{m_1}^1,...,y_{m_p}^p)] \bullet$$
$$S_B = \lambda y_1^1 ... y_{n_1}^1 ... y_{n_q}^q \bullet [S_{B_1}(y_1^1,...,y_{n_1}^1) \wedge\ ......\ \wedge$$
$$S_{B_q}(y_1^q,...,y_{n_q}^q) \wedge\ K(y_1^1,..,y_{n_1}^1,..,y_{n_q}^q)] \bullet$$

S_A contains $(p + 1)$ terms and S_B contains $(q + 1)$ terms. Let μ be a maximal sub-expression of $S_{A \otimes B}$ such that:

$$both \ \ S_A \ \rightarrow \ \mu \ \ and \ \ S_B \ \rightarrow \ \mu \tag{a}$$

where μ has the form:

$$\lambda y_1^1 ... y_{d_1}^1 ... y_{d_r}^r \bullet [S_{C_l}(y_1^1,...,y_{d_1}^1) \wedge \ ...... \ \wedge S_{C_r}(y_1^r,...,y_{d_r}^r) \wedge L(y_1^1,..,y_{d_1}^1,...,y_{d_r}^r)] \bullet$$

If μ is empty, ie. 'false', then the semantics of A and B are independent. If μ is non-empty then the semantics of A and B have something in common and A and B should be joined with a maintenance link.

Now examine μ to see *why* A and B should be joined. If μ is non-empty and if both A and B are items in the basis then:

A and B are a pair of basis items with logically dependent semantics   (b)

If μ is non-empty and if A is *not* in the basis then there are three cases. First, if:

$$S_A \leftrightarrow S_B \leftrightarrow \mu \tag{c}$$

then items A and B are equivalent and should be joined with an *equivalence link*. Second if (c) does not hold and:

$$either \ \ S_A \leftrightarrow \mu \ \ or \ \ S_B \leftrightarrow \mu \tag{d}$$

then either A is a sub-item of B, or B is a sub-item of A and these two items should be joined with a *sub-item link*. Third, if (c) and (d) do not hold then if Δ is a minimal sub-expression of S_A such that $\Delta \rightarrow \mu$. Then:

$$either \ \ S_{A_j}(y_1^j ,...,y_{m_j}^j) \in \Delta, \text{ for some j} \tag{e}$$

$$or \ \ J(y_1^1 ,...,y_{m_j}^1 ,...,y_{m_p}^p) \in \Delta \tag{f}$$

Both (e) and (f) may hold. If (e) holds then items A and B share one or more component items to which they should each be joined with a *component link*. If (f) holds then items A and B may be constructed with two object operators whose respective semantics are logically dependent. Suppose that item A was constructed by object operator C then the semantics of C will imply:

$$\Phi = \lambda Q_1{:}X_1^{i_1} \ Q_2{:}X_2^{i_2} ...Q_j{:}X_j^{i_j} \bullet \lambda y_1^1 ... y_{d_1}^1 ... y_{d_r}^r \bullet [$$
$$S_{P_1}(y_1^1 ,...,y_{d_1}^1) \wedge \ ..... \ S_{P_r}(y_1^r ,...,y_{d_r}^r) \wedge$$
$$L(y_1^1 ,...,y_{d_1}^1,...,y_{d_r}^r)] \bullet$$

where the Q_i's take care of any possible duplication in the P_j's. Let E be the object $E[\Phi, T, \varnothing]$ then C is a sub-object of E; that is, there exists a non-tautological object F such that:

$$C \cong_W E \otimes_M F \tag{g}$$

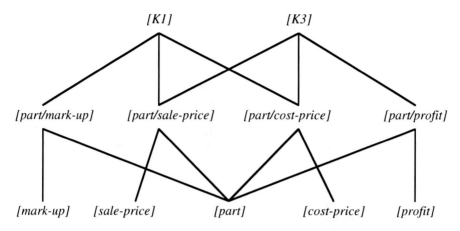

Fig. 3. Maintenance links for [K1] and [K2].

for some set M and where the join is not necessarily monotonic. Items *A* and *B* are *weakly equivalent*, written $A \simeq_w B$, if there exists a permutation π such that:

$$(\forall x_1 x_2 ... x_n)[S_A(x_1, x_2, ..., x_n) \leftrightarrow S_B(\pi(x_1, x_2, ..., x_n))]$$

where the x_i are the n_i variables associated with the i'th component of *A*. If *A* is a sub-item of *B* and if *B* is a sub-item of *A* then items *A* and *B* are weakly equivalent.

If (g) holds then the maintenance links are of three different kinds. If the join in (g) *is* monotonic then (g) states that *C* may be decomposed into *E* and *F*. If the join in (g) is *not* monotonic then (g) states that either $C \simeq_w E$ or $C \simeq_w F$. So, if the join in (g) is not monotonic then *either E* will be weakly equivalent to *C, or C* will be a sub-object of *E*.

It has been shown above that sub-item links between non-data items may be reduced to sub-type links between data items. So if:

- the semantics of the items in the basis are all logically independent;
- all equivalent items and objects have been removed by re-naming, and
- sub-item links between non-data items have been reduced to sub-type links between data items

then the maintenance links will be between nodes marked with:

- a data item that is a sub-type of the data item marked on another node, these are called the *sub-type links*;
- an item and the nodes marked with that item's components, these are called the *component links*, and
- an item constructed by a decomposable object and nodes constructed with that object's decomposition, these are called the *duplicate links*.

If the objects employed to construct the conceptual model have been decomposed then the only maintenance links remaining will be the sub-type links and the component links. The sub-type links and the component links cannot be removed from the conceptual model.

4 Conclusion

A very high level conceptual model represents each chunk of knowledge as a single item. A rule of decomposition is applied to reduce [K2] above to [K1] and [K3], so removing [K2] from the conceptual model. Maintenance links join two items in the conceptual model if modification of one of these items could require that the other item should be checked for correctness if the validity of the conceptual model is to be preserved. The efficiency of maintenance procedures depends on a method for reducing the density of the maintenance links in the conceptual model.   One kind of maintenance link is removed by applying the rule of knowledge decomposition [11]. Another is removed by reducing sub-item relationships to sub-type relationships [2]. And another is removed by re-naming. In the simple example given the conceptual model consists only of [K1] and [K3], and the maintenance links are just the component links as shown in Fig. 3. So what? Because the model can not be decomposed it means that the maintenance links in Fig. 3 are *complete*. These links may then be mapped to the imperative programs that implement the knowledge in chunks [K1] and [K2].

References

[1]   Debenham, J.K.   "Knowledge Object Decomposition" in *proceedings 12th International FLAIRS Conference*, Florida, May 1999, pp203–207.
[2]   Mayol, E. and Teniente, E. "Addressing Efficiency Issues During the Process of Integrity Maintenance" i*n proceedings Tenth International Conference DEXA99*, Florence, September 1999, pp270–281.
[3]   Katsuno, H. and Mendelzon, A.O. "On the Difference between Updating a Knowledge Base and Revising It", in *proceedings Second International Conference on Principles of Knowledge Representation and Reasoning, KR'91*, Morgan Kaufmann, 1991.
[4]   Barr, V. "Applying Reliability Engineering to Expert Systems" in *proceedings 12th International FLAIRS Conference*, Florida, May 1999, pp494–498.
[5]   Jantke, K.P. and Herrmann, J.. "Lattices of Knowledge in Intelligent Systems Validation" in *proceedings 12th International FLAIRS Conference*, Florida, May 1999, pp499–505.
[6]   Darwiche, A. "Compiling Knowledge into Decomposable Negation Normal Form" in *proceedings International Joint Conference on Artificial Intelligence, IJCAI'99*, Stockholm, Sweden, August 1999, pp 284–289.
[7]   Johnson, G. and Santos, E. "Generalizing Knowledge Representation Rules for Acquiring and Validating Uncertain Knowledge" in *proceedings 13th International FLAIRS Conference*, Florida, May 2000, pp186–2191.
[8]   Debenham, J.K. *"Knowledge Engineering"*, Springer-Verlag, 1998.
[9]   Ramirez, J. and de Antonio, A. "Semantic Verification of Rule-Based Systems with Arithmetic Constraints" in *proceedings 11th International Conference DEXA2000*, London, September 2000, pp437–446.
[10] Kern-Isberner, G. "Posulates for conditional belief revision" in *proceedings International Joint Conference on Artificial Intelligence, IJCAI'99*, Stockholm, Sweden, August 1999, pp 186–191.
[11] Debenham, J.K. "From Conceptual Model to Internal Model", in *proceedings Tenth International Symposium on Methodologies for Intelligent Systems ISMIS'97*, Charlotte, October 1997, pp227–236.

Image Retrieval by Web Context: Filling the Gap between Image Keywords and Usage Keywords

Koji Zettsu[12], Yutaka Kidawara[1], and Katsumi Tanaka[2]

[1] Communications Research Laboratory
4-2-1 Nukui-Kitamachi, Koganei,
Tokyo, 184-8795 Japan
{zettsu,kidawara}@crl.go.jp
[2] Graduate School of Informatics,
Kyoto University
Yoshida-Honmachi, Sakyo-ku,
Kyoto, 606-8501 Japan
tanaka@dl.kuis.kyoto-u.ac.jp

Abstract. The Web contains a wide variety of images published by the general public. Because the image is exposed as part of a Web page, the image is specified by not only the image content, but also the Web content using the image. This generates a gap between the content keywords and the usage keywords of the image. To fill the gap, we propose a concept of "context" of images in the Web. The context of an image is the set of Web contents (e.g. text and images) surrounding the image. We extend the notion of surroundings to include Web contents associated with the image by Web document structure and hyperlinks. We define different types of contexts for an image in accordance with types of associations between the image and the surrounding content. By visualizing context of each image, users can distinguish reliable image content among similar images based on the usage and/or reputation of the image. In this paper, we propose methods for searching and visualizing the context of images. We also propose a method for retrieving images based on their context.

1 Introduction

The Web contains a wide variety of images published by the general public. The ability to retrieve images from the Web by keywords, in the same way as Web pages, is an emerging requirement. In the conventional keyword-based image retrieval approach, the images are retrieved by image keywords that represent specific image content. This approach treats each image as individual Web content. However, the images are exposed part of Web pages. Therefore, it often happens that users search for images based on Web content surrounding the images. Here are some motivating examples:

V. Mařík et al. (Eds.): DEXA 2003, LNCS 2736, pp. 579–588, 2003.
© Springer-Verlag Berlin Heidelberg 2003

Q1: select images in preferred usage :

When a user only has partial knowledge about content of the target image, the user cannot have enough confidence about the images retrieved by image keywords. In this case, the user selects the image in preferred usage from the retrieval results. For example, among the images retrieved for the image keyword "dolphin", the user distinguishes the images used for introducing animal-assisted therapy from the images used for advertising a marine cruise. Under the conventional approach, the user would have to visit the Web page containing the result image to understand the usage.

Q2: search for images suitable for a specific part of a document :

This is analogous to clip art retrieval. A user searches for images frequently used in a similar context for a specific part of a document. However, it is difficult for a user to specify keywords to find the image.

Q3: search for images typically used in a specific context :

Let us consider retrieving images for the keyword "environment pollution". The keyword "environment pollution" does not represent the specific image content, but indicates the subject in which the target image is typically used. Under the conventional approach, the user must devise image keywords that represent the image content typically used for environment pollution. Examples could be "foul river", "floating refuse", "smoking factory", and so on. However, there are few or perhaps no images whose content is described by all of these keywords. Therefore, the user must continue to modify image keywords by trial and error until preferred images are retrieved.

All of the above search scenarios require information about the **context** of each image. The *context* is represented by the Web content surrounding the image and indicates how the image is used in the Web. In this paper, we introduce a concept of *"context"* of images in the Web, and propose an image retrieval approach based on the *context*. We propose methods for searching and visualizing the *context* and we also propose a method for retrieving images by their *context*.

The rest of this paper is organized as follows. Section 2 describes the basic concepts of image retrieval based on the *context*. Section 3 explains methods for searching and visualizing the *context* of an image. Section 4 explains about retrieving images by their *context*. Section 5 describes related work. Finally, Section 6 provides concluding remarks and our future work.

2   Basic Concepts

2.1   Retrieving Context for Image

At first, let us consider the search scenario described in Q1 of Section 1. This concerns retrieving the *context* for the given images. In order for a user to select an image based on its *context*, it is necessary to extract the context of each image from the Web and visualize it along with the image content. The *context* of an image is characterized not only by its neighboring text and/or images, but also by the headings and sub-headings that contain the image, and the titles

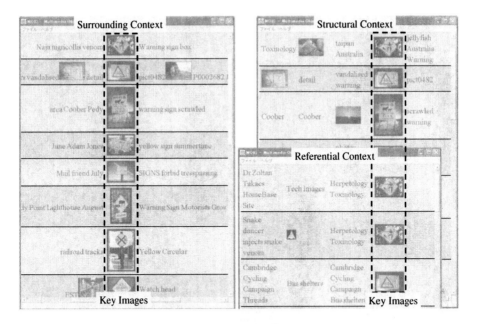

Fig. 1. Visualizing context of images extracted from the Web.

of the Web pages that link to the image. Therefore, we extend the concept of "surroundings" to include those Web content for representing the *context*.

Figure 1 shows an example of visualized *context* of images extracted from the Web. The details are described in Section 3. Each list shows three types of *context* for the same images: surrounding *context*, structural *context* and referential *context*. Each line shows the *context* of the image, denoted as the *key image*. The key images were retrieved by a search engine [1] using the keyword "warning sign". Looking at the *context* at the top of the list, the surrounding *context* indicates that the image is used together with text such as "warning sign", "venom", and so on. Furthermore, the structural *context* indicates that the key image is used in a paragraph describing toxinology, specifically for jellyfish in Australia. The referential *context* indicates that the key image is used in a Web page about the subjects of herpetology and toxinology. It is linked to from Dr Zoltan's home page and a page about injecting snake venom by a snake dancer. The former gives some credit to the key image, while the latter clarifies the subject using the key image. These three types of *contexts* give different aspects of the key image. Each means something more than the image keyword "warning sign". By browsing these *contexts*, a user can immediately understand what kind of "warning sign" each image represents.

---

[1] Google image search: http://www.google.com

2.2   Retrieving Image for Context

Let us consider the search scenario Q2. This search scenario concerns retrieving images for the given *context*. In order to search suitable images for a specific part of a Web page, it is necessary to retrieve the images in the similar context to the part of a Web page. Similarity in *context* intuitively means how much of the surroundings are characterized by similar content.

Figure 2 shows the prototype application. The image retrieval is done as follows.

1. A user specifies a place on a Web page where the target image is to be used.
2. The retrieval mechanism extracts the *context* of the place as a **query context** using the *context* extraction method (see Section 3.2 for details).
3. The retrieval mechanism retrieves *contexts* similar to the query *context* from the Web (see Section 4 for details). The retrieved *contexts* are listed in the order of similarity to the query *context* by the *context* visualization method (see Section 3.3 for details).
4. The user selects the preferred image from the result list.

In the result list of Figure 2, the keywords contained in the query *context* are underlined. Looking at the first result, the *context* shares the keywords "warning" and "motorists" with the query *context*. These keywords appear close to both the image and the target spot, while the keyword "motorists" rarely appears in other *contexts*. Therefore, these keywords characterize the *context* of the image for the query *context*. If the user agrees with both the content and *context* of the image, he/she can select the image.

Finally, let us consider the search scenario Q3. This also retrieves images by their *contexts* but differs slightly to the scenario Q2. In Q3, an image is retrieved by usage keywords that represent some typical *context* the image is used in, such as "environment pollution". This is done by clustering images used in similar *contexts*. As a result of this *context* clustering, each cluster represents a typical usage of all the images included within. The cluster label (typically, cluster centroid) represents the usage keywords.

3   Extracting and Visualizing Context of Image

3.1   Context Types

We define the following types of *context* for an image on the Web. Here, an image whose *context* is discussed is called a **key image**.

Surrounding context: This consists of neighboring text and/or images and represents the kind of content used together with a key image. For a given key image I, words and/or images that precede and follow the key image are extracted: $\ldots, s_{-2}, s_{-1}, I, s_1, s_2, \ldots$. Here, s_i represents an individual word or image.

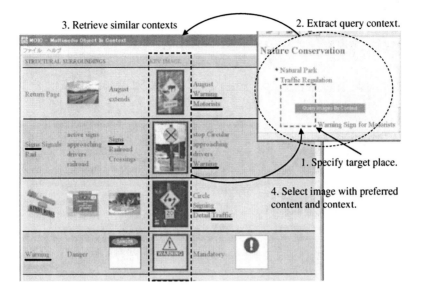

3. Retrieve similar contexts

2. Extract query context.

1. Specify target place.

4. Select image with preferred content and context.

Fig. 2. Retrieving images for given context.

Structural context: A Web page consists of paragraphs in a nested structure. The paragraphs contain some sub-paragraphs. A structural *context* represents the paragraphs that contain a key image. For a given key image I, words and/or images in paragraphs at upper levels from the key image are extracted: ..., P_3, P_2, P_1, I. Here, P_i represents a paragraph. The paragraph P_{i+1} is at an upper level (i.e. contains) of paragraph P_i. Paragraph P_1 contains the key image I. A nested structure of paragraphs is represented as a tree structure in a Web page. That is, each tree node represents a paragraph and a parent (ancestor) node represents an upper paragraph.

Referential context: This consists of link anchors that refer to the key image and the titles of the Web pages containing those link anchors. The referential *context* indicates from what kind of content the key image is referred. For a given key image I, words and/or images in the titles and link anchors in a backward link path from the key image are extracted: ..., T_2, A_1, T_1, I. Here, T_i is the Web page title and A_i is a link anchor. The anchor A_i links to the page titled T_i, while the anchor A_i is contained in the page titled T_{i+1}. T_1 contains the key image I.

Figure 3 illustrates the three types of *contexts*. In Figure 3, the surrounding *context* indicates that the key image is used together with texts about deforestation and CO2 reduction. The structural *context* indicates that the key image is included in paragraphs about nature conservation in the Kyoto protocol. The referential *context* indicates that the key image is quoted from a Web page on the Kyoto protocol, which is so famous that a United Nations Web page refers to it.

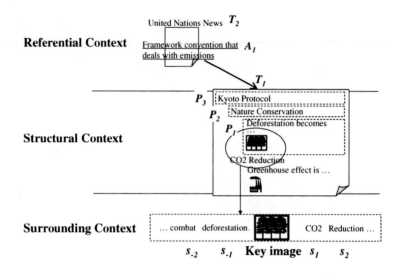

Fig. 3. Three types of image contexts.

3.2   Extraction Algorithm

For each type of *context*, the *context* extraction method extracts a minimal range of the surrounding content that contains just enough words and/or images to characterize the *context*. Intuitively, the *context* of an image is characterized by the surrounding content that (1) appear close to the image and (2) appear frequently near the image but less frequently around other images.

Let us consider each word or image in the surrounding content of the key image I as a **surrounding object**, denoted by o. The set of I's surrounding objects is extracted as the *context* of the key image I, denoted by $C(I)$, that satisfies the following:

1. Every surrounding object appears at least once in a region R that contains the image I.
2. The summation of the **context–contribution degrees** of all surrounding objects in $C(I)$ exceeds a predefined threshold.
3. No proper subregion R' of R satisfies both of 1 and 2.

Context–contribution degree of the surrounding object o for the *context* $C(I)$ is defined as follows:

$$ccontrib(o, C(I)) = \frac{adensity(o, C(I))}{distance(o, I)} \tag{1}$$

Here, $adensity(o, C(I))$ is the **appearance density** of the surrounding object o for the *context* $C(I)$, and $distance(o, I)$ is the distance between the surrounding object o and the key image I. Appearance density $adensity(o, C(I))$ intuitively means how intensively the same words or images as the surrounding object o

appear in the *context* $C(I)$. If the same words or images as the object o appear frequently in the *context* $C(I)$ but less frequently in other *contexts*, the appearance density $adensity(o, C(I))$ becomes a large value. Supposing that the image I is the k-th key image I_k among all key images (to be retrieved), the appearance density of the surrounding object o in the *context* $C(I_k)$ is calculated as follows:

$$adensity(o, C(I_k)) = \frac{N_{E(o,C(I_k))}}{N_{E(o,U))}} \tag{2}$$

Here, $E(o, C(I_k))$ is a set of surrounding objects representing the same words or images as the object o in the *context* $C(I_k)$, and $E(o, U)$ is a set of such surrounding objects in the *contexts* of all key images: $U = C(I_1) \cup C(I_2) \cup \dots$. $N_{E(o,C(I_k))}$ and $N_{E(o,U)}$ represent the number of objects in $E(o, C(I_k))$ and $E(o, U)$, respectively. Because it was difficult to identify the set U previously due to mutual dependencies between the *contexts*, we approximate the set U as a set of surrounding objects in Web pages containing all the key images.

The distance $distance(o, I)$ indicates the strength of the associations between the surrounding object o and the key image I. It is defined for each type of *context* as follows:

Distance in surrounding context: Number of objects between the key image I and the surrounding object o.

Distance in structural context: Number of parent nodes to be followed from the key image I to the surrounding object o.

Distance in referential context: Number of links to be followed from the key image I to the surrounding object o.

3.3   Visualizing Context

The visualization method visualizes relationships between an image and its surrounding content. We take advantage of the KWIC metaphor[1] for visualizing *contexts* of images.

The visualization method generates a list of *contexts* for each type of *context*. Each *context* is shown in a line. A key image and its surrounding content are serially aligned as follows:

Surrounding context: The key image I and the neighboring content $\{s_i\}$ are aligned in sequential order: $\dots, s_{-2}, s_{-1}, I, s_1, s_2, \dots$.

Structural context: The key image I and content in its upper paragraphs $\{P_i\}$ are aligned in nesting order: $\dots, P_3, P_2, P_1, I$. For each paragraph, the visualization method displays the specified number of words and/or images in the order of their context–contribution degree, because this characterizes the *context*.

Referential context: The key image I, content in Web page titles $\{T_i\}$, and link anchors $\{A_i\}$ are aligned in referencing order: $\dots, T_2, A_1, T_1, I$. For each title or link anchor, the visualization method displays words and/or images in the order of their context–contribution degrees, in the same manner as the structural *context*.

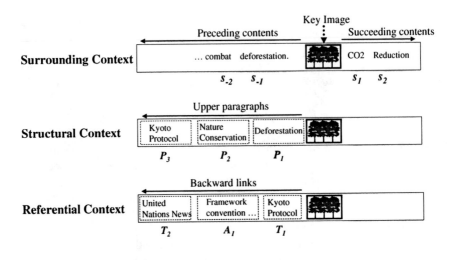

Fig. 4. Visualizing each context type.

Figure 4 illustrates how each type of *context* in Figure 3 is visualized.

The visualization method then lists the serialized *contexts* so that their key images are aligned in a single column. This makes it easier to compare the surrounding content between the *contexts*. The list is sorted by the similarity between the key images. In order to list visually-similar key images close to each other, similarity is evaluated by the image content (e.g. color histograms). As a result, a user can acquire various *contexts* of similar images at a glance.

4   Searching for Images in Similar Context

Basically, retrieving images by *context* is done to find images used in similar *contexts* to the specified *context*. Intuitively, similarity between *contexts* indicates how much of the surroundings of the key image are characterized by similar content. This is evaluated based on the similarity in context–contribution degrees between similar surrounding content. Let us calculate the similarity between the *context* $C(I_i)$ and the *context* $C(I_j)$. Let $E = \{e_1, e_2, \ldots, e_n\}$ be a set of discrete words and images in the $C(I_i)$ and $C(I_j)$. The *context* $C(I_i)$ is represented by the *context* feature vector $f(C(I_i)) = (v_1, v_2, \ldots, v_n)$, where v_k is a summation of the context–contribution degrees of the surrounding objects in $C(I_i)$, each of which represents the same word or image as e_k. In the same way, the *context* $C(I_j)$ is also represented by the *context* feature vector $f(C(I_j))$. Similarity between the *context* $C(I_i)$ and the *context* $C(I_j)$ is calculated as the cosine correlation value[2] between their *context* feature vectors: $f(C(I_i))$ and $f(C(I_j))$.

$$similarity(C(I_i), C(I_j)) = \frac{f(C(I_i)) \cdot f(C(I_j))}{|f(C(I_i))|\,|f(C(I_j))|} \tag{3}$$

The retrieval mechanism assumes that all images are previously indexed by their *context*. The retrieval method evaluates similarity between the *context* specified in a query and the *context* extracted from the Web for each image. The similarity is evaluated individually for each type of *context*. The retrieval method returns images whose similarity values exceed a predefined threshold.

5   Related Work

Although using *context* information for Web searches is not a new idea, the meaning of "*context*" in our approach is significantly different from conventional approaches[3,4,5]. In these approaches, *context* means the domain of a search. They extract information on a search user's activity (e.g. Web browsing history, previous search requests) and infer the search user's interest. As a result, keywords related to the user's interest are added to the user's query and/or the user's query is routed to domain-specific search engines. On the other hand, *context* in our approach means the relation between Web content. Our approach extracts a set of Web content associated with a target image and visualizes the associations. In our approach, *context* is used to represent the usage of an image on the Web.

In conventional Web image retrieval, the surrounding text of image is utilized for extracting the image keywords in order to improve the retrieval performance[6,7,8,9]. In contrast, in our approach, the surrounding text (and images) is utilized separately from the image keywords for representing the *context* of the image. The *context* shows the usage and/or reputation of the image. The conventional approaches assume that users can specify image keywords precisely. However, it is hard for users to specify appropriate image keywords for distinguishing among a wide variety of images on the Web Therefore, our approach focuses on making users select reliable images from the retrieval results for the imperfect image keywords by providing the context of the result image.

The Focus+context views (F+C views)[10,11,12,13] are the information visualization methods that show detailed view of target information and coarse grained view of its surrounding information simultaneously. They enable to capture interested information in detail without losing its *context*. Our approach extends conventional F+C view approaches for comparing multiple surrounding information (i.e. *contexts*) more effectively.

6   Conclusion and Future Work

In this paper, we proposed basic concepts *context* of images. The *context* of an image is represented by its surrounding content. We defined three types of *contexts* for an image: surrounding *context*, structural *context*, and referential *context*. We explained methods for extracting and visualizing *contexts* with the prototype implementations. We also explained a method for retrieving images based on their *context*.

In our future work, we will develop a method for retrieving images by usage keywords, as described in Section 2. We will also develop a method to evaluate the search performance of image retrieval by *context*. It is difficult to apply conventional precision-recall criteria to image retrieval by *context* because the set of relevant images for a query is not predefined. Relative measures, like novelty, relative recall and recall effort[14], should be considered.

Acknowledgement. This research is partly supported by the cooperative research project with Communications Research Laboratory and Kyoto University. This research is partly supported by the research for the grant of Scientific Research (14019048 and 15017249) form Ministry of Education, Culture, Sports, Science and Technology of Japan.

References

1. H. P. Luhn. Keyword in context index for technical literature (kwic index). *American Documentation*, (11):288–295, 1960.
2. G. Salton and M. McGill. Introduction to modern information retrieval. In *McGraw Hill*, 1983.
3. Steve Lawrence. Context in web search. In *IEEE Data Engineering Bulletin*, volume 23, pages 25–32, 2000.
4. Lev Finklstein, Evgeniy Gabrilovich, Yossi Matias, Ehud Rivlin, Sach Solan, Gadi Wolfman, and Eytan Ruppin. Placing search in context: The concept revisited. In *ACM Transactions on Information Systems*, volume 20, pages 116–131, 2002.
5. J. Budzik and K. J. Hammond. User interactions with everyday applications as context for just-in-time information access. In *Proceedings of the 2000 International Conference on Intelligent User Interfaces*, pages 41–51. ACM Press, 2000.
6. *Google Image Search FAQ, http://www.google.com/help/faq_images.html.*
7. *Altavista Help – Image Search, http://www.altavista.com/help/search/help_img.*
8. *Frequently Asked Questions – Picture Search, http://www.alltheweb.com/help/faqs/picture_search.html.*
9. V. Harmandas, M. Sanderson, and M. D. Dunlop. Image retrieval by hypertext links. In *Proceedings of the ACM SIGIR '97 Conference on Research and Development in Information Retrieval*, pages 296–303, 1997.
10. G. Furnas. Generalized fisheye views. In *Proceedings of the ACM SIGCHI '86 Conference on Human Factors in Computing Systems*, pages 16–23, 1986.
11. S. Mukherjea and Y. Hara. Focus+context views of world-wide web nodes. In *Proceedings of ACM Hypertext '97 Conference*, pages 187–196, 1997.
12. J. Lamping, R. Rao, and P. Pirolli. A focus+context technique based on hyperbolic geometry for visualizing large herarchies. In *Prceedings of the ACM SIGCHI '95 Conference on Human Factors in Computing Systems*, pages 401–408, 1995.
13. S. Björk. Hierarchical flip zooming: Enabling parallel exploration of hierarchical visualizations. In *Proceedings of the Working Conference on Advanced Visual Interfaces*, pages 232–237, 2000.
14. Robert Korfhage. *Information Storage and Retrieval.* John Wiley & Sons, Inc., 1997.

Query-by-Humming on Internet

Naoko Kosugi, Hidenobu Nagata, and Tadashi Nakanishi

NTT Cyber Space Laboratories,
NTT Corporation, Japan
nao@isl.ntt.co.jp

Abstract. We present a query-by-humming system on the Internet. It is fundamentally a content-based music retrieval system based on multi-dimensional spatial indices for high speed similarity searching. This paper discusses technical goals and approaches that will make it possible to use the system on the Internet. The keywords that indicate our goals are retrieval accuracy, quick response, large database, scalability, flexibility, robustness, and usability. We realize these by using some new technologies such as beat-based music data processing, music data splitting by a sliding-window method, database downsizing based on repetitive structure of songs, feature vectors based on timely transition of tones, or-retrieval with multiple feature information, duplicated registration of songs in doubled/halved tempo for a database, and a high-speed retrieval engine with distributed indices. Finally, we present our query-by-humming system, SoundCompass/Humming, that includes these technologies, using our latest GUI.

1 Introduction

Internet use is increasing rapidly as the network expands and becomes faster. Thus, search service on it is absolutely essential as a tool to obtain information efficiently. In addition, the use of multimedia data such as images and music, is expanding widely with the availability of low-cost and high-performance personal computers. Thus, multimedia data retrieval is now becoming ever-more important[2,8].

General retrieval systems on the Internet accept only letter strings as queries. However, formulating a query in words is often difficult for multimedia data retrieval. Typical situations are the retrieving of songs whose name we are not sure of. Enabling users input hummed tunes as queries to find songs would thus be very convenient. We call this content-based retrieval, in which same type of media data held in the database is accepted as query inputs.

In content-based retrieval, feature information is used for matching, and so the way in which data features are expressed is important. The feature information should represent media characteristics and input attributes, and also cover the many errors included in hummed tunes. The matching should also be robust against such errors. Accuracy and speed are also necessary for a practical retrieval system.

V. Mařík et al. (Eds.): DEXA 2003, LNCS 2736, pp. 589–600, 2003.

The goal of our work is to develop an effective content-based music retrieval system for query-by-humming that finds the target song efficiently. At the early stage of our work, we developed a prototype retrieval system and verified its effectiveness[6]. However, the retrieval accuracy, search speed and user-interface of this prototype system need to be improved to enable it to be widely used by many Internet users. Towards this end, we have analyzed the prototype's properties and performance, and developed new technologies such as feature-or retrieval and a high-speed retrieval engine with distributed indices to make a highly sophisticated retrieval system that provides superior performance.

In this paper, Section 2 describes the goals and approaches of a query-by-humming system on the Internet. Solutions are proposed in detail in Section 3 and the whole system is introduced in Section 4. Section 5 evaluates each solution quantitatively. Finally, conclusions are provided in Section 6.

2   Goals and Approaches

1. Retrieval accuracy $\cdots$ Users always expect correct answers.
2. Quick response $\cdots$ Users expect to receive answers within a few seconds.
3. Large database $\cdots$ It is said that radio stations in general have a daytime playbase of about 5,000 songs, while a typical karaoke parlor in Japan has one of about 30,000 songs. This implies a practical music retrieval system should be able to deal with a database that holds at least 5,000 songs, ideally much more than that.
4. Scalability $\cdots$ The system has to expand/reduce according to the number of queries.
5. Flexibility $\cdots$ Users should be able to select speed, length, part, and key height of their hummings.
6. Robustness $\cdots$ The system must be robust against errors of tone, note-integration, and so on that may be included in queries[7]. Errors will mainly occur by mis-singing of users and mis-processing for pitch tracking of vocal signals.
7. Usability $\cdots$ A common goal for systems that are directly used by users. Since query-by-humming systems are not well known yet, a GUI that can be of direct help to users is particularly needed.

This paper describes our development of a high-speed similarity retrieval system based on a k-nearest neighbor search on multi-dimensional spatial indices[1] of feature vectors to address points 2 and 6. Beat is the basic unit used for music data processing to address points 5 and 6 (Section 3.1). Melody data is split by a sliding-window method to address point 5 (Section 3.2). In addition, the storage cost of the database is reduced to address points 2 and 3 (Section 3.3). Feature vectors that represent music characteristics well and that are robust against errors are introduced to address points 1, 5, and 6 (Section 3.4). Or-retrieval with multiple feature information is introduced to address point 1. Moreover, duplicated registration of songs in doubled/halved tempo for a database is introduced to address point 5 (Section 3.5). We also make a high-speed similarity retrieval engine with distributed indices to address points 2 and 4 (Section 3.6). A GUI is implemented to address point 7 (Section 4).

3 Proposed Method

3.1 Beat-Based Music Data Processing

Since music in fact comprises time series data, it is difficult to use it as a basis for data processing because users will hum music at various speeds. Consequently, some traditional systems[4,5] have used "notes" in this regard. However, as noted in point 6 above, there are many note errors in humming inputs, and thus the use of note-based music data processing degrades the retrieval accuracy and speed of query-by-humming systems. Thus, we employ "beat" instead of "notes" as a basis for processing music data. This makes our system more robust against note errors and allows users to hum in any tempo they wish to.

3.2 Segmenting Music Data with the Sliding-Window Method

Users should be allowed to hum any part of a song they desire, and to make melody data matching efficient and fair, each data should contain the same quantity of information. This can be achieved by splitting melody data into subdata of constant length and then storing them in the database. In addition, database flexibility can be improved by using a sliding-window method for data splitting and setting the slide length shorter than the window length.

3.3 Reducing Database Storage Cost

Music is generally self-similar[3], and many songs have a repetitive structure consisting of two or three similar verses. Figure 1 shows the duplication ratio of all 21,804 songs in our music database. Duplication ratio is defined as the percentage of subdata that generates identical feature vectors[1] in each song. Four beats for the slide length and 16 beats for the window length are used in this analysis. The x-axis shows the duplication ratio and the y-axis shows the number of songs.

The figure shows that about 50% of the songs have duplication ratio ranging from 30% to 60%. The problem is that a high duplication ratio raises the storage cost of the database and reduces the retrieval speed. To overcome this problem, we propose a method where, in case subdata generate identical feature vectors for all features, only the feature vectors of the first appearing subdatum are stored in the database. The effectiveness of this method is evaluated in Section 5.2.

---

[1] ETT and PTT (Section 3.4) are used here.

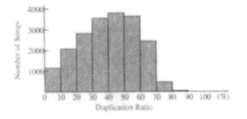

Fig. 1. Duplication Ratio of Songs

3.4   Feature Vectors

Feature vectors are one of the most important ingredients for achieving accuracy in retrieval systems. This section proposes an *Entire Tone Transition Feature Vector, "ETT"*, which characterize music data very well, and a *Partial Tone Transition Feature Vector, "PTT"*, which improves flexibility. Both are robust against note errors.

Timely Tone Transition. One of the sheerest pleasures of music appreciation is listening to timely changes in the heights and lengths of tones. Thus, we propose a type of feature vector that represents the transition of tones in a timely fashion. We call this the "Entire Tone Transition Feature Vector" (ETT). It is defined as tone values in a line that are extracted for every constant beat. We refer to the constant beats as *beat resolution*. Each vector element is represented by differences within a given tone, which we call the *base tone*, to make it possible to search for songs with various key heights (see no.5 in Section 2.) Figure 2 shows an image for making an ETT whose beat resolution is a quaver. An eight-dimensional feature vector can be made from this four-beat tune. E4, F4, and G4 are MIDI codes, and the numbers to their right are the MIDI note number. A feature vector, (-1, -1, 0, 0, 2, 2, 0, 0), can be generated from the tune if the most frequent tone, F4 (65), is defined as the base tone.

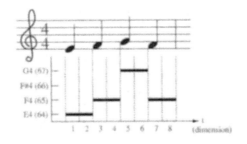

Fig. 2. Making an Entire Tone Transition Feature Vector.

Representative Tones for Vector Elements. Musical performance often requires the humming of very short notes or very minor shifts in notes. However, few people can hum them correctly. Moreover, many note errors are made in the hummings described in Section 2. Thus, feature vectors that accurately describe such short notes and small note-shifts are not particularly effective.

Consequently, the method we propose is to select a representative note for every beat resolution and to let the notes be vector elements. A representative note is defined as the longest note[2] rendered within the beat resolution. As a result, robust feature vectors are made because errors occurring in the representative notes do not affect the generation of feature vectors.

Achieving Matching with Vector Heads. Splitting melodies redundantly by the sliding-window method allows users greater song part flexibility in humming melodies. With this method, however, there may be variance of as much as half the slide length between the music subdata vector heads and those from the hummed tunes. For feature vectors that represent tone sequences, the mismatching of vector heads used for matching is a critical problem. This is particularly important in pop music, since in many recent pop hits the beat at the beginning of the song differs from that at the beginning of the song's bridge. As an example, let us consider the tune shown in Figure 3. The bridge part (B) of

Fig. 3. A tune in which the beat at the start (A) of the song differs from that at the start of the bridge part (B).

this tune starts on the fourth beat in the third bar. This means the bridge part is an auftact. If this tune were split at every fourth beat by the sliding-window method, all of the heads of the subdata would be the heads of bars. Thus there would be no subdata whose head matches that of the hummed tunes if the user hums the bridge part of the tune.

To solve this problem, we propose a method to determine vector heads independently of the heads of subdata and hummed tunes. A partial vector whose head is the dimension that contains the maximum value, in other words, the highest tone, within the slide length is extracted from each ETT. This vector is called a "Partial Tone Transition Feature Vector" (PTT). Reducing the slide length is another solution, however, it is not an attractive one because it enlarges the database.

Getting back to the tune in Fig. 3, though four subdata generate vectors whose heads are the same as the subdata heads, the fifth vector's head (C in the figure) is not the same as that of the subdata. This means if a user hums

---

[2] If there are multiple longest notes, the highest one is selected as the representative note.

the bridge part, including the fifth bar, there is a PTT in the database whose head matches with the vector head of the hummed tune. Thus with PTT, it is highly possible to achieve accurate matching with vectors whose heads match. The effectiveness of this method is evaluated in Section 5.3.

3.5   Duplicated Registration of Songs in Doubled/Halved Tempo

Since our music data is timely normalized based on the beat (Section 3.1), tempo is important information as the basis of the data processing. However, the faster a song is, the more people will use a tempo that is half the correct one and the slower a song is, the more people will use a tempo that is double the correct one. We call the former case *half-tempo error* and the latter case *double-tempo error*. In both cases, a correct matching cannot be performed because the amount of information per beat is doubled or halved.

Accordingly, we propose duplicated song registration in the database, whereby a fast tempo song is duplicated in halved tempo and both are stored in the database, and a slow tempo song is duplicated in doubled tempo and both are stored in the database. The effectiveness of this method is evaluated in Section 5.3.

3.6   "Keren" – Retrieval Engine with Distributed Indices

To achieve scalability and high-speed similarity retrieval, we built a search engine with distributed indices, which we call *Keren*. Keren is an abbreviation of "**Ker**nelized r**e**trieval e**n**gine". It reduces the retrieval cost because it uses small databases loaded in multiple machines instead of a large monolithic database. Moreover, all queries are processed in parallel with multiple threads. Threads are generated when Keren is initialized and are continuously waiting for queries.

Keren comprises a Global Manager (GM) and multiple Database Managers (DM). GM accepts retrieval requests from clients and sends queries to DMs. It also receives retrieval results from DMs, merges and formats them, and sends them to clients. In the database update phase, GM distributes input songs to DMs equally and requests database update. DM, in the retrieval phase, accepts queries from GM, then retrieves them, and sends results to GM. In the update phase, DM processes data distributed by GM and updates its indices. Figure 4 shows a query-by-humming system with Keren. By duplicating the system for the retrieval and update phases, in the retrieval phase, Keren can concentrate on searching to respond quickly. For the updating phase, Keren's indices are restructured so as to make them well-balanced. This ensures that Keren is able to conduct efficient searches.

4   SoundCompass/Humming System

Database Construction. MIDI music data is used for the database elements. The database is constructed as follows:

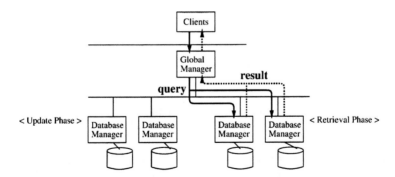

Fig. 4. The "Keren" high speed similarity retrieval engine

1. Melody data is extracted from songs.
2. Melodies are analyzed according to their tempos. Two copies of the melody data are made: one at the original tempo and another at half/double tempo for songs whose tempo is fast/slow.
3. The melody data is split into subdata by the sliding-window method.
4. Feature information is extracted from each subdatum. Multiple features are extracted and converted into multi-dimensional feature vectors.
5. Subdata that produce the same feature vectors are deleted.
6. Feature vectors are individually indexed according to feature.

Hummed Tune Processing. The hummed tune is recorded through a microphone. The user is required to clearly hum the song notes using only the syllable "ta" to transcribe pitches as accurately as possible. In addition, users are required to hum following the beats of a metronome. This is done to enable people to hum in constant tempo. The user may adjust the speed of the metronome to the desired tempo.

The acoustic data is processed based on FFT to track the fundamental frequency (F0) of each frame. The sampling rate of the acoustic data is 11kHz. For FFT, the window size is 512 and the shift length is 256. The F0 data is converted into a MIDI-like format. Then, the hummed tune is split into hummed pieces of the same window length and slide length as that of the subdata. The same kinds of features as those extracted from subdata are extracted from each hummed piece. These are also converted to feature vectors and used for queries.

Similarity Measurement, Similarity Retrieval. The similarity retrieval finds vectors in each feature's vector space that are close to the vectors generated by the hummed tune. Dissimilarity is calculated for each subdatum by using the weighted linear summation of the distance between the vectors. City block distance is used for the measurement. The shorter the distance to the subdata is, the more the subdata resembles the hummed piece. The final retrieval result is a weighted combination of the search results from individual feature vector spaces and is presented as a ranked list of songs.

User Interface. We have developed the SoundCompass/Humming system which integrates all technologies described in this paper. There are 21,804 songs in the database and only a 16-beat humming is needed to get the right song name in a few seconds. Information provided in this way makes it easy for users to use the Internet to purchase a CD, to get information about a song, or to access the artist's homepage. Since today there are many detailed song titles and artist names, if users can obtain the song name and more information only by inputting humming, it makes things easier for them and frees them from worries of mis-typing.

Figure 5 shows the GUI for the SoundCompass/Humming system. Figure 4 is a screen for adjusting the tempo of a metronome and recording a humming. This scene shows that 11 beats of the humming have been recorded already. Explanations for each button can be seen in the lower part of the screen. Thus, beginners can easily use the system by referencing them. Figure 4 shows a retrieval result example and web sites associated with the first ranked song. It shows songs whose hummed parts closely matched the 100-point score that SoundCompass/Humming awards for perfect humming and lists them according to the closeness of the match. In query-by-humming systems, accepting hummed tunes and retrieving similar songs are the most fundamental services that can be provided. After getting the results, even though there are a variety of options on how to utilize them on the Internet, this paper illustrates some example screens of CD purchase and text information retrieval in addition to playing and download service of the retrieved songs. The advantage of the services is that users can easily access information about songs and artists merely by humming a few bars without inputting the correct song names and artist names. In particular, information about major world-wide hits made in other countries can be accessed easily without any worries about mis-spelling.

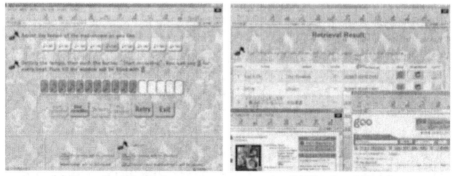

(a) Recording Humming   (b) Retrieved Result

Fig. 5. SoundCompass/Humming on Internet

Table 1. Retrieval Accuracy by Entire/Partial Tone Transition Feature Vector

	1st rank	within 5th rank	within 25th rank
ETT	151 (62.9%)	161 (67.1%)	169 (70.4%)
PTT	152 (63.3%)	173 (72.1%)	190 (79.2%)

Table 2. Number of hummings whose vector heads are consistent/inconsistent with those of subdata for ETT and PTT.

		ETT	
		consistent	inconsistent
PTT	consistent	160	59
	inconsistent	14	7

5 Evaluation

5.1 Experimental Environment

In our experiments, the database comprised 21,804 MIDI songs. Most of them are Japanese pop hits; however, about 6,000 of them are foreign songs, simple nursery songs, and folk songs. In retrieval accuracy experiments, 240 tunes hummed by 39 people (30 males and nine females) were used. All the tunes were of good enough quality that people can recognize them as a part of a song. The retrieval time experiment was conducted on four PentiumIV 1.5GHz PCs with 1GB RAM, running RedHat Linux 7.3.

5.2 Database Downsizing

When the melodies of the 21,804 songs are split by the sliding-window method of 16-beat window length and four-beat slide length, 3,241,038 subdata are generated. This includes the duplicated songs mentioned in Section 3.5. These subdata take up about 1.01GB. Deleting subdata by the method mentioned in Section 3.3 reduces the number of subdata to 1,858,115 and reduces the database size by 42.7%. Even with these reduction, there is no negative impact on retrieval accuracy.

5.3 Retrieval Accuracy

Entire/Partial Tone Transition Feature Vector. Table 1 shows retrieval accuracy using the ETT or the PTT. According to the table, the feature vectors that represent timely transition of tones can provide correct song names within the 5th rank about 70% of the queries. PTT can provide higher accuracy because it can cover the cases where the vector heads of subdata are not consistent with those of hummed pieces, described in Section 3.4.

Table 2 shows the cases where the vector heads of subdata are consistent/inconsistent with those of hummed pieces in each feature vector. Table

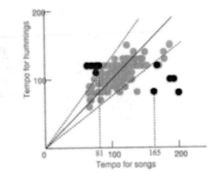

Fig. 6. Tempos of hummed parts of songs and hummings

2 shows that there are 66 hummed tunes whose vector heads are not consistent with those of subdata for ETT; however, PTT solved 59 of them. On the contrary, there are 14 tunes whose vector heads are not consistent with those of subdata for PTT even though they are consistent with each other for ETT. Among the 66 hummed tunes, the vector heads of 48 of them are not consistent with those of subdata in the music scores, where the other 18 tunes of them are not consistent with those of subdata because of errors of pitch extraction or tempo distortion. The PTT made it possible to achieve consistency between the vector heads of the hummed tunes and those of the subdata in 44 of the 48 former cases and 15 of the 18 latter cases.

Duplicated Registration of Songs of Doubled/Halved Tempo. Among 240 hummed tunes, tempo errors occurred in 11 tunes (Fig. 6). The x-axis represents the correct tempo of songs and the y-axis represents tempo that users selected. Across the solid diagonal line, the black circles on the right side show the cases where half-tempo error occurred. Such errors occurred for songs whose tempo is more than 165. The black circles on the left side show the cases where double-tempo error occurred. Such errors occurred for songs whose tempo is less than 81. The grey circles show songs where no such errors occurred. Thus, for songs whose tempo is less than 85 and is more than 160, songs whose tempo is doubled and halved are generated, and both are stored in the database.

As a result, the correct answer is obtained within the 6th rank for eight of the 11 hummed tunes. For the remaining three tunes, the vector heads are not consistent for two of them, and the other one is simply out of tone in its latter part.

Total Retrieval Accuracy. Table 1 and 2 show that both types of feature vectors should definitely be used for retrieval, and the better results obtained from either type of feature vector should be used as the final result. We call this method *feature-OR retrieval*. The retrieval accuracy with this method for ETT and PTT can be seen in the following table. A song database that holds the previously-mentioned duplicated songs of their doubled/halved tempo was used for the investigation.We found that feature-OR retrieval and the duplicated-song database improves the retrieval accuracy.

Table 3. Retrieval Accuracy of Feature-OR Retrieval with Duplicated Songs

	1st rank	within 5th rank	within 25th rank
ETT or PTT	162 (67.5%)	184 (76.7%)	205 (85.4%)

5.4 Retrieval Time

Figure 7 shows the retrieval times achieved with Keren. The x-axis represents the number of songs in a database and the y-axis represents the time to retrieve songs. Songs to make subsets of the database for this experiment were chosen randomly. We measured the time from the instant that the client submitted a query to Keren to the instant that the result from Keren was received. The dotted line represents the time without indices, the thin line represents that using one Database Manager with indices, and the thick line represents that using four of them with indices.

This figure reveals that the greater the size of the database is, the higher the efficiency the retrieval with indices, is and the more efficient the distributed indices are.

6 Concluding Remarks

This paper described a query-by-humming system available on the Internet. The system can retrieve correct songs within the 5th rank of 76.7 % accuracy in about 400 msec. This was achieved by using a number of new technologies, such as beat-based music data processing to adapt note errors and tempo flexibility, music data splitting by a sliding-window method to allow users to hum any part of

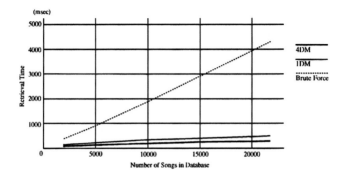

Fig. 7. Retrieval Time Evaluation.

songs, database downsizing based on repetitive structure of songs to reduce data storage cost, feature vectors based on tone transition that represent music characteristics well, partial feature vectors to determine vector heads independently from music data and hummed tunes, feature-OR retrieval with multiple feature information to improve retrieval accuracy, duplicated registration of songs in doubled/halved tempo for database to solve tempo errors. Furthermore, Keren, a high-speed retrieval engine with distributed indices was provided to attain quick response and the scalability with Internet use. We incorporated these technologies with our latest GUI into SoundCompass/Humming, our query-by-humming system.

References

1. K. Curtis, N. Taniguchi, J. Nakagawa, and M. Yamamuro. A comprehensive image similarity retrieval system that utilizes multiple feature vectors in high dimensional space. In *Proceedings of International Conference on Information, Communication and Signal Processing*, pages 180–184, September 1997.
2. J. Foote. An overview of audio information retrieval. In *Multimedia Systems 7*, pages 2–10. ACM, January 1999.
3. J. Foote. Visualizing Music and Audio using Self-Similarity. In *Proc. ACM Multimedia 99*, pages 77–80, November 1999.
4. A. Ghias, J. Logan, and D. Chamberlin. Query By Humming. In *Proc. ACM Multimedia 95*, pages 231–236, November 1995.
5. Jyh-Shing Roger Jang and Hong-Ru Lee. Hierarchical Filtering Method for Content-based Music Retrieval via Acoustic Input. In *Proc. of the 9th ACM International Conference on Multimedia*, pages 401–410, 2001.
6. N. Kosugi, Y. Nishihara, T. Sakata, M. Yamamuro, and K. Kushima. A Practical Query-By-Humming System for a Large Music Database. In *Proc. of the 8th ACM International Conference on Multimedia*, pages 333–342, 2000.
7. Rodger McNab. INTERACTIVE APPLICATIONS OF MUSIC TRANSCRIPTION. Master's thesis, Computer Science at the University of Waikato, 1996.
8. A. Yoshitaka and T. Ichikawa. A Survey on Content-Based Retrieval for Multimedia Databases. *IEEE Trans. Knowledge and Data Engineering*, 11(1):81–93, Feb. 1999.

Efficient Indexing of High Dimensional Normalized Histograms*

Alexandru Coman, Jörg Sander, and Mario A. Nascimento

Department of Computing Science,
University of Alberta,
Canada
{acoman,joerg,mn}@cs.ualberta.ca

Abstract. This paper addresses the problem of indexing high dimensional normalized histogram data, i.e., D-dimensional feature vectors H where $\sum_{i=1}^{D} H_i = 1$. These are often used as representations for multimedia objects in order to facilitate similarity query processing. By analyzing properties that are induced by the above constraint and that do not hold in general multi-dimensional spaces we design a new split policy. We show that the performance of similarity queries for normalized histogram data can be significantly improved by exploiting such properties within a simple indexing framework. We are able to process nearest-neighbor queries up to 10 times faster than the SR-tree and 3 times faster than the A-tree.

1 Introduction

Histograms, and normalized histograms in particular, have been extensively used as abstractions of multimedia objects in order to process similarity queries. A histogram for an object is a D-dimensional vector $H = (H_1, H_2, \ldots, H_D)$ where each coordinate value measures how much of each feature component is expressed in the object. In multimedia applications histogram are typically normalized, i.e., $\sum_{i=1}^{D} H_i = 1$.

A typical application of normalized histograms is the use of global color histograms as a means to represent images. In this case, each bin H_i represents the probability of a pixel being of color C_i, assuming a D-color space [6]. Even though we focus on normalized color histograms as the application of choice, the arguments presented throughout this paper apply to any type of normalized histogram. For instance, in [1] different methods for decomposing the enclosing sphere of an object into a number of cells (e.g., concentric shells), corresponding to histogram coordinates, are proposed. The value of a coordinate in these histograms is the percentage of the object that falls into the corresponding cell.

Using D-dimensional histograms for modelling multimedia objects enables a fairly effective and efficient processing of similarity queries. Since D-dimensional histograms can be viewed as points in a D-dimensional space, a distance function such as the Euclidean distance can be used to measure the dissimilarity

---

* This work was partially supported by NSERC Canada.

between objects. One important type of similarity query in multimedia information retrieval is the *K-nearest neighbor query*. Given a query object, the goal is
to retrieve the K objects that are closest (i.e., most similar) to the query object.
Although the efficient execution of this query, using a multidimensional index,
has well known solutions for lower dimensional data (e.g., [9]) the performance
of this type of query degenerates rapidly with increasing dimensionality of the
data space (e.g., [5]). Those effects have been observed in many applications,
e.g., it has been proven that they have to occur when the data is *uniformly* distributed [4,11]. However, the observed effects for high-dimensional normalized
histogram data have been much weaker than what the theoretical model would
suggest. Typically, it has been assumed that the underlying data set is highly
clustered so that the negative effects of high-dimensionality occurred to a much
lesser extent than expected.

In this paper we argue that this is not the only, nor the main reason. This
unexpected behavior can be observed for histograms obtained from real data
sets as well as for synthetically generated and completely unclustered histogram
data. We will show that this is a consequence of the constraint

$$\sum_{i=1}^{D} H_i = 1 \tag{1}$$

for normalized histograms $H = (H_1, H_2, \ldots, H_D)$ which induces additional constraints on both the point and the distance distribution in the whole data set.
For instance, unlike in the general unconstrained case, the maximum distance
between two points is now bounded. As well, the ratio of the average distance
between the farthest and the closest neighbor exhibits different behavior.

Based on our observations we derive a data-oriented split policy for data
pages in an simplified X-tree [3], which clearly outperforms even sophisticated
state-of-the-art multidimensional indexing structures when applied to histogram
data sets.

The rest of the paper is organized as follows: In Section 2 we briefly review the
related work on multi-dimensional indexing structures. In Section 3 we analyze
the multidimensional normalized histogram space and discuss the consequences
of its properties on similarity query processing. The design of a specialized split
policy for normalized histogram data is also presented in that section. Extensive
experimental results are presented in Section 4. Section 5 concludes the paper.

2   Related Work

Based on the general ideas of the R-tree [7] several access structures have
been proposed in recent years, aiming particularly at indexing points in high-
dimensional spaces, e.g., the X-tree, the SR-tree, and the A-tree.

The X-tree [3] is based on the observation that, for a large number of dimensions, the overlap introduced by the R-tree family of structures is very high
and large portions of the whole structure have to be searched for the majority of

queries. Therefore, a linear organization of the directory may be more efficient. Depending on the dimensionality of the feature space, the X-tree uses a hybrid approach to organize the directory as hierarchically as possible without introducing overlap. For very low dimensionality the X-tree is similar to an R-tree, for very high dimensionality the X-tree's directory consists of only one large supernode (root). Experimental performance shows that, on high-dimensional data, the X-tree outperforms the R*-tree by up to two orders of magnitude.

The SR-tree [8] improves on the SS-tree [12], which proposed the use of minimum bounding spheres (MBSs) instead of minimum bounding rectangles (MBRs). A minimum bounding sphere has a shorter diameter than the diagonal of the corresponding MBR for the same underlying objects, but its volume is generally much larger than the volume of the MBR. A careful combination of both MBSs and MBRs gives the SR-tree the advantage from both abstractions. The performance evaluations in [8] have shown that nearest neighbor queries are specially effective using the SR-tree for high-dimensional and non-uniform data sets, which is the general case for real data in image retrieval.

An approach that combines both data and space partitioning techniques is the A-tree [10]. The basic idea of this structure is to combine both the pruning advantages of tree-like indexes and the compact representation of vector approximations as in the VA-file [11]. The main contribution in this respect is the introduction of Virtual Bounding Rectangles (VBRs), which are approximate representation of MBRs or data objects. Since VBRs can be represented compactly, the fanout of nodes in the tree becomes larger, and the search speed increases. The reported results show that the A-tree is about three times faster than both the SR-tree and the VA-file for 64 dimensions.

As we discuss in Section 3.1, a fundamental difference between our new approach and the ones above is the data-oriented split policy, which, to the best of our knowledge, has received relatively little attention. As we shall see, the X-tree equipped with our specialized split policy outperforms the SR-tree and the A-tree by a factor of up to 10 and 3 respectively, in terms of page accesses.

3   Indexing the Normalized Histogram Space

In what follows we examine interesting properties of the normalized histograms data space and study the effect they have when processing similarity queries.

Each feature vector satisfies Equation 1, hence the value of any dimension can be determined by the values in the other $D - 1$ dimensions. That is, the data points are located in the intersection of a particular $D - 1$ dimensional hyper-plane with the unit cube, as illustrated in Figure 1 (the for 3D case). The most important consequence of the orientation of this hyper-plane is that the maximum possible distance between any two points in a normalized histogram space does not grow steadily with the dimension D as it does in an unconstrained data space. In fact, $d_{L2}(p,q) \leq \sqrt{2}$, for any two normalized histograms p and q — independent of their dimensionality. As a further consequence, nearest neighbor distances and the size of minimum bounding rectangles (MBRs) in an index

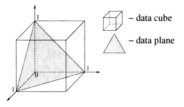

Fig. 1. The normalized histogram data space in 3D.

structure do not grow in the same way with increasing dimension as they do in an unconstrained data space.

Another important observation is related to the "meaningfulness" of nearest-neighbor queries in high dimensional space. In [4] the authors argue that for many high-dimensional scenarios the notion of nearest neighbor has little meaning since the nearest neighbor of a query point is likely to be as close as its farthest neighbor. If we denote the distance to an object's farthest neighbor by MaxDist and the distance to its closest neighbor by MinDist, the authors prove that for several scenarios the ratio MaxDist/MinDist approaches 1 with increasing dimensionality. For the case of feature vectors uniformly distributed in the unit cube, i.e., $U = (U_1, U_2, \ldots, U_D)$ where $U_i \sim \text{Unif}(0, 1), i = 1, \ldots, D$, this ratio converges to 1 extremely fast. This is not true for normalized histograms.

Figure 2 shows experimental results using synthetically generated data. For uniform data, doubling the dimensionality from 4 to 8 dimensions causes the ratio to decrease by one order of magnitude (note that both axis are in a log scale). A very distinct behavior can be observed for normalized histograms. For instance, even for a extremely high dimensionality such as 1024, the ratio MinDist/MaxDist for normalized histograms, is still as high as the same ratio for an only 4 dimensional Uniform space. The fact that for high-dimensional normalized histograms the data points are as far apart from each other as in the case of very low dimensional uniformly distributed data means that nearest neighbor queries in the normalized histogram space *are* meaningful. This may also explain why multidimensional indexing structures have been observed to yield acceptable performance for this type of data.

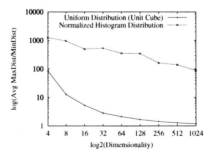

Fig. 2. Convergence rate of closest to farthest object distance.

Typical multidimensional indexing structures partition the data space using recursive splits and represent the resulting partitions by MBRs. A partition P, represented by an MBR B, is split into 2 new partitions P_1 and P_2 by choosing a split dimension and a split value which are used to distribute the data points within P into P_1 and P_2. Then, the resulting MBRs B_1 and B_2, for P_1 and P_2 respectively, are computed. The split value is typically chosen as the median, i.e., the value that divides the number of data points in two equally sized sets.

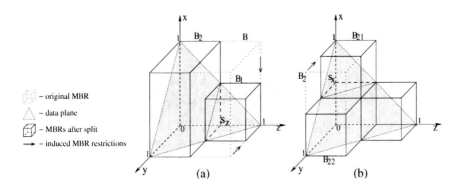

Fig. 3. Illustration of the effect yielded by *induced* restrictions.

When applying this split procedure to unconstrained uniform data the sum of the volumes of the resulting MBRs is approximately the same as the volume of the original MBR. This is very different for normalized histogram data as illustrated, using the 3-dimensional space, in Figure 3. Figure 3(a) shows the resulting MBRs B_1 and B_2 after splitting MBR B at value S_z along dimension Z, and Figure 3(b) shows the resulting MBR B_2 being split into B_{21} and B_{22}. Even though only one dimension is split in each case, the constraint on the data space (c.f., Equation 1) can lead to additional restrictions in other dimensions in at least one of the resulting MBRs. We refer to these as *induced restrictions*. A direct consequence is that a query range may be less likely to intersect MBRs in the index, yielding less pages accessed during query processing, compared to the uniform unconstrained case. Again, this may be a factor why existing structures behave acceptably when indexing normalized histograms. Note that the induced restrictions depicted in the figure assume that the data is evenly distributed in the normalized histogram data space. Depending on the actual data distribution, the resulting MBRs may shrink even further.

A final observation regarding the normalized histogram dataspace is with respect to the marginal distributions, i.e., the distribution of values along each dimension. In the unconstrained uniform data, the average value (0.5) in each dimension does not depend on the dimensionality, whereas in the uniform normalized histogram space it does depend on it – the higher the dimensionality D the smaller the average values ($1/D$) for each dimension. The properties of the marginal distributions and the induced restrictions allow us to determine better split values than the median split.

3.1   A New Split Policy for Normalized Histograms

In the following we will show that the distribution of the feature values for normalized histograms allows us to design a new and very efficient split policy. We assume static datasets and use a bulkload construction technique (e.g., [2]) that yields overlap-free partitions and a near 100% node storage utilization. A typical bulkloading algorithm partitions the dataset recursively choosing a split dimension and then a split value until objects fit on a page. In order to measure the effect of our split policy without the interference of other effects, e.g., the directory structure, and because we deal with high dimensional feature vectors, we assume a simplified version of the X-tree that consists of a large supernode and a list of leaf nodes.

A common choice for the split dimension is the one with the maximal extension, i.e., the dimension with the largest difference between the minimum and maximum value (e.g., [2]). This allows more freedom for choosing the split value, which can lead to stronger induced restrictions on the resulting MBRs.

For the split value there are several possibilities. The usual choice in most indexing structures, is the median, i.e., the value that divides the objects into partitions with equal cardinalities. This is not the optimal choice for normalized histograms, due to the properties of the marginal distributions for this space.

Our observation about the induced restrictions on MBRs suggest that a high split value leads to stronger induced restrictions. On the other hand if the split value is too high, one of the resulting MBRs will have a very narrow extension in the split dimension. This may degrade query performance because a query range falling into such a narrow MBR is then more likely to intersect its neighboring MBRs, leading to an increased number of page accesses. To better determine the effect of different split values let us further investigate the marginal distributions of the normalized histogram datasets.

The marginal distribution in each dimension for a (synthetically generated) uniform normalized histogram data space as well as for most dimensions in real datasets (e.g., color histograms) is as depicted in Figure 4(a). Note that the vast majority of values is close to zero, with an average of $1/D$ as discussed earlier. For real color histograms, however, a few colors are (naturally) more common than others yielding a marginal distribution as the one depicted in Figure 4(b). An extreme case of a more frequent color is(are) background color(s), which have a very different marginal distribution (Figure 4(c)).

As a consequence, for most colors, the median split value corresponds to a value very close to the lower end of the extension on the split dimension, which is contrary to our argument above.

A choice that follows our intuition of a high split, but ignores the narrowness of the upper MBR, is to choose a value so that the objects in the upper partition fit in one disk page. We call this approach the *Last Page Split* (LP-split). Another possibility is to choose a fixed ratio r so that the extension of the lower partition is r times the total extension, and the extension of the upper partition is $(1-r)$ times the total extension. We call this approach the R(r)-*split*. The LP-split

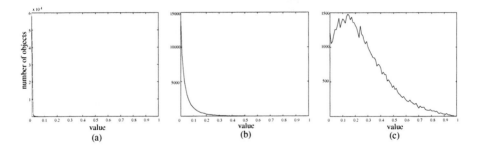

Fig. 4. Marginal value distribution for real (color) histograms in 64 dimensions.

generally corresponds to an R(r)-split with a high value of r, whereas the median typically corresponds to an R(r)-split with a very low value of r.

4   Experimental Results

In order to evaluate the efficiency of the proposed split policies we used two real datasets and one synthetically generated dataset. One real dataset was obtained by extracting color histogram from 60,000 images from a set of COREL CDs, and the other dataset consists of color histograms for approximately 100,000 TV snapshots. Since the relative performance of all methods for the TV dataset was very similar to the relative performance for the COREL dataset, due to space limitations, we show only the results for the synthetic dataset and for the COREL dataset. The synthetic dataset has 100,000 data points following an even distribution in the constrained normalized histogram space (referred to as *histogram-uniform dataset*). We used the Euclidean distance as the similarity measure. Since the distance evaluation is relatively inexpensive, we assume that the number of page accesses dominates query processing time. To compare the performance of the investigated indexing structures, we measure and average the number of accessed disk pages over 100 20-nearest neighbor queries.

We integrated both the LP-split and R(0.8)-split into the simple framework discussed in Section 3.1 – called LP-split Index and R(0.8)-split Index, respectively. The simplified X-tree using a median split is denoted as Median-split Index in the following.

We first compare the effect of varying the split ratio r in the R(r)-split with the LP-split and the usual median split. Figure 5(a) shows that when indexing the histogram-uniform dataset, the LP-split performs best. As expected, for high r values, the R(r)-split performs similar to the LP-split. Both clearly outperform the median split by up to one order of magnitude. Figure 5(b) shows that for the real data set the R(r)-split outperforms the other split policies for all tested split ratios (by a factor of 2 to 3) with the best split ratio being 80%, i.e., $r = 0.8$. (The same best r value was also found for the TV dataset.) The reason why the LP-split is not as good as the R(0.8)-split for the real data is that splitting the background color(s) using the LP-split will partition those colors on an extremely high value. This creates very narrow upper partitions, leading to reduced performance as discussed earlier. The figure also shows that the median split, which must correspond to a very low r value as previously discussed, is clearly the worst choice.

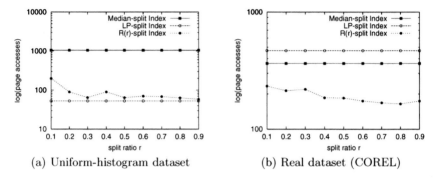

(a) Uniform-histogram dataset   (b) Real dataset (COREL)

Fig. 5. Gain (or loss) factor when using R(r)-split instead of LP-split.

We also compare all split policies to the SR-tree [8] and to the A-tree [10]. The SR-tree has been widely used as a comparison in the literature, and the A-tree is the current state-of-the-art multidimensional index. It integrates sophisticated ideas such as data quantization and MBR approximations and it has been shown to outperform other efficient indexing methods. In particular it outperforms the SR-tree and the VA-file by a factor of 3. For both the SR-tree and A-tree the number of pages accessed is the number reported by the provided source code[1].

For the case of uniform-histogram data, Figure 6(a) shows that the LP-split was up to 3 times faster than the A-tree, about 10 times faster than the SR-tree, and up to 20 times better than the median split. When indexing real datasets (Figure 6(b)) the R(0.8)-split showed more modest gains. The R(0.8)-split index was around 2 times faster than the A-tree and the median split (for 60,000 objects) and 7 faster than the SR-tree. In both cases we observed a relative gain in performance with increasing size of the dataset.

We have also investigated the performance of all access methods as a function of the data dimensionality (Figures 7(a) and (b)). For uniform data and 16 dimensions the LP-split Index performs slightly better than the A-tree, whereas for 64 dimensions it is 3 times faster. It is important to note that this gain increases significantly with the dimensionality because our technique is very stable with increasing dimensionality. When indexing real data (Figure 7(b)) the R(0.8)-split was up to 2 times faster than the A-tree. Compared to the SR-tree, the LP-split was over 10 times faster for uniform-histogram data and the R(0.8)-split was 7 times faster when indexing real data. Again, the LP-split was much faster than the median split (10 to 20 times) for uniform-histogram data, and twice as fast for real data.

---

[1] The source codes for the SR-tree and A-tree were kindly provided by their respective authors.

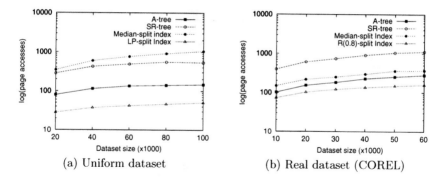

Fig. 6. Number of page access (log-scale) when varying the size of the dataset.

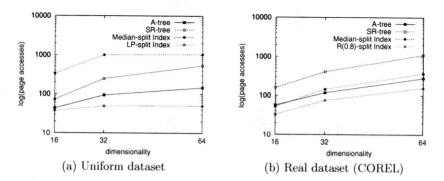

Fig. 7. Number of page access (log-scale) when varying the data dimensionality.

5   Conclusions and Future Work

Normalized histograms can be used to model object features and are usually of high dimensionality. Processing a similarity search within such a space can be seen as performing a nearest-neighbor search in the corresponding Euclidean space. In this paper we investigated the properties of the normalized histogram data space and subsequently how to take advantage of special properties of this data space when indexing it.

We proposed and investigated two node split policies, the LP-split and R(r)-split for normalized histogram data, which clearly outperform the typical median split. Using a simplified version of the X-tree as a framework we found that the LP-split was more suitable for evenly distributed histogram data, and the R(0.8)-split performed better for real data. When compared to the more complex A-tree and the SR-tree, both split policies were shown to be consistently more efficient (up to 3 times faster than the A-tree and up to 10 times faster than the SR-tree) and more robust with respect to dimensionality.

We are currently investigating an adaptive split policy that automatically takes the data distribution into account to determine the optimal split ratio for each page. In the future we will also investigate combining similar optimized

A. Coman, J. Sander, and M.A. Nascimento

split policies within more sophisticated techniques, such as data quantization and MBR approximation as in the A-tree, as well as dynamic insertions and deletions.

References

1. M. Ankerst et al. 3d shape histograms for similarity search and classification in spatial databases. In *Proc. of the Intl. Symp. on Advances in Spatial Databases*, pages 207–226, 1999.
2. S. Berchtold, C. Böhm, and H.-P. Kriegel. Improving the query performance of high-dimensional index structures by bulk load operations. In *Proc. of the Intl. Conf. on Extending Database Technology (EDBT)*, pages 216–230, 1998.
3. S. Berchtold, D.A. Keim, and H.-P. Kriegel. The X-tree: An index structure for high-dimensional data. In *Proc. of the Intl. Conf. on Very Large Databases*, pages 28–39, 1996.
4. K. S. Beyer et al. When is nearest neighbor meaningful? In *Proc. of the 7th Intl. Conf. on Database Theory*, pages 217–235, 1999.
5. C. Böhm, S. Berchtold, and D. A. Keim. Searching in high-dimensional spaces: Index structures for improving the performance of multimedia databases. *ACM Computer Surveys*, 33(3):322–373, 2001.
6. A. Del Bimbo. *Visual Information Retrieval*. Morgan Kaufmann Publishers, Inc., 1999.
7. A. Guttman. R-trees: A dynamic index structure for spatial searching. In *Proc. of ACM SIGMOD Intl. Conf. on Management of Data*, pages 47–57, 1984.
8. N. Katayama and S. Satoh. The SR-tree: An index structure for high-dimensional nearest neighbor queries. In *Proc. of the ACM SIGMOD Intl. Conf. on Management of Data*, pages 369–380, 1997.
9. N. Roussopoulos, S. Kelley, and F. Vincent. Nearest neighbor queries. In *Proc. of the ACM SIGMOD Intl. Conf. on Management of Data*, pages 71–79, 1995.
10. Y. Sakurai et al. The A-tree: An index structure for high-dimensional spaces using relative approximation. In *Proc. of the Intl. Conf. on Very Large Data Bases*, pages 516–526, 2000.
11. R. Weber, H. Schek, and S. Blott. A quantitative analysis and performance study for similarity-search methods in high-dimensional spaces. In *Proc. of the Intl. Conf. on Very Large Databases*, pages 194–205, 1998.
12. D. A. White and R. Jain. Similarity indexing with the SS-tree. In *Proc. of the IEEE Intl. Conf. on Data Engineering*, pages 516–523, 1996.

Implementation of a Stream-Oriented Retrieval Engine for Complex Similarity Queries on Top of an ORDBMS

Andreas Henrich and Günter Robbert

University of Bayreuth,
Faculty of Mathematics and Physics,
D-95440 Bayreuth, Germany
{andreas.henrich,guenter.robbert}@uni-bayreuth.de

Abstract. When dealing with structured multimedia documents the typical query is no longer an exact match query, but a best match or similarity query yielding a ranking for the required objects. To process such queries different components are needed — namely, *rankers* delivering a sorting of objects of a given type with respect to a single similarity criterion, *combiners* merging multiple rankings over the same set of objects and *transferers* transferring a ranking for objects of a given type to related objects. In the literature various approaches for these single components have been presented. However, the integration of the components into a comprehensive approach for complex similarity queries has hardly been addressed. In this paper we propose IRstream as a retrieval engine for the stream-oriented processing of complex similarity queries. This retrieval engine is intended to complement traditional query processing techniques for queries dominated by similarity conditions. It utilizes rankers, combiners and transferers and it is implemented on top of an ORDBMS. We describe the concept and the architecture of the system and state some experimental results.

1 Motivation

In recent years structured multimedia data has become one of the most challenging application areas for database systems and retrieval services for structured multimedia data are an important research topic in this respect. To emphasize the key problems in this field let us assume tree structured multimedia documents, where the internal nodes represent intermediate components, such as chapters or sections, and where the leaves represent single media objects such as text objects, images, videos, or audios.

In order to support the search for documents in this scenario we need a powerful retrieval service, which has to fulfill the following requirements [6]:

Dealing with Structured Documents: The fact that in our scenario documents are complex structured objects brings up various interesting research issues. (1) A retrieval service must allow to search for arbitrary granules ranging from

V. Mařík et al. (Eds.): DEXA 2003, LNCS 2736, pp. 611–621, 2003.

whole documents over intermediate chunks to single media objects. (2) Many properties of an object are not directly attached to the object itself, but to its components. For example, the text of a chapter will usually be stored in separate text objects associated with the chapter object via links or relationships. (3) Additional information about an atomic media object can be found in its vicinity. Exploiting the structure of a multimedia document this "vicinity" can be addressed navigating one link up and then down to the sibling components.

Feature Extraction and Segmentation: With multimedia data the semantics is usually given implicitly in the media objects. For example, an image might represent a certain mood. Therefore the retrieval service should allow to extract features from the media objects potentially describing their semantics. Furthermore it should provide means to subdivide media objects such as images or videos into semantically coherent segments.

Similarity Queries: Because of the vagueness in the interpretation of the media objects and in the expression of the users information need similarity queries should be facilitated. The retrieval service should provide the definition of ranking criteria for media objects. For example, text objects can be ranked according to their content similarity compared to a given query text. To this end, e.g. the well known vector space model can be applied [12]. Images can be ranked with respect to their color or texture similarity compared to a sample image [10,13].

Combination of Several Similarity Queries: Images are an example for a media type, for which no single comprehensive similarity criterion exists. Instead different criteria addressing e.g. color, texture and shape similarity are applicable. Hence, features to combine multiple ranking criteria and to derive an overall ranking are needed. Since each similarity criterion yields some type of similarity value — usually called *Retrieval Status Value* (RSV) — for each object, a weighted average over multiple similarity values can be applied to derive an overall ranking [3]. Other approaches are based on the ranks of the objects with respect to the single criteria [8]. To calculate such a combined ranking algorithms such as Nosferatu, Quick-Combine or J^* have been proposed [11,4,9].

Transfer of Ranking Values between Different Object Types: With structured documents ranking criteria are often not defined for the required objects themselves, but for their components or other related objects. An example arises when searching for images where the text in the "vicinity" (e.g. in the same subsection) has to be similar to a given sample text. Another example would be a query searching for chapters containing images similar to a given sample image. In such situations the ranking defined for the related objects has to be transferred to the required result objects. However, since there will usually be a 1:n-relationship or even a n:m-relationship between the objects, neither the semantics nor the implementation of such a "transfer" is self-evident. As a solution for this problem we have proposed an *RSV-transfer* algorithm in [7].

Extensibility and Scalability: In order to be applicable to a wide range of different application areas the retrieval service has to be extensible in many directions. It should be possible to integrate new feature extractors and similarity measures addressing specific characteristics of multimedia documents. Furthermore, the retrieval service should offer possibilities to integrate index structures which can accelerate the query execution.

Performance: The retrieval service should offer a good performance for all types of queries. In this respect a pull-based approach might be useful to process similarity queries, because it allows to deliver the first elements of the query result as fast as possible.

In the following, we propose a retrieval service for structured multimedia documents, which fulfils most of the requirements mentioned above, and elucidate its architecture.

2   The IRstream Architecture

The main idea behind IRstream is the stream-oriented realization of complex queries for structured multimedia documents. "Stream-oriented" means that the whole query evaluation process is based on components producing streams one object after the other. Usually the stream production will be implemented realizing a lazy approach — i.e. objects are produced only on demand, and if only k objects are required by the consumer this will usually induce less effort than the production of $k + 1$ objects.

The concrete architecture for our IRstream system is based on the idea that the data is maintained in one (or more) external data sources. In our implementation, an objectrelational database (ORDBMS) is used for this purpose. The stream-oriented retrieval engine is implemented in Java on top of this data source and provides an application programming interface (API) to facilitate the realization of similarity based retrieval services. Figure 1 depicts this architecture which will be explained in more detail in the rest of this section.

The core IRstream system — shaded grey in figure 1 — comprises four main parts: (1) Implementations for rankers, combiners, transferers, and filters. (2) Implementations of various methods for the extraction of feature values for different object types as well as corresponding similarity measures. (3) A component maintaining meta data for the IRstream system itself and for the applications willing to use IRstream. (4) Wrappers needed to integrate external data sources, access structures and stream implementations.

Let us now explain the main parts of our IRstream system in more detail. Note, that the addressed components are realized as interfaces, by this way each of these components can be implemented in different kinds. For example, in our prototype implementation we implemented Combiners using the algorithms Nosferatu and Quick-Combine.

2.1   Feature Extractors and Similarity Measures

A feature extractor receives an object of a given type (e.g., an image) and extracts a feature value for this object (e.g., color or texture information). The similarity measures are methods which receive two feature representations — usually one representing a query object and the other representing an object

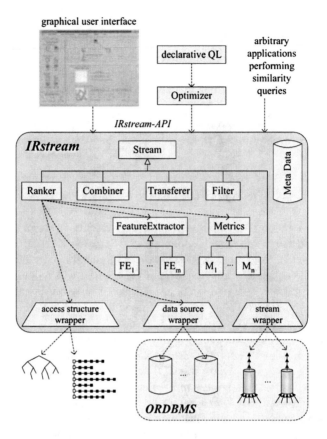

Fig. 1. Architecture of the IRstream system

for which the similarity compared to the query object has to be calculated. The result of such a similarity measure is a corresponding *retrieval status value*.

2.2   Ranker, Combiner, Transferer, Filter, ...

All these components are extensions of the interface "Stream". The interface of these classes mainly consists of a specific constructor and a getNext method.

Ranker: The starting point for the stream-oriented query evaluation process is formed by rankers which are streams generated for a set of objects based on a given ranking criterion. As mentioned earlier, text objects can be ranked according to their content similarity compared to a given query text and images can be ranked with respect to their color or texture similarity.

Such "initial" streams can be efficiently implemented by various access structures supporting similarity searches, such as the M-tree, the X-tree, the LSD^h-tree or the VA-file [16,1,5,15].

The constructor of a ranker receives a specification of the data source — in our system this is usually a table in the underlying ORDBMS —, a feature extractor, a similarity measure and a query object. Then the constructer inspects the meta data to see if there is an access structure for this similarity query. In case the access structure is employed to speed up the ranking. Otherwise, a table scan with a subsequent sorting is performed.

Combiner: A combiner merges multiple streams providing the same objects ranked with respect to different ranking criteria. For example with images, two rankings sorting the images with respect to their color and texture similarity, respectively, can be combined into a single ranking. Hence, components which merge multiple streams representing different rankings over the same base set into a combined ranking are needed. Since each element of each input stream is associated with some type of retrieval status value (RSV), a weighted average over the retrieval status values in the input streams can be used to derive the combined ranking [3]. Other approaches are based on the ranks of the objects with respect to the single criteria [8,6]. To calculate such a combined ranking efficient algorithms, such as Fagin's algorithm, Nosferatu, Quick-Combine or J^* have been proposed [2,11,4,9].

For the construction of a combiner two or more incoming streams with corresponding weights have to be defined. Here it is important to note that combiners such as Fagin's algorithm or Quick-Combine rely on the assumption that random access is supported for the objects in the input streams. This means that an input stream has to provide the opportunity to calculate efficiently the retrieval status value of a concrete element which has not yet been delivered by this input stream. The reason for this requirement is simple. When these algorithms receive an object on one input stream, they want to calculate the mixed retrieval status value of this object immediately. To this end, they perform random accesses on the other input streams. Unfortunately, some input streams do not provide such random access options or a random access would require an unreasonable high effort. In these cases, other combine algorithms — such as Nosferatu or J^* — have to be applied.

Transferer: As mentioned in the motivation, with structured documents ranking criteria are sometimes not defined for the required objects themselves but for their components or other related objects. An example arises when searching for images where the text nearby (for example in the same section) should be similar to a given sample text. The problem can be described as follows: We are concerned with a query which requires a ranking for objects of some desired object type ot_d (*image* for example). However, the ranking is not defined for the objects of type ot_d, but for related objects of type ot_r (*text* for example).

We assume that the relationship between these objects is well-defined and can be traversed in both directions. This means that we can determine the concerned object — or objects — of type ot_d for an object of type ot_r and that we can determine the related objects of type ot_r for an object of type ot_d. The concrete characteristics of these "traversal operations" depend on the database or object store used to maintain the documents. In objectrelational databases join indexes and index structures for nested tables are used to speed up the traversal of such relationships. For a further improvement additional path index structures can be maintained on top of the ORDBMS (cf. section 3).

Furthermore, we assume there is an input stream yielding a ranking for the objects of type ot_r. For example, this stream can be the output of a ranker or combiner.

To perform the actual transfer of the ranking we make use of the fact that each object of type ot_r is associated with some type of retrieval status value (RSV_r) determining the ranking of these objects. As a consequence, we can transfer the ranking to the objects of type ot_d based on these retrieval status values. For example, we can associate the maximum retrieval status value of a related object of type ot_r with each object of type ot_d. Another possibility would be to use the average retrieval status value over all associated objects of type ot_r. The retrieval status value calculated for an object of type ot_d according to the chosen semantics will be called RSV_d in the following.

Based on these assumptions, the "transfer algorithm" can proceed as follows: It uses the stream with the ranked objects of type ot_r as input. For the elements from this stream, the concerned object — or objects — of type ot_d are computed traversing the respective relationships. Then the retrieval status values RSV_d are calculated for these objects of type ot_d according to the chosen semantics and the object of type ot_d under consideration is inserted into an auxiliary data structure maintaining the objects considered so far. In this data structure, each object is annotated with its RSV_d value. Now the next object of type ot_r from the input stream is considered. If the RSV_r value of this object is smaller than the RSV_d value of the first element in the auxiliary data structure which has not yet been delivered in the output stream, this first element in the auxiliary data structure can be delivered in the output stream of the transfer component [7].

For the construction of a transferer, an incoming stream, a path expression and a transfer semantics have to be defined. In our implementation, references and scoped references provided by the underlying ORDBMS are used to define the path expressions.

Filter: Of course, it must be possible to define filter conditions for all types of objects. With our stream-oriented approach this means that filter components are needed. These components are initialized with an input stream and a filter condition. Then only those objects from the input stream which fulfill the filter condition are passed to the output stream. To construct a filter, an incoming stream and a filter predicate have to be defined.

2.3   Meta Data

This component maintains data about the available feature extractors, similarity measures, access structures, and so forth. On the one hand, this meta data is needed for the IRstream system itself in order to decide if there is a suitable access structure for example. On the other hand, the meta data is also available via the IRstream-API for applications.

2.4   Extensibility and Scalability

IRstream allows for the extension of the retrieval service in various directions by the use of wrappers and interfaces:

Data source wrappers are needed to attach systems maintaining the objects themselves to our retrieval system. At present, objectrelational databases can be attached via JDBC.

Access structure wrappers can be used to deploy access structures originally not written for our system. For example, we incorporated an LSD^h-tree written in C++ via a corresponding wrapper. In general this interface should be used to attach access structures which can maintain collections of feature values and perform similarity queries on these values. Such an access structure is used to speed up the ranking of objects maintained in separate data sources. In contrast, the *stream wrapper* interface is used to incorporate external sources for streams into our system. It can be used to incorporate external stream producers. At present, the text module of the underlying ORDBMS is integrated via a stream wrapper. In contrast to an access structure, such an external stream producer provides not only a ranking but also access to the maintained objects themselves. This means that an external stream producer is aware of the objects themselves, whereas an external access structure does only maintain feature values and associated object references.

Whereas wrappers allow for the integration of external data sources, index structures and stream providers, IRstream also supports internal extensions by the use of interfaces. For all components predefined interfaces are provided for the integration of new feature extractors, similarity measures, combiners etc. As an example we consider the following interface for similarity measures which defines the methods a measure has to implement:

```
public interface MeasureMethod {
    public double Distance(GenericValue param1, GenericValue param2)
                  throws IRStreamException;
    public String[] getSupportedDatatypes();
    public boolean isDatatypeSupported(String typename);
    public double getBestMatch();
    public double getWorstMatch();
}
```

This interface requires that a method named `Distance()` has to be implemented which determines the distance between two parameters of type `GenericValue`. This data type encapsulates all data types which can be handled by IRstream for retrieval purposes. In general, a distance measure can be applied only on some subtypes of `GenericValue`, therefore it has to implement the methods `getSupportedDatatypes()` and `isDatatypeSupported(String typename)`, which deliver information about the supported data types. Furthermore, a measure has to provide the methods `getBestMatch()` and `getWorstMatch()`. These methods indicate which result values can be seen as a best or worst match.

2.5 Programming API

As mentioned, IRstream provides an API for the development of new retrieval services. To give a flavor of this API we will briefly discuss the following program code fragment.

```
public void retrieveSimilarSegments() {
    // generate connection information for IRstream server
    ServerConnectionInfo sci =
        new ServerConnectionInfo("132.180.192.17","ai1k2",1521,"dexa","****");

    // generate connection information for data source
    ORDBMSWrapper ow =
        new ORDBMSWrapper(new DBConnectionInfo("132.180.192.9","ai1x2",1521,"dexa","****"));
    sci.connect();    // connect to IRstream server
    Image img = new Image(); // load query image from file
    img.loadImageFromFile("c:\\example.tif",sci.getConnection());

    // define Ranking condition for Ranker 1:
    RankingCondition rc1 = new RankingCondition(new TextureVector(),new e_dist(),
                                new IMAGEValue(img),StreamInfo.ASCENDING);
    // instantiate Ranker 1
    Ranker r1 = new Ranker(sci,ow,"dexa","segments","texture",rc1);

    // define Ranking condition for Ranker 2:
    RankingCondition rc2 = new RankingCondition(new MunsellColorVector(),new e_dist(),
                                new IMAGEValue(img),StreamInfo.ASCENDING);
    // instantiate Ranker 2
    Ranker r2 = new Ranker(sci,ow,"dexa","segments","color",rc2);

    Stream[] st = {r1, r2}; // define input streams for combine operation
    double[] wt = {0.3, 0.7}; // define weighting of the streams

    // use QuickCombine for merging
    QuickCombine cc = new QuickCombine(st,wt,Combiner.MERGE,StreamInfo.ASCENDING);
    cc.init(); // initialize the streams

    while(cc.getNext()!=null) { // incremental access to the result stream
        /* do something ... */
    } // while
} // retrieveSimilarSegments
```

This program code can be used to search for image segments similar to a given query image with respect to color and texture. In the first step the connections to the IRstream server and the external data source are established. Thereafter, two ranking conditions and associated rankers are defined. These rankers produce two ranking streams containing ascending similarity values with respect to the color and texture similarity. Then a combiner implementing the algorithm *QuickCombine* is used to merge the two incoming streams. To this end, the incoming streams are weighted with weights of 0.3 and 0.7. Finally, the stream processing is started calling init() at the combiner level. Now the elements of the result stream can be accessed incrementally using the getNext()-Method.

3 Experimental Results

To assess the performance of our IRstream approach, we performed tests on a document collection containing more than 12000 articles from the IEEE computer magazine in XML format. The collection comprises 12565 color images

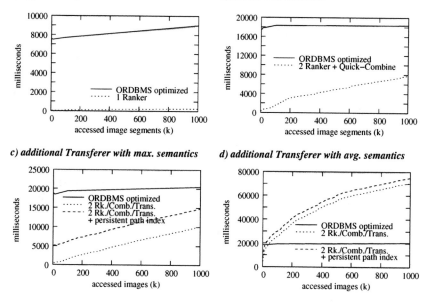

Fig. 2. Performance results for different query types

and about 50000 image segments. The documents where inserted into the OR-DBMS underlying our system. Furthermore, two LSD^h-trees were maintained as access structures for feature vectors representing the color and the texture characteristics of the image segments. For the color similarity 10-dimensional Munsell color histograms were used [14]. For the texture similarity 4-dimensional feature vectors comprising homogeneity, energy, contrast and entropy are used. We performed three different query types:

In the first query we searched for the k most similar image segments compared to a query image with respect to color similarity. As a consequence, only one ranker had to be used. Figure 2a shows that the performance of the IRstream system is far better than the performance of the ORDBMS in this case.

In the second query we searched for the k most similar image segments compared to a query image with respect to color and texture similarity. IRstream performed this query based on two rankers and a combiner. Figure 2b shows the performance results for this scenario.

Finally, the third query is based on the second query and additionally transfers this ranking to the corresponding images according to the maximum semantics and the average semantics (cf. figure 2c+d). Here the performance of two variants of our approach is given. The upper curve gives the performance when a path index for the traversal of the relationships between the image segments and the images is computed on the fly during the query execution. The lower curve gives the performance, when the path index is maintained persistently and updated every time the concerned tables are changed. The curves show that the performance achieved with the maximum semantics is by far better than the performance of the ORDBMS. With the more costly average semantics only for the first 30 accessed images our system shows a better performance than the ORDBMS. Here it has to be noted that our system is implemented in Java and is by no means optimized. An IRstream approach implemented directly into an ORDBMS would be much faster. Nevertheless, it becomes obvious that the transfer semantics has a dramatic influence on the performance. An in depth evaluation of this aspect will be part of our future research.

4   Conclusion and Future Work

In this paper we have presented IRstream as a retrieval engine for the stream-oriented processing of complex similarity queries. This retrieval engine is intended to complement traditional query processing techniques for queries dominated by similarity conditions. Our IRstream approach has been implemented as a prototype in Java on top of an ORDBMS and first experimental results achieved with this prototype are promising.

In the near future, we will address the optimization of the prototype implementation and experiments with larger test collections. Furthermore, we will develop a query language for this approach and consider optimization issues.

References

1. S. Berchtold, D. A. Keim, and H.-P. Kriegel. The X-tree : An index structure for high-dimensional data. In *VLDB'96, Proc. 22th Intl. Conf. on Very Large Data Bases*, pages 28–39, Mumbai, India, 1996.
2. R. Fagin, A. Lotem, and M. Naor. Optimal aggregation algorithms for middleware. In *Proc. 10th ACM Symposium on Principles of Database Systems: PODS*, pages 102–113, New York, USA, 2001.
3. R. Fagin and E. L. Wimmers. A formula for incorporating weights into scoring rules. *Theoretical Computer Science*, 239(2):309–338, 2000.
4. U. Güntzer, W.-T. Balke, and W. Kießling. Optimizing multi-feature queries for image databases. In *VLDB 2000, Proc. 26th Intl. Conf. on Very Large Data Bases*, pages 419–428, Cairo, Egypt, 2000.
5. A. Henrich. The LSD^h-tree: An access structure for feature vectors. In *Proc. 14th Intl. Conf. on Data Engineering, Orlando, USA*, pages 362–369, 1998.
6. A. Henrich and G. Robbert. Combining multimedia retrieval and text retrieval to search structured documents in digital libraries. In *Proc. 1st DELOS Workshop on Information Seeking, Searching and Querying in Digital Libraries*, pages 35–40, Zürich, Switzerland, 2000.
7. A. Henrich and G. Robbert. An approach to transfer rankings during the search in structured documents (in german). In *Proc. 10. GI-Fachtagung Datenbanksysteme für Business, Technologie und Web, BTW'03*, Leipzig, Germany, 2003.
8. J. H. Lee. Analyses of multiple evidence combination. In *Proc. 20th Annual Intl. ACM SIGIR Conference on Research and Development in Information Retrieval*, pages 267–276, Philadelphia, PA, USA, 1997.

9. A. Natsev, Y.-C. Chang, J. R. Smith, C.-S. Li, and J. S. Vitter. Supporting incremental join queries on ranked inputs. In *Proc. 27th Intl. Conf. on Very Large Data Bases*, pages 281–290, Los Altos, USA, 2001.

10. W. Niblack et al. The QBIC project: Querying images by content, using color, texture, and shape. In *SPIE Proc. Vol. 1908*, pages 173–187, San Jose, 1993.

11. U. Pfeifer and S. Pennekamp. Incremental Processing of Vague Queries in Interactive Retrieval Systems. In *Hypertext – Information Retrieval – Multimedia '97: Theorien, Modelle und Implementierungen*, pages 223–235, Dortmund, 1997.

12. G. Salton. *Automatic Text Processing: the Transformation, Analysis, and Retrieval of Information by Computer*. Addison-Wesley, Reading, Mass., 1989.

13. J. Smith and S.-F. Chang. VisualSEEk: A fully automated content-based image query system. In *Proc. of the 4th ACM Multimedia Conf.*, pages 87–98, New York, USA, 1996.

14. J. Sturges and T. Whitfield. Locating basic colours in the munsell space. *Color Research and Application*, 20:364–376, 1995.

15. R. Weber, H.-J. Schek, and S. Blott. A quantitative analysis and performance study for similarity-search methods in high-dimensional spaces. In *Proc. 24th Intl. Conf. on VLDB, New York City, USA*, pages 194–205, 1998.

16. P. Zezula, P. Savino, G. Amato, and F. Rabitti. Approximate similarity retrieval with M-trees. *VLDB Journal*, 7(4):275–293, 1998.

GFIS Pro – A Tool for Managing Forest Information Resources

Thanh Binh Nguyen[1] and Mohamed T Ibrahim[2]

[1] IUFRO,
Vienna, Austria
binh@ifs.tuwien.ac.at
[2] University of Greenwich,
London UK SE10 9LS
M.T.Ibrahim@greenwich.ac.uk

Abstract. The Global Forest Information Service (GFIS), an initiative of internationally recognized forestry institutions lead by the International Union of Forest Research Organizations (IUFRO), primarily aims as an electronic system that utilises the Internet to facilitate forest information resource discovery. For describing the content of resources, the GFIS metadata has been designed and implemented as a generalization of the Dublin Core metadata element set. In this context, a set of multilingual controlled forest vocabularies has been established that allows GFIS to focus on a forest special application domain. Hereafter, we have studied and implemented the GFIS prototype, which supports interoperability search among a class of GFIS nodes by means of GFIS-Dublin Core Metadata and the multi host search (MS) tool.

Keywords: Metadata, Interoperability, Multihost search

1 Introduction

Information systems are rapidly being influenced by web technologies and are driven by their growth and proliferation to create next generation web information systems. The World Wide Web is a distributed global information resource. It contains a large amount of information that have been placed on the web independently by different organizations and thus, related information may appear across different web sites. Different search engines (Alta Vista, Hot Bot, Lycos, Yahoo!, etc.) provide keyword-based search facilities to help users to retrieve information and the results come as HTML pages [3]. From one or several words, such engines collect a whole range of information from web documents that use these words, but results are often limited. The search engines do not take account of the semantics of the documents.

On the other hand, in forestry and related disciplines, it is widely recognized that rapid, reliable and universal access to quality information is essential for informed decision-making concerning forests and all their inherent values. The volume of forest-related information generated globally is enormous, and the number of sources of information is equally overwhelming [10]. The major problem facing information-seekers world-wide is the location of information sources corresponding to their needs. Equally important, information-providers often do not easily find appropriate fora for presenting their information, which then remains inaccessible to others.

V. Mařík et al. (Eds.): DEXA 2003, LNCS 2736, pp. 622–630, 2003.

To help address these problems, an Internet-based metadata service, namely GFIS is studied and developed to provide coordinated world-wide access to forest-related information. GFIS is envisaged primarily as an electronic system that utilises the Internet to facilitate information resource discovery, through access to a distributed network of information providers. The evolution of GFIS has been taking place during a period of very rapid changes in the technologies associated with the Internet and the World Wide Web. Both the GFIS community and the web technologies are now sufficiently mature to move from proof of concept towards a semi-operational prototype. Key components of GFIS are metadata standards, and database interoperability [9]. For describing the content of resources, the GFIS system uses the Dublin Core metadata element set. By using the same metadata standard information providers would improve interoperability. In the GFIS context, interoperability is the ability for the user interface to operate with multiple disparate metadata repositories in a transparent manner. The use of universally accepted terminologies to describe information resources furthers the objective of interoperability [12].

This paper describes the present state and discusses some of the most relevant technical issues encountered in the process of establishing the Global Forest Information Service. The remainder of this paper is organized as follows. Section 2 presents related works. In Section 3 we introduce GFIS conceptual model, i.e. system architecture, GFIS-Dublin Core metadata standard. Hereafter, we apply the concepts to implement the GFIS prototype including GFIS Nodal package and the information server with the multi-host search. The conclusion and future works appear in Section 5.

2   Related Works

Our work is related to research within the area of metadata for federated database systems, mediation between multiple information systems, especially distributed forest information systems.

The DARPA Agent Markup Language (DAML) [14] developed by DARPA aims at developing a language and tools to facilitate the concept of the *Semantic Web* [15]: the idea of having data on the Web defined and linked in a way that it can be used by machines not just for display purposes, but for automation, integration and reuse of data across various applications. The DAML language is being developed as an extension to XML and the Resource Description Framework (RDF). The latest extension step of this language (DAML + OIL - Ontology Inference Layer) provides a rich set of constructs to create ontologies and to markup information so that it is machine readable and understandable.

The Ontology Inference Layer (OIL) [4] from the On-To-Knowledge Project is a proposal for such a standard way of expressing ontologies based on the use of web standards like XML schema and RDF schemas. OIL is the first ontology representation language that is properly grounded in W3C standard such as RDF/RDF-schema and XML/XML-schema. DAML and OIL are general concepts not specifically related to database or forest information interoperability.

In the research area of formal ontologies the authors of [4] propose the use of similarity relations in order to find out whether (and how) elements from different schemas are related (involving human supervision). They then use reasoning systems (such as PowerLoom) to merge ontologies – but they do not try to detect or resolve mismatches between ontologies.

The library community has much to offer in this regard and a mature protocol know as Z39.50 [16]is in use by many libraries, providing a standard interface to heterogeneous library catalogue systems. However Z39.50 has been somewhat obscure outside of the library community and has been difficult to configure.

In forest information systems, since its establishment in September 1998, the basic elements of such an information service have been proposed and discussed [8, 10]. In addition, two GFIS-related projects have been established in Africa [13] and Europe, and more are in preparation.

3 Conceptual Model

The GFIS is based upon the notion of a distributed network of databases which catalogue the information resources of contributing GFIS partners using a common metadata standard. The Internet and WWW are used to facilitate the location and searching of metadata items. It is proposed that the GFIS will function by providing a standardised core of metadata (catalogue) elements, a standardised set of key words. This will facilitate interoperability among metadata databases, namely GFIS nodes. The envisioned structure and information flow within the GFIS is illustrated in Figure 1 and presented in the following section.

3.1 GFIS System Architecture

GFIS is conceived as a distributed system whereby member organisations remain responsible for the generation and maintenance of their information content. GFIS enables users to locate that content and, where appropriate, to access it in term of GFIS node as represented in figure 1. Another component to GFIS is the GFIS Information Server that is the central component of the GFIS. It collects GFIS metadata from the nodes, thus enabling global interoperability searching. It also provides house-keeping functionality, maintaining records of GFIS members, organizations, events, announcements, and projects.

Data/Information Object (DO): these are the items that the user want to find using metadata. These items have different contents, spatial and temporal scales, format and other attributes specific to each database.

Metadata: these are Data about Data. Each metadata item is used to describe a data/information object. The GFIS metadata definition is based on the Dublin Core metadata standard, and is used to describe specific GFIS DOs.

GFIS Node: a GFIS partner institution that collects, maintains and manages GFIS metadata submitted by data provider(s) or others. Nodes also collect regional information about their members, organizations, events and activities.

GFIS Affiliated Node: an institution offering a forest-related website which metadata may not be GFIS-Dublin Core standard. To be integrated to GFIS system, the metadata can be converted to GFIS-Dublin Core metadata by using GFIS conversion tool.

GFIS Information Server (IS) is the central component of the GFIS. It collects GFIS metadata from the nodes, thus enabling global searching. It also provides house-keeping functionality, maintaining records of GFIS members, organizations, events, announcements, and projects.

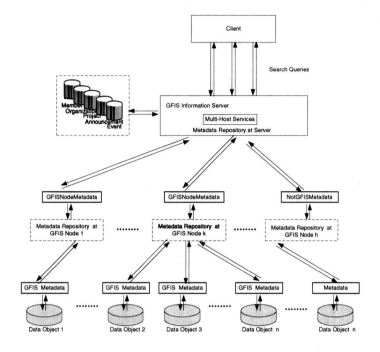

Fig. 1. System Architecture- Federated Approach

3.2   GFIS Metadata

GFIS-Dublin Core Metadata

Key components to organising information, whether it is on electronic or paper media, are metadata – "data about data" [5,6,7]. Furthermore, the Dublin Core Metadata Initiative is literally a core set of metadata elements for electronic information resources that have been agreed by consensus [15]. The elements are generic and non-subject specific, but can be qualified to add subject richness. The Dublin Core Element Set is attractive because it is simple and manageable with just fifteen basic elements, but also extensible via qualifications. The GFIS has adopted the following approach on metadata:

- adopt the Dublin Core as a basic core set of metadata elements
- 15 elements of the Dublin Core can be repeated in use.
- qualify the Dublin Core with additional elements as required by the forest community
- provide controlled forest vocabularies for certain metadata elements, for example subject and keywords

Standardisation enables interoperability between heterogeneous systems, thereby fostering information exchange and collaboration.

Modelling GFIS-Dublin Core Metadata with UML

The Unified Modelling Language (UML) is a graphical notation based upon the object-oriented paradigm for modelling systems [11]. UML is being utilised by GFIS to graphically specify the GFIS system and API (Application Programming Interface).

The GFIS API class diagram is designed and implemented for the various GFIS projects in the programming environment of their choice. Versions in Java, JSP, PHP and ASP are being discussed.

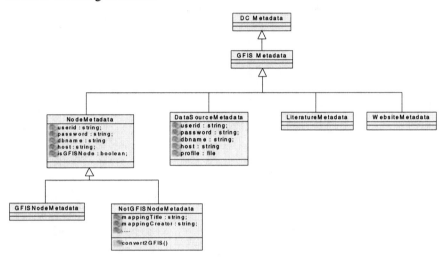

Fig. 2. GFIS-Dublin Core Metadata Class Diagram.

GFIS-Dublin Core Metadata Design and Implementation

An object-oriented approach is being taken with the GFIS design, including the GFIS metadata standard. The starting point for the GFIS metadata is the fifteen Dublin Core Elements. However, the GFIS is using these attributes to compile a data dictionary of standard elements and qualifiers, augmented by additional GFIS specific elements and qualifiers. These attributes, together with a content attribute, are taken as the data members of a *GFIS Metadata Class*. The data dictionary, which is stored in a database and can easily be modified and added to, is then being used as the basis for an XML Document Type Definition (DTD). By defining an XML DTD for forest information we are starting to define a GFIS specific XML dialect – ForestML. ForestML will be used as the information transport mechanism within GFIS [9]. A DTD explicitly defines the elements and attributes that are allowable in a ForestML metadata document and can be used for validating ForestML documents for "well formedness".

The Metadata Element Class, which is generic, can be replicated to accommodate the full GFIS element set, comprised of Dublin Core plus GFIS qualifications, or other more extended standards such as the ISO geo-spatial standard, when it is published. An XML example of GFIS-Dublin Core can be seen in the appendix A.

3.3 GFIS Interoperability Search

Conforming to a GFIS-Dublin Core metadata standard, by using the same standard elements and controlled vocabularies as others, means that the meta-databases or nodes can be searched in the same way as those of other organizations. This provides a degree of interoperability and enables the same search query to be submitted to many organizations and meaningful results returned. As a result, a multi-host searching engine has been studied and implemented. The full description of the multi-host search is presented in section 4, GFIS prototype.

4 GFIS Prototype

The main reason for developing a prototype is to resolve uncertainties early in the development cycle. In the context of GFIS, a prototype is also an excellent way to reveal and resolve ambiguity in the requirements. The GFIS prototype has been implemented. There are two main packages: GFIS Information Server and Node.

Each time query is posed for the GFIS system, the following 5 steps are required (see figure 3).

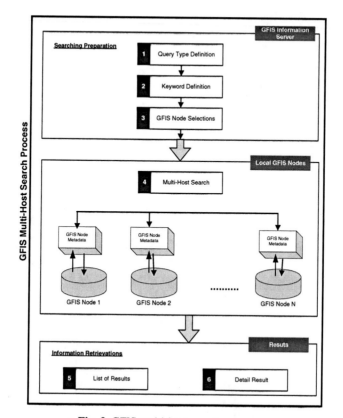

Fig. 3. GFIS multi-host search process.

Steps 1-3 belong to the build-time stage at the global Information Server. This stage covers the modeling and the design of the search metadata. In this stage all definitions for the required metadata are completed which are required to search into GFIS Nodes. The next step 4 belongs to the run-time stage or searching processes at local GFIS Node systems by means of GFIS-Dublin Core Metadata. Steps 5 and 6 are used to display retrieved information. All steps are described following in more detail.

Query Type Definitions. Dependent on the characteristics of the required metadata, two types of query, namely *simple* and *advanced search*, can be defined at the GFIS Information Server.

Keyword Definition. Based on the tree representation of the GFIS controlled forest vocabularies (figure 5), user can roll up or drill down to select keyword(s) for searching. The selected keyword(s) will be used to for query in local GFIS Node(s).

Local MetaCube-X Selections. This step provides flexibility in support of interoperability searching among multiple heterogeneous GFIS Nodes (figure 4). User can select one or more local GFIS Nodes from the tree.

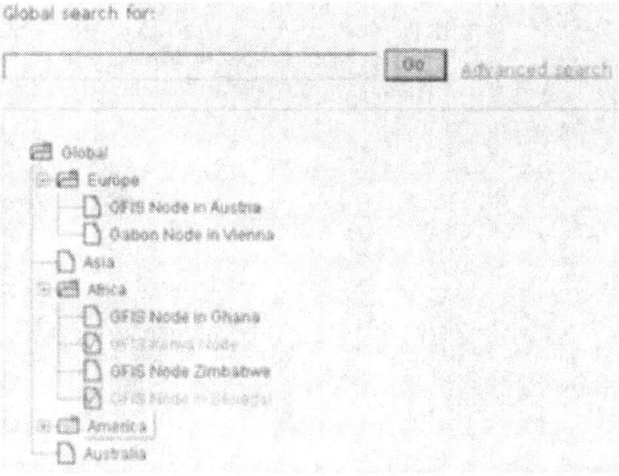

Fig. 4. GFIS query type and node selections.

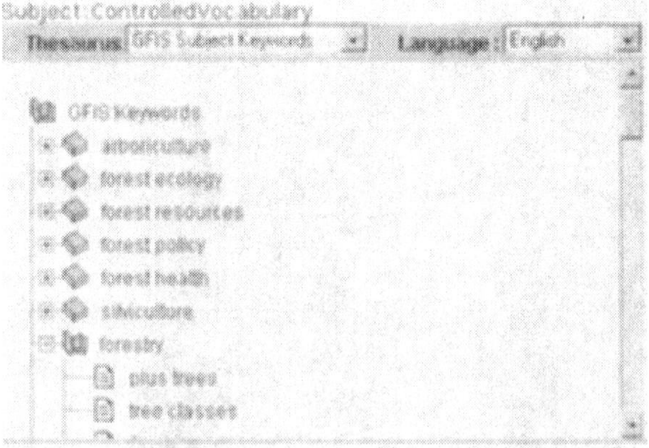

Fig. 5. GFIS Controlled Vocabulary selections.

Multi-Host Search. In this step, the request will be delivered to the selected local GFIS Nodes. At each local node, keywords and other parameters are derived and then used to select metadata items in the node database.

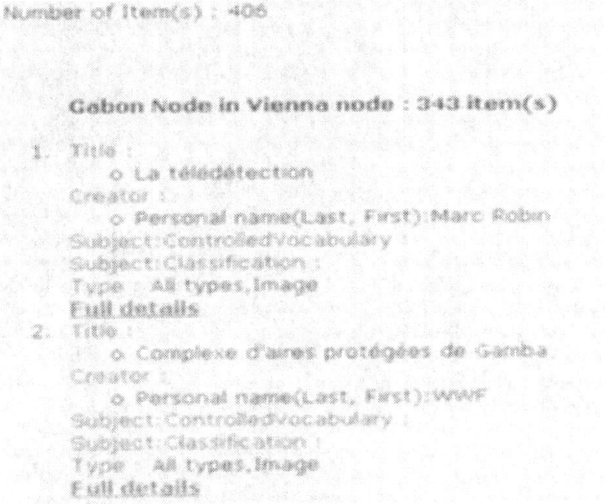

Fig. 6. GFIS query results.

5   Conclusion and Future Works

GFIS has had a long gestation and has been a learning process for all involved. The GFIS prototype has been built and provided useful vehicles for discussion and development of ideas. GFIS has considered standardization and metadata, linking metadata to the data/information [9].

In the next step, a GFIS Metadata repository will be studied and implemented as a component to store integrated metadata from multiple nodes for efficient querying and analysis. The metadata is extracted from heterogeneous nodes as it is generated or updated. When a user query is submitted to the metadata repository, the required information is already there, with inconsistencies and differences already resolved. This makes it much easier and more efficient to run queries over data that originally came from different nodes.

References

1. Fensel D., I. Horrocks, F. Van Harmelen, S. Decker, M. Erdmann, and M. Klein. OIL in a Nutshell. In: Knowledge Acquisition, Modeling, and Management, Proc. of the 12th European Knowledge Acquisition Conference (EKAW-2000), R. Dieng et al. (eds.), Springer-Verlag LNAI 1937, pp. 1-16, Oct. 2000.
2. Hakimpour F., and A. Geppert. Resolving Semantic Heterogeneity in Schema Integration: an Ontology Based Approach. Proc. of the Intl. Conf. On Formal Ontologies in Information Systems (FOIS-2001), ACM Press, Ogunquit, Maine, Oct. 2001.

3. Hocine A. & M. Lo, FRANCE. Modeling and information retrieval on XML-based dataweb. In Proc. of First Biennial International Conference on Advances in Information Systems(ADVIS'2000), Izmir, TURKEY, October 2000. Lecture Notes in Computer Science (LNCS), Springer, 2000.
4. Horrocks, D. Fensel, J. Broekstra, S. Decker, M. Erdmann, C. Goble, F. van Harmelen, M. Klein, S. Staab, R. Studer, and E. Motta. The Ontology Inference Layer OIL.
5. Meta Data Coalition. Metadata Interchange Specification (MDIS) Version 1.1, August 1997.
6. Meta Data Coalition. Open Information Model XML Encoding. Version 1.0, December 1999. http://www.mdcinfo.com/.
7. Meta Data Coalition. Open Information Model. Version 1.1, August 1999. http://www.mdcinfo.com/.
8. Mills, R.A. 2000. The role of libraries and information centres in the global forest information service. Abstract, p. 403, in: Krishnapillay, Baskaran et al. (eds). 2000. Forests and Society: the role of researcy. Abstracts of group discussions, vol. 2. .XXI IUFRO world congress, 7-12 August 2000, Kuala Lumpur. ISBN 983-2181-09-7.
9. Päivinen, R., , Richards T., Thanh Binh Nguyen, Richard Wood. The IUFRO Global Forest Information Service – Towards a Common Resource. Proceedings of a IUFRO 4.11 conference held at the University of Greenwich, June 2001.
10. Päivinen, R., Iremonger, S., Kapos, V., Landis, E., Mills, R., Petrokofsky, G., Richards, T. and Schuck, A. . "Better access to information on forests", http://iufro.boku.ac.at/iufro/taskforce/tfgfis/icris-gfis.pdf (233 kb). (The document is also available at EFI: http://www.efi.fi/files/icris.pdf.) 1998
11. Rational. *Unified Modeling Language, Version 1.3* http://www.rational.com/uml
12. Saarikko, J., Päivinen, R., Richards, T., and Sini, M. 2000. Information server prototype for Global Forest Information Service (GFIS). In: Joint FAO/ECE/ILO Committee on Forest Technology, Management and Training Workshop: Forestry Information Systems 2000, 16-20 May 2000, Hyytiälä, Finland. 7pp. http://iufro.boku.ac.at/iufro/taskforce/tfgfis/FIS2000-hyytiala-paper.pdf (61 kb)
13. Szaro, R. et al. 2000. Mobilising and Disseminating information on forests to promote sustainable management in Africa. Abstract, pp. 404–405. In: Krishnapillay, Baskaran et al. (eds). 2000. Forests and Society: the role of researcy. Abstracts of group discussions, vol. 2. .XXI IUFRO world congress, 7–12 August 2000, Kuala Lumpur. ISBN 983-2181-09-7; http://iufro.boku.ac.at/iufro/taskforce/tfgfis/IUFRO2000-Szaro-et-al.pdf (59kb)
14. The DARPA Agent Markup Language Homepage. http://daml.semanticweb.org/
15. The Dublin Core Metadata Initiative (DCMI). http://www.dublincore.org/about/
16. The Semantic Web Homepage. http://www.semanticweb.org
17. The Z39.50 Gateway to Library Catalogs. http://www.loc.gov/z3950/agency.

FDRAS: Fashion Design Recommender Agent System Using the Extraction of Representative Sensibility and the Two-Way Combined Filtering on Textile

Kyung-Yong Jung[1], Young-Joo Na[2], and Jung-Hyun Lee[1]

[1] Department of Computer Science & Engineering
[2] Department of Clothing and Textiles
Inha University, Inchon, Korea
dragon@nlsun.inha.ac.kr, {youngjoo,jhlee}@inha.ac.kr

Abstract. It is important for the strategy of product sales to investigate the customer's sensibility and preference degree in the environment that the process of material development has been changed focusing on the customer center. In this paper we identify collaborative filtering and content-based filtering as independent technologies for information filtering. We propose the Fashion Design Recommender Agent System of textile design applying two-way combined filtering technologies as one of methods in the material development centered on customer's representative sensibility and preference. We build the database founded on the sensibility adjective to develop textile design by extracting the representative sensibility adjective form user's sensibility and preference about textiles. Our system recommends textile designs to a customer who has a similar propensity about textile. Ultimately, this paper suggests empirical applications to verify the adequacy and the validity on this system.

1 Introduction

Information filtering techniques fall in two combined filtering categories: content-based filtering and collaborative filtering. Content-based filtering is based on content analysis of the considered objects. It is therefore necessary that the results of content analysis and user preferences can reliably and automatically be determined. While recent research shows good results for the content-based filtering of text document, filtering of other media, as video and audio, is hard due to the limitations of content analysis technology available. On the other hand, collaborative filtering does not show this limitation. In collaborative filtering, objects are selected for a particular user when they are also relevant to similar users and, in general, the content of the object is ignored. Therefore, collaborative filtering is especially interesting for objects for which content analysis is difficult or impossible. However, the performance of collaborative filtering relies in the amount of available opinions on the considered objects and it therefore performs poorly when few or no opinions are known. In order to build better performing filtering systems both techniques can be combined [1,7].

The purpose of our research is to explore the combination of collaborative filtering and content-based filtering on textiles. We used content-based criteria to textile

V. Mařík et al. (Eds.): DEXA 2003, LNCS 2736, pp. 631–640, 2003.

design content predictors. These predictors were then linearly combined with collaborative filtering predictor. Our approach extends by the use of *Sarwar*[4], in such using content-based criteria to create artificial rating, but it differ as to we create many artificial user profiles, whose ratings are derived by content-based filtering and corresponding original users profiles, which are similar to the selection agents of *Fab*[1], which specialize to the preferences of specific users. We have implemented our idea in a prototype called the Fashion Design Recommender Agent System.

2   System Overview

The Fashion Design Recommender Agent System(FDRAS) is a project that aims at study how the two-way combination of collaborative filtering and content-based filtering can be used to build user-adapting recommender agent system. Fig. 1 shows system overview for FDRAS using the extraction of representative sensibility and the two-way combined filtering on textile. This system consists of server and client module. We use filtering techniques to create a user-adapting textile design, in which the hypertext structure is created for each specific user, based on prediction of what this user should prefer. The basic idea that the user is asked to provide rating for the textiles that he views during his login. The system then selects textiles similar to textiles with high ratings. Collaborative filtering is also used to make prediction based on the rating that other users have provided during previous visits. These predictions are then used to present textiles to the user accordingly, so that more relevant textiles are seen first.

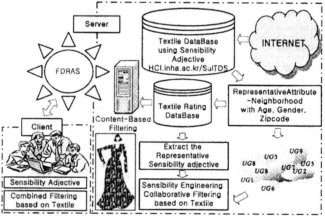

Fig.1. System overview for Fashion Design Recommender Agent System

For collaborative filtering based on textile, Representative-Attribute Neighborhood is adapted to determine the number of neighbors that will be used for preferences[5,6]. Pearson Correlation Coefficient is used to calculate similarity weights among users. We build the database founded on the sensibility adjective to develop textile designs by extracting the representative sensibility from users' sensibility and preferences about textile designs. FDRAS recommends textile designs to a customer who has a similar propensity about textile. Therefore, users evaluate the sensibility of each textile through the representative sensibility adjectives at the client module of FDRAS using two-way combined predictor. The server classifies the users having similar sensibility into several groups with based on Representative Attribute-Neighborhood of age, gender and zipcode[5,6]. FDRAS recommends the proper 5 textiles designs to user with certain sensibility after the combination of collaborative filtering and content-based filtering.

3   Sensibility Engineering Collaborative Filtering Based on Textile

3.1   Construction of Textile Database Using Sensibility Adjective

We decide 18 pairs of the sensibility adjective by using a method that extracts adjectives from a dictionary, the magazine, the literature and etc. The pairs of sensibility adjective about textile used in questionnaire are shown {(Spaced, Compact), (Dark, Bright), (Rural, Urban), (Childish, Adult), (Ungraceful, Graceful), (Pure, Sexy), (Conservative, Progressive), (Female, Male), (Curve, Linear), (Dull, Clear), (Cold, Hot), (Simple, Complicated), (Mechanical, Natural), (Old, New), (Static, Active), (Retro, Modern), (Oriental, Western), (Soft, Hard)}. 512 users (259 males and 253 female) evaluated each textile according to type of the meaning division scale from –2 to +2 rating(5 phases). The textile database by the sensibility adjective consists of the user ratings, user-profiles, and information about textile. All the textiles are classified each 20 textile with 4 categories of Imaginal, Natural, Geometry, and Artificial. After selecting each pair of adjective, which expresses sensibility, we decided 36-sensibility adjective. The questionnaires on web are based on the degree of the sensibility that the users feel about 60 textiles. The composition of questionnaires based on web follows to answer 10 phases on 6 textiles in one page.

3.2   The Extraction of Representative Sensibility Adjective on Textile

It is difficult to evaluate the sensibility of the human objectively due to the ambiguity and qualitatively. In addition, it is difficult to grasp the image of abstract users because the expression comes out by the restrict adjectives only.

In this paper, we tried to grasp the general sensibility of users through a method that extracts the representative sensibility adjective about textile. Rough algorithm is below which draws representative sensibility adjective based on the data evaluated on each textile by users.

[Step 1] classifying the sensibility data on each textile.
[Step 2] calculating means and standard deviations of each sensibility adjective.
[Step 3] sorting sensibility adjective by its mean.
    (Selecting top 5 adjectives in descending).
[Step 4] establish database of sensibility adjectives on textiles.

The reason of using 5 adjectives is that one adjective is not sufficient for expressing the sensibility of textiles. The results of survey on the sensibility adjective are open on http://hci.inha.ac.kr/SulTDS/result.htm.

3.3   Textile Based Collaborative Filtering

Collaborative filtering technique selects items for a user based in the opinions of other users. Generally, collaborative filtering techniques do not rely on content-based information about items, considering only human judgments on the value of items[6]. Collaborative filtering technique consider every user as an expert for his taste, so that personalized recommendations can be provided based on the expertise of taste-related users. Collaborative filtering has been applied to several domains of information. For example, MovieCritic, Music, Ringo[2,3], GroupLens[8]. Most collaborative filtering systems collect the user opinions as ratings on a numerical scale, leading to a sparse matrix rating (*user*, *item*) in short $r_{u,i}$. Collaborative filtering technique then uses this rating matrix in order to derive predictions. Several algorithms have been proposed on how to use the rating matrix to predict rating[2,3,6]. In our FDRAS, we apply a commonly used algorithm, proposed in the GroupLens project and also applied in Ringo, which is based on vector correlation using the Pearson correlation coefficient.

Usually the task of a collaborative filtering technique is to predict the rating of a particular user u for an item i. The system compares the user u's rating with the rating of all other users, who have rated the considered item i. Then a weighted average of the other users rating is used as a prediction. If I_u is set of items that a user u has rated then we can define the mean rating of user u by Equation (1).

$$\overline{r_u} = \frac{1}{|I_u|}\sum_{i\in I_u} r_{u,i} \tag{1}$$

Collaborative filtering algorithms predict the rating based on the rating of similar users. When Pearson correlation coefficient is used, similarity is determined from the correlation of the rating vectors of user u and the other users a by Equation (2).

$$w(u,a) = \frac{\sum_{i\in I_u\cap I_a}(r_{u,i}-\overline{r_u})(r_{a,i}-\overline{r_a})}{\sqrt{\sum_{i\in I_u\cap I_a}(r_{u,i}-\overline{r_u})^2 \bullet \sum_{i\in I_u\cap I_a}(r_{a,i}-\overline{r_a})^2}} \tag{2}$$

It can be noted that $w(u,a)\in[-1,+1]$. The value of $w(u,a)$ measures the similarity between the two users' rating vectors. A high absolute value signifies high similarity and low absolute value dissimilarity. The general predict formula is based in the assumption that the prediction is a weighted average of the other users rating. The weights refer to the amount of similarity between the user u and the other users by Equation (3). The factor k normalizes the weights.

$$p^{collab}(u,i) = \overline{r_u} + k\sum_{a\in U_i} w(u,a)(r_{a,i}-\overline{r_a}) \qquad k = \frac{1}{\sum_{a\in U_i} w(u,a)} \tag{3}$$

Sometimes the correlation coefficient between two users is undefined because they not rated common objects ($I_u \cap I_a = \emptyset$). In such cased the correlation coefficient is estimated by a default voting ($w_{default} = 2$), which is the measured mean of typically occurring correlation coefficient. The $w_{default}$ is defined as 2 because the sensibility data evaluated on textiles has the distribution of bimodal distribution in Fig. 4.

4   Content-Based Filtering on Textile

It is reasonable to expect that textiles with similar content will be almost equally interesting to users. The problem is that defining textile content and textile similarity is still an open problem. Ongoing research in multimedia indexing is focusing on two directions. First, each textile is described by a textual caption, and captions are compared using techniques derived from document retrieval. Second, analysis and recognition technique are applied to the textile pixels to extract automatically features that are compared using some distance measure in the feature space. We focus on the latter approach, because it can be entirely automated. In our prototype, we have currently implemented two feature extraction components, derived from the work described in color histograms and textile design coefficients.

4.1   Color Histograms

The original textiles are available in RGB format, where each pixel is defined by the value(0-255) of the three components red, blue, and green. We project these values in the HSV(Hue, Saturation, Value) space which models more accurately the human perception of colors. The HSV coefficients are quantized to yield 166 different colors. For each textile, the histogram of these 166 colors is computed(proportion of pixels with a given quantized color).

To compare two textiles design, we compute the L_1 distance between their color histograms with the following Equation (4). $h_i(j)$ represents the percentage of number of pixels of textile i with the color j.

$$d^{color}(k,l) = L_1(h_k, h_l) = \sum_j |h_k(j) - h_l(j)| \qquad d^{color} \in [0..2] \qquad (4)$$

4.2   Textile Design Coefficients

While color histograms do not take into account the arrangement of pixel, textile design coefficients can be computed to characterize local properties of the textile. We are using a wavelet decomposition using the two-dimensional Haar transform, by which a number of sub-textiles corresponding to frequency decomposition are generated. These sub-textiles are quantized to binary values, so that each pixel of the original textile is associated with binary vector of length 9. The histogram of these vectors(length $512 = 2^9$) is the feature vector associated to analysis of the textile. As previously for color distance, the L_1 distance is used to measure the distance between textiles by Equation (4). As shown in Fig. 2, in order to determine the similarity between textiles design, all the textiles in the database are decomposed into sub textiles using wavelet decomposition. From the decomposition a feature histogram is derived, which can then be compared by the use a vector metric.

636   K.-Y. Jung, Y.-J. Na, and J.-H. Lee

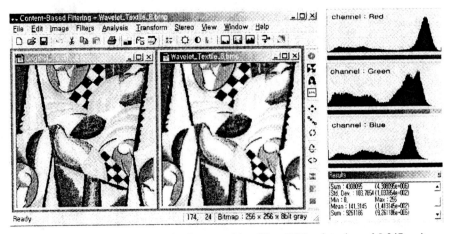

Fig. 2. Original textile / Wavelet decomposition (Haar 2 Wavelet: elapsed 0.047 sec)

We use a linear estimated for the content-based prediction, which is illustrated in the following Equation (5). $p^{color}(u,i)$ represents the prediction for textile i for user u.

$$p^{color}(u,i) = \sum_{j} \lambda_j \frac{\sum_{a \in C_j(i)} r_{u,a}}{|C_j(i)|} \qquad (5)$$

If a prediction is to be made for a user u and a target textile i, all the textiles previously rated by user u are grouped into distance classes $C_j(i)=\{a \in I_u : d^{color}(k,l)\}$ according to color-based distance to target textile i. Each class is associated with a weight λ_j. The prediction is then the weighted sum of the mean ratings of each class. The weights λ_j are estimated through linear regression by using a separated subset of the rating.

5   An Approach Combining Collaborative Filtering and Content-Based Filtering on Textile

In cases where collaborative filtering is limited by an insufficient amount of users and ratings, a combination of collaborative filtering and content-based filtering should lead to better filtering performance. Besides the improvements of performance for case of *sparsity*, a system which uses the two-way combined filtering approach can also recommended items which have not yet received any ratings e.g., new items, which is not possible for a system relying only on collaborative filtering. In the following we present the combination of collaborative filtering and content-based filtering.

5.1   Deriving Artificial Users from Textile Design Metrics

We pursue to extend the database used for collaborative filtering technique, so that artificial ratings are inserted, which are coherent with the content-based distances. For each described distance metric of section 4 and for each real user u a corresponding artificial user u^{color} and $u^{textile}$ is derived. The artificial users are assigned the same rating as the original user u, so that if $r_{u,i}$ is defined, then $r_{u^{color}}_{,i} = r_{u^{textile}}_{,i} = r_{u,i}$.

Additionally, artificial ratings are derived for some textiles, which the original user u had not rated. The artificial ratings are content-based predictions for that particular user. That means that some un-rated items are assigned a predicted rating, based on similarity between the rated items and the item whose score should be predicted. In order to perform a content-based prediction, we define a restricted neighborhood for of a textile i within user-profile of a user u, which contains textiles rated by user u, which distance is below a threshold T by Equation (6).

$$N_{u,i}^{color} = \{j \in I_u \mid d^{color}(i,j) \le T^{color}\} \tag{6}$$

These neighboring textiles are then user to predict a score for the artificial ratings. The prediction formula for color is shown in Equation (7).

$$p^{color}(u,i) = mean_{j \in N_{u,i}^{color}}(r_{u,j}) \tag{7}$$

In this perspective, the database is extended for color as following Equation (8).

$$r_{u^{color},i} = \begin{cases} r_{u,i} & \text{if } r_{u,i} \text{ is defined.} \\ p^{color}(u,i) & \text{if } N_{u,i}^{color} \text{ is not empty} \\ undefined & eles \end{cases} \tag{8}$$

The extended database is then used with collaborative filtering algorithm, which has been described earlier. By extending existing users the possibility of correlation with the artificial users is increased. In fact, a user u correlates perfectly with his counterparts u^{color} and $u^{textile}$, which causes the content-based prediction to be strong part of the collaborative prediction of user u and transitively also all other users according to their similarity to user u.

5.2   The Two-Way Combined Filtering on Textile

For the following considerations we assume an existing collaborative filtering system, as Fashion Design Recommender Agent System. The combination with content-based filtering is therefore rather an extension of collaborative filtering. As research leads to additional content-analysis tools, the extension approach should not limit the number of content-based extensions. Therefore we combine the content-based predictors with the collaborative filtering predictor $p^{collab}(u,i)$, as described in section 3, linearly using the following Equation (9).

$$p^{comb}(u,i) = \mu^{collab} p^{collab}(u,i) + \mu^{color} p^{color}(u,i) + \mu^{textile} p^{textile}(u,i) \qquad \sum \mu = 1 \tag{9}$$

The weights $\mu^{\{collab,color,textile\}}$ are estimated by the use of linear regression with a set-aside subset of the rating.

5.3   FDRAS: Fashion Design Recommender Agent System

Fig. 3 shows Fashion Design Recommender Agent System(FDRAS) using the extraction of representative sensibility and the two-way combined filtering on textile. The two-way combined filtering consists of collaborative prediction and content-based prediction. The questionnaire is through http://hci.inha.ac.kr/SulTDS in Korean users, this site can download FDRAS client program. [Sensibility adjective] is the part that the users enter his/her preferred sensibility in the order and its degree by moving the control bar. The user has the 18 adjective pairs shown in drop-down list. The selected 5 adjectives are each given weights: first weight, 100%; second weight, 50%; third weight, 30%; fourth weight 15%; and fifth weight, 5%. FDRAS runs its engine to recommend the five textiles as fitting the preferred sensibility to the user. If there in no proper textiles in database, [Combined predictor based on textile] will recommend 5 textiles according to the sensibility adjectives of others based on collaborative predictor on the user's attributes, through the content-based predictor.

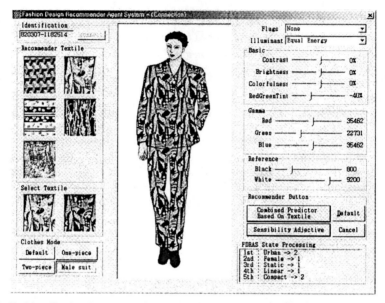

Fig. 3. Fashion Design Recommender Agent System using the extraction of representative sensibility and the two-way combined filtering

The determination of user's attributes includes the process, which let him/her evaluate the sensibility on 3 textiles among 60 textiles. Though this step, similar class of database showing the similar evaluation to his/her will be referred to predict the sensibilities on other 57 textiles using collaborative predictor and determine the user's attributes. The users can control the textile design with view factor control window, this input will change the textile of apparel on visual model to approach the sensibility preferred by him/herself. View factor control includes Illuminant, Flags[None, Negative, Logarithmic Filter, Negative & Logarithmic Filter], Reference[Black, White], Basic[Contrast, Brightness, Colorfulness, RedGreenTint], Gamma[Red, Green, Blue]. This gives the tool controlling in detail on the hue, chroma, and value of textile design. Therefore, our fashion design recommender agent system will become the referencing tool on planning sensibility product to the merchandisers or buyers of textiles and apparel industry.

6 Evaluation

After the questionnaire based on web has been online for 3 months (2002.1~2002.4), 31232 ratings by 512 users(259 males and 253 female) were collected. Fig. 4 shows the bimodal distribution of data that users rating.

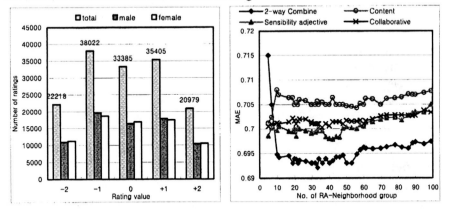

Fig. 4. Histogram of the user ratings   **Fig. 5.** MAE performance of prediction method

According to the histogram of the user ratings about textile in Fig. 4, we can see the fact there are a number of ratings in both -1 and +1. This is considered as the bimodal distribution that expresses the total of the distribution, which is biased to right, and distribution to left. As a matter of convenience of calculation and an economy of memory, this paper uses the user ratings as mapping values on 1, 2, 3, 4, and 5 instead of –2, -1, 0, +1, and +2. This is to expresses the vocabulary pair that has an opposite propensity([-2, -1, 0, +1, +2]→[1, 2, 3, 4, 5] ‖ [-2, -1, 0, +1, +2]→[5, 4, 3, 2, 1]). The user ratings on both –1 and +1 are manifested as mapping value 2. According to the bimodal distribution of the user ratings, we define 2 as the default voting ($w_{default} = 2$).

For the measurements 10 ratings for each user of a subset of 15 users were randomly separated in a test-set of ratings. Then the system was used to predict ratings in the test-set, using various prediction methods with the remaining ratings as a training set. The predictions are then compared to the original test-set to derive prediction errors. Fig. 5 shows the histogram of the absolute prediction errors created by using only collaborative predictor and using the two-way combined predictor. It can be noted that while the collaborative predictor shows more frequent smaller errors, the two-way combined predictor avoids large errors. However, it is hard to judge which one should be better. Also since the data set is rather small the histograms of absolute errors the result changes depending on the selected test-set. In order to measure the performance of the prediction more robustly, the division into test-set and training set was repeated five times. After each run the prediction is evaluated using mean absolute error(MAE) and correlation as distances between the test-set and predicted set. These measurements were then averaged[2,5,6,7].

Table 1 lists the measured precision for the previously discussed predictors. Here, it is interesting to note the improvements of the two-way combined filtering approach compared to the collaborative filtering, content-based filtering, and representative sensibility approach. An improvement of mean absolute prediction error is the two-way combined prediction over the collaborative prediction can be identified. Further, an improvement of standard deviation of the absolute error(DEV) can be observed indicating, that the predictions are more robust using the combination, i.e. large prediction errors are likely avoided.

Table 1. Prediction precision of collaborative, content-based, representative sensibility, and two-way combined predictor

Prediction method	MAE	DEV
Collaborative filtering	0.704	1.397
Content-based filtering	0.735	1.405
Representative Sensibility	0.709	1.301
Two-way combined filtering	0.681	1.159

7 Conclusion

In this paper we identify collaborative filtering and content-based filtering as independent technologies for information filtering. However, filtering is a hard problem, and cannot be addressed by one filtering technology alone. Due to limitations of both collaborative and content-based filtering, it is useful to combine these independent two-way combined filtering approaches to achieve better filtering results and therefore better the Fashion Design Recommender Agent System. In the future, we plan evolve the extension algorithm to achieve better performance.

Reference

1. M. Balabanovic, and Y. Shoham, *"Fab*: Content-based, Collaborative Recommendation," Communication of the Association of Computing Machinery, 40(3), pp. 66–72, 1997.
2. J. S. Breese, D. Heckerman, C. Kadie, "Empirical Analysis of Predictive Algorithms for Collaborative Filtering," Proc. of the 14th Conference on Uncertainty in AI, 1998.
3. J. Herlocker, et al., " An Algorithm Framework for Performing Collaborative Filtering," In Proc. of ACM SIGIR'99, 1999.
4. Badrul M. Sarwar, Joseph A. Konstan, Al Bochers, Jon Herlocker, Bral Miller, and John Riedl, "Using filtering agents to improve prediction quality in the grouplens research collaborative filtering system," In Proc. of ACM CSCW'98, 1998.
5. K. Y. Jung, J. K. Ryu, and J. H. Lee, "A New Collaborative Filtering Method using Representative Attributes-Neighborhood and Bayesian Estimated Value," Proc. of ICAI'02, USA, pp. 709–715, 2002.
6. K. Y. Jung, J. H. Lee, "Prediction of User Preference in Recommendation System using Association User Clustering and Bayesian Estimated Value," LNAI 2557, 15th Australian Joint Conference on Artificial Intelligence, pp. 284–296, 2002.
7. M. Pazzani, "A Framework for Collaborative, Content-Based and Demographic Filtering," AI Review, pp. 393–408, 1999.
8. P. Resnick, et. al., "GroupLens: An Open Architecture for Collaborative Filtering of Netnews," Proc. of ACM CSCW'94, pp. 175–186, 1994.

An Explanation-Based Ranking Approach for Ontology-Based Querying

Nenad Stojanovic

AIFB Institute
University of Karlsruhe
Germany
nst@aifb.uni-karlsruhe.de

Abstract. One of the main strengths of an ontology-based system is the intensional description of the knowledge (information) about a domain, which is used in an inferencing process as a means of implying new domain knowledge. This inferencing process is very efficiently used for the explanation how an answer to a user's query was derived, increasing the trust of a user in the answers of the query. Moreover, such a derivation tree can be treated as an evidence of the relevance of an answer for the user's query. In this paper we present an approach which combines the derivation tree with the factual information in order to support the ranking of the results of an ontology-based query. Moreover, we discuss the possibilities to use such a ranking for clustering query's results. The approach has been implemented in the Ontobroker system, a main memory deductive database system.

1 Introduction

In lots of applications related to the searching for information, a user wants to select only some of the results returned for his query. For example, in an e-commerce application a user inspects just a few products in more details. In a skill-management application, a user wants to find/consult just several experts. Obviously, a user is interested in those results which are the most relevant to his query and consequently, the results of a query have to be ordered according to their relevance to the query. Since an average searcher on the Web reads only the first page of results (about ten results), the ranking is even more important for the web-based applications.

Although the determination of the relevance of a result for a query is a long debate in various communities, especially in information retrieval (IR) [1] and natural language processing (NLP) [2], the powerful formal framework is still missing. The relevance of a result for a query is commonly defined as the similarity between that result and the query [3]. The calculation of such a similarity depends on the model used for the representation of the information objects e.g. the vector space model or the semantic networks. Obviously, the precision of the calculation increases with the amount of the background information incorporated in the model. The best example is the Google Search Engine (www.google.com), whose powerful ranking algorithm, PageRank, benefits from the exploitation of the hyperlink structure of the web documents.

V. Mařík et al. (Eds.): DEXA 2003, LNCS 2736, pp. 641–650, 2003.

In the ontology-based applications an explicit and formal model of the domain (an ontology) is used as the backbone for information processing. Usage of more semantics about the domain in the information processing, results in better performances of the whole system, for example in the increasing precision and recall of the searching for information [4]. Moreover, this explicit semantics can be used for determining the relevance of a retrieved result for the initial query, i.e. for the ranking of the results of the searching. Since the information from the model of the domain (e.g. hierarchies of terms, axioms) is extensively used in the searching process in order to infer new information, an efficient ranking approach has to exploit the characteristics of the searching (inferencing) process. The inferencing process can be presented as the sequence of the evaluation of the domain rules – so called derivation tree [5]. Up to now, the derivation trees were used for generating human-understandable explanations of the inferencing process, i.e. how a result was inferred [6]. In this paper we have extended this research in order to use a derivation tree for the ranking results of an ontology-based query. We have developed a novel ranking approach that combines the characteristics of the inferencing process and the capacity of the information repository used for querying. It means that the ranking algorithm exploits the specificity of the domain model as well as its concrete instantiation for a given task, enabling in that way a simulation of the ranking process used by humans. We call it *ranking based on the background information*.

The ranking algorithm has been implemented in the Ontobroker inferencing system [7] and applied in the ontology-based Portal of our Institute [8], which is driven by Ontobroker. The initial evaluation study has shown very high precision (relevance) of our ranking approach.

The paper is organised in the following way: In the second section we define the basic terminology we use in the paper. In the section 3 we present the ranking approach, whereas the section 4 contains the details about its implementation and evaluation. Related work is presented in the section 5 and section 8 contains some concluding remarks.

2   Background

In this subsection we give the basic terminology we use in this paper. Due to lack of space some definition of lower importance for understanding this paper are omitted.

Let $\Re$ and $\aleph$ denote real and natural numbers, respectively. All subscripts are in $\aleph$, unless otherwise specified. If S is a set, 2^S denotes its power set, i.e., the set of all subsets of S, and $|S|$ denotes its cardinality.

Definition 1: Ontology
A core ontology is a structure $O := (C, \leq_c, R, \sigma, \leq_r)$ consisting of

- two disjoint sets C and R whose elements are called concept identifiers and relation identifiers, resp.,
- a partial order $\leq_c$ on C, called concept hierarchy or taxonomy
- a function $\sigma: R \to C^+$, called signature

- a partial order $\leq_r$ on R called relation hierarchy, where $r_1 \leq_r r_2$ implies $|\sigma(r_1)| = |\sigma(r_2)|$ and $\pi_i(\sigma(r_1)) \leq_c \pi_i(\sigma(r_2))$ for each $1 \leq i \leq |\sigma(r_1)|$

Often we call concept identifiers and relation identifiers concepts and relations, respectively, for the sake of simplicity.

An ontology with *L*-axioms is a pair *(O, A)*, where *O* is an ontology and *A* is an *L*-axiom system for *O*.

Definition 2: Knowledge Base

A Knowledge Base is a structure $KB := (C_{KB}, R_{KB}, I, l_c, l_r)$ consisting of

- two disjoint sets C_{KB} and R_{KB}
- a set *I* whose elements are called instance identifiers (or instances or objects in brief)
- a function $l_C : C_{KB} \rightarrow I$ called concept instantiation

- a function $l_r : R_{KB} \rightarrow I^+$ called relation instantiation

A relation instance can be depicted as $r(l_1, l_2, ..., l_n)$, where $r \in R_{KB}, l_i \in I$. *r* is called a predicate and l_i is called a term.

Definition 3: Ontology-Based Query

A (conjunctive) query is of the form or can be rewritten into the form:

$$forall\ \overline{X}\quad \overline{P}(\overline{X}, \overline{k})\ \text{and}\ not(\overline{N}(\overline{X}, \overline{k}))$$

with $\overline{X}$ being a vector of variables $(X_1, ..., X_n)$, $\overline{k}$ being a vector of constants (concept instances), $\overline{P}$ being a vector of conjoined predicates (relations) and $\overline{N}$ a vector of disjoined predicates (relations). A query can be viewed as an axiom without a head.

For example, for the query "*forall x workIn(x, KM) and researchIn(x, KMsystems)*" we have

$\overline{X} := (x)$, $\overline{k} := (KM, KMsystems)$, $\overline{P} := (P_1, P_2)$, $P_1(a,b,c) := worksIn(a,b)$,

$P_2(a,b,c) := researchIn(a,c)$.

Note: In this paper we consider only conjunctive queries. Since a disjunctive query can be represented as a disjunction of several conjunctive queries our approach can be easily extended to disjunctive queries.

Definition 4: Answers (Results) of a Query

Let Ω be the set of all relation instances which can be proven in the given ontology (this set can be obtained by the materialisation of all rules).

For a query *Q* "$forall\ \overline{X}\quad \overline{P}(\overline{X}, \overline{k})$ and $not(\overline{N}(\overline{X}, \overline{k}))$ " an answer is an element (tuple) in the set $R(Q) = \{\overline{X}\} = \{(x_1, x_2, ..., x_n)\}$, such that $\overline{P}(\overline{X}, \overline{k})$ and $not(\overline{N}(\overline{X}, \overline{k}))$ is provable, i.e. each of the relation instances $r(x_1, x_2, ..., x_n, k_1, ..., k_l)$, $r \in \overline{P}$ exists in the set Ω and each of $l(x_1, x_2, ..., x_n, k_1, ..., k_l), l \in \overline{N}$ does not exist in Ω.

Although a query returns the set of concept instances as an answer, the relevance of these answers is defined on the level of the relation instances. The reason is that the concept instance is treated as the identifier of an object (e.g. rst), whereas the relation instance (e.g. `researchIn(rst, KM]`) represents the property of that object whose relevance for the query can be determined. It means that the relevance of an answer a = $\overline{X}_1$ = ($x_1, x_2, ..., x_n$) for the query Q will be calculated on the substitution of this answer in the query Q, i.e. by considering the $\overline{P(\overline{X}_1, \overline{k})}$: $P_1(\overline{X}_1, \overline{k}), P_2(\overline{X}_1, \overline{k}), ..., P_k(\overline{X}_1, \overline{k})$ - the set of *returned relation instances*, depicted as $\Lambda(a)$, for an answer a. It is clear that $\forall a, \Lambda(a) \supset \Omega$.

3 Ranking Based on the Background Information

The task of a ranking schema is to measure the relevance of an answer for the given query. Generally, such a relevance is determined by analysing some properties of an answer regarding the query, e.g. syntactical similarity between an answer and the query 3: the answer which is more similar to the query is treated as a more relevant answer. Since an ontology-based querying process is realised as an inferencing process which "generates" a list of answers (relation instances), each of them matches the query perfectly, such a similarity measurement cannot be established easily. For example, the answers: `researchIn(rst,KM)` and `researchIn(nst,KM)` are "ideal-answers" for the query *"forall x* `researchIn(x,KM)`*"* and are, consequently, equally relevant for that query. In order to see the difference between answers on a query, one has to consider additional properties of an answer, first of all properties related to the inferencing process and to the capacity of the knowledge base.

We see two differences between relation instances for two answers to a query:
(i) the specificity of the instantiation of the ontology (the content of the knowledge base)

   e.g. for a query about researchers in the KM, a useful information for ranking is that a researcher works in three projects about KM and gives two lectures regarding KM
(ii) the inferencing process in which an answer is implied - the derivation tree of an answer (a returned relation instance)

   e.g. the query for researcher who research in KM will return the researcher who research in the DataMining as well, since the DataMining is a subtopic of KM

Therefore, we introduced the relevance function $\sigma: \Omega \rightarrow \Re$ that computes the relevance of a relation instance returned in the querying process, based on analysing (i) the knowledge base (criteria i) and the inferencing process (criteria ii). The relevance of an answer a, $\rho(a)$, $a \in R(Q)$, is the geometrical mean of the relevancies of the returned relation instances for that answer, i.e. $\rho(a) = \sqrt[|\Lambda(a)|]{\prod_{x \in \Lambda(a)} \sigma(x)}$. Finally, the ranking of the answers for a query is achieved by ordering these answers according to their relevance.

In the following two subsections we describe in detail the calculation of the above mentioned relevancies.

3.1 The Content of the Knowledge Base

In this subsection we explain the calculation of the relevance of a relation instance for the user's query.

Definition 5: The Ambiguity of a Term in a Relation Instance

The ambiguity of a term (a concept instance) in a relation instance is defined as the number of interpretations of the given relation instance with respect to that term (i.e. when all other terms in the relation instance, except the considered term, are substituted with a variable).

$$Amb(I_j, r(I_1, I_2, ..., I_j, ..., I_n)) = |\{x, y, ..., w| \exists x, y, ...w \ r(x, ..., I_j, ..., w)\}| \tag{1}$$

For example, in the case that person gst works in three projects: OntoWeb, DotCom, WonderWeb, then the ambiguity of the term gst in the relation instance work_in(gst, OntoWeb) is

$$Amb(gst, work\_in(gst, OntoWeb)) = |\{x| \exists x, work\_in(gst, x)\}| = 3.$$

Definition 6: The Specificity/Relevance of a Relation Instance

The specificity of a relational instance is the reciprocal value of the ambiguity of each of its terms (concept instances). It is calculated as:

$$Spec(r(I_1, I_2, ..., I_n)) = \frac{1}{Amb(I_1, r(I_1, I_2, ..., I_n))} \cdot ... \cdot \frac{1}{Amb(I_n, r(I_1, I_2, ..., I_n))} \tag{2}$$

Continuing the above example, in the case that there are two persons who work in the project OntoWeb, the specificity of the instance work_in(gst, OntoWeb) is as follows:

$$Spec(work\_in(gst, OntoWeb)) = \tag{3}$$

$$\frac{1}{Amb(gst, work\_in(gst, OntoWeb))} \cdot \frac{1}{Amb(OntoWeb, work\_in(gst, OntoWeb))} = \frac{1}{3} \cdot \frac{1}{2} = \frac{1}{6}$$

The specificity is maximal (i.e. = 1) when no one of the terms from the relational instance can be found in any other relation instance of the same type. For example, if there is only one relation instance for the relation teaches which contains either meh or InfoA then the relation instance teaches(meh, InfoA) has the maximal specificity.

The specificity of a relation instance can be interpreted as the measure of its relevance for the user's query. If the specificity of a relation instance is higher, then the relevance is greater. Therefore $Rel(r(I_1, I_2, ..., I_n)) = Spec(r(I_1, I_2, ..., I_n))$ (4)

The treatment of factors which determine the relevance is task-relevant. The formula (2) can be adapted to such task-dependent customisation by changing the reciprocity impact of the ambiguity of a term on the relevance of the whole relation instance. For example, when the number of the participant on a project increases the relevance of a participant for the research related to that project, than the statement (3) can be changed into:

$$Spec(work\_in(gst, OntoWeb)) =$$

$$\frac{1}{Amb(gst, work\_in(gst, OntoWeb))} \cdot Amb(OntoWeb, work\_in(gst, OntoWeb)) = \frac{1}{3} \cdot 2 = \frac{2}{3}$$

Our approach supports this kind of parameterised calculation of the relevance.

3.2 The Characteristics of the Inferencing Process

As showed in the motivating example, in querying an ontology the background knowledge about the domain is used for implying new, implicitly stated facts in the knowledge base. Therefore, the query results might be extended by inferencing which uses rules from the domain ontology, i.e. the query process includes an ontology-based inferencing. We avoid here the detailed description of the different types of the inferencing process (evaluations) [9], but present the common inferencing structure which can be used for the proof of the returned results. Such a proof structure enables the reconstruction of the inferencing steps for a query's result and consequently the calculation of its relevance. This structure is described in the next three definitions.

Definition 7: AND-OR Tree
An AND-OR tree is a tree structure, defined as the set $T = \{root, N, v\_and, v\_or\}$, where

root is the root of the tree,
N is the set of nodes in the tree,
v_and and v_or are (irreflexive, anti-symmetric) relations between nodes.
    They define links in the tree and are called parent-child relations in the text.
v_and: $N \rightarrow N$, such a link is called an and_link and the node is called an and_connector.
    v_or: $N \rightarrow N$ *, such a link is called an or_link and the node is called an or_connector.

Definition 8: Derivation Tree of an Answer on the Query
Given an ontology O with axioms, the derivation tree of the query Q is an AND-OR tree whose root plays the role of an or_connector between the derivation trees of each result (resulting relation instance) for the query Q, i.e. for the elements from $R(Q)$.

$DTree(Q) = \{root, N, v\_and, v\_or\}$,
$N = \bigcup_{r \in A(a) \wedge a \in R(Q)} DTree(r)$
v_or: root$\rightarrow$N
$v\_and = \{\}$

Definition 9: Derivation Tree of a Relation Instance (Creating)
The derivation tree of a relation instance $r(l_1, l_2, ..., l_n)$ is defined as follows:

- every relation instantiation l from KB is a derivation tree for itself; a single node with label l.
- Let A be the set of axioms from the given ontology O, whose heads contain the atomic formula which can be unified with the relation r..

- Let $A = p:-q_1,...,q_n$, be an axiom from the A, let d_i, $1 \le i \le n$, be relation instances with derivation trees T_i, let θ be the mgu[1] of $(q_1,...,q_n)$ and $(d_1,...,d_n)$. Then the following is a derivation tree for $p[\theta]$ (relation instance) : the root is a node labelled with $p[\theta]$ and each T_i, $1 \le i \le n$, is a child of the root. The root plays an and_connector role.
- The derivation tree for r is the tree with the root which plays the role of an or_connector between the derivation trees for all axioms from A. It is labelled with $p[\theta]*$

It is clear that a derivation tree represents the manner in which a result was inferred. The root is the disjunction of all results. Each node in a tree is a relation instance. Each or_connector node connects various ways in which a relation instance is derived, whereas an and_connector node defines a way in which the relation instance is derived. For a relation instance there are several and_connector nodes (the number is equal to the number of rules, whose head parts unify with that relation instance) and an or_connector, which connects those and_connector nodes.

For each and_connector node it is possible to define the query specificity as a measure of the relevance of that relation instance (using formula (2)). From the definition of the derivation tree it is clear that the relevance of a node depends on the relevance of its children's nodes. A relevance is propagated in two ways depending on the type of nodes:

- an and_connector multiplies the relevancies of its children (because each child is a part of a rule that infers the parent)
- an or_connector makes a sum of the relevances of its children (because children make an impact on the parent independently)

The following formulas describe the processing done by a node:
(i) for an and_connector node :

$$Rel\_and(node_i) = Rel(node_i) \cdot \sum_{v\_or(node_i,node_j)} Rel\_or(node_j) \quad (5)$$

for the root node $root$, we set $Rel(root)=1$.

(ii) for an or_connector node: $Rel\_or(node_j) = \prod_{v\_and(node_j,node_l)} Rel\_and(node_l) \quad (6)$

(iii) for leaf nodes: $Rel\_and(node_i) = Rel(node_i) \quad (7)$

Each node is in the form $r(l_i, l_2,..., l_n)$, $Rel(node)$ is the initial relevance, defined with formula (7), $Rel\_and(node)$ is the calculated relevance of the relation instance corresponding to $node$. Therefore, the relevance of a returned relation instance r for the answer a, i.e. $r \in \Lambda(a)$, is calculated as follows: $\sigma(r) = Rel\_and(r)$.

Finally, the relevance of the answer a is $\rho(a) = \sqrt[|\Lambda(a)|]{\prod_{r \in \Lambda(a)} Rel\_and(r)}$. $\quad (8)$

---

[1] A substitution is a mapping from the set of variables of the language under consideration to the set of terms. Two terms t1 and t2 are said to be unifiable if there is a substitution σ such that $t1[\sigma] = t2[\sigma]$; σ is said to be a unifier of t1 and t2. Note that if two terms have a unifier, they have a most general unifier (mgu) that is unique up to renaming of variables.

4 Implementation

In this section we give some details about the current implementation of our ranking approach. Since the focus of the paper is not on the implementation issues, we mention just the most important ones.

We implemented the presented ranking approach in the Semantic Portal of our Institute. The Semantic Portal (SEAL) [8] is an ontology-based application, which provides a "single-click" access to almost all information related to the organisation, people, researches and projects of our Institute. It is widely used by our research and administrative staff as well as by our students. One of the most usable features is the possibility to search for people, research areas and projects on the semantic basis, i.e. using corresponding Institute Ontology. The hierarchy of research areas is especially comprehensive – more than 130 instances. The example from section 3 is a part of it. The portal provides a very user-friendly interface, which enables formation of arbitrary queries using entities from the underlying ontology. The search is performed as an inference through metadata, which is crawled from Portal pages. As an inference mechanism we use the Ontobroker system [7], a deductive, object-oriented database system operating either in the main memory or on a relational database (via JDBC). It provides compilers for different languages to describe ontologies, rules and facts. More details about Ontobroker can be found in [7]. We mention here only several details relevant for the inferencing process. Ontobroker uses the bottom-up fix-point evaluation procedure. It allows general recursion and the negation is allowed in the clause body. If the resulting program, is stratified, a simple stratified semantic is used and evaluated with the technique called dynamic filtering [Kif86]. To deal with non-stratified negation we have adopted the well-founded model semantics [VGe91] and compute this semantics with an extension of dynamic filtering. The native logical language of the Ontobroker is F-Logic.

The latest version of Ontobroker (www.ontoprise.com) has a powerful explanation facility, which tracks the evaluation of the rules and the substitutions applied in them. The ranking approach is based on processing this explanation file. Out of it, the derivation tree for a query, according to the definition 8 and 9 is generated.

The ranking approach is developed as an additional module for the Ontobroker system. The ranking module takes the list of results for the query and the explanation file as inputs. The output is the ranked list of results. The time delay introduced in the answering process is not significant.

5 Related Work

There are several research areas we can relate to our research and in this section we mention only two most important aspects.

Similarity measures in the ranked retrieval. Ranked retrieval plays an important role in IR and NLP. In IR, the closest match to a query is often chosen by ranking the database objects by their similarity to the query [10]. Many IR systems retrieve objects from a universe represented as a vector space whose dimensions are the features of the retrievable objects, e.g., terms found in document collections. The ranking functions in these systems utilize feature frequency counts, boolean feature combinations or probabilistic feature distributions [3]. In NLP, the best interpretation of an input is frequently selected by ranking the interpretations induced by the input in the available knowledge base [2]. Many NLP systems retrieve objects from a universe represented as a semantic network. The ranking functions in these systems utilize numerical spreading activation levels [11], shapes of activation paths [2] or node activation sequences [12]. All of these approaches have introduced some interesting similarity properties we use in our approach (e.g. node activation sequences). However, all of them use a shallow domain model which does not allow comprehensive calculation of the relevance.

The closest approach to our calculation of the specificity of a relation instance (formula (5)) is the research related to the similarity between two concepts in a isA-taxonomy such as the WordNet or CYC upper ontology [13], which uses edge weights between adjacent nodes as an estimator of semantic similarity. Our approach differs from this notion of similarity in a hierarchy in two main aspects: Firstly, our similarity measure is applicable to a hierarchy which may, but need not be a taxonomy and secondly it takes into account not only commonalties but also differences between the items being compared, expressing both in semantic-cotopy terms. The second property enables the measuring of self-similarity and subclass-relationship similarity, which are crucial for comparing results derived from the inferencing processes, executed in the background.

However, our research was subsequently considerably influenced by that of Sussna,[14], about the automatic edge weighting in the massive semantic networks.
Ontologies. A very interesting approach for processing ontology-based information is given in [15]. It exploits the connectionistic structure of an ontology in order to define connectedness metrics between instances in the ontology. The approach is applied for defining communities of practice in the system called ONTOCOPI. The insight behind the approach ONTOCOPI is that if an ontology of the working domain of an organisation is created, then the links between the instances can be measured to indicate which are closely related. This approach does not exploit all the semantic which is behind an ontology (e.g. rules) or which can be induced from the usage of the link structure.

6   Conclusion

Since the strength of an ontological structure lies in the formal and explicit semantics of the relationships between ontological entities, an ontology-based information retrieval has to exploit the full potential of the semantic-based link structure between information objects, in order to improve the efficiency of object retrieval. We see two types of the linkage between objects: (i) one implied by the capacity of the knowledge base and (ii) one derived in the inferencing process. In this paper we presented an approach which uses both types of the semantic relation between objects in order to calculate the relevance of a result for a user's query.

The ranking algorithm has been implemented in the Ontobroker inferencing system and applied in the ontology-based Portal of our Institute, which is driven by Ontobroker. The initial evaluation study has shown very high precision (relevance) of the ranked retrieval.

The approach can be easily extended with application-specific information, such as the frequency of the usage of a result for the given query, in order to generate more relevant ranking. Moreover, the semantics used in the ranking process enables the grouping of the calculated relevancies according to some properties, which, additional to ranking, enables the efficient clustering of the results of a query.

Acknowledgement. The research presented in this paper would not have been possible without our colleagues and students at the Institute AIFB, University of Karlsruhe. Special thanks to Ontoprise GmbH Karlsruhe, for support in using Ontobroker. Research for this paper was partially financed by BMBF in the project "SemiPort" (08C5939).

References

1. Saracevic, T. Relevance: A Review of and a framework for the thinking on the notion in information science. Journal of the American Society for Information Science, 26, (6), 321–343, 1975.
2. Norvig, P. From A Unified Theory of Inference for Text Understanding, UC Berkeley Computer Science Technical Report CSD-87-339, 1987
3. Kulyukin, V., Settle, A Ranked retrieval with semantic networks and vector spaces. JASIST 52(13): 1224–1233 (2001)
4. Guarino, N., Masolo, C. and Vetere, G. "OntoSeek: Content-Based Access to the Web", IEEE Intelligent Systems, 14(3), pp. 70–80, (May 1999).
5. Ramakrishnan, R., Srivastava, D. and Sudarshan S. Rule Ordering Bottom-Up Fixpoint Evaluation of Logic Programs. In Proceedings of the International Conference on Very Large Data Bases, Brisbane, Australia (1990), 359–371
6. Arora, T., Ramakrishnan, R., Roth, W.G., Seshadri, P. and Srivastava, D. Explaining program execution in deductive systems. In S. Ceri, K. Tanaka, and S. Tsur, editors, Proceedings of the Deductive and Object-Oriented Databases Conference, number 760 in Lecture Notes in Computer Science. Springer-Verlag, December 1993.
7. Decker, S., Erdmann, M., Fensel, D. and Studer, R. Ontobroker: Ontology Based Access to Distributed and Semi-Structured Information. In R. Meersman et al., editors, *Database Semantics: Semantic Issues in Multimedia System*s, pages 351–369. Kluwer, 1999.
8. Stojanovic, N., Maedche, A., Staab, S., Studer, R., Sure, Y., SEAL — A Framework for Developing SEmantic PortALs, ACM K-CAP 2001. October, Vancouver, 2001.
9. Ullman J. D. Principles of Database and Knowledge-based Systems. Computer Science Press, Rockville.
10. Aalbersberg, I.J. A document retrieval model based on term frequency ranks. In Proceedings of the 17th International Conference on Research and Development in Information Retrieval (ACM SIGIR. '94) (pp. 163–172), Dublin, Ireland: ACM.
11. Charniak, E. Passing markers: A theory of contextual influence in language comprehension. Cognitive Science, 7, 171–190.
12. Martin, C. Direct memory access parsing (Tech. Rep. No. CS93–07). Chicago, IL: The University of Chicago, Department of Computer Science.
13. Richardson, R., Smeaton, A.F. and Murphy, J. Using Wordnet as knowledge base for measuring semantic similarity between words. Technical Report CA–1294, Dublin City University, School of Computer Applications, 1994.
14. Sussna M. (1993). Word Sense Disambiguation for Free-text Indexing Using a Massive Semantic Network, *Proceedings of CIKM*.
15. O'Hara, K., and Alani, H. and Shadbolt, N. Identifying Communities of Practice: Analysing Ontologies as Networks to Support Community Recognition, IFIP-WCC 2002, Montreal, 2002

Visual Querying with Ontologies for Distributed Statistical Databases

Yaxin Bi[1], David Bell[1], Joanne Lamb[2] and Kieran Greer[3]

[1] School of Computer Science,
Queen's University of Belfast,
Belfast, BT7 1NN, UK
{y.bi,da.bell}@qub.ac.uk
[2] CES, University of Edinburgh,
St John's Land, Holyrood Road,
Edinburgh, EH8 8AQ, UK
j.m.lamb@ed.ac.uk
[3] Faculty of Informatics,
University of Ulster,
Newtownabbey, Co. Antrim, BT37 0QB, UK
krc.greer@ulster.ac.uk

Abstract. In this paper we describe a visual, ontology-based query paradigm. It has two novel features: visually specifying aggregate table queries and table layout in a single process, and providing users with an ontology guide for formulating statistical data analysis tasks as table queries which are composed of the terms defined in ontologies. We describe the role of the fundamental concept of ontology in the content representation of distributed databases with large numbers of multi-valued attributes, along with the methods and techniques developed for representing and manipulating ontologies, and for understanding semantics of database contents and query formulation and processing.

1 Introduction

The concept of "ontology" has been much used in discussions on data integration in recent years. Ontologies are useful because they provide a commonly agreed understanding of a domain for integrating separate databases through the identification of semantic connections or constraints between the data or pieces of information.

There exist some approaches for ontology-based data integration [1]. In all these cases, the ontology is mainly used to define the meaning of terms used in data sources, and to ensure the consistent use of terminology in order to cope with semantic heterogeneity reflected in heterogeneous data sources. But the way they use can be different. Three major approaches can be identified: single ontology [2], multiple ontologies [3] and hybrid approaches. From the query processing point of view, these ontologies act as query views which correspond to three query models of *global as view*, *local as view*, and *hybrid views*. Through one of these views, the user can understand the contents of diverse databases via the semantics of the data and

V. Mařík et al. (Eds.): DEXA 2003, LNCS 2736, pp. 651–661, 2003.

formulate queries using terms from the ontology. As indicated in [1], one of the difficult problems related to these query models is how the ontologies can be visualized as query views in terms of their structure and content.

In the MISSON* project, we provide an ontology-based solution to the integration of distributed databases in the context of statistical databases. This work extends the MIMAD (Micro-Macro Data) model by incorporating ontologies to achieve interoperation and integration between diverse data sources instead of metadata [4, 5, 6], and by replacing a *global as view* with *local as view*. It also enhances the preliminary macro table query with a visual, table-driven query paradigm in the QBE (Query-by-Example) style [7]. The ontologies are constructed on the basis of metadata associated with data sources and stored in a range of relations. Such ontologies are called *source ontologies*. To visualize the ontologies as views (*local as views*) and facilitate query processing, an XML-based data model is developed to hold some information from the *source ontology*. The ontology constructed in this way is called *query ontology*. The significant advantage of this model is to allow the content of data sources to be described more precisely, and in turn to be visualized to end-users on the fly and to be incorporated into a macro summary table query formulation and processing.

To achieve the best performance in the exploitation of the ontology for representing contents of databases, and query formulation and processing in an integrated environment, by taking account of the two phase query paradigm [8] and DataGuide [9], and by extending QBE, we develop a visual and ontology-based query paradigm. The underlying characteristics of our approach are as follows:

- Provide the query ontology with a well-defined XML data model, allowing the content of statistical databases with a large number of attributes to be represented and to be visualized with a hierarchical structure.
- Support aggregate table-driven querying by means of QBE
- Incorporate ontological information into query formulation and facilitate the processing queries by the agents
- Enable users to formulate complex queries with heterogeneous data sources using multi-query ontologies without prior knowledge about databases
- Adapt implicit Boolean connectives within ontology hierarchies based on two operations: *aggregation* and *generalization*.

This paper presents part of the MISSION client work and high-level query processing, the details about the system client design and ontology construction can be found in [10, 11].

2   Data Model for Ontologies

An ontology is defined as a shared formal conceptualization of a particular domain [12]. In practice, an ontology can be regarded as a controlled vocabulary providing a concrete specification of term names and term meanings with hierarchical structure, and can be represented in various ways, such as description logic [3] and frames [12]. To address issues in the content representation of databases, ontology visualization,

---

* MISSON: Multi-Agent Integration of Shared Statistical Information Over the [inter]Net

query formulation and processing, we employ XML to represent ontologies, because it deals well with hierarchies, variable length attributes and large numbers of attributes. In particular, it is more suited to the generation of hierarchies on the fly, as required by the system client, than relational models.

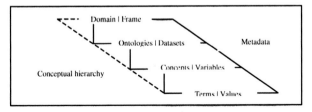

Fig. 1. Correspondence between conceptual hierarchy and metadata

In our case, an ontology is defined as a set of variables (concepts or nomenclatures) with a hierarchical structure. Each variable may consist of a set of category values. To make an ontology more understandable, we put high level information about application domains on the ontology using the ontology constructor, called *frame*, e.g. Catewe (Comparative Analysis of Transitions from Education to Work in Europe). Fig.1 illustrates the correspondence between the general concept of ontology and the specific application. As mentioned previously, a source ontology is stored in relations and encompasses more ingredients such as mappings of nomenclatures with classification schema, etc. than a query ontology does. At the heart of this paper is the query ontology. In the following, we will interchangeably use these names, and *concept* and *variable,* etc. when we are not interested in distinguishing between them.

In the MISSION project, for representing ontologies we have refined the DTD (Document Type Definition) developed in our previous work [5]. Fig. 2 illustrates a fragment of the DTD. As we see, the FRAME is the root element, and there are four high level elements under it, i.e. TITLE, SUBJECT, DESCRIPTION, and ONTOLOGY. The first three of these represent the conceptual frame, indicating application domains to which ontologies are related. The last element, ONTOLOGY, is broken down into smaller elements: DESCRIPTION, CLASSIFICATION, and VARIABLE, to cover essential information required in the system. In particular, the element VARIABLE is used to define the meanings of concepts which are associated with the attributes within data sets, and constraints indicating the properties of the concepts.

```
<!ELEMENT FRAME (TITLE?, SUBJECT, DESCRIPTION?, ONTOLOGY+)>
<!ELEMENT ONTOLOGY (DESCRIPTION?, CLASSIFICATION?, VARIABLE+)>
<!ELEMENT VARIABLE (SET+)>
<!ATTLIST VARIABLE vartype (numeric I categorical I geographical I temporal) #REQUIRED
                name CDATA #REQUIRED
                mnemonic CDATA #REQUIRED>
<!ELEMENT SET EMPTY>
<!ATTLIST SET label CDATA #REQUIRED
                value CDATA #REQUIRED>
```

Fig. 2. A DTD definition for the simplified ontology ('*': zero or more elements, '+': one or more elements, '?': optional, and 'I': or)

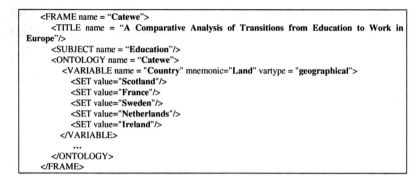

```
<FRAME name = "Catewe">
    <TITLE name = "A Comparative Analysis of Transitions from Education to Work in
Europe"/>
    <SUBJECT name = "Education"/>
    <ONTOLOGY name = "Catewe">
        <VARIABLE name = "Country" mnemonic="Land" vartype = "geographical">
            <SET value="Scotland"/>
            <SET value="France"/>
            <SET value="Sweden"/>
            <SET value="Netherlands"/>
            <SET value="Ireland"/>
        </VARIABLE>
        ...
    </ONTOLOGY>
</FRAME>
```

Fig. 3. An example fragment of XML data

To demonstrate how the metadata can be specified using XML, let us see the general structure of the metadata based on Fig.1. Assuming that the frame and ontology use the same name, i.e. Catewe. The ontology Catewe is composed of a set of concepts: {*Country, Year left school, Age at interview time, Gender, Type of school*}, where each concept in turn contains a set of values. For example, the *country* contains {*Ireland, Netherlands, Scotland, France, Sweden*}. Such structures perfectly match the structure that the DTD affords and can easily be specified by the DTD. Fig. 3 gives a fragment of the ontology of "Catewe" to show how the ontology is modelled (represented) in the DTD. In order to visualize and manipulate ontology information in the user interface, we make extensive use of the DOM model (Document Object Model).

3   Posing Queries against Ontologies

The use of ontology to represent the content of data sources is an alternative to schema and the views-based representations. In this sense, queries will be composed using the terms defined in the ontologies, and posed against the ontologies, instead of schemas or views. In order to answer the queries, there needs to be a relationship defined between the ontology and the schema, and a methodology for ontology-based query processing that efficiently converts the query expressions derived from the ontologies into the internal expressions of the queries. Research on this aspect has not been extensively investigated yet. Some relevant issues are addressed in [13]. In our work, the solutions to the issues of relations between ontologies and database schemas, along with mappings between ontologies have been described in [14]. In this section, we discuss the other two important aspects: operations on ontologies and a table query language for expressing ontology-based queries.

3.1   Operations on Ontologies

The development of effective operations on ontologies with hierarchical structure is essential for incorporating the ontologies into query formulation and processing. We develop three functions in terms of *browsing*, *aggregation* and *generalization* in our work. The first of these is mainly used for discovering fundamental concepts and relationships embedded in the hierarchy. The other two are developed for the purposes of query composition and processing. The idea behind both these functions is to map the nodes in the hierarchies of the ontologies onto the Boolean operations of intersection and union by means of the *aggregation* and *generalization* respectively, as proposed in [8]. We use these operations in different ways. In this context, an *aggregation* represents a relationship between concepts. The aggregation operations are *count*, *sum*, and *sum of square* which are performed to generate macro object tables. A *generalization* represents a combination of conceptual categories. Notice that different categories within a generalization must be disjoint. These operations constitute important operands in the function of *query construction*.

3.2 Query Language

To express ontology-based queries, we adapt a table query language [14]. The table query language consists of the ten operators and the brief descriptions of the function of each operator are given in Table 1. To handle ontologies, we define two additional operators to express the aggregation and generalization. To ease query processing and enhance syntactic interoperability with ontologies encoded in XML, we have developed a markup language based on the table query language – DTD (Document Type Definition). The operators of the query language are directly used to define the tag names in the DTD. Fig.2 gives the DTD for this query language.

Table 1. Table query language

Operator	Operand	Example of operand
COMPUTE	Table	Table, graph or model
OF	Count	Count, sum or sum of square
ON	Frame	Survey, e.g. LFS
MERGE	Shallow	Merge t1 and t2 in shallow or deep
FOR	Target concept	Numerical attribute e.g. salary
WITH	Predicate	GENDER=Female
BROKEN-DOWN-BY	Cross-product of categorical attributes	GENDER by JOB
OVER	Geo-referenced categorical attribute(s)	Countries e.g. Scotland
IN	Temporal-referenced categorical attribute(s)	YEAR =1980 thru 1999
Ontology	Ontology	Catewe, etc.

```
    <!ELEMENT TQUERY (COMPUTE, OF, ON, MERGE, FOR, WITH, BROKENDOWNBY, OVER, IN,
ONTOLOGY)>
    <!ELEMENT COMPUTE EMPTY>
    <!ATTLIST COMPUTE operand CDATA #REQUIRED>
    <!ELEMENT ON EMPTY>
    <!ATTLIST ON operand CDATA #REQUIRED>
    ...
    <!ELEMENT WITH (VARIABLE+)>
    <!ELEMENT VARIABLE (SET+)>
    <!ATTLIST VARIABLE vartype (numeric I categorical I geographical I temporal) #REQUIRED>
                operand (generalization) #REQUIRED
    ...
    <!ELEMENT BROKEN-DOWN-BY (VARIABLE+)>
    <!ATTLIST BROKEN-DOWN-BY operand (aggregation) #REQUIRED>
    ...
```

Fig. 4. An XML DTD for the table query language

The table query language is integrated into the system client. It provides a well-formed internal expression of ontology-based queries, and an underlying basis for converting the internal expression of the queries to executable queries and for query validation. Also this query language is visible in the query editor – a client function window – allowing users to express their information needs with minimum understanding of the query procedure and the syntax of the query language. In particular, its advantage over SQL-like languages is the capability of composing a range of the commands and structural data into objects such as frames, ontologies, attributes, and the expressiveness of statistical analysis required to generate aggregate table objects.

4 Visual Query Formulation

In this section, we investigate how the query ontology is involved in query formulation and processing. Before looking at a process with respect to visual specification of queries, we begin with a brief description of macro table objects.

4.1 Macro Table Object and Table-Driven Queries

A macro object is defined as follows [4]:

$MacroObject$: $\{C_1, C_2, ..., C_n; N_1, N_2, ..., N_m\}$, count, sum, sum-of-squares
where $C_1, ..., C_n$, are categorical attributes with disjoint categories of values, N_1 to N_m are numeric attributes, and $V_{C1}, ... V_{Cn}$ are attribute values, i.e. $V_{C_i} = \{V_{C_{i1}}, ..., V_{C_{aik}}\}$ is the domain of attribute C_i. Now we stipulate that the functions of the *count, sum, sum-of-squares* are operations to be performed on the Cartesian product of the categorical values of attributes, denoted by $V_{C1} \times \times V_{Cn}$, and on numeric attributes. For example, if $C_1 = Gender$, $C_2 = Employment$ and $N_1 = Salary$, along with $V_{C1} = \{Male, Female\}$, and $V_{C2} = \{Full-time, Part-time\}$, then the macro table object together with the total income of individuals who are combined together is given in Table 2(a). When no numerical attributes exist, the *count* operation will be applied to C_1 and C_2, producing the group cardinalities.

Table 2. The macro object table (a:left, and b: right with layout it)

Gender	Employment	Income_SUM
Male	Full-time (F)	2,122,000
Male	Part-time (P)	1,422,000
Female	Full-time	1,922,000
Female	Part-time	1,122,000

		Gender	
		Male	Female
Employment	F	2,122,000	1,922,000
	P	1,422,000	1,122,000

For queries which produce macro objects as illustrated in Table 2(a), we need a mechanism to formulate queries in a tabular QBE style. A complete configuration of table queries consists of three separate expressions in terms of *horizontal header*, *vertical stub* and *data cells*. Two of the expressions define the configuration of the x and y axes of the table, partitioning the table into rows and columns. The third expression defines the data points that hold aggregated values, corresponding to the

Cartesian product of the value sets of categorical attributes. The table configuration provides the layout definition, and implicitly restricts attributes to be placed in either the *header* or *stub* only. For example, in formulating the preceding macro query, the attribute *Gender* is placed on the header and *Employment* is put on the stub, and the cells hold aggregated values produced using the *sum* operation, as illustrated in Table 2 (b).

4.2 The User Interface

Fig. 5 shows a visual and interactive user interface, integrating the features of ontology visualization, visual query formulation, aggregate table-driven querying and extension of QBE to achieve three major functions: *browsing*, *query construction* and *publishing*. These functional constituents are clearly important for supporting the broader user activities in flexible ways, such as interrogating semantics of database contents. As illustrated in the screenshot, the two functions of *browsing* and *query construction* are displayed on three sub-windows. Users can interleave the functions through their views and track their progress. At the top of the query constructor, there exist two combo-boxes, one is to store numerical attributes (users can choose from them to compose queries), and the other presents a choice from the aggregation functions *count*, *sum*, *sum-of-squares*, which will be integrated into queries of macro tables.

The function of query construction provides a novel mechanism to bring query composition and table layout definition together in a single process of query formulation. Defining a layout and style on the one hand and a query on the other hand are usually seen as two different tasks which should be done in two different ways. However, the two tasks are indeed related. It is difficult to define a layout without also defining the related query. In the system client, the *query construction* component expands the QBE style as a way of query formulation, and incorporates the layout definition into the query formulation process, which acts as the client publishing function.

4.3 Visual Specification

From the visual specification of queries to the executable queries, it involves three key steps: (a) converting visual specifications to the expressions of the table query language, (b) decomposing a query expressed by the table query language into a set of sub-queries expressed by SQL statements, and (c) grouping, sorting and aggregating the data drawn from different data sources and filling the results into the macro object tables. We go through these steps below.

Suppose an information need is to count "different types of school by gender within the countries of Scotland and Ireland". The user begins with the user interface. He/she first opens the browser to obtain a list of frames, selects one frame of interest such as Catewe, and then gets a list of ontologies e.g. *Catewe Scotland*, etc. which are stored in the combo-box on the ontology browser. According to the above request, the user chooses the master ontology of Catewe. After that, as illustrated in Fig. 5(a), he/she starts to navigate the ontology information to locate the three concepts "country, type of school and gender", respectively, and drags an individual node of

Scotland and *Ireland* from the ontology tree and drops them on the Geographical field, drags *gender* onto the header, places *type of school* on the stub, and selects the *count* operator. When complete, the query is sent for execution. Simultaneously the visual expression formulated in the query constructor is internally converted into the expression of the table query language, a fragment of it is shown in Fig. 6.

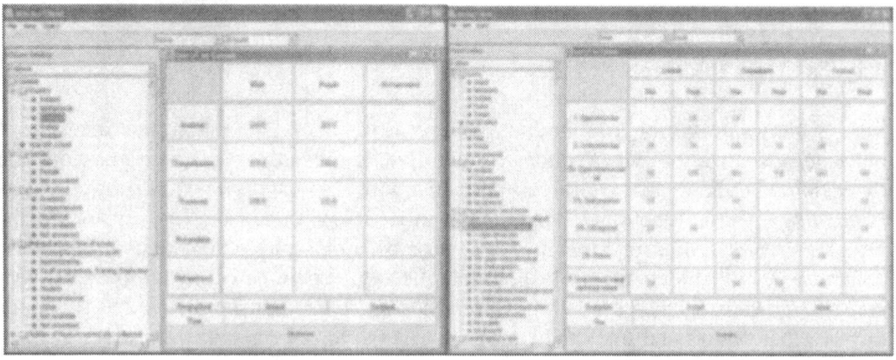

Fig. 5. The query formulation and querying result (a: left, b: right)

Fig. 6. depicts the query expression in the table language, which is derived from the visual specification of the query. The query parameters (bold pieces) dropped in the query constructor and the commands of the table query language have been integrated together, and conform to the syntax defined in Fig. 4. The conversion process from visual specifications to the expressions in the query language is determined by the commands selected, the node structures of the concepts dragged from the ontology trees and their configuration of the concepts on the query constructor. The major conversion processes include:

1. Map a selected command to the OF clause, e.g. Count.
2. Map the concepts' values constrained by the concept hierarchy from the header and stub to the WITH clause. Notice that the restrictions on the concepts and their values are implicitly linked by the *generalisation* operator, the form of query expressions is disjunction, i.e. $<concept = value_1> \vee <concept = value_2>$ ....
3. Map the concepts from the header and stub to the BREAKDOWNBY clause. In this case, the concepts on the header and stub are implicitly restricted by the *aggregation* operator, and the form of query expressions is conjunction, i.e. $<concept_1> \wedge <concept_2>$ ....
4. The same rules are applied to the cases of nested concepts as shown in Fig. 5(b). The conjunction operations on two nested concepts are treated as the conjunction of two concepts in our cases. For example, *Gender* (*male* and *female*) is nested in *Type of School* (*Academic*), so that they are a conjunction of *Gender* $\wedge$ *Type of School*.

In Figure 6, note that the attribute names, such as SCHTYPE, defined in the schemas along with their encoding values are left blank; these data will be filled during query processing. Internally the query expression is passed as an object to the agents held in the library, and then the agents perform the reformulation tasks.

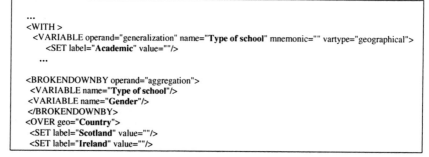

Fig. 6. A query expressed in the table query language

5 Query Reformulation

During the query process, a query composed using the ontology will be processed and reformulated into executable source-level queries. The agents first take as input a query as shown in Fig. 6, extract the frame, and the geo- and temporal-referenced categorical attributes, and match them against the frames and geo- and temporal-referenced data stored in the ontology server to prune the data sources to obtain a list of source ontologies. Then the matches of the query ontology with the list of the source ontologies are made and finally the ordinary categorical attributes are matched with the source ontologies to examine whether the attributes are included in the source ontologies to decide where the query will be executed.

If the source ontology is different from the query ontology then a heterogeneous match will be made, where categorical attributes will be reclassified and the numerical attribute will be converted by means of the mappings established beforehand. More description of heterogeneous query processing using the agents can be found in [15].

When there are enough data sources found which cover the whole query, the query will be reformulated into a set of source-level subqueries to be sent to the local databases for execution. From the definition of the macro object, we can see that the macro aggregations with the functions of *count*, *sum* and *sum-square* can be implemented using a SELECT-FROM-WHERE-GROUPBY pattern. Consequently, the task of translating the query expressions to SQL statements is to map the commands denoted by the tags to the above pattern of the SQL clauses.

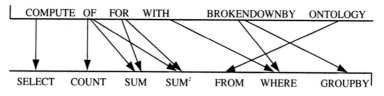

Fig. 7. Translation from the tag names to the SQL clauses

Fig.7 gives an idea of translations from the tag names defined in the table query language to the SQL clauses required by the macro aggregations. An important part is the predicate formulation in the WHERE clause. This formulation combines the query parameters and operand values (*generation* and *aggregation*) included in the VARIABLE (WITH) and BROKENDOWNBY tags to form a general form of a conjunction of disjunctions.

Fig. 8 shows the result of decomposing the query shown in Fig. 6. The query is reformulated into two subqueries. One is sent to the database that contains the "Scotland" data and the other to the "Ireland" data. In the reply process, the agent collects the answers to the query supplied by the individual database and returns to the client site. The client then presents the result to the user by filling in the macro object table as shown in Fig. 5(a).

```
Subquery1:
SELECT 0, COUNT(*), sex, schtype
FROM Scotland
WHERE   ((sex=0) ∨ (sex=1) ∨ (sex=-9)) ∧ ((schtype=1) ∨ (schtype=2) ∨ (schtype=3) ∨ (schtype=-8) ∨
(schtype=-9))
GROUP BY sex, schtype
Subquery2:
    ...
```

Fig. 8. The subqueries derived from Fig. 6

6 Conclusion

In this work we use a visual, ontology-based query paradigm to reduce the burden on novices in understanding semantics of database contents and identifying pertinent attributes for expressing information needs. A user-friendly graphical interface built on such a query paradigm by the extension of the QBE style has fulfilled this requirement. For more advanced users, this interface offers a powerful means of composing complex queries and publishing their analysis results, thereby supporting decision making and sharing expertise.

The methods and techniques developed for this query paradigm, including the data model for representing and manipulating ontologies, ontology-based query language, query formulation and processing, and translating ontology-based queries into a set of executable sub-queries provide valuable experience for research in data integration in a broad sense. In particular, XML has been utilized effectively in this work. The approach we have taken significantly enhances the user's ability to visualize ontologies, to express queries, and to perform validation and integrity checks. In particular, the demarcation of query parameters with the tags of the table query language provides a novel mechanism for query expression and processing. In this sense, a query expressed in XML can be regarded as a data object. Further, the tags are treated as the operators of the query languages, in such a way that the tag names can be directly mapped to the corresponding SQL statements, significantly reducing the complexity of decomposing queries.

Acknowledgement. The work is partially supported by the MISSION project (IST 1999-10655) and partially supported by the ICONS project (IST-2001-32429), which are funded by the European Framework V. The authors would like to acknowledge the contributions made the MISSION client development team.

References

1. Wache, H., Vogele, T. Visser, U. Stuckenschmidt, H., Schuster, G., Neumann, H. and Hubner, S. (2001). Ontology-based integration of information – a survey of existing approaches. In Stuckenschmidt, H., ed., IJCAI-01 Workshop: Ontologies and Information Sharing, 108–117.
2. Yigal Arens, Craig A. Knoblock, and Wei-Min Shen. Query reformulation for dynamic information integration. Journal of Intelligent Information Systems, 6(2/3):99–130, 1996.
3. Eduardo Mena, Arantza Illarramendi, Vipul Kashyap, Amit P. Sheth (2000). OBSERVER: An Approach for Query Processing in Global Information Systems Based on Interoperation Across Pre-Existing Ontologies. Distributed and Parallel Databases 8(2): 223–271
4. Sadreddini, M. N. Bell, D. A. and McClean, S. I. (1992b) A Model for Integration of Raw Data and Aggregate Views in Heterogeneous Statistical databases. Database Technology, Vol 4, part 2, pp115–127.
5. Bi, Y., Murtagh, F. and McClean, S.I. (1999). Metadata and XML for Organising and Accessing Multiple Statistical Data Sources. Proceedings of ASC International Conference, Edinburgh, 393–404.
6. Scotney, B.W., McClean, S.I. & Rodgers, M. C. Optimal and Efficient Integration of Heterogeneous Summary Tables in a Distributed Database. The Journal of Data and Knowledge Engineering, Vol.29, pp337–350.
7. Zloof, M. (1975) Query by Example. AFIPS, 44.
8. Shneiderman, B. (1994). Dynamic Queries: for visual information seeking, IEEE Software, vol. 11, 6, 70–77.
9. Goldman, R. and Widom, J. (1997). DataGuides: Enabling Query Formulation and Optimization in Semi-structured Databases. Proceedings of the Twenty-Third International Conference on Very Large Data Bases, 436–445, Greece.
10. Bi, Y., Bell, D. and Lamb, J. Aggregate Table-driven Querying Via Navigation Ontologies in Distributed Statistical Databases. To appear in Twentieth British National Conference on Databases (BNCOD), 2003.
11. Bi, Y., Bell, D. and Lamb, J., Greer, K. Ontology-based Access to Distributed Statistical Databases. To appear in The Fourth International Conference on Web-Age Information Management (WAIM), 2003.
12. Gruber,T. (1993). A translation Approach to Portable Ontology Specifications. Knowledge Acquisition. Vol. 5(2), 199–220.
13. Cui, Z., Jones, D., and O'Brien, P. (2002). Semantic B2B integration: issues in ontology-based approaches. ACM SIGMOD Record, Vol.31 (1), pp43–48.
14. Froeschl, K.A. (1997) Metadata management in statistical information processing, New York: Springer Wien.
15. McClean, S., Páircéir, R., Scotney, B. and Greer, K. (2002). A Negotiation Agent for Distributed Heterogeneous Statistical Databases. 14th International Conference on Scientific and Statistical Database Management (SSDBM), pp 207–216.

DOEF: A Dynamic Object Evaluation Framework

Zhen He[1] and Jérôme Darmont[2]

[1] Department of Computer Science
The Australian National University
Canberra, ACT 0200, Australia
zhen@cs.anu.edu.au
[2] ERIC, Université Lumière Lyon 2
5 avenue Pierre Mendès-France
69676 Bron Cedex, France
jerome.darmont@univ-lyon2.fr

Abstract. In object-oriented or object-relational databases such as multimedia databases or most XML databases, access patterns are not static, i.e., applications do not always access the same objects in the same order repeatedly. However, this has been the way these databases and associated optimisation techniques like clustering have been evaluated up to now. This paper opens up research regarding this issue by proposing a dynamic object evaluation framework (DOEF) that accomplishes access pattern change by defining configurable styles of change. This preliminary prototype has been designed to be open and fully extensible. To illustrate the capabilities of DOEF, we used it to compare the performances of four state of the art dynamic clustering algorithms. The results show that DOEF is indeed effective at determining the adaptability of each dynamic clustering algorithm to changes in access pattern.

Keywords: Performance evaluation, Dynamic access patterns, Benchmarking, Object-oriented and object-relational databases, Clustering.

1 Introduction

Performance evaluation is critical for both designers of Object Database Management Systems (architectural or optimisation choices) and users (efficiency comparison, tuning). Note that we term Object Database Management Systems (ODBMSs) both object-oriented and object-relational systems, indifferently. ODBMSs include most multimedia and XML DBMSs, for example. Traditionally, performance evaluation is achieved with the use of benchmarks. While the ability to adapt to changes in access patterns is critical to database performance, none of the existing benchmarks designed for ODBMSs incorporate the possibility of change in the pattern of object access. However, in real life, almost all applications do not always access the same objects in the same order

V. Mařík et al. (Eds.): DEXA 2003, LNCS 2736, pp. 662–671, 2003.
© Springer-Verlag Berlin Heidelberg 2003

repeatedly. Furthermore, none of the numerous studies regarding dynamic object clustering contain any indication of how these algorithms are likely to perform in a dynamic setting.

In contrast to the TPC benchmarks [13] that aim to provide *standardised* means of comparing systems, we have designed the *Dynamic Object Evaluation Framework* (DOEF) to provide a means to explore the performance of databases under *different* styles of access pattern change.

DOEF contains a set of protocols which in turn define a set of styles of access pattern change. DOEF by no means has exhausted all possible styles of access pattern change. However, it makes the first attempt at exploring the issue of evaluating ODBMSs in general and dynamic clustering algorithms in particular, with respect to changing query profiles.

DOEF is built on top of the *Object Clustering Benchmark* (OCB) [8], which is a generic benchmark that is able to simulate the behavior of the *de facto* standards in object-oriented benchmarking (namely OO1 [5], HyperModel [1], and OO7 [3]). DOEF uses both the database built from the rich schema of OCB and the operations offered by OCB. DOEF is placed into a non-intrusive part of OCB, thus making it clean and easy to implement on top of an existing OCB implementation. Furthermore, we have designed DOEF to be open and fully extensible. First, DOEF's design allows new styles of change to be easily incorporated. Second, OCB's generic model can be implemented within an object-relational system and most of its operations are relevant for such a system. Hence, DOEF can also be used in the object-relational context.

To illustrate the capabilities of DOEF, we benchmarked four state of the art dynamic clustering algorithms. There are three reasons for choosing to test the effectiveness of DOEF using dynamic clustering algorithms: "ever since the early days of object database management systems, clustering has proven to be one of the most effective performance enhancement techniques" [10]; the performance of dynamic clustering algorithms are very sensitive to changing access patterns; and despite this sensitivity, no previous attempt has been made to benchmark these algorithms in this way.

This paper makes two key contributions: (1) it proposes the first evaluation framework that allows ODBMS and associated optimisation techniques to be evaluated in a dynamic environment; (2) it presents the first performance evaluation experiments of dynamic clustering algorithms in a dynamic environment.

The remainder of this paper is organised as follows: Section 2 describes the DOEF framework in detail, we present and discuss experimental results achieved with DOEF in Section 3, and finally conclude the paper and provide future research directions in Section 4.

2 Specification of DOEF

2.1 Dynamic Framework

We start by giving an example scenario that the framework can mimic. Suppose we are modeling an on-line book store in which certain groups of books are popular at certain times. For example, travel guides to Australia during the 2000 Olympics may have been very popular. However, once the Olympics is over, these books may suddenly or gradually become less popular. Once the desired book has been selected, information relating to the book may be required. Example required information includes customer reviews of the book, excerpts from the book, picture of the cover, etc. In an ODBMS, this information is stored as objects referenced by the selected object (book), thus retrieving the related information is translated into an object graph navigation with the traversal root being the selected object (book). After looking at the related information for the selected book, the user may choose to look at another book by the same author. When information relating to the newly selected book is requested, the newly selected object (book) becomes the root of a new object graph traversal. We now give an overview of the five main steps of the dynamic framework and in the process show how the above example scenario fits in.

1. **H-region parameters specification:** In this step we divide the database into regions of homogeneous access probability (H-regions). In our example, each H-region represents a different group of books, each group having its own probability of access.
2. **Workload specification:** H-regions are responsible for assigning access probability to objects. However, H-regions do not dictate what to do after an object has been selected. We term the selected objects *workload root*, or simply *root*. In this step, we select the type of workload to execute after selecting the root from those defined in OCB. In our example, the selected workload is an object graph traversal from the selected book to information related to the selected book, e.g., an excerpt.
3. **Regional protocol specification:** Regional protocols use H-regions to accomplish access pattern change. Different styles of access pattern change can be accomplished by changing the H-region parameter values with time. For example, a regional protocol may initially define one H-region with high access probability, while the remaining H-regions are assigned low access probabilities. After a certain time interval, a different H-region may become the high access probability region. This, when translated to the book store example, is similar to Australian travel books becoming less popular after the 2000 Olympics ends.
4. **Dependency protocol specification:** Dependency protocols allow us to specify a relationship between the currently selected root and the next root. In our example, this is reflected in the customer deciding to select a book which is by the same author as the previously selected book.
5. **Regional and dependency protocol integration specification:** In this step, regional and dependency protocols are integrated to model changes in dependency between successive roots. An example is a customer using our on-line book store, who selects a book of interest, and then is confronted with a list of *currently* popular books by the same author. The customer then selects one of the listed books (modeled by dependency protocol). The set of *currently* popular books by the same author may change with time (modeled by regional protocol).

2.2   H-Regions

H-regions are database regions of homogeneous access probability. The parameters that define H-regions are listed below.

- *HR_SIZE:* Size of the H-region (fraction of the database size).
- *INIT_PROB_W:* Initial probability *weight* assigned to the region. The actual probability is equal to this probability weight divided by the sum of all probability weights.
- *LOWEST_PROB_W:* Lowest probability weight the region can go down to.
- *HIGHEST_PROB_W:* Highest probability weight the region can go up to.
- *PROB_W_INCR_SIZE:* Amount by which the probability weight of the region increases or decreases when change is requested.
- *OBJECT_ASSIGN_METHOD:* Determines the way objects are assigned into the region. *Random* selection picks objects randomly from anywhere in the database. By *class* selection first sorts objects by class ID and then picks the first *N* objects (in sorted order), where *N* is the number of objects allocated to the H-region.
- *INIT_DIR:* Initial direction that the probability weight increment moves in.

2.3   Regional Protocols

Regional protocols simulate access pattern change by first initialising the parameters of every H-region, and then periodically changing the parameter values in certain predefined ways. This paper documents three styles of regional change. For every regional protocol, a user defined parameter H is used to control the rate at which access pattern changes. More precisely, H is defined as one divided by the number of transactions executed between each change of access pattern. Three regional protocols are listed below:

- **Moving Window of Change Protocol:** This regional protocol simulates sudden changes in access pattern. In our on-line book store, this is translated to books suddenly becoming popular due to some event (e.g., a TV show). Once the event passes, the books become unpopular very fast. This style of change is accomplished by moving a window through the database. The objects in the window have a much higher probability of being chosen as root when compared to the remainder of the database. This is done by breaking up the database into N H-regions of equal size. Then, one H-region is first initialised to be the hot region (i.e., a region with high probability of reference), and after a certain number of root selections, a different H-region becomes the hot region.
- **Gradual Moving Window of Change Protocol:** This protocol is similar to the previous one, but the hot region cools down gradually instead of suddenly. The cold regions also heat up gradually as the window is moved onto them. This tests the dynamic clustering algorithm's ability to adapt to a more moderate style of change. In our book store example, this style of change may depict travel guides to Australia gradually becoming less popular

after the Sydney 2000 Olympics. As a consequence, travel guides to other countries may gradually become more popular. Gradual changes of heat may be more common in the real world. This protocol is implemented in the same way as the previous protocol except the H-region that the window (called the hot region in the previous protocol) moves *into* gradually heats up and the H-region that the window moves *from* gradually cools down.

- **Cycles of Change Protocol:** This style of change mimics something like a bank where customers in the morning tend to be of one type and in the afternoon of another type. This, when repeated, creates a cycle of change. This is done by break up the database into three H-regions. The first two H-regions represent objects going through the cycle of change. The third H-region represent the remaining unchanged part of the database. The first two H-regions alternates at being the hot region.

2.4   Dependency Protocols

There are many scenarios in which a person executes a query and then decides to execute another query based on the results of the first query, thus establishing a dependency between the two queries. In this paper, we have specified four dependency protocols. All four protocols functions by finding a set of candidate objects that maybe used as the next root. Then a random function is used to select one object out of the candidate set. The selected object is the next root. An example random function is a skewed random function that selects a certain subset of candidate objects with a higher probability than others. The four dependency protocols are listed below:

- **Random Selection Protocol:** This method simply uses some random function to select the current root. This protocol mimics a person starting a completely new query after finishing the previous one.
- **By Reference Selection Protocol:** The current root is chosen to be an object referenced by the previous root. An example of this protocol in our on-line book store scenario is a person having finished with a selected book, who then decides to look at the next book in the series.
- **Traversed Objects Selection Protocol:** The current root is selected from the set of objects that were referenced in the previous traversal. An example is a customer requesting in a first query a list of books along with their author and publisher, who then decides to read an exerpt from one of the books listed.
- **Same Class Selection Protocol:** The currently selected root must belong to the same class as the previous root. Root selection is further restricted to a subset of objects of the class. The subset is chosen by a function that takes the previous root as a parameter. That is, the subset chosen dependent on the previous root object. An example of this protocol is a customer deciding to select a book from our on-line book store which is by the same author as the previous selected book. In this case, the same class selection function returns books by the same author.

Hybrid Setting. The hybrid setting allows an experiment to use a mixture of the dependency protocols outlined above. Its use is important since it simulates a user starting a fresh random query after having followed a few dependencies. Thus, the hybrid setting is implemented in two phases. The first *randomisation phase* uses the random selection protocol to randomly select a root. In the second *dependency phase*, one of the dependency protocols outlined in the previous section is used to select the next root. R iterations of the second phase are repeated before going back to the first phase. The two phases are repeated continuously.

2.5   Integration of Regional and Dependency Protocols

Dependency protocols model user behavior. Since user behavior can change with time, dependency protocols should also be able to change with time. The integration of regional and dependency protocols allows us to simulate changes in the dependency between successive root selections. This is easily accomplished by exploiting the dependency protocols' property of returning a candidate set of objects when given a particular previous root. Up to now, the next root is selected from the candidate set by the use of a random function. Instead of using the random function, we partition the candidate set using H-regions and then apply regional protocols on these H-regions.

3   Experimental Results

3.1   Experimental Setup

We used DOEF to compare the performance of four state of the art dynamic clustering algorithms: Dynamic, Statistical, and Tunable Clustering (DSTC) [2], Detection & Reclustering of Objects (DRO) [6], dynamic Probability Ranking Principle (PRP) [12], and dynamic Graph Partitioning (GP) [12]. The aim of dynamic clustering is to automatically place objects that are likely to be accessed together in the near future in the same disk page, thereby reducing the number of I/O. The four clustering techniques have been parameterized for the same behaviour and best performance.

We chose simulation for these experiments, principally because it allows rapid development and testing of a large number of dynamic clustering algorithms (all previous dynamic clustering papers compared at most two algorithms). The experiments were conducted on the Virtual Object-Oriented Database discrete-event simulator (VOODB) [7]. Its purpose is to allow performance evaluations of OODBs in general, and optimisation methods like clustering in particular. VOODB has been validated for real-world OODBs in a variety of situations. The VOODB parameter values we used are depicted in Table 1 (a).

Since DOEF uses the OCB database and operations, it is important for us to document the OCB settings used for these experiments (Table 1 (b)). The size of the objects used varied from 50 to 1600 bytes, with an average of 233 bytes. A total of 100,000 objects were generated for a total database size of 23.3 MB.

Table 1. VOODB and OCB parameters

Parameter Description	Value
System class	Centralized
Disk page size	4096 bytes
Buffer size	4 MB
Buffer replacement policy	LRU-1
Pre-fetching policy	None
Multiprogramming level	1
Number of users	1
Object initial placement	Sequential

(a) VOODB parameters

Parameter Description	Value
Number of classes	50
Maximum number of references, per class	10
Instances base size, per class	50
Total number of objects	100000
Number of reference types	4
Reference types distribution	Uniform
Class reference distribution	Uniform
Objects in classes distribution	Uniform
Objects references distribution	Uniform

(b) OCB parameters

Although this is a small database size, we also used a small buffer size (4 MB) to keep the database to buffer size ratio large. Clustering algorithm performance is indeed more sensitive to database to buffer size ratio than database size alone. The operation used for all the experiments was a simple, depth-first traversal of depth 2. We chose this simple traversal because it is the only one that always accesses the same set of objects given a particular root. This establishes a direct relationship between varying root selection and changes in access pattern. Each experiment involved executing 10,000 transactions. The main DOEF parameter settings used in this study are shown in Table 2. These DOEF settings are common to all experiments in this paper. The *HR_SIZE* setting of 0.003 creates a hot region about 3% the size of the database. This fact was verified from statistical analysis of the trace generated. The *HIGHEST_PROB_W* setting of 0.8 and *LOWEST_PROB_W* setting of 0.0006 produce a hot region with 80% probability of reference, the remaining cold regions having a combined reference probability of 20%. These settings are chosen to represent typical database application behaviour [11,4,9].

Table 2. DOEF parameters

Parameter Name	Value
HR_SIZE	0.003
HIGHEST_PROB_W	0.80
LOWEST_PROB_W	0.0006
PROB_W_INCR_SIZE	0.02
OBJECT_ASSIGN_METHOD	Random object assignment

As we discuss the results of these experiments, we focus our discussion on the relative ability of each algorithm to adapt to changes in access pattern, i.e., as rate of access pattern change increases, we seek to know which algorithm exhibits more rapid performance deterioration. This contrasts from discussing which algorithm gives the best absolute performance. All the results presented here are in terms of total I/O (transaction I/O plus clustering I/O).

3.2   Moving and Gradual Moving Regional Experiments

In these experiments, we tested the dynamic clustering algorithms' ability to adapt to changes in access pattern by varying the rate of access pattern change (parameter H). The results of these experiments (Figure 1) induce three main conclusions. First, when rate of access pattern change is small (H lower than 0.0006), all algorithms show similar performance trends. Second, when the more vigorous style of change is applied (Figure 1 (a)), all dynamic clustering algorithms' performance quickly degrades to worse than no clustering. Third, when access pattern change is very vigorous (H greater than 0.0006), DRO, GP, and PRP show a better performance trend, implying these algorithms are more robust to access pattern change. This is because these algorithms choose only a relatively few pages (the worst clustered) to re-cluster. This leads to greater robustness. We term this flexible conservative re-clustering. In contrast, DSTC re-clusters a page even when there is only small potential gain. This explains DSTC's poor performance when compared to the other algorithms.

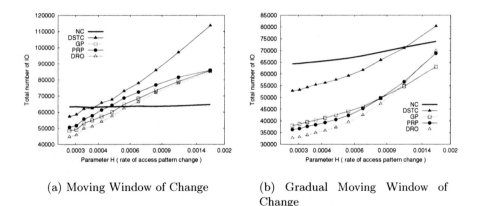

(a) Moving Window of Change   (b) Gradual Moving Window of Change

Fig. 1. Regional dependency results

3.3   Moving and Gradual Moving by Reference Experiments

These experiments, used the integrated regional dependency protocol method outlined in Section 2.5 to integrate *by reference dependency* with the *moving* and *gradual moving window of change regional* protocols. We also used the hybrid dependency setting detailed in Section 2.4. The random function we used in the first phase partitioned the database into one hot (3% database size and 80% probability of reference, which represents typical database application behaviour) and one cold region. The results for these experiments are shown on Figure 2. In the moving window of change results (Figure 2 (a)), DRO, GP and, PRP were again more robust to changes in access pattern than DSTC. However, in contrast to the previous experiment, DRO, GP, and PRP never perform worse than NC by much, even when parameter H is 1 (access pattern changes after every transaction). The reason is the cooling and heating of references is a milder form of access pattern change than the pure moving window of change regional protocol of the previous experiment. As in the previous experiment, all dynamic clustering algorithm show approximately the same performance trend for the gradual moving window of change results (Figure 2 (b)).

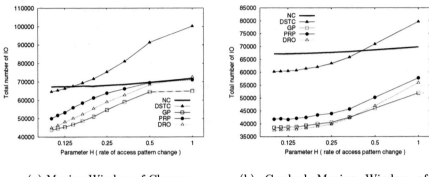

(a) Moving Window of Change

(b) Gradual Moving Window of Change

Fig. 2. S-reference dependency results

4   Conclusion

In this paper we presented a new framework for object benchmarking, DOEF, which allows ODBMSs' designers and users to test the performances of a given system in a dynamic setting. This is an important contribution since almost all real world applications exhibit access pattern changes, but no existing benchmark attempt to model this behavior.

We have designed DOEF to be extensible along two axes. First, new styles of access pattern change can be defined, through the definition of H-regions. We encourage other researchers or users to extend DOEF by making the DOEF code freely available for download[1]. Second, we can apply the concepts developed in this paper to object-relational databases. This is made easier by the fact OCB (the layer below DOEF) can be easily adapted to the object-relational context[2].

Experimental results have demonstrated DOEF's ability to meet our objective of exploring the performance of databases within the context of changing patterns of data access. Two new insight were gained: dynamic clustering algorithms can cope with moderate levels of access pattern change but performance rapidly degrades to be worse than no clustering when vigorous styles of access pattern change is applied; and flexible conservative re-clustering is the key in determining a clustering algorithm's ability to adapt to changes in access pattern.

This study opens several research perspectives. The first one concerns the exploitation of DOEF to keep on aquiring knowledge about the dynamic behavior

---

[1] *http://eric.univ-lyon2.fr/~jdarmont/download/docb-voodb.tar.gz*

[2] Even if extensions would be required, such as abstract data types or nested tables.

of various ODBMSs. Second, adapting OCB and DOEF to the object-relational model will enable performance comparison of object-relational DBMSs. Since OCB's schema can be directly implemented within an object-relational system, this would only involve adapting existing and proposing new OCB operations relevant for such a system. Lastly, the effectiveness of DOEF at evaluating other aspects of database performance could be explored. Optimisation techniques, such as buffering and prefetching could also be evaluated.

References

1. ANDERSON, T., BERRE, A., MALLISON, M., PORTER, H., AND SCHEIDER, B. The HyperModel benchmark. In *2nd International Conference on Extending Database Technology (EDBT)* (March 1990), vol. 416 of *LNCS*, pp. 317–331.
2. BULLAT, F., AND SCHNEIDER, M. Dynamic clustering in object databases exploiting effective use of relationships between objects. In *10th European Conference on Object Oriented Programming (ECOOP)* (1996), vol. 1222 of *LNCS*, pp. 344–365.
3. CAREY, M., DEWITT, D., AND NAUGHTON, J. The OO7 benchmark. *ACM SIGMOD International Conference on Management of Data* (May 1993), 12–21.
4. CAREY, M. J., FRANKLIN, M. J., LIVNY, M., AND SHEKITA, E. J. Data caching tradeoffs in client-server DBMS architectures. In *ACM SIGMOD International Conference on Management of Data* (1991), pp. 357–366.
5. CATTELL, R. An engineering database benchmark. In *The Benchmark Handbook for Database Transaction Processing Systems* (1991), pp. 247–281.
6. DARMONT, J., FROMANTIN, C., REGNIER, S., GRUENWALD, L., AND SCHNEIDER, M. Dynamic clustering in object-oriented databases: An advocacy for simplicity. In *International Symposium on Object and Databases* (June 2000), vol. 1944 of *LNCS*, pp. 71–85.
7. DARMONT, J., AND SCHNEIDER, M. VOODB: A generic discrete-event random simulation model to evaluate the performances of OODBs. In *25th International Conference on Very Large Data Bases (VLDB)* (September 1999), pp. 254–265.
8. DARMONT, J., AND SCHNEIDER, M. Benchmarking OODBs with a generic tool. *Journal of Database Management 11*, 3 (Jul-Sept 2000), 16–27.
9. FRANKLIN, M. J., CAREY, M. J., AND LIVNY, M. Local disk caching for client-server database systems. In *19th International Conference on Very Large Data Bases (VLDB)* (1993), R. Agrawal, S. Baker, and D. A. Bell, Eds., pp. 641–655.
10. GERLHOF, C., KEMPER, A., AND MOERKOTTE, G. On the cost of monitoring and reorganization of object bases for clustering. *ACM SIGMOD Record 25* (1996), 28–33.
11. GRAY, J., AND PUTZOLU, G. R. The 5 minute rule for trading memory for disk accesses and the 10 byte rule for trading memory for cpu time. In *ACM SIGMOD International Conference on Management of Data* (1987), pp. 395–398.
12. HE, Z., MARQUEZ, A., AND BLACKBURN, S. Opportunistic prioritised clustering framework (OPCF). In *International Symposium on Object and Databases* (June 2000), vol. 1944 of *LNCS*, pp. 86–100.
13. TRANSACTION PROCESSING PERFORMANCE COUNCIL. TPC home page. http://www.tpc.org, 2002.

Object Oriented Mechanisms to Rewriting Queries Using Views

Abdelhak Seriai

Ecole nationale supérieure des mines de Douai
Département Génie informatique et productique
941, rue Charles Bourseul
BP 838 – 59508 Douai Cedex, France
seriai@ensm-douai.fr

Abstract. In this article, we propose an object-oriented approach to rewrite queries using views. Our approach is based on the object-oriented classification reasoning mechanism which is possible thanks to the representation of queries as classes. In our approach, we used results of classification of query-classes, to generate possible rewritings for the corresponding queries. We have proposed two types of rewritings: elementary rewritings and recursive rewritings. Then, query rewriting is possible without limitation of query types. In fact, authorized queries are OQL expressions and query rewriting process can generate query expressions using all existing views.

1 Introduction

1.1 Problem

The importance of query rewriting using views is not any more to be illustrated [Calvanese00a, Qian96]. This technique has multiple applications for data integration, query optimisation or for maintenance of physical data independence [Millstein00]. Consequently, many approaches have been proposed to rewriting queries using views in object-oriented contexts. From them, we distinguish mainly three categories: bytransformation, algorithmic and heterogeneous approaches.

The by-transformation approach is based on the use of the same techniques suggested for relational [Levy95, Qian96, Pottinger01] or deductive database [Beeri97, Deen99, Calvanese00b] contexts. Thus, although conceptually elegant, this approach has an evident disadvantage: it requires the translation of object concepts to be left towards a target representation (logical or descriptive). Moreover, it is limited to queries which can be expressed via logical or descriptive representations. For example, queries with embedded structures, conjunction of functions or aggregations are not easily represented in logic (e.g. Datalog) [Folerescu96].

Concerning the algorithmic approach, a query rewriting is obtained using a procedural reasoning. In this way, *Florescu* and *al.* have proposed in [Florescu96] a method based on algorithms that intended to decide about containment of *OQL* queries and their rewriting using views. The disadvantage of this method consists in

V. Mařík et al. (Eds.): DEXA 2003, LNCS 2736, pp. 672–682, 2003.

the absence of an abstract reasoning mechanism. Indeed, the related reasoning is carried out through ad-hoc algorithms aiming to compare queries and detecting their containments, in order to rewrite them. The noticeable disadvantage is that algorithmic reasoning is known to be difficult to check, to adapt and to re-use.

The third approach (i.e. heterogeneous one) is related to a query model where queries are represented by multiple facets. In fact, *Buchheit* and *al.*[Buchheit94] have proposed an approach to rewrite queries using views based on their query-model named *ConceptBase* [Jarke95]. Using this query-model, queries are represented at the same time as concepts, rules and classes.

In this approach and compared to the by-transformation one, query rewriting is carried out without translation in another target model. Moreover, it is made in an abstract way (i.e. existence of an abstract reasoning mechanism: the descriptive logic). Nevertheless, the disadvantage of this approach is the heterogeneity of the used query and view models. This heterogeneity is due to the integration of multiple paradigms representing query facets (i.e. concept, rule and class).

1.2 Proposal Principle

We think that the weaknesses underlined above can be alleviated by exploiting all power of the object-oriented representation and reasoning. Thus, we propose, on the one hand, an object-oriented representation model of queries and views, and on the other hand, the exploitation of the object-oriented classification mechanism to rewrite, using views, complex OQL queries. In fact, a query is represented as an objectoriented class. The latter is classified in an inheritance hierarchy which organises queries defining existing views. This classification is exploited to deduce containment links between query to rewrite and the ones defining existing views. These links are used to generate possible rewritings of the query in question.

We underline here, that we do not address here the problem of optimal rewriting of a query. Our principal goal is to generate all possible rewritings of a query, basing only on the object-oriented concepts and mechanisms.

The rest of the paper is organized as follows. Section 2 presents our representation model of queries and views. Sections 3 presents the related query containment reasoning. Section 4 presents stages permitting to generate possible rewritings of a query, according to its containment results. Section 5 concludes the paper.

2 Query and View Object-Oriented Representation Model

The representation model is based on the one hand, on three concepts: *query*, *queryresult* and *view*, and on the other hand, on object-oriented representation of these concepts as object-oriented classes and their organisation in specific inheritance hierarchies.

2.1 Query-Class

A Query-class is the result of an object-oriented representation of a query. It is a composite class whose components are classes representing algebraic operations used in this query (e.g. restriction, join, etc.). As a consequence, structural properties of these component classes describe sources classes, properties of sources objects to be selected, source collections, as well as restrictions to be applied to these collections. As examples, a *Select-From-Where* query is represented as a composite class. Their component classes are both, the object-oriented representation of the algebraic projection operator and the collections from which attributes are selected.

Example 1. The expression described below is an OQL *Select-From-Where* query which selects peoples who are project heads. *Project-Head* query-class described in figure *1a* is the representation of this query in our model.

Project-head **populated with {**
Select   *Employee.name, Employee.age, Project.title, Project.duration*
From   *Employee in Employees, Project in Projects*
Where   *Employee.age <30 AND Project.head = Employee*

Figure 1b describes *Employee_Restriction* class, which is the object-oriented representation of the attribute *"Collection1"* used in the *Project-Head* query-class.

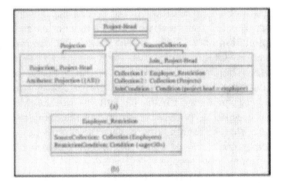

Fig. 1. An example of a query representation

2.2 Query-Result Class

A query-result class is the representation model of data selected by a query. Figure 2 represents query-result class related to query presented in *Example 1*.

Project-Head
Name :   String Age :   Integer ProjectTitle: String ProjectDuration:Date

Fig. 2. An example of a query-result class

2.3 View Class

We consider that a view is defined through two parts: the query defining this view (view intension) and the data resulting from its evaluation (view extension). Thus, we represent a view as a composite class, whose components are classes representing equivalent queries defining this view, and at most one class representing the corresponding query-result data (cf. Figure 3). When a view class is not composed of any query-result class this means that extension of this view is not calculated and the view is not materialized.

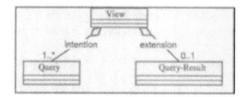

Fig. 3. The view model

3 Query Containment Reasoning

Determining containment between a determined query and other ones defining existing views is a necessary way to rewrite this one. In fact, determining a query containment permits to detect link between, on the one hand, collection representing result of this query to be rewritten, and on the other hand, collections representing extensions of existing views.

To determine these containment links, we proceed following two steps: first, the canonical transformation of queries, and next the classification of classes representing these queries in an inheritance hierarchy.

3.1 Query Canonical Transformation

Using a complex query language as OQL, several queries which are syntactically different can be semantically equivalent. For example, in some cases, it is possible to express an existential quantifier using either by an explicit existential operator or a join operator. In a similar way, join operation can be expressed either using navigation through object links or by explicitly join operator. Thus, to determine these semantically equivalences between queries, we proceed to their transformation in a canonical format.

Example 2. Let consider Q_{user} query, calculating "Researchers who are assistant professors in a French laboratory, having published at least a book and participating to a financed project".

This query can be transformed to an equivalent query written in a canonical format ($Q_{canonical}$). The latter is obtained by application of transformations concerning object properties.

Q_{user}:	**SELECT**	x **FROM** x *in Researchers, y* **in** *x.publications*
	WHERE	*x.grade =* «*Assistant Professor*»
	AND	*x.laboratory.country = "France" AND y.type =* « *book* »
	AND	**EXISTS** *z* **in** *x.projects (z.type="financed")*

$Q_{canonical}$:	**SELECT**	x
	FROM	x *in Researchers, y* **in** *Publications, w* **in** *Laboratories, z in Projects*
	WHERE	*x.grade =* «*Assistant Professor*»
	AND	*x .laboratory = w* AND *w.Country =* «*France*»
	AND	*y* **in** *x.publications* AND *y.type =* «*book*»
	AND	*z in x.projects* AND *z.type="financed"*

In fact, $Q_{canonical}$ is obtained from Q_{user} by:
- Changing the implicit join (i.e., *x.laboraory.country*) into an explicit join (i.e. *x.laboratory = w* AND *w.Country =* «*France*»),
- Separating dependent join collections used in the *From* clause (i.e. *x in Researchers, y in x.publications*) to making them independents (i.e. *x in Researchers, y in Publications)*
- Changing existential quantifier (i.e. *EXISTS z in x.projects (z.type=1 ="Financed")*) into an explicit join (i.e. *z in Projects, z in x.projects* AND *z.type="financed")*.

3.2   Query Containment Reasoning

The next stage in query rewriting reasoning, after canonical transformations, is thequery containment detection.

To determine this containment we exploit object-oriented classification mechanism. The last permits to detect links between query-class representing a query to be rewritten and query-classes representing queries defining existing views. Then, these links are used to deduce inclusion relationships existing between the corresponding query-result collections. This passage is possible as a result of the duality property announced below.

Duality Property: Links between Query-Classes vs. Links between Query-Result Classes

The property of duality concerns, one the one hand, specialization/generalization links existing between query-classes, and on the other hand, inclusion links between collections of objects resulting from evaluation of the corresponding queries.

This property is made possible thanks to our query and view representation model.[1]

Duality property: Are C_{Q1} and C_{Q2} two query-classes whose corresponding query-result classes are respectively C_{R1} and C_{R2}. If C_{Q1} specializes C_{Q2}, then the list of attributes of C_{R1} is included in the list of attributes of C_{R2} and the extension collection of C_{R1} is included in the extension collection of C_{R2} (cf. Figure 4).

---

[1] Proof of this property for OQL queries is presented in [Seriai01].

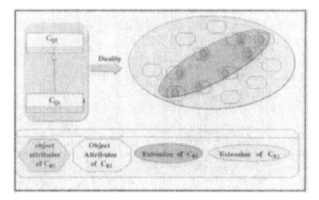

Fig. 4. Links between query-classes versus links between query-result classes

Query-Class Classification vs. Query Containment

Query-classes are organized in an inheritance hierarchy representing existing links between these ones. These links are specialisation/generalisation or/and share of component classes.

Thus, the result of the classification of a query-class C_Q can be one of the following list (cf. Figure 5):

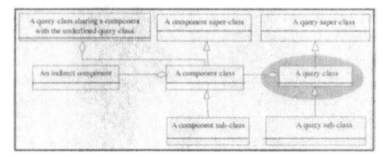

Fig. 5. Possible links between query classes

- Equality between C_Q and another existing query-class.
- Specialisation/generalisation of C_Q by other query-classes.
- Specialisation or generalisation between certain component classes of C_Q and other query-classes or their component classes.
- Share of certain component classes of C_Q with other existing query-classes.
- Absence of any direct links between C_Q and existing query-classes.

To determine the mentioned links, we have developed a classification algorithm based on two stages. The first one consists of determining most specific classes generalizing a query-class (MSG). The second stage aims to determine most general query-classes specializing the underlined query-class (MGS). The placements in the inheritance hierarchy of classes MSG and MGS are shown in figure 6.

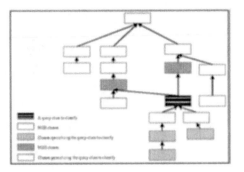

Fig. 6. MSG et MGS of a query class

4 Query Rewriting Reasoning

We have based the rewriting of a query on both the deduced links of this query and the property of duality. Therefore we distinguish, following these links, two types of rewriting: elementary and complex rewritings.

Summary of all cases related to elementary and complex query rewritings is specified in Figure 7. Details are given below.

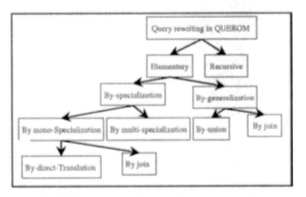

Fig. 7. Elementary and recursive query rewriting

4.1 Elementary Query Rewritings

Elementary rewriting of a query consists of exploiting views which are directly related to query to be rewritten. Thus, we distinguish two sorts of elementary rewritings: by specialization and by generalization query rewritings.

By-specialization Query Rewriting

By-specialization query rewriting concerns the case when the query-class corresponding to a query to be rewritten is a subclass of some other query-classes.

Example 3. Let given queries Q$_{user}$ and Q$_{view}$ presented below. Q$_{user}$ calculates "Names of teachers and courses where teachers have necessary competences to teach the selected courses, and have more than five years experiences ".

Q$_{view}$ calculates "Name, age and address of teachers and name of courses where teachers have necessary competences to teach the selected courses"

Q$_{user}$:	SELECT	x.name, y.name
	FROM	x in Teachers, y in Courses
	WHERE	y. NecessaryCompetences in x.competences AND x.experience > 5

Q$_{view}$:	SELECT	x.nam, x.age, x.adress, y.name
	FROM	x in Teachers, y in Courses
	WHERE	y. NecessaryCompetences in x.Competence

The query-class representing Q$_{user}$ is classified as a subclass of that representing Q$_{view}$. The rewritten query Q$_{ByRewriting}$, presented below, is obtained by the join of the source class (*Teachers*) and the query-result instances (C$_{QView}$) corresponding to Q$_{view}$.

Q$_{ByRewriting}$: SELECT x.name, x.age, x.adress, x.CourseName
FROM x in Extent(CQView), Y in Teachers
WHERE x.name=y.nom And x.age=y And age And x.address=y.address AND y.experience<5

By-generalization Query Rewriting
The by-generalization rewriting of a query is possible when its corresponding queryclass is a super-class of some others query-classes.

Example 4. Consider two queries Q1$_{view}$ and Q2$_{view}$ whose corresponding queryresult classes are respectively C$_{Q1}$ and C$_{Q2}$. Q$_{user}$ is a query to be rewritten.

Q1$_{view}$:	SELECT	x.name, y.name
	FROM	x in Teachers, y in Courses
	WHERE	y in x.courses AND x.age>= AgeRetirement – 2

Q2$_{view}$:	SELECT	x.name, y.name
	FROM	x in Teachers, y in Courses
	WHERE	y in x.courses AND x.age < AgeRetirement – 2

The by-union rewriting of Q$_{user}$ is obtained as it is shown through Q$_{ByRewriting}$ query. This rewriting is possible because the query-class representing Q is a super-class of those representing Q1$_{view}$ and Q2$_{view}$, and conditions related to selected attributes are verified too.

Q$_{user}$:	SELECT	x.name, y.name
	FROM	x in Teachers, y in Courses

WHERE	*y* **in** *x.courses*

$Q_{ByRewriting}$:	*(Extent(CQ1)* **Union** *Extent(CQ2))*

4.2   Recursive Query Rewriting

Compared to elementary query rewriting, the recursive one is characterized by considering all existing views. The latter can be directly or indirectly linked to the query to be rewritten. In fact, components of a query-class are usually intermediate results in its computation (e.g. join, restriction or embedded queries).

In addition, classification of this query-class permits to deduce all existing links between its components and either query-classes defining existing views or component-classes composing other query-classes.

Starting from these assets, we propose to exploit links concerning component-classes to rewrite sub-query expressions forming part of a query to be rewritten and which are represented by components.

The rewriting of a sub-query expression is achieved with the same manner of a query rewriting (i.e. elementary or recursive query rewritings). Thus, for each rewritten subexpression representing a component, its new rewritten expression is replaced in the starting query expression.

This process can be applied in a recursive way to rewriting expression representing indirect components of a starting query-class. Therefore, generated rewritings can use queries defining views which have not direct links with the query to be rewritten.

Example 5. Let consider Q_{user} and Q_{view} two queries, where the first one calculates "Names of temporary teachers intervening in a Master training", and the second calculates "Courses given in all Master trainings".

Q_{user}:	**SELECT**	*teacher. name*
	FROM	*teacher* **in** *Teachers, training* **in** *Trainings, course* **in** *Courses*
	WHERE	*Teacher. status= « Temporary » **AND** course* **in** *teacher. Courses*
	AND	*course* **in** *training. Courses **AND** training. name=«Master»*

Q_{view}:	**SELECT**	*course **FROM** course* **in** *Courses, formation* **in** *Formations*
	WHERE	*course* **in** *formation. Courses **AND** formation. type=«Master»*

Using recursive query rewriting principle, Q_{user} can be rewritten by exploiting Q_{view}, as it's shown by $Q_{byRewriting}$ query. This is possible because the object collection resulting from the evaluation of Q_{view} is an intermediate result in the calculation of Q_{user}. This situation is deduced from the result of the classification of query-class corresponding to Q_{user} (cf. Figure 8). The shared component is thus rewritten according to Q_{view} and it is replaced in the expression of Q_{user}.

$Q_{ByRewitting}$: **SELECT** *teacher. Name **FROM** course* **in** *Extent(CQView), teacher* **in** *teachers* **WHERE** *teacher. status= « Temporary » **AND** course* **in** *teacher. Course*

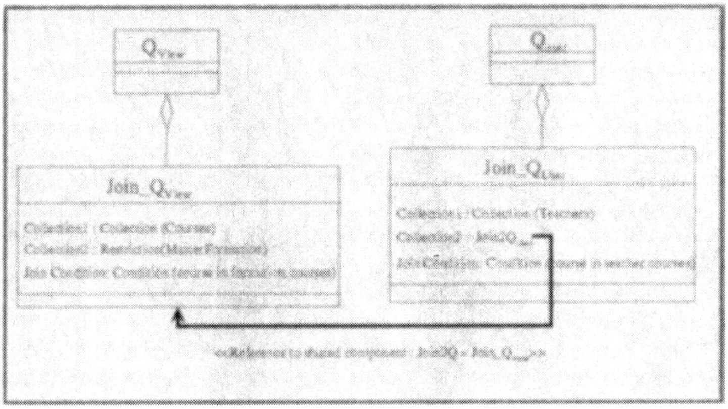

Fig. 8. Example of recursive rewriting

5   Conclusion

We have proposed in this paper an object-oriented approach to rewrite queries using views. Our approach is based on the object-oriented classification reasoning mechanism which is possible thanks to the representation of queries as classes. In our approach, we used results of classification of query-classes, to generate possible rewritings for the corresponding queries. We have proposed two types of rewritings: elementary rewritings and recursive rewritings. Compared to the existing approaches, ours has the following characteristics:

1. Containment and rewriting of a query are obtained by a uniform reasoning mechanism with reference to object-oriented model.
2. Query rewriting is possible without limitation of query types. In fact, authorized queries are OQL expressions.
3. Query rewriting process can generate query expressions using all existing views.
4. Query rewriting process is recursive. It permits to generate complex rewritings starting from elementary ones.

In this paper we only illustrated the validity and principles of our object oriented query rewriting approach. We not addressed the performance problem, and the choice of the optimal rewriting is not addressed either. We are working to consider these issues.

References

1. [Beeri97] C.Beeri, A.Levy: Rewriting Queries Using Views in Description Logics. PODS 1997: 99–108
2. [Booch00] G. Booch, J. Rumbaugh, I. Jacobson The UML user guide ISBN 0-201-57168-4, Addison-Wesley.
3. [Buchheit94] M. Bucheit, M.A Jeusfled, W. Nutt, M. Staudt: Subsumption between Queries to Object-Oriented Databases. EDBT 1994: 15–22

4. [Calvanese00b] D. Calvanese, G. Giacomo, M. Lenzerini: Answering Queries Using Views over Description Logics Knowledge Bases. AAAI/IAAI 2000: 386–391
5. [Calvanese 00a] D. Calvanese, G. Giacomo, M. Lenzereni, M.Y Vardi: What is View-Based Query Rewriting? KRDB 2000: 17–27
6. [Deen 99] S.M. Deen, Mohammed Al-Qasem: A Query Subsumption Technique. DEXA 1999: 362–371
7. [Florescu96] D. Florescu, L. Raschid, P. Valduriez: Answering Queries Using OQL View Expressions. VIEWS 1996: 84–90
8. [Jarke95] M. Jarke, R. Gallesdörfer, M.A Jeusfeld, M. Staudt: ConceptBase - A Deductive Object Base for Meta Data Management. JIIS 4(2): 167–192 (1995)
9. [Levy95] A. Y. Levy, A. O Mendelzon, Y. Sagiv, D. Srivastara: Answering Queries Using Views. PODS 1995: 95–104
10. [Millstein00] T.D Millstein, A. Y. Levy, M. Friebman: Query Containment for Data Integration Systems. PODS 2000: 67–75
11. [Pottinger01] R. Pottinger, A.Y. Levy: MiniCon: A scalable algorithm for answering queries using views. VLDB Journal 10 (2-3): 182–198 (2001)
12. [Qian96] X. Qian: Query Folding. ICDE 1996: 48–55
13. [Seriai01] A. Seriai, QUERYAID : an Object-Oriented model for query and query-result representation and management, PHD thesis, Nantes university (in French).

TVL_SE – Temporal and Versioning Language for Schema Evolution in Object-Oriented Databases

Renata de Matos Galante, Nina Edelweiss, and Clesio Saraiva dos Santos

Instituto de Informática
Universidade Federal do Rio Grande do Sul
{galante,nina,clesio}@inf.ufrgs.br

Abstract. This paper presents a language designed for the description of both temporal schema versioning and schema modification in object-oriented databases. The language supports temporal and versions features in both schemata and data levels. An extension of the ODMG standard is presented in order to incorporate temporal and versioning features into ODL language to properly manage the schema evolution mechanism. Thus, this proposal improves the database environment with temporal and versioning features concerning database modification. The solution to the problem is shown to be feasible since it is defined in terms of the ODMG standard.

1   Introduction

Due to the nature of the design process, a schema may need to be dynamically modified in several ways, reflecting new specifications and user requirements. Schema evolution is an essential feature for supporting design methodology management in an evolving environment. In this way, much research [1,2,3,4,5] has been done in the area of schema evolution since Banerjee et. al [1] presented the first taxonomy for schema updates.

Object-oriented databases offer powerful modeling concepts as those required by advanced application domains like CAD and Case tools. Typical applications handle large and complex structured objects, which frequently change their value and structure. As the structure is described in the database schema, support to schema evolution is a highly required feature. This fact led to researches concerning the schema versioning [1, 4] which keep all the history of the database evolution. On the other hand, the conceptual schema and its data are evolving entities, which require adequate support for past, present and future data. Temporal databases with schema versioning support [2,3,5] have been developed to fulfill this need.

The Object Data Management Group (ODMG) [6] has proposed a standard for object-oriented databases, including a standard object model, a query language (OQL), and an object definition language (ODL). The definition of such a standard represents an important step toward the diffusion of object-oriented databases. Some works extend one or more components of the ODMG architecture, with schema versioning [3,5] or with database transformations [4]. However, they do not include both schema and object versioning as well as the temporal dimension, like transaction and valid time.

In [7], a schema versioning mechanism (*TV_SE Evolution*) to manage the schema evolution in temporal object-oriented database is presented. Its definition is based on an

V. Mařík et al. (Eds.): DEXA 2003, LNCS 2736, pp. 683–692, 2003.
© Springer-Verlag Berlin Heidelberg 2003

object-oriented data model that supports temporal features and versions definition - the *Temporal Versions Model* - TVM [8]. This work specifies a versioning and modification language for *TV_SE Evolution*. New features are added to handle schema versioning as well as schema modification during schema evolution. An extension of the ODMG standard is also presented in order to standardize the main feature of the proposed language.

The rest of this paper is structured as follows. Section 2 briefly exposes TVM. Section 3 shows an overview of the key concepts of the temporal and versioning approaches to schema evolution. Section 4 specifies the language for schema versioning and modification through a series of examples and illustrates how it can be used to express a wide variety of versioning and schema update operations, while section 5 presents the ODMG extension. Section 6 provides a comparison with other ongoing researches, and the main ideas of this paper including future work are summarized in section 7.

2   Temporal Versions Model

The *Temporal Versions Model* (TVM) is proposed as an object-oriented (OO) data model that extends a version model by adding the temporal dimension to the *instance versioning level* [8]. Indeed, the user can model the database considering the design alternatives as well as the data evolution. TVM does not require all classes to be temporal and versionable, which allows the integration into existing applications.

TVM supports the storage of different designed versions along with all updates of those attributes and relationships defined as temporal. Different versions may coexist, representing branching time order. These features are not usual in other data models, since the time order is almost always linear. The updates of temporal attributes and relationships vary in linear order within a version.

3   An Overview of the TV_SE Evolution Environment

The following introduction to the elements of the *Temporal and Versioning Approach to Schema Evolution* (TV_SE *Evolution Environment*) is sightly simplified, and restricted to the focus of this paper. The interested reader is referred to [7] for an extensive motivation of the introduced concepts and for a complete explanation of the model.

Fig. 1. Schema evolution environment

The general architecture of the approach is depicted in figure 1, split into four main parts. First, the *TV_SE Versioning* implements the schema versioning through TVM features. Second, the *Schema Evolution Manager* controls the schema evolution management through two modules: *TV_SE Modification* controls modifications in the schema versions, and *TV_SE Propagation* accomplishes instance update according to schema transformation. Third, the *TV_SE Manipulation* controls schema changes, change propagation and data manipulation through transaction processing. Fourth, the *TV_SE Storage* controls the storage of schema and its corresponding data. This module is divided into: *Metadata Structure*, that keeps track of the information about the schema modification and the schema version derivation, and *Intention and Extension Storage*, a database that stores the user's applications and their associated data.

4 Temporal and Versioning Language for Schema Evolution

After a brief outline of TV_SE, this section presents its language for versioning schema and modification, *Temporal and Versioning Language for Schema Evolution* (TVL_SE). The language is separated into two parts: *Schema Versioning Language*, that controls the process of the schema version derivation, and *Schema Modification Language*, that handles schema update operations under schema versions.

A Concrete Example. In order to illustrate the proposal described in this paper, TV_SE is used to model a simple application [1]: the *Academic System* at the Federal University of Rio Grande do Sul (UFRGS), which controls all undergraduate activities. The Academic System is a mission-critical legacy system, and its database has an approximate 25-year historical data. For a more concrete example, let´s consider the Academic System database and the outcome of two schema modifications. Both modifications are applied to an initial schema version SV0 (figure 2-(b)) producing schema version SV1 (figure 2-(c) and schema version SV2 (figure 2-(d)). Figure 2-(a) has the versions graph derivation with all schema versions. SV1 is obtained from SV0 by adding a new class (Student), forming a relationship between Student and Degree classes, and SV2 is obtained from SV0 by adding a new attribute concentration to the Degreeclass.

4.1 Schema Versioning Specification

Versioning is associated with schemata. When a new schema version is created from a schema yet without version, this schema becomes the first version and the new version is derived from it (implicitly the versioned schema is created). To this end, the following simplified syntax defines the *create schema* operation:

```
createSchema::= CREATE SCHEMA [ TEMPSV schemaVersionName schemaSpec
   [VALIDITY INTERVAL definedInterval]
definedInterval::=[iInstant ..[fInstant]] | [..fInstant]
```

By default, the CREATE SCHEMA clause allows the specification of a schema without versions, i.e. a conventional schema of databases. The user's schema specification can be made in the schemaSpec clause.

---

[1] The example only shows a piece of the database as a matter of simplification.

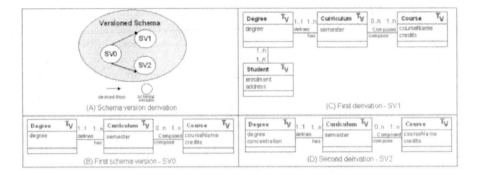

Fig. 2. Schema version derivation for the Academic System at UFRGS

Considering the temporal and versioning features, TVL_SE offers properties for handling bitemporal schema versioning, as follows. The TEMPSV terminal symbol allows to specify a schema version that will be temporal and versionable. Besides specifying the TEMPSV schema, the class definition language of TVM must be used in order to specify attributes and relationships as temporal as well as temporal and versionable class specification, allowing versioning features in the extensional data levels. Through the optional VALIDITY INTERVAL clause, the validity of the schema can be specified, enabling retro and pro-active navigation among schema versions. When the VALIDITY INTERVAL is not specified, the validity is assumed to be '$[now, \infty]$'. It is important to notice that the validity time of the schema versions has been only restricted to present and future. The hypothesis of modifying the past was discarded because this kind of change has no sense, once the schema models the reality, and the schema version is the representation of that reality. Besides, if modifying the past were allowed, the query processing would not retrieve the reality anymore, since the past would have changed.

Example 1. Suppose that as a first step, an initial curriculum structure (schema) is specified, previously shown in figure 2-b. The CREATE SCHEMA statement would be:

```
CREATE SCHEMA TEMPSV sv0
   class Degree {
      attribute string degree };
   class Curriculum {
      attribute integer semester };
   class Course {
      attribute string courseName,
      attribute integer credits };
VALIDITY INTERVAL ['01 jan 2003', '30 set 2003']
```

Note that since the TEMPSV is specified, the new created schema is defined as the first version and the versioned schema is also created. The validity interval for the new created schema is supplied.

Schema Version Status Specification. The schema versions have a *status*, and they reflect its robustness. Depending on its status, operations can or cannot be applied to a schema version. The status and operations are shown in figure 3.

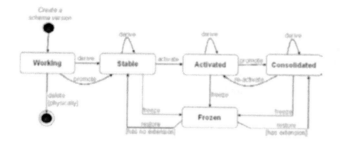

Fig. 3. Schema version status

New versions are created in the *working* status. When a version is derived from another one, its predecessor is automatically promoted to *stable*, thus avoiding modifications on versions that were important from a historical point of view. Only in the *working* status the version can be physically modified, otherwise a new version is created from this one as successor . *Activated* versions represent ready versions, which is the unique status in which the schema version can be populated. Finally, while *frozen* versions represent a logical exclusion (only used to solve queries), *consolidated* versions cannot be populated, but can be used as a base for a new derivation, and to solve queries. The following simplified syntax shows the status operation specification:

```
derive::= DERIVE schemaVersionName FROM (identificSV | {identificSV}) [schemaSpec]
promote::=PROMOTE [ALLPREDECESSORS] identificSV TO status [iValidity]
activate::=ACTIVATE identificSV [iValidity]
delete::=DELETE identificSV
freeze::=FREEZE (ALL |[CASCADE] identificSV) [iValidity]
restore::=RESTORE (ALL
   | ALLVERSIONS [VALIDITY INTERVAL definiedInterval])
   | [TOP] identificSV [VALIDITY INTERVAL definiedInterval]) iValidity
identificSV ::= current | schemaVersionName | schemaSelection
```

The DERIVE operation creates a new version as a successor of one or more versions. In the FROM clause the user can specify the schema in which the versioning process begins. Since the new version is created in the *working* status, the time interval does not need to be specified. The PROMOTE operation promotes the schema version from the *working* status to *stable*, or from *activated* to *consolidated*. Since the status represents the development phases, each version must be at least in the same status of its predecessor versions. The optional ALLPREDECESSORS clause recursively promotes not only the schema version selected but also all its predecessors to the same status. The ACTIVATE operation defines a version as usable (instantiated schema version), connecting a data extension and allowing to insert new data. The DELETE operation physically excludes the schema version, and may be used only for versions in the *working* status. The FREEZE operation logically excludes the schema version, closing its validity time (if there is no successive version). The optional CASCADE clause excludes the selected schema version as well as all its successor versions and the ALL clause excludes the versioned schema and all its versions. The RESTOREoperation restores the schema version to the *stable* status if there are not associated data; otherwise the schema version is restored to *consolidated*.

In order to restore one version, the `identificSV` clause must be specified. However, if its predecessor is also frozen, it must be restored before in order to keep track of derivation (this procedure must be recursively performed until there are not excluded schema versions). The optional `TOP` clause allows to restore recursively all predecessor versions of the selected schema version. The `ALL`clause restores all schema versions of the versioned schema, since another sequence of derivation has not been generated.

In order to retrieve schema versions, the `identificSV` clause can be used according to three ways: *(i)* `current` clause - the current schema version is selected; *(ii)* `schemaVersionName` - the user is able to select a specific schema version through its name; and *(iii)* `schemaSelection` - it is basically the same statement defined by TSQL2 [9], in which the `SET SCHEMA` clause is executed in order to retrieve a schema version by specifying the date time expression for transaction time or valid time (or both). The `iValidity` clause is usually supplied by the user in order to specify the instant in which the new status shall be assumed (initial validity time). When it is not specified, the `ivalidity` is assumed to be *now*.

Example 2. Suppose that the new schema version is derived from sv0 . The `DERIVE` statement would be:

```
DERIVE sv1 FROM SVO
    class Student {
        attribute string enrolment,
        attribute string address }
        relationship 1:n Degree ;
```

Note that the new schema version `sv1` will be created keeping its schema specification, and adding the new specifications as the `Student` class and its relationship. The validity interval is not necessary since the schema version is created in *working* status.

4.2   Schema Modification Language

Banerjee [1] defines a complete collection of primitive updates that can be applied to a schema. In order to accommodate the requirements of *TV_SE*, these primitives were extended considering relationship operations as follows: inheritance, association, aggregation, composition and extension inheritance relationship (a special relationship of TVM), as well as the possibility of defining relationship and attributes as temporal or non temporal. Besides, the validity interval changes are also specified (and consequently a new schema version is derived), since the schema is changed and the correct treatment during instance propagation is required. The simplified syntax of the resultant language for schema modification is presented as follows:

```
primitiveUpdate::= (add | delete | modify | changeValidityDefinition) identificSV
 [newSV schemaVersionName [VALIDITY INTERVAL definedInternval]]
add::=ADD (CLASS className specificClass
 |ATTRIBUTE attributeName specificClass
 |RELATIONSHIP relationshipName specificRelationship
 |OPERATION operationName specificOperation )
delete::=DELETE (CLASS className
 |ATTRIBUTE attributeName FROM className
 |RELATIONSHIP relationshipName FROM className relatedClass
 |OPERATION operationName )
modify::= MODIFY (CLASS name className INTO className
```

```
|CLASS type className INTO (hasVersions|normal)
|ATTRIBUTE name attributeName INTO attributeName className
|ATTRIBUTE type attributeName INTO (temporal|normal) className
|OPERATION name operationName INTO operationName)IN className
|RELATIONSHIP name [inverse] relationshipName INTO relationshipName) relatedClass
|RELATIONSHIP cardinality [inverse] relationshipName (1:1|1:n|n:1|n:n)relatedClass
|RELATIONSHIP type relationshipName INTO (temporal|normal) relatedClass
changeValidityDefinition::= modify identificSV
[newSV schemaVersionName [VALIDITY INTERVAL definedInterval]]
```

When applied to an existing schema version, each schema change leads to the creation of a new schema version. All changes are required to be exclusively performed through the update primitives to guarantee the schema consistency. The primitive updates are classified in three categories: *add* includes an element of the schema; *delete* excludes an element to the schema; and *modify* changes an element of the schema. The *specificSV* clause allows defining the schema version in which the primitive update will be performed. The *newSV* clause specifies the new schema version that will be created due to the changes.

Example 3. Suppose that the address attribute is included in Student class in sv1 schema version, previously shown in figure 2-d. The ADD ATTRIBUTE statement would be:

```
ADD ATTRIBUTE string concentration IN Degree sv0 NEWSV sv2
    VALIDITY INTERVAL ['01 oct 2003', '20 dec 2003'];
```

Note that since the sv0 indicates the schema version that was used as derivation basis, the new schema version will be the sv2 . The validity interval to the new created schema version is also supplied.

It is important to notice that when a schema version is modified, extensional data has to be adapted to assure consistency between the new schema version and data. In this case, the modification language needs to know the difference between the schema versions along the version derivation graph. Concerning physical implementation, two kinds of function have been defined [7]: *propagation* and *conversion*. These functions have been specified to assure the correct instance propagation and to allow the user to handle all instances consistently in both backward and forward schema versions.

5   An ODMG Extension for Temporal Schema Evolution Language

ODMG object model encompasses the most commonly used object model and standardizes its features into one object model, thus increasing the portability and applicability of out applications. Due to space restrictions we do not discuss the ODMG here, rather the reader is referred to [6]. In this section, an extension of the ODMG standard is presented in order to incorporate temporal and versioning features into ODL language for properly managing the schema evolution mechanism.

Figure 4 depicts the general architecture of SE_Evolution in terms of ODMG. The main components of the architecture are listed below and represent the use of the typical ODBMS products. The components listed at the top of the figure make up the *Temporal Versions Environment*: classes management, schema evolution and data manipulation.

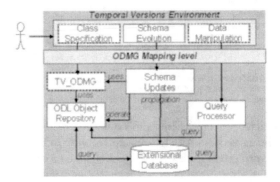

Fig. 4. TVSE_ODMG Architecture

The components listed in the *ODMG level* represent system components that the OODB system must provide. Figure 4 also shows the interaction of the modules during the application execution. The query language is used to query over metadata (metadata presented in section 3 were mapped to *ODL Object repository* in ODMG standard) and to handle extensional data for running applications. The *schema updates* also use the query language in order to invoke the schema updates and for propagating changes to the database. The dotted lines present the modules that have been implemented in TVM environment.

5.1   TV_ODMG

TV_ODMG [10] proposes an extension of ODMG [6] standard for object versioning with temporal features (as transaction time and valid time) based on TVM. The following components of the ODMG architecture were extended: the Object Model, the ODL and the OQL. These extensions are respectively called as: *TV_OM*, *TV_ODL* and *TV_OQL*. TV_ODL adds new rules to ODL, and modifies the existing ones. Class specification [2] is shown as follows:

```
(2a#) class ::= class_dcl | class_forward_dcl | tv_class_dcl
(2c#) class_forward_dcl ::=class identifier|class tv_class_name hasVersion
(2T1) tv_class_dcl ::= tv_class_header {tv_interface_body}
(2T2) tv_class_header ::= class tv_class_name hasVersion
                         [byExtension tv_ascendant][([extent_spec])]
(2T3) tv_class_name ::= identifier
(2T4) tv_ascendant ::= tv_class_name [correspondence corresp_options]
(2T5) corresp_options ::= 1:1 | 1:n | n:1 | n:m
(8T1)tv_interface_body ::= tv_export | tv_export tv_interface_body
(9T1)tv_export ::= temp_attr_dcl;| temp_rel_dcl;| aggr_dcl;| temp_aggr_dcl;|export
```

The *hasVersion* term indicates the temporal versioned classes, the *byExtension* indicates extension inheritance relationship and *correspondence* specifies the cardinality among class objects with their ascendants in the superclass. Besides, it is possible to specify an *extent* for these classes. New rules are added for supporting the temporal classes properties.

---

[2] The changed rules are pointed by *(nx#)+* or *(n#)*, in which *n* and *x* show the modified rules, and # indicates the changes.

5.2   ODL Extension for Schema Versioning Manipulation and Modification

ODL extension for schema evolution is handled by two categories: *schema versioning manipulation* and *schema versioning modification*. The former integrates schema versioning characteristics in order to allow the versions manipulation concerning the derivation relationship among schema versions (forming a directed acyclic graph). The latter is related to elements of the ODMG Object Model: attributes, relationships, operations, classes and interface. All these changes act on the schema version selected during the performed operation (*identificSV* clause in section 4.1). The language presented in section 4 is mapped for ODL specification. There is insuficient space in this paper to completely show the syntax of the ODL extension, but the resultant syntax is very similar that presented in section 4. Schema and class specifications are defined through interface and class respectively. Primitive updates are specified by modifying of the interface elements as attributes, relationships, operations and exception.

6   Comparison with Other Ongoing Research

A survey of schema versioning issues can be found in [2]. The Database Systems Research Group led by Elke Rundensteiner was the first to propose a comprehensive support for relationship evolution [4]. The main difference in the *TV_SE Evolution* is that the change management handles temporal attributes and relationships and derives versions in order to keep track of the evolution. In the temporal database context, [3] defines a formal model for the support of temporal schema versions in object-oriented databases. The model is also provided with extensions to the definition and manipulation language of the standard object-oriented data model ODMG for a generalized schema versioning support.

Alternative approaches with different goals to define a new language for specifying the database transformation have been explored in the literature. WOL [11] is a declarative language designed to allow transformations between the complex data type structures and reasoning about the interactions between database transformation and constraints. In [12] a new methodology that supports the schema modification in temporal object database is proposed. The class and the instance structures of the existing data model are extended to maintain historical information about the schema modification. Also, [5] describes a strategy in which the evolution of objects databases can be controlled by enhanced versioning, and an extension of the notions of ODMG is proposed in order to capture temporal versions.

7   Summary and Concluding Remarks

The development of *TV_SE Evolution* was in part motivated by a project that aims at implementing an integrated environment for class specification, object versioning, versions management, query and visualization. In [7] we propose a schema versioning approach to manage schema evolution on temporal object-oriented databases. This paper deals with a language to accommodate both temporal schema versioning and schema modification.

Besides, an extension of the ODMG standard is presented in order to incorporate temporal and versioning features into the ODL language for properly managing the schema evolution mechanism. We have applied our work in the legacy systems described in section 4. Legacy systems undergo frequent schema evolution and the ability to handle schemata and their data according to multiple versions is thus essential.

This work leaves an open field for future work toward indexes and clustering directives because they can be affected by schema modifications. For instance: removing a class that has an index or removing an attribute that is a component of an index (and others); this may need to rebuild or redefine an index after the schema changes propagation is complete. In this way, we intend to extend our approach in order to fulfill this requirement.

References

1. J. Banerjee, W. Kim, H. F. Korth, Semantics and implementation of schema evolution in object-oriented databases, in: ACM Sigmod Intl. Conf. on Management of Data, San Francisco, CA, 1987, pp. 311–322.
2. J. Roddick, A survey of schema versioning issues for database systems, Information and Software Technology 37 (7) (1995) 383–393.
3. F. Grandi, F. Mandreoli, A formal model for temporal schema versioning in object-oriented databases, Tech. Rep. TR-68, Time Center (jan 2002).
4. K. T. Claypool, E. A. Rundensteiner, G. T. Heineman, ROVER: flexible yet consistent evolution of relationships, Data & Knowledge Engineering 39 (1) (2001) 27–50.
5. H. Riedel, Outdating outdated objects, in: Workshop on Object-Oriented Databases, Vol. 1743 of LNCS, springer, Lisbon, Portugal, 1999, pp. 73–83.
6. R. G. G. Cattell, et al., The Object Data Standard: ODMG 3.0, Morgan Kaufmann Publishers, San Francisco, 2000, 280p.
7. R. M. Galante, N. Edelweiss, C. S. dos Santos, Change management for a temporal versioned object-oriented database, in: Intl. Workshop on Evolution and Change in Data Management, Intl. Conf. on Conceptual Modelling, Tampere, Finland, 2002, pp. 1–12.
8. M. M. Moro, S. M. Saggiorato, N. Edelweiss, C. S. dos Santos, Adding time to an object-oriented versions model, in: Intl. Conf. on Database and Expert Systems Applications, Vol. 2113 of LNCS, Springer, Munich, Germany, 2001, pp. 805–814.
9. R. T. Snodgrass (Ed.), The TSQL2 Temporal Query Language, Kluwer Academic Publishers, 1995.
10. P. C. Gelatti, C. S. dos Santos, N. Edelweiss, An extension to the ODMG standard for time and versioning support, Tech. rep., UFRGS (2003).
11. S. B. Davidson, A. Kosky, Specifying database transformations in wol, IEEE Data Engineering Bulletin 22 (1) (1999) 25–30.
12. W. S. Kim, D. C. Chang, T. Y. Lim, Y. H. Shin, Temporal object-oriented data model for the schema modification, in: Intl. Conf. on Database Systems for Advanced Applications, World Scientific, Singapore, 1995, pp. 422–429.

Building Conceptual Schemas by Refining General Ontologies

Jordi Conesa, Xavier de Palol, and Antoni Olivé

Universitat Politècnica Catalunya
Departament de Llenguatges i Sistemes Informàtics
Jordi Girona 1-3 E08034 Barcelona (Catalonia)
{jconesa,xdepalol,olive}@lsi.upc.es

Abstract. In practice, most conceptual schemas of information systems and databases are developed essentially from scratch. This paper deals with a new approach to that development, consisting on the refinement of a general ontology. We identify and characterize the three activities required to develop a conceptual schema from a general ontology, that we call refinement, pruning and refactoring. The focus of the paper is on the differences of the new approach with respect to the traditional one. The pruning activity may be automated. We formalize it and present a method for its realization. Besides, we identify a particular problem that appears during the refactoring activity, determining whether two types are redundant, and provide two sufficient conditions for it. We illustrate the approach with the development of a conceptual schema by refinement of the Cyc ontology. However, our results apply to any general ontology. The conceptual modeling language we have used is the UML, but we believe that our results could be applied to any similar language.

1 Introduction

Information systems (IS) must embody some general knowledge about its domain in order to be able to perform their functions. The specification of that knowledge in some language is the conceptual schema. Conceptual schemas are elaborated during the conceptual modeling activity, which is a part of the requirements engineering phase [13].

There are several definitions of the term 'ontology'. We adopt here the one proposed in [20], in which an ontology is defined as the explicit representation of a conceptualization. A conceptualization is the set of concepts (entities, attributes, processes) used to view a domain, including their definitions and their relationships. An ontology is the specification of a conceptualization in some language.

According to these definitions, it is clear that there is a strong similarity between the terms 'conceptual schema' and 'ontology'. In this paper, we consider a conceptual schema as the ontology that an information system needs to know.

Ontologies can be classified in terms of their level of generality into [8]:

- *Top-level* ontologies, which describe very general, domain-independent concepts such as space, time, etc.

V. Mařík et al. (Eds.): DEXA 2003, LNCS 2736, pp. 693–702, 2003.

- *Domain* and *Task* ontologies, which describe, respectively, the vocabulary related to a generic domain (medicine,...) and a generic task or activity (selling,...). These ontologies can be very large.
- *Application* ontologies, which describe concepts depending on a particular domain and task.

Top-level ontologies tend to be more abstract and smaller than domain and task ontologies [19].

A conceptual schema may include parts of all the above ontologies, depending on the kind of knowledge that needs to have the corresponding information system. We call top-level, domain and task ontologies *general* ontologies.

General ontologies may play several roles in conceptual modeling of information systems. One of them is the base role. We say that a general ontology plays a base role when it is the basis from which the conceptual schema is derived. The conceptual schema is then just a specialization or refinement of a general ontology.

The approach of deriving conceptual schemas of information systems and databases from general ontologies has not been explored in detail in the literature, yet we believe it may yield important benefits. To the best of our knowledge, the existing work most relevant to that approach is: (1) [7], which suggests that requirements models should be "developed by specializing, refining or adapting selected parts of the relevant domain model, if this is appropriate"; (2) [19], which uses the SENSUS ontology to derive the conceptual schema for an air campaign planning system; and (3) The Knowledge Bus [16], a system which generates database and programming interfaces, having as input a conceptual schema derived from the Cyc ontology. Much more work needs to be done to achieve the full potential of that approach.

Development of conceptual schemas by refining general ontologies is not the same as the development from scratch. Of course many tasks are alike in both cases, but the overall main activities are very different. The main contribution of this paper is the identification and characterization of the three activities required to develop a conceptual schema from a general ontology, that we call refinement, pruning and refactoring. The focus of the paper is on the differences of the new approach with respect to the traditional one. In particular, we point out two problems (almost) exclusive of the new approach, and provide an initial solution to them.

The structure of the paper is as follows. In the next section we review the roles that ontologies may play in conceptual modeling. Section 3 identifies and characterizes the three main activities in the development of conceptual schemas from general ontologies. We exemplify them by means of small excerpts from an in-depth case study (taken from [1,ch.10]), which deals with bus management in a bus company. Space constraints prevent us from including here more details, but the interested reader may find the complete case study in [5]. As general ontology, we have chosen the public version (OpenCyc [15]) of Cyc. The main reason for this choice has been that Cyc is probably the largest general ontology in use (more than 10^5 general concepts) [10]. The Cyc ontology is specified in the CycL language. However, in this paper we aim at practical applications of the new approach, and for this reason we find it convenient to use as conceptual modeling language the UML [14].

Section 4 formalizes one of the exclusive problems in the new approach, pruning ontologies, and presents a method to solve it. Section 5 does the same for a problem found during the refactoring activity, determining whether two types are redundant, and proposes two sufficient conditions for it. Section 6 gives the general conclusions, and points out future work.

2 Roles of Ontologies in Conceptual Modeling

The activity of conceptual modeling is performed using a conceptual modeling environment, which includes one or more CASE tools [2]. Currently, most environments do not use any ontology. This means that, in these cases, conceptual schemas must be developed each time from scratch.

The general trend towards software reusability has also had its impact on conceptual modeling, and there have been many efforts trying to reuse existing ontologies in the development of new conceptual schemas [12]. The approaches taken by these efforts can be classified in several ways [8]. We focus here on the role played by the ontologies in the conceptual modeling activity, and we distinguish three roles: building block, support and base role. A given ontology may play one or more of these roles.

An ontology plays a *building block* role if it provides blocks (fragments) that can be reused in new conceptual schemas, possibly after an adaptation or customization. For example, we may have a general ontology including, among others, financial concepts. In a particular conceptual schema, we may be interested in the concept of *Money* as defined in that ontology. We can then take it from there, adapt it to our particular needs and incorporate it into our conceptual schema. When an ontology plays a building block role, the environment must provide facilities for finding the blocks that meet the requirements and for their adaptation [12, 2]. Among the reported efforts of use of ontologies in the building block role there are [4] and [17].

An ontology plays a *support* role if it can be used by the environment in a way that supports the designer in the development of new conceptual schemas. For example, an ontology may help designers become familiar with a domain by browsing the ontology to learn the basics of that domain [19]. As another example, an environment may suggest the cardinality constraints of a relationship type, if they can be inferred from the ontology. Among the reported efforts on the use of ontologies in the support role there are [18] and [11].

Finally, an ontology plays a *base* role when it is the basis from which the conceptual schema is derived. The conceptual schema can then be seen as a specialization (refinement or extension) of the ontology. The task of the designer is to extend the ontology until it includes (as a subset) the conceptual schema. In the literature, the base role has been much less studied than the other two, at least in the development of information systems and data bases. In this paper, we focus on this role.

3 Developing Conceptual Schemas from General Ontologies

In the general case, the development of a conceptual schema from a general ontology requires three main activities: refinement, pruning and refactoring. Normally, these activities will be performed sequentially (see Fig. 1), but an iterative development is also conceivable. In particular circumstances, some of the above activities may not be needed. In the following we briefly characterize the three activities.

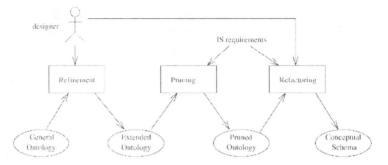

Fig. 1. The three activities in the development of conceptual schemas from general ontologies.

3.1 Refinement

Normally, a general ontology O_G will not include (as a subset) the conceptual schema *CS* required by a particular information system. The objective of the refinement activity is then to obtain an extended ontology O_X such that:

- O_X is an extension of O_G, and
- O_X includes the conceptual schema *CS*.

The refinement is performed by the designer. S/he analyzes the IS requirements, determines the knowledge the system needs to know to satisfy those requirements, checks whether such knowledge is already in O_G and, if not, makes the necessary extensions to O_G, thus obtaining O_X. Refinement is not needed in the rare case that *CS* is already included in O_G.

In our example, the IS requirements include storing data about the company's drivers (name, license type,…) and the drivers' absences (date, cause,…). If we assume that our general ontology O_G defines the concepts shown at the top of Fig. 2, we need to extend it with the concepts shown at the bottom. We have defined entity type *Driver* as subtype of *Person*, with attribute *licenseType*. Note that attribute *name* is already defined by O_G in *Person*. Similarly, we have defined entity type *DriverAbsence*, as subtype of *Event*, and with attribute *cause*. Note also that attribute *date* of absence is already defined in *Event*. The absent driver is given by the *actor* association between *SomethingExisting* (an indirect generalization of *Person*) and *Event*. See [5] for the complete specification (in the UML) of the extended ontology in the case study. We have refined the OpenCyc ontology with over 40 entity types, attributes and associations.

3.2 Pruning

Normally, an extended ontology O_X will contain many irrelevant concepts for a particular information system. The objective of the pruning activity is then to obtain a pruned ontology O_P such that:

- O_P is a subset of O_X, and
- O_P includes the conceptual schema *CS*, and
- The concepts in O_X but not in O_P would have an empty extension in the information system (i.e. they are irrelevant).

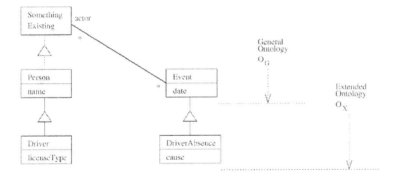

Fig 2. Example of refinement of a general ontology

In the case study, we find that the OpenCyc ontology contains thousands of concepts irrelevant for bus management purposes. For example, the entity and relationship types dealing with Chemistry. Our information system is not interested in these concepts and, therefore, their extension in the information base would be empty. The objective of the pruning activity is to remove such concepts from O_X.

In general, the concepts in O_X but not in O_G (i.e. those added during refinement) will not be pruned. On the other hand, pruning is not needed in the rare case that all concepts in O_X are relevant to our information system.

When the IS requirements are formalized, the pruning activity may be automated. In section four, we describe a method for pruning an ontology when the requirements are expressed as system operations defined by formal pre and postconditions.

3.3 Refactoring

Normally, a pruned ontology O_P cannot be accepted as a final conceptual schema because it can be greatly improved. The objective of the refactoring activity is then to obtain a conceptual schema CS that is externally equivalent to O_P yet improves its structure. The purpose of ontology (or conceptual schema) refactoring is equivalent to that of software system refactoring [6].

The refactoring is performed by the designer, but important parts of the activity can be automated, provided that the IS requirements are formalized. Refactoring consists in the application of a number of refactoring operations to parts of an ontology. Most of these operations are similar to those applicable to software. An important issue is to remove from O_P those concepts that have the same extension as other concepts also present in O_P. In Section 5 we provide sufficient conditions for two types to be redundant.

In the case study, we have the set of generalizations *Driver* → *Person* → *LegalAgent* → *SocialBeing* → *Agent* → *CompositeTangibleAndIntangibleObject* → *PartiallyTangible* → *SomethingExisting* (shown partly in Figure 2). Most of these entity types would have exactly the same extension in our information base, and they should be removed to improve the quality of the conceptual schema.

4 Pruning Ontologies

Many of the problems faced by a designer, when developing a conceptual schema from a general ontology, are similar to those faced in other development approaches. However, there are a few problems exclusive to that approach. One of them is pruning ontologies, as explained above. In this section, we formalize the problem and present a method to solve it.

4.1 The Problem

The inputs to the pruning activity are: an extended ontology O_x and a set of requirements for an IS S. We deal here with ontologies and requirements defined in the UML. In this language an ontology O_x consists of:
- A set of entity types. We allow multiple classification and, therefore, an entity may be direct instance of several entity types.
- A set of attributes and associations.
- A set of generalizations links of entity types. An entity type may have multiple generalizations.
- A set of generalizations links of associations. An association may have multiple generalizations. In the UML, attributes cannot be generalized.
- A set of integrity constraints, defined as invariants of entity types, and formalized in the OCL.

On the other hand, we assume that requirements are formalized as system operations [9]. Each of them consists of:
- Its signature (name, parameters, result and their types)
- Its preconditions, formalized in the OCL.
- Its postconditions, formalized also in the OCL.

Given these inputs, the problem is to select from O_x those entity types, associations and attributes which may have instances in the IS S, and the relevant integrity constraints. The result is called a pruned ontology.

4.2 The Method

Our method for pruning ontologies consists of the following six steps:
1. Select all entity types referred to in the signature or in the pre/postconditions of system operations.
2. Select all attributes referred to in the pre/postconditions of system operations. Select also the source and target entity types of these attributes.
3. Select all associations referred to in the pre/postconditions of system operations. Select also the participant entity types of these associations.
4. Select all associations that are direct or indirect supertypes of the above associations, and the corresponding generalization links. Select also the participant entity types of these associations.
5. Select all entity types that are direct or indirect supertypes of the ones selected in the four previous steps, and the corresponding generalization links.

6. Select the integrity constraints such that all their participant elements (entity types, attributes, associations) have been selected in the previous steps.

As an example, consider the system operation that adds a new driver's absence (see Figure 2). Its formal specification, in OCL, could be:

```
context System::DriverAbsence (driverName:String, cause:String)
   pre:  Driver.allInstances() -> exists (name = driverName)
   post: abs.oclIsNew() and abs.oclIsTypeOf(DriverAbsence) and
         abs.cause = cause and abs.date = Today and
         let d:Driver = Driver.allInstamnces() ->
                         any (name = driverName) in
         abs.actor = Set {d}
```

Using this operation only, step 1 selects entity types *String*, *Driver*, and *DriverAbsence*. Step 2 selects attributes *name, cause* and *date*, as well as entity types *Person, DriverAbsence, Event, String* (the target type of attributes *name* and *cause*) and *Date* (the target type of attribute *date*). Step 3 selects the association *actor* between *Event* and *SomethingExisting*, as well as these two entity types. Note that the five entity types in the chain of generalization links between *Person* and *SomethingExisting* would not be selected in the steps 1, 2 and 3.

The rationale for steps 1, 2 and 3 is that all types referred to in the system operations must be present in the final conceptual schema. Steps 4 and 5 add the supertypes of the types selected in the previous steps. Some of these added types will be removed in the refactoring activity. Step 6 adds the integrity constraints that can be enforced by the information system because all their types have been selected.

In our case study, the extended ontology consists of 2268 entity types and 1191 attributes or associations. After the application of the above pruning method, the resulting ontology has 200 entity types and 85 attributes or associations [5].

4.3 Comparison with Previous Work

To the best of our knowledge, the work most similar to ours, with respect to pruning ontologies, has been reported in [19, 16, 21]. Our method contributes to this work in two aspects: (1) The selection of concepts is automatic, while in the mentioned works the selection must be done manually, and (2) We deal with richer ontologies, including entity types, attributes, associations, generalization of entity types and associations, and integrity constraints, while in the mentioned works one or more of these elements are not considered.

5 Redundant Types

Another particular problem of conceptual schema development from general ontologies is that of redundant types. We say that two entity or relationship types are redundant (or equivalent) in a conceptual schema if they must have the same extension in all possible states of the corresponding information base [3]. Naturally, the general problem of redundancy may appear in any conceptual schema, and several methodologies provide some guidance on how to detect and remove it. However, in our context we find very often a particular class of redundancy: two entity or relationship types related by a generalization link. For example, in Figure 2, if drivers are the only persons in which we are interested, then *Driver* and *Person* are redundant. Given that hierarchies in general ontologies tend to be very deep, the number of redundant types may be very large.

In principle, redundant types must be removed during the refactoring activity. This can be done by the application of the well-known operation called "*collapse hierarchy*" [6, p. 344], whose purpose is to empty a type (by pulling up or pushing down its associations) and then remove it from the ontology.

The application of the collapse hierarchy operation requires the detection of the redundant types. In general, this detection is done manually. However, in our context many redundant types can be detected automatically. We define below two sufficient conditions for two types to be redundant.

5.1 The Problem

We assume we have a pruned ontology O_p in the UML, that includes, among other things: a set of entity types, a set of associations, and a set of generalizations between pairs of entity types and pairs of associations.

Given these inputs, the problem is to determine whether two entity types or two associations are redundant or not.

5.2 Sufficient Conditions for Redundancy

We have defined two similar, but independent conditions for redundancy. Both are sufficient conditions. Let A and B be two types (entity types or associations), such that there is a direct generalization link from B to A. The first condition applies when A is a direct supertype of only one type (B), and in this case we say that A has a single child. The second condition applies when B is a direct subtype of only one type (A), and in this case we say that B has a single parent.

Our conditions for redundancy require to know the value of attribute *isAbstract* for single child and single parent types. This is a boolean attribute that the UML metamodel defines for entity types and associations. A true value for this attribute means that an instance of the entity type or association must be also an instance of a child. False indicates that there may be an instance of the entity type or association that is not an instance of the child [14, p.2-43]. A type for which *isAbstract* has the value true is called abstract. For the purposes of our redundancy conditions, we make the conservative assumption that a single child or single parent type in a pruned ontology O_p is abstract if it is never referenced in the specification of the system operations. That is, if it has not been selected in steps 1-3 of pruning activity.

In this context, our two conditions for redundancy become simple. The first one states that when type A is the supertype of type B only, A and B are redundant if A is abstract. Similarly, the second one states that when type B is the subtype of type A only, A and B are redundant if B is abstract. Both are not necessary conditions for redundancy, but sufficient ones.

As an example, in our case study we have the generalization *PartiallyTangible* → *SomethingExisting*, where *SomethingExisting* is supertype of *PartiallyTangible* only, and *SomethingExisting* is not referenced in any system operation (and, therefore, it is abstract). Then, by the application of the first condition we conclude that *Partiall-Tangible* and *SomethingExisting* would be redundant in our information system.

As another example, consider the generalization *MathematicalThing* → *Intangible*, where *MathematicalThing* is subtype of *Intangible* only, and *MathematicalThing* is not referenced in any system operation. Then, by the application of the second condition we conclude that *MathematicalThing* and *Intangible* are redundant.

The above conditions for redundancy are very effective in the refinement and pruning of large ontologies. In our case study, the conditions have determined that over 70% of the entity types and associations in the pruned ontology are redundant (in absolute numbers, over 155 entity types and 40 associations) [5]. The automatic removing of these redundant types is a significant refactoring operation.

6 Conclusions

This paper deals with a new approach to the development of conceptual schemas of information systems and databases, consisting in the refinement of a general ontology. We believe that this approach may yield important benefits, although this has not been explored here. Instead, we have focused on the identification and characterization of the main activities required by that approach, which we have called refinement, pruning and refactoring. The pruning activity may be automated. We have formalized it and have presented a method for its realization. On the other hand, we have identified a particular problem that appears during the refactoring activity, determining whether two types are redundant, and we have provided two sufficient conditions for it.

We have illustrated the approach with the development of a conceptual schema by refinement of the Cyc ontology, described in full in [5]. However, our results apply to any general ontology. As conceptual modeling language we have used the UML, but we believe that our results apply to any similar language.

We hope that our work will be a step forward in the development of conceptual schemas from general ontologies. Nevertheless, more work needs to be done for the new approach to be widely used in practice. The main directions of our future work will be the formalization of refinement operations (focusing on those more used during refinement), the improvement of our pruning method (increasing the expressiveness of the language), and the formalization of refactoring operations (again focusing on those more used in our approach). We also plan to develop CASE tools to be integrated in existing UML-based conceptual modeling environments.

Acknowledgments. This work has been partly supported by the Ministerio de Ciencia y Tecnologia and FEDER under project TIC2002-00744.

References

1. Batini, C.; Ceri, S.; Navathe, S.B. Conceptual Database Design. An Entity-relationship Approach. The Benjamin/Cummings Publishing Co., 1992, 470 p.
2. Bouzeghoub, m.; Kekad, Z.; Métais, E. "CASE Tools: Computer Support for Conceptual Modeling", in Piattini, M.; Díaz, O. (Eds). "Advanced Database Technology and Design", Artech House, 2000.
3. Calvanese, D.; Lenzerini, M.; Nardi, D. "Description Logics for Conceptual Data Modeling". In Chomicki, J.; Saake, G. (eds). Logics for Databases and IS, Kluwer, 1998, pp. 229–263.
4. Castano, S.; De Antonellis, V.; Zonta, B. "Classifying and Reusing Conceptual Schemas", Proc. ER'92, LNCS 645, pp. 121–138.
5. Conesa, J.; de Palol, X. "A Case Study on Building Conceptual Schemas by Refining General Ontologies", UPC, 2003, http://www.lsi.upc.es/~jconesa/casestudy.html.
6. Fowler, M. Refactoring. Improving the Design of Existing Code. Addison-Wesley, 2000.
7. Gibson, M.D.; Conheeney, K. "Domain Knowledge Reuse During Requirements Engineering". Proc. CAiSE 1995, LNCS 932, pp. 283–296
8. Guarino, N. "Formal Ontology and Information Systems", FOIS'98, IOS Press, pp. 3–15.
9. Larman, C. Applying UML and Patterns. Prentice Hall, Second Edition, 2002.
10. Lenat, D.B.; Guha, R.V.; Pittman, K.; Pratt, D.; Shepherd, M. "CYC: Towards Programs with Common Sense", Comm. ACM, 33(8), pp. 30–49.
11. Lloyd-Williams, M. "Exploiting domain knowledge during the automated design of O-O databases", Proc. ER'97, LNCS 1331, pp. 16–29.
12. Mili, H.; Mili, F.; Mili, A. "Reusing Software: Issues and Research Directions", IEEE TSE, 21(6), pp. 528–562.
13. Olivé, A. "An Introduction to Conceptual Modeling of Information Systems", in Piattini, M.; Díaz, O. (Eds). "Advanced Database Technology and Design", Artech House, 2000.
14. OMG. "Unified Modeling Language Specification", Version 1.4, September 2001, http://www.omg.org/technology/documents/formal/uml.htm
15. Opencyc, http://www.opencyc.org.
16. Peterson, B.J.; Andersen, W.A.; Engel, J. "Knowledge Bus: Generating Application-focused Databases from Large Ontologies". Proc. 5th KRDB Worshop Seattle, WA. 1998
17. Ruggia, R.; Ambrosio, A.P. "A Toolkit for Reuse in Conceptual Modelling" Proc. CAiSE 1997, LNCS 1250, pp. 173–186.
18. Storey, V.; Chiang, R.; Dey, D.; Goldstein, R.; Sundaresan, S. "Database Design with Common Sense Business Reasoning and Learning", ACM TODS 22(4), 1997 pp. 471–512.
19. Swartout, B.; Patil, R.; Knight, K.; Russ, T. "Toward Distributed Use of Large-Scale Ontologies", Proc. 10th. KAW, 1996, Canada.
20. Uschold, M.; Gruninger, M. "Ontologies: principles, methods and applications", The Knowledge Engineering Review, 11(2), 1996, pp. 93–136.
21. Wouters, C.; Dillon, T.; Rahayu, W.; Chang, E. "A Practical Walkthrough of the Ontology Derivation Rules", Proc. DEXA 2002, LNCS 2453, pp. 259–268.

Semantics for Interoperability
Relating Ontologies and Schemata

Trevor Bench-Capon, Grant Malcolm, and Michael Shave

Department of Computer Science,University of Liverpool
PO Box 147,Liverpool L69 3BX, UK

Abstract. We present a formal approach to ontologies that supports reuse and sharing of information through relationships between compatible conceptualisations. This general approach is extended to database schemata, which allows us to characterise precisely the relationships between schemata and ontologies, and to give some foundations for interoperability of heterogeneous information systems. Our main results give a correctness criterion for relationships between schemata, and show that compatible schemata can be combined to provide an appropriate language for interoperation at an abstract, conceptual level.

1 Introduction

Through the WWW information has become accessible in ever increasing quantities. In consequence the potential benefits of information reuse have become increasingly important, as is recognised by initiatives such as the Semantic Web [1]. The major obstacle to reuse is that information is produced according to the varying conceptualisations of the many designers and the many purposes for which it is gathered and represented. It thus embodies a number of assumptions reflecting the background, experience and needs of its producers. For reuse to be possible these assumptions must be made as available as the information itself. In the case of fully specified information systems, most typically relational databases, the existence of schemata provide the required basis for reuse, and interoperability of databases through integration schemata is now commonplace. For less tightly specified information sources, these assumptions very often remain implicit. The response to this has been the development of ontologies, intended to supply formal expressions of the conceptualisations of a domain of knowledge. Even when an ontology is available, however, the need to recast information developed according to one ontology in a form usable by a system developed using a different ontology remains. The solution is the use of a shared ontology which captures what is common between the two conceptualisations, but this may still need procedural information to render it usable by an application: this, to provide parallels with database systems, we refer to as an integration schema. In this paper we attempt to make precise the relationship between ontologies and schemata, so as to provide a formal basis for the reuse of information, regardless of the type of system from which it is derived.

V. Mařík et al. (Eds.): DEXA 2003, LNCS 2736, pp. 703–712, 2003.

In Sect. 2 we give formal description of ontologies, and in Sect. 3 we provide a compatible description of schemata, and show how this can be used to describe relations between schemata and between schemata and ontologies. For reasons of space, we give only brief motivations for definitions, and omit proofs; these proofs, more extensive motivations, and some technical details we have omitted here for brevity's sake, are given in a technical report [2].

2   Specifying and Relating Ontologies

In this section we give a formal account of specifications of ontologies, and summarise some results from [3] that provide support for knowledge reuse.

Throughout this paper, we assume a given collection, D, of data types with names (always in italics) such as *String*, providing standard data representations for attribute values. Note that [2,3] take a more general approach to the use of data types in specifying both ontologies and schemata.

Definition 1. *An* **ontology signature**, *or just* **signature** *for short, is a pair* (C, A), *where* $C = (C, \leq)$ *is a partial order, called a* **class hierarchy**, *and* A *is a family of sets* $A_{c,e}$ *of* **attribute symbols** *for* $c \in C$ *and* $e \in C + D$. *This family of sets is such that* $A_{c',e} \subseteq A_{c,e'}$ *whenever* $c \leq c'$ *in* C *and* $e \leq e'$ *in* $C + D$.

(We write $C + D$ for the disjoint union of classes and data types; i.e., an attribute might take values in either a class or a data type.)

Example 1. The following is an ontology that might be used by a second-hand car dealer. There are four classes, Car, Estate-Car, Saloon-Car and Model. Each class is followed by an indented list of its attributes and their result types.

Car
   colour : {*white, red, blue*}
   model : Model
   price : *Pounds*

Estate-Car < Car
   rear-space : *SquareMetres*

Saloon-Car < Car
   hatchback : {*y, n*}

Model
   name : *String*
   manufacturer : {*maker1, maker2*}
   photo : *Gif*

The class Car has three attributes, e.g., model, which takes values in the class Model (i.e., model $\in A_{\mathsf{Car},\mathsf{Model}}$). The class Estate-Car has four attributes: three inherited from Car plus rear-space, which takes values in a data type *SquareMetres*.

The semantics of signatures is given by *models*: essentially, a model M interprets each class name c as a set M_c, and each attribute $\alpha \in A_{c,e}$ as a function M_α of the appropriate type ($M_c \rightarrow M_e$, if e is a class name; $M_c \rightarrow D_e$, where D_e is the set of appropriate data values, if e is a data type), subject to certain monotonicity requirements (see [3,2] for details). While models provide a notion of interpretation, the following gives a notion of translation:

Definition 2. *An* **ontology signature morphism** $\chi : (C, A) \rightarrow (C', A')$ *is a pair* $\chi = (f, g)$, *where* $f : C \rightarrow C'$ *is a morphism of partial orders, and* g *is a family of functions* $g_{c,e} : A_{c,e} \rightarrow A'_{f(c),f(e)}$, *where* $f(e) = e$ *if* e *is a data type in* D, *such that if* $c \leq c'$ *and* $e \leq e'$ *then* $g_{c',e}(\alpha) = g_{c,e'}(\alpha)$ *for all* $\alpha \in A_{c',e}$.

Interpretations can work backwards along translations, in the following sense: given a morphism $\chi : (\mathsf{C}, A) \to (\mathsf{C}', A')$, and given a (C', A')-model M, we define the (C, A)-model χM by

- $(\chi M)_c = M_{f(c)}$ for $c \in C$, and
- $(\chi M)_\alpha = M_{g_{c,e}(\alpha)}$ for $\alpha \in A_{c,e}$.

An ontology consists of a signature together with some axioms that constrain the values of attributes (see Example 2 below). A **morphism** of ontologies $\chi : \mathcal{O} \to \mathcal{O}'$ is a signature morphism such that whenever M is a model of $\mathcal{O}'$ (i.e., M satisfies the axioms of $\mathcal{O}$) then χM satisfies the axioms of $\mathcal{O}$. Intuitively, this means that $\mathcal{O}'$ has more constraints than $\mathcal{O}$ has.

Example 2. As an example, we give an ontology for models of cars that might be used for a buyers' guide:

Model
    name : *String*
    type : {*estate, saloon*}
    hatchback : {$y, n, n/a$}
    picture : *Gif*
    rear-space : *SquareMetres*
    manufacturer : Motor-maker
    price : *Pounds*

Car
    colour : {*white, red, blue*}
    model : Model

Motor-Maker
    name : {*maker1, maker2*}
    dealer : Dealer

Dealer
    name : *String*
    address : *String*

Axioms
hatchback(M) = n/a if type(M) = *estate*

The axiom constrains the value of hatchback depending on the type of model.

Morphisms express relationships between ontologies; the 'cocompleteness theorem' in [3] states that ontologies can be combined without duplicating shared components:

Theorem 1. *The category of ontologies and their morphisms is cocomplete.*

In the terminology of category theory, a combination of related ontologies produces a 'colimit'; the following illustrates what this means:

Example 3. Consider the following ontology, which provides a common subcomponent for the ontologies of Examples 1 and 2.

Car
    colour : {*white, red, blue*}
    model : Model

Model
    name : *String*
    manufacturer : {*maker1, maker2*}
    photo : *Gif*

There is an inclusion from this ontology (call it $\mathcal{O}$) to the ontology (call it $\mathcal{O}_1$) of Example 1. This gives us $\chi_1 : \mathcal{O} \to \mathcal{O}_1$. To relate $\mathcal{O}_1$ to the ontology (call it $\mathcal{O}_2$) of Example 2, we construct a morphism $\chi_2 : \mathcal{O} \to \mathcal{O}_2$ as follows. The class Car and its attributes are simply included in $\mathcal{O}_2$. The class Model and its attribute name are likewise included, and the attribute photo is mapped to the attribute picture in $\mathcal{O}_2$. The attribute manufacturer is treated in a more complex manner: it is mapped to the *compound* attribute manufacturer;name in $\mathcal{O}_2$, i.e., take the manufacturer attribute, giving a value in the class Motor-Maker, then take the attribute name of that class, giving a value in $\{maker1, maker2\}$.

In the colimit of this relation the attribute photo represents both the photo attribute of $\mathcal{O}_1$ and the picture attribute of $\mathcal{O}_2$. This is because these two attributes are the image of photo in $\mathcal{O}$ under χ_1 and χ_2 respectively, so this attribute is shared between the two ontologies, just as all the attributes of the class Car are shared. However, there are two manufacturer attributes in the colimit; one representing the attribute of the same name from $\mathcal{O}_1$, and the other (which we call manufacturer2) representing the attribute from $\mathcal{O}_2$. The morphisms χ_i state that manufacturer and manufacturer2;name should be the same, so in the colimit there is an axiom that constrains all models to treat them in the same way:

```
manufacturer(M) = name(manufacturer2(M)) .
```

The colimit of our two related ontologies is given in full below.

Car
    colour : $\{white, red, blue\}$
    model : Model
    price : $Pounds$

Estate-Car < Car
    rear-space : $SquareMetres$

Saloon-Car < Car
    hatchback : $\{y, n\}$

Dealer
    name : $String$
    address : $String$

Model
    name : $String$
    type : $\{estate, saloon\}$
    hatchback : $\{y, n, n/a\}$
    picture : Gif
    rear-space :
    manufacturer : $\{maker1, maker2\}$
    manufacturer2 : Motor-maker
    price : $Pounds$

Motor-Maker
    name : $\{maker1, maker2\}$
    dealer : Dealer

Axioms
    manufacturer(M) = name(manufacturer2(M))
    hatchback(M) = n/a if type(M) = $estate$

In general, colimits combine the constraints of the related ontologies; the following gives a sufficient condition for these constraints to be consistent (i.e., satisfiable):

Proposition 1. *Let* $\chi_i : \mathcal{O} \rightarrow \mathcal{O}_i$ *for* $i = 1, 2$ *and let* M_i *be a model of* $\mathcal{O}_i$ *for* $i = 1, 2$ *such that* $\chi_1 M_1 = \chi_2 M_2$; *then the colimit of* χ_i *has a model, and so* $\mathcal{O}_1$ *and* $\mathcal{O}_2$ *are compatible over* $\mathcal{O}$.

In summary, colimits provide a way of combining ontologies by providing a 'superlanguage' in which related ontologies can be embedded. The next section shows that similar support for interoperability can be provided for schemata, and gives a formal relation between ontologies and schemata.

3   Relating Ontologies and Database Schemata

We turn now to conceptual modeling by relational schemata. We give a formal account of schemata and relate these to ontologies. Our main contribution is a cocompleteness result that supports interoperability through merging related schemata.

Definition 3. *A* **schema** *consists of:*

- *a partially ordered set E of* **entity class names***;*
- *a typed collection A of* **attribute names***, i.e., sets $A_{e,s}$ for $e \in E$ and $s \in S$ such that $A_{e,s'} \subseteq A_{e',s}$ whenever $e \leq e'$ and $s \leq s'$;*
- *a partially ordered set R of* **relationship names***;*
- *a typed collection B of* **role names** *for relationships, i.e., sets $B_{r,w}$ for $r \in R$ and $w \in E+D$ (i.e., roles can also be data-valued attributes of relationships), such that $R_{r,w'} \subseteq R_{r',w}$ whenever $r \leq r'$ and $w \leq w'$;*
- *for each class $e \in E$ a set* keys(e)*, giving* **candidate keys***, which are sets of attributes of e, including a designated primary key denoted* pk(e)*;*
- *a set Fk of* **foreign keys***, which are triples (k, e_1, e_2) with $e_1, e_2 \in E$, and k a set of attributes of e_1 which is the primary key of e_2; we write Fk_{e_1,e_2} for the set of foreign keys in Fk of the form (k, e_1, e_2) for some k; and*
- *a set F of functional dependencies $\beta \rightarrow_e \alpha$, indicating that for $e \in E$, the value of the attribute α depends on the value of the attributes β.*

We denote such a schema by $(E, A, R, B, \text{keys}, Fk, F)$, and often we will just write S or S' for a schema and refer to its components as E or E', A or A', etc.

This definition is based on the Enhanced Entity-Relation model (see, e.g., [4]), and errs on the side of simplicity. For example, we omit weak entities and cardinalities of relationships, although it would be fairly straightforward to include these. Similarly, while all attributes of a class $e \in E$ are required to take values in data types, it is a simple matter to extend the definition with 'entity-valued' attributes; this is allowed for the relationship classes R, for which we also allow data-valued attributes (our use of the term 'role' for the attributes of relationships is not standard, but we adopt it in order to distinguish between attributes of entities and of relationships). We also do not provide for integrity constraints: the only 'axioms' allowed by our definition are functional dependencies. Again, it would be fairly straightforward to allow more expressive constraints by allowing, for example, arbitrary axioms as we do for ontologies.

Example 4. Consider the ontology of Example 2. An entity-relation diagram based on this ontology is shown in Figure 1 below. A schema corresponding to the diagram has entity classes for cars, models, motor-makers and dealers, i.e., the set of class names is $E = \{\text{Car}, \text{Model}, \text{MotorMaker}, \text{Dealer}\}$. The class MotorMaker has a single attribute name taking values in the datatype $d = \{maker1, maker2\}$, so $A_{\text{MotorMaker},d} = \{\text{name}\}$, and $A_{\text{MotorMaker},d'} = \emptyset$ for all other data types d'. There are three relation types, corresponding to the diamond-shaped boxes in

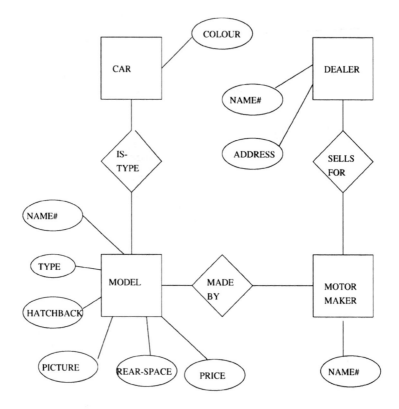

Fig. 1. A diagramatic schema

the diagram, i.e., $R = \{\mathsf{IsType}, \mathsf{MadeBy}, \mathsf{SellsFor}\}$, each of which has two roles; for example, $B_{\mathsf{SellsFor},\mathsf{Dealer}} = \{\mathsf{dealer}\}$ and $B_{\mathsf{SellsFor},\mathsf{MotorMaker}} = \{\mathsf{maker}\}$, with $B_{\mathsf{SellsFor},w} = \emptyset$ for all other w. Keys and functional dependencies would depend on some conception of how these entities and relations were to be stored; but $\{\mathsf{name}\}$ would presumably be a key for Model.

One notion of semantics for such schemata is much the same as that of models for ontologies: the semantics gives sets for entities and relationships, and functions for attributes and roles, and is intended to capture the semantics of actual databases that implement a schema:

Definition 4. *A **realisation** ρ of a schema S consists of:*

- *sets ρ_e for $e \in E$ such that $\rho_e \subseteq \rho_{e'}$ whenever $e \leq e'$;*
- *functions $\rho_\alpha : \rho_e \to D_d$ for each attribute name $\alpha \in A_{e,d}$ (where D_d is the set of appropriate data values for the data type d);*
- *sets ρ_r for $r \in R$ such that $\rho_r \subseteq \rho_{r'}$ whenever $r \leq r'$;*
- *functions $\rho_\alpha : \rho_r \to \rho_w$ for each role name $\alpha \in R_{r,w}$;*
- *functions $\rho_k : \rho_{e_1} \to \rho_{e_2}$ for each foreign key $(k, e_1, e_2) \in Fk$.*

In addition, we require that:

- *keys uniquely identify elements of ρ_e:*

$$x = y \quad \text{if} \quad \rho_k(x) = \rho_k(y)$$

for all $x, y \in \rho_e$ and all $k \in \mathsf{keys}(e)$, where the condition in the above equation is an abbreviation for $\rho_{\alpha_1}(x) = \rho_{\alpha_1}(y)$ and ... and $\rho_{\alpha_n}(x) = \rho_{\alpha_n}(y)$, where $\mathsf{keys}(e) = \{\alpha_1, \ldots, \alpha_n\}$; and
- *functional dependencies are observed:*

$$\rho_\alpha(x) = \rho_\alpha(y) \quad \text{if} \quad \rho_\beta(x) = \rho_\beta(y)$$

for all $x, y \in \rho_e$, whenever the functional dependency $\beta \rightarrow_e \alpha$ is in F (and using the same abbreviation as in the previous equation in case β is a set of attributes).

There are standard techniques for translating a conceptual schema to a relational database schema (see, e.g., [4]). It would be possible to formalise such relational schemata and their realisations in the spirit of Definitions 3 and 4, and then show that the realisations of a relational schema are realisations of the original conceptual schema. We do not do so here, however, prefering instead to concentrate on the relationships between conceptual schemata and ontologies; in particular, we obtain a broader view of the realisations of a schema by relating schemata to ontologies:

Definition 5. *Given a schema S, let $\mathcal{O}_S = (D, \mathsf{C}, A^S, Ax)$ be the ontology constructed as follows:*

- *the classes are (the disjoint union of) the entities and the relationships, i.e., $C = E + R$;*
- *the attributes are the attributes, roles and foreign keys of S, i.e.,*

$$A^S{}_{v,w} = \begin{cases} A_{v,w} & \text{if } v \in E \text{ and } w \text{ is a data type} \\ B_{v,w} & \text{if } v \in R \\ Fk_{v,w} & \text{if } v, w \in E \\ \emptyset & \text{otherwise;} \end{cases}$$

- *the axioms are the key and functional dependency axioms; i.e., for every $e \in E$ with primary key $\mathsf{pk}(e) = \alpha$, Ax contains an axiom of the form*

$$X = Y \text{ if } \alpha(X) = \alpha(Y),$$

where X and Y are variables ranging over the class e, and for every functional dependency $\beta \rightarrow_e \alpha$ in F, Ax contains an axiom of the form

$$\alpha(X) = \alpha(Y) \text{ if } \beta(X) = \beta(Y),$$

where X and Y range over the class e.

The relationship between schemata and ontologies is very straightforward; essentially, both specify classes of entities with attributes, together with some axioms constraining their behaviour. The major difference is that a schema makes a distinction between entities and relationships, and also specifies keys that uniquely identify entities. In other words, a schema is an ontology with a little extra structure consisting of keys and the division of classes into entities and relationships. The directness of this relationship is reflected with a correspondingly straightforward relationship between their semantics, stated in Proposition 2 below. However, the directness of the relationship is by no means trivial: if the recipe given in Definition 5 is applied to the schema of Example 4, the resulting ontology is different from the ontology of Example 2 on which the schema was based. The reason for this is that, as the diagram in Example 4 makes clear, new relationship classes have been introduced in moving from the ontology to the schema. A further difference is that the ontology $\mathcal{O}_S$ does not have the axioms of the ontology of Example 2. We discuss these important issues in the final section.

Proposition 2. *There is a one-to-one correspondence between realisations of S and models of $\mathcal{O}_S$.*

Note that this does not say that ontologies and schemata are the same thing; the translation $S \mapsto \mathcal{O}_S$ gives an ontology by 'forgetting' the extra structure of a schema. While it is possible to move in the other direction, i.e., to construct a schema from an ontology, any recipe for doing so involves artificial concoctions for the extra structure. For example, a key could be created for a class that consists of all the attributes of that class, or might be added as a new attribute that gives a unique identifier for members of the class. The very artificiality of such resorts suggests that moving from an ontology to a schema is part of a design process best left to the informed designer.

What the above proposition *does* say is that the translation $S \mapsto \mathcal{O}_S$ strongly preserves the semantics of the schema. In Section 2, we saw that morphisms between ontologies played an essential role in sharing and combining ontologies. We begin our investigation of interoperability of schemata with an appropriate definition of morphism:

Definition 6. *A* **schema morphism** *(or* **view***)* $\mu : S \to S'$ *is a tuple* $\mu = (fA, gA, fB, gB)$*, where*

- $fA : E \to E'$ *is a monotone map of partial orders;*
- gA *is a family of maps* $gA_{e,d} : A_{e,d} \to A'_{fA(e),d}$ *for* $e \in E$ *and data type* d*, taking attributes to attributes;*
- $fB : R \to R'$ *is a monotone map of partial orders;*
- gB *is a family* $gB_{r,w} : B_{r,w} \to B'_{fB(r),fB(w)}$ *for* $r \in R$ *and* $w \in E+D$ *(where* $fB(d) = d$ *for data types* d*), taking roles to roles.*

We also require that $(gA(k), fA(e_1), fA(e_2)) \in Fk'$ *whenever* $(k, e_1, e_2) \in Fk$ *(i.e., foreign keys are preserved), and that for every* $k \in \mathsf{keys}(e)$*, there is some* $k' \in \mathsf{keys}'(fA(e))$ *with* $gA(k) \subseteq k'$ *(i.e., every key in* S *forms part of a key in* S'*).*

Example 5. Suppose we have a schema S with a class c, which has five attributes α, β, γ, δ and ϵ, with primary key $\{\alpha, \beta\}$, and suppose that γ functionally depends on β, and ϵ on δ. A second normal form for this schema, call it S_2, will have classes d_1 and d_2, where d_1 has attributes α, β, δ and ϵ, with primary key $\{\alpha, \beta\}$, and where d_2 has attributes β and γ, with primary key $\{\beta\}$. Moreover there is a foreign key (which we denote $f\beta$) from d_1 to d_2. The view from the original schema to S_2 is characterised as follows:

- fA maps c to d_1;
- gA maps α to α, etc., but maps γ to $f\beta; \gamma$, where $f\beta; \gamma$ is a *compound attribute* as in Example 3.

Starting again with the schema S, we could eliminate the non-key dependency $\delta \rightarrow \beta$ by factoring c into classes e_1 (with attributes α, β, γ and δ) and e_2 (with attributes δ and ϵ). Call this schema S_3. Again, there is a view $S \rightarrow S_3$, the details of which we leave as an exercise for the reader.

As this example suggests, views express the sort of 'refinement' relationships between schemata that are captured by ontology morphisms. In other words, the view of the above example expresses the semantic correctness of reduction to second normal form. However, the notion of correctness here is much weaker than in the case of ontologies, as we explain in the concluding section.

We can now state a major result of our approach: schemata can be 'merged' across common sub-schemata:

Theorem 2. *The category of schemata and views is cocomplete.*

As with Theorem 1, the intuition behind this is that any collection of schemata, given explicit descriptions of their shared concepts, can be merged in a way that preserves their shared components. Roughly speaking, this merging corresponds to integrating schemata by taking their union while preserving commonalities.

Example 6. Consider the schema S and its related schemata S_2 and S_3 from Example 5; the views from S to these latter schemata express the 'lossless decomposition' of eliminating, respectively, partial-key and non-key functional dependencies. The schema S_3, however, is not in 3rd Normal Form, as it is not in 2nd Normal Form (S_2 on the other hand, is in 2nd Normal Form). The colimit given by Theorem 2 gives a (the obvious) schema that is in 3rd Normal Form, by merging the two refinements to remove both functional dependencies.

4   Conclusions

We have given formal definitions of ontology and schema, described how the two concepts are related, and shown that both enjoy 'cocompleteness' properties that support reuse and interoperability. We believe the definitions of schema and realisation are new, and will prove useful in providing a formal basis for the notions of correctness that must be a cornerstone to any body of work on interoperability. While the results of the present paper are just the beginnings of such a body of work, we suggest they represent promising beginnings.

Interoperability of schemata and sharing of knowledge in ontologies both arise naturally in our approach as cocompleteness properties, and their naturality resides in the algebraic nature of our approach. Algebra is, after all, the mathematics of (re)combination, and the results presented here bring algebraic techniques to bear on the important topics of knowledge sharing and interoperability (similar in spirit to recent work by Schorlemmer et al., which places more emphasis on logical morphisms [5,6]) and suggest avenues of further research that should be very rewarding. For example, an 'amalgamation' property for schemata along the lines of Proposition 1 would get to the heart of operational solutions to interoperating complex databases (Such a property should not be too hard to prove; a similar property is given in an abstract logical setting in [7]). It should be stressed however, that the body of work adumbrated here is still speculative, and there are important technical issues to be addressed.

The most pressing is the nature of the relationship between ontologies and schemata. Proposition 2 gives a very elegant relationship, but the preceding comments suggest that it is not the relationship required in practice. If we begin with an ontology O, and use this to construct a schema S, as in Example 4, then the ontology $\mathcal{O}_S$ differs from O in having both *more* structure (more classes arising from the relationships), and *less* structure (the axioms of O are lost). This describes exactly the situation of ontologies being related: O and $\mathcal{O}_S$ are related through their 'common denominator' — an ontology without the axioms of O and without the extra classes of $\mathcal{O}_S$. Our future studies of the semantical bases for interoperability will centre on how colimits of schemata and ontologies interact with such relations, and in particular on how these figure in the design of integration schemata.

References

1. Berners-Lee, T., Hendler, J., O. Lassila: The semantic web. Scientific American **279** (2001)
2. Bench-Capon, T., Malcolm, G., Shave, M.: Semantics for interoperability: relating ontologies and schemata. Technical Report ULCS-02-029, Dept. of Computer Science, Univ. Liverpool (2002)
3. Bench-Capon, T., Malcolm, G.: Formalising ontologies and their relations. In Bench-Capon, T., Soda, G., Tjoa, A.M., eds.: Proc. 10th International Conf. on Database and Expert Systems Applications (DEXA'99), Springer Lecture Notes in Computer Science volume 1677 (1999) 250–259
4. Elsmari, R., Navathe, S.B.: Fundamentals of Database Systems. 2nd edn. Addison-Wesley (1994)
5. Schorlemmer, M.: Duality in knowledge sharing. Technical Report EDI-INF-RR-0134, Division of Informatics, Univ. Edinburg (2002)
6. Kalfoglu, Y., Schorlemmer, M.: Information-flow-based ontology mapping. Technical Report EDI-INF-RR-0135, Division of Informatics, Univ. Edinburg (2002)
7. Alagić, S. Bernstein, P.A.: A model theory for generic schema management. In Grahne, G., Ghelli, eds.: DBLP 2001. Volume 2397 of Springer Lecture Notes in Computer Science (2002) 228–246

Multiple Views with Multiple Behaviours for Interoperable Object-Oriented Database Systems

M.B. Al-Mourad[1], W.A. Gray[2], and N.J. Fiddian[2]

[1] Aston University,
Computer Science Dept.,
B4 7ET UK
m.b.al-mourad@aston.ac.uk
[2] Cardiff University,
Computer Science Dept.,
CF24 3XF, UK
{w.a.gray,n.j.fiddian}@cs.cf.ac.uk

Abstract. There is increasing interest from large organisations who are requiring access to and manipulation of data distributed over the multiple sites of a computer network, and furthermore, they want to share and reuse database resources and services that are not available in their original systems. In the context of *Object-Oriented Database Systems* (OODBSs), services are the set of methods that describe the behaviour of a particular class in a database system. Sharing these services saves effort, cost and time where the investment made in developing them can be exploited again by the original owner of these services and also by new users in the interoperation context. Different users have different needs for data integration, and the same user might want to integrate the same data with different services (i.e. behaviours). Therefore, multiple integration views with multiple behaviours are required to capture this diversity. This paper describes the theoretical framework we are using in the construction of the (MVMBS) *Multiple Views supported by Multiple Behaviours System.* MVMBS offers the potential for users to work in terms of integrated and customised global views supported by multiple behaviours. Our goals for MVMBS include flexibility and customisability, to this end we have developed a semantically-rich integration operator language. The user is able to generate global view(s) from scratch by means of these operators.

1 Introduction

The creation of an environment that permits the controlled sharing and exchange of information among multiple heterogeneous databases has been identified as a key issue in the future of database integration research [19,10]. Systems that support database interoperability are called *Multidatabase Systems* (MDBS) [12,

V. Mařík et al. (Eds.): DEXA 2003, LNCS 2736, pp. 713–723, 2003.

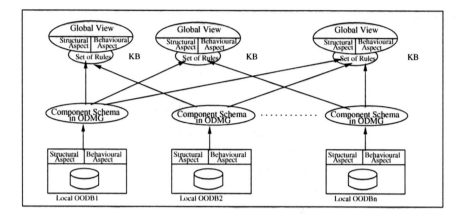

Fig. 1. Multiple Views supporting Multiple Behaviours

11,17]. Their architectures range from tightly coupled to loosely coupled [18], and they employ static [5,14,4] or dynamic [13,22,9] views in accessing data from multiple databases. Both approaches have a number of disadvantages. For instance, the global schema may become huge and very difficult to maintain, also it may not meet all user requirements. Likewise, multidatabase language users must have sufficient skills to reconcile the heterogeneity encountered in such an environment. These previous disadvantages led to the multiple global schema approach, which is more flexible to support multidatabase interoperability [1, 23,3,7]. The emphasis of all these approaches has traditionally been placed on the structural aspects of data integration. Even though the use of an *Object-Oriented* (OO) data model as the canonical data model for database integration has been widely favoured [8], attention to behavioural aspects of such models has been ignored. Object-oriented multidatabase systems generally do not present object methods other than those implementing generic query and transaction facilities to a global user, in spite of the fact that component databases may have implemented application-specific methods with their local objects. Reuse or sharing of these methods by other users in a MDBS environment saves effort, cost and time where the investment made in developing them can be exploited again by the original owner of these methods and also by new users in the interoperation context.

For example, when two bank databases are integrated due to merger, management might require that the loan-granting services/procedures in one bank will be adhered to by both databases. We argue the importance of the behavioural part (behavioural semantics), i.e. that both structural and behavioural semantics are important [6] in the object-oriented schema integration context. We suggest that interoperability between a set of heterogeneous object-oriented databases is best achieved by building several tailored global views supporting multiple behaviours to fully meet user requirements and this allows local conflicts to be resolved in various ways (Fig. 1). These views are defined in terms of *virtual classes* and *materialisation rules* and they are created by applying a set of semantically-rich integration operators to local database schemas represented in the ODMG standard. The operators comprise a language we call the *Multiple Views supporting Multiple Behaviours Language* (MVMBL).

Section 2 of this paper presents the basic characteristics of the *Object Model* (OM) used in our research. In section 3 we explain the concept of reusing and sharing behaviours at the global level and we give a formal definition for this concept as this is essential to explain the definition of MVMBL operators. In section 4 we explain the characteristics of properties in global view(s). In section 5 we describe our schema integration language (MVMBL). Finally, section 6 contains the conclusion of this paper.

2   The Object Model

Real-world entities are modelled as a set of objects (O). An object $o_i \in O$ consists of *structure properties* (attributes of the object) and *behaviour properties* (the methods that can be executed on or by the object). We will refer to the attributes and behaviours of an object as *object properties* [2] and together they identify the object's *Type*. Each object has an *object identifier* (OID). Objects that have the same properties (Type) are grouped into sets called classes C. A class $c \in C$ has a unique class name, Properties(c), Type(c), and a set of instances Ext(c). We will refer to the properties of a class by (*classname.propertyname*), which can be applied as a predicate. Formally, Properties(c)={A, M}, where:

- A is the set of all attributes of class c: $A = \{a_1 : D_1, ..., a_n : D_n\}$; where D_i $(i = 1, n)$ is the type of attribute a_i.
- M is the set of all methods of class c: $M = \{m_1, m_2, ..., m_j\}$; where m_i $(i = 1, j)$ is the signature of method i and has the form: Name $(Arg_1 : T_1, ..., Arg_k : T_k) \rightarrow$ $(R_1 : S_1, ..., R_p : S_p)$ where Name is the method name; Arg_i is an input parameter and T_i is the type of $Arg_i((i = 1, k)$, k$\geq$ 0); and R_j is a return value and S_j its type $((j = 1, p)$, p$\geq$ 0).

The domain of each method is a cross-product of the domains of its result values: dom(m) $\subseteq \{\times_{i=1,p} dom(R_p)\}$ and the domain of c is: dom(c) $\subseteq \{\times_{i=1,n} dom(a_i)\}$ $\times \{(\times_{i=1,j} dom(m_i)\}$. For two classes c_1 and $c_2 \in$ C: we call c_1 a *subset* of c_2, denoted as $(c_1 \subseteq c_2)$, if and only if: $((\forall$ o $\in O$ and o $\in c_1) \Rightarrow$ o $\in c_2)$. We call c_1 a *subtype* of c_2, denoted as $(c_1 \preceq c_2)$, if and only if: Properties$(c_1) \supseteq$ Properties(c_2) and $(\forall$ p $\in$ Properties$(c_2)) \Rightarrow dom_{c_2}(p) \subseteq dom_{c_1}(p))$. We will call c_1 a *subclass* of c_2, denoted by $(c_1$ is a $c_2)$, if and only if $(c_1 \subseteq c_2)$ and $(c_1 \preceq c_2)$.

Methods of a class can do several tasks, they can be classified as: *Constructor*, *Update*, *Access* and *Computation Methods*. We are interested in computation methods, which are designed to provide services that are able to perform an efficient computation on an object of a class.

3   Sharing Behaviour - Scope and Requirements

Let us consider the classes EMPLOYEE and WORKER in DB1 and DB2, respectively (Fig. 2). Assume that both classes are semantically related and ideal for

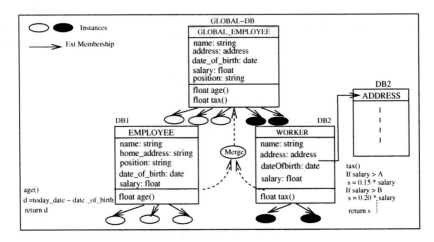

Fig. 2. Method property requirements

integration by merging into a global class GLOBAL-EMPLOYEE where its extension is the union of both EMPLOYEE and WORKER extensions [14]. Typically, reusing the tax() method defined in local class WORKER at the global level offers an additional feature to the global users. So they can share this method by applying it to instances derived from the EMPLOYEE class in DB1 as well as instances derived from class WORKER in DB2 . From the previous example we can differentiate between two different meanings, *reusing* and *sharing* behaviour at the global level. Reusing behaviour is the ability to use the behaviour defined in a component database class on instances of this class but at global schema level. In contrast, sharing behaviour is the ability to use the same behaviour but on instances belonging to other component database classes.

3.1   Semantic Requirements for Reusing and Sharing Behaviour in MDBS

We found that sharing behaviour at the global level implies three basic semantic requirements: *property, property assertion validity* and *property value validity* requirements. For the sake of space limitations we will briefly describe the property requirement alone as it is fundamental to this paper, and the reader is invited to review [16] for fuller details. The global class that wishes to reuse or share a method should ensure the properties required by the method in order to perform its functionality. For example, the method (tax) in WORKER requires the data represented in an attribute (salary) in order to perform its functionality, which is calculating employee income tax based on salary. The global class GLOBAL_EMPLOYEE (which is a merger of both classes in the global schema) must have the attribute salary in order to share the method (tax) defined in the WORKER class.

Formally: for semantically related classes c_1 and c_2 in DB1 and DB2 respectively, with: Properties(c_1)={$A1, M1$} and Properties(c_2)={$A2, M2$} Let us have m $\in M_1$ a method available in the class c_1 and the global user would like to reuse this method on the global class G_c that is an integration of the classes c_1 and c_2 by applying one of the integration operators (see section 5). The extension of the class G_c could be either $\text{Ext}(c_1) \cup \text{Ext}(c_2)$; $\text{Ext}(c_1) \cap \text{Ext}(c_2)$; $\text{Ext}(c_1)$ or $\text{Ext}(c_2)$.

We define the function MethodProperties(m,c) which returns a set of properties (Properties(c*)) from class c that is required by the method m in order to perform its functionality: MethodProperties(m,c) = Properties(c*) = {A*,M*} $\subseteq$ Properties(c). Assuming that c is an integration of c_1 and c_2, we can formally recognise three cases:

- If MethodProperties(m,c) $\subseteq$ {Properties(c_1) $\cap$ Properties(c_2)} and dom(m) $\subseteq$ (dom(c_1) $\cup$ dom(c_2)) this means the method m is applicable on instances retrieved from both class c_1 and class c_2. This corresponds to both Reusing and Sharing at the same time.
- If ((MethodProperties(m,c) $\subseteq$ Properties(c_1) and dom(m) $\subseteq$ dom(c_1)) and (MethodProperties(m,c) $\not\subseteq$ Properties(c_2) or dom(m) $\not\subseteq$ dom(c_2))). The method m is applicable only on instances retrieved from class c_1 ($\text{Ext}(c_1)$), and corresponds to Reusing only.
- If ((MethodProperties(m,c) $\subseteq$ Properties(c_2) and dom(m) $\subseteq$ dom(c_2)) and (MethodProperties(m,c) $\not\subseteq$ Properties(c_1) or dom(m) $\not\subseteq$ dom(c_1))). The method m is applicable only to instances retrieved from class c_2 ($\text{Ext}(c_2)$), and corresponds to Reusing only.

4 Characteristics of Properties in Global View(s)

In section 2, we defined the predicate *classname.propertyname*, this can be used to check whether a property is defined for a class (c) or not. We will differentiate between two cases: first, when the property (p) represents an attribute (a), this predicate will check if this attribute is defined for the class or not; second, when the property (p) represents a method (m), this predicate not only checks the availability of this method in the class, it also checks the method property requirement defined earlier, in other words: c.m = true. This means that MethodProperties(m,c) $\subseteq$ Properties(c).

We will refer to an object property in a particular class (c) as follows:

$$\text{PropertyName(ObjectReference in ClassName)}$$

A property in general takes its values from its domain class (primitive or non-primitive). There are two special values for a property in a global class, ('**undefined**') and ('**unknown**') and they play an important role at the global level. The value 'undefined' means that the property is not defined for a given object in a particular class, which implies that this property is not defined in the local class these objects are derived from, while the value 'unknown' means that the property is defined but no value has been assigned to it[1]. In general, if a

---

[1] When the property (p) represents a method (m), the value m(o in c) = 'unknown' means that c.MethodProperties(m,c) is false (i.e. MethodProperties(m,c) $\not\subseteq$ Properties(c)).

property (p) is not defined for a class (c) then the value of the property (p) will be 'undefined' for all instances of the class (c). Formally this can be stated as follows:

$$(c.p? = false) \Rightarrow (\forall o \in c)\ (p(o\ in\ c) = \text{'undefined'})$$

On the other hand, if a property (p) is defined for a class (c) then all instances of the class (c) will take some value (not equal to 'undefined') for the property (p). This value will be either 'unknown' or a value from the property domain class (D). This can be stated formally as follows:

$$(c.p? = true) \wedge (dom_c(p) = D) \Rightarrow (\forall o \in c)$$

$$(\text{either}\ p(o\ in\ c) = \text{'unknown'}\ \text{or}\ p(o\ in\ c) \in D\ \text{or}\ p(o\ in\ c) \subseteq D)$$

5 MVMBL Operators

MVMBL is an OO schema integration language that is capable of reconciling conflicting local classes and constructing homogeneous and customised global classes. It is based on a set of fundamental operators that integrate local classes according to their semantic relationships (e.g. equivalence, inclusion, overlap, etc.) and on integrator preferences. Therefore, establishing real-world semantic relationships between these classes is an essential task of the functionality of the operators [15]. The operands of any operator are typically the local classes which are located in several autonomous databases and the result will be a set of virtual classes and their materialisation rules. These virtual classes provide a consistent and integrated global view of the distributed and heterogeneous local information augmented with preferred behaviours.

We will show the specification of the global classes and how each operator determines their derived instances (set aspect of the class) and their properties (type aspect of the class). The instances of the global class derived by one of the operators are based on the object identities of the objects involved. A definition that covers treatment of global property values is given next, based on the assumption that conflicts between properties are detected and resolved. We define a **property Union** function which describes how a particular global property is to be constructed by the global class materialisation rules. In particular the values for a global property (P) are combined into one global property by collecting and/or calculating property values that an object acquires for a local property (p) while it is member of c_1 and/or c_2.

For a global class G_c a property (P) is determined from the local classes c_1 and c_2 by using the property Union function as follows:

$$P(o\ in\ G_c) = \underline{Union}(p(o\ in\ c_1), p(o\ in\ c_2))$$

We can identify three main cases:

1. $P(o\ in\ G_c) = \underline{Union}(p(o\ in\ c_1), p(o\ in\ c_2)) = function(p(o\ in\ c_1), p(o\ in\ c_2))$ if $(o \in c_1 \wedge c_1.p? \wedge p(o\ in\ c_1) \neq \text{'unknown'}) \wedge (o \in c_2 \wedge c_2.p? \wedge p(o\ in\ c_2) \neq \text{'unknown'})$

In this case, the local property (p) is defined in both local classes c_1, c_2 and the object (o) is a member of both classes and acquires known values for (p) as an object of both classes. The function that takes as its parameters the values of property (p) in both local classes could be either a decision function, which assigns one of these properties to the (P) in the global class[2], or a function like sum, average, max, min,..,etc. [5] which assigns its result to the property (P) in the global class[3]. When both local properties are methods and a function like sum is defined to compute the sum of the result of the two methods, this implies that a global method is implicitly implemented by given local methods in the component databases [21].

2. $P(o$ in $G_c) = \underline{Union}(p(o$ in $c_1),p(o$ in $c_2)) = p(o$ in $c_1)$
   if $(o \in c_1 \wedge c_1.p? \wedge p(o$ in $c_1) \neq$ 'unknown' $\wedge (o \notin c_2 \vee Not(c_2.p?) \vee (c_2.p?$ $\wedge p(o$ in $c_2) =$ 'unknown')))
   In this case, (p) is defined for c_1, the object (o) is a member of c_1, and it takes a known value for (p) as a member of c_1 (e.g. the position attribute in Fig. 2). However, either (p) is not defined for c_2; the object (o) is not a member of c_2; or (o) does not acquire a known value for (p) as a member of c_2. Consequently, the value $p(o$ in $c_1)$ is assigned to the global class property (P).

3. $P(o$ in $G_c) = \underline{Union}(p(o$ in $c_1),p(o$ in $c_2)) = p(o$ in $c_2)$
   if $(o \in c_2 \wedge c_2.p? \wedge p(o$ in $c_2) \neq$ 'unknown' $\wedge (o \notin c_1 \vee Not(c_1.p?) \vee (c_1.p?$ $\wedge p(o$ in $c_1) =$ 'unknown'))) This is similar to the previous case, with the role of classes c_1 and c_2 interchanged.

Merge: This operator is used to combine two equivalent or synonymous local classes by generating a global class G_c, whose properties are the combination of local class properties and determined by using the <u>Union</u> function. In addition, it has a set of methods which are able to be reused on the global class. The extension of this class is the union of both extents (e.g. GLOBAL_EMPLOYEE in Fig. 2). Formally, if c_1 and c_2 are local classes in DB1 and DB2 respectively, $G_c = Merge(c_1,c_2)$ will add a global class G_c to the current view, where:

- $Ext(G_c) = \{o \mid o \in Ext(c_1) \cup Ext(c_2)\}$
- $Properties(G_c) = Properties(c_1) \cup Properties(c_2)$, where:
  $((\forall o \in G_c) (\forall P \in Properties(G_c)) \Rightarrow P(o$ in $G_c) = \underline{Union}(p(o$ in $c_1),p(o$ in $c_2)))$
- $SharableMeth(G_c) = Method(M_1*,c_1) \cup Method(M_2*,c_2)$, where:
  $M_1* \subseteq M_1$ (M_1 is the set of methods in c_1 and the condition: $G_c.MethodProperties(m,c_1)$ is valid for every $m \in M_1*$, in other words

---

[2] This implies that $p(o$ in $c_1) = p(o$ in $c_2)$, for example the name property in EMPLOYEE and WORKER (Fig. 2) can be retrieved from one of the classes; and in the case where (p) represents a method, this means that both methods are semantically equivalent and hence we will include one of them in the global schema.

[3] This implies that the value of the global property is determined by both local values, for example if a person works in two places and has two salaries (Fig. 2). The global salary could be the sum of both salary properties whether the property be an attribute and/or a method in the local databases.

MethodProperties(m,c_1) $\subseteq$ Properties(G_c));
$M_2{}^* \subseteq M_2$ (M_2 is the set of methods in c_2 and the condition:
G_c.MethodProperties(m,c_2) is valid for every m $\in$ $M_2{}^*$, in other words
MethodProperties(m,c_2) $\subseteq$ Properties(G_c)).

Union: This operator is used to integrate two equivalent local classes by generating a common superclass. It creates a global class G_c, whose properties are the set of properties that belong to the local classes and determined by using the Union function, and it has a set of methods which are able to be reused and shared by the global class. The extension of this class is the combination of the extents of the two local classes.

Formally, if c_1 and c_2 are local classes in DB1 and DB2 respectively, $G_c =$ Union(c_1,c_2) will add a global class G_c to the current view, where:

- Ext(G_c) = {o | o $\in$ Ext(c_1) $\cup$ Ext(c_2)}
- Properties(G_c) = Properties(c_1) $\cap$ Properties(c_2), where:
  ((∀ o $\in$ G_c) (∀ P $\in$ properties(G_c)) $\Rightarrow$ P(o in G_c) = Union(p(o in c_1),p(o in c_2)))
- SharableMeth(G_c) = Method($M_1{}^*$,c_1) $\cup$ Method($M_2{}^*$,c_2), where:
  $M_1{}^* \subseteq M_1$ (M_1 is the set of methods in c_1 and the condition:
  G_c.MethodProperties(m,c_1) is valid for every m $\in$ $M_1{}^*$, in other words
  MethodProperties(m,c_1) $\subseteq$ Properties(G_c));
  $M_2{}^* \subseteq M_2$ (M_2 is the set of methods in c_2 and the condition:
  G_c.MethodProperties(m,c_2) is valid for every m $\in$ $M_2{}^*$, in other words
  MethodProperties(m,c_2) $\subseteq$ Properties(G_c)).

Intersect: This operator is used to generate a common subclass for two overlapping local classes. It creates a global class G_c, whose properties are the set of properties that belong to the combination of local classes and are determined by the Union function. The extension of this class is the intersection of the extents of the two classes. With this operator, it is not required to specify the sharable methods, as the Union function will already import all the methods defined for the intersection extent of both classes. Formally, if c_1 and c_2 are local classes in DB1 and DB2 respectively, $G_c=$ Intersect(c_1,c_2) will add a global class G_c to the current view, where:

- Ext(G_c) = {o | O $\in$ Ext(c_1)$\cap$ Ext(c_2)}
- Properties(G_c) = Properties(c_1) $\cup$ Properties(c_2), where:
  ((∀ o $\in$ G_c) (∀ P $\in$ Properties(G_c)) $\Rightarrow$ P(o in G_c) = Union(p(o in c_1),p(o in c_2)))

Include: This operator is used to import local classes into a global view. It is useful if the integrator is interested in forming a set of local classes without actually integrating them:

- Ext(G_c) = {o | O $\in$ Ext(c)}
- Properties(G_c) = Properties(c), where:
  ((∀ o $\in$ G_c) (∀ P $\in$ Properties(G_c)) $\Rightarrow$ P(o in G_c) = p(o in c))

- SharableMeth(G_c) = Method(M,c), where:
  M is the set of all methods in the local class c.

Note that for all operators, the integrator has the flexibility to choose a subset of the properties and/or methods available as a result of operator application.

5.1 Global Class Materialisation Rules

The instances of the generated virtual classes are derived from their corresponding local ones. This is done by possibly aggregating several local instances where the same instance may have heterogeneous representations in different databases. Specifying the rules that derive the global class instances and reconciling heterogeneous representations is the task of the set of materialisation rules that augments each global view. MVMBS generates such rule sets automatically as a result of applying one of the MVMBL operators. When a query is posed against a global class, the query processor uses its corresponding materialisation rules to decompose the global query into local sub-queries. The following is the general syntax of an MVMBS rule, which is an upgraded version of [20]:

Rule<name> on retrieve to <virtual class properties>,
apply <virtual class methods>
do instead: retrieve <local corresponding properties>,
apply <local corresponding methods>
where <condition>

where: <condition> is the condition under which the rule is executed.

6   Conclusion

This paper is concerned with the creation of multiple integration views supporting multiple behaviours over a set of heterogeneous Object-Oriented databases available across a computer network. We described the theoretical framework we used to construct the (MVMBS) *Multiple Views supported by Multiple Behaviours System*. MVMBS offers the potential for users to work in terms of integrated and customised views augmented with their preferred behaviours. We have shown the requirements of reusing and sharing behaviours in a global view. The characteristics of properties at the global level have been described and the definitions of a number of MVMBL operators, namely: merge, union, intersect and include, have been given. These operators enable a user to construct a global schema by generalising, specialising, merging and importing local database classes. Finally, we explained the general syntax of materialisation rules which map queries against global concepts into queries against local ones.

References

1. E. Bertino. Integration of heterogeneous data repositories by using object-oriented views. *Proc. 1st International Workshop on Interoperability in Multidatabase Systems, Kyoto, Japan*, pages 22–29, 1991.

2. S. Castano, V. De Antonellis, and M. G. Gugini. Conceptual schema analysis: Techniques and applications. *ACM Transactions on Database Systems*, 23, September 1998.
3. D. Clements and et al. Myriad: Design and implementation of a federated database prototype. Technical report, University of Minnesota, U.S.A., 1993.
4. C. Collet, M. N. Huhns, and W. Shen. Resource integration using a large knowledge base in carnot. *IEEE Computer*, pages 55–62, December 1991.
5. U. Dayal and H. Hwang. View definition and generalization for database integration in a multidatabase system. *IEEE Transactions on Software Engineering*, SE-10(6):628–645, November 1984.
6. Pam Drew, Roger King, Dennis McLeod, Marek Rusinkiewicz, and Avi Silberschatz. Report of the workshop on semantic heterogeneity and interoperation in multidatabase systems. *ACM SIGMOD RECORD*, 22(3), September 1993.
7. G. Fahl. *Object Views of Relational Data in Multidatabase Systems*. PhD thesis, Linkoping University, Sweden, 1994.
8. Manuel Garcia-Solaco, Felix Saltor, and Malu Castellanos. Semantic heterogeneity in multidatabase systems. In O. A. Bukhres and A. K. Elmagarmid, editors, *Object-Oriented Multidatabase Systems, A Solution for Advanced Applications*. Prentice-Hall, 1996.
9. F. Gingras and L. V. S. Lakshmanan. nd-sel: A multi-dimensional language for interoperability and olap. *Proc. 24th International Conference on Very Large Data Bases*, pages 134–145, 1998.
10. Joachim Hammer and Dennis McLeod. An approach to resolving semantic heterogeneity in a federation of autonomous, heterogeneous database systems. *International Journal of Intelligent & Cooperative Information Systems, World Scientific*, 2(1):51–83, 1993.
11. W. Kim and J. Seo. Classifying schematic and data heterogeneity in multidatabase systems. *IEEE Computer*, 24(12):12–18, December 1991.
12. W. Litwin. From database systems to multidatabase systems: Why and how. In *Proceedings of BNCOD6, Cardiff, Wales*, 1988.
13. W. Litwin. O*sql: A language for object oriented multidatabase interoperability. In D. K. Hsiao, E. J. Neuhold, and R. Sacks-Davis, editors, *Interoperable Database Systems (DS-5) (A-25)*. North Holland, 1993.
14. A. Motro. Superviews: Virtual integration of multiple databases. *IEEE Transactions on Software Engineering*, SE-13(7):785–798, 1987.
15. M. B. Al Mourad, W. A. Gray, and N. J. Fiddian. Detecting object semantic similarity by using structural and behavioural semantics. In *Proc. 5th World Multiconference on Systemics, Cybernetics and Informatics*, Orlando, USA, July 2001.
16. M. B. Al Mourad, W. A. Gray, and N. J. Fiddian. Semantic requirements for sharing behaviours in federated object-oriented database systems. Ukraine, June 2001.
17. E. Pitoural, O. A. Bukhres, and A. K. Elmagarmid. Object-oriented multidatabase systems: An overview. In O. A. Bukhres and A. K. Elmagarmid, editors, *Object-Oriented Multidatabase Systems: A Solution for Advanced Applications*, pages 347–378. Prentice Hall, 1996.
18. A. P. Sheth and J. A. Larson. Federated database systems for managing distributed, heterogeneous and autonomous databases. *ACM Computing Surveys*, September 1990.
19. Avi Silberschatz, Michael Stonebraker, and Jeffrey D. Ullman. Database systems: Achievements and opportunities. *ACM SIGMOD RECORD*, 19(4):23–31, December 1990.

20. M. Stonebraker, L. A. Rowe, and M. Hirohama. The implementation of POST-GRES. *IEEE Transactions on Knowledge and Data Engineering*, 2(1):125–142, 1990.

21. Mark W. W. Vermeer and Peter M. G. Apers. Behaviour specification in database integration. *Proc. Conference on Advanced Information System Engineering (CAISE 97), Barcelona, Spain*, June 1997.

22. A. Watters. Incremental data integration of federated databases. *Proc. Research Issues in Data Engineering: Interoperability in Multidatabase Systems (RIDE-IMS93), Vienna, Austria*, pages 78–85, 1993.

23. K. Zhao, R King, and A. Bouguettaya. Incremental specification of views across databases. *Proc. 1st International Workshop on Interoperability in Multidatabase Systems, Kyoto, Japan*, pages 187–190, 1991.

Integrating Association Rule Mining Algorithms with the F2 OODBMS

Lina Al-Jadir[*]

Department of Mathematics and Computer Science
American University of Beirut, P.O. Box 11-0236, Beirut, Lebanon
lina.al-jadir@aub.edu.lb

Abstract. In this paper, we integrate two association rule mining algorithms, Apriori and TRAND, with the F2 object-oriented database system (DBMS). The advantages of our integration are the following. Both algorithms do not need to maintain complicated data structures and use only database classes. Both algorithms do not need to manage the buffer since it is handled by the DBMS. Both algorithms store frequent itemsets in the database which can be retrieved later using the DBMS data manipulation language. In addition to that, the TRAND algorithm takes advantage of the transposed storage supported in F2. To compute the support of candidate itemsets, it applies logical AND on boolean attributes, implemented in F2 as vectors, and avoids scanning the database. This reduces significantly the number of block accesses and consequently the execution time.

1 Introduction

Mining association rules, a successful data mining task, was introduced in [1] ten years ago. The initial research on association rule mining was concentrated on developing efficient algorithms. Most of these algorithms (e.g. Apriori [1], DHP [10], Partition [14]) do not take into account *where* data is stored (in a file, in a database) and *how* data is stored (data format). They are neutral to the representation of data. Later, other algorithms designed for vertical data layout (i.e. an item is associated with a list of transactions instead of a transaction being associated with a list of items) were proposed (e.g. Intersect [8], Eclat/Clique [17], CW-Apriori [6], Boolean [16], VIPER [15], MAFIA [4]). They are not integrated with a DBMS (except Intersect with Monet). New algorithms for mining a reduced set of association rules based on frequent closed itemsets were proposed (e.g. A-Close [11], CHARM [18], CLOSET[12]). The issue of integrating mining with databases has not been widely addressed. Extensions of SQL were proposed to support mining operators (e.g mine rule operator [9]). In [13] the authors studied several architectural alternatives for integrating Apriori with relational DBMS: loose-coupling through SQL cursor interface, encapsulation in a stored procedure, caching data to a file system on-the-fly and mining, tight-coupling using user-defined functions, and SQL implementations.

---

[*] This work was partly supported by a grant from the AUB University Research Board.

V. Mařík et al. (Eds.): DEXA 2003, LNCS 2736, pp. 724–736, 2003.
Springer-Verlag Berlin Heidelberg 2003

In this paper, we integrate two association rule mining algorithms with the F2 object database system [2] [3] as pre-defined methods (like the stored procedure approach in [13]). The first is the famous Apriori [1], and the second is TRAND a new algorithm that we will present. The advantages of our integration are the following. First, for both algorithms, only classes in the database are used, no data structures (such as hash-trees [1], FP-trees [7]) and no extra storage are required. The buffer is managed by the DBMS and not by the mining algorithms. Consequently, coding these algorithms becomes much easier. Second, the generated frequent itemsets (and association rules) are stored as objects in the database classes with their support (and confidence). Consequently, one can query them later using the F2 data manipulation language (F2-DML). One can also use them later after the database is updated to mine association rules using an incremental updating technique (such as FUP [5]). Third, the TRAND (TRansposed AND) algorithm takes advantage of the transposed storage in F2 [3] where attributes are stored as vectors. Support counting is simple and fast, done by ANDing bit vectors (like in CW-Apriori [6], Boolean [16], MAFIA [4]). Consequently, the database is not scanned for support counting. Through experiments and cost analysis we show that TRAND requires less block accesses than Apriori and consequently outperforms it.

In this paper, we focus on the consuming step in mining association rules: find all frequent itemsets wrt. a minimum support. The paper is organized as follows. In section 2, we describe the transposed storage in F2. In section 3, we review the Apriori algorithm but integrated within F2. In section 4, we present the TRAND algorithm integrated within F2. In section 5, we run experiments and compare the performance of TRAND with that of Apriori in terms of block transfers, buffer replacements, and block accesses. Finally, we conclude this paper in section 6.

2   Background: Transposed Storage

The idea of transposed storage is to vertically partition the objects of a class according to each attribute of the class. The values on an attribute of all objects are grouped together in a *vector*. In the classical horizontal storage, an object o of a class C having n attributes att_1, att_2,..., att_n is stored in a record containing its n attribute values. In the transposed

Fig. 1. Storage format of a Person object

storage, it is spread over n vectors: each vector v_i contains its value on the attribute att_i. There is a $(n+1)$th vector for the state attribute, used to determine whether an object is present in the class or deleted from it. The oid of o is a pair $<I_C, i>$ where I_C is the class identifier and i the instance identifier within C. All the attribute values of o are stored in the vectors at the same logical offset i. Figure 1 shows the storage of two *Person* objects (class *Person* has three attributes). Since the domain class of the *spouse* attribute is *Person*, the values on this attribute are oids. The employee named "Paul" is married to the student and musician "Pauline". A disk block contains the values of only one vector. If the block size is smaller than the vector size, the vector is stored in several blocks not necessarily contiguous. Moreover, blocks corresponding to different attributes of the same class need not to be contiguous. A map in the database files indicates the blocks for each attribute.

The transposed storage is advantageous for access operations (queries, navigations) that need to access a small part of objects value. For any operation, only the blocks of involved attributes are loaded into main memory instead of blocks of whole objects as with the classical storage. This reduces the number of I/O operations and the I/O time. Our results of the OO7 benchmark on F2 confirm it [3]. The transposed storage is also interesting when retrieving the values on the same attribute of many objects (e.g. aggregate functions such as average). Moreover, the transposed storage has two major advantages for schema evolution operations. It reduces I/O operations and requires no database reorganization as shown in [3]. The transposed storage can be disadvantageous when retrieving many (n) attribute values of an object, since it requires to load n blocks instead of one. It is the same when creating/deleting an object with n attribute values. This explains why the transposed storage is not widely used. Nevertheless we think that loading n blocks could be done in parallel and this issue deserves to be investigated. In the next sections, we show that the transposed storage can be advantageous for association rule mining.

3   Integrated Apriori

In this section, we first describe the database schema used by Apriori. Then, we present the Apriori algorithm integrated within F2 (we assume that the reader is familiar with Apriori [1]).

3.1   F2 Database Schema

The initial database schema for Apriori has two classes: *Item* and *Transaction*. Class *Transaction* has two attributes: *transaction_id* and *items* (multi-valued attribute). Thus a transaction object has an id and is associated with a list of item objects (see example in fig. 2).

Example DB
minsup = 50%

TID	Items
100	$i_1\ i_3\ i_4$
200	$i_2\ i_3\ i_5$
300	$i_1\ i_2\ i_3\ i_5$
400	$i_2\ i_5$

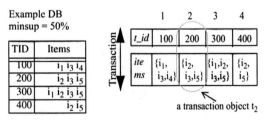

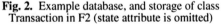

a transaction object t_2

Fig. 2. Example database, and storage of class Transaction in F2 (state attribute is omitted)

At each pass k of the Apriori algorithm, the classes C_k and F_k are created in the database (see fig. 3) to store the candidate k-itemset objects and the frequent k-itemset objects respectively. Each candidate and frequent k-itemset object is associated with k item objects and has a support. A candidate k-itemset object is also associated with the two frequent $(k-1)$-itemset objects that generated it.

3.2   Apriori Algorithm

Figure 4 shows the integrated Apriori algorithm. For finding frequent itemsets it makes multiple passes. A pass k of the algorithm consists of two phases. First, the frequent itemsets in class F_{k-1} (found in pass k-1) are used to generate the candidate itemsets in class C_k, using the *apriori-gen* method. Next, the

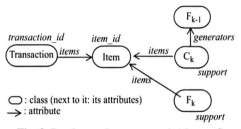

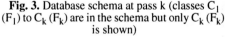

Fig. 3. Database schema at pass k (classes C_1 (F_1) to C_k (F_k) are in the schema but only C_k (F_k) is shown)

Transaction class is scanned to count the support of candidates in class C_k, using the *getF* method. Candidates which have minimum support are stored in class F_k. The algorithm terminates when F_k becomes empty.

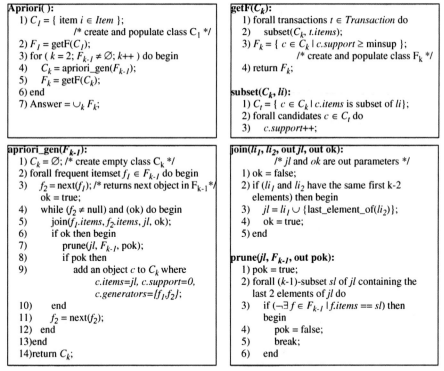

```
Apriori( ):
1) C_1 = { item i ∈ Item };
                        /* create and populate class C_1 */
2) F_1 = getF(C_1);
3) for ( k = 2; F_{k-1} ≠ ∅; k++ ) do begin
4)     C_k = apriori_gen(F_{k-1});
5)     F_k = getF(C_k);
6) end
7) Answer = ∪_k F_k;
```

```
getF(C_k):
1) forall transactions t ∈ Transaction do
2)     subset(C_k, t.items);
3) F_k = { c ∈ C_k | c.support ≥ minsup };
                        /* create and populate class F_k */
4) return F_k;

subset(C_k, li):
1) C_t = { c ∈ C_k | c.items is subset of li};
2) forall candidates c ∈ C_t do
3)     c.support++;
```

```
apriori_gen(F_{k-1}):
1) C_k = ∅; /* create empty class C_k */
2) forall frequent itemset f_1 ∈ F_{k-1} do begin
3)     f_2 = next(f_1); /* returns next object in F_{k-1}*/
       ok = true;
4)     while (f_2 ≠ null) and (ok) do begin
5)         join(f_1.items, f_2.items, jl, ok);
6)         if ok then begin
7)             prune(jl, F_{k-1}, pok);
8)             if pok then
9)                 add an object c to C_k where
                       c.items=jl, c.support=0,
                       c.generators={f_1,f_2};
10)        end
11)        f_2 = next(f_2);
12)    end
13)end
14)return C_k;
```

```
join(li_1, li_2, out jl, out ok):
                        /* jl and ok are out parameters */
1) ok = false;
2) if (li_1 and li_2 have the same first k-2
      elements) then begin
3)     jl = li_1 ∪ {last_element_of(li_2)};
4)     ok = true;
5) end

prune(jl, F_{k-1}, out pok):
1) pok = true;
2) forall (k-1)-subset sl of jl containing the
      last 2 elements of jl do
3)     if (¬∃ f ∈ F_{k-1} | f.items == sl) then
          begin
4)         pok = false;
5)         break;
6)     end
```

Fig. 4. Integrated Apriori

Our implementation of the integrated Apriori algorithm differs from the implementation in [1]. First, frequent itemsets and candidate itemsets are stored in the database, and the buffer is handled by the F2 DBMS. In [1] they are kept in main memory and if they do not fit in it then the Apriori algorithm has to handle the buffer. Second, frequent itemsets and candidate itemsets are stored as objects of a class, while in [1] they are stored in a hash table and a hash-tree respectively. To test membership of a k-itemset in class C_k (*subset* method, line 1) or in class F_k (*prune* method, line 3) a binary search is applied on the class objects indexed by their oids. Third, the join and prune steps are grouped, i.e. a candidate obtained by the join step is added to C_k only if it can not be pruned (as in [13]), while in [1] all candidates obtained by the join step are added to C_k, then those which can be pruned are deleted from C_k. Fourth, when pruning a candidate k-itemset c, only the $(k-1)$-subsets that contain the last two items of c are checked; the other $(k-1)$-subsets are the generators of c and need not to be checked (as in [13]).

The advantages of the integrated Apriori algorithm are the following. First, since it does not handle neither data structures nor the buffer, developing and maintaining its code is much easier. Second, since it stores the frequent itemsets in the database, one can retrieve and query them later using the F2-DML. For example, one can find the frequent 2-itemsets which contain the item i_3 (in F2-DML: `result  :=  F2'[items contains Item'[item_id: "i3"]];`), or find the frequent 2-itemsets and 3-itemsets whose support is greater than 0.5 (in F2-DML: `s := 0.5 * size(Transaction'[ ]); result := union(F2'[support > s] F3'[support > s]);`). The stored frequent itemsets can also be used later, after the database is updated, to mine association rules using an incremental updating algorithm (e.g. FUP [5]) instead of rerunning a mining algorithm from scratch.

4   Integrated TRAND

In this section, we propose TRAND, an efficient algorithm for mining association rules. We first describe the database schema used by it. Then, we present the TRAND algorithm integrated within F2 and show how it takes advantage of the transposed storage.

4.1   F2 Database Schema

The initial database schema for TRAND has two classes: *Item* (containing the item objects i_1, i_2,..., i_n) and *Transaction$_1$* (containing the transaction objects t_1, t_2,..., t_m). Class *Transaction$_1$* has the *transaction_id* attribute and n boolean attributes Ai_1, Ai_2,..., Ai_n that correspond to the n objects in *Item*. A transaction object t_k takes 1 on the attribute Ai_j if the transaction contains the corresponding item, other-wise it takes 0. For example, in figure 5 transaction object t_2 takes the values *transaction_id*=200, Ai_1=0, Ai_2=1, Ai_3=1, Ai_4=0, Ai_5=1, since the second transaction contains the items $\{i_2, i_3, i_5\}$.

Example DB
minsup = 50%

TID	Items
100	$i_1\ i_3\ i_4$
200	$i_2\ i_3\ i_5$
300	$i_1\ i_2\ i_3\ i_5$
400	$i_2\ i_5$

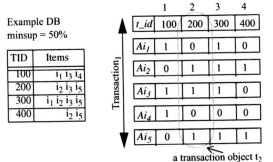

Fig. 5. Example database, and storage of class Transaction$_1$ in F2 (state attribute is omitted)

At each pass k ($k > 1$) of the TRAND algorithm, the classes F_k and $Transaction_k$ are created in the database (see fig. 6). Class F_k contains the frequent k-itemset objects $f_1, f_2, ..., f_p$. Each of them is associated with k objects in *Item* (its items) and two objects in F_{k-1} (its generators), and has a support. In addition to that, it is associated with an attribute of

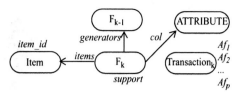

Fig. 6. Database schema at pass k (classes F_1 (Transaction$_1$) to F_k (Transaction$_k$) are in the schema but only F_k (Transaction$_k$) is shown)

class $Transaction_k$ (note that the domain of the *col* attribute is the meta-class *ATTRIBUTE*). Class $Transaction_k$ has p boolean attributes $Af_1, Af_2, ..., Af_p$ corresponding to the p objects in F_k, and contains m objects for the m transactions. An object in $Transaction_k$ takes 1 on the attribute Af_j if the transaction contains the corresponding frequent k-itemset.

4.2 TRAND Algorithm

Figure 7 shows the TRAND algorithm. It first generates frequent 1-itemsets, and then iterates to generate all frequent k-itemsets, $k > 1$, until no frequent itemset is found.

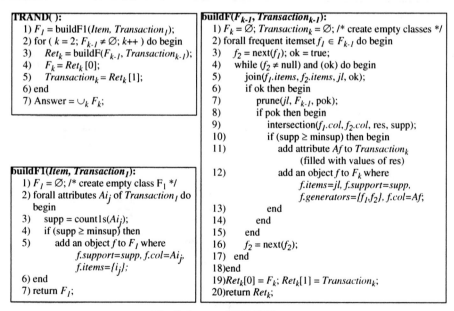

Fig. 7. Integrated TRAND

A pass k of the algorithm consists of only one phase: candidate generation and support counting are performed in the *buildF* method. In this method, the *join* step builds a candidate k-itemset using frequent $(k-1)$-itemsets found in the previous pass. The *prune* step ensures that every subset of a frequent itemset is frequent, and so discards the candidate itemset if it does not satisfy this property. The *intersection* step counts the support of the candidate itemset.

The *buildF1* method (fig. 7) creates a new class F_1 [line 1]. It computes the support *supp* of each item by counting the number of '1's on the corresponding attribute Ai_j of *Transaction$_1$* [line 3]. If it is greater than or equal to *minsup* then the method adds an object *f* to F_1 (with values *supp*=*supp*, *col*=Ai_j, *items*={i_j}, *f* has no generators) [line 5]. The method returns class F_1 (i.e. its oid). The result of applying *buildF1* on our example database is shown in figure 8.

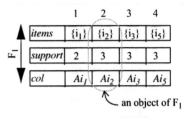

Fig. 8. Applying TRAND on the example database (pass 1)

The *buildF* method (fig. 7) creates two new classes F_k and *Transaction$_k$* [line 1]. The outer for loop [line 2] scans class F_{k-1}. For each of its objects f_1, the inner while loop [line 4] scans class F_{k-1} starting from the next object f_2. If f_1 and f_2 can be *joined* [line 5], i.e. if f_1.*items* and f_2.*items* have the same first (k-2) elements, then a join list *jl* is created with the common (k-2) items and the last item of f_1 and the last item of f_2. This list represents a candidate k-itemset. *jl* is *pruned* [line 7] if it contains a (k-1)-subset *sl* and there is no object *p* in class F_{k-1} such that *p.items*==*sl*. If *jl* is not pruned, then the attributes of *Transaction$_{k-1}$* corresponding to f_1 and f_2, i.e. f_1.*col* and f_2.*col*, are *intersected* [line 9] by applying logical AND on them. The result is stored in a temporary array *res*, and the number of '1's (*supp*) in this array is counted. If *supp*, the support of the candidate itemset, is greater than or equal to *minsup* then an attribute *Af* is added to class *Transaction$_k$* (values on this attribute are values of the array) [line 11], and a frequent k-itemset object *f* is added to F_k (with values *items*=*jl*, *support*=*supp*, *generators*={f_1,f_2}, *col*=*Af*) [line 12]. The while loop is exited when all objects in F_{k-1} have been examined or when f_1 can not be joined. At the end of the *buildF* method, classes F_k and *Transaction$_k$* are returned (i.e. 2 oids returned in an array). The next passes on our example database are shown in figure 9.

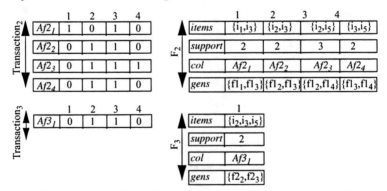

Fig. 9. Applying TRAND on the example database (passes 2 and 3)

Like the integrated Apriori algorithm, TRAND does not require complicated data structures, does not handle the buffer, and stores frequent itemsets in the database. Consequently, it has the same advantages. Another important advantage in TRAND is that the database is not scanned for support counting. To compute the support of a candidate itemset (e.g. $\{i_2,i_3,i_5\}$) only the attributes corresponding to the itemsets that generated it (e.g. $\{i_2,i_3\}$, $\{i_2,i_5\}$) are loaded into memory. This reduces the I/O time and the processing time since not the whole database is accessed, but only a very small part of it (see experiment results and cost analysis in section 5.2). This is possible thanks to the transposed storage. TRAND applies then logical AND on the two boolean attributes and counts the '1's in the result. ANDing bit vectors is a fast operation, during which TRAND uses low-level primitives of the F2 DBMS to read/write the contents of a block at once. Finally, adding the resulting attribute to the schema or deleting it are not expensive operations, because the database is not reorganized thanks to the transposed storage [3].

5   Experiments and Results

To evaluate the performance of the TRAND algorithm we ran several experiments on a laptop with CPU clock rate 800 MHz, 128 MB of main memory, and running Microsoft Windows 2000 Professional. The F2 buffer size was set to 60 MB, and the F2 block size was set to 1 KB. The algorithms were coded in Ada. In this section, we first describe the databases used in our experiments. Then we compare the performances of TRAND and Apriori in experiment 1, and explain these performances. Then we propose the TRAND-del algorithm, and compare it with TRAND in experiment 2.

5.1   Generation of Synthetic Data

The databases used in our experiments were synthetically generated using the technique described in [1][1]. The parameters used in the experiments are summarized in table 1a. We generated 6 databases whose sizes are given in table 1b. In [1], the size of T5.I2.D100K is 2.4 MB only, while in F2 it is 7.5 MB for the Apriori algorithm. The average size of the transactions is 5 but the biggest size of the transactions is 17. In F2, for a multi-valued attribute of class C (e.g. *Transaction.items*) which has a maximal cardinality m, space is reserved to store a set-value of size m for every object of C even if an object takes a set-value of size less than m (this is a limitation of F2). This explains the difference in size. Note that for Apriori the size of databases increases when |T| increases, while for TRAND it does not change since there are N boolean attributes containing bits for |D| transactions; the only change is that there will be more '1's on the attributes (T5.I2.D100K is smaller because the synthetic data generation program did not create exactly 100,000 transactions but 97,155 for T5.I2.D100K and 99,917 for T10.I2.D100K).

---

[1] We downloaded the synthetic data generation program from www.almaden.ibm.com/cs/quest/ syndata.html. We used the data files produced by this program to create F2 databases.

Table 1. a) Parameters

Parameter symbol	Parameter meaning	Parameter values
N	Nb. of items	1,000
IDI	Nb. of transactions	100,000
ITI	Average size of the transactions	5 / 10 / 20
ILI	Nb. of maximal potentially frequent itemsets	2,000
III	Average size of maximal potentially frequent itemsets	2 / 4 / 6

Table 1. b) Synthetic DB

DB name	DB size (MB) TRAND	DB size (MB) Apriori
T5.I2.D100K	13.3	7.5
T10.I2.D100K	14.3	12.4
T10.I4.D100K		
T20.I2.D100K	14.3	19.2
T20.I4.D100K		
T20.I6.D100K		

5.2   Experiment 1

Table 2 and figure 10A (top) show the execution times of TRAND and Apriori for T5.I2.D100K and T10.I2.D100K for decreasing values of minimum support. Note that our execution times include I/O time. The table shows also the number of generated frequent itemsets, and the greatest k for which F_k is not empty. This experiment shows that for TRAND and Apriori: (i) when the minimum support decreases, the execution time increases (because the number of frequent itemsets increases); (ii) when the average size of the transactions |T| increases (for same value of |I|), the execution time increases (same reason). It shows also that for both databases and for all the supports TRAND beats Apriori significantly.

Table 2. Execution times of TRAND and Apriori (in seconds)

	T5.I2.D100K				T10.I2.D100K			
minsup	TRAND time	Apriori time	Nb. frequent itemsets	Max k	TRAND time	Apriori time	Nb. frequent itemsets	Max k
2.00%	3	85	34	1	6	411	173	1
1.50%	3	103	84	1	10	709	264	3
1.00%	6	118	184	1	19	1,462	429	4
0.75%	10	161	271	3	30	2,054	622	4
0.50%	19	233	430	4	40	8,663	1,081	6
0.33%	29	336	751	4	65	10,486	1,856	6
0.25%	38	528	1,054	6	93	14,366	2,647	6

Explanation of Performance. To explain the difference in the execution times of TRAND and Apriori, we measured: (i) the number of block transfers from disk to the buffer; (ii) the number of buffer replacements (when the buffer is full, p blocks are transferred from the buffer to disk using the Least Recently Used technique; p was set to 3,000); (iii) the number of block accesses (to read or write a value); the block can be either in the buffer or on disk. The obtained results are given in table 3. Firstly, blocks are transferred from disk to the buffer once when computing F_1. Secondly, the databases fit in the buffer (there is no buffer replacement). Thirdly, the number of block accesses is much higher in Apriori than in TRAND. We explain this difference with the cost analysis. Figure 10A (bottom) shows the number of block accesses for T5.I2.D100K and T10.I2.D100K, and thus the similarity between these curves and the ones of the execution time.

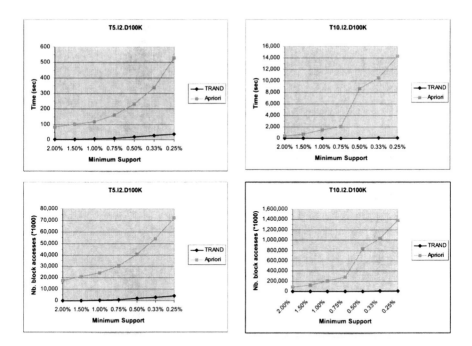

Fig. 10A. Execution times and number of block accesses of TRAND and Apriori

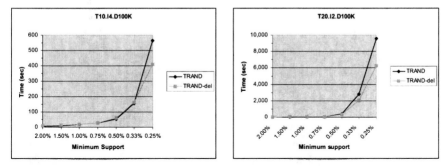

Fig. 10B. Execution times of TRAND and TRAND-del

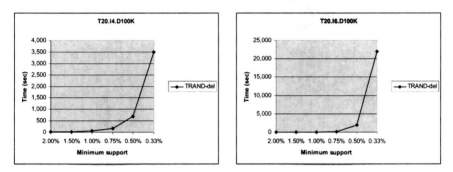

Fig. 10C. Execution times of TRAND-del

Table 3. Number of block transfers and block accesses in TRAND and Apriori

		T5.I2.D100K		T10.I2.D100K	
	minsup	TRAND	Apriori	TRAND	Apriori
Nb. block transfers disk → buffer	all	12,049	6,870	13,049	11,748
Nb. block transfers buffer → disk	all	0	0	0	0
Nb. block accesses	2.00%	33,001	17,565,422	452,679	82,714,714
	1.50%	112,826	21,079,090	967,544	121,620,053
	1.00%	474,976	24,423,142	2,079,179	203,989,095
	0.75%	957,498	30,699,237	2,910,600	280,985,403
	0.50%	1,987,479	40,482,169	4,317,449	835,360,430
	0.33%	3,079,351	54,214,110	6,886,365	1,024,915,830
	0.25%	4,030,888	72,208,969	9,630,177	1,387,212,895

Cost Analysis. Let us compare the cost of TRAND and Apriori algorithms with respect to the number of block accesses in pass k. Reading an attribute value of an object (e.g. $f_1.items$) costs one block access. Creating or modifying an object may cost several block accesses (attribute values are checked, reference counters are updated, then attribute values are stored in different blocks). Instead of including the number of *all* block accesses, we include only those terms that help us distinguish between the two algorithms. $|C_k|$ (resp. $|F_k|$) is the number of candidate (resp. frequent) k-itemsets.

The *buildF* (fig. 7) and *apriori_gen* (fig. 4) methods have a for loop over F_{k-1}, with a nested while loop over F_{k-1} containing the same join and prune operations. In *buildF*, the intersection operation [line 9] is done $|C_k|$ times, and requires reading the blocks of 2 boolean attributes (each occupies $(|D| / 8192)$ blocks, since the block size is 1KB i.e. 8192 bits). Storing the resulting attribute [line 11] is done $|F_k|$ times, and requires writing the blocks of one boolean attribute. Creating this attribute as object in the meta-class ATTRIBUTE costs 17 block accesses. Finally, creating an object in class F_k [line 12] is done $|F_k|$ times and costs 26 block accesses. This gives a total: $(|C_k| * 2 * (|D| / 8192)) + (|F_k| * ((|D| / 8192) + 17 + 26))$.

In *apriori_gen*, creating an object in class C_k [line 9] is done $|C_k|$ times and costs 21 block accesses. In *getF*, scanning class *Transaction* [line 1] costs $(2 * |D|)$ block accesses ($t.items$ and $t.state$ are read). For each transaction, we get the k-itemsets contained in it, i.e. $C(|T|, k)$ subsets (where $|T|$ is the average size of the transactions, and $C(|T|, k) = |T|! / (k! * (|T|-k)!))$. Checking whether a subset is a candidate [*subset*, line 1] costs $\log_2(|C_k|)$ block accesses (binary search on *c.items*). Incrementing the support of candidates [*subset*, lines 2,3] costs $(2 * \Sigma_{c \in Ck} c.support)$ block accesses (2 because the old support is read then modified). In the last step of *getF* [line 3] scanning class C_k costs $(2 * |C_k| + |F_k|)$ block accesses (*c.support* and *c.state* are read $|C_k|$ times, *c.items* is read $|F_k|$ times) and creating objects in class F_k costs $(12 * |F_k|)$ block accesses. This gives a total: $(21 * |C_k|) + (2 * |D|) + (|D| * C(|T|, k) * \log_2(|C_k|)) + (2 * \Sigma_{c \in Ck} c.support) + (2 * |C_k| + 13 * |F_k|)$

The cost of TRAND is dominated by the cost of intersecting boolean attributes: $|C_k| * 2 * (|D| / 8192)$, while the cost of Apriori is dominated by the cost of scanning the *Transaction* class and searching for candidates in it: $|D| * C(|T|, k) * \log_2(|C_k|)$. For example, for D = T5.I2.D100K, *minsup* = 0.25%, and $k = 2$, $|C_2|$ is found to be 134,421 and the dominant term becomes $|D| * 33$ for TRAND and $|D| * 170$ for Apriori.

5.3   Experiment 2

Since TRAND adds a boolean attribute to the database schema for each generated frequent itemset, the buffer may become full at some point in time. F2 applies then buffer replacements. We met this situation with the databases T10.I4.D100K ($minsup \leq 0.33$), T20.I2.D100K, T20.I4.D100K and T20.I6.D100K ($minsup \leq 0.50$). Therefore, we propose the TRAND-del algorithm, a variant of TRAND. The TRAND-del algorithm deletes the boolean attributes when they are no longer used. In the *buildF* method (fig. 7), after the while loop [line 17], we add a statement to delete $f_l.col$ (only if $k \geq 3$, since we should not delete the attributes of class *Transaction$_1$*). Buffer replacements can not be avoided during the second pass, but their number can be reduced in subsequent passes. We ran the TRAND-del algorithm on the mentioned databases (see figures 10B and 10C). For T10.I4.D100K, *minsup*=0.25%, TRAND required 21 buffer replacements (9 times when k=3, 7 times when k=4, 3 times when k=5, 2 times when k=6) and 565 seconds as execution time, while TRAND-del required no buffer replacements and 408 seconds. For T20.I2.D100K, *minsup*=0.25%, 137 buffer replacements (57 when k=2, 76 when k=3, 4 when k=4) occurred for TRAND and 63 for TRAND-del (57 when k=2, 6 when k=3) resulting in 9,617 seconds for TRAND and 6,278 seconds for TRAND-del. Multiplying the number of buffer replacements by 3,000 gives the number of block transfers from the buffer to disk. Note that some blocks which are transferred to disk may be needed later and will be transferred again to the buffer.

6   Conclusion

In this paper, we integrated two association rule mining algorithms, Apriori and TRAND, with F2 a general-purpose object-oriented database system. In our integration, both algorithms do not need to maintain complicated data structures. Both do not need to manage the buffer. Consequently, coding and maintaining these algorithms becomes much easier. Both store frequent itemsets in the database. Consequently, one can retrieve and query the mined frequent itemsets using the F2-DML. One can also use them later for association rule incremental updating algorithms. In addition to that, TRAND takes advantage of the transposed storage supported in the F2 DBMS. To compute the support of candidate itemsets, it applies simple and fast logical AND on boolean attributes, implemented in F2 as vectors, and avoids scanning the database. Moreover, adding the resulting attributes is not expensive since it does not require reorganizing the database. Consequently, TRAND gains a significant performance improvement over Apriori as shown in our experiments and cost analysis. We also proposed the TRAND-del algorithm, a variant of TRAND, which reduces the number of buffer replacements.

Extensions to this work include the compression of bit vectors which would reduce the number of block accesses and the number of buffer replacements. Parallel computation of candidate itemset support is another issue which deserves to be investigated. For example, if we have four frequent 1-itemsets *A, B, C, D*, one can compute the support of candidates $\{A,B\}$ and $\{C,D\}$ at the same time, since it involves ANDing different bit vectors.

Acknowledgements. The author would like to thank Wael Marji, Housam Takkoush, Hilal Issa, Mohammad Kanj, Mirna Nahhas, and Rima Mansour, for their assistance in coding the algorithms.

References

1. Agrawal R., Srikant R., "Fast Algorithms for Mining Association Rules in Large Databases", Proc. Int. Conf. on Very Large Data Bases (VLDB), 1994.
2. Al-Jadir L., Estier T., Falquet G., Leonard M., "Evolution Features of the F2 OODBMS", Proc. Int. Conf. on Database Systems for Advanced Applications (DASFAA), 1995.
3. Al-Jadir L., Leonard M., "Transposed Storage of an Object Database to Reduce the Cost of Schema Changes", Proc. Int. ER Workshop on Evolution and Change in Data Management, 1999.
4. Burdick D., Calimlim M., Gehrke J., "MAFIA: A Maximal Frequent Itemset Algorithm for Transactional Databases", Proc. Int. Conf. on Data Engineering (ICDE), 2001.
5. Cheung D., Han J., Ng V., Wong C.Y., "Maintenance of Discovered Association Rules in Large Databases: An Incremental Updating Technique", Proc. Int. Conf. On Data Engineering (ICDE), 1996.
6. Dunkel B., Soparkar N., "Data Organization and Access for Efficient Data Mining", Proc. Int. Conf. on Data Engineering (ICDE), 1999.
7. Han J., Pei J., Yin Y., "Mining Frequent Patterns without Candidate Generation", Proc. Int. Conf. on Management of Data (ACM SIGMOD), 2000.
8. Holsheimer M., Kersten M., Mannila H., Toivonen H., "A Perspective on Databases and Data Mining", Proc. Int. Conf. on Knowledge Discovery and Data Mining (KDD), 1995.
9. Meo R., Psaila G., Ceri S., "A New SQL like Operator for Mining Association Rules", Proc. Int. Conf. on Very Large Data Bases (VLDB), 1996.
10. Park J.S., Chen M.-S., Yu P.S., "An Effective Hash-Based Algorithm for Mining Association Rules", Proc. Int. Conf. on Management of Data (ACM SIGMOD), 1995.
11. Pasquier N., Bastide Y., Taouil R., Lakhal L., "Discovering Frequent Closed Itemsets for Association Rules", Proc. Int. Conf. on Database Theory (ICDT), 1999.
12. Pei J., Han J., Mao R., "CLOSET: An Efficient Algorithm for Mining Frequent Closed Itemsets", Proc. ACM SIGMOD Workshop on Research Issues in Data Mining and Knowledge Discovery, 2000.
13. Sarawagi S., Thomas S., Agrawal R., "Integrating Association Rule Mining with Relational Database Systems: Alternatives and Implications", Proc. Int. Conf. on Management of Data (ACM SIGMOD), 1998 (extended version in: Data Mining and Knowledge Discovery, vol. 4, no 2/3, 2000).
14. Savasere A., Omiecinski E., Navathe S., "An Efficient Algorithm for Mining Association Rules in Large Databases", Proc. Int. Conf. on Very Large Data Bases (VLDB), 1995.
15. Shenoy P., Bhalotia G., Haritsa J.R., Bawa M., Sudarshan S., Shah D., "Turbo-charging Vertical Mining of Large Databases", Proc. Int. Conf. on Management of Data (ACM SIGMOD), 2000.
16. Wur S-Y., Leu Y., "An Effective Boolean Algorithm for Mining Association Rules in Large Databases", Proc. Int. Conf. on Database Systems For Advanced Applications (DASFAA), 1999.
17. Zaki M.J., Parthasarathy S., Ogihara M., Li W., "New Algorithms for Fast Discovery of Association Rules", Proc. Int. Conf. on Knowledge Discovery and Data Mining (KDD), 1997.
18. Zaki M.J., Hsiao C.-J., "CHARM: An Efficient Algoithm for Closed Association Rule Mining", Tech. Report 99-10, Computer Science Dept., Rensselaer Polytech. Institute, 1999.

Using User Access Patterns for Semantic Query Caching

Qingsong Yao and Aijun An

Department of Computer Science,
York University,
Toronto M3J 1P3 Canada
{qingsong,aan}@cs.yorku.ca

Abstract. In this paper, we propose a solution that partly solves the selection and replacement problems for semantic query caching. We believe that the queries submitted by a client are not random. They have certain meaning and may follow certain rules. We use *user access graphs* to represent the query execution orders and propose algorithms that use such information for semantic query caching. Unlike the previous approaches, ours anticipates incoming queries based on the queries that have been submitted, analyzes the semantic relationship between them, and rewrites and caches the current query to answer multiple queries. Our initial experimental result shows that our solution improves cache performance.

1 Introduction

Semantic query caching (SQC) [3,5,6] assumes that the queries submitted by a client are related to each other semantically. Therefore, grouping tuples according to the semantic meaning can provide better performance than other caching approaches (i.e., page-based or tuple-based caching). Previous research considers every submitted query as a cache candidate. Such solution is not extendable since the number of cache candidates for a given client application is quite large. The cache replacement algorithms are based on the statistics (i.e., query result size, query referencing frequency or underlying data updating frequency). The replacement algorithms may not provide good performance since they do not take query locality into account. Meanwhile, in order to find and retrieve the answer of a query from caches, an algorithm is needed to examine how they are related semantically. A special case is that the query is semantically contained in the caches, which is called *query containment*. There are many studies in this field, but the execution time of the algorithms cannot be ignored when the number of caches is large.

In this paper, we use *user access patterns* to describe how a user or a client accesses the data of a database, and explore ways to use such information for semantic query caching. We can anticipate the queries to be submitted by using the query execution patterns. We found that a user always accesses the same part of the data within certain time interval. Thus, semantic relationships exist

V. Mařík et al. (Eds.): DEXA 2003, LNCS 2736, pp. 737–746, 2003.

738 Q. Yao and A. An

between the corresponding queries, and can be used to rewrite and cache a query
to answer multiple queries. The rewritten queries save both the network load and
the processing cost of the server.

The rest of the paper is organized as follows. User access patterns and related issues are presented in Sect. 2. In Sect. 3, we propose three caching solutions: *sequential-execution*, *union-execution* and *probe-remainder-execution*. We
present the evaluation strategies and experimental results in Sect. 4. We describe
related work in Sect. 5. Sect. 6 is the conclusion.

2 User Access Patterns

We can transform a SQL query into an *SQL template* and a set of *parameters*.
We treat each integer value or string value of a given SQL query as a parameter,
and the SQL template can be obtained by replacing each parameter in the SQL
with a wildcard character (%). Database users often submit *similar queries* to
retrieve certain information from the database. We use a *user access event* to
represent a set of similar queries which share the same SQL template. A user
access event contains an SQL template and a set of parameters.

The query execution order, represented by a directed graph, is called a *user
access graph*. The graph has one start node and one or many end nodes, and
cycles may exist in a graph. Each node is a user access event. An edge is rep-
resented by $e_k : (v_i, v_j, \sigma_{v_i \to v_j})$, where $\sigma_{v_i \to v_j}$ is the probability of v_j following
v_i, which is called the confidence. The graph associates with a support value τ_g
which describes how often it is executed[1]. For example, table 1 lists an instance
of a patient information model which retrieves a given customer's information.
Fig. 1 shows the corresponding user access graph. The graph is a special graph
since it contains no branches or cycles. It is called a *user access path*.

Table 1. An instance of patient information model

Label	Statement
30	select authority from *employee* where employee_id ='**1025**'
9	select count(*) as num from *customer* where cust_num = '**1074**'
10	select card_name from customer t1,member_card t2 where t1.cust_num = '**1074**' and t1.card_id = t2.card_id
20	select contact_last,contact_first from *customer* where cust_num = '**1074**'
47	select t1.branch ,t2.* from *record* t1, *treatment* t2 where t1.contract_no = t2.contract_no and t1.cust_id ='**1074**' and check_in_date = '**2002/03/04**' and t1.branch = '**scar**'

The graph may contain a set of global variables: employee id (*g_eid*), customer id (*g_cid*), branch id(g_bid) and check-in date (*g_date*). Variable *g_date*
is a system variable which equals to today's date, and we call it as a constant

---

[1] The support and the confidence have the same meaning in the field of association
rule mining.

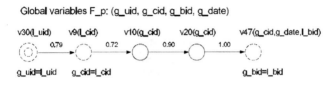

Global variables F_p: (g_uid, g_cid, g_bid, q_date)

v30(l_uid)   v9(l_cid)   v10(g_cid)   v20(g_cid)   v47(g_cid,q_date,l_bid)

g_uid=l_uid   g_cid=l_cid   g_bid=l_bid

Fig. 1. User access path for patient information module

global variable. Meanwhile, g_cid is unknown before event $v9$ is submitted, so the parameter of $v9$ is a local variable($L cid$). When $v9$ is submitted, g_cid is set to the value of $L cid$, then event $v10,v20$ are determined since their parameters are known. Thus, some nodes in the graph associate with a set of actions which change the value of global variables according to the values of its local variables.

There are two kinds of events: *determined event* and *undetermined event*. An event is a determined event if and only if each parameter is either a constant or a global variable. Otherwise, it is undetermined. Three kinds of determined events, graph-determined event, parameter-determined event and result-determined event, exist in a graph. If every parameter of an event is a constant or a constant global variable, we call it a graph-determined event. Event v_j is result-determined by v_i, if and only if one or more parameters of v_j are unknown until v_i finishes execution[2]. Event v_j is parameter-determined by v_i, if and only if one or more parameters are unknown until v_i is submitted. For example, $v30$, $v9$ and $v47$, represented by dotted cycles in the graph, are undetermined events, and $v10$ and $v20$ are parameter-determined by $v9$.

We use *user access patterns* to describe how a client application or a group of users access the data of a database. User access patterns include a collection of *frequent* user access graphs whose support is bigger than a given threshold τ, and a collection of user access events associated with the occurrence frequency and the parameter distribution. In this paper, we assume that the user access graphs are already obtained from database workload files or from the corresponding business logic, and the graphs are broken into several user access paths which can be processes efficiently. We are interested in finding and using the semantic relationship between the events of the user access path.

3   SQC Selection and Replacement

3.1   SQC Selection Problem

The SQC selection problem is defined as follows. Given a user access path p and a cache pool of size δ, find a set of query rewriting rules (for semantic query caching) to minimize the total execution cost of p. During the execution of the queries of path p, the size of the cached data should not exceed the cache size δ. In this section, we call a user access query a parameterized query, referred to as a query.

---

[2] The difference between an undetermined event and a result-determined event is that the parameters of the latter can be derived from the query result of other queries.

We first consider to generate rewriting rules for two consecutive queries u and v, and then extend the solutions to the whole path. We assume that the queries are *SPJ (select-project-join)* queries which can be written in the form $\{\alpha, \gamma, \delta\}$, where $\alpha = \{\alpha_1, \alpha_2, ...\alpha_m\}$ is a set of *selection attributes*, $\gamma = \{\gamma_1, ..\gamma_k\}$ is a set of relations and δ is the predicate. The attributes involved in the query predicate are called *search attributes.*

We use R_u to represent the answer of u. When query u is submitted, three solutions can be used to retrieve R_u and R_v. The first solution is to pre-fetch R_v, which is called the *sequential-execution (SEQ)* solution since we execute u and v sequentially. We may also submit the union query $(u \cup v)$ to answer both u and v together, and it is called the *union-execution (UNI)* solution. In order to retrieve the answer of the two queries from the cached data, the union query must include both the selection attributes of them and some search attributes. The third solution is called *probe-remainder-execution (PR)* solution. In this solution, an extended version of query u, referred as to u', is submitted and cached which includes columns needed by query v. To answer v, the solution retrieves part of the answer from $R_{u'}$, as well as submitting a remainder query v' to the server to retrieve the tuples which are not in the cache. The *UNI* and *PR* solutions are not applicable when two queries do not access the same relations.

The *SEQ* solution pre-executes queries to shorten the latency between the request and the response, while the *UNI* and *PR* solution aim to improve response time by decreasing the network transmission cost and the server processing cost. The *SEQ* has extra network transmission and server processing cost when query v isn't submitted. The *UNI* may improve server performance by accessing the base relation only once, and the *PR* may cause the server to access less data. But, the *UNI* and *PR* solutions may introduce "*disjunction*" and "*negation*" operations respectively which may cause the server to generate different query execution plans and increase the server processing cost. The *SEQ* and *UNI* solutions have extra network transmission cost when query v isn't submitted, but the *PR* solution may save the cost by retrieving part of the query answer from the caches.

3.2   Semantic Relationship between Parameterized Queries

We use the similar idea presented in [5] to illustrate the possible semantic relationships between two parameterized queries u and v in Fig. 2. Each query result can be viewed as an abstract relation which is represented by a box in the figure. The x-axis corresponds to the columns or the selection attributes, and the y-axis corresponds to the corresponding rows of the original relations. We are interested in the relationship between the rows since we can rewrite queries to include more columns. We summarize these cases as:

– *containing-match.* In case 1, the rows of u contains those of v. The union and the probe query are both u', and there is no remainder query. Thus, the *UNI* solution and the *PR* solution become the same. The solution usually does not generate worse query execution plans compared to the original queries, and the overall result size determines whether the solution is applicable.

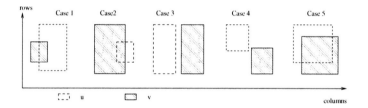

Fig. 2. Semantic relationship between two parameterized queries

- *contained-match.* In case 2, the rows of v contain those of u. The *UNI* and *PR* solutions are the possible solutions. When $\sigma_{u \to v}$ is small, we choose *PR* solution since *UNI* solution has extra costs when v isn't submitted.
- *horizontal-match (h-match).* In this case, u and v have the same set of rows, but may have different columns. The *UNI* and the *PR* solution usually do not generate worse query plans and have better query performance than the *SEQ* solution. When v has more columns than u and $\sigma_{u \to v}$ is small, we choose the *PR*. Otherwise, we choose *UNI*.
- *u disjoint with v.* In this case, there is no common rows between R_u and R_v (case 4). The *PR* solution is not suitable, but the *UNI* solution is applicable since it may save the server cost by only accessing the base relation once.
- *u partial-match with v.* That is, R_u and R_v have common rows (case 5). All three solutions may be applicable in this case.
- *u and v are irrelevant.* Two queries are irrelevant if their base relations are different, and the only possible solution is *SEQ*.

3.3 Algorithms

In this section, we propose an off-line algorithm, *rewriting-one*, to solve the SQC selection and replacement problem. The algorithm tries to find the semantic relationship between u and v, builds up rewriting queries and chooses an optimal rewriting query based on the costs. The *rewriting_one* algorithm is described in Figure 3.

We assume that the predicates of u and v are both the conjunction of basic predicate units which have the following format: *"var op constant"* or *"var op var + constant"*, where the operators are $\{=, <, >, \leq, \geq\}$ and the domain of each variable is integer. The algorithm first transforms a query predicate into an expression that only contains $\leq$ operators, and builds a weighted directed graph which describes the range of the search attributes and the relationship between them[3]. An edge $e(x, y, c)$ of the graph means that $x \leq y + c$ holds. For example, given queries:

- u1: *"select a1 from r1 where a2=1 and a3≤3"*
- u2: *"select a1 from r1 where a2=1"*
- u3: *"select a1 from r1 where a2=1 and a3≥1"*,

---

[3] Weighted directed graph was first introduced in [8]

Algorithm: rewriting_one(u,v).
Input: two queries u and v.
Output: query rewriting solution.

1. $solutions = \{\};$
2. if v is *undetermined*, $solutions=\{\};$
3. else if v is *result-determined* by u, $solutions= \{SEQ\};$
4. else if u and v are *irrelevant*, solutions $= \{SEQ\};$
5. else $G_u = weighted\_directed\_graph(\delta_u);$
6. $G_v = weighted\_directed\_graph(\delta_v);$
7. $comm\_diff(G_u, G_v, comm, diff);$
8. $rel = relation(comm, diff);$
9.   switch $(rel):$
10.   case $containing:solutions = \{UNI\};$
11.   case $contained,h\_match:solutions = \{UNI, PR\};$
12.   case $disjoint:$ solutions $= \{SEQ, UNI\};$
13.   case $partial\text{-}match:$ solutions $= \{SEQ, UNI, PR\}$
14. $build\_queries(\alpha_u, \alpha_v, comm, diff);$
15. select a solution based on the overall costs.

Fig. 3. Algorithm rewriting_one

and we want to generate query rewriting rules for query pair *u1* and *u2*, and for query pair *u2* and *u3*. The graphs are listed in Figure 4, where the dotted edges are marked as *derived* since they are derived from other edges.

In step 7, the algorithm builds the common edges set (*comm*) and the different edges set (*diff*) between two graphs. For each edge in G_u, the algorithm tries to find the corresponding edge in G_v, or vice versa. If the weights of two edges are the same, we add them to *comm* set, otherwise we add them to *diff* set. For example, *u1* and *u2* have the same predicate unit *a2=1* which corresponds to two identical edges in the graphs. In step 8 of the algorithm, we find the relationship between two queries by testing each pair of edges in the *diff*

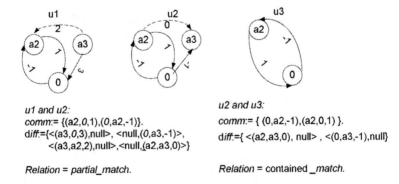

u1 and u2:
comm:= {(a2,0,1),(0,a2,-1)}.
diff:={<(a3,0,3),null>, <null,(0,a3,-1)>,
         <(a3,a2,2),null>,<null,(a2,a3,0)>}

Relation = partial_match.

u2 and u3:
comm:= { (0,a2,-1),(a2,0,1) }.

diff:={ <(a2,a3,0), null> , <(0,a3,-1),null}

Relation = contained _match.

Fig. 4. Weighted directed graphs for query u1, u2, and u3

set. If two queries have *h-match* relationship, the *diff* set is empty. If they have *contained-match* relationship, then for each edge pair $< e_u, e_v >$ in the *diff* set, either e_v is *null* or e_v has a larger weight than e_u. The *containing-match* can be tested in a similar way. The *disjoint-match* is obtained by testing whether $u \cap v$ has an answer, which in turn tests whether there is a negative circle in the graph of $u \cap v$. In step 9, we convert the edges of the *diff* and the *comm* set into corresponding predicate units, and use logic conjunction, disjunction and negation operators to connect them.

In the previous example, *u1 partial-matches* with *u2*, and *u2* is contained by *u3*. The rewriting queries for *u1* and *u2* are:

- union query: *"select a1,a3 from r1 where a2=1"*
- probe query: *"select a1,a3 from r1 where a2=1 and a3 ≤3"*
- remainder query: *"select a1 from r1 where a2=1 and t3 >3"*.

The *rewriting-one* algorithm can also process queries which contain join operations. For example, query *10* in Figure 1 is a join query, which can be rewritten as *"select card_name from member_card where card_id in (select card_id from customer t1 where t1.cust_num ='1074')"*, and the sub-query has *h-math* with queries *9* and *20*. Algorithm *rewriting-one* only considers two consecutive queries in a path, and in many cases, two consecutive queries do not have a *strong* relationship, such as *h-match*, *containing-match*, or *contained-match*. Thus, we suggest a *rewriting-n* algorithm which can generate global optimal plans by considering all queries in the path together. The algorithm finds a candidate set for every query, and analyzes the relationship between them. Then the algorithm sorts the set according to the rank of the relationships, and an optimal plan is generated by applying a heuristic method based on accumulative costs and available spaces.

4   Performance Evaluation and Experiments

We propose and implement a database proxy program *SQL-Relay*, to be the platform of our SQC solution. *SQL-Relay* is an event-driven, rule-based database proxy program which intercepts every message sent from the client or the server, and treats it as an event. It traces the user request sequence for each connected client. When the sequence matches one user access path, a set of pre-defined rewriting rules are applied. The *SQL-Relay* cache manager manages two kinds of caches: the global caches and the local caches. All connected clients share a global cache pool which is managed by using the LRU replacement policy. Meanwhile, each client also has a local cache pool. Each local cache entry has a *reference count* which indicates how many queries can be (partly) answered currently. When the *reference count* of an entry becomes zero, it is moved to the global cache pool, and we move all local caches into the global cache pool when a path finishes execution. To maintain the caches efficiently, we use the similar idea in [6] to describe the contents of each cache entry by using a predicate description, and discard the cache when the content of it is changed.

Table 2. Comparison of cache performance (per 100 queries).

	response time (s)	global cache hit	local cache hit	queries sent to server	network traffic(K bytes)	server I/O (K blocks)
case 1	11.4	N/A	N/A	100	61.0	1,390
case 2	11.2	19.1	N/A	100	62.1	1,182
case 3	10.8	20.2	10.5	82.6	63.7	1,207
case 4	10.3	21.3	6.4	78.2	50.6	1,108

Now, we present the experimental result of an OLTP application. A clinic office has a client application, *Danger Front*, which helps the employee check in patients, make appointments and sell products. After preprocessing one day's database queries log, we found 12 instances of the application. The query log has 9,344 SQL statements in 190 SQL templates, where 72% (136) of queries are *SPJ* queries. 718 sequences are found from the log. They belong to 21 user access paths which have support bigger than 10. We generate 19 *SEQ* rules, 4 *UNI* rules and 3 *PR* rules by using the rewriting-n algorithm.

We use *MySQL* as our database server which features a server-side *query cache* function, and compare the performance of server caching with our approach. The connection speed between the database and the *SQL-Relay* is 56 Kbps, and the speed between the clients and the *SQL-Relay* is 10 Mbps. We synthesize 300 client request sequences based on the path supports, and compare the cache performance under the following conditions: (1) executing queries without cache, (2) executing queries with 128K server cache, (3) pre-fetching queries based on user access patterns, and (4) using rules generated by using *rewriting-n*. In case 3 and 4, the caching function of *MySQL* is disabled and the *SQL-Relay* configures with a 128K cache. Each connected client has 4K local caches, and the size of global caches dramatically changes as more clients get connected or disconnected.

The result is listed in Table 2. The query response time is calculated at the client side. It includes server processing time, network transmission time, cache processing and maintaining time. We found 87% of queries are selection queries which did not change the state of the server. Thus the cache maintenance cost is not too high. The response time of our solution is the shortest since it saves both network transmission time and server processing time. The pre-fetching case has better response time than the server caching, but it doesn't improve server performance and has heavier network traffic than the latter.

Figure 5 shows the cache performance when the support of a path or the confidence of an event changes. We decrease the support of paths by increasing the frequency of random paths. The result is shown on the left of the figure. It shows that the network load decreases, and so does the local cache hits, since the paths are not frequent. Then we do not change the support of the paths, but decrease the confidence of queries in a path by increasing the frequency of the random queries. The result is shown on the right of the figure. It shows that the network load as well as the local cache hits also decrease since we cannot find suitable rules.

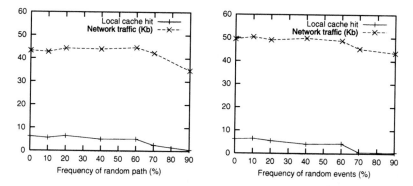

Fig. 5. Cache performance with different support or confidence. (per 100 queries)

5   Related Work

The cache selection and replacement problem has been extensively studied in
[11]. Sellis proposes the cache selection algorithms for both the *unbounded space*
where the available cache space is infinite and the *bounded space* where there is
limited space. Sellis suggests various *rank* functions for an LRU-like replacement
policy. Dar *et al* [3] use a semantic region as the unit of cache replacement. Their
replacement policies can be based on temporal locality or spatial locality. Keller
and Basu [6] use predicate descriptions to describe the cached data for each
previously-asked query. They focus on using server-side and client-side predicate
description to maintain the cached data efficiently. Godfrey and Gryz [5] provide
a comprehensive logic-based framework of semantic query caching by using *Datalog*, and introduce the concepts of semantic overlaps, semantic independence
and semantic query remainder.

Similar studies focus on using database access patterns to predict the buffer
hit ratio [1,2], to improve caching performance of OLAP systems [10], and to
generate global optimal query execution plans [4,9]. In [10], Sapia discusses the
PROMISE approach which provides the cache manager with access patterns to
make prediction in the OLAP environment. Finkelstein [4] describes an algorithm to detect common expressions between a set of queries. Multiple query
optimization [9] generates global optimal query execution plans for multiple
queries. Their solutions are server-side solutions which help the server to process multiple queries, but the intermediate results may be too large to be cached
by a client or a mediator.

6   Conclusion

In this paper, we propose a method that preforms semantic query caching by
using user access patterns. To our knowledge, it is the first attempt to make use
of such information for semantic query caching. Compared with other semantic
query techniques, our SQC approach has several advantages. Our caching algorithms are based on the query execution orders and the semantic relationship

between queries, which are better than the selection policies based on the global query reference statistics. The pre-defined query writing rules simplify the cache finding and replacing procedure. Our SQL-Relay application is flexible and extendable where various caching and rewriting rules can be added and tested. We would like to thank Professor Jarek Gryz for providing valuable feedback on this paper.

References

1. A. Dan, P. S. Yu, and J. Chung. Database Access Characterization for Buffer Hit Prediction. ICDE 1993: 134–143.
2. A. Dan, P. S. Yu, and J. Chung. Characterization of Database Access Pattern for Analytic Prediction of Buffer Hit Probability. VLDB Journal 4(1) 1995.
3. S. Dar, M. J. Franklin, B. T. Jonsson, D. Srivatava and M. Tan. Semantic Data Caching and Replacement. Proc. VLDB Conf, 1996.
4. S. Finkelstein. Common Expression Analysis in Database Application. In Procs. of ACM SIGMOD, 1987.
5. P. Godfrey and J. Gryz. Answering Queries by Semantic Caches. DEXA 1999: 485–498.
6. A. M. Keller and J. Basu. A predicate-based caching scheme for client-server database architectures. In Proc VLDB Conf.,1996.
7. MySQL Reference Manual (*http://www.mysql.com*).
8. D. J. Rosenkrantz and H. B. Hunt. Processing Conjunctive Predicates and Queries. In Proceedings of VLDB, 1980
9. T. Sellis and S. Ghosh. On the multiple-query optimization problem. TKDE,2(2), June 1990.
10. C. Sapia. PROMISE: Predicting Query Behavior to Enable Predictive Caching Strategies for OLAP Systems. In Proc. DAWAK 2000, 224–233.
11. T. K. Sellis. Intelligent caching and indexing techniques for relational database systems. Inform. Systems,13(2), 1988.

Exploiting Similarity of Subqueries for Complex Query Optimization[*]

Yingying Tao[1], Qiang Zhu[1], and Calisto Zuzarte[2]

[1] Department of Computer and Information Science
The University of Michigan,
Dearborn, MI 48128, USA.
[2] IBM Toronto Laboratory[***]
Markham, Ontario, Canada L6G 1C7

Abstract. Query optimizers in current database management systems (DBMS) often face problems such as intolerably long optimization time and/or poor optimization results when optimizing complex queries. To tackle this challenge, we present a new similarity-based optimization technique in this paper. The key idea is to identify groups of similar subqueries that often appear in a complex query and share the optimization result within each group in the query. An efficient algorithm to identify similar queries in a given query and optimize the query based on similarity is presented. Our experimental results demonstrate that the proposed technique is quite promising in optimizing complex queries in a DBMS.

1 Introduction

Query optimization is vital to the performance of a database management system (DBMS). The main task of a query optimizer in a DBMS is to seek an efficient query execution plan (QEP) for a given user query. Extensive study on query optimization has been conducted in the last three decades [2,3,6]. However, as database technology is applied to more and more application areas, user queries become increasingly complex in terms of the number of operations (e.g., more than 50 joins) and the query structure (e.g., star-schema queries with snowflakes). The query optimization techniques adopted in the existing DBMSs cannot cope with the new challenges.

As we know, the most important operation for a query is the join operation. A query typically involves a sequence of joins. To determine a good join order for the query, which is an important decision in a QEP, two types of algorithms are adopted in the current DBMSs. The first type of algorithms is based on dynamic programming or other exhaustive search techniques. Although such an algorithm can guarantee to find an optimal solution, its worst-case time complexity is

---

[*] Research supported by the IBM Toronto Lab and The University of Michigan.
[***] IBM is a registered trademark of International Business Machines Corporation in the United States, other countries, or both.

V. Mařík et al. (Eds.): DEXA 2003, LNCS 2736, pp. 747–759, 2003.

exponential. The second type of algorithms is based on heuristics. Although such algorithms have a polynomial time complexity, they often yield a suboptimal solution.

Hence, the above techniques cannot handle complex queries with a large number of joins, which occur more and more often in the real world. For an algorithm with exponential complexity, it may take months or years to optimize such a complex query. On the other hand, although a heuristic-based algorithm takes less time to find a join order for a complex query, the efficiency difference between a good solution and a bad one can be tremendous for a complex query. Unfortunately, the heuristics employed by current systems do not take the characteristics of a complex query into consideration, which often leads to a bad solution.

Therefore, we need a technique with a polynomial time complexity to find an efficient plan for a complex query. Note that the general query optimization problem has been proven to be NP-complete [4]. Hence, it is generally impossible to find an optimal plan within a polynomial time. Several studies have been reported to find a good plan for a large query (i.e., involving many joins) within a polynomial time in the literature, including the iterative improvement (II), simulated annealing (SA) [5], Tabu Search (TS) [7], AB algorithm (AB) [9], and genetic algorithm (GA) [1]. These algorithms represent a compromise between the time the optimizer takes for optimizing a query and the quality of the optimization plan. However, these techniques are mostly based on the randomization method. One advantage of this approach is that it is applicable to general queries, no matter simple or complex. On the other hand, a method only based on randomization has little "intelligence". It does not make use of some special characteristics of the underlying queries.

In our recent work [11], we introduced a technique to optimize a complex query by exploiting common subqueries that often appear in such a query. This technique is shown to be more effective than a pure randomization based method since it takes the structural characteristics of a complex query into consideration when optimizing the query. However, since this technique requires existence of common subqueries in a query, its application is limited.

We notice that many complex queries often contain similar substructures (subqueries) although they may not be exactly the same (i.e., common). This phenomenon appears more often when predefined views are used in the query, the underlying database system is distributed, or some parts of the query are automatically generated by programs. The more complex the query is, the more similar subqueries there will possibly be. As an example, consider a UNION ALL view defined as a fact table split up by years. Assume that dimension tables are to be joined with the view. To avoid materializing the view, a DBMS usually pushes down the dimension tables into the view, resulting in similar UNION ALL branches (subqueries).

Based on the above observation, we introduce a new similarity-based technique to reduce optimization time for a complex query by exploiting its similar subqueries in this paper. It is a two-phase optimization procedure. In the first phase, it identifies groups of similar subqueries in a given query. For each group of subqueries, it performs optimization for one representative subquery and share the optimization result with other member(s) within the group. After each similar subquery is replaced by its (estimated) result table obtained by using the corresponding execution plan in the original query, the modified query is then optimized in the second phase. Since the complexities of similar subqueries and the modified final query are reduced, they have a better chance to be optimized by a conventional approach (e.g., dynamic programming) or a randomization approach (e.g., AB) efficiently and effectively.

The rest of this paper is organized as follows. Section 2 introduces the concepts of a query graph and its similar subqueries. Section 3 gives the details of an algorithm to identify similar subqueries in a given query and optimize the query based on similarity. Section 4 shows some experimental results. Section 5 summarizes the conclusions.

2 Query Graph and Similar Subquery

In this section, we introduce the definitions of a query graph and its similar subquery graphs, which are the key concepts for our query optimization technique.

2.1 Query Set Considered

Most practical queries consist of a set of selection (σ), join ($\bowtie$), and projection (π) operations. These are the most common operations studied for query optimization in the literature, which are also the ones to be considered in this paper. Note that π is usually processed together with other operations (σ or $\bowtie$) it follows in a pipelined fashion. For simplicity, we assume that there is always a projection operation following each $\sigma/\bowtie$ operation to filter out the columns that are not needed for processing the rest of the given query. We also assume that the query condition is a conjunction of simple predicates of the following forms: $R.a \ \theta \ C$ and $R_1.a_1 \ \theta \ R_2.a_2$, where R, R_1 and R_2 are tables (relations); a, a_1 and a_2 are columns (attributes) in the relevant tables; C is a constant in the domain of $R.a$; and $\theta \in \{=, \neq, <, \leq, >, \geq\}$. Another assumption is that joins are executed by the nested-loop method. Under this assumption, we can simply consider one cost model. However, our technique can be extended to include other join methods by adopting multiple cost models.

2.2 Query Graph

Let Q be a query, $T = \{R_1, R_2, ..., R_m\}$ be the set of (base) tables referenced in Q, and $P = \{p_1, p_2, ..., p_n\}$ be the set of predicates referenced in Q. We call each table reference in Q a table instance. The logical structure of query Q can be represented by a query graph, based on the following rules:

- Each table instance in Q is represented by a vertex in the query graph G for Q. Let V be the set of vertices in G. Since several table instances may reference the same base table, there exists a many-to-one mapping $\delta : x \mapsto R$, where $x \in V$ and $R \in T$. In G, each $x \in V$ is labeled with $\delta(x) = R$.
- For any table instances (vertices) x and y, if there is at least one predicate in P involving x and y, then query graph G has an edge between x and y, with the set of all predicates involving x and y labeled on the edge. If x and y are the same table instance, the edge is a self-loop for the vertex in query graph G. Let E be the set of all edges in G. There exists a mapping $\varphi : e \mapsto c$, where $e \in E$ and $c \in 2^P$. $\varphi(e)$ gives the set of all simple predicates involving the (both) vertices of edge e. In G, each $e \in E$ is labeled with $\varphi(e) = c$.

Therefore, a query graph for query Q is a 6-tuple $G(V, E, T, P, \delta, \varphi)$, with each component defined as above. For the rest of the paper, we use the following notation: $edge(x, y)$ denotes the edge between vertices x and y in a query graph, $vertices(e)$ denotes the set of (one or two) vertices connected by edge e in a query graph. $sizeof(x)$ denotes the size of the table represented by x, $sel(e)$ denotes the selectivity of $\varphi(e)$, i.e., the selectivity of the conjunction of all the simple predicates in $\varphi(e)$.

Without loss of generality, we assume our query graph is connected in this paper. Otherwise, each isolated component graph can be optimized first and a set of Cartesian products are then performed to combine the results of the component graphs.

For our query optimization technique, we adopt a data structure called the ring network representation to represent a query graph. In such a representation, every vertex x in query graph G has a node x. Assume that node x has a set of adjacent nodes $y_1, y_2, ..., y_n$. We use a closed link list (i.e., a ring): $x \rightarrow y_1 \rightarrow y_2 \rightarrow ... \rightarrow y_n \rightarrow x$ to represent such an adjacency relationship. Node x is called the owner (node) of the ring, while nodes $y_1, y_2, ..., y_n$ are called the members of the ring. Each node in the ring network for G is the owner of one ring, and it also participates in other rings as a member.

2.3   Similar Subquery Graphs

Let $V' \subseteq V$ be a subset of vertices in the query graph $G(V, E, T, P, \delta, \varphi)$ for query Q. Let $E|_{V'} = \{ e \mid e \in E \text{ and } vertices(e) \subseteq V' \}$; $T|_{V'} = \{ R \mid R \in T \text{ and there exists } x \in V' \text{such that } x \text{ is an instance of } R \}$; $P|_{V'} = \{ p \mid p \in P \text{ and } p \in w \text{ and } w \text{ is the set of predicates labeled on } e \in E|_{V'} \}$; $\delta|_{V'} : x \mapsto R$, where $x \in V'$, $R \in T|_{V'}$ and $\delta(x) = R$; and $\varphi|_{V'} : e \mapsto c$, where $e \in E|_{V'}$, $c \in 2^{P|_{V'}}$and $\varphi(e) = c$. Clearly, $G'(V', E|_{V'}, T|_{V'}, P|_{V'}, \delta|_{V'}, \varphi|_{V'})$ is a subgraph of G. If G' is connected, we call it a subquery graph in G. The corresponding query is called a subquery of Q.

Let $G'(V', E|_{V'}, T|_{V'}, P|_{V'}, \delta|_{V'}, \varphi|_{V'})$ and $G''(V'', E|_{V''}, T|_{V''}, P|_{V''}, \delta|_{V''}, \varphi|_{V''})$ be two subquery graphs in G. r_t and r_s are two given error bounds for table sizes and condition selectivities, respectively. Assume that every table size and selectivity are non-zero. Otherwise, the result of the entire query will be empty, in which case no optimization is needed. If G' and G'' satisfy the following conditions, we regard them as a pair of similar subquery graphs with respect to error bounds r_t and r_s, denoted as $G' \approx |_{(r_t, r_s)} G''$:

- There exists a one-to-one mapping f between V' and V'', such that for any $x \in V'$ and $f(x) \in V''$, we have $\varepsilon_t(x, f(x)) < r_t$, where $\varepsilon_t(x, f(x)) = max\{\frac{|sizeof(x) - sizeof(f(x))|}{sizeof(x)}, \frac{|sizeof(x) - sizeof(f(x))|}{sizeof(f(x))}\}$.
- There exists a one-to-one mapping g between E' and E'', such that, for any $e \in E'$ and $g(e) \in E''$, if $vertices(e) = \{x, y\}$, then $vertices(g(e)) = \{f(x), f(y)\}$, and $\varepsilon_s(e, g(e)) < r_s$, where $\varepsilon_s(e, g(e)) = max\{\frac{|sel(e) - sel(g(e))|}{sel(e)}, \frac{|sel(e) - sel(g(e))|}{sel(g(e))}\}$.

Let us consider an example. Given a query graph G in Fig. 1 (the size of the table represented by each node and the selectivity of the predicates on each edge are marked in parentheses), using error bounds $r_t = r_s = 0.3$, the similar subqueries are shown in the dotted circles marked as G' and G''. Intuitively, a pair of similar subquery graphs have the same inner graph structure, and the table sizes for the corresponding vertices and the selectivities for the corresponding edges in the pair are within error bounds r_t and r_s, respectively.

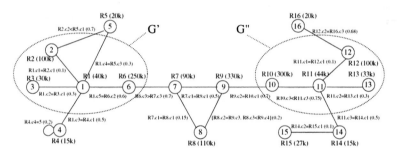

Fig. 1. Example of a query graph with similar subqueries

3 Query Optimization via Exploiting Similarity of Subqueries

In this section, we will introduce a technique to perform query optimization via exploiting similarity of subqueries in a given complex query. Due to the paper length limitation, we only discuss the technique making use of pairs of similar queries. However, the technique can be generalized to utilize more than two similar subqueries in each group (with one representative subquery)[12].

3.1 Basic Idea

The basic idea of the technique is as follows: (1) identify pairs of similar subqueries with respect to the given error bounds r_t and r_s; (2) optimize one subquery in a similar pair, and map and apply the resulting execution plan to the other subquery, which would reduce the optimization time by sharing the same (mapped) plan between two similar subqueries; and (3) replace similar subqueries with their (estimated) result tables in the query graph and optimize the resulting modified query. As the number of tables/vertices in the query graph is reduced, less overhead is needed to optimize the modified query.

3.2   Algorithm Description

The description of the algorithm for our technique is given below. Note that if there is a self-loop on a node/vertex, it is usually a good strategy to perform such a unary subquery first to reduce the operand table size. Hence we assume that all self-loops are removed in such a way for a given query graph.

ALGORITHM 1 Query Optimization Based on Similar Subqueries
Input: query graph $G(V, E, T, P, \delta, \varphi)$ for user query Q, and error bounds r_t and r_s.
Output: Execution plan for query Q.
Method:
1.   Initialize flag selected(x)=0 for each node x;
2.   Initialize the sets of identified pairs of similar subquery graphs $S_{accept} = S_{hold} = \emptyset$;
3.   **while** there are unselected node pairs with similar table sizes within r_t **do**
4.   Pick up nodes x and y following the rules for choosing starting nodes in Sect. 3.3;
5.   Let V_1={x}; V_2={y};
6.   Record one-to-one mapping $f:$ $x \mapsto y$;   /* i.e., $y = f(x)$ */
7.   Let selected(x)=selected(y)=1;
8.   **while** V_1 and V_2 have unexpanded nodes **do**
9.   Pick the next pair $x \in V_1$ and $y \in V_2$ based on FIFO order for expanding;
10.   **for** each member x_1 with selected(x_1)=0 in the ring owned by x **do**
11.   **for** each member y_1 with selected(y_1)=0 & $y_1 \neq x_1$ in the ring owned by y **do**
12.   **if** $\varepsilon_t(x_1, y_1) < r_t$ and   [$edge(x_1, x')$ exists for any $x' \in V_1$ if and only if
13. $edge(y_1, y')$ exists for $y' = f(x') \in V_2$ & $\varepsilon_s(edge(x_1, x'), edge(y_1, y')) < r_s$]
14.   **then** $V_1 = V_1 \cup \{x_1\}$; $V_2 = V_2 \cup \{y_1\}$; selected(x_1)=selected(y_1)=1;
15.   Record one-to-one mapping $f:$ $x_1 \mapsto y_1$;
16.   Record one-to-one mapping $g:$ $edge(x_1, x') \mapsto edge(y_1, y')$
                       if such edges exist for any $x' \in V_1$ and $y' = f(x') \in V_2$
17.   Break;
18.   **end if**
19.   **end for**
20.   **end for**
21.   **end while**;
22.   Evaluate the resulting pair of similar subquery graphs $< G_1, G_2 >$;
23.   **if** it is worth to accept $< G_1, G_2 >$
24.   **then** Remove any $< G_1', G_2' >$ from S_{hold} that shares node(s) with $< G_1, G_2 >$;
25. $S_{accept} = S_{accept} \cup \{< G_1, G_2 >\}$;
26.   **else if** it is worth to hold $< G_1, G_2 >$
27.   **then** Reset selected(x) = 0 for all x in G_1 or G_2;
28. $S_{hold} = S_{hold} \cup \{< G_1, G_2 >\}$;
29.   **else** Reset selected(x)=0 for all x in G_1 or G_2;
30.   Discard $< G_1, G_2 >$;
31.   **end if**;

32.   **end while**;
33. $S_{accept} = S_{accept} \cup S_{hold}$;
34.   **for** each similar subquery pair $< G_1, G_2 > \in S_{accept}$ **do**
35.   Optimize G_1 and share the execution plan with G_2;
         /* after an appropriate mapping using f and g */
36.   Replace G_1 and G_2 in original G with their (estimated) result tables;
37.   **end for**;
38.   Optimize the modified G to generate an execution plan;
39.   **return** the execution plan for Q, which includes the plan for the modified G
         and the plans for all accepted similar subqueries.

Lines 3 - 32 search for all pairs of similar subquery graphs in query Q. Lines 8 - 21 expand the current pair of similar subquery graphs using the ring network. Lines 22 - 31 determine if we should accept, hold, or reject the pair of identified subquery graphs. Line 33 accepts the remaining pairs of held similar subquery graphs, which are not overlapped with any accepted similar subquery graphs as guaranteed by Line 24. Lines 34 - 38 optimize all similar subquery graphs and the modified final query graph. Line 43 returns the execution plan for the given query.

More details of some steps and the reasons why some decisions in the algorithm were made are discussed in the following subsection.

3.3   Detailed Explanation of the Algorithm

Choosing Starting Nodes
For a given query Q, when we construct its ring network, we also construct a set of similarity starting lists. Each list in the set is for one base table in the query, which has a header containing the base table name R_i and two sublists – one OL_i contains all its instances (nodes) in the query and the other SL_i contains other table instances whose sizes are within error bound r_t with respect to the size of R_i. For example, for the query graph in Fig. 2 (selectivities on the edges are omitted), using error bound parameter $r_t = 0.3$, its similarity starting lists set is shown in Fig. 3.

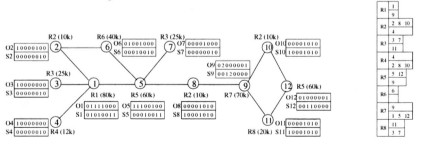

Fig. 2. Example of indicator arrays

Fig. 3. Example of similarity lists set

In principle, any node in OL_i together with another node in OL_i or SL_i can be used as a pair of potential starting (similar) nodes. However, our goal is to find a pair of as large as possible similar subquery graphs. This is because the larger the similar subquery graphs in a pair, the more the optimization work can be shared.

Unfortunately, we cannot predict how the subquery graphs will grow from a pair of starting nodes. Hence, a greedy approach is adopted. We attempt to choose a pair of nodes with the maximum number of adjacent node pairs which satisfy: (1) the adjacent nodes in each pair are unselected and different, and (2) the sizes of tables represented by the adjacent node pair are within the given error bound r_t.

To efficiently search for such a pair of starting nodes from the set of similarity starting lists, we attach two indicator arrays O (occurrence) and S (similarity) to each table instance in the query. The lengths of arrays O and S are the size of T for the given query. Let x be a table instance vertex in the given query graph, and R_i be a base table. Array element $O_x[i]$ indicates how many current adjacent nodes representing base table R_i that x has. Array element $S_x[i]$ indicates how many current adjacent nodes whose table sizes are within the given error tolerance with respect to R_i that x has, excluding $O_x[i]$. Fig. 2 shows examples of indicator arrays O and S.

Let m be the size of set T for query Q. For any pair of potential starting nodes x and y selected from a similarity starting list, we can calculate the following value:

$$matching\_pairs(x, y) = \sum_{i=1}^{m} w(x, y, i), \qquad (1)$$

where $w(x, y, i)$ is defined as follows:

$$w(x, y, i) = \begin{cases} O_x[i] + min\{O_y[i] - O_x[i], S_x[i]\}, & O_x[i] \leq O_y[i], \\ O_y[i] + min\{O_x[i] - O_y[i], S_y[i]\}, & otherwise. \end{cases} \qquad (2)$$

If we first match the adjacent table instances representing the current i-th base table for the starting pair and then match the remaining such table instances for one node (if any) in the pair to the other table instances whose sizes are within the given error bound for the other node, formula (2) gives the total number of such matchings for the current base table. Note that arrays O and S need to be updated every time when matched nodes are removed from consideration based on (2) before the next new base table is considered in (1).

Formula (1) essentially gives the total number of matching pairs of adjacent nodes for the pair of starting nodes x and y in a matching way described above. Our heuristic for choosing a pair of starting nodes is to choose the pair that maximizes the value of formula (1). If there is a tie, we pick up a pair with the smallest difference of table sizes. If there is still a tie, a random pair is chosen.

Searching for Similar Subquery Graphs

In Algorithm 1, we use the breadth-first search strategy to expand a pair of similar subquery graphs G_1 and G_2. That is, all adjacent nodes for the current pair of expanding nodes x and y are considered before a new pair of nodes is selected in the first-in first-out (FIFO) fashion for further expansion. This procedure is repeated until no pair of nodes can be expanded.

We use a nested-loop method to check all the unselected nodes (x_1 and y_1) in the two rings owned by the current pair of expanding nodes (x and y). If the table sizes of this new pair of nodes x_1 and y_1 are within error bound r_t, then we check all nodes that are already in similar subquery pair G_1 and G_2 to see if adding x_1 and y_1 into the current subquery pair will violate the similarity of subqueries or not.

There are two cases in which the similarity of G_1 and G_2 may be violated if we add x_1 and y_1 into them: (i) there exists a pair of $x' \in V_1$ and $y' = f(x') \in V_2$ such that $edge(x_1, x')$ exists, but $edge(y_1, y')$ does not, or vice versa; and (ii) there exists a pair of $x' \in V_1$ and $y' = f(x') \in V_2$ such that there exist both $edge(x_1, x')$ and $edge(y_1, y')$, but $sel(edge(x_1, x'))$ and $sel(edge(y_1, y'))$ are not within error bound r_s.

Selecting Similar Subquery Graphs

If the similar subquery graphs in an identified pair are very small (in terms of the number of nodes in each graph), e.g., containing only 2 nodes, not much optimization work can be shared between them. Furthermore, if we use them in optimization, their nodes cannot participate in other possibly larger similar subquery graphs. In such a case, it is better not to use them (Lines 29-30). If the pair is worth to keep, we remove all nodes in the subquery graph pair from the original query graph by setting their "selected" flag to 1.

If the sizes of similar subquery graphs in a pair are marginal, it is uncertain if it is worth to use it in optimization. In this case, we hold this pair, but allow other similar subquery graphs to use their nodes. If we can find a pair of larger similar subquery graphs using some of the nodes, we adopt the new similar subqueries and discard the held ones. Otherwise, we will still use the held similar subquery graphs (Line 33).

To determine whether to accept, reject, or hold a pair of similar subquery graphs, we use two threshold values c_1 and c_2, where $c_1 < c_2$. Let n be the number of nodes in a similar subquery graph (note that G_1 and G_2 are of the same size). The following rules are used to decide the fate of a pair of similar subquery graphs: (1) if $n \geq c_2$, then the new pair of similar subquery graphs is accepted; (2) if $c_1 \leq n < c_2$, then we put this pair on hold; and (3) if $n < c_1$, then the new pair is rejected.

Optimizing Query

After all similar subquery pairs are selected, we can apply an optimization algorithm, such as AB or II, to optimize one of the subquery graphs in each pair. As all corresponding relationships of the nodes in each pair of similar subqueries are recorded during searching them, we can map the execution plan for one subquery to the one for its partner. For example, consider a pair of similar subqueries G_1 and G_2 that have the following corresponding relationship for the nodes: $x_1 \leftrightarrow y_1, x_2 \leftrightarrow y_2, x_3 \leftrightarrow y_3$, where x_1, x_2, x_3 are in G_1, and y_1, y_2, y_3 are in G_2. By optimizing G_1, assume that we get such a plan: $((x_1 \bowtie x_2) \bowtie x_3)$. The mapped plan for G_2 is $((y_1 \bowtie y_2) \bowtie y_3)$.

By replacing all accepted similar subqueries with their result tables in the original query graph, we reduce the number of nodes in it. Since the complexities of the similar subqueries and the modified final query are less than that of the original query, many existing query optimization techniques (such as AB and II) usually perform well for them. If a similar subquery or the modified final query is sufficiently small (e.g., less than a chosen small constant), a dynamic-programming-based optimization technique could also be used to find a truly optimal plan for it.

It is not difficult to see that the time complexity of the algorithm is $O(max\{n^4, T(n)\})$, where n is the number of tables instances (vertices) in the query graph for input query Q, and $T(n)$ is the complexity of the optimization technique used to optimize the similar subqueries and the modified final query. As mentioned before, unless n is less than a small constant, we employ a polynomial-time technique such as AB or II with our algorithm. Therefore, our technique is of polynomial time complexity.

4   Experiments

As mentioned above, our technique is an efficient polynomial-time technique suitable for optimizing complex queries. Although our technique may not be more efficient than a randomization method or a heuristic-based technique in the worst case, it is expected that our technique usually generates a better execution plan for a complex query since it takes some complex query characteristics into account. To examine the quality of the execution plans generated by our technique, we have conducted some experiments.

In the experiments, we chose to compare our technique with the most promising randomization technique, i.e., the AB algorithm, for optimizing complex queries. To make a fair comparison, we employ the same AB algorithm with our technique for optimizing similar subqueries and the modified final query (i.e., Lines 35 and 38 in Algorithm 1). It is assumed that the nested-loop join method is used to perform joins in a query for all the techniques.

The experiments were conducted on a SUN UltraSparc 2 workstation running Sun OS 5.1. All techniques were implemented in C. Test queries and their operand tables in the experiments were randomly generated.

Let n be the number of nodes in a query graph. In the experiments, the following threshold values were used to accept, hold, or reject a pair of identified similar subquery graphs: (1) If $n < 25$, we set $c_1 = c_2 = 3$. That is, similar subquery graphs with $>= 3$ nodes are accepted; otherwise, they are rejected. (2) If $n >= 25$, we set $c_1 = 3$ and $c_2 = 4$. That is, similar subquery graphs with $>= 4$ nodes are accepted; similar subquery graphs with < 3 nodes are rejected; and similar subquery graphs with 3 nodes are put on the hold list.

We focused on comparing the I/O costs (i.e., the number of I/O's) when queries were performed by using the execution plans generated from different techniques. Table 1 shows such a comparison for a set of randomly-generated

Table 1. Comparison of I/O costs for execution plans generated by two techniques

Q#	# of table instances in Q	I/O# by AB algo	I/O# by similarity tech	improve %
1	29	0.1161e+37	0.4730e+36	59.3%
2	21	0.7514e+25	0.3615e+25	51.9%
3	28	0.9714e+38	0.2313e+38	76.2%
4	34	0.8102e+42	0.7046e+41	91.3%
5	24	0.1649e+30	0.5320e+29	67.7%
6	26	0.1107e+31	0.6304e+30	43.1%
7	15	0.1308e+18	0.2218e+17	83.0%
8	23	0.5953e+27	0.1726e+27	71.0%
9	37	0.8535e+47	0.6774e+46	92.1%
10	14	0.7197e+17	0.1089e+17	84.9%

test queries. The error bounds used for the similarity-based technique in the experiments are $r_s = r_t = 0.3$.

From the experimental results, we can see that the performance of our similarity-based technique is better than that of the AB algorithm. In fact, it reduces the query costs (on average) by 72.1%. Although AB can improve its results by taking longer time to try more random plans, our experiments showed that with the same number of tries our technique is always superior to the AB algorithm. This observation verifies that making use of the characteristics of a complex query can improve the quality of its execution plan.

To examine the effect of error bounds on the performance of our technique, we conducted an experiment, in which a typical test query (i.e., query # 9 in Table 1) was used, and the error bounds r_t and r_s were changed from 0.1 to 1. The result is shown in Fig. 4. From the figure, we can get the following

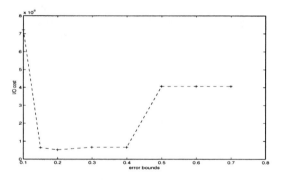

Fig. 4. Effect of changing error bounds on I/O costs

observations: (1) very small error bounds cannot yield good performance, since the smaller the error bounds, the smaller the similar subqueries; (2) moderate error bounds (0.15 ∼ 0.40) yield the best performance, since similar subqueries with reasonable sizes can be found; and (3) large error bounds lead to poor performance, since subqueries are less similar in such cases, which makes that sharing execution plans between them may not be appropriate; and (4) when the error bounds are very large (close to 1), the performance of the similarity-based technique stays at the same level. The reason for (4) is that similar subqueries must have the same query structure, and the sizes of similar subqueries may reach their maximums when the error bounds are beyond a certain limit.

In summary, the similarity-based technique with moderate error bounds can significantly improve the performance of complex queries.

5   Conclusions

As database technology is applied to more and more application domains, user queries become increasingly complex. Query optimization for such queries becomes very challenging. Existing query optimization techniques either take too much time (e.g., dynamic programming) or yield a poor execution plan (e.g., simple heuristics). Although some randomization techniques (e.g., AB, II, and SA) can deal with this problem to a certain degree, the quality of the execution plan generated for a given query is still unsatisfactory since these techniques do not take the special properties of a complex query into consideration.

In this paper, we propose a new technique for optimizing complex queries by exploiting their similar subqueries. The key idea is to identify pairs (groups) of similar subqueries for a given query, optimize one subquery in each pair, share the optimization result with the other similar subquery, reduce the original query by replacing each similar subquery with its result, and then optimize the modified final query. An efficient technique such as the AB algorithm can be used together with our technique for optimizing identified similar subqueries as well as the modified query. It has been shown that our technique is efficient and can usually generate good execution plans for complex queries since it takes the structural characteristics of a query into account and divides a large query into small parts. Our experimental results demonstrate that the proposed technique is quite promising in optimizing complex queries.

References

1. Bennett, K., Ferris, M.C., Ioannidis, Y. A genetic algorithm for database query optimization. In *Proc. of Int'l Conf. on Genetic Algorithms*, pp. 400–07, 1991.
2. Chaudhuri, S. An overview of query optimization in relational systems. In *Proc. of ACM PODS*, pp. 34–43, 1998.
3. Graefe, G. Query Evaluation Techniques for Large Databases. In *ACM Comp. Surveys*, 25(2) 111–152, 1993.
4. Ibaraki, T., Kameda, T. On the optimal nesting order for computing N-relational joins. In *ACM Trans. on DB Syst.*, 9(3) 482–502, 1984.
5. Ioannidis, Y. E., Wong, E. Query Optimization by Simulated Annealing. In *Proc. of ACM SIGMOD*, pp. 9–22, 1987.
6. Jarke, M., Koch, J. Query Optimization in Database Systems. In *ACM Comp. Surveys*, 16(2) 111–52, 1984.
7. Matysiak, M. Efficient Optimization of Large Join Queries Using Tabu Search. In *Infor. Sci.*, v83, n1–2, 1995.
8. Selinger P. G., *et al.* Access Path Selection in a Relational Database Management System. In *Proc. of ACM SIGMOD*, pp. 23–34, 1979.

9. Swami, A., Iyer, B. R. A polynomial time algorithm for optimizing join queries. In *Proc. of IEEE ICDE*, pp. 345–54, 1993.
10. Swami, A., Gupta, A. Optimization of Large Join Queries. In *Proc. of ACM SIGMOD*, pp. 8–17, 1988.
11. Tao, Y., Zhu, Q., Zuzarte, C. Exploiting Common Subqueries for Complex Query Optimization. In *Proc. of CASCON*, pp. 21–34, 2002.
12. Tao, Y., Zhu, Q., Zuzarte, C. Optimizing Complex Queries by Exploiting Similarities of Subqueries. *Technical Report CIS-TR-0301-03*, CIS Dept, U. of Michigan, Dearborn, MI 48128, USA, March 2003.

Process Data Store: A Real-Time Data Store for Monitoring Business Processes

Josef Schiefer[1], Beate List[2], and Robert M. Bruckner[3]

[1] IBM Watson Research Center
Hawthorne, NY 10532
josef.schiefer@us.ibm.com
[2] Women's Postgraduate College for Internet Technologies
Institute of Software Technology and Interactive Systems
Vienna University of Technology
list@wit.tuwien.ac.at
[3] Institute of Software Technology and Interactive Systems
Vienna University of Technology
bruckner@ifs.tuwien.ac.at

Abstract. With access to real-time information on critical performance indicators of business processes, managers and staff members can play a crucial role in improving the speed and effectiveness of an organization's business operations. While the investments in data warehouse technologies have resulted in considerable information processing efficiencies for the organizations, there is still a significant delay in the time required for mission critical information to be delivered in a form that is usable to managers and staff. In this paper we introduce an architecture for business process monitoring based on a process data store which is a data foundation for operational and tactical decision-making by providing real-time access to critical process performance indicators to improve the speed and effectiveness of workflows. The process data store allows to identify and react to exceptions or unusual events that happened in workflows by sending out notifications or by directly changing the current state of the workflow. Our proposed architecture allows to transform and integrate workflow events with minimal latency providing the data context against which the event data is used or analyzed.

1 Introduction

As businesses are being forced to become much more operationally efficient, enterprises are turning their attention toward implementing solutions for real-time business activity monitoring (BAM) [2]. These initiatives require enterprise data to be captured and analyzed in real-time from a wide variety of enterprise applications, operational data stores (ODS) and data warehouses. While traditional data integration approaches, built on top of core ETL (extraction, transformation, loading) solutions, are well suited for building historical data warehouses for strategic decision support initiatives, they do not go far enough toward handling the challenge of integrating data with minimal latency and implementing a closed loop for business processes.

V. Mařík et al. (Eds.): DEXA 2003, LNCS 2736, pp. 760–770, 2003.
© Springer-Verlag Berlin Heidelberg 2003

Separated from operational systems, data warehouse and business intelligence applications are used for strategic planning and decision-making. As these applications have matured, it has become apparent that the information and analyses they provide are vital to tactical day-to-day decision-making, and many organizations can no longer operate their businesses effectively without them. Consequently, there is a trend toward integrating decision processing into the overall business process. Workflow audit trail information is a good example for this trend because it provides the most value to the users and process analysts if it is embedded into the decision-making processes of workflows and if it is available with minimal delays.

In this paper, we propose a process data store (PDS) which aims to support business processes with a near real-time business intelligence. The main data source is a workflow audit trail that is propagated and transformed with minimal delay into valuable business information. The PDS involves several challenges:

Real-time data propagation. Delays in propagating a workflow audit trail from workflow management systems (WFMSs) to the PDS can significantly decrease the value of the audit trail information for the users. When workflow audit trail information is available in near real-time in the PDS, it gives managers and the operational staff accurate and detailed information about current business situations. In addition, it allows them to identify weaknesses and bottlenecks in the process handling earlier.

Adding business process context. The calculation of workflow metrics often requires additional information from other data sources. For instance, in the case of an order process, the workflow events do not include detailed information about the corresponding orders and customers. Nevertheless, order and customer information might be needed for the calculation of workflow metrics about order transactions. Therefore, during data integration the workflow audit trail has to be merged with additional information from other data sources.

Automated response mechanisms. The monitoring or analysis of workflow audit trails often entails a direct or indirect feedback into WFMSs or operational systems. This response can be done manually or automatically and enhances the operational system with business intelligence. This is usually referred to as closed loop analysis. In the case where an automatic response is required, the ETL process or an active PDS has to evaluate workflow metrics and trigger business operations.

The remainder of this paper is organized as follows. In section 2, we discuss the contribution of this paper and related work. In section 3, we present an architecture for integrating workflow audit trail into a data warehouse environment. In section 4, we discuss the real-time integrating of workflow audit trail information into the PDS. Section 5 discusses in detail the ETL container which is the core component for the integration of workflow events. In section 6, we discuss data management issues of the PDS. Section 7 presents a case study and examples for the PDS. Finally, in section 8 we present our conclusion.

2 Related Work and Contribution

Although monitoring and analysis are considered as important tasks of the workflow management system (e.g. [4]), and the Workflow Management Coalition has already published a standard for workflow logs [9], little work has been done in integrating and analyzing the workflow audit trail information. Some approaches emphasize the need for integrating audit trail into data warehouse systems (e.g. the process data warehouse in [7]), others are limited to a smaller set of workflow history that is managed within a workflow management system. To our knowledge there has been no work that thoroughly discusses an end-to-end solution for propagating, transforming and analyzing large amounts of workflow events in near real-time.

Sayal et al. present in [7] a set of integrated tools that support business and IT users in managing process execution quality. These tools are able to understand and process the workflow audit trail from HP Process Manager (HPPM), and can load them into the process data warehouse using a particular loader component. Sayal et al. provide a high-level architecture and a data model for the process data warehouse, but they do not discuss the problem of integrating and analyzing the workflow audit trail in near real-time. An approach for history management of audit trail data from a distributed workflow system is also discussed in [5]. The paper describes the structure of the history objects determined according to the nature of the data and the processing needs, and the possible query processing strategies on these objects. These strategies show how to write queries for retrieving audit trail information. Unlike our approach, neither the transformation and aggregation of audit trail data, nor the analytical processing of this data is considered.

Geppert and Tombros [3] introduce an approach for the logging and post-mortem analysis of workflow executions that uses active database technology. The post-mortem analysis is accomplished through querying the event history, which is stored in an active database system supporting Event-Condition-Action (ECA) rules. Various types of events (e.g., database transitions, time events, and external signals) in the event history can trigger the evaluation of a condition. If the condition evaluates to true, the action is executed.

Most of the existing WFMSs offer only basic monitoring and analytical capabilities, such as the retrieval of status information about process instances or summary information about cycle times. While this supports basic reporting, it requires considerable configuration effort and assumes the existence of comprehensive knowledge of the users to write reasonable queries. Furthermore, it does not provide active mechanisms for automated intelligent responses of currently running workflows. Our contribution in this paper is the characterization of the PDS, the identification of technologies that can support it, and the composition of these technologies in an overall architecture. We also show examples how the PDS can be applied to a real world scenario.

3   Architectural Overview

The main rationale of a PDS is to provide real-time information about business processes that can be used for monitoring purposes. It is conceptually equivalent to traditional operational data stores (ODSs) with the only difference being that it is used to store process and workflow data. The PDS can be combined with a process warehouse (PWH) [6] which is part of the enterprise data warehouse system and which is used for storing a rich set of historical process control data for the strategic decision support. The combination of the PDS and the PWH forms a process information factory, which is a data foundation for a process-driven decision support system to monitor and improve business processes continuously. It is a global process information repository, which enables process analysts and software agents to conveniently access comprehensive information about business processes very quickly, at different aggregation levels, from different and multidimensional points of view, over a long period of time, using a huge historical data basis prepared for analyzing purposes to effectively support the management of business processes.

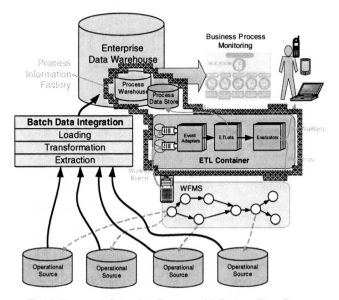

Fig. 1. Process Information Factory with Process Data Store

The PDS is the component which includes very detailed up-to-date process data of currently running processes and also allows real-time access for the tactical and operational decision support. Fig. 1 shows the PDS as part of the process information factory. In our architecture, we are using an ETL container for integrating event data continuously from a workflow management system. Arrows indicate a flow of data or control among these components. The components on the left highlight the extensions to a conventional (passive) data warehouse environment. The ETL container ultimately transforms on-the-fly workflow events into metrics that are stored in the PDS. Since the workflow events are continuously integrated, the data of the PDS can be used to create *automated intelligent responses* (e.g. sending out notifications to business people or triggering business operations) in near real-time. Therefore, the PDS addresses the need for collective, integrated operational, DSS/informational processing. A PDS is a hybrid structure that has equally strong elements of operational processing and DSS processing capabilities. This dual nature of the PDS easily makes it one of the most complex architectural structures in the process information factory.

A PDS is a collection of detailed data that satisfies the collective, integrated, and operational needs of the organization. Generally, these needs arise in the following situations: 1) as integrated operational monitoring and tactical decision support is needed for workflow management systems and also across multiple but related operational systems, 2) as strategic decisions are made using the PWH and action is required. A PDS is 1) subject-oriented, 2) integrated, 3) volatile, 4) current-valued, 5) detailed, and 6) adaptive to workflow changes. The PDS and the PWH are identical when it comes to being *subject oriented* and *integrated*. There are no discernible differences between the two constructs with regard to those characteristics. However, when it comes to transaction support, level of integration with source systems, volatility, currency of information, history and detail, the PDS and the PWH differ significantly.

History of Data. In contrast to a PWH that is rich in history, a PDS generally does not maintain a rich history of process data, because it can be used within WFMSs and operational environments, and often has tight requirements for query response times. Consequently, a PDS is highly volatile in order to reflect the current status and information of business processes.

Data Propagation. For a PDS it is common that data records are updated. A PDS must stay in sync with the WFMSs to be able to respond to active workflows and to consistently operate within its environment. A PDS has predictable arrival rates for workflow event data and includes sync points or checkpoints for the ETL process.

Transaction Support. Data in a PDS is subject to change every time one of its underlying details changes. An advantage of the PDS is that it is integrated and that is can support both decision support and operational transaction processing. A PDS often requires a physical organization which is optimal for updates and flexible processing of data (e.g. "close" to a WFMS) while the PWH is not interwoven with the WFMS or other operational systems and requires a physical organization which is optimal for strategic analyses of processes.

Detailed Data. The PDS contains data that is very detailed, while a PWH contains a lot of summary data. The PDS also stores all workflow events with their attributes. The persisted event data is used to extract valuable business information which is stored in separated tables. Usually, the detailed event data is removed after a workflow instance has completed and all workflow metrics for this workflow instance have been calculated. Data in the PDS can also be summarized, but, because the summarized values are subject to immediate change (PDSs are highly volatile), it has a short effective lifetime.

Adaptive to Workflow Changes. Changes of the workflow or settings in the workflow management settings must not disrupt the interoperability with the PDS. The PDS must be able to adapt to such changes. Therefore, the schema and data propagation components for the PDS must stay in sync with the operational environment. This requires the PDS to be very adaptive to changes of the workflow models and settings in the workflow management system.

4   Real-Time Data Integration

Traditional data warehouse systems are refreshed, at best, on a daily basis and assume that data in the data warehouse can lag at least a day if not a week or a month behind the actual operational data. That was based on the assumption that business decisions do not require up-to-date information but very rich historical data. Existing ETL

(Extraction, Transformation, Loading) tools often rely on this assumption and achieve high efficiency in loading large amounts of data periodically into the data warehouse system. While this approach works well for a wide range of data warehouse applications, the new desire for monitoring information about business processes in real-time requires new mechanisms for propagating and processing data in near real-time. Workflow audit trail is a good example for data that provides the most value to the users and process analysts if it is available with minimal delays.

The processing steps for continuously integrating workflow data are not equivalent to the traditional ETL systems because the underlying assumptions for the data processing and the latency requirements are different. Traditional ETL tools often take for granted that they are operating during a batch window and that they do not affect or disrupt active user sessions. If data is integrated continuously, a permanent stream of data must be integrated into the data warehouse environment while users are using it. The data needs to be trickle-fed continuously from the source systems and therefore differs from traditional batch load data integration. The data integration process has to use regular database transactions (i.e. generating *inserts* and *updates* on-the-fly), because in general database systems do not support block operations on tables while user queries simultaneously access these tables. In addition, the data rate of continuously integrated workflow data is usually low with an emphasis on minimized latency for the integration. In contrast, bulk-loading processes buffer datasets in order to generate larger blocks, and therefore, the average latency for data integration with bulk loading increases. Data integration based on frequent bulk loads can exceed the data latency requirements.

Since data in the PDS changes in near real-time, the data integration process and the PDS themselves can monitor the data and the corresponding metrics, automatically detect conditions that are likely to interest various users, and proactively communicate these conditions to the business users. This is usually referred to as *active* decision-making [8]. The detection of situations and exceptions in the PDS often indicates a condition that requires action. With this fact in mind, users should not only receive alerts, but should also have the ability to respond to an existing business situation. The purpose of alerting could also be merely to ensure that appropriate personnel are notified about an important situation or exception. In this case, the required action in the workflow could be the simple acknowledgement of the alert. Other actions could include forwarding the information to someone else, flagging as unimportant, or increasing the threshold before future alerts are triggered. In choosing these follow-up options, users can help the system learn over time to improve the accuracy of detecting future situations and exceptions.

Workflow rules can also be enabled by the PDS. For example, if an alert is not acted upon within a certain timeframe, it may automatically escalate to another event or change the priority of a workflow instance. Or, if recipients reply that they will take action on an alert, they may need to follow up with more details on the status of the resolution within a certain period of time.

5   Real-Time Data Integration with an ETL Container

We built an ETL container for the integration of workflow events which provides a robust, scalable, and high-performance data staging environment, and which is able to handle a large number of workflow events in near real-time. In [1] we proposed the architecture for an ETL container, which provides services for the execution and monitoring of event processing tasks. The core services are responsible for creating, initializing, executing and destroying the managed components that are used for the event data extraction, data processing and evaluation. In this paper, we want to focus our discussion on integrating data into the PDS and the advantages of using an ETL container for this task. Therefore, we only briefly discuss the components and services provided by the ETL container.

An ETL container is part of a Java application server and manages the lifecycle of ETL components. There are three component types that are managed by the container: 1) event adapters, 2) ETLets, and 3) evaluators. Event adapters are used to extract or receive data from a WFMS (e.g. utilizing a JMS-based interface), and they unify the extracted event data in a standard XML format. ETLets use the extracted XML event data as input and perform the data processing tasks. ETLets also publish workflow metrics that can be evaluated by evaluator components. Figure 2 shows how these ETL components work together.

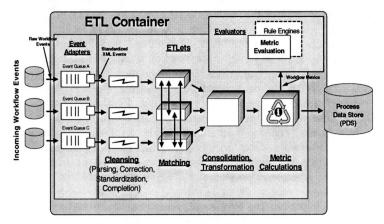

Fig. 2. ETL Container – Architecture [1]

The ETL container handles incoming events with a lightweight Java thread, rather than a heavyweight operating system process. The event processing can be performed without using intermediate storage. When new events arrive, the ETL container decides which ETL components are called, in what sequence these components are executed, and which business metrics are evaluated. The ETL container is a crucial component for feeding data into the PDS and providing active mechanisms for automated responses based on the integrated event data. The main advantages for using the ETL container are summarized as follows:

- The separation of the extraction logic (event adapters), transformation logic (ETLets) and evaluation logic (evaluators) is very critical for the extendibility and configurability of the ETL components. It facilitates the maintenance and synchronization of the PDS with the workflow management system.
- ETLet components are used for the event data processing that can include complex calculations and aggregations of workflow metrics. During the data processing,

ETLets can collect supplementary data from various data sources (e.g. ERP or legacy systems) that can be used for the calculation of workflow metrics.

• The scalability of the ETL container allows the processing of a large number of workflow events concurrently in near real-time.

• Mechanisms for evaluating fresh calculated and changed workflow metrics can be used for sending notifications or triggering business operations with minimal latency. The ability of directly responding to incoming workflow events can be utilized for modifying currently running workflows (e.g. trigger an activity, increase the priority). The PDS contains all details about currently running workflow instances in order to enable automated actions and responses.

6 Data Management

The management of data that is integrated in near real-time raises some challenging data modeling issues. For instance, if the PDS includes aggregated workflow metrics at various levels based on a time dimension, the aggregates may be out of sync with the real-time data. Also, some metrics such as month-to-date and week-to-date metrics are permanently updated during the data integration.

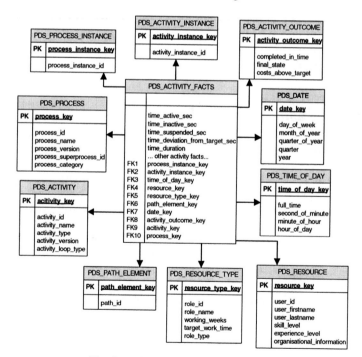

Fig. 3. Activity-Level Facts of the PDS

The process data store includes two types of data: 1) very detailed event data, which is stored as workflow events streams into the PDS via the ETL container, and 2) detailed up-to-date process data at various granularity levels. For storing the workflow events in the PDS, the ETL container uses ETLet components to map all attributes of the workflow events in one or more database tables. Various XML technologies are available to perform this mapping (e.g. DB2 XML Extender, Oracle XML SQL Utility for Java). The detailed event data normally only resides in the PDS as long as it is needed for future metrics calculations. The time to live for event data is usually quite short since it has only limited use as direct input for the data analysis.

A process is a set of one or more linked process activities, which may result in several work items. Processes and activities have hierarchical dependencies and therefore a lot of attributes in common such as workflow participants, but differ in other aspects like instance states. Therefore, the PDS has to maintain separate process, and activity fact tables. Those dimensions, which are needed by all fact tables, enable a drill-across between the fact tables. The fact tables of the PDS look similar to the fact tables of the PWH with the only difference that they capture values of current running process instances. The PDS also uses accumulated fact tables for process instances, whose records are updated for status changes in the business process. Furthermore, the PDS fact tables often include a status dimension which allows to easy filtering or sorting of the process or activity instances by their current state.

Fig. 3 shows a detailed logical data model for a star schema that supports the analysis of activity durations of currently running workflows. The model includes various dimensions that form the context of activity instances. The dimensions are used to show the activity facts from various perspectives. The schema illustrated in Fig. 3 can be used to find out the status of a workflow instance by querying the last performed activity of a workflow instance. Furthermore, analysts can ask questions like what are the workflow instances that completed certain steps in the business process (e.g. an approval step).

7 Case Study and Examples

In this section, an example business process for a mobile phone company is presented. The business process demonstrates how the PDS supports the competitiveness of the entire organization. The business processes to be analyzed is the mobile phone activation process of a telecommunication company. Organizations or private individuals can be customers of the mobile phone activation process. The deliverable of the process is an activated mobile phone connection for a new customer. The mobile phone activation process includes the following three activities: (1) registration, (2) debt and liability examination, and (3) clearing and connecting or refusal. The activity 'registration' includes the registration of the customer's personal data and terms and conditions. The data is submitted to the organization via fax or e-mail. Within the activity 'debt and liability examination', the customer is examined in terms of his/her credit-worthiness. Therefore, the Debt Collection Order System, a system for credit assessment is used. The activity 'clearing and connecting or refusal' includes the clearing of the request and the connection to the mobile phone system or the refusal of the phone service.

The mobile phone activation process is carried out about 1000 times a day and the number of personnel engaged in this process is about 30. The business process is a so-called core business process and generates value to the company. The overall goal of the mobile phone activation process is *low process duration*. The customer is assured that thirty minutes after registration at the latest, the mobile phone connection is established. This is an objective with highest priority. The entire business process is carried out by a WFMS, and workflow events are captured by the PDS. The PDS is used for monitoring the current status of the activation process. If a mobile phone activation process instance is running out of time, an event is sent to the workflow engine and the priority of the process instance is increased. As a result, the process instance has a higher priority and it is therefore moved to the top of the process performer's worklist, ready for processing in time. Further, the process owner of the business process is also notified. Due to an unexpected peak, additional process performers might be required.

As demonstrated, the PDSs main area of application is a highly competitive and fast-paced market with low margins like the Telecom or the Grocery sector. The PDS approach is especially suited for production workflows, because they generate a high business value, have a high degree of repetition, are customer focused and often time critical. Very tight task supervision that can be observed, reminds on the era of scientific management methods. The number of measures in the PDS is very low compared with the PWH. Measures are either time or frequency based and have a very low level of granularity as well as a short-term focus. Basically, measures can be characterized as quantitative and unbalanced. However, process cycle times, working times and waiting times are not sufficient key figures to assure long-term process quality. But, nevertheless they can be described as the most important performance drivers, which support long-term performance results. The analysis of these short-term performance drivers are the main objectives of the PDS.

8   Conclusion

A traditional data warehouse focuses on strategic decision support. A well-developed strategy is vital, but its ultimate value to an organization is only as good as its execution. As a result, deployment of data warehouse solutions for *operational* and *tactical* decision-making is becoming an increasingly important use of information assets. In this paper we have discussed the process data store, which is a part of the solution for the challenge of continuously integrating workflow event data and enables access to workflow metrics with minimal latency. A process data store is well integrated with the operational environment for business processes and is a data foundation that supports these processes with near real-time business intelligence.

References

1. Bruckner, R. M., Jeng, J. J., Schiefer, J.: Real-time Workflow Audit Data Integration into Data Warehouse System. ECIS, Naples, 2003.
2. Dresner, H.: Business Activity Monitoring: New Age BI?, Gartner Research LE-15-8377, April 2002.
3. Geppert, A., Tombros, D.: Logging and Post-Mortem Analysis of Workflow Executions based on Event Histories. Proc. 3rd Intl. Conf. on Rules in Database Systems (RIDS), Springer LNCS 1312, pp. 67–82, Skövde, Sweden, June 1997.

4. Jablonski, S., Bussler, C.: Workflow Management. Modeling Concepts, Architecture, and Implementation. Thomson Computer Press, London, 1996.
5. Koksal, P., Alpinar, S. N., Dogac, A.: Workflow History Management. ACM SIGMOD Record Vol. 27(1), pp. 67–75, 1998.
6. List, B., et al., The Process Warehouse – A Data Warehouse Approach for Business Process Management, MiCT 1999, Copenhagen, Denmark, 1999.
7. Sayal, M., Casati, F., Dayal, U., Shan M.: Business Process Cockpit. Proc. of VLDB 2002, Peking, 2002.
8. Thalhammer, T., Schrefl. M.: Realizing Active Data Warehouses with Off-the-shelf Database Technology. In Software - Practice and Experience, Vol. 32(12), pp. 1193–1222, 2002.
9. Workflow Management Coalition Audit Data Specification, Document Number WFMC-TC-1015, 1998.

Integrated Workflow Planning and Coordination

Hilmar Schuschel and Mathias Weske

Hasso-Plattner-Institute for Software Systems Engineering,
Prof.-Dr.-Helmert-Straße 2-3,
14482 Potsdam, Germany,
{Hilmar.Schuschel,Mathias.Weske}@hpi.uni-potsdam.de

Abstract. Two major tasks in process management are the planning of a process and the coordination of its execution. Workflow management systems support and automate the coordination of a process, but planning the process remains a manual task. This paper argues that planning and coordination are closely interrelated and therefore restricting the attention to the automation of coordination can lead to problems concerning consistency and performance. A concept is presented to avoid these problems by adding automated planning. It is shown how planning algorithms from Artificial Intelligence can be combined with workflow management concepts to build an integrated workflow planning and coordination system. Advantages, limitations and areas of application of this approach are discussed.

1   Introduction

Competition in dynamic markets forces organizations to take advantage of information technology to improve their business. A crucial point for the competitiveness of organizations is the performance of their processes [7,18]. Two major tasks in process management are the planning of a process and the coordination of its execution. Workflow management systems [6,9,11] support and automate the coordination of a process, but planning the process remains a manual task. This paper argues that planning and coordination are closely interrelated and therefore concentrating on the automation of coordination and disregarding planning aspects can lead to problems concerning consistency [14, 16,19] and performance. In this paper, a concept is presented to avoid these problems by adding automated planning and building an integrated workflow planning and coordination system.

A *process* is a defined set of partially ordered steps intended to reach a goal [4]. It is the means to change a given situation in order to fulfill a company's goal. The information about this situation including all relevant documents is called a *case*. Examples of cases are an incoming purchase order that has to be handled or a sick patient who has to be cured. From an organizational point of view, the life cycle of a process includes the phases planning and coordination. *Planning* is the development of a description called a *process definition* of what has to be done in which order to reach a particular goal. The subsequent phase

V. Mařík et al. (Eds.): DEXA 2003, LNCS 2736, pp. 771–781, 2003.

is *coordination*, which is the organizational task to schedule the work in accordance to the process definition. Workflow management systems take a process definition as input and use it to support and automate coordination. In contrast, there is rarely any automated planning of business processes. Planning and supplying the process definition to the workflow management system has to be done manually. Manual planning is a time intensive work of specialists and thus a costly task. For this reason, it is not economically advantageous to plan an individual process definition for every case. Instead, similar cases are grouped together and planned conjointly. For example, there is only one generic process definition used for all incoming purchase orders. Finding a process definition that copes with all possible variants of purchase orders becomes more difficult the more the structure of the cases varies. Normally one process definition is used to coordinate a process, but if something unanticipated occurs threatening the achievement of the goal, it becomes necessary to react by changing the process definition. This *replanning* has to be done manually and, thus, delays execution. Afterwards the workflow management system has to adapt its coordination to the changed process definition. This change of process definition at run time has already been investigated [3,16,8,19]. It proves to be a difficult task for the workflow management system to assure consistency, because it does not have all the required information on the dependencies between process steps.

This paper describes how these problems can be avoided by an integrated planning and coordination system. Since automated planning is done without human effort, it changes the possibilities to organize planning and coordination. Instead of planning just one process definition for a group of similar cases, automated planning allows to individually plan every case. This can result in an optimized process definition taking into account all the specific properties of the case. This capability can realize a competitive advantage, since individual treatment of cases and thereby of costumers becomes increasingly important [7]. Furthermore, an integrated planning and coordination system can automatically trigger and perform replanning if necessary. Thus, a delay of the process execution can be avoided. If a process definition has to be changed at runtime, consistency can be assured, because all necessary information on the dependencies between the process steps is available for the planning system. To automate planning, algorithms are needed that take case and goal as input and deliver an appropriate process definition. Such planning algorithms exist in Artificial Intelligence (AI) [5]. This paper describes how these planning algorithms can be combined with workflow management concepts, to build an integrated workflow planning and coordination system. In Section 2 the relevant foundations on AI planning algorithms and workflow management concepts are introduced. Section 3 describes the functional integration and behavior of the overall system and deduces the advantages and limitations of this approach. Finally, in Section 4, related work, areas of application, and unsolved problems are discussed.

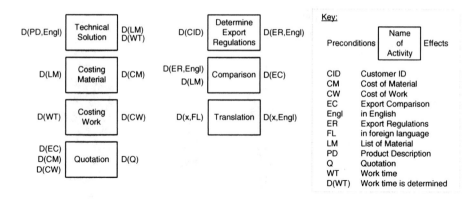

Fig. 1. Activities with Preconditions and Effects

2 Preliminaries

The integrated planning and coordination system presented in this paper is based on the planner and the coordinator as the two main sub-systems. On planning and coordination there has already been done a lot of research in the areas of AI planning algorithms and workflow management systems respectively. This section presents the concepts from both research areas that are important for an integration. Common concepts of both areas are described using one continuous terminology, instead of applying the area specific terminology at each case. The example introduced in this section will be used throughout the paper to illustrate the integration to an overall system.

2.1 Planning Algorithms

Planning algorithms [5,12] take a description of the current state of a case, a goal and a set of activities as input. The *goal* constitutes the wanted state of the case. The means to transform the case from its actual state to the goal are the activities. An *activity* is a piece of work that forms one logical step within a process. The conditions under which an activity can be executed are called *preconditions* and its impacts on the state of the case are called *effects*. *Planning* is defined as a search problem, which is to find an partially ordered set of activities that when executed transforms the case from its current state to the goal. The description of this set of activities and their ordering – the process definition – is the output of the planning algorithm.

To illustrate the basic procedure of a planning algorithm and the relationship between its input and output, the planning of a simplified process in a company that manufactures individual products for international customers is presented. The process is the handling of a request for quotation. Thereby, a customer describes a desired product and asks the company to propose a price. To model the input of the planning algorithm a formal description of the current state of the case, the goal and the activities is needed. The initial state of the case and the goal are described using a set of ground clauses in first order logic [5]. The initial state of the case is that the customers identity (CID) and a product description (PD) in English are determined (D). The terms D(CID) and D(PD, Engl) formally describe this state. The goal D(Q) is the determination of the quotation (Q) for the customer. The available activities with their preconditions and effects can be found in Fig. 1. The activities are depicted by rectangles. The clauses on the left hand side of the activities are their preconditions and the clauses on the right hand side are their effects. *Technical Solution* can only be executed if a product description in English is available. As the effect of this activity a list of material and the expected time to build the product are determined. Based on this information *Costing Material* and *Costing Work* can determine the original costs for the manufacturing. *Determine Export Regulations* determines the export regulations for the country of the customer. *Comparison* checks if material needed for the manufacturing of the product breaches the export regulations. *Quotation* determines the price and the delivery terms of the product. *Translation* takes any document – indicated by the variable x – in a foreign language as input and delivers a translation of that document into English. To complete the input of a planning algorithm, two extra activities are introduced: an activity *Start* that has no preconditions and whose effect is the initial state of the case and an activity *Finish* that has the goal as a precondition and no effects. The task of a planning algorithm is to find a process definition that allows to reach the goal. A solution is depicted in Fig. 2. The activities are partially ordered in a way that the effects of preceding activities satisfy the preconditions of subsequent activities. For example the list of material needed by *Costing Material* is determined in *Technical Solution*. This directed relationship between two activities is called a causal link and is displayed as an arrow. A causal link always implies a temporal ordering. Therefore, *Technical Solution* has to be executed before *Costing Material*. If the coordination of the process follows this ordering, all preconditions are satisfied when their corresponding activities are executed and the goal will be reached. The effects of the activities are not displayed in the process definition, because the causal links combined with the preconditions of the subsequent activities make them a redundant information.

2.2   Workflow Management

The purpose of workflow management systems [6,9,11,17] is to support and automate the coordination of business processes. Coordination means that pieces of work have to be passed to the right participant at the right time with the support of the right tool. A central property of a workflow management system is that this functionality is not hard coded for a specific process, but implemented in a way that the system can take any process definition as input. For a workflow management system the relationship between effects and preconditions as the causal origin of the ordering of the activities is not relevant. Therefore, a process definition that a workflow management system takes as an input only contains

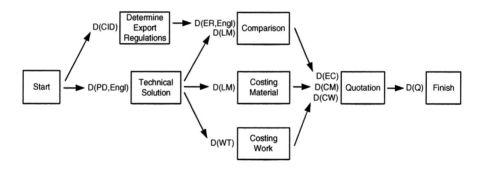

Fig. 2. Process Definition: Request for Quotation

ordering constrains instead of causal links. As a causal link always implies an ordering constraint, a corresponding process definition can be derived from the process definition in Fig. 2 by omitting the effects of the activities and changing the semantics of the arrows from causal links to ordering constraints. Next to the process definition the workflow management system needs information on the potential participants of the process and the available tools.

The execution of a process starts with the activities in the process definition that have no predecessors. In the process definition in Fig. 2 the activities *Technical Solution* and *Determine Export Regulations* are scheduled first. When an activity is executed the workflow management systems automatically starts the appropriate tool with the data that has to be processed in this activity. After the execution of an activity its subsequent activities are started. This iterates until all activities are executed and the process is completed. An execution is *consistent*, if all preconditions of each activity are satisfied when it is executed and the execution leads to the achievement of the goal. To guarantee consistency, an appropriate process definition has to be planned and the activities have to be scheduled accordingly. Planning takes the dependencies between the activities and their contribution to the achievement of the goal into account. The workflow management system maintains consistency by following the ordering in the process definition when scheduling the activities.

3   Integration of Planning and Coordination

In this section a conceptual framework for an integrated planning and coordination system is outlined. Then the resulting ability to plan case-individual process definitions is presented. Finally the framework will be enhanced by the factor of uncertainty to make it more realistic and to show the potential of the integrated approach in this concern.

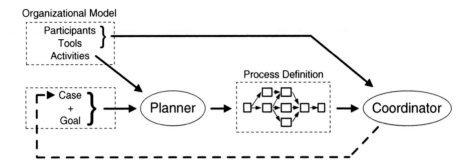

Fig. 3. Integrated Planner and Coordinator

3.1   Framework

The two central sub-systems of the framework are the planner and the coordinator. For each case the planner generates a process definition, that is used by the coordinator to schedule the work steps. In the following the basic functional and behavioral aspects of the interaction of these components are described. Fig. 3 gives an overview of the interrelation of input and output between planner and coordinator. The basis for the overall system is the formal description of the activities, the participants and the tools. They describe the means of the company to process individual cases. To handle a case it has to be associated with a goal. The planner takes a case, the associated goal and the activities as input and generates a process definition as output. The process definition combined with information about participants and tools builds the input of the coordinator. This allows the coordinator to schedule the execution of the activities in accordance to the process definition using the company's resources until the goal is reached. The dashed arrow from the coordinator to the case depicts the effects of the activities on the case, which are scheduled by the coordinator.

To illustrate the behavior of the overall system the example of a request for quotation is carried on. Before cases can be handled, the organization has to be modeled by defining activities, tools, and participants. The activities shown in Fig. 1 are a subset of a company's set of activities. They have in common that they are usually needed to handle a request for quotation, but they represent self-contained business rules that can be used to handle all kinds of cases. For example the activities *Determine Export Regulations* or *Comparison* can be part of every process dealing with export. After the organizational model is defined, the system is ready to process individual cases. In our example the trigger for processing is a request for quotation arriving in the company. The participant who handles the incoming request has to build a corresponding case by defining its initial state and assigning a goal. This means he has to enter the customers identity and the product description into the system. Then he assigns the goal of determining the quotation to the case. When this initial work is done the planner is triggered to find a process definition to handle this case. The planner delivers the process definition shown in Fig. 2 and passes it on to the coordinator. The coordinator starts the execution of the process by enabling the activities *Technical Solution* and *Determine Export Regulations*.

3.2   Individual Planning

An important feature of the integrated planning and coordination system is that each case is planned individually. Using a classical workflow management system, the participant who handles an incoming request has to assign a predefined process definition matching more or less the requirements of the case. With integrated planning, for each case an individual process definition is generated, taking into account all particularities of the case. For example, a customer wants to buy only the necessary material and to assemble the product on his own. In this case no work costs have to be calculated. This can be easily taken into account when defining the initial state of the case by setting the work costs as already determined. As a result the planner delivers a process definition without the activity *Costing Work*, because its effect D(CW) is already set and thus this precondition of *Quotation* is already satisfied. Another example for an individual customization of the process definition is the handling of a product description written in a foreign language (FL). Thereby, the initial state is formally described by D(CID) and D(PD,FL). To reach the goal starting from this initial state the activity *Translation*, shown in Fig. 1, is needed. When generating the process definition the planner inserts this activity between *Start* and *Technical Solution*. In this way the precondition of *Technical Solution* that the product description is in English, will be satisfied.

Using a classical workflow management system only predefined process definitions are available. Thereby, particularities of cases have to be taken into account by anticipating possible variants of cases and modelling alternative execution paths. Often this can not be done completely because not all possible variants are known when the process definition is planned. A conceptual problem lies in the fact that the process definition has to be planned before the cases are known. An integrated planning and coordination system avoids this problem, by planning after the state of the case is known. No predefined process definitions exist. They are planned when they are needed to handle a given case. Therefore, all particularities of a case can be considered and no unnecessary alternatives have to be defined. Thus, the resulting process definitions are only as complex as a given case requires and potentially more concise.

3.3   Automated Replanning

The interaction between planner and coordinator becomes more interlaced if the aspect of uncertainty is taken into account. Until now it was assumed that the planner always had full knowledge about the effects the activities will have. To be more realistic it is necessary to deal with partial knowledge in this concern. Modeling an activity, effects are assigned that are anticipated from the execution of this activity. For example, the anticipated effects of *Technical Solution* are the determination of the list of material and the work time. But it is possible that the activity has other, unanticipated effects. For example, the participant executing *Technical Solution* remembers that recently a technical solution for a similar product was determined. Therefore, the old solution can be reused, i.e. the list of material and the work time. Furthermore, even the cost for material and work of the old case can be adopted. Thus, *Technical Solution* has the two additional effects D(CM) and D(CW), which makes executing the activities *Costing Material* and *Costing Work* redundant.

In general, the coordinator has to compare the actual effects with the effects described in the activity's definition. If they differ, the current process definition becomes invalid, because it was planned based on wrong assumptions concerning the effects of activities. For this reason the coordinator has to trigger a replanning, which is the development of a new process definition based on the current state of the case. This implies considering the previously unanticipated effects. In the example the new process definition misses the activities *Costing Material* and *Costing Work*. The coordinator has to adopt the new process definition by leaving out these activities. The alternating phases of planning and coordination are iterated whenever an unanticipated effect occurs. In contrast to the example above, activities can also have unanticipated effects that endanger the achievement of the goal. For example, the participant executing *Determine Export Regulations* is unable to find an English version of the export regulations, i.e. the effect of the activity is D(ER,FL) instead of D(ER,Engl). *Compare Material* can not be executed because its preconditions are not satisfied. This problem can also be solved by triggering replanning, which delivers a new process definition with *Translate Document* as predecessor of *Compare Material*. Next to unanticipated effects, there can be other reasons for replanning. For instance unavailable activities, a change in the preconditions of an activity, or a change of the goal. All of these possibilities can be handled by triggering replanning.

A prerequisite to allow replanning when using a workflow management system is the support of dynamic change [3,16,8,14,19]. This means the ability to adopt a new process definition during process execution. Nevertheless, replanning has to be done manually. While the initial process definition usually is developed, checked and optimized by specialists, who spend a lot of time and effort on this task, replanning often has to be done in an ad-hoc manner and is time critical. This is especially problematic, if temporarily no specialist is available. Hence, an integrated planning system helps to save time and costs. A more conceptual problem when using a workflow management system, is assuring consistent execution when replanning is necessary. Without replanning one process definition is valid from the beginning of the process until the goal is reached and the workflow management system can maintain consistency by scheduling the activities in accordance to the process definition as described in Subsection 2.2. This becomes more complex if replanning is necessary, because the coordinator has to switch from one process definition to another. A classical workflow management system knows nothing about the dependencies causing the ordering of the activities. Thus, its ability to check the consistency, when adopting a new process definition is limited. The integration of a planner solves this problem. The planner always has the necessary information to guarantee consistency when replanning, because it takes the current state of the case and thereby the effects of already executed activities into account.

4 Discussion

Only recently there has been interest in the application of AI techniques to workflow management. PLMFlow [20] avoids the use of predefined process definitions in order to be independent from the availability of specific activities. Instead, this approach combines activities by considering sets of possible predecessor and successor activities. A goal driven backward chaining algorithm is used to determine process definitions, but the state of the case is not taken into consideration. In [13] the application of contingent planners to existing workflow management systems is discussed. Oz Collaborative Workflow Environment [1] stems from the automation of building software products. Dependencies between software components are mapped into preconditions and effects.

In this paper we outlined a framework for an integrated planning and coordination system, which shows how AI planning algorithms and workflow management concepts can be combined to improve the support of business processes. The integration facilitates individual planning of cases and improves the handling of uncertainty by supporting automated and consistent replanning. A limitation of this approach is that automated replanning only works if a new process definition can be found. In contrast there can be situations in which the available set of activities proves to be insufficient to reach the goal. In such cases user intervention is still necessary to define missing activities or to declare the case as unsolvable. Areas of application for the presented approach are indicated by strong varying case structures and a high amount of uncertainty concerning the effects of activities. Especially if replanning is time crucial or has to be done without human interaction, the integration of automated planning can be beneficial. However, if process definitions seldom change and cases are very uniformly structured, the presented approach offers few additional value. But with indications given, integration of automated planning seems to have the potential to establish new areas of application for workflow management systems.

Future work includes the choice and adaptation of appropriate AI planning algorithms. One aspect is that alternatives are a typical element of organizational processes. As shown in Section 3.2, individual planning avoids alternative branches that result from uncertainty about the initial state of a case. To also handle uncertainty about the effects of activities, a conditional planner that is able to generate and join alternative branches seems appropriate. C-BURIDAN [2] for instance is a planner based on BURIDAN [10] and CNLP [15] that satisfies this requirement and has to be checked for its suitability.

References

1. I. Z. Ben-Shaul, G. T. Heineman, S. S. Popovich, P. D. Skopp, A. Z. Tong, and G. Valetto. Integrating groupware and process technologies in the Oz Environment. In *9th International Software Process Workshop: The Role of Humans in the Process*, pages 114–116, Airlie VA, 1994. IEEE Computer Society Press.
2. D. Draper, S. Hanks, and D. Weld. Probabilistic planning with information gathering and contingent execution. In K. Hammond, editor, *Proceedings of the Second International Conference on AI Planning Systems*, pages 31–36, Menlo Park, California, 1994. American Association for Artificial Intelligence.
3. C. Ellis, K. Keddara, and G. Rozenberg. Dynamic change within workflow systems. In *Proceedings of conference on Organizational computing systems*, pages 10–21. ACM Press, 1995.
4. P. H. Feiler and W. S. Humphrey. Software process development and enactment: Concepts and definitions. In *Proceedings of the Second International Conference on Software Process*, pages 28–40. IEEE CS Press, 1993.
5. R. E. Fikes and N. Nilsson. Strips: A new approach to the application of theorem proving to problem solving. *Artificial Intelligence*, 2:189–208, 1971.
6. D. Georgakopoulos, M. F. Hornick, and A. P. Sheth. An overview of workflow management: From process modeling to workflow automation infrastructure. *Distributed and Parallel Databases*, 3(2):119–153, 1995.
7. M. Hammer and J. Champy. *Reengineering the corporation*. Harper Collins Publishing, New York, 1993.
8. S. Horn and S. Jablonski. An approach to dynamic instance adaption in workflow management applications. In *Conference on Computer Supported Cooperative Work (CSCW)*, 1998.
9. S. Jablonski and C. Bussler. *Workflow Management: Modeling Concepts, Architecture, and Implementation*. International Thomson Computer Press, 1996.
10. N. Kushmerick, S. Hanks, and D. S. Weld. An algorithm for probabilistic planning. *Artificial Intelligence*, 76(1–2):239–286, 1995.
11. F. Leymann and D. Roller. *Production workflow: concepts and techniques*. Prentice Hall, 2000.
12. D. McAllester and D. Rosenblitt. Systematic nonlinear planning. In *Proceedings of the Ninth National Conference on Artificial Intelligence (AAAI-91)*, volume 2, pages 634–639, Anaheim, California, USA, 1991. AAAI Press/MIT Press.
13. MD R-Moreno, D. Borrajo, and D. Meziat. Proces modelling and AI planning techniques: A new apporach. In *Proceedings of the 2nd International Workshop on Information Integration and Web-based Applications Services*, 2000.
14. G. J. Nutt. The evolution towards flexible workflow systems. *Distributed Systems Engineering*, 3:276–294, Dec 1996.
15. M. Peot and D. Smith. Conditional nonlinear planning. In *Proceedings of the First International Conference on AI Planning Systems*, pages 189–197. Morgan Kaufmann, 1992.
16. M. Reichert and P. Dadam. ADEPT flex-supporting dynamic changes of workflows without losing control. *Journal of Intelligent Information Systems*, 10(2):93–129, 1998.
17. A. P. Sheth, D. Georgakopoulos, S. Joosten, M. Rusinkiewicz, W. Scacchi, J. C. Wileden, and A. L. Wolf. Report from the NSF workshop on workflow and process automation in information systems. *SIGMOD Record*, 25(4):55–67, 1996.

18. D. Wastell, P. White, and P. Kawalek. A methodology for business process re-design: experiences and issues. *Journal of Strategic Information Systems*, 3(1):23–40, 1994.
19. M. Weske, J. Hündling, D. Kuropka, and H. Schuschel. Objektorientierter Entwurf eines flexiblen Workflow-Management-Systems. *Informatik Forschung und Entwicklung*, 13(4):179–195, 98. (in German).
20. L. Zeng, D. Flaxer, H. Chang, and J.-J. Jeng. PLMflow – Dynamic business process composition and execution by rule inference. In *TES*, volume 2444 of *LNCS*. Springer, 2002.

Block Optimization in the Teradata RDBMS

Ahmad Ghazal, Ramesh Bhashyam, and Alain Crolotte

NCR Corporation, Teradata Division
100 N. Sepulveda Blvd.
El Segundo, CA, 90245
{ahmad.ghazal,ramesh.bhashyam,alain.crolotte}@ncr.com

Abstract. Block optimization involves several techniques used to avoid optimizing blocks or parts of a query separately. This process may involve integrating views, derived tables, and subqueries with the rest of the query. For those query blocks that cannot be integrated with the rest of the query, the Teradata optimizer tries to simplify and optimize these blocks. Such optimizations can be achieved using the satisfiability test (checking if a set of conditions are satisfiable) and generating transitive closure, which allows pushing constraints into and out of query blocks. Several new Block Optimization techniques, added to the new release of Teradata DBMS (V2R5), are described.

1 Introduction

Block optimization or **BO** is concerned with optimizing queries as whole and not isolating different blocks (pieces) from the rest of the query. Query blocks refer to views, derived tables, subqueries or joins prior to an aggregate. The optimizer chooses not to integrate blocks (opposite of **BO**) because the block is either **complex** or **impossible** to integrate with other pieces of the query. We refer to block integration as **BI**.

The need for more BO techniques for optimization is because of the ever-increasing query complexity. This complexity is due to the generated SQL. Less and less of SQL is directly entered by a user, but rather generated by various front end tools employed by the user to ease the querying and analysis of data. The trend in this generated SQL is towards more complex queries. In many cases, a simpler physical or logical database model offsets the complexity of the query.

There are several **BI** techniques applied in Teradata prior to V2R5. Examples are view integration and subquery un-nesting. In V2R5 a new **BI** technique is applied to aggregate queries where the optimizer attempts to apply aggregations prior to joins, by moving the aggregation fully or partially before a join. This optimization technique is discussed in section 2.1

Another crucial aspect of **BO** is to try to push constraints into and out of query blocks and use integrity constraints (like check and referential constraints) for query optimization. Most of the features in this paper fall into this category. The rest of this paper is organized as follows.

V. Mařík et al. (Eds.): DEXA 2003, LNCS 2736, pp. 782–791, 2003.

Chapter 2 is the main chapter with a description of all the BO features implemented in Teradata V2R5. The partial group by optimization is described in section 2.1 and as mentioned before the main purpose is to try to apply early aggregations prior to joins. Section 2.2 discusses the use of check constraints in query optimization and horizontal partitioning. Check constraints refers to domain constraints on database table columns. Section 2.3 describes the satisfiability test, which deals with checking if a set of SQL conditions is contradictory. Transitive closure solutions are shown in section 2.4. This feature deals with deriving new conditions from the query conditions. These new conditions may provide a better execution plans for the query. A special case of transitive closure where new conditions are derived across query blocks is also explained in this section. Section 2.5 discusses the algorithms used to implement satisfiability and transitive closure. Join elimination based on RI is listed in section 2.6. This feature is based on the fact that under certain conditions a join between a parent & and a child tables could be eliminated. Vertical partitioning of tables is shown as an application of this feature.

Chapter 3 gives some preliminary performance results realized by these features. Finally, chapter 4 is the summary. Note that all the examples in this paper refer to the TPC-H database. The TPC-H [16] database is not described in this paper since it is very well known in the database community. We will use a little bit of variation of the orders table where this table is horizontally partitioned according to the month of the order date. The 12 fragments of the order table are called: orders1, orders2, orders12. A view called ordertbl is defined as a union of the 12 tables.

2 Description of Features

2.1 Partial Group by

DBMS systems typically execute database operations in the same order as is specified in the query. However, relational algebra provides the freedom to execute these operations in any order as long as the mathematical rules of algebra are strictly followed. For example even though a query implicitly specifies a join order by virtue of how it lists the joins most database systems would pick a join order that may be different and that is considered optimal for that DBMS implementation.

Similarly, when a query specifies joins and aggregation, the normal method is to perform the aggregation on the join result. In some cases this operation can be reversed. Such transformation can significantly benefit complex queries with aggregation and joins. There is some work in this area in the literature. [17] is one of the earliest works on pushing group by past a join. It discusses the transformation of "performing group by before joins" and specifies necessary conditions for performing transformation. [4] is another work in this area and discusses how to make the transformations based on cost. It is outside the scope of this paper to reiterate when the transformation is appropriate but intuitively it can be performed if the join does not change the number of rows per group over which aggregation is performed.

When is this transformation beneficial? This transformation is beneficial in cases where the aggregation reduces significantly the number of rows being joined. In general it is not beneficial when the join cardinality is very low and/or the aggregation does not significantly reduce the number of rows being joined. For example a Partial

Group By will not provide any benefit if the aggregation is on a unique column. In fact it will hurt since two aggregations will have to be performed (partial group by and final group by) before the query is completed. Partial Group By is beneficial when the number of groups is small, the number rows per group are large, and the join cardinality is high. When an early aggregation reduces the number of rows it also reduces the preparation cost for the join. This is especially relevant in MPP architectures where preparation might include relocating one or both tables.

The basic goal of the transformation is to reduce the cost of performing two relatively popular operations in complex queries. The idea of performing aggregation before join(s) is to reduce the number of rows being joined. For example, consider two large tables - *sales* with ten billion rows and *inventory* with 100 million rows. In order to determine the cost of sales and inventory by state it may be necessary to join these two tables and aggregate by state. The billion row joins can be replaced with a 50 row join if each of the tables can first be aggregated individually. Please note that the transformation may not always be advantageous, for example when the aggregation does not substantially reduce the input cardinalities to the join. Therefore the Teradata technique is based on a cost model.

We refer to this transformation as "partial group by". The following example illustrates a simple Partial Group By example. One interesting implementation note is about how the early aggregation is performed in Teradata. It can be performed either as an explicit aggregation step or it can be performed as part of the preparatory step to a join such as during the redistribution and sort process. Another technique for performing aggregation has also been added to further improve the efficiency of transformation. Aggregation can also be performed, where appropriate, as part of the sort operation instead of as a separate distinct operation.

Using the TPC-H model consider the following query on partsupp and lineitem tables.

Q: SELECT l_partkey SUM(l_quantity),
*   SUM(ps_supplycost)*
* FROM   partsupp, lineitem*
* WHERE   l_partkey = ps_partkey*
GROUP BY 1;

The normal method would be to redistribute lineitem on the join column (l_partkey), perform the join with partsupp and then perform the aggregations on the result of the join. With a TPC-H scale factor of 1000 or 1TB database this will redistribute 6 billion rows and perform the join with partsupp to produce a 6 billion-row result set on which the specified aggregation operations will be performed.

With "partial early group by" this same query will be performed as follows. For purposes of explanation views are used to denote the partial results with aggregation even though Teradata does not implement those using views.

CREATE VIEW S1
* (ps_partkey, sumsupcost, count1) AS*
SELECT ps_partkey, SUM (ps_supplycost),
*   count(*)*
FROM   partsupp
GROUP BY 1;

CREATE VIEW S2
  (l_partkey, sumlqty, count2) AS
SELECT l_partkey, SUM (l_quantity),
    count(*)
FROM   lineitem
GROUP BY 1;

*Q': SELECT l_partkey, sumlqty*count1,*
     *sumsupcost*count2*
FROM   S1, S2
WHERE   l_partkey = ps_partkey;

Views S1 and S2 will be materialized first into a spool. The materialized spools S1 and S2 will be joined together, as shown in Q', to get the final result set. Note that S1 would be performed using local aggregation. S2 will be performed as part of the redistribute and sort process required for the join.

The partial-group-by transformation will provide significant performance improvement for this query. Without the transformation approximately 85 billion rows will be read and written. This is largely because the join of the 6 billion-row lineitem table is joined to the 800 million-row partsupp table to produce a 24 billion-row join result spool for aggregation. With the transformation the lineitem table is aggregated as part of the sort/redistribution operation to produce a 200M-row spool. The partsupp table is locally aggregated to produce a 200M-row spool also. These are joined to produce a 200M-row result. Overall there is a reduction of about 3X in the number of rows read and written.

2.2   Use of Check Constraints

In general, the optimizer does not use or include check constraints on a table as part of the query plan to access that table. This is because semantically these constraints are redundant while accessing the table since all tuples added to the table was verified to satisfy these constraints. However, in some cases adding these constraints to the query allows the optimizer to find more optimal execution plans. For example assume that a user would like to list all orders made in the first three months of the year. Assuming that the user has access only to the ORDERTBL view (the union of the 12 tables partitioned by month as described see description in chapter 1), the query will be like this:

*Select * from* ORDERTBL where extract(month from o_orderdate) <= 3; For this query, the DBS will access all the tables orders1, … orders12 with the constraint "extract(month,o_orderdate) <= 3" where in reality it only needs to access orders1, orders2 and orders3. The only way the optimizer will filter out the other nine tables is to add the check constraints for every table to the query and to figure out the contradiction between the check constraint and the query constraint. For example, if the check constraint on order4 is added to the corresponding step, the optimizer will have "extract(month, o_orderdate) <= 3 and extract(month, o_orderdate) = 4" which is a contradiction. For this example the optimizer can simply eliminate this step. As noted in this example the optimizer needs to know if a set of constraints is satisfiable. This feature is discussed in the next section.

2.3   Check if a Set of Constraints Is Satisfiable

So far there was no need in the Teradata optimizer to check if a set of constraints are contradictory (the opposite is called satisfiable) regardless of the data. The reason is that it will be very rare for a user to submit a contradictory query that does not return results regardless of the data like a=1 and a=2. The example in the previous section shows the need for such checks. Such problem will be called the satisfiability problem or **SAT**. Any solution to **SAT** will get a set of constraints and either declare FALSE to denote that they are contradictory and TRUE which means for some specific data the set of constraints are satisfiable.

There are two more applications to **SAT** in the usage and maintenance of materialized views or **MAT**. The first problem is to find if a **MAT** requires maintenance for a maintenance operation for one of its base tables (see [1] for detailed analysis of the problem). This problem can be solved by calling SAT for the conjunction of the MAT conditions and the condition applied in the base table maintenance.

The second problem in **MAT** subsystem that uses **SAT** is the problem of checking if a **MAT** covers a query or part of the query. This problem could be solved in general as a number of **SAT** problems. The details of the exact relationship between **SAT** and **MAT** coverage test are outside the scope of this paper and shown in part in [8,15].

2.4   Transitive Closure

Transitive closure or **TC** of a set of constraints S1 denoted by **TC**(S1) is the set of all possible derivable constraints from S1. For example if S1 is (a=b and a=1) then **TC**(S1) will be (b=1). Prior to V2R5, the Teradata optimizer finds transitive closure but limited to the simple cases like the previous example. It only finds **TC**(S1) only if S1 is a conjunction of constraints and it only derives new ones for a sequence of equality constraints.

In many DSS and CRM applications, **TC** is needed for date ranges and IN clause and therefore there is a need to extend the current **TC** implementation to cover these cases. The following example, a subset of TPC-H Q12, illustrates one of these cases:

SELECT l_shipmode,
      SUM (CASE WHEN
          o_orderpriority = '1-URGENT'
      OR o_orderpriority = '2-HIGH'
      THEN 1 ELSE 0 END)
FROM lineitem
WHERE l_commitdate < l_receiptdate
  AND l_shipdate < l_commitdate
  AND l_receiptdate >= '1994-01-01'
  AND l_receiptdate < ('1994-06-06')
GROUP BY l_shipmode;

From the example above one can obtain constraint set S1=(L_SHIPDATE <= L_COMMITDATE-1   and   L_COMMITDATE   <=   L_RECEIPTDATE-1   and L_RECEIPTDATE <= '1994-06-05'). The new set constraints that can be derived from S1 or **TC**(S1) is (L_COMMITDATE <= '1994-06-04' and L_SHIPDATE <= '1994-06-03'). These conditions are useful, if either of the derived conditions have indexes defined on them.

2.5 Two Algorithms for SAT & TC

The problem of **SAT** and **TC** are inherently related. For example, we could figure out that (a=1) and (a=2) are contradictory to TC{(a=1) and (a=2)} = {(1=2)}. Another example, **TC**{(a >= 2 and a <=b and b <= 1} = {b>=2 and a<=1 and 2<=1} which has the contradiction of (2<=1). The two previous examples suggest that **SAT** is actually a by-product of **TC**.

There are many algorithms in the research to solve **TC** and **SAT** [3,5,6,13]. We implemented two separate algorithms for SAT & TC that suits the type of conditions that Teradata users deal with.

The first algorithm is based on the work done by Rosenkrantz and Hunt [13]. This algorithm considers conjunctive conditions, where each condition is of the form (X op Y + C) or (X op C). Both X and Y are integer variables and op ∈ {<,=,>,≥,≤}. We implemented this algorithm with some modification to suit the real domain and include some limited form of ≠.

The second algorithm was designed and implemented in Teradata. It addresses what we consider a more common and practical conditions we have noticed in user's queries. It solves equality conditions between columns, comparisons between a column and a constant, and IN list for a column. The details of the algorithm are beyond the scope of this paper and the conditions are formally shown below:

- *(X=Y)*

- *X IN (value1,value2, …), where all value1, value2, … valuen are constants.*

- *X op Constant, where op ∈ {<,=,>,≥,≤,≠}*

We also applied the two previous algorithms to cross-query transitive closure, i.e. transitive closure between outer and inner query blocks. This allowed pushing conditions into and out of subqueries. The basic approach is to combine the query blocks conditions before computing the transitive closure. The IN and NOT IN clauses are handled as = and ≠. The derived conditions are added appropriately to each block.

2.6 Eliminate Joins Based on Referential Integrity (RI)

Primary key – foreign key relationships between tables are very common in normalized data models and their corresponding physical databases. We will denote these tables as PK-tables and FK-tables. These relationships can be explicitly defined by the user and are called RI constraints.

Eliminating redundant PK-FK joins can reduce query execution cost. [7] is one of the earliest reliable works on join elimination. [2] has detailed analysis on eliminating joins using referential integrity constraints. Also, the concept of join elimination was implemented in IBM DB2 universal database [3].

Redundant joins frequently occur in views, tool generated SQL, and even in user written queries. Views generally join across PK-FK as part of a complex generic data model. The users of the views do not have access to the underlying tables and therefore cannot detect or alter redundant joins. Application tools used to generate SQL queries often have a preset query generation capability that automatically generates redundant PK-FK joins. PK-FK joins can be considered redundant when the query does not reference columns from the PK-table other than PK-columns themselves. Recognizing and eliminating such redundant joins could significantly reduce the query execution time.

The following is an example of RI based joins elimination using the TPC-H [16] data model. Query 3 in the TPC-H benchmark is called the Shipping priority query. It retrieves the shipping priority and potential revenue of the orders having the largest revenue among those that had not been shipped as of a given date in a specific market segment. If the query were changed to require the same information across all market segments, i.e. remove the constraint on c_mktsegment, from the original query then it would look like:

```
Q: SELECT l_orderkey,
          sum(l_extendedprice*
          (1-l_discount)),
          o_orderdate, o_shippriority
FROM      customer, orders, lineitem
WHERE     c_custkey = o_custkey
AND       l_orderkey = o_orderkey
AND       o_orderdate < date '[DATE]'
AND       l_shipdate > date '[DATE]'
GROUP BY  l_orderkey, o_orderdate,
          o_shippriority
ORDER BY 2 desc, o_orderdate;
```

Note that the TPC-H model specifies a PK-FK relationship between the customer and order table on c_custkey and o_custkey. The optimizer would use this information and remove the join with the customer table. The query would become:

```
Q': SELECT l_orderkey,
           sum(l_extendedprice*
           (1-l_discount))
           o_orderdate, o_shippriority
FROM       orders, lineitem
WHERE      l_orderkey = o_orderkey
AND        o_orderdate < date '[DATE]'
AND        l_shipdate > date '[DATE]'
GROUP BY   l_orderkey, o_orderdate,
           o_shippriority
ORDER BY 2 desc, o_orderdate;
```

Another benefit of RI based redundant join elimination is to enable vertical partitioning of tables. Tables with wide rows can be vertically split (partitioned) into two tables one with "frequently accessed" columns and the other with the rest of the "infrequently accessed" columns. In order to insure consistency an RI is specified between the two tables. The choice of which one is a PK-table and which one is a FK-table is arbitrary but it is advisable to have the table with the frequently accessed columns as the FK-table in order to achieve join elimination as explained earlier. To hide the artificial partitioning a view with a PK-FK join that selects all the columns from both tables is defined. When a query is submitted on the view that only references columns from the FK-table the join in the view is obviously redundant and the optimizer eliminates the join. Note that without the intervention of the optimizer the user has no way of removing the join.

As an example, the order table from the TPC-H example [16] can be split into two vertically partitioned tables - one consisting of column o_clerk and o_comment which not only make up the majority of the bytes in a row but are also infrequently accessed and the other consisting of all the other columns which are frequently accessed. This will make the vertical partition table with the frequently accessed columns to be about a fourth of the size of the original table. This reduction will improve the overall IO performance of the system. This efficiency is made possible without any application changes - the application continues to use the view called order table.

When can we consider a FK-PK join as redundant? We currently consider the following conditions to be sufficient:

1. There is an RI defined between the two tables.
2. The query conditions are conjunctive.
3. No columns from the PK-table other than the PK-columns are referenced in the query. That includes the SELECT, WHERE, GROUP BY, HAVING, ORDER BY, etc
4. The PK-columns in the WHERE clause can only appear in PK=FK joins

If the above conditions are met then the PK and PK- join will be removed from the query and all references to the PK columns in the query will be mapped to the corresponding FK columns. Also, "NOT NULL" condition on the FK columns will be added if they are nullable.

Removing a PK-FK join can sometimes be not cost effective. In cases where the PK column is further constrained using a specific value the overall execution plan can be much more efficient. For example in the query mentioned earlier if the user was interested in only one customer then Teradata would pick a nested join with order table instead of a scan of the order table. Our implementation captures such considerations by imposing the restriction mentioned under item 4 when removing a join. Removing this restriction and applying costing to join elimination is considered for future releases.

3   Performance Results

Preliminary tests of the new Teradata software release V2R5 at some beta customer sites show queries where the techniques described in this paper can be applied, run time improvements of 25-50% have been achieved. Also, three TPC-H queries benefited from these features. Table 1 below shows the reduction in execution time for these queries in a recent internal TPC-H test using a 200GB TPC-H database. The machine used was a 4-node 5250 configured with one disk array per node (i.e. two generations old). The results are taken from the power test. The queries were run in single-user mode.

Table 1. Block optimization impact on TPC-H

TPC-H Query	% of execution time reduction
Q10	22%
Q12	40%
Q13	23%

4 Summary

In summary, five block optimization techniques were implemented in Teradata V2R5. These techniques are necessary due to the increased complexity of the queries from SQL generated by front-end tools. In many cases, these techniques are expected to improve the query performance significantly.

References

1. J. A. Blakeley, N. Cobum, and P. A. Larson. Updating derived relations: Detecting/Irrelevant and autonomously computable updates. VLDB 12, pages 457–466, 1986. Kyoto.
2. U. Chakravarthy, J. Grant, and J. Minker. Logic-based approach to semantic query optimization. *ACM TOD, 15(2):162–207, June 1990.*
3. Q. Cheng, J. Gryz, and F. Koo. Implementation of Two Semantic Query Optimization Techniques in DB2 Universal Database. VLDB 25, 1999. Edinburgh.
4. S. Chaudhuri and K. Shim. Including Group By in Query Optimization. VLDB 20 Santiago Chile 1994
5. A. Ghazal and A. Ouksel, Termination of Programs in Constraint Query Languages, 1994 Symposium on Applied Computing, Special Track on Computational Logic, Phoenix, Arizona, March 1994.
6. A. Ghazal and A. Ouksel, Subsumption in Constraint Query Languages Involving Disjunctions of Range Constraints, Fort Lauderdale, Florida, January 1994.
7. J. J. King. Query Optimization by semantic reasoning Dept of Computer Science Stanford University. 1981
8. P. A. Larson and H. Z. Yang. Computing queries from derived relations. VLDB 11, pp. 259–269, 1985.
9. A.Y. Levy, I. Mumick, and Y. Sagiv Query optimization by predicate move-around. In *Proc. of VLDB,* pages 96–108, 1994.
10. I. Mumick and H. Pirahesh. Implementation of magic sets in Starburst. In *Proc. SIGMOD,* 1994.
11. G. Paulley and P. Larson. Exploiting uniqueness in query optimization. In *Proceeding of ICDE,* pages 68–79, 1994.
12. H. Pirahesh, J. M. Hellerstein, and W. Hasan. Extensible/rule based query rewrite optimization in Starburst. In *Proc. SIGMOD,* pages 39–48, 1992.
13. D. Rosenkrantz and H. I. Hunt, Processing conjunctive predicates and queries. VLDB 80, pp 64–72.
14. S.T. Shenoy and Z.M. Ozsoyoglu. Design and implementation of a semantic query optimizer. *IEEE Transactions on Knowledge and Data Engineering,* 1(3): 344–361, September 1989.

15. X. H. Sun, N. Kamel, and L. Ni. Processing implications on queries. IEEE Transactions on Software Engineering, 15(10): 1168–1175, October 1990.
16. Transaction Processing Performance Council, 777 No. First Street, Suite 600, San Jose, CA 95112 6311, www.tpc.org. *TPC Benchmark H*, 1.5.0 edition, 12 July 2002.
17. Weipeng P. Yan and Per-Ake Larson. Performing Group By Before Join. Proceedings of the 10th IEEE International Conference on Data Engineering, p89–100, Houston, TX 1994.

Selecting Topics for Web Resource Discovery: Efficiency Issues in a Database Approach*

Abdullah Al-Hamdani and Gultekin Ozsoyoglu

Electrical Engineering and Computer Science Dept,
Case Western Reserve University,
Cleveland, Ohio 44106
{abd,tekin}@eecs.cwru.edu

Abstract. This paper discusses algorithms for topic selection queries, designed to query a database containing metadata about web information resources. The metadata database contains topics and relationships, called metalinks, about topics. Topics in the database contain associated importance scores.

The topic selection operator TSelection selects, within time T, topics that satisfy a given selection formula and having output importance scores above a given threshold value or in the top-k. The selection formula contains expensive predicates, in the form of user-defined functions.

To minimize the number of expensive predicate evaluations (probes) in the TSelection algorithm, we introduce and evaluate three heuristics. Also, due to the time constraint T, the TSelection algorithm may terminate without locating all output tuples. In order to maximize the number of output tuples found, we introduce and evaluate three heuristics to locate a tuple to evaluate at a given time.

1 Introduction

Search engines such as *Yahoo!* use topics and topic hierarchies, extracted as metadata from the web, in order to allow for keyword-based searches over the entire web. We propose (i) restricting the scope of metadata extraction to specific web information resources such as the ACM Digital Library [1], and (ii) extending the metadata extraction process to include automatic extraction of topics *and* relationships among topics (called *metalinks* in this paper). Such metadata is stored in a database, and employed for ad hoc querying of web information resources [4, 5].

Data Model. To model the metadata extracted from a web information resource, we have recently used [3, 4, 5] a topic maps-based [9] data model with topic entities (a keyword or a phrase) and metalinks. Examples of topics for the DBLP Bibliography [6] and the ACM SIGMOD Anthology [7] are T1: "query optimization" (a "phrase"), T2: "database dependency theory" (a phrase), and T3: "The Interaction between Functional Dependencies and Template Dependencies" (the title of a paper by Sadri and Ullman [8] in ACM SIGMOD Anthology). Topics and metalinks have associated "importance scores", which may be obtained using data mining techniques (e.g.,

---

* This research is supported by the National Science Foundation grants INT-9912229 and DBI-0218061.

V. Mařík et al. (Eds.): DEXA 2003, LNCS 2736, pp. 792–802, 2003.

association rule-based mining), derived by information retrieval techniques (e.g., the vector space model [10] and cosine similarities) [14], or others (e.g., [12]). Each topic has one or more *topic sources*; for example, the pdf file for paper with title T3 in the ACM SIGMOD Anthology constitutes a topic source for both topics T2 and T3. Note that topics and metalinks are metadata, (e.g., information about the web resource) whereas topic sources constitute data. Maintaining topics and metalinks as metadata in a database allows for ad hoc queries to locate relevant topic sources.

Normally, the number of topics satisfying a user request is quite large. Therefore, an algebra-based way of ranking topics and returning only a small number of highly important topics (and their topic sources) is needed. Towards this goal, we have proposed [4] a sideway value algebra (SVA) for object-relational databases. This paper investigates the evaluation of one SVA operator for web computing, namely, the SVA selection operator that implements *topic selection queries*.

Topic Selection (TS) Queries. Given a database of topics, metalinks, and topic source URLs, a TS query takes (i) a single topic relation R with each tuple t containing information about topics and having an importance score $Imp(R(t))$, (ii) a (propositional calculus) selection formula C with predicates on topic similarity, (iii) an output importance score computation function $f_{out}(t)$, (iv) a query stopping condition β in terms of top-k importance-scored output tuples or output tuples whose importance scores are above a given threshold, and (v) a query response time limit T. The TS query returns within time T those tuples t of R satisfying the selection formula C and with output importance scores computed as $f_{out}(t)$ satisfying β.

Example 1. (*TS query*). Consider the web resources DBLP Bibliography and the ACM SIGMOD Anthology, and the associated metadata database at www.DBLPandAnthology.com. Assume that the relation *RelatedToPapers*, extracted from DBLP and Anthology, has the schema *RelatedToPapers*(Pid$_1$, Title$_1$, Abstract$_1$, Pid$_2$, Title$_2$, Abstract$_2$, ...) where the importance score of each *RelatedToPapers* tuple t can be obtained through the function $Imp(RelatedToPapers(t))$. Topics/metalinks/topic source *importance scores* are reals in the range [0,1]. The paper type is a specialization of the topic type, and a paper (instance) is an object/entity with an object-id (i.e., Pid).

A user is interested in selecting, within 2 minutes, the top 10 papers in DBLP and Anthology that are related to the paper [8] by Sadri and Ullman (say, with Pid of p23) with a *RelatedToPapers* importance score of 0.8 or above; and selected papers have either title-similarity of 0.9 or above to the paper p23, or an abstract-similarity to p23 of 0.95 or above. Such a query can be expressed using an SQL-like syntax as:

select * **from** RelatedToPapers RT
where RT.Pid1= "p23" **and** Imp(RT) $\geq$ 0.8
    and (Sim (RT.Title1, RT.Title2)> 0.9 **or** Sim(RT.Abstract1, RT.Abstract2)$\geq$0.95)
propagate importance within selection as min **for** conjunctions **and** avg **for** disjunctions
stop after 10 **most important and within time** 2 min

where Sim() denotes a similarity function. *Propagate importance* clause defines the output tuple importance score computation function f_{out} which, in this case, is defined as

$$f_{out}() \equiv Imp(RT()) * AVG [Sim(RT.Abstract_1, RT.Abstract_2), Sim(RT.Title_1, RT.Title_2)]$$

Issues addressed in this paper. We investigate two query processing issues for TS queries:

(a) *Expensive metalink importance score computation*: Some of the metalink types such as *RelatedTo* are *expensive* [13] in that their importance score computations are time-consuming *executions*. We call such functions *expensive functions,* and any predicate that contains an expensive function an *expensive predicate*. As an example, the importance score of the metalink type *RelatedToPapers,* given papers pid_1 and pid_2, can be computed [14] by the function

$$Imp(RelatedToPapers(pid_1, pid_2)) = w_{Title}* Sim_{Title}(pid_1.title, pid_2.title) + w_{Authors}*$$
$$Sim_{Authors}(pid_1.authors, pid_2.authors) + w_{Abstract}*$$
$$Sim_{Abstract}(pid_1.abstract, pid_2.abstract) + w_{IndexTerms}*$$
$$Sim_{IndexTerms}(pid_1.index\text{-}terms, pid_2.index\text{-}terms) + w_{Body}*$$
$$Sim_{Body}(pid_1.body, pid_2.body) + w_{References}*$$
$$Sim_{References}(pid_1.references, pid_2.references). \tag{1}$$

where $Sim_{Title}(\ )$, $Sim_{Authors}(\ )$, $Sim_{Abstract}(\ )$, $Sim_{IndexTerms}(\ )$, $Sim_{Body}(\ )$, and $Sim_{References}(\ )$ denote similarity functions for pairs of paper titles, authors, abstracts, index terms, paper body, and references, respectively; and w terms constitute weight terms with the constraint

$$w_{Title} + w_{IndexTerms} + w_{Authors} + w_{Body} + w_{References} + w_{Abstract} = 1.$$

We refer to a metalink importance score evaluation as a *probe*. Clearly, a *RelatedToPapers* probe (i.e., the computation of $Imp(RelatedToPapers(pid_1, pid_2))$ in equation (1)) is expensive, and the system must attempt to minimize the number of such probes. We assume that (i) all probes of a given metalink type have the same cost, and (ii) there is a total ordering to the probe costs of different metalink types.

We make the assumption that it is *not* expensive to compute topic importance scores, and topic importance scores are computed a priori (using pre-collected topic source data) and maintained in the metadata database.

(b) *Time Constraints.* TS query computation times can be too high. Therefore, such queries may have a time constraint clause of the form, say, *"Time=2 minutes"*. Time constraints can be transformed into constraints on the number of expensive predicate evaluations (i.e., probes). Time-constrained query evaluation algorithms must be "correct"; i.e., given a top-k query with a time constraint, all output tuples must be in the top-k; and, for a threshold query with a threshold τ and a time constraint, importance scores of output tuples must be greater than τ.

In the ideal case, a TS query evaluation performs *only* the probes needed for the output tuples, i.e., the *positive* probes. In general there will be some probes that will not contribute towards an output tuple, resulting in wasted time. In such cases, there can be multiple goals such as maximizing the number of highest importance-scored output tuples, or maximizing the number of output tuples satisfying an importance score threshold, etc. We present different heuristics and their evaluations for different goals.

Contributions. We discuss TS algorithms for evaluating the SVA Topic Selection operator. The algorithms are pipelined: they continuously generate output, and attempt to maximize the number of positive probes they make. In section 2, we present the top-k and threshold-based TS algorithms. Section 3 briefly presents the experimental evaluations. Section 4 concludes.

2 Top-k and Threshold-Based Topic Selection Algorithms

In this section, we use an operator-based specification of the topic selection query (instead of the SQL-like syntax) as $\sigma^*_{C, f_{out}, \beta, T}(R)$ where each tuple r of the relation R has an input importance score $Imp_{in}(r)$, C is the selection condition with *only* expensive predicates, $f_{out}()$ is the output importance score function, β is the *output threshold* which is either a positive integer k as the *ranking threshold*, a real-valued *importance score threshold* V_t in the range [0, 1], or the two-tuple (k, V_t), and T is the time constraint. The operator σ^* returns, in decreasing order of output importance scores and within time T, either (i) top k f_{out}-ranking output tuples that satisfy the selection condition C (when β is k), or (ii) all tuples of R with an f_{out}-importance score greater than V_t and satisfy the selection condition C (when β is V_t), or (iii) top k f_{out}-ranking output tuples that satisfy the selection condition C and with an f_{out}-importance score greater than V_t (when β is the two-tuple (k, V_t)). When the time constraint T is not sufficient to get the answer, the selection query evaluation becomes a *"best-effort"* evaluation. We assume that the input relation R is sorted in decreasing order by the input importance scores Imp_{in} of its tuples.

Example 2. In the selection query of example 1, after eliminating inexpensive predicates, we have C as C = $Imp(RT) \geq 0.9$ **and** [Sim(RT.Title$_1$, RT.Title$_2$) $\geq$ 0.9 **or** Sim(RT.Abstract$_1$, RT.Abstract$_2$) $\geq$ 0.95)] = $C_1 \cap (C_2 \cup C_3)$ = $(C_1 \cap C_2) \cup (C_1 \cap C_3)$ = term$_1 \cup$ term$_2$.

Using the importance score functions *Min* and *Avg* as specified in the query, we have, for a given tuple r, $Imp(C, r)$ = $AVG(Imp(\text{term}_1, r), Imp(\text{term}_2, r))$ = $AVG(MIN(Imp(C_1, r), Imp(C_2, r)), MIN(Imp(C_1, r), Imp(C_3, r)))$. If a predicate C_i in a given term t is *"false"* (i.e., $Imp(C_i, r)$=0) then term t is "false" (i.e., Imp(t, r)=0). Therefore, we do not need to evaluate the unevaluated predicates in term t.

Note that, in our environment, the expensive predicates are either importance score computation functions (e.g., *Imp(RelatedToPapers())*) or similarity computation predicates (e.g., Sim() > 0.9). Without losing generality, we assume that the selection condition C is in the disjunctive normal form C = $\cup_i$ term$_i$ where term$_i$ = $\cap_j C_j$ and C_j is an atomic expensive predicate. The output importance score $f_{out}(r)$ for a given tuple r is computed as $f_{out}(r)=Imp_{in}(r) * Imp(C,r) = Imp_{in}(r) * g_1(g_2(\text{term}_1,r), g_2(\text{term}_2,r),....)$ where $g_1( )$ and $g_2( )$ are monotone functions that are used to incorporate the effects of the disjunctions and the conjunctions, respectively, on the output importance score computation.

When $g_1( )$ and $g_2( )$ are monotone, the decision that a given tuple is not in the top-k or does not satisfy the threshold value V_t can be derived *without evaluating all of its atomic expensive predicates*. The monotonicity of a given function is defined below.

Definition 1 (*Monotone Function*). A given function g( ) with n parameters is monotone iff it satisfies the following two conditions:

(a)   If $a_i \geq b_i$ for all $1 \leq i \leq n$ then $g(a_1,..,a_n) \geq g(b_1,..,b_n)$, and

(b) $g(a_1,...,a_n)=1.0$ iff $a_i=1.0$ for all $1 \leq i \leq n$.

Some examples of monotone functions are $PRODUCT(a_1, \ldots, a_n) = \Pi_{i=1}^{n} a_i$, $MIN(a_1, \ldots, a_n) = a_i$ where $a_i \leq a_j$ for all $1 \leq j \leq n$, and $AVG(a_1, \ldots, a_n) = (a_1+a_2+...+a_n)/n$. In this paper, we assume that $g_1(\ )$ and $g_2(\ )$ functions are monotone.

2.1   Fixed Order Probe-Optimal Topic Selection Algorithm

Chang and Hwang [2] have proposed the *MPro* algorithm to evaluate the top-k Selection operator with *only* conjunctive expensive predicates using *only* one monotone function $F(x,p_1,p_2,...,p_n)$, where x is a pre-computed inexpensive predicate (i.e., with zero cost) and $p_1,p_2,..,p_n$ are expensive predicates. They have proven that *MPro* algorithm is "probe-optimal" *assuming that* there is a *pre-defined* and *fixed* *evaluation ordering* of the predicates. The problem with the *MPro* algorithm is that usually there is no fixed "optimal" predicate evaluation order, and the best predicate evaluation order dynamically changes with respect to the tuple being evaluated.

In the rest of this section, assuming a fixed pre-defined predicate evaluation ordering, we adapt and extend the minimal probing algorithm *MPro* in order to evaluate the top-k or threshold-based topic selection operator with two evaluation functions g_1 and g_2. Then, in section 2.2, we eliminate the fixed predefined predicate ordering assumption, and revise the algorithms with dynamically chosen predicates to evaluate. First, we define the evaluation cost of a given expensive predicate.

Definition 2 (*Expected Evaluation Cost*). Let $Cost(C_i)$ be the expected evaluation (time) cost of C_i where C_i is a conjunct in a selection formula C, $1 \leq i \leq n$, which is in the disjunctive normal form. Then the *expected evaluation cost* of C is defined as $Cost(C) = \Sigma_{i=1}^{n} Cost(C_i)$.

Assume, at a given time, the predicates C_1 to $C_{current}$, $1 \leq current \leq n$, have been evaluated using *Imp*( ), here referred to as *EvaluatedImp*( ).

Definition 3 (*Unevaluated Predicate Cost*). Let C_1, C_2, C_3, $\ldots$, C_n be the pre-defined evaluation ordering for computing f_{out} for a topic selection operator on relation R, and $Cost(C_i)$ be the expected evaluation cost of a given predicate C_i. The *unevaluated predicate cost* $UCost(r)$ for a given tuple r *after* computing the predicate $C_{current}$ with tuple r in relation R is defined as $UCost(r) = \Sigma_{i=current+1}^{n} Cost(C_i)$.

Definition 4 (*Imp(C_j,r)*). Let C_1, C_2, C_3, $\ldots$, C_n be the pre-defined evaluation ordering for computing f_{out} for a topic selection operator on relation R. The importance score for the jth expensive predicate C_j *after* computing the predicate $C_{current}$ with tuple r in relation R is defined as:

$$Imp(C_j,r) = \begin{cases} EvaluatedImp(C_j,r) & \text{if } j \leq current \\ 1 & \text{otherwise} \end{cases}$$

When j>current, we refer to C_j as an unevaluated expensive predicate; otherwise it is an evaluated expensive predicate.

Definition 5 (*Current Output Importance Score*). Consider a topic selection operator with the selection condition $C = \bigcup_{i=1}^{m} term_i$ and $term_i = \bigcap_j C_j$. The *current output importance score* of a tuple r on a relation R using the topic selection operator after evaluating the expensive predicate $C_{current}$ is

$$Imp_{current}(r) = Imp_{in}(r) * g_1(g_2(term_1,r), g_2(term_2,r), \ldots, g_2(term_m,r)),$$

where $g_1( )$, $g_2( )$ are monotone functions, n is the number of atomic selection predicates, $1 \leq current \leq n$, m is number of terms, $g_2(term_i,r) = g_2(Imp(C_j,r)$, $Imp(C_{j+1},r),\ldots)$, and $Imp(C_j,r)$ is as defined in definition 4.

Proofs of all lemma and theorems are presented in [11].

Lemma 1.   (a) For $1 \leq current < n$, $f_{out}(r) \leq Imp_{current}(r)$
　　　　　 (b) When $current=n$ then $f_{out}(r) = Imp_{current}(r)$

For the threshold-based TSelection algorithm, lemma 2 states *the early termination criteria* for a tuple to be dropped from the output.

Lemma 2. Assume that the threshold-based topic selection operator is to be applied to tuple r in relation R with atomic expensive predicates C_1, C_2, ..., C_n. During the evaluation of expensive predicates, if $Imp_{current}(r)$ becomes less than the threshold value V_t then the tuple r cannot be in the output.

Note that, in comparison, the top-k based TSelection algorithm does not have *the early termination criteria*. A tuple r can be dropped from the output only if $Imp_{current}(r)$ less is than the importance score f_{out} of k fully evaluated tuples.

Fig.1 illustrates the threshold-based topic selection *Threshold-TSelection* algorithm. In each iteration, the algorithm finds a tuple r for evaluation using the *LocateTuple( )* function, and finds an unevaluated predicate C_j of tuple r using the *LocatePredicate( )* function. It evaluates the predicate C_j for tuple r and computes $Imp_{current}(r)$ using $g_1( )$ and $g_2( )$ functions. If $Imp_{current}(r)$ is less than the threshold value V_t then tuple r is discarded. If all predicates are evaluated for tuple r and $Imp_{current}(r) \geq V_t$ then tuple r is added to the output. The algorithm stops when all output tuples are found or when the time T runs out.

We assume in this section that the *LocatePredicate( )* function locates the next predicate to evaluate by using the *same pre-defined predicate evaluation ordering* for all tuples.

```
Algorithm Threshold-TSelection (Vt,R,C,g1,g2,T)
For each tuple r in R do{ Imp_current(r)=Imp_in(r);
    Set Imp(C_i,r)=1.0 for all expensive predicates C_i;
    if(Imp_in(r)≥ V_t)then Add r into PossibleOutput;}
While(PossibleOutput is not empty)and(Time T is sufficient)do{
    r=LocateTuple(PossibleOutput);
    C_j=LocatePredicate(r);//C_j     is     an     unevaluated     expensive
predicate
    Imp(C_j,r)=Probe(C_j); Compute Imp_current(r)using g_1 and g_2;
    if(Imp_current(r)< V_t) then remove r from PossibleOutput
```

Fig. 1. Threshold-TSelection Algorithm

Theorem 1. *Threshold-Selection* algorithm has no false drops; i.e., it does not output tuples that are not in the output of the *TSelection* operator. And, when T is sufficiently large to evaluate all tuples in *PossibleOutput*, the algorithm has no false dismissals; i.e., it outputs all tuples that are in the output of the *TSelection* operator.

Fig. 2 illustrates the top-k topic selection *Top-k-TSelection* algorithm.

```
Algorithm Top-k-TSelection (k,R,C,g₁,g₂,T)
For each tuple r in R do{
   Set Imp(Cᵢ,r)=1.0 for all expensive predicates Cᵢ;
   Imp_current(r)=Imp_in(r); Add r into PossibleOutput;}
While (|Output|<k) and (Time T is sufficient) do{
   Let CurrentTopK be (k-|Output|) tuples in PossibleOutput with
   the highest Imp_current.
   r=LocateTuple(CurrentTopK);
   if(there exist an unevaluated expensive predicate in tuple r)
   then{Cⱼ=LocatePredicate(r);//Cⱼ is an unevaluated expensive predicate
        Imp(Cⱼ,r)=Probe(Cⱼ); Compute Imp_current(r)using g₁ and g₂;}
   if(all r's predicates are evaluated)and(r is current top-k tuples)
   then add r into Output;}
```

Fig. 2. Top-k-TSelection Algorithm

Theorem 2. *Top-k-Selection* algorithm has no false drops. And, when T is sufficiently large to evaluate all tuples in *PossibleOutput*, the algorithm has no false dismissals.

2.2 Time-Constrained Query Evaluation Heuristics

Due to the time constraint T, *TSelection* algorithm is terminated at time T, possibly before locating all output tuples that satisfy the given threshold value V_t. There are multiple possible query evaluation goals:

(1) Maximize the number of highest importance-scored output tuples.
    MaxImpLT (Locate Tuple) Heuristic: Locate the tuple r with the highest $Imp_{current}(\ )$ from PossibleOutput.
(2) Maximize the number of higher (but, not the highest) importance-scored output tuples with lower unevaluated predicate costs.
    HigherImpLT Heuristic: Locate the tuple r with the highest $Imp_{current}(\ )$ / $UCost(\ )$ from PossibleOutput.
(3) Maximize the size of the query output.
    MaxSizeLT Heuristic: Locate the tuple r with the lowest $UCost(\ )$ from PossibleOutput. If two or more tuples have the lowest $UCost(\ )$ then locate among them the tuple with the highest $Imp_{current}(\ )$.

In section 3.2, we present comparative evaluations of the three heuristics.

2.3 Dynamic Predicate Evaluation Order Heuristics

Next, we discuss heuristics for the *LocatePredicate()* function. The *"best"* predicate evaluation order may change with respect to the tuple chosen with *LocateTuple( )* while evaluating the expensive predicates. For example, assume that the importance score of a given evaluated expensive predicate C_i is very small (say, $Imp(C_i)=0.05$) for a given tuple r. Therefore, the remaining unevaluated predicates in the same conjunctive term with C_i possibly have a very small effect on the overall output importance score $Imp_{current}(r)$. Therefore, after computing $Imp(C_i)=0.05$ for r, it is better to evaluate an expensive predicate in another term. Thus, the best order of the expensive predicates for a given tuple should be dynamically computed. Next, we define the heuristic *(Predicate-Selection-by-)D(ynamic-)E(ffect-On-)C(ost)1* that locates the next expensive predicate to be evaluated in a dynamic manner for a given tuple r.

DEC1-LP (LocatePredicate) **Heuristic:** Assume that, at a given time, the predicates $C_1, C_2, \ldots, C_{current}$ in the selection condition C are evaluated for a given tuple r in a given relation R. We choose the unevaluated expensive predicate C_i with the highest *"max-effect-On-Cost"* as the next predicate in the *dynamic evaluation order*. The *max-effect-On-Cost*(C_i) for each unevaluated predicate C_i is computed as follows: Let $Imp_{min}(C_i, r)$ be computed as $Imp_{current}(r)$ after assigning $Imp(C_i, r)=0$ and $Imp(C_j, r)=1$ for unevaluated predicates C_j, $j \neq i$.

$$Max\text{-}Effect\text{-}On\text{-}Cost(C_i, r) \equiv [Imp_{current}(r) - Imp_{min}(C_i, r)]/Cost(C_i)$$

It is easy to prove that if the importance score of the predicates of a given selection condition C are uniformly distributed and independent from each other then the *DEC1* heuristic gives the optimum order of predicate evaluation for a given tuple r.

If the importance scores of predicates are not uniformly distributed or their distribution is not known then we may take a small sample of the tuples from relation R.

DEC2-LP Heuristic. At a given time, let the predicates $C_1, C_2, \ldots, C_{current}$ be evaluated for a given tuple r in a given relation R. The heuristic chooses the unevaluated expensive predicate C_i with the highest *"Max-Effect-On-Cost2"* as the next predicate in the *dynamic evaluation order*. The *Max-Effect-On-Cost2*(C_i) for each unevaluated predicate C_i is computed as follows: Let $Imp_{min}(C_i, r)$ be computed as $Imp_{current}(r)$ after assigning $Imp(C_i, r)=0$ and $Imp(C_j, r)=1$ for unevaluated predicates C_j, $j \neq i$. Also, let *SampleSel*(C_i) be the selectivity of the importance scores of predicate C_i using a sample from relation R.

$$Max\text{-}Effect\text{-}On\text{-}Cost2(C_i, r) = [(Imp_{current}(r) - Imp_{min}(C_i, r)) + (1 - SampleSel(C_i))]/Cost(C_i)$$

The following heuristic *(Predicate-Selection-by-)D(ynamic-)A(vg-)E(ffect-On-)C(ost)* uses the average expected *"Effect-On-Cost"* for each unevaluated predicate, and chooses the predicate with the highest *"Avg-Effect-On-Cost"* as the next predicate to evaluate.

DAEC-LP Heuristic. Assume that, at a given time, the predicates $C_1, C_2, \ldots, C_{current}$ are evaluated in the selection condition C for a given tuple r in a given relation R. The heuristic chooses the next predicate to evaluate as the predicate C_i with the highest *"Avg-effect-On-Cost"*. The *Avg-effect-On-Cost*(C_i, r) for each unevaluated predicate C_i

is computed as follows: Let $Imp_{avg}(C_i,r)$ be computed as $Imp_{current}(r)$ after assigning $Imp(C_i,r)$= expected average of $Imp(C_i)$, computed using sampling, and $Imp(C_j,r)$=1 for unevaluated predicates C_j, j≠i.

$$Avg\text{-}Effect\text{-}On\text{-}Cost(C_i) = [Imp_{current}(r) - Imp_{avg}(C_i,r)]/\ Cost(C_i)$$

3 Experimental Evaluations of TSelection Algorithms

We have implemented *Top-k-TSelection* and *Threshold-TSelection* algorithms using synthetic data. The importance scores for the expensive predicates are generated using uniform distribution, and normal distributions.

We compute the selectivity of predicates by randomly evaluating the predicates for 1% of the tuples from a relation R. For each tuple t, we compute its derived importance score $Imp(t)$ using $g_1(\ )$ and $g_2(\ )$ functions. Let Imp_{max} be the tuple with the highest Imp on the sample S. The selectivity $Sel(P)$ of a predicate P is established as the number of tuples in S with $Imp(t, P) > Imp_{max}$ divided by the total number of tuples in S.

3.1 Locate-Predicate Heuristics

We compare the performances of the *MPro, DEC1, DEC2* and *DAEC* heuristics in terms of the time differences between their evaluation times and the evaluation time of the *Best* heuristic. For the *Best* heuristic, we assume that at a given time we know the actual truth values and importance scores for all predicates for a given tuple t. As in [2], the *fixed predicate ordering* for *MPro* heuristic is the descending ordering of the predicates by their ranks, where the rank of a predicate P is $(1 - Sel(P)) / Cost(P)$.

We use the selection condition $(C_1 \cap C_2) \cup (C_3 \cap C_4 \cap C_5)$ with the expected evaluation cost $Cost(C_i)$={0.5, 0.3, 1.0, 0.4, 0.1} seconds, respectively. That is, C_1 takes 0.5 seconds to evaluate, C_2 takes 0.3 seconds to evaluate and so on. The size of the input relation R is 1000 tuples. We compute the derived importance score $Imp(t)$ of a given tuple t using the average function as g_1 and the minimum function as g_2.

a) Uniform distribution: The importance scores of all expensive predicates have been generated using the uniform distribution. We have observed that the *dynamic predicate evaluation order* heuristics improve the performances of the top-k and threshold based *TSelection* algorithms by 8% to 20%. The time difference between the *MPro* heuristic evaluation time and that using other dynamic heuristics increases as the threshold V_t decreases or k increases. As expected, the *DEC1* heuristic has lower total cost (i.e., faster) than other heuristics for both top-k and threshold based TSelection algorithms. The DEC1 heuristic is (14, 20)% better than the *MPro* heuristic. The evaluation time using the *DAEC* heuristic is very close to that using the *DEC1* heuristics, whereas, the *DEC2* heuristic has a higher evaluation time. The increase in the evaluation time for threshold-based *TSelection* is almost linear with respect to the decrease threshold V_t.

b) Combinations of distributions: The distributions of the importance scores for the expensive predicates C_1 and C_3 are chosen as uniform, and C_2, C_4, and C_5 are chosen as normal with a mean of 0.7 and a standard deviation of 0.2.We have observed that the evaluation time differences between the *MPro* heuristic and other dynamic heuristics is small as compared to those in other distributions. The difference decreases when k increases or threshold V_t decreases. The dynamic heuristics are (0, 9)% better than the *MPro* heuristic for threshold-based and *top-k* algorithms. Also, the *DEC2* heuristic has the best performance for both top-k and threshold based TSelection algorithms.

In conclusion, using any distribution to generate the importance scores of the expensive predicates, the *dynamic predicate evaluation order* heuristics improve the performances of the top-k and threshold based *TSelection* algorithms. If the importance scores for all expensive predicates have the same distribution then the best heuristic is the *DEC1* heuristic. If the importance scores have different distributions then the *DEC2* heuristic has the best performance.

3.2   Time Constraints

We have evaluated top-k and threshold based *TSelection* algorithms with a time constraint T and by using different distributions to generate importance scores for expensive predicates. We used the *MaxImpLT HigherImpLT,* and *MaxSizeLT* heuristics to locate the tuple from which an unevaluated expensive predicate is to be evaluated at a given time. For a given time constraint T, we compare the performances of the three heuristics in terms of the *precision* and *wasted time ratio.*

Definition 6 (*Wasted Time Ratio, Precision*): Let T be a query evaluation time limit, and t_{useful} be the time spent, out of time T, to completely evaluate those tuples that are verified to be in the output. Then,
Wasted time ratio $= 1 - (t_{useful} / T)$, and
Precision =(No. of output tuples found within time T)/(No. of tuples in the fully evaluated output).

We used an input relation R of size 500 tuples. We used the selection condition $(C_1 \cap C_2) \cup (C_3 \cap C_4 \cap C_5)$ with the expected evaluation cost $Cost(C_i) = \{0.5, 0.3, 1.0, 0.4, 0.1\}$ seconds, respectively. The derived importance score $Imp(t)$ of a given tuple t is computed using the average function as g_1 and the minimum function as g_2. For the threshold-based *TSelection* algorithm, we located the tuples that satisfy the threshold value V_t of 0.5. For the *top-k TSelection* algorithm, we computed the top-50 tuples. Let $T_{Required}$ be the required time to fully evaluate a given query. We used 0.5, 0.6, 0.7, 0.8 and 0.9 of $T_{Required}$ as the time constraint T, and computed the precision and wasted time ratio.

First, the importance scores for all expensive predicates are generated using the normal distribution with a mean of 0.7 and a standard deviation of 0.2. The *MaxImpLT* heuristic has the worst performance as compared to the other heuristics. It has (14, 54)% lower precision and (20,63)% higher wasted time ratio. The *MaxSizeLT* has the best performance for all values of the time constraint T: it has (0, 23)% higher precision and (0, 42)% wasted time ratio as compared to the HigherImpLT heuristic.

As for the performance for the *top-k TSelection* algorithm using the normal distribution, the *MaxImpLT* has the worst performance and there is a small difference between its performance and that of other heuristics: it has (0, 20)% lower precision and (0, 4)% higher wasted time ratio. The *HigherImpLT* heuristic has the best performance, it has (0, 6)% higher precision and (0, 2)% lower wasted time ratio as compared to the *MaxSizeLT* heuristic.

In conclusion, using any distribution to generate the importance scores for expensive predicates, the *MaxImpLT* heuristic has the worst performance for the *top-k* and *threshold-based TSelection* algorithms. In the *threshold-based* algorithm, there is a large difference between the performances of the *MaxImpLT* heuristic and that of other heuristics. And, at a given time T, *MaxSizeLT* has the best performance. In the *top-k based* algorithm, there is no large difference in the performances of the *MaxImpLT* heuristic and that of other heuristics, and *HigherImpLT* has the best performance.

4   Conclusions

We have presented algorithms to evaluate the topic selection *TSelection* operator for information resource discovery. We have proposed and evaluated heuristics to locate tuples and to evaluate expensive predicates.

References

1.   ACM Digital Library, at http://www.acm.org/dl.
2.   Chan, K., C-C, Hwang, S-W., "Minimal Probing: Supporting Expensive Predicates for Top-k Queries", ACM SIGMOD, 2002.
3.   Altingovde, I.S., et al, "Topic-Centric Querying of Web Information Resources", Proc, DEXA 2001.
4.   Ozsoyoglu, G, Al-Hamdani, A, Alt•ngovde, I.S, Ozel, S.A, Ulusoy, O, Ozsoyoglu, Z.M., "Sideway Value Algebra for Object-Relational Databases", VLDB Conf., 2002.
5.   Ozsoyoglu, G., Altingovde, I. S., Al-Hamdani, A., Ozel, S. A., Ulusoy, O., Ozsoyoglu, M., "Extending SQL for Metadata-based Querying", Submitted for journal publication, 2003.
6.   DBLP Bibliography, by Michael Ley, at http://www.acm.org/sigmod/dblp/db.
7.   ACM SIGMOD Anthology, at http://www.acm.org/sigmod/dblp/db/anthology.html.
8.   Sadri, F., Ullman, J., "The Interaction between Functional Dependencies and Template Dependencies", SIGMOD Conf., 1980.
9.   Biezunski, M., Bryan, M., Newcomb, S., editors, ISO/IEC 13250, Topic Maps, available at http://www.ornl.gov/sgml/sc34/document/0058.html, 1999.
10. Salton, G., "Automatic Text Processing", Addison-Wesley, 1989
11. Al-Hamdani, A., Ozsoyoglu, G., "Selecting Topics for Web Resource Discovery: Efficiency Issues in a Database Approach", technical report, EECS, CWRU, 2003.
12. Agichtein, E., Gravano, L., "Snowball: Extracting Relations from Large Plain-Text Collections", Proc. of the 5th ACM International Conf. on Digital Libraries, 2001.
13. Hellerstein, J.M, Stonebraker, M., "Predicate Migration: Optimizing queries with expensive predicates", ACM SIGMOD 93.
14. Li, Li, "Finding Related Papers in a Digital Library", MS Thesis, CWRU, June 2003.

Integrating Quality of Service into Database Systems*

Haiwei Ye[1], Brigitte Kerhervé[2], and Gregor v. Bochmann[3]

[1] Département d'IRO,
Université de Montréal, CP 6128
Succ. Centre-ville,
Montréal Québec, Canada H3C 3J7
ye@iro.umontreal.ca
[2] Département d'informatique,
Université du Québec à Montréal, CP 8888,
Succ. Centre-ville,
Montréal Québec, Canada H3C 3P8
Kerherve.Brigitte@uqam.ca
[3] School of Information Technology & Engineering,
University of Ottawa
P.O. Box 450, Stn A,
Ottawa Ontario, Canada K1N 6N5
bochmann@site.uottawa.ca

Abstract. Quality of Service (QoS) management has attracted a lot of research interests in the last decade, mainly in the fields of telecommunication networks and multimedia systems. With the recent advance in e-commerce deployment, it clearly appears that today's web applications will require the integration of QoS mechanisms to specify, declare and support the different service levels they can provide. Such mechanisms should therefore be integrated in the different components of the core technology and more specifically in database systems. In this paper, we present an approach to push QoS inside database systems. This approach integrates QoS requirements into distributed query processing and considers also the dynamic properties of the system. We propose a query optimization strategy where multiple goals may be considered with separate cost models.

1 Introduction

To support QoS activities, mechanisms have been mainly provided for individual components such as operating systems, transport systems, or multimedia storage servers and integrated into QoS architectures for end-to-end QoS provision [1]. None of these proposals takes database systems into consideration. However, database systems are an important component of today's distributed systems. We consider them a major player in QoS management.

* This work was supported by a grant from the Canadian Institute for Telecommunication Research (CITR), under the Network of Center for Excellence Program of the Canadian Government, a collaborative research and development grant from NSERC No. CRD-226962-99, by a student fellowship from IBM and an individual research grant from NSERC No. RGPIN138210.

V. Mařík et al. (Eds.): DEXA 2003, LNCS 2736, pp. 803–812, 2003.
© Springer-Verlag Berlin Heidelberg 2003

In the context of a research project funded by the Canadian Institute for Telecommunication Research (CITR), we investigate how to support different QoS levels in distributed systems [2] and more specifically for e-commerce applications. We address two complementary issues. On one hand, we study the management of QoS information to support distributed QoS decision models. For that purpose, we are currently designing and implementing an extensible QoS Information Base (QoSIB) manager offering basic services to store, access, share, transfer, produce or analyze QoS information [3]. On the other hand, we work on pushing QoS inside database systems [4][5][11]. More specifically, we propose an approach to integrate user-defined QoS requirements, in addition to the dynamic properties of the system components involved, into a distributed query processing environment.

In this paper, we focus on the second issue of our research. We present the general principles of our approach and we describe the query optimization strategy we propose where multiple goals may be considered with several cost models. A complete description of this work, together with experimental results can be found in [6].

The rest of the paper is organized as follows. The next section introduces the QoS concepts related to the proposed approach. Section 3 describes our QoS-based distributed query processing strategy. Section 4 provides a short conclusion.

2   Pushing QoS inside Database Systems

Many efforts have been directed at the provision of QoS at the network level. We believe that QoS concepts could and should be broadened from networking to the database area. However, there has been a lack of discussion of QoS issues in database systems. This observation opens possibilities to introduce QoS concepts in database systems.

What are the QoS issues in database system? The quality of service provided by the database systems in an e-commerce application is less likely perceivable by the end user. However, the implementation of QoS for the whole system requires each system component to be QoS responsive. In our work, different QoS requirements and constraints specified by end users are mapped to different optimization goals for the database system. Traditional database systems cannot be directly used for this purpose since they are designed to provide a single optimization goal. Another reflection of QoS requirements is the integration of dynamic system properties. The consideration of the user's QoS preferences is modeled into user classes. In this section, we concentrate on concepts that are important to our work: classes of users, multiple optimization goals, and dynamic system properties.

2.1   Classes of Users

The involvement of the user is crucial in e-commerce applications; accordingly various user requirements and QoS should also be available from the underlying DBMS. Defining user classes is a way of differentiating users according to their QoS expectation in order to provide different levels of service. A user class is a generalization of a number of users sharing common characteristics. Classification of the users may be based on different policies and criteria [7]. For example, different users may exhibit various patterns of navigation through an e-commerce site, therefore based on the user's *navigation behavior*, we may segregate users into two classes: *buyer* and *browser*. Another example of segregating users could be based on *priority*. In this classification, we differentiate users into different classes according to, for example, their profit brought to an e-store. Thus an e-commerce site tries to provide *higher priority* users with better service than *lower priority* users.

2.2 Various Optimization Goals

Conventional distributed/parallel database query optimization was primarily aimed at either minimizing the response time or system resource utilization. However, in the context of emerging applications, such as e-commerce, this provision of a single optimization goal is not adequate. Therefore, other possible optimization goals should be proposed and integrated into the optimizer. Table 1 lists some optimization goals that are useful for our study. They are grouped into different categories. Some optimization goals are *performance oriented*, for example, the response time, and the throughput of the database system. Others are *money oriented*, one example is the service charge for a particular service.

Table 1. Example of optimization goals

Optimization category	Optimization goal
Performance oriented	- Minimize response time - Maximize DB throughput
Money oriented	- Minimize the cost of a service - Maximize the benefit of the database system
Data quality	- Multimedia vs. Plain text - Recency of data
System oriented	- Minimize resource utilization

When various optimization goals exist along multiple QoS dimensions, we should find an *optimal* solution that satisfies all of them, optimal either from the user perspective or the system perspective, or both. One way of combining various optimization objectives is to use *weighted combination* (for example, a weighted sum) of different goals. The weight assigned to each goal is explicitly specified by the user.

The satisfaction for each optimization goal or QoS metric can be captured by using a *utility* function. By indicating different utility functions, the user expresses his/her individual tastes. Usually the utility function maps the value of one QoS dimension to a real number, which corresponds to a satisfaction level. For example, the following formulas give the utility functions for the response time and the service charge:

$$u_t(t) = 1 / t, \ u_\${(x)} = 1 / x$$

where t is the response time for a query access plan and x is the corresponding service charge for that plan. Utility functions are used in our cost model to achieve an overall optimization since they are used to compare the quality of the access plans. Utility functions also provide an important link between the quality of a query plan and the user satisfaction.

2.3 Dynamic System Properties

Two main challenges imposed by today's e-commerce applications are *diversity* and *unpredictability*. Diversity includes various user expectations and the heterogeneity of the database systems, network types and the machine power. The unpredictable nature comes from the varying network performance (especially for the Internet-based networks) and server load at different times. To capture these dynamic properties of the systems, we rely on the QoS monitor to offer the time-changing information. This information is then modeled in the relevant cost models of query processing.

2.4 An Example

In order to illustrate the idea of user classes and multiple optimization goals, we give an example. Assume we are interested in two QoS dimensions: response time and money. Suppose that the query optimizer compares two query access plans. The related information is given in Table 2.

Table 2. An example of related information for two query plans

	Plan a	Plan b	User 1 Weight	User 2 Weight
Response time	0.01s	0.009s	0.8	0.2
Money	$0.05	$0.10	0.2	0.8

Also assume that the utility functions are the formula defined in Section 2.2, that is $u_t(t) = 1 / t$ and $u_s(x) = 1 / x$. In our approach, weighed sum of utilities is used to achieve the overall optimization. For each user, the optimizer selects the maximum utility values between two query access plans. For User 1, the overall utilities for Plan *a* and *b* are 84 and 90.8, respectively. Accordingly, Plan *b* will be chosen for User 1 since it has higher utility. Similarly, Plan *a* is optimal from User 2's perspective.

From this example, we can see that corresponding to different user's QoS requirements/preferences, the optimizer should be able to choose different query access plans.

3 QoS-Based Query Processing

To support QoS in database systems, we propose to enrich query processing by investigating how the construction and the selection of query access plans can be enriched with QoS features. We build our framework along the issues addressed above. More specifically, we consider QoS factors such as user requirements, dynamic network performance and dynamic server load in the procedure of global query processing. The main objective is to provide a flexible QoS model for multidatabase management systems and to offer differentiated services. Due to space limitation, in this section we present the general principles of our approach, addressing relevant issues and sketching the general methodology used to tackle the problem. The reader can refer to [6] for a detailed presentation of the approach and corresponding algorithms.

3.1 Query Processing and Optimization Revisited

To address the dynamically changing requirements of the user and the unpredictable performance of the underlying systems, we propose the integration of QoS within distributed query processing. Specifically, we are guided by two main goals when designing the QoS-based query processor: 1) recognition of individual user requirements, and 2) consideration of the dynamic nature of the underlying system. A logical architecture is proposed in Figure 1, which shows the relationships between QoS management and distributed query processing.

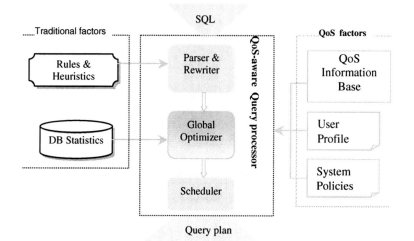

Fig. 1. A big picture for QoS-aware distributed query processor

We follow the conventional steps for distributed query processing: parsing, optimizing, and scheduling. In this framework, we include the typical components introduced in [8]. We keep the traditional factors (such as table, column, and index statistics) considered in the query processor. More importantly, we include the QoS factors, which are information from the *QoS Information Base* (QoSIB), *User Profile* and *System Policies*. The QoS information base (QoSIB) stores information about the service level offered by the different system components. A user profile is built to 1) store the user's QoS expectation for a particular service, and 2) to derive the trade-off between QoS dimensions, which is represented by the weight assigned to each dimension. The class of a user is used in the system policies. The system policies also determine the constraints under which the system resources can be used for providing services to the users. Although our focus is to push these QoS factors in the phase of optimization, the similar treatment can be applied to other steps. As a result, the global optimizer chooses a query access plan which will satisfy multiple optimization objectives derived from the user's requirements specified by the user. The dynamic system status is captured by QoS monitoring such that the selected query access plan takes into consideration the available system resources.

Adding QoS factors into a distributed query processing environment has several impacts and requires to provide new optimization goals, to modify the corresponding cost models, and to propose new algorithms for the query optimization. We address these problems in [6]. In this paper, we give a brief discussion on cost models used in our work and general description of our approach.

3.2 Cost Models

We propose a new approach to the problem of evaluating the cost of a query plan in a multidatabase system. Our approach relies on QoS monitoring to provide dynamic system status and on user profiles. The novelty of our approach lies in the consideration of user requirements, user classes as well as the way to deal with dynamic network performance. In our work, three levels of cost models are used. The first level is the global cost model, which is used to calculate the overall utility of a query access plan. The second level is used to calculate the cost for each node in a query access plan. The last level is the local cost model, which is used to estimate the cost of an operator locally.

Global cost model. Global optimization involves evaluation of the trade-offs between the amount of work to be done by the global level and the amount of communication and processing done by different component databases. Similar trade-offs exist in a distributed DBMS, but the heterogeneity and autonomy add considerably to the complexity.

Global cost models are the essential parts for the global query optimizer. Therefore, the information for network performance and load of database server is more crucial for the global cost model. The global cost model is defined as follows:

$$max\ \{ \sum_{i=1}^{n} \omega_i \cdot u_i(C_i)\}\ ,$$

where $u_i()$ is the utility function for cost component C_i (based on one of the QoS dimensions i); ω_i is the weighting factor assigned to the cost component C_i, where $0 \leq \omega_i \leq 1$ and the sum of ω_i equals to 1.

Plan cost model. A query access plan is represented by a binary tree. Each internal node is an inter-site binary operation (such as join or union) and each leaf node is the subquery executed at one database server. Since we consider several cost components, the cost of each node is also expressed according to multiple dimensions. For example, if we select the response time, the service charge, and the availability as our cost components, then the cost information recorded in each node will include three parts: time, dollar, and availability. The cost information for leaf nodes is based on the local cost model and the QoS Information Base (e.g. availability). The cost information for the internal node is calculated as a combination of the cost information of its left and right child nodes. The cost formula for each QoS dimension is different. Table 3 lists the cost functions for time, dollar, and availability. We use join operation as our study focus. The join time for each node is determined by the load of the server and the current TCP performance. Note that the QoS monitor captures this information. The formula for each join is:

$$T_{join} = local\ (site, query) + net\ (site_i, site_j)$$

where local (*site*, *query*) represents the local execution time for the *query* at *site*, net (*site_i*, *site_j*) represents the data transfer time spent over the network.

Table 3. Cost functions for each cost component

Cost Component	Cost function	Brief Description
Response time	Join-time + max (left.respose_time, right.response_time)	The join time is the response time to perform the join between the left and the right child.
Service Charge	Join-charge + left.charge + right.charge	The join charge is the money cost to perform the join between the left and the right child.
Availability	Left.availability * right.availability	The probability that both servers are available.

Local cost model. As just mentioned, the local cost information relies on the estimation of the execution of a query at a local server, the pricing policy applied by the local server for a service charge, and the server availability. The price and the availability must be reported by each local database server. However, the execution strategy, and therefore the execution time, of a query is hard to obtain since local database systems do not report the needed statistical information. To estimate the local database cost, we adopt the sampling method[9], where multiple regression models are used to guess the local cost structure (in terms of time). Due to space limitation, we will not give detailed information here. A complete discussion can be found in[6].

3.3   System Overview

After we have obtained the user's SQL query and QoS requirements, two major steps are used in our approach. One is the selection of the cost model, the other one is the global query processing.

The selection of the cost model includes the selection of cost components and the choice of utility functions. Different optimization goals may correspond to different cost models or query processing strategies. Our general heuristic for the selection of the cost model is that one optimization goal usually corresponds to one cost component. Therefore, how many cost components are included in the general cost model is determined by the number of optimization goals. For example, in the performance category given in Table 1, the cost factors comprise the measures of local processing time, communication time as well as some overhead due to parallelism. For the optimization goals related to cost (in terms of dollars), the cost measures include information on the resource usage and the pricing scheme. For the category of data quality, special attention should be given to query rewrite techniques to locate the best target databases. The selection of utility functions relies on the cost component and the application. For example, if the cost component is the image resolution, the available utility functions are usually non-decreasing (which means the more the better). On the other hand, if the cost components involve time or money, the utility functions are usually decreasing (which means the less the better).

Three steps are deployed for global query processing. They are global query decomposition, join ordering and join site selection. The main task of the global query decomposition is to break down a global query into several subqueries so that the tables involved in each subquery target one location. The cost model used for this step mainly depends on the local information, depending on the optimization goal selected. For example, if the optimization goal is the response time, the cost model could be the response time for each subquery under various server loads. We do not consider data transfer in this step; therefore communication cost is not involved. The QoS factor considered is mainly the system performance information from QoS information base.

Global query decomposition generates a set of subqueries with location information. In the following join ordering step, the optimizer tries to come up with a good ordering of how to combine these joins between subqueries. The algorithms for join ordering are based on the traditional algorithms [10] but enriched with QoS features. The cost models used in this step consist of both global cost model and local cost model. A new transformation rule, called flex-transformation, is defined for the step of bushy tree generation as discussed above. The algorithms for global query decomposition and third site consideration for join site selection are new. The QoS aspects include the provision of different query execution plans for different user classes. The construction of the global query plan also takes into consideration the dynamic system properties, such as server load and network available throughput, with the help of QoS monitoring. Some of this support comes from our QoS-based cost model used in the algorithm, others are directly infused in the algorithms.

In case of data duplication, one subquery might have several potential locations, thus the optimizer should decide at which location this subquery would be executed. Like the join ordering problem, all the QoS metrics are taken into account. The key issue in the site selection is to decide which site is the best (depending on how the user defines his or her optimization goal) for each binary operator. Traditionally, the possible site to perform the join or the union is chosen from one of the operand sites, i.e. the site where one of its operands is located. However, there may be circumstances when shipping the two operand tables to a third site is a better solution, in terms of response time. We call the join site to be a *third* site if the selected site is neither of the operand sites. This process may be done in a bottom-up fashion. We propose a new algorithm where we use post order tree traversal to visit the internal nodes of the tree[6].

3.4 Prototype Implementation

In order to validate our approach, we implemented a prototype where we concentrated on those aspects that are representative for the QoS-based distributed query processing we propose. For simplicity, we only integrate two QoS dimensions in the prototype. However, the implementation is not limited to these two dimensions, the modules implementing other dimensions can be easily plugged into our prototype. Highlights of the implementation are given below.

1) User classes: In order to show the differentiated services in our prototype, we have adopted the priority-based user classification and considered two user classes, namely *VIP user* and *normal user*.

2) Optimization goal. For our prototype implementation, we focus on two optimization goals: minimize the response time and/or the service charge. Basically, we want to demonstrate the integration of the criteria of *time* and *money* into our prototype. Accordingly the overall optimization goal is calculated by the following formula:

$$\text{Min} \{ \omega_t u_t (\text{response\_time}) + \omega_s u_s (\text{service\_charge}) \}$$

where ω_t and ω_s are the weights specified by the users for the response time and service charge, respectively; u_t and u_s are utility functions used for the response time and service charge respectively. For the purpose of simplicity, we adopt the utility functions given in the example in section 2.3.

3) Cost models. The general cost model contains two cost components: response time and service charge. Depending on the optimization goals, three cost models can be selected:

    i. C_{time} = response_time;
    ii. C_{dollar} = service_charge;
    iii. $C_{overall} = W_{time} * u_t(\text{response\_time}) + W_{dollar} * u_s(\text{service\_charge})$

We also evaluate the performance of our QoS-based query processing strategy according to the framework proposed in the previous sections. The objective of our experiment is to show that our query optimizer can adapt to workload changes (both server load and network load) and always chooses the best plan for different user classes. In the experiment we simulate two classes of users: *VIP* user and *normal* user. Under different system loads, the results [6] show that the VIP user always enjoy the fast response time while the normal user will get slower response when the system is heavily loaded.

4 Conclusions

In this paper, we have presented a general framework for integrating QoS requirements in a distributed query processing environment. This framework is based on user classes, cost models, utility functions, and policy-based management. Our approach allows offering differentiated services to different classes of users according to their expectations in terms of QoS. We also developed a prototype to verify the effectiveness of the idea. Our current prototype supports two QoS dimensions: response time and service charge. In the future, we will consider other QoS dimensions to be specified by the user, such as data quality or freshness. We will also be interested in working on rewriting rules to transform specifications on these dimensions into optimization goals and corresponding cost models.

References

[1] C. Aurrecoechea, A. Campbell, L Hauw, A Survey of QoS Architectures. ACM Multimedia Journal, 6, May 1998, pp. 138–151

[2] G. v. Bochmann, B. Kerhervé, H. Lutfiyya, M. M. Salem, H. Ye, Introducing QoS to Electronic Commerce Applications, Second International Symposium, ISEC 2001 Hong Kong, China, April 26–28, 2001, pp 138–147

[3] K.K. Nguyen, F. Fetjah, B. Kerhervé, Quality of Service Information Base (QoSIB) Manager for Electronic Commerce Applications, Poster presented at the CITR Annual Conference, August 2001

[4] H. Ye, B. Kerhervé, G. v. Bochmann, QoS-aware distributed query processing, DEXA Workshop on Query Processing in Multimedia Information Systems (QPMIDS), Florence, Italy, 1–3 September, 1999

[5] H. Ye, B. Kerhervé, G. v. Bochmann, V. Oria, Pushing Quality of Service Information and Requirements into Global Query Optimization, the Seventh International Database Engineering and Applications Symposium (IDEAS 2003), Hong Kong, China, July 16–18

[6] H. Ye, Integrating Quality of Service Information and Requirements in a Distributed Query Processing Environment, Ph.D. thesis, University of Montreal, May 2003

[7] D. A. Menasce, V. A. F. Almeida, Scaling for E-Business Technologies, Models, Performance, and Capacity Planning, Prentice Hall Canada, 2000

[8] D. Kossmann, The state of the art in distributed query processing, ACM Computing Surveys (CSUR), Volume 32, Issue 4, December 2000, pp 422–469

[9] Q. Zhu, Y. Sun and S. Motheramgari, Developing Cost Models with Qualitative Variables for Dynamic Multidatabase Environment, Proceedings of IEEE Int'l Conf. On Data Eng. (ICDE2000), San Diego, Feb 29-March 3, 2000, pp 413–424

[10] W. Du, M.-C. Shan, U. Dayal, Reducing Multidatabase Query Response Time by Tree Balancing. SIGMOD Conference 1995, pp 293–303

[11] H. Ye, B. Kerhervé, G. v. Bochmann, Revisiting Join Site Selection in Distributed Database Systems. International Conference on Parallel and Distributed Computing, 26th–29th August 2003, Klagenfurt, Austria

Handling Dynamic Changes in Decentralized Workflow Execution Environments*

Vijayalakshmi Atluri[1] and Soon Ae Chun[2]

[1] CIMIC and MS/IS Department,
Rutgers University,
USA
{atluri,soon}@cimic.rutgers.edu
[2] Department of Computing and Decision Sciences,
Seton Hall University,
USA

Abstract. Often, real world business processes are constantly changing and dynamic in nature. These runtime changes may stem from various requirements, such as changes to the goals of the business process, changes to the business rules of the organization, or exceptions arising during the workflow execution. Unfortunately, traditional workflow management systems do not provide sufficient flexibility to accommodate such *dynamic* and *adaptive* workflows that support run-time changes of in-progress workflow instances. Moreover, traditional workflow management is accomplished by a single centralized workflow management engine, which may not only be a performance bottleneck, but also unsuitable for the emerging internet-based commerce and service environments where workflows may span many organizations that are autonomous. In this paper, we propose a formal model for a *decentralized workflow change management* (DWFCM) that uses a rules topic ontology and a service ontology to support the needed run-time flexibilty. We present a system architecture and the workflow adaptation process that generates a new workflow that is *migration consistent* with the original workflow.

1 Introduction

With the internet-based commerce and service environment, business processes often cross organizational boundaries, as can be seen in *virtual enterprise* and *digital government* services. A workflow management system that supports these inter-organizational processes needs to address the following challenges: (1) The execution of these processes needs to be scalable and honor the autonomy of the participating organizations; (2) The definition of inter-organizational processes needs to be dynanmic and *ad hoc*, providing customization considering diverse user requirements and variations; (3) The workflow management should have sufficient flexibility to handle dynamic changes at run-time.

* This work is partially supported by the National Science Foundation under grant EIA-9983468 and by MERI (the Meadowlands Environmental Research Institute).

We have proposed a *decentralized workflow management model* (DWFMS) [1,2], and a model for customized workflow generation (WFGM) [6] to address the first two challenges. In this paper, we present a *dynamic, decentralized workflow change management model* (DWFCM) based on ontologies. The ontologies provide controlled vocabulary to specify different types of changes, and allow the system to automatically identify and incorporate necessary *migration rules*. The significant components of our DWFCM include: (1) *workflow context manager* (ConMan) that monitors changes in the user profiles, rules, and exceptions during task execution and (2) a *Self adaptor* that identifies the necessary migration rules, based on workflow composition rules, and performs the workflow migration such that changes are, as much as possible, local and minimal.

This paper is organized as follows. In section 2, we present different types and sources of dynamic changes. In section 3, we present a decentralized workflow execution model, followed by a workflow generation model in section 4. In section 5, our change management model is presented, followed by algorithms and methods to manage the dynamic changes in section 6[1].In section 7, our approach to automatic exception handling is presented. We discuss related work in section 8, followed by conclusions in section 9.

2   Dynamic Change Types

Dynamic changes to a workflow may occur due to (1) changes to the goals of the business process, that is, changes to the user profile, (2) unanticipated exceptions that arise during a task execution, and (3) changes to the business rules and regulations. Consider the following land development permit process:

An entrepreneur, Bill, wishes to build a car wash on a 5-acre vacant property that is 400 feet from the bank of the Hackensack River in Little Ferry, New Jersey. The zoning for this area is "neighborhood commercial," as designated by the New Jersey Meadowlands Commission (NJMC). In this example, the developer needs to perform tasks that are shown as solid lines in figure 1.

1. **Profile Change:** While a zoning certificate (task t_2 in figure 1) is under review, assume that Bill submits a request to add a storage mezzanine. This change in Bill's profile requires additional parking on the property, and assuming that the property does not have enough space for additional parking, variance-related tasks t_6 and t_7 need to be inserted, as shown in figure 1.

2. **Exceptions:** While reviewing the stream encroachment permit application (t_5), suppose that the engineers found some hazardous substances underground. According to the regulations, this would require a task t_9 (*notify to remove hazardous materials*) needs to be added before t_5 into the original workflow, as shown in figure 1.

---

[1] Due to the space limitation, we did not include the algorithms and proofs of theorems. See [5]

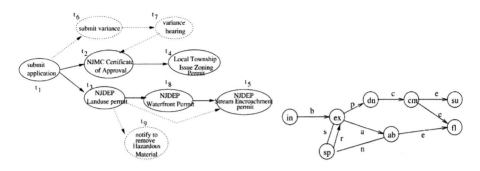

Fig. 1. Examples of Workflow Changes   **Fig. 2.** States of a Task

3. **Rule Change:** Assume that while the development application review is under way, the waterfront regulation which requires a developer to obtain a Waterfront permit that applies to all the developments within 500 feet from the water has changed to apply to all the lots within 300 feet. As a result, the Waterfront permit task (t_8) needs to be deleted since this rule is no longer applicable.

As can be seen from the above examples, the dynamic changes result in restructuring of the workflow, which can either be done as an insertion or a deletion of a task t_j. Such insertions can either be sequential or parallel to a task t_i that has not started its execution yet, or to a task t_k that has completed its execution. In some cases, the changes require to undo an already completed task and to redo it. If it is possible to undo or compensate for a completed task, then this change can be accommodated. On the other hand, change requests requiring to undo a completed task that does not have a compensating task will be rejected. Table 1 categorizes these various cases of structural workflow adaptation based on the type of operation.

The types of adaptation that can be accommodated are marked "yes," while the ones that cannot be accommodated are marked "no." The categories marked with "limited" indicate that the adaptation occurs if certain conditions are met, such as when redoing and compensating for a task is possible. The others, marked with "N/A," are cases that do not occur.

Table 1. Adaptation Types w.r.t uncompleted task t_i and completed task t_k

Operation	Sequential		Parallel
	before t_i	after t_i	
insert t_j	yes	yes	yes
delete t_j	yes	yes	N/A
	before t_k	after t_k	
insert t_j	limited	limited	N/A
delete t_j	no	no	N/A

Restructuring of a completed part of the workflow does not occur in case of a rule change or of changes due to exceptions. This is, because changes in rules are always applicable from the time of change onwards. Exceptions are encountered only when a task is executing, so they do not affect the part of the workflow that has already been executed.

3   Decentralized Workflow Model

A workflow and a task are formally defined as follows:

Definition 1. [Workflow] *A workflow W can be defined as a directed graph (T, D), where T, the set of nodes, denotes the tasks $t_1, t_2...t_n$ in W, and D, the set of edges, denotes the intertask dependencies $t_i \xrightarrow{x} t_j$, such that $t_i, t_j \in T$ and x is the type of the dependency.*

Definition 2. [Task] *Each task $t_i \in T$ is a 5-tuple $\langle$ A, Ω, Input, Output, EOutput $\rangle$, where A denotes the execution agent of t_i (denoted as $A(t_i)$), $\Omega = OP \cup PR$ is operations, Input the set of objects allowed as inputs to t_i, Output and EOutput are the set of objects expected as output from t_i and their expected values, respectively.*

Each task has internal structure represented as a state transition diagram (figure 2) with a set of states ST = {initial (in), executing (ex), done (dn), committed (cm), aborted (ab), succeeded (su), failed (fl), suspended (sp)}, and a set of primitive operations PR={b (begin), p (precommit), a (abort), c (commit), e (evaluate), s (suspend), r (resume), n (cancel)}.

The DWFMS enforces inter-task dependencies without a centralized WFMS. This model uses the notion of *self-describing workflows (Self)* and *WFMS stubs*. Self-describing workflows are partitions of a workflow that carry sufficient information so that they can be managed by a local task execution agent rather than the central WFMS. A WFMS stub is a light-weight component that can be attached to a task execution agent, which is responsible for receiving the self-describing workflow, modifying it and re-sending it to the next task execution agent.

When the *WFMS stub* at the first task agent receives a *Self*, it unpacks the information in *Self*, checks preconditions for its task and executes the task. Once the task agent finishes its task, it partitions the remaining workflow and generates *Selfs* and forwards them to the subsequent task agents. This process continues until all tasks are executed and returned to the central WFMS stub.

4   Ontology-Based Generation of Customized Workflows

Our earlier work [6] proposed a customized workflow generation model (WFGM). Workflow composition (generation) is achieved with the ontology of tasks, shown in figure 3, that captures the knowledge of available tasks and their relationships (definition 3), and the ontology of composition rules, shown in figure 5, that captures and organizes rules and regulations that prescribe how to compose tasks (definition 4).

Definition 3. [Domain Tasks Ontology] *A domain service ontology* SO *is defined as a set of services* $\{s_1, s_2, ... \}$. *Each* $s_i \in$ SO *is defined as a pair* $\langle SA, SR \rangle$, *where* SA *is a set of service attributes and* $SR = \{rel_1, rel_2, ...\}$ *a set of relationships. Each* $rel_i = \{c_1, c_2, ...\}$ *is a set of concepts that* s_i *bears the relationship to.*

Definition 4. [Rules Topic Ontology] *A rules topic ontology* RO *is defined as a set of rule topics* RO $= \{to_1, to_2, ...\}$. *Each* $to_i \in$ RO *is defined as a triple* $\langle RA, Rel, R \rangle$, *where* RA *denotes a set of attributes, Rel a set of relationships that* to_i *bears to other concepts, and* $R = \{r_1, r_2, ...\}$ *a set of composition rules associated with* to_i.

The relationships *has-subtopic*(to_i) define a set of subtopic concepts that are related to to_i, and *isa-subtopic*(to_i) defines a topic concept that is the super-topic of to_i.
Each composition rule is represented as a condition-action pair, which is defined below.

Definition 5. [Composition Rule] *Given a task* $t \in$ SO *and a composition operation cop* $\in COP = \{insert, order, parallelize\}$, *a composition rule r is defined as a pair* $r = \langle c, a \rangle$ *where c is the condition and* $a = cop(t)$ *is the action.*

Example 1. $r_1 = \langle distance(river) \leq 300\ feet,\ insert(obtain\ Waterfront\ permit) \rangle$: r_1 *states that if the distance from river is less than 300 feet, then insert task obtain Waterfront permit into the workflow and add distance(river)* $\leq$ *300 feet as the precondition for the task.*

5   Decentralized Workflow Change Management Model

In this section, we present our Decentralized Workflow Change Management model (DWFCM) that allows a workflow executing under decentralized control to transparently adapt to run-time changes and exceptions so as to provide the needed flexibility. Our approach to managing dynamic changes includes (1) specify change requests, and exceptions, (2) identify tasks and operations for structural modification, and (3) apply migration of workflow partitions to new ones. Figure 4 shows the architecture of our dynamic workflow change management system.

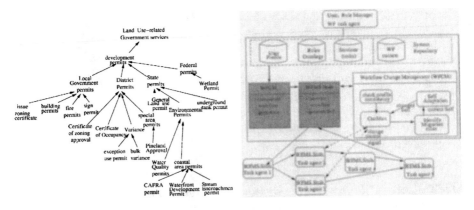

Fig. 3. Service Ontology

Fig. 4. The Dynamic Workflow Change
Management System

5.1   Change Request

A change request can be made by a change agent, e.g. a user or a task agent or
a rule administrator. A set of change request operators $ROP \subseteq \{insert, delete,$
$change\}$ is provided for a change agent to place a request to insert, delete or
change a profile, a rule or a workflow condition at run time. The following defines
a change operand and a change request.

Definition 6. [**Change Operand**] *Given a Rules topic ontology* $RO=\{to_1, to_2,$
$\ldots\}$, *a service ontology* $SO=\{s_1, s_2, \ldots\}$, *and a composition operator cop* $\in COP$,
a change operand co is defined as follows:

  – *If* $at=to_i \in RO$ *and* $v=to_j \in$ *has-subtopic* (to_i), *then a pair* $\langle at, v \rangle$ *is a change*
    operand.
  – *If c is a condition and* $a=cop(t_i)$, *then* $\langle c, a \rangle$ *is a change operand.*

Definition 7. [**Change Request**] *Given a workflow* $W = (T, D)$, *a set of*
user preferences $PRO =\{pro_1, pro_2, \ldots\}$, *a set of domain composition rules*
$R=\{r_1, r_2, \ldots\}$, *and a set of change request operators* $ROP =\{insert, delete,$
$change\}$, *a change request cr is defined as a tuple,* $\langle obj, \delta, co \rangle$ *where obj* $\in$
$PRO \cup R \cup T$ *is an object to be changed,* $\delta \in ROP$ *is a change request op-*
erator and co is a change operand.

Example 2.   – $\langle pro_{12}, change, \langle \ business.type, restaurant \rangle \rangle$ *where* $pro_{12} = \langle$
   $business.type, automobile \ service \ station \rangle \rangle$. This is a change request to change
   a business type from an automobile service station to a restaurant.
  – $\langle r_{11}, \quad change, \quad \langle (coastal\text{-}development=yes) \quad \land \quad (buffer\text{-}area \quad \leq 500ft),$
   $insert(Wate\text{-}rfront \quad Development \quad permit) \rangle \rangle$ *where* $r_{11} = \langle (coastal\text{-}$
   $development=yes) \land buffer\text{-}area \leq 300ft, insert(Waterfront \ Development$
   $permit) \rangle$. This example illustrates that the current rule r_{11} is changed for a
   coastal area development to expand the Waterfront buffer area to 500 ft.

5.2   Workflow Context

Each workflow is associated with a sequence of contexts, which keeps track of the changes in workflow execution from the initial workflow up to the current time. Following formally defines a workflow context.

Definition 8. [Workflow Context] *A workflow W is associated with a sequence of workflow contexts, denoted as $CN(W) = \{cn_0, cn_1, \ldots cn_n\}$. Each context cn_i is defined as a tuple $\langle ts, PRO, CR, WF \rangle$ where ts is a timestamp for the context switch time from cn_{i-1} to cn_i, PRO is the user profile, $CR \subset R$ is the set of composition rules used in generating W, and WF is the set of self describing workflows ($Self_c$) active at time ts.*

We use $PRO(cn_i)$, $CR(cn_i)$ and $WF(cn_i)$ to denote the user profile, the set of rules applied in generating W, and the set of *self describing workflows* (Selfs) in currently executing task agents at context cn_i, respectively. Each *Self* in $WF(cn_i)$ contains the current task t_i, the precondition set (*PreSet*) for t_i, an *OutState* with the execution state and the output generated from the task t_j before t_i. We use $cn_j(W)$ to denote the jth context for workflow W.

A *context switch* from cn_i to cn_{i+1} occurs whenever a task agent $A(t_i)$ finishes its task and forwards its execution environment and workflow partitions to the next task agents, $Self_{j_1}, \ldots, Self_{j_k}$, resulting in $WF(cn_{i+1}) = WF(cn_i) - \{Self_i\} \cup \{Self_{j_1}, \ldots Self_{j_k}\}$. Also, when one of the context components, $PRO(cn_i)$, $CR(cn_i)$ or $WF(cn_i)$ is updated, a context switch occurs.

The following defines change control signals that are used to communicate with the WFMS stubs at various task agents, to suspend, resume or cancel tasks.

Definition 9. [Change Control Signal] *Given a task change primitive $cpr \in CPR = \{s, r, n\} \subset PR$, a task $t_i \in W$, and its task agent $A(t_i)$, a change control signal signal is defined as a triple $\langle cpr, t_i, A(t_i) \rangle$.*

Depending on the type of change primitive *cpr*, a change control signal is referred to as *suspend-signal, resume-signal,* or *cancel-signal.*

Example 3. $\langle s, t_2, A(t_2) \rangle$ is an example of a suspend signal to notify the task agent $A(t_2)$ that it should suspend t_2.

5.3   Migration Rules

The adaptation process takes a change request and a set of workflow contexts, identifies a set of *migration rules* and applies them to transform the current workflow partitions. Our approach to identifying these migration rules is to use the regulatory ontology. The migration rules are extensions of compositional rules in a rules ontology that are used for generating a customized workflow. The migration rules are defined as follows:

Definition 10. [Migration Rule] *Given a set of composition rules $R = \{r_1, r_2, \ldots\}$ in the rules topic ontology* RO, *where each rule $r_i = \langle c, a \rangle$ is a condition action pair, and a set of migration operators $MOP = COP \cup \{delete, redo, compensate\}$, where $COP = \{insert, order\}$, a migration rule mr is defined as follows: If $r_i = \langle c, a \rangle$ is a composition rule where $a = cop(t)$ with $cop \in COP$ and a task $t \in T$, then $\langle c, a' \rangle$ is a migration rule where $a' = mop(t)$ such that $mop \in MOP$.*

An example migration rule: $mr_1 = \langle$ coastal water $=$ tidally flowed waterway, delete(obtain Waterfront permit) $\rangle$ states that the task of obtaining a Waterfront permit needs to be deleted.

Definition 11. [Workflow Migration Consistency] *Let $W = (T, D)$ be the workflow before a change, $W' = (T', D')$ be the workflow after the change, and R be the set of composition rules in the rules topic ontology. We say that the changed workflow W' is* migration consistent *with W,*

1. *if R does not change, then W' satisfies R or*
2. *if R changes to R', then W' satisfies R'.*

6   Handling Dynamic Changes

6.1   Ensuring Consistency in Profile Changes

The vocabulary used in the change operand specification may vary widely. In our approach, we avoid the individual variability and ambiguities in the operand specification by restricting the specification to only the vocabulary from the topic concept nodes of the composition rule topic ontology as shown in figure 5. For example, when a user wants to change his development location from "Neighborhood Commercial zone" to "Park and Recreations zone," the change operand $\langle$ *zone, Park and Recreation* $\rangle$ can be formed using the concepts from the rules ontology, i.e. *zone* and *Park and Recreation*. The use of the rules topic ontology also ensures that change requests are consistent. For example, the change of *location* from *Neighborhood Commercial zone* to *Park and Recreation zone* also imposes changes to all the subtopic nodes. The neighborhood commercial zone-related attributes such as water quality and flood zone become relevant. The following defines the profile change consistency constraint. We have developed an algorithm, a theorem and its proof to ensure profile change consistency [5].

Definition 12. [Profile Change Consistency] *Let* RO $= \{to_1, to_2, \ldots\}$ *be the rules topic ontology, PRO be the user profile, cr be the change request and to_i be the topic attribute in cr. We say that the new profile PRO' is* profile change consistent *with PRO if PRO' contains to_i and all subtopic descendants of to_i.*

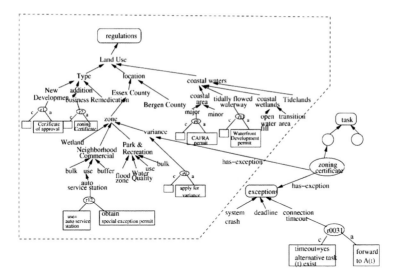

Fig. 5. A Rules Topic Ontology for land development

6.2 Ontology-Based Identification of Migration Rules

In order to identify the necessary migration rules, Self Adaptor first examines the change request $cr = \langle obj, \delta, co \rangle$. For each type of change (user profile, rule, or workflow exception), a composition rule that satisfies the change operand co is selected from the rule ontology. If the attribute at in $co = \langle at, v \rangle$ matches a topic concept in the ontology, then the composition rules are evaluated against v. The composition rules that satisfy co are identified and converted into migration rules. We describe below how the migration rules are identified for each type of change request.

Case 1: Profile Change and Workflow Condition Change: If the change operation δ in $cr = \langle obj, \delta, co \rangle$ is 'insert', Self Adaptor first identifies a topic node in the rules topic ontology RO that matches the attribute at in the change operand $co = \langle at, v \rangle$. If there is any rule associated with the topic node, the rule is inserted into the set of insert rules. It does the same for all the subtopic nodes under this topic node to meet the profile change consistency constraint defined in definition 12.

When the change operation is 'delete,' Self Adaptor identifies the topic node, as in the case of insert, and applicable rules are added into a set of delete rules. However, Self Adaptor checks if the task to be deleted has already finished its execution. If this is the case, it checks whether there is any compensating rule or task, and adds that to the insertion rules.

When the change operation is 'change,' Self Adaptor needs to identify an existing profile attribute value pair to be replaced. It then identifies insertion rules using the new profile values, as in the case of 'insert,' and it identifies deletion rules using old profile values as in the case of 'delete.' Then these sets of insertion and deletion rules are returned as a set of migration rules. For example, in figure 5, the user can request a change in his profile $\langle\,p_{12}$, delete, $\langle$ use, automobile service station $\rangle\rangle$ that was previously assumed. In this case, the system finds a node that matches the topic *use*, and the regulatory rule that is relevant to this topic $(r_{12} = \langle\, c$, insert(t) $\rangle$ in the figure) is identified, where t is to obtain a special exception permit. Thus, the migration rule $\langle c, delete(t)\rangle$ is identified and inserted to be used to transform the current workflow partitions into new ones.

Similarly, the workflow condition change request is made by a task agent with $cr=\langle t_2$, *insert*, $\langle toxic\ waste\ site,\ yes\rangle\rangle$ to add a toxic waste site related task. In the same fashion as above, the composition rule related to the topic "toxic waste site" in the rules ontology is added as a migration rule.

Case 2: Rule Change: When a rule change request $cr=\langle obj, \delta, co\rangle$ is made, the change operand is in the form of a condition action pair, $co=\langle c, a\rangle$. In case of a rule to be inserted, Self Adaptor checks if the existing profile $PRO(ccn)$ satisfies the condition c in the changed rule. If the condition is satisfied and a is an insertion of a task t, then it checks if t is already in the current workflow. If such a task t exists, then Self Adaptor checks if it was already executed. If t was already executed, then no migration is necessary and the rule is not inserted into the set of migration rules. This avoids redoing the task t twice. Otherwise, it inserts the rule into the insertion migration operation. If there is no profile that satisfies this new rule, then there is no need to transform the workflow. The changed rule simply does not apply to the current workflow.

6.3   Self Migration

Once the migration rules are identified, Self Adaptor applies these rules to workflow partitions in $Self_c$. We call this migration process *Self adaptation* or *Self migration*. The Self migration process considers different types of migration operations, *compensate, redo, order, insert,* and *delete*. Every change is either adapted in the workflow generating the modified Self(s), denoted as $Self_{new}$, or a flag to reject the change is returned to ConMan. ConMan sends signals to the appropriate task agents to either resume or cancel $Self_c$ or restart execution with $Self_{new}$.

The following describes Self migration. Let the current workflow partitions be $\{P_1, P_2, \ldots\}$ and a set of migration rules be $MR = \{mr_1, mr_2, \ldots\}$, where each $mr_i = \langle c, a\rangle$ is a condition action rule with $a = mop(t_c)$. Self Adaptor goes through each migration rule in MR and applies migration operation mop to W in the applicable current partition P_i. If a *point-of-no-return* signal is returned during the migration rule identification process, the change is rejected. First, Self Adaptor looks at all the *compensation* rules, and puts them into a partition in P_c. Then, it goes through the *redo* rules, and puts them into another partition P_r.

The other migration rules are subsequently incorporated into partitions P_i in the current $Self_c$. Each time when a migration rule applies to P_i, the partitions are updated to P^i_{new}. For an insertion rule (e.g. insert(t)), Self Adaptor checks if the task to be inserted has any ordering relationships to be met (e.g. order (t, t') or order(t', t)). If there is such a t', then t will be inserted into all the partitions with t'. For a deletion rule, Self Adaptor considers whether it is the first task, last task or a task between two tasks, and incorporates the rule in all the applicable partitions. Once the current partitions are updated with insertion and deletion migration rules, compensation and redo partitions are combined together, P_c followed by P_r. This combined partition is attached into one of the updated current partitions, P_{new}^i. The updated partitions are returned to ConMan for resuming the execution.

6.4 Workflow Context Management (ConMan)

When ConMan receives a change request for a workflow W, it sends suspend control signals to WFMS stubs that are currently executing W. Upon receiving a suspend control signal, t_i at $A(t_i)$ makes a transition from its current state to suspended (sp). When ConMan receives an acknowledgment from the currently active WFMS stubs, it invokes the migration process, *Self Adaptor*, to handle the change in the current self-describing workflows, $Self_c$ in $WF(ccn)$. The updated self-describing workflows $Self_{new}$ in WF_{new} are sent to appropriate task agents to resume the execution with updated self-describing workflows.

7 Automatic Exception Handling

Our approach to dynamic changes uses a change request initiated by a change agent, such as a task agent, the user or the rule administrator. This section provides an approach how the change request is automatically formulated by a WFMS stub, and submitted to ConMan for adaptation. In order to achieve the automatic identification of change needs and to formulate a change request automatically, a WFMS stub has to recognize whether the current workflow execution condition is considered an exception or not.

Recall from section 3 that in our workflow model, a task t is modeled as $\langle A, \Omega, Input, Output, EOutput \rangle$. When there are discrepancies between the actual output produced in *Output(t)* and the expected output *EOutput(t)*, the WFMS stub recognizes that there is an exception. In order for the WFMS stub to handle these exception, the WFMS stub suspends its execution, and notifies ConMan about the exceptions. ConMan sends suspend signals to active task agents, while the exception is being handled.

For exception handling, our approach uses the task ontology. Each task in the task ontology has a set of attributes and relationships. One relationship that a task may have is *has-exception*, which points to a topic node in the rules ontology. In other words, each task may have associations with specific exception-related rules topics. Figure 5 shows that a task (*obtain zoning certificate*) has exception rules that are related to the topic *variances*. The task also has other generic exceptions, such as deadline or timeout, with a relationship link *has-exception* to a rule topic *exception*. These other exception rules, related to external exceptions, such as system connection failure within timeout period, are also considered.

The WFMS stub formulates a change request cr by comparing the *Output* and *EOutput*. If the output is different from the expected output, or an output parameter and its values are not expected, then a WFMS stub sets cr $=\langle t_i, insert, co \rangle$, where co is the pair $\langle$ output parameter, unexpected result $\rangle$. For example, the *toxic waste site* was not in the expected output, but occurred in the output. This is an exception that will be incorporated into the change request cr. Once the change request has been formulated, it is sent to ConMan and the exception handling process begins. ConMan first locates t_i in the service ontology and follows the link (relationship) *has-exception(t_i)* to locate exception-related rules. If co satisfies the condition of a rule r, then the action of r is added as a migration rule, and the Self migration begins.

8   Related Work

Several techniques for handling dynamic changes and exceptions in workflow management systems exist. Some approaches address correctness issues in conjunction with dynamic structural changes [7,3,10]. They are concerned with dynamic changes of the control flow and the handling of in-progress workflow instances when the schema is modified. Some *ad hoc* changes are handled by late modeling strategies, i.e. the workflow definition contains incomplete nodes that can be fully specified at run-time [4].

In HEMATOWork [9] the system tries to achieve automatic decisions on which instances need to be changed and what modification actions are needed using a rule knowledge base. It is different from our approach in that they do not utilize the hierarchical conceptual organization of rules. In [8], exceptions in collaborative processes between contractors and subcontractors in Electronic Commerce are handled with a generic process type hierarchy (called *process template*). Each template type is annotated with characteristic exception types. Every exception type has an associated knowledge base entry that provides information for what situations it is critical, and how it can be handled. This approach is close to our approach with respect to its unexpected exception handling. They do not address explicit change requests.

9   Conclusions and Future Research

We have provided an ontology-based framework for Decentralized Workflow Change Management (DWFCM), called "Self Migration," for automatic runtime adaptation of decentralized workflows (called Self), in response to changes in both the execution environment and user requirements as well as changes in rules and policies that govern the workflow. We also provide a mechanism for exception handling. Our change management framework provides a model to manage workflow contexts, called ConMan, that includes not only the workflow execution status and the partition locations, but also keeps track of a set of user profiles and rules that are used in defining the customized workflow. Our model for Self adaptation allows 1) to express a change request, 2) to automatically identify, with the help of the rules ontology, migration rules necessary for accommodating changes, 3) to automatically apply these migration rules to generate a runtime customized workflow, and 4) resume and restart the execution.

Our approach is different from other studies on workflow adaptation, which assume the user's or a workflow designer's knowledge of the internal structure of the workflow or change knowledge. We intend to extend this work by pursuing the issues of workflow change authorization and accommodating simultaneous change requests from different sources.

References

1. Vijayalakshmi Atluri, Soon Ae Chun, and Pietro Mazzoleni. A Chinese Wall Security Model for Decentralized Workflow Systems. In *Proceedings of the 8th ACM Conference on Computer and Communications Security*, pages 48–57. ACM Press, 2001.
2. Vijayalakshmi Atluri, Soon Ae Chun, and Pietro Mazzoleni. Chinese Wall Security for Decentralized Workflow Management Systems. *Journal of Computer Security*, 2003. (in press).
3. F. Casati, S. Ceri, B. Pernici, and G. Pozzi. Workflow Evolution. *Data & Knowledge Engineering*, 24:211–238, 1998.
4. Fabio Casati, Ski Ilnicki, Li jie Jin, Vasudev Krishnamoorthy, and Ming-Chien Shan. Adaptive and Dynamic Service Composition in eFlow. In *Proceedings of CAiSE 2000*, pages 13–31, 2000.
5. Soon Ae Chun. *Decentralized Management of Dynamic and Customized Workflow*. PhD thesis, Department of Mangement Science and Information Systems, Rutgers University, Newark, 2003.
6. Soon Ae Chun, Vijayalakshimi Atluri, and Nabil R. Adam. Domain Knowledge-based Automatic Workflow Generation. In *Proceedings of the 13th International Conference on Database and Expert Systems Applications (DEXA 2002)*, Aix-en-Province, France, September 2002.
7. Clarence Ellis, Karim Keddara, and Grzegorz Rozenberg. Dynamic change within workflow systems. In *Proceedings of Conference on Organizational Computing Systems*, 1995.
8. Mark Klein and Chrysanthos Dellarocas. A Knowledge-Based Approach to Handling Exceptions in Workflow Systems. *Journal of Computer-Supported Collaborative Work. Special Issue on Adaptive Workflow Systems*, Vol 9(No 3/4), August 2000.
9. R. Muller, B. Heller, M. Loffler, E. Rahm, and A. Winter. HematoWork: A Knowledge-based Workflow System for Distributed Cancer Therapy. In *Proc. GMDS98*, Bremen, September 1998.
10. Shazia Sadiq. On Capturing Exceptions in Workflow Process Models. In *Proceedings of the 4th International Conference on Business Information Systems*, Poznan, Poland, April 2000. Springer-Verlag.

A QoS Oriented Framework for Adaptive Management of Web Service Based Workflows

Chintan Patel, Kaustubh Supekar, and Yugyung Lee

School of Computing and Engineering
University of Missouri-Kansas City
{copdk4,kss2r6,leeyu}@umkc.edu

Abstract. Web Services are emerging technologies that enable application-to-application communication and reuse of autonomous services over Web. Traditional Workflow Management Systems fail to provide a comprehensive solution for a Web Service based Workflow. A framework that meets the quality of service (QoS) requirements for ad hoc Internet based Services is rarely provided. Considering the increasing demand for expanding services and application requirements coupled with use of Web Services, it is a challenging task to develop a QoS model as a framework for Web Service based Workflows. In this paper, we have proposed a QoS oriented Framework, called WebQ, that is capable of conducting the adaptive selection process and simultaneously provides binding and execution of Web Services for the underlying workflow. To achieve these objectives, as the first step, we have designed a QoS model for Web Service selection, binding, and execution. We, then, develop a set of algorithms to compute QoS parameters and implement them using a rule-based system. A series of experiments performed on workflows composed of real Web Services have confirmed that the proposed framework is very effective in improving the overall QoS of the system.

1 Introduction

Web Services have been used to achieve system interoperability over the Web through exchange of application development and service interactions using the standards like Web Services Description Language (WSDL), Universal Description, Discovery and Integration (UDDI)[1], and Simple Object Access Protocol (SOAP)[2].

While current Web Service technologies show much progress, they are mainly limited to atomic services[3]. Thus, it is not adequate to handle autonomous and complex services in realistic settings. In dealing with this problem, some researchers [1] have developed languages to compose the individual Web Services

---

[1] http://www.uddi.org/pubs/Iru_UDDI_Technical_White_Paper.pdf
[2] www.w3.org/TR/SOAP
[3] http://www.w3.org/TR/ws-arch

V. Mařík et al. (Eds.): DEXA 2003, LNCS 2736, pp. 826–835, 2003.

into transactions or workflows. Web Services Flow Language (WSFL) was designed for service compositions in the form of a workflow[4], XLANG[5] for the behavior of a single Web Service. However, these works are insufficient for providing the adaptive Web Services generated from a particular context.

In fact, the automatic or semi-automatic management of service flows over the Web has not been achieved. For the purpose, we need to examine the characteristics of the composition model of Web Services. In the Web Services model that is quite different from traditional one, there is the large number of similar or equivalent services which user can freely select and use for their application. Second, since the service is developed and deployed by the third party, the quality of service is not guaranteed. Third, the services may not be adequate as per service requestor's requirements and kept evolving, without notification to service requestors, according to the provider's requirements and computing environment. Thus, it is important to provide adaptability to evolving services as well as diverse context of services.

Kammer et al. [2] suggested workflow to be dynamic, which allows changes with minimal impact to the ongoing execution of underlying workflow, as well as be reflexive, which provides knowledge about a workflow's applicability to the context and the effectiveness of its deployment evaluated over time. Understanding context associated with services may affect the quality of service. From this perspective, optimization may occur through the evaluation and refinement of a previous service flow. Facilitating service composition may not be difficult if one knows which Web Services and in which order to compose. However, automatic composition of services is challenging. This is because it is difficult to capture semantics and context of services and measure the quality of services. One exemplary effort that aims for this function is DAML-based Web Service Ontology (DAML-S)[6], describing the properties and capabilities of Web Services [3].

The goal of this paper is to develop a QoS-based Web Service framework, called WebQ, that enables to select appropriate Web Services, dynamically bind the services with the underlying workflow, and perform the refinement of existing services. Our definition of QoS considers the criteria with respect to Web Services and Workflow that renders a smooth and efficient execution of tasks. Since evaluation and refinement of services tend to be subjective, the generation of them needs a formal matrix, which can measure the requirements and quality of services. In the WebQ Framework, criteria is quantitatively set to evaluate whether a particular service is appropriate for specific service flow and to define service quality. This generic framework can be applicable to the various domains, such as e-commerce, medicine, and bioinformatics.

---

[4] http://www-3.ibm.com/software/solutions/webservices/pdf/WSFL.pdf
[5] http://www.gotdotnet.com/team/xml_wsspecs/xlang-c/default.htm
[6] http://www.daml.org/services/

2   Related Work

Workflow technology has been around since a decade and has been successful in automating many complex business processes. A significant amount of work has been done to deal with different aspects of workflow technology viz process modeling, dynamic workflows [4], and distributed workflows [5]. Process modeling languages such as IDEF, PIF [6], PSL [7] or CIMOSA [8] and frame based models of services were used to design process typing, resource dependencies, ports, task decomposition and exception.

On the other hand Web Services are emerging resources on the Web and have received a great deal of attention from the industry. Standards such as WSDL, SOAP, and UDDI are being developed for low-level descriptions of Web Services. Web Services Description Language (WSDL) provides a communication level description of the messages and protocols of services[7]. Simple Object Access Protocol (SOAP) invokes services through remote method invocations over HTTP. Universal Description, Discovery and Integration (UDDI) announces and discovers services which are registered by their providers at a logically central registry. Some emerging approaches include additional features through the use of ontologies, describing and indexing services based on process models [9].

Current research on Web Services paves way for Web Service based workflows, which has obvious advantages pertaining to scalability, heterogeneity, reuse and maintenance of services. Major issues in such inter-organizational service based workflows are service discovery, service contracts [10] and service composition. Service composition aids such as BizTalk[8] and WSFL were proposed to overcome the limitations of traditional workflow tools [8] which manually specify the composition of programs to perform some task. Other industrial initiatives such as BPEL4WS[9], XLANG concentrate on service representation issues to tackle the problem of service contracts, compositions and agreements. Current efforts [11] are to automate the complete process of service discovery, composition and binding using machine understandable languages. Some other recent advances are WS-Transaction[10] and WS-Coordination[11] which defines protocols for executing Transactions among Web Services. [12] focuses on modeling QoS of workflows, [13] defines a QoS based middleware for services associated with the underlying workflow, but it doesn't take into account QoS factors related to Internet based services. [14] describes QoS issues related to Web Services from the provider's perspective. We believe that the current research has not delved into QoS issues related to Web Service based workflows, many critical issues related to the availability, reliability, performance and security of Web Services need to be handled. Our approach tactfully utilizes and monitors these QoS parameters

---

[7] http://www.w3.org/TR/wsdl

[8] http://www.microsoft.com/biztalk/

[9] http://www-106.ibm.com/developerworks/webservices/library/ws-bpel/

[10] http://www-106.ibm.com/developerworks/webservices/library/ws-transpec/?dwzone=webservices

[11] http://www-106.ibm.com/developerworks/library/ws-coor/

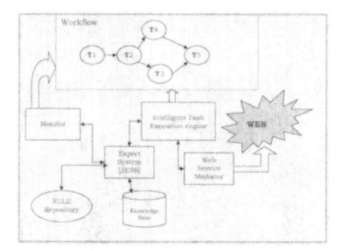

Fig. 1. The WebQ Architecture

to provide a consistent service interface to other applications in the workflow through adaptive QoS based selection, binding and execution of Web Services.

3   WebQ Framework

3.1   Architecture

WebQ architecture depicted in Fig. 1 is comprised of gamut of collaborative components that allows for QoS oriented adaptive management of Web Service based workflows. *Workflow*, the process under execution, is a collection of tasks that can either be accomplished by in-house services or third party services. DAML-S specification is used to specify workflow. *Web Service Mediator* queries UDDIs to retrieve Web Services for given tasks. *Monitor* is responsible for monitoring, measuring and asserting facts about the WebQ QoS parameters. *Intelligent Task Execution Engine* manages execution of tasks that are part of underlying workflow. The engine utilizes the DAML-S workflow specification to coordinate the execution of tasks, providing input to a task, binding and execution of a Web Service associated with the task, routing the request to appropriate task depending upon the output obtained. *Expert System* allows assertion of facts in the knowledge base depending upon the rules fired. WebQ uses JESS[12] which reduces the overhead associated with dynamic selection and binding of Web Service to a task at runtime. *Knowledge Base* is a repository of facts about Web Service related parameters (i.e., QoS parameters). *Rule Repository* collects rules used to specify user specific QoS requirements, available workflow QoS and elicitation of steps to be taken for achieving specified QoS requirement. We use a multi-level approach wherein firing of a set of atomic rules leads to composite rule being executed. For further details, please refer to [15].

---

[12] http://herzberg.ca.sandia.gov/jess/

We now illustrate various phases of workflow management in WebQ.

Phase 1: Workflow Modelling. A workflow is defined, using DAML-S, as a collection of tasks accomplished using in-house services-components or through third party services.

Phase 2: QoS Requirements Setting. QoS parameters associated with the underlying workflow are specified. In this paper, three QoS categories (task-specific, Internet service specific and general parameters) were introduced. Designer specifies QoS requirements in rule forms [15].

Phase 3: Initialization. WebQ fetches set of Web Services for every task in the underlying workflow. Each Web Service is assigned a uniform fitness value Ω. Fitness value Ω is defined as *how fit a web Service is for executing a task for given QoS requirement.* Initially, we randomly select m services per task as every Web Service has a uniform fitness value. It could be noted here that absence of apriori knowledge about third party services calls for assignment of uniform fitness value.

Phase 4: Execution and Monitoring. In the execution phase load per task is divided across m selected Web Services associated with that task. Rationale behind selecting best m Web Services and load distribution methodology is discussed in Section 3.3. Task is accomplished on execution of selected Web Services. During execution associated QoS parameters are monitored, recorded and asserted as facts in Knowledge Base.

Phase 5: Dynamic and adaptive Web Service selection. The process of continuous monitoring of workflow under execution updates related QoS parameters by updating associated fitness value. Deteriorating QoS of a selected Web Service triggers *Rule* that forces de-selecting poorly performed services and re-selecting m best services. The dynamic service selection process accounts for the adaptability of the framework to an ad-hoc environment where quality of a Web Service changes stochastically.

3.2   QoS Based Service Selection and Execution

Our QoS model proposed in this paper dynamically selects the best among the available services and performs parallel execution of services. The goal of the adaptive selection and execution is to maximize the overall QoS. For the purpose, we carefully reviewed QoS parameters and classified them into the following three categories: General, Internet Service Specific and task specific QoS parameters.

In order to design the Quality of Service for Web Service based workflow, multiple perspectives of the stakeholders of the system were considered. This task can be achieved by maintaining separate set of QoS management rules per user per task node, which would sum up to meet the overall desired QoS requirements. QoS model should be flexible and extensible enough to capture the fine granularity of requirements that could arise in any given domain. [13] considers only generalized QoS features for traditional Workflow Management Systems, an Internet based Service Workflow requires a comprehensive QoS model that also incorporates task specific QoS requirements. Tables 1 - 3 show a QoS model which captures all these essential features.

Table 1. General QoS parameters

QoS Parameter	Description
Performance (Latency)	The time taken to deliver services between service requestors and providers. $t_{latency} = t_{o/p}(X) - t_{i/p}(X)$, $t_{i/p}(X)$ is the timestamp when the service X is invoked and $t_{o/p}(X)$ is timestamp when the service X is delivered.
Performance (Throughput)	The number of requests served in a given period [13]. $t_{throughput} = \#$Service invocations in time T.
Reliability	This parameter is related to the number of failures of a service in a time interval. $R = 1 - P(success)$ where $P(success)$ is probability of successful executions, $P(success) = \#$successful executions$/\#$TotalInvocations
Cost	The cost of the service execution including the enactment cost (management of workflow system and monitoring [13]) and licensing fees of Web Services. $C = C(Enactment) + C(Licensing)$

Table 2. Internet-Service Specific QoS

QoS Parameter	Description
Availability	The probability that the service will be available at some period of time. An associated parameter is time-to-repair, the time taken to repair a service [14]. $P_{availability} = \#$SuccessExec$/\#$TotalInvoc $TTR = t_{restart}(X) - t_{failed}(X)$, where TTR represents Time To Repair, t_{failed} is timestamp when the service X failed, $t_{restart}$ is timestamp when service was restarted.
Security	Confidentiality, non repudiation message encryption and access control [14]. Values assigned by the workflow designer depending upon the strength of the Encryption technology used, PKI, Kerberos etc.
Accessibility	Instances when a particular service is not accessible even if its available because of high volume of requests. $P_{accessibility} = P_{availability}$ at Time $T = t$
Regulatory	A quality aspect which deals with issues of conformance of service with the rules, the law, compliance with standard, and the established Service Level Agreement [14]. Specific in-house ratings by the workflow designer at design time.

Table 3. Task Specific QoS

QoS Parameter	Description
Task specific	Related to the quality of the output or the type of service offered etc. $E(TaskQoS) = w_1 * f(p_1) + w_2 * f(p_2) + \ldots + w_n * f(p_n)$ where $f(p_i)$ refers to the probability function that maps the output of parameter p_i to a specific value depending upon how close the output is to the desired value w_i is the weight assigned to p_i.

3.3   Best One v/s Best m Approach

The WebQ QoS model allows selecting best service that fits the QoS requirement. The approach of selecting a single third party service to accomplish a task is inherently unreliable. Consider a scenario where we have n available services for a given task. Our Best One QoS model approach would select one service for that task. Most of Web Services used in the workflow are third party services that cannot be trusted. It is quite possible that the execution of workflow is in jeopardy because of failure of best available service. The problem can be accounted for single point dependency between the workflow task and third party service. Our model accommodates for such problem, we advocate selection of best m against single best service. The WebQ framework allows selection of best m services based on fitness value Ω. Selection of m allows load distribution across these services. One of approach is to equally distribute load across m services. In this way better service can take more load than an average service hence a weighted average approach can distribute the load across m best services.

The load distribution function (ldf) can be expressed as a function of fitness value Ω associated with Web Service. Load per Web Service $= ldf(X_i) = L_i = N * w_i; 1 < i < m; \sum w_i = 1$, X_i is the i_{th} service from set of m best services, N is the total number of inputs at a given time t. w_i is weight associated with Web Service X_i. It is function of fitness value Ω_i of X_i. $w_i = $ f (Ω_i). A Web Service X_i with a high fitness value Ω would have high weight w_i, $w_i = \Omega_i/\sum \Omega_i$. Consider an example where N $= 1000$ (weather information request), $n = 5$ (Weather Information Web Services), $m = 3$(The best selected Web Services). Assume observed fitness values on scale of 100 as $\Omega_1 = 95$, $\Omega_2 = 35$, $\Omega_3 = 85$, $\Omega_4 = 60$, $\Omega_5 = 50$. Three best Web Services are selected: X_1, X_3 and X_4. We assign weight to each Web Service $w_1 = 95/(95+85+60) = 0.395$, $w_3 = 85/(95+85+60) = 0.355$, $w_4 = 60/(95+85+60) = 0.25$. Based on this load distribution function, load per Web Service $L_1 = w_1 * N = 395, L_3 = w_3 * N = 355, L_4 = w_4 * N = 250$.

The Best m approach has a two-fold advantage. First, it makes the workflow fault-tolerant. Probability of failure of the workflow is now distributed across m services against a single point dependency. Failure of one or more Web Services would not completely jeopardize the execution of underlying workflow. Second, distributing load across m services improves efficiency of overall system as similar tasks can be concurrently executed. Thus, the concurrent, load distributed QoS model can render a fault tolerant, efficient and reliable workflow.

4   Implementation and Experimental Results

We implemented and deployed a Java based prototype of the proposed framework on Linux. The JESS rule-based QoS management system was constructed through Java implementation which reads the process specifications in DAML-S, selects, binds and executes Web Service from a service pool associated with each task. Monitor component asserts QoS measurements in the logDB, JESS Knowledge base. JESS Rules, measures of QoS requirements, are triggered by deteriorating Quality of Service. Dynamic service selection leads to the refinement of the workflow for maximizing the overall QoS. Java Web Services toolkit (JAX-RPC) was used for implementing the in-house Web Services and for interactions with third party Web Services.

A set of experiments have been conducted to validate the proposed QoS oriented framework for adaptive management of Web Service based workflows. In these experiments actual services available on the Internet were used. We focussed on a single task in the underlying workflow. The *weather information retrieval* task was selected as the basis of our experiments. The choice of task was dictated by the amount of freely available third party services for that task. The main goal of the tests was to determine the performance gain by our approach of distributing load per task across m task specific services and to illustrate how the dynamic service refinement process renders an efficient, high performance and a fault tolerant workflow. Following Web Services were selected to accomplish the task of retrieving weather information.

Table 4. Input for the Performance Gain Experiments

ID	Provider[1]	WSDL
WS1	www.xmethods.net	http://www.xmethods.net/sd/2001/TemperatureService.wsdl
WS2	www.ejse.com	http://www.ejse.com/weatherservice/service.asmx?WSDL
WS3	www.juice.com	http://webservices.juice.com:4646/temperature.wsdl
WS4	FastWeather	http://ws2.serviceobjects.net/fw/FastWeather.asmx?WSDL

We validate the proposed QoS based selection approach, a set of Web Services (Table 4) were tested rigorously across Internet and their QoS parameters were measured over a period of time. In these tests, we monitored a subset of QoS parameters - availability, latency, throughput, and performance gain.

QoS requirements on selecting the task node were services which are 1) highly available 2) handle large number of inputs and 3) provide maximum throughput. The experimental results (Fig. 2(a), 2(b), 2(c)) at instances $t = t_1$ and $t = t_2$ show the associated QoS parameter values for Web Services WS_1, WS_2, WS_3 and WS_4 at time t_1 and t_2 respectively. The number of inputs(load) at time $t = t_1$ were 30 and $t = t_2$ were 50. JESS Rules, measure of aforementioned QoS requirements, were triggered to select services WS_1, WS_3 (m=2) at $t = t_1$ and WS_1, WS_2($m = 2$) at $t = t_2$. It is important to note that the failure of service WS_3 that was selected at time $t = t_1$ doesn't effect quality of the underlying workflow. It is because our dynamic Web Service selection at $t = t_2$ leads to selection of the new set of best m (=2) services, WS_1 and WS_2.

Moreover our research into existing Web Services revealed a highly important factor concerning the Availability parameter. Many Web Services listed on UDDIs were not available for most of time, hence we assert that Availability is an important QoS factor to take into consideration for selection of services.

---

[1] The services were used for just experimental analysis but we do not intent to endorse or discriminate between providers.

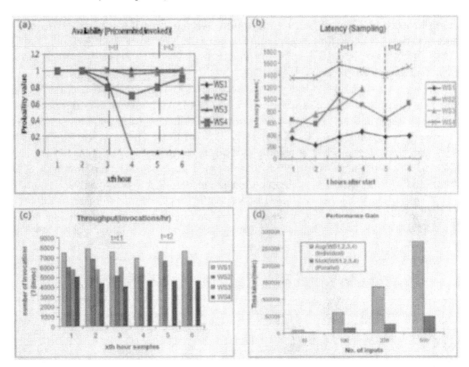

Fig. 2. Experimental Results:(a) Availability (b)Latency (c) Throughput (d) Performance Gain

Our results confirmed that Performance is also an important parameter for selection for the service. Tests revealed a large amount of variation in the performance of the Web Services. For Web Services WS_2 (mean latency = 800ms) and WS_3(mean latency = 775 ms) we observed there are very high values of variance, 110 ms and 132 ms respectively. Hence in such unpredictable Internet environment, creating a Internet based workflow demands strict performance monitoring and subsequent dynamic modification of the workflow execution.

Finally, we tested each of the services individually, then incorporated them into our Workflow, and compared the difference in their performances. Performance gain, G, is ratio of total time taken for single Web Service (n inputs) to the time taken when all services in set S are executed simultaneously with n inputs being divided among them. We conducted tests for 10, 100, 250 and 500 inputs, corresponding performance gain was calculated, $G = 3.28, 4.31, 5.38, 5.62$ respectively. Results indicate an average performance gain of 400% ($G = 4$). Higher values of ($G > 4$) can be attributed to the fact that WebQ uses weighted average load distribution function against uniform load distribution. The results as depicted in Fig. 2(d) strengthen our hypotheses that the WebQ approach of load distribution renders a high performance and fault-tolerant workflow.

5   Conclusions

We proposed a Web Service based framework for adaptive workflow management. A comprehensive QoS model can provide consistent interface of Web Services to workflow-based applications. Incorporated rules in the framework helped to establish a dynamic workflow by achieving a fine-grained control over service selection. The experimental results confirmed the effectiveness of the framework in enhancing the overall QoS of the system. As an ongoing work, we have extended the rule-base system to achieve automatic Web Service composition using advanced Semantically enriched Web Services model, that allows semantic service matching, composition and choreography.

References

1. V. Benjamins et al., Ibrow3: An intelligent brokering service for knowledge-component reuse on the world-wide web, In The 11th Banff Knowledge Acquisition for knowledge-Based System Workshop, 1998.
2. P. Kammer, G. Bolcer, R. Taylor, M. Bergman, Techniques for Supporting Dynamic and Adaptive Workflow, J of Computer Supported Cooperative Work, 269–292.
3. D. McDermott, M. Burstein, D. Smith, Overcoming ontology mismatches in transactions with self-describing agents, Proc. of the First International Semantic Web Working Symposium, 285–302, 2001
4. J. Meng, S. Su, H. Lam, A. Helal, Achieving Dynamic Inter-organizational Workflow Management by Integrating Business Processes, Events, and Rules, Proc. of the Thirty-Fifth Hawaii International Conference on System Sciences, 2002.
5. J. A. Miller, D. Palaniswami, A. Sheth, K. Kochut, H. Singh. WebWork: METEOR 2's web-based workflow management system. Journal of Intelligent Information Systems, 10(2):185–215, 1998
6. J. Lee et al. The PIF process interchange format and framework. Technical Report 180, MIT Center for Coordination Science, 1995.
7. C. Schlenoff et al., The essence of the process specification language, Transactions of the Society for Computer Simulation, 16(4), pp. 204–216, 1999.
8. K. Kosanke, CIMOSA – Open System Architecture for CIM; ESPRIT Consortium AMICE, Springer-Verlag 1993.
9. M. Klein, A. Bernstein, Searching for services on the semantic web using process ontologies, Proc. of the International Semantic Web Working Symposium, 2001
10. Y. Hoffner, H. Ludwig, P. Grefen, K. Aberer, Crossflow: Integrating Workflow Management and Electronic Commerce, SIGeCOM, 2001
11. S. McIlraith, T. Son, H. Zeng, Semantic Web services, IEEE Intelligent Systems, 16(2), 46–53, 2001.
12. J. Cardoso, A. Sheth, J. Miller, Workflow Quality Of Service, Proc. Enterprise Integration and Modeling Technology and Intern. Enterprise Modeling, 2002.
13. A. Sheth, J. Cardoso, J. Miller, K. Koch, QoS for Service-oriented Middleware, Proc. of the Conference on Systemics, Cybernetics and Informatics, 2002.
14. A. Mani, A. Nagarajan, Understanding quality of service for Web services, http://www-106.ibm.com/developerworks/library/ws-quality.html
15. C. Patel, K. Supekar, Y. Lee, Adaptive Workflow Management for Web Service using QoS Framework, Technical Report TR030103, University of Missouri – Kansas City, 2003.

Discovering Role-Relevant Process-Views for Recommending Workflow Information

Minxin Shen and Duen-Ren Liu

Institute of Information Management,
National Chiao-Tung University
1001 Ta Hsueh Road,
Hsinchu 300, Taiwan
{shen,dliu}@iim.nctu.edu.tw

Abstract. Workflow technology automates business processes to increase managerial efficiency. However, workers (representing organizational roles) cannot easily obtain a global view of a complex and large workflow. This work proposes a process-view based recommendation of workflow information to address this problem. A process-view is an abstracted process derived from a physical process, and can provide adaptable task granularity. The relationships among tasks, roles and operations, as specified in role-based access control systems, are used to evaluate the degrees of relevance between roles and tasks. Next, a novel algorithm is proposed to generate automatically role-relevant process-views based on degrees of relevance. Workflow systems can thus recommend abstracted workflow information through process-views for those roles in a complex workflow.

1 Introduction

As an effective process management tool, workflow management systems (WfMS) allow a business to analyze, simulate, design, enact, control and monitor the processes involved in its general business [3, 4]. Despite notational differences, activity-based methodologies [3] are extensively used process modeling techniques. A typical activity-based approach designs a workflow though a top-down decomposition procedure. This stepwise refinement allows a modeler to define a process more easily and completely than do one-step approaches.

In practice, workflow participants possess different needs and types of authority when obtaining information on business processes. For example, a high-level manager may need aggregated information of a process, and a marketing manager may not have the authority and need to know each specific step of production flow. However, the activity-based model cannot flexibly alter task granularity of a process based on role characteristics. Therefore, WfMS may not provide each organizational level and unit with an appropriate view of that process. This work aims to develop a method that can recommend workflow information at a customized granularity to workers.

Recommending relevant and necessary documents to workers in order to accomplish their tasks in a workflow environment has been addressed in Refs. [1, 6].

V. Mařík et al. (Eds.): DEXA 2003, LNCS 2736, pp. 836–845, 2003.

However, these studies suggested task-specific information, rather than process-oriented knowledge, such as of the progress status of an entire workflow. Our earlier study [5] described a process-view model that enhances the ability of conventional activity-based process models to abstract processes, and can present a process definition at adaptable task granularity. A process-view, i.e., a virtual process, is abstracted from an actual process. According to the requirements of distinct organizational roles, a process modeler can design various process-views, providing the process information suitable for each participant. However, the preliminary process-view model requires process modelers (domain experts) to define various process-views for distinct roles. Process-view design is complex and time-consuming. Therefore, this work proposes a novel approach to assisting the discovery of *role-relevant* process-views and applies the results to recommend workflow information.

This work first presents a quantitative method for evaluating the degrees of relevance between tasks and organizational roles. Different roles may perform different workflow operations on tasks, under the restriction of permission rules in role-based access control systems [2]. Thus, permission rules, which prescribe the authorization relationships among roles, tasks and operations, and audit logs of task execution are utilized to measure the degrees of relevance between roles and tasks. Based on the relevance degrees and the granular threshold, novel algorithms are proposed herein to derive role-relevant process-views. Process designers or workers specify the granular threshold to control the granularity of generated process-views. Thus, during workflow enactment, WfMS can recommend workflow information at a suitable granularity to participants; that is, more relevant parts are presented with a finer resolution and less relevant parts are presented more coarsely.

The rest of this paper is organized as follows. Section 2 presents the process-view based recommendation of workflow information. Formal definitions and the means of constructing an order-preserving process-view, as presented in [5], are also summarized. Next, Section 3 presents the procedure for evaluating relevance degrees between roles and tasks. The algorithms for discovering role-relevant process-views are also presented. Section 4 draws conclusions.

2   Recommendation of Workflow Information

A process-view - an abstracted process derived from a physical process - reveals abstracted process information. Process designers can define various role-relevant process-views, according to the characteristics of participating roles, to achieve different levels of information concealment. The following presents process-view based recommendation of workflow information, and then formally defines base processes, process-views and order-preserving process-views.

2.1   Process-View Based Recommendation

A process that may have multiple process-views is referred to herein as a *base process*. A process-view is generated from either base processes or other process-views and is considered a *virtual process*. From the users' perspective, a process-view resembles a typical process that consists of activities (tasks) and dependencies although it is an abstracted form of an implemented process.

Fig. 1 illustrates process-view based recommendation of workflow information. Assume that the base process is a manufacturing process. Marketers do not need to know every step in the process, although they must know the progress of order fulfillment to serve their customers. A process modeler can design an appropriate process-view for the marketing department as follows: a_1, a_2, and a_3 are mapped into va_1; a_4 and a_5 are mapped into va_2; a_6 and a_7 are mapped into va_3. Thus, WfMS can recommend workflow information at the granularity suitable for marketers to serve their customers.

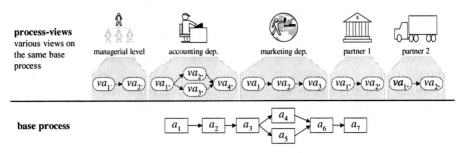

Fig. 1. Process-view based recommendation of workflow information

2.2   Basic Definitions: Base Process and Process-View

Fig. 2 illustrates how the components of our model are related. To differentiate the terminology used in base process and process-view, this work uses the terms *virtual activity/dependency* for the process-view while the terms *base activity/dependency* are used for the base process. A virtual activity is an abstraction of a set of base activities and corresponding base dependencies. A virtual dependency connects two virtual activities in a process-view.

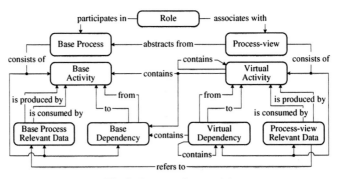

Fig. 2. Process-view model

The following summarizes basic definitions of base process and process-view. Please refer to [5] for detailed definitions, semantics and examples.

Definition 1 (Base process). A base process *BP* is a 2-tuple $\langle BA, BD \rangle$, where

1. *BD* is a set of dependencies. A dependency is denoted by $dep(x, y, C)$. Condition *C* represents the constraints, such as time or events, that determine whether routing can proceed from activity *x* to activity *y*.

2. *BA* is a set of activities. An activity is a 3-tuple $\langle SPLIT\_ \ flag, JOIN\_ \ flag, SC \rangle$, where (a) *SPLIT_ flag/JOIN_ flag* may be "NULL", "AND" or "XOR", respectively, representing *sequence, AND-split/join* and *XOR-split/join* as specified by the Workflow Management Coalition (WfMC) [8]. (b) *SC* is the *starting condition* of this activity. A workflow engine evaluates *SC* to determine whether this activity can be started. If *JOIN_ flag* is NULL, *SC* equals the condition associated with its incoming dependency. If *JOIN_ flag* is AND/XOR, *SC* equals Boolean AND/XOR combination of the conditions of all incoming dependencies.

3. For x, $y \in BA$: (a) If there is a path from *x* to *y* in *BP*, then the ordering of *x* is higher than *y*, i.e., *x* precedes *y*. Their ordering relation in *BP* is denoted by $x > y$ or $y < x$. (b) If no path exists from *x* to *y* or from *y* to *x* in *BP*, then *x* and *y* are ordering independent, i.e., *x* and *y* proceed independently. Their ordering relation in *BP* is denoted by $x \infty y$.

Definition 2 (Process-view). A process-view is a 2-tuple $\langle VA, VD \rangle$, where (1) *VA* is a set of virtual activities. (2) *VD* is a set of virtual dependencies. (3) Analogous to base process, $\forall va_i$, $va_j \in VA$, the *ordering relation* between va_i and va_j may be ">", "<", or "∞".

2.3 Order-Preserving Process-View

According to the different properties of a base process, various approaches can be developed to derive a process-view. A novel *order-preserving* approach to derive a process-view from a base process has been presented in [5] and is summarized below. This approach ensures that the original execution order in a base process is preserved. A *legal* virtual activity in an order-preserving process-view must follow three rules: membership, atomicity, and order preservation rules [5]. The following defines virtual activities and virtual dependencies in an order-preserving process-view.

Definition 3 (Virtual Activity). For a base process $BP = \langle BA, BD \rangle$, a virtual activity *va* is a 5-tuple $\langle A, D, SPLIT\_flag, JOIN\_flag, SC \rangle$, where

1. *A* is a nonempty set, and its members follow three rules:
   a. Members of *A* are base activities that are also members of *BA* or other previously defined virtual activities that are derived from *BP*.
   b. *va* is started if one member activity is started, and is completed if all member activities are completed. (Note: this is a simplified expression of the original definition in [5])
   c. For any $x \in BA$, $x \notin A$, $\Re \in \{<, >, \infty\}$: if existing $y \in A$ such that $x \ \Re \ y$ holds in *BP*, then $x \ \Re \ z$ holds in *BP* for all $z \in A$. That means the ordering relations between *x* and all members (base activities) of *A* are identical in *BP*.

2. $D = \{dep(x, y, C_{xy}) \mid dep(x, y, C_{xy}) \in BD \text{ and } x, y \in A\}$.

3. *SPLIT_ flag/JOIN_ flag* may be "NULL" or "MIX". NULL suggests that *va* has a single outgoing/incoming virtual dependency while MIX indicates that *va* has multiple outgoing/incoming virtual dependencies.
4. *SC* is the starting condition of *va*.

The *SPLIT_ flag* and *JOIN_ flag* cannot simply be described as AND or XOR since *va* is an abstraction of a set of base activities that may be associated with different ordering structures. Therefore, MIX is used to abstract the complicated ordering structures. A WfMS evaluates *SC* to determine whether *va* can be started. Members of *A* are called *va*'s *member activities*, and members of *D* are called *va*'s *member dependencies*. To save space, the abbreviated notation $va = \langle A, D \rangle$ is employed below to represent a virtual activity.

Definition 4 (Virtual Dependency). For two virtual activities $va_i = \langle A_i, D_i \rangle$ and $va_j = \langle A_j, D_j \rangle$ that are derived from a base process $BP = \langle BA, BD \rangle$, a virtual dependency from va_i to va_j is $vdep(va_i, va_j, VC_{ij}) = \{ dep(a_x, a_y, C_{xy}) \mid dep(a_x, a_y, C_{xy}) \in BD, a_x \in A_i, a_y \in A_j \}$, where the virtual condition VC_{ij} is a Boolean combination of C_{xy}.

3   Discovering Role-Relevant Process-Views

This section first describes the measurement of the relevance degrees between roles and tasks, and then proposes three algorithms to generate automatically process-views for workflow participants.

3.1   Role-Task Relevance

The crucial part of process-view design is finding the relevance degree between each activity (task) and each role in a given base process. Based on these relevance degrees, process designers can define appropriate process-views for different organizational roles. Consequently, WfMS can recommend workflow information at a suitable granularity to participants, i.e., more relevant parts are presented with a finer resolution and less relevant parts are coarser.

Process designers can directly evaluate the relevance degrees between tasks and roles. However, inconsistency and bias may occur without criteria for evaluating relevance degrees. Moreover, as the number of tasks grows, the evaluation becomes excessively complex. Besides, knowledge embedded in access control systems is not utilized. WfMC has defined several *workflow operations* for controlling and monitoring task execution [7]. For example, *WMFetchActivityInstanceState* returns an activity state, and *WMReassignWorkItem* reassigns an activity from one participant to another. Whether a role is authorized to perform an operation on a task object is determined by the organization's security systems, or more specifically, by *role-based access control* systems [2]. Hence, this work applies these different operations as the criteria for evaluating degrees of relevance since their number is finite, and the relationships among tasks, roles and operations are specified by security constraints.

The associations between roles and tasks are established based on workflow operations. Each task is associated with a set of operations that participating roles may perform on it. For example, a role may perform *WMChangedActivityInstance-*

State operation on a task. Therefore, if participating roles evaluate the relevance degrees of these operations, then the role-task associations can be quantified. However, security constraints are such that roles cannot perform operations on tasks arbitrarily. Accordingly, the relevance degrees between roles and tasks are evaluated

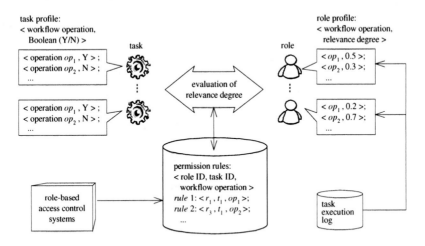

Fig. 3. Evaluating role-task relevance

based on the usage of workflow operations and the access control policies. Fig. 3 depicts the framework for evaluating role-task relevance. For example, if the relevance degree of role *r* with respect to operation *op* is 0.4 (role profile); task *t* supports operation *op* (task profile), and *r* is authorized to perform *op* on *t* (permission rule), then the relevance degree between role *r* and task *t* is assessed as 0.4. The main components are as follows.

Task profile. Different tasks may be associated with different operations. A task profile records which operations can be performed on a given task.

Role profile. A role has different degrees of relevance to its authorized operations. A role *r*'s profile includes a set of pairs ⟨operation *op*, relevance degree *deg* ⟩, which indicates that the relevance degree of role *r* with respect to operation *op* is *deg*.

Permission rules. These rules are derived from access control systems, and govern which role is authorized to perform which workflow operation on which task. Namely, a permission rule ⟨role *r*, task *t*, operation *op* ⟩ states that role *r* is authorized to perform operation *op* on task *t*.

Task execution log. Each record in this database is a 3-tuple ⟨TaskInstNo, RoleInstNo, operation name⟩, where TaskInstNo/RoleInstNo is a task/role instance identifier. A log record states that a role instance has performed a specific operation on a task instance.

Construction of role profile. Initially, role profiles are constructed by analyzing these logs. Let *M* denote the number of tasks on which operation *op* is performed, and let *N* denote the number of tasks on which role *r* performs operation *op*. The default degree of relevance of *r* with respect to *op* is *N/M*. For example, if the

ChangedActivityInstanceState operation is performed on 100 tasks, and the *IT manager* executes 20s of them, then the relevance degree of *IT manager* with respect to the *ChangedActivityInstanceState* operation is 0.2. Several factors can also be considered to enrich the role profiles. Intuitively, a higher frequency or cost associated with an operation performed by a role corresponds to a higher relevance degree of the operation to the role. Let Q denote the number of tasks executed by role r. The frequency that r performs operation *op* is N/Q. Meanwhile, cost can be measured by the time and money consumed by roles in performing operations on tasks.

Evaluation of role-task relevance. The relevance degrees between a given role and tasks of a workflow can be derived from the role/task profiles and permission rules. For example, given a permission rule $\langle$role r, task t, operation op_1 $\rangle$, role r's profile $\{\langle op_1, 0.4 \rangle, \langle op_2, 0.8 \rangle, ... \}$, and task t's profile $\{\langle op_1, Y \rangle, \langle op_1, Y \rangle, ... \}$, the relevance degree between role r and task t is 0.4. However, if another rule $\langle r, t, op_2 \rangle$ is added, then the relevance degree is $\max(0.4, 0.8) = 0.8$. That is, the maximum relevance degree is selected when a role is authorized to perform multiple operations on a single task.

3.2 Algorithms for Generating Process-Views

This section presents three algorithms to generate automatically process-views based on the relevance degrees derived as described above.

3.2.1 Generating Virtual Activities of a Process-View

Algorithm 1 determines the virtual activity set of a process-view definition from a base process. The process of generating virtual activities begins with the *highest ordering* activities in the base process. When the total relevance degree of a set of base activities approximates the *granular threshold* TH, as specified by the process designer, a virtual activity is found. The above steps are repeated against residual base activities until virtual activities cover all base activities of the base process. Consequently, the virtual activity set of the target process-view is found. The following explains four important parts of algorithm 1, including the granular threshold, the total relevance degree, the virtual activity generator (algorithm 2), and the verification of order-preserving property (algorithm 3).

Algorithm 1 (The generation of virtual activity set)

```
1:  input: a base process BP = ⟨BA, BD⟩.
2:  output: the virtual activity set (VA) of a process-view VP = ⟨VA, VD⟩
3:  require: f_RD (a_i) ≤ TH for all activities of BP.
4:
5:  procedure main(base process BP = ⟨BA, BD⟩)
6:  begin
7:      i ← 1;
8:      repeat
9:          va_i = ⟨A_i, D_i⟩ ← ⟨∅, ∅⟩;
```

```
10:          residual activity set RAS ← BA−{x | x belongs to one of A_j, j = 1.. i };
11:          select a highest ordering activity x from RAS;
12:          va_i ← VAGenerator(x, RAS, BP);
13:          i ← i + 1;
14:      until  for all x∈ BA, x belongs to one of A_j, j = 1.. i
15:      return VA ← { va_j }, j = 1.. i;
16: end
```

Granular threshold TH. This parameter determines the granularity of generated process-view. A virtual activity is an aggregation of a set of base activities. When the sum of the relevance degrees of some base activities approximates the threshold value, these activities can form a virtual activity, which is seen as relevant enough to the role. A larger TH corresponds to the generation of fewer virtual activities (and more base activities included in a virtual activity). Notably, TH must be larger than or equal to the maximum relevance degree between roles and tasks (line 3).

Total relevance degree $F_{RD}(\ )$. Simply, if the function f_{RD} (base activity ba) returns the relevance degree of ba and function F_{RD} (activity set A) returns the total relevance degree of A, then $F_{RD}(A) = \Sigma f_{RD}(a_i)$ for all $a_i \in A$.

However, ordering structures should be considered. Consider an example in which the threshold value equals 1, a base activity a_1 splits into a_2 and a_3, and their relevance degrees to a role are 0.6, 0.3, and 0.4, respectively. Clearly, the three activities do not belong to the same virtual activity, according to the above formula $(f_{RD}(a_1)+f_{RD}(a_2)+f_{RD}(a_3) >$ threshold). However, during run-time, all activities that follow *AND-split* are executed while only one activity is executed after *XOR-split*. Thus, if the split structure is *XOR-split* in the example, then the maximum relevance degree of the three activities is expected to be 0.6+0.4, rather than 0.6+0.3+0.4 or 0.6+0.3. Namely, the total relevance degree $F_{RD}(A)$ is the maximum expected value of $\Sigma f_{RD}(a_i)$ for all $a_i \in A$. The above discussion also holds for *XOR-join*.

Virtual activity generation. Algorithm 2 discovers a virtual activity that contains a given base activity and has approximately the maximum degree of relevance below the granular threshold TH. For a virtual activity $va = \langle A, D \rangle$, the members of A must be identified first, since D can be derived from A. Initially, A contains only the given activity a (line 3). Algorithm 2 then determines whether the activities adjacent to members of A can be added to maximize its total relevant degree $(F_{RD}(A))$ to approximate TH. A is updated during the *while* loop (lines 7 ~ 15) by adding the adjacent activities that cause A to satisfy three conditions: A conforms to the order-preserving property (line 10, see algorithm 3); total relevance degree of A does not exceed the threshold ($F_{RD}(A_{tmp}) \leq$ TH); A does not overlap with previously derived virtual activities $(A_{tmp} \subseteq RAS)$. The *repeat-until* loop (lines 4 ~ 16) continues until no other adjacent activity is added to A (line 16, $A = TAS$), i.e., no more adjacent activity can be added to A while still satisfying the threshold limit and maintaining order-preservation.

Following the determination of A, the members of D are those dependencies whose succeeding and preceding activities are both members of A (Definition 3.2). Thus, the virtual activity of $va = \langle A, D \rangle$ is generated (lines 17 ~ 18).

Algorithm 2   (The generation of a virtual activity whose total relevance degree approximate granular threshold)

```
1:   procedure VAGenerator(seed activity a, residual activity set RAS, BP=⟨BA,BD⟩)
2:   begin
3:       va = ⟨A, D⟩ ← ⟨{a}, ∅⟩;
4:       repeat
5:           temp activity set TAS ← A;
6:           adjacent activity set AAS ←{ x | x, y∈ RAS, x∉ A, y∈ A, and dep(x, y)∈ BD };
7:           while AAS is not empty do
8:           select an activity x from AAS;
9:           remove x from AAS;
10:          A_tmp ← OP(A ∪ {x}, BP);           /* check order-preserving property */
11:          if ( F_RD(A_tmp) ≤ TH ) and (A_tmp ⊆ RAS ) then        /* check threshold */
12:              A ← A_tmp;
13:              AAS ← AAS − {y | y∈ AAS ∩ A};
14:          end if
15:          end while
16:  until A = TAS
17:  a dependency set D ← { dep(x, y) | x, y∈ A, and dep(x, y)∈ BD };
18:  return va = ⟨A, D⟩;
19:  end
```

Verification of order-preserving property. For a given activity set AS, algorithm 3 is capable of obtaining the member activities of a minimum and order-preserving virtual activity. According to the definition of a virtual activity (Definition 3.1.c), a legal virtual activity $va = ⟨A, D⟩$ must satisfy the order-preserving condition: the ordering relations between x and all members of A that belong to BP are identical for any base activity $x∈ BA$ and $x∉ A$.

Algorithm 3 (The generation of a legal virtual activity)

```
1:   procedure OP (activity set AS, base process BP = ⟨BA, BD⟩)
2:       begin
3:       repeat
4:           temp activity set TAS ←AS;
5:           adjacent activity set AAS ← { x | x, y∈ BA, x∉ AS, y∈ AS and dep(x, y)∈ BD };
6:           while AAS is not empty do
7:               select an activity x from AAS;
8:               remove x from AAS;
9:                   if ∃y, z∈ AS, and x, y, z∈ BA such that (x ℜ y holds in BP but x ℜ z
10:                      does not holds in BP, where ℜ∈ {<, >, ∞} ) then
11:                  /* the ordering relations between x and all base activities of AS are
12:                      not identical */
13:                      add x to AS;
14:               end if
15:           end while
16:  until AS = TAS
17:  return AS;
18:  end
```

3.2.2 Generating Virtual Dependencies
The derivation of virtual dependencies and *SPLIT/JOIN_ flag* of virtual activities are omitted herein and similar to those in Ref. [5].

4 Conclusions

This work presents a process-view based recommendation of workflow information. Task granularity of recommended information is adapted to the needs of workflow participants. Workers can thus obtain helpful views of a large and complex workflow. This work proposes a systematic procedure for measuring the degrees of relevance between roles and tasks to support the discovery of role-relevant process-views. Role-based access control systems formally authorize roles to perform workflow operations on tasks. The relationships among roles, tasks and operations are listed in permission rules. Therefore, this work uses workflow operations as criteria to evaluate role-task relevance. Role-relevant process-views are automatically generated based on evaluation results using the proposed algorithms. Accordingly, WfMS can recommend workers with process-oriented knowledge at the granularity suitable for their organizational role.

Acknowledgements. This research was supported by the National Science Council of the Republic of China under the grant NSC 91-2416-H-009-008.

References

[1] A. Abecker, A. Bernardi, H. Maus, M. Sintek, and C. Wenzel, "Information Supply for Business Processes: Coupling Workflow with Document Analysis and Information Retrieval", *Knowledge-Based Systems*, 13(5), pp. 271–284, 2000.

[2] D. F. Ferraiolo, R. Sandhu, S. Gavrila, D. R. Kuhn, and R. Chandramouli, "Proposed NIST Standard for Role-Based Access Control", *ACM Transactions on Information and Systems Security*, 4(3), pp. 224–274, 2001.

[3] D. Georgakopoulos, M. Hornick, and A. Sheth, "An Overview of Workflow Management - from Process Modeling to Workflow Automation Infrastructure", *Distributed and Parallel Databases*, 3(2), pp. 119–153, 1995.

[4] F. Leymann and W. Altenhuber, "Managing Business Processes as an Information Resource", *IBM Systems Journal*, 33(2), pp. 326–348, 1994.

[5] D.-R. Liu and M. Shen, "Workflow Modeling for Virtual Processes: An Order-Preserving Process-View Approach", *Information Systems*, 28(6), pp. 505–532, 2003.

[6] S. Staaba and H.-P. Schnurr, "Smart Task Support through Proactive Access to Organizational Memory", *Knowledge-Based Systems*, 13(5), pp. 251–260, 2000.

[7] Workflow Management Coalition, "Workflow Management Application Programming Interface (Interface 2&3) Specification", Technical report WFMC-TC-1009, 1998.

[8] Workflow Management Coalition, "The Workflow Reference Model", Technical report WfMC TC-1003, Jan. 19, 1995.

Termination Analysis of Active Rules with Priorities

Alain Couchot

Conservatoire National des Arts et Métiers,
Paris, France
couchot-a@wanadoo.fr

Abstract. This paper presents an algorithm for termination static analysis of active rules with priorities. Active rules termination is an undecidable problem. Several recent works have suggested proving termination by using the concept of triggering graph. We propose here a refinement of these works, exploiting the priorities defined between rules. We introduce the notions of path set and destabilizing set. We show how to determine the priority of a path set. The triggering graph can then be reduced thanks to considerations about priorities of the path sets. Much more termination situations can be detected, since priorities are exploited.

1 Introduction

Databases are now endowed with a reagent behavior. They can react to variations of the environment, and modify the stored data according to these variations. This results from two technological tendencies: on the one hand, the development of the rules languages (production rules, active rules, deductive rules), and, on the other hand, the development of object oriented technologies. Rules languages and object oriented technology play additional roles : the object oriented technology allows to integrate into the same entity the structural aspects and the behavioral aspects, and the rules languages allow to describe the reaction of an entity according to its environment.

However, although the vocation of rules is to facilitate design and programming, writing a rules set is still a delicate work, reserved for specialists. Indeed, a rules set is not a structured entity : the global behavior of a rules set is difficult to foresee and to control [1]. Two important points were underlined by research works concerned with rules : the *termination* problem (the rules execution can sometimes be infinite), and the *confluence* problem (the same rules do not necessarily provide the same results, according to the order of rules execution).

We are here interested in the active rules termination problem. The active rules are structured according to paradigm Event-Condition-Action. Event is an immediate fact, which can arise inside or outside of the system. Condition is a predicate or a request on the database. Action is generally composed of a sequence of database updates, or of a procedure containing database updates. Coupling modes allow to specify the evaluation moment of the Condition part, or the execution moment of the Action part. The most frequent modes are immediate mode and deferred mode. A rule can be triggered by a single occurrence of an event: *instance oriented rule*, or by a set of occurrences of an event: *set oriented rule*.

V. Mařík et al. (Eds.): DEXA 2003, LNCS 2736, pp. 846–855, 2003.

In the section 2, we present the previous work on the subject; in the section 3, we expose a motivating example; in the section 4, we introduce the path sets of a rule and the path sets of a path; in the section 5, we propose a reduction of the triggering graph based on the consideration of the prioritites defined for the active rules; the section 6 ends.

2   Previous Works

The active rules termination is an undecidable problem. The previous works on the active rules analysis generally propose criteria supplying sufficient conditions allowing to guarantee termination.

The majority of works on active rules termination exploit the concept of *triggering graph*.

[1] defines the notion of *triggering graph* ; a such graph is built by means of a syntactic analysis of rules ; the nodes of the graph are rules. Two rules *r1* and *r2* are connected by a oriented edge from *r1* to *r2* if the action of *r1* can provoke a triggering event of *r2*. The presence of cycles in such a graph means a risk of non-termination of the rules set. The absence of cycles in the triggering graph guarantees the termination of the rules set. However, the possible deactivation of the rule condition is not taken into account by this analysis. Some techniques refine the triggering graph analysis, taking into account the condition part of the rules [2, 4, 5, 6, 7, 8]. [3] studies the influence of composite events on the termination property. The influence of the priorities on the termination property are considered by [2]. A self-deactivating rule *R* can be removed from the triggering graph, if the priorities of the rules included in the paths from *R* to the rule which can reactivate the condition of *R* (the paths do not include *R*) is strictly lower than the priorities of the rules included in the paths from *R* to the rule which can trigger *R* (the paths include *R*).

Our work is based on the following observation : priorities between rules can be used to refine termination analysis. This observation has just partially been taken into account by [2], within the framework of the self-deactivating rules. We show in this paper that much more termination cases can be detected using the priorities between rules.

The aim of our work is to reduce the triggering graph, thanks to the priorities of the rules. We first introduce the notions of *path set of a rule* and *path set of a path*. The path set includes the paths which are executed before a rule (or before a path). We determine then the priority of a path set. We also propose the notion of *destabilizing set of a path*. The destabilizing set of a path includes the rules which oppose the deactivation of the path. Thanks to the priorities of a path set, we can sometimes reduce the destabilizing sets of a path. This can lead to reduce the path set of a rule. When the path set of a rule is empty, the rule can be removed from the triggering graph.

3 Motivating Example

We propose in this section an example which illustrates the motivation of our work. We take place within the framework of a banking application. An object oriented database is used. Four active rules are defined. We suppose that the coupling modes of the rules are immediate.

Rule R_1: When the loan capacity of an account is updated, if the loan rate of the account is equal to "low", the allowed overdraft of the account is set to "low". The priority of this rule is strong.

Rule R_2: When the allowed overdraft of an account is updated, if the loan rate of the account is equal to "high", the loan capacity of the account is set to "high". The priority of this rule is strong.

Rule R_3: When the loan capacity of an account is updated, the loan rate of the account is set to "low". The priority of this rule is weak.

Rule R_4: When the allowed overdraft of an account is updated, the loan rate of the account is set to "high". The priority of this rule is weak.

Rule:	R_1	R_2
Priority:	strong (numeric value: 2)	strong (numeric value:2)
Event:	*account_capacity_update_event(A_1)*	*account_overdraft_update_event(A_2)*
Condition:	A_1.*rate* = "low"	A_2.*rate* = "high"
Action:	A_1.*overdraft* = "low"	A_2.*capacity* = "high"
Raised event:	*account_overdraft_update_event(A_1)*	*account_capacity_update_event(A_2)*

Rule:	R_3	R_4
Priority:	weak (numeric value: 1)	weak (numeric value: 1)
Event:		*account_capacity_update_event(A_3)* *account_overdraft_update_event(A_4)*
Condition:	-	-
Action:	A_3.*rate* = "low"	A_4.*rate* = "high"
Raised event:	*account_rate_update_event(A_3)*	*account_rate_update_event(A_4)*

Let us try to guarantee termination of this rules set using the algorithms proposed in the literature. The triggering graph is represented by figure 1.

The Refined Triggering Graph method [5] is unable to remove any edge of the cycle $(R_1 \rightarrow R_2 \rightarrow R_1)$. Indeed, the attribute *rate* can be updated by rule actions and cannot be included in a triggering formula.

If we use the improvement of the RTG method proposed by [4] (which allows to include in a triggering formula attributes which can be updated by rule actions), we obtain the following triggering formula for the edge $R_1 \rightarrow R_2$:

$$((A_1.rate = \text{"low"}) \lor ((A_1 = A_4) \land (A_4.rate = \text{"high"}))) \land (A_1 = A_2) \land (A_2.rate = \text{"high"})$$

This formula can be satisfied, and termination cannot be guaranteed.

The algorithm [2], which considers rules with priorities, just considers self-deactivating rules. It cannot guarantee termination in this case, since no rule is self-deactivating.

However, this rules set cannot exhibit an infinite processing. Let us suppose that an infinite process occurs. There is an infinite number of instances of R_1 and an infinite number of instances of R_2 (else, R_1 or R_2 would be removed from the triggering graph, and the process would be finite).

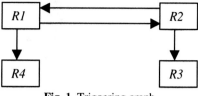

Fig. 1. Triggering graph.

But no instance of R_3 can occur between two instances of R_1, and no instance of R_4 can occur between two instances of R_1. Indeed, let us take place at the moment where an instance of R_4 is evaluated and executed. At this moment, R_2 is not triggered (else R_2 would be evaluated and executed before R_4). If R_2 is not triggered, R_1 is not triggered. Since the action of R_4 triggers no rule, the rules process stops. We can do the same reasoning for R_3. As we have supposed that an infinite rules process occurred, we obtain a contradiction. Thus no instance of R_3 can occur between two instances of R_1, and no instance of R_4 can occur between two instances of R_1. That is the attribute *rate* cannot be updated between two instances of R_1.

So, we can build the following triggering formula for the edge (R_1, R_2) by using the RTG method, since we know now that the attribute *rate* cannot be updated between the evaluation of the condition of R_1 and the evaluation of the condition of R_2:

$$(A_1.rate = \text{"low"}) \wedge (A_1 = A_2) \wedge (A_2.rate = \text{"high"})$$

This formula cannot be satisfied. So, an infinite rules process is impossible for this rules set. An algorithm could draw this conclusion, if this algorithm would consider the priorities between rules.

4   Path Sets

The utility of this section is to introduce the notions of *path set of a rule* and *path set of a path*. The path set serves for replacing the notion of cycle, used in the previous termination algorithms.

4.1   Considered Active Rules

The active rules that we consider in this paper are defined according to the paradigm Event-Condition-Action. The database model is a relational model or a model object. We suppose that the database is treated in a transactional context. Triggering events are either data operation events *(internal* events), or events reported to the system by the outside *(external* events), or a disjunction of internal and external events. The rule condition is a request expressed with some requests language. The rule action is a sequence of database updates, or, more generally, a procedure containing database updates.

We suppose that each rule is defined with a numeric priority. The rules process is the following:

1. Choose a rule instance with the strongest priority in the set of triggered rules instances.
2. Remove the chosen rule instance from the set of the triggered rule instances.
3. Evaluate the condition.
4. If the condition is false : go to step 1.
5. If the condition is true, execute the action.
6. Update the set of triggered rules instances.
7. Go to step 1.

4.2 Path Set of a Rule

We replace the classic notion of cycle (used by the previous termination algorithms) by the notion of *path set of a rule*. The path set of a rule captures the rules paths which are executed before a rule instance.

We first recall the notion of triggering graph. The nodes of the triggering graph are the active rules. There is an oriented edge from a rule R_1 to a rule R_2 if the rule R_1 can trigger the rule R_2.

Let G be a triggering graph. We first precise the notion of *path*. Let N_1 , N_2... N_i... N_n be n *nodes* (not necessarily all different) of G, such as there is a oriented edge since N_{i+1} towards N_i. The tuple $(N_1$, N_2... $N_n)$ constitutes a *path*. We adopt the following notation : $N_n \rightarrow N_{n-1} \rightarrow ... \rightarrow N_i \rightarrow ... \rightarrow N_1$. N_1 is called the *last node* of the path. N_n is called the *first node* of the path.

The *path set* of the rule R *Path_Set(R ; G)* is the set of the paths *Path* of G which satisfy the following properties:
1. The last rule of the path *Path* is R.
2. The path *Path* does not contain twice the same node.
3. The path *Path* is not included in a path which satisfies the properties 1 and 2 (except itself).

The path set of R is built performing a "depth search" in the opposite direction of the edges. The procedure is the following : (the first path provided to the procedure is the path (R))

Path_Set_Building_Procedure $((R))$
Path_Set_Building_Procedure (incoming variable : *Path*_{in})
>   Let *N* be the first node of *Path*_{in}
>   Let N_1, N_2, ... N_p be the nodes of G such as there is an edge from N_i to N
>   **FOR** each node N_i $(1 \leq i \leq p)$
>>   **IF** N_i is not in *Path*_{in}
>>>   **Path_Set_Building_Procedure** $(N_i \rightarrow Path_{in})$
>>   **ELSE**
>>>   Add *Path*_{in} to *Path_Set(R ; G)*
>>   **ENDIF**
>   **ENDFOR**

Example. See the figure 1. $Path\_Set(R_4 ; G) = \{(R_2 \rightarrow R_1 \rightarrow R_4)\}$

4.3 Path Set of a Path

We generalize now the notion of path set, defining the *path set of a path*. The path set of a path corresponds to the set of the paths which are executed before an occurrence of the path. Let us consider a path :

$$Path = N_n \rightarrow N_{n-1} \rightarrow ... \rightarrow N_i \rightarrow ... N_2 \rightarrow N_1.$$

   Let us suppose that:

$$Path\_Set(N_n ; G) = \{ Path_1 , Path_2 ,... , Path_p \}$$

   The path set of the path *Path* is:

$$Path\_Set(Path ; G) = \{ (Path_1 \rightarrow N_{n-1} \rightarrow ... \rightarrow N_i \rightarrow ... \rightarrow N_1),$$
$$(Path_2 \rightarrow N_{n-1} \rightarrow ... \rightarrow N_i \rightarrow ... \rightarrow N_1), ..., (Path_p \rightarrow N_{n-1} \rightarrow ... \rightarrow N_i \rightarrow ... \rightarrow N_1) \}$$

Example. See figure 1. $Path\_Set((R_1 \rightarrow R_4) ; G) = \{ R_2 \rightarrow R_1 \rightarrow R_4 \}$

4.4 Priority of a Path / Path Set

We introduce here the notion of *priority of a path*. The priority of a path is the weakest priority of the rules of the path. The priority of the path corresponds to a narrow gorge: this is the priority which will delay the execution of the path.

   We use the notion of priority of a path to define now the *minimal priority* of a path set: this is the weakest priority of the paths of the path set. We adopt the following notation: $m\_p(Path\_Set(Entity ; G))$. (*Entity* is a path or a rule).

   We also define the *maximal priority* of a path set: this is the stronger priority of the paths of the paths set. We adopt the following notation: $M\_p(Path\_Set(Entity ; G))$.

5 Reduction of the Triggering Graph

This section introduces our termination algorithm. The previous termination algorithms exploit the following principle: when every cycle containing the rule R contains a deactivated path, the rule R can be removed from the triggering graph. Our termination algorithm suggests improving this principle: the rule R will be removed by our algorithm when the path set of R will be empty. Considerations about priorities of the rules will allow to reduce the path set of a rule.

5. 1 Destabilizing Set of a Path

In order to refine the deactivation of a path, we introduce the notion of *destabilizing set*. The utility of this notion is to list the rules which can oppose the deactivation of the path. A *destabilizing set of a path* is a set of rules. Informally, the conjunction of the conditions of the rules of the path is **TRUE** only a finite number of times, if there is only a finite number of occurrences of the rules of the destabilizing set.

Definition. Let *Path* be a path of the triggering graph *G*. Let R_1, R_2, ..., R_s be *s* rules of *G*.

We say that the set $\{R_1, R_2, ... , R_s\}$ is a *destabilizing set* of *Path* iff the following property holds for each rules process *P*:

(A finite number of instances of the rules R_1, R_2, ..., ..., R_s occur during *P*) $\Rightarrow$ (There is only a finite number of occurrences of *Path* during *P*).

For a destabilizing set, we will use the following notation: *Desta_Set(Path ; G)*. The destabilizing sets can be used in conjunction with all the deactivation cases of path listed by the previous algorithms [2, 5, 6, 7].

For example, if it is possible to establish a generalized triggering formula along a path which cannot be satisfied [5, 7], but if this formula contains attributes which can be updated by the database, a destabilizing set of the path contains all the rules R_i such as the action of the rule R_i can modify attributes contained in the generalized triggering formula.

Note that a path can have zero or several destabilizing sets.

Example. See the motivation example and figure 1. $\{R_3, R_4\}$ is a destabilizing set of $(R_2\rightarrow R_1)$. Indeed, we can establish a triggering formula along the edge $(R_2\rightarrow R_1)$ using the "Refined Triggering Graph" Method [5] :

$$(A_1.rate = \text{"low"}) \wedge (A_1 = A_2) \wedge (A_2.rate = \text{"high"})$$

This triggering formula can not be satisfied. But the attribute *rate* can be updated by the rules R_3 and R_4. If there is just a finite number of instances of R_3 and R_4 during a rules process, there is just a finite number of occurrences of the path $(R_2\rightarrow R_1)$ during the rules process.

5.2 Reduction of the Triggering Graph

We can reduce the triggering graph thanks to the four following considerations:
  (1) The rule *R* can be removed from the triggering graph if *R* has no incoming edge. Indeed, *R* will be just triggered a finite number of times.
  (2) Let *R* be a rule. Let $Path_j$ be a path of *Path_Set(R ; G)*. We can remove $Path_j$ from *Path_Set(R ; G)* if $\emptyset$ is a destabilizing set of $Path_j$. Indeed, in this case, it is impossible for the rules process to go through the path $Path_j$ an infinite number of times.
  (3) The rule *R* can be removed from the triggering graph if *Path_Set(R ; G)* $= \emptyset$. Indeed, in this case, it is impossible for the rules process to reach the rule *R* an infinite number of times, since all the paths which lead to *R* are deactivated after a finite time.
  (4) Let us consider now a destabilizing set $\{R_1, R_2, ... , R_s\}$ of the path *Path*.
If we observe one of the following properties :
  (i) the maximal priority of *Path_Set(Path ; G)* is strictly smaller than the minimal priority of *Path_Set(R_i ; G)* or:
  (ii) the maximal priority of *Path_Set(R_i; G)* is strictly smaller than the minimal priority of *Path_Set(Path ; G)*,

then the rule R_i can be removed from the destabilizing set $\{R_1, R_2, \ldots, R_s\}$.

Proof of (4). Let us consider the case (i). We show that there is no occurrence of *Path* between two instances of R_i. Let us suppose that there is an occurrence of *Path* between two instances of R_i. This means that there is a rule R' which belongs to the path set of *Path* and which is evaluated and executed before a rule R'', which is triggered and which belongs to the path set of R_i. But the priority of R' is strictly smaller than the priority of R'' (since each rule of the path set of R_i has a priority stronger than each rule of the path set of *Path*). This leads to a contradiction. So, since there is no occurrence of *Path* between two instances of R_i, there is no instance of R_i between two occurrences of *Path*. Thus, R_i can be removed from the destabilizing set. We can do the same type of reasoning for the case (ii).

5.3 Termination Algorithm

We can now sketch the termination algorithm. The termination algorithm captures the four properties which we have shown above :
    (1) We can remove a rule from the current graph if the rule has no incoming edge.
    (2) We can remove a path *Path* from a path set if $\emptyset$ is a destabilizing set of *Path*.
    (3) We can remove a rule from the current graph if the path set of the rule is empty.
    (4) We can remove a rule from a destabilizing set depending on the priorities.

```
REPEAT
  REPEAT
      Remove the nodes without incoming edge
      Remove the edges without origin node
  UNTIL (no node is removed)

  FOR EACH rule R of G
      Determine Path_Set(R ; G)
      FOR EACH path Path of Path_Set(R ; G)
          Determine Path_Set(Path ; G)
          Determine the sets Desta_Set(Path ; G)
          FOR EACH set Desta_Set(Path ; G)
              FOR EACH rule Rᵢ of Desta_Set(Path ; G)
                  IF (M_p(Path_Set(Path ; G)) < m_p(Path_Set(Rᵢ ; G)))
                  OR (M_p(Path_Set(Rᵢ ; G)) < m_p(Path_Set(Path ; G)))
                      Remove Rᵢ from Desta_Set(Path ; G)
                  ENDIF
              ENDFOR
          ENDFOR
          IF there is a set Desta_Set(Path ; G) such as Desta_Set(Path ; G) = ∅
              Remove Path from Path_Set(R ; G)
          ENDIF
      ENDFOR
      IF Path_Set(R , G) = ∅
          Remove R from G
      ENDIF
  ENDFOR
UNTIL (no entity is removed)
```

If the final triggering graph is empty, termination is guaranteed. Else, the remaining rules can possibly be triggered an infinite number of times. Note that our termination algorithm can discover the termination situations detected due to the self-deactivating rules [2], due the RTG method [5], due to the deactivation of a condition because of the action of a rule [6], and the termination situations detected by the "Path Removing Technique " [7].

Much more termination situations can in fact be discovered by our algorithm, since our termination algorithm exploits the priorities of the active rules.

Example. Let us study the termination of the set of rules of our motivating example. $\{R_3, R_4\}$ is a destabilizing set of the path $(R_2 \rightarrow R_1)$ (see section 5.1). We have:

$Path\_Set((R_2 \rightarrow R_1); G) = \{(R_2 \rightarrow R_1)\}$
$Path\_Set(R_3 ; G) = \{(R_1 \rightarrow R_2 \rightarrow R_3)\}$
$Path\_Set(R_4 ; G) = \{(R_2 \rightarrow R_1 \rightarrow R_4)\}$

We determine the priorities of the path sets:

$m\_p(Path\_Set((R_2 \rightarrow R_1) ; G)) = 2$
$M\_p(Path\_Set(R_3 ; G)) = 1$
$M\_p(Path\_Set(R_4 ; G)) = 1$

We observe that:

$M\_p(Path\_Set((R_3) ; G)) < m\_p(Path\_Set((R_2 \rightarrow R_1) ; G))$
and that:
$M\_p(Path\_Set((R_4) ; G)) < m\_p(Path\_Set((R_2 \rightarrow R_1) ; G))$

So, we can remove R_3 and R_4 from the destabilizing set of the path $(R_2 \rightarrow R_1)$.

Thus, $\emptyset$ is a destabilizing set of $(R_2 \rightarrow R_1)$. The path set of R_1 is $\{(R_2 \rightarrow R_1)\}$. Since $\emptyset$ is a destabilizing set of $(R_2 \rightarrow R_1)$, we can remove the path $(R_2 \rightarrow R_1)$ from the path set of R_1. The path set of R_1 is then $\emptyset$. This leads to remove the rule R_1 from the triggering graph. Once the rule R_1 is removed, we can remove the other rules of the triggering graph.

The termination of this rules set can be guaranteed by our algorithm. Note that no previous algorithm is able to detect this termination situation.

6 Conclusion

We have presented a significant improvement of the termination analysis of the active rules defined with priorities. We have developed the notions of path set of rule and path set of a path. The notion of destabilizing set has allowed us to represent the deactivation cases of a condition listed by the previous algorithms [2, 5, 6]. We can then reduce the destabilizing set of a path thanks to the priorities of the path sets. When the destabilizing set of a path is empty, the path can be removed from the path set of a rule. When the path set of a rule is empty, the rule can be removed from the triggering graph. So, the triggering graph can be reduced thanks to considerations about the priorities of the rules.

In the future, we plan to conceive an algorithm which proposes priorities between rules, when the termination can not be guaranteed.

References

1. A. Aiken, J. Widom, J.M. Hellerstein. Behavior of Database Production Rules : Termination, Confluence and Observable Determinism. In *Proc. Int'l Conf. on Management of Data (SIGMOD)*, San Diego, California, 1992.
2. E. Baralis, S. Ceri, S. Paraboschi. Improved Rule Analysis by Means of Triggering and Activation Graphs. In *Proc. Int'l Workshop Rules in Database Systems (RIDS)*, Athens, Greece, 1995.
3. A. Couchot. Improving Termination Analysis of Active Rules with Composite Events. In *Proc. Int'l Conf. on Database and Expert Systems Applications (DEXA)*, Munich, Germany, 2001.
4. A. Couchot. Improving the Refined Triggering Graph Method for Active Rules Termination Analysis. In *Proc. British National Conf. on Databases* (*BNCOD*), Sheffield, United Kingdom, 2002.
5. A.P. Karadimce, S.D. Urban. Refined Triggering Graphs : a Logic-Based Approach to Termination Analysis in an Active Object-Oriented Database. In *Proc. Int'l Conf. on Data Engineering (ICDE)*, New-Orleans, Louisiana, 1996.
6. S.Y. Lee, T.W. Ling. Refined Termination Decision in Active Databases. In *Proc. Int'l Conf. on Database and Expert Systems Applications (DEXA)*, Toulouse, France, 1997
7. S.Y. Lee, T.W. Ling. A Path Removing Technique for Detecting Trigger Termination. In *Proc. Int'l Conf. on Extended Database Technology (EDBT)*, Valencia, Spain, 1998.
8. S.Y. Lee, T.W. Ling. Unrolling Cycle to Decide Trigger Termination. In *Proc. Int'l Conf. on Very Large Databases (VLDB)*, Edinburgh, Scotland, 1999.

A Toolkit and Methodology to Support the Collaborative Development and Reuse of Engineering Models

Zdenek Zdrahal[1], Paul Mulholland[1], Michael Valasek[2], Phil Sainter[1],
Matt Koss[1], and Lukas Trejtnar[1]

[1] Knowledge Media Institute,
The Open University,
Walton Hall, Milton Keynes, UK
{Z.Zdrahal,P.Mulholland,P.Sainter,M.Koss,L.Trejtnar}
@open.ac.uk
[2] Faculty of Mechanical Engineering
Czech Technical University,
Karlovo nam. 13, 12135 Praha 2
Czech Republic
valasek@felbr.fsik.cvut.cz

Abstract. Engineering design is a knowledge intensive activity. Design is characterized as comprising a number of phases from requirements to detailed specification. Transitions between the design phases stem from decision-making processes supported both by generally available domain and design knowledge and from unique and original knowledge worth of recording for future reuse. The Clockwork project addresses the problems of representing, sharing and reusing knowledge in a collaborative design engineering environment. The Clockwork knowledge management methodology is supported by a web-based toolkit that allows designers to share, formally and informally annotate and reuse engineering models. Reuse is supported through the semantic search of engineering models and of the design rationale by which the engineering models were developed. The approach has been successfully deployed in two industrial organisations.

1 Introduction

Clockwork is a European Union funded R&D project whose aim is to develop methodology and software tools for capturing and sharing valuable engineering knowledge generated and used in design processes. There is increasing pressure to reuse design knowledge in order to expedite the design process and reduce time to market. Generally, design models have to be described and annotated in order that they can be effectively understood and reused. Annotating design models and capturing design rationale imposes additional overheads. It can disrupt the design process, and can require the designer to spend a significant amount of time off task. Clockwork provides methodology and supporting tools for efficient, semantic based annotation of design knowledge focused around crucial decisions in the design process. The Clockwork toolkit includes a powerful knowledge retrieval mechanism

V. Mařík et al. (Eds.): DEXA 2003, LNCS 2736, pp. 856–865, 2003.

which combines semantic web technologies with informal description of engineering models.

The Clockwork approach has been tested on two pilot applications: modeling and simulation of dynamic systems in mechanical engineering and the development and support of specialized thermal technologies. Both applications have been developed in collaboration with Clockwork industrial partners, INTEC GmbH and ELOTHERM, GmbH.

2 Modelling Design Processes

Design is considered to be an ill-structured problem [5], [9]. This means that prior to the start of the design process the goal specification is not completely known and requirements are often inconsistent. The task specification and its solution are therefore worked out simultaneously.

For ill-structured problems only "weak" problem solving methods (such as generate-and-test) exist and weak methods provide only weak results [5]. By applying domain knowledge, ill-structured problems can be converted into a number of well-structured problems - "the problem is well-structured in the small, but ill-structured in the large" [9, p.190]. For well-structured problems "strong" problem solving methods i.e. specialised algorithms exist which offer much better solution. For this reason knowledge plays a crucial role in design.

In engineering, design processes have been studied [1], [2], [8] with the aim to better understand the underlying activities, organize them and, whenever possible, provide methodological support. Two types of design processes are distinguished in [1]:

- *descriptive* design processes are focused on the analysis of the tasks and their sequences as they typically occur in design processes, and
- *prescriptive* design processes, which, in addition, attempt to provide a sound methodological guidance for these tasks.

Knowledge plays an important but different role in descriptive and prescriptive types of design process. The former rely mainly on heuristic knowledge while the latter ones emphasize the role of logical reasoning as the major inference vehicle for design reasoning. Though individual types differ, they subscribe to a similar set of constituent tasks which divide the design process into four *phases*. They are: *requirement specification*, *conceptual design*, *embodiment design* (preliminary design) and *detailed design*. Each design phase constitutes a design task, each task results in an *engineering model*. The tasks are executed sequentially each task refining the model produced by the previous task. The design process is nonlinear: the designer backtracks or iterates in a loop if he or she finds out that the current solution has reached a dead end. This is a consequence of design being an ill-structured problem and therefore search being an appropriate problem solving method. However, regardless of the sequence of steps taken in the design process the final design must include all phases.

Each task is self-contained in the sense that it has an associated set of objects from which the solution is constructed and a language for expressing the solution. The design process can be viewed as a sequence of transformations between representations of the design phases, i.e. based on the requirements specification the designer constructs a conceptual model which is further elaborated into an embodiment model and eventually to the final detailed design. Each of these transformations refines the outcome of the previous phase by imposing additional assumptions and by reasoning supported by design and domain knowledge. The design result is associated with assumptions and justifications for each individual decision made along the design process. A generic model for design reasoning includes a structured account for design hypotheses, goals, actions and justifications [3].

Though it has been accepted that knowledge plays an essential role in design, support for knowledge reuse in practical applications is still insufficient. Standard design packages do not include suitable tools and therefore valuable design knowledge situated in the context of a concrete problem and solution is usually lost. Despite the obvious benefits, design rationale is rarely recorded. Often, even the results of the intermediate design phases, such as the conceptual design, are discarded. Designers tend not to make their decisions explicit because the design tools usually do not provide user-friendly facilities for annotation and knowledge capture and without proper tools and methodology, such activity would distract them from designing and consume their time [7]. However, despite of the obvious lack of support, knowledge reuse is a standard and widely used design technique.

Attempts have been made to tackle the problem by allowing the designer to carry on his/her work and to reconstruct the design reasoning in a non-intrusive way.

The Rationale Construction Framework (RCF) project at SRI International aims at inducing and interpreting design rationale from the trace of designer's activities when interacting with the CAD tool [4]. The project is focused on detailed design, i.e. the last of the design phases. From the design event log, RCF abstracts a symbolic model of the emerging design which is used to reason about designer's intent.

The ASSISTANCE system, under development at MIT [6], applies similar ideas at the other end of the "design phase" sequence. The system interprets designer's sketches and spoken comments to derive a causal model of the conceptual design and allows reasoning about the structure and behaviour of the designed artifact.

Unlike RCF and ASSISTANCE, the Software Integration and Design Rationale Capture Tool SSPARCY [10] supports only semiautomatic annotation of design rationale. The tool has been developed to support simulation and modeling of aerospace design. Similarly as RCF, the system is linked to low level design tools, such as MATLAB and Excel, from which it extracts, parses and organizes design data and records the design history. The designer is encouraged to associate textual annotation with the data as design rationale.

3   Clockwork Knowledge Modeling

Clockwork addresses the problem of sharing and reuse of design knowledge based on the following philosophy: If professional designers document their reasoning to communicate their ideas among themselves or to reuse them in the future, they record only decisions which are valuable. These are for example: new and unique design "tricks" discovered when solving the case; decisions which are meaningful only within the specific context; decisions which relate to an assumption made earlier or which respond to a concrete design requirement imposed by the client or a collaborating partner. Standard design knowledge which can be found in any textbook is not recorded, because it would only increase the complexity of documentation, decrease the efficiency of information retrieval and take designer's time. Moreover, this knowledge is implicitly represented in the design and each experienced designer can immediately find it. Clockwork therefore focuses only on important knowledge, and does it across all design phases.

Design phases are represented by *engineering models* and transitions between them. Engineering models are the result of work of design engineers, when designing cars, complex technologies, control systems or simulation models. They embody an implicit form of design knowledge. Engineering models often need additional information to define their applicability. For example, control systems or simulation models are designed for certain input and performance criteria. This contextual information propagates in the design process and is refined together with the engineering model. In Clockwork, we introduce the concept of *design world* which includes the engineering model and all associated contextual information. Therefore we say we have a requirement world, conceptual world etc.

Knowledge description is constructed on the following principles:

- Depending on the problem and the available support, engineering models are developed using different tools, such as CAD packages, MATLAB/Simulink, Solid Edge or they might be just hand-drawn sketches. However, at the knowledge level engineering models are represented in a unified way as *knowledge models* in terms of ontologies and knowledge bases. Ontology is an explicit conceptualisation of the domain. It is a dictionary of engineering concepts i.e. formally defines all available concepts in terms of their properties and relation with other concepts. Concepts are represented as classes of an object oriented language. Knowledge bases contain instances of classes pertinent to a specific case.

- The association of knowledge models with engineering models allows for reasoning about the engineering models. Knowledge models need not describe engineering models completely, only important model components need to be included. The selected components are associated with classes in the corresponding ontology by means of class instances created in the knowledge base. The instances are called *semantic indexes* because by associating objects of the engineering model with concepts in the ontology they assign the meaning to the object.

- Refinement of engineering models can be described as relations between corresponding formal knowledge models.

- Formal knowledge models can be further supported by informal text annotations or sketches.

An example of a knowledge model and its associations with the engineering model is shown in Fig. 1. The class "Lever" has two instances, L1 and L2 and the class "Joint" has an instance J. These are used as semantic indexes describing the components of the lower left arm of the mechanism shown in Fig. 1. Though the drawing is a non-executable conceptual model, the association with a formal knowledge model makes it possible to reason about the three model components.

Based on these principles the Clockwork methodology for sharing and reuse of engineering knowledge has been developed and a support toolkit has been implemented. Core to our approach is the web-based Clockwork Knowledge Management Tool (CKMT) that allows designers and other stakeholders such as customers and domain experts to explain, share, discuss and collaboratively develop

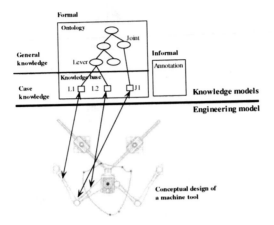

Fig. 1 Clockwork knowledge types.

engineering models. Engineering models stored in the CKMT repository can be annotated formally by association with domain ontologies or informally using notes or sketches.

For developing ontologies, Clockwork provides the Apollo ontology editor, which allows the user to define classes, their structure and hierarchies and create instances. The ontology and knowledge base created by Apollo can be exported into various formats including XML, RDF, Lisp and Operational Conceptual Modelling Language (OCML). The current version of Apollo is available at http://apollo.open.ac.uk.

CKMT has been tested on two case studies.

4   Case Study 1: Simulation and Modelling of Dynamic Systems

The knowledge sharing and reuse framework introduced in the previous section has been instantiated for the design of simulation models of dynamic systems and implemented using the CKMT. Since this is a typical design problem, the four design phases introduced in Section 2 have a straightforward interpretation in the simulation and modeling context. They are:

Requirement analysis. When constructing a simulation model, the real world system to be modeled specifies the requirement for the model design task.

Conceptualisation. From the real world system, the conceptual model is elaborated. Conceptual model specifies the components which will be included in the design, their properties and interactions accompanied by the description of their function from which causal and functional explanation can be inferred. For example, for the horizontal machine tool DYNA-M (real world system) the conceptual model shown in Fig. 1 consists of two arms in the lower part, a spindle in the middle and two moving screws with drives in the upper part. Drives and moving screws convert rotation to translation and allow positioning of the spindle.

Modelling. In the next step the conceptual model is converted into the corresponding physical model composed of ideal modelling objects. The physical model is still independent of the simulation environment which will be used for implementation.

Simulation. Finally, the physical model is implemented in a selected simulation package such as MATLAB/Simulink or Simpack. The four design worlds shown in Fig. 2 are called Real World Object (RWO), Conceptual Model Object (CWO), Model World Object (MWO) and Simulation World Object (SWO).

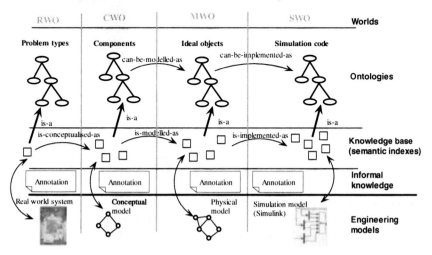

Fig. 2. Four-world simulation and modeling framework

Developing Knowledge Models

Each world includes additional information needed as a context for model development: The question to be answered by the modeling experiment, is associated with the Real World Object, converted into the modeling objective at the conceptual level and further refined as input and output specification for the physical model. Results of the simulation experiment are interpreted in terms of the physical and conceptual models and the real world system. Assumptions under which the model has been elaborated are associated with each world.

Fig. 2 also shows relations between pairs of knowledge models. Relation *is-conceptualised-as* is one-to-many, relations *is-modelled-as* and *is-implemented-as* can be in general many-to-many, though the model refinement usually means that one object of conceptual/physical model is modeled/implemented as several objects of physical/simulation world and therefore these relations are one-to-many. Other predefined relations included are *is-part-of* for membership of an object to the model and *has-status* to indicate whether the model was a success or failure. The user can define additional relations for problem description.

Relations across worlds capture important modeling knowledge. For example, we may express that a shaft of the conceptual model *is-modelled-as* three masses and two ideal springs in the physical model. When the designer builds a model of any of the worlds, he/she selects the object which carries interesting design knowledge, gives it a name and associates it with the corresponding class in the ontology, i.e. creates a semantic index. Then the object becomes a part of the knowledge model, can be included in relations and can be used by the reasoning algorithm. An example of the annotation of a revolute joint in a physical model is shown in Fig. 3.

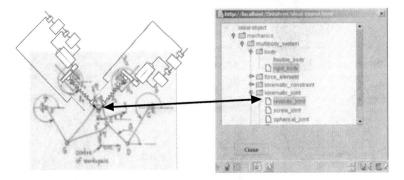

Fig. 3. Defining semantic index in the physical model

In accord with Fig.1 and 2, CKMT also allows the designer to provide informal annotation in the form of plain text or sketches. The annotation is included as one of the documents associated with each world and text can be accessed by keyword search.

Querying Knowledge Models

CKMT query engine offers a number of options which can be combined. The simplest query is the keyword search which can be applied to all annotations and assumptions. However, this mechanism is usually not powerful enough and therefore does not provide good results. For this reason CKMT introduces semantic search which exploits ontologies, semantic indexes and inter-world relations described above.

Semantic indexes and ontologies allow the query engine to reason in class hierarchies and use relations as executable rules. For example, the query "Show me an example of modelling kinematic joint" will retrieve the model of DynaM shown in Fig.3, because the semantic index for a revolute joint has been created (see the arrow in Fig.3) and a revolute joint is a kind of kinematic joint. The underlying representation of knowledge models in OCML allows for defining complex relations. For example, the user can define a new relation *successful-simulation-of-component* for models ?x and component ?y as follows:

> ?x *is-successful-simulation-of-component* ?y
> if
> component ?y *is-part-of* conceptual model ?z, and
> ?z *is-modelled-as* ?w, and
> ?w *is-implemented-as* ?x, and
> ?x *has-status* success.

If the variable ?y is instantiated to an object describing a shaft, the relation returns all available successful simulation models of a shaft. If ?y is left uninstantiated, the query returns all successful simulation models of all components. The CKMT query tool is shown in Fig. 4.

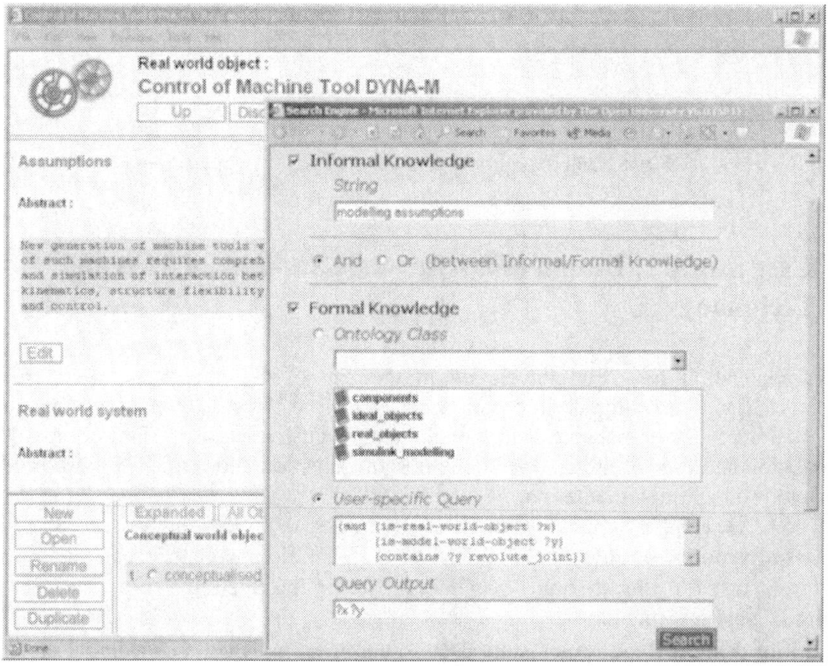

Fig. 4. Query tool

5 Developing New Clockwork Applications

Though the underlying processes of design problems have much in common, the applications differ depending on the engineering domain, goals, the range of activities which need to be supported and other factors. In order to seamlessly support existing work practices the new application must include existing knowledge management tools and legacy tools of the company. The same knowledge modeling technology used for semantic search can support the development of a new application. The analysis of the design process identifies the number of worlds and their structure needed to represent the problem. A model of the design process is constructed in terms of a *backbone ontology* and serves as an input for the *CKMT generator* which designs the client and server component of the CKMT tool. An application developer then integrates these components with existing knowledge management and legacy tools. The overall architecture is shown in Fig. 5.

By introducing the modeling approach this methodology significantly simplifies and speeds up the application development. This approach has been used to develop customized CKMT's in a number of applications including the one described in Case Study 2.

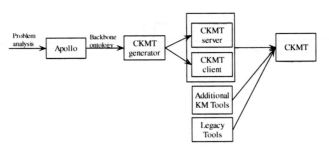

Fig. 5. Ontology driven generation of CKMT application

6 Case Study 2: Design and After-Sale Support of Thermal Technology

This application has been developed at the site of Clockwork industrial partner ELOTHERM. The company's products are industrial thermal technology, developed for customers, and installed and maintained at customer sites. The company use simulation and modelling to support the design, selection and tuning of these products prior to product implementation.

The ELOTHERM application can be described by the following four worlds:

Requirements world: ELOTHERM in collaboration with the customer develop requirements for the thermal machine, covering productivity, cost and relevant technological parameters.

Initial design: Requirements are used to construct or select a conceptual model for the design. The conceptual model takes the form of an abstracted physical model of the machine. For example, the designer may think, a machine is required of the type '20 coil inductor'.

Detailed design: For the detailed design components and their parameters are selected. This step may raise further questions (e.g. acceptable range in the rate of heating) to be discussed with the customer. ELOTHERM have a set of available models and simulation and modelling software. The proposed model is then tested. A range of parameters are then tried and the values which ensure that the model functions satisfactorily are selected.

Product world: The thermal technology has been designed, manufactured and installed at the customer site. Details of the installation procedure are recorded in the Product World. ELOTHERM provide maintenance for the machine in the long term. Fault reports are used to document this process and provide additional feedback to the design department.

7 Conclusions

Design is characterized as comprising a number of phases from requirement specifications to detailed design. In Clockwork, these phases are described as "worlds". Crucial design knowledge supports transitions between the worlds. The Clockwork toolkit makes it possible to record important knowledge concerning the construction of each world and its transformations. In addition, the toolkit allows the user to analyze the design process, describe it in terms of a backbone ontology and use the knowledge model to generate the structure of the tool.

The Clockwork knowledge modelling approach produces a minimal design history but provides a sufficient level of description to support its reuse. Engineering models such as sketches, diagrams and executable simulation models are integrated with knowledge models described in terms of knowledge bases, ontologies and text annotations. Recorded knowledge is used to guide semantic search in retrieving relevant engineering models which can be reused in a new design task.

Clockwork can be contrasted with many previous design rationale approaches which impose too high an annotation burden to the designer. The methodology and tools have been successfully tested in two industrial applications.

References

1. Cross N.: Engineering Design Methods. John Wiley & Sons. (1989).
2. Hubka V. and Eder E.W.: Design Science : Introduction to the Needs, Scope and Organization of Engineering Design Knowledge. Springer-Verlag Berlin and Heidelberg. (1995)
3. Louridas P. and Loucopoulos P.: A generic Model for Reflexive Design. ACM Transactions on Software Engineering and Methodology, Vol.9. No.2. pp. 199–237, (2002)
4. Myers K.L., Zumel N.B. and Garcia P.: Automated Capture of Rationale for the Detailed Design Process. In Proceedings of the Eleventh Conference on Innovative Applications of Artificial Intelligence (IAAI99). Pp. 1–8. (1999)
5. Newell A.: Artificial Intelligence and the Concept of Mind. In Computer Models of Thought and Language (R.C.Schank and K.M.Colby eds.). W.H.Freeman and Company. San Francisco. 1973. pp. 1–60. (1973)
6. Oltmans M. and Davis R.: Naturally Conveyed Explanations of Device Behavior. PUI 2001 Orlando FL, USA (2001)
7. Ormerod T.C., Mariani J., Ball L.J. and Lambell N.: Desperado: Three-in-one indexing for innovative design. Proceedings of Interact '99. Edinburgh. (1999)
8. Schön, D. A.: The Reflective Practitioner: How Professionals Think in Action. New York, Basic Books. (1983)
9. Simon H. A.: The Structure of Ill Structured Problems. Artificial Intelligence 4 (1973). pp. 181-201. (1973)
10. Yeung J.: SSPARCY: A Sofrware Integration and Design Rationale Capture Tool. Space System Policy Architecture Research Center. MIT. Bitstream (2002)

Secure Interoperability between Cooperating XML Systems by Dynamic Role Translation

Somchai Chatvichienchai, Mizuho Iwaihara, and Yahiko Kambayashi

Department of Social Informatics,
Kyoto University
Yoshida Sakyo Kyoto 606-8501 Japan
somchai@db.soc.i.kyoto-u.ac.jp
{iwaihara,yahiko}@i.kyoto-u.ac.jp

Abstract. The integration of XML data among organizations is essential for providing information infrastructure for global e-services. Secure data sharing and interoperability among cooperating XML systems is a major concern. Role-based access control (RBAC) models appear to be the most attractive solution for providing fine-grained access control on shared XML data among cooperating XML systems. In this paper we propose a dynamic role translation in order to provide secure data sharing among systems while preserving necessary autonomy of each individual system. We address security violation caused by associating roles among XML systems and give our solution.

1 Introduction

The increasing use of XML, e.g. in B2B applications, suggests that XML data is suitable for interchanging and sharing information among organizations. The interchange of XML data among organizations in both commercial and government sectors is necessary for providing information infrastructure for global e-services. Our previous work [4] has addressed problems of translating access control policies of an XML document when the document structure is transformed to match with that of another system. Recently, some work has been done on inter-connected and large-scale cooperating XML systems [5,14]. From the viewpoint of security, secure data sharing and interoperability among XML systems is a major concern. Among XML access control models that are recently proposed [1,6,9], the RBAC model of Hitchens et al. [9] appears to be the most attractive model for providing fine-grained access control on shared XML data among XML systems. Their RBAC model provides a very flexible set of mechanisms for managing access control of a complex system with many users, objects and applications. Users can be easily reassigned from one role to another. Roles can be granted new permissions as new applications and systems are incorporated, and permissions can be revoked from roles as needed. We call roles of local system *local roles*. We also call roles of remote systems *foreign roles*. To provide data sharing among XML systems, we propose an approach that allows the security manager of the local system to map some foreign roles to certain local roles. If foreign role *A* is mapped to local role *B*, foreign role *A* can access data of the local system on behalf of local role *B*. Another benefit of role mapping is to

V. Mařík et al. (Eds.): DEXA 2003, LNCS 2736, pp. 866–875, 2003.

relieve the security manager of the local system from the task of assigning local roles to users of other systems. To support secure interoperability between cooperating XML systems by role mapping, each system needs some authentication technologies (such as digital certificate, etc) to identify users of other systems and the foreign roles assigned to the users. We observe that mapping roles of the systems having different access control policies may cause security violation in the systems. A user of a role may be able to acquire privileges illegally from the role of higher level in the same system through the mapped foreign roles of other systems.

The objective of this paper is to present a model that maps foreign roles to local roles by knowledge of semantic equivalence relationship between schema elements of *export schemas* of local and remote systems to provide fine-grained access control on shared XML data among the systems. Export schemas of a system are derived from the conceptual schemas of the system to define the data that the system is willing to share with other systems. We focus on the cases when semantic equivalence relationship between export schemas of the systems is given and the finest granularity of access control of the RBAC model is the schema element level. We show an algorithm detecting security violation in the systems. If a security violation is found, we may try to remove several semantic equivalence relationships to acquire security. However, finding a maximum non-violating subset of a given role mapping is proven to be NP-complete. We also show that this problem is solvable in polynomial time if of the systems have graph structures of bounded treewidth [2,13].

Related Work

Federated Database Systems (FDBSs) have been recognized as a practical approach to integrate traditional databases while retaining the autonomy and security of each participant. Jonscher et al. [10] have examined management of global and local identities and their authentication. Bonatti et al. [3] have considered the combination of mandatory policies, where the goal is to define an ordered set combining different security label orderings in such a way that a set of security constraints among them is satisfied. Osborn [12] has proposed an algorithm for merging two role graphs into one graph. The main difference between our work and the previous work is that our technique does not change roles and role hierarchical structure of each system. Moreover we discuss role mapping by knowledge of semantic equivalence relationship between schema elements of export schemas while no previous work discusses this issue.

The rest of the paper is organized as follows. Section 2 presents basic concepts of XML and the RBAC for XML documents. Section 3 discusses role mapping and security violation problem. Section 4 presents complexity analysis of the security violation problem. Finally, Section 5 presents our conclusions.

2   Basic Concepts

An XML document is composed of a sequence of nested elements, each delimited by a pair of start and end tags or by an empty tag. An element can have attributes attached to it. Both elements and attributes are allowed to contain values. The original XML 1.0 specification used document type definitions (DTDs) [15] to describe

868   S. Chatvichienchai, M. Iwaihara, and Y. Kambayashi

structures of XML documents, and a more advanced version XML Schema is
proposed. We model a DTD or a schema of XML documents as a tree of labelled
nodes. Each node denotes a schema element. Figure 1 depicts a sample of XML
document (*client.xml*) and DTD (*client.dtd*) of the sample document.

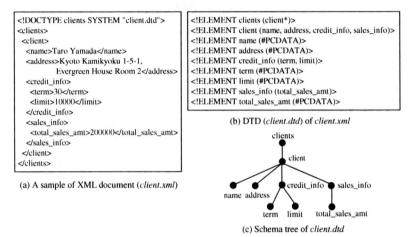

```
<!DOCTYPE clients SYSTEM "client.dtd">
<clients>
 <client>
  <name>Taro Yamada</name>
  <address>Kyoto Kamikyoku 1-5-1,
         Evergreen House Room 2</address>
  <credit_info>
   <term>30</term>
   <limit>10000</limit>
  </credit_info>
  <sales_info>
   <total_sales_amt>200000</total_sales_amt>
  </sales_info>
 </client>
</clients>
```

(a) A sample of XML document (*client.xml*)

```
<!ELEMENT clients (client*)>
<!ELEMENT client (name, address, credit_info, sales_info)>
<!ELEMENT name (#PCDATA)>
<!ELEMENT address (#PCDATA)>
<!ELEMENT credit_info (term, limit)>
<!ELEMENT term (#PCDATA)>
<!ELEMENT limit (#PCDATA)>
<!ELEMENT sales_info (total_sales_amt)>
<!ELEMENT total_sales_amt (#PCDATA)>
```

(b) DTD (*client.dtd*) of client.xml

(c) Schema tree of *client.dtd*

Fig. 1. A sample of an XML document and its DTD

In this paper, we formalize the RBAC model proposed by Hitchens et al. [9] to
match the objective of the paper. The actual authorizations in the model are expressed
in *permissions*, which are then grouped together within the roles themselves. A
permission indicates the right to perform a specific operation on a particular data
object. Permissions in the model can be fine-grained (e.g. at the element level) or
coarse-grained (e.g. at the level of entire document).

Definition 1 (Permissions): A permission is a 7-tuple of the following form:
<pname, target, path, action, sign, prop, priority>,
    where pname is a permission name, target is a list of XML documents or a DTD or
a schema, path is an optional set of path expressions of XPath identifying elements to
which the permission apply, action ∈ {read, write, create, delete}, sign ∈ {•+•, •-•}
specifies whether the permission grants (•+•) or disallows (•-•) access, prop ∈ {local,
recursive}, and priority is an optional value specifying the priority of the permission.
                                                                                       □

If *target* is a DTD (or a schema) then the permission applies to all instances of the
DTD (or the schema, respectively). If the *prop* is *local* then the permission only
applies to the attributes, links and data of the specified elements (as defined by *path*).
Otherwise, permission applies to the specified elements, their direct and indirect subelements and attributes. Conflict resolution of the model is based on *priority* of
permissions. If there is a conflict among a set of permissions on an element then the
permissions with the highest priority are selected. If the permissions have the same
priority, negative permissions override positive permissions. Another important
feature of the role concept is *role hierarchy*. The security manager defines a role
hierarchy by the following role definition.

Definition 2 (Roles): A role is a 3-tuple of the form:

(role_name, child_roles, pnames),

where *role_name* is a role name, *child_roles* is an optional list of child roles, and *pnames* is an optional list of permission names. The parent role inherits access privileges from its child roles. Therefore, the parent role is *senior* to the child role since the set of access privileges of the child role is a subset of those of the parent role.   □

Example 1: Consider the following permissions and roles defined for all instances of *client.dtd* depicted in Figure 1(b). Role *a1* is permitted to read name and address information of *client.dtd* instances. Role *a3*, which is senior to roles *a1* and *a2*, is permitted to read all information of *client.dtd* instances.

Permissions:*<p1,client.dtd,{/clients, //client, //name, //address}, read, +, local, 0>*
<p2, client.dtd, {//client/credit_info}, read, +, recursive, 0>
<p3, client.dtd, {//client/sales_info}, read, +, recursive, 0>

Roles: *(a1, , {p1}), (a2, {a1}, {p2}), (a3, {a2}, {p3})*

3   Role Mapping by Knowledge of Semantic Equivalence Relationship between Schema Elements of Export Schemas

Similar to FDBSs, the autonomy of an individual system is essential. Namely, each system may be administrated independently. To obtain this feature, secure interoperation must enforce the following two principles.

- **Autonomy Principle,** which states that if access is permitted within an individual system, it must also be permitted under secure interoperation.
- **Security Principle,** which states that if an access is not permitted within an individual system, it must not be permitted under secure interoperation.

Any other new access introduced by interoperation should be permitted unless explicitly denied by the specification of secure interoperation.

Our role translation methodology applies semantic equivalence relationship between schema elements of export schemas to define the relationship of roles among cooperating XML systems. This semantic equivalence relationship can be obtained by schema matching tools [7,11] which use matching technologies, such as automated linguistic matching of schema element names, similarity of atomic elements, and context-dependent mappings. Figure 2 depicts a sample of semantic equivalence relationship between schema elements of two export schemas. Schema element *term* of schema *client* has semantic equivalence relationship with schema element *c_term* of schema *customer*. We consider terminal elements of a schema because their instances contain text data that has meaningful information. For example, *term* and *limit* of schema *client* are terminal elements while *credit_info* is a non-terminal element.

Based on semantic equivalence relationship between schema elements of export schemas, condition for role mapping is defined as follows. For simplicity, we focus on mapping roles of the same *action* (read, write, create or delete).

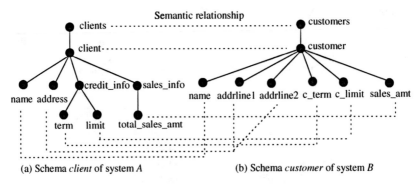

(a) Schema *client* of system *A*   (b) Schema *customer* of system *B*

Fig. 2. A sample of semantic equivalence relationship

Definition 3 (Role mapping condition): Let S and T be export schemas of systems A and B, respectively, where instances of S and T are shared by both systems A and B. Let r_x and r_y be roles of systems A and B, respectively. Suppose that X (resp. Y) is the set of terminal elements of S (resp. T) that can be accessed by role r_x (resp. r_y). Role r_x *can be mapped* to role r_y if each element of Y is given semantic equivalence relationship with each element of X.   □

Example 2: Suppose that permissions and roles of Example 1 are defined for system A. The sets of terminal elements of schema *client.dtd* accessed by roles $a1$, $a2$ and $a3$ of system A are $E1$, $E2$, and $E3$, respectively, where $E1 = \{name, address\}$, $E2 = E1 \cup \{term, limit\}$ and $E3 = E2 \cup \{total\_sales\_amt\}$. Suppose that the sets of terminal elements of schema *customer.dtd* accessed by roles $b1$, $b2$, $b3$ and $b4$ of system B are $F1$, $F2$, $F3$ and $F4$, respectively where $F1 = \{name, addrline1, addrline2\}$, $F2 = F1 \cup \{c\_term\}$, $F3 = F2 \cup \{c\_limit\}$, and $F4 = F3 \cup \{sales\_amt\}$. Based on semantic equivalence relationship between schema elements of schemas *client.dtd* and *customer.dtd* depicted in Figure 2, role $a1$ can be mapped to role $b1$, and vice versa. Role $a2$ can be mapped to roles $b2$ and $b3$. Role $b3$ can be mapped to role $a2$. Role $a3$ can be mapped to role $b4$, and vice versa.

Definition 4 (Role hierarchies): A *role hierarchy* is a directed graph $G = <V, E>$ where V is a set of roles and E is a binary relation •senior on V where E is irreflexive and anti-symmetric.   □

For role hierarchy $G = <V, E>$, an edge (u, v) from node u to node v means ˙u is senior to v . We call (u, v) in E a *senior-edge*. Two separate role hierarchies $G_1 = <\{a1, a2, a3\}, \{(a3, a2), (a2, a1)\}>$ and $G_2 = <\{b1, b2, b3, b4\}, \{(b4, b3), (b3, b2), (b2, b1)\}>$ are shown in Figure 3(a).

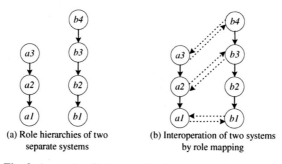

(a) Role hierarchies of two
separate systems

(b) Interoperation of two systems
by role mapping

Fig. 3. A sample of interoperation between two systems

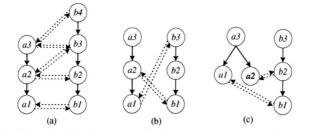

(a)   (b)   (c)

Fig. 4. Samples of security violation problems caused by role mapping

Let $G = <V, E>$ be a role hierarchy. We say that a relation (u, v) is *legal* in G if and only if there is a path of senior-edges from u to v in G. Otherwise, (u, v) is called *illegal*. For instance, $(a3, a1)$ is legal in G_1, while $(a1, a2)$ is illegal. Suppose that we have h systems where each system has a role hierarchy $G_i = <V_i, E_i>$, $i=1, 2, ..., h$. For simplicity, we assume that all nodes are distinctly named. Namely, $V_i \cap V_j = \emptyset$, for $i \neq j$. (Here $\emptyset$ denotes the empty set). To facilitate interoperation, mapping of roles between different systems must be introduced to reflect desired data sharing though interoperation. Such mappings can be represented by a set of cross-system role mappings R, which are defined by a committee of security managers from the individual systems.

Definition 5 (Role mapping): *Role mapping* is a binary relation R on $\cup_{i=1}^{h} V_i$ where for each $(u, v) \in R$ and $i \neq j$, $u \in V_i$ and $v \in V_j$ hold. We call (u, v) in R a *role-edge*. □

For $u \in V_i$, $v \in V_j$, and $i \neq j$, the fact that role-edge $(u, v) \in R$ indicates that role u (in role hierarchy G_i of system i) is permitted to access information of system j on behave of role v (in role hierarchy G_j of system j). Note that it is possible to have both $(u, v) \in R$ and $(v, u) \in R$. Based on application requirement, the committee of the security managers may define role mapping of Example 2 as $R = \{(a1, b1), (b1, a1), (a2, b3), (b3, a2), (a3, b4), (b4, a3)\}$. Figure 3(b) shows the graphical representation of the interoperation of the two systems by R. The edge connecting from a role of a system to a role of another system is represented as a dotted line.

We now discuss a security violation problem caused by role mapping. Figure 4 shows samples of security violations. In Figure 4(a), system B has a security violation because role *b2* can illegally acquire privilege of role *b3* through role-edges (*b2*, *a2*) and (*a2*, *b3*). In Figure 4(b), role *b1* can illegally acquire privilege of role *b3* through role-edge (*b1*, *a2*), senior-edge (*a2*, *a1*) and role-edge (*a1*, *b3*). In Figure 4(c), privilege of role *a1* is different from that of role *a2*. However, role *a2* can illegally acquire privilege of *a1* through role-edge (*a2*, *b2*), senior-edge (*b2*, *b1*) and role-edge (*b1*, *a1*). Note that *a2-b2-b1-a1* is a *violation path* for illegal relationship (*a2*, *a1*).

We now give the definition of a secure interoperation of a federated consisting of h systems. Recall that the autonomy principle requires that interoperation should not violate the security of an individual system.

Definition 6 (Secure interoperation): Given role hierarchies G_1, G_2, .. , G_h where G_i = $<V_i, E_i>$ where $1 \leq i \leq h$, role mapping R, and $Q = <V, E>$ where $V = \bigcup_{i=1,...,h} V_i$ and $E = (\bigcup_{i=1,...,h} E_i) \cup R$, Q is a secure interoperation if for each path from u to v in Q there is a path u to v consisting of role-edges of a system G_i. □

4   Complexity of Security Violation Problems Caused by Role Mapping

The first problem we encounter is to decide whether an interoperation Q is secure. We show algorithm *CheckSecurity* depicted in Figure 5, which detects security violations caused by role mapping in Q. *CheckSecurity* carries out standard reachability analysis from a single node, and the following is straightforward:

Theorem 1. Given role hierarchies G_1, G_2, .. , G_h, role mapping R, and $Q = <V, E>$ where $V = \bigcup_{i=1}^{h} V_i$ and $E = (\bigcup_{i=1}^{h} E_i) \cup R$, *CheckSecurity* detects security violation of Q in time $O(|V|(|E|+|V|))$. □

CheckSecurity(R, G_1, G_2, .. , G_h, Q)
For each G_i ($1 \leq i \leq h$), do the following:
  For each node $v \in G_i$), do the following:
    Find the set V_r of nodes reachable from v through directed paths on E-E_i.
    Let $V_r = V_r \cap V_i$
    If there is a node u in V_r such that u is not a descendant v in the role hierarchy G_i,
    then
      report security violation and quit.
report there is no security violation.

Fig. 5. The algorithm *CheckSecurity*

If a security violation is caused by a role mapping R, it is useful to find a subset R' of R such that R' causes no security violation. Finding a maximum non-violating subset of R is desirable, because we need the smallest number of changes to the original R. However, this optimization is NP-complete.

Theorem 2. Given role hierarchies G_1, G_2, .. , G_h, role mapping R, and positive integer $K \leq |R|$, finding subset $R \subseteq R$ such that $K \leq |R|$ is NP-complete.

Proof Outline: Transformation from FEEDBACK ARC SET [8].   □

Since finding a maximum non-violating subset of a role-mapping is NP-complete, we would like to know special cases where the problem can be solvable in polynomial time. For example, it is known that finding FEEDBACK ARC SET for *undirected* graphs is solvable in linear time. However, simple restrictions to role hierarchies do not reduce complexity (proof is omitted):

Theorem 3. Given role hierarchies G_1, G_2, .. , G_h, role mapping R, and positive integer $K \leq |R|$, finding subset $R' \subseteq R$ such that $K \leq |R|$ is NP-complete, even if one of the following restrictions is applied:

Each role hierarchy G_i consists of only one edge connecting two nodes.

Each role hierarchy G_i is a linear path (no branching), and each node in G_i is adjacent to at most one edge of R.

The role mapping R is bidirectional in the sense that if edge (u, v) is in R, then edge (v, u) is in R, and the subset $R' \subseteq R$ must also be bidirectional.

The number of role hierarchies is limited to 2.   □

We now consider restriction on role mapping. It is known that many NP-complete problems on graphs become polynomial-time solvable if the graphs are restricted to trees. This property can be extended to graphs having *bounded treewidths* [2]. In the following, we formulate this idea for our security violation problem.

Definition 7 (Tree decomposition) [13]: Let $Q = \langle V, E \rangle$ be a directed graph. A *tree decompotition* of Q is any pair $\langle \{X_i | i \in I\}, T \rangle$ with $\{X_i | i \in I\}$ a family of subsets of V and $T = \langle V, E \rangle$ a tree with the elements of I as nodes, such that the following properties hold:

- $\cup_{i \, I} X_i = V$,
- for every edge $e = (u,v) \in E$ there is an $i \in I$ such that $u \in X_i$ and $v \in X_i$, and
- for all $i,j,k \in I$, if j lies on the path (direction ignored) between i and k in T, then $X_i \cap X_k \subseteq X_j$.

The *width* of a tree decomposition $\langle \{X_i | i \in I\}, T \rangle$ is equal to $\max_{i \, I} \{|X_i|-1\}$. The *treewidth* of Q, denoted by *treewidth(Q)*, is the minimum value of k such that Q has a tree decomposition of width k.   □

There is a polynomial-time algorithm to decided for arbitrary graphs Q whether *treewidth(Q)* $\leq k$ for any fixed k. Now, suppose that a federated system $Q = \langle V, E \rangle$ has *treewidth(Q)=k*, where k is a fixed positive number. We show algorithm *MaximumRoleMapping* for computing a maximum non security-violating subset of role-mapping R. *MaximumRoleMapping* has time bound polynomial to the size of Q. Let $Q(X)$ denote the subgraph induced by a node set X.

Theorem 4. Given a federated system $Q = \langle V, E \rangle$ consisting of role hierarchies G_1, G_2, .. , G_h and role mapping R, assume that *treewidth(Q)=k* is a fixed positive number. Then *MaximumRoleMapping* computes a maximum non-violating subset of R in time

$$O(4^{k^2} |V|^k).$$

MaximumRoleMapping(R, G_1, G_2, .. , G_h, Q, k)

1.   Compute tree decomposition $<\{X_i \mid i \in I\}, T>$.
2.   For an arbitrary node $i \in I$ as a root of T, perform the following.
3.   Let F_i be *outer edges* $\{(u,v) \mid u,v \in X_i$, both adjacent to edges in $Q - Q(X_i)\}$.
4.   Let R_i be $R \cap Q(X_i)$.
5.   **for each** subset S of $F_i \cup R_i$
6.   **for each** subset $F'_i \subseteq F_i$, mark F'_i ($\subseteq S$) as role-edges
7.   Run *CheckSecurity* on *projection* $P_i = (Q(X_i) - R) \cup S$.
8.   If P_i has security violation, go to Step 6 to process next subset of F_i.
9.   **for each** child j of i
10.   Look up table B by $Q(X_j) \cap S$ as a key and obtain $rmax_j$.
11.   If $rmax_j$ is not defined, recursively call Step 2 with j as root and obtain $rmax_j$.
12.   Let r_i be $|S \cap R_i|$ plus the sum of $rmax_j$'s for all children j.
13.   Let $rmax_i$ be the maximum r_i during the loop of Steps 5 and 6.
14.   Register $rmax_i$ to table B with key $Q(X_i) \cap S$.

Fig. 6. The algorithm *MaximumRoleMapping*

Proof: We remove a subset of R from Q, and test whether Q is secure. We have to test every subset of R to find a minimum subset R_m. Then $R - R_m$ is the solution. By tree decomposition, if there is a path from v to u such that $v \in X_i$ and $u \in X_j$ for some $i,j \in I$, then an edge in the path is contained in $Q(X_l)$, for any l which is on the path between i and j in T. Using this property, we decompose the maximization problem into subproblems. For any $i \in I$, we compute *projection* P_i by X_i such that $Q(X_i)$ is added with edges such that if there is a path from v to u such that $v,u \in X_i$ and the path consists of edges in $Q - Q(X_i)$, then we add an *outer* edge (v,u) to P_i. We need one-bit information on whether the path contains edges of role hierarchies, since a loop of non-role hierarchy edges is not a violation. Then, if there is no violation in P_i and $Q - Q(X_i)$, we can conclude that Q has no violation. We carry out the series of tests by dynamic programming. The table B is used to avoid repeated computation on the same subgraph.

By tree decomposition, $|X_i| < k$ holds for $i \in I$. Then the number of edges of P_i is bounded by $2k(k-1)$. Since $|R| \leq k(k-1)$, Step 5-6 is repeated $O(2^{2k(k-1)})$ times. *CheckSecurity* at Step 7 runs in time $O(k^2)$. Looking up table B takes time $O(k^2)$. Since table B is used, $rmax_i$ is computed only once for each i and each distinct projection P_i. The number of nodes of T is bounded by ${}_nC_k = O(n^k)$, where $n = |V|$. Overall, we have time bound $O(2^{2k(k-1)} k^2 |n|^k) = O(4^{k^2} |V|^k)$.   □

5   Conclusion

In this paper, we have presented a model that maps foreign roles to local roles by using knowledge of semantic equivalence relationship between schema elements of export schemas of local and remote systems. Our model can provide fine-grained access control on shared XML documents among cooperating XML systems. Since each system may have different access control policies, role mapping may cause security violation in the cooperating systems. We have shown that finding optimum non-violating role mapping is NP-complete, but solvable in polynomial time if the graphs of cooperating systems have bounded treewidth.

References

1. E. Bertino, S. Castano, S.Ferrari and M. Mesiti, Specifying and Enforcing Access Control Policies for XML Document Sources, World Wide Web, Baltzer, Vol. 3, No. 3, 2000.
2. H.L. Bodlaender, Dynamic programming on graphs with bounded tree-width, Proc. ICALP, Springer LNCS 317, pp. 103–118, 1988.
3. P.A. Bonatti, M.L. Sapino and V.S. Subrahmanian, Merging heterogeneous security orderings, Proc. Computer Security – ESORICS96, LNCS1146, pp. 183–197, 1996.
4. S. Chatvichienchai, M. Iwaihara, Y. Kambayashi, •Towards Translating Authorizations for Transformed XML Documents, Proc. 3rd Int. Conf. Web Info. Systems Engineering (WISE), pp.291–300, Dec.2002.
5. E. Damiani, S. De Capitani di Vimercati, S. Paraboschi, and P. Samarati. •Fine Grained Access Control for SOAP e-Services, 10th Int. World Wide Web Conf., pp. 504–513, ACM Press, 2001.
6. E. Damiani, S. De Capitani di Vimercati, S. Paraboschi, and P. Samarati. •A Fine-grained Access Control System for XML Documents, ACM Trans. Info. and Syst. Security (TISSEC), 5(2), pp. 169–202, 2002.
7. A.H. Doan, P. Domingos, A. Halevy. •Reconciling Schemas of Disparate Data Sources: a Machine-Learning Approach, Proc ACM SIGMOD Conf, pp. 509–520, 2001.
8. M. R. Garey and D. S. Johnson, *"Computers and Intractability, A Guide to the Theory of NP-Completeness,"* pp. 192, Freeman, 1979.
9. M. Hitchens and V. Varadharajan, RBAC for XML Document Stores Information and Communications Security, 3rd Int. Conf., pp. 131–143, 2001.
10. D. Jonscher and K.R. Dittrich, •An Approach for Building Secure Database Federations, Proc. 20th VLDB Conference, pp. 24–35, 1994.
11. J. Madhavan, P.A. Bernstein and E. Rahm, Generic Schema Matching with Cupid, Proc. 27th VLDB Conference, pp.49–58, Roma, Italy, 2001.
12. S. Osborn, Database Security Integration Using Role-Based Access Control, Proc. TC11/ WG11.3 14th Ann. Working Conf. Database Security, pp.245–258, Aug. 2000.
13. J. van Leeuwen (ed.), *Handbook of Theoretical Computer Science, Volume A: Algorithm and Complexity,* MIT Press, pp. 549, 1990.
14. L. Wang, D. Wijesekera, S. Jajodia, •Towards Secure XML Federations, 16th IFIP WG11.3 Working Conf. Database and Application Security, 2002.
15. W3C (2000). Extensible Markup Language (XML) 1.0 (Second Edition). http://www.w3c.org/TR/REC-xml (October 2000).

A Flexible Database Security System Using Multiple Access Control Policies*

Min-A Jeong[1], Jung-Ja Kim[1], and Yonggwan Won[2]

[1] Research Institute of Electronics and Telecommunications Technology,
Chonnam National University
300 Yongbong-Dong Buk-Gu
Kwangju, Republic of Korea
{majung,jjkim}@grace.chonnam.ac.kr
[2] Department of Computer Engineering,
Chonnam National University
300 Yongbong-Dong Buk-Gu
Kwangju, Republic of Korea
ykwon@chonnam.ac.kr

Abstract. Due to various requirements for the user access control to large databases in the hospitals and the banks, database security has been emphasized. There are many security models for database systems using wide variety of policy-based access control methods. However, they are not functionally enough to meet the requirements for the complicated and various types of access control. In this paper, we propose a database security system that can individually control user access to data groups of various sizes and is suitable for the situation where the user's access privilege to arbitrary data is changed frequently. Data group(s) in different sizes d is defined by the table name(s), attribute(s) and/or record key(s), and the access privilege is defined by security levels, roles and polices. The proposed system operates in two phases. The first phase is composed of a modified MAC(Mandatory Access Control) model and RBAC(Role-Based Access Control) model. A user can access any data that has lower or equal security levels, and that is accessible by the roles to which the user is assigned. All types of access mode are controlled in this phase. In the second phase, a modified DAC(Discretionary Access Control) model is applied to re-control the '*read*' mode by filtering out the non-accessible data from the result obtained at the first phase. For this purpose, we also defined the user group s that can be characterized by security levels, roles or any partition of users. The policies represented in the form of ***Block***(s, d, r) were also defined and used to control access to any data or data group(s) that is not permitted in '*read*' mode. With this proposed security system, more complicated 'read' access to various data sizes for individual users can be flexibly controlled, while other access mode can be controlled as usual. An implementation example for a database system that manages specimen and clinical information is presented.

---

* This study was supported by a grant of the International Mobile Telecommunications 2000 R&D Project, Ministry of Information & Communication, Republic of Korea.

V. Mařík et al. (Eds.): DEXA 2003, LNCS 2736, pp. 876–885, 2003.

1 Introduction

Database security becomes more crucial as the scale of database for public and private organizations is growing and the various user access schemes are required. Recently, most relational database management systems(RDBMS) provide only some limited security techniques, which generally use a policy-based access control[1].

The most popular access control policies currently used are Mandatory Access Control(MAC), Discretionary Access Control(DAC), Role-Based Access Control(RBAC). MAC policy designates a security level to data and users, and therefore makes it possible to control the abnormal flow of information. However, the MAC policy lacks the flexibility to fulfill the conditions for a complex access control[2]. While DAC policy can control the access flexibly rather than the MAC policy, it cannot control an illegal flow of information to unauthorized users[3]. RBAC policy assigns the users to applicable roles, and the users can access to data by the access right assigned to each role. Therefore, RBAC policy can provide simple security management methods and also prevent the abused access right by allowing only least privilege to the users[4][5].

With respect to the characteristics of each access control policy above, some security models using one or two policies were proposed for the database system. Some models using the MAC policy are Access Matrix model, Task-Grant model, Action-Entity model, Wood and so on[6]. Jojodia-sandhu model and Smith-Winslett model adopt the DAC policy[7][8][9]. Sea View model is a suggestion to combine both policies[10]. Additionally, there are researches referring to the RBAC techniques that provide simple security management by Sandhu-Bhamidipati and Ferraiolo[11][12].

Those security models extend the standard relational database model, and have a drawback that a modification or alternation is not easy when security requirements are frequently changed. That is, they are not suitable to the situations when the user's access right on a data changes at any time, and also have difficulty in performing different access control for each user to the same data. For example, if two users have same access right on the same attributes but have different access right on the different tuples in a table of medical information database, it is not easy to control the individual access by the existing security models. In some situations, it is frequently required that the user who has access right on specific patient data should grant access right to some users who does not have. Consequently, a special access control is necessary for each data group of different sizes, which is formed by a combination of various tuples and attributes.

In this paper, we propose a system for user-specific access control to data groups of various sizes. The proposed system operates in two phases. The first phase is composed of a modified MAC model and RBAC model. A user can access any data that has lower or equal security levels, and that is accessible by the roles to which the user is assigned. All types of access mode are controlled in this phase. In the second phase, a modified DAC model is applied to re-control the 'read' mode by filtering out the non-accessible data from the result obtained at the first phase. For these procedures, user groups and data groups were firstly defined and then an access rule was set up on the basis of the defined groups of user and data. The system does not extend a standard relational model but makes it possible to handle complex access control by providing different access rules to each user or user groups.

This paper is composed of six chapters. Chapter 2 describes the research related to previous access control policies and database security models, and chapter 3 shows the definitions of users, data and access control rule for the specific access control suggested in this paper. The definition of a security policy for the specific access control is shown in chapter 4. The system architecture to support the suggested security policy and the implementation results are illustrated in chapter 5. Finally, this paper is finished with the conclusion in chapter 6.

2 Access Control Policies and Database Security Models

2.1 MAC Policy

Mandatory Access Control(MAC) policy is based on a security model designed by Bell and LaPadula for an operating system[2]. This policy controls the access according to the classification of subjects and objects in a system. The security levels of subjects and objects are assorted into TopSecret(TS), Secret(S), Confidential(C), and Unclassified(U) in the relations of TS > S > C > U. This access control policy defines two basic rules: a subject can read only objects in the equal or lower levels than itself, and a subject can record only objects in the equal or higher levels than itself. This policy is usually applied to mass data, which generally needs to be strong protection. It is also designed to protect the data from intrusion via Trojan horse or covert channel. However, the data integrity cannot be maintained because a lower level user possibly write on the higher level objects. There are some typical MAC-based security models; Jajodia-Sandhu model that proposed a formalized relational model regarding security classification levels, Smith-Winslett model based on a trustworthy theory, and Sea View model that is an integration of the MAC and DAC polices[7][8][9][10].

2.2 DAC Policy

Discretionary Access Control(DAC) policy controls the data access according to the user's identity and rules. It can be discretionary in the view point that a user can grant the access right to another user[3]. Owing to the flexibility of this policy, most of previous DBMSs adopt it. However, the access right can be transferred to other users avoiding the data owner's recognition. Therefore, this policy is vulnerable to malicious attack like an innate virus in the program. A model proposed by Wood *et al* considered a grant problem in a multi-level relational database[6].

2.3 RBAC Policy

Role-Based Access Control(RBAC) policy permits access to information in a specific mode only through the roles to which the user is assigned[4][5]. The hierarchical relation between roles should be maintained to create inheritance of the access right, and a security policy is essential in separation of tasks by the role characteristics. This policy makes it possible to simplify the security management and to prevent the abuse of rights by allowing only least privilege to users. Nevertheless, it is not practically applicable to a large-scale database system due to a vast set of the complex relations between huge volume of roles and the role grants. Nowadays, this policy is widely used and many modified ones have been proposed along with new issues [11][12].

3 Preliminary Definition

3.1 User

A user u_i, referred to as a *subject*, is a database user, and characterized as follows.
- User set $U = \{u1, u2, u3, ..., up\}$, p = number of users.
- User subset $S = \{S1, S2, S3, ..., St\}$, $Sq \subset U$, t = number of user subsets.
- User group by security level $H = \{H1, H2, H3, ..., Hm\}$, m = number of security levels.
- User group by role $R = \{R1, R2, R3, ..., Rn\}$, n = number of roles.
- $ui \in Hk$ and $ui \in Rl$
- $1 \leq N(Hk) \leq p, 1 \leq N(Rj) \leq p$

In this notations, $N(\cdot)$ indicates the total number of users.

3.2 Data

Data, referred to as a *object*, is information item. As similar to the user group, the data if grouped in different sizes using table name, attribute name(s) and record key(s). The record key implies any information with which the records to be retrieved can be uniquely identified. The data group DG is defined as follows:
- $DG = \{ DG1, DG2, DG3, ..., DGn \}$, n = number of data groups
  $DGi = \{Table\ Name,\ Attribute\ Name(s),\ Record\ Key(s)\}$

According to the above definition, the data groups are in three different types.

① Table: $DG_i^1 = \{Table\ Name,\ NULL,\ NULL\}$

② Table and Attribute: $DG_i^2 = \{Table\ Name,\ Attribute\ Name(s),\ NULL\}$

③ Table Attribute and Record Key:

  $DG_i^3 = \{Table\ Name,\ Attribute\ Name(s),\ Record\ Key(s)\}$

The superscript is only for discriminating the three types. We are going to use this superscript only when it is necessary to resolve any confusion.

The first type sets a whole table as one data group while the second type determines data groups by a partial set of attributes for a table designated by table name. Data groups defined by the third type are in various sizes. It can define any size of data by the combination of table name, attribute names and record keys. The figure 1 illustrates some examples of the data groups defined by the third type. As shown in the figure 1, the data group DG_1 has only a single entry represented by $\{Table\ Name, A_3, R_2\}$. Other examples are expressed as;

$DG_2 = \{Table\ Name,\ A_4,\ \{R_2,\ R_3\}\},\quad DG_3 = \{Table\ Name,\ \{A_5,\ A_6\},\ R_3\}$

$DG_4 = \{Table\ Name,\ A_6,\ \{R_2,\ R_4\}\},\quad DG_5 = \{Table\ Name,\ \{A_2,\ A_4\},\ R_5\}$

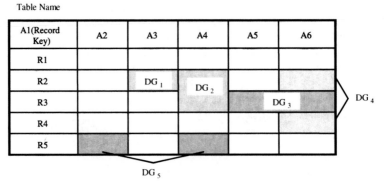

A1~A6 : Attribute Name, R1~R5 : Record Key value

Fig. 1. Examples of data groups

4 Security Requirements

The system proposed in this paper was initially designed to satisfy the following security policies. The security policies were defined in order to effectively manage the specimen and clinical information in a genomic research center. In the following policies, $SL(\cdot)$ represents the security level, and

[Policy 1]

$$SL(H_k) \geq SL(DG_i^2) \rightarrow \{u_i \in H_k, DG_i^2, \{I, U, D\}\}$$

A user u_i can insert(I), update(U), and delete(D) an entry in DG_i^2 if the security level of the user group is equal to or higher than that of the data group.

[Policy 2]

$$\{u_i \in \{R_c \rightarrow DG_i^2\}\} \rightarrow \{u_i \in R_c, DG_i^2, \{I, U, D\}\}$$

A user u_i can insert, update, and delete an entry in DG_i^2 accessible by the corresponding role.

[Policy 3]

A data group is only readable by a designated user or user groups only if the previous policies are satisfied.

To satisfy the above security policies, the access control is performed by two phases. In the first phase, execution of query is determined by the combination of a modified MAC and the RBAC. If the security level of a user dominates the security level of a data group, user can perform the access modes of 'insert', 'update' and 'delete' according to the application of the MAC policy. The drawback of the original MAC policy is that the data integrity is not guaranteed because a lower level subject can execute an access to a higher level object. However, the proposed system guarantees the data integrity by blocking the lower level subjects from accessing the higher level objects. Besides, the application of RBAC policy allows an access to higher objects exceptionally only when the user is assigned to the role by which the objects can be accessible. Control on the execution of insert, update and delete is completed in the second phase, a modified DAC policy is applied to meet the 'Policy 3' described above. Details of the operations are explained in the next chapter. The data access control for the second phase, **Block**(s, d, r) is defined as following;

- Block(s, d, r)

   $s \in S_j$, $j = \{1, 2, \dots, u\}$, u = number of user subsets

   $d \in DG_r$, $r = \{1, 2, \dots, v\}$, v = number of data groups

   r : read mode

For example, an access control policy **Block(S_l, DG_q, r)** indicates that a user in S_l cannot read the data entry in DG_q. In summary, the second phase performs the selective read-access by the policies described **Block(s, d, r)**.

The *selective* read-access control can be implemented by a step-wise filtering process. In the first   phase, all the users are controlled in access to objects according to their security levels and assigned roles. In other words, access control for read mode is conducted based on the roles and security levels by the modified MAC and the RBAC in the first phase. The selective access control for the read mode is actually completed in the second phase by the policies described by a set of **Block(s, d, r)**. If there is any policy that the user and the part of the data group is involved, the data is filtered out by encoding the values.

5   Architecture and Operations

In this chapter, we will first describe the system architecture and operational flow. An implementation result for the *selective* read-access control will be also presented.

5.1 System Architecture

The security administrator creates and store several things such as user groups S_c, H_j, and R_j, security levels for tables and attributes, role assignments, data groups DG_j, and **Block(s, d, r)** policies. The functional modules in the system will use those stored informations. The system architecture is shown in the figure 2.

In the first phase, the user identification is first obtained. The access request submitted is examined if it is an ordinary SQL statement or invocation of a role. If the request is a SQL statement, the information for access mode, table names and attributes are extracted from the query statement. Based on the first policy described in the chapter 4, a new query statement is created. In the case of role invocation, user's role assignment information is examined and the RBAC module is called if assigned to that role (see the second policy). If the request does not meet any policy, the request will be denied. In the second phase, the query result produced in the first phase will be filtered by the S-DAC(*Selective* DAC) module using the third policy represented by **Block(s, d, r)**. Any data that is not blocked by the policies will be viewed finally.

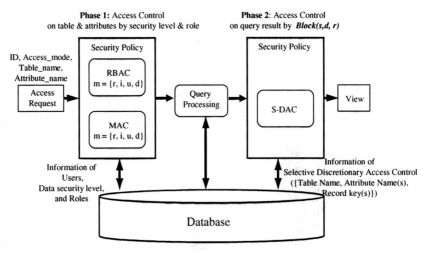

Fig. 2. System Architecture

5.2 Operations of the Modules

We here described the detailed functional description and operational flow for the MAC, RBAC, and S-DAC modules.

RBAC Module

When an access to a role is requested, the RBAC module first checks if the user is a member of the user group classified the role assignment. Assuming that a role in R_l is invoked by user $u_i \in R_l$, the role is then invoked and the access operation that is pre-defined for the role will be performed.

MAC Module

When the access is requested by SQL statement, the MAC module compares the user's security level with those of the tables and each attribute in the SQL statement. For each accessible table, the MAC module calculates the number of the attributes which has the security level equal to or lower than that of the user, and extracts those attribute names. Based on the result of this procedure, a new query(SQL) statement is generated, which meets the first policy shown in the chapter 4. The figure 3 shows the diagram for the operational flow of the MAC and RBAC module.

S-DAC Module

The S-DAC module first selects the S-DAC policies **Block(s, d, r)** where s includes the user. **d**, Data groups in the collected polices is then examined. For the tuple list resulted from the first phase, the value of any data item presented in the data groups will be encoded or scrambled into a designated character string, which is a process of filtering the blocked data items. The figure 4 shows the diagram for the operational flow of the S-DAC module.

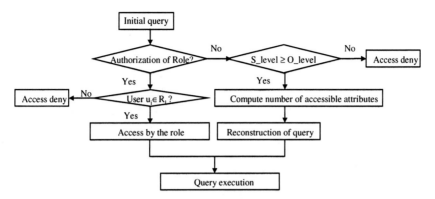

Fig. 3. The diagram for the operational flow of the MAC and RBAC module

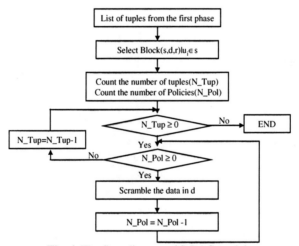

Fig. 4. The flow diagram of S-DAC module

5.3 Implementation Results

Since the implementation for the MAC and the RBAC can be found in many literatures, we only focus on the second phase where the *selective* read-access control is performed. The figure 5 shows the result of the query "SELECT * FROM Patient_info;" submitted by a user. The user does not have read-access right to the information of 'Diagnosis Hospital' for the patient '1-2001-1' and 'Doctor' for '1-2002-3', which is set as a policy ***Block(s, d, r)***. Note that the values for those items are encoded into '*****'. All other tuples have a higher security level than that of the user.

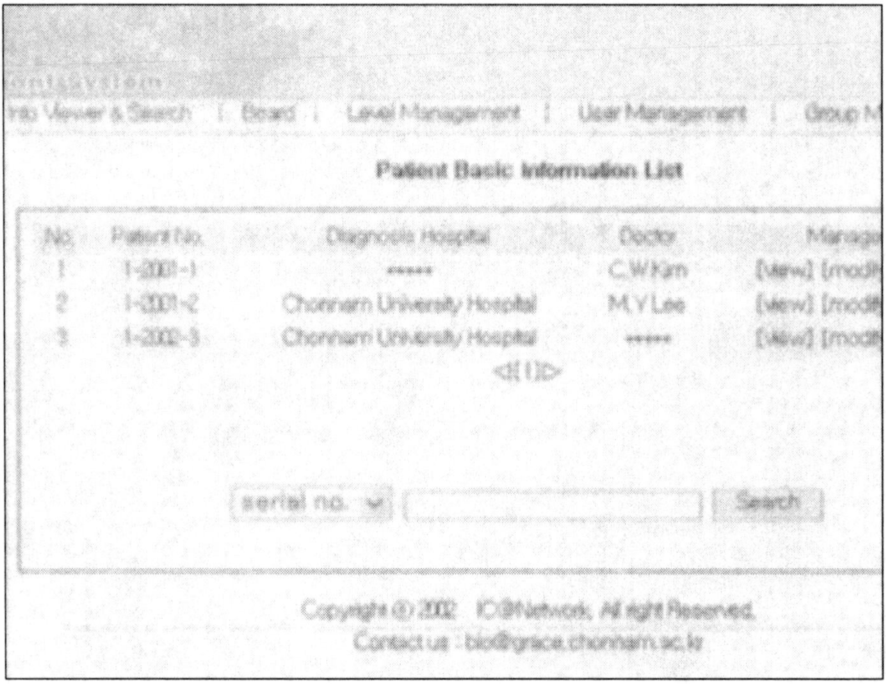

Fig. 5. An example of the S-DAC result

6   Conclusion

As the scale of the database become larger and the user access control is complicated, database security becomes more crucial. There are many security models for database systems using wide variety of policy-based access control methods. However, they are not functionally enough to meet the requirements for the complicated and various types of access control. Especially in the situation when the security policies change frequently, the existing security models are not suitable to provide a proper security mechanism.

In this paper, we proposed a database security system that can individually control user access to data groups of various sizes and is suitable for the situation where the user's access privilege to arbitrary data is changed frequently. The proposed system operates in two phases. The first phase is composed of a modified MAC model and the RBAC model. A user can access any data that has lower or equal security levels, and that is accessible by the roles to which the user is assigned. In the second phase, a modified DAC model, named in S-DAC which performs a *selective* read-access control, is applied to re-control the '*read*' mode by filtering out the non-accessible data from the result obtained at the first phase.

With this proposed security system, more complicated 'read' access to various data sizes for individual users can be flexibly controlled and managed, while other access mode can be controlled as usual. Although we applied the system to securely manage the specimen and clinical information, the methodology used in this paper can be applied to other systems that require different security policies.

Even though the proposed security system can flexibly control more complicated 'read' access to various data sizes for individual users, it is obvious that there is an extra overhead which may degrades the system performance. We should do further study to minimize the overhead. Also, there is a possibility that a new policy can be a duplication of existing policies. Therefore, a policy reduction methodology should be considered.

References

1. M. Piattini and E. Fernandez-Medina, "Secure databases: state of the art," Security Technology, Proc. Of the IEEE 34th Annual 2000 International Carnahan Conference, pp. 228–237, 2000
2. R. Lindgreen and I. Herschberg, "On the Validity of the Bell-LaPadula Model," Computer & Security, Vol.13, pp.317–338, 1994.
3. S. Lewis and S. Iseman, "Securing an object relational database," Computer Security Applications Conference, 1997.
4. D. Ferraiolo, R. Sandhu, S. Gavrila, D. Kuhn, and R. Chandramouli, "Proposed NIST Standard for Role-Based Access Control," ACM Transactions on Information and Systems Security, Vol. 4, No. 3, pp.224–274, Aug. 2001.
5. R. Sandhu, E. Coyne, H. Feinstein, and C. Youman, "Role-based access control models," IEEE Computer, Vol. 29, Issue 2, pp.38–47, 1996.
6. C. Wood, R. Summers, and E. Fernandez, "Authorization in multilevel database models," Information Systems, Pergamon Press, 4(2), 1979.
7. S. Jajodia and R. Sandhu, "Enforcing primary key requirements in multilevel relations," In Proc. 4th RADC Workshop on Multilevel Database Security, Little Compton, Rhode Island, 1991.
8. R. Sandhu and S. Jajodia, "Polyinstantiation for cover stories," In Proc. European Symposium on Research in Computer Security, Toulouse, France, Springer-Verlag LNCS 648, 1992.
9. M. Winslett, K. Smith, and X. Qian, "Formal query language for secure relational databases, ACM-TODS, 1994.
10. D. Denning et al., "The Sea View Security Model," In Proc. IEEE Symp. on Security and Privacy. Oakland, CA, pp. 218–233, 1988.
11. R. Sandhu and V. Bhamidipati, "The URA97 model for role-based user-role assignment," Database Security XI: Status and Prospects, Chapman and Hall, London, pp. 262–275, 1997.
12. D. Ferraiolo, J. Barkley, and R. Kuhn, "A role-based access control model and reference implementation within a corporate intranet," ACM Transactions on Information and Systems Security, Vol. 2, No.1, pp. 34–64, 1999.

Designing Secure Databases for OLS*

Eduardo Fernández-Medina and Mario Piattini

Escuela Superior de Informática.
University of Castilla-La Mancha.
Paseo de la Universidad 4,
13071, Ciudad Real. Spain
Tel: 34 926 29 53 00
{Eduardo.FdezMedina,Mario.Piattini}@uclm.es
http://www.inf-cr.uclm.es

Abstract. Some Database Management Systems (DBMS) allow to implement multilevel databases, but there are no methodologies for designing these databases. Security must be considered as a fundamental requirement in Information Systems (IS) development, and has to be taken into account at all stages of the development. We propose a methodology for designing secure databases, which allows to design and implement secure databases considering constraints regarding sensitive information from the requirements phase. The models and languages included in the methodology provide tools to specify constraints and to classify the information into different security levels and to specify which roles users need to play to access information. The methodology prescribes rules to specify the database and the security information with the Oracle9*i* Label Security (OLS) DBMS. It also has been applied in an actual case by the Data Processing Center of the Ciudad Real Provincial Government.

1 Introduction

The modern society forces companies and enterprises to evolve, and to manage information properly in order to achieve their objectives and survive in the digital era. Organizations depend increasingly on IS, which rely upon large databases, and these databases need increasingly more quality and security. Indeed the very survival of the organization depends on the correct management, security and confidentiality of this information [1].

Databases are present in many situations of our real life, managing and storing a huge amount of important information. So, it is important to protect databases and IS [2]. Sometimes, databases also store information regarding private or personal aspects of individuals, like identification data, medical data or even religious beliefs, ideologies, or sexual tendencies. Because of this, there are laws to protect the individual privacy (e.g., *Spanish Constitutional Law for the Personal Data Protection*

---

* This research is part of the DOLMEN project (TIC2000-1673-C06-06) and RETISSI project (TIC2001-5023-E) supported by the Research Projects Subdirection of the Ministry of Science and Technology.

V. Mařík et al. (Eds.): DEXA 2003, LNCS 2736, pp. 886–895, 2003.

(LOPD)[1] – [3]). Failure to comply with these laws used to be very strict, enforcing severe penalties. That information should then be equipped with mechanisms that prevent non-authorized access, fulfilling the existing Data Protection Laws.

As some authors remarked [5, 6], we think that database protection is a serious requirement which must be considered carefully, not as an isolated aspect, but as an element present in all stages of the database life cycle, from the requirement analysis to implementation and maintenance. For this purpose, different ideas for integrating security in the system development process are proposed [7], but they only considered database security from a cryptographic point of view. Chung et al. also insist on integrating security requirements in the design, by providing the designers with models specifying security aspects, but they do not deal with database specific issues [8].

There are a few proposals that try to integrate security into conceptual modeling such as the Semantic Data Model for Security [9] and the Multilevel Object Modeling Technique [10], but they have not been very spread. One more recent proposal is UMLSec [11] where UML is extended to develop secure systems. This approach is very interesting, but it -again- only deals with IS in general, whilst conceptual and logical database design, and secure database implementation are not considered. Moreover Castano et al. presents a very interesting methodological approach for designing security in databases, but it does not consider the integration with the database development process [12]. Also, traditional database methodologies, do not consider security in their proposals [13, 14].

To overcome this problem, we propose a methodological approach, which allows us to design databases taking into consideration security aspects from the earliest stages, until the end of the development. This approach could also be an extension of the existing methodologies and modeling standards, since the organizations who are really interested in database security would not have to make a great effort to adapt to a new methodology. The methodology we proposed extends different UML models and the Object Constraint Language (OCL). It allows us to create conceptual and logical model of multilevel databases, and to implement them by using Oracle 9i Label Security [15].

In order to develop the methodology, we have used the '*Action Research*' method [16], applying the methodology to the redesign of a database for the Ciudad Real Provincial Government (Spain). This database was managed by an application, called SALA (System for the Accounting of the Local Administration), that had different confidentiality problems, which we have solved through a new secure design. The general aim of this application is to control the budget and the accounting of the Provincial Government. This application manages not only economic information about companies and individuals, but also *personal information of individuals*. If minimal security measures are taken into account, someone could illegally explore economic and personal information, by collecting addresses, account numbers, telephone numbers, information about economic transactions, etc. It is possible to know the habits of companies and individuals, and therefore to get a profile of them. In this case the organization would have to face up to legal responsibilities.

---

[1] LOPD is an adaptation of the European Union Directive 95/46/CE of the European Parliament and Council about people protection regarding the personal data management and the free circulation of these data [4].

In the next section we present an overview of the secure database design methodology, including the models and languages that have been defined. Finally in section 3 we comment conclusions and future work.

2 Methodology Overview

This methodology allows us to classify the information according to its confidentiality properties and to which user roles will have access permissions. It is also possible to specify security constraints on that classification. The methodology ends defining rules to specify the database, the security information and the security constraints with OLS.

The methodology be iterative and incremental, driven by use cases, and centered on the architecture. The stages of the methodology are *Requirements Gathering*, *System Analysis*, *Multilevel Relational Logical Design*, and *Specific Logical Design*.

In order to give support to the methodology, we have extended Rational Rose, to include and manage the security information of the elements into the use case and class diagrams. It also permits definition of security constraints and their lexical and syntactical checking.

In the following sections, we present each stage in more detail, illustrating them with a portion of the case study.

2.1 Requirements Gathering

As in any other development methodology, the goal of this stage is to collect and represent requirements, with the particularity that we also have to consider security requirements. The most important artifact of this stage is the *extended use case model*, which allows us to indicate special security characteristics of actors and use case through stereotypes. The extended use case model introduces the concept of *secure use case* and *authorized actor*. A secure use case is a use case that should be deeply studied from the point of view of security. An authorized actor is an actor that must have special authorizations in order to execute a particular use case.

This stages consists of the following activities: Gathering initial requirements, creating the business model and the system glossary, looking for actors, looking for use cases, looking for persistent elements, describing use cases, analyzing security in actors and in use cases, defining priorities in use cases, structuring the use case model, looking for relationships between use cases, and reviewing use cases.

For space reasons it is not possible to develop in detail the extended use case model. More details can be found in [17].

2.2 System Analysis

The aim of this stage is to build the database conceptual model, considering all the requirements that have been collected in the previous activities. The conceptual model will be composed of the *extended class diagram*, and a set of *security constraints* that are expressed through the OSCL language [18].

The extended class diagram makes possible to specify security information in classes, attributes and associations, which indicates the conditions that the subjects have to fulfill to access them, regarding *security levels* and *roles of authorized users.* If one security level, for instance, is assigned to a class, it means that subjects have to be classified in at least the same level in order to access the information. If a set of roles is assigned to an element, it means that the subjects have to play at least one of those roles to access the element.

The OSCL language allows the specification of security constraints that define the information about security of classes, attributes or associations, depending on a particular condition. For instance, in the following example:

Context CreditorOfTheExpenseBudget **inv**:
    self.SL=if Refunds <= 3000 then U else if Refunds <= 10000 then S else T

The constraint specifies that the security level of the objects belonging to the class *CreditorOfTheExpenseBudget* will be more restrictive if the value of the attribute *Refunds* have one particular value. As we can see the syntax of OSCL is easy to understand, because this language is based on the well-known OCL.

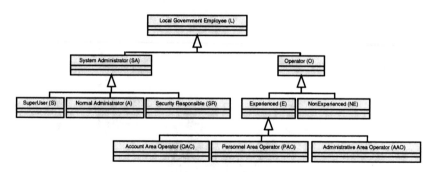

Fig. 1. Roles Hierarchy

The activities of this stage are architecture analysis, use case analysis, classes analysis, security analysis, and package analysis. All of these activities are composed of many more tasks. The components of the security analysis activity are as follows:

- Defining the valid security levels for the system.
- Assigning security levels to the classes, attributes and associations, taking into account the security properties of the information, and the *inherent constraints*[2] of the extended class model.
- Classifying classes, attributes and associations into different authorized user roles, if necessary.
- Specifying security constraints, which define the security information of different model elements.
- Analyzing other kinds of security constraints (not only about confidentiality).

---

[2] The extended class model has different inherent constraints that all instances must fulfill. For example, the security level of the attributes should be equal to or more restricted than the security level of the class to they belong.

- Defining the authorization information of the users, which is composed of the security level and the roles that users play.

Part of the hierarchy of roles that has been defined for the case study database is shown in Figure 1. Figure 2 illustrates an example of an extended class diagram. The security levels[3] that have been defined for this database are Unclassified (U), Confidential (C), Secret (S), and Top Secret (T). For each role, a short name is also defined, which is used in the diagrams. For instance, the class 'EconomicalData' has defined the security level 'T' and the role 'OAC' (Account Area Operator). This means that the information of the objects that belongs to that class will only be accessible to users who have security level 'Top Secret' and who play role 'Account Area Operator'. If there is no security information associated to a class, then all users can access it.

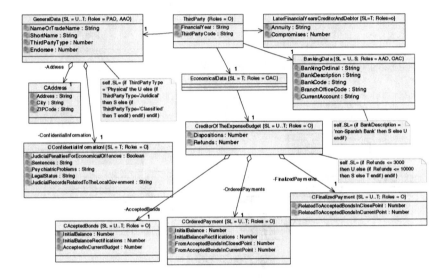

Fig. 2. Third Parties Class Diagram

We can also observe in Figure 2 three OSCL constraints, which define the security level of the objects, depending on the value of different attributes. For instance, the security constraint associated with class 'BankingData' indicates that the security level of its objects will be 'Secret' if the value of the attribute 'BankDescription' is equal to 'Non-Spanish Bank', and 'Unclassified', in any other case.

2.3 Multilevel Relational Logical Design

This stage is the bridge between the conceptual model and the implementation with a specific logical model. We think it is very important to keep the independence

---

[3] In this methodology it is possible to define a particular set of security levels, depending on the complexity of the database.

between a "general logical model" and the different specific logical models because multilevel and other authorization issues vary considerably from one product to another. For the moment we have considered only a general relational security database model because relational databases are the most used and widespread at present [19], but it could be possible to develop secure object-relational or object oriented databases.

The three components of the general multilevel relational model are:

- Database relational model: This component includes the definition of each relation of the database, considering the necessary attributes for representing the confidentiality information
- Meta-information of the model: Each relation has associated a meta-information tuple, which includes the data type of the attributes, and the valid values of the attributes related to security information of the tuple and attributes.
- Security Constraints: All the security constraints defined in the conceptual model are specified in this model without losing or modifying their semantics.

The activities of this stage deal with the transformation of all elements in the extended class diagram into the multilevel relational model.

Database Relational Model
BankingData(Id, BankOrdinal, BankDescription, BankCode, BranchOfficeCode, CurrentAccount, TFinancialYear, TThirdPartyCode, SecurityLevel)
ThirdParty(FinancialYear, ThirdPartyCode)
LaterFinancialYearsCreditorAndDefaulter (Annuity, Compromises)
CreditorOfTheExpenseBudget(Id, Dispositions, Refunds, Bon_InitialBalance, Bon_InitialBalanceRectifications, Bon_AcceptedInCurrentBudget, Ord_Pay_InitialBalance, Ord_Pay_InitialBalanceRectifications, Ord_Pay_BondsClosedPoints, Ord_Pay_BondsCurrentPoints, Fin_Pay_ClosedPoints, Fin_Pay_CurrentPoints, SecurityLevel)

Meta-information
<BankingData, U..S, AAO, OAC, Id: VarChar; BankOrdinal: VarChar; BankDescription: VarChar; BankCode : VarChar; BranchOfficeCode:VarChar; CurrentAccount: VarChar; TfinancialYear: VarChar; TThirdPartyCode : VarChar; SecurityLevel : SL>
< LaterFinancialYearsCreditorAndDefaulter, T, O, Annuity: VarChar; Compromises: Real>
< CreditorOfTheExpenseBudget,U..T, O, Id :VarChar; Dispositions: Real; Refunds :Real; Bon_InitialBalance: Real; Bon_InitialBalanceRectifications: Real; Bon_AcceptedInCurrentBudget : Real; Ord_Pay_InitialBalance :Real; Ord_Pay_InitialBalanceRectifications: Real; Ord_Pay_BondsClosedPoints : Real; Ord_Pay_BondsCurrentPoints :Real; Fin_Pay_ClosedPoints : Real; Fin_Pay_CurrentPoints : Real; SecurityLevel : LS>

Security Constraints

Context BankingData **inv:**
    Self.SecurityLevel = (if self.BankDescription = "Non-Spanish bank" then S else U endif)
Context CreditorOfTheExpenseBudget **inv:**
    Self.SecurityLevel = (if Refunds <= 3000 then U else (if refunds <= 10000 then S else T endif) endif)

Fig. 3. Multilevel Relational Model

A fragment of the multilevel relational model of our example can be seen in Figure 3. For space reasons, we have selected only a subset of the classes of the class diagram. We can observe that each class appears in the relational model and in the metainformation section, and the constraint section includes the security constraints related to the considered classes. Obviously, we have done a translation of the data types used in the conceptual model into logical data types.

892   E. Fernández-Medina and M. Piattini

2.4 Specific Logical Design

In this stage we specify the secure database in a particular logical model: Oracle Label Security (OLS). We have chosen this model because it is part of one of the most important database management systems, that allows the implementation of label-based databases; and because the organization wanted to support the new database in this DBMS.

In the context of OLS, a security policy is the most important element, and includes different parameters, such as valid security levels, groups and compartments, and different options that define the way of managing the security. Taking that into account, the activities of this stage are as follows: Defining the database model (all the tables), defining the security policy and their default options, defining the security information in the security policy, creating the authorized users and assigning their authorizations, defining security information for tables through labeling functions, implementing security constraints through labeling functions and access control predicates, and finally, if necessary, implementing operations and controlling their security.

```
CREATE_POLICY('SecurityPolicy','SecurityLabel', 'HIDE, CHECK_CONTROL,
       READ_CONTROL, WRITE_CONTROL')

CREATE_LEVEL('SecurityPolicy', 1000, 'U', 'Unclassify')
CREATE_LEVEL('SecurityPolicy', 2000, 'C', 'Confidential')
CREATE_LEVEL('SecurityPolicy', 3000,'S', 'Secret')
CREATE_LEVEL('SecurityPolicy', 4000, 'T', 'Top Secret')

CREATE_GROUP('SecurityPolicy', 1, 'L', 'LocalGovermmentEmployee')
CREATE_GROUP('SecurityPolicy', 2, 'O', 'Operator', 'L')
CREATE_GROUP('SecurityPolicy', 3, 'SY', 'SystemAdministrator', 'L')
CREATE_GROUP('SecurityPolicy', 4, 'S', 'SuperUser', 'SA')
CREATE_GROUP('SecurityPolicy', 5, 'A', 'NormalAdministrator', 'SA')
CREATE_GROUP('SecurityPolicy', 6, 'SR', 'SecurityResponsible', 'SA')
CREATE_GROUP('SecurityPolicy', 7, 'E', 'Experienced', 'O')
CREATE_GROUP('SecurityPolicy', 8, 'NE', 'Non-Experienced', 'O')
CREATE_GROUP('SecurityPolicy', 9, 'AAO', 'AccountAreaOperator', 'E')
CREATE_GROUP('SecurityPolicy', 10, 'PAO', 'PersonnelAreaOperator', 'E')
CREATE_GROUP('SecurityPolicy', 11, 'OAC', 'AdministrativeAreaOperator', 'E')
```

Fig. 4. Security Policy, Levels and Groups Definition

In Figure 4, we show the way of defining the security policy, the security levels and the user groups in OLS. 'SecurityLabel' is the name of the column that stores the sensitive information in each table, which is associated with the security policy. The option 'HIDE' indicates that the column 'SecurityLabel' will be hidden, so that users will not able to see it in the tables. The Option 'CHECK_CONTROL' forces the system to check that when a subject introduces or modifies a row, the user has reading access. The option 'READ_CONTROL' applies a policy read enforcement for select, update and delete operations. Finally, the option 'WRITE_CONTROL' applies policy write enforcement for insert, delete and update operations.

When a new security level is defined, we have to specify the name of the policy, a number -which indicates the order of the levels-, a short name, and the name of the security level. Also, when a new group is created, we have to specify the name of the policy, the number of the group, a short name, the name of the group, and the short name of its father in the hierarchy.

```
SET_LEVELS('SecurityPolicy', 'User1', 'T', 'S', 'S')
SET_GROUPS('SecurityPolicy', 'User1', 'O', 'O', 'O')
SET_USER_PRIVS('SecurityPolicy', 'User1', 'FULL, WRITEUP, WRITEDOWN, WRITEACROSS')
```

Fig. 5. User definition

Once the security policy, the levels and groups have been defined, we can identify the users in the system, and assign them privileges if necessary. In Figure 5 the user 'User 1' is defined with the following information: Max security level 'T', default security level 'S', minimum security level 'S', read access groups 'Operator', write access groups 'Operator', and default groups 'Operator'. Since it is not usual to assign special privileges to users, we show how this is possible. The description of all the possible options can be seen in [15].

```
CREATE FUNCTION Function1 (BankDescription: VarChar) Return LBACSYS.LBAC_LABEL
As MyLabel varchar2(80);
Begin
   If BankDescription='Non-Spanish bank' then MyLabel := 'S::AAO,OAC'; else MyLabel := 'U::OAA,OAC';
   end if;
   Return TO_LBAC_DATA_LABEL('SecurityPolicy', MyLabel);
End;
CREATE FUNCTION Function2( ) Return LBACSYS.LBAC_LABEL
As   MyLabel varchar2(80);
Begin
   MyLabel := 'T::O' ;
   Return TO_LBAC_DATA_LABEL('SecurePolicy', MyLabel);
End;
CREATE FUNCTION Function3(Refunds: Real) Return LBACSYS.LBAC_LABEL
As MyLabel varchar2(80);
Begin
   If Refunds <=3000 the MyLabel := 'U::O';
     else if Refunds <= 10000 then MyLabel := 'S::O'; else MyLabel := 'T::O';
        end if;
   end if;
   Return TO_LBAC_DATA_LABEL('SecurityPolicy', MyLabel);
End;

APPLY_TABLE_POLICY ('SecurityPolicy', 'BankingData', 'Scheme', , 'Function1')
APPLY_TABLE_POLICY ('SecurityPolicy', 'LaterFinancialYearsCreditorAndDefaulter', 'Scheme', , 'Function2')
APPLY_TABLE_POLICY ('SecurityPolicy', 'CreditorOfTheExpenseBudget', 'Scheme', ,'Function3')
```

Fig. 6. Labeling Functions

The way of assigning security information to the row, once they are inserted, is through labeling functions. When there are no security constraints associated with a table, the labeling function always assigns the same security information to the row. The security constraints are also implemented by the labeling function. Figure 6 shows three labeling functions, and the command by which they are assigned to the tables, which are associated with the relations that have been defined in Figure 3. 'Function1' creates the security information, depending on the value of the column 'BankDescription'. 'Function2' always creates the same security information, and finally, 'Function3' creates the security information depending on the value of the column 'Refunds'. These functions are associated with tables; therefore it is possible to reuse the same labeling function for several tables.

3   Conclusions

The criticality of IS, and specially databases for modern business, together with new requirements of laws and governments, make necessary more sophisticated approaches to ensure database security.

Traditionally, information security deals with different research topics, like access control techniques, cryptographic methods, etc. Although all these topics are very important, we think that it is fundamental to use a methodological approach, where security-at different levels- is taken into consideration at all stages of the database development process. In this paper we have summarized a methodology, which extends the most accepted modeling languages, process models, constraint languages and security models in the industrial and research community. The methodology has been refined and proved in the design of a secure database in a Spanish local government, solving its confidentiality problems. We have also developed a CASE tool to automatically support the management of use case and class diagrams and OSCL security constraints.

There are several interesting directions in which we are extending the proposal presented in this paper: It could be interesting to improve and extend the languages and techniques involved in this methodology, for example, to consider new kinds of security constraints, such as temporal, integrity or availability constraints [20]. We are also improving the gathering requirements stage in order to reuse legal requirements [21].

References

1.   Dhillon, G. & Backhouse, J. (2000). Information system security management in the new millennium. *Communications of the ACM,. 43, 7,* 125–128.
2.   Brinkley, D. & Schell, R. (1995). What is there to worry about? An introduction to the computer security problem. In Abrams, M., Jajodia, S. & Podell (Eds.), *Information security, an integrated collection of essays* (Chapter 1). California, IEEE Computer Society.
3.   Spanish Constitutional Law (15/1999). *December 13th, on personal data protection.* BOE no. 298, 14/12/1999 (in Spanish).
4.   Directive (95/46/CE). Directive 95/46/CE of the European Parliament and Council, dated October 24th, about People protection regarding the personal data management and the free circulation of these data. DOCE no. L281, 23/11/1995, P.0031–0050.
5.   Devanbu, P. & Stubblebine, S. (2000). Software engineering for security: a roadmap. The future of software engineering. In proceedings of the Finkelstein, A. (ed.) 22nd International Conference on Software Engineering (pp. 227–239).
6.   Ferrari, E. & Thuraisingham, B. (2000). Secure Database Systems. Advanced Databases: Technology Design. Eds.: Piattini, M. and Díaz, O. Artech House. London.
7.   Hall, A. & Chapman, R. (2002). Correctness by construction developing a commercial secure system. IEEE Software, 19, 1, 18–25.
8.   Chung, L., Nixon, B., Yu, E. & Mylopoulos, J. (2000). Non-functional requirements in software engineering. Boston/Dordrecht/London, Kluwer Academic Publishers.
9.   Smith, G.W. (1991). Modeling security-relevant data semantics. In proceedings of the IEEE Trans. On Software Engineering, 17, 11, 1195–1203.

10. Marks, D., Sell, P. & Thuraisingham, B. (1996). MOMT: A multilevel object modeling technique for designing secure database applications. Journal of Object-Oriented Programming.9, 4, 22–29.
11. Jürjens, J. (2002). UMLsec: Extending UML for secure systems development. In Jézéquel, J., Hussmann, H. & Cook, S. (Eds.), UML 2002 – The Unified Modeling Language, Model engineering, concepts and tools (pp. 412–425). Germany, Springer.
12. Castano, S., Fugini, M., Martella, G. & Samarati, P. (1994). Database Security. Addison-Wesley
13. Batini, C., Ceri, S. & Navathe, S. (1991). Conceptual database design. An entity-relationship approach. New York, Addison-Wesley.
14. Connolly, T. & Begg, C. (2002). Database systems. A practical approach to design, implementation, and management. Addison Wesley.
15. Levinger, J. (2002). Oracle label security. Administrator's guide. Release 2 (9.2). Retrieved July 1, 2002, from
   http://www.csis.gvsu.edu/GeneralInfo/Oracle/network.920/a96578.pdf.
16. Avison, D., Lau, F., Myers, M. & Nielsen, A. (1999). Action research. Communications of the ACM, 42(1), 94–97.
17. Fernández-Medina, E., Martínez, A., Medina, C. and Piattini, M. (2002). Integrating Multilevel Security in the Database Design Process. In proceedings of the 6th International Conference on Integrated Design and Process Technology (IDPT'2002). June. Pasadena, California.
18. Piattini, M. & Fernández-Medina, E. (2001). Specification of security constraints in UML. In proceedings of the 35th Annual 2001 IEEE International Carnahan Conference on Security Technology (ICCST 2001), pp. 163–171. October, 2001. London (UK).
19. Leavitt, N. (2000). Whatever happened to Object-Oriented Databases?. Industry Trends, IEEE Computer Society, August, 16–19.
20. Conrad, C. & Turowski, K. (2001). Temporal OCL: Meeting specification demands for business components. In Siau, K. & Halpin, T. (Eds.), Unified modeling language: Systems analysis, design and development issues (Chapter 10). Hersey, PA., Idea Group Publishing.
21. Toval, A., Olmos, A & Piattini, M. (2002). Legal Requirements Reuse: A Critical Success Factor for Requirements Quality and Personal Data Protection. IEEE Joint International Requirements Engineering Conference (RE'02). IEEE Computer Society, 95–103.

CAML – A Universal Configuration Language for Dialogue Systems

Gergely Kovásznai[1,2], Constantine Kotropoulos[1], and Ioannis Pitas[1]

[1] Dept. of Informatics,
Aristotle Univ. of Thessaloniki,
Thessaloniki, Greece
{kovasz,costas,pitas}@zeus.csd.auth.gr
[2] On leave from the Institute of Mathematics and Informatics,
Univ. of Debrecen,
Debrecen, Hungary
kovasz@math.klte.hu

Abstract. In this paper, a novel architecture of a universal dialogue system and its configuration language, so-called Conversational Agent Markup Language (CAML), is proposed. The dialogue system embodies a CLIPS engine in order to enable CAML to formulate procedural and heuristic knowledge. CAML supports frames, functions, and categories that enable it: (a) to process wildcards, to control the inner state through variables, and to formulate procedural knowledge in contrast to Phoenix/CAT Dialog Manager; (b) to support nested macros, to control the inner state through variables, to assign priorities and weights to states, and to interface with external databases in contrast to Dialog Management Tool Language (DMTL); (c) to implement context-free grammars, to extract semantic content from user input through frames, to allow numeric variables, and to interface with external databases as opposed to Artificial Intelligence Markup Language (AIML). The proposed system is extensible in the sense that it can be embedded in any conversational system that receives and emits XML content. Such a dialogue system can be incorporated in multimodal interfaces, such as talking head applications, conversational web interfaces, conversational database interfaces, and conversational programming interfaces.

1 Introduction

Nowadays, human-machine interaction is changing dramatically toward spoken dialogue. Many dialogue systems (DSs) or conversational agents have been developed for web applications, database interfaces or even chat bots [2]. State-of-the-art DSs vary in their architecture, aims, and configuration. All of them include three basic modules, namely a dialogue manager, a language parser, and a language generator. Henceforth, the aforementioned modules will be referred to as the DS core.

The features of any state-of-the-art DS core depend highly on the application they have been designed for. Usually, the application is well-defined, but limited

V. Mařík et al. (Eds.): DEXA 2003, LNCS 2736, pp. 896–906, 2003.

to a restricted domain, e.g. train/airplane reservation systems. Furthermore, the core is highly influenced by the additional modules embedded in the same DS (e.g., speech recognizer, speech synthesizer) in terms of the structure of input (output) data received (emitted). Accordingly, any state-of-the-art DS core cannot be used as a universal one, that can be embedded in any DS. For example, the core of a chat bot cannot be transformed to the core for a conversational database interface. The aim of this paper is to propose an architecture for a DS core which is arbitrarily *extensible*, i.e., it can be extended with any external resource and external module in order to be embedded in any DS. Another aim of the paper is to design a novel configuration language for the core, which is *universal* in the sense that it can be attached to any spoken language or any possible topic offering syntactic and semantical independence. Other strong points of the configuration language are the low-level procedural knowledge formulation (for experienced users) and its facilities to perform tasks closely related to dialogue management (for naive users) that make it easily used. We call the proposed configuration language Conversational Agent Markup Language (CAML). It is an XML-compliant language. A DS core configured by CAML is called a CAML core.

2   Overview of a Dialogue System Core

A general architecture of a DS core is shown in Figure 1. Its three modules perform language parsing, dialogue management, and language generation. The configuration language of the core must manage all the aforementioned tasks and interrelate them.

Several techniques have been applied to these tasks. Since CAML is designed to be a universal language, it supports the most flexible, commonly used techniques. Although the use of fixed techniques may limit the utility of CAML, its

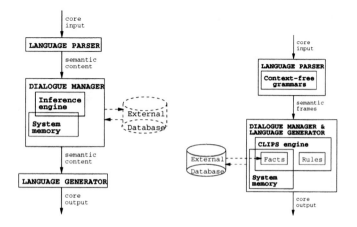

Fig. 1. Architecture of a dialogue system core and the CAML core (on the right).

extensibility makes it possible to replace these techniques with external ones, as explained in Section 4.

2.1   Language Parsing

Language parsing extracts semantic information from the core input. Language parsers employ several techniques. CAML supports *robust parsing* [1]. To configure a robust language parser, a grammar must be specified in order to analyze the core input. In terms of the grammar used, several types of language parsers exist. CAML uses context-free (CF) grammars [3]. Since CF grammars are not able to formulate complex data and relations that are common in real life, CAML provides also facilities to combine CF grammars with procedural data in order to alleviate the just described deficiency of CF grammars. In a CF grammar, a set of non-terminal symbols and a set of CF rewriting rules are specified. If the user input can be derived by a CF grammar, one or more parse-trees can be constructed for it. Language parsers vary even in the representation of semantic information extracted from a parse-tree. CAML uses the *semantic frames* [1]. CAML provides a facility for users to define the frames used in the extraction of semantic information.

A CAML core analyzes the input in the following way: (1) it checks whether the input can be derived from a non-terminal symbol in the grammar; (2) if it can be derived, it constructs one of the possible parse-trees based on the priorities of non-terminal symbols that are employed to define the tree having the highest priority; (3) it extracts the semantic information from the parse-tree into frames.

2.2   Dialogue Management and Language Generation

Dialogue management determines the next state of the DS core according to its current state and the currently extracted semantic information. It is also responsible for generating the semantic content used during language generation in order to provide a spoken output. The CAML core contains only one module to perform the tasks related to these two phases, i.e., (1) to load the frames extracted during language parsing; (2) to trace the inner state of the core (to place the data into the system memory and to retrieve them if needed); (3) to infer the next state of the core (i.e., the content of the system memory) from its current state and the frames loaded; and (4) to generate output. Some dialogue managers provide an interface for external databases, i.e., to perform queries in the databases and to load the results into the system memory.

The CAML core contains a *CLIPS engine*. CLIPS is a tool for building expert systems [9]. As a part of the CAML core system memory, CLIPS facts are specified during the dialogue management and they are modified by CLIPS rules defined by the user.

The system memory is a set of variables. A variable can get either a literal or a frame value. A frame value is implemented as a CLIPS fact. CAML provides the users facilities to formulate the procedural knowledge inherent in CLIPS language and heuristic knowledge by defining CLIPS rules. CAML provides the

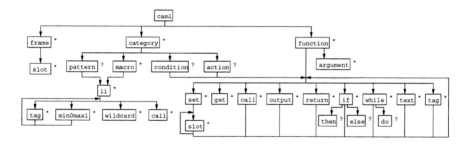

Fig. 2. CAML DTD

following facilities in order to perform the aforementioned tasks: (1) it loads the extracted frames into variables; (2) it declares variables, it sets and gets their values; (3) it formulates the procedural and heuristic data in order to specify CLIPS rules and to execute them; (4) it formulates the procedural data in order to specify core output. CAML provides facilities to query in external databases and to load the results into variables.

3   Specification of CAML

In this section, the syntactic elements of CAML are introduced. Since CAML is an XML-compliant language, its structure can be specified by a Document Type Definition (DTD) as can be seen in Figure 2. The use of syntactic elements is demonstrated by examples which belong to a simple DS providing information about museums.

3.1   Top Level Syntactic Elements

Three syntactic elements of CAML are accentuated, namely the frames, the functions, and the categories. They are located on the highest syntactic level, while the rest can be located only within another syntactic element. A frame used during language parsing can be defined by the use of a `<frame>` tag containing zero or more `<slot>` tags. As part of procedural knowledge, functions are defined as parameterizable units of procedural data. They are implemented by `<function>` tags.

```
<frame name="query">
  <slot name="museum"/>
  <slot name="monument"/>
</frame>
```

```
<function name="display-museum">
  <output>
    The following information was found about the museum
    <argument number="1"/> located in <argument number="2"/>.
    <argument number="3"/>
  </output>
</function>
```

Fig. 3. Frames and functions.

The most important syntactic element of CAML is the category. A category can be defined by a `<category>` tag. Categories contain all parse-specific and heuristic data on the points where the execution of procedural data starts. Each category contains some rewriting rules, a condition on its validity, and an action (i.e., procedural data) to be executed if the category is valid. Actually, two types of categories can be defined by using the same syntax. If the given category specifies at least one rewriting rule, it formulates parse-specific and strictly procedural data. Otherwise, it formulates heuristic data, a CLIPS rule. The execution of a CAML content attaches to the categories inside, and comprises the following tasks: (1) to read core input; (2) to find the category having the highest priority to which the input fits; (3) to construct the parse-tree having the highest priority for the input and the category; (4) to extract the frames from the parse-tree; (5) to execute the actions of the categories within the parse-tree; (6) to instruct the CLIPS engine to start the rule execution.

The tags `<pattern>` and `<macro>` contain so-called patterns, i.e., the right-hand-side of rewriting rules. Within a pattern a non-terminal symbol can be specified by the use of a: (1) `<call>` referring to a `<category>` or a `<macro>`; (2) `<opt>` specifying an optional pattern; (3) `<wildcard>` which can be matched with any text. The use of `<wildcard>` tags is a very important facility to define partially specified patterns. The text matched with a wildcard can be stored in a variable. Accordingly, we may check in a `<condition>` tag, whether its value is equal to the value of another variable or can be found in an external database. The tags `<condition>` and `<action>` contain procedural data. Each `<condition>` tag must return a boolean value TRUE or FALSE.

By the use of the parameter `priority`, a priority number can be assigned to a category, which is used to define the parse-tree having the highest priority or to schedule the execution of CLIPS rules. The parameter `extracted` determines whether the category takes part in the extraction of frames [6]. A set of categories, a constructed parse-tree, and an extracted frame are shown as examples in Figure 4.

3.2 Procedural Knowledge

Procedural data can be specified within either a `<function>`, or a `<condition>`, or an `<action>` tag. Procedural data is a set of CLIPS function calls, e.g., `(str-cat "Hi" " Joe")` or `(= (+ 2 2) (- 7 3))`. CAML provides some tags to ease the situation of naive users, that is, to exempt them from using CLIPS language, e.g., `<output>` for sending data to core output, `<if>` for checking a conditional statement, `<while>` for making a loop in the execution, `<call>` for calling an arbitrary CLIPS function or command, `<return>` for returning a value from a CLIPS function, `<text>` for specifying a CLIPS string literal.

Special tags are needed to control variables. The tags `<set>` and `<get>` are used to read and write a value in an object referred by a qualified name, i.e., a name consisting of segments separated by dots. The first segment is the name of a variable, the rest is a sequence of names of slots. E.g., `person.name.surname` refers to the slot "surname" of the slot "name" of the variable "person". The

```
<category name="tell museum" priority="10">      <category name="museum" extracted="museum">
  <pattern>                                        <pattern>
    <li><call>speak</call>                           <li>
      about <call>museum</call></li>                   <opt>museum called</opt>
  </pattern>                                           <call>museum name</call>
  <macro name="speak">                                 <opt>located</opt> in
    <li>speak</li>                                     <call>museum location</call>
    <li>tell me</li>                                 </li>
  </macro>                                         </pattern>
</category>                                       </category>

<category name="museum name"                     <category name="museum location"
      extracted="name" priority="9">                   extracted="city" priority="9">
  <pattern>                                        <pattern>
    <li><wildcard name="museum_name"/></li>          <li><wildcard name="museum_city"/></li>
  </pattern>                                       </pattern>
  <condition>...</condition>                       <condition>...</condition>
</category>                                       </category>
```

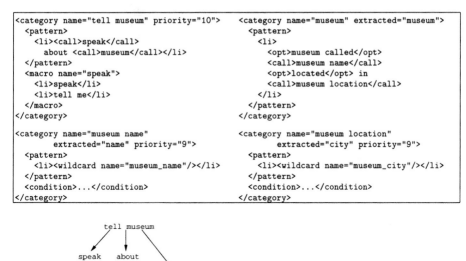

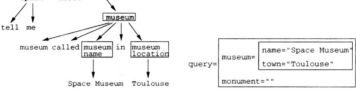

Fig. 4. A parse-tree and an extracted frame for a set of categories related to the input "tell me about museum called Space Museum in Toulouse".

referred object can get either a literal or a frame value. A frame value can be formulated by the use of `<slot>` tags. In Figure 5, the use of `<set>` and `<get>` is shown. Below each `<get>`, the value returned by the tag is written.

In order to read the content of a frame extracted during language parsing, a `<get>` with the parameter `type="frame"` can be used. In this case, the first segment of the qualified name is interpreted as the name of the given frame. An example is shown in Figure 5.

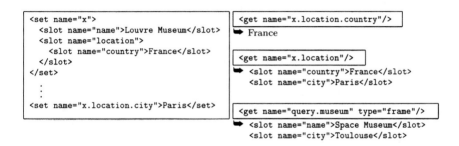

Fig. 5. Controlling variables.

```
<category name="museum_rule">
  <condition>
    <return>
      <call name="neq">
        <get name="query.museum" type="frame"/>
        <text></text>
      </call>
    </return>
  </condition>
  <action>
    <set name="museum_query" type="sql"
      database="jdbc:mysql://zeus.csd.auth.gr/museumdb?user=visitor&password=04eg35">
        select name,city,text from museums where
          name='<get name="query.museum.name" type="frame"/>' and
          city='<get name="query.museum.city" type="frame"/>'
    </set>
    <while>
        <call name="neq">
          <get name="museum_query"/>
          <text></text>
        </call>
      <do/>
        <call name="display-museum">
          <get name="museum_query.name"/>
          <get name="museum_query.city"/>
          <get name="museum_query.text"/>
        </call>
        <get name="museum_query" type="sql"/>
    </while>
  </action>
</category>
```

Fig. 6. Interfacing an external database and formulating complex procedural data in a category specifying a CLIPS rule.

In order to interface an external database, the parameter `type="sql"` can be used in a `<set>` or a `<get>`. In this case, the content of a `<set>` is interpreted as an SQL command. The database is accessed through JDBC interface, so it is addressed by a JDBC URL. The first result of the SQL query is loaded into the object referred by the qualified name. The next result can be loaded by the use of a `<get>` with `type="sql"`. An example can be found in Figure 6.

4   Extensibility of the CAML Core

One of the aims of the CAML core is its extension by external resources if needed. The DS core reads a text input and emits a text output, traditionally in a spoken language. The CAML core uses the same input channel and the same output channel in order to be extensible. In order to communicate with external resources through these channels, the CAML core reads *structured text-typed input* and emits *structured text-typed output*. A quite easy way to structure text data is the use of an *XML*-compliant language, e.g., if an external language parser is used to extract semantic information from a user input, this information can be easily incorporated in the input of the CAML core by the use of XML tags. Similarly, semantic content can be embedded in the output of the CAML core in order to make it accessible for an external language generator. The most important reason of making a DS core able to read structured input and to emit

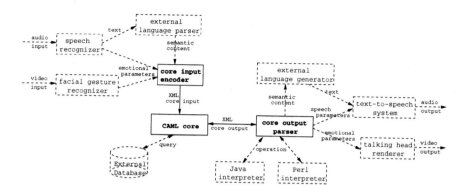

Fig. 7. Architecture of a possible dialogue system including the CAML core.

structured output is the *multi-modal nature of human communication*. Humans communicate by expressing their thoughts in several ways simultaneously, i.e., not only by the words uttered, but also by prosody of speech, facial gestures, hand movements, etc. Three possible applications are:

1. *Talking head applications*: an animated human head which the user can conduct a dialogue with. The core output could be in Virtual Human Markup Language (VHML) [5] in order to incorporate information about emotions, gestures, movements, etc.
2. *Web pages with conversational interfaces*: a web page which provides a natural language interface to help web navigation. Core output could be in Hypertext Markup Language (HTML) in order to generate whole web pages or web page segments, and to execute scripts.
3. *Conversational programming interfaces*: a DS which can "translate" user requests into procedural data in a programming language and execute them. The source code in a given programming language could be encapsulated by an XML tag in core output, e.g., `<cplusplus>...</cplusplus>` for C++, `<java>...</java>` for Java, etc.

In order to embed the CAML core in a DS, two modules are necessary. The first module encodes the core input in XML (core input encoder) and the second module parses the core output (core output parser). In Figure 7, a possible architecture of such a DS is shown.

In order to support XML core input and core output, CAML allows embedding XML tags in patterns of categories and within `<output>` tags. Since not every XML tag is included in the CAML DTD, its reserved characters must be encoded into XML standard entities (e.g., "<" into "<", """ into "&quote;"). CAML provides a tag called `<tag>` to exempt naive users from encoding them manually. In Figure 8, the use of `<tag>` is demonstrated by two examples with inputs that should be matched and the output that is generated.

Bi-directional communication is needed through the output channel of a CAML core in some cases. A typical example is the case of conversational programming interfaces, because there we need to load the results of operations

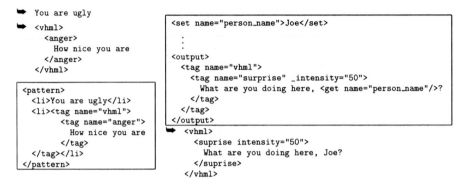

Fig. 8. Structured core input and core output.

implemented in any programming language back into the core. To implement this, the core output parser must be able to specify return values for all XML tags embedded in core output and then to load them back through the output channel of the CAML core, as return values of the given `<output>` tags. The specification of these return values is a technical problem which has to be solved by the core output parser, hence it does not belong to the CAML and the CAML cores.

5   Comparison with Other Configuration Languages

In this section, the abilities of CAML are compared to the abilities of three state-of-the-art configuration languages for a DS core according to six aspects, presented in Table 1. CAML has been inspired by these languages. Any of them is used in a specific area. CAML can be conceived as a superset of these languages, with respect to universality and abilities.

Table 1. Abilities of other configuration languages.

	Language parsing	Controlling inner state	Procedural knowledge	Heuristic knowledge	Language generation	Interfacing databases
Phoenix/CAT	good	good	no	poor	poor	yes
DMTL	poor	poor	no	medium	poor	no
AIML	poor	medium	medium	no	medium	no

The *Phoenix Semantic Parser* [6] was developed by the Center of Spoken Language Research and used in *CAT Dialog Manager*, which was incorporated in CU Communicator [7] for flight, car, and hotel rental agents. The configuration language of the Phoenix Semantic Parser provides facilities to specify a set of context-free grammars and to extract the semantic information from the core input into frames. Only fully-specified core inputs can be formulated. The CAT Dialog Manager provides facilities to load the frames extracted by the Phoenix

Semantic Parser and to perform dialogue management tasks on them. These tasks can be specified in CAT's proprietary configuration language, which assigns so-called text templates to the slots of the frames. The inner state of the system is controlled through frames and global variables. The level of determination to display text templates is not specified by the CAT documentation, but it could be non-deterministic. System-defined weights are assigned to parse-trees, but user is not able to specify weights. Only three types of text templates (core outputs) can be assigned to the slots: prompts, confirmations, and sql queries.

The *Dialogue Management Tool Language (DMTL)* is the configuration language for the *Dialog Management Tool (DMT)* [8]. This language was tested embedding VHML content in talking head applications. Context-free grammars can be specified, but there is no facility to generate parse-trees higher than three levels. Only fully-specified core inputs can be formulated. There is no facility to extract semantic information from inputs. The states of the system can be defined and linked to each other, but no data can be placed into the system memory by the user. Validity conditions can be attached to the states, however it is not real procedural knowledge. Weights can be assigned to core outputs, but not to states or core inputs. Two types of core outputs can be specified, namely responses and signals.

The *Artificial Intelligence Markup Language (AIML)* was developed by A. L. I. C. E. AI Foundation as the configuration language of *Alicebot systems*, which are used in chat bots. AIML parsing is not based on context-free grammars, but rather on simple, linear pattern matching. Partially specified core inputs can be formulated. There is no facility to extract semantic content from the core input. Variables can be used, but only text values can be assigned to them. Procedural data can be formulated mostly to read, write or check the value of a variable. There are only a few facilities to operate with such a value. These is no possibility to operate with numeric values. Patterns are matched with the core input in alphabetic order, there are no facilities to set their priority. The core output is generated by the execution of procedural data. Only text output can be emitted.

Conclusions

We have designed a novel universal configuration language and an extensible architecture for a dialogue system core. We have outlined several state-of-the-art areas, where such a core can be used. The proposed language has been compared to other state-of-the-art configuration languages and its features are found to comprise a superset of those offered by the other configuration languages. After the design phase, we have developed the first version of the proposed CAML core.

Acknowledgement. This work has been supported by the European Union funded Research Training Network "Multi-modal Human-Computer Interaction" (MUHCI).

References

1. R. Suereth, *Developing Natural Language Interfaces.* N.Y., McGraw-Hill, 1997.
2. N. Ole Bernsen, H. Dybkjær, and L. Dybkjær, *Designing Interactive Speech Systems.* London, Springer-Verlag, 1998.
3. X. Huang, A. Acero, and H.-W. Hon, *Spoken Language Processing.* Upper Saddle River, N.J., Prentice Hall PTR, 2001.
4. A. L. Gorin, A. Abella, T. Alonso, G. Riccardi, and J. H. Wright, "Automated Natural Spoken Dialog", *IEEE Computer*, vol. 35, no. 4, pp. 51–56, April 2002.
5. A. Marriott, "VHML – Virtual Human Markup Language", in *Proc. OzCHI 2001 Workshop*, 2001.
6. W. Ward, "Understanding Spontaneous Speech: the Phoenix System", in *Proc. ICASSP 91*, 1991, pp. 365–367.
7. B. Pellom, and W. Ward, S. Pradhan, "The CU Communicator: An Architecture for Dialogue Systems", in *Proc. ICSLP*, Beijing China, November 2000.
8. C. Gustavsson, L. Strindlund, and E. Wiknertz, "Dialogue Management Tool", in *Proc. OzCHI 2001 Workshop*, 2001.
9. CLIPS, *http://www.ghg.net/clips/CLIPS.html.*

NLC: A Measure Based on Projections*

Roberto Ruiz, José C. Riquelme, and Jesús S. Aguilar-Ruiz

Departamento de Lenguajes y Sistemas,
Universidad de Sevilla
Avda. Reina Mercedes S/N.
41012 Sevilla, España
{rruiz,riquelme,aguilar}@lsi.us.es

Abstract. In this paper, we propose a new feature selection criterion. It is based on the projections of data set elements onto each attribute. The main advantages are its speed and simplicity in the evaluation of the attributes. The measure allows features to be sorted in ascending order of importance in the definition of the class. In order to test the relevance of the new feature selection measure, we compare the results induced by several classifiers before and after applying the feature selection algorithms.

1 Introduction

The selection of relevant features is a central problem in machine learning. If a relevant feature is removed, the measure of the remaining features will deteriorate. In order to identify relevant attributes, we need to address what a good feature is for classification. Without defining the *goodness* of a feature or features, it does not make sense to talk about best or optimal features. The algorithms evaluate the attributes based on general characteristics of the data.

Feature Selection can be viewed as a search problem, where each state in the search space specifies a subset of the possible features. The need for evaluation is common to all search strategies.

In this paper, we propose a new feature selection criterion not based on calculated measures between attributes, or complex and costly distance calculations. This criterion is based on a unique value called NLC. It relates each attribute with the label used for classification. This value is calculated by projecting data set elements onto the respective axis of the attribute (ordering the examples by this attribute), then crossing the axis from the beginning to the greatest attribute value, and counting the Number of Label Changes (NLC) produced.

---

* This work has been supported by the Spanish Research Agency CICYT under grant TIC2001-1143-C03-02, and Junta Andalucia under coordinated action ACC-1021-TIC-2002.

V. Mařík et al. (Eds.): DEXA 2003, LNCS 2736, pp. 907–916, 2003.
© Springer-Verlag Berlin Heidelberg 2003

2   Related Work

Feature selection algorithms use different evaluation functions. Functions are based in criterions to measure the relevance of the attributes. There are several taxonomies of these evaluation measures in previous work, depending on different criterions: Langley [9] group evaluation functions into two categories: filter and wrapper. Blum y Langley [3] provide a classification of evaluation functions into four groups, depending on the relation between the selection and the induction process: embedded, filter, wrapper, weight. Another different classification, Doak [5] and Dash [4] provide a classification of evaluation measure based on their general characteristics more then in the relation with the induction process. The classification realized by Dash, separate five different types of measures: distance, information, dependence, consistency y accuracy. Feature Selection can be viewed as a search problem, where each state in the search space specifies a subset of the possible features. The need for evaluation is common to all search strategies. In general, attribute selection algorithms perform a search through the space of feature subsets, and must address four basic issues affecting the nature of the search: 1) Starting point: forward and backward, according to whether it began with no features or with all features. 2) Search organization: exhaustive or heuristic search. 3) Evaluation strategy: wrapper or filter. 4) Stopping criterion: a feature selector must decide when to stop searching through the space of feature subsets. A predefined number of features are selected, a predefined number of iterations reached. Whether or not the addition or deletion of any feature produces a better subset, we also stop the search, if an optimal subset according to some evaluation function is obtained.

3   Feature Evaluation

3.1   Observations

To discover main idea of the algorithm we base on the data sets IRIS and WINE, because of the easy interpretation of their two-dimensional projections.

In Figure 1(a) it is possible to observe that if the projection of the examples is made on the ordinate axis we can not obtain intervals where any class is a majority. Nevertheless, for the Petalwidth attribute it is possible to appreciate some intervals where the class is unique: [0,0.6] for Setosa, [1.0,1.3] for Versicolor and [1.8,2.5] for Virginica. This is because when projecting the examples on this attribute the number of label changes is minimum. For example, it is possible to verify that for Petalwidth the first label change takes place for value 1 (setosa to Versicolor), the second in 1.3 (Versicolor to Virginica). There are other changes later and the last one is in 1.8.

In Figure 1(b) the same conclusion is reached with data set WINE. We analyze the projection of data set elements onto C8 and C7 attributes. We identify intervals where one class is a majority when crossing the abscissas axis from the beginning to the greatest attribute value: [0,1] for class 3, [1.5,2.3] for

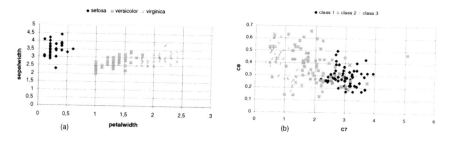

Fig. 1. (a) IRIS. Representation of Attributes *Sepalwidth-Petalwidth* (b) WINE. Representation of Attributes *C8-C7*

class 2 and [3,4] for class 1. Nevertheless, for C8 attribute on the ordinate axis it is not possible to observe any intervals where the class is unique.

We conclude that it will be easier classify by attributes with the smallest number of label changes. If the attributes are in ascending order according to the NLC, we obtain a ranking list with the better attributes from the point of view of the classification, in Iris this would be: Petalwidth 16, Petallength 19, Sepallenth 87 and Sepalwidth 120. This result agrees with what is common knowledge in data mining, which states that the width and length of petals are more important than those related to sepals.

Classifying IRIS with C4.5 by Sepalwidth only, we obtain 59% accuracy and by Petalwitdth 95%. The attributes used in Figure 1(b) are the first and the last on the ranked list, with a NLC value of 43 and 139 respectively. Applying the classifier C4.5, we obtain 80.34% accuracy by C7 and 47.75% by C8.

3.2 Definitions

Definition 1: An *example* e ∈ E is a tuple formed by the Cartesian product of the value sets of each attribute and the set C of labels. We define the operations *att* and *lab* to access the attribute and its label (or class): att: E x N → A and lab: E → C, where N is the set of natural numbers.

Definition 2: Let the *universe* U be a sequence of example from E. We will say that a database with n examples, each of them with m attributes and one class, forms a particular universe. Then U=<u[1],...,u[n]> and as the database is a sequence, the access to an example is achieved by means of its position. Likewise, the access to j-th attribute of the i-th example is made by att(u[i],j), and for identifying its label lab(u[i]).

Definition 3: An *ordered projected sequence* is a sequence formed by the projection of the universe onto the i-th attribute. This sequence is sorted out in ascending order.

Definition 4: A partition in *constant subsequences* is the set of subsequences formed from the ordered projected sequence of an attribute in such a way as to maintain the projection order. All the examples belonging to a subsequence have the same class and every two consecutive subsequences are disjoint with respect to the class.

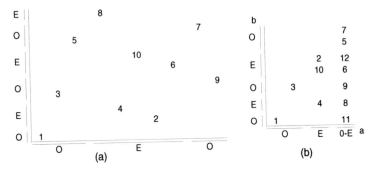

Fig. 2. Data set with (a) ten and (b) twelve elements and two classes

Definition 5: A *subsequence of the same value* is the sequence composed of the examples with identical value from the i-th attribute within the ordered projected sequence. This situation can be originated in continuous variables, and it will be the way to deal with the discrete variables.

Definition 6: two examples are *inconsistent* if they match except for the class label.

3.3 Description

The algorithm is based on this basic principle: to count the label changes of examples projected onto each feature. If the attributes are in ascending order according to the NLC we will have a list that defines the priority of selection, from greater to smaller importance.

Before formally exposing the algorithm, we will explain in more detail the main idea. Let us consider the situation depicted in Figure 2(a), with ten elements numbered and two labels (O-odd numbers and E-even numbers): the projection of the examples on the abscissas axis produces three constant subsequences {O,E,O} corresponding to the examples {[1,3,5][8,4,10,2,6][7,9]}. Identically, with the projection on the ordinates axis we can obtain six constant subsequences {O,E,O,E,O,E} formed by the examples {[1][2,4][3,9][6,10][5,7][8]}. We check that the first attribute has two label changes and the second one has five. Applying our hypothesis, the first attribute is more relevant than the second one, because it has a smaller NLC.

4 Algorithm

The algorithm is very simple and fast (Table 1). It has the capacity to operate with continuous and discrete variables as well as with databases which have two classes or multiple classes. For each attribute, the training-set is ordered (QuickSort [7], this algorithm is O(n log n), on average and we count the NLC throughout the ordered projected sequence.

Table 1. Main Algorithm

```
Input: E training (N examples, M attributes)
Output: E reduced (N examples, K attributes)
    for each attribute Aᵢ ∈ 1..M
      QuickSort(E,i)
      NLCᵢ ← NumberChanges(E,i)
    NLC Attribute Ranking
    Select the k first
```

Table 2. NumberChanges function

```
Input: E training (N examples, M attributes), i
Output: number of label changes
    for each example eⱼ ∈ E with j in 1..N
      if att(u[j],i) ∈ subsequence of the same value
        changes = changes + ChangesSameValue()
      else
        if lab(u[j]) <> lastLabel)
          changes = changes + 1
    return(changes)
```

Applying the algorithm to the example of the Figure 2(b) we obtain the ordered projected sequences:

$$\{1,3,4,10,2,11,8,9,6,12,5,7\}$$

$$\{1,11,4,8,3,9,10,6,2,12,5,7\}$$

and the partitions:

$$\{[1,3][4,10,2][11,8,9,6,12,5,7]\}$$

$$\{[1,11][4,8][3,9][10,6,2,12][5,7]\}$$

The elements' projections onto the first attribute produce two constant subsequences and one subsequence of the same value with different labels. The elements' projections onto the second attribute produces five constant subsequences.

NumberChanges considers whether we deal with different values from an attribute, or with a subsequence of the same value (this situation can be originated in continuous and discrete variables). In the first case, it compares the present label with the last one. Whereas in the second case, where the subsequence is of the same value, it counts the maximum possible changes by means of the function *ChangesSameValue*.

In the attribute represented on the ordinates axis (*b*) in Figure 2(b), we see several subsequences of the same value with the same label, then, we deal with constant subsequence, and the result is four label changes (NLC=4). In the attribute on the abscissas axis (*a*), the first two partitions are constant subsequences, and the third is a subsequence of the same value with two labels. Therefore, we consider the maximum possible NLC.

In the previous case, we have the subsequence [11,8,9,6,12,5,7] where four elements are class O (odd) y three class E (even). There are two reasons for counting the maximum NLC: first, we want to penalize the attribute in these inconsistency situations; and second, we want to avoid ambiguities that could be produced depending on the elements order after algorithm QuicSort is applied. For example, in different independent executions, we could obtain these situations: [E,E,E,O,O,O,O], [E,E,O,O,O,O,E], [O,O,E,E,O,O,E],... with NLC equal to 1, 2 and 3 respectively. *ChangesSameValue* returns 5, the maximum. The situation is: [O,E,O,E,O,E,O]. This can be obtained with low cost. It can be deduced counting the class' elements in the subsequence without resorting the elements.

We conclude that the attribute *b* with four NLC is more relevant that the attribute *a* with seven NLC.

5   Experiments

In this section we compare the quality of selected attributes by the NCL measure with the selected attributes by the other two methods: Information Gain (IG) [10] and the ReliefF method [8]. IG has been chosen because it is the more popular concept and it is used more when you want to evaluate the relevance of an attribute. And the ReliefF method has been chosen because it is widely referenced in other papers. The ReliefF method is a version of the Relief method by Kononenko, wich permits attributes with missing values and multiclass problems. The quality of each selected attribute was tested by means of three classifiers: the Naive Bayes [6], C4.5 [10] and 1-NN [1]. The implementation of the induction algorithms and the others selectors was done using the Weka library[1] and the comparison was performed with eighteen databases of the University from California Irvine [2]. The data sets were chosen with few missing values.

The process followed to test the quality of the attributes selected with the NCL measure was the following. For all original data sets, we obtained the accuracy using the three classifiers and the size of the decision trees induced by C4.5. We obtained the same measures after applying each selector algorithm, recording the number of attributes selected.

To asses the obtained results, two paired t statistical tests with a confidence level of 95% were realized

In order to establish the number of attributes in each case, we obtain a ranked list of features with the three method and we use the learning curve to observe the effect of added features. Starting with one feature (the most relevant one first) and gradually adding next most relevant feature one by one, we calculate its accuracy rate. We select the set of attributes with the best accuracy. Applying a different classifier, we obtain a different set.

---

[1] http://www.cs.waikato.ac.nz/ ml

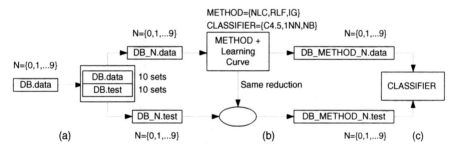

Fig. 3. Cross-validation process

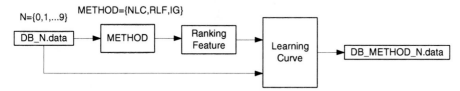

Fig. 4. Reduction method: feature ranking and learning curve

For each database (DB), the measures were estimated taking the mean of a ten fold cross validation. A ten-fold cross-validation is performed by dividing the data into ten blocks of cases that have an approximately similar size, and for each block in turn, testing the model constructed from the remaining nine blocks on the unseen cases in the hold-out block (Figure 3(a)). The same folds were used for each algorithm training-sets.

Each reducing method was given a training set (DB_N.data) consisting of 90% of the available data, from which it returned a subset DB_METHOD_N (Figure 3(b)), where METHOD is one of NLC, RLF, IG, N is a value in 0,1,...,9 and includes a classifier to obtain the learning curve (Figure 4). We use the same classifier that we are going to classify the test set. For example, from DB_1.data we would obtain DB_IG_1.data by applying the IG method. The remaining 10% of the unseen data (DB_N.test) was also reduced (DB_METHOD_N.test) (Figure 3(b)) and tested on the instances of DB_METHOD_N.data using a classifier (Figure 3(c)). For example, we obtain iris_ig_1.data by applying the IG method to the iris_1.data file generated by the cross validation. Afterwards, we use iris_ig_1.data to classify iris_ig_1.test by means of the nearest neighbor technique. When we deal with the learning curve, we also apply 1NN (Figure 4).

As a further comparison, another widely-used learner, C4.5 and NB, was run on these data sets (Figure 3(c)). For example, after reducing iris_3.data with NLC, iris_nlc_3.data was generated, it was given as input to C4.5 and the decision tree generated was used to classify the iris_nlc_3.test file (test files are reduced too).

If we consider all the possible results that we get using the original data, the three selection methods (NLC, RLF and IG) and the three classifiers (C4.5, 1NN and NB) with eighteen data sets taking the mean of a 10-fold cross validation,

Table 3. Accuracy obtained with *C4.5*, *1NN* and *naive Bayes*, selecting the subset with the best accuracy

Data	C4.5	NLC	1 2 3	RLF	IG	1NN	NLC	1 2 3	RLF	IG	NB	NLC	1 2 3	RLF	IG
anne	98.6	98.4		98.4	98.0	99.3	99.0		98.9	98.9	86.3	89.2	∘ •	90.0	92.4
bala	78.4	78.4		78.4	78.4	86.9	86.9		86.9	86.9	88.8	88.8		88.8	88.8
germ	71.1	73.8	∘ ∘	70.5	74.5	72.4	69.7		70.8	71.0	74.8	75.5		73.4	74.7
diab	76.7	75.1		75.9	75.5	70.9	68.2		66.7	68.5	76.2	75.6		75.8	76.5
glas	69.2	70.1		71.0	67.3	70.5	71.9	•	75.1	74.2	45.8	56.6	∘ ∘	47.7	51.0
gla2	77.8	79.6		79.2	79.0	79.2	78.3	• •	89.0	89.0	61.9	69.9	∘ ∘	64.4	69.9
h-st	78.5	83.7	∘	80.4	85.2	74.4	79.3	∘ •	79.6	83.3	84.1	81.9	•	85.2	84.4
iono	88.6	89.7	•	92.6	91.2	86.6	87.2	•	91.4	89.2	83.2	84.6		89.7	87.2
iris	94.0	92.7		94.0	92.7	95.3	93.3		93.3	93.3	95.3	92.7	•	94.0	92.7
kr-v	99.5	99.3		99.5	99.5	96.5	97.4	∘ ∘	98.3	96.9	88.0	90.4	∘ •	94.0	90.4
lymp	78.3	74.9		77.7	76.3	79.7	77.0		83.0	77.8	83.8	83.8		81.8	83.8
segm	97.0	96.9		96.8	96.9	97.0	97.1		97.1	97.1	80.0	87.2	∘	87.2	87.2
sona	72.6	73.5		75.0	72.2	85.5	84.6		81.3	87.5	67.8	73.5		74.9	73.5
spli-2	94.4	94.0		94.0	94.2	73.9	90.0	∘	90.0	90.0	95.3	96.1		96.3	95.8
vehi	73.5	72.6		72.7	73.7	70.1	70.7		71.2	69.3	44.3	44.3	•	48.5	44.3
vowe	82.9	81.7		82.7	81.0	99.4	99.2		99.0	99.2	66.1	68.7	∘	69.2	69.1
wave	76.6	77.6		78.1	77.4	73.8	79.1	∘	78.2	79.1	80.0	80.7	•	81.4	80.7
zoo	93.1	94.1		93.1	92.1	96.0	97.0		95.0	95.0	95.0	95.0		91.0	92.1

we get two hundred and eighteen results $((1+3) \times 3 \times 18 = 216)$. Now we are going to analyze these results to obtain some conclusions about the performance of the different methods.

Table 3 shows a summary of the results of the classification using C4.5, 1NN and NB. Table shows how often each method performs significantly better (denoted by ∘) or worse (denoted by •) than data without reduction (column named 1), and better or worse than ReliefF (RLF) and Information Gain (IG) (column 2 and 3 respectively). Then, we obtain fifty four results comparing NLC with data without reduction (18 data sets × 3 classifiers = 54) and one hundred and eight comparing NLC with RLF and IG (18 data sets × 3 classifiers × 2 = 108). NLC measure is better than data without reduction in twelve of the fifty four cases, and in forty one are equal and only in one is worse than data without reduction. Furthermore, in four of the one hundred and eight cases, the set of attributes selected by the NLC measure yields better accuracy than the two other methods. In ninety three they are equal, and in eleven they are worse than the other.

We select the set of attributes with the best accuracy. Applying each classifier, we obtain a different set. Therefore, we get three set of attributes for each reduction method for each data set. We obtain the percentage of the original features retained and we calculate the average over the eighteen data sets (nine results). All the methods are between 50% and 60% of the original features.

The experiments show that by applying NLC, the knowledge attained in the original training file is conserved into the reduced training file, and the

Table 4. Accuracy obtained with *C4.5*, *1NN* and *naive Bayes*, selecting the three first attributes of the ranked list

Data	C4.5	NLC	1	2	RLF	IG	1NN	NLC	1	2	RLF	IG	NB	NLC	1	2	RLF	IG
anneal	98.6	89.9	•		92.5	90.6	99.3	91.1			91.6	91.6	86.3	84.0	•	•	90.0	88.9
balance	78.4	69.4			69.4	69.4	86.9	68.0			69.6	67.7	88.8	74.2			73.6	73.3
g_credit	71.1	70.9			71.5	72.2	72.4	61.2	•	•	70.6	70.6	74.8	71.6			71.3	73.9
diabetes	76.7	74.6			74.7	75.1	70.9	69.8			66.7	69.3	76.2	77.1			76.4	76.8
glass	69.2	71.9			67.7	65.4	70.5	66.3			66.3	64.5	45.8	53.8	○		45.8	49.1
glass2	77.8	81.4			77.9	81.4	79.2	77.9			83.4	77.9	61.9	68.7			63.8	68.7
heart-s	78.5	72.6	•		73.3	85.2	74.4	67.8	•	•	73.3	84.8	84.1	74.8	•		74.8	79.6
ionosphe	88.6	80.4	•	•	88.3	90.0	86.6	84.3			85.7	88.6	83.2	78.3	•		83.5	86.6
iris	94.0	94.0			94.0	94.0	95.3	95.3			95.3	95.3	95.3	95.3			95.3	95.3
kr-vs	99.5	90.4			90.4	90.4	96.5	90.4			90.4	90.4	88.0	90.4			90.4	90.4
lymph	78.3	77.7			79.7	77.7	79.7	75.7			83.7	75.0	83.8	75.0			80.3	72.3
segment	97.0	90.5	○	○	85.6	85.5	97.0	91.8	○	○	85.3	88.5	80.0	77.0	○	○	72.5	64.3
sonar	72.6	68.8			70.2	70.7	85.5	73.1			66.8	70.2	67.8	73.1			70.6	70.6
splice-2	94.4	80.5			81.4	80.8	73.9	80.2			81.2	80.6	95.3	79.6			81.1	80.7
vehicle	73.5	53.5	•	•	62.4	61.4	70.1	53.7			56.0	57.7	44.3	40.4			42.8	40.8
vowel	82.9	69.1			70.6	72.1	99.4	79.6			80.1	82.8	66.1	57.9			56.0	58.7
waveform	76.6	66.2			64.5	65.3	73.8	57.0			56.3	56.4	80.0	65.1			66.1	64.9
zoo	93.1	84.2	○		72.3	85.2	96.0	83.2	○		71.3	87.2	95.0	84.2	○		71.3	84.2

dimensionality of data is reduced significantly. We obtain similar results with the other method, but needing much more time.

It is very interesting to compare the speed of attribute selection techniques. We measured the time taken in milliseconds to select the ranking of attributes. NLC is an algorithm with a very short computation time. NLC takes 792 milliseconds in reducing 18 data sets whereas ReliefF takes 566 seconds and IG 2189 milliseconds. We obtain the percentage of reduction time of each data sets, and we calculate the average. NCL reduce the computational cost to the 99% of the time needed by ReliefF and 50% of the time needed by IG.

In order to compare the first attributes in the ranking list of each method, we obtain Table 4 where the data sets are reduced to the first three attributes of each ranking list. we observe the accuracy for each reduction method applying the three classifiers. We obtain similar results with the three methods. Table shows how often each method performs significantly better or worse than ReliefF (RLF) and Information Gain (IG) (column 1 and 2 respectively). In ten of the one hundred and eight cases, the set of attributes selected by the NLC measure yields better accuracy than the two other methods. In eighty they are equal, and in fourteen they are worse than the other.

6   Conclusions

In this paper we present a deterministic attribute selection criterion. The main advantages are its speed and simplicity in the evaluation of the attributes. The measure allows features to be sorted in ascending order of relevance. A considerable reduction of the number of attributes is produced. It is not based on calculated measures between attributes, or complex and costly distance calculations. The computational cost is lower than other methods $O(m \times n \times \log n)$.

We conclude that by applying NLC, the knowledge attained in the original training file is conserved into the reduced training file, and the dimensionality of data is reduced significantly. We obtain similar results with the other method, but needing much more time.

References

1. Aha, D., Kibler, D., & Albert, M. Instance-based learning algorithms. Machine Learning, 6, 37–66 (1991).
2. Blake, C., & Merz, E. K. Uci repository of machine learning databases (1998).
3. Blum, A., & Langley, P. Selection of relevant features and examples in machine learning. Artificial Intelligence, pp. 245–271 (1997).
4. Dash, M., & Liu, H. Feature selection for classification. Intelligent Data Analisys, 1 (1997).
5. Doak, J. An evaluation of search algorithms for feature selection. Technical Report, Los Alamos National Laboratory (1994).
6. Duda, R., & P. Hart. Pattern classification and scene analysis. John Willey and Sons (1973).
7. Hoare, C. A. R. Quicksort. Computer Journal, 5, 10–15 (1962).
8. Kononenko, I. Estimating attributes: Analysis and estensions of relief. European Conference on Machine Learning, pp. 171–182 (1994).
9. Langley, P. Selection of relevant features in machine learning. Procs. Of the AAAI Fall Symposium on Relevance, pp. 140–144 (1994).
10. Quinlan, J. Induction of decision trees. Machine Learning, 1, 81–106 (1986).

Decentralized Temporal Authorization Administration

Chun Ruan[1] and Vijay Varadharajan[1,2]

[1] School of Computing and Information Technology
University of Western Sydney,
Penrith South DC, NSW 1797 Australia
{chun,vijay}@cit.uws.edu.au
[2] Department of Computing
Macquarie University,
North Ryde, NSW 2109 Australia
vijay@ics.mq.edu.au

Abstract. Access control is a significant issue in any secure database system. In this paper, we develop a logic programming based approach for temporal decentralized authorization administration in which users can be delegated, granted or forbidden some access rights for restricted periods of time. Three major aspects are taken into consideration for the semantics of the program, the temporal authorization delegation correctness, temporal authorization propagation and temporal authorization conflict resolution. In particular, a conflict resolution method based on the underlying delegation relation and temporal relation is presented, which can support controlled temporal delegation, temporal authorization suspension or exception and the automatic authorization update. The approach provides users a useful way to express complex security policy with time constraints.

1 Introduction

In the real world, there are many situations in which users may need to be granted some authorizations for limited periods of time. For example, a contract staff in a university can access the university network for the length of his/her contract. A part time programmer in a company is allowed to work only during his/her permitted working hours, such as 9AM to 1PM. There are also many situations in which users may need to be delegated some administrative privileges for a certain duration. For example, a contract database administrator can grant, revoke or possibly delegate authorizations for the database to other users only within his period of contract. *Temporal authorizations* have been used for this purpose. By using temporal authorizations, subjects may grant permissions to others for a certain duration, and these permissions are automatically revoked on the expiration of the time intervals, beginning from the instant they were initially permitted.

Temporal authorizations have been recognized as an important practical security policy to adopt. It has been studied under a Discretionary Access Control

V. Mařík et al. (Eds.): DEXA 2003, LNCS 2736, pp. 917–926, 2003.

(DAC) and Role-based Access Control (RBAC) Models. In [3], Bertino et al presented an authorization model with temporal capabilities. Both positive and negative authorizations are supported in their model, and derivation rules can be expressed in which four temporal operators can be used. However it doesn't support authorization delegations and thus is mainly suitable for a centralized authorization model. In [4], Bertino et al introduced a temporal RBAC model, which supports both periodic activations and deactivations of roles, and temporal dependencies among such actions. In [2], Barker presented a temporal RBAC model. The model is based on logic programs which incorporate the Simplified Event Calculus and can support time-constrained permissions and membership

This paper presents a temporal decentralized authorization model for DAC in which temporal authorization delegations and negations are allowable. When temporal authorizations are delegated in a model, not only the facts such as who owns the authorizations but also the facts such as who owns the administrative privileges in a period of time are derived from the system. A conflict resolution method based on the underlying delegation relation and temporal relation is proposed, which can support controlled delegation, temporal suspension and the automatic authorization update.

To take advantage of strong expressive and reasoning power of logic programming, we will develop our temporal authorization framework based on extended logic programs [5], which supports both negation as failure and classical negation. Logic based approaches have been developed by many researchers recently for the purpose of formalizing authorization specifications and evaluations. The advantage of this methodology is to separate policies from implementation mechanisms, give policies precise semantics, and provide a unified framework that can support multiple policies. We show how extended logic programs may be used to specify complex security policies which support time constrained permissions. In our framework, authorization rules are specified in a temporal delegatable authorization program (TDAP) which is an extended logic program associated with different types of partial orderings on the domain, and these orderings specify various inheritance relationships among subjects, objects and access rights in the domain. A set of domain-independent temporal rules can be defined to achieve the property of temporal delegation correctness, temporal authorization propagation and temporal conflict resolution.

2   Motivation

2.1   Administration of Authorizations

A key issue for discretionary access control is related to the authorization administration policy, which refers to the function of granting and revoking authorizations. Centralized and decentralized administration are two possible approaches to policy management.

With centralized administration, conceptually a single central authorization authority has the privilege to grant and revoke authorizations. It usually reflects the situation in a single enterprize where authorization is controlled by a single authority. But it is rather inflexible, since usually no individual can know what controls are appropriate for every object/system when the number of objects/systems is very large.

With decentralized administration, on the other hand, multiple authorities (subjects) may have the privilege to grant and revoke authorizations, and the ability to manage administrative privilege can be delegated to multiple subjects. Decentralised authorization usually follows the ownership paradigm; i.e. every creator of an object possesses rights to access them as well as the ability to grant and delegate authorizations on this object to other subjects. It is rather flexible and apt to the particular requirements of individual subjects. Many commercial systems adopt such a decentralised approach to authorization. Nevertheless, the authorizations become more difficult to control since multiple subjects can grant and revoke authorizations, and the problem of cascading and cyclic authorization may arise. Further more, when both positive and negative authorizations are allowed in a decentralized authorization model, conflict problem becomes crucial because multiple administrators greatly increase the chance of conflict and cyclic authorizations may lead to unexpected situations. Although the issue of temporal conflict resolution in a decentralized environment is important, we have found that it has not been explored considerably by researchers and hence will investigate it in this paper.

2.2   Extended Logic Program

Traditional logic programming language does not contain classical negation ¬. The declarative semantics of logic programming automatically applies the *closed world assumption* to all predicates, and each ground atom that does not follow from the facts included in the program is assumed to be false. Procedurally, the query evaluation give the answer no to every query that does not succeed. A limitation of this method is that logic programming does not allow us to deal directly with incomplete information. Extended logic programs are proposed by M.Gelfond and V.Lifschitz in [5] to overcome this limitation, which contain classical negation ¬ in addition to negation-as-failure. While traditional logic programs provide negative information implicitly through closed-world reasoning, an extended program can include explicit negative information. In the language of extended programs, we can distinguish between a query which fails in the sense that it does not succeed and a query which fails in the stronger sense that its negation succeeds. In access control context, for example, we can distinguish between the situation that a person is not granted to read a file (negation-as-failure) and the situation that a person is granted "not read" (classical negation, or strong negation) for a file. Classical negation allows us to explicitly express that some access is forbidden. On the other hand, the extended logic programs can deal directly with incomplete information in reasoning. Since the incomplete information is a common issue in the security world, many access control policies are easier to specify in extended logic programs. There are two leading semantics for extended logic programs: well-founded semantics and stable model

semantics [5]. We select answer set semantics for TDAPs because it provides a
more flexible manner to deal with contradicted or incomplete information.

3   Syntax of TDAP

3.1   Time Points and Intervals

Two important and often used representations of time are the time point and
temporal interval [1]. A time point is a zero-length moment in time, such as
"1:00 PM." By contrast, a temporal interval consists of time duration, such as
"5 hours". Intervals can be represented by modelling their endpoints, or instants
such as "9:00 AM to 4:00 PM.". Interval and instant-based representation of
time are widely investigated in the study of time. Assuming a model consisting
of a fully ordered set of points of time, an interval is an ordered pair of points a
and b, denoted by [a,b], with the first point a less than the second b. The length
of such an interval is identified by $b - a$. Although relative timing between two
intervals can be determined from these endpoints, in many cases, sometimes it
is more convenient to specify intervals with respect to each other. Given any
two intervals, there are 13 distinct ways in which they can be related [1]. These
relations indicate how two intervals relate in time; whether they overlap, equal,
before, etc. The 13 relations can be represented by seven cases because six of
them are inverses.

- Time point predicates and functions: $=, <, \leq, +$.
- Interval predicates and function: their use and definitions are those developed
  by Allen in [1].

Relation	Symbol	Pictorial Example
x before y	$\prec$	$xxx\ yyy$
x equal y	$=$	xxx
		yyy
x meets y	m	$xxxyyy$
x overlaps y	o	xxx
		yyy
x during y	d	xxx
		$yyyyyy$
x starts y	s	xxx
		$yyyyy$
x finishes y	f	xxx
		$yyyyy$

$x\,dur\,y = x\,d\,y \vee x\,s\,y \vee x\,f\,y$.
We will use $\sqsubset$ to denote dur, and $x \sqsubseteq y = x \sqsubset y \vee x = y$
$\cap$ is the interval intersection function; $\emptyset$ is the empty interval. Open ended
intervals are also allowed. $(-\infty, t] = \{x | x <= t\}$, $[t, +\infty) = \{x | x >= t\}$, and
$(-\infty, +\infty) = (-\infty, t] \cup [t, +\infty)$
- Mixed point-interval predicates: in with type $\mathcal{T} \times \mathcal{I}$. $in(t, i)$ is true if t is
  inside i, which formally is defined as $in(t, i) = [t, t] \sqsubset i$.

3.2   TDAP Programs

Our language $\mathcal{L}$ is a many-sorted first order language, with six disjoint *sorts* $\mathcal{S}, \mathcal{O}, \mathcal{A}, \mathcal{T}, \mathcal{TI}$, and $\mathcal{I}$ for subjects, objects, access rights, authorization types, time points and time intervals respectively. Variables are denoted by strings starting with lower case letters, and constants by strings starting with upper case letters.

In addition, three partial orders $<_S, <_O$ and $<_A$ are defined on sorts $\mathcal{S}, \mathcal{O}$ and $\mathcal{A}$ respectively, which are used to represent the inheritance hierarchical structures of subjects, objects and access rights. There are three authorization types denoted by $-, +$ and $*$, where $-$ means *negative*, $+$ means *positive*, and $*$ means *delegatable*. A negative authorization specifies that the access must be forbidden, while a positive authorization specifies that the access must be granted. A delegatable authorization specifies that the administrative privilege for the access as well as the access itself must be granted. In other words, $*$ means $+$ plus administrative privilege on the access. The functions are user-defined functions plus time and interval functions given in the last subsection.

The predicates are typed with fixed arity. It consists of a set of ordinary predicates defined by users, the time and interval predicates introduced in last section and two built-in predicate symbol for delegatable authorizations, *grant* and *own*. *grant* is a 6-term predicate symbol with type $\mathcal{S} \times \mathcal{O} \times \mathcal{T} \times \mathcal{A} \times \mathcal{S} \times \mathcal{I}$. The first argument is the *grantee*, the second is the *object*, the third is the *authorization type*, the fourth is the *access right*, the fifth is the *grantor* and the sixth is the *time interval* of this authorization. Intuitively, $grant(s, o, t, a, g, i)$ means s is granted by g the access right a on object o with authorization type t for a period of i. *grant* is called *authorization predicate*. *own* is a 2-term predicate symbol with type $\mathcal{S} \times \mathcal{O}$. Intuitively, $own(s, o)$ means s is the owner of o. A variable or a constant is a *term*. If f is a n-ary function symbol and $t_1, ... t_n$ are terms then $f(t_1, ..., t_n)$ is a term. An *atom* is a construct of the form $p(t_1, ..., t_n)$, where p is a predicate of arity n in P and $t_1, ..., t_n$ are terms. A *literal* is either an atom p or the negation of the atom $\neg p$, where the negation sign $\neg$ represents classical negation. Specially, we forbid the negation form of the authorization predicate grant, since we can use the argument of authorization type in grant to express the opposite meaning. Two literals are *complementary* if they are of the form p and $\neg p$, for some atom p. A *rule r* is a statement of the form:

$b_0 \leftarrow b_1, ..., b_k, not\ b_{k+1}, ..., not\ b_m, m >= 0$

where $b_0, b_1, ..., b_m$ are literals, and not is the negation as failure symbol. The b_0 is the *head* of r, while the conjunction of $b_1,...,b_k,not,\ b_{k+1},...,not,\ b_m$ is the *body* of r. Obviously, the body of r could be empty. A *Temporal Delegatable Authorization Program*, denoted as TDAP, consists of a finite set of rules. A term, an atom, a literal, a rule or program is *ground* if no variable appears in it.

Example 1. Information security concerns that arise in the context of e-consent in health care system relate to: personal health data, temporal consents and denials given by patients, the capacity to create a temporal consent(i.e. temporal consent delegation). Various forms of patient consent can be supported in our model. Consider the following situation. A patient John delegates a temporal consent for reading and writing of his Health Data (HD) to his hospital Doctor (Dr) and his Family GP (FGP) from Jan. 01, 2002 to Dec. 31, 2002, but denies disclosure to his Immediate Family (IF) during this period (because for example, HD contains information about STD condition). This situation can be represented by the following TDAP Π.

(r_1) $own(John, HD) \leftarrow$
(r_2) $grant(Dr, HD, *, Write, John, [01/01/2002, 31/12/2002]) \leftarrow$
(r_3) $grant(FGP, HD, *, Write, John, [01/01/2002, 31/12/2002]) \leftarrow$
(r_4) $grant(IF, HD, -, Read, John, [01/01/2002, 31/12/2002]) \leftarrow$

Please note that, in order to have more expressive examples, we introduce user-defined intervals such as hours and dates. The authorizations to John's hospital doctor and family GP for "reading" of his health data are implied by rules (r_2) and (r_3), which will be explained in more detail later.

4   Semantics of TDAP

Three major aspects are taken into consideration: temporal delegation correctness, temporal authorization propagation and temporal authorization conflict resolution.

4.1   Temporal Delegation Correctness

To make the authorization delegation effective, specific constraints are needed to be enforced on it. Firstly, it is natural to require that authorization grantors own the relative administrative privileges for the effective periods of those authorizations. In our model, the privileged grantors include the owners of objects and the subjects that hold $*$ type of authorizations during those periods. Secondly, cyclic authorizations should be avoided at any time, which usually do not make sense. To illustrate the problem, consider Example 1 again. John has delegated his hospital doctor the capacity to further create a temporal consent on his health data. What happens if the doctor denies disclosure to John by giving him a negative authorization on his health data? This is clearly undesirable. It does not make much sense too if the doctor grants John to read his health data. The constraints are formally specified in the following definition.

Definition 1. *(Temporal delegation correctness) An authorization set is temporal delegation correct if it satisfies the following two conditions: (a) subject s can grant other subjects an access right a over object o for an interval i if and only if s is the owner of o or s has been granted a over o with a delegatable type $*$ for an interval i' such that $i \sqsubseteq i'$; (b) if a subject s receives a delegatable authorization directly or indirectly from another subject s' on some object o and access right a with time interval i, then s cannot grant s' any further authorization on the same o and a for any time period i' such that $i' \cap i \neq \emptyset$.*

4.2   Temporal Authorization Propagations

Next we consider the authorization propagations along hierarchies of subjects, objects and access rights represented by the corresponding partial orders. It has been widely recognized that these propagations can greatly reduce the amount of authorizations that need to be explicitly specified, and thus can simplify the work by a great deal.

Example 2. In Example 1, usually we need to give every person in John's immediate family an explicit negative authorization. However, if authorization inheritance along the subject hierarchy is supported, we just need to indicate who belongs to his immediate family (through " $<$ " relation in our model), and the negative authorization defined by (r_4) will automatically propagate to each member of his immediate family. On the other hand, John's health data may consist of personal detail and health detail which may further consist of clinic related detail and treatment detail. By supporting authorization inheritance along the object hierarchy, rules (r_2) to (r_4) will automatically propagate to all these data. In addition, with the support of authorization inheritance along the access right hierarchy, by defining $Write < Read$, rule $(r_2) and (r_3)$ will propagate to "Read" automatically.

4.3   Temporal Authorization Conflict Resolution

Since both positive and negative authorizations are acceptable in our framework, conflicts among authorizations may arise. As we mentioned before, allowing authorization delegation greatly increases the chance of conflict since there may exist multiple administrators for an access right on an object. For example, in Example 1, the patient John, his hospital doctor and his family GP are all administrators for his health data. Furthermore, since the authorizations have time intervals associated with them, the conflicts are also time related. They may conflict all the time, or only some time in the spans of their intervals. Two temporal authorizations are considered to be conflicting if they are on the same object and access right, and their intervals are intersected, and they have different authorization types. Note that types $*$ and $+$ are considered to be conflicting in the sense that $*$ holds the administrative privilege while $+$ does not.

Since both positive and negative authorizations are acceptable in our framework, conflicts among authorizations may arise. Furthermore, since the authorizations have time intervals associated with them, the conflicts are also time related. They may conflict all the time, or only some time in the spans of their intervals. Two temporal authorizations are considered to be conflicting if they are on the same object and access right, and their intervals are intersected, and they have different authorization types. Note that types $*$ and $+$ are considered to be conflicting in the sense that $*$ holds the administrative privilege while $+$ does not.

Currently the major proposed conflict resolution policies can be summarized as follows

- *Negative-take-precedence*: If a conflict occurs on some subject, the negative authorization will take precedence over positive one.
- *Positive-take-precedence*: If a conflict occurs on some subject, the positive authorization will take precedence over negative one.
- *Strong-and-Weak*: Authorizations are classified into two types, strong and weak. Strong authorizations can not be overridden. Conflicts between strong authorizations are not permitted. The strong authorizations will always override the weak ones when conflict occurs between strong and weak authorizations. When conflict occurs between weak authorizations, the negative one will take precedence.
- *More specific-take-precedence*: The authorization granted to a subject will take precedence over the authorizations granted to a group to which the subject belongs when conflict occurs. This policy is useful for supporting exceptions.
- *Time-take-precedence*: The new authorization will take precedence over the old one.

While the existing conflict resolution methods meet the requirements in most centralized administration models, they may cause problems when the delegation of administrative privilege is taken into consideration. For example, they could not prevent the following undesirable situation from happening. That is, if a subject $s1$ delegates an administrative privilege on a file to another subject $s2$, then $s1$ might be denied to access the file by $s2$ later on. Thus, our conflict resolution policy will first consider the temporal delegation relation.

The basic idea of our method of resolving conflicts is outlined in terms of the following five principles.

Principle 1: Solving conflicts based on the underlying temporal delegation relation by giving higher priorities to the predecessors. Along the delegation path, we give higher priorities to the predecessors. In particular, if subject s delegates to a subject s' directly or indirectly an authorization on object o and access right a at time ti, then, when a conflict w.r.t o and a occurs at ti, the authorization from s (i.e. s is the grantor) will override the one from s' at ti. In other words, the priorities of grantors decrease along the delegation path. Therefore, despite delegation, the owners can still take control of the objects. We believe that this controlled delegation can take advantage of both centralized and decentralized control.

Example 3. In Example 1, John has the highest priority on his health data and his authorizations can never be overridden. Suppose John's family GP try to disclosure his health data to his immediate family by giving them an positive authorization as follows:

(r_5) $grant(IF, HD, +, Read, FGP, [01/01/2002, 31/12/2002]) \leftarrow$

(r_5) conflicts with rule (r_4) and is overridden by (r_4) since the grantor of (r_5), FGP, get his/her capacity to grant from the grantor of (r_4), the patient John.

Principle 2: Smaller time intervals take precedence. If the grantors of two conflicting authorization are identical, then we consider time intervals of the authorizations. If one interval is contained within the other, then we use the *smaller time interval-take-precedence* principle, which means that the authorization with smaller time interval will override the one with the larger interval. This principle can be used to support temporary suspension or exception of an authorization.

Example 4. In Example 1, suppose John does not want his family GP to be involved in his treatment during the period from June 01, 2002 to Oct. 31, 2002. Then he may issue the following authorization:

(r_6) $grant(FGP, HD, -, Write, John, [01/06/2002, 31/10/2002])$ ←

(r_6) conflicts with (r_3) and will override (r_3) during the period from June 01, 2002 to Oct. 31, 2002 according to Principle 2.

Principle 3: Newer intervals take precedence. If the grantors of two conflicting authorization are identical, and the two intervals are overlapping, then we will let the authorization with newer interval dominate. This principle can support automatic update of authorizations without revoking the old ones.

Example 5. In Example 1, suppose John moved to another hospital later and therefore refuses his previous doctor to write on his health data from Sep. 01, 2002 to Sep. 30, 2003. The following rule expresses his denial:

(r_7) $grant(Dr, HD, -, Write, John, [01/09/2002, 30/09/2003])$ ←

(r_7) conflicts with (r_2) during the period from Sep. 01, 2002 to Dec. 31, 2002 and will override it according to Principle 3.

Principle 4: Solving conflicts according to the types of authorizations. If all the above policies fail to solve the conflict between two authorizations, then we will solve the conflict in a pessimistic manner by using the negative-take-precedence principle. This will help to achieve the maximum degree of security. We solve the conflict based on the authorization type, by giving the authorization type − the highest priority followed by + and then by *.

Principle 5: Cascade overriding. When a delegatable authorization is overridden in a period, the authorizations granted by the grantee of that authorization should also be overridden in that period. In other words, we support cascade overriding.

4.4   Formal Semantics of TDAP

We can define a set of domain independent rules to capture the features of temporal delegation correctness, temporal conflict resolution and temporal authorization propagation along the hierarchies of subjects, objects and access rights. Suppose they are TDCP, TCRP and TAPP respectively. The basic idea is to combine these general rules with the domain-specific TDAP program defined by users to derive the authorizations holding in a period of time. Figure 1 illustrates the method to evaluate the semantics of a user program TDAP. The rules in TDCP, TCRP and TAPP are omitted here because of the space limit.

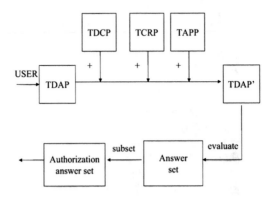

Fig. 1. Evaluating the Semantics of TDAP

Definition 2. *Let Π be a TDAP. We say that M is an answer set for Π if M is an answer set for $\Pi \cup TDCP \cup TCRP \cup TAPP$. If M is an answer set for Π, then its subset of all the authorization literals is called temporal authorization answer set for Π.*

5   Conclusions

In future work, we are interested in developing a dynamic conflict resolution method which can support different policies in terms of various temporal properties of subjects, objects and access rights. We also intend to implement a prototype of our framework based on logic programming technique.

References

1. Allen, J.F.: Towards a general theory of action and time. *Artificial Intelligence*, **23** (1984) 123–154
2. Barker, S.: Data protection by logic programming. *Lecture Notes in Computer Science*, **1861** (2000) 1300–1314
3. Bertino, E., Bettini, C., Ferrari, E., Samarati, P.: A temporal access control mechanism for database systems, *IEEE Trans. on KDE*, 8(**1**) (1996) 67–80
4. Bertino, E., Bonatti, P.A., Ferrari,E.: TRBAC: A temporal role-based access control model,*ACM Trans. on Information and System Security*, 4(**3**) (2001) 191–233
5. Gelfond, M., Lifschitz, V.: Classical negation in logic programs and disjunctive databases. *New Generation Computing*, **9** (1991) 365–385

Mobile Agent Watermarking and Fingerprinting: Tracing Malicious Hosts

Oscar Esparza, Marcel Fernandez, Miguel Soriano,
Jose L. Muñoz, and Jordi Forné

Department of Telematics Engineering
Universitat Politècnica de Catalunya
C/ Jordi Girona 1 i 3
Campus Nord, Mod C3, UPC
08034 Barcelona, Spain
{oscar.esparza,marcelf,soriano,jose.munoz,jforne}@entel.upc.es

Abstract. Mobile agents are software entities consisting of code and data that can migrate autonomously from host to host executing their code. Despite its benefits, security issues strongly restrict the use of code mobility. The protection of mobile agents against the attacks of malicious hosts is considered the most difficult security problem to solve in mobile agent systems.

The approach that is presented here detects manipulation attacks performed during the agent's execution. Software watermarking techniques are used in order to embed a mark into the agent. The agent's execution creates marked results. When the agent returns to the origin host, these results are examined in order to find the embedded mark. If the mark has changed, this means that the executing host has modified the agent. Colluding hosts can also be identified by using codes with the identifiable parent property (IPP) as marks, i.e. mobile agent fingerprinting.

1 Introduction

Mobile agents are software entities that move code and data to remote hosts. Mobile agents can migrate from host to host performing actions autonomously on behalf of a user. The last host that executes the agent sends the processed results to the agent sender, i.e. the origin host as it is also called. The use of mobile agents saves bandwidth and permits off-line and autonomous execution in comparison with habitual distributed systems based on message passing. Mobile agents are especially useful to perform functions automatically in almost all electronic services, like data mining, e-commerce and network management. Despite their benefits, massive use of mobile agents is restricted by security issues.

This paper introduces a new approach that detects manipulation attacks by making the origin host to embed a mark into the agent. This approach also traces the malicious hosts that are responsible for the attack. During execution, the mark is transferred to the agent's results. When the agent returns to the origin host, these results are examined in order to find the embedded mark. If

V. Mařík et al. (Eds.): DEXA 2003, LNCS 2736, pp. 927–936, 2003.

the mark has changed or has dissapeared, this means that the executing host has modified the agent. This scheme is based on software watermarking models. Colluding hosts can be identified by using codes with the *identifiable parent property* (IPP)[6] as marks.

The rest of the paper is organized as follows: Section 2 describes the existing approaches to protect mobile agents; Section 3 details how to trace malicious hosts and finally, some conclusions can be found in Section 4.

2   Malicious Hosts

The attacks to a mobile agent performed by a malicious host that is executing the mobile agent are considered, by far, the most difficult problem to solve regarding mobile agent security. On one hand, it is possible to assure the integrity and authentication of code, data or results that come from other hosts by using digital signature or encryption techniques. On the other hand, it is difficult to detect or prevent the attacks performed by a malicious host during the agent's execution, i.e. execution integrity. Malicious hosts could try to get some profit of the agent reading or modifying the code, the data, the communications or even the results due to their complete control on the execution. The agent cannot hold a decryption key because the hosts could read it. Furthermore, it is not sure that the host runs the complete code in a correct manner, or it simply does not permit the migration to other hosts.

The rest of the section enumerates some published approaches that aid to solve the problem of malicious hosts.

In [11], Vigna introduces the idea of cryptographic traces. The running agent takes traces of instructions that alter the agent's state due to external variables. The host sends a hash of the traces with the results because the complete traces are too large. If the agent owner wants to verify execution, it asks for the traces and executes the agent again. If new execution does not agree with the traces, the host is cheating. This approach has various drawbacks: (1) Verification is only performed in case of suspicion; and (2) Each host must store the traces for an indefinite period of time because the origin host can ask for them.

In [12], Yee introduces the idea of a closed tamper-proof hardware subsystem where agents can be executed in a secure way. This forces each host to buy a hardware equipment and to consider the hardware provider as trusted.

In [8], Roth presents the idea of mutual protection. In the author's opinion, in an open environment like the Internet it can be assumed that trustworthy relationships are limited, so collusion between hosts is difficult. For this reason, the agent's results are saved in a cooperative agent that has a disjunct itinerary. This approach presents two drawbacks: (1) The loss of the cooperative agent implies the loss of the results; (2) The possibility of collusion does not dissappear.

The Environmental Key Generation presented in [7] makes the agent's code impossible to decipher until the proper conditions happen on the environment, so previous analysis from hosts is avoided. The main drawback of this proposal is that the malicious hosts can attack the agent once it has been deciphered.

A Blackbox is a software environment that only allows to read the inputs and the outputs, but no internal data can be read or modified. There is no known algorithm that has this properties. The Time Limited Blackbox [5] has this security level but only for a period of time. After this time, the privacy or a proper execution of the agent cannot be assured. Hohl's mechanism is based on a mess-up algorithm that obfuscates the code and data. The main difficulty in this case is how this security time can be estimated as it depends on the capacity of the malicious host to analize the obfuscated code.

The use of encrypted programs [9] is proposed as the only way to give privacy and integrity to mobile code. Hosts execute the encrypted code directly. A decryption function is used when the agent reaches the origin host to recover the results. The difficulty here is to find functions that can be executed in an encrypted way.

3   Tracing Malicious Hosts

This paper introduces a new approach that detects manipulation attacks performed during the agent's execution. The approach also traces the malicious hosts responsible for the attack. Software watermarking and fingerprinting techniques are used in order to place a embedded mark into the agent. The running of the agent creates marked results. When the agent returns to the origin host, these results are examined in order to find the embedded mark. If the mark has changed or dissapeared, the executing host modified the agent.

3.1   Software Watermarking

Watermarking is used to provide copyright protection for digital contents. A distributor embeds a mark into a digital object, so its ownership can be proved. This mark is usually a secret message that contains the distributor's copyright information. The mark is normally embedded into the digital object by exploiting the usually inherent information redundancy. The problem arises when a dishonest user tries to delete the mark in the digital object before redistribution in order to claim authorship. In consequence, the strength of watermarking schemes must be based on the difficulty of locating and changing the mark. There are many watermarking approaches that try to protect the intellectual property of multimedia objects, specially images, but unfortunately very little attention has been paid to software watermarking. However, there are some published approaches that describe how to embed a mark into a piece of code [10].

In [1] a taxonomy of software watermarking models can be found. Tree main parameters are defined for a software watermarking scheme: (1) *the data rate* expresses the quantity of hidden data that can be embedded within the digital object; (2) *the stealth* expresses how imperceptible the embedded data is to an observer; and (3) *the resilience* expresses the hidden message's degree of immunity to attacks by an adversary. In [1], the definition of the two main kinds of software watermarking techniques can also be found: (1) static watermarking, in which marks are stored directly into the data or the executable code itself; and (2) dynamic watermarking, in which marks are stored in the program execution state. In Collberg's et al opinion, static watermarks seem to be easy to delete by using semantic preserving program transformations, like obfuscation, translation or optimization. Published dynamic watermarking schemes are resilient to some of these transformations, but not all of them.

3.2   Software Fingerprinting

The aim of fingerprinting is not only protecting the intellectual property, but also tracing the dishonest users. For this reason, a different mark is placed in each copy of the digital object. However, fingerprinting schemes are vulnerable to collusion attacks, i.e. a group of dishonest users compare their copies, and by changing the marks where their copies differ, they create a new copy that conceals their identities.

Software fingerprinting uses software watermarking techniques in order to embed a different mark for each user. Software fingerprinting shares the same weaknesses than these of software watermarking: marks must be imperceptible for observers and resilient to transformation attacks.

3.3   Mobile Agent Watermarking

The authors of this paper introduce a new approach that uses software watermarking techniques in mobile agents, that is to say mobile agent watermarking. Mobile agent watermarking can be used not for property right protection, but for the assurance of the integrity of the execution. The aim of mobile agent watermarking is detection of manipulation attacks performed during the mobile agent's execution. For this reason, a mark is embedded into the mobile agent by using software watermarking techniques. This mark is transferred to the agent's results during the execution. Obviously, the mark is disguised as part of the real results to the executing hosts. When the agent returns to the origin host, the results of each host are verified in order to locate the mark. If the mark differs from the expected mark, this means that the executing host has modified the agent, so it should be treated as malicious. The alteration of the mark not only detects manipulation attacks, but also proves the malicious behavior of the host. This tampered results can be used as proofs in order to punish the malicious host by using a Third Trusted Party (TTP from here on) [3].

As opposed to software watermarking schemes, where the aim of the malicious users is trying to modify or delete the mark (for instance by using semantic preserving program transformations, like obfuscation, translation or optimization), in mobile agent watermarking, the aim of malicious hosts is to try to modify the code, the data and/or the results, but without modifying the embedded mark, because any change in the mark will reveal that the agent was modified.

For this reason, software watermarking schemes with little resilience can be used because malicious hosts cannot use program transformation without changing directly the mark. The stealth must be the main property in the software watermarking scheme used, because malicious hosts with no knowledge about where the mark is can only try random changes in the agent.

The rest of the section describes the tasks that must be performed in order to protect a mobile agent by using mobile agent watermarking techniques.

Mark Embedding. As it is said, mobile agents consist mainly of code and data, so the origin host must embed the mark inside of them. These are the main possibilities in order to embed the mark into the mobile agent:

- Marking the code: the origin host embeds the mark into the code, so all the hosts in the agent's itinerary run the same marked code.
- Marking the input data: the origin host can assign different input data for each host. This is the way that the origin host uses in order to personalize the execution for each host. Embedding the mark into these input data forces the origin host to place the mark inside several digital objects. Furthermore, malicious hosts have the possibility of comparing these different input data in order to locate the mark. For this reason, we consider that marking the data in a mobile agent watermarking scheme is not a good choice.
- Marking the obfuscated code: another possibility is obfuscating the code and the data before embedding the mark. Obfuscation makes the code harder to analyze, so malicious hosts cannot easily understand it, so it is difficult to modify in order to take some profit. Placing the mark in an obfuscated code makes difficult the task of discriminating which parts are normal code from those parts that contain the mark. This way is the most secure, but also the most computationally expensive. Hohl in [5] also used obfuscation as a way of protecting mobile code, as was pointed in section 2. In [2] a taxonomy of obfuscation techniques is provided.

Mark Transference. The agent's code must transfer the mark to the results, because the origin host will verify the integrity of the mark when the agent returns to home. The way the mark is transferred can be as easy as printing the mark inside the result in some places previously known by the origin host, the same places for the results of all hosts. Obviously the mark must seem part of the real results to the executing hosts.

Figure 1 shows how the mark is embedded in the agent's code and the way the mark is transferred to the results of each host. Remember that the mark is the same for all hosts and it is embedded in the same places into the results.

Mark Verification. When the agent's execution finishes in the last host of the itinerary and it returns to the origin host, the mark must be verified in order to assure the execution integrity.

The origin host gets the information of the previously chosen places in the results in order to reconstruct the mark. Verification consists in comparing the mark embedded in the results with the expected mark. If the mark has changed or has disappeared, the executing host has modified the agent, so it is malicious.

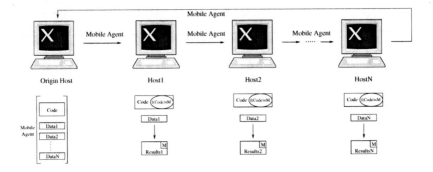

Fig. 1. Mark Embedding and Transference in Mobile Agent Watermarking

The alteration of the mark not only detects manipulation attacks, but also proves the malicious behavior of the host. This tampered results can be used as proofs in order to punish the malicious host by using a TTP [3].

Attacks. These are the main attacks that malicious hosts can perform to the mobile agent watermarking approach:

- Eavesdropping: all non-encrypted data in an agent can be read by the host.
- Manipulation: malicious hosts can try to manipulate any part of the mobile agent in order to take some profit. The aim of malicious hosts is modifying the mobile agent without altering the mark, because any change in the mark can be used as a proof in order to punish them. For this reason, the strength of the mobile agent watermarking approach is based on making the mark imperceptible enough to an observer, that is to say, the mark must be disguised as part of the real results to the executing hosts. The use of obfuscation makes harder the work of an observer.
- Collusion: as all the hosts share the same mark and it is embedded into the same places of the results, a group of colluding hosts can try to locate the mark by comparing those bits that are equal in their results. Therefore, malicious hosts can change those bits that are different in their results without altering the mark. Using mobile agent fingerprinting avoids this possibility and permits the detection of the colluding hosts.

3.4   Mobile Agent Fingerprinting

The aim of mobile agent fingerprinting is the same as the aim of mobile agent watermarking: detection of manipulation attacks performed during the mobile agent's execution. Furthermore, mobile agent fingerprinting can detect collusion attacks performed by a group of dishonest users.

In the mobile agent fingerprinting approach, the embedded mark is different for each host. The corresponding mark is transferred to the agent's results during the execution of each host. When the agent returns to the origin host, the results are verified in order to locate these marks. If the mark in the results of a host has changed, this host is malicious because it modify the agent's execution. The fact that each host has a different mark makes harder the possibility of collusion. Colluding hosts can also be identified by using trazable codes with the *identifiable parent property* (IPP)[6] as marks.

IPP Codes. Let $\mathbf{F}_q^n$ be a vector space, then $C \subseteq \mathbf{F}_q^n$ is called a **code**. A code C is called a **linear code** if it forms a subspace of $\mathbf{F}_q^n$. If the dimension of the subspace is k, then we call C a $[n, k, d]$-code.

A well known class of linear codes are Reed-Solomon codes that can be defined as follows. Take n distinct elements $P = \{\alpha_1, \dots, \alpha_n\} \subseteq \mathbf{F}_q$. Then a **Reed-Solomon code** of length n and dimension k, consists of all codewords of the form $(f(\alpha_1), \dots, f(\alpha_n))$ where f takes the value of all polynomials of degree less than k in $\mathbf{F}_q[x]$: $\mathrm{RS}(P, k) = \{(f(\alpha_1), ..., f(\alpha_n)) | f \in \mathbf{F}_q[x] \wedge \deg(f) < k\}$

For any two words $\mathbf{a}$, $\mathbf{b}$ in $\mathbf{F}_q^n$ we define the *set* of *descendants* $D(\mathbf{a}, \mathbf{b})$ as $D(\mathbf{a}, \mathbf{b}) := \{\mathbf{x} \in \mathbf{F}_q^n : x_i \in \{a_i, b_i\}, 1 \leq i \leq n\}$.

For a code C, the *descendant code* C^* is defined as: $C^* := \bigcup_{\mathbf{a} \in C, \mathbf{b} \in C} D(\mathbf{a}, \mathbf{b})$.

If $\mathbf{z} \in C^*$ is a descendant of $\mathbf{a}$ and $\mathbf{b}$, then we call $\mathbf{a}$ and $\mathbf{b}$ *parents* of $\mathbf{z}$. If for every descendant in C^*, at least one of the parents can be identified, we say that code C has the *identifiable parent property* (IPP).

Theorem 1. *Let q be a prime power. If $q \geq n - 1$, then there exists a (shortened, extended or doubly extended) Reed-Solomon code over $\mathbf{F}_q$ with parameters $[n, \lceil n/4 \rceil, n - \lceil n/4 \rceil + 1]$ that has IPP [6].*

The rest of the section describes the tasks that must be performed in order to protect a mobile agent by using mobile agent fingerprinting techniques.

Mark Embedding. In the mobile agent fingerprinting approach, the embedded mark is different for each host. The way that marks are embedded in the mobile agent watermarking approach can also be used in the mobile agent fingerprinting. Obviously, marks must be imperceptible for observers in order to avoid that malicious hosts can locate them. The resilience of the mark is not as important as the stealth, because malicious hosts cannot use semantic preserving program transformations to modify the mobile agent.

The difference between mobile agent watermarking and fingerprinting is the fact that it is possible to detect collusion attacks performed by a group of dishonest hosts. Furthermore, it is possible to trace the colluding hosts by using IPP codes as marks. An IPP tracing algorithm can be found in [4]

These are the main possibilities in order to embed the mark into the agent:

– Marking the code: embedding a different mark in the code for each host makes that each host has a different marked code. In this case, malicious hosts have the possibility of comparing their different codes in order to locate their marks. For this reason, we consider that marking the code in a mobile agent fingerprinting scheme is not a good choice.

- Marking the data: the data are usually different for each host. Embedding a different mark in each data seems logical because the malicious hosts cannot locate the marks by comparing their data. Remember that the marks are different and the cover digital objects are also different, so it is difficult to know which bits are part of the mark and which bits are part of the real data.
- Marking the obfuscated code: we consider that using obfuscated code and data is not a good choice because there are several marks to embed into a unique cover digital object. Furthermore, malicious hosts could try to compare the set of instructions that have executed in order to locate which instructions are different.

Mark Transference. In the mobile agent fingerprinting approach, the agent transfers its own mark to its results while it is running the mobile agent. The way the mark is transferred can be as easy as printing the mark inside the result in some places previously known by the origin host, the same places for all hosts. Obviously the mark must seem part of the real results to the executing hosts. In this sense, it is recommended that the mark in the mobile agent does not coincide exactly with the mark that is transferred to the results, in order to avoid that a malicious host match the mobile agent with the results to locate the mark.

Mark Verification. The procedure is similar to the mobile agent watermarking approach. When the agent's execution finishes in the last host of the itinerary and it returns to the origin host, the marks must be verified in order to assure the execution integrity. The origin host must know what the marks were and where they were embedded. So the marks can be reconstructed by catching the information of the previously chosen places in the results. Verification consists in comparing the marks embedded in the results with the expected marks. If one mark has changed or has disappeared, the executing host has modified the agent, so it is malicious.

The alteration of the mark not only detects manipulation attacks, but also proves the malicious behavior of the host. This tampered results can be used as a proof in order to punish the malicious host by using a TTP [3].

Additionally, using IPP codes [6] as marks permits the origin host to trace the colluding hosts. Error correcting codes fit naturally in fingerprinting schemes, since one can take advantage of their structure. If the minimum distance of the code meets certain conditions then the code has the identifiable parent property (IPP). If a mark has changed, the IPP code properties permit locating the colluding hosts.

Figure 2 shows the complete process of embedding, transference and verification of the marks.

Attacks. These are the main attacks that malicious hosts can perform to the mobile agent fingerprinting approach:

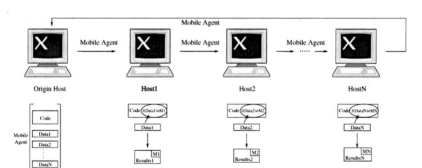

Fig. 2. Mark Embedding and Transference in Mobile Agent Fingerprinting

- Eavesdropping: all non-encrypted data in an agent can be read by the host.
- Manipulation: malicious hosts can try to manipulate any part of the mobile agent, including the results, in order to take some profit. The aim of malicious hosts is modifying the mobile agent without altering the mark, because any change in the mark can be used as a proof in order to punish them. For this reason, the mark must be imperceptible enough to an observer, i.e. the mark must seem part of the normal code.
- Collusion: colluding hosts comparing their data or results cannot extract any information about the mark, because all hosts have a different input data and a different embedded mark.

3.5 Drawbacks

These are the main drawbacks that can be found in the approach presented:

- There is an increase in the code and data size. Embedding a mark always means that some overhead is added to the mobile agent.
- Similar to all attack detection approaches, a TTP is needed in order to punish malicious behaviors [3].
- We use a mobile agent model that it is not general because always assume that the mobile agent must return to the origin host. In our opinion, a secure mobile agent system can only be achieved by making the agent returning home. For instance, a denial of service attack cannot be detected if the agent does not return to the origin host.

4 Conclusions

This paper introduces two new schemes for detection of manipulation attacks. Both of them make the origin host to embed a mark in the mobile agent. During the execution, the mark is transferred to the agent's results. When the agent returns to the origin host, these results are examined in order to find the embedded mark. If the mark has changed or has dissapeared, this means that the executing host has modified the agent, so it is malicious.

Mobile agent watermarking detects manipulation attacks by embedding the same mark in the results of all the executing hosts. Unfortunately, watermarking schemes are not resilient to collusion attacks. For this reason, mobile agent fingerprinting is presented as the way to detect collusion attacks. A different mark is embedded in the mobile agent in order to detect manipulation and collusion attacks.

Acknowledgments. This work is supported by the Spanish Research Council under the project DISQET CICYT TIC2002-00818.

References

1. C. Collberg and C. Thomborson. Software watermarking: Models and dynamic embeddings. In *Principles of Programming Languages 1999, POPL'99*, 1999.
2. C. Collberg, C. Thomborson, and D. Low. A taxonomy of obfuscating transformations. Technical Report 148, The University of Auckland, 1997.
3. O. Esparza, M. Soriano, J.L. Muñoz, and J. Forné. Host Revocation Authority: a Way of Protecting Mobile Agents from Malicious Hosts. In *International Conference on Web Engineering (ICWE 2003)*, LNCS. Springer-Verlag, 2003.
4. M. Fernandez and M. Soriano. Algorithm to decode identifiable parent property codes. *Electronics Letters*, 38(12):552–553, June 2002.
5. F. Hohl. Time Limited Blackbox Security: Protecting Mobile Agents From Malicious Hosts. In *Mobile Agents and Security*, volume 1419 of *LNCS*. Springer-Verlag, 1998.
6. H. Hollmann, J. van Lint, J. Linnartz, and L. Tolhuizen. On codes with the identifiable parent property. *Journal of Combinatorial Theory*, 82(2):121–133, May 1998.
7. J. Riordan and B. Schneier. Environmental Key Generation Towards Clueless Agents. In *Mobile Agents and Security*, volume 1419 of *LNCS*. Springer-Verlag, 1998.
8. V. Roth. Mutual protection of cooperating agents. In *Secure Internet Programming: Security Issues for Mobile and Distributed Objects*, volume 1906 of *LNCS*. Springer-Verlag, 1999.
9. T. Sander and C.F. Tschudin. Protecting mobile agents against malicious hosts. In *Mobile Agents and Security*, volume 1419 of *LNCS*. Springer-Verlag, 1998.
10. J.P. Stern, G. Hachez, F. Koeune, and J.J. Quisquater. Robust object watermarking: Application to code. In *Information Hiding*, volume 1768 of *LNCS*. Springer-Verlag, 1999.
11. G. Vigna. Cryptographic traces for mobile agents. In *Mobile Agents and Security*, volume 1419 of *LNCS*. Springer-Verlag, 1998.
12. B.S. Yee. A sanctuary for mobile agents. In *DARPA workshop on foundations for secure mobile code*, 1997.

A Quick Review: What Have Been Presented at DEXA International Conferences?

Tran Khanh Dang[1], Roland Wagner[1], and A Min Tjoa[2]

[1] Institute of Applied Knowledge Processing
University of Linz,
Austria
{khanh,rrwagner}@faw.uni-linz.ac.at
[2] Institute of Information and Software Engineering
Technical University of Vienna,
Austria
amin.tjoa@ifs.tuwien.ac.at

Abstract. Things have been changing increasingly since the first DEXA events due to the new challenges posed by new issues ubiquitously appearing in modern application domains nowadays. In this paper, a quick review of contributions to the DEXA international conferences will be given. The different research trends and challenges that have been posed are succinctly analysed. Some predictions about the future trend of the DEXA events are also presented.

1 Introduction

Until the 14th DEXA events held this year – DEXA 2003, many things have been changing increasingly compared to the first DEXA events held in 1990. In the beginning, the DEXA conference was just a forum for researchers to exchange and disseminate knowledge and research results in the area of Database and Expert Systems Applications. As we know, however, with the increasing production and exchange of multimedia information through the Internet, the need of effective information retrieval (IR) systems and other modern database applications is a crucial issue nowadays [18]. Therefore, going along with these trends, the DEXA events are expanded as well to meet with the new challenges introduced by new issues in the modern application domains.

Regardless of plenty of difficult facts, the DEXA events have been still annually organized and widely accepted in the scientific community [1, 2, 3, 4, 5, 6, 7, 8, 9, 10, 11, 12, 13]. In this paper, we give a brief overview of the development of the DEXA events by means of the scientific contributions accepted.

The rest of this paper is organized as follows: Section 2 shortly presents the scientific history of the DEXA events since the first DEXA conference was held. Then, in section 3, we shall elaborate on recent trends in the contributions to the DEXA events and some predictions about their future trend.

V. Mařík et al. (Eds.): DEXA 2003, LNCS 2736, pp. 937–941, 2003.

2 A Short History Since DEXA 1990

In a previous review [19], the authors already presented the development of the DEXA events since 1990. This section is to summarize the key points with respect to the scientific contributions to the DEXA events.

In the first DEXA conference held in 1990, as non-standard applications, object-oriented technology, and other advanced systems for management applications were extensively developing, a number of important and related trends in the original scope of the DEXA events were discussed. In that year, there were nearly 90 accepted papers. Most of them were focused on (advanced) applications in the area of database and expert systems and close to commercial products. Even then, in the beginning stage of the DEXA events, there were also papers dealing with modern database applications emerging such as IR systems and computer integrated manufacturing (CIM), etc.

Following DEXA 1990, the DEXA events later in years 1991, 1992, 1993 and 1994 were also mainly focus on the area of database and expert systems. However, some new research topics come and were more and more apparent. Such new topics come from new research challenges and real-world application demand, e.g. active databases and their applications, the interoperability between heterogeneous database systems, data extraction techniques and data mining, metadata management, etc. Specially, modern application domains such as IR systems, multimedia databases, object-oriented technology based systems, spatial and geographical databases, etc. had been always included and become more and more important during the DEXA events. Such things, as we are seeing, lead to a wider and not "obsolete" DEXA conference nowadays in whatever sense.

In 1995, the DEXA events started a very important direction: the DEXA workshops were organized in order to allow researchers to discuss about very specialized research areas relevant to the main scope of the DEXA conference [17]. Also, at the DEXA 1995, some new research areas were introduced as Computer Supported Cooperative Work (CSCW) systems, parallel and distributed database applications and relevant query processing aspects, etc. In our perspective, most contributions tended to focus more on advanced aspects of modern and emerging database applications.

In 1996, many accepted papers discussed object-oriented and active databases aspects. Besides, parallel architectures for database and expert systems applications can also be observed apparently by its increasing interest as well as the increase of valuable articles. Furthermore, CSCW and work flow systems together with many other theoretical aspects were discussed as well.

In the DEXA 1997, it is the first time that an invited presentation mentioned about the connection between databases with the Web. Except for that, the contributions also showed that in the area of database and expert systems applications aspects like object-oriented, active and temporal are very important. In this year, modern application domains, which together with the Web, were more apparent. They included image processing, multimedia databases, digital libraries, deductive databases, query languages, federated databases, etc.

Generally, in 1998, the contributions to the DEXA events were quite similar to those of the last year. However, we should note here that some modern application domains become the most important research areas during the DEXA 1998, including data warehouses and knowledge discovery, information retrieval, spatial and temporal databases, etc. Specially, because of the emerging trend in knowledge discovery and data mining, it was clear that an own conference on this "hot" topic should be planned and this turned out to be true one year later, i.e. at the DEXA 1999. Besides, the scientific contributions at the DEXA workshops were also very valuable. They focused on lots of concrete and more deeply problems related mostly to modern application domains emerging. We can name some of the most important workshops as follows: Query Processing and Multimedia Issues in Distributed Systems, Data Warehouse Design and OLAP Technology, Storage and Retrieval Issues in Image and Multimedia Databases, Parallel Databases: Innovative Applications and New Architectures, and so forth.

In DEXA 1999, the object-oriented databases one more time proved their importance in the area of database and expert systems applications because there were a lot of valuable articles accepted and they discussed about many advanced important aspects relevant. Moreover, further advanced query aspects were also introduced together with heterogeneous, distributed and federated database and expert systems. It is not less important to mention that although there was an own conference on Data Warehousing and Knowledge Discovery (DaWaK) [14], many papers in the field of data warehousing and data mining were still accepted in this 10th DEXA conference. Furthermore, as previous DEXA events, the contributions to the DEXA workshops are always the state of the arts in the relevant fields. Several of such important workshops can be named, e.g. Similarity Search, Web-Based Information Visualization, Spatio-Temporal Data Models and Languages, Information Technologies for Electronic Commerce, International Workshop on Internet Data Management, Electronic Commerce and Security, and more others.

In the DEXA 2000, one fact should be memorized is that the first papers in the direction of Web based systems were accepted and discussed. Besides, important problems related to query aspects, data warehouses and knowledge discovery, multimedia databases, multidimensional index structures, and other modern application domains were still at the center of this 11th DEXA conference. Coming along with the Web technology, the e-commerce systems, e-government and relevant issues have also got special attention from the research community. This was, as usual, reflected via the contributions to the DEXA workshops this year, e.g. Workshop on Trends in Electronic Government Managing Distributed Knowledge, Workshop on Negotiations in Electronic Markets - Beyond Price Discovery - E-Negotiations, etc. However, more importantly, the first international conference on Electronic Commerce and Web Technologies (EC-Web) [15] was started in this year. Besides them, other workshops relevant to advanced/modern database applications were still in great progress.

In 2001, the DEXA events continued gaining lots of contributions related to modern application domains such as modern information retrieval systems, advanced query aspects, and (high-dimensional) indexing techniques, etc. Until this year, the DEXA events included three conferences (DEXA, DaWaK, and EC-Web) and lots of workshops. In this year, a new research area got much attention from the researchers, that is "e-Government" (the 2nd International Workshop on Electronic Government was organizing at this 12th DEXA conference and become the most important one [19]). This built the base to organize the first international conference on "e-Government" one year later [16], i.e. at the DEXA 2002.

Except for those, in 2001, the DEXA events also observed several other new workshops established for research and commercial problems and systems of great interest such as Dlib - First International Workshop on Digital Libraries, INBOSA - First International Workshop on Internet Bots: Systems and Applications, WBC - First International Workshop on Web Based Collaboration, WEBH - First International Workshop on Electronic Business Hubs: XML, Metadata, Ontologies, and Business Knowledge on the Web, and so on.

The last DEXA conference – DEXA 2002, held in Aix-en-Provence, accepted many papers in the fields and research topics related to Web-based systems, indexing techniques, XML, advanced query aspects, data warehouses and data mining, and information retrieval. In the scope of the workshops, the notable fact is that they mainly focused on Web-based systems, e.g. e-commerce systems. Besides, the "hot" research topics were also reflected immediately therein: First International Workshop on Web Semantics – WebS, International Workshop on Very Large Data Warehouses – VLDWH, etc.

This year, 2003, the DEXA conference is held in Prague and we accepted 91 papers among 236 papers submitted. Except for other contemporary research topics that had been accepted at the previous DEXA events, in this year we also accepted lots of papers in other new research areas such as mobile computing, bioinformatics, etc. More importantly, a new international conference is organizing in parallel to our DEXA events: The 1st International Conference on Industrial Applications of Holonic and Multi-Agent Systems - HoloMAS 2003. Therefore, at the moment, the DEXA events include 5 international conferences and many satellite workshops as follows:

- DEXA conference
- DaWaK conference
- EC-Web conference
- eGOV conference
- HoloMAS conference
- and the DEXA workshops

3   Recent and Future Trends of the DEXA Events

Not only the DEXA conference, but any other conference also has to found a forum for researchers to discuss problems of interest and to exchange information they all consider. The problems and information of interest usually come together with the development of the technology and the requirements from the human society. They are always changing and the change is even faster in the digital era nowadays. To aim at satisfying such requirements, a professional international conference must be flexible to cope with the changes.

From the beginning, the DEXA events have completely satisfied such things, leading to an increasingly wider DEXA conference as proven. Recent (and previous) DEXA events have always brought a very good forum to the researchers to discuss and debate the concerned state of the art problems. This is also the main aim of the DEXA organizers. In the future, any new research area relevant to the scope of the DEXA events will also be welcome to join to our forum.

References

1. M. Tjoa, R. Wagner (Eds.): Proceedings of the 1st International Conference on Database and Expert Systems Applications – DEXA 1990, Springer-Verlag, 1990, Austria.
2. D. Karagiannis (Ed.): Proceedings of the 2nd International Conference on Database and Expert Systems Applications – DEXA 1991, Springer-Verlag, 1991, Germany.
3. M. Tjoa, I. Ramos (Eds.): Proceedings of the 3rd International Conference on Database and Expert Systems Applications – DEXA 1992, Springer-Verlag, 1992, Spain.
4. V. Marík, J. Lazanský, R. Wagner (Eds.): Proceedings of 4th International Conference on Database and Expert Systems Applications – DEXA 1993, Lecture Notes in Computer Science, Springer-Verlag 1993, Czech Republic.
5. D. Karagiannis (Ed.): Proceedings of the 5th International Conference on Database and Expert Systems Applications – DEXA 1994, Lecture Notes in Computer Science, Springer-Verlag 1994, Greece.
6. N. Revell, A. M. Tjoa (Eds.): Proceedings of the 6th International Conference on Database and Expert Systems Applications – DEXA 1995, Lecture Notes in Computer Science, Springer-Verlag 1995, United Kingdom.
7. R. Wagner, H. Thoma (Eds.): Proceedings of the 7th International Conference on Database and Expert Systems Applications – DEXA 1996, Lecture Notes in Computer Science, Springer-Verlag 1996, Switzerland.
8. Abdelkader Hameurlain, A. Min Tjoa (Eds.): Proceedings of the 8th International Conference on Database and Expert Systems Applications – DEXA 1997, Lecture Notes in Computer Science, Springer-Verlag 1997, France.
9. G. Quirchmayr, E. Schweighofer, T. J. M. Bench-Capon (Eds.): Proceedings of the 9th International Conference on Database and Expert Systems Applications – DEXA 1998, Lecture Notes in Computer Science, Springer-Verlag 1998, Austria.
10. T. J. M. Bench-Capon, G. Soda, A. M. Tjoa (Eds.): Proceedings of the 10th International Conference on Database and Expert Systems Applications – DEXA 1999, Lecture Notes in Computer Science, Springer-Verlag 1999, Italy.
11. M. T. Ibrahim, J. Küng, N. Revell (Eds.): Proceedings of the , 11th International Conference on Database and Expert Systems Applications – DEXA 2000, Lecture Notes in Computer Science, Springer-Verlag 2000, United Kingdom.
12. H. C. Mayr, J. Lazanský, G. Quirchmayr, P. Vogel (Eds.): Proceedings of the 12th International Conference on Database and Expert Systems Applications – DEXA 2001, Lecture Notes in Computer Science, Springer-Verlag 2001, Germany.
13. Hameurlain, R. Cicchetti, R. Traunmüller (Eds.): Proceedings of the 13th International Conference on Database and Expert Systems Applications – DEXA 2002, Lecture Notes in Computer Science, Springer-Verlag 2002, France.
14. Data Warehousing and Knowledge Discovery (DaWaK): http://www.informatik.uni-trier.de/~ley/db/conf/dawak/index.html
15. Electronic Commerce and Web Technologies (EC-Web): http://www.informatik.uni-trier.de/~ley/db/conf/ecweb/index.html
16. Electronic Government: http://www.informatik.uni-trier.de/~ley/db/conf/egov/index.html
17. DEXA Workshops: http://www.informatik.uni-trier.de/~ley/db/conf/dexa/index.html
18. T. K. Dang: Semantic Based Similarity Searches in Database Systems (Multidimensional Access Methods, Similarity Search Algorithms). PhD Thesis, May 2003, Johannes Kepler University of Linz, Austria.
19. M. Tjoa, R. Wagner: Database and Expert Systems 2002 "Quo vadis"?, DEXA 2002, pp. 945–948

Author Index

Aguilar-Ruiz, Jesús S.   907
Al-Hamdani, Abdullah   792
Al-Jadir, Lina   724
Al-Mourad, M.B.   713
An, Aijun   737
Aramburu, María José   109
Asano, Yasuhito   558
Atallah, Mikhail   223
Atluri, Vijayalakshmi   813

Bacon, Liz   8
Baptista, Cláudio S.   548
Behrendt, Wernher   423
Bell, David   651
Bench-Capon, Trevor   703
Berardi, Margherita   256
Berger, Helmut   474
Berlanga, Rafael   109
Bhashyam, Ramesh   782
Bhowmick, Sourav S.   350, 392
Bi, Yaxin   651
Blok, H.E.   67
Bochmann, Gregor v.   803
Böhm, Christian   504
Bortenschlager, Manfred   423
Bressan, Stephane   454
Bruckner, Robert M.   760
Butler, Alun   8

Ceci, Michelangelo   256
Chang, Elizabeth   88, 148
Chatvichienchai, Somchai   866
Che, Dunren   18
Choi, Byron   28
Chun, Soon Ae   813
Comai, Sara   171
Coman, Alexandru   601
Conesa, Jordi   693
Couchot, Alain   846
Crolotte, Alain   782

Dang, Tran Khanh   937
Darmont, Jérôme   662
Debenham, John   569
Dekhtyar, Alex   527
Dervos, Dimitrios   464

Dillon, Tharam S   88, 148
Ding, Zhiming   444
Dittenbach, Michael   474
Dohnal, Vlastislav   484

Edelweiss, Nina   683
Enokido, Tomoya   340
Erwig, Martin   494
Esparza, Oscar   927
Evangelidis, Georgios   464

Feng, Ling   88, 148
Fernandez, Marcel   927
Fernández-Medina, Eduardo   886
Fiddian, N.J.   713
Fierbinteanu, Cristina   57
Finin, Timothy   276
Flokstra, J.   67
Forné, Jordi   927
Franco, Annalisa   119
Frikken, Keith   223
Fry, Andrew G.   318
Fu, Yongjian   350

Gennaro, Claudio   484
Ghazal, Ahmad   782
Goda, Kazuo   202
Goldsmith, Judy   527
Gray, W.A.   713
Greer, Kieran   651
Gruenwald, Le   371

Hahn, Karl   212
He, Jianglin   494
He, Zhen   662
Henrich, Andreas   611
Hidayanto, Achmad Nizar   454
Höfling, Gabriele   212
Hong, Bonghee   308
Horng, Jorng-Tzong   297
Hou, Wen-Chi   18
Huang, Yu-Cheng   297
Hwang, San-Yih   287
Hwang, Sohyun   403

Ibrahim, Mohamed T   8, 622

Imai, Hiroshi   558
Iwaihara, Mizuho   866

Jeong, Min-A   876
Jin, Ming-Hui   297
Joshi, Anupam   276
Jun, Bonggi   308
Jung, Kyung-Yong   631
Jung, Sungwon   433

Kambayashi, Yahiko   866
Kameyama, Keisuke   517
Kao, Cheng-Yan   297
Kerhervé, Brigitte   803
Keulen, M. van   67
Kidawara, Yutaka   579
Kim, Jung-Ja   876
Kim, Sang-Kyun   98
Kitagawa, Hiroyuki   517
Kitsuregawa, Masaru   202, 537, 558
Koss, Matt   856
Kosugi, Naoko   589
Kotropoulos, Constantine   896
Kovásznai, Gergely   896
Krebs, Florian   504
Kwan, Paul W.H.   517

Lam, Nicole   266
Lamb, Joanne   651
Lau, Ho Lam   182
Laud, Amey   392
Laur, P.A   38
Lechner, Stephan   46
Lee, Byungkyu   433
Lee, Jung-Hyun   631
Lee, Kyu-Chul   98
Lee, Myungcheol   98
Lee, Sukho   129, 139
Lee, Taewon   129
Lee, Yugyung   381, 826
Li, Quanzhong   160
Liau, Chu Yee   454
Lim, Ee-Peng   287
List, Beate   760
Liu, Duen-Ren   836
Lumini, Alessandra   119

Ma, Ling   360
Madria, Sanjay Kumar   350
Maekawa, Mamoru   57

Mahoui, Malika   28
Maio, Dario   119
Malcolm, Grant   703
Malerba, Donato   256
Marrara, Stefania   171
Matos Galante, Renata de   683
Mehrotra, Sharad   192
Meng, Xiaofeng   444
Merkl, Dieter   474
Milner, Ben   360
Mohania, Mukesh   1
Mondal, Anirban   202
Moody, Daniel L.   77
Moon, Bongki   129, 160
Mulholland, Paul   856
Muñoz, Jose L.   927

Na, Young-Joo   631
Nagata, Hidenobu   589
Nakanishi, Tadashi   589
Narang, Inderpal   1
Nascimento, Mario A.   601
Ng, Wilfred   182, 244
Nguyen, Thanh Binh   622
Nitsos, Ilias   464

Olivé, Antoni   693
Ozsoyoglu, Gultekin   233, 792
Ozsoyoglu, Z. Meral   233

Palol, Xavier de   693
Park, Myungsun   139
Park, Seong-Bae   403
Park, Sung-Hee   413
Patel, Chintan   826
Pérez, Juan Manuel   109
Perich, Filip   276
Piattini, Mario   886
Pitas, Ioannis   896
Poncelet, P.   38
Pramudiono, Iko   537

Rajugan, Rajagopal   148
Ray, Indrakshi   330
Rehrl, Karl   423
Reich, Sigi   423
Reiner, Bernd   212
Rho, Hongsik   18
Rieser, Harald   423
Riquelme, José C.   907
Robbert, Günter   611

Ruan, Chun   917
Ruiz, Roberto   907
Ryu, Keun Ho   413

Sainter, Phil   856
Sampaio, Marcus Costa   548
Sander, Jörg   601
Sanz, Ismael   109
Saraiva dos Santos, Clesio   683
Schiefer, Josef   760
Schrefl, Michael   46
Schuschel, Hilmar   771
Seriai, Abdelhak   672
Shave, Michael   703
Shen, Minxin   836
Shiraishi, Masashi   340
Silva, Fábio Soares   548
Singh, Dadabhai T   392
Singh, Sachin   381
Smith, Dan   360
Son, Hyeon S.   413
Soriano, Miguel   927
Stojanovic, Nenad   641
Supekar, Kaustubh   826

Takizawa, Makoto   340
Tanaka, Katsumi   579
Tanca, Letizia   171
Tao, Yingying   747
Teisseire, M.   38
Tjoa, A Min   937
Toraichi, Kazuo   517
Toyoda, Masashi   558
Trejtnar, Lukas   856

Vajirkar, Pravin   381

Valasek, Michael   856
Varadharajan, Vijay   917
Vonk, J.   67
Vries, A.P. de   67

Wagner, Roland   937
Wang, Chih-Fang   18
Wang, Kuo   57
Wang, Yida   287
Weigand, Hans   88
Weske, Mathias   771
Westenthaler, Rupert   423
Williams, Hugh E.   318
Won, Yonggwan   876
Wong, Raymond K.   266
Wood, Derick   28
Wu, Eric Hsiao-Kuang   297

Xin, Tai   330

Yao, Qingsong   737
Ye, Haiwei   803
Yesha, Yelena   276
Yu, Byunggu   308
Yu, Wei   233
Yu, Xingbo   192

Zdrahal, Zdenek   856
Zettsu, Koji   579
Zezula, Pavel   484
Zhang, Byoung-Tak   403
Zhang, Jianting   371
Zhao, Wenzhong   527
Zhu, Qiang   747
Zuzarte, Calisto   747

Lecture Notes in Computer Science

For information about Vols. 1–2704
please contact your bookseller or Springer-Verlag

Vol. 2705: S. Renals, G. Grefenstette (Eds.), Text-and Speech-Triggered Information Access. Proceedings, 2000. VII, 197 pages. 2003. (Subseries LNAI).

Vol. 2706: R. Nieuwenhuis (Ed.), Rewriting Techniques and Applications. Proceedings, 2003. XI, 515 pages. 2003.

Vol. 2707: K. Jeffay, I. Stoica, K. Wehrle (Eds.), Quality of Service – IWQoS 2003. Proceedings, 2003. XI, 517 pages. 2003.

Vol. 2708: R. Reed, J. Reed (Eds.), SDL 2003: System Design. Proceedings, 2003. XI, 405 pages. 2003.

Vol. 2709: T. Windeatt, F. Roli (Eds.), Multiple Classifier Systems. Proceedings, 2003. X, 406 pages. 2003.

Vol. 2710: Z. Ésik, Z, Fülöp (Eds.), Developments in Language Theory. Proceedings, 2003. XI, 437 pages. 2003.

Vol. 2711: T.D. Nielsen, N.L. Zhang (Eds.), Symbolic and Quantitative Approaches to Reasoning with Uncertainty. Proceedings, 2003. XII, 608 pages. 2003. (Subseries LNAI).

Vol. 2712: A. James, B. Lings, M. Younas (Eds.), New Horizons in Information Management. Proceedings, 2003. XII, 281 pages. 2003.

Vol. 2713: C.-W. Chung, C.-K. Kim, W. Kim, T.-W. Ling, K.-H. Song (Eds.), Web and Communication Technologies and Internet-Related Social Issues – HSI 2003. Proceedings, 2003. XXII, 773 pages. 2003.

Vol. 2714: O. Kaynak, E. Alpaydin, E. Oja, L. Xu (Eds.), Artificial Neural Networks and Neural Information Processing – ICANN/ICONIP 2003. Proceedings, 2003. XXII, 1188 pages. 2003.

Vol. 2715: T. Bilgiç, B. De Baets, O. Kaynak (Eds.), Fuzzy Sets and Systems – IFSA 2003. Proceedings, 2003. XV, 735 pages. 2003. (Subseries LNAI).

Vol. 2716: M.J. Voss (Ed.), OpenMP Shared Memory Parallel Programming. Proceedings, 2003. VIII, 271 pages. 2003.

Vol. 2718: P. W. H. Chung, C. Hinde, M. Ali (Eds.), Developments in Applied Artificial Intelligence. Proceedings, 2003. XIV, 817 pages. 2003. (Subseries LNAI).

Vol. 2719: J.C.M. Baeten, J.K. Lenstra, J. Parrow, G.J. Woeginger (Eds.), Automata, Languages and Programming. Proceedings, 2003. XVIII, 1199 pages. 2003.

Vol. 2720: M. Marques Freire, P. Lorenz, M.M.-O. Lee (Eds.), High-Speed Networks and Multimedia Communications. Proceedings, 2003. XIII, 582 pages. 2003.

Vol. 2721: N.J. Mamede, J. Baptista, I. Trancoso, M. das Graças Volpe Nunes (Eds.), Computational Processing of the Portuguese Language. Proceedings, 2003. XIV, 268 pages. 2003. (Subseries LNAI).

Vol. 2722: J.M. Cueva Lovelle, B.M. González Rodríguez, L. Joyanes Aguilar, J.E. Labra Gayo, M. del Puerto Paule Ruiz (Eds.), Web Engineering. Proceedings, 2003. XIX, 554 pages. 2003.

Vol. 2723: E. Cantú-Paz, J.A. Foster, K. Deb, L.D. Davis, R. Roy, U.-M. O'Reilly, H.-G. Beyer, R. Standish, G. Kendall, S. Wilson, M. Harman, J. Wegener, D. Dasgupta, M.A. Potter, A.C. Schultz, K.A. Dowsland, N. Jonoska, J. Miller (Eds.), Genetic and Evolutionary Computation – GECCO 2003. Proceedings, Part I. 2003. XLVII, 1252 pages. 2003.

Vol. 2724: E. Cantú-Paz, J.A. Foster, K. Deb, L.D. Davis, R. Roy, U.-M. O'Reilly, H.-G. Beyer, R. Standish, G. Kendall, S. Wilson, M. Harman, J. Wegener, D. Dasgupta, M.A. Potter, A.C. Schultz, K.A. Dowsland, N. Jonoska, J. Miller (Eds.), Genetic and Evolutionary Computation – GECCO 2003. Proceedings, Part II. 2003. XLVII, 1274 pages. 2003.

Vol. 2725: W.A. Hunt, Jr., F. Somenzi (Eds.), Computer Aided Verification. Proceedings, 2003. XII, 462 pages. 2003.

Vol. 2726: E. Hancock, M. Vento (Eds.), Graph Based Representations in Pattern Recognition. Proceedings, 2003. VIII, 271 pages. 2003.

Vol. 2727: R. Safavi-Naini, J. Seberry (Eds.), Information Security and Privacy. Proceedings, 2003. XII, 534 pages. 2003.

Vol. 2728: E.M. Bakker, T.S. Huang, M.S. Lew, N. Sebe, X.S. Zhou (Eds.), Image and Video Retrieval. Proceedings, 2003. XIII, 512 pages. 2003.

Vol. 2729: D. Boneh (Ed.), Advances in Cryptology – CRYPTO 2003. Proceedings, 2003. XII, 631 pages. 2003.

Vol. 2730: F. Bai, B. Wegner (Eds.), Electronic Information and Communication in Mathematics. Proceedings, 2002. X, 189 pages. 2003.

Vol. 2731: C.S. Calude, M.J. Dinneen, V. Vajnovszki (Eds.), Discrete Mathematics and Theoretical Computer Science. Proceedings, 2003. VIII, 301 pages. 2003.

Vol. 2732: C. Taylor, J.A. Noble (Eds.), Information Processing in Medical Imaging. Proceedings, 2003. XVI, 698 pages. 2003.

Vol. 2733: A. Butz, A. Krüger, P. Olivier (Eds.), Smart Graphics. Proceedings, 2003. XI, 261 pages. 2003.

Vol. 2734: P. Perner, A. Rosenfeld (Eds.), Machine Learning and Data Mining in Pattern Recognition. Proceedings, 2003. XII, 440 pages. 2003. (Subseries LNAI).

Vol. 2735: F. Kaashoek, I. Stoica (Eds.), Peer-to-Peer Systems II. Proceedings, 2003. XI, 316 pages. 2003.

Vol. 2736: V. Mařík, W. Retschitzegger, O.Štěpánková (Eds.), Database and Expert Systems Applications. Proceedings, 2003. XX, 945 pages. 2003.

Vol. 2737: Y. Kambayashi, M. Mohania, W. Wöß (Eds.), Data Warehousing and Knowledge Discovery. Proceedings, 2003. XIV, 432 pages. 2003.

Vol. 2738: K. Bauknecht, A M. Tjoa, G. Quirchmayr (Eds.), E-Commerce and Web Technologies. Proceedings, 2003. XII, 452 pages. 2003.

Vol. 2739: R. Traunmüller (Ed.), Electronic Government. Proceedings, 2003. XVIII, 511 pages. 2003.

Vol. 2740: E. Burke, P. De Causmaecker (Eds.), Practice and Theory of Automated Timetabling IV. Proceedings, 2002. XII, 361 pages. 2003.

Vol. 2741: F. Baader (Ed.), Automated Deduction – CADE-19. Proceedings, 2003. XII, 503 pages. 2003. (Subseries LNAI).

Vol. 2742: R. N. Wright (Ed.), Financial Cryptography. Proceedings, 2003. VIII, 321 pages. 2003.

Vol. 2743: L. Cardelli (Ed.), ECOOP 2003 – Object-Oriented Programming. Proceedings, 2003. X, 501 pages. 2003.

Vol. 2744: V. Mařík, D. McFarlane, P. Valckenaers (Eds.), Holonic and Multi-Agent Systems for Manufacturing. Proceedings, 2003. XI, 322 pages. 2003. (Subseries LNAI).

Vol. 2745: M. Guo, L.T. Yang (Eds.), Parallel and Distributed Processing and Applications. Proceedings, 2003. XII, 450 pages. 2003.

Vol. 2746: A. de Moor, W. Lex, B. Ganter (Eds.), Conceptual Structures for Knowledge Creation and Communication. Proceedings, 2003. XI, 405 pages. 2003. (Subseries LNAI).

Vol. 2747: B. Rovan, P. Vojtáš (Eds.), Mathematical Foundations of Computer Science 2003. Proceedings, 2003. XIII, 692 pages. 2003.

Vol. 2748: F. Dehne, J.-R. Sack, M. Smid (Eds.), Algorithms and Data Structures. Proceedings, 2003. XII, 522 pages. 2003.

Vol. 2749: J. Bigun, T. Gustavsson (Eds.), Image Analysis. Proceedings, 2003. XXII, 1174 pages. 2003.

Vol. 2750: T. Hadzilacos, Y. Manolopoulos, J.F. Roddick, Y. Theodoridis (Eds.), Advances in Spatial and Temporal Databases. Proceedings, 2003. XIII, 525 pages. 2003.

Vol. 2751: A. Lingas, B.J. Nilsson (Eds.), Fundamentals of Computation Theory. Proceedings, 2003. XII, 433 pages. 2003.

Vol. 2752: G.A. Kaminka, P.U. Lima, R. Rojas (Eds.), RoboCup 2002: Robot Soccer World Cup VI. XVI, 498 pages. 2003. (Subseries LNAI).

Vol. 2753: F. Maurer, D. Wells (Eds.), Extreme Programming and Agile Methods – XP/Agile Universe 2003. Proceedings, 2003. XI, 215 pages. 2003.

Vol. 2754: M. Schumacher, Security Engineering with Patterns. XIV, 208 pages. 2003.

Vol. 2756: N. Petkov, M.A. Westenberg (Eds.), Computer Analysis of Images and Patterns. Proceedings, 2003. XVIII, 781 pages. 2003.

Vol. 2758: D. Basin, B. Wolff (Eds.), Theorem Proving in Higher Order Logics. Proceedings, 2003. X, 367 pages. 2003.

Vol. 2759: O.H. Ibarra, Z. Dang (Eds.), Implementation and Application of Automata. Proceedings, 2003. XI, 312 pages. 2003.

Vol. 2761: R. Amadio, D. Lugiez (Eds.), CONCUR 2003 - Concurrency Theory. Proceedings, 2003. XI, 524 pages. 2003.

Vol. 2762: G. Dong, C. Tang, W. Wang (Eds.), Advances in Web-Age Information Management. Proceedings, 2003. XIII, 512 pages. 2003.

Vol. 2763: V. Malyshkin (Ed.), Parallel Computing Technologies. Proceedings, 2003. XIII, 570 pages. 2003.

Vol. 2764: S. Arora, K. Jansen, J.D.P. Rolim, A. Sahai (Eds.), Approximation, Randomization, and Combinatorial Optimization. Proceedings, 2003. IX, 409 pages. 2003.

Vol. 2765: R. Conradi, A.I. Wang (Eds.), Empirical Methods and Studies in Software Engineering. VIII, 279 pages. 2003.

Vol. 2766: S. Behnke, Hierarchical Neural Networks for Image Interpretation. XII, 224 pages. 2003.

Vol. 2769: T. Koch, I. T. Sølvberg (Eds.), Research and Advanced Technology for Digital Libraries. Proceedings, 2003. XV, 536 pages. 2003.

Vol. 2776: V. Gorodetsky, L. Popyack, V. Skormin (Eds.), Computer Network Security. Proceedings, 2003. XIV, 470 pages. 2003.

Vol. 2777: B. Schölkopf, M.K. Warmuth (Eds.), Learning Theory and Kernel Machines. Proceedings, 2003. XIV, 746 pages. 2003. (Subseries LNAI).

Vol. 2779: C.D. Walter, Ç.K. Koç, C. Paar (Eds.), Cryptographic Hardware and Embedded Systems – CHES 2003. Proceedings, 2003. XIII, 441 pages. 2003.

Vol. 2782: M. Klusch, A. Omicini, S. Ossowski, H. Laamanen (Eds.), Cooperative Information Agents VII. Proceedings, 2003. XI, 345 pages. 2003. (Subseries LNAI).

Vol. 2783: W. Zhou, P. Nicholson, B. Corbitt, J. Fong (Eds.), Advances in Web-Based Learning – ICWL 2003. Proceedings, 2003. XV, 552 pages. 2003.

Vol. 2786: F. Oquendo (Ed.), Software Process Technology. Proceedings, 2003. X, 173 pages. 2003.

Vol. 2787: J. Timmis, P. Bentley, E. Hart (Eds.), Artificial Immune Systems. Proceedings, 2003. XI, 299 pages. 2003.

Vol. 2789: L. Böszörményi, P. Schojer (Eds.), Modular Programming Languages. Proceedings, 2003. XIII, 271 pages. 2003.

Vol. 2790: H. Kosch, L. Böszörményi, H. Hellwagner (Eds.), Euro-Par 2003 Parallel Processing. Proceedings, 2003. XXXV, 1320 pages. 2003.

Vol. 2794: P. Kemper, W. H. Sanders (Eds.), Computer Performance Evaluation. Proceedings, 2003. X, 309 pages. 2003.

Vol. 2795: L. Chittaro (Ed.), Human-Computer Interaction with Mobile Devices and Services. Proceedings, 2003. XV, 494 pages. 2003.

Vol. 2796: M. Cialdea Mayer, F. Pirri (Eds.), Automated Reasoning with Analytic Tableaux and Related Methods. Proceedings, 2003. X, 271 pages. 2003. (Subseries LNAI).

Vol. 2803: M. Baaz, J.A. Makowsky (Eds.), Computer Science Logic. Proceedings, 2003. XII, 589 pages. 2003.

Vol. 2805: K. Araki, S. Gnesi, D. Mandrioli (Eds.), FME 2003: Formal Methods. Proceedings, 2003. XVII, 942 pages. 2003.

Vol. 2810: M.R. Berthold, H.-J. Lenz, E. Bradley, R. Kruse, C. Borgelt (Eds.), Advances in Intelligent Data Analysis V. Proceedings, 2003. XV, 624 pages. 2003.

Vol. 2817: D. Konstantas, M. Leonard, Y. Pigneur, S. Patel (Eds.), Object-Oriented Information Systems. Proceedings, 2003. XII, 426 pages. 2003.

CPSIA information can be obtained at www.ICGtesting.com
Printed in the USA
LVOW09s0746120616
492225LV00002B/9/P

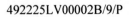